ENGLISH LITERATURE

English Literature Romanticism to 1945

Edited by
FRANK N. MAGILL

Derived from Library Editions
Published by Salem Press, Inc.

SALEM SOFTBACKS
Pasadena, California

LIBRARY OF CONGRESS CATALOG CARD NUMBER: 81-51766

ISBN 0-89356-309-9

Some of this material has appeared previously in
works published under the titles *Masterplots*: Revised Edition, *Cyclopedia of World Authors*, *Cyclopedia of Literary Characters*, and *Magill's Bibliography of Literary Criticism*.

First Printing

PUBLISHER'S NOTE

MAGILL SURVEYS form a series of integrated study guides designed to provide sources for augmenting classroom work in the Humanities. These guides offer ready-reference information about authors and their works and are structured with classroom requirements strictly in mind. Articles include biographical information about authors and their total canon, and, where appropriate, they provide plot summaries, character studies, critical evaluations, and extensive bibliographical references.

Magill Surveys are intended to take the student far beyond the immediate assignment. For example, if the program calls for the study of "a Dickens novel," the appropriate Survey will present to the student half a dozen or more pages on each of several Dickens novels, including a critical biography of Dickens, plot summaries and critical evaluations of the novels, individual character analyses of scores of the characters appearing in these novels, and finally an average of about twenty bibliographical references for *each* of the novels—the latter element a highly valuable resource whether for class work or term papers. Thus, the student may gain extensive background information about the author and his canon while concentrating on in-depth study of a particular work. When dealing with poetry or works of nonfiction, an essay-review is employed, offering the reader a concise evaluation of content and structural elements of the author's work.

The text for this Survey derives from a series of extensive library references in world literature edited by Frank N. Magill, including the following sources: *Masterplots*, *Cyclopedia of World Authors*, *Cyclopedia of Literary Characters*, and *Magill's Bibliography of Literary Criticism*.

All the material drawn from the above sources has been revised and supplemented where necessary to reflect current critical opinion. The text has been arranged to provide convenient access to a great amount of basic information condensed in one handy volume. Elaborate indexing techniques have been employed to assure information retrieval with a minimum of time and effort.

The original material reproduced in *Magill Surveys* has been developed through consultations with and contributions by hundreds of professors and scholars throughout the United States and abroad over a period of years. Its authoritativeness is attested by the thousands of academic and public libraries where the basic works from which this material is drawn will be found. The student who wishes to go beyond his assignment will find here ample means to satisfy his desire.

CONTENTS

The Romantic Age

The Victorian Age

CONTENTS

The Twentieth Century

CONTENTS

Special Consultant

Leslie B. Mittleman

List of Contributors

Walter Allen
Eric J. Batson
Joseph L. Blotner
Judith Bolch
Peter A. Brier
Edward E. Foster
Alice Guise
Wayne E. Haskin
James Marc Hovde
George Burke Johnston
Joanne G. Kashdan
David L. Kubal

Margaret McFadden-Gerber
Francis Claiborne Mason
Leslie B. Mittleman
Catherine E. Moore
Ann E. Reynolds
Mary Rohrberger
Tench Francis Tilghman
Carl J. Weber
Janet Wester
John Wilson
Morton Dauwen Zabel

ENGLISH LITERATURE

THE ROMANTIC PERIOD

Literary Forms
Criticism: Coleridge's *Biographia Literaria*; Hazlitt's *Characters of Shakespeare's Plays*; Shelley's *A Defence of Poetry*
Drama (Verse): Byron's *Manfred*; Shelley's *The Cenci, Prometheus Unbound*
Essays: Hazlitt's *Table Talk*; Lamb's *Essays of Elia*; De Quincey's *The English Mail Coach*; Landor's *Imaginary Conversations*
Lyric Poetry: by Blake, Byron, Coleridge, Moore, Shelley, Keats, Landor, Wordsworth
Elegy: Shelley's *Adonais*
Ode: Coleridge's "Dejection: An Ode"; Keats's "Ode on a Grecian Urn," "Ode to a Nightingale"; Shelley's "Ode to the West Wind"; Wordsworth's "Ode: Intimations of Immortality"
Reflective and Philosophical Verse: Shelley's "Alastor"; Wordsworth's "Lines Composed a Few Miles Above Tintern Abbey"
Sonnets: Keats's "When I Have Fears"; Shelley's "Ozymandias"; Wordsworth's "The World is Too Much with Us"
Narrative Poetry: Coleridge's "The Rime of the Ancient Mariner"; Byron's *The Corsair*; Keats's *The Eve of St. Agnes*, "Lamia"; Scott's *The Lady of the Lake*
Novel: Austen's *Pride and Prejudice*; Scott's *Kenilworth, Quentin Durward*
Satire (Verse): Byron's *Don Juan*, "The Vision of Judgment"

Thematic Characteristics
Reaction against Neo-Classic conventions of order, regularity, restraint, and decorum with emphasis instead upon originality, spontaneity, boldness, and vigor (See Basil Willey's *Nineteenth Century Studies: Coleridge to Matthew Arnold*, 1949)
Nature: Romantic emphasis on rugged power, irregularity, rather than on static order; a feeling for the mysterious spiritual power of wild nature that, especially in Wordsworth and Coleridge, approaches Pantheistic worship (see H.W. Piper, *The Active Universe: Pantheism and the Concept of Imagination in the English Romantic Poets*, 1962)
The Supernatural: Interest in non-rational states of consciousness, visionary experiences (see M. H. Abrams' *Natural Supernaturalism: Tradition and Revolution in Romantic Literature*, 1971)
Romantic Hero: Concern for the uniqueness of the individual; nonconformity. Emphasis upon originality, creativity, self-knowledge, often in defiance of society. The hero endowed with great potential, whether for good or evil (see Mario Praz's *The Romantic Agony*, 1951)
Exotic lands and the past: Interest in travel and adventure, especially in remote places; glorification of the Middle Ages and the Renaissance.

2

Isolation: A counter-impulse, emphasizing the solitary, reclusive, or alienated individual; interest in the psychology of the social outcast, including the criminal and sinner (see Peter Thorslev's *The Byronic Hero*, 1962)

Romantic revolt against political and social constraints: Emphasis upon the ideal of liberty, the worth and dignity of all classes and conditions of people (see Carl Woodring's *Politics in English Romantic Poetry*, 1970)

THOMAS LOVELL BEDDOES

Born: Clifton, England (June 30, 1803)
Died: Basle, Switzerland (January 26, 1849)

Principal Works

POEMS: *Poems of the Late Thomas Lovell Beddoes*, 1851.
PLAYS: *The Bride's Tragedy*, 1822; *Death's Jest-Book*, 1850.

Thomas Lovell Beddoes, son of the well-known British physician, Dr. Thomas Beddoes, was also the nephew of Maria Edgeworth, the novelist. He was educated at Bath Grammar School, Charterhouse, and Pembroke College, Oxford. As early as his student years he wrote poetry and drama, finding praise for his work as soon as it was published, especially *The Bride's Tragedy* (1822), which established him as a dramatist working in the traditions of the Jacobean dramatists of the early seventeenth century. Beddoes took his degree at Oxford a year late, in 1825, having been called to Italy during his examinations the previous year because of his mother's fatal illness. Shortly after taking his degree, Beddoes left England for the Continent, where he lived for most of the remaining years of his life. During 1825–1829 he studied medicine, specializing in anatomy and taking his medical degree at Würzburg in 1832. During the years of his medical study he worked on *Death's Jest-Book*, completing it in its initial form as early as 1829. He also became active as a writer on political matters, taking the liberal side. Because of this activity, Beddoes was forced to leave Bavaria shortly after taking his medical degree in 1832, and he then took up residence in Zurich, Switzerland. He became involved in politics there and was forced to flee Zurich for Berlin in 1840. Then came a period of wandering. He practiced medicine at various places and visited briefly in England, where he revealed himself as having become highly eccentric. He also continued to work on his poetry and plays, including revisions of *Death's Jest-Book*. In July, 1848, he attempted suicide at Basle, by cutting open an artery in his leg. He survived this attempt on his life, although he lost his leg. Six months later a second attempt, this time by poison, was successful. His suicide was kept a secret for many years, but more recently biographers have uncovered the evidence which proves that he took his own life. In obedience to Beddoes' written wishes, Thomas Forbes Kelsall, a long-time friend of the poet, published *Death's Jest-Book, or The Fool's Tragedy* in 1850, the year after the author's death. This is a play based upon thirteenth century German history and is considered Beddoes' best piece of work. In 1851 Kelsall also published *Poems by the Late Thomas Lovell Beddoes*, with a memoir written by Kelsall for that edition.

Bibliography

The definitive edition is *The Works*, edited by H. W. Donner, 1935. Donner also edited *Plays and Poems* for the Muses Library edition, 1950. For criticism see H. W. Donner, *Thomas Lovell Beddoes: The Making of a Poet*, 1935; Royall H. Snow, *Thomas Lovell Beddoes, Eccentric and Poet*, 1928; Charles Alva Hoyt, "Theme and Imagery in the Poetry of T. L. Beddoes," *Studia neophilologica*, XXXV (1963), 85–103; and Lytton Strachey, "The Last of the Elizabethans," *Books and Characters*, 1922. Donner's *The Browning Box*, 1935, contains letters relating to Beddoes.

Especially helpful are the brief discussion of Beddoes and the short bibliography in Ian Jack, *English Literature, '815–1832*, 1963.

THE POETRY OF BEDDOES

Author: Thomas Lovell Beddoes (1803–1849)
Principal published works: The Brides' Tragedy, 1822; *Death's Jest-Book,* 1850;
Poems, 1851

Essay-Review

The life and works of Thomas Lovell Beddoes were failures of which he is largely the cause. His life was spent as a perpetual medical student, even after he qualified for his degree at universities in Germany and Switzerland; he ended it by poison at the age of forty-five.

Apart from two books of juvenile poems Beddoes published only one work in his lifetime, *The Brides' Tragedy,* which made him a best seller in London when he was a nineteen-year-old undergraduate at Oxford. Early success with this poetical drama suggested to him the notion of "reviving" the English drama, a desire shared by many English writers between the successes of Dryden and W. B. Yeats or T. S. Eliot—witness the impossible verse dramas of Wordsworth, Shelley, Browning, Tennyson, Hardy. The shadow of Shakespeare and the Elizabethans lay long across the centuries, but unlike the Elizabethans the great English poets had very little practical experience of the stage. Thus it is that Beddoes' two most complete works are verse dramas, *The Brides' Tragedy* and *Death's Jest-Book,* which he completed in the four years ending in 1828 and spent the rest of his life revising.

Beddoes enjoyed a competent income all his life and suffered no attachments; he seems to have spent his years on the Continent, between 1825 and 1848, as a graduate student and political radical; a favorable rate of exchange and the reputation of a free Englishman made him a well-known figure among students and the secret police abroad. He seems to have been fortunate in his friends, especially his literary executor, Thomas Forbes Kelsall, but to have suffered a grand dyspepsia for life, of which he was thoroughly conscious:

> For death is more "a jest" than Life, you see
> Contempt grows quick from familiarity,
> ... Few, I know,
> Can bear to sit at my board when I show
> The wretchedness and folly of man's all
> And laugh myself right heartily.

Beddoes' long self-exile is perhaps the clearest indication of his malaise and the cause of his fragmentary work: he was unable to grasp the realities of life around him. A gentleman, a student, a foreigner, he sought an effective means of communication in a totally unrealistic medium, the poetic drama. Having little to say and no way of saying it, he turned ever inward, exploring his own melancholy and recording it in an outworn medium he acquired not from the stage but from books.

But for all this perversity, eccentricity, and tragedy, no anthology of nineteenth century English poetry can afford to omit at least two of Beddoes' lyrics: "Old Adam, the carrion crow" from the final scene of *Death's Jest-Book* and "Dream-Pedlary" from *The Ivory Gate*, the title of a collection of the poems written on the Continent. The fact that he was removed from the country of his speech—the events and literature of his time—may have been the precondition of his unique tone, which escapes finer definition as does that of his place in English literature. The situations of his lyrics are always slightly strange, for it is the style that marks their individuality. Along with much conventional language there are turns in the lines that can either be crass or inspired phrasing:

> And through every feather
> Leaked the wet weather. . . .

The second line is ironic and realistic. This is the effect Beddoes was always trying to bring off, a *danse macabre* in polka time which forces his lines to try to outdo one another often in a succession of compounds. When the inspiration fails, crassness results. These terrible alternatives are more or less described in the words of Wolfram which introduce the lyric:

> When I am sick o' mornings,
> With a horn-spoon tinkling my porridge-pot,
> 'Tis a brave ballad: but in Bacchanal night,
> O'er wine, red, black, or purple-bubbling wine,
> That takes a man by the brain and whirls him round,
> By Bacchus' lip! I like a full-voiced fellow,
> A craggy-throated, fat-cheeked trumpeter,
> A barker, a moon-howler. . . .

There is more triumph than failure of these startling effects in the last poems of "The Ivory Gate," and the range is much larger. Beddoes can satirize Britannia from a penny:

> O flattering likeness on a copper coin!
> Sit still upon your slave-raised cotton ball,
> With upright toasting fork and toothless cat.

He concludes "Silenus in Proteus" with the wit of

> I taught thee then, a little tumbling one,
> To suck the goatskin oftener than the goat?

"An Unfinished Draft," beginning "The snow falls by thousands into the sea," shows his lyric powers, as does the striking image in "The Phantom-Wooer":

> Sweet and sweet is their poisoned note,
> The little snakes of silver throat, . . .

Similarly, the lyrics in the verse-dramas are now best remembered. The larger effect Beddoes was trying for by constructing plot, character, and situation never quite came off; the fault mainly lies in the plots of the dramas together with their settings and the distrait emotions of the speakers. The two brides of *The Brides' Tragedy* are Floribel and Olivia; the latter's brother, Orlando, has forced Floribel's wooer, Hesperus, to promise marriage to Olivia so that Orlando himself can wed Floribel. Hesperus decides both shall be the "brides" of Death. In Act III he stabs Floribel when she keeps his tryst; as Olivia is preparing for her wedding to Hesperus his deed is discovered and the Duke orders his arrest at the marriage feast. When he is condemned to die, Olivia dies, too, and Floribel's mother (having poisoned Hesperus with the scent of flowers at the place of execution) precedes Hesperus to the grave in a general holocaust that includes the fathers of Floribel and Hesperus. Most of the action takes place offstage, the characters making the most of the marvelous situations, such as a suicide's grave, for verbal arias which furiously imitate the clotted passages of witty exchange in the Elizabethan play. The play is moment by moment effective, but as a whole it is impossible. Much the same can be said for *Death's Jest-Book* or "The Fool's Tragedy." Wolfram goes to the Holy Land to rescue Duke Melveric from the Saracens. The two fight over the love of Sibylla and Melveric kills Wolfram, whose body is returned to Grussau accompanied by the Duke, in the disguise of a friar, and Sibylla. There the Duke finds his two sons, Adalmar and Athulf, plotting rebellion against the Duke's Governor, Thorwald, and fighting each other for the love of Thorwald's daughter, Alama. The rebellion is led by Isbrand, Wolfram's vengeful brother, who has substituted a clown, Mandrake, for Wolfram's corpse, so that when the Duke, despairing of his present troubles, asks his African slave to raise the dead, first Mandrake, then Wolfram come from the sepulchre. The wedding of Adalmar and Alama is planned. Isbrand agrees to marry Sibylla; Athulf appears to commit suicide by drinking poison as the musicians, come to lead Alama to her marriage, sing the beautiful song, "We have bathed, where none have seen us." The scene ends with Athulf killing Adalmar. In the fifth act the events are most complicated, for the ghost of Wolfram is seeking revenge and the conspirators have decided to kill Isbrand. Sibylla dies but Athulf does not. The conspiracy first succeeds and then is overthrown. In the end the Duke loses both his sons, resigns his crown to Thorwald, and makes a marvelous final exit, going into the sepulchre with Wolfram. The play is saturated in echoes of Shakespeare, both in the language ("O Arab, Arab! Thou dost sell true drugs") and situation of a Duke in disguise, and but for Beddoes' obvious gravity the situation would amount to a parody. Many of the situations and passages play on death, but apart from a soliloquy by Isbrand, the "Fool" of the subtitle, do little more than weave around the subject. The soliloquy in Act V, Scene 1, begins:

> How I despise
> All you mere men of muscle! It was ever
> My study to find out a way to godhead,
> And on reflection soon I found that first
> I was but half created; that a power
> Was wanting in my soul to be its soul,
> And this was mine to make.

This passage carries the ring of reality and makes us see Isbrand as a *persona* for Beddoes, one of the rare moments when he speaks recognizable truth. In the "Lines written in Switzerland," after a passage that plays with the notion of Truth, Beddoes again speaks out in what may well be his epitaph:

> Not in the popular playhouse, or full throng
> Of opera-gazers longing for deceit; . . .
> May verse like this e'er hope an eye to feed on't.
> But if there be, who, having laid the loved
> Where they may drop a tear in roses' cups,
> With half their hearts inhabit other worlds; . . .
> Such may perchance, with favorable mind,
> Follow my thought along its mountainous path.

WILLIAM BLAKE

Born: London, England (November 28, 1757)
Died: London (August 12, 1827)

Principal Works

POEMS (Lyric, Symbolic, Didactic): *Poetical Sketches*, 1783; *There Is No Natural Religion*, c. 1788–1794; *All Religions Are One*, c. 1788–1794; *Songs of Innocence*, 1789; *The Book of Thel*, 1789; *The Marriage of Heaven and Hell*, c. 1790; *The French Revolution*, 1791; *For the Sexes: The Gates of Paradise*, 1793; *Visions of the Daughters of Albion*, 1793, *America, A Prophecy*, 1793; *Songs of Experience*, 1794; *Europe, A Prophecy*, 1794; *The First Book of Urizen*, 1794; *The Song of Los*, 1795; *The Book of Ahania*, 1795; *The Book of Los*, 1795; *Milton*, 1804–1808; *Jerusalem, The Emanation of the Giant Albion*, 1804–1820; *Laocoön*, c. 1820; *The Ghost of Abel*, 1822.

ILLUSTRATIONS AND ENGRAVINGS: *The Complaint and the Consolation, or Night Thoughts*, by Edward Young, 1797; *Blair's Grave*, 1808; *The Prologue and Characters of Chaucer's Pilgrims*, 1812; *The Pastorals of Virgil*, 1821; *Illustrations of the Book of Job*, 1825; *Illustrations of Dante*, 1827.

ESSAY: *A Descriptive Catalogue*, 1809.

William Blake, the greatest visionary poet in English, was born on November 28, 1757, the second son of James Blake, a London native of obscure origin who was a hosier by occupation. A few remarkable incidents of Blake's childhood have been recorded, among them the manifestation of his first known vision, when, at the age of four, he beheld God's head at a window and was seized with a fit of screaming. On other occasions he informed his parents that during his walks about the fields he had seen angels; and once he returned to say that the prophet Ezekiel had appeared to him under a tree. He was so fiery-tempered that his father preferred not to send him to school, where he might be whipped, but chose to give him elementary instruction at home. At the age of ten he was enrolled in Henry Pars' drawing school, from which, at fourteen, he advanced to a formal apprenticeship in the engraver's trade under James Basire. He was already writing verse, and several of the pieces collected in *Poetical Sketches* were composed when he was only twelve. Although he passed his early youth in studious application to his technical work, he found time also to increase his familiarity with literature. He read modern philosophers and the poets, far outdistancing his Swedenborgian father. In 1778, having qualified as an engraver, he began to accept commissions from booksellers and was quickly able to assert his professional competence.

In 1781, jilted by a certain Polly Wood, he fell in love with Catherine Boucher; reaching an understanding almost at once, he married her the following year. At their first meeting she had been suddenly overwhelmed with the intuitive knowledge that she had met her destined husband, and she had been forced to leave the room to keep from fainting. The match so easily made was in all respects ideal: Blake taught her to read, write, sketch, and paint, and she became skillful enough to assist his labors. In his transports of artistic and visionary rapture, which often roused him from sleep and sent him irresistibly to his worktable, she would sustain him by sitting immobile for hours at his side. He found that her presence helped him subdue his wilder emotions, thus bringing order to his mind. Perhaps no artist ever had a more affectionately docile wife.

In the closing decade of the century, Blake, working almost frenziedly under the pressure of visionary experience while perfecting his mastery of artistic media, published his lyric *Songs of Innocence* and *Songs of Experience* in such a way as to co-ordinate his different talents. Using a writing substance impervious to acid, he prepared for each page a copper plate inscribed in reverse with the text of a poem and with a decorative frame, and having etched the plate he made impressions in color, afterward in some cases adding other tints by hand. This method he called illuminated printing. He employed it further in issuing his didactic and prophetic works, from *There Is No Natural Religion*, to *The Ghost of Abel*. His final masterpieces, however, the illustrations for the Book of Job and his illustrations of Dante, were engraved from watercolor drawings, as were the illustrations for Young's *Night Thoughts*, Virgil's *Pastorals*, and for numerous other books.

In 1800, Blake formed an association with William Hayley, who engaged him to illustrate a *Life of Cowper*, and he moved from London to Felpham, Sussex, in order to work there with Hayley. The scheme proved unsatisfactory; after three years he went back to London to set up as a publisher of his own writings, for which the commercial arrangement with Hayley had made no provision. Since his works were not in demand, his new venture failed; and as a result he and his wife lived in straitened circumstances, subsisting on commissions from Thomas Butts, already for some years Blake's patron. Butts was the first Blake collector and enthusiast. For an exhibition of his works in 1809, Blake issued a *Descriptive Catalogue* in which, analyzing his painting of the Canterbury Pilgrims, he expounded his artistic theories.

Few traces exist of Blake's activities between 1809 and 1818; but between the latter year and his death in London on August 12, 1827, he emerged as one of the most respected artists in London, where he had many friends, including the well-known painter John Linnell. In this period he attained his zenith as a designer and engraver. Since his lifetime, his work has become more and more a topic of specialized study, and the mystical symbolism of his prophetic books in particular has been subjected to much exegesis.

Bibliography

The standard text is *The Complete Writings of William Blake, with All the*

Variant Readings, edited by Geoffrey Keynes, 1957. This edition supersedes the same editor's *The Writings of William Blake*, 3 vols., 1925, and *The Poetry and Prose of William Blake*, 3 vols., 1927. *The Letters of William Blake* were edited by Geoffrey Keynes, 1956. An earlier edition of the *Works* was edited by E. J. Ellis and William Butler Yeats, 3 vols., 1893. *The Prophetic Writings of William Blake* have been edited by D. J. Sloss and J. P. R. Wallis, 2 vols., 1926.

THE MARRIAGE OF HEAVEN AND HELL

Type of work: Prophetic satire
Author: William Blake
First published: c. 1790

Essay-Review

In 1968 Allen Ginsberg recorded a number of Blake's lyric poems, sung to simple tunes of his own improvising. (Blake sang his own poems to his friends, without accompaniment.) Ginsberg wanted "to articulate the significance of each holy & magic syllable ... as if each syllable had intention." There is no better way to begin studying Blake than to speak his poems aloud. Only after he has learned to breathe with Blake in the lyrics should the student proceed to the Prophetic Books. "Man has no Body distinct from his Soul; for that call'd Body is a portion of Soul discern'd by the five Senses, the chief inlets of Soul in this age." Sound is the body of language, and the reader must train himself on the lyrics, where each syllable has intention, to breathe with Blake. Otherwise he will turn to the Prophetic Books—parts of which are not truly poems—and read them with his discursive intelligence only.

The Marriage of Heaven and Hell is not, for the most part, poetry. T.S. Eliot called it "naked philosophy, presented." (His essay, "William Blake," in the *Selected Essays*, is very short but very rich, essential reading.) It combines prose (the greatest part), poetry, and—on the borderline between poetry and prose—striking aphorisms with biblical cadences. The result is a mixture which distinguishes it, despite many affinities, from all of the other Prophetic Books.

Although the form of *The Marriage of Heaven and Hell* is unique among Blake's works, it shares the visionary experience which informs everything Blake wrote. "Visionary" is really an inadequate word here, a cover for perplexity, and before considering *The Marriage of Heaven and Hell* in particular we should give some attention to the ambiguous status of Blake's "visions." Repeatedly in his poems, Blake says that he has seen and talked with angels and demons, with Old Testament prophets, with his beloved dead brother, Robert.

> What to others a trifle appears
> Fills me full of smiles and tears;
> For double the vision my eyes do see,
> And a double vision is always with me.

In one sense, readers are quite willing to grant "double vision" to any poet, but it is clear that by "double vision" Blake means more than the license to speak in metaphors. For example, he wrote to his patron, Thomas Butts, in April, 1803, to explain why he was returning to live in London: "That I can alone carry on my visionary studies in London unannoy'd, & that I may converse with my friends in Eternity, See Visions, Dream Dreams, & prophesy and speak Parables unobserved & at liberty from the Doubts of other Mortals. . . . "

Several generations ago most readers did Blake the honor of taking his statements at face value: they judged that he was mad. Many contemporary critics, on the other hand, "allegorize" away all of Blake's embarrassing visions, claiming that he was actually talking about poetry and the creative process. A good example of this approach is Harold Bloom's commentary to the Erdman text of *The Poetry and Prose of William Blake*, which competes with the text of Geoffrey Keynes as the standard edition. Bloom comments on the second "Memorable Fancy" in *The Marriage of Heaven and Hell*: "One risks redundance in observing again how far this passage (and everything else in Blake) is from mysticism of any kind. It is Blake's work *as a creative artist* that will expunge the notion of dualism, and cleanse the doors of perception, the infinitely expandable senses of man."

There is an alternative between these extremes. Blake did not accept the dichotomy between "literal" and "metaphorical" which many modern readers accept as simply "common sense." He believed that the Imagination *participates* in the creation of the world; he was primarily concerned, in the words of Czeslaw Milosz, "with the *energy* which reveals itself in a constant interaction of Imagination with the things perceived by our five senses." Many readers will dismiss this as nonsense (Blake would say they suffered from single vision, from idolatry of the literal), but this is what Blake believed; and if one wishes to fully understand Blake's beliefs before finally judging them, the best guide is Owen Barfield.

Barfield is not a Blake scholar; although he only occasionally mentions Blake, his books explore again and again the false "common sense" against which Blake warned, "the premise that literalness of meaning is some kind of unclouded correspondence with a mindless external reality which was given from the start. . . . " With Blake, Barfield believes that "neither nature nor man will ever be understood . . . until we accept that nature is the reflected image of man's conscious and unconscious self." Barfield's books, among them *The Rediscovery of Meaning*, *History, Guilt, and Habit*, and *Saving the Appearances*, are invaluable.

Finally, in considering Blake's visions, one should never forget that he was a Christian—a heretic, yes, but a *Christian* heretic. This is undeniable (his letters alone provide ample evidence: a typical passage runs: "I still & shall to Eternity Embrace Christianity and Adore him who is the Express image of God"), although nothing can prevent men from denying—as they have done—what is obviously true but uncongenial to their presuppositions. Pascal carried with him to his death, sewn into his clothing, a scrap of parchment on which he had recorded the decisive experience of his life: on the night of November 23, 1654, Jesus Christ revealed himself to Pascal, in a personal form. Simone Weil recorded a similar experience of personal revelation. George Fox conversed with angels and was guided by them. Whether the reader himself is a believer or not, he must acknowledge Blake's belief, and consider Blake's visions not only in the context of poetic tradition, but in the context of a tradition which runs continuously from St. Paul to Thomas Merton (whose thesis at Columbia University was written on

Blake): a tradition in which diverse men and women have seen visions, dreamed dreams, and prophesied.

Indeed, although Blake is notorious as a self-taught, idiosyncratic genius, he was acutely conscious of tradition, and many of his works are "dialogues" with his predecessors. *Milton* is an obvious example; less obvious is the "dialogue" in *The Marriage of Heaven and Hell*, where Blake is conversing ("Opposition is true Friendship") with Swedenborg.

Swedenborg (1688–1772) was a Swedish scientist of astonishingly wide learning and great practical accomplishment when, like Pascal, he experienced a personal revelation which changed his life. He gave up his scientific studies and his administrative duties and wrote book after book describing his spiritual experiences, including visits to Heaven and Hell and conversations with angels. Shortly after his death, his works were translated into English; in London, a small group of converts formed the Swedenborgian Church of New Jerusalem, to which Blake belonged for an undetermined, but probably short, time. Swedenborg had a surprisingly wide circulation in the nineteenth century, but in the twentieth century few have read him outside the byways of the occult. For Blake, he was both a master (many of Blake's ideas can be traced to Swedenborg) and an opponent to wrestle with.

Blake's *The Marriage of Heaven and Hell* wrestles with a book of Swendenborg's called *Heaven and Hell*, in which there is the most explicit statement of the doctrine of "correspondences"—the doctrine best known through Baudelaire, who took it from Swedenborg. According to Swedenborg, in *Heaven and Hell*, "the whole natural world corresponds to the spiritual world, and not merely the natural world in general, but also every particular of it; and as a consequence everything in the natural world that springs from the spiritual is called correspondent." Such a teaching was obviously influential on Blake, yet he did not accept Swedenborg without reservations. For example, Swedenborg believed in Hell as the eternal punishment of the damned; Blake did not. The doctrine of eternal damnation was for Blake merely the most extreme expression of a misguided religion which dominated the church in his time. *The Marriage of Heaven and Hell* is a polemic against Swedenborg and against the corrupt church as well.

It is essential not to lose sight of the polemical and strongly satirical intention of *The Marriage of Heaven and Hell*, which is no more straightforward than Swift's *A Modest Proposal*. Blake began the work in 1790, which explains the otherwise puzzling lines: "As a new heaven is begun, and it is now thirty-three years since its advent, the Eternal Hell revives. And lo! Swedenborg is the Angel sitting at the tomb: his writings are the linen clothes folded up." Swedenborg had announced that the Last Judgment was beginning in 1757. Thirty-three years later, in 1790, Blake was mocking Swedenborg's excessively literal apocalyptic predictions. He was *not*, as some critics have suggested, falling into the same trap, predicting the imminent end of the Age.

Because of its suddenly shifting tones and forms, *The Marriage of Heaven and*

Hell is one of Blake's most difficult works, yet its central message is clear enough. In fact, there is another difficulty posed by this very "clarity." Many of the ideas which were revolutionary in Blake's time have become, in our time, the unexamined dogmas against which we must struggle. In the typical English church of Blake's time, as Czeslaw Milosz has observed, the clergy devoted their sermons to a veritable orgy of terror, threatening the worshippers with infernal punishments. Religion consisted of prohibitions, above all against sexuality, and the role of the church as guardian of the status quo was unquestioned.

In this context, Blake's beliefs—which included his faith in the great Restoration (*apokatastasis*), in which every human being and the very substance of the world will be redeemed and cleansed—were truly revolutionary: "every thing that lives is Holy." Nowadays it is all too easy to pay lip-service to such a belief. However, Blake paradoxically believed that ultimately all men would be redeemed, yet he never ceased to struggle, to wrestle—he struggled against falsehood, and he exalted all that was holy against doubt and poverty and fatigue. In the last year of his life, he wrote that "since the French Revolution Englishmen are all intermeasurable by one another: certainly a happy state of agreement, in which I for one do not agree. God keep you and me from the divinity of yes and no too. . . ."

THE POETRY OF BLAKE

Author: William Blake (1757-1827)
Principal published works: Poetical Sketches, 1783; *There Is No Natural Religion,* c. 1788-1794; *All Religions Are One,* c. 1788-1794; *Songs of Innocence,* 1789; *The Book of Thel,* 1789; *The Marriage of Heaven and Hell,* c. 1790; *The French Revolution,* 1791; *For the Sexes: The Gates of Paradise,* 1793; *Visions of the Daughters of Albion,* 1793; *America, A Prophecy,* 1793; *Songs of Experience,* 1794; *Europe, A Prophecy,* 1794; *The First Book of Urizen,* 1794; *The Song of Los,* 1795; *The Book of Ahania,* 1795; *The Book of Los,* 1795; *Milton,* 1804-1808; *Jerusalem, The Emanation of the Giant Albion,* 1804-1820; *Laocoön,* c. 1820; *The Ghost of Abel,* 1822

Essay-Review

The poetry of William Blake—artist, printer, prophet, and revolutionary—varies widely in style and substance, from youthful imitations of Spenser to lyrics of seemingly naïve childish wonder to symbolic verse of extraordinary complexity. Apart from his earliest productions, his work shows a powerful originality in form, images, and technique.

His juvenile work, written between the ages of twelve and twenty, was published in 1783 as *Poetical Sketches.* The poems, which are slight and at times even crude, show a strong Elizabethan influence. Occasional flashes of lyrical brilliance are visible, however, such as this stanza from a song known to have been written before he was fourteen:

> With sweet May dews my wings were wet,
> And Phoebus fir'd my vocal rage;
> He caught me in his silken net,
> And shut me in his golden cage.

Although he remained poor and generally unknown throughout his life, Blake was well acquainted with a number of leading social and political radicals, and he belonged to a discussion group which included Henry Fuseli, Thomas Holcroft, Mary Wollstonecraft, Thomas Paine, and others. Through such stimulation he was able to develop his own radical views about Christianity, Swedenborgianism, and the American and French revolutions. His dual concern with mysticism and political radicalism about 1788-1789 marks his intellectual and artistic maturity. These two strains were immediately evident in Blake's two major collections of lyrics, *Songs of Innocence* (1789), and *Songs of Experience* (1794), printed together in 1794 as *Songs of Innocence and Experience.* All three volumes were illustrated by the author's powerfully imaginative engravings, which contribute greatly to the reader's appreciation of the text. By "innocence" and "experience" Blake means two contrary, though not clearly defined, states of the human soul.

The two groups of poems directly oppose their subject matter. We are given "Infant Joy" against "Infant Sorrow," "The Blossom" against "The Sick Rose," "The Lamb" against "The Tiger," "The Divine Image" against "The Human Abstract," and opposed treatments of "The Chimney Sweeper," "A Little Boy Lost," and others. The poems are remarkable for their simple grace and direct emotional expression. "Innocence" is something like happiness, a state of wonder and acceptance and endurance of life. The "innocent" chimney sweep, for example, although aware of his misery, retains his vision and faith:

> There's little Tom Dacre, who cried when his head,
> That curled like a lamb's back, was shaved: so I said
> "Hush Tom! never mind it, for when your head's bare
> You know that the soot cannot spoil your white hair."

In contrast, the chimney sweep of the opposed poem in *Songs of Experience* understands the earth-bound social cause and the destructive aspects of life. His complaint is bitter:

> And because I am happy and dance and sing,
> They think they have done me no injury,
> And are gone to praise God and His Priest and King.
> Who make up a Heaven of our misery.

The poet's opposition of "innocence" and "experience" reflects the development of his Doctrine of Contraries, a philosophical view which was to dominate his poetry for the rest of his life. He defines this doctrine in *The Marriage of Heaven and Hell* (c. 1790): "Without Contraries is no progression. Attraction and repulsion, reason and energy, love and hate, are necessary to human existence." Elsewhere in the same work he casts these oppositions as a "Prolific Force" against a "Devouring Force":

> But the Prolific would cease to be prolific unless the Devourer, as a sea, received the excess of his delights. Some will say: 'Is not God alone the Prolific?' I answer: 'God only acts and is in existing beings, or men.'

Blake apparently viewed progress as cyclical, as a period of creation following one of destruction. Such a view is present in the mythology of his later works. Specifically, *The Marriage of Heaven and Hell* attacks the rationalism of eighteenth century Protestantism, which, Blake felt, reduced complex moral problems to over-simplified formulas. By means of paradox he hoped to stress a truer and more complicated awareness of the human condition. In "The Little Vagabond," for example, a later lyric associated with *Songs of Experience*, the young narrator complains: "Dear mother, dear mother, the Church is cold,/But the Ale-house is healthy and pleasant and warm." Although apparently uncomplicated, Blake's lyrics are written in a complex vision.

Blake's prophetic and mystical writings include *The Book of Thel* (1789); *Tiriel* (c. 1789); *Visions of the Daughters of Albion* (1793); *America, A Prophecy* (1793); *Europe, A Prophecy* (1794); *The First Book of Urizen* (1794); *The Song of Los* (1795); *The Book of Ahania* (1795); *The Four Zoas* (c. 1797); *Milton* (1804–1808); *Jerusalem* (1804–1820); and *The Ghost of Abel* (1822). These poems generally employ a kind of free verse, although there are some memorable lyrical passages, and an obscure and at times incomprehensible personal mythology. Various critics have produced widely differing interpretations.

These writings may be profitably divided into four groups which indicate different directions in the author's thought. The first such group contains *Thel* and *Tiriel*, works that are allegorical rather than symbolic. *Thel* argues for a benevolent providence found in all things. *Tiriel* is an Ossianic imitation with the theme of defiant children against a tyrannical father. Neither poem shows the paradoxical views Blake was soon to develop.

The second group marks the beginning of Blake's characteristic mystical thought. It includes the prose work, *The Marriage of Heaven and Hell*, and two subgroups of related poems. The first group, consisting of *A Song of Liberty; Visions of the Daughters of Albion; America, A Prophecy; Europe, A Prophecy*; and *The Song of Los*, employs relatively uncomplicated symbolism. They stress the doctrine of man's regeneration through a revolt against common moral standards to produce an apparently anarchical society. The second group, which includes *The First Book of Urizen, The Book of Los* (1795), and *The Book of Ahania*, introduces a myth which challenges the Hebraic-Christian and Miltonic views of cosmology, man, and sin. These poems are intellectually significant in that the action is set against a background of blind fate. The power of God to direct the universe is implicitly denied.

Vala, an earlier form of *The Four Zoas*, is representative of a third development in Blake's mythology. To his earlier symbolism he added new qualities and powers. Urizen, Luvah, Tharmas, and Urthona or Los are associated respectively with the intellect or the Brain, the affections or the Heart, the appetite or the Tongue, and the Ear or the prophetic and creative activity. He apparently wished either to base his myth in psychology or to include human attributes in a story about the origins of the universe.

About 1797, however, while still working on *Vala*, Blake radically shifted his views to a belief in a beneficent God, although he maintained his attack against conventional theology and moral codes. *The Four Zoas, Milton*, and *Jerusalem* belong to the fourth group, which features a more extensive use of symbols derived from Christianity and a more elaborate view of his theories about reality and knowledge. His theory of salvation through revolt, as well as Orc, its symbol, finally disappears. At the same time Blake more closely identifies his mysticism with art. Instead of creating a new mythology to express his new views, Blake rewrote and patched up the old symbolism, inevitably confusing it still further. He left no fully coherent myth.

Milton consists of two separate parts, the obscure and shadowy Satan-Palama-bron myth, and the descent of Milton into the world to correct his theological errors in *Paradise Lost*, such as having regarded Satan as punished by God for his sins. Blake often claimed to have spoken to Milton in visions. Crabb Robinson, an acquaintance of Blake, wrote to Dorothy Wordsworth: "Now, according to Blake, atheism consists in worshipping the natural world, which same natural world, properly speaking, is nothing real but a mere illusion produced by Satan. Milton was for a great part of his life an atheist, and therefore his fatal errors in *Paradise Lost*, which he often begged Blake to refute." *Milton* is also noteworthy for the striking lyric with which it begins, "And did those feet in ancient time."

Jerusalem deals with Albion's (man's) conquest of error on earth and with his return to Eternity. It celebrates the law of Forgiveness of Sins. The text as we have it is obscured by many revisions, but in 1809 the poet published a clear description of its theme: "(The Strong Man, the Beautiful Man, and the Ugly Man) were originally one man who was fourfold; he was self-divided, and his real humanity slain on the stems of generation, and the form of the fourth was like the Son of God . . . it is voluminous, and contains the ancient history of Britain and the world of Satan and of Adam."

Bibliography

Aers, D. "William Blake and the Dialectics of Sex," in *ELH*. XLIV (Fall, 1977), pp. 500–514.

Bentley, Gerald E., Editor. *William Blake: The Critical Heritage*. Boston: Routledge and Kegan Paul, 1975.

————. *Blake Records*. Oxford: Clarendon Press, 1969.

Bronowski, Jacob. *William Blake and the Age of Revolution*. London: Routledge and Kegan Paul, 1972.

Chayes, I.H. "Blake and the Seasons of the Poet," in *Studies in Romanticism*. XI (Summer, 1972), pp. 225–240.

Damon, Samuel F. *William Blake: His Philosophy and Symbols*. London: Dawsons, 1969.

Erdman, David V. *Blake, Prophet Against Empire: A Poet's Interpretation of the History of His Own Times*. Princeton, N.J.: Princeton University Press, 1969.

Fisher, Peter F. "Blake's Attacks on the Classical Tradition," in *Philological Quarterly*. XL (1961), pp. 1–18.

Frye, Northrop. *Fearful Symmetry: A Study of William Blake*. Princeton, N.J.: Princeton University Press, 1969.

Gilchrist, Alexander. *The Life of William Blake.* New York: Phaeton Press, 1969.

Gleckner, R.F. "Most Holy Forms of Thought: Some Observations on Blake's Language," in *ELH.* XLI (Winter, 1974), pp. 555–577.

Heinzelmann, K. "Blake's Golden Word," in *English Language Notes.* XV (1977), pp. 33–38.

Hirst, Désirée. *Hidden Riches: Traditional Symbolism from the Renaissance to Blake.* New York: Barnes & Noble, 1964.

Lefcowitz, B.F. "Blake and the Natural World," in *PMLA.* LXXXIX (January, 1974), pp. 121–131.

Murray, R. "Blake and the Ideal of Simplicity," in *Studies in Romanticism.* XIII (Spring, 1974), pp. 89–104.

Paley, Morton D., Editor. *William Blake: Essays in Honor of Sir Geoffrey Keynes.* Oxford: Clarendon Press, 1973.

Raine, Kathleen. *Blake and Tradition.* London: Routledge and Kegan Paul, 1969.

————. "Blake's Christ-consciousness," in *Studies in Comparative Religion.* X (Autumn, 1976), pp. 213–218.

Rosenfeld, Alvin H., Editor. *William Blake: Essays for Samuel Foster Damon.* Providence, R.I.: Brown University Press, 1969.

Sutherland, J. "Blake: A Crisis of Love and Jealousy," in *PMLA.* LXXXVII (May, 1972), pp. 424–431.

Wilson, Mona. *The Life of William Blake.* New York: Oxford University Press, 1971.

Witcutt, William D. *Blake: A Psychological Study.* Folcroft, Pa.: Folcroft Library Editions, 1974.

Witke, J. " 'Jerusalem': A Synoptic Poem," in *Comparative Literature.* XXII (Summer, 1970), pp. 265–278.

Wright, Thomas. *The Life of William Blake.* New York: A. Schram, 1972.

ROBERT BURNS

Born: Alloway, Ayrshire, Scotland (January 25, 1759)
Died: Dumfries, Scotland (July 21, 1796)

Principal Works

POEMS: *Poems, Chiefly in the Scottish Dialect*, 1786 (Kilmarnock Edition); 1787 (Edinburgh Edition); 1793, 2 volumes.

Although Robert Burns lived only to the age of thirty-seven, he lived with more intensity and produced more memorable writing than most authors who have lived twice as long. He became acquainted with hard work early, on his father's farm in Ayrshire where he was born, January 25, 1759. William Burnes, as he chose to spell it, was a poor tenant farmer who was kept in constant poverty by high rents and poor soil. Robert was put to work in the fields by the age of twelve, and he was doing a man's work at fifteen. Even while laboring strenuously, however, Burns was an avid reader, stealing moments whenever possible to read Pope, Shakespeare, Milton, Dryden, and any other author whose works he could get.

The two major influences on Burns's early years, aside from his reading, were his father, whom Burns immortalized in *The Cotter's Saturday Night* (1786), and the local folk songs and legends. His earliest schooling he received from John Murdoch, a scholar hired by the farmers of the district, and at the parish school in Dalrymple. In 1773 he was sent to Murdoch's school at Ayr for a brief period. The old notion that Burns was an uneducated clod is quite inaccurate. He learned French well enough to read in that language and he was well grounded in English grammar. During the summer of 1777, while living with an uncle at Ballochneil, he studied mathematics and surveying under High Rodger, schoolmaster at nearby Kirkoswald.

Throughout Burns's early life the history of his family was the story of moving from one poor farm to another. Thus they moved from Mount Oliphant to Lochlie in 1777, and from Lochlie to Mossgiel in 1784, at the death of Burns's father. As a possible source of income, Robert had tried to learn to dress flax in Irvine, but the work was uncongenial; when the flax shop burned down, he returned home immediately. He then spent four years with his younger brothers, trying to make the farm at Mossgiel pay. By this time Burns had already started those romantic activities for which he is perhaps needlessly famous. He had had affairs with Jean Armour and Mary Campbell by this period in his life, but far more important, he had also started writing verse. He began "The Jolly Beggars" (1799) as early as 1785, and he had done some short songs and poems before that date.

By the time he was twenty-five many of Burns's most strongly expressed ideas were beginning to take shape in his mind. One of the most important of these was his mocking attitude toward Calvinism. Burns devoted much of his verse to exposing what he considered the hypocrisies and pomposities of Calvinism, and he was ever an enemy of the false, seemingly devout ministers, one of whom he pictures mercilessly in "Holly Willie's Prayer" (1799). Of equal importance, and of superior fame, was Burns's love of the countryside and its people. He was always primarily interested in the human significances of things; so, while he was not a nature poet in the Wordsworthian cause, he tried to show the effects of the rural environment on his countrymen.

After several years of fruitless and back-breaking work at the Mossgiel farm, Burns suddenly achieved success. The first edition of his poems came out in the nearby town of Kilmarnock in 1786, and overnight Burns became famous. That he should achieve fame with this group of poems is only fitting, since it contained some of his best work: "The Holy Fair," "The Cotter's Saturday Night," and "Address to the Deil." In this volume, *Poems, Chiefly in the Scottish Dialect*, Burns expressed his love of simple folk and his hate of specious religion.

Owing to the success of this first edition, Burns went to Edinburgh, where he comported himself well and was applauded by the critics. He also had there another love affair, with a Mrs. M'Lehose; this was not a hearty country romance, but an artificial, rather conventional one. Burns had received only twenty pounds for the first edition of the Kilmarnock poems, but he got four hundred for the second edition in 1787. With this money he traveled, had the leisure in which to write, and was able to marry and buy property of his own. In 1788 he made Jean Armour, mother of his four children, his wife and settled down on a farm at Ellisland, near Dumfries. In the next year he was given a post as an excise officer, and in 1791 he moved to Dumfries, where he remained for the rest of his life.

The last years of Burns's life were spent in further writing, including the three hundred songs which he contributed to two collections of Scottish songs, Johnson's *Musical Museum* (1787–1797) and Thomson's *Select Collection of Original Scottish Airs* (1793–1805), and in a fevered defense of the French Revolution and its principles. This latter enthusiasm is evidence of another of his traits, for Burns was a social rebel, never accepting blindly the traditional order of things. In the matter of the revolution, however, his outspoken advocacy earned him only contempt from his fellow citizens. There is considerable doubt about the last five years of Burns's life. Some biographers picture it as a time of dissipation and increasing ill temper, while others paint Burns as a tired but respected member of society. Probably parts of both stories are true. But it is certain that he suffered from melancholy and fits of extreme depression during his last years. His health never having been completely restored after the rigors of his youth and having declined rapidly in his mature years, he died in Dumfries on July 21, 1796.

Burns led a far from happy life. He was always under the burden of poverty, and, although he was socially minded and always a social success, he saw too realistically the faults and weaknesses of his fellow man ever to enjoy complete happiness. His love affairs, too, often gave him pain, and in his poems about the women involved the reader can detect a note of sadness and regret. But his warm and often tender poetry has earned for him a high place among writers of his own time and has made him the national poet of Scotland. Burns was not a great original thinker; he owes much to Robert Fergusson and Allan Ramsay, both for content and style. But his absolute sincerity, his moral honesty and rough ethical code, and his power to supply telling and vivid poetic details place him high in the first ranks of romantic poets. Perhaps the one quality of Burns's verse that appeals most strongly to the reader is the prominent personal note. Burns was a poet for everyone. His little songs or longer poems all speak directly to the reader directly from Burns. In poetry, a type of writing which tends to be most exclusive, Burns was probably the most un-exclusive writer of all. For this reason he has been widely read and admired by people of all ages and from all parts of the world.

Bibliography

The basic edition for all Burns studies is the Library Edition of *The Life and Works of Robert Burns*, edited by Robert Chambers, 4 vols., 1856–1857, and revised by William Wallace, 1896. The standard edition of the *Poems* is that edited by William E. Henley and T. F. Henderson, 4 vols., 1896–1897. See also the *Works*, edited by W. S. Douglas, 6 vols., 1877–1879; the *Poetical Works*, edited by J. L. Robertson, Oxford Standard Authors Series, 1904; *Selected Poems of Robert Burns*, edited by John De Lancey Ferguson, 1926; *Robert Burns: The Poems*, edited by Charles S. Dougall, 1927; *Poems of Robert Burns*, edited by Lawrence Brander, World's Classics series, 1950; and *Poems and Songs*, edited by James Kinsley, 3 vols., 1968. Burns's letters are included in many of the editions of his works. The most reliable modern editions are the *Letters*, edited from original mss. by John De Lancey Ferguson, 2 vols., 1931, and *idem, Selected Letters*, World's Classics Series, 1953.

Many of the early biographies of Burns are inaccurate and biased. The standard biography is Franklyn B. Snyder, *The Life of Robert Burns*, 1932. See also Hans Hecht, *Robert Burns*, 1919 (trans., 1936); Catherine Carswell, *The Life of Robert Burns*, 1930; John De Lancey Ferguson, *Pride and Passion: Robert Burns*, 1939; David Daiches, *Robert Burns*, 1952; E. S. Rae, *Poet's Pilgrimage: A Study of the Life and Times of Robert Burns*, 1960; G. Ross Roy, *Robert Burns*, 1966; and Robert T. Fitzhugh, *Robert Burns: The Man and the Poet*, 1971. A useful brief critical study is David Daiches, *Robert Burns*, 1957.

POEMS, CHIEFLY IN THE SCOTTISH DIALECT

Type of work: Poetry
Author: Robert Burns (1759–1796)
First published: 1786

Essay-Review

Since the first publication of Burns's verse in the famous Kilmarnock edition entitled *Poems, Chiefly in the Scottish Dialect*, the poet's fame has increased and spread. Other editions of his work, containing later poems, only enhanced his reputation.

At least part of the reason for the continuing appreciation of Burns's verse is that the poet is essentially a transitional figure between the eighteenth century neoclassicists and the Romantics who were soon to follow. Possessing some of the qualities of each school, he exhibited few of the excesses of either. He occasionally used the couplet that had been made a skillful tool by Pope and his followers, but his spirit was closer to the Romantics in his attitude toward life and his art.

Although he occasionally displayed a mild conservatism, as in the early "The Cotter's Saturday Night," he was fundamentally a rebel—and rebellion was a basic trait of the Romantics. It would have been hard for Burns to be a true neoclassicist because his background, which figures constantly in his poems, simply did not suit him for this role. He had a hard early life and a close acquaintanceship with the common people and the common circumstances of life. He was certainly not the uneducated, "natural" genius that he is sometimes pictured—having had good instruction from his father and a tutor and having done considerable reading on his own—but he lacked the classical education that earlier poets thought necessary for the writing of true poetry.

Like the neoclassicists, however, he was skillful in taking the ideas and forms of earlier poets—in Burns's case, particularly, the Scottish poets Ramsay and Fergusson as well as the anonymous balladists and writers of folk songs—and treating them in his own individual way. Thus his verse has a wide variety of stanza forms and styles.

Despite the variety of his techniques, his basic outlook in his poems is remarkably consistent. This outlook also may have a great deal to do with his popularity. Perhaps more than any other poet since Chaucer, Burns possessed the personal insight and the instinct for human feelings that can make a poem speak to all men's hearts. Burns always saw the human aspect of things. His nature poetry, for instance, marks a departure from the precise appreciation of the eighteenth century poets; Burns's lines about nature treat it primarily as a setting in which people live.

The warmth of his verse arises from this attitude combined with the experience he had of being in close personal contact with the people about whom he wrote.

His writing never deals with subjects that he did not know intimately. Burns loved several women and claimed that they each served as great poetic inspiration. The reader may well believe this statement when he encounters the simple and clearly sincere little poems "Highland Mary," "Mary Morison," and the well-known song "Sweet Afton." It was this quality of sincerity that another great Scot, Thomas Carlyle, found to be Burns's greatest poetic value.

Burns was not an original thinker, but he had a few strong convictions about religion, human freedom, and morality. His condemnation of Calvinism and the hypocrisy it bred is accomplished with humor and yet with sharpness in two of his best poems, "The Holy Fair" and the posthumously published "Holy Willie's Prayer." In these and several other poems Burns pokes occasionally none too gentle fun at the professional religionists of his time without ever seeming didactic. Here his intensely personal viewpoint saved him from preaching in the style of earlier eighteenth century versifiers. It is to be expected that the few poems that contain examples of his rare attempts to be lofty are unsuccessful.

Having grown up in a humble environment, Burns was especially sensitive to social relations and the value of human freedom and the equality of men. On this subject, too, he is never didactic, but few readers have remained unmoved by the lines of probably his most famous poem in defense of the lower classes, "A Man's a Man for A' That":

> Is there, for honest poverty
>   That hings his head, an' a' that?
> The coward slave, we pass him by—
>   We dare be poor for a' that!
> For a' that and a' that,
>   Our toil's obscure and a' that;
> The rank is but the guinea's stamp,
>   The man's the gowd for a' that.
>
>   . . . . . .
>
> Then let us pray that come it may,
>   As come it will for a' that,
> That sense and worth, o'er a' the earth,
>   Shall bear the gree, an' a' that.
> For a' that, an' a' that,
>   It's coming yet for a' that,
> That man to man, the warld o'er,
>   Shall brithers be for a' that.

It was this powerful feeling for democracy that led Burns, in his later years, to a tactless advocation of the principles of the French Revolution, a crusade that did his career as a minor government official no good.

It is questionable whether Burns's heated protest against Calvinism and the strict morality it proclaimed was simply a rationalization of his own loose behavior. However many the romances he had, and however many the illegitimate children he fathered, there can be little doubt of Burns's sincere devotion, at least at the time, to the woman of his choice. In a larger sense, too, the poet's warm sympathy for his fellow man is evidence of a sort of ethical pattern in his life and work that is quite laudable.

The poetic techniques in Burns's poems are unquestionably a chief reason for his popularity. Few poets have so well suited the style to the subject, and his use of earlier stanza forms and several kinds of poetic diction has a sureness and an authority that are certain to charm even the learned student of poetry.

There are three types of diction in his poetry: Scottish dialect, pure English, and a combination of the two. In "Tam O' Shanter," a later work that is perhaps his masterpiece, Burns used dialect to tell an old legend of the supernatural with great effect. The modern reader who takes the trouble to master the dialectal terminology will be highly rewarded. In this, as in most of Burns's poems, the pace and rhythm of the lines are admirably well suited to the subject.

His use of the purely English idiom, as in "The Vision," was seldom so successful. Usually Burns wrote in pure English when he had some lofty purpose in mind, and with the exception of "The Cotter's Saturday Night" this combination was nearly fatal to the poetic quality of these poems.

For the general reader, probably the most enjoyable and rewarding reading consists of the poems and songs that Burns did in English, with occasional Scottish touches here and there in the lines. Most happy is this joining of language and dialect in such a poem as the famous little love lyric, "A Red, Red Rose." These three kinds of poetic diction can be found side by side in one of Burns's best poems, the highly patriotic "The Jolly Beggars," which gives as fine a picture of Scottish low life as can be found anywhere.

Naturally, Burns was most at home when he wrote in his native dialect; and, since one of the most striking characteristics of his verse is the effortless flow of conversational rhythms, it is not surprising that his better poems are those that came as natural effusions in his most familiar diction.

The total achievement of Burns is obviously great, but it should not be misunderstood. Burns lacked the precision and clarity of his predecessors in the eighteenth century, and he never was able to reach the exalted heights of poetic expression attained by Shelley and Keats not long after him. For vigor and the little touches that breathe life into lines of poetry, however, he was unexcelled by earlier or later poets.

The claim that Burns wrote careless verse has been perhaps too much emphasized. His poems and songs are surely not carefully carved jewels, but neither are they haphazard groupings of images and rhymes. The verses seem unlabored, but Burns worked patiently at them, and with considerable effort. That they seem to have been casual utterances is only further tribute to his ability.

It may be that the highest praise of all was paid to Burns, both as man and poet, by Keats when the great Romantic said that we can see in Burns's poems his whole life; and, though the life reflected was not an altogether happy one, the poet's love of freedom, people, and of life itself appears in nearly every line.

Bibliography

Tam O'Shanter

Campbell, Ian.   "Burns's Poems and Their Audience," in *Critical Essays on Robert Burns*. Edited by Donald A. Low. London: Routledge & Kegan Paul, 1975, pp. 42–46.

Crawford, Thomas.   *Burns: A Study of the Poems and Songs*. Stanford, Calif.: Stanford University Press, 1960, pp. 220–236, 358–361.

Daiches, David.   *Robert Burns*. New York: Macmillan, 1966, pp. 249–260.

Kinsley, James.   "A Note on *Tam O'Shanter*," in *English*. XX (1967), pp. 213–216.

Kroeber, Karl.   *Romantic Narrative Art*. Madison: University of Wisconsin Press, 1960, pp. 3–11.

Mackensie, M.L.   "A New Dimension for *Tam O'Shanter*," in *Studies in Scottish Literature*. I (1964), pp. 87–92.

MacLaine, Allan H.   "Burns's Use of Parody in *Tam O'Shanter*," in *Criticism*. I (Fall, 1959), pp. 308–316.

Morton, Richard.   "Narrative Irony in Robert Burns's *Tam O'Shanter*," in *Modern Language Quarterly*. XXII (1961), pp. 12–20.

Thomas, W.K.   "Burns' *Tam O'Shanter*, 57–58," in *Explicator*. XXVIII (1969), item 33.

Troutner, Jack.   "*Tam O'Shanter*'s Path of Glory: Tone in Robert Burns's Narrative," in *Massachusetts Studies in English*. I (1968), pp. 69–74.

Weston, John C.   "The Narrator of *Tam O'Shanter*," in *Studies in English Literature, 1500–1900*. VIII (1968), pp. 537–550.

White, Gertrude M.   "Don't Look Back: Something Might Be Gaining on You," in *Sewanee Review*. LXXXI (1973), pp. 870–874.

"To a Mouse"

Baird, John D.   "Two Poets of the 1780's: Burns and Cowper," in *Critical Essays on Robert Burns*. Edited by Donald A. Low. London: Routledge & Kegan Paul, 1975, pp. 116–117.

Brooks, Cleanth and Robert P. Heilman.   *Understanding Drama*. New York: Holt, 1945, pp. 19–22.

Bruce, George.   "Burns: A Comparative View," in *Robert Burns, New Judgments; Essays by Six Contemporary Writers*. Edited by William Montgomerie. Glasgow, Scotland: W. MacLellan, 1947, pp. 19–20.

Crawford, Thomas.   *Burns; A Study of the Poems and Songs*. Stanford, Calif.: Stanford University Press, 1960, pp. 164–168.

Daiches, David.   *Robert Burns*. New York: Macmillan, 1966, pp. 151–154.

Highet, Gilbert.   *Powers of Poetry*. New York: Oxford University Press, 1960, pp. 74–81.

GEORGE GORDON, LORD BYRON

Born: London, England (January 22, 1788)
Died: Missolonghi, Greece (April 19, 1824)

Principal Works

POEMS: *English Bards and Scotch Reviewers*, 1809; *Childe Harold's Pilgrimage*, 1812 (Cantos I and II); *The Giaour*, 1813; *The Bride of Abydos*, 1813; *The Corsair*, 1814; *Lara*, 1814; *Hebrew Melodies*, 1815; *The Siege of Corinth*, 1816; *Parisina*, 1816; *Childe Harold's Pilgrimage*, 1816 (Canto III); *The Prisoner of Chillon*, 1816; *Beppo*, 1818; *Childe Harold's Pilgrimage*, 1818 (Canto IV); *Don Juan*, 1819–1824; *The Vision of Judgment*, 1822; *The Island*, 1823.
PLAYS: *Manfred*, 1817; *Cain*, 1821; *Marino Faliero*, 1821; *Sardanapalus*, 1821; *The Two Foscari*, 1821; *Werner*, 1823; *Heaven and Earth*, 1824.

More than 150 years after his death the name of George Gordon, Lord Byron, can still evoke all that was poetic, dramatic, and scandalous about the Romantic Period. But instead of just one Byron, there seem to have been three (and perhaps more): Byron the Adventurer, Byron the Lover, Byron the Poet.

Adventurer he was, with exploits not confined to the drawing-room, and a revolutionist who fought not only with words but with a physical bravery that led to his death.

Born in London on January 22, 1788, Byron was the son of a spendthrift father and a mother whose alternating moods of affection and wild anger left him bewildered. His life was tempestuous from the beginning. Lame, handsome, and with a personality magnetic to both men and women, he embarked in 1809 on a trip to the Near East. His adventures included a shipwreck, a bout with fever, the swimming of the Hellespont, and the rescue of a girl who was about to be drowned. When he returned to England his first speech in the House of Lords was in defense of the working man—a radical start for a young lord. Later, when the scandal of his personal life broke over his head, he was advised not to appear in public, for fear the very sight of him might cause a riot. When he left England for his exile in Europe, friends had to protect his life with firearms.

In Italy, at Ravenna, Byron became again the adventurer. Probably joining the revolutionary Carbonari, he bought guns and ammunition for a revolt against Austrian tyranny. His death at Missolonghi, in Greece, on April 19, 1824, was the result of a fever caught while fighting against the Turks for Greek independence.

There was also Byron the Lover. "Mad, bad, and dangerous to know"—thus Lady Caroline Lamb summed up her first impression of him. Byron's love affairs started early, while he was a student at Harrow, and they continued through Cambridge and the period when he was a darling of London society. In 1814 he married Anne Isabella Milbanke, and his friends thought the match might calm the wild lord; it failed to do so. After the birth of his daughter Ada, he and Lady Byron separated; rumors spread over England, rumors of an incestuous relationship between Byron and his half-sister, Augusta Leigh. No public explanation of their separation was ever advanced by either Byron or his wife, and so the society that had idolized him now turned him, on the basis of rumor alone, into a monstrous villain. He virtually went into exile when he left England in 1816. In Venice, in 1818, Byron the Lover became Byron the Debauchee. Then he met the Countess Teresa Guiccioli, the beautiful young wife of an old man. His love for the Countess was no idle affair of a confirmed libertine. Byron followed her from Venice to Ravenna, from Pisa to Genoa. The arrangements for such a lovelife were complicated but in part regularized by Teresa's separation, by Papal decree, from her husband, but it seems characteristically Byronic that his one real love could never be completely his own. Yet he remained her faithful paramour until his death.

Out of these conflicting personalities there was enough left over for Byron the Poet, who remains, after the drama and the swashbuckling are stripped away, a truly major figure among the English Romantics. Certainly the early Byron who awoke to find himself famous was not then a great poet but a versifier who shocked and insulted. His first volume, *Hours of Idleness* (1807), came out while Byron was at Cambridge and the *Edinburgh Review* criticized it scathingly; Bryon retaliated with *English Bards and Scotch Reviewers*, equally as scathing. From his trip to the Near East he brought back the first two cantos of *Childe Harold's Pilgrimage*. They made him famous and extremely popular. Volume followed volume until he reached, in 1814, a peak of popularity with *The Corsair*, which sold 10,000 copies on the day of publication. To the second edition Byron added "Lines to a Lady Weeping," which disparaged the Prince Regent. This insult provoked a revolt against him. Next came the scandal in his personal life, and Byron went into the exile that turned him from a weak sensationalist into a great lyric and narrative poet.

On the site of the Battle of Waterloo he composed the famous stanza for a new canto of *Childe Harold*. In Venice (sandwiched between his notorious affairs) he wrote more cantos, and *Manfred*, and the beginning of *Don Juan*, the greatest of his narrative poems. Starting out like a slapstick bedroom farce, *Don Juan* slowly emerges as a beautiful romance between its protagonist and Haidée, a native girl. Along with his newfound poetic strength Byron kept his talent for invective: the dedication of *Don Juan* insults Robert Southey (then Poet Laureate), Coleridge, and Wordsworth, among others.

The charge has been brought that Byron is too topical, too stale for our time. Yet his *The Vision of Judgment*, one of his last works, makes history sound as fresh as a clipping from this morning's newspaper.

The poetry of Byron is as many-sided as the man himself. It ranges from gentle love lyrics like "She Walks in Beauty" and "When We Two Parted" to the pure narrative of "The Prisoner of Chillon" and the biting satire of *The Vision of*

Judgment. Byron might well be a product of our own times, so twentieth century in spirit are his love of athletics, his disillusionment, his laughing satire, his genuine spirit of revolt.

England refused this stormy Poet, Adventurer, and Lover a burial in Westminster Abbey; he lies in the family vault at Hucknall-Torkard Church, near Newstead. But time, which may wash away the muck of sensationalism from his life, will thereby more fully reveal the sparkling facets of his best verse.

Bibliography

The collected works of Byron comprise the *Poems*, edited by E. H. Coleridge, and the *Letters and Journals*, edited by R. E. Prothero, 13 vols., 1898–1904. Important among the volumes of selections are the *Poetical Works*, edited by Paul Elmer More, 1905, and *Don Juan and Other Satirical Poems*, edited by L. I. Bredvold, 1935.

The standard biography is Ethel C. Mayne, *Byron*, 2 vols., 1912, but this work must now be supplemented by Leslie A. Marchand, *Byron: A Biography*, 3 vols., 1957, a monumental and authoritative study incorporating the results of recent Byron scholarship. The best short work is *ibidem, Byron: A Portrait*, 1971. For biographical studies of Byron as presented by his contemporaries see Thomas Medwin, *Journal of the Conversations of Lord Byron*, 1824; Leigh Hunt, *Lord Byron and Some of His Contemporaries*, 1828; John Galt, *The Life of Lord Byron*, 1830; Thomas Moore, *The Life of Lord Byron with His Letters and Journals*, 1830; and Teresa Guiccioli, *My Recollections of Lord Byron*, 1869. Other studies include Richard Edgecombe, *Byron: The Last Phase*, 1909; Harold Nicolson, *Byron: The Last Journey, April 1823–April 1824*, 1924; Sir John C. Fox, *The Byron Mystery*, 1925; André Maurois, *Byron*, 1930; Peter Quennell, *The Years of Fame*, 1935; *idem, Byron in Italy*, 1941; and Iris Origo, *The Last Attachment: The Story of Byron and Teresa Guiccioli*, 1949; Doris Langley Moore, *The Late Lord Byron*, 1961; and Malcolm Elwin, *Lord Byron's Wife*, 1962. See also E. W. Marjarum, *Byron as Skeptic and Believer*, 1938; Elizabeth Boyd, *Byron's Don Juan*, 1945; Paul Trueblood, *The Flowering of Byron's Genius*, 1945; W. H. Marshall, *The Structure of Byron's Major Poems*, 1962; and Paul West, editor, *Byron: A Collection of Critical Essays*, 1963.

CAIN

Type of work: Drama
Author: George Gordon, Lord Byron (1788–1824)
Type of plot: Romantic tragedy
Time of plot: The period of Genesis
Locale: Outside Eden
First published: 1821

Byron, religiously unorthodox and bitterly critical of his society's mores, managed to adapt this Biblical tale to an expression of his own temperament. Cain's motivation in murdering his brother lies deep within his tortured soul, which lusts for a truth that is constantly denied. Byron's Cain is the eternal romantic rebel.

Principal Characters

Adam, the first man. He orders Cain to leave the family after the murder of Abel.

Eve, Adam's wife, the first woman. Because she was bitter at the expulsion from Eden, Cain blames her for his undying bitterness against God and death and claims this bitterness was transmitted to him before birth.

Cain, Adam's elder son. He refuses to pray because of the expulsion from Eden and is sullen at the loss of immortality. He hates work and doubts God's goodness. Tempted, he follows Lucifer and expresses a wish to remain in Hades. Jealous of his brother Abel, Cain strikes him a blow, killing him. Marked by an angel, Cain leaves his family. Destined to grow no living thing, he is a bitter man.

Abel, Cain's young brother and victim. He is a good man who worships God sincerely. He is killed for telling Cain that he loves God more than life.

Adah, Cain's wife. She tries to keep her husband from following Lucifer to Hades. When her husband is banished from the family, she accompanies him, taking their children. She is a faithful wife.

Zillah, Abel's wife, a good woman.

Lucifer, the fallen angel. He says he did not appear as a snake to tempt Eve. He exults that Cain shares his misery.

Enoch, the son of Cain and Adah.

The Story

While Adam, Eve, Abel, Zillah and Adah prayed to God, Cain stood sullenly by and complained that he had nothing to pray for, since he had lost immortality when Eve ate the fruit from the tree of knowledge. He could not understand why, if knowledge and life were good, his mother's deed had been a deadly sin. Abel, Adah, and Zillah urged him to cast off his melancholy and join them in tending the fields.

Alone, Cain deplored his worldly toil. Tired of the repetitious replies to all his questions, replies which refused to challenge God's will, he was no longer sure that God was good.

At the conception of this thought, Lucifer appeared to explain that Cain's mortality was only a bodily limit. He would live forever even after death. Cain, driven by instinct to cling to life, at the same time despised it. Lucifer admitted that he also was unhappy in spite of his immortality, which was a cursed thing in his fallen state. He launched into a bitter tirade against God, whom he described as a tyrant sitting alone in his misery, creating new worlds because his eternity was otherwise expressionless and boring to him. Lucifer exulted that his own condition was at least shared by others. These words echoed for Cain his own beliefs about the universe. Long had he pitied his relatives for toiling so hard for sustenance, as God had decreed when he had banished Adam and Eve from Eden.

Lucifer confessed that the beguiling snake had not been a disguise for himself; the snake was merely a snake. He predicted, however, that later generations of man would array the fall of Adam and Eve in a cloak of fable.

Cain then asked his mentor to reveal the nature of death, which held great terrors for Cain. Lucifer promised to teach Cain true knowledge if Cain would worship him. But Cain, having refused to worship even God, would not worship any being. His refusal was, according to Lucifer, in itself a form of worship.

Adah came to ask Cain to go with her, but he claimed that he must stay with Lucifer, who spoke like a god. She reminded Cain that the lying serpent, too, had spoken so. Lucifer insisted that the serpent had spoken truly when it had promised knowledge from the fruit of the forbidden tree; man's grief lay not in the serpent's so-called lie but in man's knowledge of evil. Lucifer said he would take Cain with him for an hour, time enough to show him the whole of life and death.

Traveling with Lucifer through the air, Cain, watching with ecstasy the beauty around him, insisted upon viewing the mystery of death, which was uppermost in his mind. The travelers came at last to a place where no stars glittered and all was dark and dreadful. As they entered Hades, Cain voiced again his hatred of death, the end of all living things.

In the underworld he saw beautiful and mighty shapes which, Lucifer explained, had inhabited the world and died by chaotic destruction in an age before Adam had been created. When Lucifer taunted Cain with his inferiority compared to those other beings of an earlier age, Cain declared himself ready to stay in Hades forever. Lucifer confessed, however, that he had no power to allow anyone to remain in Hades. When he pointed out to Cain that the spirits of the former inhabitants of the earth had enjoyed a beautiful world, Cain said that earth was still beautiful. His complaint was against man's toil for what the earth bore, his failure to obtain knowledge, and his unmitigated fear of death.

Cain, bewailing the trade man had made of death for knowledge, asserted that man knew nothing. Lucifer replied that death was a certainty and therefore truth and knowledge. Cain thought that he had learned nothing new from his journey, but Lucifer informed him that he had at least discovered that there was a state beyond his own.

They discussed Cain's relative state of happiness in life, which, Cain asserted, was dependent upon his love for his family. Lucifer hinted that Abel, favored by the others and by God, caused Cain some jealousy. Cain then asked his guide to show him where Lucifer lived, or else God's dwelling place. It was reserved for those who died, Lucifer claimed, to see either one or the other, not both.

As Lucifer prepared to return his pupil to earth, Cain complained that he had learned nothing. He had, Lucifer said, discovered that he was nothing. With a warning to distinguish between real good and evil, and to seek his own spiritual attachment, Lucifer transported the mortal back to earth.

Standing over their son Enoch, who was asleep under a tree, Adah and Cain discussed their ever-present sorrow: they must all die. When Adah said she would gladly die to save her parents, Cain agreed only if his own death might save everyone else. Adah prophesied that such a gift might some day be rendered. Seeing the pair of altars Abel had erected for a sacrifice, Cain uttered his first evil thought by muttering a denial that Abel was his brother.

Abel insisted that Cain share in the sacrificial rites he was about to perform. While Cain impiously stood by, Abel knelt in eloquent prayer. Cain's prayer was a defiant challenge to the omnipotent to show his preference for one of the altars. His own offerings were scattered to the earth, while Abel's sacrifice burned in high flames toward the heavens. In anger Cain attacked his brother's altar, and when Abel protested that he loved his God more than life, Cain struck him a mortal blow.

Adam, Eve, Adah, and Zillah, rushing to the scene of the murder, accused Cain of murdering his brother. Eve uttered loud imprecations against her guilty son. Adam ordered him to depart. Only Adah remained by his side. The Angel of the Lord then appeared to confront Cain and ask the whereabouts of his brother. The Angel predicted that henceforth Cain's hand would cultivate no growing things from the earth and that he should be a fugitive. Lest the man guilty of fratricide be the cause of another murder, the Angel branded Cain with a mark on his forehead, to warn the beholder that to kill Cain would engender a seven-fold vengeance. Cain blamed his evil deed upon Eve, who bore him too soon after her banishment from Eden, when her own mind was still bitter over the lost paradise.

Adah offered to share her husband's fate. Carrying their children with them, she and Cain traveled eastward from Eden.

Critical Evaluation

Byron suffered from excessive guilt over a sin he never clearly identified in any of his works or letters. But biographers are almost in universal agreement that the sin was incest with his half sister, Augusta. Whether this sin, or the many others he indulged in as a student and continental traveler, is the shaping force in his poetry is largely a matter of conjecture. Nevertheless, from his early melodramatic verse tales such as *The Giaour* (1813) to his later dramatic poems, *Manfred* (1817) and *Cain,* the protagonist is always haunted by a sense of his corruption and at the same time sustained by strong feelings of individual power, uniqueness, and worth.

In *Manfred,* for example, the hero dies refusing to acknowledge the power of Death over his soul. Although suffering from remorse, Manfred cannot accept any jurisdiction over his soul other than the judgment of his own mind. *Cain* begins by establishing the protagonist's anger, his indignation at the injustice of his fate. Why should his mother Eve's eating of the forbidden fruit have cost him his immortality? Cain's complaint has the same urgency and authority that animated the political and social revolutions of Byron's time. Why should the forms of the past dictate the possibilities of the future? What distinguishes *Cain* from Byron's other works on the remorseful hero is that whereas in the others the hero's individual sense of power compensates him for the self-loathing of his guilt, in *Cain* the protagonist discovers his uniqueness through the help of Lucifer and then plunges into the action—the killing of his brother—which stamps him with everlasting guilt.

Byron could not separate man's genius from his propensity toward evil. Like Blake, Byron understood the misplaced energy in so much of man's misguided actions. To adapt a phrase of Blake, Byron "was of the devil's party *with* knowing it." But he lacked a mystical vision like Blake's to explain the paradox of his own sensibility. It was Byron's fate, like Cain's, to live a life of exile, literally and spiritually.

Bibliography

Blackstone, Bernard. *Byron: A Survey.* London: Longmans, 1975, pp. 244–250.

Bostetter, Edward E. *The Romantic Ventriloquists: Wordsworth, Coleridge, Keats, Shelley, Byron.* Seattle: University of Washington Press, 1963, pp. 282–292.

Calvert, William J. *Byron: Romantic Paradox.* New York: Russell and Russell, 1962, pp. 174–196.

Chew, Samuel C., Jr. *The Dramas of Lord Byron: A Critical Study.* New York: Russell and Russell, 1964, pp. 118–134.

Cooke, Michael G. *The Blind Man Traces the Circle: On the Patterns and Philosophy of Byron's Poetry.* Princeton, N.J.: Princeton University Press, 1969, pp. 74–81.

Elledge, W. Paul. *Byron and the Dynamics of Metaphor.* Nashville, Tenn.: Vanderbilt University Press, 1968, pp. 139–151.

Gleckner, R.F. *Byron and the Ruins of Paradise.* Baltimore: Johns Hopkins University Press, 1967, pp. 323–327.

Joseph, M.K. *Byron the Poet.* London: Victor Gollancz, 1964, pp. 116–130.

Jump, John D. *Byron.* London: Routledge and Kegan Paul, 1972, pp. 166–182.

McGann, J.J. *Fiery Dust: Byron's Poetic Development.* Chicago: University of Chicago Press, 1968, pp. 245–273.

Marchand, Leslie A. *Byron's Poetry: A Critical Introduction.* Boston: Houghton Mifflin, 1965, pp. 84–91.

Marshall, William H. *The Structure of Byron's Major Poems.* Philadelphia: University of Pennsylvania Press, 1962, pp. 136–154.

Michaels, Leonard. "Byron's *Cain*," in *PMLA.* LXXXIV (January, 1969), pp. 71–78.

Thorslev, P.L. *The Byronic Hero: Types and Prototypes.* Minneapolis: University of Minnesota Press, 1962, pp. 176–184.

Trueblood, Paul G. *Lord Byron.* New York: Twayne, 1969, pp. 109–111.

CHILDE HAROLD'S PILGRIMAGE

Type of work: Poem
Author: George Gordon, Lord Byron (1788–1824)
First published: Cantos I and II, 1812, Canto III, 1816; Canto IV, 1818

Essay-Review

Childe Harold's Pilgrimage is the poem which brought instant fame and notoriety to its author. In Byron's often quoted phrase: "I awoke one morning and found myself famous." The reasons why the virtually unknown poet should suddenly take the world by storm with this poem are obvious. It is a travel poem written at a time when the English were eager for travel literature. It is about places of interest to the English, especially Portugal and Spain. Further, the poem is sinewed and enriched by the character of the traveler, the Byronic hero who is dark and melancholy, haughty, diffident, jaded, introspective, wicked, and successful.

The first two Cantos were begun in 1809, when Byron was actually traveling through the countries described: Portugal, Spain, the Mediterranean, Constantinople, Albania, Asia Minor, Troas, and Greece. The term "Childe" for the designation of the hero, Byron says in the Preface to the first two Cantos, was used in accordance with the old structure of versification; it is used in the medieval sense of a young noble who is waiting to be knighted. The poem, a so-called Romaunt, that is, a romance or narrative of adventure, runs to 156 Spenserian stanzas. This particular stanzaic form was chosen, Byron said, because, traditionally, it admits of all kinds of variation.

The first two Cantos cover the author's journey through Portugal, Spain, the Ionian Isles, Albania, and Greece. In the Preface Byron insists that the poem is not autobiographical and that "Childe Harold" should not be misinterpreted as a person for the writer. He kept up this pretense through the publication of the third Canto, but in the fourth Canto Byron dropped his pretense and spoke out in his own person. That the poem was autobiographical from the first is demonstrated by the fact that in the manuscript version of Cantos I and II Byron called his hero "Childe Burun," which was the early form of his own name.

The first two Cantos are well directed and tightly controlled. The general tone of the poem and the stance of the Byronic hero is set at the very beginning. In an "Addition to the Preface" Byron apologizes for his hero by saying that he is in effect no worse than the knights of old, Sir Tristram and Sir Lancelot, for example, who surely were no better than they should have been. Therefore his hero is not to be censured for his character. This character is sketched in, beginning with the second stanza. Byron begins by saying that this Childe once lived in Albion's isle and did not take delight in virtue, but passed his days in dissipation, especially at night, and delighted in evil company and loose women. He sinned widely without atonement, and therefore fortunate was the virtuous girl who escaped his wicked influence.

Then, sick at heart, jaded, Harold sails from England and his father's house, where, although he had reveled with many acquaintances, he had not been loved by any of them. His antifeminist pose is reiterated, for the women he had enjoyed were dissolute and vain. Therefore, revolting from this dissolute life, or tired of it, Harold, that is, Byron, departs without remorse to visit other lands:

> And now Childe Harold was sore sick at heart,
> And from his fellow bacchanals would flee;
> 'Tis said, at times the sullen tear would start,
> But Pride congealed the drop within his ee:
> Apart he stalked in joyless reverie,
> And from his native land resolved to go,
> And visit scorching climes beyond the sea;
> With pleasure drugged, he almost longed for woe,
> And e'en for change of scene would seek the shades below.

His first stop is Portugal, a lovely land to him. Almost immediately his travels have a therapeutic effect. His melancholy pose is kept up by constant restatement of his troubles and his need for a cure. As he gazes on beautiful Portugal, he broods on his misspent youth and realizes that there is more to life than the ease of his early years.

In addition to the pose of the Byron hero that permeates the poem, there is another strain that constantly energizes it: Byron's real zeal for liberty. Throughout his life he had a genuine dedication to the freedom of both individuals and nations. In his own words: "There are but two sentiments to which I am constant—a strong love of liberty, and a detestation of cant." This strong love of liberty is immediately manifest in Spain, the second land Childe Harold visits, a romantic land teeming with songs, pregnant with glorious tale. Harold addresses himself to the proud Spain of yesteryear and to the liberty she then enjoyed.

From Spain he travels to Greece and Albania. A considerable amount of interest is maintained in these later sections by Byron's stirring up of classical memories. Here, for example, he sails past the spot where "sad Penelope" waited for the return of her husband, Ulysses, and where "dark Sappho" wrote. In writing of Greece, he addresses himself further to liberty. His feeling for the freedom of Greece was so genuine and so intense that he finally gave up literature for revolution. At his own expense he organized an expedition to help free the Greeks from the Turks, and in the town of Missolonghi, after an excellent display of military skill and leadership, he grew sick of fever and died just after his thirty-sixth birthday.

Canto III is generally felt to be superior to the other three. It begins with an affirmation of the Byronic pose. The hero is driven by fate to continue his travels. He is a weed washed by the seas of life whenever the waves of the ocean roll. He is the "wandering outlaw of his own dark mind," and he has grown old in this woeful world. One of the major characteristics of the third Canto is the poet's romantic love of nature, which sounds amazingly Wordsworthian. Byron had always maintained that he detested all the Romantic poets except Shelley. Shelley, however, had read Wordsworth aloud to Byron and had changed his mind about this poet. Consequently, there are beautiful passages in this Canto that sound Wordsworthian.

Historical associations are maintained in this Canto. Byron visits Waterloo, a battle which constituted a victory for the opponents of liberalism:

> And Harold stands upon this place of skulls,
> The grave of France, the deadly Waterloo!
> How in an hour the power which gave annuls
> Its gifts, transferring fame as fleeting too!
> In "pride of place" here last the eagle flew,
> Then tore with bloody talon the rent plain,
> Pierced by the shaft of banded nations through;
> Ambition's life and labors all were vain;
> He wears the shattered links of the world's broken chain.

The poet wonders if the earth is more free after Napoleon's fall, a lesson for all tyrants; he hopes that the answer is in the affirmative. In this Canto he continues his travels, going next to the Rhine, to the Alps, and to the Jura.

Canto IV, the longest of the four, was written eight years after the first. In it Byron abandons his pose of distinguishing between himself and Childe Harold; as he admits in a preface dedicated to John Hobhouse, with whom he had begun his European travels in 1809, the public refused to accept his statement that he was not writing autobiography but was fictionalizing a character. Byron says in this dedication that in this last Canto he had wanted to write on Italian literature and manners but could not do so under his former disguise. Therefore he had abandoned it.

Byron's comments on Italian literature constitute one of the major interests in this Canto. Venice, the first city visited, is still a beautiful place, though Tasso's echoes are no longer heard. The mountain village of Arqua sepulchers the bones of Petrarch, where he lived during his later years. Tasso is the glory of Ferrara. Dante sleeps far from "ungrateful Florence." Rome is haunted by the ghosts of her great men, stretching historically from the Scipios to Rienzi. But even more, Byron is moved by the romantic aspects of nature:

> There is a pleasure in the pathless woods,
> There is a rapture on the lonely shore,
> There is society where none intrudes,
> By the deep sea, and music in its roar:
> I love not Man the less, but Nature more,
> From these our interviews, in which I steal
> From all I may be, or have been before,
> To mingle with the Universe, and feel
> What I can ne'er express, yet can not all conceal.

The poem ends as it began, with the pose of the Byronic hero. He is weary of travel, jaded and wasted. He has written what he had to write. He wishes he could have done better, but he could not. With an irony that must have pleased him, he says that the pain of the travels of the Pilgrim must be his, but the moral should be the reader's:

> Farewell! a work that must be, and hath been—
> A sound which makes us linger—yet—farewell!
> Ye! who have traced the Pilgrim to the scene
> Which is his last, if in your memories dwell
> A thought which once was his, if on ye swell
> A single recollection, not in vain
> He wore his sandal shoon and scallop shell;
> Farewell! with *him* alone may rest the pain,
> If such there were—with *you*, the moral of his strain!

Childe Harold's Pilgrimage is today a work of more than mere historical interest, more than one of the most characteristic books of the Romantic movement or important for its characterization of the Byronic hero. It is the revelation of one of the most whimsical, paradoxical, and gifted minds of the nineteenth century, and as such the poem remains stimulating and fascinating.

Bibliography

Berry, Francis.   "The Poet of *Childe Harold*," in *Byron: A Symposium*. Edited by John D. Jump. New York: Barnes & Noble, 1975, pp. 35–51.

Blackstone, Bernard.   *Byron: A Survey*. London: Longmans, 1975, pp. 79–105, 184–230.

Bostetter, Edward E.   *The Romantic Ventriloquists: Wordsworth, Coleridge, Keats, Shelley, Byron*. Seattle: University of Washington Press, 1963, pp. 271–277.

Calvert, William J.   *Byron: Romantic Paradox*. New York: Russell and Russell, 1962, pp. 111–113, 144–151.

Chew, Samuel C.   "Introduction," in *Childe Harold's Pilgrimage and Other Romantic Poems*. New York: Odyssey, 1936, pp. ix–xxxiv.

Cooke, Michael G.   *The Blind Man Traces the Circle: On the Patterns and Philosophy of Byron's Poetry*. Princeton, N.J.: Princeton University Press, 1969, pp. 38–60, 122–126.

————.   *The Romantic Will*. New Haven, Conn.: Yale University Press, 1976, pp. 216–222.

Elledge, W. Paul.   *Byron and the Dynamics of Metaphor*. Nashville, Tenn.: Vanderbilt University Press, 1968, pp. 54–81.

Gleckner, R.F.   *Byron and the Ruins of Paradise*. Baltimore: Johns Hopkins University Press, 1967, pp. 53–90, 225–250, 271–297.

Joseph, M.K.   *Byron the Poet*. London: Victor Gollancz, 1964, pp. 13–102.

Jump, John D.   *Byron*. London: Routledge and Kegan Paul, 1972, pp. 75–84.

McGann, J.J.   *Fiery Dust: Byron's Poetic Development*. Chicago: University of Chicago Press, 1968, pp. 31–138, 301–318.

Marchand, Leslie A.   *Byron's Poetry: A Critical Introduction*. Boston: Houghton Mifflin, 1965, pp. 38–59.

Marshall, William H.   *The Structure of Byron's Major Poems*. Philadelphia: University of Pennsylvania Press, 1962, pp. 36–39, 72–81.

Rutherford, Andrew.   *Byron: A Critical Study*. London: Oliver and Boyd, 1962, pp. 26–35, 48–65, 93–102.

Thorslev, P.L.   *The Byronic Hero: Types and Prototypes*. Minneapolis: University of Minnesota Press, 1962, pp. 127–145.

Trueblood, Paul G.   *Lord Byron*. New York: Twayne, 1969, pp. 46–53, 76–80, 85–90.

DON JUAN

Type of work: Poem
Author: George Gordon, Lord Byron (1788–1824)
Type of plot: Social satire
Time of plot: Late eighteenth century
Locale: Spain, Turkey, Russia, England
First published: By Cantos, 1819–1824

This unfinished epic satire is written in ottava rima *and contains 16,000 lines in its sixteen cantos. Rather than following the epic tradition, the poem becomes a vehicle for digression on any subject; Byron, through his hero, gives his views on wealth, power, society, chastity, poets, diplomats, and England. For this reason the poem holds a high place among literary satires.*

Principal Characters

Don Juan, the young son of Donna Inez and Don José, a hidalgo of Seville. He is a handsome, mischief-making boy whose education, after his father's death, is carefully supervised by his mother, who insists that he read only classics expurgated in the text but with all the obscenities collected in an appendix. He is allowed to associate only with old or ugly women. At the age of sixteen he learns the art of love from Donna Julia, a young matron. The ensuing scandal causes Donna Inez to send her son to Cadiz, there to take ship for a trip abroad. The vessel on which he is a passenger sinks after a storm; he experiences a romantic interlude with the daughter of a Greek pirate and slave trader; he is sold to the Turks; he takes part in the siege of Ismail, a Turkish fort on the Danube River; he becomes the favorite of the Empress Catherine of Russia; and he is sent on a diplomatic mission to England, where he becomes a critical observer of English society.

Donna Inez, Don Juan's mother, a domineering and short-sighted woman who first tries to protect her son from the facts of life but later rejoices in his good fortune and advancement when he becomes the favorite of Empress Catherine of Russia.

Don José, Don Juan's father, a gallant man often unfaithful to his wife, with whom he quarrels constantly. He dies while his son is still a small boy.

Donna Julia, Don Juan's first love, a woman of twenty-three married to a fifty-year-old husband, Don Alfonso. She is forced to enter a convent after her irate husband discovers his wife and her young lover in her bedchamber. In a long letter, written on the eve of Don Juan's departure from Spain, she professes her undying love for him.

Don Alfonso, the cuckold husband who discovers Don Juan hiding in a closet in his wife's bedroom.

Haidée, the second love of Don Juan. A tall, lovely child of nature and passion, she finds him unconscious on the seashore following the sinking of the ship on which he had sailed from Spain. Filled with love and sympathy, she hides and protects him. This idyllic island romance ends when Lambro, her pirate father, returns from one of his expeditions and finds the two sleeping together after a great feast which Lambro has watched from a distance. Don Juan, wounded in a scuffle with Lambro's men, is bound and put aboard one of the pirate's ships. Shortly afterward Haidée dies lamenting her vanished lover, and his child dies with her.

Lambro, Haidée's father, "the mildest-manner'd man that ever scuttled ship or cut a throat." Returning from one of his piratical expeditions, he surprises the young lovers and sends Don Juan, wounded in a fight with Lambro's men, away on a slave ship. Later he regrets his hasty action when he watches his only child die of illness and grief.

Gulbeyaz, the Sultana of Turkey. Having seen Don Juan in the slave market where he is offered for sale, along with an Italian opera troupe sold into captivity by their disgusted impresario, she orders one of the palace eunuchs to buy the young man. She has him taken to the palace and dressed in women's clothes. Even though she brings her strongest weapon, her tears, to bear, she is unable to make Don Juan her lover.

The Sultan of Turkey, the father of fifty daughters and four dozen sons. Seeing the disguised Don Juan in his wife's apartments, he orders the supposed female slave to be taken to the palace harem.

Baba, the African eunuch who buys Don Juan at the Sultana's command. He later flees with Don Juan and John Johnson from Constantinople.

Lolah,
Katinka, and
Dudú, three girls in the Sultan's harem. Dudú, lovely and languishing, has the disguised Don Juan for her bed fellow. Late in the night she awakes screaming after a dream in which she reached for a golden apple and was stung by a bee. The next morning jealous Gulbeyaz orders Dudú and Don Juan executed, but they escape in the company of Johnson and Baba.

John Johnson, a worldly Englishman fighting with the Russians in the war against the Turks. Captured, he is bought in the slave market along with Don Juan. The two escape and make their way to the Turkish lines before Ismail. Johnson is recognized by General Suwarrow, who welcomes him and Don Juan as allies in the attack on Ismail.

Leila, a ten-year-old Moslem girl whose life Don Juan saves during the capture of Ismail. He becomes her protector.

General Suwarrow (Souvaroff), the leader of the Russian forces at the siege and taking of Ismail.

Catherine, Empress of Russia, to whose court Don Juan is sent with news of the Turkish victory at Ismail. Voluptuous and rapacious in love, she receives the young man with great favor and he becomes her favorite. After he becomes ill she reluctantly decides to send him on a diplomatic mission to England.

Lord Henry Amundeville, an English politician and the owner of Norman Abbey. Don Juan meets the nobleman in London and the two become friends.

Lady Adeline Amundeville, his wife, who also becomes Don Juan's friend and mentor. She advises him to marry because she is afraid that he will become seriously involved with the notorious Duchess of Fitz-Fulke. During a house party at Norman Abbey she sings a song telling of the Black Friar, a ghost often seen wandering the halls of the Abbey.

The Duchess of Fitz-Fulke, a woman of fashion notorious for her amorous intrigues. She pursues Don Juan after his arrival in England and finally, disguised as the ghostly Black Friar of Norman Abbey, succeeds in making him her lover.

Miss Aurora Raby, a young Englishwoman with whom Don Juan contemplates matrimony. Although she seems completely unimpressed by his attentions, he is piqued by her lack of interest.

Pedrillo, Don Juan's tutor. When the ship on which he and his master sail from Cadiz sinks after a storm, they are among those set adrift in a longboat. When the food runs out, the unlucky pedagogue is eaten by his famished companions. Although Don Juan considers the man an ass, he is unable to help eat the hapless fellow.

Zoe, Haidée's maid.

Lady Pinchbeck, a woman of fashion who, after Don Juan's arrival in London, takes Leila under her protection.

The Story

When Don Juan was a small boy, his father died, leaving the boy in the care of his mother, Donna Inez. Donna Inez was a righteous woman who had made her husband's life miserable. She had her son tutored in the arts of fencing, riding, and shooting, and she herself attempted to rear him in a moral manner. But even though young Don Juan read widely in the sermons and lives of the saints, he did not seem to absorb from his studies the qualities his mother thought essential.

At sixteen, he was a handsome lad much admired by his mother's friends. Donna Julia, in particular, often looked pensively at the youth. Donna Julia was just twenty-three and married to a man of fifty. Although she loved her husband, or so she told herself, she thought often of young Don Juan. One day, finding herself alone with him, she gave herself to the young man.

The young lovers spent long hours together during the summer, and it was not until November that Don Alfonso, her husband, discovered their intrigue. When Don Alfonso found Don Juan in his wife's bedroom, he tried to throttle him. But Don Juan overcame Don Alfonso and fled, first to his mother's home for clothes and money. Then Donna Inez sent him to Cadiz, there to begin a tour of Europe. The good lady prayed that the trip would mend his morals.

Before his ship reached Leghorn a storm broke it apart. Don Juan spent many days in a lifeboat without food or water. At last the boat was washed ashore, and Don Juan fell exhausted on the beach and slept. When he awoke, he saw bending over him a beautiful girl who told him that she was called Haidée and that she was the daughter of the ruler of the island, one of the Cyclades. Her father, Lambro, was a pirate, dealing in jewels and slaves. Because she knew her father would sell Don Juan to the first trader who came by, Haidée hid Don Juan in a cove and sent her maids to wait on him.

When Lambro left on another expedition, Haidée took Don Juan from the cave and they roamed together over the island. Haidée heaped jewels and fine foods and wines on Don Juan, for he was the first man she had ever known except her father and her servants. Although Don Juan still tried to think of Donna Julia, he could not resist Haidée. A child of nature and passion, she gave herself to him with complete freedom. Again Don Juan lived an idyllic existence, until Haidée's father returned unexpectedly. Don Juan again fought gallantly, but at last he was overcome by the old man's servants and put aboard a slave ship bound for a distant market. He never saw Haidée again, and he never knew that she died giving birth to his child.

The slave ship took Don Juan to a Turkish market, where he and another prisoner were purchased by a Negro eunuch and taken to the palace of a sultan. There Don Juan was made to dress as a dancing maiden and present himself to the sultana, the fourth and favorite wife of the sultan. She had passed by the slave market and had seen Don Juan and wanted him for a lover. In order to conceal his sex from the sultan, she forced the disguise on Don Juan. But even at the threat of death, Don Juan would not become her lover, for he still yearned for Haidée. Perhaps his constancy might have wavered, if the sultana had not been an infidel, for she was young and beautiful.

Eventually Don Juan escaped from the palace and joined the army of Catherine of Russia. The Russians were at war with the sultan from whose palace Don Juan had fled. Don Juan was such a valiant soldier that he was sent to St. Petersburg, to carry the news of a Russian victory to Empress Catherine. Catherine also cast longing eyes on the handsome stranger, and her approval soon made Don Juan the toast of her capital.

In the midst of his luxury and good fortune, Don Juan grew ill. Hoping that a change of climate would help her favorite, Catherine resolved to send him on a mission to England. When he reached London he was well received, for he was a polished young man, well versed in fashionable etiquette. His mornings were spent in business, but his afternoons and evenings were devoted to lavish entertainment. He conducted himself with such decorum, however, that he was much sought after by proper young ladies and much advised by older ones. Lady Adeline Amundeville, made him her protégé, and advised him freely on affairs of the heart. Another, the Duchess of Fitz-Fulke, advised him too, but her suggestions were of a more personal nature and seemed to demand a secluded spot where there was no danger from intruders. Because of the Duchess of Fitz-Fulke's attentions to Don Juan, Lady Adeline began to talk to him about selecting a bride from the chaste and suitable young ladies attentive to him.

Don Juan thought of marriage, but his interest was stirred by a girl not on Lady Adeline's list. Aurora Raby was a plain young lady, prim, dull, and seemingly unaware of Don Juan's presence. Her lack of interest served to spur him on to greater efforts, but a smile was his only reward from the cold maiden.

His attention was diverted from Aurora Raby by the appearance of the ghost of Black Friar, who had once lived in the house of Lady Adeline, where Don Juan was a guest. The ghost was a legendary figure reported to appear before births, deaths, or marriages. To Don Juan, the ghost was an evil omen, and he could not laugh off the tightness about his heart. Lady Adeline and her husband seemed to consider the ghost a great joke. Aurora Raby appeared to be a little sympathetic with Don Juan, but the Duchess of Fitz-Fulke merely laughed at his discomfiture.

The second time the ghost appeared, Don Juan followed it out of the house and into the garden. It seemed to float before him, always just out of his reach. Once he thought he had grasped it, but his fingers touched only a cold wall. Then he seized it firmly and found that the ghost had a sweet breath and full, red lips. When the monk's cowl fell back, the Duchess of Fitz-Fulke was revealed.

On the morning after, Don Juan appeared at breakfast, wan and tired. Whether he had overcome more than the ghost, no one will ever know. The duchess, too, came down, seeming to have the air of one who had been rebuked. . . .

Critical Evaluation

Don Juan, an "epic" poem written in *ottava rima,* is permeated throughout with Byronic philosophy. Its episodic plot, narrated in first person by its author, tells the story of young Juan, who, victimized by a narrow-minded and hypocritical mother, an illogical educational system, and his own fallible humanity, loses his innocence and faith and becomes disillusioned with man and his institutions. The poem's rambling style allows for Byron's numerous digressions, in which he satirizes many aspects of English life: English government and its officials, religion and its confusions and hypocracies, society and its foibles, war and its irrationality, woman and her treachery, man and his inhumanity to his fellows. Even English poets feel the fire of Byron's wrath. Thus Byron has been accused of a completely negative view in *Don Juan*— anti-everything and pro-nothing. And though it is true that to Byron all is relative because there can be no absolutes in a world without reason, sanity, or justice and where the precepts of Christianity are so contradictory that they offer no panacea for life's problems, the philosophy of *Don Juan* is not wholly pessimistic. Admittedly, the undertone, especially in the digressions, is often sardonic; yet the overtone, created by a flippant refusal to take Juan's story (or life) too seriously and by extensive use of exaggerated feminine rhyme, such as "intellectual" and "hen-peck'd you all," is essentially comic. Thus the zest and the laughter in *Don Juan* belie the idea of total despair and lend an affirmation of life despite its ironies; the lapses into lyricism reveal a heart that sings despite the poet's attempt to stifle emotion with sophistication.

In *Don Juan,* Byron's philosophical confusion seems to be caused by his natural affinity for a Platonic, idealistic view, which has been crushed under the weight of a realism he is too honest and too perceptive to ignore. Though he denies that he discusses metaphysics, he comments that nothing is stable or permanent; all is mutable and subject to violent destruction. Yet Byron, in calling the world a "glorious blunder," is not totally blind to its temporary beauties. During the Juan-Haidée romance, the lovers live in an Edenic world of beautiful sunsets and warm, protective caves. Still, Juan's foreboding and Haidée's dream are reminders that nature's dangers always lurk behind its façade of beauty. And even Haidée, "Nature's bride," pursued pleasure and passion only to be reminded that "the wages of sin is death."

Byron's view of the nature of man is closely akin to his complex view of natural objects. Man has his moments of glory, integrity, and unselfishness. For example, Juan, the novice, does not flee from the horror of battle; he shuns cannibalism even though he is starving; he refuses to be forced to love the sultana; he risks his life to save young Leila. Often Byron emphasizes man's freedom of mind and spirit. Yet he believes that man's self-deceit is the chief factor in his decadence; his false ideas of glory lead to bloodshed. Ironically, Surrow lectures his soldiers on "the noble art of killing"; man kills because "it brings self-approbation." In fact, Byron suggests that man is more destructive than nature or God. Still, he does not condemn man; some taint at the heart of nature and of man turns "simple instinct and passion" to guilt; besides, society's corruption in turn corrupts man. Lord Henry as the elder sophisticate is perhaps the best example of man's inability to retain his innocence; caught in the trap of his own greed and hypocrisy and of society's political game, Lord Henry finds that he cannot turn back, even though "the fatigue was greater than the profit." Byron also strikes out against political corruption. He had strong hopes for England's budding liberalism: a "king in constitutional procession" had offered great promise in leading the world to political freedom and morality. Yet Byron boldly declares England's failure to fulfill this promise.

Byron does, however, offer positive values in *Don Juan*. He believes that momentary happiness and glory and love *are* worth living for. Although "A day of gold from out an age of iron/ Is all that life allows the luckiest sinner," it is better than nothing. Man must fight, though he knows that he can never redeem the world and that defeat and death are certain. Since hypocrisy is one of the worst sins, man should be sincere. To Byron, the creative act is especially important, for it is man's only chance to transcend his mortality.

Throughout *Don Juan,* then, one follows man through his hapless struggle with life. Born in a fallen state, educated to hypocrisy and impracticality, cast out into a world of false values and boredom, man follows the downward path to total disillusionment. He learns, however, to protect himself from pain by insulating himself with the charred shell of burned-out passion and crushed ideals. Blindly, he stumbles toward that unknown and unknowable end— death. Yet he goes not humbly but defiantly, not grimly but with gusto.

Therefore, Byron's philosophy, despite its harshness, is one which embraces life, seeking to intensify and electrify each fleeting, irrevocable moment. It is a philosophy of tangibles, though they are inadequate; of action, though it will not cure man's ills; of honesty, though it must recognize man in his fallen state. And, though death is inevitable and no afterlife is promised, Byron maintains his comic perspective: "Carpe diem, Juan, . . . play out the play."

Bibliography

Blackstone, Bernard. *Byron: A Survey.* London: Longmans, 1975, pp. 287–344.

Bostetter, Edward E. *The Romantic Ventriloquists: Wordsworth, Coleridge, Keats, Shelley, Byron.* Seattle: University of Washington Press, 1963, pp. 241–253.

Boyd, Elizabeth F. *Byron's* Don Juan: *A Critical Study.* New Brunswick, N.J.: Rutgers University Press, 1945. Partially reprinted in *Twentieth Century Interpretations of* Don Juan: *A Collection of Critical Essays.* Edited by Edward E. Bostetter. Englewood Cliffs, N.J.: Prentice-Hall, 1969, pp. 98–99.

Bredvold, Louis I. "Introductory Essay," in *Lord Byron: Don Juan and Other Satirical Poems.* New York: Odyssey Press, 1935, pp. v–xxxv.

Calvert, William J. *Byron: Romantic Paradox.* New York: Russell and Russell, 1962, pp. 182–210. Reprinted in *Byron*: Childe Harold's Pilgrimage *and* Don Juan—*A Casebook.* Edited by John D. Jump. London: Macmillan, 1973, pp. 111–131.

Cooke, Michael G. *The Blind Man Traces the Circle: On the Patterns and Philosophy of Byron's Poetry.* Princeton, N.J.: Princeton University Press, 1969, pp. 128–174.

Gardner, Helen. "Don Juan," in *London Magazine.* V (July, 1958), pp. 58–65. Reprinted in *Byron: A Collection of Critical Essays.* Edited by Paul West. Englewood Cliffs, N.J.: Prentice-Hall, 1963, pp. 113–121. Also reprinted in *English Romantic Poets: Modern Essays in Criticism.* Edited by M.H. Abrams. New York: Oxford University Press, 1975, pp. 303–312.

Gleckner, R.F. *Byron and the Ruins of Paradise.* Baltimore: Johns Hopkins University Press, 1967, pp. 329–347. Reprinted in *Twentieth Century Interpretations of* Don Juan: *A Collection of Critical Essays.* Edited by Edward E. Bostetter. Englewood Cliffs, N.J.: Prentice-Hall, 1969, pp. 109–112.

Hirsch, E.D., Jr. "Byron and the Terrestrial Paradise," in *From Sensibility to Romanticism.* New York: Oxford University Press, 1965, pp. 467–486. Reprinted in *Twentieth Century Interpretations of* Don Juan: *A Collection of Critical Essays.* Edited by Edward E. Bostetter. Englewood Cliffs, N.J.: Prentice-Hall, 1969, pp. 106–108.

Joseph, M.K. *Byron the Poet.* London: Victor Gollancz, 1964, pp. 149–333. Partially reprinted in *Twentieth Century Interpretations of* Don Juan: *A Collection of Critical Essays.* Edited by Edward E. Bostetter. Englewood Cliffs, N.J.: Prentice-Hall, 1969, pp. 29–37.

Jump, John D. *Byron.* London: Routledge and Kegan Paul, 1972, pp. 103–151.

Kernan, Alvin B. *The Plot of Satire.* New Haven, Conn.: Yale University Press, 1965, pp. 171–222. Partially reprinted in *Twentieth Century Interpretations* *of* Don Juan: *A Collection of Critical Essays.* Edited by Edward E. Bostetter. Englewood Cliffs, N.J.: Prentice-Hall, 1969, pp. 85–93.

Kroeber, Karl. *Romantic Narrative Art.* Madison: University of Wisconsin Press, 1960, pp. 135–167. Reprinted in *Twentieth Century Interpretations of* Don Juan: *A Collection of Critical Essays.* Edited by Edward E. Bostetter. Englewood Cliffs, N.J.: Prentice-Hall, 1969, pp. 103–105.

Lovell, Ernest J., Jr. "Iron and Image in Byron's *Don Juan,*" in *The Major English Romantic Poets: A Symposium in Reappraisal.* Edited by Clarence C. Thorpe, Carlos Baker and Bennett Weaver. Carbondale: Southern Illinois University Press, 1957, pp. 129–148. Reprinted in *Twentieth Century Interpretations of* Don Juan: *A Collection of Critical Essays.* Edited by Edward E. Bostetter. Englewood Cliffs, N.J.: Prentice-Hall, 1969, pp. 21–28.

McGann, J.J. *Fiery Dust: Byron's Poetic Development.* Chicago: University of Chicago Press, 1968, pp. 186–188, 199–201, 294–298.

Marchand, Leslie A. *Byron's Poetry: A Critical Introduction.* Boston: Houghton Mifflin, 1965, pp. 157–234.

Marshall, William H. *The Structure of Byron's Major Poems.* Philadelphia: University of Pennsylvania Press, 1962, pp. 174–177.

Ridenour, George M. *The Style of* Don Juan. New Haven, Conn.: Yale University Press, 1960. Partially reprinted in *Byron: A Collection of Critical Essays.* Edited by Paul West. Englewood Cliffs, N.J.: Prentice-Hall, 1963, pp. 122–137.

Robson, W.W. "Byron as Poet," in *Critical Essays.* London: Routledge and Kegan Paul, 1966, pp. 148–190. Reprinted in *Byron: A Collection of Critical Essays.* Edited by Paul West. Englewood Cliffs, N.J.: Prentice-Hall, 1963, pp. 88–95. Also reprinted in *Byron:* Childe Harold's Pilgrimage *and* Don Juan—*A Casebook.* Edited by John D. Jump. London: Macmillan, 1973, pp. 132–152.

Rutherford, Andrew. *Byron: A Critical Study.* London: Oliver and Boyd, 1962, pp. 125–217. Partially reprinted in *Twentieth Century Interpretations of* Don Juan: *A Collection of Critical Essays.* Edited by Edward E. Bostetter. Englewood Cliffs, N.J.: Prentice-Hall, 1969, pp. 51–62.

Steffan, Guy. *Byron's* Don Juan, *Volume I: The Making of a Masterpiece.* Austin: University of Texas Press, 1957, pp. 278–296. Reprinted in *Byron: A Collection of Critical Essays.* Edited by Paul West. Englewood Cliffs, N.J.: Prentice-Hall, 1963, pp. 96–112.

Trueblood, Paul G. *The Flowering of Byron's Genius: Studies in Byron's* Don Juan. New York: Russell and Russell, 1962.

————. *Lord Byron.* New York: Twayne, 1969, pp. 97–103, 135–161.

MANFRED

Type of work: Poem
Author: George Gordon, Lord Byron (1788–1824)
Type of plot: Romantic tragedy
Time of plot: No set time
Locale: The Alps
First published: 1817

Manfred *is Byron's first presentation of the revolt theme that became so central to his poetry. Stimulated by his own experiences and feelings—social ostracism, the outraged virtue of English society, separation from Augusta Leigh—Byron shaped them into a passionate, brooding study of the individual who cannot seek deliverance from any social institution, but must work out his own destiny in isolation.*

Principal Characters

Manfred, a magician who summons the spirits of the universe, asking them for knowledge and oblivion. Although he contemplates suicide, mourning his limited powers, he is saved by a chamois hunter. He continues to raise other spirits and refuses the help of the Church. Since he does not give his loyalty to the Church or the powers of evil, he dies conquered by nothing but death.

The Spirit of Air, who asks Manfred what he wants to forget, a question the magician cannot answer.

The Spirit of Interior Fire,
The Spirit of Ocean,
The Spirit of Earth,
The Spirit of Exterior Fire, and
The Spirit of Night, spirits summoned by Manfred.

The Spirit of Manfred's Destiny, summoned by Manfred. It takes on the bodily shape of a beautiful woman who eludes the magician's embrace.

The Chamois Hunter, who saves Manfred from death. Seeing Manfred preparing to leap to his death on the Jungfrau Mountain, the hunter prevents the suicide. He feels sorry for Manfred but cannot help the magician solve his problems.

The Witch of the Alps, summoned by Manfred. She offers to share the beauties of nature with the magician and to aid him, if he agrees to obey her. She departs when Manfred refuses.

The Abbot of St. Maurice. He tries to save Manfred's soul for God but fails.

Astarte, whom Manfred has wronged. She is summoned from her tomb at Manfred's request by spirits in the Hall of Arimanes. She prophesies that his despair will end the next day. Death fulfills her prophecy.

The Story

Alone in a Gothic gallery at midnight, Manfred meditated deeply about his life. He had undergone many experiences, but none had profoundly affected him. When he called upon the spirits of the universe to appear before him, none came.

Three times he summoned them. At the third call, a summons in the name of his own cursed soul, the spirits arose.

The first was the Spirit of Air. The Spirit of Interior Fire next appeared, followed by the Spirit of Ocean. The spirits of Earth, Exterior Fire, and Night arose in succession, each demanding to know what the mortal magician wished. Finally the star, Manfred's own star of ill-fated destiny, joined the spirits.

Manfred's reply was that he desired forgetfulness. When the Spirit of Air sought further explanation, Manfred could not reveal what he wanted to forget. Surely, he insisted, spirits that controlled earth, sky, water, mountains, winds, night, and destiny, could bring the oblivion he sought. But the spirits replied that they had no powers beyond their own realms. When Manfred, failing in his hopes, asked the spirits to take bodily forms, the seventh spirit, the star of his destiny, took the shape of a beautiful woman. At sight of her, Manfred, hinting at a former love, attempted to hold her; but she vanished, leaving him senseless. In her place came a formless voice, the voice of himself as a magician, uttering a long incantation, mysterious and despairing.

Next morning, alone on a cliff of the Jungfrau Mountain, Manfred mourned the failure of his magic powers to assist him. Marveling at the surrounding beauty of the mountain, he weighed the possibility of leaping from the cliff. A passing hunter saw the lonely man and wondered what Manfred was doing so high on the mountain, where even the best hunters could not climb. Fearing that Manfred would lose his footing when the morning mist arose, the hunter approached him cautiously, for Manfred appeared to be tottering. Actually Manfred was about to jump when the hunter caught hold of him and led him down the steep slope.

In his cottage in the Bernese Alps, the hunter urged Manfred to rest a while before journeying on. Manfred, refusing guidance, declared that he would go on alone. When the hunter offered Manfred his best wine, Manfred exclaimed in horror that he saw blood, symbolic of Manfred's alienation from social contact, on the rim of the cup. The hunter, thinking Manfred mad, suggested that the wretched man seek comfort in contemplation and in the Church. Manfred, spurning the suggestion, said that he wished he were mad, for then his mind would be tortured by unrealities instead of the truths which now beset him. He envied the hunter's simple life, but when the hunter, noting Manfred's high-born appearance, wonderingly asked if his guest would then wish to change stations in life, Manfred replied that he would not wish any human to suffer his own wretchedness. To this the hunter said that surely a man capable of such tenderness could not harbor a soul belabored by evil. Manfred, departing, protested that the evil was not within himself; he had destroyed those whom he loved.

Below, the Witch of the Alps answered Manfred's summons that she share the loveliness of nature with him. To her he described his past spiritual life, when he had lived among men but not with them. Preferring solitude, he had studied ancient mysteries and had loved and destroyed with love a woman said to have resembled him. The Witch promised to aid him if he would swear obedience to her, but he refused her offer and she left him.

The three destinies and Nemesis gathered for a festival in the Hall of Arimanes, Spirit of Evil, Prince of Earth and Air. Manfred, daring to approach, was recognized as a magician. He told them he had come in quest of Astarte, the symbol of his sin. When she had been summoned from her tomb, she prophesied only that the next day would end his despair.

Back in his castle, Manfred felt a sublime calm. The Abbot of St. Maurice, having heard that Manfred had practiced witchcraft, arrived to save his soul. To Manfred's bitter assurance that his sins lay between heaven and himself, the abbot urged that Manfred turn to the Church for help. Manfred explained that he had always lived alone and would remain alone. The abbot mourned that he could not help such a noble man.

While the servants gossiped about their master's strange behavior, Manfred stood alone in his tower. There the abbot came once more in a last vain attempt to save Manfred. Warned that a dangerous spirit was approaching, the abbot insisted that he would confront the spirit, who had come to summon Manfred. Manfred, however, defied the summons; he was willing to die but not to join the spirits of hell, to whom he owed nothing.

As the demon disappeared, Manfred died, still lonely and unconquerable to all but death itself.

Critical Evaluation

Lame, handsome, and with a personality magnetic to both men and women, Byron lived three lives: adventurer, lover, and poet. His adventures included a shipwreck, a bout with fever, the swimming of the Hellespont and the rescue of a girl about to be drowned. His first speech in the House of Lords was in defense of the working man—a radical position at the time.

Byron the lover was dubbed "mad, bad and dangerous to know" by Lady Caroline Lamb, darling of London society. His presumed incestuous relationship with his half-sister Augusta Leigh caused society to turn against him. Later the sight of him could cause a riot.

Byron the poet is a major figure. *Childe Harold's Pilgrimage* and *Don Juan* are classics. *Manfred*, a shorter work, is important as a transition piece because it was written in Venice following *Childe Harold* and just prior to *Don Juan*.

Manfred is Byron's first great poem of revolt, spurred by an autobiographical urge. It is a rationalization of social ostracism, an explanation of the failure to cope with the outraged virtues of English society. Byron was perhaps also disturbed by separation from Augusta Leigh at the time.

The dramatic poem parallels Goethe's *Faust* with its wild mountain scenery and its theme of man learning to summon spirits. Manfred's adventures are symbolic ones, and the play is full of philosophical references. Unlike Faust, Manfred makes no contact with the devil. Therefore he dies free of hell's powers.

Manfred is a study of an isolated individual who cannot seek deliverance from any external social machinery, but who must work out his own destiny.

Bibliography

Blackstone, Bernard. *Byron: A Survey.* London: Longmans, 1975, pp. 152–154, 231–238.

Bostetter, Edward E. *The Romantic Ventriloquists: Wordsworth, Coleridge, Keats, Shelley, Byron.* Seattle: University of Washington Press, 1963, pp. 278–282.

Calvert, William J. *Byron: Romantic Paradox.* New York: Russell and Russell, 1962, pp. 139–144.

Chew, Samuel C., Jr. *The Dramas of Lord Byron: A Critical Study.* New York: Russell and Russell, 1964, pp. 59–84.

Cooke, Michael G. *The Blind Man Traces the Circle: On the Patterns and Philosophy of Byron's Poetry.* Princeton, N.J.: Princeton University Press, 1969, pp. 64–74.

Elledge, W. Paul. *Byron and the Dynamics of Metaphor.* Nashville, Tenn.: Vanderbilt University Press, 1968, pp. 81–94.

Gleckner, R.F. *Byron and the Ruins of Paradise.* Baltimore: Johns Hopkins University Press, 1967, pp. 256–265.

Joseph, M.K. *Byron the Poet.* London: Victor Gollancz, 1964, pp. 103–108.

Jump, John D. *Byron.* London: Routledge and Kegan Paul, 1972, pp. 84–87.

Marchand, Leslie A. *Byron's Poetry: A Critical Introduction.* Boston: Houghton Mifflin, 1965, pp. 75–84.

Marshall, William H. *The Structure of Byron's Major Poems.* Philadelphia: University of Pennsylvania Press, 1962, pp. 97–110.

Rutherford, Andrew. *Byron: A Critical Study.* London: Oliver and Boyd, 1962, pp. 76–92.

Thorslev, P.L. *The Byronic Hero: Types and Prototypes.* Minneapolis: University of Minnesota Press, 1962, pp. 165–176.

Trueblood, Paul G. *Lord Byron.* New York: Twayne, 1969, pp. 81–84.

West, Paul. *Byron and the Spoiler's Art.* London: Chatto and Windus, 1960, pp. 102–104.

THE POETRY OF BYRON

Author: George Gordon, Lord Byron (1788–1824)
First published: Hours of Idleness, 1807; *English Bards and Scotch Reviewers,*
1809; *Hebrew Melodies,* 1815; *The Prisoner of Chillon,* 1816

Essay-Review

Byron's lyric poems are uneven in subject matter and execution, a quality accounted for, perhaps, by their intensely personal nature and by the fact that in some instances they look back toward the eighteenth century, in others toward the nineteenth. At their best they exhibit depth of feeling, simplicity of structure, and quality of style; at their worst they are squibs and occasional pieces which bite and sting but accomplish little.

The first volume of his lyric poems received greater attention than it deserved. Published originally as *Fugitive Pieces,* it was soon withdrawn and then reissued a year later as *Hours of Idleness.* In his preface Byron struck a pose that was to grow through the years into the character of the dark, melancholy, brooding Byronic hero. Apparently the foreword was intended to anticipate criticism, but its tone was intolerably condescending. These verses, said the author, were written by a young man who had just completed nineteen years of life; they might afford some amusement to other nineteen year olds, and probably they would be the last given to the public by the young nobleman.

The literary critic of the *Edinburgh Review* attacked the volume viciously, hoping that indeed this would be the last publication by the young nobleman, who must be thought an intruder in the groves of literature. This slashing attack elicited from Byron his own vicious *English Bards and Scotch Reviewers,* in which he attacked not only his critic but innocent bystanders against whom he held harsh feelings, including Wordsworth, Coleridge, and Southey.

The poems of his first volume are indeed slight. There are numerous pieces such as "Translation from Catullus," "Translation of the Epitaph on Virgil and Tibullus," "Imitation of Tibullus," and "Imitated from Catullus." There are also numerous poems addressed to young ladies. Most are conventional and worthless. Occasionally there are pieces which promise a more vigorous and individualized poet. Such is "When I roved a Young Highlander," which reveals at least the presence of the life, muscle, and vigor that would subsequently drive the poet hectically through life.

The lyrics of later years are still in every way occasional, covering virtually all aspects of Byron's life. Though they all show a development over the juvenilia of the first volume, they too vary widely in quality.

On the weaker side is "To a Vain Lady," in which he pleads to a young girl not to disclose the foolish and deceitful compliments and pledges made to her by men, who, as is well known, are insincere in their protestations. The poet ends his plea with the statement that for the girl who reveals these amorous nothings he can have pity, but he cannot love her.

A considerably better poem is the direct and economically executed "When We Two Parted," though it is on the same subject as the poem mentioned above. The poet and his love parted tearfully but silently. The author asks how he should greet her if they should meet now after all these years; his feeling is still one of tears and silence.

An infinitely superior poem is the justly famous "Maid of Athens, Ere we Part," one of Byron's best. The poem was written to Theresa Macri, a young girl whom he met in Athens while on the Grand Tour. A brief work of only four stanzas, with a refrain in Greek ("My life, I love you"), is a clean, honest statement of love and of the continuation of this love:

> Maid of Athens, ere we part,
> Give, oh give me back my heart!
> Or, since that has left my breast,
> Keep it now, and take the rest!
> Hear my vow before I go,
> Ζωή μον, σάς ἀγαπω.
>
> By those tresses unconfined,
> Woo'd by each Agean wind;
> By those lids whose jetty fringe
> Kiss thy soft cheeks' blooming tinge;
> By those wild eyes like the roe,
> Ζωή μον, σάς ἀγαπω.
>
> By that lip I long to taste;
> By that zone-encircled waist;
> By all the token-flowers that tell
> What words can never speak so well;
> By love's alternate joy and woe,
> Ζωή μον, σάς ἀγαπω.
>
> Maid of Athens! I am gone:
> Think of me; sweet! when alone.
> Though I fly to Istambol,
> Athens holds my heart and soul:
> Can I cease to love thee? No!
> Ζωή μον, σας αγαπω.

Another effective lyric is "So, We'll Go No More A-Roving," which is informed by a genuine and unmaudlin nostalgia for the joys of the past strengthened by the realization that all things, even love, must end.

> I
> So, we'll go no more a-roving
> So late late into the night,
> Though the heart be still as loving,
> And the moon be still as bright.

II

For the sword outwears its sheath,
  And the soul wears out the breast,
And the heart must pause to breathe,
  And love itself have rest.

III

Though the night was made for loving,
  And the day returns too soon,
Yet we'll go no more a-roving
  By the light of the moon.

Some of Byron's best lyrics are those addressed to his very good friend, the poet Thomas Moore. These lyrics are masculine, lively, and expressive of genuine good spirits. Perhaps the best is entitled "To Thomas Moore," in which Byron says that his boat is on the shore and his bark is on the sea, but before he sails away he will drink a double health to Tom Moore.

Without question, several of Byron's most superb lyrics are the so-called "Hebrew Melodies," which according to Byron's prefatory remarks were written at the request of a friend, Douglas Kinnaird, and were to be set to traditional Hebrew tunes, as arranged by a young musician named Isaac Nathan. "She Walks in Beauty," one of the best of these, was written the morning after Byron met a beautiful young cousin, Mrs. Robert John Wilmot, who was wearing a black mourning gown, the beauty of which was highlighted with spangles. The poem is a genuine, unposed, tender, and honest compliment to beauty and innocence.

I

She walks in beauty, like the night
  Of cloudless climes and starry skies;
And all tha's best of dark and bright
  Meet in her aspect and her eyes:
Thus mellow'd to that tender light
  Which heaven to gaudy day denies.

II

One shade, the more, one ray the less,
  Had half impair'd the nameless grace
Which waves in every raven tress,
  Or softly lightens o'er her face;
Where thoughts serenely sweet express
  How pure, how dear their dwelling-place.

III

And on that cheek, and o'er that brow,
  So soft, so calm, yet eloquent,
The smiles that win, the tints that glow,
  But tell of days in goodness spent,
A mind at peace with all below,
  A heart whose love is innocent!

Another famous lyric from "Hebrew Melodies" is the well-known, "The Destruction of Sennacherib," with the beginning lines that compare the onset of the Assyrian to that of the wolf on the fold, with the cohorts gleaming in gold and purple, with spears shining like stars on the sea of Galilee.

In both such pieces Byron was at his best, vigorous, fluent, easy, direct, honest, and without the pose that characterized his longer works and often his short ones as well.

One of Byron's pieces that should be included in this discussion is scarcely a lyric at all except in the sheer power of the subject and of the author's execution. It is "Darkness," dated at Diodati in July, 1816. Written in blank verse, it depicts the end of the world, the final destruction of life on earth. It is a dream but more than a dream. The sun is extinguished; the stars wander in space. The earth is icy and swings back and forth aimlessly, cold and killing. The people are dying. The lucky ones are those who can warm themselves by volcanoes. All men are enervated by despair. Wild animals are tamed by the terror of their situations. Even the vipers are without sting, and are slain and eaten. War, which had been stilled a moment, broke out again in a struggle for the survival of the strongest. Finally, in this world of despair and tearing of the weak by the strong, only two persons survive, enemies. They meet beside an altar. Surviving for a moment on the ashes around that holy place, they suddenly look up and see each other, then shriek and die, slain by the hideousness of each other's visage. The world is left in blackness and desolation, with Darkness the mistress of all:

> Ships sailorless lay rotting on the sea,
> And their masts fell down piecemeal: as they dropp'd
> They slept on the abyss without a surge—
> The waves were dead; the tides were in their grave,
> The moon, their mistress, had expired before;
> The winds were wither'd in the stagnant air,
> And the clouds perish'd; Darkness had no need
> Of aid from them—She was the Universe.

This poem, like Byron's lyrics at their best, is powerfully imagined and executed with true poetic skill and restraint.

Byron's great lyrics are not numerous. Often they are weak or mediocre because of the speed of their writing; Byron once said that he had written most of his poetry while either dressing or undressing. Often they suffer from the nature of the subject, being trivial treatments of trivial themes. But when he exercised his best skill on worthy topics the results rank high indeed among lyric poems of the early nineteenth century.

Bibliography

English Bards and Scotch Reviewers

Blackstone, Bernard. *Byron: A Survey*. London: Longmans, 1975, pp. 43–54.

Calvert, William J. *Byron: Romantic Paradox.* New York: Russell and Russell, 1962, pp. 42–45.

Gleckner, R.F. *Byron and the Ruins of Paradise.* Baltimore: Johns Hopkins University Press, 1967, pp. 27–31.

Joseph, M.K. *Byron the Poet.* London: Victor Gollancz, 1964, pp. 131–133.

Marchand, Leslie A. *Byron's Poetry: A Critical Introduction.* Boston: Houghton Mifflin, 1965, pp. 21–28.

Marshall, William H. *The Structure of Byron's Major Poems.* Philadelphia: University of Pennsylvania Press, 1962, pp. 27–36.

Mayne, Ethel C. *Byron.* New York: Scribner's, 1924, pp. 80–85.

Rutherford, Andrew. *Byron: A Critical Study.* London: Oliver and Boyd, 1962, pp. 20–24.

Trueblood, Paul G. *Lord Byron.* New York: Twayne, 1969, pp. 33–36.

Yarker, P.M. "Byron and the Satiric Temper," in *Byron: A Symposium.* Edited by John D. Jump. New York: Barnes & Noble, 1975, pp. 76–93.

The Prisoner of Chillon

Cooke, Michael G. *The Blind Man Traces the Circle: On the Patterns and Philosophy of Byron's Poetry.* Princeton, N.J.: Princeton University Press, 1969, pp. 87–88.

Elledge, W. Paul. *Byron and the Dynamics of Metaphor.* Nashville, Tenn.: Vanderbilt University Press, 1968, pp. 45–54.

Gleckner, R.F. *Byron and the Ruins of Paradise.* Baltimore: Johns Hopkins University Press, 1967, pp. 191–199.

McGann, J.J. *Fiery Dust: Byron's Poetic Development.* Chicago: University of Chicago Press, 1968, pp. 165–173.

Marchand, Leslie A. *Byron's Poetry: A Critical Introduction.* Boston: Houghton Mifflin, 1965, pp. 69–70.

Marshall, William H. *The Structure of Byron's Major Poems.* Philadelphia: University of Pennsylvania Press, 1962, pp. 82–96.

Rutherford, Andrew. *Byron: A Critical Study.* London: Oliver and Boyd, 1962, pp. 66–75.

Trueblood, Paul G. *Lord Byron.* New York: Twayne, 1969, pp. 72–75.

Wood, Gerald C. "Nature and Narrative in Byron's *The Prisoner of Chillon*," in *Keats-Shelley Journal.* XXIV (1975), pp. 108–117.

JOHN CLARE

Born: Helpston, England (July 13, 1793)
Died: Northampton, England (May 20, 1864)

Principal Works

POEMS: *Poems Descriptive of Rural Life and Scenery*, 1820; *The Village Minstrel and Other Poems*, 1821; *The Shepherd's Calendar*, 1827.

John Clare, who became known as a "peasant poet," was born into the family of an almost illiterate farmer, Parker Clare, in Northamptonshire. The child was one of a pair of twins; the other twin, a girl, died shortly after birth. As a child he spent his time playing in the countryside with his surviving sister. Only about three months a year did he attend school, a dame-school of the time, in the nearby village of Glinton. At the age of twelve he went to work, attending school at night until his fourteenth year. As a young lad he worked in the fields at haying time and tended cattle, later finding work as a gardener at Burghley House, owned by the Marquis of Exeter. This was a life which gave the young man time to wander, to read, and to think. He also found time to write poetry, sometimes nature poems and sometimes drinking songs.

Fame came to Clare immediately after the publication of *Poems Descriptive of Rural Life and Scenery* in 1820. On the title page of this volume the poet was described as "a Northamshire peasant." The volume brought John Clare influential friends, as well as fame. It also brought him some friendly reviews in the important periodicals of the time. Lord Radstock became Clare's patron, and the poet, assured of an income, married Martha Turner, whom he had known for some time prior to his success as a published poet. In 1821, a year after his first volume, he published *The Village Minstrel and Other Poems*. As time passed, the poet's family grew in size, and so did his problems. Quarrels with his publishers, need of more and more money, and poor mental helath, as well as physical disability, plagued the poet. After the publication of *The Shepherd's Calendar* in 1827, Clare still found himself in such need of immediate funds that he took to selling his poems from house to house. His mental illness increased in intensity, with attacks recurring with greater frequency until he had to be placed in an asylum in Epping Forest in 1837. Unusual for the time, he was permitted to continue to write while in the asylum. He escaped custody briefly in 1841, but was found and placed in another asylum in Northampton, where he remained until his death in 1864. During his last years he wrote a great deal of poetry, most of it revealing his mental state.

Clare's fame, which declined greatly during the latter years of his life, rose again after his death. To the present time he has retained some significance as a minor poet for his exact and detailed descriptions of nature.

Bibliography

The *Selected Poems and Prose* were edited by Eric Robinson and Geoffrey Summerfield, 1966. The basic biography is J. L. Cherry, editor, *Life and Remains of John Clare*, 1873. Later works are J. W. and A. Tibble, *John Clare: A Life*, 1932; and *ibidem, John Clare: His Life and Poetry*, 1956; Frederick Martin, *Life of John Clare*, with an introduction and notes by Eric Robinson and Geoffrey Summerfield, second edition, 1964; C. Xenophantos, editor, *Life and Letters of John Clare*, 1966; and *Letters*, edited by J. W. and Ann Tibble, 1970.

THE POETRY OF CLARE

Author: John Clare (1793–1864)
Principal published works: Poems of Rural Life, 1820; *The Village Minstrel*,
1821; *The Shepherd's Calendar*, 1827; *The Rural Muse*, 1834

Essay-Review

Country-born and country-bred, enjoying literary success in London until the late 1820's, ending his days in a madhouse—the curve of John Clare's life is important to appreciate in any reading of his poetry. That Clare is rooted in the language and customs of the country, more specifically of the little village of Helpstone on the borders of the Lincolnshire Fens, is immediately evident in his earlier poems, as are his extremely delicate perceptions, the totalism of a sensibility nearly always hovering on the edge either of ecstasy or despair. Less evident are his strong literary affiliations with the Thomson of *The Seasons*, the Wordsworth of the "Ode: Intimations of Immortality," the Byron of *Childe Harold*. With Burns, Clare is one of the finest of the "original geniuses" of the late eighteenth and early nineteenth centuries, writing in a vein more authentic and serious than most of the other poetical plowboys, threshers, milkmaids, or cobblers then in vogue. His own Northamptonshire version of the conserving myth of the countryside, eloquently expressed in his lament for the loss of Swordy Fell by the enclosures of the 1820's, is in the line of Gray and Wordsworth and points directly to the writings of Barnes and Hardy later in the nineteenth century.

Clare's provincialism, his distance from the literary fashions of his early manhood, permitted him to mine his slender gift deeply. Again and again he returns to the themes, the moral and technical elements which are present in his earliest poems. The same subjects are to him always new and pressing: the importance of place, the loss of childhood innocence, the destruction of the countryside, absence in love, the poet as nature's spokesman. There is an uncomplicated resting in nostalgic description rather than a thrusting and exploratory meditation; there is no Wordsworthian straining after the philosophical poem, and Clare's successes are therefore more limited but purer than Wordsworth's.

Clare's ordinary medium is the loosened heroic couplet, the informal ballad stanza, the simple quatrain of the later Augustans, and he is not above using the "poetic diction" which Wordsworth explicitly rejected. Clare's originality was not one of perspective or technique so much as it was the focusing of a single-minded intensity upon the problems and perceptions of the countryman. The "ecstasy" Clare so often alludes to explains much in the tone of his poems on nature and on human love; but it is also directly related to a personal instability, the delicacy or fragility which led to the madness he himself had been anticipating.

Clare begins one of his best poems thus: "Hail, humble Helpstone.... Unletter'd spot! unheard in poet's song." The peculiarly Romantic celebration of the local and unique is here, but also a sense that the obscure village may be taken as standing for hundreds of others like it, places finally being encroached upon by wealth and civilization. The enclosure of the common forage lands, and the leveling of the woodlands, are Clare's concern even as early as this poem of 1809:

> How oft I've sigh'd at alterations made,
> To see the woodman's cruel axe employ'd
> A tree beheaded, or bush destroy'd. . . .

The resulting conviction that nature is herself somehow threatened accounts for some of the loving anxiousness in Clare's descriptions of both landscape and village life. One may take for an instance the fine stanza from "Summer Images":

> To note on hedgrow baulks, in moisture spent,
>   The jetty snail creep from the mossy thorn,
> With earnest heed and tremulous intent,
>   Frail brother of the morn,
> That from the tiny bent's dew-misted leaves
>   Withdraws his timid horn,
>   And fearful vision weaves.

The descriptive vignette, complete in a stanza, is characteristic. Clare is a cataloguer, a poet who, with an evocative title ("Morning," "Autumn") or a generalizing opening, launches a poem organized mainly into a progression of instances. "Noon" begins multiplying instances and images with the second line of the poem:

> All how silent and how still;
> Nothing heard but yonder mill:
> While the dazzled eye surveys
> All around a liquid blaze;
> And amid the scorching gleams,
> If we earnest look, it seems
> As if crooked bits of glass
> Seemed repeatedly to pass. . . .
> Not a twig is seen to shake,
> Nor the smallest bent to quake;

"Liquid blaze," though obviously a piece of poetic diction, is nevertheless a small triumph of authenticity.

In line with this effect is Clare's inclination to relate human moods to the four seasons. One remembers his comment that the first poetry which genuinely moved him was Thomson's *The Seasons*. Perhaps the finest of his nature poems is "Autumn," written in the unrhymed stanza of Collins' "Ode to Evening":

> Soon must I view thee as a pleasant dream

> Droop faintly, and so reckon for thine end,
>   As sad the winds sink low
>   In dirges for their queen;
>
> While in the moment of their weary pause,
> To cheer thy bankrupt pomp, the willing lark
>   Starts from his shielding clod,
>   Snatching sweet scraps of song.

Here as elsewhere we find comparisons made between nature and human nature. This analogy works both ways; sometimes there are such phrases as "wind-enamoured aspen" ("Summer Images"). At other times childhood and virginity find images in the blooming of trees or flowers: "Young Jenny blooming in her womanhood/That hides from day like lilies while in bud." In the poems of Clare's madness, when he writes of the impossibility of recovering his childhood, or of repossessing the unblemished love of his first sweetheart, Mary Joyce, he unconsciously connects his loss with the moods of the natural world. He longs "for scenes, where man hath never trod," where he can

> ... sleep as I in childhood sweetly slept,
> Untroubling, and untroubled where I lie,
> The grass below—above the vaulted sky.

In such poems as "The Village Minstrel," "To the Rural Muse," "Pastoral Poesy," and "The Progress of Rhyme," Clare sets forth the naïve poetics which informs all his lyric utterance. He engages in a radical but fruitful confusion of the process of writing and the observation of natural phenomena: "Wordsworth I love, his books are like the fields" ("To Wordsworth"); "True poesy is not in words,/But images that thoughts express," and observation affords "A language that is ever green. . . . As hawthorn blossoms, soon as seen,/Give May to every heart." ("Pastoral Poesy"). It is one indication of Clare's provinciality that he meant these lines quite literally.

The most important result of this assumption about the nature and function of poetry is Clare's accuracy of image and phrase. Where the countryman's English is most apt, he will use it though the effect is idiosyncratic:

> —And never choose
> The little sinky foss,
> Streaking the moors whence spa-red water spews
> From pudges fringed with moss. . . .

No animal, insect, or scene is too insignificant to bear description: "I see. . . . I see" is one of Clare's most habitual phrases, and when he writes of "shower-bedimpled sandy lanes," "smoke-tanned chimney tops," or "broad old cesspools" which "glittered in the sun," he is bringing new veridical images into English poetry. In "Eternity of Nature," Clare praises the Power behind nature by a marvelously convincing collection of the ways the number five recurs in the phenomena of the world:

> So trailing bindweed, with its pinky cup,
> Five leaves of paler hue go streaking up;
> And many a bird, too, keeps the rule alive,
> Laying five eggs, nor more nor less than five.

Keats thought that Clare was too descriptive, that the images from nature tend in his poetry to remain instances rather than being integrated with sentiment and meditation. The judgment is correct as far as it goes; we must allow Clare his visual accuracy but we must finally match his descriptive success against the larger enterprise of Wordsworth, who risked his poetry itself to make it a moral and teaching medium. In Wordsworth and Keats, observation leads more quickly to meditation than in Clare, a poet who does not explore the more symbolic uses of the natural image.

Clare is best known for lyric poetry which poses serious questions about life and death and eternity. His longer works have many of the same qualities of observation to recommend them. "The Village Minstrel" is autobiographical, charged with the same kind of visual acuity one finds in the shorter poems. One gets from "The Village Minstrel" some sense of what the "Eden" of Clare's humble childhood was like in a poor agricultural community. Clare himself never tires of emphasizing that it was in fact a genuine community; this is the burden of the excellent poem on the labors and customs of a country village presented in *The Shepherd's Calendar*. Here Clare describes the work, the sport, the violence, and the frank sexuality of provincial farm communities in the early nineteenth century (the honesty of his genre scenes, like the impetuous couplets of the poem, stand in vivid contrast to the centuries earlier *The Shepheardes Calendar* of Edmund Spenser). Clare's "Poems Written in Madness" remain to be described, yet there is no way to describe them in terms or categories other than those used above to discuss poems written before his confinement for madness. The fact is that the superb poems from this period—"To Wordsworth," "Written in a Thunderstorm," "I've Wandered Many a Weary Mile," "I Am," "Hesperus"—represent only an unconscious focusing on the elements of despair and absence already conveyed earlier in Clare's work.

SAMUEL TAYLOR COLERIDGE

Born: Ottery St. Mary, England (October 21, 1772)
Died: Highgate, London, England (July 25, 1834)

Principal Works

POEMS: *Poems on Various Subjects*, 1796; *Poems: Second Edition*, 1797; *Lyrical Ballads*, 1798 (with Wordsworth); *Christabel*, 1816; *Sibylline Leaves*, 1817; *Poetical Works*, 1828 (3 vols.).

ESSAYS AND STUDIES: *Addresses to the People*, 1795; *The Friend*, 1809–1810; *The Statesman's Manual*, 1816; *Biographia Literaria*, 1817; *Aids to Reflection*, 1825; *On the Constitution of Church and State*, 1830; *Confessions of an Inquiring Spirit*, 1840.

PLAYS: *The Fall of Robespierre*, 1794 (with Southey); *Remorse*, 1813; *Zapolya*, 1817.

TRANSLATIONS: Schiller's *Wallenstein*, 1800 (*The Piccolomini* and *The Death of Wallenstein*).

Samuel Taylor Coleridge, English poet, critic, and amateur philosopher, was born in Ottery Saint Mary, in Devonshire, on October 21, 1772. In 1782, at the death of his father, a Church of England clergyman, he was sent to the Christ's Hospital school in London. After eight years there he went to Jesus College, Cambridge. Charles Lamb, who wrote an essay about Coleridge as a boy, said that he had a tendency to monopolize conversation, and was interested in metaphysical discussions. His school fellows considered him impractical and eccentric.

In the fall of 1793 Coleridge left Cambridge and enlisted in the Light Dragoons. Discharged the following spring, he traveled in England and Wales. On a visit to Oxford he met Robert Southey, another young radical of the day. Both were sympathetic to the principles of the French Revolution and together they devised the idea of starting a new social settlement free from the prejudices and influences of the English political system. This settlement, to be called a "Pantisocracy," was to be on the banks of the Susquehanna River in America; but lack of funds doomed the plan. Coleridge left Cambridge without a degree in 1794. His marriage in 1795 to Sarah Fricker came about because the pantisocratic plan called for married emigrants.

In 1796 he published *Poems on Various Subjects* and for a few weeks edited the periodical, *The Watchman*, in which he voiced the principles of the French Revolution and of Godwinism. In the next year he settled in Nether Stowey, Somerset, and formed an intimate friendship with Wordsworth. Together they conceived the idea of publishing the *Lyrical Ballads*, which, appearing in 1798, is considered a landmark in English literature and the beginning of nineteenth century Romanticism.

The original plan of *Lyrical Ballads* was to upset and defy the old literary standards of the didactic school of Pope. Wanting poetic diction synonymous with ordinary speech, Wordsworth and Coleridge dropped the couplet form and adapted the ballad form from folk songs of the countryside. A new type of character, the peasant, was introduced. *Lyrical Ballads* is simple in language and verse forms, and presents simple characters. Coleridge's contribution, *The Rime of the Ancient Mariner*, is its best ballad. He took preternatural events with the intention of making them seem natural, just as Wordsworth took natural events and put over them a screen of imaginative wonder.

During a trip with the Wordsworths to Germany, Coleridge attended lectures at the universities and became a student of German literature and philosophy. This interest led to his introduction of German philosophy into England. After his return to England in 1799 he produced a translation of Schiller's *Wallenstein*.

Coleridge acquired the habit of taking opium, which took firm hold on him in 1801. In 1802 he wrote "Dejection, an Ode," in which he seems to make up his mind he never can be a great poet, and at the time he lived in a state of great depression. His attempt to recover his health at Malta, where he was secretary to Governor Sir Alexander Ball, failed. At home he became estranged from his friends and separated from his wife and children. He lived with friends until his death.

In 1808 he delivered a series of lectures at the Royal Institution of London, a course on Shakespeare and Milton, and one on the history of literature. Most of these exist today in fragmentary form only (Vols. I and II of the *Literary Remains*, 1836–1838).

The Friend, a periodical he began after five months of procrastination, is characteristic of the sick and destitute Coleridge. Advertised as a "weekly" essay on philosophical questions, politics, and allied subjects, it rarely came out on time and folded with the twenty-seventh issue. Coleridge published a revised edition of *The Friend* in 1818.

He had his first definite quarrel with Wordsworth in 1810 and left the Lake Country for good. Some of the most acute criticism of Wordsworth comes from Coleridge. He attacks Wordsworth's extreme primitivism in *Biographia Literaria*, but praises his high degree of imagination. Considered one of the foremost literary critics of the time, in his later years Coleridge set himself up as a kind of London sage, and with partial control over opium he began republishing in 1816, when his two most famous unfinished poems, *Christabel* and "Kubla Khan," along with "Pains of Sleep," appeared. *Christabel* is an example of pseudo-medievalism popular with Romantic poets. In descriptive detail and ballad meter Coleridge creates an atmosphere of superstition and pleasing horror. He tried to develop poetry in which the intellect is consciously left out, poetry of imagination and sensibility producing sheer mood.

During his last years he published *Sibylline Leaves, Aids to Reflection*, and *On the Constitution of the Church and State*. Today he is recognized as one of the

most important Church of England thinkers before the Oxford Movement.
He died in poverty at Highgate, London, on July 25, 1834.

Bibliography

The standard edition of the poems is the *Complete Poetical Works*, 2 vols.,
edited by E. H. Coleridge, 1912. The best edition of the *Biographia Literaria* is
that edited by J. Shawcross, 1907. The *Notebooks* have been edited by Kathleen
Coburn, 2 vols., 1957–1962; the *Collected Letters* by E. L. Griggs, 4 vols., 1956–
1959; and the *Shakespearean Criticism* by T. M. Rayson, 2 vols., 1930. The *Collected Edition of The Works*, edited by Kathleen Coburn, is in progress, 1969ff.
The standard biographies are J. D. Campbell, *Samuel Coleridge: A Narrative of
Events in His Life*, 1894; E. K. Chambers, *Samuel Taylor Coleridge*, 1938; and
Lawrence Hanson, *The Life of Samuel Taylor Coleridge: The Early Years*, 1939.
All critical studies have been overshadowed by John Livingston Lowes, *The Road
to Xanadu: A Study in the Ways of the Imagination*, 1927. See also J. H.
Muirhead, *Coleridge as Philosopher*, 1930; I. A. Richards, *Coleridge on Imagination*, 1934; Robert Penn Warren, "A Poem of Pure Imagination: An Experiment
in Reading," in *The Rime of the Ancient Mariner*, 1946; Patricia M. Adair, *The
Waking Dream: A Study of Coleridge's Poetry*, 1967; Walter J. Bate, *Coleridge*,
1968; Richard Haven, *Patterns of Consciousness: An Essay on Coleridge*, 1969;
and Thomas McFarland, *Coleridge and the Pantheist Tradition*, 1969.

BIOGRAPHIA LITERARIA

Type of work: Intellectual autobiography
Author: Samuel Taylor Coleridge (1772–1834)
First published: 1817

Essay-Review

Samuel Taylor Coleridge's *Biographia Literaria* begins as an account of the major influences on the development of his philosophy and his literary technique, but the total effect of the work is considerably less coherent than this plan would indicate. As he progressed the author apparently altered his purpose, and he discussed at considerable length intellectual problems of special interest to him and gave some of his standards of literary criticism with comments on specific works. In his opening paragraph he speaks of his work as "miscellaneous reflections"; the description seems appropriate.

The loose rambling structure of the *Biographia Literaria* accords well with the picture of Coleridge that has been handed down, that of a man of great intellectual and poetic gifts who lacked the self-discipline to produce the works of which he seemed capable. Charles Lamb and William Hazlitt both characterized him as an indefatigable and fascinating talker, full of ideas, and this trait, too, plays its part in the creation of the *Biographia Literaria*, which is, in essence, a long conversation, ranging widely over the worlds of poetry, drama, philosophy, and psychology. However, the lack of a tight organizational plan in no way prevents the book from being both readable and profound in its content; Coleridge's comments on the nature of the poetic imagination have never been surpassed, and his criticism of Wordsworth's work is still perhaps the most balanced and judicious assessment available, a model for all scholars who seek to form general views on the basis of close examination of individual texts.

In the opening chapter Coleridge pays tribute to his most influential teacher, the Reverend James Bowyer of Christ's Hospital, who insisted that his students learn to think logically and use language precisely, in poetry as well as in prose. Coleridge also discusses the poetry he preferred in the years when his literary tastes were being formed; he turned toward the "pre-romantic" lyrics of minor writers rather than to the terse, epigrammatic intellectual poems of the best-known of the eighteenth century literary men, Alexander Pope and his followers. At an early stage he developed sound critical principles, looking for works that gained in power through rereading and for words that seemed to express ideas better than any phrases substituted for them could, and he quickly learned to distinguish between the virtues of works of original ideas and the faults of those that made their effect through novel phraseology. He confesses, however, that his critical judgment was better than his creative talent: his own early poems, though he thought highly of them when he wrote them, left much to be desired.

The harshness of critics in his time is a recurrent theme throughout Coleridge's autobiography, and in his second chapter he ponders on the tendency of the public to side with them rather than with the poets, who are considered to be strange, irritable, even mad. Yet the greatest writers, Chaucer, Shakespeare, Spenser, and Milton, seem to him unusually well-balanced, and he suggests that the popular heresy results from the frustrations of the second-rate writer who pursues fame without real talent. These general comments are closely linked to Coleridge's sense of injustice at the vituperative attacks on him that issued regularly from the pages of the popular reviews, partly as a result of his association with Wordsworth and Robert Southey. The three poets were accused of trying to revolutionize, to vulgarize, poetry; they were avowedly interested in freeing poetry from the limitations of the eighteenth century poetic tradition. Coleridge denies that they deserved the abuses hurled at them.

After making some comments on the works of Wordsworth and Southey, Coleridge turns to a number of philosophical problems that fascinated him, questions of perception, sensation, and the human thought processes. It is this section of his work that provides the greatest difficulty for the uninitiated reader, for he assumes considerable familiarity with the works of German philosophers and English psychologists and mystics. He surveys the theories of Thomas Hobbes, David Hartley, Aristotle, Descartes, and others as they relate to problems of perception and of the development of thought through the association of ideas, and he assesses the influence of Immanuel Kant on his own philosophy.

Coleridge digresses from the complex history of his intellectual growth to describe his first literary venture into the commercial side of his world, his publication of a periodical called *The Watchman.* His attempts to secure subscriptions were ludicrous, and his project met with the failure that his friends had predicted; one of them had to pay his printer to keep Coleridge out of debtors' prison.

One of the most important periods in Coleridge's life was his 1798 trip to Germany, where he widened his knowledge of the literature and philosophy of that country. He returned to England to take a position with a newspaper, writing on literature and politics; he attacked Napoleon so vociferously that the French general actually sent out an order for his arrest while he was living in Italy as a correspondent for his paper. Coleridge evidently enjoyed his journalistic work, and he advises all would-be literary men to find some regular occupation rather than to devote all their time to writing.

Returning to his philosophical discussion, Coleridge lists several of his major premises about truth and knowledge. He is particularly concerned with distinguishing between the essence of the subject, the perceiver, and of the object, that which is perceived. Related to this distinction is the nature of the imagination, which Coleridge divides into two parts. The primary imagination is that power in man which perceives and recognizes objects; the secondary imagination acts on these initial perceptions to produce new thoughts: "It dissolves, diffuses, dissipates, in order to re-create."

Coleridge next turns to a presentation of his literary standards, referring especially to the *Lyrical Ballads*, the volume containing much of Wordsworth's poetry and some of his own. He tries to define poetry, pointing out that it has as its "immediate object pleasure, not truth," and that it delights by the effect of the whole, as well as of individual parts. In one of the most famous passages in the book he discusses the function of the poet, who, by the power of his imagination, must bring unity out of diversity, reconciling "sameness, with differences; of the general, with the concrete; the idea, with the image; the individual, with the representative; the sense of novelty and freshness, with old and familiar objects; a more than usual state of emotion, with more than usual order; judgment ever awake and steady self-possession, with enthusiasm and feeling profound or vehement."

Coleridge applies these general tenets to specific works, analyzing Shakespeare's early poems, *The Rape of Lucrece* and *Venus and Adonis* to determine what in them reveals genius and what is the result of the poet's immaturity. He praises particularly Shakespeare's musical language and his distance from his subject matter, saying, with reference to the latter point, that the average youthful writer is likely to concentrate on his own sensations and experiences. Shakespeare's greatness seems to him to lie, too, in the vividness of his imagery and in his "depth, and energy of thought."

While he was closely associated with Wordsworth in the creation of the *Lyrical Ballads*, Coleridge does not hesitate to indicate the points at which he differed from his colleague. He takes issue most strongly with Wordsworth's assertion that the speech of low and rustic life is the natural language of emotion and therefore best for poetry. Coleridge stresses rather the choice of a diction as universal as possible, not associated with class or region, and he says that it is this kind of language that Wordsworth has, in fact, used in almost all of his work. He feels that in the preface to the *Lyrical Ballads* Wordsworth was, to a certain extent, exaggerating in order to make clear advantages of natural, clear language over the empty poetic diction of the typical poetry of the time.

Coleridge's comments on Wordsworth lead him to an extended attack on the practices of the critical reviews, whose commentary on his friend's works seems to him both biased and absurd. He ridicules the tendency of anonymous reviewers to offer criticism without giving examples to support their assertions; they hardly seem to have read the works they lampoon. So as to counteract their ill-tempered, inconsistent judgments he sets down his own views on Wordsworth's most serious flaws and his outstanding talents. He criticizes his "inconstancy of the style," a tendency to shift from a lofty level to a commonplace one; his occasionally excessive attention to factual details of landscape or biography; his poor handling of dialogue in some poems; his "occasional prolixity, repetition, and an eddying instead of progression of thought" in a few passages; and, finally, his use of "thoughts and images too great for the subject."

With these defects in mind Coleridge commends Wordsworth's work for the purity and appropriateness of its language, the freshness of the thoughts, the "sinewy strength and originality of single lines and paragraphs," the accuracy of the descriptions of nature, the pathos and human sympathy, and the imaginative power of the poet.

The major portion of the *Biographia Literaria* ends with a final assessment of Wordsworth's work. To this material Coleridge has added, in order to give the reader a picture of his early maturity, a group of letters written to friends while he was traveling in Germany, containing amusing accounts of his shipboard companions, his meeting with the famous poet Klopstock, and some of his literary opinions. To show how little his critical standards had changed, he also included a long and devastating critique of a contemporary melodrama, *Bertram, or the Castle of St. Aldobrand*, an essay published just before the *Biographia Literaria*.

Coleridge's concluding chapter, as rambling in subject matter as the rest of the book, treats briefly the harsh critical reaction to his poem *Christabel*, then turns to his affirmation of his Christian faith and his reasons for holding it. He makes no attempt to summarize his volume, which has presented a remarkably full portrait of his wide-ranging, questioning mind.

Bibliography

Abrams, M.H. "Coleridge and the Romantic Vision of the World," in *Coleridge's Variety: Bicentenary Studies*. Edited by John Beer. Pittsburgh: University of Pittsburgh Press, 1974, pp. 102–133.

Appleyard, J.A. "Coleridge and Criticism: I. Critical Theory," in *Writers and Their Background: S.T. Coleridge*. Edited by R.L. Brett. London: Bell, 1971, pp. 135–140.

Barth, J. Robert. *The Symbolic Imagination: Coleridge and the Romantic Tradition*. Princeton, N.J.: Princeton University Press, 1977, pp. 22–23, 44–49.

Bate, Walter Jackson. *Coleridge*. New York: Macmillan, 1968, pp. 130–131.

Brett, R.L. *Fancy & Imagination*. London: Methuen, 1969, pp. 31–53.

Cooke, Michael G. "Quisque Sui Faber: Coleridge in the *Biographia Literaria*," in *Philological Quarterly*. L (1971), pp. 208–229.

Fields, Beverly. *Reality's Dark Dream: Dejection in Coleridge*. Kent, Oh.: Kent State University Press, 1967, pp. 104–108.

Fruman, Norman. *Coleridge, the Damaged Archangel*. New York: George Braziller, 1971, pp. 69–107.

Gilpin, George H. "Coleridge and the Spiral of Poetic Thought," in *Studies in English Literature, 1500–1900*. XII (1972), pp. 639–652.

_____. "Coleridge: The Pleasure of Truth," in *South Central Bulletin*. XXX (1970), pp. 191–194.

Harding, Anthony John.   *Coleridge and the Idea of Love: Aspects of Relationship in Coleridge's Thought and Writing.* London: Cambridge University Press, 1974, pp. 36–37, 84–85, 179–180, 200–201.

McFarland, Thomas.   *Coleridge and the Pantheist Tradition.* Oxford: Clarendon Press, 1969, pp. 40–44.

————.   "The Origin and Significance of Coleridge's Theory of Secondary Imagination," in *New Perspectives on Coleridge and Wordsworth: Selected Papers from the English Institute.* Edited by Geoffrey H. Hartman. New York: Columbia University Press, 1972, pp. 195–226.

Mallette, Richard.   "Narrative Technique in the *Biographia Literaria*," in *Modern Language Review.* LXX (1975), pp. 32–40.

Prickett, Stephen.   *Coleridge and Wordsworth: The Poetry of Growth.* Cambridge: University Press, 1970, pp. 70–81.

Read, Herbert.   "Coleridge as Critic," in *Coleridge: A Collection of Critical Essays.* Edited by Kathleen Coburn. Englewood Cliffs, N.J.: Prentice-Hall, 1967, pp. 94–111.

Shaffer, Elinor S.   "The 'Postulates in Philosophy' in the *Biographia Literaria*," in *Comparative Literature Studies.* VII (1970), pp. 297–313.

Teich, Nathaniel.   "Coleridge's *Biographia* and the Contemporary Controversy About Style," in *The Wordsworth Circle.* III (1971), pp. 61–70.

Whalley, George.   "On Reading Coleridge," in *Writers and Their Background: S.T. Coleridge.* Edited by R.L. Brett. London: Bell, 1971, pp. 32–35.

Willey, Basil.   *Samuel Taylor Coleridge.* New York: Norton, 1972, pp. 188–205.

Yarlott, Geoffrey.   *Coleridge & the Abyssinian Maid.* London: Methuen, 1967, pp. 280–282.

THE POETRY OF COLERIDGE

Author: Samuel Taylor Coleridge (1772–1834)
First published: Poems on Various Subjects, 1796; *Poems: Second Edition*, 1797;
  Lyrical Ballads, 1798 (with Wordsworth); *Christabel*, 1816; *Sibylline Leaves*,
  1817; *Poetical Works*, 1828

Essay-Review

Samuel Taylor Coleridge is one of the most complex and richly suggestive writers in English. Poet, philosopher, critic, and, not infrequently, genius, he has left an indelible mark on the history of English poetry and criticism. His major critical work, *Biographia Literaria*, stands as the source of much modern critical theory. With William Wordsworth, Coleridge led the "Romantic revolt" in English poetry. They asserted not only that the source of poetry is the ordinary life and language of men, but also reasserted the validity and beauty of the imagination. Coleridge's poetry is not voluminous, and the great pieces were nearly all written in a space of from two to five years, but at his best his poems are rich in their concrete, forthright evocation of the psychological and the mysterious.

Coleridge believed in the "feeling heart," in the spiritual power of the individual imagination to apprehend, in images of beauty, the completeness and harmonious beauty of God's creation. He was, therefore, the first of the English idealistic Romantics who asserted the primacy of the inner vision in the face of eighteenth century theories of materialism and mechanical, sense-bound perception. He derived from the German idealists—notably the Schlegels and Schelling and through them, Kant—many of his ideas of reason and imaginative vision, both of which qualities free men from bondage to the senses alone.

His earlier poetry is notable for its subtly patterned use of ordinary speech and its quiet, imaginative manipulation of scene and mood.

> Low was our pretty cot; our tallest Rose
> Peeped at the chamber-window. We could hear
> At silent noon, and eve, and early morn,
> The sea's faint murmur: In the open air
> Our myrtles blossomed; and across the porch
> Thick jasmins twined: The little landscape round
> Was green and woody, and refreshed the eye.

Here is a distinctive ease of manner, of rhythm and direct observation which, as in Wordsworth's verse and according to the credo announced in his Preface to their *Lyrical Ballads*, replaces the artificially poetic, "literary" manner of much eighteenth century verse. An example of how Coleridge can develop a passage of such simplicity into a more elaborate vision may be found in "The Nightingale." He does so without sacrificing the basic tone and texture of ordinary speech. Here, he writes disapprovingly of the closeted, ink-horn poet:

> Poet who hath been building up the rhyme
> When he had better far have stretched his limbs
> Beside a brook in mossy forest-dell,
> By Sun or Moon-light, to the influxes
> Of shapes and sounds and shifting elements
> Surrendering his whole spirit, of his song
> And of his name forgetful! so his fame
> Should share in Nature's immortality,
> A venerable thing!

The alliteration and the repetition of prepositional phrases create a heightened effect, expressive of Coleridge's faith, not in a poetry of midnight oil, but of a direct, spiritual connection between man and actual nature. As Coleridge's poetry developed, however, he became even more strikingly the poet of the imagination, of the supernatural, as is evidenced in such poems as "Kubla Khan" and *The Rime of the Ancient Mariner*.

For though Coleridge shared with Wordsworth a desire to return poetry to the ordinary, the concrete, and the language of speech, he was also desirous of discovering the spiritual, supernatural principles of unity within, and lying behind, the concretely sensed multiplicity of ordinary experience. Thus, he writes, the best style is that written "when the author has had his own eye fixed steadily on the abstract, yet permits his readers to see only the concrete." Accordingly, Coleridge expresses his conception of poetry in terms of a synthesis of imaginative vision and of actual perception, of "outer" and "inner," in other words, or of "object" and "subject." His earlier verse usually had nature as the "object," but later poems approach treatment of the symbolic, mythic, and general consciousness of the inner man. Myths of death and symbolic rebirth predominate.

Historically, this conception of poetry, a synthesis of the individual and subjective with the concrete and objective, moves sharply away from neoclassic doctrines of a poetry as imitation governed by rules. To Coleridge, art is less imitative than "organic"; a poem is a growing unity, the parts related to one another and all comprising a whole. The "end" of poetry is pleasure, not instruction, and yet a poem tells a higher truth. A poem expresses "a more than usual state of emotion with more than usual order." The order, however, is not imposed from without, by aid of rules for writing poems, nor according to agreed-upon "laws" of nature. The order grows out of the synthesizing power of the individual imagination. Indeed, according to Coleridge's notion, the creative act of the imagination is first a breaking down of the usual sensations and perceptions of outward reality, and then a synthesizing, a reconstruction of that outward reality by means of an inner vision to produce "a new unity, a new reality." This conception of the "creative imagination" and of "organic unity" underlies nearly all modern criticism.

Coleridge's desire for synthesis and unity marked all his thinking and writing. Any tendency toward isolation or fragmentation, whether in idea or in his personal life, was an occasion for regret and even despair. Many of his best poems lament a fall from communion, a loss of harmony, and celebrate a revival of companionship, of unity both personal and moral. He ever tried to express his sense of the underlying Oneness of the world, the great created Cosmos of God, Who is, in these terms, the original and most sublime Artist. The poet-as-seer and idealist must try to achieve a vision, however partial, of this divine wholeness.

"Dejection, an Ode" records a sense of failure in trying to achieve such harmony, and the poem marks the approximate end of Coleridge's brief and brilliant "great period" as a poet. "Dejection" was first published on Wordsworth's wedding day. Perhaps there is some significance in that fact, for their vital partnership, which had helped both so much, was ending. "Dejection" begins in the conversational tone noted earlier.

> Well! If the Bard was weather-wise who made
> The grand old ballad of Sir Patrick Spence,
> This night, so tranquil now, will not go hence
> Unaroused by winds....

The tone sounds somewhat rueful, a trifle bitter; one notices, too, the firmer cadence of this mature poetry: simple, yet beautifully molded. Coleridge refers here to the prophecy of storm in that ballad ("And I fear, I fear, my Master Dear!/We shall have a deadly Storm"), and the disarming tone of the opening lines gives way, naturally and "organically," to the dirgelike cadences which express the poet's inner turmoil:

> My genial spirits fail,
> And what can these avail
> To lift the smothering weight from off my breast?

Disharmony has soured the visionary's glimpse of Nature's goodness:

> Hence viper thoughts, that coil around my mind,
> Reality's dark dream!

Coleridge, like Wordsworth, had often felt that Nature brought him solace and pleasure. Nature was an "Eolian Harp," making a kind of cosmic music. Now, he welcomes the storm, whose sound had before "sent my soul abroad." He hopes that the sounds

> Might now their wonted impulse give,
> Might startle the dull pain, and make it move and live!

But the poet has lapsed into a state of alienation from Nature, and from his most natural self. His inner sadness has closed him off, isolated him. Addressing his "lady," he describes the beauty of the evening sky and stars:

> I see them all so excellently fair,
> I see, not feel, how beautiful they are!

The old source of solace, wonder and "feeling" is shut off from him. His inner self has shrunken, and so he can no longer make, personally, that vital synthesis between inner and outer vision. He makes, instead, a poem out of the failure, a poem which still deals, negatively, with the old harmony.

> O Lady! We receive but what we give,
> And in our life alone does nature live.

Coleridge next writes a stanza which is, in effect, a hymn to joy, and he states that man and nature are wedded in joy, and as a dowry man gets "A new Earth and new Heaven." But the poet has lost such capacity for joy and has, as well, lost "my shaping spirit of imagination." Stoically, then, he will take refuge in patience and "abstruse research" in an attempt to escape the personal pain. He turns to the wild mountain storm for some solace, and calls the wind a "mad lutanist," befitting his dark soul. Silence comes, and then a softer sound, or moan, appears to sing sadly of a lost child. The image of that lost child, growing organically out of both the theme and imagery of the poem, becomes on a deeper level symbolic of Coleridge himself, lost, afraid, cut-off. Like the ancient mariner, he is adrift, at sea, and such images are recurrent in the poetry. The child-wanderer and the spellbound damsel symbolize both Coleridge's creative imagination and his fear of losing that creative power of attaining unity. So "Dejection" ends poignantly enough with an appeal to the stars to bring his "lady," his friend, joy—for they remind him only of sorrow.

The Rime of the Ancient Mariner also deals with the theme of isolation, frustration, and symbolic renewal. The ballad form of the poem indicates Coleridge's preference for the poetry of the folk, dealing often mysteriously but always concretely with significant human actions. Ballads preserve the supernatural within the ordinary, and their simple yet highly patterned form and language appealed to Coleridge, and his most memorable verse is built on the ballad form.

The story of the mariner who shoots the albatross, symbol of divine beneficence, and who thereby brings upon himself a curse, but who is finally released from the curse by blessing in his heart, in spite of his lonely suffering, the beauty of the mysterious water-snakes, is familiar to all readers. What should be emphasized is that it is through the mariner's opening of his heart to God's created creatures that his release from the curse is brought about. His tale sobers the wedding guests, for it warns of how the "wedding" of man and woman, man and nature, is dependent, as both image and idea repeat in "Dejection," on a creative, joyful communion with all of nature. The springs of life lie under the surface and are mysterious, and such is the effect of the mariner's experience and tale.

Formally, *The Rime of the Ancient Mariner* is notable for its swiftness of narration, its vivid imagery, and Coleridge's sure-handed use of a modified ballad measure. Important and dramatic details are given quickly, increasing both the economy and dramatic effect of the poem. Thus, when a wedding guest wonders why the tormented old mariner tells this tale, the crucial fact is abruptly supplied.

> God save thee, ancient mariner!
> From the fiends, that plague thee thus!
> Why look'st thou so?—With my crossbow
> I shot the Albatross.

The visual detail is suggestive and mysterious:

> About, about, in reel and rout
> The death-fires danced at night;
> The water, like a witch's oils,
> Burnt green, and blue and white.

Repetition, alliteration, and the subtle use of refrain, often incremental, produce the eerie, chanting effect of the masterwork, in which the symbolic meanings of spiritual death and rebirth find fully adequate objective terms, both in the imagery and in the dramatic situation of the mariner and the wedding guest.

Christabel, written earlier but left incomplete, was not published until 1816. In a preface to the poem, Coleridge explains how the meter is based on the number of accents, regardless of the number of unaccented syllables. This, in fact, is the simple principle behind Gerard Manley Hopkins' "sprung" rhythm. Again, the form and effect is that of a modified ballad-narrative, and the story is both swiftly told and richly endowed with imaginative detail. Christabel, while praying in the woods at night for her betrothed, is interrupted by Geraldine, who is, in fact, a supernatural creature, a witch, apparently bent on doing harm. Geraldine herself is deformed and isolated, cut off from human sympathy. Christabel is permitted to see through the disguise when the two spend a night together, but she is silenced by a spell.

Bracy, the bard, is sent to tell Geraldine's supposed father, Lord Roland, that the young woman is well. As in *The Rime of the Ancient Mariner*, the theme of estrangement and reunion is touched on here, for Sir Leoline and Lord Roland, once friends, are now estranged, and on this occasion Sir Leoline suddenly desires a reconciliation. But Bracy as poet-seer, has also felt the evil presence, and is reluctant to leave on his mission. Sir Leoline is angered at his daughter Christabel's inhospitality; he appears to have fallen in love with Geraldine. The poem is incomplete, and the short conclusion to Part Two really solves none of the logical or narrative questions. Thus, the poem lurks in the imagination, somehow mysterious, psychologically profound, haunting. Themes of purity and guilt, of isolation, estrangement, and reunion are all working, but *Christabel* remains an enigma.

The same is true of Coleridge's most famous fragment, the drug-induced "Khubla Khan." This poem expresses a dream-vision in which Coleridge's genius for weird, mysterious, and yet concretely realized poetic effects is most in evidence. Coleridge himself claimed no "poetic" merits for the piece (having in mind, no doubt, the requirement that a poem be a whole), and he published it as a "curiosity" at Byron's request. Dreamed while Coleridge was ill and under the influence of a prescribed anodyne, its "two or three hundred" subconscious lines became, upon wakeful reconstruction, the fifty-four or so that we know. These describe a sacred river, a fountain, "a sunny pleasure-dome with caves of ice," where Kubla Khan hears "ancestral voices prophesying war!" As in most of Coleridge's great poems, perhaps it is that the mysterious evocations rouse, in our "collective unconscious," "ancestral voices."

At any rate, the fragment is a vivid image of the mysterious vitality of nature set against the recurring and conflicting paroxysms of human dreams, desires, and actions. It is, in a sense, the epitaph of a dejected genius.

Bibliography

Christabel

Adair, Patricia M.   *The Waking Dream: A Study of Coleridge's Poetry.* New York: Barnes & Noble: 1967, pp. 144–171.

Adlard, John.   "The Quantock *Christabel*," in *Philological Quarterly.* L (1971), pp. 230–238.

Alley, Alvin D.   "Coleridge and Existentialism," in *Southern Humanities Review.* II (Fall, 1968), pp. 459–460.

Angus, Douglas.   "The Theme of Love and Guilt in Coleridge's Three Major Poems," in *Journal of English and Germanic Philology.* LIX (October, 1960), pp. 655–668.

Basler, Roy P.   "Christabel," in *Sewanee Review.* LI (Winter, 1943), pp. 73–95.

————.   *Sex, Symbolism, and Psychology in Literature.* New Brunswick, N.J.: Rutgers University Press, 1948, pp. 25–51.

Bate, Walter Jackson.   *Coleridge.* New York: Macmillan, 1968, pp. 65–74.

Beer, J.B.   *Coleridge the Visionary.* New York: Collier, 1962, pp. 185–208.

Cornwell, John.   *Coleridge: Poet and Revolutionary, 1772–1804; A Critical Biography.* London: Allen Lane, 1973, pp. 287–291.

Farrison, W. Edward.   "Coleridge's *Christabel*, 'The Conclusion to Part II,' " in *College Language Association Journal.* V (December, 1961), pp. 83–94.

Fields, Beverly.   *Reality's Dark Dream: Dejection in Coleridge.* Kent, Oh.: Kent State University Press, 1967, pp. 56–86.

Flory, Wendell Stallard.   "Fathers and Daughters: Coleridge and *Christabel*," in *Women & Literature: A Journal of Women Writers and the Literary Treatment of Women up to 1900.* III (1975), pp. 5–15.

Harding, Anthony John. *Coleridge and the Idea of Love: Aspects of Relationship in Coleridge's Thought and Writing.* London: Cambridge University Press, 1974, pp. 66–74.

Holstein, Michael E. "Coleridge's *Christabel* as Psychodrama: Five Perspectives on the Intruder," in *Wordsworth Circle.* VII (1976), pp. 119–128.

Hunting, Constance. "Another Look at 'The Conclusion of Part II' of *Christabel,*" in *English Language Notes.* XII (1975), pp. 171–176.

Radley, Virginia L. "*Christabel*: Directions Old and New," in *Studies in English Literature, 1500–1900.* IV (Autumn, 1964), pp. 531–541.

Spatz, Jonas. "The Mystery of Eros: Sexual Initiation in Coleridge's *Christabel,*" in *PMLA.* XC (1975), pp. 107–116.

Tomlinson, Charles. "*Christabel,*" in *Interpretations: Essays on Twelve English Poems.* Edited by John Wain. London: Routledge and Kegan Paul, 1955, pp. 103–112.

Twitchell, James. "Coleridge's *Christabel,*" in *Explicator.* XXXV (1976), pp. 28–29.

Walsh, William. *Coleridge: The Work and the Relevance.* New York: Barnes & Noble, 1967, pp. 109–112.

Wormhoudt, Arthur. *The Demon Lover: A Psychoanalytic Approach to Literature.* New York: Exposition, 1949, pp. 29–42.

Yarlott, Geoffrey. *Coleridge & the Abyssinian Maid.* London: Methuen, 1967, pp. 176–202.

"Dejection: An Ode"

Bate, Walter Jackson. *Coleridge.* New York: Macmillan, 1968, pp. 106–110.

Bowra, C.M. *The Romantic Imagination.* Cambridge, Mass.: Harvard University Press, 1949, pp. 85–92.

Brett, R.L. "Coleridge and Wordsworth," in *Writers and Their Background: S.T. Coleridge.* Edited by R.L. Brett. London: Bell, 1971, pp. 186–188.

Fields, Beverly. *Reality's Dark Dream: Dejection in Coleridge.* Kent, Oh.: Kent State University Press, 1967, pp. 105–167.

Fogle, Richard H. "The Dejection of Coleridge's Ode," in *Journal of English Literary History.* XVII (March, 1950), pp. 71–77.

Fruman, Norman. *Coleridge, the Damaged Archangel.* New York: George Braziller, 1971, pp. 422–429.

Gay, R.M. "'Dejection: An Ode,'" in *Explicator.* II (November, 1943), item 14.

Harding, Anthony John. *Coleridge and the Idea of Love: Aspects of Relationship in Coleridge's Thought and Writing.* London: Cambridge University Press, 1974, pp. 74–78.

Jones, A.R. "Coleridge and Poetry: I. The Conversational and Other Poems," in *Writers and Their Background: S.T. Coleridge*. Edited by R.L. Brett. London: Bell, 1971, pp. 116–122.

Knight, G. Wilson. *The Starlit Dome: Essays in the Poetry of Vision*. New York: Oxford University Press, 1941, pp. 105–107.

Lefebure, Molly. *Samuel Taylor Coleridge: A Bondage of Opium*. New York: Stein and Day, 1974, pp. 355–358.

Mays, Morley J. " 'Dejection: An Ode,' " in *Explicator*. II (February, 1943), item 27.

Parker, Reeve. *Coleridge's Meditative Art*. Ithaca, N.Y.: Cornell University Press, 1975, pp. 180–209.

Prickett, Stephen. *Coleridge and Wordsworth: The Poetry of Growth*. Cambridge: Cambridge University Press, 1970, pp. 110–113.

Smith, James. "The Poetry of Coleridge," in *Scrutiny*. VIII (March, 1940), pp. 416–420.

Stallknecht, Newton Phelps. "The Doctrine of Coleridge's *Dejection* and Its Relation to Wordsworth's Philosophy," in *PMLA*. XLIX (March, 1934), pp. 196–207.

Thompson, William I. "Collapsed Universe and Structured Poem: Essay in Whiteheadian Criticism," in *College English*. XXVIII (October, 1966), pp. 27–29.

Walsh, William. *Coleridge: The Work and the Relevance*. New York: Barnes & Noble, 1967, pp. 131–136.

Yarlott, Geoffrey. *Coleridge & the Abyssianian Maid*. London: Methuen, 1967, pp. 248–274.

"Kubla Khan"

Adair, Patricia M. *The Waking Dream: A Study of Coleridge's Poetry*. New York: Barnes & Noble, 1967, pp. 108–143.

Angus, Douglas. "The Theme of Love and Guilt in Coleridge's Three Major Poems," in *Journal of English and Germanic Philology*. LIX (October, 1960), pp. 655–668.

Bate, Walter Jackson. *Coleridge*. New York: Macmillan, 1968, pp. 75–84.

Beer, John. "Coleridge and Poetry: I. Poems of the Supernatural," in *Writers and Their Background: S.T. Coleridge*. Edited by R.L. Brett. London: Bell, 1971, pp. 60–70.

————. *Coleridge the Visionary*. New York: Collier, 1962, pp. 209–240.

Bodkin, Maud. *Archetypal Patterns in Poetry*. London: Oxford University Press, 1934, pp. 90–116.

Cornwell, John. *Coleridge: Poet and Revolutionary, 1772–1804; A Critical Biography*. London: Allen Lane, 1973, pp. 181–190.

England, A.B.   " 'Kubla Khan' Again: The Ocean, the Caverns, and the Ancestral Voices," in *Ariel: A Review of International English Literature.* IV (1973), pp. 63–72.

Fleissner, Robert F.   "Shakespeare Again in Xanadu," in *Research Studies.* XLIII (1975), pp. 193–196.

Fogle, Richard Harter.   "The Romantic Unity of 'Kubla Khan,' " in *College English.* XIII (October, 1951), pp. 13–18.

Gerber, Richard.   "Keys to 'Kubla Khan,' " in *English Studies.* XLIV (October, 1963), pp. 321–341.

Hoffpauir, Richard A.   " 'Kubla Khan' and the Critics: Romantic Madness as Poetic Theme and Critical Response," in *English Studies in Canada.* II (1976), pp. 402–422.

Meier, Hans Heinreich.   "Ancient Lights on Kubla's Lines," in *English Studies.* XLVI (February, 1965), pp. 15–29.

Mercer, Dorothy F.   "The Symbolism of 'Kubla Khan,' " in *Journal of Aesthetics and Art Criticism.* XII (September, 1953), pp. 784–801.

Patterson, Charles I., Jr.   "The Daemonic in 'Kubla Khan': Toward Interpretation," in *PMLA.* LXXXIX (1974), pp. 1033–1042.

Piper, H.W.   "Two Paradises in 'Kubla Khan,' " in *Review of English Studies.* XXVII (1976), pp. 148–158.

Raine, Kathleen.   "Traditional Symbolism in 'Kubla Khan,' " in *Sewanee Review.* LXXII (Autumn, 1964), pp. 626–642.

Sloane, Eugene H.   "Coleridge's 'Kubla Khan': The Living Catacombs of the Mind," in *American Imago.* XXIX (1972), pp. 97–122.

Smith, James.   "The Poetry of Coleridge," in *Scrutiny.* VII (March, 1940), pp. 411–414.

Starr, Nathan Comfort.   "Coleridge's Sacred River," in *Papers on Language and Literature.* II (Spring, 1966), pp. 117–125.

Stevenson, Warren.   " 'Kubla Khan' as Symbol," in *Texas Studies in Literature and Language.* XIV (1972), pp. 605–630.

Walsh, William.   *Coleridge: The Work and the Relevance.* New York: Barnes & Noble, 1967, pp. 111–122.

Woodring, Carl R.   "Coleridge and the Khan," in *Essays in Criticism.* IX (October, 1959), pp. 361–368.

Yarlott, Geoffrey.   *Coleridge & the Abyssinian Maid.* London: Methuen, 1967, pp. 126–154.

THE RIME OF THE ANCIENT MARINER

Type of work: Poem
Author: Samuel Taylor Coleridge (1772–1834)
Type of plot: Ballad fantasy
Time of plot: Late medieval period
Locale: A voyage around the Horn into the Pacific and thence home
First published: 1798

Coleridge's intention in writing The Rime of the Ancient Mariner *was to make the supernatural seem real. To do so he carefully moves his reader from a realistic sea voyage, reinforced by concrete details from the everyday world, to a nightmarish otherworldly setting, where supernatural powers force the Ancient Mariner to undertake an allegorical quest for understanding and redemption.*

The Story

Three young gallants on their way to a wedding were stopped by an old gray-headed sailor who detained one of them. The Ancient Mariner held with his glittering eye a young man whose next of kin was being married in the church nearby and forced him to listen, against his will, to the old seaman's tale. The Ancient Mariner told how the ship left the home port and sailed southward to the equator. In a storm the vessel was blown to polar regions of snow and ice.

When an albatross flew out of the frozen silence, the crew hailed it as a good omen. The sailors made a pet of the albatross and regarded it as a fellow creature. One day the Ancient Mariner killed the bird with his crossbow. The superstitious sailors believed bad luck would follow.

Fair winds blew the ship northward until it reached the equator, where it was suddenly becalmed and lay for days without moving. The thirsty seamen blamed the Ancient Mariner and hung the dead albatross about his neck as a sign of his guilt.

In the distance a ship appeared, a skeleton ship which moved on the still sea where no wind blew. On its deck Death and Life-in-Death were casting dice for the crew and the Ancient Mariner. As a result of the cast, Death won the two hundred crew members, who dropped dead one by one. As the soul of each dead sailor rushed by, the Ancient Mariner was reminded of the whiz of his crossbow when he shot the albatross. Life-in-Death had won the Ancient Mariner, who must now live on to expiate his sins. Furthermore, the curse lived on in the eyes of the men who died accusing him. One night the Ancient Mariner, observing the beauty of the water snakes around the ship, blessed these creatures in his heart. The spell was broken. The albatross fell from his neck into the sea.

At last the Ancient Mariner was able to sleep. Rain fell to quench his thirst. The warped vessel began to move, and the bodies of the dead crew rose to resume their regular duties as the ship sailed quietly on, moved by a spirit toward the South Pole.

The Ancient Mariner fell into a trance. He awoke to behold his own country, the very port from which he had set sail. Then the angelic spirits left the dead bodies of the crew and appeared in their own forms of light. Meanwhile, the pilot on the beach had seen the lights and he rowed out with his son and a holy Hermit to bring the ship in to harbor.

Suddenly the ship sank, but the pilot pulled the Ancient Mariner into his boat. Once ashore, the old man asked the Hermit to hear his confession and give him penance. The Ancient Mariner told the Wedding Guest that at uncertain times since that moment, the agony of his guilt returned and he must tell the story of his voyage to one who must be taught love and reverence for all things God has made and loved.

The merry din of the wedding had ceased, and the Wedding Guest returned home a sadder and a wiser man.

Critical Evaluation

Critical opinion about *The Rime of the Ancient Mariner* runs the gamut from the sublime to the ridiculous; one commentator gives each line a gloss from the Bible, while another wonders why all the fuss is made about a bird. A modern critic (David Beres) finds in the poem a systematic description of an orally fixated, homosexual personality; another (Elder Olson) declares that the poem does not have to mean anything, that it stands simply as a beautiful object. A beautiful object it undeniably is, for read aloud its stanzas fall on the ear like music. But to view the poem simply as a travelog is perverse. Coleridge's contemporaries, for all their bewilderment about it, never doubted its high import; Coleridge himself added the gloss to the fifth edition in order to make the allegory more accessible, so it seems reasonable to conclude that he did not intend it merely as a Gothic horror tale.

But what did he intend? Born the son of an Anglican minister, he turned to Unitarianism at Cambridge, but before writing *The Rime of the Ancient Mariner* he had returned to orthodox belief. But he had absorbed certain tenets of Neoplatonism which clearly helped to shape *The Rime of the Ancient Mariner*; for example, Coleridge and other Romantics believed that men were united with all living things in having been divinely created. They thought that palpable reality was but a screen beyond which a higher reality existed. In addition, the notion that places and elements were inhabited by tutelary spirits had acquired a vogue in literary circles at least at that time. Elements of Protestantism and Neoplatonism, then, formed the philosophical impulses of the poem.

The physical circumstance and details that are their vehicle are equally easy to trace. At the time of composition Coleridge had never been to sea, but it is known that some years previously, perhaps in preparation for a voyage to North America where he and the poet Southey intended to set up a utopia, he had begun to read accounts of voyages around Cape Horn and to the hot climes of the Pacific. Navigational details of such voyages were familiar to everybody; the greater part of the descriptions of natural things, such as the green color of the polar ice and the sounds it makes, the phosphorescence clothing the "water-snakes," and the abrupt onset of night in the tropics, can be found almost verbatim in one or another chronicle or traveler's memoir of the time. The plot evolved strangely, from the smallest of seeds. A friend told the poet of a dream he had had of a skeleton craft worked by a ghostly crew. Coleridge decided to write a poem about this in collaboration with Wordsworth, in order to earn five pounds to pay for a walking tour. Wordsworth contributed a few lines and the suggestion that an albatross be the victim of the mariner's crime, before dropping out of the project, and Coleridge thereafter, in four months of sustained effort most uncharacteristic of him, completed the poem. It was and is the greatest of his poems, mysterious, ambiguous, and deliciously terrifying, defying pat interpretation.

Coleridge wanted to write a poem of which the virtue would "consist in the interesting of the affections by the dramatic truth of such emotions, as would naturally accompany [supernatural] situations, supposing them real." (Coleridge, quoted in *The Annotated Ancient Mariner* by Martin Gardner.) His first object, then, was to anchor the physical circumstances firmly in the known. To begin with, he employed the ballad form and strategic archaisms, as evocative and familiar as "Once Upon a Time." Then he set the tale upon the sea. No one in England can live farther from the sea than a hundred miles or so, and all Englishmen look on seafaring as their birthright. (At the same time, none would venture to point out the exact latitude or hour of the day when the sea ceases to be a mere element and becomes a force in itself.) In addition, the navigational details in the poem are flawlessly correct: the sun overhead at noon when the ship is on the Equator, the frightful cold and emptiness of the polar passage, the sudden glare of the sun when the ice-fog is left behind, the trade winds blowing northeasterly that carried the ship north to the line again. Other details too: the warping of the deck in the calm, the thin rotting sails at the end of the voyage, all help to anchor the story in quotidian reality. At what point, then, does the ship pass into the spirit-haunted world of guilt, retribution, and rebirth? At the point farthest from home, the passage around Cape Horn. It is here that the Albatross appears, that Christlike creature that "loved the man/who shot him with his bow." The act of shooting the albatross is so boldly stated, without any attempt at motivation or explanation, that it packs a tremendous emotional punch. Upon this act as on a pivot the entire plot turns; it is the reason for everything that follows. The reader is given notice that he is entering the realm of the supernatural. Yet it all happens so gradually that the sense of reality is preserved. The ship is becalmed in the tropics; what could be more ordinary?

The kind of suffering experienced by the mariner leaves no doubt about the Christian character of the allegory. The albatross is hung from his neck as a Christian wears a cross. He suffers the agonies of thirst, dryness being a universal symbol of spiritual drought, separation from the creative principle. He is brought by the grace of God to understand his kinship to the monsters of the calm, and so to all living things ("Sure my kind saint took pity on me,/ and I blessed them *unaware*"). He is refreshed with rain, baptised anew when, by supernatural agency, the ship sinks in the home harbor. He is shriven of the guilt but not the memory of his crime, and like the Wandering Jew roams the world, telling his tale of death-in-life and rebirth in love.

Bibliography

Alley, Alvin D.   "Coleridge and Existentialism," in *Southern Humanities Review*. II (Fall, 1968), pp. 456–458.

Angus, Douglas.   "The Theme of Love and Guilt in Coleridge's Three Major Poems," in *Journal of English and Germanic Philology*. LIX (October, 1960), pp. 655–668.

Bosletter, Edward E.   "The Nightmare World of *The Ancient Mariner*," in *Coleridge: A Collection of Critical Essays*. Edited by Kathleen Coburn. Englewood Cliffs, N.J.: Prentice-Hall, 1967, pp. 65–77.

Brett, R.L.   *Reason and Imagination: A Study of Form and Meaning in Four Poems*. London: Oxford University Press, 1960, pp. 78–107.

Buchan, A.M.   "The Sad Wisdom of the Mariner," in *Studies in Philology*. LXI (October, 1964), pp. 669–688.

Creed, Howard.   "*The Rime of the Ancient Mariner*: A Rereading," in *English Journal*. XLIX (April, 1960), pp. 215–222.

Delson, Abe.   "The Symbolism of the Sun and Moon in *The Rime of the Ancient Mariner*," in *Texas Studies in Literature and Language*. XV (1974), pp. 707–720.

Dyck, Sarah.   "Perspective in *The Rime of the Ancient Mariner*," in *Studies in English Literature, 1500–1900*. XIII (1973), pp. 591–604.

Ebbatson, J.R.   "Coleridge's Mariner and the Rights of Man," in *Studies in Romanticism*. XI (1972), pp. 171–206.

Empson, William.   "The Ancient Mariner," in *Critical Quarterly*. VI (Winter, 1964), pp. 298–319.

Fulmer, O. Bryan.   "The Ancient Mariner and the Wandering Jew," in *Studies in Philology*. LXVI (October, 1969), pp. 797–815.

Gibbons, Edward E. "Point of View and Moral: *The Ancient Mariner*," in *University Review.* XXXV (June, 1969), pp. 257–261.

Gose, Elliot B., Jr. "Coleridge and the Luminous Gloom: An Analysis of the 'Symbolic Language' in *The Rime of the Ancient Mariner*," in *PMLA.* LXXV (June, 1960), pp. 238–244.

Harding, D.W. "The Theme of *The Ancient Mariner*," in *Coleridge: A Collection of Critical Essays.* Edited by Kathleen Coburn. Englewood Cliffs, N.J.: Prentice-Hall, 1967, pp. 51–64.

Littman, Mark. "*The Ancient Mariner* and Initiation Rites," in *Papers on Language and Literature.* IV (Fall, 1968), pp. 370–389.

Lupton, Mary Jane H. "*The Rime of the Ancient Mariner*: The Agony of Thirst," in *American Imago.* XXVII (1970), pp. 140–159.

McDonald, Daniel. "Too Much Reality: A Discussion of *The Rime of the Ancient Mariner*," in *Studies in English Literature.* IV (Autumn, 1964), pp. 543–554.

May, Charles E. "Objectifying the Nightmare: Cain and the Mariner," in *Ball State University Forum.* XIV (1973), pp. 45–48.

Owen, Charles A. "Structure in *The Ancient Mariner*," in *College English.* XXIII (January, 1962), pp. 261–267.

Pafford, Ward. "Coleridge's Wedding-Guest," in *Studies in Philology.* LX (October, 1963), pp. 618–626.

Piper, H.W. "*The Ancient Mariner*: Biblical Allegory, Poetic Symbolism and Religious Crisis," in *Southern Review.* X (1977), pp. 232–242.

Rowell, Charles H. "Coleridge's Symbolic Albatross," in *College Language Association Journal.* VI (December, 1962), pp. 133–135.

Stevenson, Warren. "*The Rime of the Ancient Mariner* as Epic Symbol," in *Dalhousie Review.* LVI (1976), pp. 542–547.

Ware, Malcolm. "*The Rime of the Ancient Mariner*: A Discourse on Prayer?," in *Review of English Studies.* XI (August, 1960), pp. 303–304.

THOMAS DE QUINCEY

Born: Manchester, England (August 15, 1785)
Died: Edinburgh, Scotland (December 8, 1859)

Principal Works

ESSAYS AND STUDIES: *Confessions of an English Opium Eater*, 1822; *The Logic of Political Economy*, 1844; *Collected Writings*, edited by David Masson, 1889–1890 (14 vols.).
NOVEL: *Klosterheim*, 1832.

Thomas De Quincey, a close associate of Coleridge and Wordsworth, deserved to be near the center of the great Romantic Movement in England. Like the other Romantics, he placed great emphasis on feeling; like some of them, he was a master of the curious and obscure in literature; and he was a creator of a poetic prose that, in its range of diction and display of surprising fancy, is the equal of any writing of his time. It is prose written by an isolated man, a man in whom dream and vigor are not antithetical.

De Quincey was born in Manchester, August 15, 1785, the fifth child in a family of eight children. His busy and stern parents soon alienated De Quincey, who was a sensitive and quiet child much in need of understanding. The boy's only comfort within his own family was an unusually close devotion to one of his sisters, whose untimely death left him alone, disturbed, and morose.

Since both of De Quincey's parents were well-educated and interested in scholarship, he at least did not lack for opportunity of study. A brilliant if somewhat unbalanced boy, he could read, write, and speak Greek "as though it were his native tongue" by the age of fifteen. Dissatisfied with the restrictions of his home and also by his own shortcomings, De Quincey ran off at the age of seventeen. For almost a year he hid in London, where he led a frugal and difficult life of study and introspection. Here he performed his deep reading of English poets, a reading characteristic of all the Romantics. This period he later called an "impassioned parenthesis of my life." Reunited with his family, he was allowed to enter Oxford in 1803. There he quickly won the reputation of brilliant scholar and conversationalist, but left without taking a degree in 1808.

When De Quincey was about twenty he became subject to severe pain. Some say it was a stomach disorder; others, that it was a combination of eyestrain and astigmatism. Upon a friend's suggestion, he started to use laundanum for relief from his discomfort. Apparently as a child he had been subject to deep dreams or visions; and since he was not adjusted either to himself or the people around him, it is natural to suppose that he welcomed the artificial, remote dream world that the continued use of opium led him into. It was a habit he submitted to for over twenty years; then, for no explainable reason, he disciplined himself and ceased its use. This was a period of immeasurable physical and emotional torture for De Quincey; but world literature is the richer for it.

After college he made the acquaintance of the Lake poets and, in 1816, married; both relations were happy ones, in part because of the charm of De Quincey's own nature, which was courteous, playful, and firm. His life was one of much literary toil, he supported himself and his large family by contributions to *Blackwood's, Hogg's Weekly Instructor*, and other magazines, whose editors gave him—as must seem to readers of modern periodicals—very free rein. He touched a wide variety of topics and—as in the celebrated "Flight of a Tartar Tribe"—in a way quite imaginative and fanciful.

De Quincey moved to Edinburgh, leaving behind such London friends as Lamb and Hazlitt, like him masters of a colored and personal style. (It was these friends who encouraged him to write the *Confessions of an English Opium Eater*, the work that brought him fame and assured him the attention of editors and publishers.) De Quincey continued his periodical writing until his death in Edinburgh: December 8, 1859. It is said that when the quantity of his writing became too voluminous for his lodgings, he would simply move away from the mass and start fresh elsewhere.

Representative samples of his ability to take an assigned topic and effect a personal transmutation of it appear in "Joan of Arc" (1847) and "On Murder Considered as One of the Fine Arts" (1827). De Quincey's reminiscences of the Lake poets reveal a unique view of the great men of his day. In all his writing De Quincey well illustrates a famous literary distinction of his own creation between the literature of knowledge and the literature of power. He may begin on a theme which suggests that the writer will convey knowledge (information or instruction); but few essays conclude without creating in the reader a sense of unexpected and, indeed, ungovernable fantasy at work.

Bibliography

For many years the standard biographical and critical study was David Masson, *De Quincey*, 1887; but this work has now been superseded by Horace Ainsworth Eaton, *Thomas De Quincey*, 1936, and Edward Sackville-West, *Thomas De Quincey: His Life and Work*, 1936. See also Malcolm Elwin, *De Quincey*, 1935; John C. Metcalf, *De Quincey: A Portrait*, 1940; Sigmund K. Proctor, *Thomas De Quincey's Theory of Literature*, 1943; John E. Jordan, *Thomas De Quincey: Literary Critic*, 1952, and *De Quincey to Wordsworth: A Biography of a Relationship*, 1962; and Judson S. Lyon, *Thomas De Quincey*, 1969.

CONFESSIONS OF AN ENGLISH OPIUM EATER

Type of work: Essays
Author: Thomas De Quincey (1785–1859)
Type of treatise: Confession and fantasy
Time of treatise: Early nineteenth century
Locale: England and Wales
First published: 1821

> *Because De Quincey was a conscious stylist who attempted to charge his prose with the imagination and emotional qualities of poetry, this work is often difficult for the modern reader to appreciate, in spite of its sensational subject matter. The essays abound in deliberate displays of erudition, protracted sentimentality, latinate diction and sentence structures, and apostrophes to inanimate objects or abstract ideas.*

The Story

When Thomas De Quincey was about twenty-eight years of age, intense stomach pains drove him to take opium for relief. These stomach pains were a legacy from hardships that he endured as an adolescent.

De Quincey's father had died when the boy was seven. Thomas, the joint responsibility of four guardians, was sent to school, where he became an excellent Greek scholar. Later, at the Manchester Grammar School, he was so superior to his teachers in Greek that he soon felt a desire to leave the school. His guardians being against this plan, however, he asked an old friend for money, received it, and planned to make his escape from a school which he felt had nothing to offer him intellectually.

The day of his escape came. When the groom of his hall was carrying his book-laden trunk down a narrow stairway, the man slipped and fell, the trunk clattering noisily to the floor below. Young De Quincey was sure he would be caught. But the incident, miraculously, did not arouse the curiosity of the resident master, and the youth was able to get away.

Seventeen-year-old De Quincey headed westward, walking through Wales, where, in Bangor, he took a room. His landlady was the ex-servant of a bishop's family. On one of her regular visits to the bishop's house, she disclosed that she was taking in lodgers. When she reported her disclosure to De Quincey, he took exception to the tenor of her remarks concerning him, moved out of her house at once, and found lodging in inns. That type of lodging being relatively expensive, the young man soon found himself reduced to eating only once a day, and this a meal of only coffee or tea. The mountain air of Wales and the walking made him abnormally hungry, so that his having to subsist off berries and charitable handouts hurt him physically. As time went by, he managed to earn a meager living by writing letters for the illiterate and by doing odd jobs. But the damage to his health had been done.

His travels then took him from Wales to London, where, utterly destitute and afraid to reveal himself to any friends of his family, he lived for several months on little more than a small ration of bread; also, at that time, he slept out of doors. At last, in cold weather, an acquaintance gave him shelter in a large, almost empty house, where De Quincey's companion was a ten-year-old girl. Pains in his stomach prevented his ever getting a proper night's sleep; consequently, he slept by fits and snatches both day and night. The master of the house was a legal representative of moneylenders, but despite the man's apparent lack of principles De Quincey found him generous in his way. The little girl appeared to be a servant in the large house, which was situated near Soho Square.

De Quincey walked the streets and often sat all day in parks, until Ann, a sixteen-year-old streetwalker, befriended him. One night, when he had a violent attack of his stomach complaint, Ann spent part of her scant savings on wine and spices for him.

Soon afterward he met an old family acquaintance who gave him money, thus ending De Quincey's period of extreme poverty. Previously, he had been afraid to appeal to family friends for help for fear that his guardians would send him back to the grammar school. That he might have taken on literary work of some kind never occurred to him. Now, solvent for the moment, he made arrangements to get an advance on his patrimony, which would not be legally his until his twenty-first birthday.

After saying goodbye to Ann, he took a coach to Eton to get a signature that was required for an advance on his patrimony. At Eton he called upon an acquaintance, young Lord Desart, who invited him to breakfast. Finding that he could not keep down the food, he took wine to his great comfort. Lord Desart, who was only eighteen, was reluctant to sign for security, but he finally consented. De Quincey returned to London, where he found that Lord Desart's signature did not impress the moneylenders with whom he was negotiating for the advance. Again he was threatened with hardship; again, however, he was saved, for his reconciled relatives sent him to Oxford University. Meanwhile, before he left London, he searched unsuccessfully for Ann. She was nowhere to be found, and he never saw her again.

De Quincey, now nineteen, made frequent weekend trips to London from Oxford. One Sunday, while in the metropolis, he suffered agonies from neuralgic pains in the head, and a fellow student whom he encountered recommended opium for relief. He thereupon bought a small amount of laudanum, the tincture of opium, from an apothecary. He returned to his room and took the prescribed amount. The result seemed phenomenal to him; all his pain ceased, and he knew boundless pleasure. There was no intoxication, as from wine or spirits; there was only a protracted sense of being utterly at peace with the world and with himself. The opium uplifted the intellect rather than the animal spirits, and when its effect wore off there was no period of depression such as spirits induced.

As a college student, De Quincey's two great pleasures were to hear Grassini, an Italian soprano who often sang in London, or to take opium and afterward join the Saturday night crowds in the London markets. Even greater than these pleasures, however, was that of withdrawing himself at the time when the opium had reached its maximum effect on his mind, so that he could get the most complete enjoyment from his opium-induced dreams and visions.

De Quincey left Oxford. In 1812 he took a cottage, where he studied German metaphysics and continued to take opium once a week. His health was apparently never better. Even after eight years of taking opium, he was able to say that he had not become a slave to the drug; he was still able to control the amount taken and the intervals between doses.

But a recurrence, in 1813, of his old stomach disorder led him to take the drug every day. That he was already partially addicted was a secondary reason for his increased use of opium. For two years he took three hundred and twenty grains of opium daily, but at last he was able to reduce the amount to forty grains. Staying on that allowance, he experienced the happiest year of his life.

About that time a Malay, traveling afoot, stopped for a night at the cottage. De Quincey was impressed by the aspect and garb of the Oriental. Before the man left the next morning, De Quincey gave him enough opium, divided into three parts, to kill a man if taken all at once. The Malay clapped all three pieces into his mouth and departed. De Quincey felt concern for several days, but to his relief he never heard or read of the untimely death of a Malay in his part of Great Britain.

In his little cottage in the mountains of northern England, De Quincey, in the winter of 1816–1817, knew complete happiness in his experience with opium. Deep snows, heavy rains, a snug cottage, a roaring fire, a large collection of good books, plenty of tea, and daily consumption of laudanum brought him idyllic happiness.

But matters changed. Having become addicted to the daily taking of opium, it became impossible for him to reduce his daily allowance without bringing on abnormal perspiration and excruciating abdominal pains. He soon lost interest in reading and the study of mathematics and philosophy. A friend sent him David Ricardo's *Principles of Political Economy and Taxation.* The book aroused him from his lethargy long enough to write for publication on that popular subject. Then, unable to write a preface for his work, he shelved the project. He neglected household responsibilities. At night he lay awake in his bed, processions of visions passing through his mind. These visions consisted largely of scenes from the English Civil War and from ancient Rome. Soon he found it difficult to distinguish between the real and the unreal. Furthermore, other dreams and visions took him into frightful abysses. Constantly depressed, he lost all normal sense of space and time, and he often had the sensation of having lived through a millennium. Also, he found himself able to recall insignificant events of his childhood, details which he had never been conscious of remembering.

The opium dreams were periodic in subject matter: there were nights during which he dreamed historical scenes; then there was a period of architectural dreams—vast piles of buildings and enormous cities; these were followed by dreams of water—lakes, lagoons, vast oceans; and next a period of dreams in which countless human faces presented themselves in peculiar situations to his mind's eye.

In May, 1818, his dream visions took on an Oriental theme. At times he was in Egypt, then in China, or in India. Where in previous dream sequences he had known only spiritual horrors, in these Oriental ones he sensed physical horror from reptiles and frightful birds.

In the summer of 1819, De Quincey, still addicted to opium, dreamed of a graveyard in his own little valley. In the dream he arose and walked out of his cottage yard to enjoy the air. He thought he saw an Oriental city and, beneath a palm tree, Ann, the streetwalker friend of his youth. She did not speak; the dream faded and he found himself walking with her in the streets of London. In 1820 one vision was so terrifying in its profundity and breadth that he awoke and declared that he would never sleep again.

Finally, he reasoned that he would surely die if he continued to take opium and that he might die in the attempt to break the habit. With so little choice, he decided to try, at least, to free himself from opium. He reduced his ration gradually and finally broke free, thus proving to himself that an addict may end a habit of seventeen years' duration.

Critical Evaluation

In 1821, at the age of thirty-six, Thomas De Quincey was an unemployed writer with a wife and a family to support. Married "beneath his station" to a farmer's daughter, Margaret Simpson, in 1817 (a few months after their first child was born), he would eventually father eight children, whose needs kept him working at Grub Street journalism for thirty years. A self-styled philosopher, he never managed to finish the ambitious books he contemplated; their grandiose titles—such as a *Prolegomena to All Future Systems of Political Economy*—recall Coleridge's lists of projected works. In 1921, De Quincey had published nothing but a Postscript to a pamphlet by Wordsworth and some pieces, mostly unsigned, in a country newspaper. It was in these circumstances that De Quincey published, anonymously, the *Confessions of an English Opium Eater*, in two installments, in the September and October, 1821, issues of the *London Magazine*.

The *Confessions of an English Opium Eater* was an immediate sensation, arousing both commentary in many journals and extraordinary public interest. The author's identity was soon disclosed. De Quincey himself responded to many of the reactions to his work, promising also a third installment which, characteristically, he never finished. The work appeared in book form in 1822 and was reprinted many times; although De Quincey did not make a great deal of money directly, he was launched on his public career as an essayist, occasional novelist, and pen-for-hire. At the age of seventy, De Quincey undertook for inclusion in his collected works a revision of the *Confessions of an English Opium Eater*, and a number of editions print this inferior version, which is nearly three times the length of the original. But this leisurely reshaping by the aged, eminent man of letters could hardly have been imagined by his harried younger self.

It is helpful when beginning to read this work to bear in mind the circumstances of its composition. De Quincey begins in an insufferably sanctimonious tone, reminiscent of Coleridge at his worst: "I have for many months hesitated about the propriety. . . ." The introductory section, "To the Reader," gives the impression that one is about to read a sort of tract on the evils of opium. Hypocrisy? De Quincey was probably not consciously dishonest. In his day it was not the custom to confess one's sins and weaknesses publicly in order to prove good faith, while religiously avoiding any explicit claim to virtue. De Quincey was no more hypocritical than the contemporary writer who regards the chaos of his inner life with a practiced eye, judiciously selecting certain "sins" to confess, while keeping silent about others which might appear too mean, petty, or simply boring in print.

Nevertheless, there is a duplicity to the *Confessions of an English Opium Eater*, for it surely does not preach its ostensible moral. De Quincey was quite aware of the sensational market value of his material; he must have been at least subliminally aware that his account of the pleasures of opium was the most persuasive, evangelical, section of the work, as even his metaphors suggest: after contrasting the ill-effects of liquor (which encourages brutality) with the benefits of opium (under the influence of which "the moral affections are in a state of cloudless serenity; and over all is the great light of the majestic intellect"), he pronounces: "This is the doctrine of the true church on the subject of opium: of which church I acknowledge myself to be the only member—the alpha and the omega. . . ."

"Duplicity" implies a policy of deception; what one actually senses, reading the *Confessions of an English Opium Eater*, is an intense inner conflict, a "split" in the self such as is found later in the century in the case of Charles Dodgson/ Lewis Carroll and in the character of Sherlock Holmes. Thus De Quincey insistently characterizes himself as a "philosopher," a characterization so inept that it arouses pity, anger, and laughter all at once, as when he solemnly explains that, while stoned on opium, for "nearly two years I believe I read no book but one," which turns out to be David Ricardo's *Principles of Political Economy and Taxation*. He read lyric poets "by snatches," he adds, but "my proper vocation, as I well knew, was the exercise of the analytic understanding." His very name points to a contradiction: born Thomas Quincey, he added the "De" himself; always suffering from feelings of inferiority, he nevertheless included sententious passages in which he disavowed any desire to be an aristocrat.

His narrative account of the circumstances which led to his addiction has the logic of paranoia. He explains that although he had used opium sparingly, for pleasure, for some years, he did not begin to use it daily until he was twenty-eight, when a stomach ailment forced him to it. This ailment was caused, he writes, by "extremities of hunger, suffered in my boyish days," about ten years earlier. He then proposes to explain how these "youthful sufferings" came about. Quite simply, De Quincey left school when he was seventeen, striking out on his own to enter the university. He would have done so in a year in any case, but he was so superior in intellect to his schoolmaster, he explains, that he could not endure another year as a "schoolboy." His guardians would not approve his desire, so he left, apparently with the intention of borrowing enough money against his inheritance to begin at the university immediately. He ended up, broke and hungry, in London, where he met the young prostitute Ann, who was to haunt his imagination and his dreams for the rest of his life.

This crucial section of the *Confessions of an English Opium Eater* which purports to explain how he came to be an addict, is maddening, disturbing, and undeniably powerful. The narrative has a plausible surface, it has the linking devices of conventional narrative, yet something is wrong. As a rational explanation it is entirely unsatisfactory, yet the emotional logic is clear: De Quincey's value (his brilliance, his superiority as a Greek scholar in particular) was not sufficiently recognized; therefore he became an opium addict.

For a number of literary generations the work had a quaint exotic quality which it no longer has today, when drug abuse of all kinds is so terribly familiar. A line of descent can be traced from De Quincey's London to the drug culture of recent times; but there are other claims to be made on behalf of the *Confessions of an English Opium Eater*, along with the eccentric essays which are still anthologized. De Quincey's interest in dreams, his introspection, and the "illogical" structure of his prose anticipate the work of many modern writers. Yet his most enduring claim is that great indefinable, style.

Seventy-five years ago De Quincey, like Macaulay, was prominently featured—in what we now call Composition courses—as a model, a master to imitate. Today, under the tyranny of the "plain style," all that has changed: the editors of the influential *Norton Anthology*, for example, find De Quincey's prose "too contrived to sustain his reputation as one of the supreme prose stylists," and suggest that we should read him for other reasons: his exploration of the "night-side of human consciousness" and the "novel principles" which govern the structure of his prose. Both approaches to style are incorrect. *Every* style is contrived: the dialogue of Hemingway, as many readers have observed, now sounds as stylized as that of John Webster. Style is the gift of projecting an individual world; it is ultimately as indefinable as an individual human being is indefinable: only as an American, male, a steelworker—a member of a group—can he be defined. De Quincey has the gift of style, not a technique to be imitated, but a world to be inhabited, for as long as we are reading his marvelous sentences.

Bibliography

Abrams, M.H.   *The Milk of Paradise: The Effect of Opium Visions on the Works of De Quincey, Crabbe, Francis Thompson, and Coleridge.* Cambridge, Mass.: Harvard University Press, 1934, pp. 6–13.

Bett, Walter R.   *The Infirmities of Genius.* London: Christopher Johnson, 1952, pp. 91–102.

Bilsland, John W.   "De Quincey's Opium Experiences," in *Dalhousie Review.* LV (1975), pp. 419–430.

Blake, Kathleen.   "The Whispering Gallery and Structural Coherence in De Quincey's Revised *Confessions of an English Opium Eater*," in *Studies in English Literature.* XIII (1973), pp. 13, 632–642.

Bolitho, William.   "Introduction," in *Confessions of an English Opium Eater.* Oxford: Shakespeare Head Press, 1930, pp. i–vii.

Cooke, Michael G.   "De Quincey, Coleridge, and the Formal Uses of Intoxication," in *Yale French Studies.* L (1974), pp. 26–40.

Davies, Hugh Sykes.   *Thomas De Quincey.* London: Longmans, Green, 1964, pp. 5–35.

Elton, Oliver.   "Thomas De Quincey," in his *A Survey of English Literature, 1780–1830*, Volume II. London: Edward Arnold, 1912, pp. 312–333.

Elwin, Malcolm.   "Introduction," in *Confessions of an English Opium Eater.* London: MacDonald, 1956, pp. vii–xx.

Grant, Douglas.   "Thomas De Quincey," in *Some British Romantics: A Collection of Essays.* Edited by James V. Logan, John E. Jordan and Northrop Frye. Columbus: Ohio State University Press, 1966, pp. 143–166.

Hayter, Althea.   "Introduction," in *Confessions of an English Opium Eater.* Harmondsworth, England: Penguin, 1971, pp. 7–24.

Jack, Ian.   *English Literature, 1815–1832.* Oxford: Clarendon Press, 1963, pp. 292–311.

Lyon, Judson S.   *Thomas De Quincey.* New York: Twayne, 1969, pp. 91–97, 177–179.

Mayoux, Jean-Jacques.   "De Quincey: Humor and the Drugs," in *Veins of Humor.* Edited by Harry Levin. Cambridge, Mass.: Harvard University Press, 1972, pp. 109–129.

Miller, J. Hillis.   *The Disappearance of God: Five Nineteenth-Century Writers.* Cambridge, Mass.: Harvard University Press, 1963, pp. 17–80.

Porte, Joel. "In the Hands of an Angry God: Religious Terror in Gothic Fiction," in *The Gothic Imagination: Essays in Dark Romanticism*. Edited by G.R. Thompson. Pullman: Washington State University Press, 1974, pp. 45–50.

Rubenstein, Jill. "The Curse of Subjectivity: De Quincey's *Confessions of an English Opium Eater* and Baudelaire's *Paradis Artificiels*," in *Romance Notes*. XV (Autumn, 1973), pp. 68–73.

Sackville West, Edward. *Thomas De Quincey: His Life and Work*. New Haven, Conn.: Yale University Press, 1936.

Woolf, Virginia. *The Common Reader*. New York: Harcourt, Brace, 1948, pp. 141–149.

WILLIAM HAZLITT

Born: Maidstone, England (April 10, 1778)
Died: London, England (September 18, 1830)

Principal Works

INFORMAL AND LITERARY ESSAYS: *The Round Table*, 1817; *Table Talk*, 1821–1822; *The Spirit of the Age, or Contemporary Portraits*, 1825; *The Plain Speaker*, 1826; *Winterslow*, 1839; *Sketches and Essays*, 1839.
CRITICAL STUDIES: *Characters of Shakespeare's Plays*, 1817; *Lectures on the English Poets*, 1818; *Views of the English Stage*, 1818; *Lectures on the English Comic Writers*, 1819; *Dramatic Literature of the Age of Elizabeth*, 1821.
AUTOBIOGRAPHY: *Liber Amoris, or the New Pygmalion*, 1823.
BIOGRAPHY: *Life of Napoleon*, 1828.

One of the great English Romantic critics, William Hazlitt, born in Maidstone, England, on April 10, 1778, was also one of the first great journalistic essayists. He was a political liberal, writing eloquent defenses of the principles of the French Revolution, and he replied savagely to the attacks of the Scottish Tory reviewers, though he himself was not free from politically prejudiced literary criticism. He attacked the later work of the Lake Poets, mainly because they had turned politically conservative. All his work is marked by a complete independence of spirit. He cannot be classed with any particular "school" of criticism; he is simply a courageous, honest, and sensitive man who brought his serious mind to bear upon literature.

Hazlitt inherited his liberalism from his father, a Unitarian minister who sympathized with the American fight for independence. In 1783 the Rev. William Hazlitt emigrated with his family to America, but after an unsuccessful struggle he returned to England in the winter of 1786. He took a small parish in Wem, Shropshire, where young William Hazlitt attended school. In 1793 Hazlitt was sent to the Hackney Theological College to become a dissenting minister. He soon decided against that profession and returned to Wem. He heard Coleridge preach at Shrewsbury in 1798, and the poet's influence and example after their meeting encouraged him in his study of metaphysics. The next year he visited Coleridge and met Wordsworth.

In 1802 Hazlitt decided to become a portrait painter like his brother John, and he went to Paris to copy pictures at the Louvre. Four months later he returned to London; he had decided that he could never be a very good painter. He lectured for a time on modern philosophy but later turned to journalism. He was a Parliamentary reporter and then the drama critic for the *Morning Chronicle*; he also contributed articles to Leigh Hunt's *Examiner*. His *Characters of Shakespeare's Plays* is a basic work in Shakespearean criticism, and his *Dramatic Literature of the Age of Elizabeth* directed attention toward some of the more neglected playwrights of that period.

Hazlitt's marriage to Sarah Stoddart in 1808 was a miserable match of two opposed temperaments. He had a passionate affair with the ignorant daughter of his landlord; *Liber Amoris* records the history of the attachment. He finally freed himself from the girl, divorced his wife, and married a Mrs. Bridgewater. Toward the end of his life his publisher suffered financial difficulties, and Hazlitt died in poverty, on September 18, 1830, in London. Modern criticism regards him as an important critic, a master of the familiar essay, and a distinguished prose stylist.

Bibliography

The *Complete Works of Hazlitt* have been edited by P. P. Howe, 21 vols., 1933. A useful volume is *The Essays: A Selection*, edited by C. M. Maclean, 1949; see also H. M. Sikes, ed., *The Hazlitt Sampler: Selections from His Familiar, Literary and Critical Essays*, 1961. There is a *Bibliography of Hazlitt* by Geoffrey Keynes, 1931. At least three good biographies have been published: Augustine Birrell, *Hazlitt*, English Men of Letters Series, 1902; P. P. Howe, *Life of William Hazlitt*, 1922; and C. M. Maclean, *Born Under Saturn: A Biography of William Hazlitt*, 1944. More recent is H. C. Baker, *William Hazlitt*, 1962. Good material on Hazlitt appears in M. H. Law, *The English Familiar Essay in the Early Nineteenth Century*, 1934. Worthwhile critical judgments appear in the essays included in George Saintsbury, *Collected Essays and Papers*, 1924; H. W. Garrad, *The Profession of Poetry, and Other Lectures*, 1929; and Virginia Woolf, *The Second Common Reader*, 1935. See also C. I. Patterson, "William Hazlitt as a Critic of Prose Fiction," *Publications of the Modern Language Association*, LXVIII (1953), 1001–1016.

THE CRITICAL ESSAYS OF WILLIAM HAZLITT

Author: William Hazlitt (1778–1830)
First published: Characters of Shakespeare's Plays, 1817; *Lectures on the English Poets,* 1818; *Views of the English Stage,* 1818; *Lectures on the English Comic Writers,* 1819; *Dramatic Literature of the Age of Elizabeth,* 1821.

Essay-Review

There were two pre-eminent literary critics in the second decade of the nineteenth century, Samuel Taylor Coleridge and William Hazlitt. While the former developed his critical principles in his early philosophical studies and in a decade of splendid poetic creation, the latter had no such period of creativity to look back on when he began his career as journalist-critic in 1813, at the age of thirty-six. His early life was a series of failures. Neither his earnest attempts to become a portraitist nor equally earnest attempts to make a reputation as a political and philosophical writer had borne fruit. In 1812, he and his family lived in London almost without funds until a series of lectures helped set the family on its feet. Hazlitt then served an important apprenticeship as a journalist in Parliament and, in 1813, found the work which exactly suited him: writing dramatic criticism and essays on many topics for various periodicals.

Within a decade Hazlitt ranked with Coleridge as literary critic as a result of both his lectures and his essays. Hazlitt's popular series *Lectures on the English Poets* was given early in 1818; *English Comic Writers* was delivered late that year. The following year he delivered the series *The Dramatic Literature of the Age of Elizabeth*. These lecture series were duly issued in book form. His most important written criticism includes *View of the English Stage*, which covers the years 1813–1818, and the *Characters of Shakespeare's Plays*.

Hazlitt was one of the first professional critics to have a significant identity as a critic. In the previous century, when the monthly reviews were established, most criticism was anonymous and probably no critic was half so well known for his criticism as Hazlitt became. One reason is that earlier writers on literature, such as Tobias Smollett and Samuel Johnson, relied largely on original compositions for their livelihood and reputations, while Hazlitt, through his essays and lectures, built his reputation as an essayist-critic.

He made his critical reputation largely by reviewing contemporary drama and by lecturing, often on Elizabethan poetry and drama. Thus, like most literary critics, he had his feet planted in both past and present. He often tried to explain the difference between the contemporary and the Elizabethan, the antipodes of literary creation in Hazlitt's mind. He admired the work of several Renaissance writers basically for their objectivity. As he wrote of Shakespeare in "On Shakespeare and Milton," "He was the least of an egotist that it was possible to be." Or, as the Hazlitt-inspired John Keats was to write later the same year: "the poetical Character . . . is not itself—it has no self—it is every thing and nothing." Hazlitt admired Shakespeare for keeping his self out of his poetry and for his genius in leaving his own consciousness behind in order to enter the consciousness of his characters. It is understandable, therefore, that Hazlitt would find serious flaws in the poetry of his own age. It was for him, generally, unbearably narcissistic. In a review of *Childe Harold's Pilgrimage*, he lashes out at the ennui and world-weariness of Byron's self-contemplative hero. From such a position it is a small step to this assessment of Byron's famous contemporary: "Mr. Wordsworth, to salve his own self-love, makes the merest toy of his own mind,—the most insignificant object he can meet with,—of as much importance as the universe." It was the subjectivity or the egotism of the moderns that revolted Hazlitt, as he clearly revealed in his review of *The Excursion*. Despite his high praise for the poem "in power of intellect, in lofty conception, in the depth of feeling, at once simple and sublime," he finds fault with both the descriptions of nature and the handling of human nature since "an intense intellectual egotism swallows up every thing." Nevertheless, it would be wrong to conclude that Hazlitt was unfairly prejudiced against the poets of his day; he was neither blind to the originality and power of his contemporaries nor unwilling to praise their works.

The reasons behind Hazlitt's mixed feelings regarding the poets of his day and his preference for the writings of Shakespeare and Milton are suggested by an essay in *The Examiner* for October 2, 1814, in which he alludes to an important distinction between different kinds of poets and the poetry they write. Poetry is of two classes, "the poetry of imagination and the poetry of sentiment." The former "consists in the power of calling up images of the most pleasing or striking kind; the other depends on the strength of the interest which it excites in given objects." Naturally, the greatest writers possess both powers, but in his opinion such poets as Young and Cowley instance "the separation of feeling from fancy" and Wordsworth "is certainly deficient in fanciful invention."

Hazlitt's thoughts on criticism and the critic were never systematically formulated at any length, but certain essays give us some insights on how he regarded his calling, as, for example, "On Criticism," which is primarily an attack on modern criticism. In it, he reveals his admiration for certain aspects of eighteenth century criticism and his awareness of the critical drift since then. Critics of the preceding century were "gentle almost to a fault" and there was "no scalping of authors, no hacking and hewing of their Lives and Opinions," except in the case of Laurence Sterne and *Tristram Shandy*. But in Hazlitt's day critics were somewhat less gentle, and somewhat more anxious to utter dogmatic, sometimes violent, evaluations of works. Hazlitt had still other objections to certain modern critical methods. The scholarly investigator aroused Hazlitt's ire when he was guilty of employing "the dry and meagre mode of dissecting the skeletons of works, instead of transfusing their living principles." Other critics to be despised are the "mere word-catchers" who object to tiny flaws in usage, those who let their personal biases establish the criteria for literary excellence, and the men of peevish genius who are delighted by nothing.

In considering Hazlitt's own criticism, one should remember how he wrote much of it. Most of it, especially that on the drama, was produced for instant publication. He wrote rapidly, quoting freely from his amazing memory and gave little thought to structure or revision. As a result, many of the critical essays have great spontaneity and verve, but they often lack structure. Of his many critical essays which might be chosen to show how well he measured up to the standards which he suggested in "On Criticism," "On Milton's Sonnets" is a fair representation of his method. He frankly admits his deep admiration for the sonnets. After comparing Milton's achievement in this genre with that of Shakespeare, Sir Philip Sidney, and Wordsworth, in all cases to Milton's advantage, he launches into the essay by a long paragraph that loads statement on statement concerning Milton's "*ideal* faculty in his composition" and then quotes the Cyriac Skinner sonnet in its entirety. After the barest commentary about its beauties he turns to the sonnet to Cromwell, quotes it, and then quotes the entire Piedmont Massacre sonnet. In all, he quotes six sonnets of Milton (and one of Shakespeare) in a seven page essay. Naturally a critic may use extensive quotation to support his assertions, but Hazlitt has little to assert except rather commonplace generalizations. Of the sonnet "On his Blindness" Hazlitt says that "we see the jealous watchfulness of his mind over the use of his high gifts, and the beautiful manner in which he satisfies himself that virtuous thoughts and intentions are not the least acceptable offer to the Almighty." In this kind of "appreciation criticism" the use of large quantities of quotations to illustrate obvious comments is quite common in British criticism. But there is a fault in the essay often met in Hazlitt's writing, and one that cannot so easily be blamed on tradition: there is no logic whatever in its order. Hazlitt simply moves from favorite sonnet to favorite sonnet with no progression, no development. In many of his critical essays the same qualities appear: the piling of statement on statement, the lack of logical structure, the use of extensive, one might say excessive, quotations.

But not all that one says of his critical essays is on the debit side of the ledger. Sudden insights illuminate nearly all of his essays as, for instance, this striking explanation of one of Milton's paradoxes: "Milton has borrowed more than any other writer, and exhausted every source of imitation, sacred or profane; yet he is perfectly distinct from every other writer." "In reading his works, we feel ourselves under the influence of a mighty intellect, that the nearer it approaches to others becomes more distinct from them." Part of the worth of Hazlitt's critical essays, moreover, is due to his style. He may have overloaded occasional paragraphs with allusions and quotations, but his own words were thoughtfully chosen. He is sincere, candid, and vigorous. He is a voice of experience that has not lost all the warmth and passion of youth. Even in the essay "On Reading Old Books," in which he laments the loss of his youth and with it much of the pleasure of reading, he is still capable of this kind of writing, at once warm, and sincere. Old books, Hazlitt notes, "bind together the different scattered divisions of our personal identity." "They are pegs and loops on which we can hang up, or from which we can take down, at pleasure, the wardrobe of a moral imagination, the relics of our best affections, the tokens and records of our happiest hours." "They are like Fortunatus's Wishing Cap—they give us the best riches—those of Fancy; and transport us, not over half the globe, but (which is better) over half our lives, at a word's notice!"

Bibliography

Albrecht, W.P. *Hazlitt and the Creative Imagination.* Lawrence: University of Kansas Press, 1965, pp. 149–171.

Baker, Herschel C. *William Hazlitt.* Cambridge, Mass.: Harvard University Press, 1962, pp. 385–403, 448–462, 469–474.

Brett, R.L. *Hazlitt.* Harlow, England: Longmans, 1977.

Cecil, David. "Hazlitt's Occasional Essays," in his *The Fine Art of Reading and Other Literary Studies.* London: Constable, 1957, pp. 189–199.

Clutton-Brock, Arthur. "William Hazlitt," in his *Essays on Literature and Life.* New York: Books for Libraries, 1968, pp. 155–167.

Coburn, Kathleen. "Hazlitt on the Disinterested Imagination," in *Some British Romantics: A Collection of Essays.* Edited by James V. Logan, John E. Jordan and Northrop Frye. Columbus: Ohio State University Press, 1966, pp. 167–188.

Dobrée, Bonamy. "William Hazlitt, 1778–1830," in *Review of English Literature.* II (January, 1961), pp. 30–37.

Elton, Oliver. *A Survey of English Literature, 1780–1880*, Volume II. New York: Macmillan, 1920, pp. 357–377.

Faverty, Frederick E. "William Hazlitt and the Familiar Essay," in his *Your Literary Heritage.* Philadelphia: Lippincott, 1959, pp. 96–98.

Garrod, H.W. "The Place of Hazlitt in English Criticism," in his *The Study of Good Letters.* Oxford: Oxford University Press, 1925, pp. 1–19.

Howe, W.D. "Hazlitt," in *Cambridge History of English Literature*, Volume XII. Edited by A.W. Ward and A.R. Waller. Cambridge: Cambridge University Press, 1933, pp. 180–198.

Jack, Ian. *English Literature, 1815–1832.* Oxford: Clarendon Press, 1963, pp. 260–277.

Klingopulos, G.D. "Hazlitt as Critic," in *Essays in Criticism.* VI (October, 1956), pp. 385–403.

Maclean, Catherine MacDonald. "Which Hazlitt?," in *Essays by Divers Hands: Being the Transactions of the Royal Society of Literature of the United Kingdom*, Volume XXIV. Edited by Clifford Bax. London: Oxford University Press, 1948, pp. 88–104.

More, Paul Elmer. "The First Complete Edition of Hazlitt," in his *Shelburne Essays*. New York: Putnam's, 1909, pp. 73–86.

Park, Roy. *Hazlitt and the Spirit of the Age*. London: Oxford University Press, 1971, pp. 161–236.

Priestley, J.B. *William Hazlitt*. London: Longmans, Green, 1960, pp. 22–32.

Rubinstein, Annette T. "William Hazlitt—1778–1830," in her *The Great Tradition in English Literature from Shakespeare to Shaw*. New York: Citadel, 1953, pp. 457–493.

Saintsbury, George. *A History of Criticism and Literary Taste in Europe, from the Earliest Texts to the Present Day*, Volume III. Edinburgh: Blackwood, 1904, pp. 251–266.

Stapleton, Laurence. "William Hazlitt: The Essayist and the Moods of the Mind," in his *The Elected Circle: Studies in the Art of Prose*. Princeton, N.J.: Princeton University Press, 1973, pp. 93–119.

Sykes, W.J. "Hazlitt's Place in Literature," in *Queen's Quarterly*. LIII (Spring, 1946), pp. 69–80.

Walker, Hugh. *The English Essay and Essayists*. New York: Dutton, 1923, pp. 173–185.

Wardle, Ralph M. *Hazlitt*. Lindoln: University of Nebraska Press, 1971, pp. 498–508.

Wellek, René. *A History of Modern Criticism, 1750–1950*, Volume II. New Haven, Conn.: Yale University Press, 1955, pp. 188–191, 195–212.

Zeitlin, Jacob. "Introduction," in *Hazlitt on English Literature: An Introduction to the Appreciation of Literature*. New York: Oxford University Press, pp. xi–lxxiii.

THE FAMILIAR ESSAYS OF WILLIAM HAZLITT

Author: William Hazlitt (1778–1830)
First published: The Round Table, 1817; *Table Talk*, 1821–1822; *The Spirit of the Age, or Contemporary Portraits*, 1825; *The Plain Speaker*, 1826; *Winterslow*, 1839; *Sketches and Essays*, 1839

Essay-Review

William Hazlitt came to be regarded as one of the nineteenth century's most gifted essayists, but he did not arrive at this mode of expression by any systematic or logical process. As George Bernard Shaw came to writing drama only after long experience as a musical and dramatic critic and a novelist, Hazlitt discovered his true vocation only at the age of thirty-five, and only after years of trying, in turn, to become a painter, a political writer, and a philosopher. He had talent as a painter, as his portrait of Charles Lamb in the National Gallery shows, but his literary gifts were not displayed to good advantage in his writing until 1811. In that year he and his family (he had married Sarah Stoddart in 1808, and had one son by then) were clinging to an impecunious existence in London when a series of lectures helped relieve his financial worries. Through the aid of Charles Lamb, Hazlitt entered, at the age of thirty-four, a crucial apprenticeship as a reporter for the *Morning Chronicle*. He worked for a year in the gallery of the House of Commons. By the next year he had finished his apprenticeship and had begun the career as an essayist that was to suit him so well. His books up to now, among which may be mentioned *An Essay on the Principles of Human Action* and the *Life of Holcroft*, had brought him little fame or fortune, but in the shorter essay he found the kind of form that suited him ideally.

Hazlitt's familiar essays appeared in numerous periodicals between 1812 and his death in 1830. Many of them were reprinted in his lifetime but even in the Centenary Edition they are scattered over twenty-one volumes. Some of the major periodicals for which he wrote were Leigh Hunt's *The Examiner*, 1814–1817; Constable's *Edinburgh Magazine*, 1818; John Scott's *London Magazine*, 1820–1822; Colburn's *New Monthly Magazine*, 1822; and Lord Byron and Leigh Hunt's *The Liberal*, 1822. Important collections containing his familiar essays which were published during his life include *The Round Table* (with Leigh Hunt), 1815; *Table Talk* (2 volumes), 1821–22; and *The Plain Speaker*, 1826.

It is nearly impossible to give an accurate idea of the range of Hazlitt's interests, but literature, painting, the drama, travel, and the oddities of human behavior were chief among them. While he wrote familiar essays on subjects within all of these areas, those on literary or art topics are not ordinarily treated with those on human experience, men, manners, and customs of different countries—his favorite areas for exploration.

Like all great familiar essayists, Hazlitt had but one subject: himself. Whether writing of books, a prizefight, or the necessity of hating things, his own reaction to his material was his subject. Thus Hazlitt continues to be read because of the intriguing quality of mind revealed in the essays, a strange mixture of vivacity and gloom. He said of himself in "On Depth and Superficiality": "I am not, in the ordinary acceptation of the term a good-natured man. . . ." This assessment may be taken as an understatement. Although cheerful and happy as a child, he passed through some crisis in adolescence that left him gloomy and morose. Irascibility alone is probably as dull as superficial optimism, but in Hazlitt it was coupled with an amazingly vivacious intellect, stocked with vivid recollections of a staggering number of books, penetrating in vision, and never tired of examining all aspects of existence. That such a mind should be linked with such a temperament perhaps accounts for the remarkable productions of his pen, which in their diversity, penetration, and vivacity of expression are unequaled. His unusual temperament affected several aspects of his essays: it lent a distinctive cast to his style and it made him eschew rigid, formal structure in favor of a more casual organization.

One objection to his informal essays is their lack of structure. Perhaps Hazlitt's inability to succeed as a writer of books may be traced to the same deficiency. In any case it is a rare Hazlitt essay that seems tightly structured. His famous "Merry England" will serve as an example. He suggests his thesis in the first paragraph: English merriment is deeper than that of other countries because the English are forced to overcome gloom in the attainment of it. Merriment in England is not a sort of National Constant as it is, according to Hazlitt, in Spain and other southern nations; it is "that sort of intermittent, fitful, irregular gaiety." The paragraphs that follow, however, seem inspired by whatever aspects of English life moved Hazlitt to speak, not by any conscious attempt to support his generalization logically. From this development, Hazlitt's basic writing scheme may be suggested. After stating a purpose or a case for investigation, he built his essay not by the use of a point-by-point argument or even by the careful organization of evidence but by a spirited though unmethodical piling up of examples. When the pile grew great enough, he simply stopped writing. He was saved from this structural embarrassment when his subject naturally lent form to his writing. "The Fight," perhaps his most famous familiar essay, is an account of his journey to Hungerford in Berkshire to see a prizefight involving Neate and Hickman. The chronological nature of the experience, which involved several clearly separate stages in addition to the fight itself, led Hazlitt to structure the essay in a somewhat relaxed chronological order and so produce one of his few tightly knit essays.

One is hardly conscious of Hazlitt's structural lapses in his best essays for two intimately connected reasons: his style and his attitude toward his readers. His style was the mirror of the man: restless, impetuous, virile. In "On Reading Old Books" he revealed several of his ideas on style; he called true eloquence "a man pouring out his mind on paper." He disliked the refined, polished, balanced style of Dr. Johnson or Junius. His stylistic mentor, he says, was Burke, whose "style was forked and playful as lightning, crested like the serpent." Like his mentor, Hazlitt admired warmth of expression, and there is a definite degree of emotion in all his writings. He is rarely gay and never asks us to weep; but sorrow, joy, and anger in subdued forms do lend warmth to his essays, as in this frank expression of emotion from "On the Spirit of Obligations."

> In all these pretended demonstrations of an overanxiety for our welfare, we may detect a great deal of spite and ill-nature lurking under the disguise of a friendly and officious zeal. It is wonderful how much love of mischief and rankling spleen lies at the bottom of the human heart, and how a constant supply of gall seems as necessary to the health and activity of the mind as of the body.

Hazlitt's style is also distinguished by the feeling of sincerity it establishes. The language is that of a cultured man of wide experience; he uses many quotations and allusions to writers from ancient Greece to those of his own day. Above all, Hazlitt manages nearly always to avoid the common pitfalls of the familiar essayist: glib superficiality and pompous sentimentality. He was able to move on a safe course by means of his hard, bright intellect which helped create an attractive, sincere style.

In his relationship with his audience, Hazlitt neither condescends nor is overly familiar. He is frank and engaging, but never whispers "dear reader" in our ear. The "I" of the familiar essays belongs to a well-read, well-traveled student of life who expresses his beliefs boldly.

It may be, as Geoffrey Keynes expressed it, that Hazlitt's personality was as prickly as a quilled porcupine, giving pointed sharpness to everything he wrote. But neither Hazlitt's prickliness nor his lack of modern structural ideals seriously obstructs our appreciation of the products of a most remarkable mind that was honest, inquisitive, sensitive, and keen.

Bibliography

Albrecht, W.P. *Hazlitt and the Creative Imagination.* Lawrence: University of Kansas Press, 1965, pp. 149–171.

Baker, Herschel C. *William Hazlitt.* Cambridge, Mass.: Harvard University Press, 1962, pp. 385–403, 448–462, 469–474.

Brett, R.L. *Hazlitt.* Harlow, England: Longmans, 1977.

Cecil, David. "Hazlitt's Occasional Essays," in his *The Fine Art of Reading and Other Literary Studies.* London: Constable, 1957, pp. 189–199.

Clutton-Brock, Arthur. "William Hazlitt," in his *Essays on Literature and Life.* New York: Books for Libraries, 1968, pp. 155–167.

Coburn, Kathleen. "Hazlitt on the Disinterested Imagination," in *Some British Romantics: A Collection of Essays.* Edited by James V. Logan, John E.

Jordan and Northrop Frye. Columbus: Ohio State University Press, 1966, pp. 167–188.

Dobrée, Bonamy. "William Hazlitt, 1778–1830," in *Review of English Literature.* II (January, 1961), pp. 30–37.

Elton, Oliver. *A Survey of English Literature, 1780–1880*, Volume II. New York: Macmillan, 1920, pp. 357–377.

Faverty, Frederick E. "William Hazlitt and the Familiar Essay," in his *Your Literary Heritage.* Philadelphia: Lippincott, 1959, pp. 96–98.

Garrod, H.W. "The Place of Hazlitt in English Criticism," in his *The Study of Good Letters.* Oxford: Oxford University Press, 1925, pp. 1–19.

Howe, W.D. "Hazlitt," in *Cambridge History of English Literature*, Volume XII. Edited by A.W. Ward and A.R. Waller. Cambridge: Cambridge University Press, 1933, pp. 180–198.

Jack, Ian. *English Literature, 1815–1832.* Oxford: Clarendon Press, 1963, pp. 260–277.

Klingopulos, G.D. "Hazlitt as Critic," in *Essays in Criticism.* VI (October, 1956), pp. 385–403.

Maclean, Catherine MacDonald. "Which Hazlitt?," in *Essays by Divers Hands: Being the Transactions of the Royal Society of Literature of the United Kingdom*, Volume XXIV. Edited by Clifford Bax. London: Oxford University Press, 1948, pp. 88–104.

More, Paul Elmer. "The First Complete Edition of Hazlitt," in his *Shelburne Essays.* New York: Putnam's, 1909, pp. 73–86.

Park, Roy. *Hazlitt and the Spirit of the Age.* London: Oxford University Press, 1971, pp. 161–236.

Priestley, J.B. *William Hazlitt.* London: Longmans, Green, 1960, pp. 22–32.

Rubinstein, Annette T. "William Hazlitt—1778–1830," in her *The Great Tradition in English Literature from Shakespeare to Shaw.* New York: Citadel, 1953, pp. 457–493.

Saintsbury, George. *A History of Criticism and Literary Taste in Europe, from the Earliest Texts to the Present Day*, Volume III. Edinburgh: Blackwood, 1904, pp. 251–266.

Stapleton, Laurence. "William Hazlitt: The Essayist and the Moods of the Mind," in his *The Elected Circle: Studies in the Art of Prose.* Princeton, N.J.: Princeton University Press, 1973, pp. 93–119.

Sykes, W.J. "Hazlitt's Place in Literature," in *Queen's Quarterly.* LIII (Spring, 1946), pp. 69–80.

Walker, Hugh. *The English Essay and Essayists.* New York: Dutton, 1923, pp. 173–185.

Wardle, Ralph M. *Hazlitt.* Lindoln: University of Nebraska Press, 1971, pp. 498–508.

Wellek, René. *A History of Modern Criticism, 1750–1950,* Volume II. New Haven, Conn.: Yale University Press, 1955, pp. 188–191, 195–212.

Zeitlin, Jacob. "Introduction," in *Hazlitt on English Literature: An Introduction to the Appreciation of Literature.* New York: Oxford University Press, pp. xi–lxxiii.

LEIGH HUNT

Born: Southgate, Middlesex, England (October 19, 1784)
Died: Putney, England (August 28, 1859)

Principal Works

JOURNALISM: *The Examiner*, 1808–1822; *The Indicator*, 1819–1821; *The Liberal*, 1822.
BIOGRAPHY: *Lord Byron and Some of His Contemporaries*, 1826.
POETRY: *The Story of Rimini*, 1816; *Poetical Works*, 1860.
PROSE: *Christianism*, 1832; *Imagination and Fancy*, 1844; *Wit and Humor*, 1846; *Men, Women and Books*, 1847; *Autobiography*, 1850.

James Henry Leigh Hunt, editor, essayist, poet, and dramatist, was the youngest son of Isaac Hunt, a former student and lawyer in Philadelphia, and of Mary Shewell Hunt, a kindhearted, conscientious woman of Quaker ancestry. Persecuted in revolutionary America for his loyalist views, Isaac Hunt had moved his family to England, where he adopted liberal views and became a popular Unitarian preacher.

In 1792 Leigh Hunt was sent to Christ's Hospital School, which Coleridge and Lamb had attended. As a student, he admired Collins and Gray and composed poems in imitation of their work. Upon leaving school, he haunted various bookstalls, read avidly, and continued to write poetry. The publication of his juvenile poems reached a fourth edition in 1804. He began to write essays, and in 1808 joined his brother John in the publication of a weekly independent newspaper, *The Examiner*. As an editor, Hunt was drawn into the arena of political opinion and became a consistent, courageous, but tolerant exponent of parliamentary reform and the liberal point of view. In 1809 he married Marianne Kent.

Having been several times acquitted in trials for political offenses in *The Examiner*, the Hunt brothers were convicted in December, 1812, of publishing an article disloyal to the Prince Regent. During his two unusually interesting years in Surrey jail, Leigh Hunt continued to write poetry and to edit *The Examiner*. His visitors included Hazlitt, Lamb, Bentham, and Byron, the last becoming a lifelong friend. Upon release from prison, Hunt renewed his acquaintance with Shelley, who became his most valued friend, and he soon formed a new friendship with Keats.

In 1816, Hunt published *The Story of Rimini*, his best-known long poem. Despite severe attacks from Tory journals, he continued to edit *The Examiner* until 1822, when he moved his large family to Italy and began editing *The Liberal*, a quarterly magazine sponsored by Byron and Shelley. But Shelley's death intervened, and the periodical survived for only four numbers. Returning to England in 1825, Hunt found his views increasingly tolerated and lived to become a sage counselor, sought out by aspiring young liberal thinkers and writers. Throughout his life he continued his journalistic, editorial, and creative ventures, the masterpiece of which is his *Autobiography*, published in 1850 and later edited by his writer-son, Thornton. Among Leigh Hunt's greatest contributions are the elevation of the tone of newspaper writing and the friendship, encouragement, and guidance which he gave to the noted literary men who were his associates.

Bibliography

The Poetical Works have been edited by H. S. Milford, 1923; the *Dramatic Criticism* by L.H. and C. W. Houghton, 1949; and the *Literary Criticism, ibidem*, 1956. Of primary importance is Leigh Hunt's *Autobiography*, 1850, revised 1859 (The best later edition is that by J. E. Morpurgo, 1948). See also Edmund Blunden, *Leigh Hunt: A Biography*, 1930; G. D. Stout, *The Political History of Leigh Hunt's Examiner*, 1949; and Kenneth Neill Cameron, ed., *Shelley and His Circle*, Vol. I, 1961.

THE AUTOBIOGRAPHY OF LEIGH HUNT

Author: Leigh Hunt (1784–1859)
Time: 1784–1850
Locale: England and Italy
First published: 1850

Essay-Review

Seldom has a creative man, notable in his own right, been so fortunate in his association with great men as was Leigh Hunt. To have known intimately all three of the leading "younger generation" English Romantic poets—Byron, Shelley, and Keats—and to have been well acquainted with Wordsworth, Coleridge, Hazlitt, Lamb, and Carlyle is a social and intellectual privilege not in any sense usual.

The *Autobiography* of James Henry Leigh Hunt, to give him his full name, is far more than a chronological account of the life of an important essayist and minor poet. It is a sorting out of vivid impressions from past experiences and associations, impressions which delineate Hunt's lifelong passion for human advancement as well as his ability in old age to evaluate objectively the way he has come, the influences he has experienced, and those he has exerted.

Published in 1850, nine years before Hunt's death, the *Autobiography* was hailed by Thomas Carlyle as the best autobiographical writing in the English language. This opinion was widely shared by reviewers, and the book has become a classic of its kind. Its quality derives largely from its emphasis on human values and on the interactions between the author and his various notable friends. Leigh Hunt, therefore, can afford to be neglectful of mere dates and mundane details; he has matters of present and future value to impart.

The *Autobiography* begins with a survey of the author's ancestry, largely Anglican ministers with strong Tory leanings. In the seventeenth century the family, seeking to avoid harassment by the Puritans, had moved to the West Indies but had returned to England in the following century. Leigh Hunt's father, Isaac Hunt, had gone to Philadelphia for an education and had narrowly escaped being tarred and feathered during the American Revolution for the Tory views he expressed in various pamphlets. Having returned to England with his wife and children, he had encountered severe financial difficulties and had abandoned the Tory cause to assume more liberal opinions. With his wife's enthusiastic support, Isaac Hunt had become a Unitarian minister and strong advocate of political reform.

After the Hunts had settled in the Middlesex village of Southgate, their youngest son Leigh was born on October 19, 1784. With his brothers, he was brought up in an atmosphere pervaded by the newly adopted liberalism of both parents, the general improvidence of his father, and the kindliness and near pacifism of his mother. Yet, despite the appeal of Hunt's reminiscences about his youth and his schooling at Christ's Hospital, which Coleridge and Lamb had attended earlier, the *Autobiography* achieves its greatness only in its dealing with the adult life of Leigh Hunt, for it is not in and of itself that Hunt's life demands the memorial; it is the interaction of this life with others that draws our attention.

Having, through his father's efforts, had his first volume of poetry published when he was sixteen, Leigh Hunt continued to follow a literary career. His editing of the weekly *Examiner* in collaboration with his politically minded brother John, made of the young Hunt a resolute champion of liberal politics. Not long after *The Examiner* was founded, Hunt married Marianne Kent, who not only became the devoted mother of a large family but also proved an undaunted partner throughout the difficulties which his open pronouncements for reform brought upon Hunt. Its expression of these liberal views made *The Examiner* attractive to Byron, Shelley, Keats, and Hazlitt, who all soon published in it and thus made the acquaintance of Leigh Hunt.

Its unreserved political criticisms repeatedly involved *The Examiner* in legal prosecutions by the government. After three acquittals, the Hunt brothers, who had called the Prince Regent "a libertine over head and ears in disgrace ... the companion of gamblers and demireps," were sentenced to two years' imprisonment and were each fined five hundred pounds. The chapter in which Hunt describes his strange imprisonment has become something of a classic. Its most excellent features are the humanly humorous character sketch of "honest old Cave," the jailor; the account of various visitors, including Byron, Lamb, and Hazlitt; and the description of the previously unused rooms of the prison infirmary which Hunt charmingly redecorated for himself and his family and in which one of his daughters was born. Despite such notes of pleasantness, however, the concluding comments on the author's release from imprisonment in 1815 bear an interesting resemblance to Byron's account of the freeing of Bonnivard in "The Prisoner of Chillon."

After regaining their freedom, John and Leigh Hunt gave clear indications in *The Examiner* that their imprisonment had not mellowed their political enmity toward the Prince Regent. His health having declined during his imprisonment, Leigh Hunt continued to enjoy Byron's visits and was especially pleased by an unannounced visit from Wordsworth, during which he characteristically drew his visitor's attention to a volume of Wordsworth and one of Milton side by side on the bookshelf. Although Hunt was frequently critical of Byron, the *Autobiography* gives evidence of a genuine respect for Byron's poetry and a sincere appreciation of the poet's attractive qualities.

Byron soon left England, and Hunt did not hear from him again until Byron some years later invited him to Italy. At this point the *Autobiography* takes up the author's association with Shelley, Keats, Lamb, and Coleridge. Of these, Shelley is singled out as a true friend and as a spirit who, although he professed antagonism to the Established Church, was the most "Christian" of men. Hunt was the most loyal of Shelley's friends, standing by him without reservation or doubt during the ordeal of Harriet Shelley's suicide and the government's subsequent action which deprived Shelley of the custody of his two children. Hunt's anecdotes and descriptions of Shelley have become valuable portions of the biography.

Hunt declares his love for Keats to have been second only to that for the "heart of hearts," Shelley. He finds both poets to have had that greatness which renders it delightful to be obliged by them and an equal but not greater delight to oblige them. It is evident that only Hunt's modesty prevents him from writing freely of the extent to which his friendship was a molding influence on the poetic development of Keats. With Byron and Shelley, Hunt (quite mistakenly) believes that the vitriolic attack by the *Quarterly Review* against *Endymion* was largely responsible for the early death of Keats.

Although Hunt pays little attention to the dates of his various activities and enterprises, he discusses his editorship not only of *The Examiner* but also of *The Indicator* and *The Liberal*. He was co-editor of *The Examiner* from 1808 to 1822. Meanwhile, from 1819 to 1821, he also edited *The Indicator*, in which his personal essays drew praise from his close friends, William Hazlitt and Charles Lamb. Hunt, in his turn, gives favorable accounts of the personalities of Hazlitt and Lamb. Especially appreciative is his presentation of the latter as a tender-hearted but witty "Lamb-punner." Coleridge, incidentally, was less well known to Hunt than were the two Romantic essayists; yet Coleridge, especially his trait of talkativeness, receives interesting treatment in the *Autobiography*.

An important event in Hunt's life was his decision to accept the invitation of Byron and Shelley to move his family to Italy and there, under their sponsorship, edit a new periodical, *The Liberal*. Hunt soon left *The Examiner*, now in decline, to accept this new post. He gives a graphic description of the voyage to Italy, a journey which repeatedly tried both the patience and stamina of the Hunt family. A highlight of the *Autobiography* is the narrative of Hunt's first weeks in Italy. The reunion with Byron, Thomas Moore, and especially Shelley at Leghorn, and the few days he spent with Shelley before the latter's tragic drowning, are described so as to leave no doubt of Hunt's selflessness and capacity for genuine friendship. One of the most memorable scenes in biographical prose is that of the gathering of Shelley's friends, including Trelawney, Byron, and Hunt, for the cremation of Shelley's body.

After the death of Shelley, Byron's enthusiasm for *The Liberal* waned, and the periodical survived for only four numbers, all published in 1822. But the Hunt family, although in difficult financial circumstances, remained in Italy until 1825, when they returned to England and Hunt resumed his literary and editorial profession. The *Autobiography* contains a lengthy account of the more pleasant voyage back to England and concludes with a modest review of the author's numerous, and now more generally accepted, literary and journalistic endeavors, none of which, except the *Autobiography* itself, has achieved the status of his earlier essays and poems.

The final view Leigh Hunt gives us of himself is that of a man of letters who has come through a storm of struggle and controversy upon which he can look back without either regret or malice. He appears finally as an unselfish friend and a fair evaluator of his important inspirational function among men of generally greater literary talent than his own.

JOHN KEATS

Born: Moorfields, London, England (October 29 or 31, 1795)
Died: Rome, Italy (February 23, 1821)

Principal Works

POEMS: *Poems,* 1817; *Endymion,* 1818; *Lamia, Isabella, The Eve of St. Agnes, and Other Poems,* 1820.

John Keats, English poet, was born October 29 or 31, 1795, in Moorfields, London, where his father managed a livery stable. John, the eldest child, had two brothers, George and Tom, and a sister Fanny. After the death of their father in 1804, and of their mother in 1810, the children were under the care of guardians. The boys attended school at Enfield where John became a close friend of Charles Cowden Clarke, the headmaster's son. Clarke introduced Keats to Spenser's *Faerie Queene,* which became the inspiration for his own first poetry.

In 1811 Keats was apprenticed to a surgeon in Edmonton. About this time he finished his first translation of the *Aeneid.* As a young medical student he worked steadily and passed his examinations before the Court of Apothecaries in 1816. Although he continued his studies in Guy's and St. Thomas's hospitals briefly, he was more interested in writing poetry.

In London Clarke showed Keats' verses to Leigh Hunt, who published in his newspaper Keats' first important poem, "On First Looking into Chapman's Homer" (1815). Hunt was a worthy man and kind to Keats, but from him Keats acquired many words and turns of phrase not considered "good" in the best English tradition. "Cockney," it was termed by the reviewers of Keats' first volume, *Poems,* published in 1817. He eventually overcame a great many of these faults, but the fact was that he was an urban Londoner associated in the minds of his contemporaries with the "cockney" world of Hunt. His consequent struggle was with his own natural virtues and talents and his opposing environmental factors.

His first work showed promise, though it was immature. He delighted in the world of eye, ear, and touch, and he made a constant effort to make the senses talk. Seeming to have hated abstractions of all sorts, his tendency was toward the concrete, individual object, rather than to use an image abstracted from many things and presented as a generality. In his imaginative projection of sensation into various other forms, Keats would ask, for example, how it might feel to be a ripple of water—and then proceeded to record his impression with intense poetical feeling.

In 1817 he went alone to the Isle of Wight and began work on *Endymion,* published the following year. Endowed with common sense and a decided critical ability, Keats tells us in the preface that *Endymion* is a splendid failure. But it is an excellent example of Keats' Hellenism at a time when Greek art was on exhibition in England. Hunt had earlier introduced him to Benjamin Robert Haydon, a painter who took Keats to see the Elgin marbles. Keats himself had some knowledge of Latin but none of Greek. He took from translations certain emotional elements of Greek civilization; the more unrestricted side intoxicated with beauty and color. The first line of *Endymion* is one of his most famous: "A thing of beauty is a joy forever."

After a walking tour of Scotland with Charles Armitage Brown in the summer of 1818, Keats developed tuberculosis. Prior to this his brother Tom had developed tuberculosis and brother George and his wife were starting to America to live. After Tom's death Keats lived with Brown at Hampstead and began work on *Hyperion*. There he fell completely in love with Fanny Brawne, an attractive seventeen-year-old girl who lived close by. Even though his health was failing rapidly, Keats, consumed with passionate love, began the most creative period of his life. Within the period of a year he completed "The Eve of St. Agnes," "La Belle Dame sans Merci," and the odes "To a Nightingale," "On a Grecian Urn," "To Psyche," and "On Melancholy." At Winchester he finished "Lamia" and wrote the ode "To Autumn." In February, 1820, Keats realized his illness was fatal. His last volume, *Lamia, Isabella, The Eve of St. Agnes, and Other Poems*, appeared in July, 1820.

An advance in technique can be seen in all these poems, especially in the narrative ones. "Isabella," started six months before the first draft of "The Eve of St. Agnes," shows the romantic tendency to dwell on detail rather than the telling of the story. Also, with Keats as an impassioned advocator of Isabella's cause, the story loses the classical aloofness of Boccaccio, from whom Keats took the tale. Ottava rima is its measure, suggestive of Chaucer, one of Keats' models along with Spenser (especially in his first works), Shakespeare, Milton, Dryden, and others. "The Eve of St. Agnes" uses medieval motifs, makes little attempt at narration, but is successful pictorially. "Lamia" is generally considered the most successful of these three narratives. The story is told in a classical, forthright manner and with vigor. "To Autumn" is viewed by most critics as a classic of pure description. It is his most impersonal poem, an example of how, as his art developed, he became less emotionally involved. Keats began with sensuousness, but throughout the short career of this extraordinarily talented young man, he tried to arrive at the best poetry he was capable of writing, not simply to force his art to serve any particular personal whimsies.

During the earlier part of his career he had arranged a sort of program of what he hoped to do in "Sleep and Poetry." For a time he would content himself with poetry of beautiful things that the senses can perceive. Afterward he would write noble poetry of agonies and strife. Never did he write didactic or moralistic poetry. Also, he had what may be called an anti-intellectual attitude toward poetry; he attempted to feel his way into the matter of the poem. The end result was that his later works were poetry of the highest order. He was the most promising of the Romantic poets.

Keats sailed in September, 1820, for Rome with his friend, Joseph Severn, an artist. He had a final relapse in Rome on December 10, and on February 23, 1821, he died. He was buried in the Roman Protestant Cemetery. At his wish his non-prophetic epitaph was, "Here lies one whose name was writ in water."

Bibliography

The standard edition of the poems is H. W. Garrod, *The Poetical Works of John Keats*, 1939. H. B. Forman, *The Poetical Works and Other Writings of John Keats*, was revised by M. B. Forman, 8 vols., 1938–1939. M. B. Forman has also edited *The Letters of John Keats*, 1931 (rev. ed., 1947). Sidney Colvin, *John Keats: His Life and Poetry, His Friends, Critics, and After-Fame*, 1917, is the standard critical biography. Robert Gittings, *John Keats: The Living Year*, 1954, is a valuable work of criticism.

See also Amy Lowell, *John Keats*, 2 vols., 1925; J. Middleton Murry, *Keats and Shakespeare: A Study of Keats's Poetic Life from 1816 to 1820*, 1925; *idem, Studies in Keats, New and Old*, 1930; H. W. Garrod, *Keats*, 1926; C. D. Thorpe, *The Mind of John Keats*, 1926; M. R. Ridley, *Keats' Craftsmanship: A Study in Poetic Development*, 1933; C. L. Finney, *The Evolution of Keats' Poetry*, 2 vols., 1936; Douglas Bush, *Mythology and the Romantic Tradition in English Poetry*, 1937; W. J. Bate, *Negative Capability: The Intuitive Approach to Keats*, 1939; *idem, The Stylistic Development of John Keats*, 1945; R. H. Fogle, *The Imagery of Keats and Shelley: A Comparative Study*, 1949; W. J. Bate, *John Keats*, 1963; Aileen Ward, *John Keats: The Making of a Poet*, 1963; and Judith O'Neill, ed., *Critics on Keats*, 1969.

THE EVE OF ST. AGNES

Type of work: Poem
Author: John Keats (1795–1821)
Type of plot: Chivalric romance
Time of plot: Middle Ages
Locale: A castle
First published: 1820

The plot of Keats's poem is built around an ancient superstition that a maiden who retires to her bed on St. Agnes Eve after practising a particular ritual will be awakened in her dreams by her lover. An example of English Romanticism at its best, the poem is matchless in its musical verse and vivid in its descriptions of color, sight, and sound.

Principal Characters

Madeline, a young virgin, first shown preoccupied at a ball given in the castle of her noble father. Eager to carry out the ritual of St. Agnes' Eve and thereby see her future husband in a dream, she leaves the revelry and retires to her room where, falling asleep, she dreams of Porphyro, the son of an enemy house. Awaking to find him beside her bed, she is at first frightened; but after he tells her, "This is no dream, my bride," she steals with him out of the castle, past the sleeping, drunken wassailers, and away into the stormy night.

Porphyro (pôr′fĭ·rō), her gallant young knight, who comes from his home across the moors, slips into the castle full of his enemies, and with the aid of Angela, an understanding old nurse, goes to Madeline's chamber before she prepares for bed. After she is asleep he emerges from the closet where he has hidden himself, sets a table loaded with exotic foods, and wakes his beloved with a song, "La belle dame sans mercy," to the accompaniment of Madeline's lute. He persuades his beloved to leave her home of hate and flee with him.

Angela, an old beldame, Madeline's nurse and Porphyro's friend. Convinced, after Porphyro has revealed his plan, that the young lover's intentions are honorable, she hides him in Madeline's bedchamber and provides the dainties for a feast. She dies "palsy-twitched."

The Beadsman, an aged supplicant who at the beginning of the poem is telling his rosary with cold-numbed fingers in the castle chapel. He closes the story by sleeping forever unsought for "among his ashes cold."

The Story

A cold St. Agnes' Eve it was—so cold that the owl with all its feathers shivered, so cold that the old Beadsman's fingers were numb as he told his rosary and said his prayers. Passing by the sculptured figures of the dead, he felt sorry for them in their icy graves. As he walked through the chapel door, he could hear the sound of music coming from the castle hall. He sadly turned again to his prayers.

The great hall of the castle was a scene of feasting and revelry, but one among the merry throng was scarcely aware of her surroundings. The lovely Madeline's thoughts were on the legend of St. Agnes' Eve, which told that a maiden, if she followed the ceremonies carefully and went supperless to bed, might there meet her lover in a dream.

Meanwhile, across the moonlit moors came Porphyro. He entered the castle and hid behind a pillar, aware that his presence meant danger, because his family was an enemy of Madeline's house. Soon the aged crone, Angela, came by and offered to hide him, lest his enemies find him there and kill him.

He followed her along dark arched passageways, out of sight of the revelers. When they stopped, Porphyro begged Angela to let him have one glimpse of Madeline. He promised on oath that if he so much as disturbed a lock of her hair, he would give himself up to the foes who waited below. He seemed in such sorrow that the poor woman gave in to him. She took Porphyro to the maiden's chamber and there hid him in a closet where was stored a variety of sweet meats and confections brought from the feast downstairs. Angela then hobbled away, and soon the breathless Madeline appeared.

She came in with her candle, which blew out, and kneeling before her high arched casement window, she began to pray. Watching her kneel there, her head a halo of moonlight, Porphyro grew faint at the sight of her beauty. Soon she disrobed and crept into bed, where she lay entranced until sleep came over her.

Porphyro stole from the closet and gazed at her in awe as she slept. For an instant a door opened far away, and the noises of another world, boisterous and festive, broke in; but soon the sounds faded away again. In the silence he brought dainty foods from the closet—quinces, plums, jellies, candies, syrups and spices that perfumed the chilly room. Madeline slept on, and Porphyro began to play a soft melody on a lute. Madeline opened her eyes and thought her lover a vision of St. Agnes' Eve. Porphyro, not daring to speak, sank upon his knees until she spoke, begging him never to leave her or she would die.

St. Agnes' moon went down. Outside the casements, sleet and ice began to dash against the windowpanes. Porphyro told her that they must flee before the house awakened. Madeline, afraid and trembling, followed her lover down the cold, gloomy corridors, through the wide deserted hall, and past the porter, asleep on his watch. So they fled—into the wintry dawn.

Critical Evaluation

Keats wrote "The Eve of St. Agnes" in January and February of 1819, the first of an astonishing spate of masterpieces that belied his failing health and emotional turmoil, and which ended abruptly one year later when it became apparent that his illness was mortal. "La Belle Dame Sans Merci," "Lamia," and six great odes were all written before October of that year. The near circumstance of his death seems to throw into a kind of relief the luscious descriptions of physical reality in this and other poems. More striking still is the poet's refusal to take comfort in the simplistic assurances of any religious or philosophical system that denied either the complexity of mind or the reality and importance of sense. "The Eve of St. Agnes" manifests Keats's characteristic concern with the opposition and subtle connection of the sensual world to the interior life. He shared this preoccupation with other Romantic poets, notably Coleridge and Wordsworth, taking as his subject the web of an antithesis at the heart of human experience; like them, he cloaked his meditations in sensuous imagery.

In this and other ways, Keats and all the Romantics abandoned the poetic theory of the century before. Eighteenth century poetry was formal, didactic, and objective in stance. Its chief aim was to show to the world (that is, to mankind) a picture of itself for its own improvement and edification. Its chief ornament was art: puns, wordplay, satiric description, and so forth. In short, what eighteenth century poets saw as virtue in poetry was logic and rigid metrics. Nineteenth century poets wrote from a radically different philosophical base, due in part to the cataclysmic political changes surrounding the American and French Revolutions. Before these upheavals occurred, a belief in order and measure extended into all facets of life, from social relations to literature; extremes were shunned in all things as unnatural, dangerous, and perhaps blasphemous.

After 1789, when the social order in France turned upside down, an expectation of the millennium arose in England, especially in liberal intellectual circles; the old rules of poetry were thrown off with the outworn social strictures, and a new aesthetic bloomed in their place. Its ruling faculty was imagination. The world seemed made new, and poetry released from bondage. Romantic poets frequently stated that poems ought to be composed on the inspiration of the moment, thereby faithfully to record the purity of the emotion. In fact, Keats and his contemporaries labored hard over their creations; they exerted themselves not to smoothness of meter but to preserving the grace of spontaneity while achieving precision in observation of natural and psychological phenomena. Poets saw themselves as charting hitherto unexplored reaches of human experience, extremes of joy and dejection, guilt and redemption, pride and degradation. They wrote meditations, confessions, and conversations, in which natural things were seen to abet internal states. And they wrote ballads and narratives, such as "The Eve of St. Agnes," set in the past or in distant parts of the world and using archaic language and rhythms to make the events related seem even more strange and wonderful. And over and over they described epiphanous moments when the human consciousness becomes one with nature, when all is made new, when divinity animates the inanimate, and the lowest creature seems wondrous. This way of seeing was thought to be a return to an earlier consciousness lost in early childhood, and is the theme of Wordsworth's seminal "Ode: Intimations of Immortality."

In "The Eve of St. Agnes," Keats attempts, among other things, to maintain this elevated state of mind throughout the narrative. He sets the story in medieval times, so that the familiar Romeo-and-Juliet characters take on charm from their quaint surroundings, and from the archaic language in which they speak and are described. Its verse form is the Spenserian stanza, smooth yet free, with its slightly asymmetric rhyme scheme that avoids the monotony of couplet or quatrain, and the piquant extension of the ninth line which gives to the whole an irregularity echoing ordinary speech. The first five stanzas contrast the Beadsman, coldly at his prayers, with the "argent revelry" making gaudy the great hall. This imagery of cold and warmth, silver and scarlet, chastity and sensuality continues throughout the poem, a comment on the plot.

That the poem is named for a virgin martyr yet tells the story of an elopement is likewise significant; for the point of the poem, on the one hand, is that piety and passion are opposing but inseparable drives. Each without the other has no point of reference. Porphyro without Madeline becomes the gross Lord Maurice, the savage Hildebrand; Madeline without Porphyro becomes the Beadsman with his deathlike abrogation of sense. Instead, Porphyro is made to faint at the celestial beauty of Madeline at her prayers, Madeline to be wooed by songs and colors and things to eat. But what fruits! Not mere groceries, but the glowing essence of fruitfulness, tribute to a love match of the meditative and emotional faculties that, when accomplished in one individual, fulfills the whole human potential.

The other theme, or perhaps the other face of the same theme, is the relentless press of quotidian misery on the poetic personality, another favorite arena of reflection among the Romantics, and one that was poignantly near Keats's heart, menaced by tuberculosis as he was, and his younger brother having died of the disease the previous winter. The lovers are shown, unearthly fair, escaping from a house where wrath and drunkenness hold sway, bound for a dream-vision of happiness. But significantly the poet does not follow them to their southern sanctuary. Instead he relates the wretched end of Angela, who dies "palsy-twitched" in her sleep; the cold sleep of the Beadsman among the ashes; the drunken nightmares of the Baron and his guests. The ending, in short, is not unreservedly happy, but partakes of that bittersweet emotion which in the midst of joy acknowledges wretchedness, the mark of a mind that strives for aesthetic detachment while believing in its duty to the rest of human kind.

Bibliography

Clark, E. "Of Graves and Poets," in *Commentary*. LVIII (November, 1974), pp. 61–73.

Colvin, Sidney. *John Keats: His Life and Poetry, His Friends, Critics, and After-Fame.* New York: Octagon, 1970. Reprint of 1917 Edition.

Danzig, Allan, Editor. *Twentieth Century Interpretations of the* Eve of St. Agnes*: A Collection of Critical Essays.* Englewood Cliffs, N.J.: Prentice-Hall, 1971.

Dickstein, Morris. *Keats and His Poetry: A Study in Development.* Chicago: University of Chicago Press, 1971.

Ende, Stuart A. *Keats and the Sublime.* New Haven, Conn.: Yale University Press, 1976.

Finney, Claude Lee. *The Evolution of Keats's Poetry.* 2 Volumes. London: Russell, 1936.

Gittings, Robert. *The Mask of Keats.* London: Hillary, 1956.

Goslee, N.M. "Under a Cloud in Prospect: Keats, Milton, and Stationing," in *Philological Quarterly.* LIII (Spring, 1974), pp. 205–219.

Hewlett, Dorothy. *A Life of John Keats.* New York: Barnes & Noble, 1970.

Hilton, Timothy. *Keats and His World.* New York: Viking, 1971.

Jones, James L. *Adam's Dream: Mythic Consciousness in Keats and Yeats.* Athens: University of Georgia Press, 1975.

Kavvar, Gerald P. *The Other Poetry of Keats.* Rutherford, N.J.: Fairleigh Dickinson University Press, 1969.

Kinnaird, J. "Hazlitt, Keats, and Poetics of Intersubjectivity," in *Criticism.* XVIII (Winter, 1977), pp. 1–16.

Little, Judy. *Keats as a Narrative Poet: A Test of Invention.* Lincoln: University of Nebraska Press, 1975.

Matthews, G.M., Editor. *Keats: The Critical Heritage.* London: Routledge and Kegan Paul, 1971.

Murry, John Middleton. *Keats.* New York: Octagon, 1975. Reprint of 1930 Edition.

Patterson, Charles I. *The Daemonic in the Poetry of John Keats.* Urbana: University of Illinois Press, 1970.

Pettet, E.C. *On the Poetry of Keats.* Cambridge: Cambridge University Press, 1970.

Ragussis, M. "Narrative Structure and the Problem of the Divided Reader in the *Eve of St. Agnes*," in *ELH.* XLII (Fall, 1975), pp. 378–394.

Ricks, Christopher.   *Keats and Embarrassment.* Oxford: Clarendon Press, 1974.

Simpson, D.   "Keats's Lady, Metaphor, and the Rhetoric of Neurosis," in *Studies in Romanticism.* XV (Spring, 1976), pp. 265–288.

Sperry, Stuart M.   *Keats the Poet.* Princeton, N.J.: Princeton University Press, 1973.

————.   "Some Versions of Keats," in *Modern Language Quarterly.* XXXVII (June, 1977), pp. 178–185.

Stillinger, Jac.   *The Hoodwinking of Madeline, and Other Essays on Keats's Poems.* Urbana: University of Illinois Press, 1971.

Zeff, J.   "Strategies of Time in Keats's Narratives," in *Studies in English Literature.* XVII (Autumn, 1977), pp. 621–637.

THE LETTERS OF JOHN KEATS

Author: John Keats (1795–1821)
First published: Life, letters, and Literary Remains of John Keats, edited by R. M. Milnes, 1848; *Letters of John Keats to Fanny Brawne*, edited by H. B. Forman, 1878; *Letters of John Keats to His Family and Friends*, edited by Sidney Colvin, 1891; *The Letters of John Keats*, edited by M. B. Forman, 1931, 1935, 1947

Essay-Review

The letters of John Keats begin in 1816 and end with his death in 1821. They are very much a personal record, so much so that their publication in the nineteenth century occasioned notable critical hostility. The Victorians were shocked by these letters. Men like Matthew Arnold and even Algernon Swinburne stated that they were too emotional and should not be presented to public view. Modern criticism has taken a completely different viewpoint; the love letters are acknowledged to be among the greatest of their kind and the passages on criticism are now thought to be major documents of Romantic aesthetics.

The correspondents of Keats were Benjamin Bailey (1791–1853), a friend to whom Keats addressed a number of letters with matters of importance from a critical point of view; Fanny Brawne (1800–1865), the subject of the famous love letters; Charles Armitage Brown (1786–1842), himself a writer; Charles Wentworth Dilke (1789–1864), a generous friend and admirer of the poet; Charles Cowden Clarke (1787–1877), an early friend and literary influence; William Haslam (1795–1851), a schoolfellow friend and a financial supporter of Keats; Benjamin Haydon (1786–1846), a painter much admired by the poet; Leigh Hunt (1784–1859), essayist and an early influence on Keats and other writers of the time; Fanny Keats (1803–1889), sister of the poet; George Keats (1797–1841), a brother; Joseph Severn (1793–1879), the poet and diplomat in whose arms Keats died; and Percy Bysshe Shelley (1792–1822), an admirer of his brother poet.

Throughout the letters there are many references to the great men who created the literature of England. Keats, although not formally educated in literary studies, was conscious of his heritage as a writer. One of the great themes of these letters is therefore English literature itself and Keats's relationship to it. He mentions the names of Shakespeare and Milton often, and he continually tries to orient his own attitudes and work toward the great works of the past. In writing to his brother he goes through a whole catalogue of poets and essayists, in the process showing his strong sense of belonging to a community of the literate. He reveals that he reads matter outside what might be thought of as the range of poetry: the works of Voltaire, Gibbon, and Rabelais. In addition to these he reveals that he is interested in and indeed familiar with the work of Swift among the older writers, and with the whole spectrum of literature in his century: Words-worth, Byron, Shelley, Hunt, Scott, and Hazlitt. Keats mentions these men and others often, and generally he reveals the operation of a strong critical sense. He tries not only to understand what these writers represent, but in what ways he himself can come to terms with them as a writer.

Shakespeare is certainly one of the great to whom his letters make important reference. In a significant letter of 1818 he states that he can read and under-stand Shakespeare "to his depths." The importance of Shakespeare to Keats was profound; he classified him as among those ultimate realities of life, like the exis-tence of the sun and stars themselves.

If the letters have a good deal to say about Keats' vocation, they have perhaps even more to say about his feelings. The letters to Fanny Brawne express many emotions: perhaps the most constant themes are the depth of his love, his feelings of inadequacy in that love, and the sense he attains of the meaning this love has in establishing new conditions for his existence. Keats admits that his contemplation of Fanny prevents his obsessive preoccupation with himself: with his ego, his work, and, ultimately, with his death. The luxuries over which he broods are, he says, the beauty of this woman and the hour of his death. The letters are not full of elaborate, reasoned, and eloquent statement, but give the appearance of the irresistible, disordered, and even hasty expression of deep feelings. They move very rapidly from expressions of joy to those of sadness, from talk of self to dis-cussion of things more abstract. There is a good deal of news in these letters, even of gossip. Keats's own phrase describing his state is that of "uneasy spirits," and the letters convey these feelings directly and forcefully. There is a strong element of consciousness in these letters. Keats strives to create for the object of these letters the tone and appearance of the world through which he moves, and of the things which he experiences.

His letters to friends reveal a strong sense of the obligations of friendship. It is one of the great topics to which he returns again and again. He asks forgiveness time after time for putting the demands of art ahead of those of friendship, and he states the impossibility of rationally dividing himself between the art of writ-ing and that of friendship. He writes, with some pride, that he is glad not to be a burden to his friends. Yet, increasingly as the time of his death approached, he did become dependent on them for financial aid and for comfort of a less material kind. That they responded to his need is to their lasting honor.

When Keats writes about his friendships he continually takes a conciliatory and even humble tone. He begins by asking whether he can, in fact, allow himself to intrude upon his friends to the extent of imposing his problems, even his sense of self, upon them. Yet when Keats writes of his art there is a difference in tone. He has a firm conviction of the essential rightness of criticism, and, even when writing about Milton and other figures in the Pantheon of letters, he is honest about what he thinks are their failings. He believes, for example, that in many ways Wordsworth is to be preferred to Milton, because the former supplies a sense of "the human heart." Yet, to balance and give equal critical judgment, he adds that Milton was a much better thinker. In commenting on his own dedication to writing he said very strongly that he preferred his own criticism to that of others. Society mattered very little to him, and its opinions of art even less.

The letters have far more variety in them than the textbooks mention. They are in effect a calendar of events for Keats, in which he brings to his own mind and that of his correspondent the nature of those things which have affected his train of thought. They are in a sense both journals and letters, full of references to the dramas he has seen and the opinions he has formed about them; about the books he has read and the comparisons he has drawn from them; about the people he has met, and the way their characters have engaged him. Perhaps the outstanding trait of these letters is simply their universality. one letter to his brother, for example, covers everything from Freemasonry to fairy tales, and it is written in lively and expressive metaphors drawn from all the experiences of life. In fact, the letters are a kind of factory of language in that they reveal the same kind of experimentation with the possibilities of language as do the poems.

Throughout the letters Keats refuses to deceive himself. He does not hide the meaning of his brother's symptoms, and he acknowledges that this fatal sickness has its own place in the scheme of things. Perhaps the most famous letters deal with his awareness of his own approaching death; their rigorous honesty and insight are, one grants, unique. He wishes for death every day, a letter of 1820 admits, yet he wishes too that the pains of life might continue because they may be all he has. With almost scientific objectivity he considers the thought of his death, but wastes very small self-pity on it. As in most of his earlier letters, those of his later life are centered not on the problem of the end of things but on their creation. The work must continue, and it must endure.

A summary of the meaning of the letters must take account of the complexity of their response to life. They are chronicles as well as criticisms, and they require attention to details as well as emotional responses in their readers. Keats himself remarked that he may not have left anything immortal behind him, except the memories of his friends. He was wrong in this belief. But he was right when he intimates that his friendships, of which his letters are the concrete expression, were themselves of tremendous importance.

Bibliography

Clark, E. "Of Graves and Poets," in *Commentary.* LVIII (November, 1974), pp. 61–73.

Colvin, Sidney. *John Keats: His Life and Poetry, His Friends, Critics, and After-Fame.* New York: Octagon, 1970. Reprint of 1917 Edition.

Danzig, Allan, Editor. *Twentieth Century Interpretations of the* Eve of St. Agnes: *A Collection of Critical Essays.* Englewood Cliffs, N.J.: Prentice-Hall, 1971.

Ende, Stuart A.   *Keats and the Sublime.* New Haven, Conn.: Yale University Press, 1976.

Gittings, Robert.   *The Mask of Keats.* London: Hillary, 1956.

Goslee, N.M.   "Under a Cloud in Prospect: Keats, Milton, and Stationing," in *Philological Quarterly.* LIII (Spring,1974), pp. 205–219.

Hewlett, Dorothy.   *A Life of John Keats.* New York: Barnes & Noble, 1970.

Hilton, Timothy.   *Keats and His World.* New York: Viking, 1971.

Jones, James L.   *Adam's Dream: Mythic Consciousness in Keats and Yeats.* Athens: University of Georgia Press, 1975.

Kavvar, Gerald P.   *The Other Poetry of Keats.* Rutherford, N.J.: Fairleigh Dickinson University Press, 1969.

Kinnaird, J.   "Hazlitt, Keats, and Poetics of Intersubjectivity," in *Criticism.* XVIII (Winter, 1977), pp. 1–16.

Little, Judy.   *Keats as a Narrative Poet: A Test of Invention.* Lincoln: University of Nebraska Press, 1969.

Matthews, G.M., Editor.   *Keats: The Critical Heritage.* London: Routledge and Kegan Paul, 1971.

Murry, John Middleton.   *Keats.* New York: Octagon, 1975. Reprint of 1930 Edition.

Ricks, Christopher.   *Keats and Embarrassment.* Oxford: Clarendon Press, 1974.

Simpson, D.   "Keats's Lady, Metaphor, and the Rhetoric of Neurosis," in *Studies in Romanticism.* XV (Spring, 1976), pp. 265–288.

Sperry, Stuart M.   "Some Versions of Keats," in *Modern Language Quarterly.* XXXVII (June, 1977), pp. 178–185.

Trilling, Lionel.   "The Poet as Hero: Keats in His Letters," in his *The Opposing Self.* New York: Columbia University Press, 1955, pp. 69–82.

Zeff, J.   "Strategies of Time in Keats's Narratives," in *Studies in English Literature.* XVII (Autumn, 1977), pp. 621–637.

CHARLES LAMB

Born: London, England (February 10, 1775)
Died: Edmonton, England (December 27, 1834)

Principal Works

ESSAYS: *Essays of Elia*, 1823; *Last Essays of Elia*, 1833.
CRITICISM: *Specimens of English Dramatic Poets, Who Lived about the Time of Shakespeare, with Notes*, 1808.
POEMS: *Blank Verse*, 1798 (with Charles Lloyd); *Poetry for Children*, 1809 (with Mary Lamb); *Album Verses*, 1830; *The Poetical Works of Charles Lamb*, 1836.
TALES AND STORIES: *A Tale of Rosamund Gray and Old Blind Margaret*, 1798; *Tales from Shakespeare*, 1807 (with Mary Lamb); *Adventures of Ulysses*, 1808; *Mrs. Leicester's School*, 1809 (with Mary Lamb).
PLAYS: *John Woodvil, A Tragedy*, 1802; *Mr. H.*, 1806.

Charles Lamb was born in Crown Office Row, Inner Temple, London, on February 10, 1775. His father, described under the name Lovel in Lamb's essay "The Old Benchers of the Inner Temple," was an assistant and servant to Samuel Salt, a member of Parliament. Through the generosity of Salt, Lamb in 1782 was allowed to enroll in the celebrated charity school, Christ's Hospital, where he continued for seven years; among his fellows was Samuel Taylor Coleridge. In 1789 he left school and became a clerk in the South Sea House. In 1792 he went to work for the East India Company, first in the accountant's office and later, on the recommendation of Salt, in the examiner's office. Here, except for a six-week period of derangement (1795–1796), when he was confined in a madhouse, he was employed for thirty-three years, the span of time coinciding with his principal literary activities. In 1796 his sister Mary, ten years his senior, who shared with him a hereditary mental disorder marked by recurrent mania, stabbed their mother to death. The responsibility of caring for Mary devolved upon Charles and proved a source of anxiety for the rest of his life; she survived him, dying in 1847.

To Lamb's close friendship with Coleridge is to be credited his emergence as a poet, and in Coleridge's *Poems on Various Subjects* (1796) were included four sonnets by Lamb. Through Coleridge, Lamb established friendships with Dorothy and William Wordsworth, with Robert Southey, and with Charles Lloyd. In 1798, under the joint authorship of himself and Lloyd, appeared a volume entitled *Blank Verse*, assembling some of his best lyrics, among them "The Old Familiar Faces." The same year saw the publication of his prose romance *A Tale of Rosamund Gray*, a melodramatic and sentimental story with sources in Lamb's family misfortunes. The income from his clerkship at the East India House, though assured, was small, and Lamb augmented his means by writing humorous sketches for newspapers. Aspiring to less transitory fame, he composed and offered to the actor John Kemble a tragedy, *John Woodvil*, which drew heavily on his favorites, the Elizabethans. Undeterred by indifference to this effort, he wrote a farce, *Mr. H.*, and enjoyed enthusiastic hopes when it was scheduled to be staged at Drury Lane. Produced in December, 1806, it was greeted with derision; Lamb added his own hisses to those of the audience.

Mary Lamb had been approached by the wife of William Godwin (later Shelley's father-in-law) with the request that she prepare for Godwin, who was publishing books for children, a collection of prose versions of Shakespeare's plays. Accordingly, with her brother's help, she wrote *Tales from Shakespeare*. The work achieved instant success, and Godwin got out a complete two-volume edition of the twenty tales, as well as several illustrated sixpenny pamphlets each containing one. Charles Lamb wrote paraphrases of six tragedies; Mary, the remainder. He had already conceived one slight juvenile story for Godwin's list, and afterwards he furnished others, including *Adventures of Ulysses*, based on the *Odyssey*, and *Mrs. Leicester's School*, the latter being chiefly the work of Mary Lamb.

Leigh Hunt, in 1810, began to edit a quarterly magazine, *The Reflector*. To this Lamb contributed some of his finest critical pieces, notably the essays on Hogarth and on Shakespeare's tragedies. His steady absorption in the works of the old dramatists had resulted in his *Specimens of English Dramatic Poets*, appreciatively annotated; the essays published through Hunt brought out even more distinctly his genius as an interpreter of the English literary past. Unfortunately, *The Reflector* was short-lived, and this fact, with the improvement in Lamb's salary from the East India Company, diminished his incentive to write. Until 1820 he wrote little else, though the publication of his *Works* (1818), in two volumes, attracted favorable notice. Upon the inauguration of the *London Magazine*, he found a new outlet for his ideas, and in the next four or five years he wrote industriously. His pseudonym "Elia" he took, without asking leave, from an Italian fellow clerk. In the popular mind, Lamb is best known for the essays published under this name. In 1825, he was pensioned by the Company and almost at once redoubled his studies in the drama. But his writing days were near their end. As Mary Lamb's mental instability grew, his worries multiplied. In 1834 Coleridge died. Two months later Lamb fell while walking in the London road near his house at Edmonton, Middlesex, and a few days later, December 27, 1834, he died of an infection, diagnosed as erysipelas, spreading from a facial scratch. He was in his sixtieth year.

The friends of Charles Lamb knew him as a convivial man of placid temper. Coleridge, with a hint of a pun on Lamb's surname, characterized him as "gentle-hearted Charles." Such indeed is the impression conveyed by the Elia essays, which are blended of graciousness and humor. No reader ever forgets "The Praise of Chimney-Sweepers," "Witches and Other Night Fears," "Christ's Hospital Five and Thirty Years Ago," "The Two Races of Men," "Sanity of True Genius,"

"Dream Children: A Reverie," or "Confessions of a Drunkard." These desultory familiar essays, numbering several of his best, reveal Lamb's sentiment. They also exemplify the scope of his fancy, and so does his style, with its histrionic mannerisms and its quaint archaic terms learned from Sir Thomas Browne, Robert Burton, and other seventeenth century originals. But Lamb was no mere amiable eccentric: his intelligence, as manifested in his voluminous letters and in his formal criticism, was of extremely high quality. He far surpassed Coleridge in orderliness of mind and may possibly have equaled him in sensibility. The proof of Lamb's powers lies in his remarkable insight into the minor Elizabethan and Jacobean drama, which, by his critical evaluations, he revived from its two centuries of neglect as literature

Bibliography

The standard edition is *The Works of Charles and Mary Lamb*, edited by E. V. Lucas, 7 vols., 1903, reissued in 6 vols., 1912. Another edition is the *Works in Prose and Verse*, edited by Thomas Hutchinson, 2 vols., 1909. Useful one-volume editions of selections include *Twenty Essays of Elia*, edited by Daniel Varney, 1932; *Essays and Letters*, edited by J. M. French, 1937; and *The Portable Charles Lamb*, edited by J. M. Brown, 1949. Of particular interest for its combination of selections and biographical text is *Charles Lamb and Elia*, edited by J. E. Morpurgo, 1948.

The standard biography is E. V. Lucas, *The Life of Charles Lamb*, 2 vols., 1905 (rev. ed., 1921), supplemented by the same writer's edition of the *Letters*, 3 vols., 1935. Other biographical studies include F. V. Morley, *Lamb Before Elia*, 1932; Edmund Blunden, *Charles Lamb and His Contemporaries*, 1933; A. C. Ward, *The Frolic and the Gentle: A Centenary Study of Charles Lamb*, 1934; J. May Lewis, *Charles Lamb*, 1934; E. C. Ross, *The Ordeal of Bridget Elia: A Chronicle of the Lambs*, 1940; Katharine Anthony, *The Lambs*, 1945; and Edmund Blunden, *Charles Lamb*, 1954. For criticism see M. H. Law, *The English Familiar Essay in the Nineteenth Century*, 1934; G. L. Barnett, *The Evolution of Elia*, 1952; and William K. Seymour, *Charles Lamb as a Poet*, 1953.

ESSAYS OF ELIA and LAST ESSAYS OF ELIA

Type of work: Essays
Author: Charles Lamb (1775–1834)
First published: 1823 and 1833

Essay-Review

Among modern platitudes at least half true is the assertion that conversation is a lost art. Certainly more than half true is a similar statement: that the art of the personal essay as practiced by Charles Lamb in *The Essays of Elia* is an art that few modern writers practice. Both conversation and the personal essay—as might be pointed out by persons who lived at other stages of our culture—depend on periods of quiet, periods of boredom, and finally mental action that is various and witty, the display of riches that have been laid up in periods of quiet and refined in periods of apparent boredom. The personal essay, at any rate, can be only the product of a person who has followed from his youth onward the dictum of Dr. Samuel Johnson and read five hours a day and who, in his middle years, takes delight in displaying, sometimes with mock modesty, the fruits of silent study. Lamb's essays are, at any rate, a kind of conversation with the unhurried reader; and the reader's part, though mute, is essential. He must be a "good listener"; he must be patient and allot to Lamb time enough to play with a thought as well as to develop it; he must award a smile to the poor "jokes" that mingle with the good ones told by Elia; he must be able to follow the quick alternations of mood that appear in such essays as "The South-Sea House," "Dream-Children," and "The Superannuated Man." He must be willing to be irresponsibly playful along with the author who is, at a particular moment, writing "A Dissertation on Roast Pig" or "A Chapter on Ears."

For these reasons it is obvious that the old-style personal essay, as written by Lamb and his great contemporary William Hazlitt, is a form of writing to which hasty readers, readers for information, will continue to remain indifferent. Such readers read essays as they attend lectures. They wish to be informed about a topic on which, it is supposed, the speaker is an expert. Or they hope to be given a new set of ideas; and they scan these ideas energetically to see whether the lecturer is unsound on crucial issues. Lamb demands no such attention; indeed, he suffers from it. Lamb does not write to convey ideas or facts or convictions even though his essays are full of all these. But his ideas are mostly playful, as in "Sanity of True Genius"; he aims not to persuade the reader of the truth of a concept but chiefly to provide temporary entertainment by presenting a startling assertion. And though his essays abound in facts about old houses and old relatives and old clerks, they are not facts that "prove" anything; they simply stand as reminders of mileposts along which "Elia" (Lamb's pen name) has passed in his journey—mileposts of which it is amusing to speak. Finally, Elia-Lamb is not without convictions, but they are not ideas that command attention because they belong to the abstract level of philosophy. The true, the beautiful, and the good do not exist in Lamb's essays and demand our assent or denial. Lamb's mind seizes little portions of truth that turn up in the daily round. In his world virtue is not a system; it is a fleeting deed or a glance of affection detected in a parlor, over a game of whist. Nor is beauty an intellectual entity; it is, at the most, a hundred tiny little impressions recorded during a summer stroll and now shared with us.

By such perceptions we can come to understand what Lamb's essays offer to us. Originally written for the *London Magazine*, the essays survive their first appearance in a modest but insistent way. Weightier writing of the time—Coleridge's essays, for example, which were not conversations but lectures and "final" philosophical pronouncements, and similar writings—survive in the "complete works" and become the subject of graduate study. Lamb's essays continue to speak to a small but faithful company of readers who are more drawn by a tone, a sensibility delicate and yet robust, hinting rather than explicit. (Some of this company are probably readers of Jane Austen also, whose ideas may fade but whose perceptions of truth are deathless.)

Doubtless the conditions of Lamb's life, once they are known, add to the interest of the essays. That Lamb had a stammer and could not find a way to complete his education, that he worked through a hundred folios of bookkeeping for the East India Company, that violence and insanity threatened the good cheer of his life, that "Dream-Children" was written by a man condemned to solitary life, that "Old China" speaks of luxury that Lamb himself could never possess, that many essays explore old books that Lamb haunted bookstalls to buy—all such knowledge adds to our response to the blend of whimsy, outright jest, and fleeting sentiment in the essays.

This blend was Lamb's own. But it is not without its models in language and form, as Lamb would be ready to admit. It might be said that Lamb's literary tastes caused him to leap backward more than a century. He ignored the essays of Addison and Steele and even more those of Dr. Samuel Johnson; these were writers who tended toward public address, public instruction, and public betterment, whatever they treated. Lamb, who sought an audience of friends rather than a cluster of worshipful inferiors, turned to such seventeenth century masters as Sir Thomas Browne and Robert Burton, men who wrote before English prose had taken on a cold, instructing, and regular form. Sir Thomas Browne said, "I love to lose myself in O Altitudos"; and in such spirit does Lamb love to pursue the small ecstasies of his daily life: the middle-class jaunts, the excitements of the card table, and the thrills of inexpensive theatrical attendance. "T'is all mine, none mine," wrote Robert Burton of his disorderly masterpiece, *The Anatomy of Melancholy*, that vast tissue of quotation and opinionated comment. So might Lamb say; whatever he treats, there are ancient echoes. In these echoes sound the quaint, crabbed spirits of Browne and Burton, and the more generous and still more undisciplined natures of Elizabethan dramatists who, though "minor," were one and all great to Lamb, one of their first "discoverers."

No analysis or digest can suggest to the reader the charm of the *Essays of Elia* or the *Last Essays*. They must, if we may use a wordplay that would please Lamb, not be *dig*ested but digested, and that again and again.

Bibliography

Barnett, George L. *Charles Lamb: The Evolution of Elia.* Bloomington: Indiana University Press, 1964.

————. "Elia," in *Charles Lamb.* Twayne, 1976, pp. 89–113.

Blunden, Edmund. "Elia," in his *Charles Lamb and His Contemporaries.* New York: Macmillan, 1933, pp. 149–175.

————. "Elia's Farewell," in his *Charles Lamb and His Contemporaries.* New York: Macmillan, 1933, pp. 176–206.

Fukuda, Tsutomu. *A Study of Charles Lamb's* Essays of Elia. Tokyo: Hokuseido Press, 1964.

Haven, Richard. "The Romantic Art of Charles Lamb," in *Journal of English Literary History.* XXX (June, 1963), pp. 137–146.

Iseman, Joseph Seeman. *A Perfect Sympathy: Charles Lamb and Sir Thomas Browne.* Cambridge, Mass.: Harvard University Press, 1937.

Johnson, Edith Christina. *Lamb Always Elia.* Boston: Marshall Jones, 1936.

Mulcahy, Daniel J. "Charles Lamb: The Antithetical Manner and the Two Planes," in *Studies in English Literature.* III (Autumn, 1963), pp. 512–542.

Nabholtz, John. "Drama and Rhetoric in Lamb's Essay of the Imagination," in *Studies in English Literature.* XII (1972), pp. 683–703.

Pater, Walter. "Charles Lamb," in his *Appreciations.* London: Macmillan, 1889.

Randel, Fred V. *The World of Elia: Charles Lamb's Essayistic Romanticism.* Port Washington, N.Y.: Kennikat, 1975.

Reiman, Donald H. "Thematic Unity in Lamb's Familiar Essays," in *Journal of English and Germanic Philology.* LXIV (July, 1965), pp. 470–478.

Scoggins, James. "Images of Eden in the *Essays of Elia*," in *Journal of English and Germanic Philology.* LXXI (1972), pp. 198–210.

Tillotson, Geoffrey. "The Historical Importance of Certain *Essays of Elia*," in *Some British Romantics.* Edited by James Logan, *et al.* Columbus: Ohio State University Press, 1966, pp. 89–116.

WALTER SAVAGE LANDOR

Born: Warwick, England (January 30, 1775)
Died: Florence, Italy (September 17, 1864)

Principal Works

DIALOGUES: *Imaginary Conversations*, 1824–1848; *The Citation and Examination of William Shakespeare . . . Touching Deer-Stealing*, 1834; *Pentameron and Pentalogia*, 1837.
LETTERS. *Pericles and Aspasia*, 1836.
POEMS: *Poems*, 1795; *Gebir*, 1798; *Hellenics*, 1847; *Italics*, 1848; *Heroic Idylls*, 1863.
PLAY: *Count Julian*, 1812.

Seldom does a man of wealth, without a degree or a profession, become an outstanding poet, but this in brief is the life of Walter Savage Landor, born at Warwick, England, on January 30, 1775. His education was irregular at best; he was early removed from Rugby in favor of a private tutor, and in 1794 he was rusticated from Trinity College, Cambridge, for firing a shot in a political dispute. At the age of twenty, after his father had given him an independent allowance, he brought out his first poems. In these he immediately established his reputation as satirist and epigrammatist. Shortly afterward he inherited a fortune from his father and removed to fashionable Bath. Much of his inheritance he squandered by outfitting a regiment and fighting with the Spaniards against the French at La Coruña. From this experience came the lofty and heroic closet-drama, *Count Julian.*

His domestic life was stormy at best. Having married Julia Thuillier in 1811, he removed to the Continent after domestic and legal strife in 1818, and was finally separated from his wife in 1835. In the meantime, he was writing his best work. The *Imaginary Conversations*, written over a period of some twenty years, range widely in theme and time and present such figures as Diogenes and Plato, Lucullus and Caesar, Henry VIII and Anne Boleyn, Rousseau and Malesherbes. The *Pentameron* records conversations between Boccaccio and Petrarch. *Pericles and Aspasia* purports to be an exchange of letters which mirror the life of Athens in its golden age.

Landor's career continued stormy, and in his old age he became embroiled in litigation over libelous writings as well as his contested estate. During these latter years he did many of his Latin poems and epigrams as well as dramatic dialogues. He was friendly with such writers as Robert Southey, Charles Lamb, and Robert Browning, and for a time he carried on a literary feud with Lord Byron. Always the hothead and incendiary, he was in turn gentle to children and animals, a nature lover, and generous to a fault. He died in Florence, Italy, September 17, 1864.

His literary life, from the time he was twenty until he was nearly ninety, is hard to assess. He was a stylist in the Latin tradition, coming midway between Milton and Shelley. His drama, like that of the later Victorians, was interesting as poetry but unplayable, and his poetry sometimes degenerated into banal verse, though at its best it was heightened to sublimity. As an essayist he was irreproachable, Swiftian, satiric, incisive in his praise or condemnation. He paid tribute to the younger literary figures of his day before they were generally recognized.

Within recent years a revival of interest in Landor has become increasingly evident. This, certainly, is only poetic justice, for he remains one of the great eccentrics in English literature and a fascinating personality once the truth is separated from prejudiced opinions against him.

Bibliography

The standard edition, although not definitive, is *The Complete Works of Walter Savage Landor*, edited by T. E. Welby and Stephen Wheeler, 16 vols., 1927–1936. The *Poems* have been edited by Stephen Wheeler, 3 vols., 1937, and *Imaginary Conversations* by Ernest de Selincourt, 1915. A representative selection from his poetry and prose was included in *Selections from Landor*, edited by Sidney Colvin, 1904 (rev. ed.). Also see Charles L. Proudfit, ed., *Selected Imaginary Conversations of Literary Men and Statesmen*, 1969.

There is no standard biography, but for biographical and critical studies see John Forster, *Walter Savage Landor*, 1869, reprinted in an edition of the *Works*, 8 vols., 1876; Sidney Colvin, *Landor*, English Men of Letters Series, 1881; H. C. Minchin, *Last Days, Letters and Conversations with Walter Savage Landor*, 1934; Michael Elwin, *Savage Landor*, 1942; and Robert H. Super, *Walter Savage Landor: A Biography*, 1954. See also Malcolm Elwin, *Landor: A Replevin*, 1958; and Pierre Vitaux, *L'Œuvre de Walter Savage Landor*, 1964. Briefer studies include Stephen Leslie, *Hours in a Library, Third Series*, 1879; George Saintsbury, *Essays in English Literature, 1780–1860*, 1895; and Helene Richter, "Walter Savage Landor," *Anglia*, L (1926), 123–152, 317–344, and LI (1927), 1–30.

IMAGINARY CONVERSATIONS

Type of work: Dialogues
Author: Walter Savage Landor (1775–1864)
First published: 1824–1848

Essay-Review

Landor once said, "Poetry was always my amusement, prose my study and business." When he was forty-five, after having devoted many years to poetic composition, he began the *Imaginary Conversations*, and in this work he found the form best suited to the peculiar aim and direction of his art.

By the very nature of his character Landor was drawn for guidance and inspiration to the classical tradition. One side of his personality admired balance, moderation, and precision: qualities admirably displayed in his writing. The other side was irascible, impractical, and impulsive; these traits are revealed in some of his personal relationships. Like Mozart, Landor appears to have found in his restrained and faultless art a counterpoise to his external world of turbulence.

Landor was a true classicist, not a belated adherent of neo-classicism with its emphasis on rules over substance. He was rigorously trained in youth and continued his scholarly pursuits throughout his adult life. His knowledge was no mere surface phenomenon; he was so immersed in the ancients that he took on their characteristic habits of thought. Thus the volumes of the *Imaginary Conversations* not only make use of events and characters from the Greco-Roman civilization, but are infused with classical ideals of clarity and precision in style and tough intellectualism in content.

The *Imaginary Conversations*, written in five series, are grouped into classical dialogues, dialogues of sovereigns and statesmen, dialogues of literary men, dialogues of famous women, and miscellaneous dialogues. The conversations, usually between two people, cover many centuries, ranging from the time of the Trojan War to Landor's own period, and they include people from many geographical areas. Many of the scenes are based on suggestions from history or mythology, but the actual remarks of the individuals are never used. Landor did not attempt to re-create a sense of the past by use of artificial or archaic language. He did, however, endeavor to represent faithfully the spirit of the age and the essential nature of the personage presented.

In the *Imaginary Conversations*, Landor was above all concerned with interpretation of character. While he displayed brilliant insights into human nature, his aim was not toward fully developed characters, but for abstractive idealizations. They are products not of observation directly reported but of observation, especially that gained from reading, filtered through a long process of reflection. Never are the predilections of the author—his sympathies and his aversions—far from the surface.

The manly, heroic character is depicted in many of the dialogues. Two examples of this type are found in "Marcellus and Hannibal." History records the death of Marcellus in the Second Punic War and the respect paid him by Hannibal. Landor created a scene in which Marcellus survived long enough to converse with the Carthaginian leader. When the wounded Marcellus was brought to the camp, Hannibal made every effort to save his life and to make him comfortable. A contrast to Hannibal's chivalric behavior was provided by that of his ally, a Gallic chief who thought only of revenge and of glory to Gaul. Marcellus welcomed death as an escape from capture and politely declined Hannibal's request that Rome agree to a peace treaty. Although under great suffering, he avoided any outward expression of pain. In return for Hannibal's kindness, Marcellus presented him with a ring that might benefit him with the Romans, if his fortunes changed. As Marcellus was dying, the two men were more closely united by their common nobility and respect for nobility in others than were they divided by the exigencies of war.

Women of praiseworthy character are depicted in several of the conversations. In "Lady Lisle and Elizabeth Gaunt," Landor portrayed the remarkable idealism of two women who were condemned to death for sheltering adherents of Monmouth. They had acted through simple Christian charity. Confronted with a choice between the law of the king and the commandment of Jesus, they embraced the latter. Lady Lisle had no blame for the jury that under duress had convicted her. Elizabeth, serene about her own fate, felt sorrow for her companion. Betrayed by the very man she had concealed, she felt no anger toward him, but pitied him for his having to suffer a guilty conscience. Both viewed execution as the avenue to eternal bliss and wished that others might have their perfect serenity.

A more complex character study is found in "Oliver Cromwell and Walter Noble." Cromwell was controlled by conflicting emotions—ambition, pride, compassion, vindictiveness, humility, fear. In response to the practically irrefutable arguments of Noble against regicide, Cromwell constantly shifted position and even contradicted himself. As a last refuge, he justified his proposed action as the carrying out of God's will.

Although Landor sometimes used crucial situations as settings for his conversations, he seldom revealed character in truly dramatic fashion. His dialogues, unlike Browning's monologues, do not have a close causal relationship between the stresses of the moment and the disclosures of the speaker. Nor do Landor's speakers often reveal their inner natures unwittingly. While Browning's works are subtle and require reading between the lines, Landor's are direct and leave little to implication. In the treatment of characters with whom he was unsympathetic, Landor used an irony that is unmistakable, even too obvious at times.

In some of the dialogues, especially the long discursive ones, the characters are not important in themselves, but serve as vehicles for the ideas of the author. Not a systematic philosopher nor a highly original thinker, Landor was alive to the whole range of man's thought, past and present. A wise and judicious man, he expressed his opinions felicitously.

Love of freedom is a leading theme in the *Imaginary Conversations*. Fighters for liberty, such as Washington and Kosciusko, who combined modesty with valor, evoked Landor's highest admiration. Equally fervid was his detestation of tyrants, as expressed, for example, in "Peter the Great and Alexis," a dialogue in which Peter, having failed to make his son as brutal as he, callously orders the boy's execution. Landor believed in a republican form of government and opposed pure democracy because of the corruption, intemperance, and anti-intellectualism that such a system fostered. His expression of political ideas seldom went beyond a statement of general principles.

Landor was often critical of religious leaders and he showed his antipathy to fanaticism in such dialogues as "Mahomet and Sergius" and "Melanchthon and Calvin." Hypocrisy is attacked in other dialogues, such as "Fra Filippo Lippi and Pope Eugenius IV," which is, in part, a satire on the Pope, who makes an outward show of piety and displays great zeal in maintaining the forms of religion, but who is essentially a worldly and sensual man. Also, in this conversation, the Christian-spirited barbarians of Tunisia are, with heavy irony, contrasted with the barbaric Christians of Rome. Landor favored a simple religion that stayed close to its basic tenets. Believing in the limitation of human reason in such matters, he disliked dogmatism and theological quibbling.

His philosophy was influenced by Epicurus and by the Stoics. He believed in meditation, in detachment, in freedom from the ambition and envy of the world. These sentiments are expressed in "Epicurus, Leontion, and Ternissa." Feeling that man's happiness depends on his use of reason to overcome doubts and worries, in many of his character portrayals Landor revealed his belief in self-control, fortitude, sympathy, and humanitarianism.

A significant part of the *Imaginary Conversations* is devoted to literary criticism. Classical standards were Landor's guide. He disapproved of unnecessary ornamentation in writing. "Never try to say things admirably, try only to say them plainly." "Whatever is rightly said, sounds rightly." But Landor was not a narrow classicist in his tastes; he admired a variety of authors, his favorites being Milton, Bacon, Shakespeare, Dante, and Pindar. Among his contemporaries he most respected Wordsworth and Southey.

Landor predicted that only a small, select group of people would prize his writings. He was correct. One reason for the failure of the *Imaginary Conversations* to attract a large audience is the fact that the dialogues lack direction and cohesive development. The absence of dramatic motivation and the presence of disconcerting gaps and shifts in argument create difficulties for the reader.

This weakness, which is a considerable one, has prevented the high merits of the *Imaginary Conversations* from being widely appreciated. Landor's aphorisms scattered throughout the work are among the best in the language. The range of his thought is impressive and his prose style is unexcelled in vigor and purity.

Bibliography

Colvin, Sir Sidney.   *Landor.* New York: Harper, 1881.

De Selincourt, Ernest.   "Landor's Prose," in his *Wordsworthian and Other Studies.* Oxford: Clarendon Press, 1947.

Elton, Oliver.   *A Survey of English Literature, 1780–1880,* Volume II. New York: Macmillan, 1920.

Emerson, Ralph Waldo.   *The Letters of Ralph Walso Emerson.* Edited by Ralph L. Rusk. New York: Columbia University Press, 1939.

————.   *Natural History of Intellect, and Other Papers. Complete Works,* Volume XII. Edited by Edward Waldo Emerson. Boston: Houghton Mifflin, 1904.

Hamilton, G. Rostrevor.   *Walter Savage Landor.* London: Published for the British Council and the National Book League by Longmans, Green, 1960.

Mercier, Vivian.   "The Future of Landor Criticism," in *Some British Romantics: A Collection of Essays.* Edited by Jane V. Logan, John E. Jordan, and Northrup Frye. Columbus: Ohio State University Press, 1966.

Prondfit, Charles L.   "An Unrecorded Cancellans in the First Edition of Walter Savage Landor's *Imaginary Conversations of Literary Men and Statesmen,*" in *Notes and Queries.* CCXIII (September, 1968), pp. 345–346.

————.   "Landor's Hobby Horse: A Study in Romantic Orthography," in *Studies in Romanticism.* VII (Summer, 1968), pp. 207–217.

Super, R.H.   "The Fire of Life," in *Cambridge Review.* LXXXVI (January 16, 1965), pp. 170–175.

————.   "Landor," in *The English Romantic Poets and Essayists. A Review of Research and Criticism.* Edited by C.W. and L.H. Houtchens. New York: New York University Press, 1966.

————.   *Walter Savage Landor, A Biography.* New York: New York University Press, 1954.

Williams, Stanley T.   "Walter Savage Landor as a Critic of Literature," in *PMLA.* XXXVIII (December, 1923), pp. 906–928.

Wise, Thomas James.   *A Landor Library.* London: Printed for Private Circulation, 1928.

THE POETRY OF LANDOR

Author: Walter Savage Landor (1775–1864)
First Published: Poems, 1795; *Gebir,* 1798; *The Hellenics,* 1847; *Poemata et Inscriptiones,* 1847; *Italics,* 1848; *Last Fruit off an Old Tree,* 1853; *Antony and Octavius,* 1856; *Dry Sticks Fagoted by W. S. Landor,* 1858; *Heroic Idylls,* 1863

Essay-Review

Walter Savage Landor, who has been described as a classic writer in a romantic age, was an isolated figure who outlived by many years the period of the Romantic triumph in England. Possessing from his earliest youth a strong attachment to both the ideals and the styles of Greek and Latin literature, he nevertheless admired and sympathized with the artistry of Byron, Shelley, and Keats. On the whole, however, the more restrained manner of his poetry tended toward the temper best exemplified by Browning and Tennyson. Often he composed first in Latin and then translated his work into English, consciously preserving the classical qualities of the original.

Having studied at Rugby, Landor matriculated at Oxford in 1795, when the tide of republicanism and revolutionism was running high. His active sympathy with the ascendant ideals of liberty brought him into difficulties with the university officials and eventually led to his withdrawing from Oxford without a degree. But the excellent training in Latin which he received there was to leave a distinctive mark on all his writings. Unmistakably and pervasively it is evident in the noble restraint and chastened expression which give Landor's poems a typically classical touch.

At the same time, like the Romantics he was a worshiper of nature and an unflinching defender of the downtrodden and helpless. In actuality, there is in the man, as in his poetry and prose, not a diametric clash of classical and Romantic contraries but, rather, a mingling of these opposing tendencies. Landor declared sincerely that he was not seeking wide popularity as a poet. To explain this attitude he used the effective metaphor, "I shall dine late, but the dining room will be well-lighted, the guests few and select." Although their mutual influence seems not to have been great, he appreciated, and was appreciated by, such notable contemporaries as Carlyle, Dickens, Browning, and Wordsworth.

In his first volume of poetry, *Poems,* which appeared in 1795, Landor displayed considerable dignity of phrase and artistry of style. Yet this volume appears inconsequential when compared to *Gebir,* an Oriental tale in blank verse written during two solitary years in Wales and published in 1798. In its seven books this epic recounts the adventures of the mythic founder of Gibraltar. The elevated style and cadence of the poem suggest that Landor's models were Milton and classical authors such as Pindar. *Gebir* drew attention and admiration from a

number of Landor's discriminating contemporaries, but was too weak in characterization and narrative content to appeal to the general reader. The one passage
of the poem which has achieved lasting recognition is the episode of "Tamar's
Wrestling," in which the outclassed shepherd loses to the "nymph divine" both
the wrestling match and the sheep he has wagered.

> "Shepherd," said she, "and will you wrestle now.
> And with the sailor's hardier race engage?"
>   . . . .
> "Whether a shepherd, as indeed you seem,
> Or whether of the hardier race you boast,
> I am not daunted, no: I will engage."
>   . . . .
> Now she came forward, eager to engage;
> But, first her dress, her bosom then, survey'd,
> And heav'd it, doubting if she could deceive.
> Her bosom seem'd, inclos'd in haze like heav'n,
> To baffle touch; and rose forth undefined.
> Above her knees she drew the robe succinct,
> Above her breast, and just below her arms:
> "This will preserve my breath, when tightly bound,
> If struggle and equal strength should so constrain."
> Thus, pulling hard to fasten it, she spoke,
> And rushing at me, closed. I thrill'd throughout
> And seem'd to lessen and shrink up with cold.
> Again, with violent impulse gushed my blood;
> And hearing nought external, thus absorb'd,
> I heard it rushing through each turbid vein,
> Shake my unsteady swimming sight in air.
> Yet with unyielding though uncertain arms,
> I clung around her neck; the vest beneath
> Rustled against our slippery limbs entwined:
> Often mine, springing with eluded force,
> Started aside, and trembled, till replaced.
> And when I most succeeded, as I thought,
> My bosom and my throat felt so comprest
> That life was almost quivering on my lips,
> Yet nothing was there painful! these are signs
> Of secret arts, and not human might,
> What arts I cannot tell: I only know
> My eyes grew dizzy, and my strength decay'd,
> I was indeed o'ercome!—with what regret,
> And more, with what confusion, when I reached
> The fold, and yielding up the sheep, she cried,
> "This pays a shepherd to a conquering maid."
> She smil'd, and more of pleasure than disdain
> Was in her dimpled chin, and liberal lip,
> And eyes that languished, lengthening,—just like love.
> She went away . . . .

The uneven quality of *Gebir* has been best described by Coleridge, who referred to its beautiful passages as "eminences excessively bright and all the ground around and between them in darkness." Indeed, Landor's longer poems, generally, are best remembered in extract. "I must read again Landor's *Julian*," Charles Lamb wrote in 1815, "I have not read it for some time. I think he must have failed in Roderick, for I remember nothing of him, nor of any distinct character as a character—only fine-sounding passages."

Landor devoted the first twenty-six years of his literary career almost wholly to verse. He then turned for a time primarily to the writing of prose, of which his *Imaginary Conversations* and the creative romance *Pericles and Aspasia* are the most noteworthy. Then followed the period of Landor's Latin poetry, during which he produced Latin verse of all kinds—elegiac, idyllic, lyric, and satiric—directly as well as indirectly imitating various Roman writers, among them Catullus, Horace, Juvenal, and Vergil. In 1847 he published these poems under the title of *Poemata et Inscriptiones*; and that year he also published in English *The Hellenics*, a series of poems on Greek topics, many of which had been written long before. A second version appeared twelve years later.

The Hellenics contains imaginary dialogues of moderate length in poetic form. A number of them having been written, like parts of *Gebir*, first in Latin, these poems are very much like their classical models. The settings and situations generally are dramatic; the characters are harmoniously arranged to set off their distinctive qualities, and the entire design is carefully proportioned. Although the products of this craftsmanship frequently resemble sedate, cool sculpture rather than intense drama, they are not devoid of an inner life of human emotion. Two poems in the collection which especially demonstrate the latter quality are the tragic "Iphigeneia" and the idyllic "Hamadryad."

In the former poem, Iphigeneia, daughter of Agamemnon, is to be sacrificed to the gods so that her father's ships will have a safe and prosperous journey.

> Iphigeneia, when she heard her doom
> At Aulis, and when all beside the king
> Had gone away, took his right-hand, and said,
> "O father! I am young and very happy.
> I do not think the pious Calchas heard
> Distinctly what the Goddess spake. Old age
> Obscures the senses . . . ."
> The father placed his cheek upon her head,
> And tears dropt down it, but the king of men
> Replied not . . . .
> "But father! to see you no more, and see
> Your love, O father! go ere I am gone!"
> Gently he moved her off, and drew her back,
> Bending his loftly head far over her's,
> And the dark depths of nature heaved and burst.
> He turn'd away; not far, but silent still . . . .
>
> An aged man now enter'd, and without

> One word, stept slowly on, and took the wrist
> Of the pale maiden. She lookt up, and saw
> The fillet of the priest and calm cold eyes.
> Then turn'd she where her parent stood, and cried
> "O father! grieve no more: the ships can sail."

Aside from *Gebir*, *The Hellenics*, and several "closet" dramas, the most nearly successful of which is *Count Julian*, almost all of Landor's poetry was in the form of occasional lyrics. Easily and regularly over a period of more than fifty years, he produced short poems, among which are his best poetic creations. There are several hundred of these occasional verses, forming a record of cheerfulness, gallantry, and affection, as well as of sad retrospect. Some of them, notably "Rose Aylmer," have achieved lasting success. Perhaps the best and most genuinely felt words in all of Landor's poetry are these eight lines of *Rose Aylmer*:

> Ah what avails the sceptred race,
>   Ah what the form divine!
> What every virtue, every grace!
>   Rose Aylmer, all were thine.
> Rose Aylmer, whom these wakeful eyes
>   May weep, but never see,
> A night of memories and of sighs
>   I consecrate to thee.

Other lyrics possess qualities which range from engaging charm to playful triviality and roguish trifling. The verses Landor wrote in old age are majestic in their own way. Of these, "I Strove with None" is the most famous, and it is typical in the author's proclaiming his apartness of temper. His announcement, "I hate the crowd," is like Ben Jonson's pose which could not entirely hide the genuine feeling underneath. Seldom successful in spontaneous poetry, and sometimes far wide of the mark, Landor yet displays sensitiveness, mastery of the exquisitely beautiful phrase, exceptional proliferation of imagery, and graceful, though fastidious, dignity.

Landor declared: "Poetry was always my amusement, prose my study and business." Although his literary reputation is based mostly on his prose, it is in poetry that he has achieved his few works of genuine greatness. During the last decades of his life, although his disposition grew increasingly aloof, he continued to produce poetry of high quality. The volume titled *Last Fruit off an Old Tree* is notable mainly for a group of five dramatic scenes on the trial and death of Beatrice Cenci, the heroine of Shelley's poetic drama *The Cenci*. *Antony and Octavius*, a group of twelve dramatic dialogues, appeared in 1856. In 1858 he published a miscellany of poetry entitled *Dry Sticks Fagoted by W. S. Landor*. His final volume was the *Heroic Idylls*.

Landor's own proud, resonant voice was heard over an amazing span of years; and although we readily acknowledge the truth of Swinburne's epitaph,

> And through the trumpet of a child of Rome
> Range the pure music of the flutes of Greece,

we must immediately qualify it by the recollection that throughout Landor's creative life, his classically based verse idylls such as the beautiful "Hamadryad" and its sequel "Acon and Rhodope" are in essence not only Landorian but also "Romantic" and modern. Landor's works are products of the age of Keats and the age of Tennyson.

Bibliography

Aldington, Richard.   "Landor's 'Hellenics,' " in *Literary Studies and Reviews*. New York: Dial Press, 1924.

Coleridge, S.T.   *Table Talk and Omniana.* Oxford: Humphrey Milford, 1917.

Colvin, Sir Sidney.   *Landor.* New York: Harper, 1881.

Davie, Donald S.   "The Shorter Poems of Landor," in *Essays in Criticism.* IV (October, 1951), pp. 345–355.

De Quincey, Thomas.   *Essays on the Poets, and Other English Writers.* Boston: Ticknor, Reed, and Fields, 1853.

Dilworth, Ernest.   *Walter Savage Landor.* New York: Twayne, 1971.

Elwin, Malcolm.   *Landor, A Replevin.* London: Macdonald, 1958.

————.   *Savage Landor.* New York: Macmillan, 1941.

Pinsky, Robert.   *Landor's Poetry.* Chicago: University of Chicago Press, 1968.

Raleigh, Walter.   *On Writing and Writers.* Edited by George Gordon. London: Arnold, 1926.

Robinson, Henry Crabb.   *Henry Crabb Robinson on Books and Their Writers.* Edited by E.J. Morley. London: Dent, 1938.

Saintsbury, George.   *Essays in English Literature, 1780–1860.* Second Series. London: Dent, 1895.

————.   *A History of English Prosody.* London: Macmillan, 1923.

Super, R.H.   "Landor," in *The English Romantic Poets and Essayists, a Review of Research and Criticism.* Edited by C.E. and L.H. Houtchens. New York: New York University Press, 1966.

Symons, Arthur.   *The Romantic Movement in English Poetry.* New York: Dutton, 1909.

THOMAS MOORE

Born: Dublin, Ireland (May 28, 1779)
Died: Bromham, England (February 25, 1852)

Principal Works

POEMS: *Epistles, Odes and Other Poems*, 1806; *Irish Melodies*, 1807–1834; *Lalla Rookh*, 1817; *The Loves of the Angels*, 1823.
SATIRES: *The Two-Penny Post Bag*, 1813; *The Fudge Family in Paris*, 1818; *Fables for the Holy Alliance*, 1823.
BIOGRAPHY: *Life of Sheridan*, 1825; *Life of Byron*, 1830; *Life and Death of Lord Edward Fitzgerald*, 1831.

Thomas Moore was born on May 28, 1779, the son of a prosperous Dublin merchant. After study in grammar school, he entered Trinity College, Dublin, in 1794, one of the first Roman Catholic students to be admitted to that institution. In the same year two poems by Moore appeared in the periodical *Anthologia Hibernica*. During his college years, Moore made a translation of Anacreon in verse which he took with him to London in 1799, when he entered the Middle Temple to study law; *Odes of Anacreon* was published in 1800, with an accepted dedication to the Prince of Wales. In 1803 Moore set out for Bermuda as a government appointee, but he decided en route to tour the United States and Canada and then return to England, leaving his post in charge of a deputy. *Epistles, Odes and Other Poems*, published in 1806, contains references to his travels. In 1807 he began to publish a series of volumes entitled *Irish Melodies*, with music by Sir John Stevenson. These volumes, highly popular, provided Moore with about £500 a year.

During the next few years, at odds with the Regent, Moore wrote a series of satires which were collected in *The Two-Penny Post Bag* in 1813. In 1811 Moore married Bessie Dyke, a young actress, by whom he had several children, all of whom were a disappointment to their father and failed to outlive him. Real fame as a writer came to Moore with *Lalla Rookh*, a long narrative poem with Oriental flavor. Other works followed, but none was so popular or so well-remembered. A biography of Lord Byron appeared in 1830. Moore also wrote a biography of Sheridan, the famous eighteenth century playwright. A novel, *The Epicurean* (1827), was not very successful. Moore's later years, made comfortable by a government pension, were spent at Slopeton Cottage, in Wiltshire. For many non-literary people Moore remains the author of the ever-popular, romantic "Believe Me, if All Those Endearing Young Charms" and a collection of patriotic Irish airs. He also edited an edition of Byron's *Works* and *Letters and Journals* (1832–1833). He died at Bromham, England, on February 25, 1852.

Bibliography

The standard edition is *The Poetical Works of Moore*, edited by A. D. Godley, 1910. An edition of the *Memoirs, Journal and Correspondence of Thomas Moore* was edited by Lord John Russell, 8 vols., 1853–1856. A more recent but abridged edition of the journal is *Tom Moore's Diary: A Selection* edited by J. B. Priestley, 1925. For biography and criticism see Stephen Gwynn, *Thomas Moore*, English Men of Letters series, 1904; W. F. Trench, *Tom Moore*, 1934; H. M. Jones, *The Harp That Once—A Chronicle of the Life of Thomas Moore*, 1937; L. A. G. Strong, *The Minstrel Boy: A Portrait of Tom Moore*, 1937; and Robert Birley, "Thomas Moore: *Lalla Rookh.*" *Sunk without Trace: Some Forgotten Masterpieces Reconsidered*, 1962.

IRISH MELODIES

Type of work: Poetry
Author: Thomas Moore (1779–1852)
First published: 1807–1834; 1835

Essay-Review

Few men of letters have been able to write on Thomas Moore without disparaging the financial and social success of his life or the great mass of his work, mostly verse, from which so little of any worth is still remembered except the *Irish Melodies*. The quantity of his work and the ready charm which contributed to his success in London society are largely attributable to the fact that Moore, like many another aspirant from the provinces, had to get on as best he could. Starvation in a garret may be the mark of genius but only posterity can decide between the respective merits of Chatterton and Blake. Moore took no chances; he stuck by the Whigs, forswore his early Republicanism, and modulated his Irishness into its most acceptable form in the London drawing room, the real source of political power and hence patronage in Regency England. He sang Irish songs and at the same time gained practically the only claim he has on our memory and affections. The rest of his work fills up that yawning gulf of trivia which kept the publishers of London prosperous, their readers contented, the popular authors wealthy, and the best of contemporary English writers—Shelley, Keats, Blake—out of sight.

Yet Moore was in his way a pioneer. He always claimed to have originated modern Irish poetry, enjoying a personal application of the song which takes its title from the opening words:

> Dear Harp of my Country! in darkness I found thee,
>   The cold chain of silence hung o'er thee long,
> When proudly, my own Island Harp! I unbound thee,
>   And gave all thy chords to light, freedom and song!

In the rest of the lyric, Moore sums up his subjects—death, love, mirth, and patriotism—and specifies his technique: "wild sweetness." The revolutionary effect of this combination in London when he began the composition of *Irish Melodies* in 1806 (seven years after his arrival there from Dublin) was more noticeable because of the stolidity of the serious verse of the time and popular light verse, to both of which Moore had contributed enough to acquire a lucrative government post in the Bermudas. He left London in 1803 to take up the post, but soon returned and set to work on his *Irish Melodies*, exile from London having apparently sharpened his love for Ireland. The new style of drawing-room entertainment Moore often provided in person (he was an accomplished musician) was soon earning him five hundred pounds a year. The lyric was restored to popularity in English literature not by the *Lyrical Ballads* or by Burns or by Blake, all of whom came before Moore, but by the *Irish Melodies*.

Moore had given a sample of his ability to write lyrics to folk tunes in the feebly satirical *Poems Relating to America*, published in 1806: the "Canadian Boat Song" which he heard his "voyageurs" sing as they rowed all the way down the St. Lawrence from Kingston to Montreal. From 1807 to 1834, he published his songs, words and music, with editions of the words alone appearing from 1820 on. Time has established the concert repertoire selected from the songs: "The Harp That Once Thro' Tara's Halls," "Believe Me if All Those Endearing Young Charms," "She Is Far from the Land," " 'Tis the last Rose of Summer," "The Minstrel Boy," "Sweet Inishfallen, Fare Thee Well," to which may be added the "Canadian Boat Song" and two later songs, the "Vesper Hymn" and "Oft in the Stilly Night" from *National Airs*, lyrics and arrangements of folk songs from most European countries.

Generally only one of the lyrics is now anthologized as a poem apart from its setting: "The Time I've Lost in Wooing." It shows Moore's abilities to advantage: the rhymes are feminine in the longer lines and in triples (*wooing . . . pursuing . . . undoing*); the shorter lines (none is long) end in masculine rhyme; the alternations give a pleasing variation to the run of the poem; the poem in three stanzas reaches a witty conclusion that echoes the Caroline poets. In the conflict between Wisdom and Beauty the poet's time has been wasted in pursuit of the latter; he knows this but still cannot cease his pursuit:

> Poor Wisdom's chance
> Against a glance
> Is now as weak as ever.

Of the language of the lyrics Edmund Gosse observed that "words of a commonplace character are so strung together as to form poetry easily grasped and enjoyed by the ear." The secret of Moore's original and present popularity lies in providing acceptable poetry for the ear, not for the eye, and since we have largely lost that gift so enjoyed by Elizabethans it is little wonder that our ears have to be assisted by folk tunes.

In the collected editions of Moore's works the *Irish Melodies* now number one hundred and twenty-five, beginning with "Go Where Glory Waits Thee" and ending with "Silence Is in Our Festal Halls," Moore's elegy for Sir John Stevenson, who wrote the arrangements for the parts. Most of the parts as they were issued contained dedications to patrons from Moore and advertisements from his publisher, Power, to the general public insisting that there were plenty more "airs" in the treasury of Irish folk song for future parts. A certain amount of national feeling is evident in both advertisements and dedications, especially in that to the first part which includes a letter from Moore referring to the Irish reputation for song as "the only talent for which our English neighbors ever deigned to allow us any credit." A more important preface is that to the third part or number. As well as dealing with the age of Irish songs, their resemblance to Scottish song, and the harmonic peculiarities of Irish music, Moore refers to three aspects which in their way sum up much of the *Melodies*: their national feeling; their peculiar mixture of defiance and despondency; and their being lyrics to songs, not poems as such.

On the last point he begs exemption from "the rigors of literary criticism" because he can "answer for their sound with somewhat more confidence than for their sense." This statement is admirably sensible but makes it difficult to discuss the *Irish Melodies* as if they were poems. If Moore's guiding principle was to make them singable, only a singer can argue the point and many a trite phrase and conventional rhyme can be excused on this ground. Moore's other two remarks point to two obvious features in the lyrics. They often begin strongly and fade into resignation at parting, death, the passage of time, the decay of good customs. Where the poems reach a strong conclusion they do so by denying the resigned close, generally by appeal to the Divine or to Ireland. The endings to two patriotic poems illustrate the difference: "Let Erin Remember the Days of Old" declines into

> Thus, sighing, look through the waves of time
> For the long-faded glories they cover.

On the other hand "Sublime Was the Warning" challenges Irish national aspirations by appealing to the success of Spanish independence after the Napoleonic wars and concludes:

> The young spirit of Freedom shall shelter their grave
> Beneath shamrocks of Erin and olives of Spain.

The Irish quality of the poems is most apparent in their subjects. Some are taken from Irish history; others contain references to Irish legends and customs; but the one thread that runs through the volume is "Erin." Much of the reference to Ireland is a prophecy of longed-for independence; a purely poetic exercise Moore's contemporaries in London must have thought it, but history has realized Moore's longing, and it would be an interesting point to settle how much his songs had to do with maintaining Irish nationalism during the struggles of the nineteenth century—songs like "Where Is the Slave?" "Erin, Oh Erin," "Oh the Shamrock," and the better-known "Minstrel Boy" and "The Harp That Once Thro' Tara's Halls." The most curious of these is "As Vanquished Erin," which describes how the Fiend of Discord persists in sending "his shafts of desolation ... through all her maddening nation." When Erin asks the "Powers of Good" when this will end, the Demon answers "Never." This is possibly the truest statement Moore made about Ireland.

The phrase that sums up the quality of the lyrics in the *Irish Melodies* is Moore's "wild sweetness," an unusual and romantic combination of opposites, its

Irishness, one may say. But the "sweetness" of the verses is obtained by both technical dexterity (Moore maintains, as he must, the rhythm of the melody in a variety of meters) and a neatness of phrasing that might be called Irish wit were it not that, except in a few light pieces of which "The Time I've Lost in Wooing" is the best, this gift is usually spent on general topics and does not show to advantage:

> Love, nursed among pleasures, is faithless as they,
> But the love born of Sorrow, like Sorrow, is true.

Much of the "wild" note comes from the subjects of war, chains, heroic death, but also from the ecstasy of the love poems, tinged as they generally are with sadness. Oddly enough, it is probably the romantic combination Moore achieved which was responsible for the gradual disfavor into which the *Irish Melodies* fell about the turn of the century, though they are still referred to in Joyce and O'Casey. When the Gaelic Revival and the independence of Eire finally arrived, a more genuine folk song with real Irish lyrics seems to have lessened Moore's popularity and reduced it to the proportions of the man himself, whom Scott once called "a little, very little man."

THOMAS LOVE PEACOCK

Born: Weymouth, England (October 18, 1785)
Died: Lower Halliford, England (January 23, 1866)

Principal Works

NOVELS: *Headlong Hall*, 1816; *Melincourt*, 1817; *Nightmare Abbey*, 1818; *Maid Marian*, 1822; *The Misfortunes of Elphin*, 1829; *Crotchet Castle*, 1831; *Gryll Grange*, 1860.

POEMS: *The Monks of St. Mark*, 1804; *Palmyra and Other Poems*, 1806; *The Genius of the Thames*, 1810; *The Philosophy of Melancholy*, 1812; *Sir Proteus: a Satirical Ballad*, 1814; *Rhododaphne*, 1818.

Thomas Love Peacock, born at Weymouth, Dorsetshire, England, on October 18, 1785, was a literary barnacle, following the ship of English Romanticism for the ride though not a part of it. Until his early thirties he wrote poetry that was intended to inspire readers as that of the Romantics did. However, it was only the shell of poetry; it contained rhyme and meter and exotic material, but the meat—emotion—was absent. This passage from *Rhododaphne* is typical:

> All other fires are of the earth,
> And transient: but of heavenly birth
> Is Love's first flame, which howsoever
> Fraud, power, woe, chance, or fate may sever
> From its congenial source, must burn
> Unquenched, but in the funeral urn. (Canto VII)

Actually Peacock was in spirit and temperament a classicist. He was precocious as a child and although he did not attend college, he was well-read in Latin and Greek (having taught himself the two languages for pleasure's sake). Among his favorite classical authors were Sallust, Tacitus, and Lucian. Of an even disposition, he walked along country roads and stopped by graveyards and mountain streams as was the prevailing practice of the Lake poets. But he collected ideas, not emotional experiences. (One idea was that a Welsh girl whom he had met on a walking tour through Wales would be a good wife to marry; when he had advanced in the East India Company to a salary sufficient to support a family ten years later he wrote to her to be his bride. She remembered and accepted.) However, he was not ignorant of the Romantic movement; many of the poets, such as Shelley, were his good friends. And it was the combination of his practical brain, his enjoyment of literature, and his sense of humor that produced his real contribution to literature, a series of seven novels satirizing the whole intellectual and artistic movement of the day.

In reality a conservative, successful businessman, Peacock was unsympathetic to the new ideas of the time primarily because they went beyond reason, which is to say they were to him unreasonably romantic. Using the method of irony, he satirized radicalism, medievalism, and transcendentalism as well as individual Romanticists like Wordsworth, Coleridge, Byron, and Shelley. Five of the seven novels—all but *Maid Marian* and *The Misfortunes of Elphin*—follow the same plan: a group of eccentric guests at a house party reveal the folly of their romantic persuasions in witty talk and inane action. Each guest, of course, is a caricature of a contemporary figure. The other two novels are burlesques of legends, the first of Robin Hood and the second of the Welsh (supra). The critic Saintsbury felt that this last novel was the best, although *Crotchet Castle* has remained the most popular. The main purpose of all the works was "to make a joke of things." Peacock died at Lower Halliford, Chertsey, on January 23, 1866.

Bibliography

The standard edition of Peacock's works is the Halliford Edition, edited by H. F. B. Brett-Smith and C. E. Jones, 10 vols., 1923–1924; it includes a biographical introduction and full bibliographical and textual notes. J. B. Priestly, *Thomas Love Peacock* in the English Men of Letters Series, 1927 (revised edition 1966), is the most adequate biography, although Carl Van Doren, *The Life of Thomas Love Peacock*, 1911, is still important. Critical works include A. Martin Freeman, *Thomas Love Peacock, a Critical Study*, 1911; A. B. Young, *The Life and Novels of Thomas Love Peacock*, 1904; H. R. Fedden, "Peacock," in *The English Novelists*, edited by D. Vershoyle, 1936; and Olwen W. Campbell, *Peacock*, in the English Novelists Series, 1953. Recent works are Carl Dawson, *Thomas Love Peacock*, 1968; and Howard Milk, *Peacock: His Circle and His Age*, 1969. An important article is O. Burdett, "Thomas Love Peacock," *London Mercury*, VIII (1923), 21–32.

NIGHTMARE ABBEY

Type of work: Novel
Author: Thomas Love Peacock (1785–1866)
Type of plot: Social satire
Time of plot: Early nineteenth century
Locale: England
First published: 1818

Thomas Love Peacock created the novel of talk, a formula for satirizing literary and social fads, that has been frequently copied (especially by Aldous Huxley) but never duplicated. A group of eccentrics, mostly thinly disguised caricatures of contemporary celebrities, is gathered at a house party where they talk brilliantly, behave farcically, and, by the novel's end, pair up romantically. In Nightmare Abbey *Peacock utilizes this formula to perfection.*

Principal Characters

Christopher Glowry, the master of Nightmare Abbey, who is largely interested in eating and drinking. He is boorish and coarse. He refuses to allow his son to marry the woman of his choice because she has no fortune. He finally changes his mind, but by that time it is too late; the young lady has discarded his son and accepted another proposal.

Scythrop Glowry, Christopher Glowry's son, a gloomy, boorish, unmannerly young man. He has a rather morbid interest in dungeons, secret panels, and skulls. He falls in love with his cousin, but his father will not allow the marriage. Later, when he is not able to decide between two girls, the two young ladies both accept other men and he is left to drink his wine alone. He is supposed to represent Shelley.

Marionetta Celestina O'Carroll, Glowry's niece and Scythrop's cousin. She is very coquettish and Scythrop falls in love with her. She has no fortune, however, and is allowed to remain in the house only as a guest. She finally accepts the proposal of a dandy named Listless.

Mr. Toobad, Glowry's friend. He and Glowry agree that his daughter would be a good match for Scythrop. He goes to London to bring her to Nightmare Abbey, but she discovers his purpose and disappears.

Celinda Toobad (Stella), Mr. Toobad's daughter. She does not take kindly to having a husband chosen for her and runs away from her father when she learns that she is to marry Scythrop. She turns up later at Nightmare Abbey as a strange woman calling herself Stella, and moves into a secret apartment constructed by Scythrop. She discusses German metaphysics and tragedy with Scythrop, without knowing who he is. When he is slow in asking for her hand, she accepts Flosky's proposal.

Listless, a bored and languid dandy, and a friend and fellow collegian of Scythrop. He is a guest at Nightmare Abbey and is interested in Marionetta. He finally asks for her hand in marriage and is accepted.

Mr. Ferdinando Flosky, a poet, and another guest at the abbey. He is interested in the supernatural and in metaphysics. He proposes to and is accepted by Celinda. He is supposed to represent Coleridge.

Mr. Cypress, another visitor at Nightmare Abbey. He is Byron.

Mr. Asterias, another guest who is an ichthyologist tracing down rumors of a mermaid supposed to have been seen near the abbey.

Aquarius, his son.

Fatout, Listless' French valet.

Raven, a servant at Nightmare Abbey.

The Story

Refused by one young lady in his youth, Glowry immediately married another. His wife was cold and gloomy, and Nightmare Abbey was a fitting name for her house. Glowry found relief from his unhappy life in food and drink, and when his lady died, he was easily consoled by increasing his consumption of food and wine. She left one son, Scythrop, who was gloomy enough to suit his father and Nightmare Abbey. A university education had so stripped Scythrop of his thin veneer of social graces that he was rapidly becoming a country boor like his father.

While his father was away in London attending to an important lawsuit, Scythrop amused himself by constructing miniature dungeons, trapdoors, and secret panels. One day he discovered by chance an apartment in the main wing of the abbey which had no entrance or exit; through an error in construction, the apartment had remained hidden for many years. He imported a dumb carpenter and together they constructed a cunning secret panel through which one could step from the library into the hidden apartment. Then, Scythrop had a private refuge for his gloomy meditations.

Miss Emily Girouette declined decidedly to marry Scythrop. In consequence, when his cousin Marionetta came to visit, she rapidly conquered the heart of that sad young man. But Marionetta had no fortune, and Glowry refused to hear of the marriage. Scythrop, however, grew more enamored daily of his coquettish cousin.

Glowry viewed the increasing attachment of Scythrop and Marionetta with great concern. Finally, he told Scythrop the girl would have to leave. Furious, Scythrop rushed to his tower and filled a human skull with Madeira wine. Confronting his father and holding high the skull, he declared in ringing tones that if Marionetta ever left Nightmare Abbey except of her own free will, he would drink the potion. Convinced that the skull contained poison, his father consented to have Marionetta stay on as a guest. Scythrop drank the wine with gusto.

Glowry confided his troubles to his friend, Toobad, who agreed that marriage with Marionetta was unsuitable in every way. He proposed his own daughter Celinda, a young woman then studying abroad, as a good match for Scythrop. With Glowry's hearty approval Toobad went to London to meet his daughter and return with her to Nightmare Abbey. But Celinda, refusing to have a husband chosen for her, fled from her domineering father. Toobad appeared at the abbey and left again, vowing to all that he would find his unruly daughter.

The house party at Nightmare Abbey grew larger. Mr. Flosky, a poet of the supernatural, came and spread confusion with his metaphysical paradoxes. Listless, a bored dandy, came with Fatout, his French valet, who was the guardian of his mind and body. Another addition to the party was Mr. Asterias the ichthyologist, engaged in tracing down rumors of mermaids in the vicinity of the abbey. It was not clear what a mermaid would do in the fens around the abbey, but Mr. Asterias had faith. That faith was rewarded one night when dimly Mr. Asterias perceived the form of a woman clad in black. As he rushed across the moat, the mysterious figure disappeared.

Scythrop took as much delight as he could in Marionetta's company. But Listless was the gayest person in the room when Marionetta was present. As far as his languid airs would permit, he followed her about with great eagerness.

Watching Scythrop's affection for Marionetta, Glowry decided that he had been too harsh with his son, and he suddenly announced his approval of their betrothal. To his father's surprise, Scythrop stammered that he did not want to be too precipitate. So the generosity of the father went unrewarded.

There was some mystery about Scythrop. For some time he had been more distraught than usual; now he practically refused marriage with his beloved. More than that, every time Glowry went to his son's rooms, he found the door locked and Scythrop slow in answering his knock. Always before the door opened, a strange, heavy thud sounded in the room.

One evening, while the whole company was sitting in the drawing-room, a tall and stately figure wearing a bloody turban suddenly appeared. Listless rolled under the sofa. Glowry roared his alarm in Toobad's ear, and Toobad tried to run away. But he mistook a window for a door, and fell into the moat below. Mr. Asterias, still looking for a mermaid, fished him out with a landing net.

These mysteries went back to the night Mr. Asterias thought he saw the mermaid. Scythrop was sitting alone in his library when the door opened softly and in stepped a beautiful, stately woman. She looked at Scythrop carefully, and reassured by what she saw, she sat down confidently. The bewildered man could only sit and stare. Gently the mysterious stranger asked him if he were the illustrious author of the pamphlet, "Philosophical Gas." Flattered, Scythrop acknowledged his authorship of that profound work, only seven copies of which had been sold. Then the girl asked his protection from a marriage that would make her the slave of her sex. Already smitten, Scythrop agreed to hide her in his secret apartment.

Then Scythrop began his dual romance. The serious girl, who called herself Stella, talked night after night of the German metaphysicians and quoted German tragedy. On the other hand, Marionetta was always gay and lively. Scythrop did not know whom to choose.

One night his father demanded entry into his room while Stella was there. Stella decided to show herself, regardless of consequences. Toobad recognized his long-lost daughter Celinda. Scythrop now had to choose either Celinda or Marionetta. But he hesitated to make a choice, feeling that he could not relinquish either. The next day, however, the decision was made for him. Marionetta had accepted Listless and Celinda would soon be Mrs. Flosky. Stoically, Glowry reminded his son that there were other maidens. Scythrop agreed, and ordered the Madeira.

Critical Evaluation

Like Jane Austen's *Sense and Sensibility,* Thomas Love Peacock's *Nightmare Abbey* satirizes Gothic fiction, the popular and often meretricious writing that was contemporary with the best of Romantic poetry. But his satire is richer than hers because he is not restricted by the conventions of the novel of manners. His book is actually a parody: it ridicules Gothic fiction by out-gothicizing it. Few Gothic novels can approach Peacock's secret passages and mysterious maidens.

J. B. Priestley calls *Nightmare Abbey* "one of the best literary satires in the language," and so it is. Its power emanates from a very clever ruse. Although it is a parody of Gothic fiction, the brunt of its satire is directed against the ideas and poses of the major Romantic poets. Peacock murders by association. In Mr. Flosky, Gothic spiritualism is identified with metaphysical obscurity: He "unintentionally" finds himself "within the limits of common sense," and he "never (gives) a plain answer to a question." Mr. Flosky is a thinly disguised Samuel Taylor Coleridge. Peacock has him announce: "This distinction between fancy and imagination is one of the most abstruse and important points of metaphysics. I have written several hundred pages to elucidate it. . . ." The *Biographia Literaria,* where Coleridge's famous chapter on the distinction between imagination and fancy first appeared, was published a year before *Nightmare Abbey.*

Peacock is just as hard on Byron, who in the person of Mr. Cypress, is ridiculed for excesses of melancholy and iconoclasm: " . . . a man who has quarrelled with his wife is absolved from all duty to his country. I have written an ode to tell the people as much, and they may take it as they list." And finally Shelley's involvement with Harriet Westbrook, the innkeeper's daughter, and Mary Godwin, the philosopher's daughter, is the basis of Scythrop's dual infatuation with Marionetta and Stella.

MRS. ANN RADCLIFFE

Born: London, England (July 9, 1764)
Died: London (February 7, 1823)

Principal Works

NOVELS: *A Sicilian Romance*, 1790; *The Romance of the Forest*, 1791; *The Mysteries of Udolpho*, 1794; *The Italian, or, The Confessional of the Black Penitents*, 1797; *Gaston de Blondeville*, 1826.

Mrs. Ann (Ward) Radcliffe, although little known today, was considered the greatest romanticist of her age, both for her imaginative plotting and for her poetic prose. Her novels have become a minor landmark in English literary history because their author formulated a Gothic school of writing that owed more to her invention than to the influence of her contemporaries in the same genre, and her tales of terror are unblurred by the awkward supernaturalism of Walpole, the sentimentality of Clara Reeves, or the turgid horrors of Matthew Gregory Lewis.

Born in London on July 9, 1764, Ann Ward included among her ancestors the celebrated classical scholar, Dr. S. Jebb. Stimulated by her wide reading, she delighted as a child in daydreams of things supernatural; however, a shy, asthmatic girl isolated in a society of her elders, she was not encouraged to exercise her abilities or to express herself. At twenty-three, pretty and demure, she married William Radcliffe, the future editor of the *English Chronicle*. Living in London, intimate with literary people, and childless, she began to write. Her first book, *The Castles of Athlin and Dunbayne* (1789), went almost unnoticed, but her second, *A Sicilian Romance*, established her reputation as a master of suspense and description. With *The Romance of the Forest*, published in 1791, she attracted the attention of a wide reading public. For her fourth novel, *The Mysteries of Udolpho*, she received £500 before it was published.

This novel typifies the two strongest elements in Mrs. Radcliffe's fiction: the suggestion of imminent evil and the atmosphere of refinement and beauty. Juxtaposed, each element intensifies the other. Mrs. Radcliffe carries the reader into a beautiful Eden, and by contrasting excellent description with vague references to impending doom an effect of mystery and terror results. That some terrible mystery suggested by a low groan from a distant tomb or an uncertain light on a castle stairs turns out to be wind or moonlight does not alter the effect of the story. Mrs. Radcliffe discriminated carefully between terror and horror, and her ability to evoke the former while avoiding the latter points to her skillful handling of atmosphere and dramatic situation.

Mrs. Radcliffe's novels are built on the same plot: a chaste, helpless young woman achieves a good marriage after a series of attempts on her life by sinister villains in an exotic setting. Although the plots are improbable and the characters are two-dimensional to the modern reader, the novels had great influence on other writers of the time, notably Scott and Byron; early in Scott's career he was hailed as Mrs. Radcliffe's successor, and certainly Schedoni, the villain of *The Italian*, is the forerunner of the Byronic hero.

Although she was in literature a mistress of the strange and picturesque, her own biography is commonplace because of the regularity of her life, and modern scholarship now discounts the contemporary belief that madness, induced by the terrors she created, accounts for the long interval of time between the publication of *The Italian* and her posthumous *Gaston de Blondeville*. A figure deserving more attention in literary history than she has received, Mrs. Radcliffe died in London on February 7, 1823.

Bibliography

The edition of 1824 was reprinted in 1971. A modern edition of *The Italian* was issued as *The Confessional of the Black Penitents* by the Folio Society of London in 1956. For biography and criticism see Clara F. McIntyre, *Ann Radcliffe in Relation to Her Time, Yale Studies in English*, LXII, 1920; and A. A. S. Wieten, *Mrs. Radcliffe: Her Relation to Romanticism*, 1926. For more general studies of the Gothic Revival and its writers see also Dorothy Scarborough, *The Supernatural in Modern English Fiction*, 1917; Edith Birkhead, *The Tale of Terror*, 1921; Eino Railo, *The Haunted Castle*, 1927; the Rev. Montague Summers, *The Gothic Quest*, 1938, and *A Gothic Bibliography*, 1941. See further Donald Thomas, "The First Poetess of Romantic Fiction: Ann Radcliffe," *English*, XV (1964), 91–95; and Harrison Ross Steeves, "The Gothic Romance," *Before Jane Austen*, 1965, 243–271.

THE ITALIAN

Type of work: Novel
Author: Mrs. Ann Radcliffe (1764–1823)
Type of plot: Gothic romance
Time of plot: 1758
Locale: Italy
First published: 1797

As in Mrs. Radcliffe's other novels, in The Italian *she mingles the wild, idyllic beauty of nature with scenes of nightmare and terror. This is wholly a work of the romantic imagination, lacking both the fantastic supernaturalism and turgid sensationalism of her rivals in the specialized genre of the gothic novel.*

Principal Characters

Vincentio di Vivaldi, a young nobleman of Naples. Impressed by the grace and voice of the veiled Ellena di Rosalba, he is warned by a ghostly stranger not to seek her identity. Disregarding the warning, he succeeds in learning the young woman's name, falls in love with her, and determines to marry her in spite of his parents' strenuous objections because of her apparent lowly station. His mother's plottings to prevent the alliance set up a train of sinister events through which the young man passes before he is finally united with his beloved.

Ellena di Rosalba, a young girl of supposed humble origin, loved by Vincentio di Vivaldi. Before her wedding, she is abducted and carried off to a strange religious establishment, the first of a series of violent and sinister adventures which end in the revelation of her identity as the daughter of Sister Olivia and the dead Count di Bruno, and at last in her marriage to Vincentio.

The Marchesa di Vivaldi, the haughty and vindictive mother of Vincentio di Vivaldi. She plots, with the monk Schedoni, to do away with Ellena di Rosalba in order to prevent the girl's marriage to her son.

The Marchese di Vivaldi, Vincentio di Vivaldi's father.

Schedoni, the Marchesa di Vivaldi's confessor and her chief ally in the plot to murder Ellena di Rosalba. He is finally revealed as the second Count di Bruno, murderer of the first Count, his brother, and as a fugitive in the disguise of a monk.

Sister Olivia, a nun who befriends Ellena di Rosalba and is finally revealed as the former Countess di Bruno, Ellena's mother.

Signora Bianchi, Ellena di Rosalba's aunt and guardian, later revealed as the sister of the Sister Olivia.

Paulo Mendrico, Vincentio di Vivaldi's faithful servant.

Bonorma, Vincentio di Vivaldi's friend.

Beatrice, the servant of Signora Bianchi and Ellena di Rosalba.

Ansaldo di Rovalli, the grand penitentiary.

Brother Jeronimo, a monk.

Spalatro, an assassin in the pay of Schedoni.

Father Nicola, a monk who turns against the sinister Schedoni and gathers evidence against him for the Inquisition.

The Story

Vincentio di Vivaldi saw Ellena di Rosalba for the first time at the Church of San Lorenzo in Naples. So impressed was he by the sweetness of her voice and the grace of her person that at the end of the service he followed the girl and her elderly companion in the hope that the fair unknown would put aside her veil so that he might catch a glimpse of her features. When the elderly woman stumbled and fell, Vivaldi seized the opportunity to offer her his arm, a gallant gesture which gave him the excuse to accompany the two women to the Villa Altieri, their modest home on an eminence overlooking the bay of Naples.

The next day he returned to ask after the health of Signora Bianchi, as the older woman was named. Although the matron received her guest courteously, Ellena did not appear. Thrown into a mood of despondency by her absence, he inquired of his acquaintances into the girl's family, but learned only that she was an orphan, the niece and ward of her aged relative.

That night, resolved to see Ellena again, he left a reception given by his mother and repaired to the Villa Altieri. The hour was late and only one window was lighted. Through a lattice he saw Ellena playing on her lute while she sang a midnight hymn to the Virgin. Entranced, he drew near the lattice and heard her pronounce his name; but when he revealed himself the girl closed the lattice and left the room. Vivaldi lingered in the garden for some time before returning to Naples. Lost in reverie, he was passing under a shattered archway extending over the road when a shadowy figure in a monk's robe glided across his path and in a ghostly whisper warned him to beware of future visits to the villa.

Thinking that the warning had been given by a rival, he returned the next night in the company of his friend Bonorma. Again the dark figure appeared and uttered a sepulchral warning. Later, as the two young men were passing under the arch, the figure showed itself once more. Vivaldi and Bonorma drew their swords and entered the ancient fortress in search of the mysterious visitant. They found no trace of anyone lurking in the ruins.

Still believing that these visitations were the work of a rival, Vivaldi decided to end his suspense by making a declaration for Ellena's hand. Signora Bianchi listened to his proposal and then reminded him that a family as old and illustrious as his own would object to an alliance with a girl of Ellena's humble station. Vivaldi realized that she spoke wisely, but with all the fervor of a young man in love he argued his suit so eloquently that at last Signora Bianchi withdrew her refusal. After Vivaldi had made repeated visits to the villa, a night came when the aged woman placed Ellena's hand in his and gave them her blessing. To Vivaldi's great joy it was decided that the marriage would be solemnized during the coming week.

The Marchese and Marchesa di Vivaldi, in the meantime, had not remained in ignorance of their son's frequent visits at the Villa Altieri. On several occasions the Marchese, a man of great family pride and strict principles, had remonstrated with his son and assured him that any expectation of marriage to one so far below him in station was impossible. To this argument Vivaldi answered only that his affections and intentions were irrevocable. His mother, a haughty and vindictive woman, was equally determined to end what she regarded as her son's foolish infatuation. Realizing that the young man could not be moved by persuasion or threats, she summoned her confessor and secret adviser, the monk Schedoni, and consulted him on measures to separate Ellena and Vivaldi.

Schedoni, a monk at the Convent of the Santo Spirito, was a man of unknown family and origins. His spirit appeared haughty and disordered; his appearance conveyed an effect of gloom that corresponded to his severe and solitary disposition. Because of his austere manners, brooding nature, and sinister appearance he was loved by none, hated by many, and feared by most. Vivaldi disliked the monk and avoided him, even though he had no presentiment of what Schedoni was preparing for him and Ellena.

On the morning after his acceptance as Ellena's suitor Vivaldi hastened to the villa. In the darkened archway the ghostly figure again appeared and told him that death was in the house. Deeply disturbed, Vivaldi hurried on, to learn on his arrival that Signora Bianchi had died suddenly during the night. When Beatrice, the old servant, confided her suspicions that her mistress had been poisoned, Vivaldi grew even more concerned. His own suspicions falling on Schedoni, he confronted the monk in the Marchesa's apartment on his return to Venice, but the confessor cleverly parried all the questions Vivaldi put to him. Vivaldi, apologizing for his conduct and accusing speech, failed to realize that he had made an enemy of Schedoni and that the monk was already planning his revenge.

Meanwhile, it had been decided that Ellena was to find a sanctuary in the Convent of Santa Maria della Pieta after her aunt's funeral, and Vivaldi was in agreement with her desire to withdraw to that shelter during her period of mourning. While Ellena was packing in preparation for her departure the next day, she heard Beatrice screaming in another room. At that same moment three masked men seized Ellena and in spite of her protests carried her from the house. Thrust into a closed carriage, she was driven throughout the night and most of the next day into the mountainous region of Abruzzo. There her captors conducted her to a strange religious establishment where she was turned over to the care of the nuns. Almost distracted, the girl was led to a cell where she was at last able to give way to the extremities of her terror and grief.

Knowing nothing of these events, Vivaldi had decided that same night to explore the ruined fortress and to discover, if possible, the secret of the strange visitant he had encountered there. With him went Paulo Mendrico, his faithful servant. When they were within the archway the figure of the monk suddenly materialized, this time telling Vivaldi that Ellena had departed an hour before. Paulo fired his pistol, but the figure eluded them. Following drops of blood, Vivaldi and Paulo came at last to a chamber into which the figure had disappeared. As they entered, the great door shut behind them. In the chamber they found only a discarded, bloody robe. During the night they spent as prisoners in that gloomy room Paulo told his master of a muffled penitent who had appeared at the Church of Santa Maria del Pianto and made a confession apparently so strange and horrible that Ansaldo di Rovalli, the grand penitentiary, had been thrown into convulsions. During this recital they were startled by hearing groans close by, but they saw no one. In the morning the door of the chamber stood open once more, and Vivaldi and Paulo made their escape.

Alarmed for Ellena's safety, Vivaldi went at once to the villa. There he found Beatrice tied to a pillar and learned from her that her mistress had been carried off by abductors. Convinced that the strange happenings of the night were part of a plot to prevent his intended marriage, he again confronted Schedoni at the Convent of the Santo Spirito and would have assaulted the monk if others had not seized the distraught young man and restrained him by force. That night, by accident, Vivaldi heard from a fisherman that early in the day a closed carriage had been seen driving through Bracelli. Hopeful that he could trace the carriage and find Ellena, he set off in pursuit in the company of faithful Paulo.

On the fourth day of her imprisonment Ellena was conducted to the parlor of the abbess, who informed her that she must choose between taking the veil or the person whom the Marchesa di Vivaldi had selected as her husband. When Ellena refused both offers she was taken back to her cell. Each evening she was allowed to attend vespers and there her attention was attracted to Sister Olivia, a nun who tried to reconcile her to the hardships of her confinement. For this reason, perhaps, Sister Olivia was the nun chosen by the abbess to inform Ellena that if she persisted in refusing a husband proper to her station she must take holy orders immediately.

Vivaldi, meanwhile, was continuing his search for Ellena. On the evening of the seventh day he and Paulo fell in with a company of pilgrims on their way to worship at the shrine of a convent about a league and a half distant. Traveling with this company, Vivaldi arrived at the convent in time to witness the service at which Ellena was to be made a novitiate. Hearing her voice raised in protest, he rushed to the altar and caught her as she fainted. Unable to secure Ellena's freedom, Vivaldi left the convent in order to try another plan to set her free. Though he did not know it, there was need of haste; the abbess had decided to punish Ellena by confining her in a chamber from which none had ever returned alive. Alarmed for the girl's life, Sister Olivia promised to help her escape from the convent that night.

Dressed in the nun's veil, Ellena attended a program of music given in honor of some distinguished strangers who were visiting the convent. There Vivaldi, disguised as a pilgrim, passed her a note in which he told her to meet him at the gate of the nuns' garden. Guided by Sister Olivia, Ellena went to the gate where Vivaldi was waiting with Brother Jeronimo, a monk whom he had bribed to lead them from the convent by a secret path. Brother Jeronimo tried to betray them, however, and Ellena would have been recaptured if an aged monk whom they disturbed at his solitary prayers had not pitied them and unlocked the last door standing between the lovers and freedom.

Once in the open air, Vivaldi and Ellena descended the mountains to the place where Paulo waited with the horses for their escape. Instead of taking the road toward Naples, the fugitives turned westward toward Aquila. That day, as they were resting at a shepherd's cabin, Paulo brought word that they were being pursued by two Carmelite friars. Eluding their pursuers, they rode toward Lake Celano, where Ellena took refuge for the night in the Ursuline convent and Vivaldi stayed in an establishment of Benedictines.

While these events were taking place, the Marchese, who knew nothing of his wife's scheming with Schedoni, was suffering great anxiety over his son's possible whereabouts and welfare. The Marchesa, on the other hand, was apprehensive only that Ellena would be found and her plans undone. When Schedoni suggested in his sly, indirect fashion that Ellena be put out of the way for good, she was at first horrified by his suggestion. Later she reconsidered and at last she and the sinister monk came to an understanding. Ellena was to die. Schedoni, who had spies everywhere, was not long in locating the fugitives. As Vivaldi and Ellena were about to be married in the chapel of San Sebastian at Celano, armed men broke into the church and arrested the two under a warrant of the Holy Inquisition. Ellena was charged with having broken her nun's vows and Vivaldi with having aided her escape. Vivaldi, although wounded in his struggle to prevent arrest, was carried to Rome and after a short hearing before the Inquisitor was imprisoned to await future trial and possible torture to extort a confession. Paulo, protesting against separation from his master, was also confined.

After the agents of the Inquisition had taken Vivaldi and Paulo away, Ellena's guards put her on a waiting horse and set out on a road which led toward the Adriatic. After traveling with little interruption for two nights and two days they came to a lonely house on the seashore. There she was turned over to a villainous-looking man whom the guards called Spalatro and locked in a room in which the only furnishing was a tattered mattress on the floor. Exhausted, she fell asleep. Twice during the next day Spalatro came to her room, looked at her with a gaze that seemed a mixture of impatience and guilt, and then went away. At another time he took her to walk on the beach, where she met a monk whose face was hidden by his cowl. The monk was Schedoni. When he spoke to her, Ellena realized that he was neither a friend nor a protector but an enemy; and she fainted. Revived, she was returned to her room.

Schedoni was determined that Ellena should die that night. When Spalatro confessed pity for the girl and refused to be the executioner, Schedoni swore to do the deed himself. Going to the room where the girl was sleeping, he stood, dagger in hand, over her. Suddenly he bent to look closely at a miniature she wore about her neck. Agitated, he awoke Ellena and asked her if she knew whose portrait she wore. When she answered that it was the miniature of her father, Schedoni was even more shaken. He was convinced that he had discovered his lost daughter.

Overcome by remorse for his persecution of Ellena and the accusation which had exposed Vivaldi to the tortures of the Inquisition, Schedoni now tried to make amends. He and Ellena traveled as quickly as possible to Naples. After leaving the girl at the Villa Altieri, the monk hastened to the Vivaldis' palace and in an interview with the Marchesa begged, without disclosing his connection with Ellena, that objections to Vivaldi's suit be withdrawn. When the Marchesa proved inattentive, he determined to solemnize, without her consent, the nuptials of Vivaldi and Ellena.

Called a second time before the tribunal of the Inquisition, Vivaldi heard again among those present at the trial the voice which had warned him on earlier occasions against his visits to the Villa Altieri. That night a strange monk visited him in his cell and asked how long he had known Schedoni. The monk then instructed Vivaldi to reveal to the Inquisition that Schedoni was actually Count Ferando di Bruno, who had lived fifteen years in the disguise of a Dominican monk. He was also to ask that Ansaldo di Rovalli, the grand penitentiary of the Black Penitents, be called to testify to a confession he had heard in 1752. When Vivaldi was again brought before the Inquisition he did as he had been told, with the result that Schedoni was arrested on his way to Rome to intercede for Vivaldi's freedom.

At Schedoni's trial the mystery that linked the sinister father confessor and the two lovers was made clear. Years before, Schedoni, then a spendthrift younger son known as the Count di Marinella, had schemed to possess himself of his brother's title, his unencumbered estate, and his beautiful wife. He had arranged to have his brother, the Count di Bruno, assassinated by Spalatro and had contrived a story that the count had perished while returning from a journey to Greece. After a proper season of mourning he had solicited the hand of his brother's widow. When she rejected him his passion had caused him to carry her off by force. Although the lady had retrieved her honor by marriage, she continued to look on her new husband with disdain, and in his jealousy he became convinced that she was unfaithful. One day, returning unexpectedly, he found a visitor with his wife. Drawing his stiletto with the intention of attacking the guest, he struck and killed his wife instead. This was the confession which had so agitated the grand penitentiary, for he himself had been the guest and for him an innocent woman had died.

Further proof was the dying confession of Spalatro, whose death had been caused by a wound inflicted by Schedoni. Condemned to die for plotting his brother's death, Schedoni still persisted in his declaration that Ellena was his daughter. This mystery was cleared up by Sister Olivia, who in the meantime had removed to the Convent of Santa Maria della Pieta; the nun was the unfortunate Countess di Bruno and the sister of Signora Bianchi. Her wound had not been mortal, but the report of her death had been given out in order to protect her from her vengeful husband. Wishing to withdraw from the world, she had entrusted her daughter by the first Count di Bruno and an infant daughter by the second to Signora Bianchi. The infant had died within a year.

Ellena, who knew nothing of this story, had been mistaken in her belief that the miniature was that of her father, and it was on her word that Schedoni had claimed her as his daughter. It was also revealed that Father Nicola, who had collected the evidence against Schedoni, had been the mysterious monk whose ghostly warnings Vivaldi heard under the arch of the old fortress. Appalled by the father confessor's villainy, he had turned against him after being wounded by Paulo's pistol on the night of the midnight search.

Schedoni had his final revenge. In some manner he administered a fatal dose of poison to Father Nicola and then died of the same mysterious drug. In his last moments he boasted that he was escaping an ignominious death at the hands of the Inquisition.

Because of Schedoni's dying confession, Vivaldi was immediately set free. During his imprisonment the Marchesa had died repentant of the harm she had plotted against Ellena. Now the Marchese, overjoyed to be reunited with his son, withdrew all objections to Vivaldi's suit. With all doubts of Ellena's birth and goodness removed, he went in person to the Convent of Santa Maria della Pieta and asked Sister Olivia for her daughter's hand in the name of his son. Vivaldi and Ellena were married in the convent church in the presence of the Marchese and Sister Olivia. As a mark of special favor Paulo was allowed to be present when his master took Ellena for his wife. If it had not been for the holy precincts and the solemnity of the occasion the faithful fellow would have thrown his cap into the air and shouted that this was indeed a happy day.

Critical Evaluation

The Italian is one of the most skillful and successful examples of the Gothic novel, a literary sub-genre whose aim is to astound, terrify, and thrill its readers. More controlled and convincing than her earlier *The Mysteries of Udolpho,* Mrs. Radcliffe's novel is filled with the conventional Gothic qualities: a highly melodramatic (and unlikely) plot set in the remote past, a minimal degree of character development, and a painstakingly developed setting and atmosphere.

The plot is a familiar one to readers of the Gothic: a mysterious and black-hearted villain, Schedoni, plots against a beautiful damsel, Ellena, who spends most of the novel either imprisoned or in imminent danger of death, while her chivalrous and faithful lover, Vivaldi, struggles against incredible odds to rescue her. Character delineation is crude, limited primarily to blacks and whites. Predictably, the villainous monk Schedoni is much more fascinating than the somewhat vapid hero and heroine. The air of mystery and terror in the monk is strikingly described: "An habitual gloom and severity prevailed over the deep lines of his countenance; and his eyes were so piercing that they seemed to penetrate, at a single glance, into the hearts of men, and to read their most secret thoughts."

Setting is crucial to *The Italian*. Here are the gloomy monasteries, the dank dungeons of the Inquisition, the dizzying precipices and crags of Abruzzo, as well as scenes of quiet but spine-tingling terror, such as the one between Ellena and Schedoni on the deserted beach. Just as the evil characters are made even more menacing by their contrast to the good characters, the wild landscapes and brooding interiors are made even more threatening by their contrast to the beauty of Naples at the beginning and end of the novel.

The excesses and improbabilities of the lurid plot are tempered by a number of qualities. First, despite the manifold mysteries and hints of ghostly or demonic forces pervading the work, nothing magical or supernatural actually does occur; unlike the events in *The Castle of Otranto,* for instance, there is ultimately a rational explanation provided for everything. Also, Radcliffe's handling of suspense, mystery, dramatic pacing, and realistic detail and description is expert and gripping throughout. Finally, the author displays a serious concern for the main Gothic theme of man's inhumanity to man, as seen, for instance, in Vivaldi's outburst against the brutalities of the Inquisition: "Can this be in human nature!—Can such horrible perversion of right be permitted! Can man, who calls himself endowed with reason, and immeasurably superior to every other created being, argue himself into the commision of such horrible folly, such inveterate cruelty, as exceeds all the acts of the most irrational and ferocious brute . . . !"

Such novels as *The Italian* were adroitly satirized by Jane Austen in her *Northanger Abbey.* But Radcliffe's novel is significant not only in its own right, but for the influence it had on later writers, such as Scott, Charlotte Brontë, Coleridge, Keats, and Poe, all of whom made use of the mysterious and threatening Gothic settings and atmospheres in many of their own works.

SIR WALTER SCOTT

Born: Edinburgh, Scotland (August 15, 1771)
Died: Abbotsford, Scotland (September 21, 1832)

Principal Works

NOVELS: *Waverley*, 1814; *Guy Mannering*, 1815; *The Antiquary*, 1816; *The Black Dwarf*, 1816; *Old Mortality*, 1816; *Rob Roy*, 1818; *The Heart of Midlothian*, 1818; *The Bride of Lammermoor*, 1819; *A Legend of Montrose*, 1819; *Ivanhoe*, 1820; *The Monastery*, 1820; *The Abbot*, 1820; *Kenilworth*, 1821; *The Pirate*, 1822; *The Fortunes of Nigel*, 1822; *Peveril of the Peak*, 1823; *Quentin Durward*, 1823; *St. Ronan's Well*, 1824; *Redgauntlet*, 1824; *The Betrothed*, 1825; *The Talisman*, 1825; *Woodstock*, 1826; *Chronicles of the Canongate*, 1927 (*The Two Drovers, The Highland Widow, The Surgeon's Daughter*); *The Fair Maid of Perth*, 1828; *Anne of Geierstein*, 1829; *Count Robert of Paris*, 1831; *Castle Dangerous*, 1831.

POEMS: *The Lay of the Last Minstrel*, 1805; *Marmion*, 1808; *The Lady of the Lake*, 1810; *The Vision of Don Roderick*, 1811; *The Bridal of Triermain*, 1813; *The Lord of the Isles*, 1815; *Rokeby*, 1815.

MISCELLANEOUS: *The Life and Works of John Dryden*, 1808; *The Life and Works of Jonathan Swift*, 1814; *The Life of Napoleon Buonaparte*, 1827.

In spite of physical handicaps Walter Scott lived a full, varied life and created an impressive body of writings. Stricken with infantile paralysis before he was two years old, and alternating between periods of physical vigor and serious ailments throughout his life, he loved and practiced outdoor sports for most of his sixty-odd years.

Born in Edinburgh, August 15, 1771, he was a product of the eighteenth century as well as of the romantic nineteenth. As a child he was a voracious reader and avid listener to tales and legends, particularly those of his native Scotland. His copious reading was stored in a retentive memory and used to advantage in his writings; and his interest in folklore led to his collection and publication of Scottish ballads. Although not a brilliant student, he was praised for his ability to enjoy and understand the Latin poets. He entered the University of Edinburgh in 1783, but after a year at college he suffered one of his severe illnesses and had to return home. He spent his convalescence with a sympathetic uncle, Captain Robert Scott, who encouraged his literary interests.

He studied law in his father's office; and in spite of a disinclination for the profession, he was admitted to the bar in 1792. He made use of his legal experiences in his novels, especially *Redgauntlet*, in which his friend William Clerk served as model for Darsie Latimer, and Scott himself for Allan Fairford. When he was twenty he cast his eye on a lovely fifteen-year-old girl, Williamina

Belsches. After an unsuccessful courtship of five years he lost her to a rival and indulged his sorrow for a time with melancholy self-dramatization out of keeping with his usual behavior.

In 1797, when the fear of a Napoleonic invasion seized Great Britain, Scott was the moving force in forming a volunteer home-guard unit, in which he held the position of quartermaster. In spite of his crippled leg he was a bold and expert horseman, and apparently was disappointed at not engaging Napoleon's forces. In the same year, on a tour of the Lake Country with his brother John and his friend Adam Ferguson, he met Charlotte Carpenter (Charpentier), daughter of a French royalist and ward of an English nobleman. This time his courtship was both short and successful, and he married his Charlotte on Christmas Eve, 1797. Their first child died in infancy, but four children reached maturity, two sons and two daughters.

In 1799 Scott was appointed Sheriff-depute of Selkirkshire; the position brought him a steady income and not-too-onerous duties. Seven years later he became Clerk of the Session in Edinburgh, adding to his steady income and increasing his routine labors considerably.

Although he translated for publication Gottfried Bürger's *Lenore* (1799) and Goethe's *Goetz von Berlichingen* (1799) and collected and edited—often revised—ballads in his *Minstrelsy of the Scottish Border* (1802–1803), he won his first recognition as a poet in 1805 with *The Lay of the Last Minstrel* and became a major literary figure in England with *Marmion* and *The Lady of the Lake*. His subsequent long poems added little to his reputation. Shortly after the publication of *The Lay of the Last Minstrel* he formed a partnership (Scott to be a silent partner) with the printer James Ballantyne, an old school friend. During his poetic career Scott completed two major works of scholarship, an eighteen-volume edition of Dryden and a nineteen-volume edition of Swift, either of which would have made a reputation for a professional scholar.

In 1814, with the anonymous publication of *Waverley*, Scott began a new literary career and his most illustrious, for he is now considered primarily a historical novelist, more than either poet or scholar. Scott gave reasons for not acknowledging the authorship of his novels; but at least one reason was a childish delight in mystification, a puckish joy in throwing dust into the public eye. Between 1814 and his death in 1832, he completed about thirty novels and novelettes, several long poems, a large mass of miscellaneous writings, and a nine-volume *Life of Napoleon*.

Scott was the first baronet created by George IV (1820). By this time he had bought acres of land and was sinking a fortune in Abbotsford. One friend who helped plan Abbotsford and stock its library was Daniel Terry, the actor-manager who produced dramatic versions of several of Scott's works, making an especial hit as Bailie Jarvie in *Rob Roy*. Scott's publishing ventures were in bad circumstances which grew worse; in 1826 Constable and Ballantyne failed. Instead of taking refuge in bankruptcy, Scott undertook to write himself and his colleagues out of debt. Few men have displayed more fortitude under adversity. To cap the material loss he suffered a severe spiritual one in the death of his beloved wife. His grief was profound, but he continued to write. In 1830, apparently as a result of his Herculean labors under stress, he suffered his first stroke of apoplexy. He recovered and continued work until recurring strokes paralyzed him and practically destroyed his mind. He died September 21, 1832, still in debt; but his son-in-law, John Gibson Lockhart, cleared the debts with the proceeds of his superb biography of the baronet.

Scott's merits as man and writer entitle him to a position much nearer his former reputation than he now holds. One of his admirers called him a combination of Shakespeare and Samuel Johnson. Those who think of him only as a cloak-and-sword romancer overlook his remarkable gift of creating comic characters and his broad view of human nature in all walks of life. He was greatly admired by Balzac and Dumas; and wise critics from Goethe to the present have been impressed with his humane wisdom.

Bibliography

There is no recent scholarly edition of Scott's works. The Border Edition of the *Waverley Novels*, 48 vols., 1892–1894, contains notes by Andrew Lang. John Gibson Lockhart's *Memoirs of the Life of Sir Walter Scott, Bart.*, 1837–1838, is basic; the definitive modern biography is Edgar Johnson, *Sir Walter Scott: The Great Unknown*, 1969. See also John Buchan (Lord Tweedsmuir), *Sir Walter Scott*, 1932; Sir Herbert Grierson, *Sir Walter Scott, Bart.*, 1938; Hesketh Pearson, *Sir Walter Scott*, 1954; F. R. Hart, *Scott's Novels*, 1966; David Daiches, *Sir Walter Scott and His World*, 1971; and Paul N. Landis, "The Waverly Novels, or a Hundred Years After," *Publications of the Modern Language Association*, LII (1937), 461–473.

THE LADY OF THE LAKE

Type of work: Poem
Author: Sir Walter Scott (1771–1832)
Type of plot: Semihistorical romance
Time of plot: Sixteenth century
Locale: Scottish Highlands
First published: 1810

One of Scott's best-known poems, The Lady of the Lake *delves into Gaelic history, retelling a legend that had been popular for generations; Scott's poetry is in a sense painting, for his descriptions are both intense and colorful. It is obvious that he loved the locale he described and understood the people who inhabited the wild Highlands of Scotland.*

Principal Characters

Ellen Douglas, who, with her rebel father, hides from the King near Loch Katrine in the Highlands. Befriended by James Fitz-James, a powerful nobleman, she is instrumental in bringing the rebel clans and the King's forces together. In the end, her marriage to Malcolm Graeme is blessed by the monarch.

James of Douglas, Ellen's father, who once was a powerful nobleman but who now is in rebellion against the King. Finally, because he can no longer agree with one of his powerful leaders, he gives himself up to the royal court. He finally is restored to favor.

Roderick Dhu, a rebel Highland chief who befriends Ellen and her father, but whose ruthless military tactics Ellen abhors. Dhu, in the guise of a guard, fights a duel with James Fitz-James and is overcome. The rebel and loyal forces do not fight, but Dhu, in prison, dies thinking his clans fought a glorious battle.

James Fitz-James, a nobleman, friendly to Ellen, who at the poem's end is discovered to be the King.

Allan-Bane, a minstrel in the service of James of Douglas who is faithful to that nobleman even while he hides with his forces in the Highlands. The minstrel is also a prophet and seer of sorts, and he knows everything between the clans and the King will end well. It is Allan-Bane who, as a kindly gesture, gives the dying Roderick Dhu the impression that the clans fought bravely against the King.

Malcolm Graeme, a young rebel nobleman who was once the object of an attack by Dhu's forces after Ellen had refused Dhu's suit because she and Malcolm were in love. Finally, with the King's blessing, he marries Ellen.

The Story

As he followed a stag during a hunt, James Fitz-James became lost in the Highlands. He wandered around until he came to Loch Katrine, a beautiful lake surrounded by steep mountains. There he met the lovely Ellen, who told him that his coming had been foretold by Allan-Bane, an ancient minstrel who served her father. When she offered the hunter food and shelter for the night, Ellen did not volunteer to tell him her name or anything of her family history, and courtesy forbade his asking questions. Fitz-James was disturbed, however, because she bore such a marked resemblance to members of the Douglas clan, a family banished by the king. When he departed the next morning, he still knew nothing about the young girl whose beauty and grace had deeply touched his heart.

Fitz-James was correct in his fear that Ellen was of the Douglas clan. Her father was James of Douglas, once a powerful friend of the king, but now hunted and with a price on his head. He and Ellen and his sister were protected by Roderick Dhu, a rebel against the king and the leader of a large and powerful Highland clan. Roderick Dhu wanted Ellen's hand in marriage, but although she honored him for the aid he gave her father she detested him for his many cruel and merciless deeds. He killed and plundered at will, trying to avenge himself on the king and the Lowlanders who he felt had robbed him and his people of their land and wealth. Among the men he hated was Malcolm Graeme, a young nobleman, Ellen's former suitor, whom she loved. After Ellen's refusal of his proposal, Roderick Dhu called his clan together to fight Malcolm and the other supporters of the king. His excuse was that he feared Malcolm would lead the king to the hiding place of Douglas.

Like lightning, burning beacons and swift-riding messengers carried through the Highlands word that the clan was gathering. Young men left their brides at the church door and mere boys replaced fathers who had died since the last gathering. The women and children were placed on a lonely and protected island for safety, for a fierce and dangerous battle was to be fought. A hermit monk prophesied that the party who spilled the first foe's blood would be the victor. The prophecy suited Roderick Dhu, whose men had seen a spy lurking in the mountains and even now had lured the stranger into paths which would lead him into a trap. He would be killed by Roderick Dhu's men and thus the Highlanders would be assured of victory.

James of Douglas left Ellen. Although he did not tell her his destination, she knew that he had gone to give himself up to the king in order to prevent the bloodshed of a great battle. Allan-Bane tried to cheer Ellen by telling her that his harp sang of glad tidings, but she would not hear him. As she sat grieving, Fitz-James appeared again. Ellen knew that he had been tricked by Roderick Dhu's men, for no one could gain entrance to a place so hidden and secret without their knowledge. But Fitz-James, refusing to heed her warning, asked her to return to the court with him. She refused, telling him of her love for Malcolm Graeme. Then Fitz-James gave her his ring which had been given to him by the king. He said the king owed him a favor and would grant any request made by the bearer of the ring. It would also promise a safe journey through the Lowlands to anyone wearing it. Fitz-James placed the ring on Ellen's finger and then departed quickly.

His guide led him through the mountain paths until they came upon a crazed woman who sang a warning song to Fitz-James. The guide thrust his sword into her. Fitz-James then killed the guide and returned to the side of the crazed woman who, before she died, told him that Roderick Dhu had killed her lover and caused her to lose her sanity. Fitz-James vowed that he would meet Roderick Dhu and avenge the woman. Having been warned by her as well as by Ellen, he was traveling cautiously when he stumbled on a guard stationed by a watch fire. The sentry called him a spy, wanted by Roderick Dhu, but offered him rest and safety, for the laws of the clansmen demanded courtesy even to one's enemy. The guard, after promising to lead Fitz-James safely through Roderick Dhu's lines, kept his word, even though Fitz-James called Roderick Dhu a coward and a murderer. When they reached a place of safety, the sentry revealed himself as Roderick Dhu. His promise fulfilled, he then challenged Fitz-James to a duel. In personal combat Roderick Dhu proved the stronger, but Fitz-James, who was more skilled, overcame the rebel. Then Fitz-James blew his horn and called his men to carry Roderick Dhu to a prison cell.

In the meantime James of Douglas went to the court to give himself up. First, however, he took part in some games being staged that day and won every event he entered. The whisper went through the crowds that only a Douglas could possess such skill and strength. Then Douglas offered himself to the king as a ransom for his friends and clansmen. When the king ordered him thrown into prison, the people sided with Douglas and would have risen against the king. Douglas quieted them, for he would not act against his monarch, and allowed himself to be taken. The king sent messengers to the Highlanders with word that there was no need to fight; Douglas had surrendered and Roderick Dhu was a prisoner.

Ellen and Allan-Bane went to the court to seek the release of her father. The ring given her by Fitz-James afforded her safety along the way. Before news came that a truce had been arranged, Allan-Bane went to Roderick Dhu's cell and sang to him of a fierce battle that had been fought. Roderick Dhu died with a smile, for he believed that his clansmen had fought bravely.

Ellen prepared for her audience with the king. Fitz-James went to her quarters to conduct her to the court, but when they arrived she noted that everyone bowed before Fitz-James. It was not until then that she knew Fitz-James was in reality the king. He told her to claim the favor promised by the ring, but there was nothing she could ask. The king had already restored her father to favor and Roderick Dhu was dead, so that she could not plead mercy for him. She tried to stammer something about Malcolm Graeme, but the king read her heart and called Malcolm to her side. He forgave Malcolm for trying to aid the rebels and redeemed the ring Ellen wore by joining her with her beloved.

Critical Evaluation

The Lady of the Lake followed *Marmion* by merely two years and achieved instant success. Its popularity was attributable to a twofold appeal. It is a romance drawn straight from folk tradition, complete with a disguised king and an innocent maiden. Ellen Douglas, first described as a "Nymph, a Naiad or a Grace," eventually is realized in a manner less classical or pastoral than essentially Romantic. As many commentators have remarked, Ellen is one of Wordsworth's children of nature. Even more than its story or heroine, the poem's setting and scenery captured the imagination of Europe. This one poem literally opened up the Highlands to tourism. Within six months of its publication, *The Lady of the Lake* had made the Loch Katrine section of the Trossachs a literary mecca. The poem served as a dramatic guidebook and started a craze for travel in "Romantic" Scotland that included artists as well as tourists. Keats took a memorable journey to the Highlands, and Mendelssohn's Scotch Symphony is an eloquent testimonial to the hold of Scott's landscape on the European mind.

The verse is less spirited than in *Marmion,* but the story is more carefully plotted and the occasional lyrics, songs, and dirges highlighting the action are among Scott's finest. The Coronach, or dirge, in Canto III is particularly famous.

Finally, the scene painting, that is merely decorative in *Marmion,* is so expertly done here that it becomes an end in itself, a form of program music providing an intensely lush background for the action. The opening of the poem, the episode describing Fitz-James's pursuing of the stag and his accidental discovery of the lovely Ellen, guides both characters and reader through a landscape emblematic of the Romantic promise of the poem's action, a landscape where

> Each purple peak, each flinty spire,
> Was bathed in floods of living fire.

THE LAY OF THE LAST MINSTREL

Type of work: Poem
Author: Sir Walter Scott (1771–1832)
Type of plot: Semihistorical romance
Time of plot: Mid-sixteenth century
Locale: The Scottish Border
First published: 1805

This semihistorical long poem describes the manners and scenery of the Scottish Border country during the middle of the sixteenth century. As in Scott's other metrical romances, he tells a picturesque story vividly and paints scenes with the skill of a great artist.

Principal Characters

Sir William of Deloraine, a knight who has served the Lord of Branksome. When Branksome is killed in a battle against the English, Deloraine remains faithful to the memory of his leader and stays on to serve Lady Buccleuch, Branksome's widow. Returning from a mission to get a magic book, Deloraine fights Lord Cranstoun, Branksome's former enemy who is in love with Branksome's daughter—and Deloraine falls wounded. Fortunately, he recovers and lives to see harmony restored between the Scots and the English.

Lady Buccleuch, Lord Branksome's widow, the daughter of a magician. Spirits tell her that Branksome Castle is doomed unless pride dies and frees love. Lady Buccleuch does not heed the spirits at first. Finally, however, when Deloraine's life may be lost, and when her son may be taken from her, she relents. Her change of heart, shown by the blessing she gives to the love of her daughter Margaret for Lord Cranstoun, the late Lord Branksome's enemy, brings peace to Branksome Castle and the Scottish border.

Lord Cranstoun, a knight who fought against Lord Branksome, but who loves

Margaret, Branksome's daughter. Cranstoun, having wounded Deloraine, makes amends by donning Deloraine's armor and fighting, as that knight, against an English champion. When he wins, the English forces retire, Lady Buccleuch blesses his suit for Margaret's hand, and Deloraine has leisure for his wounds to heal.

The Dwarf, an evil magician devoted to Lord Cranstoun. The Dwarf causes mischief at Branksome Castle by posing as the Master of Buccleuch. At a banquet, the Dwarf is killed by a thunderbolt, and in the eerie light Deloraine sees the form of the dead wizard, Michael Scott, whose book Lady Buccleuch had sent Deloraine to bring from Melrose Abbey.

The Ghost of Michael Scott, a wraith whose activities complicate the lives of those who live at Branksome Castle. At the end, Branksome's knights make pilgrimages to pray for rest for Michael Scott's soul.

Margaret, Lady Buccleuch's daughter and Cranstoun's beloved.

The Master of Buccleuch, Lady Buccleuch's son, a small boy.

The Story

As an old minstrel, the last of his kind, wandered through the country, he was treated kindly by a duchess at whose mansion he asked food and shelter. Later he rewarded her by singing a song of days gone by. This is the tale he sang:

Bold Lord Buccleuch had been killed in battle with the English, but his widow and children were well protected in their castle at Branksome by a group of brave knights who had followed their dead leader. Although a truce had been declared, there were skirmishes between the English and the Scots throughout the Border country.

The widow, Lady Buccleuch, was the daughter of a magician; before he died he had taught her to talk with the spirits. One night she heard the spirits predicting that the stars would show no favor to Branksome castle until pride should die and make love free. Lady Buccleuch knew this omen was meant for her, for her daughter Margaret loved the young Lord Cranstoun, who had fought against Lord Buccleuch. But Lady Buccleuch swore that Margaret should never wed a foeman, no matter what the spirits might say. She sent William of Deloraine to Melrose Abbey, there to secure the mystic book of Michael Scott, a wizard long dead and buried in the abbey crypt. She ordered William of Deloraine not to look into the book on peril of his life.

The monk at the abbey, although he quavered at the request made by Deloraine, obeyed without question Lady Buccleuch's command. Leading him deep into the vaults, he took the knight to the wizard's tomb. Deloraine, bravest of knights in battle, shivered with dread as he looked at the body of the magician. The man lay as if he had not been dead a day, and when the knight took the book from his hand, he seemed to frown. As Deloraine left the vault, he heard noises like the laughter and sobbing of fiends.

On the same day, while Deloraine went to the abbey, Margaret slipped out of the castle to meet her lover, Lord Cranstoun. Cranstoun was accompanied by a Dwarf, who had some time before attached himself to Cranstoun and now would not leave his side. Since the Dwarf served him well, Cranstoun had ceased his efforts to rid himself of the little page. The Dwarf warned the lovers of the approach of a horseman. The traveler was Deloraine, returning from his mission, and while Margaret fled, the two knights battled. Deloraine was seriously wounded. Cranstoun ordered the Dwarf to take Deloraine to Branksome Hall so that his wounds could be properly tended. The Dwarf found the book but could not open it until after he had smeared the cover with the blood of Deloraine, who was almost an infidel. While he was reading one of the spells described in the book, an unseen hand struck him on the cheek and knocked him to the ground. The book snapped shut and could not be opened again. The Dwarf, hiding it under his cloak, proceeded to Branksome Hall with the wounded Deloraine.

At the castle the Dwarf spied the young Master of Buccleuch. Changing himself and the boy into dogs, he led the child into the woods. There, after they had resumed their real shapes, the child was captured by the English soldiers patrolling the Border. At the castle his absence was not known, for the Dwarf returned there and, taking the child's shape, made mischief for everyone. Lady Buccleuch, busy tending the wounds of her faithful Deloraine, failed to notice the child's strange behavior.

Suddenly watchers in the castle sighted signal fires. Their meaning was clear; the English were gathering to attack the Scots. From the castle messengers were sent hurriedly to summon friendly clans of the Border to the defense of Branksome Hall. In the confusion the Dwarf, still in the form of the Master of Buccleuch, escaped from the knight assigned to watch him.

The English, arriving before the castle, made their demands. They wanted Deloraine turned over to them, for they accused him of murdering the brother of one of their group. They also demanded that two hundred English knights be quartered in Branksome, to prevent the Scotsmen from making raids on the English side of the Border. If these demands were not met, they declared, the castle would be stormed and the young heir of Buccleuch, who was held by the English, would be sent to the English court to serve as a page.

Lady Buccleuch would not meet the demands. She could not send her faithful knight to his doom, though her deed might cost her her son, her castle, and perhaps her life. She proposed that Deloraine meet the brother of the slain man in combat and settle the dispute in that knightly fashion. The English leaders, refusing to accept these terms, were preparing to attack the castle when one of their number brought word that strong Scottish clans were approaching the castle. Fearful of a trap, the English agreed to accept the proposal for a settlement by mortal combat between the two knights concerned, or by the wronged man and a substitute for Deloraine should his wounds not be healed by the next day. Then English and Scots joined together in feasting and revelry until the time appointed for the combat.

As the time approached, other knights argued over the right to represent Deloraine, who was still weak from his wounds. But at the last minute Deloraine appeared in full armor, ready to defend himself. The fight was long and fierce, and both knights lost much blood before the Englishman fell wounded. Deloraine, standing triumphantly over his victim, did not remove his visor. Then the spectators saw with amazement that Deloraine was approaching from the castle. Quickly the supposed Deloraine was uncovered. In his place stood young Lord Cranstoun. He had stolen Deloraine's armor so that he might defend the home and save the brother of Margaret. At first Lady Buccleuch would not greet him, but at last she thought of the prophecy of the spirits and knew that she must forget pride and allow love to prevail. Yielding, she gave her daughter to the knight who had been her husband's enemy. She also swore to herself that she would return the book to Michael Scott's tomb.

At the wedding feast the Dwarf continued to make trouble. In order to undo the mischief he caused, all the minstrels sang songs of days gone past. As the last song died away, the banquet hall grew suddenly dark. A great flash of lightning streaked through the room and struck the Dwarf. The evil page was seen no more. Deloraine was terrified, for in the unearthly light he had seen the shape of the dead wizard. Lady Buccleuch renounced forever the magic of her father, and all the knights made pilgrimages to pray for peace and rest for Michael Scott's soul.

Thus ended the song of the ancient minstrel.

Critical Evaluation

In *The Minstrelsy of the Scottish Border* (1802-1803) Scott had collected authentic ballads and revised some that were imperfect. *The Lay of the Last Minstrel* (1805) was the first of his series of original "metrical histories." Although *Marmion* (1808) is of greater literary merit, *The Lay of the Last Minstrel* is the poem that changed Scott's life. The enormous popularity of the poem (it sold an astounding 30,000 copies) induced Scott to abandon his work as a lawyer and part-time antiquarian in favor of a literary career. Whatever the poem's defects of plot and structure, it was full of the mystery and the Romantic manner the public longed for and it was all the more attractive because the bizarre matter was native British lore.

The poem is a medieval romance gone wild, compounded of supernatural events, folk motifs, and loosely connected episodes, but without a central, controlling theme. Its most effective element is the narrator, who allows Scott to imitate the oral character of balladry. The origins of the poem, as described by Scott, were in a commission from the Countess of Dalkeith to render the weird story of Boblin Gilpin Horner. The poem developed randomly so that the Gilpin (or dwarf) episodes now ironically seem unassimilated excrescences.

Scott recognized the limitations of the extreme regularity of the traditional ballad meter. He was influenced by Coleridge's *Christabel* to allow himself greater freedom in the construction of rhythms and stanzas, although he does not always escape a kind of formulaic doggerel. Scott also attempted to assume the linguistic simplicity of the Lake poets and he is generally successful despite an appropriately archaic diction. The greatest virtue of *The Lay of the Last Minstrel*, removed from the context of contemporary taste, is as a finger exercise in narrative techniques for Scott's subsequent novels.

MARMION

Type of work: Poem
Author: Sir Walter Scott (1771–1832)
Type of plot: Semihistorical romance
Time of plot: Early sixteenth century
Locale: The Scottish Border
First published: 1808

Even though one of Scott's best-known dramatic poems, Marmion lacks the perfection of detail that marks his best work. Hurriedly written, largely unrevised and unpolished, and burdened with a series of irrelevant introductions to each canto, Marmion frequently seems forced and melodramatic—although it does possess much of the lyrical beauty and brisk action which we associate with Scott's metrical romances.

Principal Characters

Lord Marmion, an English nobleman whose reputation as a fine, brave knight is spotless. He is sent by the English King to try to persuade the Scots to stop raiding the border. Actually, he had declared his love for a young nun, Constance de Beverley, who renounced her vows, left the convent, and followed him. He then met a young heiress and abandoned Constance. He has fought a duel with the knight who loves the heiress, Clare, and left his adversary for dead. He is mortally wounded in battle and on his deathbed repents all his sins.

Ralph de Wilton, Marmion's foe in the duel, who is now disguised as a palmer. He loved Clare but was betrayed by Marmion with some forged papers attesting to the fact that de Wilton was not true to the King. He is finally restored to his title and lands and wins the hand of Clare.

Clare Fitz-Clare, a young novice nun who has joined the convent rather than marry Marmion after the man she really loves, de Wilton, is believed to be fatally wounded. She is finally able to marry de Wilton with the King's blessing.

Constance de Beverley, a nun who broke her vows, fled the convent, and followed Marmion for three years as a page boy. She has the papers forged by Marmion to discredit de Wilton and she begs the abbess to get them to the King so that Clare will not be forced to marry Marmion. The ecclesiastical court puts her to death.

Archibald Douglas, a Scottish nobleman who is charged with Marmion's safe conduct while he is in Scotland, and with the safekeeping of the nuns.

The Story

Wherever Lord Marmion went, he was welcomed and honored as a brave and valiant knight. The English king had sent him to the Scottish court to try to persuade that country's king to end armed raids throughout the Border country.

Marmion asked a Scottish lord to furnish him a guide, someone peaceful appearing, and since there was no one else available the lord sent a palmer, a holy man who had made many pilgrimages to religious shrines.

At the same time an abbess, accompanied by several nuns, was making a sea voyage to Cuthbert Isle to hold an inquisition over two prisoners of the Church. One of the young nuns aboard, still a novice, was Clare Fitz-Clare, a lovely young girl who entered the abbey after her lover, dishonored, was believed dead. One of the accused was Constance de Beverley, a nun who had broken her vows and run away from the convent. Before she was put to death, Constance told the abbess and her other accusers the story of her fall from grace.

Her betrayer had been Lord Marmion. Believing his protestations of love for her, she had escaped from the convent and followed him for three years as his page. Then Marmion met lovely Clare Fitz-Clare, and because she was an heiress of great wealth he abandoned Constance to seek Clare for his bride. The king promised him that he should have Clare, but she loved another knight, Ralph de Wilton. Marmion forged papers which offered false proof that Wilton was not true to the king. The two knights fought a duel, and Wilton was left for dead. Constance, soon to die, gave the papers proving the forgery to the abbess and implored her to get the papers to the king in order to save Clare from a hateful marriage. Although the girl had entered a convent rather than marry Marmion, the king would force the marriage if Clare were found, for Marmion was a great favorite at court. Even though her judges pitied her, Constance was put to a horrible death after she had told her story.

Marmion continued on his way to the court. Guilty thoughts of Constance worried him; he had been responsible for her capture by the Church. But he soothed his conscience with the belief that she would not be severely punished. One night as they stayed at an inn a young boy sang a ballad about the soul's disquiet of every man who would betray a maid. At the end of the song Marmion thought he heard the tolling of a death bell. When the knight mentioned the tolling sound he heard, the palmer spoke his first words, saying that it was the toll of death for a friend. That night Marmion, unable to sleep, went out into the dark to ride. There he was attacked by what seemed a devil, for the man had the face of Wilton, long dead. The strangest part was that Marmion's mysterious adversary could have killed him, but instead sheathed his sword and rode off into the night.

As Marmion and his men rode through the Border country, they noticed everywhere huge numbers of armed clansmen readying for battle. On their arrival at the Scottish court, Marmion could not persuade King James to halt preparations for battle. The Scots, claiming that the English had wronged them, demanded vengeance. Courtesy required that Marmion be given safe conduct during his mission, however, and so the king put him in the care of Archibald Douglas, one of the most powerful of all the lords of Scotland. Douglas also was charged with the care of the abbess and her nuns, who had been taken captive by the Scots, for they were to be returned safely to their convent. But the abbess feared for Clare's safety if Marmion should learn that she was among the party of nuns. To save Clare from a forced and hated union, the holy woman gave the papers proving Marmion's forgery to the palmer and begged him to deliver them to the English king.

Marmion, learning the girl's identity, secured an order directing him to take Clare to her home, with Douglas for an escort. Separated from the abbess, Clare feared for her safety with Marmion, but he planned not to press his suit until she had been returned to her kinsmen, who would be dominated by the king. Marmion and Clare were quartered in Tantallon Castle, owned by Archibald Douglas, Earl of Angus, to await the impending battle between English and Scottish troops.

Clare, lonely and afraid, walked out onto the battlements of the castle. There she met a young knight who proved to be de Wilton. From his lips Clare heard his story. He had not been mortally wounded in his combat with Marmion, but had been healed and cared for by one of his servants. The loyal servant asked one boon for saving his life, that should de Wilton's deadliest enemy fall beneath his sword that enemy should be spared. The young knight wandered far, his name scorned by all who once loved him because he was now branded as a traitor. At last he disguised himself so well that no one recognized in the lowly palmer the once-proud knight. It was de Wilton who had so frightened Marmion during his midnight ride, but he had kept his promise to his old servant and spared the life of the man who had ruined him. The young man had told Douglas his story, which was confirmed by the papers given him by the abbess. That night Douglas restored de Wilton to his knightly honors, and the next day de Wilton would join the English troops.

Marmion, unable to resist the spectacle of troops drawn up for battle, defied Douglas and rode off to join the fight. Having learned from one of his company the palmer's true identity and fearing that he would lose Clare, he took the girl to a place of safety behind the English lines. When the battle began, Marmion was mortally wounded. Clare, pitying the man she hated, tended him gently. Before he died, Marmion learned of the death of Constance and repented all his sins.

The English defeated the Scots in that bloody battle on Flodden Field. De Wilton was everywhere in the thick of the fighting. After the battle, his lands and his titles were returned to him and Clare was given to him with the king's blessing. The proud name of de Wilton was known again through the land. Marmion, as he deserved, lay in an unmarked grave.

Critical Evaluation

Well known for his ability to depict the action and glory of battle and human turmoil in historical novels such as *Old Mortality* and *The Heart of Midlothian,* Sir Walter Scott was able to do the same thing even better in narrative poetry. Oliver Elton *(Survey of English Literature from 1780-1830,* Vol. I, 1912) writes that "for actual fighting, for duels to the death, for downright taunting and 'flyting,' Scott's verse is a better vehicle than his prose."

The passionate thrust of his octosyllabic rhymes carries the action forward at an exciting pace. Ears accustomed to the rhymed heroic couplets of Alexander Pope were startled by the tonal versatility of Scott's verse. Not only did it capture the color and speed of battle, as in the famous description of the fighting on Flodden Field in Canto IV of *Marmion,* but it also managed panoramic and stately effects such as the scene painting in the introductory letter to Canto I and the view to Edinburg as seen by Marmion over Blackford Hill.

Unfortunately, the descriptive passages in *Marmion* often appear merely decorative—ostentatious victories in verse technique. The plot is disjointed and characterization is very weak. Roughly similar to *Ivanhoe* (both works include an unscrupulous knight, a pilgrim guide who is no pilgrim, chivalric combat between the rivals), the plot of *Marmion* turns on the stock device of a forged letter; the introductory epistles give us, as David Daiches (*Sir Walter Scott and His World,* London, 1971) says "an account of the development of his [Scott's] sensibility," but they do not exactly propel the cumbersome parts of the story forward. Marmion himself is a pasteboard villain; he scowls to order like the melodramatic antagonist of a cheap Gothic tale. He affects but has none of the genuine Satanism of the dark heroes in Byron's verse tales that followed in the years shortly after the publication of *Marmion.* Nevertheless, the sheer vigor, ease, and drive of the verse is impressive. It drove Thomas Hardy to describe *Marmion* as the most Homeric poem in the language.

PERCY BYSSHE SHELLEY

Born: Field Place, Sussex, England (August 4, 1792)
Died: Off Viareggio, Italy (July 8, 1822)

Principal Works

POEMS: *Queen Mab*, 1813; *Alastor, or The Spirit of Solitude*, 1816; *The Revolt of Islam*, 1818; *Rosalind and Helen*, 1819; *Epipsychidion*, 1821; *Adonais*, 1821; *Hellas*, 1822; *Posthumous Poems*, 1824; *Poetical Works*, 1839.
PLAYS: *The Cenci*, 1820; *Prometheus Unbound*, 1820.
TRACTS AND STUDIES: *The Necessity of Atheism*, 1811; *An Address to the Irish People*, 1812; *A Refutation of Deism*, 1814; *A Defence of Poetry*, 1840.

Percy Bysshe Shelley, English poet, was born at Field Place, near Horsham, Sussex, August 4, 1792, the eldest son of a landed country squire. After some tutoring he was sent to Syon House Academy, where this shyness exposed him to brutal bullying. Entering Eton in 1804, he lived as much apart as possible, a moody, sensitive, and precocious boy with the nickname of "mad Shelley." Here he wrote *Zastrozzi* (1810), a wild Gothic romance, *Original Poetry by Victor and Cazire* (1810), and another inferior Gothic romance, *St. Irvyne, or The Rosicrucian*, published in 1811.

Shelley matriculated at University College, Oxford, in 1810. He and Thomas Jefferson Hogg were expelled the following year for publishing and sending to bishops and heads of colleges their pamphlet, *The Necessity of Atheism*. At this time Shelley fell in love with Harriet Westbrook, daughter of a retired hotel-keeper. They eloped, and despite Shelley's open break with the conventions of the Christian religion and particular scorn for the marriage ceremony, they were married in Edinburgh in August, 1811. Both fathers contributed to their support for the next three years, spent wandering in southern England, Ireland, and Wales.

In 1813 their first child was born in London and Shelley's first long poem, *Queen Mab*, was published. Meanwhile, marriage with Harriet was proving a failure. In May, 1814, Shelley met Mary, the daughter of William and Mary Wollstonecraft Godwin. Mary shared his belief that marriage was only a voluntary contract. Harriet left for her father's home, and Shelley and seventeen-year-old Mary eloped to Switzerland, accompanied by Claire Clairmont, Mary's half-sister. When they returned to England in September, Shelley proposed to Harriet that she come live with Mary and him; however, there was no reconciliation.

Mary bore a son in 1816 (the year of *Alastor, or The Spirit of Solitude*). They, with Claire, spent the summer in Switzerland and became close friends of Byron. Soon after they returned to England in the autumn, they heard Harriet had drowned herself. Shelley was now free to marry Mary Godwin (December 30,

1816), but a court order denied him the custody of his two children by Harriet.

After he had completed *The Revolt of Islam*, revised version of his earlier *Laon and Cythna*, the Shelleys and Claire Clairmont, with her child by Byron, went to Italy. There Shelley remained the rest of his life, wandering from Lake Como, Milan, Venice, Este, Rome, Florence, and Pisa to other cities and sections. Much time was spent with Byron. *Julian and Maddalo* (1818) is a poem in the form of a conversation between Shelley (Julian) and Byron (Maddalo). Next followed *The Masque of Anarchy* (1819), a revolutionary propaganda poem; *The Cenci*, a realistic tragedy; and *Prometheus Unbound*, a lyric tragedy completed in 1819 and published in 1820. Earlier in the same year, at Pisa, he wrote some of his most famous lyrics, "The Cloud," "Ode to the West Wind," and "Ode to a Skylark."

The chief productions of 1821 were *Epipsychidion*, a result of his platonic relationship with Countess Emilia Viviani; an uncompleted prose work, *A Defence of Poetry*, published after his death, and *Adonais*, an elegy inspired by the death of John Keats. From his wide reading, he was most greatly influenced by Plato, Lucretius, Spinoza, Rousseau, Hume, and Southey. Godwin's influence lasted until Shelley's death.

His final poem, *The Triumph of Life*, was incomplete at the time he was drowned, July 8, 1822, while sailing off Viareggio. His body was first buried in the sand, then cremated. The ashes were buried in the Protestant cemetery at Rome, January 21, 1823.

The nineteenth century notion of the sensitive poetic soul owes a great deal to the ideal young man (*Alastor*—"the brave, the beautiful—the child of grace and genius") built up largely by Shelley of Shelley. Yet in the history of English literature, Shelley is not as important as Wordsworth or as influential as Byron (more popular as a poet) or Keats. The public was shocked at his defiance of the conventions of life. Today he has many admirers, but for those who dislike Romantic poetry in general, Shelley is a particularly vulnerable target. Unquestionably he could give a songlike character to his verse, for his was the light, lyrical tone. He was a lover of unusual colors, blurred outlines, and large effects. He was also a lover of startling and frank realism and had an obvious passion for the mysterious and far away. In technique he illustrated something more concrete by the less concrete. What Shelley starts to define often results in vague though pretty images. He offers emotion in itself, unattached, in the void.

Because of his sensibility, perhaps, he was at war with the conventions of society from childhood. As a political dreamer he was filled with the hope of transforming the real world into an Arcadia through revolutionary reform. As a disciple of Godwin he directed *Queen Mab* against organized religion. The queen shows the human spirit that evil times, in the past and present, are due to the authority of Church and State. In the future, however, when love reigns supreme, the chains of the human spirit will dissolve; mankind will be boundlessly self-assertive and at the same time temper this self-assertion by a boundless sympathy for others. Then a world will be realized in which there is neither inferior nor superior classes or beings. The end of *Prometheus Unbound* gives this vision of humanity released from all evil artificially imposed from without (one of Rousseau's main tenets), a humanity "where all things flow to all, as rivers to the sea," and "whose nature is its own divine control."

Shelley sets up a humanity glorified through love; he worships in the sanctuary left vacant by "the great absence of God." (His youthful atheism lacked warmth and in the end he turned to a type of pantheism.) Love, as exemplified in his personal life, is a passionate kind of sensuality which becomes his simple moral code with no duty, blame, or obligation attached. The reign of love when no authority was necessary was his millennium.

Bibliography

The best editions of Shelley are the Julian Edition of the *Complete Works*, edited by Roger Ingpen and Walter E. Peck, 10 vols., 1926–1930; and the *Complete Poetical Works*, edited by Thomas Hutchinson, 1933. The standard biography is Newman I. White, *Shelley*, 2 vols., 1940. See also Thomas Medwin, *The Life of Percy Bysshe Shelley*, 1847 (rev. ed., 1913); Edward Dowden, *The Life of Percy Bysshe Shelley*, 2 vols., 1886; André Maurois, *Ariel*, 1923; Edmund Blunden, *Shelley: A Life Story*, 1946; and Jean O. Fuller, *Shelley: A Biography*, 1968. Of great importance are K. N. Cameron, gen. ed., *The Esdaile Notebooks: A Volume of Early Poems*, 1964; and *idem*, gen. ed., *Shelley and His Circle, 1773–1822*, 1961*ff.* See also Louise Schultz Boas, *Harriet Shelley: Five Long Years*, 1962.

For criticism see H. L. Hoffman, *An Odyssey of the Soul: Shelley's Alastor*, 1933; C. H. Grabo, *The Magic Plant*, 1936; Carlos Baker, *Shelley's Major Poetry*, 1948; R. H. Fogle, *The Imagery of Keats and Shelley*, 1949; K. N. Cameron, *The Young Shelley*, 1950; Sylva Norman, *Flight of the Skylark: The Development of Shelley's Reputation*, 1954; and Neville Rogers, *Shelley at Work*, 1957; also David L. Clark, "Shelley and Shakespeare," *Publications of the Modern Language Association*, LIV (1939), 261–287; E. K. Gibson, "*Alastor*: A Reinterpretation," *ibid.*, LXII (1947), 1022–1046; and Bennett Weaver, "*Prometheus Bound* and *Prometheus Unbound*," *ibid.*, LXIV (1949), 115–133.

THE CENCI

Type of work: Dramatic poem
Author: Percy Bysshe Shelley (1792–1822)
Type of plot: Romantic tragedy
Time of plot: 1599
Locale: Rome and the Apennines
First published: 1819

This is the tale of a cruel and brutal father whose torment of his family reaches demonic proportions. When Cenci ends by raping his daughter Beatrice, the heroine, she plots his murder, for which she is at last executed. Often considered lurid sensationalism, the poem actually shares the same characteristics of tragedy found in Prometheus Unbound.

Principal Characters

Count Francesco Cenci (frän·chäs′kō chĕn′chē), a Roman nobleman who lives to make people suffer. His special target for punishment is his family. He persecutes his sons—two of whom are sent to Salamanca to die—his wife, and his daughter Beatrice, against whom he commits unmentionable crimes. Finally, he is assassinated; but even in death his baleful influence continues, for his wife and daughter, though literally innocent, die for his murder.

Count Orsino (ôr·sē′nō), a nobleman turned priest who is responsible for much of the scheming that takes place in the play. He loves Beatrice but betrays her when she is tried for her father's murder. He hires assassins to kill Cenci and abandons them when they are caught. He betrays Beatrice's brother, Giacomo, to the Roman police. Orsino escapes punishment by disguising himself and fleeing the scene when the officials close in.

Lucretia (lö·krē′shyä), Cenci's wife and Beatrice's stepmother. She helps the assassins by giving Cenci a sleeping potion. After languishing a long time in prison, she is executed for her part in her husband's assassination.

Beatrice (bā·ä·trē′chä), Cenci's daughter, the chief object of his persecution, who loves Count Orsino and who is executed along with her stepmother.

Giacomo (jä′kō·mō), Cenci's son, whose wife's dowry the father takes. After the assassination, Orsino tricks Giacomo, and the son is caught by the police.

Bernardo (bĕr·när′dō), Cenci's youngest son, who pleads at the papal court for the lives of his sister and stepmother. His petition is rejected.

Olimpio (ō·lēm′pyō) and
Marzio (mär′tsyō), assassins hired by Orsino to murder Cenci. After some hesitation, they strangle the sleeping nobleman.

Savella (sä·vĕl′lä), an official of the papal court who comes to arrest Cenci for his crimes. Finding the Count dead, Savella launches the investigation that exposes the Cenci family and the assassins as participants in Cenci's murder.

The Story

Count Cenci was a cruel and brutal man whose greatest delight was to make people suffer. He had sent two of his sons to Salamanca in hopes that they would starve. His daughter, Beatrice, had been in love with Count Orsino, who had entered the priesthood. She was wretched because she did not know where to turn for solace. Her father was worse than cruel to her and her lover had become a priest. Orsino promised to present to the Pope a petition in which Beatrice begged relief from the constant punishment she and the rest of her family were suffering from her father. Beatrice told Orsino of a banquet her father was giving that night in celebration of some news from Salamanca and said that she would give him the petition at that time. When she left him, Orsino contemplated his own problem and resolved not to show the Pope her petition, lest she be married by the Pope's order and Orsino be left without a chance of winning her outside wedlock. He resolved also not to ask for special permission to marry lest he lose his own large income from the Church.

At the banquet that night, Cenci announced the purpose of his celebration; his two sons had been killed by accident in Salamanca. Since they had been given to disobedience and rebellion, Cenci felt that this punishment was well deserved. At first the guests could not believe their ears. Beatrice boldly begged that the guests protect her, her stepmother, and her remaining two brothers from further cruelties at the hands of her father. Cenci, telling them she was insane, asked the guests to leave. Then he turned on his daughter, threatened her with a new cruelty, and ordered her and his wife to accompany him to his castle in the Apennines on the following Monday.

At the Cenci palace, Beatrice disclosed to her stepmother that Cenci had committed a crime against her which she dared not name. Orsino came to the women and proposed a plan for the assassination of Cenci. At the bridge on the way to the Apennines he would station two desperate killers who would be glad to murder Cenci. As the women left the apartment, Giacomo entered to announce that he had lent his father his wife's dowry and had never been able to recover it. In fact, Cenci had accused him of spending the money in a riotous night, and had suggested to Giacomo's wife that her husband was a secret wastrel. Orsino assured Giacomo that the money would never be restored and explained to him that the murder of Cenci had been planned.

Later Orsino came to report to Giacomo that his father had escaped from the plot and was safe within his castle in the Apennines. Giacomo now resolved to kill his father by his own hand, but Orsino, restraining him, said that he knew two men whom Cenci had wronged and who would be willing to rid the earth of their persecutor. At the Apennine castle, Cenci raged against the insolence of his daughter and confessed to Lucretia that he had tried to corrupt the soul of Beatrice. While he was sleeping, the two murderers, Olimpio and Marzio, appeared. Lucretia said she had put a sleeping potion in Cenci's drink so that he would be sure to sleep soundly. But the two men were hesitant. Olimpio reported that he could not kill an old man in his sleep. Marzio thought he heard the ghost of his own dead father speaking through the lips of the sleeping Cenci. Beatrice snatched a dagger from them and cried out that she herself would kill the fiend. Shamed into action, the assassins strangled Cenci and threw his body over the balustrade into the garden.

The Papal Legate, Savella, arrived with a warrant for the immediate execution of Cenci for his crimes. When Savella and his followers discovered that Cenci was already dead, they began an investigation. The guards seized Marzio on whose person they found Orsino's note introducing the two murderers. Lucretia and Beatrice denied knowledge of the handwriting, but Savella arrested them and said that they must appear before the court in Rome. Giacomo, tricked by Orsino, fell into the hands of the Roman police. Orsino escaped in disguise.

Conflicting testimony at the trial turned against the Cenci family. Beatrice appealed to Marzio to save the innocent prisoners from death, but the assassin died on the rack without changing his testimony. Consigned to cells to await the Pope's final decision, the Cenci family lived on in misery. Beatrice tried to comfort her stepmother in vain. The Pope decreed that the prisoners must die. Beatrice at first was delirious with despair. Then the young and innocent Bernardo went to beg clemency from the Pope, but later returned filled with grief that his petition had been useless. When the guards came to take them away, Beatrice and her stepmother went out to their execution with noble resignation.

Critical Evaluation

Because of its unnatural, even unseemly, themes *The Cenci* has been largely dismissed as one of the most sensational and lurid works by a young poet given to excesses in life and art. Even Shelley's admirers have tended to think of this closet drama as they do of Shelley's extravagances in living, such as his brash atheism in youth and his strange notion that his first and second wives might live in harmony together. But Shelley's idiosyncracies are deceptive. They have an inner consistency fired by his fierce idealism.

The Cenci is a "Gothic" piece in surface only. It is actually the sister work to his other famous closet drama, the epic lyric work *Prometheus Unbound*. Both works are, as his wife and editor Mary Shelley put it, "beautiful idealisms of moral excellence." Just as Prometheus rebels in his heart against the tyranny of Jupiter, Beatrice Cenci reaches the point where any further toleration of her father's tyranny becomes unthinkable. His rape of her is only the crowning act of a life devoted to Satanic evil. The difference between Beatrice and Promethcus is that the Titan conquers Jupiter through love, his love of earth and Asia, his beloved consort or, as Blake would put it, "Emanation." Beatrice has no one through whom love can release the liberating forces necessary to save her humanity. Orsino is a self-interested schemer. Left to her own devices, Beatrice's very innocence becomes the tragic instrument of her destruction. She thinks revenge enough, and experience never permits her to test that principle. Unlike Prometheus, who is chained for an eternity to the rock and suffers his way to spiritual deliverance, Beatrice is marched off to her execution.

Shelley's conception of Beatrice as a tragic heroine is absolutely sound. Not only does she meet the Aristotelian standards, but her contrast to Prometheus underscores Shelley's hope that man could move from tragedy to lyric happiness, from the contradictions of experience to the salvation of liberated hope.

Bibliography

Baker, Carlos. *Shelley's Major Poetry: The Fabric of a Vision.* New York: Russell and Russell, 1961, pp. 138–156.

Cameron, Kenneth Neill. *Shelley: The Golden Years.* Cambridge, Mass.: Harvard University Press, 1974, pp. 395–411.

Curran, Stuart. *Shelly's* Cenci: *Scorpions Ringed with Fire.* Princeton, N.J.: Princeton University Press, 1970.

Donahue, Joseph W. *Dramatic Character in the English Romantic Age.* Princeton, N.J.: Princeton University Press, 1970, pp. 157–186.

King-Hele, Desmond. *Shelley: His Thought and Work.* Rutherford, N.J.: Fairleigh Dickinson University Press, 1971, pp. 119–137.

Murphy, John V. *The Dark Angel: Gothic Elements in Shelley's Works.* Lewisburg, Pa.: Bucknell University Press, 1975, pp. 152–185.

Reiman, Donald. *Percy Bysshe Shelley.* New York: Twayne, 1969, pp. 87–94.

Reiter, Seymour. *A Study of Shelley's Poetry.* Albuquerque: University of New Mexico Press, 1967, pp. 190–204.

Wasserman, Earl R. *Shelley: A Critical Reading.* Baltimore: Johns Hopkins University Press, 1971, pp. 84–130.

Watson, Melvin R. "Shelley and Tragedy: The Case of Beatrice Cenci," in *Keats-Shelley Journal.* VII (1958), pp. 13–21.

Whitman, Robert F. "Beatrice's 'Pernicious Mistake' in *The Cenci*," in *PMLA.* LXXIV (June, 1959), pp. 249–253.

A DEFENCE OF POETRY

Type of work: Literary essay
Author: Percy Bysshe Shelley (1782–1822)
First published: 1840

Essay-Review

In this essay Shelley is defending poetry—"my mistress, *Urania*"—against the attack by Thomas Love Peacock in "The Four Ages Of Poetry," published in the first and only number of the *Literary Miscellany* in 1820. The polemical exchange came to nothing, for *A Defence of Poetry* remained unpublished until 1840. In his essay Peacock elaborated the familiar figure of the Golden and Silver Ages of classical poetry into four (Iron, Gold, Silver, and Brass), skipped over "the dark ages," and repeated the succession in English poetry. Peacock's point was that poetry never amounts to much in civilized society; Shelley's defense is that poetry is the essential man. Their views were antithetical and neither made contact with the other: Peacock's attack is a boisterous satire, Shelley's defense is an elevated discourse.

Nevertheless, Peacock's article is still a necessary preface to Shelley's arguments, not because one prompted the other or because Shelley adopted Peacock's historical method in the middle section of his essay, but because as a pair they show clearly the opposing preferences of the older public for eighteenth century wit and of the younger for enthusiasm. Peacock's "Four Ages" has also the merit of amusing; Shelley is never amusing. Peacock's argument is that poetry belongs properly to primitive societies, that as they become civilized they become rational and nonpoetical; hence it was not until the late seventeenth century that England equaled in the work of Shakespeare and Milton the Golden Age of Homeric Greece. Early nineteenth century England seemed to him to have reached the Age of Brass in poetry but a kind of Golden Age in science; therefore, he argued, leave poetry to the primitive societies where it belongs. He is most amusing in his picture of the first Age of Iron, in which the bard of the tribal chief "is always ready to celebrate the strength of his arm, being first duly inspired by that of his liquor." Apart from Homer, Peacock respects no poet, not even Shakespeare who mixed his unities and thought nothing of "deposing a Roman Emperor by an Italian Count, and sending him off in the disguise of a French pilgrim to be shot with a blunderbuss by an English archer." Peacock's jest turns sour as he tires of his figure, and his strictures on contemporary poetry become a diatribe of which the gist is that "a poet of our times is a semi-barbarian in a civilized community." Shelley, to whom Peacock sent a copy of his essay, was stirred to write his only prose statement on his craft. In it he came to the memorable conclusion that "Poets are the unacknowledged legislators of the world."

A Defence of Poetry falls into three parts. First, Shelley presents an argument that all men are poets in some degree, for poetry is an innate faculty of Man;

hence it is seen in all societies at all times and to eternity. In the second part he attempts the historical proof, which he abandons in the third to make a subjective and poetic affirmation of the perpetual presence and ennobling virtue of poetry. In presenting his beliefs, Shelley used the ideas that inspire his poems and attempted to codify them from the base Peacock had given him. But Peacock could begin at once with his first age; Shelley found it necessary to define at the outset his notion of poetry. Two major ideas run through this first section and are reflected in the rest of the essay: the Platonic idea of mimesis, in which the imagination responds to the eternal verities it glimpses behind the material form, and the eighteenth century idea of the "sympathetic imagination" which of its own initiative extends itself and assumes an empathy with external objects and beings. The first idea leads Shelley to assert the superiority of the poet as the most active in using the glimpses of truth and conveying them to lesser beings for their uplifting; for this reason the poet is the most powerful influence on mankind, a "legislator." The second idea gives the poet an insight into the ills of mankind which, once understood, can be corrected; here is the second meaning of "legislator."

The first part presented is in two sections, dealing first with the mimetic, then with the expressive powers of poetry, which powers are part of the definition of poetry; the other two parts of the definition are contained in four paragraphs on the form of poetry, especially on its use of language, the medium which makes it superior to other art media and which is called "measured" in contradistinction to "unmeasured" language or prose. But the whole essay is prefaced by four paragraphs which define poetry in the largest or organic sense, not by its mechanics. These paragraphs go to the heart of the difference between Peacock and Shelley.

Shelley begins with a distinction between reason and imagination, leaving to the former the work of numbering, analyzing, and relating objects; the imagination perceives the similitude of objects in their innate values, not in their appearance, and synthesizes these values, presumably, into a valid and Platonic One or Truth. The synthetic principle of the imagination is poetry; Man is compared to "an Aeolian lyre," subject to impressions external and internal but possessing an inner principle (poetry) which produces not simply melody but harmony, not merely the sound of poetry but the potential of the poetic product to harmonize Man or bring him closer to the poetry of being. Poetry is thus both the name of a form of language (measured) and of the power of producing it and benefiting from the poem. Here Shelley announces that poets are "the institutors of laws, and the founders of civil society" because they discover the laws of harmony and become "legislators" by giving these laws the form of a poem. The poetic product or poem may be an act of mimesis, but the act proceeds from the poetic faculty highly developed in the poet and contained in all men: "A poem is the very image of life expressed in its eternal truth."

The argument in the second section of the first part, devoted to the effects of poetry on society, has been anticipated in the foregoing analysis. *A Defence of Poetry*, as an "apologia," could well end at that point but Shelley wanted to convince Peacock that his theory has external evidence. This he offers in the second part of the essay.

The historical method had already been touched on in Shelley's example of the propensity of the savage or child to imitate the impressions it receives, like a "lyre" producing melody only. Shelley's reading of history is as willful as Peacock's in his assertion that the morality of an age corresponds to the goodness or badness of its poetry; he adduces Greek classical drama as an evidence of a healthy society and Hellenic bucolic poetry as a sign of decay when the poets ceased to be the acknowledged legislators of the Alexandrian Hellenes. In order to cope with the same progression of health and decay in the literature of Rome, which would seem to prove Peacock's scheme, Shelley shifts the whole cycle into "episodes of that cyclic poem written by time upon the memories of men." He encounters further difficulty in coping with Christianity, for by Shelley's theory Jesus must be a great poet: "The scattered fragments preserved to us by the biographers of this extraordinary person, are all instinct with the most vivid poetry." But something went wrong in the Dark Ages: ". . . the extinction of the poetic principle . . . from causes too intricate to be here discussed." Shelley feels safer with Dante and Milton: "But let us not be betrayed from a defence into a critical history of poetry. . . ."

After abandoning the historical method which, had he followed Peacock step by step, would have brought him up to his contemporaries, Shelley returns to his defence by attacking "the promoters of utility" and, by implication, Peacock. To the utilitarian objection that poetry simply produces pleasure and that pleasure is profitless, Shelley asserts that the pleasure of poetry lies not in its superficial melody but in its innate harmony, alone capable of checking "the calculating faculty" which has already produced "more scientific and economical knowledge than can be accommodated to the just distribution of the produce which it multiplies." Shelley follows this with a paragraph which summarizes the duality of the "poetic faculty"; by synthesis it "creates new materials of knowledge and power and pleasure," and by its expressive powers it reproduces those materials "according to a certain rhythm and order which may be called the beautiful and the good."

Shelley's peroration, his personal and poetic justification for poetry, opens with three paragraphs beginning: "Poetry is indeed something divine." "Poetry is the record of the best and happiest moments of the happiest and best minds." Poetry turns all things to loveliness . . ." This is the moving genius of *Adonais*. Searching for the best proof to defend poetry from the rationalizations of Peacock, Shelley followed the prompting of his own "poetic principle" in concluding *A Defence of Poetry* with a sustained lyric in prose that Peacock could never match. The power of this essay is still inspiring. It constitutes Shelley's best claim outside his verse to be a "legislator" to the world.

Bibliography

Abbey, Lloyd. "Shelley's Repudiation of Conscious Artistry," in *English Studies in Canada.* I (Spring, 1975), pp. 62–73.

Cameron, Kenneth Neill. *Shelley: The Golden Years.* Cambridge, Mass.: Harvard University Press, 1974, pp. 188–210.

Chernaik, Judith. *The Lyrics of Shelley.* Cleveland: Case Western Reserve University Press, 1972, pp. 8–30.

Delisle, Fanny. *A Study of Shelley's* A Defence of Poetry*: A Textual and Critical Evaluation.* Salzburg, Austria: Salzburg Studies in English Literature (University of Salzburg), 1974.

Jordan, John E. "Introduction," in *A Defence of Poetry.* Indianapolis, Ind.: Bobbs-Merrill, 1965, pp. vii–xxviii.

King-Hele, Desmond. *Shelley: His Thought and Work.* Rutherford, N.J.: Fairleigh Dickinson University Press, 1971, pp. 287–295.

McElderry, Bruce R., Jr. "Common Elements in Wordsworth's 'Preface' and Shelley's *Defence of Poetry*," in *Modern Language Quarterly.* V (June, 1944), pp. 175–181.

Reiman, Donald. *Percy Bysshe Shelley.* New York: Twayne, 1969, pp. 121–124.

Schulze, Earl J. *Shelley's Theory of Poetry: A Reappraisal.* The Hague: Mouton, 1966, pp. 24–37, 70–76.

Solve, Melvin T. *Shelley: His Theory of Poetry.* Chicago: University of Chicago Press, 1927.

THE POETRY OF SHELLEY

Type of work: Poetry
Author: Percy Bysshe Shelley (1792–1822)
First published: Queen Mab, 1813; *Alastor, or The Spirit of Solitude*, 1816: *The Revolt of Islam*, 1818; *Rosalind and Helen*, 1819; *Prometheus Unbound*, 1820 (lyric drama); *Epipsychidion*, 1821; *Adonais*, 1821; *Hellas*, 1822; *Posthumous Poems*, 1824; *Poetical Works*, 1839

Essay-Review

Percy Bysshe Shelley was born on August 4, 1792. He died before his thirtieth birthday, drowned with two companions when his sailboat, the *Don Juan*, was caught in a storm off the coast of Italy. He published his first book, *Zastrozzi*, a gothic novel, when he was eighteen years old. In the next eleven years, the span of his working life, he wrote an astonishing variety of poems—verse narratives, lyrics, poems philosophical, political, satirical, sentimental, and macabre—as well as essays and translations from Greek, Latin, Italian, Spanish, and German. He dashed off broadsides and pamphlets, and kept up a voluminous correspondence. He was an extraordinarily productive writer who often composed at great speed (his rapid scrawl, Trelawney said, looked "for all the world like a marsh overgrown with bulrushes and blotted with wild ducks"), yet Wordsworth called him "one of the best *artists* of us all: I mean in workmanship of style."

It is a cliché to describe any artist as a "complex, multifaceted personality." Yet Shelley, more than any of his contemporaries, has suffered from reductive criticism, from both sympathetic and antagonistic estimates of his work which simply ignore elements that do not fit their thesis. When Shelley died, he was reviled in the press for his radical politics and his sexual immorality. Many of his poems were not available in a generally accessible edition for decades after his death. His high reputation in the Victorian era rested on his lyrics: in the public imagination, Shelley incarnated the sensitive, romantic Poet.

Perhaps in overreaction to this distorted view, contemporary studies of Shelley frequently dismiss the lyrics as charming but slight, or even as merely sentimental. On the other hand, there is a tendency in Shelley studies to read his long poems—not only *Prometheus Unbound*, but the unfinished *Triumph of Life* and lesser works such as *The Revolt of Islam*—as coherent philosophical "myths" of great subtlety and power, comparable to *Paradise Lost* and Wordsworth's *Prelude*. Such criticism, which can be found in its extreme form in the work of Harold Bloom, but is also evident in more moderate work of scholars such as Donald Reiman and Neville Rogers, can take a badly flawed poem like *Epipsychidion*—a poem of uncertain and confusing structure, its rhetoric often out of control—and present it as a seamless whole. Moreover, Shelley, like Coleridge, is now frequently seen as a kind of visionary polymath who "anticipated," somehow, everything from the Freudian unconscious to Heisenberg's Uncertainty Principle.

Neville Rogers, one of the preeminent modern Shelley scholars, goes so far as to suggest that, "like Goethe, Shelley might have made some distinguished contribution to science" had he not died prematurely.

The single indispensable guide to Shelley, the work the student should begin with after a first reading of the poetry, is Richard Holmes's *Shelley: the Pursuit* (1974). The first reliable biography of Shelley, Holmes's book is one of the most brilliant modern literary biographies: it effectively does away with the idealized Shelley, once and for all. "That fluttering apparition," Holmes writes, "is not to be found here, where a darker and more earthy, crueller and more capable figure moves with swift pace through a bizarre though sometimes astonishingly beautiful landscape." In his sympathetic and extensive treatment of Shelley's radical political convictions, and in his frank account of Shelley's complicated sexual life, Holmes clarifies as no previous commentator has done the persistent conflict which informs all of Shelley's poetry: the conflict between the ideal and the actual.

Shelley had from his youth an achingly vivid sense of human possibility, of men and women politically and sexually free. He was unwilling to simply accept the gulf between this vision of possibility and "real life" as a given, "the human condition." Yet as he pursued freedom and beauty, he became increasingly aware that the means of liberation were themselves inevitably corrupt. Politically, this meant that justice and power were irreconcilable. Sexually, it meant that desire, by its very compulsive nature, was irreconcilable with freedom and "natural" ease, even in a "community" committed to "free love." Even in Shelley's early poems, where there is considerable faith in the possibility of "revolution," of the realization of the ideal, there is an awareness of this conflict, but not until *The Triumph of Life*, his last major poem, is this disillusioned judgment stated explicitly, with full consciousness.

Shelley's first major poem, *Queen Mab* (1813), is his most optimistic revolutionary work. *Queen Mab* consists of a dedication to his wife Harriet (whom he was about to leave for Mary Godwin), and nine cantos—mostly in blank verse—followed by a section of "Notes" as long as the poem itself (some of the notes are in fact complete essays). In the poem Shelley attacks established religion—particularly Christianity—political and economic tyranny, and the institution of marriage. The poem concludes with a utopian vision: the palace stands in ruin, the deserted cathedral in decay, and

> Within the massy prison's mouldering courts,
> Fearless and free the ruddy children played,
> Weaving gay chaplets for their innocent brows. . . .

Even these ruins, the Fairy Queen says,

> soon left not a wreck behind:
> Their elements, wide scattered o'er the globe,
> To happier shapes were moulded, and became
> Ministrant to all blissful impulses:

> Thus human things were perfected, and earth,
> Even as a child beneath its mother's love,
> Was strengthened in all excellence, and grew
> Fairer and nobler with each passing year.

The "Notes," which are buttressed with many long quotations in Greek, Latin, and French as well as English, include full essays on topics such as free love, atheism (a reprint of Shelley's pamphlet written at Oxford), and even a defense of vegetarianism.

Although *Queen Mab* is a very uneven work, it is not a piece of juvenilia. Taken together, the poem and the "Notes" state Shelley's mature credo. He never abandoned the values of *Queen Mab*, but he gradually lost the optimism which fired its utopian vision. Even in *Queen Mab*, it is evident that *anger* at injustice and suffering gave Shelley his clearest voice. (In a pirated edition, *Queen Mab* was one of the principal texts of English radicalism, and had a very wide circulation throughout the nineteenth century.) Shelley's most controlled, most compelling poems—*The Mask of Anarchy* and *The Triumph of Life*—speak in this angry voice, but in verse that is cold and mature. *Queen Mab* is a crude, ambitious sketch of all the themes which preoccupied Shelley until his death.

Alastor (1816) shows a greater awareness of ambiguity in the conflict between the ideal and the actual. The title does not refer to the protagonist of the poem— the Poet—but to an evil spirit, a "spirit of solitude." Solitude, because the Poet neglects the love of an Arab maiden—a "real woman," a domestic figure who brings him food—for the vision of a dancing girl with whom he makes love in a vivid dream. Unsatisfied thereafter with anything merely human, he is driven into miserable solitude by his lust for the ideal. Although Shelley intends to show that the Poet is wrong—as he explains quite clearly in a characteristically prim, didactic Preface—the energy of the poem derives from the intense hallucinatory images of the imaginary lovemaking:

> He reared his shuddering limbs and quelled
> His gasping breath, and spread his arms to meet
> Her panting bosom: ... she drew back a while,
> Then, yielding to the irresistible joy,
> With frantic gesture and short breathless cry
> Folded his frame in her dissolving arms.

This is one of many such passages throughout Shelley's works: surely he wrote about sexual intercourse far more and more often than any of his great contemporaries. The language of such passages often seem maddeningly indirect, but it would be a mistake to explain this simply by referring to censorship and the difference in standards of explicitness between Shelley's time and our own. It is characteristic of Shelley's imagination to *linger* over such descriptions, much as he indulged himself in exquisitely drawn-out midnight sessions of self-induced terror, preferably in the company of an impressionable young woman. This

Shelley appears clearly for the first time in Holmes's biography, which gives readers a chance to begin understanding the driving imagination of Shelley's poems, in which both sexual and macabre elements are prominent. This will dispel the Platonizing fog with which so many critics have obscured Shelley's work.

Prometheus Unbound (1820), Shelley's first major poem composed in Italy, has generally been considered his greatest work, yet it has a clumsy, makeshift quality which has led many critics to dismiss entirely the last two of its four acts, reserving the first two acts as a self-contained unit. A long, complex work which cannot be treated adequately in such a brief discussion, it is—with great license—a "sequel" to the *Prometheus Bound* of Aeschylus. The poem begins with Prometheus bound to the face of a rock, in punishment for his defiance of Jupiter. The subject of the poem is the endless human struggle against tyranny, external tyranny (political and economic) and spiritual tyranny (such as that exercised by the church). In a sense, *Prometheus Unbound* is midway between the optimism of *Queen Mab* and the disillusionment of *The Triumph of Life*. Although the poem concludes on a positive note—man cannot overcome death but he can cease to fear it, and he can alleviate much of the suffering which he has brought upon himself—there are new emphases. First, there is the recognition that hatred of tyranny can itself be destructive: Prometheus' curse of Jupiter and his intransigent hatred paralyze the earth. Secondly, Shelley introduces the enigmatic figure of Demogorgon, who can perhaps be identified with Necessity (or Fate): a relentless, amoral force to which all men are subject. Man must not presumptuously struggle against Necessity but rather should accommodate himself to it; if he does, he will find that much of his misery was self-inflicted. This amoral force personified in Demogorgon is a powerful new image (although Shelley's "cosmology" in the poem is often unclear), anticipating the darker vision of *The Triumph of Life*, in which "Life" itself is a relentless juggernaut.

The Mask of Anarchy (written in 1819 but not published until long after Shelley's death, in 1832, because Leigh Hunt feared prosecution) is a neglected masterpiece. It was composed in just twelve days during one of Shelley's most sustained creative bursts, a period of two months in which he also wrote "Ode to the West Wind," *Peter Bell the Third*, and a number of shorter works, both poetry and prose. The occasion of *The Mask of Anarchy* was the Peterloo massacre, in which a large crowd of English working people were brutally dispersed by mounted militiamen; a number were trampled to death, and hundreds were injured. From its opening lines, the poem (which consists of ninety-one stanzas) has an air of inevitability, of simplicity, of *rightness* which is rare in any poetry at any time:

> As I lay asleep in Italy
> There came a voice from over the Sea,
> And with great power it forth led me
> To walk in the visions of Poesy.

> I met Murder on the way—
> He had a mask like Castlereagh—
> Very smooth he looked, yet grim;
> Seven blood-hounds followed him.

The poem shows how, beneath the veneer of the government, there is the terrible power of anarchy. But the people, in their very rebellion, are in danger of falling into Anarchy's train themselves. Shelley calls for "a great Assembly" of the downtrodden to win their rights peacefully, and concludes with a rousing exhortation:

> Shake your chains to earth like dew
> Which in sleep had fallen on you—
> Ye are many—they are few.

The Triumph of Life, Shelley's last major poem, is a substantial fragment of more than five hundred lines. Composed during May and June of 1822, it was left unfinished at his death. The title is derived from the "triumphs" of Rome, ritual processions such as those in which returning generals rode in chariots amidst great pomp, while their conquered foes were drawn along the streets in chains and variously degraded. Written in terza rima, like "Ode to the West Wind," *The Triumph of Life* has the quick, compelling movement of *The Mask of Anarchy*:

> As in that wondrous thought I lay
> This was the tenour of my waking dream.
> Methought I sate beside a public way.
>
> Thick strewn with summer dust, & a great stream
> Of people there was hurrying to & fro
> Numerous as gnats upon the evening gleam,
>
> All hastening onward, yet none seemed to know
> Whither he went, or whence he came, or why
> He made one of the multitude. . . .

Amidst this procession the Chariot appears—the Chariot of Life, which crushes everyone, yet about which men and women dance and give themselves, as if in worship. Asking "what is this?" the poet gets an answer from what he had supposed was an old root on the hillside: "Life," Rousseau tells him, for the "grim feature" is indeed Rousseau, who then becomes the poet's "guide" to the procession, pointing out figures as they pass—among them Napoleon, Voltaire, Plato, Popes and Emperors, "great bards of elder time." Rousseau then tells the poet how he too came to be there, "fallen, by the wayside," to which the poet responds with the question that ends the fragment:

Then, what is life? I cried.

A few weeks after writing those words, Shelley drowned, leaving the question unanswered.

Bibliography

Baker, Carlos. "The Bottom of the Night," in *The Major English Romantic Poets: A Symposium in Reappraisal.* Edited by C.D. Thorpe, Carlos Baker and Bennett Weaver. Carbondale: Southern Illinois University Press, 1957, pp. 185–199.

Berry, Francis. *Poetry and the Physical Voice.* New York: Oxford University Press, 1962, pp. 66–82.

Bostetter, Edward E. "Shelley and the Mutinous Flesh," in *Texas Studies in Literature and Language.* I (Summer, 1959), pp. 203–213.

Delasanta, Rodney. "Shelley's 'Sometimes Embarrassing Declarations': A Defence," in *Texas Studies in Literature and Language.* VII (Summer, 1965), pp. 173–179.

Fogle, Richard Harter. "The Abstractness of Shelley," in *The Imagery of Keats and Shelley.* Chapel Hill: University of North Carolina Press, 1949, pp. 215–240. Reprinted in *Shelley: A Collection of Critical Essays.* Edited by George M. Ridenour. Englewood Cliffs, N.J.: Prentice-Hall, 1965, pp. 13–30.

Ford, Newell F. "The Wit in Shelley's Poetry," in *Studies in English Literature.* I (Autumn, 1961), pp. 1–22.

Havens, Raymond D. "Shelley the Artist," in *The Major English Romantic Poets: A Symposium in Reappraisal.* Edited by C.D. Thorpe, Carlos Baker and Bennett Weaver. Carbondale: Southern Illinois University Press, 1957, pp. 169–184.

Holloway, John. "Introduction," in *Selected Poems of Percy Bysshe Shelley.* London: Heinemann, 1960. Reprinted in *Shelley: Shorter Poems and Lyrics.* Edited by Patrick Swinden. London: Macmillan, 1976, pp. 130–144.

Leavis, F.R. *Revaluation: Tradition and Development in English Poetry.* London: Chatto and Windus, 1949, pp. 203–232. Reprinted in *English Romantic Poets: Modern Essays in Criticism.* Edited by M.H. Abrams. New York: Oxford University Press, 1975, pp. 345–365.

Matthews, G.M. "Introduction," in *Shelley: Selected Poems and Prose.* London: Oxford University Press, 1964.

Norman, Sylva. "Twentieth-Century Theories on Shelley," in *Texas Studies in Literature and Language.* IX (Summer, 1967), pp. 223–237.

Pottle, Frederick A. "The Case of Shelley," in *PMLA.* LXVII (1952), pp. 589–608. Reprinted in *English Romantic Poets: Modern Essays in Criticism.* Edited by M.H. Abrams. New York: Oxford University Press, 1975, pp. 366–383.

Raine, Kathleen. "A Defense of Shelley's Poetry," in *Southern Review.* III (Autumn, 1967), pp. 856–863, 868–873.

Reiman, Donald H. *Percy Bysshe Shelley.* New York: Twayne, 1969.

Wilcox, Stewart C. "Present Values in Shelley's Art," in *The Major English Romantic Poets: A Symposium in Reappraisal.* Edited by C.D. Thorpe, Carlos Baker and Bennett Weaver. Carbondale: Southern Illinois University Press, 1957, pp. 200–206.

PROMETHEUS UNBOUND

Type of work: Poem
Author: Percy Bysshe Shelley (1792–1822)
Type of plot: Lyric drama
Time of plot: Remote antiquity
Locale: Asia
First published: 1820

Valuable as a key to understanding Shelley's philosophy, Prometheus Unbound *uses the combined mediums of drama and poetry to expound the author's theory that universal love is the only solution to mankind's ills.*

Principal Characters

Prometheus, a titan punished by Jupiter for having befriended mankind. He is chained to a rocky cliff for three thousand years while eagles tear at his heart, but he will not repudiate the curse he has pronounced on Jupiter. Aided by spirits and gods, Prometheus is finally unbound. His freedom heralds an age of sweetness and light for mankind.

Jupiter, chief of the gods, who has had Prometheus bound to the cliff. As Prometheus is released, Jupiter loses his power and falls, impotent, into darkness.

Demogorgon, the supreme god and ruler of all gods, who finally reverses prevailing circumstances, thus causing Jupiter's downfall and Prometheus' release from torment.

**Panthea and
Ione,** two Oceanids. Panthea and Asia, Prometheus' wife, learn from Demogorgon that Prometheus will be set free. They are Demogorgon's interlocutors as he explains what will come to pass on earth.

Herakles, the hero famous for his strength. Herakles, before spirits friendly to Prometheus, releases the captive from his bonds and torment.

Mercury, the messenger of the gods, sent by Jupiter to Prometheus to learn from the captive how long Jupiter will reign.

Earth, Prometheus' mother.

Asia, Prometheus' wife.

Phantasma of Jupiter, a wraith who appears to Prometheus to repeat for him the forgotten curse he had put on Jupiter.

The Furies, agents of torment who come with Mercury to punish further the bound titan.

The Spirit of the Hour, one of a group of Hours, figures who move in Demogorgon's realm to show the passing of time by Age, Manhood, Youth, Infancy, and Death. The Spirit of the Hour announces Prometheus' release to all mankind and describes the pleasant things that will occur on earth now that the titan is free.

The Story

Prometheus, the benefactor of mankind, was bound to a rocky cliff by order of Jupiter, who was jealous of the Titan's power. Three thousand years of torture

Prometheus suffered there, while heat and cold and many torments afflicted him. An eagle continually ate at his heart. But Prometheus still defied the power of Jupiter.

At last Prometheus asked Panthea and Ione, the two Oceanides, to repeat to him the curse he had pronounced upon Jupiter when Jupiter had first begun to torture him. But neither Earth, his mother, nor the Oceanides would answer him. At last the Phantasm of Jupiter appeared and repeated the curse. When Prometheus heard the words, he repudiated them. Now that he had suffered tortures and found that his spirit remained unconquered, he wished pain to no living thing. Earth and the Oceanides mourned that the curse had been withdrawn, for they thought Jupiter had at last conquered Prometheus' spirit.

Then Mercury approached with the Furies. Mercury told the captive that he would suffer even greater tortures if he did not reveal the secret which Prometheus alone knew—the future fate of Jupiter. Jupiter, afraid, wished to avert catastrophe by learning the secret, and Mercury promised that Prometheus would be released if he revealed it. But Prometheus refused. He admitted only that he knew Jupiter's reign would come to an end, that he would not be king of the gods for all eternity. Prometheus said that he was willing to suffer torture until Jupiter's reign ended. Although the Furies tried to frighten him by describing the pains they could inflict, they knew they had no power over his soul.

The Furies mocked Prometheus and mankind. They showed him visions of blood and despair on earth; they showed the Passion of Christ and men's disregard for His message of love. Fear and hypocrisy ruled; tyrants took the thrones of the world.

A group of spirits appeared and prophesied that Love would cure the ills of mankind. They prophesied also that Prometheus would be able to bring Love to earth and halt the reign of evil and grief.

When the spirits had gone, Prometheus acknowledged the power of Love, for his love for Asia, his wife, had enabled him to suffer pain without surrendering.

While Asia mourned alone in a lovely valley for her lost husband, Panthea appeared to tell of two dreams she had had. In one, she saw Prometheus released from bondage and all the world filled with sweetness. In the other dream she had received only a command to follow. Just then the echoes in the valley broke their silence. They called Asia and Panthea to follow them. The listeners obeyed.

Asia and Panthea followed the echoes to the realm of Demogorgon, the supreme power ruling the gods. They stopped on a pinnacle of rock, but spirits beckoned them down into Demogorgon's cave. There he told them that he would answer any question they put to him. When they asked who had made the living world, he replied that God had created it. Then they asked who had made pain and evil. Prometheus had given knowledge to mankind, but mankind had not eradicated evil with all the gifts of science. They asked whether Jupiter was the source of these ills, the evil master over man.

Demogorgon answered that nothing which served evil could be master, for only eternal Love ruled all. Asia asked when Prometheus would gain his freedom and bring Love into the world to conquer Jupiter. Demogorgon then showed his guests the passage of the Hours. A dreadful Hour passed, marking Jupiter's fall; the next hour was beautiful, marking Prometheus' release. Asia and Panthea accompanied this spirit of the Hour in her chariot and passed by Age, Manhood, Youth, Infancy, and Death into a new paradise.

Meanwhile, Jupiter, who had just married Thetis, celebrated his omnipotence over all but the soul of man. Then Demogorgon appeared and pronounced judgment on Jupiter. Jupiter cried for mercy, but his power was gone. He sank downward through darkness and ruin.

At the same time Herakles approached Prometheus. In the presence of Asia, Panthea, the Spirit of the Hour, and Earth, the captive was set free. Joyfully, Prometheus told Asia how they would spend the rest of their days together with Love. Then he sent the Spirit of the Hour to announce his release to all mankind. He kissed Earth, and Love infused all of her animal, vegetable, and mineral parts.

The Spirit of Earth came to the cave where Asia and Prometheus lived and told them of the transformation that had come over mankind. Anger, pride, insincerity, and all the other ills of man had passed away. The Spirit of the Hour reported other wonders that took place. Thrones were empty, and each man was king over himself, free from guilt or pain. But he was still subject to chance, death, and mutability, without which he would oversoar his destined place in the world.

Later in a vision Panthea and Ione saw how all the evil things of the world lay dead and decayed. Earth's happiness was boundless, and even the moon felt the beams of Love from Earth as snow melted on its bleak lunar mountains. Earth rejoiced that hate, fear, and pain had left mankind forever. Man was now master of his fate and all the secrets of Earth.

Critical Evaluation

Prometheus Unbound, Shelley's first major work composed in Italy, was written between September, 1818, and the close of 1819, and was published in the summer of 1820. It is—with great liberties—a "sequel" to the *Prometheus Bound* of Aeschylus. Although it has generally been considered Shelley's greatest work, the poem suffers from a lack of structure and dramatic coherence which has led some critics to dismiss entirely the last two of its four acts, reserving the first two acts as a self-contained unit.

Prometheus Unbound is a philosophical poem, Shelley's fullest treatment of the endless human struggle for freedom. "Freedom" for Shelley was not mere license—the freedom, that is, to do as one pleases. By "freedom," Shelley meant the fulfillment of the human potential for goodness and beauty and love, a fulfillment such as he imagined in the ecstatic conclusion of *Queen Mab*. Like the

Gospels, like Rousseau and Karl Marx, Shelly in *Prometheus Unbound* acknowledges that man is in chains and proposes to show him how he can be free.

In *Queen Mab* (1813), his first major poem, Shelley had seen external authority—church and state—as primarily responsible for human misery, and the poem was fueled by bitterness against all institutions, but particularly against Christianity. However, Shelley's ideas underwent constant evolution, and by the time he was writing *Prometheus Unbound* his perspective had changed considerably. He still believed that much of human suffering was self-inflicted, and subject to correction, yet he was aware—as he had not been in *Queen Mab*—that hatred of oppressive institutions is itself corrosive, and that many reformers simply substituted one tyranny for another. While he never ceased to call for specific political reforms, Shelley began to look more deeply into the human heart for the sources of suffering. At the same time, while he continued to criticize institutionalized Christianity as a perversion of the teachings of Christ, and while he never accepted Christian doctrine as such, Shelley had become much more sympathetic to what he regarded as the essence of Christ's message; and *Prometheus Unbound* reads at many points like an essentially Christian work.

The Christian aspect of the poem is nowhere more evident than it is in the closing lines (Act IV. 570–578), which are a kind of summary of the argument that runs throughout the work:

> To suffer woes which Hope thinks infinite;
> To forgive wrongs darker than death or night;
>   To defy Power, which seems omnipotent;
> To love, and bear; to hope till Hope creates
> From its own wreck the thing it contemplates;
>   Neither to change, nor falter, nor repent;
> This, like thy glory, Titan, is to be
> Good, great and joyous, beautiful and free;
> This is alone Life, Joy, Empire, and Victory.

However, the universe which Shelley describes in *Prometheus Unbound* is not controlled by a beneficent God, nor can it be said that ultimately all things therein work together for good. There is no assurance of immortality. Shelley's conception of the universe in *Prometheus Unbound* is almost Manichaean, for this universe is subject to an amoral force beyond man's imagining (II.iv.116: "the deep truth is imageless"). Perhaps the best approach to this aspect of Shelley is through the writings of Simone Weil, whose Christianity—flavored with Manichaeanism—was deeply influenced by Classical Greece, as Shelley himself was. "Necessity," Simone Weil wrote, "is God's veil. God has committed all phenomena without exception to the mechanism of the world." Where in such a world is there room for the redemptive power of Christ—or, as Shelley had it, of love? This is an "inconsistency" which neither Shelley nor Simone Weil was able to resolve.

Act I of the poem begins with Prometheus bound to a crag "in the Indian

Caucasus," where he has been for thousands of years, in punishment for his defiance of Jupiter. In the course of Act I, Prometheus gains self-knowledge; he hears again—at his own request—his terrible curse against Jupiter (only a Phantasm of Jupiter dares to repeat it), and understands that his own hatred—however justified—is wrong. He is tortured by the Furies, yet he triumphs over them by accepting the suffering without hatred. At the end of the Act, Panthea—one of the Oceanides, who has been watching over Prometheus—goes by the power of her love to her greater "sea-sister," Asia, to seek help for him.

In Act II, Panthea and Asia are called by one of the Spirits of the Hours to visit Demogorgon, an enigmatic figure who can perhaps be identified with Necessity or Fate. Asia talks with Demogorgon, whose answers are oracular, often ambiguous: when asked "who made terror, madness, crime, remorse," Demogorgon merely replies: "He reigns" (II.iv.19–31). "He" is "Almighty God," or Jove, yet "Jove" is merely a name for the "imageless," relentless, amoral force which rules all things.

Act II continues with Asia's summary of human history in mythic terms, a history which can be read as Shelley's rewriting of Genesis. In the age of Saturn, Asia explains, man was innocent yet lacked knowledge. Prometheus, who personifies human intelligence and creativity, brings man both evil and good, as in the Christian conception of the Fall. Jupiter—to whom Prometheus gave "wisdom, which is strength"—personifies the human bent to abuse knowledge, to convert it into power and the thoughtless lust for domination, even at the cost of destroying the planet. Throughout this mythic history, Shelley suggests that much of human suffering can be traced to man's own mind: the vast hierarchies of oppression, the networks of unreal conceptions which are accepted as infallible truth—all these testify, perversely, to the enormous creative power of the imagination.

Act III describes the fall of Jupiter and Prometheus' release. In the third scene of this Act, which recalls the Incarnation, Prometheus vows to go among men. Death will remain—"What can hide man from mutability"—but through Love, through the creative power of "Painting, Sculpture, and rapt Poesy. . ."

> swift shapes and sounds, which grow
> More fair and soft as man grows wise and kind,
> And, veil by veil, evil and error fall. . .
> (III.iii.60–62)

Prometheus will help men to redeem themselves.

Act IV opens with choruses which celebrate man's freedom and the harmony which results when he accommodates himself to Necessity and accepts mutability rather than struggling vainly against the universe. The Earth herself, in some of the most beautiful lines in English poetry, celebrates the harmony of mankind ("Man, oh, not men! a chain of linked thought"), of man reconciled to himself:

Man, one harmonious soul of many a soul,
Whose nature is its own divine control,
Where all things flow to all, as rivers to the sea;
Familiar acts are beautiful through love;
Labour, and pain, and grief, in life's green grove
Sport like tame beasts, none knew how gentle they could be!
(IV.400–405)

Bibliography

Allsup, James O.   *The Magic Circle: A Study of Shelley's Concept of Love.* Port Washington, N.Y.: Kennikat, 1976, pp. 87–100.

Baker, Carlos.   *Shelley's Major Poetry: The Fabric of a Vision.* New York: Russell and Russell, 1961, pp. 89–121.

Barrell, Joseph.   *Shelley and the Thought of His Time: A Study in the History of Ideas.* New York: Archon Books, 1967, pp. 131–161.

Bloom, Harold.   *Shelley's Mythmaking.* New Haven, Conn.: Yale University Press, 1959, pp. 91–147.

————.   *The Visionary Company: A Reading of English Romantic Poetry.* Ithaca, N.Y.: Cornell University Press, 1971, pp. 306–322.

Bowra, C. Maurice.   *The Romantic Imagination.* London: Oxford University Press, 1950, pp. 103–125.

Butter, Peter.   *Shelley's Idols of the Cave.* Edinburgh: Edinburgh University Press, 1954, pp. 151–156, 165–209.

Cameron, Kenneth Neill.   *Shelley: The Golden Years.* Cambridge, Mass.: Harvard University Press, 1974, pp. 475–564.

Chernaik, Judith.   *The Lyrics of Shelley.* Cleveland: Case Western Reserve University Press, 1972, pp. 83–90.

King-Hele, Desmond.   *Shelley: His Thought and Work.* Rutherford, N.J.: Fairleigh Dickinson University Press, 1971, pp. 169–209.

McNiece, Gerald.   *Shelley and the Revolutionary Idea.* Cambridge, Mass.: Harvard University Press, 1969, pp. 218–245.

Murphy, John V.   *The Dark Angel: Gothic Elements in Shelley's Works.* Lewisburg, Pa.: Bucknell University Press, 1975, pp. 146–151.

Reiman, Donald H.   *Percy Bysshe Shelley.* New York: Twayne, 1969, pp. 75–87.

Reiter, Seymour.   *A Study of Shelley's Poetry.* Albuquerque: University of New Mexico Press, 1967, pp. 87–190.

Wasserman, Earl R.   *Shelley's* Prometheus Unbound: *A Critical Reading.* Baltimore: Johns Hopkins University Press, 1965.

Weaver, Bennett. *Prometheus Unbound.* New York: Archon Books, 1969.

Webb, Timothy. *Shelley: A Voice Not Understood.* Manchester, England: Manchester University Press, 1977, pp. 115–121, 142–150.

Wilson, Milton. *Shelley's Later Poetry: A Study of His Prophetic Imagination.* New York: Columbia University Press, 1959, pp. 56–68, 129–147, 171–174, 207–217.

Woodman, Ross Greig. *The Apocalyptic Vision in the Poetry of Shelley.* Toronto: University of Toronto Press, 1964, pp. 103–157.

DOROTHY WORDSWORTH

Born: Cockermouth, England (December 25, 1771)
Died: Rydal Mount, England (January 25, 1855)

Principal Works

JOURNALS: *The Alfoxden Journal,* 1798 *et seq; Journal of a Visit to Hamburg and of a Journey from Hamburg to Goslar,* 1798; *The Grasmere Journal,* 1800–1803; *Recollections of a Tour Made in Scotland,* 1803; *Excursion of the Banks of Ullswater,* 1805; *Excursion up Scawfell Pike,* 1818; *Journal of a Tour on the Continent,* 1820; *Journal of My Second Tour in Scotland,* 1822; *Journal of a Tour in the Isle of Man,* 1828.

Dorothy Wordsworth was the only sister of William Wordsworth, the great English Romantic poet. She was separated from her brothers at the age of six, upon the death of her mother. While living at Halifax with her mother's cousin, Elizabeth Threlkeld, she attended a day school, except for one six-month stay at a boarding school. In 1787 young Dorothy went to live with her maternal grandparents, her education at an end. Life with her grandparents was unhappy, especially as they made her four brothers unwelcome as visitors. The following year, 1788, her maternal uncle, the Rev. William Cookson, married and took his niece into his household until 1794. In 1795, through a legacy and the loan of a house, Dorothy Wordsworth finally achieved a childhood dream, living with her older brother, William. From that time to his death in 1850 she was seldom separated from him, living amicably in his household even after he was married.

In 1798, while Dorothy and William were living at Alfoxden to be near Samuel Taylor Coleridge, Dorothy began the first of her journals, from which both Coleridge and her brother drew descriptions for some of their poems in *Lyrical Ballads*. This practice continued for Wordsworth; often in later years he depended upon his sister's descriptions of people and places to furnish him with poetic material. She wrote her journals for her own pleasure and her brother William's, none of the journals being published until after her death, although she did allow some of the manuscripts to circulate among their friends. Living in his home, acting as a second mother to his children, Dorothy Wordsworth was a constant companion to her brother, except for her brief periods of travel and visiting with friends.

But this happy existence was shattered when she was stricken by illness in April, 1829. Although she recovered physically, after she had not been expected to live, she no longer had sufficient vitality for the activities she loved: walking, mountain climbing, traveling, and writing her journals. Her mind began to fail, and she became like an excitable young child. She died five years after her brother, passing away at Rydal Mount, where she and her William had lived for more than half a century.

Bibliography

The *Poetry of Dorothy Wordsworth* was edited by H. Eigerman, 1940. Important biographical materials are the *Journals of Dorothy Wordsworth*, edited by Helen Darbishire, 1958, and the *Letters of William and Dorothy Wordsworth*, edited by E. de Selincourt, 6 vols., 1935–1938.

Helpful biographical and critical studies include E. de Selincourt, *Dorothy Wordsworth: A Biography*, 1933; C. M. Maclean, *Dorothy and William Wordsworth*, 1927; *idem.*, *Dorothy Wordsworth: The Early Years*, 1932; Amanda M. Ellis, *Rebels and Conservatives: Dorothy and William Wordsworth and Their Circle*, 1967; and Margaret Willy, *Three Women Diarists: Celia Fiennes, Dorothy Wordsworth, Katherine Mansfield*, 1964.

JOURNALS OF DOROTHY WORDSWORTH

Author: Dorothy Wordsworth (1771–1855)
First published: 1874; 1889; 1897; 1904
Principal works: The Alfoxden Journal, 1798; *et seq; Journal of Visit to Hamburg and of Journey from Hamburg to Goslar,* 1798; *The Grasmere Journal,* 1800–1803; *Recollections of a Tour Made in Scotland,* 1803; *Excursion on the Banks of Ullswater,* 1805; *Excursion up Scawfell Pike,* 1818; *Journal of a Tour on the Continent,* 1820; *Journal of my Second Tour in Scotland,* 1822; *Journal of a Tour in the Isle of Man,* 1828

Essay-Review

The *Journals of Dorothy Wordsworth* offer surprising dividends to the reader who turns to them in search of information about the author's famous brother William, for Dorothy Wordsworth was herself a remarkably sensitive and perceptive observer of man and nature, as well as a gifted prose writer. Her surviving works are of two kinds. She left daily notes about her life at Alfoxden and Grasmere, where she lived with her brother between 1798 and 1803, and about holiday excursions in the Lake Country, Germany, and on the Isle of Man. Working from notes taken on two other trips, she composed long accounts of her tour of Scotland with Wordsworth and Coleridge in 1803 and of her travels on the Continent with her brother, his wife, and several friends in 1820. These journals were written simply for the entertainment of friends, but Dorothy's smooth narrative style and her gift for conveying local color make her pages worthy of comparison with Johnson's and Boswell's more famous accounts of their trip to the western isles of Scotland.

The journals of the years at Alfoxden and Grasmere inevitably have the greatest interest for the modern reader, for they reveal most clearly Dorothy's own personality and her relationship to her poet brother during the years in which he produced many of his finest works. Her description of her life during this period gives a vivid impression of her as a modest, self-effacing woman who dedicated herself to caring for her family and friends. The dominant force in her life was her passionate affection for William; at times she speaks of him in terms more applicable to a lover than to a brother. She kept house for him until his marriage to Mary Hutchinson, and she remained a beloved member of their household, helping rear several nieces and nephews and caring for the many friends who paid extended visits, among them Thomas De Quincey, Sir Walter Scott, and William Hazlitt.

Dorothy had boundless faith in William Wordsworth's genius, and she took upon herself the task of removing all the inconveniences, distractions, and practical matters that were obstacles in the way of his writing. She spent many evenings copying the poetry he had composed on his daily walks, and she indicates that she sometimes suggested improvements. Comments like these appear on almost every page of her journals: "William composing in the wood in the morning," or, "William worked all the morning at the sheepfold, but in vain," or, "William was afterwards only partly successful in composition."

Her concern for her brother's health and poetic powers was extended to his friend and colleague, Samuel Taylor Coleridge, who was an almost constant visitor at Alfoxden and Grasmere. Dorothy and William watched with great distress Coleridge's increasing lassitude, his dependence on opium and alcohol, his despair over his uncongenial marriage that sapped his creativity. Among the saddest of Dorothy's comments are her resigned statements about his work; more than once she notes, "Coleridge had done nothing for the Lyrical Ballads."

Dorothy's aid to William did not end with cooking and copying. She had a fine mind, kept alert by wide reading; she mentions at various times enjoying Henry Fielding's *Amelia*, Boswell's work, Shakespeare, and the poetry of Edmund Spenser and Ben Jonson. She shared her brother's feeling for the natural world. Often, immediately following a prosaic account of a domestic errand, will come a description of a scene she and William enjoyed on an evening walk: "A deep stillness in the thickest part of the wood, undisturbed except by the occasional dropping of the snow from the holly boughs." On another occasion she tells how they first observed the crescent moon, a silvery line, a thready bow, attended by Jupiter and Venus in their palest hues."

Dorothy shared in the early nineteenth century preoccupation with the picturesque; her evaluations of landscapes are reminiscent of the scene in Jane Austen's *Northanger Abbey* in which Henry Tilney instructs young Catherine Morland in the proper way to look at nature: "Catherine was so hopeful a scholar, that when they gained the top of Beechen Cliff, she voluntarily rejected the whole city of Bath, as unworthy to make part of a landscape." Dorothy brands a view from the top of a Lake Country hillside "mildy interesting," and commenting on a seascape she says that "had there been a vessel sailing upon it, a perfect image of delight." Touring the Alps in 1820, she was constantly in search of the sublime or the majestic scene.

Typical, too, of the Romantic frame of mind was her love for the wilder aspects of nature; she disapproved thoroughly of the "improvements" made by eighteenth century landowners who took pride in their formal gardens. She wrote after a visit to an estate near Alfoxden: "Quaint waterfalls about which nature was very successfullly striving to make beautiful what art had deformed—ruins, hermitages, etc., etc. In spite of all these things, the dell romantic and beautiful, though everywhere planted with unnaturalized trees. Happily we cannot shape the huge hills or carve out the valleys according to our fancy."

The human scene was as fascinating to Dorothy Wordsworth as the natural world. Her travel journals are filled with accounts of the individuals she met and the places where she stayed; she leaves the reader with an indelible impression of the odors and dirt of more than one inn, and she gives unforgettable descriptions of characters like the small Scottish boy who took Wordsworth to the Falls of Clyde and hid himself like a statue in a niche in the cave there. She had a housewifely interest in family customs, furnishings, and food that make her observations valuable evidence about the lives of the Scottish highlanders.

Typical is her description of the house where she waited to take a ferry across Loch Lomond; there two young girls chattered in Erse as they tried to choose a dress to lend the rain-soaked traveler; two boys played on the floor; an old woman sang doleful Gaelic songs to a fretful baby, with "all our clothes to be dried, dinner prepared and set out for us four strangers, and a second cooking for the family." The setting more than compensated for the poverty and confusion of the place; "the peep out of the open doorplace across the lake made some amends for the want of the long roof and elegant rafters of our boatman's cottage, and all the while the waterfall, which we could not see, was roaring at the end of the hut, which seemed to serve as a sounding board for its noise."

Dorothy's notes on life on the Continent are equally vivid. From her window in Cologne she watched passengers leave a ferry boat: "Peasants, male and female, sheep, and calves—The women hurrying away, with their cargoes of fruit and vegetables, as if eager to be beforehand with the market. . . . Two young ladies trip forward, their dark hair *basketed* round the crown of the head, green bags on their arms—two gentlemen of their party—next a lady with smooth black hair stretched upward from the forehead and a skull cap at the top like a small dish. The gentry passengers seem to arrange themselves on one side, the peasants on the other:—how much more picturesque the peasants!"

Dorothy had her brother's eye for the striking individual, the man or woman who stood apart from the rest of humanity by strength of character. Like William, she was drawn to the peddlers and beggars who passed by their home. She gives in the Grasmere Journal a brief sketch of the old leech gatherer immortalized in Wordsworth's "Resolution and Independence": "When William and I returned from accompanying Jones, we met an old man almost double. He had on a coat, thrown over his shoulders, above his waistcoat and coat. Under this he carried a bundle, and had an apron on and a night-cap. His face was interesting. He had dark eyes and a long nose. John, who afterwards met him at Wytheburn, took him for a Jew. He was of Scotch parents, but had been born in the army. He had had a wife, and 'a good woman, and it pleased God to bless us with ten children'. All these were dead but one, of whom he had not heard for many years, a sailor. His trade was to gather leeches, but now leeches are scarce, and he had not strength for it. He lives by begging, and was making his way to Carlisle, where he should buy a few godly books to sell."

Miss Wordsworth made no pretense of being a literary light in her day; none of her writing was meant for publication, and this fact is, in itself, a part of its charm. The journals invite the reader to share in the author's experiences and her feelings, to look at the scenes she found beautiful or sordid, to share in her fascination with all kinds of men and women, rich and poor, young and old. Dorothy

Wordsworth will never rank as a major literary figure, but she is, in the pages of her diaries, a delightful companion.

WILLIAM WORDSWORTH

Born: Cockermouth, England (April 7, 1770)
Died: Rydal Mount, England (April 23, 1850)

Principal Works

POEMS: *Lyrical Ballads*, 1798 (with Coleridge); *Lyrical Ballads*, enlarged, with Preface, 1800; *Poems in Two Volumes*, 1807; *The Excursion*, 1814; *The White Doe of Rylstone*, 1815; *Peter Bell and the Waggoner*, 1819; *The River Duddon*, 1820; *Ecclesiastical Sketches*, 1822; *Memorials of a Tour on the Continent*, 1822; *Yarrow Revisited and Other Poems*, 1835; *Sonnets*, 1838; *Poems, Chiefly of Early and Late Years*, 1842; *Collected Poems*, 1849–1850; *The Prelude*, 1850.

To compare Wordsworth with other great English poets has long been a parlor game for critics. Matthew Arnold places him below only Shakespeare and Milton; others, ranging less widely, are content to call him the greatest of the Romantics. Incontestably, however, he stands supreme among English nature poets; and the stamp of his influence so strongly marks the short, glorious period of nineteenth century Romanticism that perhaps those can be forgiven who have gone so far as to call it the Age of Wordsworth.

The second son of a lower middle-class family, William Wordsworth was born April 7, 1770, at Cockermouth in the Lake District of Cumberland. When he was eight, his mother died; the loss of his father, five years later, made him dependent upon his uncles for an education. School at Hawkshead was followed by matriculation at Cambridge, where he entered St. John's College in 1787. His career there was interrupted in 1790 by a summer tour of Switzerland, France, and Italy; and in 1791, after receiving his degree, he returned to France, ostensibly to learn the language.

Much besides language, however, quickly absorbed Wordsworth's attention. The years 1791–1792 found Wordsworth developing two passions, one for Annette Vallon and the other for the French Revolution. Both were probably sincere, while they lasted; but both were soon to suffer from a change of heart. His daughter Anne Caroline was born to Annette Vallon while Wordsworth was still in France; for reasons which have never become clear, he acknowledged the child without marrying the mother. Wordsworth's other passion, the Revolution, stirred him deeply and left an indelible impression. His enthusiasm waned chiefly because of its growing excesses and because of the accession of Napoleon. Even so, the philosophy he acquired from Michel Beaupuy and his fellow revolutionists was an important factor in making Wordsworth the great poetic spokesman for that element as yet relatively voiceless—the common man.

Back in England, Wordsworth briefly found congeniality in the circle of young freethinkers surrounding William Godwin. Godwin, future father-in-law of Percy

Shelley, was a radical philosopher and the author of *Political Justice*. Like Wordsworth himself, he was an ardent disciple of Rousseau, a fact which helps to explain his temporary hold on the young man's attention. In 1795, however, a fortunate legacy enabled Wordsworth to settle at Racedown with his devoted and talented sister Dorothy. Here occurred a brush with fate which was to change the lives of two men. In meeting Samuel Taylor Coleridge, Wordsworth formed the most significant connection of his career. Mutual intellectual stimulation and constant companionship were its immediate dividends; and when, in 1797, Coleridge moved into Somersetshire, the Wordsworths followed. The next year the two men published jointly that little volume which would eventually come into its own as one of the most magnificent milestones of English literature.

Nevertheless, the initial reception of the 1798 edition of *Lyrical Ballads* gave no clue to the status it would achieve in the future. Most of its contents came from the industrious Wordsworth, including the sublime nature poem, "Tintern Abbey," and a group of shorter, balladlike compositions in which the author undertook to preach the kindness of Nature and exalt familiar reality. Coleridge, on the other hand, attempted the project of making supernatural subjects seem real, a project carried to superb completion in his single contribution, *The Ancient Mariner*.

Laughed at by some critics and ignored by others, *Lyrical Ballads* survived its reception sufficiently well to justify a second printing in 1800. Though this edition contained some interesting new poems, its most significant feature was Wordsworth's long Preface, which amounted to a literary declaration of independence and broke completely with neo-classical theory. The main points of this credo reflected strongly the continuing influence of Rousseau and stated formally the ideals of sincerity, democracy, nature worship, and simple, natural diction to which Wordsworth and Coleridge had vowed allegiance.

With *Lyrical Ballads* as its starting point, most of Wordsworth's great poetry was compressed into the quarter century between 1798 and 1823. Many of his celebrated short poems, such as "I Wandered Lonely as a Cloud" and "The Solitary Reaper," illustrate beautiful effects and essential truths achieved through the Wordsworthian simplicity of vocabulary advocated in his famous Preface. Still, he could successfully depart from his principles when he felt the need. That he could employ more elevated diction with telling effect finds ample illustration in his excellent sonnets, as well as in such longer poems as "Tintern Abbey" and *The Prelude*. The content of his work conveys feelings of humanitarianism, liberalism, and—finally and most distinctively—a thoroughly pantheistic worship of nature. Biographical interest combined with distinguished poetry are found in *The Prelude* and, to a lesser extent, in "The Excursion"; both of these were written as parts of a longer autobiographical work, *The Recluse*, which was never completed.

If Wordsworth's work could scale the heights, it could also make inexplicable plunges into utter sterility; hardly another major poet can be named who is capable of such extremes in his published poetry. Completely devoid of a sense of humor, his tendency to complacency led him into such demonstrations of bathos and infelicity as "Andrew Jones" and "The Idiot Boy." His detractors, Byron notable among them, seized on these lapses with unholy glee; and the failure of Wordsworth's critical faculty in such instances is difficult to explain.

His failures in human relationships were sometimes equally conspicuous. The friendship with Coleridge, which had had such an auspicious beginning, tapered off during the years which followed *Lyrical Ballads*. In 1803, a misunderstanding arose during a tour of Scotland, leading to a breach between the two men which was never fully mended.

In 1802 Wordsworth married his childhood friend, Mary Hutchinson, the inspiration for "She Was a Phantom of Delight." As he grew older, Wordsworth became more and more conservative in matters of religion and politics. From the government which had once been the object of his youthful censure he now received employment, being appointed, in 1813, Distributor of Stamps in Westmorland County. In 1843, long after the passing of his really creative period, he was appointed Poet Laureate, succeeding Robert Southey. He died at Rydal Mount on April 23, 1850, and was buried in Grasmere churchyard. A monument to him was erected in Westminster Abbey.

Bibliography

The definitive edition, excluding *The Prelude*, is *The Poetical Works of William Wordsworth*, edited by Ernest de Selincourt and Helen Darbishire, 5 vols., 1940–1949. The variorum edition of *The Prelude* was edited by Ernest de Selincourt, 1926, 1932. Editions of the letters include *Letters of the Wordsworth Family*, edited by William Knight, 3 vols., 1907; H. C. Robinson, *Correspondence with the Wordsworth Circle, 1808–1866*, 1927; and Ernest de Selincourt, *The Early Letters of William and Dorothy Wordsworth, 1780–1805*, 1937, and *Letters of William and Dorothy Wordsworth: The Middle Years*, 2 vols., 1937. This editor also prepared the *Journals of Dorothy Wordsworth*, 2 vols., 1941.

The standard biography is George McLean Harper, *William Wordsworth, His Life, Works, and Influence*, 2 vols., 1916. See also Emile Legouis, *The Early Years of William Wordsworth, 1770–1798*, 1897; Edith Batho, *The Later Wordsworth*, 1933; G. W. Meyer, *Wordsworth's Formative Years*, University Publications in Language and Literature, XX (1943); and Mary Moorman, *William Wordsworth: A Biography*, Vol. I, *The Early Years*, 1957, Vol. II, *The Later Years*, 1965. For criticism see Samuel Taylor Coleridge, *Biographia Literaria*, 1817; Matthew Arnold, *Essays in Criticism: Second Series*, 1888; Alfred North Whitehead, *Science and the Modern World*, 1925; Earl Leslie Griggs, ed., *Wordsworth and Coleridge: Studies in Honor of George McLean Harper*, 1939; R. D. Havens, *The Mind of a Poet*, 1941; Helen Darbishire, *The Poet Wordsworth*, 1950; Gilbert T. Dunklin, ed., *Wordsworth: Centenary Studies Presented at Cornell and Princeton Universities*, 1951; David Ferry, *The Limits of Mortality: An Essay on Wordsworth's Major Poems*, 1959; and G. H. Hartman, *Wordsworth's Poetry, 1787–1814*, 1965.

THE POETRY OF WORDSWORTH

Author: William Wordsworth (1770–1850)
Principal published works: An Evening Walk and Descriptive Sketches, 1793; *Lyrical Ballads*, 1798, 1800; *Poems in Two Volumes*, 1807; *The Excursion*, 1814; *Poems and The White Doe of Rylstone*, 1815; *Peter Bell and The Waggoner*, 1819; *The River Duddon*, 1820; *Ecclesiastical Sketches*, 1822; *Yarrow Revisited, and Other Poems*, 1835; *Poems Chiefly of Early and Late Years*, 1842; *The Prelude*, 1850

Essay-Review

The most original genius of his age, William Wordsworth attacked the poetic diction and mannerisms fashionable in the mediocre poetry of the late eighteenth century, but his earliest poetry abounds in the personifications, hackneyed expressions, and apostrophes that he came to dislike most. His earliest poems, contained in *An Evening Walk* and *Descriptive Sketches*, reveal the careful observation of nature that he excelled in during his most productive and most creative years between 1797 and 1807. He lacked only the discipline and the vision that came to him after he discarded Godwinism and the revolutionary fervor of his youth.

In 1797 he met Samuel Taylor Coleridge, the strongest influence on his maturing style and philosophy, and entered the period of his greatest work. Through Coleridge he discovered the associational psychology of David Hartley and discarded William Godwin's rationalism. As a result of his new interest in psychology, he chose peasants, children, and mental defectives as subjects for his poetry. This choice marked a break with the decadent neoclassicism of his minor contemporaries. Many of the poems in *Lyrical Ballads*, written in conjunction with Coleridge, thus dealt with subjects from common life in order to reveal the unsophisticated operations of the human mind. For this publication Coleridge was to have written poems in the manner of "The Ancient Mariner," in which the supernatural was made believable, while Wordsworth agreed to write on basic human emotions directly and sincerely expressed in ordinary life. The volume was dominated by Wordsworth, however, and when the public encountered such poems as "We Are Seven," "The Idiot Boy," and "The Thorn," it was shocked. The reviewers were simply unable to accept such passages as the opening lines of "The Thorn":

> There is a Thorn—it looks so old,
> In truth, you'd find it hard to say
> How it could ever have been young,
> It looks so old and grey.

But much more important in *Lyrical Ballads* was Wordsworth's famous group of poems on nature, the first truly "Wordsworthian" poems. Everywhere in nature he found harmony and an active force that he identified with God. He felt no separation between Man and nature, all things joining in harmony. In "Tintern Abbey," for example, he gave full and lasting expression to the Romantic concept of nature as divinity:

> ... I have learned
> To look on nature, not as in the hour
> Of thoughtless youth; but hearing oftentimes
> The still, sad music of humanity,
> Nor harsh nor grating, though of ample power
> To chasten and subdue. And I have felt
> A presence that disturbs me with the joy
> Of elevated thoughts. ...

Nature was to him alive, powerful, and healthy; it was the panacea for man's mechanical urban life. Only the man who turned to nature, who felt the joy of nature, could find health in escape from the stagnation of contemporary life.

During the bitterly cold winter of 1798–1799, Wordsworth and his sister were isolated in Goslar, Germany, without books and friends. There he discovered a new type of poetry. Because of his circumstances, he fell back on his inner resources; he fed his imagination upon recollections of England until he was seized by emotions similar to those he had felt years before when the experience was immediate. These newly created emotions seemed to him to overflow, and from this artificially induced emotional experience he created poetry. He described this discovery in the Preface to the second edition of *Lyrical Ballads*, where he wrote that "poetry is the spontaneous overflow of powerful feelings: it takes its origin from emotion recollected in tranquillity: the emotion is contemplated till, by a species of reaction, the tranquillity gradually disappears, and an emotion, kindred to that which was before the subject of contemplation, is gradually produced, and does itself actually exist in the mind. In this mood successful composition generally begins, and in a mood similar to this it is carried on. ..." In such a mood he composed many of his finest poems; for example, "There Was a Boy," "Lucy Grey," "I Wandered Lonely as a Cloud," and "My Heart Leaps Up."

The famous Preface in which he described his newly derived theory of poetry was meant to be an answer to the critical opposition to the first edition of *Lyrical Ballads*, but it was much more. Here Wordsworth stated the doctrines upon which he built his greatest (and his worst) poetry. Negatively, he wanted to end "the deluge of idle and extravagant stories in verse." Positively, he attempted to choose incidents and situations from common life, to relate them in simple language, to give poetry a worthy purpose, and to emphasize genuine feeling. Although Coleridge (a little piqued because Wordsworth attributed these doctrines to him) unmercifully attacked these doctrines in *Biographia Literaria* in 1817, they were essentially sound and readily acceptable to the English public. Much of Wordsworth's poetry, like "Michael" and "Lines Written in Early Spring," is grounded in these doctrines and gave them additional popularity. But these doctrines, when followed too mechanically, led to dullness and flatness, the two faults most often found in Wordsworth's poetry.

The year 1802 was a landmark in Wordsworth's career. Momentous events both in his personal life (a trip to France to see his illegitimate daughter) and in European politics (Napoleon's absolute rule in France and the beginning of the Napoleonic War) widened his creative horizons. Also, his discovery of Milton's sonnets inspired him, and he began to compose in a more majestic and musical style. His visit to Calais to visit Annette Vallon and his daughter made him intimately aware of the dangers of Napoleon's tyranny, and with renewed faith in the causes of liberty he began a series of sonnets. He now believed that Nature worked through man in an unending struggle for freedom. Several of these sonnets—"London, 1802," "The World Is Too Much With Us," "To Toussaint L'Ouverture," "It Is a Beauteous Evening Calm and Free"—are among his most famous poems. His plea to return to moral virtue and to establish ordered liberty is nowhere better expressed than in these lines from "London, 1802":

> We are selfish men;
> Oh! raise us up, return to us again;
> And give us manners, virtue, freedom, power.

These sonnets established Wordsworth as the pre-eminent poet of English patriotism.

In the spring of 1802, Wordsworth began to fear that his imaginative vision might be failing. Because to him the imagination was the supreme guide to freedom and to morality, his fear led him to re-examine his concept of the role of the human imagination. This he does in the famous, "Ode: Intimations of Immortality as Recollected from Early Childhood." From Plato and the Neo-Platonists he received the notion that the child's dreamlike moments were actually carry overs from a prenatal spiritual existence and that maturation gradually caused the ecstatic vision to fade completely away. But the doctrine of preexistence led him to the pessimistic conclusion that maturity was a time of inevitable grief. He left the poem unfinished until 1804, when he added the last three stanzas. In the addition he reaffirmed the child's loss of vision, but he added that the adult has wisdom, "the philosophic mind," which gives to man "thoughts that do often lie too deep for tears." This resolution, though not the most optimistic, promised some hope to the poet who felt his own powers dwindling. Still, it marked a profound change in his view of nature, as is apparent from his revisions made in *The Prelude* during 1839, for now he placed the joyful contemplation of nature in the past, forever lost to him.

The "Ode to Duty," also written in 1804, clarified his new position. Duty replaced the rapturous visions and freedom of youth to the extent that he thought of the supreme power as moral law, not nature. In his poem Wordsworth accepted the stoic creed of Seneca and Kant according to which peace of mind is self-imposed inner control. The tragic death of his brother in 1805 brought Wordsworth's earlier and later moods into sharp antagonism. In "Elegiac Stanzas" he renounced the visions of his youth and faced the harsh reality of experience, and in "The Happy Warrior" he confirmed his newly adopted stoicism. With these two poems Wordsworth passed into the final phase of his career.

The major work of his decline was *The Excursion*. With the gradual loss of his inspiration, he became more and more conservative, accepted Christian orthodoxy, and developed the tendency to be dogmatic and sententious. He became a sage rather than a poet. These changes were marked by a change in his poetic technique, to the extent that his later poetry not only lacked inspiration but was often dull and unnecessarily heavy. These characteristics are reflected in *The Excursion*. This long poem, second in length only to *The Prelude*, was intended to be the second and middle part of a long work to be called *The Recluse: or Views on Man, on Nature, and on Human Life*, a great philosophical poem which he never finished. Despite the inferiority of the majority of *The Excursion*, there are some admirable flashes such as the moving story of Margaret in Book I, but the poem as a whole is a marked decline from the great poetry of 1797–1807. After this poem Wordsworth wrote little that was truly great, although he continued to demonstrate artistic and metrical virtuosity in the Ecclesiastical Sonnets. But the radical young men who had defended him in his youth had become more conservative adults or, like Coleridge, Shelley, Keats, and Byron, had died years before, and the new generation of young poets thought of him as a "lost leader." He remained popular and was buried in Westminster Abbey when he died, but even when he received the laureateship in 1843, his popularity was primarily based on the poems of his earlier greatness.

The problem that Wordsworth's poetry presents to a modern reader is relatively simple: he wrote too much when he was not inspired and threw too little in the fire. Too often his verse is pedestrian and prosy, even dull. A sense of humor might have saved some of his poetry, but he showed little humor, especially in the poetry after *The Excursion*. Still he presents us with a formidable canon, and few people would deny the greatness of his early poems. His best work has a calm dignity that best expresses itself in the unadorned beauty of a cleanly chiseled line, in such lines as the following stanza from the "Lucy Poems":

> A violet by a mossy stone
> Half hidden from the eye!
> —Fair as a star, when only one
> Is shining in the sky.

His worst work is marred by bathos. His view of nature was stimulating enough to save the young John Stuart Mill from committing suicide and continues to speak to the problems of a mechanical age; his observations on the human mind—though outdated by the development of depth psychology—remain vital and revealing. Matthew Arnold's praise of Wordsworth in his famous reply to

Leslie Stephen's criticism is still the most judicious:

> "To exhibit this body of Wordsworth's best work, to clear away obstructions from around it, and to let it speak for itself, is what every lover of Wordsworth should desire. Until this has been done, Wordsworth . . . has not had a fair chance before the world. When once it has been done, he will make his way best, not by our advocacy of him, but by his own worth and power."

Bibliography

"Lines Composed a Few Miles Above Tintern Abbey"

Battenhouse, Henry Martin. *Poets of Christian Thought: Evaluations from Dante to T.S. Eliot.* New York: Ronald Press, 1947, pp. 73–76.

Benzigner, James. " 'Tintern Abbey' Revisited," in *PMLA.* LXV (March, 1950), pp. 154–162.

Bloom, Harold. *The Visionary Company: A Reading of English Romantic Poetry.* Ithaca, N.Y.: Cornell University Press, 1971, pp. 131–140. Reprinted in *Wordsworth: A Collection of Critical Essays.* Edited by M.H. Abrams. Englewood Cliffs, N.J.: Prentice-Hall, 1972, pp. 95–103.

Clarke, Colin C. *Romantic Paradox: An Essay on the Poetry of Wordsworth.* London: Routledge and Kegan Paul, 1962, pp. 39–53.

Darbishire, Helen. *The Poet Wordsworth.* Oxford: Clarendon Press, 1950, pp. 57–60.

Durrant, Geoffrey. *William Wordsworth.* London: Cambridge University Press, 1969, pp. 34–44.

Empson, William. *Seven Types of Ambiguity.* New York: New Directions, 1947, pp. 151–154.

Ferry, David. *The Limits of Mortality: An Essay on Wordsworth's Major Poems.* Middletown, Conn.: Wesleyan University Press, 1959, pp. 107–110.

Foxell, Nigel. *Ten Poems Analyzed.* Oxford: Pergamon, 1966, pp. 123–142.

Hartman, Geoffrey H. *The Unmediated Vision: An Interpretation of Wordsworth, Hopkins, Rilke, and Valery.* New Haven, Conn.: Yale University Press, 1954, pp. 3–12, 23–26.

Hodgson, John A. "Wordsworth's Dialectical Transcendentalism 1798: 'Tintern Abbey,' " in *Criticism.* XVIII (1976), pp. 367–380.

Jacobus, Mary. *Tradition and Experiment in Wordsworth's Lyrical Ballads.* Oxford: Clarendon Press, 1976, pp. 104–130.

Jones, John. *The Egotistical Sublime: A History of Wordsworth's Imagination.* London: Chatto and Windus, 1954, pp. 92–95.

Maniguis, Robert M. "Comparison, Intensity, and Time in 'Tintern Abbey,'" in *Criticism.* XI (Fall, 1969), pp. 358–382.

Noyes, Russell. *William Wordsworth.* New York, Conn.: Twayne, 1971, pp. 64–68.

Ransom, John Crowe. *The New Criticism.* Norfolk, Conn.: New Directions, 1941, pp. 115–119.

Thompson, William I. "Collapsed Universe and Structured Poem: Essay in Whiteheadian Criticism," in *College English.* XXVIII (October, 1966), pp. 29–32.

Woodring, Carl. *Wordsworth.* Boston: Houghton Mifflin, 1965, pp. 59–64.

Wormhoudt, Arthur. *The Demon Lover: A Psychoanalytical Approach to Literature.* New York: Exposition Press, 1949, pp. 52–55.

Lyrical Ballads

Bannerjee, Srikumar. *Critical Theories and Poetic Practice in the* Lyrical Ballads. London: Williams and Norgate, 1931.

Darbishire, Helen. *The Poet Wordsworth.* Oxford: Clarendon Press, 1950, pp. 35–74.

Davie, Donald. "Dionysus in *Lyrical Ballads,*" in *Wordsworth's Mind and Art.* Edited by A.W. Thompson. New York: Barnes and Noble, 1970, pp. 110–139.

Jacobus, Mary. *Tradition and Experiment in Wordsworth's* Lyrical Ballads. Oxford: Clarendon Press, 1976.

Jones, Alun R. "The Compassionate World: Some Observations on Wordsworth's *Lyrical Ballads* of 1798," in *English.* XIX (1970), pp. 7–12. Reprinted in *Wordsworth:* Lyrical Ballads, *A Casebook.* Edited by Alun R. Jones and William Tydeman. London: Macmillan, 1972.

Jordan, John E. *Why the* Lyrical Ballads? *The Background, Writing, and Characteristics of Wordsworth's 1798* Lyrical Ballads. Berkeley: University of California Press, 1976.

Kreiger, Murray. *The Classic Vision: The Retreat from Extremity in Modern Literature.* Baltimore: Johns Hopkins Press, 1971, pp. 149–195.

Mayo, Robert. "The Contemporaneity of the *Lyrical Ballads,*" in *PMLA.* LXIX (1954), pp. 486–522. Reprinted in *Wordsworth: A Collection of Critical Essays.* Edited by M.H. Abrams. Englewood Cliffs, N.J.: Prentice-Hall, 1972, pp. 67–74.

Murry, Roger N. *Wordsworth's Style: Figures and Themes in* Lyrical Ballads *of 1800.* Lincoln: University of Nebraska Press, 1967.

Noyes, Russell. *William Wordsworth.* New York: Twayne, 1971, pp. 43–92.

Parrish, Stephen Maxfield. *The Art of the* Lyrical Ballads. Cambridge, Mass.: Harvard University Press, 1973.

Sheats, Paul D. "The *Lyrical Ballads*," in *The Making of Wordsworth's Poetry, 1785–1798.* Cambridge, Mass.: Harvard University Press, 1973, pp. 187–204. Reprinted in *English Romantic Poets: Modern Essays in Criticism.* Edited by M.H. Abrams. New York: Oxford University Press, 1975, pp. 133–148.

Woodring, Carl. *Wordsworth.* Boston: Houghton Mifflin, 1965, pp. 20–53.

"Ode: Intimations of Immortality"

Bateson, F.W. *English Poetry: A Critical Introduction.* London: Longmans, Green, 1950, pp. 196–205.

Bloom, Harold. *The Visionary Company: A Reading of English Romantic Poetry.* Ithaca, N.Y.: Cornell University Press, 1971, pp. 170–177.

Bowra, C.M. *The Romantic Imagination.* Cambridge, Mass.: Harvard University Press, 1949, pp. 76–102.

Brooks, Cleanth. "The Intimations of the 'Ode,' " in *Kenyon Review.* VIII (Winter, 1946), pp. 80–102.

————. *The Well Wrought Urn.* New York: Reynal and Hitchcock, 1947, pp. 114–138, 163–165.

Brooks, Cleanth and Robert Penn Warren. *Understanding Poetry.* New York: Holt, 1950, pp. 639–645.

Darbishire, Helen. *The Poet Wordsworth.* Oxford: Clarendon Press, 1950, pp. 64–74.

Durrant, Geoffrey. *William Wordsworth.* London: Cambridge University Press, 1969, pp. 99–112.

Ferry, David. *The Limits of Mortality: An Essay on Wordsworth's Major Poems.* Middletown, Conn.: Wesleyan University Press, 1959, pp. 46–50.

Hartman, Geoffrey H. *The Unmediated Vision: An Interpretation of Wordsworth, Hopkins, Rilke, and Valery.* New Haven, Conn.: Yale University Press, 1954, pp. 40–44.

King, Alec. *Wordsworth and the Artist's Vision: An Essay in Interpretation.* London: Athlone Press, 1966, pp. 104–117.

Knight, G. Wilson. *The Starlit Dome: Studies in the Poetry of Vision.* London: Oxford University Press, 1941, pp. 37–49.

Matthison, J.K. "Wordsworth's 'Ode,' " in *Studies in Philology.* XLVI (July, 1949), pp. 419–439.

Noyes, Russell. *William Wordsworth.* New York: Twayne, 1971, pp. 141–147.

Ransom, John Crowe. "William Wordsworth: Notes Toward an Understanding of Poetry," in *Kenyon Review.* XII (Summer, 1950), pp. 514–518.

Raysor, Thomas M. "The Themes of Immortality and Natural Piety in Wordsworth's Immortality 'Ode,'" in *PMLA.* (September, 1954), pp. 861–875.

Salvesen, Christopher. *The Landscape of Memory: A Study of Wordsworth's Poetry.* Lincoln: University of Nebraska Press, 1965, pp. 109–120, 122–127.

Schneider, Robert L. "Failure of Solitude: Wordsworth's Immortality 'Ode,'" in *Journal of English and Germanic Philology.* LIV (October, 1955), pp. 625–633.

Stauffer, D.A. "Cooperative Criticism," in *Kenyon Review.* IV (Winter, 1942), pp. 133–144.

Trilling, Lionel. *The Liberal Imagination.* New York: Viking Press, 1942, pp. 129–153. Reprinted in *Discussions of William Wordsworth.* Edited by Jack Davis. Boston: Heath, 1964, pp. 142–159.

Woodring, Carl. *Wordsworth.* Boston: Houghton Mifflin, 1965, pp. 89–94.

Wormhoudt, Arthur. *The Demon Lover: A Psychoanalytical Approach to Literature.* New York: Exposition Press, 1949, pp. 58–62.

THE PRELUDE

Type of work: Poem
Author: William Wordsworth (1770–1850)
First published: 1850

Essay-Review

Planned as the introductory portion of a long autobiographical and philosophi-cal poem that was never finished, *The Prelude, or, Growth of a Poet's Mind*, was not published until shortly after Wordsworth's death in 1850. The projected long poem, *The Recluse*, was to present a comprehensive development of the poet's views on man, society, and nature, but of the projected three parts, only the sec-ond, *The Excursion* (1814) was ever completed and published.

The Prelude was to provide the autobiographical introduction to *The Recluse*, tracing the development of the poet and his mind to the point where he was ready to formulate his beliefs and philosophy. Written between 1799 and 1805 and ad-dressed to Coleridge as the important "Friend," the poem is a long and ambitious work, an attempt in blank verse to trace the history and development of the poet's feelings, ideas, and convictions.

Since Wordsworth so strongly advocated the use of poetry for individual emo-tions and insights, it is appropriate that we should have such a thorough descrip-tion of the development of his mind. In addition, *The Prelude* contains some fine passages that illustrate the clarity and force of Wordsworth's use of language to convey both a precise description and a sense of the meaning of nature. Although the poem suffers from long prosaic stretches, it also contains much of the sense of the calm beauty and power of nature which distinguishes Wordsworth's verse.

The poem begins with an account of the poet's childhood in the English Lake Country, and Wordsworth, with many digressions addressed to nature and its power, wisdom, and infusing spirit, tells of the influence of nature on his solitary childhood. Some of the sense of awe and pleasure that he found in nature, as well as some of his clearest and most penetrating use of diction, is evident in the fol-lowing passage. Young Wordsworth has found a boat in a cave, unchained the boat, and rowed out into the center of a lake. He continues:

> . . . lustily
> I dipped my oars into the silent lake,
> And, as I rose upon the stroke, my boat
> Went heaving through the water like a swan;
> When, from behind that craggy steep till then
> The horizon's bound, a huge peak, black and huge,
> As if with voluntary power instinct
> Upreared its head. I struck and struck again,
> And growing still in stature the grim shape
> Towered up between me and the stars, and still,

> For so it seemed, with purpose of its own
> And measured motion like a living thing,
> Strode after me.

The image of the peak is invested with such simplicity and power that it is transformed into a kind of force holding terror and beauty for the guilty boy who has stolen a ride in a boat.

In describing his early years, the poet speaks of his youthful love of freedom and liberty. He found this sense of freedom in his rambles through the woods and on mountain paths where he did not feel fettered by the claims of society and school work. But, he reassures the reader, he was docile and obedient externally, keeping his rebellion and sense of freedom as a matter of the spirit. This mixture of the calm and docile exterior with the independent and rebellious interior seems part of the origin of Wordsworth's ability to control highly individualistic thought in calm, dignified, unostentatious verse forms and diction. It is not that, in *The Prelude*, Wordsworth uses the speech of common man. His speech is often abstract, speculative, pervaded with a sense of the mystery and meaning of nature. Rather, Wordsworth's diction, at its best, has a dignity and calm control, a lack of pretense, through which the force of his inner meaning gently radiates.

Wordsworth continues his journey through Cambridge, telling of experiences there, discussing the fact that he neither was nor cared to be a scholar. He still, despite his studies, concentrates inwardly on the spirit of things, the power of nature and the impetus nature gives to his feelings. At this point, Wordsworth begins to speculate on the differences between reason and emotion or passion, to equate the reason with the scholars and the emotion with his own apprehension of the world of nature:

> But all the meditations of mankind,
> Yea, all the adamantine holds of truth
> By reason built, or passion, which itself
> Is highest reason in a soul sublime.

Throughout the poem, Wordsworth makes the distinction between reason and passion, attributing an ultimate sterility to the quality of reason, while glorifying the element of passion or imagination.

Wordsworth tells next of his journey to the Alps after leaving Cambridge. The mountains there reminded him of the mountains familiar in his childhood, and he felt again, even more keenly, the majesty and awe of the scenery reflected in his spirit. He begins, more strongly, to feel his kinship with nature. In perhaps the dullest section of the poem, he describes his life among the crowds and industries of London, along with his tours of the historical monuments, after his return from Europe. Dissatisfied with life in London, he then went to France during the early stages of the French Revolution. In this section he expresses his feeling that he had not cared for man sufficiently, that, in his devotion to nature, he has neglected his feeling for his fellow creatures. Recalling his early love for freedom and liberty and adding his new conviction of the importance of political liberty for man, Wordsworth became strongly attracted to the cause of the French Revolution, feeling, as he said in *The Prelude*, that he was tied emotionally and spiritually to the popular struggle against the monarchy. But the bloodiness of the revolution, popular ingratitude and popular refusal to acknowledge the heroes who championed its cause with greatest fervor and sincerity, soon disillusioned Wordsworth. Beginning to feel that blood had poisoned the cause of liberty, he returned to England.

Wordsworth relates how, disillusioned and alone, he sought to bring meaning back into his life. The penultimate section of *The Prelude* is titled "Imagination and Taste, How Impaired and Restored." At that period of his life he turned back to nature, finding there not solace alone but a sense of law and order that was lacking in man. He began to realize the difference in scale between nature and man, the range and effect of nature in comparison to the tiny ineffectuality of man. His sections of resolution frequently include passages like the following interpolation in the midst of a narrative section:

> O Soul of Nature! that, by laws divine
> Sustained and governed, still dost overflow
> With an impassioned life, what feeble ones
> Walk on this earth!

In his view, nature provides not only awe and spiritual impetus for man, but also order, rules of conduct, and the means of man's molding his behavior on this planet. In the final sections of the poem, Wordsworth uses nature as the authority for his new morality and assumes a much more overtly moral tone. He didactically advocates the importance of faith, of obedience, of not relying on man's unaided reason in human affairs. What was, in the earlier sections, the praise of emotion and freedom in opposition to rational restraint becomes the praise of the restraint of faith and spirit in opposition to rational license. This change is illustrative of the change in Wordsworth's whole career from the poet advocating the simple joy and freedom of nature to the sage defending abstract and conventional truths. His attitude is demonstrated in the following passage from the conclusion of the poem:

> ... but, the dawn beginning now
> To re appear, 'twas proved that not in vain
> I had been taught to reverence a Power
> That is the visible quality and shape
> And image of right reason; that matures
> Her processes by steadfast laws; gives birth
> To no impatient or fallacious hopes,
> No heat of passion or excessive zeal,
> No vain conceits; provokes to no quick turns

Of self-applauding intellect; but trains
To meekness, and exalts by humble faith

As *The Prelude* shows Wordsworth's changing attitudes toward nature and man, both relating and illustrating the changes and development in his mind, so the poem also shows the different characteristics of Wordsworth's diction and poetic power. No other single poem has so much of his clear reverence for nature expressed with greater power and simplicity, along with so much of his moralizing expressed with repetitive flatness. *The Prelude* is truly an autobiographical poem, a monument to the career, the changing ideas, and the changing use of poetry of and by William Wordsworth.

Bibliography

Battenhouse, Henry Martin. *Poets of Christian Thought: Evaluations from Dante to T.S. Eliot.* New York: Ronald Press, 1947, pp. 70–73.

Bloom, Harold. *The Visionary Company: A Reading of English Romantic Poetry.* Ithaca, N.Y.: Cornell University Press, 1971, pp. 140–163.

Bostetter, Edward E. *The Romantic Ventriloquists: Wordsworth, Coleridge, Keats, Shelley, Byron.* Seattle: University of Washington Press, 1975, pp. 14–30, 41–52.

Burton, Mary E. *The One Wordsworth.* Chapel Hill: University of North Carolina Press, 1942.

Christensen, Francis. "Intellectual Love: The Second Theme of *The Prelude,*" in *PMLA.* LXXX (March, 1965), pp. 69–75.

Cooke, Michael G. *The Romantic Will.* New Haven, Conn.: Yale University Press, 1976, pp. 84–118.

Darbishire, Helen. *The Poet Wordsworth.* Oxford: Clarendon Press, 1950, pp. 75–143.

Durrant, Geoffrey. *William Wordsworth.* London: Cambridge University Press, 1969, pp. 113–148.

Dyson, Anthony E. and Julian Lovelock. *Masterful Images: English Poetry from Metaphysicals to Romantics.* New York: Barnes & Noble, 1976, pp. 137–174.

Everett, Barbara. *"The Prelude,"* in *Critical Quarterly.* I (Winter, 1959), pp. 338–350.

Ferry, David. *The Limits of Mortality: An Essay on Wordsworth's Major Poems.* Middletown, Conn.: Wesleyan University Press, 1959, pp. 112–171.

Havens, Raymond D. *The Mind of a Poet: A Study of Wordsworth's Thought with Particular Reference to* The Prelude. Baltimore: Johns Hopkins University Press, 1941.

Horsman, E.A. "The Design of Wordsworth's *Prelude*," in *Wordsworth's Mind and Art.* Edited by A.W. Thompson. New York: Barnes & Noble, 1970, pp. 95–109.

Lindenberger, Herbert. *On Wordsworth's* Prelude. Princeton, N.J.: Princeton University Press, 1963.

Noyes, Russell. *William Wordsworth.* New York: Twayne, 1971, pp. 93–124.

Onorato, Richard. *The Character of the Poet: Wordsworth in* The Prelude. Princeton, N.J.: Princeton University Press, 1971.

Potts, Abbie Findlay. *Wordsworth's* Prelude: *A Study of Its Literary Form.* Ithaca, N.Y.: Cornell University Press, 1953.

Ruotolo, Lucio P. "Three *Prelude* Events: The Growth of a Poet's Faith," in *College English.* XXVI (April, 1965), pp. 546–549.

Woodring, Carl. *Wordsworth.* Boston: Houghton Mifflin, 1965, pp. 96–132.

THE VICTORIAN PERIOD

Literary Forms

Criticism: Aesthetic, Literary, Historical, Social: Arnold's *Culture and Anarchy*; Carlyle's *Sartor Resartus*; Pater's *The Renaissance*; Ruskin's *Modern Painters*

Drama: (Verse Tragedy): Swinburne's *Atalanta in Calydon*

Dramatic Monologue: Browning's "My Last Duchess," "The Bishop Orders His Tomb at Saint Praxed's Church; Tennyson's "Ulysses"

Lyric Poetry: by Arnold, Browning, Fitzgerald, Meredith, C. Rossetti, D. G. Rossetti, Swinburne, Tennyson

Elegy: Arnold's "Thyrsis"; Tennyson's *In Memoriam A. H. H.*

Humorous and Nonsense Verse: by Carroll, Lear

Reflective and Philosophical Verse: Arnold's "Stanzas from the Grande Chartreuse," "Memorial Verses"; Clough's "Dipsychus"

Sonnets: E. B. Browning's *Sonnets from the Portuguese*; Meredith's *Modern Love*; Rossetti's *The House of Life*

Narrative Poetry: Morris' "The Haystack in the Floods"; Tennyson's *Idylls of the King*; Thompson's "The Hound of Heaven"

Polemical Prose: Huxley's *Science and Culture*; Mill's *On Liberty*; Newman's *The Idea of a University*

Novel: Dickens' *Great Expectations*; Eliot's *Middlemarch*; Hardy's *The Return of the Native*; Thackeray's *Vanity Fair*; Trollope's *Barchester Towers*

Thematic Characteristics

Reaction against the Romantic glorification of the hero, sensitively ego-centered, as rebel against authority, with emphasis instead upon responsible social reform, the advancement of culture and morality (see Asa Briggs, *The Age of Improvement*, 1962)

Complex, often contrasting social concerns, ranging from a basically liberal, humanitarian interest in improving the lot of the suffering or disadvantaged masses, to a complacently conservative, self-righteous view of English moral superiority (see Walter E. Houghton's *The Victorian Frame of Mind, 1830–1870*, 1957)

Progress: Contrast between those who optimistically viewed Western civilization as progressing to higher moral levels, with those who rejected the notion of meliorism and social perfectibility; Victorian ideal of earnest, strenuous effort to achieve an important goal (see Jerome Buckley, *The Victorian Temper*, 1951)

Science vs. Religion: Conflict between advocates of the new sciences (especially of the natural and physical sciences) and those who adhered to more traditional norms of religious belief; also conflict between those who continued to value biblical revelation with those who accepted a more liberal interpretation of scriptures based upon "higher" textural criticism of documents and sources (see J. Hillis Miller, *The Disappearance of God: Five Nineteenth-Century Writers*, 1963)

Liberals vs. Conservatives: Conflict between those who championed individual liberty and social justice and those who preferred a static, class-determined society with values centering around propriety and moral conventionality

Grundyism: Prudery, grounded upon the values of sexual "purity"; an essentially middle-class moral code that rejected unconventional (or socially prohibited) sexuality as depraved. Challenging the supporters of "Mrs. Grundy" were many who favored, either through public debate or by the evidence of their own secret conduct, greater sexual freedom (see Steven Marcus, *The Other Victorians: A Study of Sexuality and Pornography in Mid-Nineteenth-Century England*, 1964)

Aestheticism: Beginning with the Pre-Raphaelites, a movement that advanced the idea that art has value for its own sake, rather than for strictly cultural or moral ends

Women's Movement: First stirrings of the struggle for the rights of women; contrast between the idealized position of women as described in popular literature with their generally subservient role in real life (see Martha Vicinus, ed., *Suffer and Be Still: Women in the Victorian Age*, 1972)

MATTHEW ARNOLD

Born: Laleham, England (December 24, 1822)
Died: Liverpool, England (April 15, 1888)

Principal Works

POEMS: *The Strayed Reveller and Other Poems*, 1849; *Empedocles on Etna*, 1852; *Poems*, 1853; *Poems: Second Series*, 1855; *Merope: A Tragedy*, 1858; *New Poems*, 1867.

ESSAYS AND STUDIES: *On Translating Homer*, 1861; *Essays in Criticism*, 1865; *On the Study of Celtic Literature*, 1867; *Culture and Anarchy*, 1869; *Literature and Dogma*, 1873; *Last Essays on Church and Religion*, 1877; *Discourses in America*, 1885; *Civilization in the United States*, 1888; *Essays in Criticism: Second Series*, 1888.

Matthew Arnold, born at Laleham, December 24, 1822, was the eldest son of the famous schoolmaster, "Arnold of Rugby." The father, Dr. Thomas Arnold, had, as headmaster of that celebrated public school, brought about important changes in English education, not by spectacular reforms, but rather through the force of his character and example, both of which profoundly affected the son. Matthew attended Rugby during his father's headmastership and then matriculated (1841) at Balliol College, Oxford, where he studied classical literature and won the Newdigate Prize for poetry. While at Oxford, he was an intimate friend of Arthur Hugh Clough, whose death he mourned in the pastoral elegy, "Thyrsis" (1866).

Soon after his graduation from Oxford, Arnold became secretary to Lord Lansdowne, by whom he was appointed, in 1851, inspector of schools, a position he held until nearly the end of his life and one which provided him with an income sufficient to relieve him of financial worries. The position was, however, no sinecure; Arnold was sent to the Continent several times to investigate public secondary education in France and Germany, and the numerous volumes of his official reports testify to his industry and his conscientious discharge of his duties. In 1857 he was elected professor of poetry at Oxford and retained the professorship for ten years.

Arnold's poetry was all written during his early years; he later abandoned verse for prose. Even in his own time his poetry never attained the popularity of his great contemporaries, Tennyson and Browning, nor is it as well known today; indeed, he has been called the "great neglected Victorian." It has been said that his range was very narrow and that the "gray elegiac mood" was too pervasive for him ever to be a popular favorite, in spite of the exquisite technique that he could sometimes achieve. He could never accomplish the bravura effects that other poets used to catch the imagination of their readers; he was always calm and aloof.

Therefore, he has generally been classed as a poet of the second rank rather than as one of the great poets of his age. Yet in "Dover Beach" he wrote one of the finest poems of the Victorian era, for in it he faced squarely a major problem of the time: the ebb of faith; and in "The Scholar Gypsy" he foreshadowed much of his later criticism of the modern world, "with its sick hurry, its divided aims."

Arnold's literary criticism, to which he turned in the early 1860's and which sprang from his lectures at Oxford, represents some of the most influential writing of the second half of the century; it can even be said that he raised the art of criticism to a level it had not attained since the days of Hazlitt and DeQuincey. Although he admitted that "the critical power is of lower rank than the creative," he still claimed for criticism an important function: its aim was "to know the best that is known and thought in the world" and to "create a current of true and fresh ideas"—both of which phrases became literary bywords. His masters were Goethe and Sainte-Beuve; indeed, he was always much interested in Continental literature. In evaluating poetry, he distrusted the study of historical developments; instead, he advanced his theory of the "touchstone": the reader should have in his memory certain great passages, from Homer, Dante, Shakespeare, Milton, against which other poems could be measured. Literature, he felt, was fundamentally a "criticism of life" and must possess "high seriousness." Milton he regarded as "the one artist of the highest rank in the great style" in England; of the moderns, he was most impressed by Wordsworth.

Arnold's criticism had an enormous effect on the serious reading public of both England and America; as T. S. Eliot has pointed out, "the valuation of the Romantic poets, in academic circles, is still very largely that which Arnold made." But gradually his writing turned toward social criticism and the consideration of the complex problem created by the "ebb of faith" during his time. He was not one of those who saw Victorian England as "the best of all possible worlds"; he hated its materialism and felt that the upper class was materialized; the middle, vulgarized; and the lower, brutalized. The middle-class "Philistines," whom he felt to be the dominant group, must be turned from what he called "Hebraism," which had led to a narrow Puritanism, to "Hellenism," "an unclouded clearness of the mind." Only through culture could their salvation be accomplished. To this task the critic, with his "current of true and fresh ideas," could contribute much.

In 1883 Arnold made a lecture tour in America which furnished the material for his last important books. In 1886 he gave up his inspectorship of schools, and on April 15, 1888, he died quite suddenly in Liverpool.

Bibliography

The definitive edition of the prose is the *Complete Prose Works*, edited by R. H. Super, 1960 (in process, vol. VII, 1970). The standard edition of the poems is *The Poetical Works of Matthew Arnold*, edited by C. B. Tinker and H. F. Lowry, 1950. A more recent edition is Kenneth Allot, ed., *The Poems of Matthew Arnold*, 1965. Because Arnold requested that no biography of him be written, there is no definitive biography. Collections of letters are *The Letters of Matthew Arnold, 1848–1888*, edited by G. W. E. Russell, 1895, and *The Letters of Matthew Arnold to Arthur Hugh Clough*, edited by H. F. Lowry, 1932. *The Notebooks of Matthew Arnold* were edited by H. F. Lowry, Karl Young, and Waldo Hilary, 1952.

For critical studies and incidental biographical materials see George Saintsbury, *Matthew Arnold*, 1899; H. W. Paul, *Matthew Arnold*, 1902; G. W. E. Russell, *Matthew Arnold*, 1904; Hugh Kingsmill, *Matthew Arnold*, 1928; C. H. Harvey, *Matthew Arnold*, 1931; Sir Edmund Chambers, *Matthew Arnold*, 1932; Lionel Trilling, *Matthew Arnold*, 1939; C. B. Tinker and H. F. Lowry, *The Poetry of Matthew Arnold*, 1940; F. K. Brown, *Matthew Arnold: A Study in Conflict*, 1948; Kenneth Allot, *Matthew Arnold*, 1955; A. Dwight Culler, *Imaginative Reason. The Poetry of Matthew Arnold*, 1966; and R. H. Super, *The Time-Spirit of Matthew Arnold*, 1970.

CULTURE AND ANARCHY

Type of work: Social criticism
Author: Matthew Arnold (1822–1888)
First published: 1869

Essay-Review

In *Culture and Anarchy*, Matthew Arnold sought a center of authority by which the anarchy caused by the troubled passage of the Reform Bill of 1867 might be regulated. At its best his style is clear, flexible, and convincing; but Arnold wrote in such a complicated mood of indignation, impatience, and fear that his style and his argumentative method are frequently repetitious and unsystematic. Still, the book is a masterpiece of polished prose in which urbane irony and shafts of ridicule are used to persuade the Victorian middle class that it must reform itself before it can reform the entire nation.

Arnold primarily directed his criticism against the utilitarianism of the followers of Jeremy Bentham and John Stuart Mill and against the various movements of liberal reform. Disturbed by the social and political confusion, by Fenianism and the Hyde Park Riots of 1866, and by the inability of either the Church or the government to cope with the growing unrest both in England and on the Continent, Arnold attempted to describe an objective center of authority that all men, regardless of religious or social bias, could follow.

This center of authority is culture, which he defined on the level of the individual as "a pursuit of our total perfection by means of getting to know, on all matters which most concern us, the best which has been thought and said in the world." Because this authority is internal, it is a study of perfection within the individual, a study which should elevate the "best self" through a fresh and free search for beauty and intelligence. By following "right reason," the disinterested intellectual pursuits of the "best self," Arnold foresaw a way to overcome the social and political confusion of the 1860's and to prepare for a future in which all men could be happy and free. With this basically romantic view of man as a means and human perfectibility as the end, Arnold turned to social criticism, carefully showing that no other center of authority was tenable. The ideal of nonconformity, the disestablishment of the Church, led to confusion or, at worst, anarchy because it represented the sacrifice of all other sides of human personality to the religious. The ideal of the liberal reformers also, carried to extremes, led to anarchy because it regarded the reforms as ends rather than means toward a harmonious totality of human existence.

Arnold clarifies his definition of culture by tracing its origin to curiosity or "scientific passion" (the desire to see things as they really are) and to morality or "social passion" (the desire to do good). Christianity, as he saw it, was like culture in that it also sought to learn the will of God (human perfection) and make it prevail; but culture went beyond religion as interpreted by the Nonconformists in that it was a harmonious expansion of all human powers. In even sharper terms, culture was opposed to utilitarianism which Arnold considered "mechanical" because it worshipped means rather than ends. In fact, anything—materialism, economic greatness, individual wealth, bodily health, Puritanism—that was treated as an end except that of human perfectibility was to Arnold mere "machinery" that led to anarchy. Only culture, the harmonious union of poetry (the ideal of beauty) and religion (the ideal of morality), saw itself as a means that preserved the totality of the individual. Culture looked beyond machinery; it had only one passion—the passion for "sweetness" (beauty) and "light" (intelligence) and the passion to make them prevail. With such a passion it sought to do away with social classes and religious bias to make the best that has been thought and known in the world ("right reason") the core of human endeavor and institutions.

After establishing his definition of culture in terms of the individual, Arnold turned toward the problem of society. He saw the characteristic view of Englishmen toward happiness as the individual's desire "to do what he liked," or freedom, but he also saw that each class had its own opinion as to what it liked to do. In other words, there was a strong belief in freedom but a weak belief in "right reason" which should view freedom disinterestedly. This misplacing of belief was to Arnold one of the chief causes of anarchy; it was the mistake of acting before thinking. Ideally, "right reason" should precede action, and the State should be the disinterested union of all classes, a collective "best self." In reality, the State was being led toward anarchy by class interests because the aristocracy, or "Barbarians," were inaccessible to new, fresh ideas; the middle class, or "Philistines," had zeal but not knowledge; and the working class, or "Populace," was raw and untrained. Because culture alone could join the two sides of the individual, culture alone could overcome the narrow views of the three classes, since it was disinterested and sought only the perfection of all men. Members of the different classes possessed the same human nature and saw happiness as freedom; also, the "best self" was common to all classes. Therefore, since authority could be found neither in religion nor in politics, it could be found only in individuals who, by following "right reason" rather than class bias, could assert their "best selves" in a harmonious union that sought the best for everyone. The major impediments to such a state were what Arnold called "Atheism," the outright denial of such a thing as "right reason," and "Quietism," the utilitarian belief that reason was the result of habit. These impediments Arnold rejected on the basis of intuition and faith. Ethics can be known intuitively, and by building faith on the individual's intuition the spirit of culture could overcome the present anarchy.

The enlargement of his terms from the individual to the State naturally led Arnold to consider the historical development of the social and political confusion that he confronted. In the famous chapter titled "Hebraism and Hellenism," Arnold accounted for the very ground and cause out of which actual behavior arises, by distinguishing between (1) the energy in human affairs that drives at practice, the obligation of duty, self-control, and work (Hebraism) and (2) the energy that drives at those ideas which are the basis of right practice (Hellenism). Like the "scientific passion," Hellenism's chief function is to see things as they really are, and like the "social passion," Hebraism seeks proper conduct and obedience. In other words, what Arnold earlier analyzed as the opposing drives in the individual, he now enlarges to a historical context, all human endeavor in the Western World being associated with either the one or the other drive. Both drives aim at human perfection or salvation, but their means and ideals are sharply different. Hebraism, or "strictness of conscience," inculcates a sense of sin; but Hellenism, the "spontaneity of consciousness," teaches what Arnold has called culture.

The rise of Christianity marked the great triumph of Hebraism over Hellenism, but the Renaissance marked the resurgence of Hellenism. The anarchy of the 1860's Arnold saw as the result of Puritanism's reaffirmation of Hebraism in the seventeenth century, a reaffirmation that was against the currents of history. The problem was intensified by the Puritan belief that duty was an end in itself; whereas in reality both great drives are no more than contributions to human development. Thus, in England there was too much Hebraism, so much, in fact, that religion and politics had become mechanical. As a solution, Arnold suggested that Hellenism be imported. In Hellenism, which ultimately is a synonym for culture, the ideals of internal harmony, or the unity of the total man, and of harmony with things overcome the one-sidedness of Hebraism. The other drive, however, should not be excluded, for Hellenism alone leads to moral relaxation. There should be a harmony of both sides, a union from which would come the awakening of a healthier and less mechanical activity.

After analyzing culture in terms of the individual, the State, and history, Arnold turned to the particular issues before Parliament at the time he wrote. He directed his wit and some of his most vivacious ridicule against the four political reforms that were at the heart of liberalism—the disestablishment of the Irish Church, the Real Estate Intestacy Bill, the Deceased Sister's Wife Bill, and Free Trade—and showed that the liberal reformers lacked disinterestedness, displayed a remarkable absence of reason, and unconsciously led to anarchy. By leaving the issues that were uppermost in his mind to the last, he dramatically illustrated that culture alone could lead to perfection. For him the four bills were examples of the disbelief in "right reason" and the Philistine endeavor to act without thought. Thus, he warned that without "right reason" there could be no society and without society there could be no perfection. Only "right reason," the disinterested search for the best that has been thought or done regardless of class interests, could defeat anarchy by establishing the way to happiness through harmony.

Bibliography

Alexander, Edward.   *Matthew Arnold, John Ruskin and the Modern Temper*. Columbus: Ohio State University Press, 1973.

Anderson, Warren D.   *Matthew Arnold and the Classical Tradition.* Ann Arbor: University of Michigan Press, 1965.

Arnold Newsletter. Volume 1– Spring 1973– Ypsilanti: Eastern Michigan University Press.

Bush, Douglas.   *Matthew Arnold: A Survey of His Poetry and Prose.* New York: Macmillan, 1971.

Connell, William F.   *The Educational Thought and Influence of Matthew Arnold.* London: Routledge and Kegan Paul, 1950.

Coulling, Sidney M.   "The Evolution of *Culture and Anarchy*, in *Studies in Philology.* LX (October, 1963), pp. 637–688.

————.   *Matthew Arnold and His Critics: A Study of Arnold's Controversies.* Athens: Ohio University Press, 1974.

DeLaura, David J., Editor.   *Matthew Arnold: A Collection of Critical Essays.* Englewood Cliffs, N.J.: Prentice-Hall, 1973.

Goldberg, J.F.   "*Culture and Anarchy* and the Present Tense," in *Kenyon Review.* XXXI (1969), pp. 583–611.

Johnson, Wendell S.   *The Voices of Matthew Arnold: An Essay in Criticism.* Westport, Conn.: Greenwood Press, 1973. Reprint of 1961 Edition.

Madden, William A.   *Matthew Arnold: A Study of the Aesthetic Temperament in Victorian England.* Bloomington: Indiana University Press, 1967.

Neiman, Fraser.   *Matthew Arnold.* New York: Twayne, 1968.

Raleigh, John H.   *Matthew Arnold and American Culture.* Berkeley: University of California Press, 1957.

Rowse, Alfred L.   *Matthew Arnold: Poet and Prophet.* London: Thames and Hudson, 1976.

Super, Robert H.   *The Time-Spirit of Matthew Arnold.* Ann Arbor: University of Michigan Press, 1970.

Thorpe, Michael.   *Matthew Arnold.* London: Evans, 1969.

Trilling, Lionel.   *Matthew Arnold.* New York: Columbia University Press, 1949.

Walcott, Fred G.   *The Origins of* Culture and Anarchy: *Matthew Arnold and Popular Education in England.* Toronto: University of Toronto Press, 1970.

THE POETRY OF ARNOLD

Author: Matthew Arnold (1822–1888)
First published: The Strayed Reveller and Other Poems, 1849; *Empedocles on Etna*, 1852; *Poems*, 1853; *Poems: Second Series*, 1854; *Merope: A Tragedy*, 1857; *New Poems*, 1867; *Poems, Collected Edition*, 1869

Essay-Review

Matthew Arnold has often been called "the forgotten Victorian," and it is certainly true that his poetry is much less read than that of his two great contemporaries, Tennyson and Browning. Their vast productivity tends, as it did a century ago, to overshadow his rathoer modest accomplishment. For even if we include his two prize poems written at Rugby and at Oxford, we find that his total adult production amounts to only 129 poems, none of exceptional length by Victorian standards. "Empedocles on Etna," one of his longest, is less than a thousand lines. Also, after the publication in 1867 of his *New Poems*, when he was only forty-five, Arnold wrote very little poetry. He turned more and more to prose, and his increasing fame as a critic of literature and of society soon drove his poetic achievement into the background, so that to modern readers he is familiar, if at all, only through a few standard anthology pieces, such as "Dover Beach" and "The Scholar-Gypsy." Yet it has become almost a critical platitude to say that Arnold's poetry, in its intellectual content, is much closer to the modern mind than is that of either Tennyson or Browning.

Arnold was quite aware of the limited audience to which his poetry appealed. In 1858 he wrote to his sister, complaining that the lack of public appreciation of his work deprived him of the stimulus needed for creative effort. To write poetry with the high quality of both content and craftsmanship that he demanded of himself was, he said, an "actual tearing of oneself to pieces"; moreover, his position as an inspector of schools did not allow him the time he needed for the writing of verse. He knew also that he lacked many of the qualities possessed by Tennyson and Browning that made them so widely popular; he did not have Browning's intellectual vigor or Tennyson's musical skill. He was not capable of the strenuous affirmations of the later Browning or of the final struggle to faith that Tennyson achieved in *In Memoriam*. He had only the "gray elegiac mood," and this was not calculated to make a writer popular in nineteenth century England or America. There were Browning Societies everywhere in the English-speaking world, and Tennyson became a national institution. Arnold was ignored except by an intellectual elite.

The demands that Arnold made of poetry were high. In *The Study of Poetry* (1850) he wrote: "More and more mankind will discover that we have to turn to poetry to interpret life for us, to console us, to sustain us. Without poetry, our science will remain incomplete; and most of what now passes with us for religion and philosophy will be replaced by poetry." Poetry must have "high seriousness"; it must be "a criticism of life"; it must exhibit "the application of ideas to life." All of this is asking a great deal of poetry, perhaps asking more than it is capable of accomplishing. To expect that poetry will take the place of religion—even of "what now passes for religion"—is to place upon the poet an intolerable burden. Yet the question of religion is one that goes straight to the center of Arnold's poetry and of his intellectual and religious predicament.

Like so many of his contemporaries, Arnold had been reared in the liberal Protestantism of the early part of the nineteenth century and had, upon reaching his middle years, found this faith to be completely unsatisfactory. At Oxford he had been exposed to Newman's Tractarian Movement but had been little affected by it, perhaps because of the Low Church tradition of his youth. The crucial point in his whole religious situations may be found in the famous lines from "Stanzas from the Grande Chartreuse":

> Wandering between two worlds, one dead,
> The other powerless to be born,
> With nowhere yet to rest my head ....

In the Carthusian monastery, Arnold caught a glimpse of a faith that strangely attracted him but which his Protestant upbringing made him instinctively regard as anachronistic, as a fossilized relic of a dead past. Yet he could find no new faith to take the place of that which he had lost, for modern men have not yet found the answer:

> Achilles ponders in his tent,
> The kings of modern thought are dumb;
> Silent they are, though not content,
> And wait to see the future come.
> They have the grief men had of yore,
> But they contend and cry no more.

It was his awareness of the spiritual dilemma created by the ebbing of traditional religious faith that brings Arnold so close to the modern mind. Tennyson wrestled with the problem of faith and doubt in *In Memoriam* and finally attained to a trust in "the truths that never can be proved"; but Arnold could hear only the "melancholy, long, withdrawing roar" as the sea of faith, which had once encircled the whole world, slowly retreated like the ebbing tide at night. He saw nothing to fill the vacuum thus created and took refuge in a kind of Stoic detachment and resignation that find expression in the last stanza of Empedocles' song:

> I say: Fear not! Life still
> Leaves human effort scope.
> But, since life teems with ill,
> Nurse no extravagant hope;
> Because thou must not dream,
> Thou need'st not then despair!

We must, therefore, accept life as it is, must strive "to be *in* the world but not *of* it," neither hoping nor fearing overmuch.

This attitude of detachment and resignation gives to Arnold's poetry a curiously negative quality that is at once apparent to the reader. His view of life permitted no deep emotional involvement: for example, the poems to Marguerite are perhaps the most tepid love poems ever written by a great poet, and it is significant that even today the identity of the woman to whom they were addressed remains a mystery. In "Thyrsis," his elegy on his friend Clough and a poem of great beauty in its description of the English countryside, Clough always remains a shadowy, retreating ghost; never does the poet feel, as did Tennyson, that "the living soul was flash'd on mine." Instead, Clough has faded into classical mythology, leaving for Arnold "that lonely tree against the western sky." Yet for verbal beauty "Thyrsis" is rivaled in the English language only by "Lycidas."

In many respects Arnold resembles T. S. Eliot, and perhaps this resemblance explains why Eliot did not care greatly for Arnold's poetry. But whether his withdrawn attitude was the result of an inward weakness or of Arnold's dislike of his own age, it is impossible to say with any degree of certainty. That he despaired of the world he saw around him is sufficiently obvious; few of his lines are more often quoted than these from "The Scholar-Gypsy":

> ... this strange disease of modern life,
> With its sick hurry, its divided aims,
> Its heads o'ertaxed, its palsied hearts ....

It was from the ugliness and the materialism of the world of the Philistines that he withdrew, to seek what solace he could find in the calm, dispassionate world of the classics.

Yet it is equally clear that Arnold felt the lack of something positive in his own nature, for like most men of his time he had a great sense of responsibility. Obviously, he longed for the decisive force of his father, the famous Headmaster of Rugby and a representative of an older, more confident generation. In "Rugby Chapel," his elegy for Thomas Arnold, dead these fifteen or more years, the poet sought to express what he considered the essence of his father's greatness: "that he was not only a good man saving his soul by righteousness, but that he carried so many others along with him in his hand, and saved them ..." Or, as he contrasted the two generations in his poem:

> Yes! I believe that there lived
> Others like thee in the past,
> Not like the men of the crowd
> Who all around me to-day
> Bluster or cringe, and make life
> Hideous, and arid, and vile;
> But souls temper'd with fire,
> Fervent, heroic, and good,
> Helpers and friends of mankind.

In recent years there have been attempts to psychoanalyze the conclusion to "Sohrab and Rustum" in an effort to find in the poet's mind some record of a subconscious conflict between son and father. Such an interpretation seems unnecessary. One of the chief marks of the Victorian age was its haunting sense of "something lost"; in its own endless questionings it looked back with regret to an earlier time when traditional values seemed, at least in retrospect, to have been unquestioned. To Arnold, his father was one of those giants of old days which the mid-nineteenth century could no longer produce.

Much of what Arnold has to say is applicable to the contemporary situation, for all of the ills that he so clearly saw in nineteenth century England have been aggravated in the passage of a hundred years. His famous description of the "darkling plain" is even more appropriate today, and the lines from "The Scholar-Gypsy" might well be written of modern men:

> Of whom each strives, nor knows for what he strives,
> And each half lives a hundred different lives;
> Who wait like thee, but not like thee, in hope.

Bibliography

Allott, Kenneth, Editor. *Matthew Arnold.* Athens: Ohio State University Press, 1976.

Anderson, Warren D. *Matthew Arnold and the Classical Tradition.* Ann Arbor: University of Michigan Press, 1965.

Arnold Newsletter. Volume 1– Spring 1973– Ypsilanti: Eastern Michigan University Press.

Buckler, William E. *The Major Victorian Poets: Tennyson, Browning, Arnold.* Boston: Houghton Mifflin, 1973.

Bush, Douglas. *Matthew Arnold: A Survey of His Poetry and Prose.* New York: Macmillan, 1971.

Connell, William F. *The Educational Thought and Influence of Matthew Arnold.* London: Routledge and Kegan Paul, 1950.

Coulling, Sidney M. *Matthew Arnold and His Critics: A Study of Arnold's Controversies.* Athens: Ohio University Press, 1974.

Culler, Arthur D. *Imaginative Reason: The Poetry of Matthew Arnold.* Westport, Conn.: Greenwood Press, 1976. Reprint of 1966 Edition.

Dawson, Carl, Editor. *Matthew Arnold, the Poetry.* London: Routledge and Kegan Paul, 1973.

DeLaura, David J., Editor. *Matthew Arnold: A Collection of Critical Essays.* Englewood Cliffs, N.J.: Prentice-Hall, 1973.

242 Poetry / ARNOLD

Johnson, Wendell S. *The Voices of Matthew Arnold: An Essay in Criticism.* Westport, Conn.: Greenwood Press, 1973. Reprint of 1961 Edition.

Latham, Jacqueline, Editor. *Critics of Matthew Arnold.* London: Allen and Unwin, 1973.

Madden, William A. *Matthew Arnold: a Study of the Aesthetic Temperament in Victorian England.* Bloomington: Indiana University Press, 1967.

Malder, F.B. "Matthew Arnold and the Circle of Recurrence," in *Victorian Poetry.* XIV (Winter, 1976), pp. 293–309.

Neiman, Fraser. *Matthew Arnold.* New York: Twayne, 1968.

Rowse, Alfred L. *Matthew Arnold: Poet and Prophet.* London: Thames and Hudson, 1976.

Super, Robert H. *The Time-Spirit of Matthew Arnold.* Ann Arbor: University of Michigan Press, 1970.

Thorpe, Michael. *Matthew Arnold.* London: Evans, 1969.

Tinker, Chauncey R. *The Poetry of Matthew Arnold: A Commentary.* New York: Russell and Russell, 1970. Reprint of 1940 Edition.

Trilling, Lionel. *Matthew Arnold.* New York: Columbia University Press, 1949.

Trotter, D. "Hidden Ground Within: Matthew Arnold's Lyric and Elegaic Poetry," in *ELH.* XLIV (January, 1977), pp. 526–553.

THE BRONTËS

Charlotte Brontë

Born: Thornton, Yorkshire, England (April 21, 1816)
Died: Haworth, Yorkshire, England (March 31, 1855)

Principal Works

NOVELS: *Jane Eyre*, 1847; *Shirley*, 1849; *Villette*, 1853; *The Professor*, 1857.

Emily (Jane) Brontë

Born: Thornton, Yorkshire, England (July 30, 1818)
Died: Haworth, Yorkshire, England (December 19, 1848)

Principal Works

NOVEL: *Wuthering Heights*, 1847.
POEMS: *The Complete Poems of Emily Jane Brontë*, 1941.

Anne Brontë

Born: Thornton, Yorkshire, England (January 17, 1820)
Died: Scarborough, England (May 28, 1849)

Principal Works

NOVELS: *Agnes Grey*, 1847; *The Tenant of Wildfell Hall*, 1848.
POEMS (IN COLLABORATION): *Poems*, by Currer, Ellis, and Acton Bell, 1846.

On December 29, 1812, the Reverend Patrick Brontë, incumbent of Harts-head, Yorkshire (originally of County Down, in Ireland), was married in Guiseley Church to Maria Branwell, a Cornish lady then visiting in the home of her uncle, the Reverend John Fennell.

Little more than seven years later, having in the meantime served a ministry in Thornton, he was appointed perpetual curate of Haworth. There he re-moved his family in April 1820. Eighteen months later Mrs. Brontë died of cancer, leaving six small children: Maria, Elizabeth, Charlotte, Branwell, Emily, and Anne, ranging in age from seven years to twenty months. The emergency was solved when Elizabeth Branwell, Mrs. Brontë's eldest sister, came from Penzance to order the house and bring up the children.

In late summer of 1824, the four older girls were entered as pupils in the Clergy Daughters' School at Cowan Bridge. Precocious in mind but shy in spirit and frail in body, they fell victims to the severity of its routine. Maria and Elizabeth, ill of tuberculosis, were taken home to die, Maria on May 6, and Elizabeth on June 15, 1825. Charlotte and Emily were immediately re-called, and thereafter the Parsonage children knew no formal school room until Charlotte, near the end of her fourteenth year, entered Miss Margaret Wooler's school near Roe Head. Branwell was taught by his father, while the girls received training in household arts from their aunt. Left much to their own devices, the children found endless entertainment in creative plays continued from day to day. Shortly after Charlotte's tenth birthday, they launched a new play centering around twelve wooden soldiers, which absorbed all other household plays, and, having taken permanent form as an imaginary world of escape, nourished and shaped the genius of the family. Not only did the heroes of this play perform great deeds, but, turning authors, artists, and publishers, they recorded them in tiny volumes in proportion to their size—histories, biographies, novels, poems, and dramas.

In January, 1831, the Young Men's Play was interrupted by Charlotte's departure for Roe Head, when Emily and Anne took advantage of the break to withdraw from the family group and set up a play of their own called Gondal. Despite Charlotte's revival of the old creation on her return eighteen months later, and its expansion into a farflung empire called Angria, the younger girls stood aloof, and, from that time on the Brontë children played and wrote in pairs: Charlotte and Branwell, of Angria; Emily and Anne, of Gondal.

Through the years, 1832–1835, the game grew and matured with its creators through an astonishing number of "books." Branwell's productions, closely paralleling Charlotte's in characters and plot, betray his corrupting association with "rough lads of the Village" and the society of the Black Bull Inn. It was time for him to prepare for his chosen work of portrait painting. To help with family expenses, Charlotte, in late summer of 1835, returned to Miss Wooler's school as teacher, taking Emily with her as pupil.

The plan worked out badly. Branwell went to London but did not enter the Royal Academy, as had been planned. Charlotte and Emily, torn from their all-absorbing dream world, inseparable from home surroundings, were miserably homesick. Emily fell so ill that Charlotte sent her home and brought Anne to school in her place. Charlotte herself endured for two years until she collapsed nervously. Back home again, and lost in their writing, both regained health and courage to try again earning a living away from home, Emily in a school near Halifax, Charlotte as a nursery governess. Convinced that health and happiness were not for them away from home, the girls laid plans for a school in the Parsonage. To acquire the needed French, they borrowed from Aunt Elizabeth the money for a term of study in Mme. Héger's school in Brussels. Charlotte and Emily entered this school in February, 1842, leaving Anne in a position as governess in the Robinson family at Thorp Green, where Branwell was tutor. They were making satisfactory progress when they were called home by the death of Aunt Elizabeth in October.

The small legacies which they received from her enabled the older girls to finish out the year quietly at home. But in January, 1843, Charlotte returned to the Pensionnat Héger as teacher-pupil. Without Emily she was lonely. Worst of all, increasing weakness of overstrained eyes raised the spectre of blindness and reinforced M. Héger's frowning advice to give up Angria, the only medium she knew of creative dreaming and writing. Life stretched before her in years of unrelieved teaching, which her soul loathed.

Broken for a time in health and spirit, she returned to Haworth on New Year's Day, 1844. In the summer of 1845, Branwell, having conceived an infatuation for his employer's wife, was dismissed from his post. Already a habitué of drink and drugs, he never again rose above the piteous existence of an addict. Anne returned to the Parsonage with him.

At home the girls found alleviation of their distress in their old creative plays of Angria and Gondal. There is evidence that Charlotte tried by this means to bring her brother back to his rightful place in the group, but his manuscripts of the period show how grievously she failed.

The order was broken in the fall of 1845, when Charlotte accidentally came upon a manuscript volume of Emily's poetry, headed "Gondal Poems," which she read with astonishment at their grandeur and power, and the beauty of their "wild, wailing music." Out of this discovery, a joint volume of verse by the three girls was carefully worked out. For it, each drew from her store of verse (chiefly Angrian and Gondalan) twenty-one pieces, and chose a pseudonym to fit her own initials. The small volume was printed at the authors' expense with £31.10s. from Aunt Elizabeth's legacy: *Poems by Currer, Ellis, and Acton Bell*, London, Aylott and Jones, 8 Paternoster Row, 1846. Charlotte records that only two copies were sold. Disappointment turned the girls more determinedly to their novels already in progress, not the usual run of the Angrian and Gondal mills, but novels of realistic setting designed to please a publisher. Charlotte's, *The Professor*, was a skillful and artistic adaptation of portions of the Angrian creation to a Yorkshire-Brussels setting. Emily's, *Wuthering Heights*, showed many recognizable Gondalan features, traceable through her poems. Anne's, *Agnes Grey*, based on her own experience as a governess, had no kinship to her earlier writing. All three retained their previous pseudonyms.

After months of repeated rejection, *Wuthering Heights* and *Agnes Grey* were accepted by Thomas Cautley Newby of London. *The Professor* continued its rounds until it reached the house of Smith, Elder and Company, who returned it, but with such encouraging advice that Charlotte, on August 24, 1847, dispatched for their consideration a second novel, *Jane Eyre*, in characters and plot incidents derived directly from Angria.

Accepted, and published in October following, *Jane Eyre* was an immediate success. Newby now hastened the publication of *Wuthering Heights* and *Agnes Grey*, encouraging the surmise that they, too, were by the author of *Jane Eyre*, the three Bells being actually one person.

In the meanwhile Branwell had sunken so far out of family life that he knew nothing of his sisters' publishing ventures. Through late summer he grew rapidly worse, dying on September 24. Emily, having taken cold at his funeral, passed rapidly into tuberculosis, and followed him on December 19. Anne, already ill of the family scourge, succumbed on May 28, 1849.

Alone in the Parsonage with her father, Charlotte returned to an interrupted novel (*Shirley*) of Yorkshire local color which had been developed through fifteen years of Angrian writing. In November, 1852, she began the refining and naturalizing of yet another group of her beloved Angrians against a Belgian background. The result, *Villette*, was published in January, 1853.

On June 29 of the next year, she married her father's curate, Arthur Bell Nicholls. Her happiness was of short duration; she died on Easter Eve, March 31, 1855.

Bibliography

The Life of Charlotte Brontë, by Mrs. E. C. Gaskell, 1857, is the pioneer biography, but this work should be supplemented by later studies, which include Clement K. Shorter, *Charlotte Brontë and Her Circle*, 1896; F. Macdonald, *The Secret of Charlotte Brontë*, 1914; Rosamond Langbridge, *Charlotte Brontë: A Psychological Study*, 1929; E. F. Benson, *Charlotte Brontë*, 1932; Laura Hinkley, *The Brontës, Charlotte and Emily*, 1947; and Margaret Crompton, *Passionate Search: A Life of Charlotte Brontë*, 1955. Among the more recent specialized critical biographies of Charlotte are Winifred Gérin, *Charlotte Brontë, The Evolution of Genius*, 1967; Margot Peters, *Unquiet Soul: A Biography of Charlotte Brontë*, 1975; and Helene Moglen, *Charlotte Brontë: The Self Conceived*, 1976. See also recent studies by Earl A. Knies, *The Art of Charlotte Brontë*, 1969; and Enid L. Duthie, *The Foreign Vision of Charlotte Brontë*, 1975.

The best early biography of Emily Brontë is Charles Simpson, *Emily Brontë*, 1929; but see also A. M. F. Robinson's pioneering *Emily Brontë*, 1883. The essays on Emily and the other Brontës by Lord David Cecil, *Early Victorian Novelists*, 1934, have influenced most later studies. See Muriel Spark and Derek Stanford, *Emily Brontë: Her Life and Work*, 1960; John Hewish, *Emily Brontë: A Critical and Biographical Study*, 1969; Miriam Allott, *Emily Brontë*, 1970; and Winifred Gérin, *Emily Brontë: A Biography*, 1971.

For Anne Brontë see the early biography by Will T. Hale, *Anne Brontë: Her Life and Writings*, Indiana University Studies, XVI, No. 83, 1929. The best recent study is Winifred Gérin, *Anne Brontë*, 1959, 1976.

General studies of the Brontë family include Clement K. Shorter, *The Brontës: Life and Letters*, 2 vols., 1908; May Sinclair, *The Three Brontës*, 1912; K. A. R. Sugden, *A Short History of the Brontës*, 1929; Lawrence C. Willis, *The Brontës*, 1933; Phyllis Bentley, *The Brontës*, 1947; Ernest Raymond, *In the Steps of the Brontës*, 1948; Lawrence and E. M. Hanson, *The Four Brontës*, 1949; Margaret Lane, *The Brontë Story*, 1953; Annette B. Hopkins, *The Father of the Brontës*, 1958; Daphne Du Maurier, *The Infernal World of Branwell Brontë*, 1960; Winifred Gérin, *Branwell Brontë*, 1961; John Lock and W. T. Dixon, *A Man of*

Sorrow: The Life, Letters, and Times of the Rev. Patrick Brontë, 1777–1861, 1965; Phyllis Bentley, *The Brontës and Their World*, 1969; Nancy B. Morrison, *Haworth Harvest: The Lives of the Brontës*, 1969; Tom Winnifrith, *The Brontës and Their Background: Romance and Reality*, 1973; Maureen Peters, *An Enigma of Brontës*, 1974; and Brian Wilks, *The Brontës*, 1975.

All recent Brontë studies owe a tremendous debt to Fannie E. Ratchford, whose definitive work is *The Brontës' Web of Childhood*, 1941, supplemented by her *Two Poems by Emily Brontë*, with the Gondal Background of Her Poems and Novel, 1934; Introduction to Emily Brontë's *Gondal's Queen*, 1955, with notes; and *Legends of Angria*, edited with W. C. Devane, 1933. The most comprehensive modern critical study is Mildred G. Christian, *The Brontës in Victorian Fiction*, 1964. Other useful specialized studies include Judith O'Neil, comp., *Critics on Charlotte and Emily Brontë*, 1968; Thomas Vogler, ed. *Twentieth Century Interpretations of Wuthering Heights: A Collection of Critical Essays*, 1969; and Ian Gregor, ed., *The Brontës: A Collection of Critical Essays*, 1970. See also the early but still useful structural studies of C. P. Sanger, *The Structure of Wuthering Heights*, 1926; Leicester Bradner, "The Growth of *Wuthering Heights*," *Publications of the Modern Language Association*, XLVIII (1933), 129–146; Martine Turnell, "*Wuthering Heights*," *Dublin Review*, CCVI (1940), 134–149; and Richard Chase, "The Brontës: or, Myth Domesticated," in *Forms of Modern Fiction*, edited by W. V. O'Connor, 1948. More recent specialized studies include the *Transactions and Publications of the Brontë Society*, various dates; in particular, Hilda Marsden, "The Scenic Background of *Wuthering Heights*," Part 67, XIII, No. 2, 1957; Francis B. Pinion, *A Brontë Companion: Literary Assessment, Background, and Reference*, 1975; G. Anthony Yablon and John R. Turner, eds., *A Brontë Bibliography*, 1978; Margaret Homans, "Repression and Sublimation of Nature in *Wuthering Heights*," *Publications of the Modern Language Association*, XVIII (1978), 9–19; and William Holtz, ed., *Two Tales by Charlotte Brontë: "The Secret" and "Lily Hart"* [Facsimile, transcription and introductions], 1978.

THE POETRY OF EMILY BRONTË

Author: Emily Brontë (1818–1848)
First published: Poems by Currer, Ellis, and Acton Bell, 1846; *Selections from the Poems of Ellis Bell,* 1850; *The Complete Poems,* edited by C. W. Hatfield, 1941

Essay-Review

Emily Brontë's poems may be read simply as independent works of art; when best understood, however, as a body of work—apart from the reflection of biography or their significance as mid-nineteenth century English verse—they form not one but two larger entities. Her two hundred poems, some still in manuscript, belong to the "Gondal Chronicles" which she and her younger sister Anne composed from the summer of 1832, when Emily was fourteen and Anne twelve, until Emily's death in 1848; thirty-nine of these poems appeared in 1846 and 1850 as the work of "Ellis Bell" without any reference to Gondal. In the case of Emily Brontë, the smaller number of poems—her "selected poems"—have the greater universality of appearing as complete entities and are here treated as to all intents and purposes the collected poems of Emily Brontë as "Ellis Bell."

The moot point in such a course is whether "Ellis Bell's" poems make complete sense without the remaining poems of Emily Brontë, constituting the "Gondal Chronicles" as we have them. The affirmative depends on two grounds: how the "Ellis Bell" poems came to be published in the lifetime of Emily and her older sister Charlotte and the amount of Gondal reference in the original poems necessary to their meaning. If there is little significant reference in a poem, it can be easily released from its original frame and considered separately. *Poems by Currer, Ellis and Acton Bell* is the fourth step in transforming the Gondal poems into those of "Ellis Bell." The first and third steps were taken by Emily Brontë herself. In the winter of 1843–1844 she transcribed some of the Gondal poems from the small printed notebooks of the "Chronicles" into two manuscript books of fair copies. One is dated February, 1844. In October of the following year Charlotte accidently read one of these books and, breaking the family code of the "secret plays," began insisting that the poems be published simply as a book of verse. Emily reluctantly agreed, probably so that the poems of Charlotte ("Currer") and Anne ("Acton") could appear with hers and thus help Charlotte's desperate gamble to capitalize on the writing ability of the three sisters against the looming possibility of their father's death and their own return to teaching simply in order to live. Charlotte, as a mature literary connoisseur of thirty, was right in her belief in the imperishable quality of Emily's best verse, and her decision—the most significant event in the lives of all three sisters—had three important results: it ended the "Angrian Chronicles" on which she had labored for twenty years with Branwell—the dangerously compulsive "web of childhood" that Miss Fannie

Ratchford has shown it to be; it opened the way for the novels which did bring Charlotte money; and, in Emily's double insistence on keeping her identity secret and erasing the Gondalian references in the poems, it provided a body of her poetry which differs textually from the Gondal canon and appears before the world as the work of "Ellis Bell." The transformation was completed when twenty-one of these poems appeared in the 1846 volume and eighteen in the 1850 *Selections from the Poems of Ellis Bell*, edited considerably by Charlotte but along the lines Emily had begun.

A final reason for following Emily's decision to publish her poems as "Ellis Bell" is that the "Gondal Chronicles" are incomplete; thus the full Gondal matrix is irrecoverable. Thanks, however, to Miss Ratchford's *The Brontë's Web of Childhood* and the work of other scholars the story can be outlined.

In this outline the lonely landscapes are sometimes called "moors" in order to stress that the "Gondal Chronicles" are as much sources for *Wuthering Heights* as they are the inspiration of Emily's poems; these occur at static moments in the action and celebrate the emotions of the character concerned (identified by initials used in the headings to the poems, most of them now lost in Emily's editing the poems for publication); the poems may refer to past events in Gondal and to the present situation of the character but the emphasis of the poem is on the emotion, and this is the prime justification for treating the "Ellis Bell" poems as the "selected poems" of Emily Brontë. A comparison of two such poems, both from the 1846 volume, will show the varying amount of Gondalian reference still in the poems and pose the question whether that reference is essential to understanding the works.

The two poems entitled "Remembrance" and "Death" were written to express Queen Augusta's continuing desolation at the loss of Julius; both poems resolve to continue mourning because the first "May" ("Death") or first "morn" ("Remembrance") is the "Sweet Love of youth" ("Remembrance") and is now gone forever. The resolution is achieved only after two different temptations have been resisted. In "Remembrance" the "Sweet Love of youth" is asked to forgive "if I forget thee," not because the speaker wants to forget "memory's rapturous pain" but because she apparently cannot die until her appointed time, even though it is her "burning wish to hasten Down to that tomb already more than mine." In "Death" the speaker has been tempted by the return of Spring (or the healing passage of time):

> Little mourned I for the parted Gladness,
>   For the vacant nest and silent song;
> Hope was there, and laughed me out of sadness,
>   Whispering, "Winter will not linger long."

But the speaker rejects the available hope: "Time, for me, must never blossom more!" She asks Death to strike down the budded branch and return it to Eternity, and thus she rejects "Life's restoring tide." There are more overt references to Gondal in "Remembrance" than in "Death," but in each case they simply give the emotion of the poem an objective correlative to sustain turning the emotion into a poem. In "Death" the references to Augusta's love for Julius can be seen in the phrases "when I was most confiding/In my certain Faith of Joy to be" and "the vacant nest." In "Remembrance" they are more concrete ("that northern shore" and "fifteen wild Decembers"), but in sum the references amount to a very small percentage in poems each of more than two hundred words. In effect these references, in the versions published by "Ellis Bell," are no more essential to a satisfactory reading of the poems than is a knowledge of Arthur Henry Hallam necessary in order to understand Tennyson's *In Memoriam.*

The emotion of the speaker in the two poems is conventional in poetry and natural in life; Emily Brontë's claim to being a poet is her personal variation on that theme of loss of the loved one. In some of her other poems there is more reference to Gondalian names and situations—the mother who loses her baby on the moor in "The Outcast Mother" or the references to "Irene" in "Faith and Despondency" and to "Edward" in "A Death-Scene"—but it is still possible to see these as the necessary though extraordinary furniture of the poem.

Emily Brontë's poems depend on the conventional antithesis of inner reality to superficial appearances, a reality discovered or celebrated in the course of the poem. Her unique handling of the convention was to prefer the eccentric or perverse to that normally celebrated in poetry; she seeks the moors, not a pleasant landscape (as Charlotte observed in introducing her *Selections from the Poems of Ellis Bell*); she chooses December before May; she prefers solitude to company and does not make the conventional return to society at the close of the poem; above all she seeks death, and she really means it. She conveys the intensity of her own emotions by dramatizing the situation and focusing on concrete objects, generally aspects of nature, to sing of sorrow; as in "Song":

> The linnet in the rocky dells,
> The moor-lark in the air,
> The bee among the heather-bells
> That hide my lady fair:

Needless to say the "fair" lady is in her grave and "in her tranquil sleep" where Emily rejoiced to go; as Charlotte dryly observed "the colour and perfume of the flowers [i.e. poems] are not such as fit them for festal uses." Charlotte's famous dictum—"Liberty was the breath of Emily's nostrils"—is shown in most of the poems, where the speaker chafes against restrictions and principally that of the body itself, especially in her three most famous: "The Old Stoic" (as it is misnamed), and the stanzas beginning "Often rebuked, yet always back returning" and "No coward soul is mine." The popular choice of these is improved by acquaintance with the other "Ellis Bell" poems; together they sum up her rejection of the unreal world of "riches," "long-past history," and temporal doubts of God's being. The poet affirms her faith only in the moors "where my own nature would be leading" and, given that nature, she achieves a resounding vision of earth which "can centre both the worlds of Heaven and Hell" and of total and real existence only in God.

Bibliography

Bentley, Phyllis. *The Brontës.* New York: Haskell House, 1975, pp. 83–89.

Brown, H. "The Influence of Byron on Emily Brontë," in *Modern Language Review.* XXXIV (July, 1939), pp. 374–381.

Donoghue, Denis. "The Other Emily," in *The Brontës: A Collection of Critical Essays.* Edited by Ian Gregor. Englewood Cliffs, N.J.: Prentice-Hall, 1970, pp. 157–172.

Drew, David P. "Emily Brontë and Emily Dickinson as Mystic Poets," in *Brontë Society Transactions.* XV (1968), pp. 227–232.

Grove, Robin. " 'It Would Not Do': Emily Brontë as Poet," in *The Art of Emily Brontë.* Edited by Anne Smith. New York: Barnes & Noble, 1976, pp. 33–67.

Hardy, Barbara. "The Lyricism of Emily Brontë," in *The Art of Emily Brontë.* Edited by Anne Smith. New York: Barnes & Noble, 1976, pp. 94–118.

Livermore, A.L. "Byron and Emily Brontë," in *Quarterly Review.* CCC (1962), pp. 337–344.

Maurer, K.W. "The Poetry of Emily Brontë," in *Anglia.* LXI (1937), pp. 442–448.

Miles, Rosalind. "A Baby God: The Creative Dynamism of Emily Brontë's Poetry," in *The Art of Emily Brontë.* Edited by Anne Smith. New York: Barnes & Noble, 1976, pp. 68–93.

Ratchford, F.E. "War in Gondal: Emily Brontë's Last Poem," in *Trollopian.* II (1947), pp. 137–155.

Starzyk, Lawrence J. "Emily Brontë: Poetry in a Mingled Tone," in *Criticism.* II (Spring, 1972), pp. 119–136.

Tinker, C.B. "The Poetry of the Brontës," in *Essays in Retrospect.* Edited by C.B. Tinker. Port Washington, N.Y.: Kennikat, 1948.

Visick, Mary. "Emily Brontë's Poetry," in *Critics on Charlotte and Emily Brontë.* Edited by Judith O'Neill. London: Unwin, 1968, pp. 108–113.

Willy, Margaret. "Emily Brontë: Poet and Mystic," in *English.* VI (Autumn, 1946), pp. 117–122.

Wordsworth, Jonathan. "Wordsworth and the Poetry of Emily Brontë," in *Brontë Society Transactions.* XVI (1972), pp. 85–100.

ELIZABETH BARRETT BROWNING

Born: Coxhoe Hall, Durham, England (March 6, 1806)
Died: Florence, Italy (June 29, 1861)

Principal Works

POEMS: *The Seraphim and Other Poems*, 1838; *Poems, by Elizabeth Barrett Barrett*, 1844; *Poems* (including *Sonnets from the Portuguese*), 1850; *Casa Guidi Windows*, 1851; *Aurora Leigh*, 1857; *Poems before Congress*, 1860; *Last Poems*, 1862.

TRANSLATION: *Prometheus Bound*, 1833.

LETTERS: *Letters of Elizabeth Barrett Browning*, 1897; *Letters of Robert Browning and E. B. Barrett*, 1899.

The most famous feminine poet in English, Elizabeth Barrett Browning achieved her popularity perhaps as much through her romantic courtship and marriage as through her poetic talents, though it is, of course, on her poetry that her reputation finally rests. Hers was a minor talent, well-endowed with a lyric gift, but often lacking the technical control that could have polished her natural lyricism. In her *Sonnets from the Portuguese*, however, the strict limitations of the form gave shape to her lyric expression, and the poems have become the most popular love cycle in the language.

Elizabeth Barrett Moulton was the eldest child of Edward Barrett Moulton, a rich landowner who later changed his surname to Barrett. Born at Coxhoe Hall, Durham, England, on March 6, 1806, she was brought up in the Malvern Hills, a landscape that appears in a number of her poems. A precocious child, she was a good student of the Greek and Roman classics. In 1820, her father had fifty copies of her youthful epic, *The Battle of Marathon*, privately printed. She published anonymously *An Essay on Mind, and Other Poems* (1826), a stiff and sterile performance dominated by the influence of Pope and the classics.

In 1832 the Barretts moved to Sidmouth, Devonshire, where Elizabeth translated Aeschylus' *Prometheus Bound*. The family then made the important move to London in 1835 and soon took up permanent residence at 50 Wimpole Street. There Elizabeth made the literary friendships she needed, and her new friends encouraged her to publish her poetry more frequently. *The Seraphim and Other Poems* received good notices when it appeared in 1838, but it was not popular. But her increased literary activities proved too much for her, a riding accident as a girl and weak lungs having left her a semi-invalid, and in 1838 she was forced to go to the sea resort at Torquay for her health. Edward, her favorite brother, stayed with her and when, after a misunderstanding between them, Edward was drowned, Elizabeth was plunged into an extreme grief from which she was slow to recover.

She returned to Wimpole Street in 1841 and tried to forget her sorrow by working on a modernization of Chaucer with Wordsworth and Leigh Hunt. *Poems, by Elizabeth Barrett Barrett* was praised by the reviewers and she received flattering letters from Carlyle, Poe and Lowell. In 1845 she received her most important letter, a note of praise from Robert Browning, a little-known poet whose work she admired. They continued the correspondence and met that summer. Browning became a frequent visitor at Wimpole Street. Because Mr. Barrett had forbidden any of his daughters to marry, the pair had a secret courtship which was climaxed on September 12, 1846, when the lovers were secretly married. A week later they left for the Continent. Her father never allowed Elizabeth to see him again, and he returned all her letters unopened. He died unreconciled in 1857.

Settling, for health and economic reasons, in Florence, the Brownings stayed at Casa Guidi, near the Pitti Palace, until Elizabeth's death. Their only child, a son, was born there in 1849. One day Mrs. Browning shyly showed her *Sonnets from the Portuguese* to her husband; he persuaded her to include them in her 1850 volume. A thorough republican, Mrs. Browning next wrote *Casa Guidi Windows* in an attempt to gain English sympathy for the cause of Italian liberty. The Brownings traveled frequently and visited England in 1851, 1855 and 1856. During her last visit Mrs. Browning wrote *Aurora Leigh*, a narrative poem that has been compared to a psychological novel. Despite its slow-moving plot, the poem had a success equal almost to that of the *Sonnets from the Portuguese*. She had put out new editions of her poems in 1853 and 1856, and by now her reputation was firmly established. Her *Poems before Congress* received mixed reviews, but they did no damage to her popular fame. When she died in Florence on June 29, 1861, she was one of the best-known of Victorian poets.

Bibliography

The Complete Poetical Works has been edited by H. W. Preston, 1900. There are four collections of letters: *Letters of Elizabeth Barrett Browning*, edited by F. G. Kenyon, 1897; *The Letters of Robert Browning and Elizabeth Barrett Browning, 1845–1846*, edited by F. G. Kenyon, 2 vols., 1899 (rev. ed., 1930); also edited by Elvan Kintner, 3 vols., 1969–1971; the *Letters to Her Sister*, edited by Leonard Huxley, 1929; and *Elizabeth Barrett to Miss Mitford*, edited by Betty Miller, 1943. See also Philip Kelley and Ronald Hudson, eds., *Diary of E.B.B.: The Unpublished Diary of Elizabeth Barrett Browning, 1831–1833*, 1969.

The definitive biography is Gardner B. Taplin, *The Life of Elizabeth Barrett Browning*, 1957. Other biographical studies include J. H. Ingram, *Elizabeth Barrett Browning, 1888*; I. C. Willis, *Elizabeth Barrett Browning*, 1928; Dorothy Hewlett, *Elizabeth Barrett Browning: A Life*, 1952; and Frances Winwar, *Elizabeth: The Romantic Story of Elizabeth Barrett Browning*, 1957. The story of Robert and Elizabeth Barrett Browning has been told in Osbert Burdett, *The Brownings*, 1929; Virginia Woolf, *Flush*, 1933; Frances Winwar, *The Immortal*

Lovers, 1950; Constance Burnett, *The Silver Answer*, 1955; and Dallas Kenmare, *The Browning Love-Story*, 1957. For family background see Jeanette Marks, *The Family of the Barretts*, 1938.

SONNETS FROM THE PORTUGUESE

Type of work: Poetry
Author: Elizabeth Barrett Browning (1806–1861)
First published: 1850

Essay-Review

Elizabeth Barrett Browning's *Sonnets from the Portuguese* are among the most famous and most frequently read of all English love poems. Their popularity, originally heightened, perhaps, because they were the first products from Mrs. Browning's pen after her romantic marriage and flight to Italy with Robert Browning, has been great ever since they first appeared to the public in 1850.

The poems themselves have come, in the popular mind, to stand for the sincere love for and faith in her husband held by the woman who had previously believed herself a hopeless spinster invalid. Her devotion to her husband, her genuine and articulate thanks to him for having made her a vital woman, shine through the poems and give them a simple autobiographical value not often found in poetry In these poems, Mrs. Browning, has no poses, no artifice, little facility for exploring technique; she is simply a woman grateful for her husband's love.

Sonnets from the Portuguese consists of forty-four sonnets that Mrs. Browning wrote to her husband during the first few years of their relationship. Many of the sonnets indicate her feelings of humility, her doubts that she deserved the love and attention of such a great and strong man. Other sonnets simply tell of her gratitude, describe her deep appreciation of the fact that Browning saved her from the life of the sheltered invalid. Still other sonnets, pursuing the theme of gratitude, tell of her pleasure in living in terms of this world rather than, as she formerly did, in terms of the next. In one way, these sonnets tell the story of Mrs. Browning's growing interest in earth and its life, her growing abandonment of her former concentration on Heaven and the spiritual life. In Sonnet XXIII, after talking of her love for her husband, she concludes:

> Then my soul, instead
> Of dreams of death, resumes life's lower range.
> Then, love me, Love! look on me ... breathe on me!
> As brighter ladies do not count it strange,
> For love, to give up acres and degree,
> I yield the grave for thy sake, and exchange
> My near sweet view of Heaven, for earth with thee!

In spite of this movement toward earth and life, Mrs. Browning retained a good deal of her religious interest and religious conviction. The sonnets are full of her devotion to God and her assurance that she shall be with her husband after death as well.

Although many modern readers find these sonnets banal and undistinguished, they have always had great appeal for the popular audience, less for serious critics or practitioners of poetry. The poems are not distinguished by either sharpness or intricacy of diction to cloak unashamed expression of a woman's simple love and devotion. When the simple emotion is decorated, it is likely to be given a decoration, an applauding angel or a direct emotional address, that was a Victorian commonplace.

The limitations of the sonnet form keep these poems more technically accurate and meaningful than many of Mrs. Browning's other poems, but the form is not enough to give them any technical distinction. Mrs. Browning neglects the dramatic possibilities of the sonnet as well as the technical intricacy possible within the scope of fourteen rhyming, iambic pentameter lines. Occasionally, however, she uses some striking poetic images. Sonnet XXIV, for example, opens with the following image:

> Let the world's sharpness, like a clasping knife,
> Shut in upon itself and do no harm
> In this close hand of Love, now soft and warm,
> And let us hear no sound of human strife
> After the click of the shutting.

The "sound of human strife" may be an easy cliché, and the "soft and warm" hand of Love may sound banal to the contemporary reader, but the whole image of the clasping knife and the sense of warmth in a closed, sheltering hand of love provides an image of some power and unusual quality for the poem. Similarly, Mrs. Browning also uses floral images effectively in order to express the flowering of her love. In addition to these occasional images, Mrs. Browning's sonnets sometimes have a sense of rhetorical movement that distinguishes them from the merely pedestrian. Although she does not use the form dramatically, she often uses it with a sense of musical and emphatic movement. The emotion is still essentially simple and the clichés are still present; but the poem itself is sometimes a rhetorically emphatic statement that carries strong feeling with ease, simplicity, and grace. Such an effect is found in Sonnet XLI:

> I thank all who have loved me in their hearts,
> With thanks and love from mine. Deep thanks to all
> Who paused a little near the prisonwall,
> To hear my music in its louder parts,
> Ere they went onward, each one to the mart's
> Or temple's occupation, beyond call.
> But thou, who, in my voice's sink and fall,
> When the sob took it, thy divinest Art's
> Own instrument didst drop down at thy foot,
> To hearken what I said between my tears, . . .
> Instruct me how to thank thee!—Oh, to shoot
> My soul's full meaning into future years,

> That *they* should lend it utterance, and salute
> Love that endures, from Life that disappears!

Although the opening lines are clotted with thanks, the poem does move with grace and power, and, in the last few lines, carries its romantic theme with compression and strength.

Critics have long pointed to the fact that such distinction is rare in Mrs. Browning's work, that much in *Sonnets from the Portuguese* is sentimental, hastily written, undistinguished in diction or pace. Yet these considerations have not diminished her appeal for her many faithful followers, an appeal based on direct expression of simple and genuine emotion.

Bibliography

Baker, Harry T. "Mrs. Browning's *Sonnets*," in *Saturday Review of Literature.* V (April 13, 1929), p. 895.

Butler, Francis H. "*Sonnets from the Portuguese*," in *Academy* (London). LXVI (March 5, 1904), p. 258.

Carter, John and Graham Pollard. *An Enquiry into the Nature of Certain Nineteenth Century Pamphlets.* London: Constable, 1934, pp. 8–37.

Cunnington, S. "*Sonnets from the Portuguese*," in *Academy* (London). LXVI (February 13, 1904), p. 181.

Dodds, M.H. "*Sonnets from the Portuguese*," in *Notes & Queries.* CXCI (November 2, 1946), p. 193.

Fussell, Paul. *Poetic Meter and Poetic Form.* New York: Random House, 1965, pp. 124–128.

Gay, Robert. "Elizabeth Barrett Browning's *Sonnets from the Portuguese*," in *Explicator.* I (December, 1942), item 24.

Going, William T. "Elizabeth Barrett Browning's *Sonnets from the Portuguese*, XLIII," in *Explicator.* XI (June, 1953), item 58.

Gosse, Edmund. "The *Sonnets from the Portuguese*," in *Critical Kit-Kats.* London: Heinemann, 1913, pp. 1–17.

Hagedorn, Ralph. "Edmund Gosse and the *Sonnets from the Portuguese*," in *Papers of the Bibliographical Society of America.* XLVI (1952), pp. 67–70.

Heilman, Robert B. "Elizabeth Barrett Browning's *Sonnets from the Portuguese*," in *Explicator.* IV (October 14, 1945), item 3.

Kay, Carol M. "An Analysis of Sonnet 6 in *Sonnets from the Portuguese*," in *Concerning Poetry.* IV (1971), pp. 17–21.

O'Hagan, Thomas. *Studies in Poetry, Critical, Analytical, Interpretive.* Boston: Marlier, Callahan, 1900, pp. 38–50.

Phillipson, John S. " 'How Do I Love Thee?'—An Echo of St. Paul," in *Victorian Newsletter*. XXII (Fall, 1962), p. 22.

Radley, Virginia. *Elizabeth Barrett Browning*. New York: Twayne, 1972, pp. 90–106.

Smith, Grover. "Petronius Arbiter and Elizabeth Barrett," in *Notes & Queries*. CXCI (November 2, 1946), p. 190.

Taplin, Gardner. "Mrs. Browning's Poems in 1850," in *Boston Public Library Quarterly*. (October, 1957), pp. 181–194.

Zimmerman, Susan. "*Sonnets from the Portuguese*: A Negative and Positive Context," in *Mary Wollstonecraft Newsletter*. II (December, 1973), pp. 7–20.

ROBERT BROWNING

Born: Camberwell, London, England (May 7, 1812)
Died: Venice, Italy (December 12, 1889)

Principal Works

POEMS: *Pauline*, 1833; *Paracelsus*, 1835; *Sordello*, 1840; *Dramatic Lyrics*, 1842 (*Bells and Pomegranates III*); *Dramatic Romances and Lyrics*, 1845 (*Bells and Pomegranates VII*); *Christmas Eve and Easter Day*, 1850; *Men and Women*, 1855 (2 vols.); *Dramatis Personae*, 1864; *The Ring and the Book*, 1868–1869 (4 vols.); *Balaustion's Adventure*, 1871; *Prince Hohenstiel Schwangau*, 1871; *Fifine at the Fair*, 1872; *Red Cotton Night-Cap Country*, 1873; *Aristophanes' Apology*, 1875; *The Inn Album*, 1875; *Pacchiarotto*, 1876; *La Saisiaz* and *The Two Poets of Croisac*, 1878; *Dramatic Idylls: First Series*, 1879; *Dramatic Idylls: Second Series*, 1880; *Jocoseria*, 1883; *Ferishtah's Fancies*, 1884; *Parleyings with Certain People of Importance*, 1887; *Asolando*, 1889.
PLAYS: *Strafford*, 1837; *Pippa Passes*, 1841 (*Bells and Pomegranates I*); *King Victor and King Charles*, 1842 (*Bells and Pomegranates II*); *The Return of the Druses*, 1843 (*Bells and Pomegranates IV*); *A Blot in the 'Scutcheon*, 1843 (*Bells and Pomegranates V*); *Colombe's Birthday*, 1844 (*Bells and Pomegranates VI*); *Luria* and *A Soul's Tragedy*, 1846 (*Bells and Pomegranates VIII*).
TRANSLATION: *The Agamemnon of Aeschylus*, 1877.

The poet Robert Browning was born May 7, 1812, in Camberwell, near London, the son of a learned and genial Bank of England clerk. His father's substantial library, notable for curious history, biography, and anecdote, became an important influence upon the future poet, as were his father's instruction in languages and his mother's Evangelical piety and love of music. Private schooling and a term at the University of London had comparatively little influence on a young man who felt himself destined to be a poet and was admirably prepared for it at home.

He came early under the influence of Shelley, whose techniques and political ideas remained with him somewhat longer than the religious radicalism which Browning repudiated in his earliest significant poem, *Pauline*. After this poem of personal confession, he turned to the "chronicling" of objective characters and the use of the dramatic techniques which were to remain his characteristic concerns.

The first poem of this dramatic kind was *Paracelsus*, published in 1835. The character here examined was that of a historical person, the Renaissance scientist, who, as Browning represented him, came to know almost too late the nature of true love, without which knowledge is empty.

Turned to stage drama through his friendship with the actor Macready, Browning produced a historical play, *Strafford*, in 1837, which ran for only four nights. He was to make two more attempts at the stage without success: *A Blot in the 'Scutcheon* and *Colombe's Birthday*. But the earlier of these was to lead him toward his destined medium of the short dramatic poem, and his studies in seventeenth century history for *Strafford* confirmed him in his characteristic political liberalism and sympathy for the common man.

The promising reputation which had begun with *Paracelsus* was spoiled in 1840 by the publication of *Sordello*. Browning's changing conceptions of the central character and an excessive concern with medieval Italian history resulted in a poem which has been called "a bewildering potpourri of poetry, psychology, love, romance, humanitarianism, philosophy, fiction, and history." It continues to be regarded, in spite of modern criticism, as distinguished chiefly by its obscurity.

From 1841 to 1846 he published the inexpensive little series titled *Bells and Pomegranates,* beginning with *Pippa Passes* and including, among other titles, *Dramatic Lyrics, A Blot in the 'Scutcheon, Colombe's Birthday,* and *Dramatic Romances and Lyrics. Pippa Passes* and a number of the shorter poems show him at his best in the dramatic monologue and lyric: "My Last Duchess," "Soliloquy of the Spanish Cloister," "Porphyria's Lover," "The Bishop Orders His Tomb at St. Praxed's Church." The last of these especially is a triumph in one of Browning's special interests, the interpretation of the Italian Renaissance; and in many of the dramatic poems of the series he illustrates the characteristic purpose of his best work: the chronicling, in concrete settings, of individualized human souls in moments of crucial and revelatory experience.

In 1844 Browning noticed a compliment to himself in a poem by the invalid poetess, Elizabeth Barrett. A correspondence and visits followed, Miss Barrett's health improved, and in 1846 they were secretly married and set out for a long and happy residence in Italy, residing first in Pisa and then moving to the now famous Casa Guidi villa in Florence. They followed the revolutionary movements of 1848 with sympathetic liberalism, though Mrs. Browning was more interested in social institutions and her husband in liberty as serving individual growth. They differed more notably in Mrs. Browning's faith in spiritualism and Browning's contempt for it.

Summer visits to London brought them the friendship of Carlyle, Ruskin, Kingsley, and Rossetti. Their son was born in Florence in 1849, and Mrs. Browning died there in 1861.

In 1850 Browning published *Christmas Eve and Easter Day,* in the first of these emphasizing love rather than ecclesiastical forms as essential to Christianity and in the second dealing with religion in its individual aspects. The poems have been called Puritan in spirit.

In 1855 he issued his "fifty men and women" under the title *Men and Women*, highly individualized characters in concrete settings, expressing in their experiences various ideas about love, art, and religion. "Fra Lippo Lippi" affirms the goodness of physical beauty, "Saul" makes human love a prophecy of the revelation of divine love, "Cleon" asserts the ethical pessimism of Greece as against the upstart Christian hope, and in "An Epistle of Karshish" an Arab physician is converted by a study of the case of Lazarus.

After his wife's death Browning returned to England to edit her unpublished poems, to supervise his son's education, and to become a highly popular figure in London society. In 1864 he published *Dramatis Personae,* similar to *Men and Women* as a collection of dramatic sketches, but with even greater emphasis upon ideas and religion. He was honored by Oxford with a fellowship and by Cambridge with an honorary degree. In 1868 he published his *Poetical Works* in six volumes.

In Florence, Browning had picked up an "old yellow book" containing, in print and manuscript, the story of a seventeenth century murder trial. This became the long poem, *The Ring and the Book*, in which the poignant story, rich in Italian background, was interpreted through monologues by nine persons involved in the trial. It is his masterpiece in his most characteristic form, the dramatic monologue.

Although his best work had been done, many volumes were to follow before his death in Venice, December 12, 1889, and burial in Westminster Abbey. Italy, religion, and the world of art had provided him with his best settings; the dramatic monologue was his triumphant art form; the chronicling of souls in growth or crisis was his central substance; optimism was his philosophical bent; and his central doctrine was the "glory of the incomplete"—the supremacy of high and unfulfilled aspiration over low-level, finite achievement. He ranks with Tennyson as one of the two greatest poets of the Victorian era.

Bibliography

The standard edition is *The Complete Poetical Works of Robert Browning*, edited by Augustine Birrell, 1915. This will be superseded by *Poems* edited by Roma A. King (13 vols.) in process, 1969 (Vol. I). The standard biography is W. H. Griffin and H. C. Minchin, *The Life of Robert Browning*, 1938. Other biographical studies include Arthur Waugh, *Robert Browning*, 1900; Edward Dowden, *The Life of Robert Browning,* 1917; Lilian Whiting, *The Brownings: Their Life and Art*, 1917; Fannie Barrett Browning, *Some Memories of Robert Browning*, 1928; and Betty Miller, *Robert Browning: A Portrait*, 1952.

For criticism see E. H. Griggs, *The Poetry and Philosophy of Robert Browning*, 1905; A. K. Cook, *A Commentary upon Browning's "The Ring and the Book,"* 1920; C. W. Hodell, ed., *The Old Yellow Book*, 1927; Frances T. Russell, *One Word More on Browning*, 1927; W. L. Phelps, *Robert Browning: How to Know Him*, 1931; W. C. DeVane, *A Browning Handbook*, 1935; W. O. Raymond, *The Infinite Moment*, 1950; Philip Drew, ed., *Robert Browning: A Collection of Critical Essays*, 1966; Thomas Blackburn, *Robert Browning: A Study of His Poetry*, 1967; Norton B. Crowell, *The Convex Glass: The Mind of Robert Browning*, 1968; and Leonard Burrows, *Browning the Poet: An Introductory Study*, 1969.

A useful volume of general reference is Edward Berdoe, *The Browning Cyclopedia*, 1916.

DRAMATIC MONOLOGUES AND LYRICS

Author: Robert Browning (1812–1889)
First published: Dramatic Lyrics, 1842; *Dramatic Romances and Lyrics*, 1845; *Men and Women*, 1855

Essay-Review

Much of Browning's finest writing was done during his thirties, years which comprise most of the poems in the volumes *Dramatic Lyrics*, *Dramatic Lyrics and Romances*, and *Men and Women*. The intentions and procedures of these three volumes are similar, so that most often one's comments on the first two hold good for the third as well. In fact, Browning himself in a later collected edition reshuffled many of these poems, breaking down the divisions between individual books but preserving always the dominating premise that the poems should be, as he said, "though often Lyric in expression, always Dramatic in principle, and so many utterances of so many imaginary persons, not mine." During his middle years we see Browning striving to write poems at once less sentimental and more objective than those of his early hero, Shelley: he develops his own form of the dramatic monologue in the attempt to overcome subjectivity and vagueness, and his success here is in the nature of an overcompensation. The poems in these volumes, "always Dramatic in principle," are brilliant but somehow chilly.

Browning's verse-play, *Pippa Passes*, published in 1841, immediately precedes *Dramatic Lyrics* and by its superb rendering of the spirit of Italy—a country which is for Browning always the dialectical counterpart of England, a kind of anti-England—the play foreshadows the skeptical attitude conveyed by the poems. In "The Bishop Orders His Tomb at Saint Praxed's Church," in "My Last Duchess," and in the immense narrative poem *The Ring and the Book* the poet was later to draw implicit and explicit contrasts between contemporary England and Renaissance Italy. His habitual approach is in this way argumentative and skeptical, the counterbalancing of opposing countries, times, sexes, and beliefs which is suggested even by many of the titles in these volumes: "Meeting at Night" against "Parting at Morning," "Love in a Life" against "Life in a Love," "The Italian in England" against "The Englishman in Italy." The method permits Browning to end an elegant dialogue between two Venetian lovers, "In a Gondola," with a vicious stabbing. Alternately, he can present the interior monologue of a warped person, allowing the character to condemn himself by his (or her) words: as is the case of the female prisoner, crossed in love, in "The Laboratory," or the deranged murderer who speaks in "Porphyria's Lover." Perhaps the most often anthologized of these interior monologues is the "Soliloquy of the Spanish Cloister," in which a splenetic monk grumbles against his abbot:

> GR-R-R—there go, my heart's abhorrence!
> Water your damn flower-pots, do!

> If hate killed men, Brother Lawrence,
>   God's blood, would not mine kill you!
> What? Your myrtle-bush wants trimming?
>   Oh, that rose has prior claims—
> Needs its leaden vase filled brimming?
>   Hell dry you up with its flames!

The lines are characteristic: not only does the voice contradict the speaker's appearance and vocation, but the very exclamations and dashes render the punctuation histrionic and serve to define a particular habit of mind.

The monologues which imply a listener are psychologically more complex. "My Last Duchess" and "The Bishop Orders His Tomb at Saint Praxed's Church," appeared in 1842 and 1845, respectively, and are models, in these earlier volumes, of the kind of irony and immediacy which the dramatic method at its best is capable of generating:

> That's my last Duchess painted on the wall,
> Looking as if she were alive, I call
> That piece a wonder, now: Fra Pandolf's hands
> Worked busily a day, and there she stands.

Browning consciously follows Donne in beginning poems with arresting first lines. Here, much of the Duke's ruthlessness is conveyed at the very outset by his exquisitely casual reference, with the possessive "my," to his dead wife, by his evident pleasure at being able now to consider her as an art object, not as an intractable life-study:

> She had
> A heart—how shall I say?—too soon made glad,
> Too easily impressed; she liked whate'er
> She looked on, and her looks went everywhere.

Subtly, Browning manages to turn the Duke's criticism of his former wife, his specious yet elegantly phrased "how shall I say?" claim that she was too much alive, too indiscriminately joyous, into an exposure of his own monstrous pride in "a nine-hundred-years-old name." Flexible couplets with unobtrusive rhymes are the fit medium for his self-justifying logic and for the vicious sweetness which informs even his dealings with his present auditor, the envoy of the woman who will probably be Ferrara's next Duchess ("Will't please you rise?" addressed to the envoy is a command in the guise of a question). By tracing a logic of association in the blank verse of "The Bishop Orders His Tomb at Saint Praxed's Church," Browning focuses in a similar way on an incident of crucial importance for the self-revelation of his title character, the churchman whose dying words concern pagan luxury and wordly pomp rather than Christian salvation.

Two dramatic monologues from the *Men and Women* volume, "Fra Lippo Lippi" and "How it Strikes a Contemporary," are explicitly concerned with aesthetics and the process of composition in poetry and painting. If we read between the lines of these poems, looking for the passages which most accord with Browning's actual practice, it is clear that he believes the best art is a universalizing of individual experience; and that to this end the poet or painter must be first of all curious, pre-eminently a noticer. Indeed, the verbs "notice," "mark," "see" are common in Browning's dramatic lyrics, where to notice a unique scene or situation is to exert an individual consciousness, and where to notice intensely is the first step in separating the apparent from the real and in beginning to write a book that, in words from *The Ring and the Book*, "shall mean beyond the facts." Accordingly, a collection of "so many utterances of so many imaginary persons" would escape the charge of subjectivity, yet taken as a whole it would convey a meaning beyond the mathematical sum of the dramatic lyric voices involved. These speakers reveal themselves far beyond what the occasion warrants, and the poems are essentially more dramatic and romantic than lyric. Browning takes definite pleasure in the vivid selfhood of his speakers, and pleasure as well in the multiple vision of the artist who can create and embody conflicting viewpoints while remaining himself uncommitted.

Browning's interest in conflict, incongruity, even in the grotesque, has its natural complement in his dramatic technique. The range of styles and effects is as various as the range of complexity among his characters. "An Englishman in Italy" exhibits a cataloguing, descriptive style, for instance in the request that one observe a fishing skiff from Amalfi, with alien English eyes watching

> ... Our fisher arrive,
> And pitch down his basket before us,
>   All trembling alive
> With pink and gray jellies, your seafruit;
>   You touch the strange lumps,
> And mouths gape there, eyes open, all manner
>   Of horns and lumps. ...

In "The Pied Piper of Hamelin," and in "Incident of the French Camp," Browning manages well two very different kinds of narrative. The mode of "Pictor Ignotus," an early monologue which looks ahead to "Andrea Del Sarto" and "Fra Lippo Lippi," is one of ratiocination, following a proud artist's ebb and flux of thought:

> O human faces, hath it split, my cup?
>   What did ye give me that I have not saved?
> Nor will I say I have not dreamed (how well!)
>   Of going—I, in each new picture—forth,
> As, making new hearts beat and bosoms swell,
>   To Pope or Kaiser, East, West, South, or North. ...

There is also the lyric outcry of "Home-Thoughts, From Abroad," with its famous lines, "Oh, to be in England/Now that April's there." Browning's metrical range is diverse and experimental as well; in "Boot and Saddle" and "How They Brought the Good News From Ghent to Aix" he brilliantly turns the difficult anapestic meter to his own purposes, for both poems succeed in conveying by a kind of metrical imitation the excitement of a fast ride on a horse ("I galloped, Dirck galloped, we galloped all three"). Finally, it accords well with Browning's perspectivism, his prizing of unique objects and irreducible selfhood, that he should have created a new metrical or stanzaic form for almost every separate poem.

These earlier poems are a true representation of Browning in that they show him to be intellectually ingenious but no philosopher; an experimenter with both social and literary norms but by no standard a Victorian radical; a writer aware of evil and violence, but for the most part a cautious optimist. The later poems and *The Ring and the Book* bear out one's sense that his major achievement is in fact in these dramatic poems of his middle years, where the view of truth as relative is first impressively demonstrated in dramatic monologues. There is, of course, something deeply subversive in the notion that different points of view are equally valid, in the oblique yet damaging criticisms of Victorian sexual and religious conventions conveyed in some of these poems, in the attacks on bureaucracy such as the telling poem written against the aging establishment-approved Wordsworth, "The Lost Leader." The dramatic monologue, at once objective and subjective, public and private in its methods, was the main vehicle used by Browning for criticism of Victorian society and manners; the monologue permitted ethical pronouncements to be made through someone else's voice.

Thus in "My Last Duchess," in "Bishop Blougram's Apology," in many of his best poems Browning is a public writer with disturbing private tendencies: he never pushes exposure or criticism past the point of pleasure, and his work as a whole gives an effect of hard impersonal brilliance. Browning was typically a man of his age in believing that the poet was a moral agent in his society, one whose concerns were norms and value, the discovery and presentation of a heightened reality. Yet in wishing to write poems which would mean "beyond the facts" he settled on a method which from the start excluded personal directness. Because all his sincerities and critiques had to be conveyed indirectly, these poems for all their peculiar triumphs will be found to lack the keynote of passionate personal despair which is a profound theme in much of the finest Victorian poetry.

Bibliography

Armstrong, Isobel, Editor. *Robert Browning.* Athens: Ohio University Press, 1975.

Benvenuto, R. "Lippo and Andrea: The Pro and Contra of Browning's Realism," in *Studies in English Literature.* XIII (Autumn, 1973), pp. 643–652.

Blackburn, Thomas. *Robert Browning: A Study of His Poetry.* Totowa, N.J.: Rowman and Littlefield, 1974. Reprint of 1967 Edition.

Brooke, Stopford A. *The Poetry of Robert Browning.* New York: AMS Press, 1969. Reprint of 1902 Edition.

Bross, A.C. "Browning's Changing Concept of Faith," in *Victorian Poetry.* XIV (Spring, 1976), pp. 11–23.

Cook, Eleanor. *Browning's Lyrics: An Exploration.* Toronto: University of Toronto Press, 1974.

Drew, Philip. *The Poetry of Browning: A Critical Introduction.* London: Methuen, 1970.

Flowers, Betty S. *Browning and the Modern Tradition.* New York: Macmillan, 1976.

Hess, S.W. "Browning in Our Ear," in *Contemporary Review.* CCXVI (March, 1970), pp. 140–144.

Holmes, S.W. "Browning: Semantic Stutterer," in *ETC.* XXXI (March, 1974), pp. 73–99.

Irvine, William. *The Book, the Ring, and the Poet: A Biography of Robert Browning.* New York: McGraw-Hill, 1974.

Jack, Ian R. *Browning's Major Poetry.* Oxford: Clarendon Press, 1973.

Korg, J. "Browning's Art and 'By the Fireside,'" in *Victorian Poetry.* XV (Summer, 1977), pp. 147–158.

Langbaum, R. "Browning and the Quest of Myth," in *PMLA.* LXXXI (December, 1966), pp. 575–584.

Litzinger, Boyd, Editor. *Browning: The Critical Heritage.* New York: Barnes & Noble, 1970.

McComb, J.K. "Beyond the Dark Tower: Childe Roland's Painful Memories," in *ELH.* XLII (Fall, 1975), pp. 460–470.

Maynard, John. *Browning's Youth.* Cambridge, Mass.: Harvard University Press, 1977.

Melchiori, B. "Browning's Don Juan," in *Essays in Criticism.* XVI (October, 1966), pp. 416–440.

Mermin, D.M. "Speaker and Auditor in Browning's Dramatic Monologues," in *University of Toronto Quarterly.* XLV (Winter, 1976), pp. 139–157.

Pearsall, Robert B. *Robert Browning.* New York: Twayne, 1974.

Peterson, William S. *Robert and Elizabeth Barrett Browning: An Annotated Bibliography, 1951–1970.* New York: Browning Institute, 1974.

Poston, L. "Browning's Political Skepticism: Sordello and the Plays," in *PMLA.* LXXXVIII (March, 1973), pp. 260–270.

Preyer, R. "Two Styles in the Verse of Robert Browning," in *ELH.* XXXII (March, 1965), pp. 62–84.

Ryals, Clyde de L. *Browning's Later Poetry, 1871–1889*. Ithaca, N.Y.: Cornell University Press, 1975.

Siegchrist, M. "Thematic Coherence in Browning's Dramatic Idyls," in *Victorian Poetry*. XI (Autumn, 1977), pp. 229–239.

DRAMATIS PERSONAE

Type of work: Poetry
Author: Robert Browning (1812–1889)
First published: 1864

Essay-Review

When Robert Browning published *Dramatis Personae* he was just beginning to gain a measure of general esteem, both in the eyes of the public and of the critics. The year before its publication a three-volume collection of his earlier works had sold moderately well. *Dramatis Personae* added considerably to his popularity, and a second edition was called for before 1864 was out. It is ironic that this volume, the first that can be said to have achieved popular success, contained the first clear signs of the decline of his poetic powers.

It was his first volume of new poems since *Men and Women*, published in 1855. In the interval the pattern of Browning's life had undergone complete transformation. On June 29, 1861, his wife had died. They had made their home in Italy; after her death, Browning returned to England. For years he had been virtually out of touch with the currents of English thought. Now he plunged into a society that was perplexed by what it had learned and troubled by what it had come to doubt. Browning was soon personally involved in the intellectual and religious controversies of the day.

The changes in his life produced changes in his poetry. His love poems, understandably, became more melancholy. Many of the poems in *Men and Women* had had historical settings; all but a few of those in *Dramatis Personae* have contemporary settings. Even when he gives his version of an old tale, as in "Gold Hair: A Legend of Pornic," he manages to work in discussion of nineteenth century problems. In general, he was becoming more argumentative, more of a preacher. He still preferred the dramatic mode of utterance, but the voice of the poet is often heard behind the dramatic mask.

Two of the important themes in the volume are love and death, frequently juxtaposed. The death of Mrs. Browning may have been an influence on his choice of subjects, but it should not be overestimated; a number of the poems antedate her death. "Prospice," however, written in the fall of 1861, is clearly Browning speaking in his own voice. It is an open affirmation of belief in immortality. When death ends his life, he says, as it has ended hers,

> O thou soul of my soul! I shall clasp thee again,
> And with God be the rest!

In "Too Late" another man grieves over a dead woman, but with a difference. He had never expressed his love for her and now suffers not grief alone but regret at having missed his opportunity. It is a familiar theme in Browning, love unfulfilled through negligence, expressed earlier in "The Statue and the Bust," and, elsewhere in *Dramatis Personae*, in "Youth and Art," and in "Dîs Aliter Visum; or Le Byron de Nos Jours." If "Too Late" has an autobiographical element it is of an inverse order: Browning, unlike the speaker, had not missed his opportunity for love. The speaker of "Too Late" says it would have been better to

> ... have burst like a thief
> And borne you away to a rock for us two
> In a moment's horror, bright, bloody, and brief,
> Then changed to myself again. . . .

Browning, a sedentary man, had stepped out of character once in his life, when he had spirited a middle-aged poetess off to Italy.

Two of the finest poems in *Dramatis Personae*, also love poems, are "Confessions" and "James Lee's Wife" (originally called, misleadingly, "James Lee"). One reason why they are perennially satisfying is that, unlike many poems in the volume, they are free from topical controversy. In "Confessions," one of Browning's shortest dramatic monologues, a dying man recalls, with satisfaction, a love affair of long ago:

> How sad and bad and mad it was—
> But then, how it was sweet!

In "James Lee's Wife," as in Tennyson's "Maud," the story is that of the death of love. It is a restrained, dignified cry of heartbreak, a skillfully wrought dramatic lyric, the desolate scene and the dying year serving as mute echoes of the speaker's mood.

Of the eighteen poems originally grouped in *Dramatis Personae* (two occasional pieces were later added: "Deaf and Dumb" and "Eurydice to Orpheus"), few are not cluttered with argument. Of these, none besides "James Lee's Wife" and "Confessions" is particularly memorable. "The Worst of It" is mawkish; "May and Death" is pleasant, but slight; "A Face" and "A Likeness" are insignificant. It should not be assumed, however, that the remaining poems, those which do serve as vehicles for Browning's beliefs, can all be dismissed as inferior poems.

"Caliban upon Setebos," for example, is not only a statement of Victorian religious belief; it is as well one of Browning's successful poems of the grotesque. But the controversial element is certainly there, as indicated by the subtitle: "Natural Theology in the Island." Browning is satirizing those who, relying too closely on their own resources, posit God in their own image. And Caliban is not merely a figure taken from Shakespeare's *The Tempest*; he is also a post-Darwinian figure, a poet's version of the evolutionary "missing link." The topical references in the poem do not, however, prevent it from being rated one of Browning's best dramatic monologues.

"A Death in the Desert," another dramatic monologue, is perhaps more seriously marred by its attempts to promote certain religious ideas. Proponents of the "higher criticism" of the Bible—Strauss in *Leben Jesu* and *New Life of Jesus*, Renan in *La Vie de Jésus*—had attempted, among other things, to prove that the Gospel of St. John had not been written, as had been assumed, by the beloved disciple. Browning's poem, an imaginative re-creation of John's death, is an argument for the authenticity of the Gospel. It contains a number of Browning's religious positions (e.g., a theory about miracles). The fact that it is the dying Apostle who gives expression to these ideas is anachronistic: many of them are clearly indigenous to the middle of the nineteenth century. As a result, the dramatic effect of the poem is appreciably undercut.

The longest poem in *Dramatis Personae*, "Mr. Sludge, 'The Medium,' " its 1525 lines comprising three-eighths of the entire volume, is more successful. It is one of Browning's liveliest character studies, not unworthy of comparison with the great dramatic monologues in *Men and Women*. But it too is tinged by Browning's growing fondness for argument. Browning satirizes spiritualism, quite a fad in mid-nineteenth century England, by portraying a fraudulent medium whose character is based on an American, Daniel Dunglass Home, whom Browning had met. Moreover, Mr. Sludge gives voice, although inconsistently, to some of Browning's characteristic religious ideas. The propagandizing is done rather subtly, however, and does not strike the reader as being obtrusive.

"Rabbi Ben Ezra" and "Abt Vogler" are similar to "Mr. Sludge" in being good poems as well as statements of opinion with regard to contemporary questions. The first eight sections of "Abt Vogler" are a brilliant tour de force, a lyrical evocation of the exalted spirit of a musician improvising at the keyboard of an organ. The last four sections are not quite so successful, being too flat an exposition of one of Browning's pet theories, the "philosophy of the imperfect":

> On the earth the broken arcs; in the heaven, a perfect round.
> And what is our failure here but a triumph's evidence
> For the fullness of the days?

But the argumentative element does not predominate; sound and sense are not at odds but in harmony with each other. It was one of Browning's favorites, among his own poems, and it has since been one of the favorites of his readers.

"Rabbi Ben Ezra," another of Browning's most popular poems, is unsurpassed as an expression of Browning's own belief in God. Some have suggested that the poet intended it to be an answer to the hedonism of Edward FitzGerald's *The Rubáiyát of Omar Khayyám*, and certainly Browning's metaphor of the potter relates to Fitzgerald's verse. Above all, "Rabbi Ben Ezra" is a cogent presentation of Browning's optimistic view that mankind exists for a purpose.

Quite another theme runs through "Gold Hair: A Story of Pornic," a curious and troubling poem. The body of it relates an old story about the death of a young girl. She had been regarded virtually as a saint; years after her death, however, it is learned that she had been interested in earthly treasure far more than in a heavenly one. Some have objected to the story itself; but that, though macabre and a bit cynical, is really unobjectionable. What ruins the poem are the last three stanzas Browning has tacked on:

> Why I deliver this horrible verse?
>   As the text of a sermon, which now I preach:
> Evil or good may be better or worse
>   In the human heart, but the mixture of each
> Is a marvel and a curse.
>
> The candid incline to surmise of late
>   That the Christian faith may be false, I find;
> For our Essays-and-Reviews' debate
>   Begins to tell on the public mind,
> And Colenso's words have weight:
>
> I still, to suppose it true, for my part,
>   See reasons and reasons; this, to begin:
> 'Tis the faith that launched point-blank her dart
>   At the head of a lie—taught Original Sin,
> The Corruption of Man's Heart.

Browning makes no bones about his intention to preach, and the value of his stories begins to decline as they become more and more pointedly the texts for sermons.

"Apparent Failure," a lesser poem, again finds Browning speaking in his own voice. The story is merely the occasion for moral instruction; it is in Browning's own words, "the sermon's text."

The final poem in *Dramatis Personae*, "Epilogue," gives brief expression to three religious positions current when Browning wrote. The "First Speaker, *as David*," sums up the High Church, ritualistic position; the "Second Speaker, *as Renan*," expressed the skepticism of one familiar with the "higher criticism." The "Third Speaker," Browning himself, answers the first two, calling ceremony unnecessary and belief tenable. Browning's belief, not unlike Tennyson's, is sustained by personal feeling rather than by a process of the reason. What is really significant about the poem is that it makes no pretense of being dramatic. It sets the pattern for the bulk of his later poems, for Browning's values have changed; controversy now means more to him than writing poems, for poetry has become the vehicle for argument. Inevitably, poetry suffers, as some of the poems in this volume and virtually all of the later poems, save *The Ring and the Book*, clearly testify.

Bibliography

Armstrong, Isobel, Editor.   *Robert Browning*. Athens: Ohio University Press, 1975.

Benvenuto, R. "Lippo and Andrea: The Pro and Contra of Browning's Realism," in *Studies in English Literature*. XIII (Autumn, 1973), pp. 643–652.

Blackburn, Thomas. *Robert Browning: A Study of His Poetry*. Totowa, N.J.: Rowman and Littlefield, 1974. Reprint of 1967 Edition.

Brooke, Stopford A. *The Poetry of Robert Browning*. New York: AMS Press, 1969. Reprint of 1902 Edition.

Bross, A.C. "Browning's Changing Concept of Faith," in *Victorian Poetry*. XIV (Spring, 1976), pp. 11–23.

Cook, Eleanor. *Browning's Lyrics: An Exploration*. Toronto: University of Toronto Press, 1974.

Drew, Philip. *The Poetry of Browning: A Critical Introduction*. London: Methuen, 1970.

Flowers, Betty S. *Browning and the Modern Tradition*. New York: Macmillan, 1976.

Hess, S.W. "Browning in Our Ear," in *Contemporary Review*. CCXVI (March, 1970), pp. 140–144.

Holmes, S.W. "Browning: Semantic Stutterer," in *ETC*. XXXI (March, 1974), pp. 73–99.

Irvine, William. *The Book, the Ring, and the Poet: A Biography of Robert Browning*. New York: McGraw-Hill, 1974.

Jack, Ian R. *Browning's Major Poetry*. Oxford: Clarendon Press, 1973.

Korg, J. "Browning's Art and 'By the Fireside,' " in *Victorian Poetry*. XV (Summer, 1977), pp. 147–158.

Langbaum, R. "Browning and the Quest of Myth," in *PMLA*. LXXXI (December, 1966), pp. 575–584.

Litzinger, Boyd, Editor. *Browning: The Critical Heritage*. New York: Barnes & Noble, 1970.

McComb, J.K. "Beyond the Dark Tower: Childe Roland's Painful Memories," in *ELH*. XLII (Fall, 1975), pp. 460–470.

Maynard, John. *Browning's Youth*. Cambridge, Mass.: Harvard University Press, 1977.

Melchiori, B. "Browning's Don Juan," in *Essays in Criticism*. XVI (October, 1966), pp. 416–440.

Mermin, D.M. "Speaker and Auditor in Browning's Dramatic Monologues," in *University of Toronto Quarterly*. XLV (Winter, 1976), pp. 139–157.

Pearsall, Robert B. *Robert Browning*. New York: Twayne, 1974.

Peterson, William S. *Robert and Elizabeth Barrett Browning: An Annotated Bibliography, 1951–1970*. New York: Browning Institute, 1974.

Poston, L. "Browning's Political Skepticism: Sordello and the Plays," in *PMLA*. LXXXVIII (March, 1973), pp. 260–270.

Preyer, R. "Two Styles in the Verse of Robert Browning," in *ELH*. XXXII (March, 1965), pp. 62–84.

Ryals, Clyde de L. *Browning's Later Poetry, 1871–1889*. Ithaca, N.Y.: Cornell University Press, 1975.

Siegchrist, M. "Thematic Coherence in Browning's Dramatic Idyls," in *Victorian Poetry*. XI (Autumn, 1977), pp. 229–239.

MEN AND WOMEN

Type of work: Poetry
Author: Robert Browning (1812–1889)
First published: 1855

Essay-Review

The title *Men and Women* was originally appended to two volumes of poems containing fifty-one of Browning's most celebrated works. Beginning with the collected edition of 1863, the number of poems appearing under this title was reduced to thirteen, only eight of which had been in the 1855 edition of *Men and Women.* Of the other forty-three poems, thirty were thereafter grouped by Browning under *Dramatic Lyrics* (the most famous of these being "Love Among the Ruins," "A Toccata of Galuppi's," "Saul," " 'De Gustibus—,' " and "Two in the Campagna"); twelve became *Dramatic Romances* (including " 'Childe Roland to the Dark Tower Came,' " "The Statue and the Bust," "The Last Ride Together," and "A Grammarian's Funeral"); "In a Balcony" came eventually to be listed separately, under its own title. But those poems which remained as *Men and Women* include several of Browning's greatest dramatic monologues: "Fra Lippo Lippi," "An Epistle Containing the Strange Medical Experience of Karshish, the Arab Physician," "Bishop Blougram's Apology," "The Bishop Orders His Tomb at Saint Praxed's Church," "Andrea del Sarto," and "Cleon."

Men and Women was Browning's only important publication during the period of his marriage to Elizabeth Barrett. These were the years when Browning made Italy his home and when his output of poetry was markedly curtailed by a number of other interests: his family, his dabbling in painting and sculpture, and his study of Italian Renaissance art. But the quality of his poetry was never higher than in the poems produced during this period. It was in *Men and Women*, above all, that he brought the dramatic monologue to perfection; and, needless to say, his current reputation is largely due to his mastery of this form.

Life in Italy suited Browning, and the atmosphere of that land permeates many of the poems in this collection. Some are Italian simply in landscape, such as the humorous "Up at a Villa—Down in the City." In other poems, such as "A Serenade at the Villa," "By the Fire-Side," and "Two in the Campagna," it is apparent that Browning's primary interest is in examining human relationships which could take place anywhere; the scene is Italy but setting is incidental. Other poems, however, draw upon distinctly Italian sources: curious customs, for example ("Holy-Cross Day"), and local legends ("The Statue and the Bust"). In later years Browning would often say that "Italy was my university"; what he had studied at that university was Italian art. "Old Pictures in Florence" reflects his interest in that art, as do "Fra Lippo Lippi" and "Andrea del Sarto," both of which are imaginary character studies of real Renaissance painters. "The Guardian-Angel" is based on an actual painting (as the subtitle indicates): "A Picture at Fano. " 'De Gustibus—' " contains the clearest statement of Browning's love for Italy; there he writes:

> Open my heart and you will see
> Graved inside of it, 'Italy.'

The Italian element is, however, less important than another personal influence, that of the poet's marriage. Although the love poems in *Men and Women* are not necessarily autobiographical, they do reflect, at least indirectly, the relationship between Elizabeth Barrett and Robert Browning. In "By the Fire-Side" communication is complete; love is serene. But in "The Last Ride Together," "Andrea del Sarto," "Love in a Life," "Life in a Love," and "Any Wife to Any Husband," communication breaks down and love fails. "Two in the Campagna" deals with

> Infinite passion and the pain
> Of finite hearts that yearn.

Thus Browning indicates the gap between love in dreams and in reality. Most of these poems dramatize a love-situation and are content to evoke it without commenting on it. "The Statue and the Bust," however, includes a flatly stated moral:

> Let a man contend to the uttermost
> For his life's set prize ...

and never miss that prize because of wasted opportunities.

Some have suggested that in examining the vicissitudes of love Browning was revealing flaws in his own marriage. "A Lover's Quarrel," for example, does involve disagreement over two subjects about which he and his wife differed: spiritualism (she believed in it; he scoffed at it) and Napoleon III, Emperor of France (she was an admirer; he was not). But the evidence is by no means conclusive, and the one poem in *Men and Women* which is openly autobiographical, "One Word More: To E.B.B.," is Browning's dedication to his wife, not only of the book, but of himself.

Many of Browning's favorite themes are broached in the poems of *Men and Women*. The idea that the course of a man's life may turn upon a moment's decision is expressed in "The Statue and the Bust." The idea that "A man's reach should exceed his grasp" is the subject of "Andrea del Sarto," as well as "Old Pictures in Florence," and "A Grammarian's Funeral." Browning's attitudes towards religion and religious belief are presented in "Saul," "Cleon," "An Epistle Containing the Strange Medical Experience of Karshish, the Arab Physician," and "Bishop Blougram's Apology."

It must be admitted that the present age is little interested in most of Browning's opinions *per se;* we may be no nearer than the Victorians to solving the problems which beset Browning and his contemporaries, but we tend to prefer more recent attempts to solve them. Browning's ideas about art are, however, perfectly current; they have a bearing not only on art in general but, more particularly, on his own poetry. A number of the poems in *Men and Women* contain, implicitly or explicitly, theories of art which help to explain what Browning was attempting to do in his poetry.

"I only knew one poet in my life," says the speaker in "How It Strikes a Contemporary," and the poem itself is in many ways Browning's own description of what a poet should be. The poet, first of all, looks the world full in the face; he is no idle dreamer. He sees life and he sees it whole, taking "such cognizance of men and things" that he can truthfully be called "a recording chief-inquisitor...." This poem can be seen as a veiled defense of Browning's own tendency to write about characters and events which may not, in the dilettantish sense, have been deemed sufficiently "poetic." If, in Browning's view, the poet's proper sphere is life as it really is, the poet's function is nonetheless an exalted one: he writes in the service of God. The poet described in "How It Strikes a Contemporary"

> ... walked about and took account
> Of all thought, said and acted, then went home,
> And wrote it fully to our Lord the King ....

"Memorabilia," a slight poem, is chiefly remembered because it alludes to Shelley—one of Browning's early enthusiasms and the subject of Browning's only important prose essay. "Popularity" is a tribute to another of Browning's favorite poets, John Keats. In this poem there is further allusion to Browning's belief that the poet's role is somehow linked with the divine mission. One of Browning's most explicit statements about what poetry should aim to be is found in " 'Transcendentalism': a Poem in Twelve Books." Here he obviously prefers Keatsian or Shelleyan "song" to the over-labored, earnest "thought" which characterized so much bad Victorian poetry. One poet, speaking to another, says:

> 'Tis you speak, that's your error. Song's our art:
> Whereas you please to speak these naked thoughts
> Instead of draping them in sights and sounds.

Browning has no objection to thought in poetry, but it should not be presented baldly, for its own sake. Rather, it should be draped "in sights and sounds."

In the two dramatic monologues which are generally acknowledged to be the finest poems in *Men and Women*, "Fra Lippo Lippi" and "Andrea del Sarto," Browning gives further insights into his theories of art. It is obvious that, in bringing these two Renaissance painters to life, his own sympathies as an artist lie completely with Lippo Lippi and not at all with Andrea del Sarto. He depicts the latter as a skilled craftsman whose hand and eye are deft, but who has only "something of a heart." His paintings are accomplished, but cold-blooded and uninspired. In the poem Andrea del Sarto comes to realize that he has failed to infuse into his work the quality of a great soul. An artist's success, Browning is saying, resides not merely in his technical perfection but also in his ability to give sufficiently of himself to make his work burn with the true "light of God."

In seeing the creation of a work of art as a moral act Browning is not advocating the kind of art which merely moralizes, though Browning's own late poems, in the years after *The Ring and the Book*, frequently do just that. Fra Lippo Lippi's monastic superiors have forced him to paint pious pictures which will

> ". . . say to folk—remember matins,
> Or, mind you fast next Friday."

They have told him that his purpose is not to depict the world but to "forget there's such a thing as flesh" and "to paint the souls of men." Lippi himself, however, is too honest an artist, and too fully a man, to be content with their dictates:

> . . . zooks, sir, flesh and blood,
> That's all I'm made of!

He loves the things of the world but not merely in and for themselves. He sees the beauty of the world as God's creation and therefore not to be despised. The artist, he believes (and Browning with him), by portraying finite beauty comes closest to portraying infinite beauty as well. "I never saw," says Lippi, "beauty with no soul at all." In his characterization of this hookey-playing Italian monk, Browning has given us, at a distance, a veritable portrait of himself as an artist.

When we have sifted Browning's poems for their ideas, even those about art, we have still done him less than justice as a poet. His greatness ultimately is to be located in his creation of memorable characters: the Chaucerian Fra Lippo Lippi, the self-pitying Andrea del Sarto, the wily Bishop Blougram, the Greek Cleon, the Arab Karshish, the dying Bishop concerned about his tomb, and a whole gallery of lovers in a splendid variety of moods. Browning's early failures as a writer for the stage taught him a valuable lesson: that his abilities were suited for the delineation of "Action in Character, rather than Character in Action." His psychological studies of "Action" within his justly famous characters, particularly in the dramatic monologues, are the main basis for the reputation his name holds today.

It is interesting to note that, during his lifetime, Browning's fame came slowly. The sale of so great a collection of poems as *Men and Women* was disappointingly slow: no second edition was ever called for. It was not until the publication of *Dramatis Personae*, in 1864, that he began to receive the recognition he deserved.

Bibliography

Armstrong, Isobel, Editor. *Robert Browning.* Athens: Ohio University Press, 1975.

Benvenuto, R. "Lippo and Andrea: The Pro and Contra of Browning's Realism," in *Studies in English Literature.* XIII (Autumn, 1973), pp. 643–652.

Blackburn, Thomas. *Robert Browning: A Study of His Poetry.* Totowa, N.J.: Rowman and Littlefield, 1974. Reprint of 1967 Edition.

Brooke, Stopford A. *The Poetry of Robert Browning.* New York: AMS Press, 1969. Reprint of 1902 Edition.

Bross, A.C. "Browning's Changing Concept of Faith," in *Victorian Poetry.* XIV (Spring, 1976), pp. 11–23.

Cook, Eleanor. *Browning's Lyrics: An Exploration.* Toronto: University of Toronto Press, 1974.

Drew, Philip. *The Poetry of Browning: A Critical Introduction.* London: Methuen, 1970.

Flowers, Betty S. *Browning and the Modern Tradition.* New York: Macmillan, 1976.

Hess, S.W. "Browning in Our Ear," in *Contemporary Review.* CCXVI (March, 1970), pp. 140–144.

Holmes, S.W. "Browning: Semantic Stutterer," in *ETC.* XXXI (March, 1974), pp. 73–99.

Irvine, William. *The Book, the Ring, and the Poet: A Biography of Robert Browning.* New York: McGraw-Hill, 1974.

Jack, Ian R. *Browning's Major Poetry.* Oxford: Clarendon Press, 1973.

Korg, J. "Browning's Art and 'By the Fireside,'" in *Victorian Poetry.* XV (Summer, 1977), pp. 147–158.

Langbaum, R. "Browning and the Quest of Myth," in *PMLA.* LXXXI (December, 1966), pp. 575–584.

Litzinger, Boyd, Editor. *Browning: The Critical Heritage.* New York: Barnes & Noble, 1970.

McComb, J.K. "Beyond the Dark Tower: Childe Roland's Painful Memories," in *ELH.* XLII (Fall, 1975), pp. 460–470.

Maynard, John. *Browning's Youth.* Cambridge, Mass.: Harvard University Press, 1977.

Melchiori, B. "Browning's Don Juan," in *Essays in Criticism.* XVI (October, 1966), pp. 416–440.

Mermin, D.M. "Speaker and Auditor in Browning's Dramatic Monologues," in *University of Toronto Quarterly.* XLV (Winter, 1976), pp. 139–157.

Pearsall, Robert B. *Robert Browning.* New York: Twayne, 1974.

Peterson, William S. *Robert and Elizabeth Barrett Browning: An Annotated Bibliography, 1951–1970.* New York: Browning Institute, 1974.

Poston, L. "Browning's Political Skepticism: Sordello and the Plays," in *PMLA.* LXXXVIII (March, 1973), pp. 260–270.

Preyer, R. "Two Styles in the Verse of Robert Browning," in *ELH.* XXXII (March, 1965), pp. 62–84.

Ryals, Clyde de L. *Browning's Later Poetry, 1871–1889.* Ithaca, N.Y.: Cornell University Press, 1975.

Siegchrist, M. "Thematic Coherence in Browning's Dramatic Idyls," in *Victorian Poetry.* XI (Autumn, 1977), pp. 229–239.

THE RING AND THE BOOK

Type of work: Poem
Author: Robert Browning (1812–1889)
Type of plot: Dramatic monologues
Time of plot: Seventeenth century
Locale: Italy
First published: 1868–1869

Based upon a murder trial in the city of Florence in 1698, The Ring and the Book *probes the inner motivations of the people involved in that old, sordid tale of passion and crime. A series of dramatic characterizations and episodes carries the reader to the magnificent conclusion. Pompilia and Caponsacchi are among Browning's most notable creations.*

Principal Characters

Count Guido Franceschini (gwē′dō frän·chĕs·kē′nē), the oldest male member of a destitute noble family of Arezzo. Knowing that he is the last hope for furthering the family name, since his two brothers are priests, Guido seeks a wife to bear him a son. Impoverished, he needs a woman with an attractive dowry. His brother finds a likely prospect, and Guido's family name attracts the girl's mother. Inept as a husband and angered by denial of the dowry after the wedding, Guido abuses his wife. To retain the last vestige of honor as a husband, after he has driven her to extramarital affections, Guido, with four men from his village, kills his parents-in-law and fatally wounds his wife. The court hearings and the gossip relating to the affair, presented from various viewpoints, point to Guido's instability, he representing an old family without means of sustenance or continuation—no wealth, no prestige, no progeny. He is sentenced to be hanged, by rulings of both Church and State.

Pompilia Comparini (pôm·pē′lyä kôm·pä·rē′nē), his seventeen-year-old wife. Bought as a newborn infant from a prostitute, Pompilia was brought up by aged foster parents. Trapped in an incompatible marriage not of her choice, she flees to Rome with Caponsacchi, a priest. Overtaken, she and the priest disavow that they are lovers. After hearing that Pompilia, who has returned to her foster parents, has given birth to a son, Guido returns to Rome with four ruffians and attacks the Comparinis. Pompilia, mortally wounded, lingers for four days, time enough for her to identify her attacker.

Violante Comparini (vī·ō·län′tē), her foster mother. Violante's warped sense of values leads to bizarre behavior. She feigns pregnancy, presents Pompilia to her husband as his child, negotiates Pompilia's marriage, and convinces her husband, who has objected to the marriage, that the status achieved by the union will be worth the promised dowry. Realizing her bad bargain and attempting to keep Guido from profiting by the marriage, Violante divulges Pompilia's parentage and disqualifies her from inheriting Comparini's money.

Pietro Comparini (pyā′trō), Violante's husband. Naïve and browbeaten, he is governed by his wife's whims and desires.

Giuseppe Caponsacchi (jö·zĕp′pä käp′ən-säk·kē), a handsome priest, Pompilia's gallant lover. Excommunicated for his part in the affair, Giuseppe wishes himself dead but looks forward to the day when he will be returned to the grace of the Church.

Margherita (mär·gä·rē′tä), Pompilia's maid, who advises and encourages Pompilia to throw off the drudgery of her life with Guido by responding to Giuseppe's attentions.

Paolo (pä′ō·lō), Count Guido's brother, a priest in Rome, who makes the initial contact with Violante for the marriage of Guido and Pompilia. His description of his brother makes Guido more attractive than the Comparinis find him.

Doctor Johannes-Baptista Bottinius (yō·hän′əs-bäp·tēs′tä bōt·tēn′yŭs), familiarly called Giovambittista o' the Bottini, who variously defends Pompilia at the hearings, for her behavior in the affair, and persecutes her, as the gossips of Rome cried, by ordering her money given to a sisterhood rather than to her child.

Dominus Hyacinthus de Archangelis (dŏm′ĭ·nəs hī′ə·sĭn′thəs də är·kan′je·ləs) familiarly called Don Giacinto of the Archangeli, the Procurator of the poor in Rome. He defends Guido and his hired companions at the hearings.

Pope Innocent XII, who condemns Count Guido to die in the presence of the populace; however, before his death he prays that the condemned man may be forgiven his sin.

Gaetano (gä·ā·tä′nō), Pompilia's two-week-old son, who, she says in her dying moments, ". . . nor was, nor is, nor yet shall be/Count Guido Franceschini's child at all—/Only his mother's born of love not hate!"

Tommati (tō·mä′tē) and Venturini (vĕn·tūr·ē′nē), judges at the hearings.

The Story

Count Guido Franceschini, descended from an ancient house of Aretine, had married Pompilia Comparini, a young and beautiful Roman girl. Unhappy with her husband, the young wife fled back to Rome in the company of a young priest, Giuseppe Caponsacchi. Guido and four accomplices followed her, and on Christmas night he found his wife at the home of her parents, Pietro and Violante. He murdered the seventy-year-old man and woman and fatally wounded seventeen-year-old Pompilia.

The aged parents were laid in the church where the people of Rome came to stare and to speculate. The Comparini had been childless until somehow Violante had tricked Pietro into thinking that she had given birth to the child she had secretly bought. It was Violante's mischief which had led to evil, asserted the Roman people. She had spied Guido, of a noble family, and had persuaded him to take Pompilia for his wife. Then all three, parents and daughter, had moved to his estate in Arezzo and there learned of Guido's poverty. Leaving Pompilia behind, the Comparini returned to Rome. Back in Rome, Violante confessed to Pietro that she had bought the child from a prostitute, and by disowning her parentage the aged couple denied Guido his dowry rights. Pompilia, meanwhile, wrote a letter to the archbishop in Rome, telling him that since her parents' departure life

in Arezzo had become unbearable. In Arezzo, Pompilia had begun a flirtation
with Caponsacchi, the Roman gossipers related, and at last had run away with
him. As the guilty pair neared Rome, Guido overtook them and brought them to
Rome and to the Pope. The couple declared themselves innocent and disavowed
love letters which Guido claimed had passed between them. When the court
treated the case as a slight marriage quarrel, Guido returned to Arezzo and the
taunts of his townsmen. Soon afterward news reached him that Pompilia, who
had returned to the Comparini, had given birth to a son. Then Guido took four
men, went to Rome, killed the parents, and left Pompilia dying. The Romans
excitedly awaited the trial, for Caponsacchi would be one of the witnesses.

Another group of spectators in Rome took a different view of the murderer and
his wife. Pompilia had been a blessing to her foster parents, no matter how she
came to them. They had considered it a blessing when Guido married their
daughter, only to reach horrible disillusionment when they went to Arezzo and
saw his cruelty and poverty. She was Guido's victim, these gossips said.

The tribunal tried to determine the truth in the case. Pietro and Violante had
been poor, struggling creatures. When the mother of Pompilia was with child,
Violante had bargained with her for the baby and deceived her husband by pretending that it was she who was pregnant. Her act was judged criminal. When
Guido came to Rome to find a wife to bear him sons, and a dowry to pay his
debts, Pietro and Violante gave him their daughter so that she could rise in name
and fortune. When they learned that Guido was penniless, they cried that they
had been cheated. Meanwhile it was Pompilia who suffered between the rival
factions of parents and husband. She was tricked by Guido to trace letters to
Caponsacchi, which were offered at the trial. But Guido's friends claimed that he
could not have so mistreated his young wife, that she must have written the letters herself.

Guido told his own story. His family had once been wealthy and great, but in
his lifetime they had known only poverty. His brothers were priests; he alone
remained to carry on the Franceschini name. His brother Paul, a priest in Rome,
had advised him that Pompilia would make a suitable wife. He was to give the
girl his name and state in return for her dowry and her son. But Pompilia shirked
her wifely duties from the first. One day she caught the eye of Caponsacchi at the
opera. Afterward Caponsacchi's way to church led him past Guido's house, past
Pompilia's window. Then one night Pompilia drugged Guido and all the servants
and fled with her priest to the inn where Guido located them. He found some
letters Caponsacchi had exchanged with her, letters which she claimed had been
forged. He brought them to court to have his marriage anulled, but the court
upheld the marriage and sent Caponsacchi away for a short confinement. Pompilia returned to Pietro and Violante and there she had a child which Guido
believed Caponsacchi's. He had no other course, he said, but to go to Rome and
cleanse his family name, and he threw himself upon the justice of the court.

Caponsacchi took the stand to describe his first sight of Pompilia at the opera.

Not long after he received a letter, signed by Pompilia, confessing love and asking him to come to her window. Suspecting the letter to be a forgery, he answered it with a refusal. He received more letters. At last he became curious and went to stand outside Guido's house. Pompilia, seeing him, rebuked him for his unseemly letters to her, a married woman. They decided that they were victims of Guido's plot. Pompilia begged Caponsacchi to take her to her parents in Rome. His heart softening at her plight, he arranged for her to go away with him.

Pompilia, Caponsacchi said, had been victimized by her cruel husband. The testimony of dying Pompilia upheld what Caponsacchi had said. At the time of her marriage she had been only thirteen years old. She had been brought to Arezzo, to an impoverished home where Guido's brother had tried to seduce her. For three years she lived in misery. Then she received letters from Caponsacchi. She tried to understand the mystery, knowing that somehow she was being tricked, but finally she sent for the priest because she had decided to seek help from the outside world.

The testimony of others followed, some in defense of Guido, others exposing his carefully laid plot to rid himself of Pompilia. Testimony of Pompilia's innocence was also presented. The Pope, condemning Guido for the crime, pronounced Pompilia innocent of guilt and told the court of the tremendous burden of justice that a Pope must carry on his shoulders. Guido and his four accomplices were sentenced to be hanged.

Humbled and fearful of death, Guido made one last plea for his life. Pride and self-love colored his statements as he confessed his crime but rationalized his motive. He was to be pitied; he wanted to live. He pleaded for mercy which was not granted.

Critical Evaluation

Compared to Shakespeare's greatest plays when it first appeared, *The Ring and the Book* put the final stamp of unqualified distinction on its author and confirmed his equality with Tennyson, the other giant of Victorian poetry. The Shakespearean comparison was a tribute to Robert Browning's poetic range, his capacity to dig deep into the muck of experience only to raise up forms and people larger than life Keats had thought Shakespeare divine because he could create both an Iago and an Imogen. Similarly, Browning was admired for the variety and complexity of his characters. In *Men and Women* (1855) he had revealed his gift for penetrating character analysis in such brilliant dramatic monologues as "Fra Lippo Lippi" and "Andreo del Sarto." The joyous realism of Lippi, his relish for portraying things "just as they are," contrasts sharply with the self-delusion of del Sarto, who betrays his talent and reputation for a worthless wife.

What Browning had accomplished with individual monologues (his characteristic poetic form), became the basis for a cosmic view of human evil in

The Ring and the Book. For four years he worked on this ambitious project and published it at intervals in 1868-1869. It is a narrative poem consisting of many long monologues, each expressing a different view of the central action —Guido's murder of Pompilia and her parents. By reflecting each character in the thoughts of the other, Browning's monologues achieve dazzling effects in point of view and psychological revelation—despite the syntactical obscurity of much of the verse (Browning shares with the later Henry James that peculiar blend of impenetrable style with striking illumination). The monologue form enables each character to penetrate his own mind and speculate on the thoughts and feelings of the others with a depth denied the conventional drama. The effect is similar to what would happen if all the best soliloquies of a Shakespearean play were juxtaposed and still constituted a unified drama despite the absence of intervening dialogue and action. The analytical power of Browning's approach is reinforced by the variety of the characters themselves; they are so divergent in temperament and nature it is difficult to imagine them together in a conventional drama: ruthless, sensual, and manic-depressive Guido; saintly but dangerously immature Pompilia; the venal and pathetic parents, so petty in their thinking and so cruelly vulnerable because of it; worldly but impressionable Caponsacchi, the priest; and finally, the humanist Pope, who must judge Guido and does so with a mixture of compassion and contempt that captures perfectly the realism and tough-minded spiritualism of the Renaissance Church.

The blend of people, values, and emotions that informs this poem is anticipated by the opening part, in which the poet explains the title of his work. The "Book" is the Yellow Book, the old record of the story and trial that Browning found in a Florence book stall. The "Ring" is the result of mixing the raw gold of the Yellow Book with the alloy of his art; in other words, the "Ring" is the crafted result of the artist's sympathetic imagination—a power that penetrates the mysteries of experience with greater revelation than any other human effort. Browning's "Ring" is also a symbol of the poem's circular reflection: it is literally a house of mirrors, in which the reflections of several minds cross in the mind of the reader.

Browning's willingness to base a dramatic poem, full of what Matthew Arnold would have called "high seriousness," on a sordid story of crime and mayhem stems largely from his conviction that anything representative of life as it truly is, is worth facing. For Browning the only absolute evil is the rejection of life itself. Anything that affirms life is finally good, even if man's vileness is part of it. To recognize the existence of evil is not to condone it; Browning simply believed that an objective consideration of the vast range of evil in the world—from petty indifference to sadistic murder—only revealed in bolder terms the ultimate moral order of the universe.

Elizabeth Barrett, Browning's wife, took issue with his insistence on the relevance of the sordid and the ugly to a moral art. She wanted him to drop his "dramatis personae" and speak with his own voice. But he insisted that his objective dramatizations, his dramatic monologues, were the "best" he had to give the world. He was right. Browning had what André Gide described as an "eclectic soul." He could "put himself momentarily into someone else." Like Keats's "negative capability," Browning's ability to enter strange forms of consciousness enabled him to achieve states of perception beyond the mere self. What seemed an absence of identity, or even personal involvement on his part, became finally a means to a poetic understanding greater than that exemplified in the ardent subjectivism of his wife's poetry. Browning may have started off as an amoral dramatizer, but he ended as one of the major poet-teachers of his period.

It is the Pope, and his function in *The Ring and the Book,* that vindicated Browning's dramatic objectivism to his wife and all the other Victorians. The Pope is a spokesman for Browning's hard-won ethical vision; he represents a projection of Browning's own power to sermonize and idealize in the very act of demonstrating the venality and terrifying corruptibility of the human soul. Browning, finally, is not a tragic writer. There is too much of a sometimes naïve robustness in him; man's flaws do not define his fate. On the contrary, Browning saw in the very imperfection of life the seeds of God's power. William Clyde DeVane suggests Browning is closer to Milton than Shakespeare. Like the poet of *Paradise Lost,* Browning "justifies the ways of God to man." Man must strive to know all he can, as does the Pope in his soul-searching effort to comprehend the meaning of Guido's crime, but the Pope's limited understanding is God's design. Even as he passes judgment on Guido, the Pope realizes that his own moral vision is being tested and shaped: "All to the very end is trial in life." For the moderns this means anxiety and alienation. For Browning it merely marks off the arena.

Bibliography

Altick, Richard D. *Browning's Roman Murder Story: A Reading of* The Ring and the Book. Chicago: University of Chicago Press, 1968.

Armstrong, Isobel, Editor. *Robert Browning.* Athens: Ohio University Press, 1975.

Blackburn, Thomas. *Robert Browning: A Study of His Poetry.* Totowa, N.J.: Rowman and Littlefield, 1974. Reprint of 1967 Edition.

Brooke, Stopford A. *The Poetry of Robert Browning.* New York: AMS Press, 1969. Reprint of 1902 Edition.

Columbus, C.K. *"Ring and the Book*: A Masque for the Making of Meaning," in *Philological Quarterly.* LIII (Spring, 1974), pp. 237–255.

Cook, Eleanor. *Browning's Lyrics: An Exploration.* Toronto: University of Toronto Press, 1974.

Cundiff, Paul A. *Browning's Ring Metaphor and Truth.* Metuchen, N.J.: Scarecrow Press, 1972.

Drew, Philip. *The Poetry of Browning: A Critical Introduction.* London: Methuen, 1970.

Flowers, Betty S. *Browning and the Modern Tradition.* New York: Macmillan, 1976.

Gaylord, Harriet. *Pompilia and Her Poet.* New York: Literary Publishers, 1931.

Gross, D.H. "Browning's Positivist Count in Search of a Miracle: A Grim Parody in *The Ring and the Book*," in *Victorian Poetry.* XII (Summer, 1974), pp. 178–180.

Irvine, William. *The Book, the Ring, and the Poet: A Biography of Robert Browning.* New York: McGraw-Hill, 1974.

Jack, Ian R. *Browning's Major Poetry.* Oxford: Clarendon Press, 1973.

James, Henry. "The Novel in *The Ring and the Book*," in his *Notes on Novelists with Some Other Notes.* London: 1914, pp. 306–319.

Johnson, E.D. "Robert Browning's Pluralistic Universe: A Reading of *The Ring and the Book*," in *University of Toronto Quarterly.* XXXI (1961), pp. 20–41.

Langbaum, Robert. "The Importance of Fact in *The Ring and the Book*," in *Victorian Newsletter.* XVII (1960), pp. 11–17.

Litzinger, Boyd, Editor. *Browning: The Critical Heritage.* New York: Barnes & Noble, 1970.

Maynard, John. *Browning's Youth.* Cambridge, Mass.: Harvard University Press, 1977.

Pearsall, Robert B. *Robert Browning.* New York: Twayne, 1974.

Peterson, William S. *Robert and Elizabeth Barrett Browning: An Annotated Bibliography, 1951–1970.* New York: Browning Institute, 1974.

Ryals, Clyde de L. *Browning's Later Poetry, 1871–1889.* Ithaca, N.Y.: Cornell University Press, 1975.

Thompson, George W. "Authorial Detachment and Imagery in *The Ring and the Book*," in *Studies in English Literature.* X (Autumn, 1970), pp. 669–686.

Wasserman, George R. "The Meaning of Browning's Ring Figure," in *Modern Language Notes.* LXXVI (May, 1961), pp. 420–426.

THOMAS CARLYLE

Born: Ecclefechan, Scotland (December 4, 1795)
Died: London, England (February 4, 1881)

Principal Works

SOCIAL, PHILOSOPHICAL, AND POLITICAL ESSAYS: *Characteristics*, 1831; *Sartor Resartus*, 1835; *Chartism*, 1839; *On Heroes, Hero-Worship and the Heroic in History*, 1841; *Past and Present*, 1843; *Original Discourses on the Negro Question*, 1849; *Latter-Day Pamphlets*, 1850; *Shooting Niagara: and After*, 1867; *Last Words of Thomas Carlyle*, 1882.

HISTORY AND BIOGRAPHY: *The French Revolution*, 1837; *Oliver Cromwell's Letters and Speeches, with Elucidations*, 1845; *Life of John Sterling*, 1851; *History of Frederick II of Prussia*, 1858–1865; *The Early Kings of Norway; also an Essay on the Portraits of John Knox*, 1875.

CRITICAL ESSAYS AND STUDIES: *Essay on Goethe's Faust*, 1822; *Life of Schiller*, 1823–1824; *Essay on Richter*, 1827; *The Present State of German Literature*, 1827; *Life and Writings of Werner*, 1828; *Essay on Burns*, 1828; *Voltaire*, 1829; *Sir Walter Scott*, 1838; *Critical and Miscellaneous Essays*, 1839, 1840, 1847.

TRAVEL SKETCHES AND IMPRESSIONS: *Reminiscences of My Irish Journey*, 1849.

AUTOBIOGRAPHY: *Reminiscences*, 1881.

TRANSLATIONS: *Wilhelm Meister's Apprenticeship*, 1824; *German Romance*, 1827.

The childhood of Thomas Carlyle was spent in the village of Ecclefechan, in Dumfriesshire, Scotland, where he was born on December 4, 1795. His father, James Carlyle, was a stonemason. From the age of ten Carlyle attended the grammar school at Annan, and at fourteen he was sent, on foot, to enroll in the University of Edinburgh. Here he remained until 1814, when he left without a degree and became a teacher of mathematics at his old school. Subsequently he held the mastership of a school at Kirkcaldy. His parents, who were devout Calvinists, had wanted him to study divinity and become a minister; but in 1817 he definitely rejected this course of life. For a time he lived in Edinburgh and desultorily read law, but was unable to interest himself in any profession. Weakened by dyspepsia and much troubled in mind by his inability to achieve philosophical or religious certitude, he underwent a period of acute strain which culminated, during the summer of 1822, in his well-known spiritual crisis, recorded in *Sartor Resartus*. By now greatly under the influence of the German philosophers, especially Richter and Fichte, he was beginning to devise a set of beliefs acceptable to himself and was coming to realize that his vocation was to be literary and philosophic. He became absorbed in the poetry of Goethe, with whom he corresponded after the publication of his English translation of *Wilhelm*

Meister's Apprenticeship.

In 1826 he married Jane Welsh, an exceptionally brilliant girl who had been a pupil of his friend Edward Irving. Their life together seems to have been tempestuous in the extreme. They lived in Edinburgh two years and then moved to Craigenputtoch, an isolated farm in Dumfriesshire. There Carlyle worked painstakingly on the "clothes philosophy" of *Sartor Resartus* and consolidated his whole system of thought; his six years at Craigenputtoch were his time of intellectual self-discovery. A few journeys to London sufficed to win him a number of literary friends, including John Stuart Mill. In 1834, after another brief sojourn in Edinburgh, the Carlyles moved to Chelsea, London, so that he might have access to the London libraries to assemble material for his great historical study, *The French Revolution.* This he finally completed early in 1837, after the terrible experience of having to rewrite the whole first volume; he had lent the manuscript to Mill, and Mill had left it with his friend Mrs. Taylor, whose servant girl heedlessly used it to light fires. Carlyle had no other copy and had preserved no notes. *The French Revolution*, as soon as it appeared, established his reputation once and for all. The most important of his later works were *Chartism, On Heroes, Hero-Worship and the Heroic in History, Past and Present*, and a six-volume history of Frederick the Great. Surviving his wife by almost fifteen years, Carlyle died in London on February 4, 1881. His highly indiscreet *Reminiscences*, edited by his official biographer, James Anthony Froude, aroused much indignation when they appeared shortly after his death.

Carlyle was a bitter enemy of conformity. He extolled government by an aristocracy of talent, despised democracy and popular political institutions, and damned the French Revolution. He admired the interdependence of classes under feudalism, preached the sacredness of work in opposition to the cult of riches, and scorned mass production as the bane of fine craftsmanship. He expressed his ideas in an intense, and often somewhat raucous, literary style.

Bibliography

The standard edition is the Centenary Edition, edited by H. D. Trail, 30 vols., 1897–1901. The library of Carlyle correspondence is extensive: *Correspondence of Carlyle and Emerson*, edited by Charles Eliot Norton, 1886; *Correspondence between Goethe and Carlyle*, ed. by Norton, 1887; *Early Letters*, ed. by Norton, 1887; *Letters, 1826–1836*, ed. by Norton, 2 vols., 1888; *Letters to His Youngest Sister*, edited by C. T. Copeland, 1899; *New Letters*, edited by Alexander Carlyle, 2 vols., 1905; *Love Letters of Thomas Carlyle and Jane Welsh*, ed. by A. Carlyle, 2 vols., 1909; *Letters to John Stuart Mill, John Sterling, and Robert Browning*, ed. by A. Carlyle, 1923; *Letters and Memorials of Jane Welsh Carlyle, Prepared for Publication by Thomas Carlyle*, edited by James Anthony Froude, 3 vols., 1883; and *Jane Welsh Carlyle: Letters to Her Family*, 1839–1863, edited by Leonard Huxley, 1924. *The Collected Letters of Thomas and Jane Carlyle* under the general editorship of Charles R. Sanders, 30 vols. projected, 1971—, will be the definitive edition of the letters.

The authorized biography is James Anthony Froude, *Thomas Carlyle: History of the First Forty Years of His Life*, 2 vols., 1882, and *Thomas Carlyle: History of His Life in London*, 2 vols., 1884. For the history of this controversial work see D. A. Wilson, *Froude and Carlyle*, 1898; J. A. Froude, *My Relations with Carlyle*, 1903; J. Crichton-Browne, *Froude and Carlyle*, 1903; J. Crichton-Browne and Alexander Carlyle, *The Nemesis of Froude*, 1903; and Waldo Dunn, *Froude and Carlyle*, 1930. For additional biographical and critical studies see D. A. Wilson, *Life of Carlyle*, 6 vols., 1923–1934, a monumental and well-documented work; also, R. S. Craig, *The Making of Carlyle*, 1908; W. S. Johnson, *Thomas Carlyle: A Study of His Literary Apprenticeship, 1814–1831*, 1911; Louis Cazinmam, *Carlyle*, 1913 (trans., 1932); Osbert Burdett, *The Two Carlyles*, 1931; F. A. Lea, *Carlyle: Prophet of Today*, 1943; Julian Symons, *Thomas Carlyle: The Life and Ideas of a Prophet*, 1952; David Gascoyne, *Thomas Carlyle*, 1952; John Holloway, *The Victorian Sage: Studies in Argument*, 1953; and Thea Holme, *The Carlyles at Home*, 1965.

THE FRENCH REVOLUTION

Type of work: History
Author: Thomas Carlyle (1795–1881)
Time: Last quarter of the eighteenth century
Locale: Paris and elsewhere in France
First published: 1837

Essay-Review

The French Revolution is a landmark in the history of nineteenth-century English literature, the work that, after the comparative public failure of *Sartor Resartus*, helped to establish Carlyle's star in its ascendancy. In its dramatic picture of the French Revolution it offered the general reader an estimate of an event that had disturbed and shocked the consciences of his grandparents. It offered a measure of revolutionary and socially disruptive movements that was neither optimistic and blindly trustful of progress (here Carlyle differed from Utilitarian friends) nor pessimistic and horrified, as Edmund Burke had been at the time of the Revolution. Finally, and perhaps most important for us, *The French Revolution* was a more successful self-realization for Carlyle than the comparatively incompleted explorations of ideas which we find in *Sartor Resartus*. *The French Revolution* presents a number of the same ideas from the earlier book brought into relation to and supported by a bewilderingly rich body of facts: the day by day events of the disturbing French years.

Impressive as is Carlyle's method of digesting and arranging the body of facts, still more memorable is the way he commands the facts to do his will. Like an Old Testament prophet, Carlyle rides the hurricane and directs the storm of the fall of absolute monarchy in France. He produces not just another history of a vexed period, full of rationalized information. It is true of Carlyle that his view of one period of history is always on the verge of becoming a vision of *all* human history. The French women who march on Versailles stand for the passionate outbreak of all oppressed human beings, and the sorrows of Marie Antoinette in the Concièrgerie stand for the agonies of all trivial human beings carried to their doom by forces they cannot dominate.

It is possible to indicate some of the means that Carlyle employs to create his apocalyptic vision—a vision, not of last things, but certainly of the forces that combine to drive history onward. The arrangement of the facts is rigorously chronological. The book begins with the death-pangs of King Louis XV; these are at once represented as the death-throes not of one aged monarch but of a regime or way of life that once justified itself but which is now a hollow reality. The book continues with an account of the suicidal follies of the young king, Louis XVI, and his pretty and thoughtless wife, Marie Antoinette. It notices the efforts of some of the king's ministers, Necker, Turgot, and others, to stem the advancing tide: to restore financial soundness and yet provide money for all who thought they had a right to spend it. Carlyle, often with a somewhat uneven pace which permits him to stop for angry or compassionate meditation when he wishes to point out the "inevitable" chain of disaster and struggle, continues his year by year and month by month account. He tells of the meeting of the Estates General, the Tennis Court Oath, the march on Versailles, the various attempts to frame a constitution, the degeneration of the relation between the royal couple and the Revolutionary Government, the royal family's attempted escape to Varennes, the successive decapitations of king and queen, the succession of leaders who could not lead but had to dictate by harangue and outright terror, and, finally, the end of the revolution at the hands of Napoleon Bonaparte, who brought order with a "whiff of grapeshot" in 1795.

Carlyle, at the end of his work, speaks of a ship that finally is over the bar after much labor and peril from counter winds; and this is certainly the effect of his narrative. Despite its complexity, his story is the single account of a set of events that give a full demonstration of the glories and horrors of revolution, a period of history that was inevitable but not, because of its inevitability, admirable.

In dramatizing a mighty and perilous passage that involved not the French nation alone but all humanity, Thomas Carlyle was able to transform his account of actual events into an apocalyptic statement about man that does not seem to belong to any particular time at all. He did so by means of his style of presentation and by passages of direct, explicit interpretation. Perhaps it is the style that is most decisive. Never before or since has an English-writing historian written a book like this history of Carlyle's. The narrative is couched in the present tense; what occurs happens not in a safely distant past, but here and now. The sentimentality of the French *philosophes* and the ignorant and brutal enthusiasms of the mob threaten us the readers as Carlyle drags us through mountains of detail and event. Moreover, Carlyle frequently interrupts the forward movement of the narrative to harangue some of the chief actors in his story—Danton, Mirabeau, Marie Antoinette—and as we read it seems possible that they may listen to him and escape what we well know was their historical fate. Some of the harangues, of course, speak not to the historical personages but to us and suggest that we (even more than a century after the appearance of the book) may escape our historical fate if we will but listen to Thomas Carlyle. Or if we may not escape it, we shall understand it better after reading *The French Revolution*.

Implication becomes explicit in innumerable passages like the following brief one:

> Or, apart from all Transcendentalism, is it not a plain truth of sense, which the duller mind can even consider as a truism, that human things wholly are in continual movement, and action and reaction; working continually forward, phasis after phasis, by unalterable laws, towards prescribed issues? How often must we say, and yet not rightly lay to heart: The seed that is sown, it will spring! Given the summer's blossoming, then there is also given the autumnal withering: so is it ordered not with seedfields only, but with transactions, arrangements, philosophies, societies, French Revolutions, whatsoever man works with in this lower world.

Carlyle asserts it is the "law" of life that social forms become old clothes unless they are worn by the people who have some kind of faith: faith in duty, faith in silent work, faith in, finally, the transcendental, self-realizing movement of some force, some kind of deity which is realizing itself in the total movements of human history and particularly in the great men who rise above themselves and command the attention of the rest of mankind, pointing a finger to show the way all men should "now" go.

Carlyle devoted later books to such demonstration. Cromwell, Frederick the Great, and a whole company of great men in *On Heroes and Hero-Worship* (1841)—all of these so exhort us. The essential tragedy of the French Revolution, as Carlyle saw it, was that here was a congeries of events that cried out for a hero and found only destruction and social chaos. It lacked, among other things, a contemporary like Carlyle to annotate that chaos. But the French people's loss is our gain. Upon their agonies Carlyle rests a view of history as a scroll of events always on the verge of parting and revealing to us—in the heavens or in the depths of our beings—the essential divine plan. *The French Revolution* was actually written and rewritten at 5, Cheyne Row, in London. In spirit, however, it was written on the isle of Patmos in the Aegean where, we were told, a still more famous revelation was composed.

Bibliography

Ben-Israel, Hedva. "Carlyle and the French Revolution," in *English Historians on the French Revolution*. Cambridge: Cambridge University Press, 1968, pp. 127–147.

Bentley, Eric R. *A Century of Hero Worship*. Philadelphia: Lippincott, 1944, pp. 42–44.

Cazamian, Louis. *Carlyle*. New York: Macmillan, 1932, pp. 153–167.

Cobban, Alfred. "Carlyle's *French Revolution*," in *History*. XLVIII (October, 1963), pp. 306–316.

Harrold, Charles F. "Carlyle's General Method in *The French Revolution*," in *PMLA*. XLIII (1928), pp. 1150–1169.

Holloway, John. *The Victorian Sage*. London: Macmillan, 1953, pp. 61–74.

Ikler, A. Abbott. *Puritan Temper and Transcendental Faith: Carlyle's Literary Vision*. Columbus: Ohio State University Press, 1972, pp. 43–46.

Kusch, Robert W. "The Eighteenth Century as 'Decaying Organism' in Carlyle's *The French Revolution*," in *Anglia*. LXXXIX (1971), pp. 456–470.

La Valley, Albert J. *Carlyle and the Idea of the Modern*. New Haven, Conn.: Yale University Press, 1968, pp. 121–186.

Lea, Frank A. "Carlyle and *The French Revolution*," in *Adelphi*. XVIII (November–December, 1941), pp. 20–24, 36–38.

Leicester, H.M., Jr. "The Dialectic of Romantic Historiography: Prospect and

Retrospect in *The French Revolution*," in *Victorian Studies*. XV (1971), pp. 5–17.

Neff, Emery. *Carlyle*. New York: Norton, 1932, pp. 173–181.

Ralli, Augustus. *Guide to Carlyle*, Volume I. London: Allen and Unwin, 1920, pp. 210–226.

Rosenberg, Philip. *The Seventh Hero: Thomas Carlyle and the Theory of Radical Activism*. Cambridge, Mass.: Harvard University Press, 1974, pp. 79–107.

Symons, Julian. *Thomas Carlyle: The Life and Ideas of a Prophet*. New York: Oxford University Press, 1952, pp. 147–160.

ON HEROES, HERO-WORSHIP AND THE HEROIC IN HISTORY

Type of work: Philosophy of history
Author: Thomas Carlyle (1795–1881)
First published: 1841

Essay-Review

Thomas Carlyle's *On Heroes, Hero-Worship and the Heroic in History* serves as the best repository in English of that development in late Romanticism that Eric Bentley has called "heroic vitalism." Consisting of a series of six lectures that Carlyle delivered to London audiences in 1840, it represents not so much any soundly based ideas about the making of history as it does Carlyle's view of what the world would be if powerful and inspired men were to have the power he thought they deserved. It thus becomes England's contribution to the nineteenth century cult of the great man, a rather deadly dream most seductively attractive to intellectuals forced to huckster their ideas in the market place with all other merchants, but closed off from the real power that is exercised in this new industrial world by economic entrepreneurs.

Carlyle's basic idea is that all history is the making of great men, gifted with supreme power of vision or action. It thus becomes our duty to "worship Heroes." (Carlyle abounds in capital letters. They often serve him instead of reason.) "We all of us reverence and must ever reverence Great Men: this is, to me, the living rock amid all the rushings-down whatsoever; the one fixed point in modern revolutionary history, otherwise as if bottomless and shoreless." Clearly in the world of onrushing liberalism and industrialism, with memory of God ever dimming through the growth of science and skepticism, Carlyle needs a faith and presents us one in the worship of great men.

This faith, dubious enough under restrictions of law and order, becomes even more so in Carlyle's handling of it. As the six lectures progress, he moves from myth to history with no clear distinction and offers as equally great or heroic, leaders of religious movements, great poets, and military conquerors. Hero worship not only ought to be devout; it actually was. In Carlyle's estimation, love of God is virtually identical with loyalty to a leader. Despite his scorn for business activity and its operators, Carlyle's heroes are all men of practical intelligence. He values the same kind of industriousness, resoluteness, and obvious sincerity that could serve to build economic as well as political or clerical empires.

Carlyle begins his historical survey with the hero as prophet. Mohammed made Islam a historical force through the sword, but history sustained his vision and rewarded him; hence he is a hero in Carlyle's pantheon. The prophet as hero is a terrifying figure of a bygone age; much more in character with our spirit is the poet as hero. After discussing poetry as a romantic vision that makes the poet spiritual kinsman of the prophet, Carlyle treats Dante's *Divine Comedy* as the poem of an age of faith. He calls it "genuine song," but it is the Christian message that Carlyle really values: the literary work is an allegory of the invisible idea. As Dante gave us "Faith, or a soul," so Shakespeare gave us "Practice, or body." Poet-heroes are born, not made; thus Carlyle's Shakespeare is a romantic visionary whom we can only adore, not analyze. Shakespeare must have suffered heroically himself; otherwise he could not have created Hamlet or Macbeth.

The hero as priest is a spiritual captain, unlike the prophet who was a spiritual king. Luther and Knox are Carlyle's subjects, for, even though they were primarily reformers, they are finally more priestlike than the priests. As all his heroes, they are "sincere" visionaries who saw the truth and led their followers forth to battle for it. (Carlyle abounds in military metaphor, whether he writes of men of peace or war.) Great religious leaders battle idolatry, which of course is symbolic. But it is insincere symbolism, and therefore to be destroyed. Here Carlyle notes that the significant visionary everywhere is the man who combats delusion and outworn convention. Every hero, every image-breaker, comes to a new sense of reality that he brings to the world. He must "stand upon things, not upon the shadow of things."

Protestantism dwindled into faction in Germany, according to Carlyle, but in Scotland, with John Knox, Lutherism found its true home. (Here, and later with Boswell and Burns, Scottish Carlyle has a special fondness for his countrymen who found fame and success.) We may censure Puritanism, but it is fervent faith that brought democracy to England, through Cromwell, and colonized much of America as well. Knox was intolerant and despotic, but he was a zealot and therefore a hero for Carlyle, who distinguishes between good and bad tyrannies with reasons he never discusses.

The heroes who are closest to Carlyle's audience were Johnson, Rousseau, and Burns. As the priests are less than the prophets, so the heroic men of letters are less than the poets. For Carlyle, Goethe is the only heroic poet of the preceding century. Johnson, Rousseau, and Burns were seekers after truth rather than bringers of it. Here Carlyle delivers a famous paean of praise for learning and publishing, from the Bible to the newspaper. All our ideas are first books; then they become institutions and empires. The eighteenth century was a skeptical age, disbelieving, and therefore unheroic and insincere. Carlyles' trio all had to struggle against the climate of opinion and against poverty, as all real visionaries should. Boswell picked his hero well, for Johnson's gospel of moral prudence and practical sense was necessary in an age of cant.

Carlyle presents Rousseau doubtfully. Too complex and introspective to be a Carlyle hearty, and French as well, Rousseau stands as an ambiguous hero whom Carlyle acclaims as a zealot but blames for the fanaticism of the French Revolution. His veneration of the savage (Carlyle's conclusion) abetted the French lapse into savagery. Robert Burns is a much more engaging figure, and Scottish. But Carlyle contradicts himself by admitting that Burns' career was virtually ruined by the lionizing paid him by his hero worshippers in Edinburgh.

The last heroism for Carlyle is kingship—the leadership of people in war and politics. Interestingly, though, the leaders he specifically presents are not revolutionary heroes, but anti-revolutionaries. Heroes seek order, and order to Carlyle is discipline and peace, even at the cost of liberty and variety. Napoleon came to equate himself with France, and so fulfilled his ego at the cost of his nation. But Carlyle obviouly respects Napoleon's practical intelligence that enabled him to seize the salient factor in a situation and make fools of Europes' conventional generals and statesmen.

Throughout his presentation Carlyle never really analyzes, but exhorts, praises, and condemns. Obviously he admires the movers and shakers of the earth; his praise of Dante and Shakespeare is perfunctory compared with his veneration of Cromwell, who could barely speak coherently, but could act and did. Anti-intellectualism, veneration of power, love of enthusiasm as an end in itself are everywhere in this work.

Bibliography

Bentley, Eric R.   *A Century of Hero Worship*. Philadelphia: Lippincott, 1944, pp. 31–42.

Cazamian, Louis.   *Carlyle*. New York: Macmillan, 1932, pp. 167–181.

DeLaura, David J.   "Ishmael as Prophet: *Heroes and Hero Worship* and the Self-expressive Basis of Carlyle's Art," in *Texas Studies in Language and Literature*. XI (1969), pp. 705–732.

Donovan, Robert A.   "Carlyle and the Climate of *Hero-Worship*," in *University of Toronto Quarterly*. XLII (1973), pp. 122–141.

Holloway, John.   *The Victorian Sage*. London: Macmillan, 1953, pp. 46–49.

Ikler, A. Abbott.   *Puritan Temper and Transcendental Faith: Carlyle's Literary Vision*. Columbus: Ohio State University Press, 1972, pp. 22–24, 167–169.

Kusch, Robert E.   "Pattern and Paradox in *Heroes and Hero Worship*," in *Studies in Scottish Literature*. VI (January, 1969), pp. 146–155.

La Valley, Albert J.   *Carlyle and the Idea of the Modern*. New Haven, Conn.: Yale University Press, 1968, pp. 236–252.

Lehman, B.H.   *Carlyle's Theory of the Hero: Its Sources, Development, History, and Influence on Carlyle's Work: A Study of a Nineteenth Century Idea*. Durham, N.C.: Duke University Press, 1928, pp. 40–60.

Ralli, Augustus.   *Guide to Carlyle*, Volume I. London: Allen and Unwin, 1920, pp. 293–304.

Rosenberg, Philip.   *The Seventh Hero: Thomas Carlyle and the Theory of Radical Activism*. Cambridge, Mass.: Harvard University Press, 1974, pp. 188–193.

SARTOR RESARTUS

Type of work: Philosophical satire
Author: Thomas Carlyle (1795–1881)
First published: 1835

Essay-Review

This ecstatic, involved work—"The Life and Opinions of Herr Teufelsdröckh," to quote its subtitle—is in many ways one of the most characteristic works of Thomas Carlyle, the "sage of Chelsea" and a crusty censor of the optimistic Victorian era.

Carlyle, a familiar gibe has it, preached the virtues of silence in a long series of volumes. *Sartor Resartus* ("the tailor reclothed") is an early preachment on silence, work, duty, and the world as spirit. These were topics that Carlyle was never able to abstain from, whether he was writing about a medieval abbot (*Past and Present*), about heroes (*On Heroes, Hero-Worship and the Heroic in History*), or about fairly recent historical events (*The French Revolution*). Of Carlyle it is fair to paraphrase and say: Scratch the historian, and you will find the prophet. In *Sartor Resartus*, at any rate, Carlyle is nearly all prophet.

In a style that is crabbed, Germanic, allusive, ironic, hectoring, and paradoxical, Carlyle gave to the age of the Reform Bill (1832), John Stuart Mill, utilitarianism, and the Industrial Revolution the "gospel" he thought it needed. It was a message that, in Carlyle's opinion, the age was likely to overlook. Historically, this is one reason why *Sartor Resartus* and other of his works are worthy of attention today.

Sartor Resartus is a title pointing to the "clothes-philosophy" at the center of the book. But no reader reaches the center of the book without penetrating the formidable framework and bastion of mystification both playful and perverse that Carlyle sets up in early chapters. The author, already an admirer, translator, and popularizer of German literature when he began this work, writes much of the time as if in his own person. That is, he is supposedly the English editor who has been faced with the task of rearranging and commenting upon the mss. contents of six paper sacks which have come to him from Germany. These sacks contain the disorderly, fervid lucubrations of a learned German philosopher named Teufelsdröckh (literally, "Devil's-dung"). Out of these scrambled materials, the English "editor" and interpreter wishes to write a "life" of the German savant and also to effect a presentation of the key ideas of the great foreign thinker.

The "life," which does not come to much, is obviously a reflection of Carlyle's admiration for Goethe's *The Sorrows of Young Werther* and other *Bildungsromane* or tales of youthful growth. Teufelsdröckh has a mysterious birth and grows up lovingly cared for by foster parents. His mind soon shows its powers and feeds omnivorously on books. The future sage falls in love with a young woman named Blumine, is jilted by her, and goes on typical early nineteenth century wanderings. Driven by *Weltschmerz*, he goes to the Alps and finally to Paris; for sufficient reason, he utters his Everlasting No, his sweeping and bitter rejection of the structure of society and its conventions. Shortly thereafter, Carlyle's hero goes to Northern Scandinavia, outfaces a murderous Russian, and utters his Everlasting Yea. This is his acceptance, in a deeper sense, of the same texture of life and convention that he had rejected in Paris. After this climactic experience, Teufelsdröckh returns to his native city of Weissnichtwo (Don't-Know-Where), puffs his pipe, drinks his beer, and now and then sits at his desk in a top-floor room and meditates upon his little town and the world beyond it.

This "life," however, takes second place to the long quotations of his opinions, also deposited in the paper bags for the benefit of his English editor and, of course, England. On many pages Teufelsdröckh is allowed to speak for himself. But in almost as many pages the editor speaks for him, extending the application of the supposedly Germanic ideas to the turmoils of contemporary England. By this transparent subterfuge, the life and opinions of the imaginary German philosopher become a tract for the time, in which Carlyle is able to utter his own Everlasting No to the anti-idealist movements of the Victorian Age: the growth of democracy, the trust in utilitarian philosophy and its cold and (to Carlyle) petty calculation of pleasure and pain, profit and loss.

Carlyle is also able to utter his Everlasting Yea, which amounts to this: clothes and human institutions and religions of the past and their empty rites must be regarded, when they are properly viewed, as the obscure and yet wonderful expression of the ongoing life of the soul. And the life of the soul must be regarded in two supplementary but noncontradicting ways: It is the destiny of each man to create or re-create the "clothes" that he himself wears. It is a gift of world destiny that mankind over many generations may trace the biography of the human race itself by study of the institutions it sets up, the buildings it erects, and, most important of all, the thoughts that it thinks and, by religion and in books, transmits to future generations.

To do all this is to be a good Teufelsdröckh; but to practice an imitation of Richter and Goethe, if not Christ, each man must trace the arc of denial and affirmation in his own life. As Carlyle points out in *Sartor Resartus*, each man must deny "the dandiacal body"—a life smart, modish, and empty—and he must sink into a condition of receptive silence. Out of this silence will come the true words, the words that emancipate man from illusions and which clear the way to *work*. This work can be humble and anonymous like the digging of a gardener, or it can be noble and widely known, like the notations of Teufelsdröckh at his desk.

Bibliography

Brookes, Gerry H. *The Rhetorical Form of Carlyle's* Sartor Resartus. Berkeley: University of California Press, 1972.

Cazamian, Louis. *Carlyle.* New York: Macmillan, 1932, pp. 100–133.

Deen, Leonard W. "Irrational Form in *Sartor Resartus*," in *Texas Studies in Literature and Language.* V (1963), pp. 438–451.

Deneau, Daniel P. "Relationship of Style and Device in *Sartor Resartus*," in *Victorian Newsletter.* XVII (1960), pp. 17–20.

Harrold, C.F. "Introduction," in *Sartor Resartus: The Life and Opinions of Herr Teufelsdröckh.* New York: Odyssey, 1937. Reprinted in *A Carlyle Reader.* Edited by G.B. Tennyson. New York: Modern Library, 1969.

Holloway, John. *The Victorian Sage.* London: Macmillan, 1953, pp. 24–26, 30.

La Valley, Albert J. *Carlyle and the Idea of the Modern.* New Haven, Conn.: Yale University Press, 1968, pp. 69–118.

Levine, George. *The Boundaries of Fiction: Carlyle, Macaulay, Newman.* Princeton, N.J.: Princeton University Press, 1968, pp. 19–78.

Metzger, Lore. "*Sartor Resartus*: A Victorian *Faust*," in *Comparative Literature.* XIII (1961), pp. 316–331.

Moore, Carlisle. "*Sartor Resartus* and the Problem of Carlyle's 'Conversion,' " in *PMLA.* LXX (1955), pp. 662–681.

Neff, Emery. *Carlyle.* New York: Norton, 1932, pp. 121–126.

Peckham, Morse. *Beyond the Tragic Vision: The Quest for Identity in the Nineteenth Century.* New York: George Braziller, 1962, pp. 177–180.

————. *Victorian Revolutionaries: Speculations on Some Heroes of a Culture Crisis.* New York: George Braziller, 1970, pp. 65–82.

Ralli, Augustus. *Guide to Carlyle*, Volume I. London: Allen and Unwin, 1920, pp. 140–150.

Reed, Walter J. "The Pattern of Conversion in *Sartor Resartus*," in *Journal of English Literary History.* XXXVIII (1971), pp. 411–431.

Rosenberg, Philip. *The Seventh Hero: Thomas Carlyle and the Theory of Radical Activism.* Cambridge, Mass.: Harvard University Press, 1974, pp. 45–62.

Sanders, Charles Richard. "The Byron Closed in *Sartor Resartus*," in *Studies in Romanticism.* III (1964), pp. 77–108.

Symons, Julian. *Thomas Carlyle: The Life and Ideas of a Prophet.* New York: Oxford University Press, 1952, pp. 127–146.

Tennyson, G.B. *"Sartor" Called "Resartus": The Genesis, Structure, and Style of Thomas Carlyle's First Major Work.* Princeton, N.J.: Princeton University Press, 1965.

LEWIS CARROLL
Charles Lutwidge Dodgson

Born: Daresbury, Cheshire, England (January 27, 1832)
Died: Guildford, Surrey, England (January 14, 1898)

Principal Works

FANTASIES AND CHILDREN'S STORIES: *Alice's Adventures in Wonderland*, 1865; *Through the Looking-Glass and What Alice Found There*, 1871; *A Tangled Tale*, 1885; *Sylvie and Bruno*, 1889; *Sylvie and Bruno Concluded*, 1893.

POEM: *The Hunting of the Snark*, 1876.

MATHEMATICAL STUDIES: *Euclid and His Modern Rivals*, 1879; *Curiosa Mathematica*, Part I, 1888; Part II, 1893; *Symbolic Logic, Specimens*, 1894.

Charles Lutwidge Dodgson, who under his pseudonym of Lewis Carroll came to be known to millions as the author of *Alice in Wonderland*, was born at Daresbury, England, January 27, 1832, the son of the rector of Daresbury, the Reverend Charles Dodgson and Frances Jane Lutwidge. He was the eldest of a family of eleven children, with seven sisters and three brothers. After a pleasant and for the most part solitary childhood he attended Richmond School and then Rugby for three extremely unhappy years. In 1851, the year he formally went into residence as a student at Christ Church College, Oxford, his mother died. He was probably deeply affected by her death; his later verses show the affection he felt for his gentle mother, and in his nonsense stories some critics have claimed to find signs of a childhood love for his mother that never matured.

Dodgson spent the rest of his life at Oxford. In 1856, two years after receiving the Bacholor of Arts degree, and after serving as a tutor in mathematics, he was made a regular member of the teaching faculty at Christ Church. Although the significance of the event was unrealized at the time, it was in the previous year, 1855, that he wrote the first lines of his famous "Jabberwocky" poem: "Twas bryllyg, and the slythy toves/Did gyre and gymble in the wabe...." This was a scholar's jest, an attempt to parody Anglo-Saxon poetry. He was twenty-three years old at the time.

As a teacher and mathematician, Charles Lutwidge Dodgson was conscientious, precise, sometimes inspired, but usually dull. His students reported finding his lectures very tiresome, even during the period when he was writing *Alice's Adventures in Wonderland*. Dodgson wrote many articles and several books in mathematics and logic, but he would not have been famous if he had relied on them or on his reputation as a teacher.

The pseudonym, Lewis Carroll, was devised in 1856 to accompany a poem which appeared in the magazine *The Train*. It appears to have been derived from the names Lutwidge and Charles by some fanciful logic of his own.

Dodgson had considerable skill as a humorous artist, but his drawings—which some have regarded as comparable to the nonsense drawings by Edward Lear—were rejected when he submitted them to the *Comic Times*. Discouraged, he turned to photography and became an excellent photographer of children and one of the notable amateurs in nineteenth century photography.

In 1856 he met the children of Dean Liddell of Christ Church, and was particularly interested in Alice Liddell, then four years old. A year after his ordination (for taking Holy Orders was a condition of his staying at Christ Church as a mathematics lecturer), on a picnic with another young clergyman and three of the Liddell girls—Alice, then ten years old, among them—Dodgson began in an extemporaneous way the story of *Alice's Adventures Underground*. He wrote the story, after expanding it considerably, and presented the manuscript to Alice. An even longer version was prepared for publication and was illustrated by John Tenniel, whose drawings have become as famous as the story. The book was published by Macmillan in 1865 with the title *Alice's Adventures in Wonderland*. This extremely popular story full of nonsense and logical fancy was followed by *Through the Looking-Glass and What Alice Found There*. *The Hunting of the Snark*, perhaps the most fascinating of his nonsense poems, became a great favorite with adults and, like the Alice books, continues to be popular. But the author's own favorite work was his long and involved *Sylvie and Bruno* which appeared in two parts, the first in 1889 and the second in 1893. Unfortunately, the public never fully shared the author's love, and compared to the other books it was a failure.

Dodgson's playful temperament, seldom in evidence in the classroom and often made wicked when he turned to criticism of his colleagues at the college, found an outlet in games of logic and mathematics, many of which he invented. He was always fascinated with girls; he liked to read to them, to make up stories for them, to draw them, and to photograph them—sometimes in the nude. But somehow he managed to stay out of trouble, if not free from all criticism. In all probability, his innocence was evident. He never married, but he probably had an unhappy love affair when he was young; the evidence is inconclusive. In any case, analysts have been amusing themselves by studying him; the maker of puzzles was something of a puzzle himself.

This solitary deacon, dull teacher, clever logician, and inspired teller of nonsense tales died of influenza and bronchial complications at Guildford on January 14, 1898. He was still ambitious, with several projects under way, but since he was more and more out of touch with "real life," living, although quite sanely, in the world of his imagination, it was not entirely inappropriate that after a long creative life he finally stopped dreaming.

Bibliography

The collected edition is *The Complete Works of Lewis Carroll*, edited by Alexander Woollcott, 1939 (reprinted 1947), with a critical introduction and illustrations by John Tenniel. The standard bibliography is *A Handbook of the*

Literature of the Rev. C. L. Dodgson, 1931, by S. H. Williams and Falconer Madan. Roger L. Green has edited *The Diaries of Lewis Carroll*, 2 vols., 1953, the most complete edition to date. Standard biographies are Langford Reed, *The Life of Lewis Carroll*, 1932; Florence B. Lennon, *Victoria Through the Looking Glass: The Life of Lewis Carroll*, 1945; and Derek Hudson, *Lewis Carroll*, 1954, the first critical biography to make use of the diaries. Other critical works are Walter de la Mare, *Lewis Carroll*, 1932; R. L. Green, *The Story of Lewis Carroll*, 1949; A. L. Taylor, *White Knight: A Study of C. L. Dodgson*, 1952; and Phyllis Greenacre, *Swift and Carroll*, 1955. An important short essay is Virginia Woolf, "Lewis Carroll," in *The Moment and Other Essays*, 1948. See also S. H. Williams and F. Madan, *The Lewis Carroll Handbook*, 1962.

ALICE'S ADVENTURES IN WONDERLAND

Type of work: Imaginative tale
Author: Lewis Carroll (Charles Lutwidge Dodgson, 1832–1898)
Type of plot: Fantasy
Time of plot: Victorian England
Locale: The dream world of an imaginative child
First published: 1865

Carroll's classic fantasy can be read on many levels and appreciated by diverse audiences: it is at once a biting social and political satire sufficiently complex to satisfy the most sophisticated adult, and a delightfully whimsical fairy tale to capture the fancy of the imaginative child.

Principal Characters

Alice, a curious, imaginative, strong-willed, and honest young English girl. She falls asleep by the side of a stream in a meadow and dreams that she follows a White Rabbit down his hole. She has many adventures in a Wonderland peopled by all kinds of strange characters and animals.

The White Rabbit, anxious, aristocratic, dandified. Alice follows him down his hole, which leads to an enchanted house and garden. The White Rabbit is a Prime Minister of sorts in this Wonderland, for he has close contact with the royalty there and carries out their orders, although he does not institute policy.

The Queen of Hearts, the ill-tempered Queen of Wonderland. She constantly demands that everyone who crosses her to be beheaded. Fond of croquet, she orders Alice to take part in a game in which flamingoes are used for mallets and hedgehogs for balls. She issues an order for Alice's execution at the end of the book, but this order is never carried out because Alice accuses the Queen and all her company of being only a pack of cards, an assertion that turns out to be true.

The King of Hearts, a timid, kindly man. Although he is completely under his wife's power because of her temper, he manages to pardon all her victims surreptitiously.

The Duchess, another member of royalty in Wonderland, a platitude-quoting, moralizing, ugly old woman who lives in a chaotic house. Deathly afraid of the Queen, she is ordered to be beheaded, but the sentence is never carried out.

The Cook, the Duchess' servant. She flavors everything with pepper, insults her mistress, and throws cooking pans at her.

The Cheshire Cat, the Duchess' grinning cat. Continually vanishing and reappearing, he is a great conversationalist, and he tells Alice much of the gossip in Wonderland.

The Duchess' Baby, a strange, howling, little infant. The baby turns into a pig when the Duchess entrusts it to Alice's care.

The Knave of Hearts, a timid, poetry-writing fellow accused of stealing some tarts that the Queen has made.

The March Hare, the rude host of a mad tea party to which Alice invites herself and then wishes that she had not.

The Mad Hatter, a riddle-making, blunt, outspoken guest at the tea party. He is a good friend of the March Hare, and at the party the two try to prove to Alice that she is stupid.

The Dormouse, another guest at the tea party. He is a sleepy creature, aroused long enough to recite for Alice and then pushed headfirst into the teapot.

The Gryphon, a mythical creature, half bird, half animal, who escorts Alice to the home of the Mock Turtle so that she may hear the recital of the Turtle's life story.

The Mock Turtle, an ever-sobbing animal. He recites his life's story to Alice and everyone else within earshot.

The Caterpillar, a hookah-smoking insect who perches on the top of a magic mushroom. Officious and easily offended, he tests Alice's intelligence with a series of ridiculous riddles.

Bill, The Lizard, an unfortunate fellow picked by the other animals to go down the chimney of the White Rabbit's house and try to force out Alice, who has assumed gigantic proportions after drinking a magic potion she found on the table.

The Mouse, who greets Alice in the pool of tears which she has made by crying while she was of gigantic size. Now of minute proportions, she is almost overwhelmed by the Mouse, a creature easily offended.

The Lorry,
The Duck,
The Dodo,
The Eaglet,
The Crab, and
The Baby Crab, all creatures whom Alice meets in the pool of her tears and who swim around with her.

Father William and
His Son, characters in a poem that Alice recites. The old man, a former athlete, can still balance an eel on his nose, much to the amazement of his curious and impertinent son. The poem is a parody of Robert Southey's "The Old Man's Comforts."

The Pigeon, a bird Alice meets after she has made herself tall by eating part of the Caterpillar's mushroom.

The Fish Footman, the bearer of a note from the Queen inviting the Duchess to play croquet.

The Frog Footman, the impolite servant of the Duchess; his wig becomes entangled with that of the Fish Footman when the two bow in greeting each other.

The Puppy, a playful animal Alice meets while she is in her small state.

The Flamingo, the bird Alice uses for a croquet mallet in the game with the Queen.

The Hedgehog, the animal that acts as the ball in the croquet game.

Five,
Two, and
Seven, three quarrelsome gardeners of the Queen. When Alice meets them, they are painting red all the white roses in the garden, to obliterate the mistake someone had made in ordering white ones.

Elsie,
Lacie, and
Tillie, three sisters in the Dormouse's story. They live at the bottom of a well and exist solely on treacle.

Dinah, Alice's pet cat in real life.

Alice's Sister, the wise older sister who is charmed by Alice's tales of her adventures in Wonderland.

The Story

Alice was quietly reading over her sister's shoulder when she saw a White Rabbit dash across the lawn and disappear into its hole. She jumped up to rush after him and found herself falling down the rabbit hole. At the bottom she saw the White Rabbit hurrying along a corridor ahead of her and murmuring that he would be late. He disappeared around a corner, leaving Alice standing in front of several locked doors.

On a glass table she found a tiny golden key which unlocked a little door hidden behind a curtain. The door opened upon a lovely miniature garden, but she could not get through the doorway because it was too small. She sadly replaced the key on the table. A little bottle mysteriously appeared. Alice drank the contents and immediately began to grow smaller, so much so that she could no longer reach the key on the table. Next, she ate a piece of cake she found nearby and soon she began to grow to such enormous size that she could only squint through the door. In despair, she began to weep tears as big as raindrops. As she sat there crying, the White Rabbit appeared, bewailing the fact that the Duchess would be angry if he kept her waiting.

The White Rabbit dropped his fan and gloves. Alice picked them up and as she did so she began to grow smaller. Again she rushed to the garden door, but she found it shut and the golden key once more on the table out of reach.

Then she fell into a pool of her own tears! Splashing along, she encountered a mouse who had stumbled into the pool. Alice tactlessly began a conversation about her cat Dinah, and the mouse became speechless with terror. Soon the pool of tears was filled with living creatures, birds and animals of all kinds. An old Dodo suggested that they run a Caucus Race to get dry. Having asked what a Caucus Race was, Alice was told that the best way to explain it was to do it. Whereupon the animals ran themselves quite breathless and finally became dry.

Afterwards, the mouse told a "Tail" to match its own appendage. Alice was asked to tell something, but the only thing she could think of was her cat Dinah. Frightened, the other creatures went away, and Alice was left alone.

The White Rabbit appeared once more, this time hunting for his gloves and fan. Catching sight of Alice, he sent her to his home to get him a fresh pair of gloves and another fan. In the Rabbit's house she found the fan and gloves and also took a drink from a bottle. Instantly she grew to a giant size, and was forced to put her leg up the chimney and her elbow out the window in order to keep from being squeezed to death.

She managed to eat a little cake and shrink herself again. As soon as she was small enough to get through the door, she ran into a nearby wood where she found a caterpillar sitting on a mushroom. The caterpillar was very rude to Alice and he scornfully asked her to prove her worth by reciting "You Are Old, Father William." Alice did so, but the words sounded very strange. Disgusted, he left her after giving her some valuable information about increasing or decreasing her size. She broke off pieces of the mushroom and found to her delight that by eating from the piece in her left hand she could become taller, and from the piece in her right hand, smaller.

She came to a little house among the trees. There a footman, who looked very much like a fish, presented to another footman, who closely resembled a frog, an invitation for the Duchess to play croquet with the Queen. The two amphibians bowed to each other with great formality, tangling their wigs together. Alice opened the door and found herself in the chaotic house of the Duchess. The cook was stirring a large pot of soup and pouring plenty of pepper into the mixture. Everyone was sneezing except the cook and a Cheshire cat which sat on the hearth grinning. The Duchess herself held a sneezing, squalling baby and sang to it a blaring lullaby. Alice, in sympathy with the poor child, picked it up and carried it out into the fresh air, whereupon the baby turned slowly into a pig, squirmed out of her arms, and waddled into the forest.

Standing in bewilderment, Alice saw the grinning Cheshire cat sitting in a tree. He was able to appear and disappear at will, and after exercising his talents, he advised Alice to go to a tea party given by the Mad Hatter. The cat vanished, all but the grin. Finally that too disappeared, and Alice left for the party.

There Alice found she had to deal with the strangest people she had ever seen—a March Hare, a Mad Hatter, and a sleepy Dormouse. All were too lazy to set the table properly; dirty dishes were everywhere. The Dormouse fell asleep in its teacup; the Mad Hatter told Alice her hair needed cutting; the March Hare offered her wine and then told her there was none. They asked her foolish riddles that had no answers. Then, worse, they ignored her completely and carried on a ridiculous conversation among themselves. She escaped after the Dormouse fell asleep in the middle of a story he was telling.

Next she found herself in a garden of talking flowers. Just as the conversation was beginning, some gardeners appeared with paint brushes and began to splash red paint on a rose bush. Alice learned that the Queen had ordered a red bush to be placed in that spot, and the gardeners had made a mistake and planted a white one. Now they were busily and fearfully trying to cover their error before the Queen arrived. But the poor gardeners were not swift enough. The Queen caught them in the act, and the wretched gardeners were led off to be decapitated. Alice saved them by shoving them down into a large flowerpot, out of sight of the dreadful Queen.

A croquet game began. The mallets were live flamingoes, and the balls were hedgehogs which thought nothing of uncurling themselves and running rapidly over the field. The Duchess cornered Alice and led her away to the seaside to introduce her to the Mock Turtle and the Gryphon.

While engaged in a Lobster Quadrille, they heard the news of a trial. A thief had stolen some tarts. Rushing to the courtroom where a trial by jury was already in session, Alice was called upon to act as a witness before the King and Queen of Hearts. But the excited child upset the jury box and spilled out all its occupants. After replacing all the animals in the box, Alice said she knew nothing of the matter. Her speech infuriated the Queen, who ordered that Alice's head be cut off. The whole court rushed at her, and Alice defiantly called them nothing but a pack of cards. She awoke from her dream as her sister brushed away some dead leaves blowing over her face.

Critical Evaluation

One summer afternoon in 1862, the Rev. Charles Lutwidge Dodgson, an Oxford friend, and three little girls set out on a boat trip. Somewhere along the way *Alice's Adventures in Wonderland* was born. It was not the first story that Dodgson had told the girls, children of Henry George Liddell, dean of Christ Church, Oxford. But it was one which immediately captured Alice Liddell, the prototype for the fictional seven-year-old heroine. And her later requests for Dodgson to "write it down" were to turn him into one of the world's favorite authors, with his work translated into 47 languages and part of the heritage of most literate people.

Dodgson, who transposed his first two names into the pen name Lewis Carroll, was on the surface a shy but seemingly conventional Oxford mathematician. But today his outwardly harmless affinity for little girls is viewed as the sign of a serious neurosis, an inability to grow up, which also revealed itself in his writings. Alice was only one of many young girls who would provide Carroll with the only love—innocent and sexless as it seemed—to which he could respond. As she matured, each child was replaced in Carroll's affections by another young lady who shared the secret world of childhood in which he spent much of his adult life.

Expressing itself in many ways, this attraction to fantasy gave rise to Carroll's love of whimsical letters, gadgets, theatricals, toys, and, of course, to the Alice stories. First prepared in a handwritten manuscript book for Alice Liddell (then called *Alice's Adventures Under Ground*), the book was published in its present form in 1865 and was almost immediately popular. Adding to its originality were the famous illustrations by Sir John Tenniel who did not use the real Alice for his model. She, unlike the pictured child, had short dark hair and bangs.

Followed in 1871 by the even more brilliant sequel, *Through the Looking-Glass and What Alice Found There,* the book has always been enjoyed on several levels. Initially, of course, it is a very special children's story, but it is also a book teeming with fascination for certain specialists—mathematicians, linguists, logicians, Freudians, and even those who envision the book as an example of a drug trip. Yet perhaps its philosophical suggestions give the work most of its never-ending appeal for adults.

If we examine the book as children's literature, we see that it offered its young readers a charming new outlook dispensing with the moralistic viewpoint then prevalent in almost all tales for youngsters. Alice is neither continuously nice nor thoroughly naughty, for she is simply a curious child whose queries lead her into strange situations, and in the end she is neither punished nor rewarded. A moral proposing that she do this or that is absent. Departing even further from the saccharine stories praising standard virtues, Carroll pokes fun at many of the ideas with which Alice, a well-bred English child, has been imbued. The Mock Turtle, for instance, chides the sacred subject of learning by terming the branches of arithmetic Ambition, Distraction, Uglification, and Derision. And children who read the book are permitted to see adults quite unlike the perfect beings usually portrayed. It is the story's adults rather than Alice who are rude, demanding, and ridiculous.

As a work for the specialist, *Alice's Adventures in Wonderland* touches on many puzzles more thoroughly presented in *Through the Looking-Glass and What Alice Found There.* Its playfulness with language, for example, involves puns, parodies, and clever phrasing, but it does not deal as fully with the basic nature of language as does its sequel. Yet even in *Alice's Adventures in Wonderland,* Carroll's casual amusement with words often has deeper meaning. When he parodies the well-known poems and songs of his day, he is again questioning their supercilious platitudes. When he makes a pun (the Gryphon tells us that boots and shoes under the sea are "done" with whiting rather than blacking and are, of course, made of soles and eels), Carroll is asserting the total logic of illogic. And when he designs a Cheshire cat, he is taking a common but unclear phrase of his time ("Grin like a Cheshire cat" referred either to inn signs in the county of Cheshire depicting a grinning lion or to Cheshire cheeses modeled in the shape of a smiling cat) and turning it into a concrete reality. Logicians also find a multitude of tidbits. The Cheshire cat "proves" it is not mad by adopting the premise that if a dog is not mad, anyone who reacts in ways opposite to a dog must be. The March Hare offers a nice exercise in logic and language with his discussion of taking "more" versus taking "less" and his challenge as to whether "I mean what I say" is the same as "I say what I mean."

For mathematicians Carroll presents the Mad Hatter's watch which tells the day of the month rather than the hour. That watch does not bother with the hour since from the center of the earth the sun would always look the same whereas the moon's phases would be visible. For the Freudians, the book is also a mass of complicated mysteries. Freudians see significance in most of the characters and incidents, but the fall down the rabbit hole, the changes in size, the interest in eating and drinking, the obnoxious mature females, and Alice's continual anxiety are some of the most revealing topics suggesting Carroll's neuroses about women and sex.

The larger philosophical questions raised by Alice center on the order of life as we know it. Set in the context of the dream vision, a journey different from a conscious quest, the book asks whether there is indeed any pattern or meaning to life. Alice is the curious innocent who compares so favorably with the jaded and even wicked grown-ups. Always sensible and open to experience, she would seem the ideal messenger to bring us a true concept. Yet her adventures hint that all we may know is the ridiculousness of logic and what we imagine to be reality and the logic of nonsense. We see that Wonderland is no more incomprehensible than Victorian England, that the Mad Duchess lives next door, that as the Cheshire cat says, "We're all mad here."

To Wonderland Alice brings a strong belief in order and certain concepts, and she must continually refuse to accept the chaos which she finds there. When Wonderland turns her views askew, she can withstand the strain for only so long. Then she must rebel. The trial, which in our world is the last refuge of justice, is the key factor in Alice's rejection of Wonderland. For it is a trial of Wonderland itself, with many of the earlier encountered creatures reassembled to assert forcefully once more that expectations and rules are meaningless. Like the child of our world that she is, Alice (and Carroll) must deny the truth that there is no truth. She must shout "Nonsense" to it all. As one critic has pointed out, she rejects "mad sanity in favor of the sane madness of the ordinary existence." Facing the same confusion and frightened by what it hints, the reader also rebels. He laughs and turns to more "serious" considerations.

Bibliography

Auerbach, Nina. "Alice and Wonderland. A Curious Child," in *Victorian Studies.* XVII (1973), pp. 31–47.

Ayres, H.M. *Carroll's Alice.* New York: Columbia University Press, 1936.

Baum, Alwin L. "Carroll's Alices: The Semiotics of Paradox," in *American Imago.* XXXIV (1977), pp. 86–108.

Blake, Kathleen. *Play, Games, and Sport: The Literary Works of Lewis Carroll.* Ithaca, N.Y.: Cornell University Press, 1974, pp. 108–136.

Boynton, Mary F. "An Oxford Don Quixote," in *Hispania.* XLIV (1964), pp. 738–750.

Egoff, Sheila, G.T. Stubbs and L.F. Ashley. *Only Connect; Readings on Children's Literature.* New York: Oxford University Press, 1969, pp. 150–155.

Empson, William. "*Alice in Wonderland*: The Child as Swain," in *English Pastoral Poetry.* New York: Norton, 1938, pp. 253–294.

Fadiman, Clifton. *Party of One; The Selected Writings of Clifton Fadiman.* New York: World, 1955, pp. 404–410.

Flescher, Jacqueline. "The Language of Nonsense in *Alice*," in *Yale French Studies.* XLIII (1969), pp. 128–144.

Graham, Neilson. "Sanity, Madness and Alice," in *Ariel.* IV (1973), pp. 80–89.

Henkle, Roger B. "The Mad Hatter's World," in *Virginia Quarterly Review.* XLIX (1973), pp. 100–106, 111–117.

Holmes, Roger W. "The Philosopher's *Alice in Wonderland*," in *Antioch Review.* XIX (Summer, 1959), pp. 133–149.

Johnson, Paula. "Alice Among the Analysts," in *Hartford Studies in Literature.* IV (1972), pp. 114–122.

Jorgens, Jack J. "Alice Our Contemporary," in *Children's Literature: The Great Excluded.* I (1972), pp. 152–161.

Kibel, Alvin C. "Logic and Satire in *Alice in Wonderland*," in *American Scholar.* XLIII (1974), pp. 605–629.

Kincaid, James R. "Alice's Invasion of Wonderland," in *PMLA.* LXXXVIII (1973), pp. 92–99.

Levin, Harry, "Wonderland Revisited," in *Kenyon Review.* XXVII (Autumn, 1965), pp. 591–616.

Matthews, Charles. "Satire in the Alice Books," in *Criticism.* XII (1971), pp. 105–119.

Pattison, Robert. *The Child Figure in English Literature.* Athens: University of Georgia Press, 1978, pp. 23, 120, 151–159.

Phillips, Robert. *Aspects of Alice: Lewis Carroll's Dreamchild as Seen Through the Critics' Looking Glasses, 1865–1971.* New York: Vanguard, 1971.

Phillips, William. *Art and Psychoanalysis.* New York: Criterion, 1957, pp. 185–217.

Rackin, Donald. Alice's Adventures in Wonderland: *A Critical Handbook.* Belmont, Calif.: Wadsworth, 1969.

————. "Alice's Journey to the End of Night," in *PMLA.* LXXXI (1966), pp. 313–326.

————. "Corrective Laughter; Carroll's *Alice* and Popular Children's Literature of the Nineteenth Century," in *Journal of Popular Culture.* I (1967), pp. 243–255.

THROUGH THE LOOKING-GLASS

Type of work: Imaginative tale
Author: Lewis Carroll (Charles Lutwidge Dodgson, 1832–1898)
Type of plot: Fantasy
Time of plot: Nineteenth century
Locale: The dream world of an imaginative child
First published: 1871

> *Its plot structured around moves in a chess game, the story of this fantasy, which continues* Alice's Adventures in Wonderland, *is set in a land peopled by live chessmen and talking insects, a land where everything happens backwards. Carroll's book may be read as a madcap children's fairy tale or interpreted as a complex, sophisticated adult fable laced with subtle ironies and inspired by inimitable humor.*

Principal Characters

Alice, an imaginative English child who has fantastic adventures in Looking-Glass House.

The White Kitten, a good kitten who is not responsible for Alice's adventures.

The Black Kitten, told by Alice to pretend that they can go through the mirror to Looking-Glass House.

Dinah, the kittens' mother.

The White Queen, a live chess piece. In Alice's adventures she becomes a sheep, gives Alice some needles, and tells the little girl to knit. She reappears throughout the story in various guises.

The White King, a live chess piece. He has Alice serve a cake which cuts itself.

Tiger Lily,
Rose, and
Violet, flowers of whom Alice asks the path to take.

Gnat, a pleasant insect as big as a chicken. He melts away.

The Red Queen, a live chess piece. She tells Alice that one has to run to stay in the same place. Later she turns into the black kitten.

Tweedledum and
Tweedledee, two odd, fat, little men. They speak in ambiguities and recite poems to Alice. They fight over a rattle until frightened away by a crow.

The Red King, a live chess piece. He dreams about Alice, says Tweedledee, and thus gives her reality.

Humpty Dumpty, who has a conversation in riddles with Alice. He explains to her the Jabberwocky poem.

The Lion and
The Unicorn, who fight over the White King's crown.

The Red Knight, a live chess piece who claims Alice as his prisoner.

The White Knight, a live chess piece who also claims Alice as his prisoner. He leads Alice to a brook and tells her to jump into the next square in order to become a queen herself.

The Story

Alice was sure the whole thing was not the white kitten's fault. It must surely have been the fault of the black kitten. For Dinah, the mother cat, had been washing the white kitten's face when it happened; she certainly had had nothing to do with it. But the mischievous black kitten had been unwinding Alice's yarn and in all ways acting naughty enough to cause the whole strange affair.

While the black kitten curled up in Alice's lap to play with the yarn, Alice told it to pretend that the two of them could go right through the mirror and into Looking-Glass House. As she talked, the glass grew all misty and soft, and in a moment Alice was through the mirror and in the Looking-Glass room. The place was very strange, for although the room looked just the same as the real room she had seen in the mirror, the clock and the fire and the other things in the room seemed to be alive. Even the chessmen, for Alice loved to play chess, were alive.

When Alice picked up the White Queen and set her on the table, the White Queen screamed in terror, thinking that a volcano had shaken her about. The White King had the same fear, but he was too astonished to cry out. They seemed not to see or hear Alice, and even though she wanted to stay and watch them and read the king's rather funny poetry, she felt she must look at the garden before she had to go back through the Looking Glass. When she started down the stairs, she seemed to float, not even once touching the steps.

In the garden every path Alice took led her straight back to the house. She asked Tiger Lily and Rose and Violet whether there were any other people in the garden; she hoped they might help her find the right path. The flowers told her there was only one, and Alice found her to be the Red Queen—but a very strange chess figure, for the Red Queen was taller than Alice herself. As Alice walked toward the Red Queen, she once more found herself back at the door of the house. Then Alice figured out that in order to get to any place in this queer land one must walk in the *opposite* direction. Doing so, she came face to face with the Red Queen.

The queen took Alice to the top of a hill. There, spread out below them, was a countryside that looked like a large chessboard. Alice, delighted, said that she would love to play on this board. Then the Red Queen told her that they would play and that Alice could be the White Queen's Pawn. They would start on the Second Square and—but at that moment the Red Queen grabbed Alice's hand and they started to run. Alice had never run so fast in her life, but even though she was breathless from such fast running the things around them never changed a tiny bit. When they finally stopped running, the queen told Alice that in this land one had to run as fast as one could to stay in the same place and twice as fast as one could to get somewhere else. Then the queen showed Alice the pegs in the Second Square and told her how to move. At the last peg the Red Queen disappeared, leaving Alice alone to continue the game.

Alice started to run down the hill. The next thing she knew she was on a train filled with insects and having quite an unpleasant time because she did not have ticket. All of the insects talked unkindly to her, and to add to her discomfort the train jumped over the brook and took them all straight up in the air. When she came down, she was sitting under a tree, talking to a Gnat. Gnat was as big as a chicken but very pleasant. He told her about the other insects that lived in the woods; then he too melted away and Alice had to go on alone.

Turning a corner, she bumped into two fat little men, called Tweedledum and Tweedledee, the funniest little creatures she had ever seen. Everything they said seemed to have two meanings. It was fun to listen to the merry little men as they recited a long poem about a Walrus and a Carpenter and some Oysters. While they were explaining the poem to Alice, she heard a puffing noise, like the sound of a steam engine. Tweedledee told her it was the Red King snoring. Sure enough, they found him asleep. Tweedledee told Alice that the Red King was dreaming about her and that if he stopped dreaming Alice would be gone for good. Alice cried when they told her she was not real but only a part of the Red King's dream.

As she brushed her tears away, she saw Tweedledum staring in terror at something on the ground. It was an old broken rattle, over which the two foolish men got into a terrible fight. That is, they *talked* a terrible fight, but neither seemed very anxious to have a real battle. The Crow flew over and frightened them so that the funny men ran away into the wood. Alice ran too, and as she ran she saw a shawl blowing about.

Alice, looking for the owner of the shawl, saw the White Queen running toward her. The White Queen was a very queer person; she lived backward and remembered things *before* they happened. For example, she hurt *before* she pricked her finger. While the queen was telling these strange things to Alice, the queen turned into a Sheep and was in a shop with Alice. It was a very curious shop, the shelves full of things that disappeared when Alice looked at them. Sometimes the boxes went right through the ceiling. Then Sheep gave Alice some needles and told her to knit.

As she started to knit, the needles became oars and she found herself and Sheep in a little boat rowing in a stream. The oars kept sticking in the water. Sheep explained that the crabs were catching them. Alice picked some beautiful, fragrant rushes that melted away as soon as she picked them. Soon, to her surprise, the river and boat vanished, and Alice and Sheep were back in the shop. She bought an egg, even though in this shop two were cheaper than one, but when she started to get the egg, as Sheep would not reach it for her, the egg began to grow larger and larger and more and more real, with eyes, a nose, and a mouth. Then Alice could tell as plain as day that the egg was Humpty Dumpty.

She had a queer conversation with Humpty Dumpty, a conversation all filled with riddles. They took turns at choosing the topic to talk about, but most of the subjects turned into arguments, even though Alice tried hard to be polite. Humpty Dumpty explained to Alice what the "Jabberwocky" poem meant, the one she had seen in the White King's book. Then, while reciting another poem, he stopped right in the middle, saying that was all. Alice thought it very queer but did not tell Humpty Dumpty so. She thought it time for her to leave, but as she walked away there was a terrible crash that shook the whole forest.

Thousands of soldiers and horses came rushing toward her, the riders constantly falling off their horses. Frightened, she escaped from the wood into the open. There she found the White King, who told her that he had sent the soldiers and horses and that the loud crash she had heard was the noise of the Lion and Unicorn fighting for the crown. She went with the king to watch the fight, which was indeed a terrible one. It was really silly of them to fight for the crown, since it belonged to the White King and he had no notion of giving it away. After the fight Alice met the Unicorn and the Lion. At the king's order she served them cake, a very strange cake which cut itself when she carried the dish around.

A great noise interrupted the party. When it stopped Alice thought she must have dreamed the whole thing until the Red Knight came along, followed soon by a White Knight. Each claimed her as a prisoner. Alice thought the whole business silly, since neither of them could do anything except fall off his horse and climb back on again, over and over and over. At last the Red Knight galloped off and the White Knight told her that she would be a queen as soon as she crossed the next brook. He was supposed to lead her to the end of the wood, but she spent the whole journey helping him back on his horse each time he fell off. The trip was filled with more queer conversation. By that time Alice was used to strange talk from her Looking-Glass friends. At last they reached the brook. The knight rode away and Alice jumped over the brook and into the last square of the chess board. To her delight, when she reached that square she felt something tight on her head—a crown! She was a queen.

Soon she found the Red Queen and the White Queen confronting her, very cross because she also thought she was a queen. They gave her a test for queens which she must have passed, for before long they were calling her "Your Majesty," and inviting people to a party which she was to give. The Red and the White Queens went to sleep after a time. Alice watched them until they disappeared. Then she found herself before a doorway marked "Queen Alice." All of her new friends were there, including the queens who had just vanished. The party was the most amazing experience of all. Puddings talked, guests poured wine over their heads, and the White Queen turned into a leg of mutton. Alice was exasperated, so much so that she seized the tablecloth and jerked it and everything on it to the floor. Then she grabbed the Red Queen and shook her as she would a kitten. But what was this? It *was* a kitten she was shaking, the black kitten.

Alice talked to Dinah and both the kittens about the adventure they had all had, but the silly kittens did nothing but purr.

Critical Evaluation

It is rare for the sequel to a highly creative literary work to surpass the original. Yet such is the case with *Through the Looking-Glass and What Alice Found There,* which in 1871 followed *Alice's Adventures in Wonderland,* published seven years earlier. For most readers the two books are so closely entwined that they are considered a unit, and many of Lewis Carroll's most famous Looking-Glass creations (Tweedledee, Tweedledum, and Humpty Dumpty, for example) are often mistakenly placed in *Alice's Adventures in Wonderland.* However, each, while joined by a common heroine and themes, is a distinct entity. And it is *Through the Looking-Glass* which most attracts adults, for it is in this second fantasy that Lewis Carroll (the pen name for Oxford mathematics lecturer and tutor the Rev. Charles Lutwidge Dodgson) presented an even more sophisticated puzzle about reality and logic than he did in the earlier story. It is in *Through the Looking-Glass* that one finds conscious suggestion of the cruel questions rather delicately presented in *Alice's Adventures in Wonderland.*

Sharing many characteristics, each book has twelve chapters, and both merge the fairy tale with science. Alice, seven years old in the first book, is seven and one-half on her second venture. A slight shift in scene turns the pleasant outdoor summer setting of *Alice's Adventures in Wonderland* into the more somber indoor winter stage of *Through the Looking-Glass.* Corresponding to the card game of the first book is chess in *Through the Looking-Glass,* another game which involves kings and queens. Within the chess-and-mirror framework of the Looking-Glass world, Carroll has, however, constructed an intricate symbolic plan unlike the seemingly spontaneous movement of Wonderland.

Although medieval and Renaissance sportsmen sometimes enjoyed chess which used human players on a giant field, Carroll is apparently the first to use the idea in literature. Science fiction has since, of course, often employed the technique. In the game plan, Alice is a white pawn on a giant chessboard of life in which the rows of the board are separated by brooks and the columns by hedges. Alice never speaks to any piece who is not in a square beside her, as appropriate for the pawn who never knows what is happening except at its spot on the board. Alice remains in the queen's field except for her last move by which time she has become a queen and captures the Red Queen (and shakes her into a kitten) and as a result checkmates the Red King who has slept throughout the game. Her behavior complements the personalities assigned to the other pieces, for each assumes the qualities of the figure it represents. As in chess, the queens are the most powerful and active beings and the kings are impotent. Erratic and stumbling, the White Knight recalls the movement of the chess knight which moves two squares in any direction, then again one square in a different direction, forming a sort of spastic "L."

Critics have noted inconsistencies in the chess game, charging that the White side makes nine consecutive moves; the White King is placed in an unnoticed check; the Queens castle; and the White Queen misses a chance to take the Red Knight. But Carroll, in a later explanatory note, said that the game is correct in relation to the moves even though the alternation of the sides is not strictly consistent, and that the "castling" of the Queens is merely his phrase to indicate that they have entered the palace. Not interested in the game as an example of chess strategy, Carroll conceived of it as a learning experience for a child who was to "be" a pawn warring against all the other pieces controlled by an adult, an idea apparently stimulated by the chess tales Carroll had fashioned for Alice Liddell, a young friend who was learning the game. Alice, daughter of the dean of Christ Church, Oxford, had also, of course, been the Alice whom he had placed in Wonderland.

Arising inevitably from Carroll's use of this structure has been the proposal that Alice is Everyman and that chess is Life. Like a human being who exists from birth to death only vaguely comprehending the forces directing his moves, Alice never understands her experience. Indeed none of the pieces really assimilates the total concept of the game. Even the mobile queens do not really grasp the idea that beyond the board there is a room and people who are determining the game. Our own reality thus becomes very unreal if we, like the chess pieces, have such a limited perception of the total environment.

Carroll pursues still another definition of reality when Alice confronts the Red King and is told that she exists merely as part of his dreams, not as an objective being. Upsetting to Alice is the sage advice of Tweedledum and Tweedledee to the effect that if the king were to wake, Alice would then vanish like the flame of a candle. The incident recalls Bishop Berkeley's empirical proposal that nothing exists except as it is perceived. Alice, like Samuel Johnson who refuted Berkeley by painfully kicking a stone, insists that she is "real" for she cries "real" tears. When she leaves the Looking-Glass world and supposedly awakens, Carroll mischievously permits her to ask herself: Which dreamed it? His final poem apparently provides the answer, for the

Bibliography

Arnoldi, Richard. "Parallels Between *Our Mutual Friend* and the Alice Books," in *Children's Literature: The Great Excluded.* I (1972), pp. 54–57.

Auerbach, Nina. "Alice and Wonderland: A Curious Child," in *Victorian Studies.* XVII (1973), pp. 31–47.

Baum, Alwin L. "Carroll's *Alices*: The Semiotics of Paradox," in *American Imago.* XXXIV (1977), pp. 86–108.

Blake, Kathleen. *Play, Games and Sport: The Literary Works of Lewis Carroll.* Ithaca, N.Y.: Cornell University Press, 1974, pp. 132–148.

Boynton, Mary F. "An Oxford Don Quixote," in *Hispania*. XLIV (1964), pp. 738–750.

Ettleson, A. *Carroll's* Through the Looking-Glass *Decoded*. New York: Philosophical Library, 1966.

Gardner, Martin. "Introduction," in *The Wasp in a Wig, a "Suppressed" Episode of* Through the Looking-Glass and What Alice Found There. By Lewis Carroll. New York: Clarkson N. Potter, 1977, pp. 1–11.

Henkle, Roger B. "The Mad Hatter's World," in *Virginia Quarterly Review*. XLIX (1973), pp. 107–111.

Johnson, Paula. "Alice Among the Analysts," in *Hartford Studies in Literature*. IV (1972), pp. 114–122.

Jorgens, Jack J. "Alice Our Contemporary," in *Children's Literature: The Great Excluded*. I (1972), pp. 152–161.

Matthews, Charles. "Satire in the Alice Books," in *Criticism*. XII (1971), pp. 105–119.

Otten, Terry. "Steppenwolf and Alice—In and Out of Wonderland," in *Studies in the Humanities*. IV (1974), pp. 28–34.

Pattison, Robert. *The Child Figure in English Literature*. Athens: University of Georgia Press, 1978, pp. 152–154.

Priestley, J.B. "Walrus and Carpenter; Political Symbolism in *Through the Looking-Glass*," in *New Statesman*. LIV (August 10, 1957), p. 168.

CHARLES DARWIN

Born: Shrewsbury, England (February 12, 1809)
Died: Down, England (April 19, 1882)

Principal Works

SCIENTIFIC ESSAYS AND STUDIES: *On the Origin of Species by Means of Natural Selection,* 1859; *The Variation of Animals and Plants under Domestication,* 1868; *The Descent of Man, and Selection in Relation to Sex,* 1871.
JOURNAL: *Diary of the Voyage of H.M.S. "Beagle,"* 1839.

The work of Charles (Robert) Darwin is of inestimable importance in the history of man and the history of science, and the publication of his *Origin of Species* in 1859 marks a turning point in the thinking of the Western world. Somewhat ironically, Darwin studied for two different professions before he turned to biology and science.

Darwin, grandson of Erasmus Darwin, was born at Shrewsbury, England, on February 12, 1809; his father was a physician and his mother a daughter of the noted English potter, Josiah Wedgwood. Darwin's mother died when he was eight years old, and his rearing was largely at the hands of older sisters. As a boy he attended Shrewsbury School, then under the direction of Dr. Samuel Butler, an educator who, devoted to a classical regimen of learning, deplored young Darwin's attention to chemistry in a home laboratory. Darwin's father intended his son for the medical profession, and so young Charles Darwin entered Edinburgh University in 1825. The study of medicine proved distasteful, however, and in 1828 Darwin entered Cambridge University to prepare himself for a career as an Anglican clergyman. While at Cambridge he became friendly with John Stevens Henslow, the famous professor of botany, through whom Darwin received his opportunity to sail as a naturalist on the official British exploration ship, H.M.S. *Beagle.*

At first Darwin's father refused to consent to this change of careers, but at the urging of Josiah Wedgwood he finally withdrew his objection and young Darwin, as the unpaid naturalist, sailed on the *Beagle* for South America and the Pacific Ocean on December 27, 1831. When he left England, Darwin was practically uneducated in science, certainly untried as a specialist in science. When he returned to England in 1836, almost five years later, he had had an unequaled practical education and experience in science, having acquired firsthand experience in methodical scientific observation over a large portion of the earth's surface. His experience, by giving him a tremendous knowledge of living creatures, had already turned his thinking to the possibility of evolution. In his travels he had seen many living creatures and organisms of his own age and from earlier geological eras. In the years immediately after his return to England, Darwin spent his time disposing of his collections of specimens and writing and editing the voluminous reports that came from the five-year exploratory trip, including the *Zoölogy of the Voyage of H.M.S. "Beagle"* (1840–1846). The voyage had taken its toll of Darwin's constitution, however, and he never again experienced good health. Two years after his marriage to Emma Wedgwood, a cousin, he was forced to leave London to take up residence in the countryside near Down, where excitement and nervous tension were at a minimum. Years later, when his books created a storm of protest and controversy, ill-health required Darwin to leave the defense of his work to Thomas Henry Huxley and others. In fact, for more than forty years weakness and illness prevented Darwin's working for more than a few hours at a time.

Although it was not published until 1859, *On the Origin of Species* began to take form in Darwin's writings as early as 1842; a manuscript of 1844 clearly defines the theory. At the urging of Lyell, Darwin began to compile the results of years of research and study, but before he was finished, in June, 1858, Darwin received a manuscript from A. R. Wallace, then in Malaya, in which an identical theory of mutation was set forth. Upon the advice of fellow scientists, Wallace's paper and one by Darwin were presented to the Linnean Society in July, 1858. The full book, *On the Origin of Species*, was published the following year. In 1868 certain aspects of his theory were more fully developed in *The Variation of Animals and Plants under Domestication*. *The Descent of Man* grew in its turn out of the 1868 volume and included man as one of the animals which had evolved through the epochs of geological history. During the rest of his life Darwin gave his time to publishing papers and books on botany, works of very little interest to a general reader. He died at his home near Down, Kent, on April 19, 1882.

Darwin's most important books are remembered as landmarks in history because they gave weight to what had previously been merely hypotheses. Linnaeus had already classified man as an anthropoid, but it was left for Darwin to present evidence of an overwhelming kind for the hypothesis. Today evolution is an accepted fact; although not every biologist is a Darwinian, there is not one of stature and reputation who does not believe in some form of evolution.

Bibliography

The principal writings of Charles Darwin have now been collected in *The Darwin Reader*, edited by Marston Bates and Philip S. Humphrey, 1957. There is also a definitive edition of *Charles Darwin's Diary of the Voyage of H.M.S. "Beagle,"* edited by Nora Barlow, 1934. A collection of Darwinian excerpts, *What Darwin Really Said*, was edited by Julian Huxley, 1929.

The standard biography is Francis Darwin, *The Life and Letters of Charles Darwin*, 3 vols., 1887 (rev. ed., 1911). For other biographical and critical studies see also Leonard Huxley, *Darwin*, 1921; Gamaliel Bradford, *Darwin*, 1926; G. A. Dorsey, *The Evolution of Charles Darwin*, 1927; Geoffrey West, *Charles Darwin: The Fragmentary Man*, 1937; H. G. Wells, *Charles Darwin: A Portrait*, 1938; Sir Arthur Keith, *Darwin Revalued*, 1955; Gertrude Himmelfarb, *Darwin and the Darwinian Revolution*, 1959; and Gerhard Whickler, *Charles Darwin*, 1961.

ON THE ORIGIN OF SPECIES

Type of work: Biological study
Author: Charles Darwin (1809–1882)
First published: 1859

Essay-Review

Charles Darwin's *On the Origin of Species*—originally titled *On the Origin of Species by Means of Natural Selection, or the Preservation of Favoured Races in the Struggle for Life*—belongs to that category of books which almost every educated person knows by title and subject but which the average person has never read. This is a circumstance to be regretted, for probably no other book written in modern times has had so powerful an influence on contemporary thought, either indirectly or directly. For Darwin's report on his biological investigations came to have far-reaching importance beyond the field of biology; the evidence he presented and the implications and principles it involved came eventually to influence psychology, sociology, law, theology, educational theory, philosophy, literature, and other branches of man's intellectual endeavor.

The ideas contained in this work were not entirely new in Western culture, as Darwin himself realized. It was he, however, who put theory in definitive form, and his writings caught the public's attention, so that in the public mind his book, together with his name, came to be a symbol for an empirical, positivistic approach to problems and their study.

Scholarly opinion is somewhat divided as to Darwin's contribution to biological science. He built on the researches of his predecessors, as all scientists do, but to his studies he brought immense labors of his own. More than twenty years prior to the publication of *On the Origin of Species* he had contemplated the thory that species were not immutable. As a naturalist he had spent five years in scientific study during the voyage of H.M.S. *Beagle*. During that time he had unusual chances to observe flora and fauna around the globe; those observations led him to believe that species did change, for what he observed caused him to see the probability of common descent for all living organisms. As early as 1837 he had begun a systematic study to determine whether such hypotheses were correct, and by 1842 he had a rough draft of his theory of evolution. Wishing to conduct as exhaustive investigations as he could before publication of his theory, he postponed public statement. In 1858 a manuscript setting forth the same ideas came to him from A. R. Wallace. The two men, working independently, had come to similar conclusions. Darwin then felt obliged to publish a statement of his own work in July, 1858, at a meeting of the Linnaean Society. *On the Origin of Species* was published a little over a year later. His later books—*Variation of Animals and Plants under Domestication* (1868), *The Descent of Man* (1871), and other writings—elaborated particular aspects of the general theory promulgated in the first book.

The possibility of evolution of species goes back in the history of thought to classical times; even Aristotle hinted at it in his writings. Darwin opened his book with an account of previous thinking on the theory of evolution in which he outlined earlier statements, beginning with Buffon, in modern times, and noting such men as Lamarck, Geoffroy Saint-Hilaire, W. Herbert, von Buch, Haldeman, the anonymous author of *Vestiges of Creation*, and others. In his introduction he also exercised care in warning the reader what to expect. He wrote:

> This Abstract, which I now publish, must necessarily be imperfect. I cannot here give references and authorities for my several statements; and I must trust to the reader reposing some confidence in my accuracy. No doubt errors will have crept in, though I hope I have always been cautious in trusting to good authorities alone. I can here give only the general conclusions at which I have arrived, with a few facts in illustration, but which, I hope, in most cases will suffice. No one can feel more sensible than I do of the necessity of hereafter publishing in detail all the facts, with references, on which any conclusions have been grounded; and I hope in a future work to do this. For I am well aware that scarcely a single point is discussed in this volume on which facts cannot be adduced, often apparently leading to conclusions directly opposite to those at which I have arrived. A fair result can be obtained only by fully stating and balancing the facts and arguments on both sides of each question; and this is here impossible.

Again, in his final chapter titled "Recapitulation and Conclusion," Darwin told his readers that the book is "one long argument" in favor of the theory of mutability and evolution of species in both the plant and animal worlds. He pointed out that all the evidence had not been gathered and that even the likelihood of someday having all the evidence is so slight as to be wholly inconceivable. Darwin pointed out that there have been too many gradations, especially among broken and failing groups of organisms, including those which have in past eras become extinct.

The vast amount of information Darwin laid before readers of *On the Origin of Species* can be appreciated only by actually reading the work itself in its entirety. A partial list of the chapter headings does give an indication, however, of the kinds of evidence Darwin accumulated and presented for the reader. There are chapters on both variation in nature and under domestication; there are chapters on the struggle for existence, on natural selection, on the principles of variation, on instinct, on hybridism, and on the geographical distribution of flora and fauna. There are also chapters on various objections to the general theory of evolution, on the mutual affinities of organic beings, and on the imperfections of the geological record of the succession of organisms. These chapters, more or less interdependent, cast light on all varied aspects of the theory of progressive evolution of species. For this reason the chapters do not lend themselves to separate study. The writer's organization of his material is as complex as it is excellent.

Darwin's theory of progressive evolution has been misunderstood at times. Despite the fact that he did his best to avoid misunderstanding, there were misinterpretations. Although Darwin pointedly expressed his view that natural selection had been the *principal* means by which variation occurred, some critics objected that his theory rested on saying that natural selection was the *only* means by which variation occurred. The grossness of such misinterpretations, now that the theory can be approached in most quarters without emotion, should be obvious to any careful reader.

In spite of its length and the weight of its content, *On the Origin of Species* is a remarkably easy book to read. The credit must go to the care with which Darwin organized his materials and the lucid style in which he wrote. His writing is scientific writing at its best. Each sentence is carefully worded so that prolixity is seldom encountered. The ideas flow naturally from sentence to sentence and paragraph to paragraph. To characterize this style, one can say of it figuratively that it is lean and muscular. Living in an age when superlatives and prolixity abound, the twentieth century reader may find himself pleasantly surprised in reading Darwin's prose.

CHARLES DICKENS

Born: Landport, England (February 7, 1812)
Died: Gadshill, England (June 9, 1870)

Principal Works

NOVELS: *The Pickwick Papers*, 1836–1837; *Oliver Twist*, 1837–1839; *Nicholas Nickleby*, 1838–1839; *The Old Curiosity Shop*, 1840–1841; *Barnaby Rudge*, 1841; *Martin Chuzzlewit*, 1843–1844; *Dombey and Son*, 1846–1848; *David Copperfield*, 1849–1850; *Bleak House*, 1852–1853; *Hard Times*, 1854; *Little Dorrit*, 1855–1857; *A Tale of Two Cities*, 1859; *Great Expectations*, 1860–1861; *Our Mutual Friend*, 1864–1866; *The Mystery of Edwin Drood*, 1870.

CHRISTMAS BOOKS: *A Christmas Carol*, 1843; *The Chimes*, 1844; *The Cricket on the Hearth*, 1845; *The Battle of Life*, 1846; *The Haunted Man*, 1848.

SKETCHES AND TALES: *Sketches by Boz*, 1836; *Sketches of Young Gentlemen*, 1838; *Sketches of Young Couples*, 1840; *The Uncommercial Traveller*, 1860; *George Silverman's Explanation*, 1868.

PLAYS: *The Strange Gentleman*, 1836; *The Village Coquettes*, 1836; *Mr. Nightingale's Diary*, 1851 (with Mark Lemon); *No Thoroughfare*, 1867 (with Wilkie Collins).

TRAVEL SKETCHES AND IMPRESSIONS: *American Notes*, 1842; *Pictures from Italy*, 1846.

MISCELLANEOUS: *A Child's History of England*, 1853; *The Life of Our Lord*, 1934.

Charles Dickens, British novelist, was born at Landport, near Portsmouth, England, February 7, 1812, the son of a minor government clerk. Owing to his parents' incompetence in money matters, at the age of ten, when the family moved to London, occurred the episode that many critics have found traumatic in its effect on the emotional and creative life of the novelist: that "deep sense of abandonment," symbolized for him by his parents' complacent relegation of him to the sordid drudgery of work in Warren's blacking warehouse. One side of its effect on him is almost certainly the way in which we find, at or near the center of so many of his novels, a suffering, neglected child; another, the almost hallucinatory intensity of his rendering of the externals of human beings. The episode was brief, and he returned to school, to leave at fifteen, his real education having been gained from the novels of Cervantes, Le Sage, Fielding, and Smollett, and his exposure to the London scene during his "abandonment." He became first a lawyer's clerk and then a shorthand reporter in the courts and the House of Commons.

His first book, *Sketches by Boz*, stemmed from his work as a journalist; it led to his being commissioned to write the text accompanying a collection of comic drawings about Cockney sportsmen which was to be published in monthly parts.

"I thought," he wrote later, "of Mr. Pickwick"; and with the appearance of Sam Weller in Chapter X the success of *The Pickwick Papers* was not merely assured but unprecedentedly sensational. From then on, Dickens was the most popular of all English novelists in his lifetime and probably for posterity too.

Even while *The Pickwick Papers* was appearing, however, *Oliver Twist* was being published as a continued story in a magazine. The two novels show the two sides of Dickens' genius. *The Pickwick Papers* is a work of pure humor, in which the crudities and miseries of the real world are sterilized by laughter and the vicious are objects of comedy, good things in themselves, without reference to moral judgment, because they are seen as comic. The world of this novel is almost fairyland: in *Oliver Twist* fairyland has become the country of nightmare; the bad fairies have become ogres. There is still laughter, but it has become savage, satirical; the appeal is to derision. On the surface, *Oliver Twist* is an exposure novel, an attack on the working of the poor law of the day, but its real theme is the fate of innocence and weakness. The savage comedy, seen in a character like Bumble, is accompanied by equally savage melodrama, the melodrama of the Jew Fagin and the robber Bill Sikes.

From then on, fairyland and nightmare exist side by side in Dickens' novels. During the first part of his career, these novels are naïve in form, based on eighteenth century picaresque, in which we follow the fortunes of the hero who gives his name to the book, as in *Nicholas Nickleby* and *Martin Chuzzlewit*. The weaknesses of structure inherent in picaresque fiction were accentuated by Dickens' practice of writing for serialization and by his lack of what today would be called the artistic conscience: Martin Chuzzlewit was sent to America not because the pattern of the novel demanded it but because sales were falling off and an element of novelty seemed called for to revive interest. Today we read the earlier novels for their incidentals, not for their plots; for the scenes at Dotheboys Hall and the character of Mrs. Nickleby in *Nicholas Nickleby*; for the wonderful Pecksniff and the sublime Mrs. Gamp—as a comic creation second only to Falstaff in English literature—in *Martin Chuzzlewit*.

The masterpiece of this first part of Dickens' career is the semi-autobiographical *David Copperfield*, the most varied of the earlier works and the best proportioned, containing, too, some of his most delightful characters, among them Mr. Micawber, modeled on his father. The darkening of his genius is already apparent, however, in *Dombey and Son*; and henceforth his criticism of the age, which up to then had largely dealt with specific abuses, becomes general, focusing on the theme of money. The humor is no longer that of delighted appreciation of the absurd, but bitterly sardonic, as in the rendering of Mr. Podsnap in *Our Mutual Friend*. Plot becomes much more highly organized; and at the same time a rich symbolism enters his fiction, sometimes as an extraordinary intensification of atmosphere, as in the description of Dombey's house in *Dombey and Son*, sometimes as a feature of the London scene, like the dust-piles which dominate *Our Mutual Friend*, sometimes even as an atmospheric condition, as in the fog that enshrouds the beginning of *Bleak House*. Symbolism of this kind was something almost entirely new in English fiction; and while his contemporaries preferred the earlier books, where he is "the unique portrayer of comical eccentrics" and the stress is on high spirits and the gospel of kindliness, critics in our time have tended more to admire the later novels, with their dark poetic sweep, the passionate intensity of their symbolism, and their affinity, in mood engendered, both with the later Elizabethan tragedy and with Dostoevski. Outstanding also among the later works are *Little Dorrit*, which is partly autobiographical in inspiration, and *Great Expectations*. His mystery story, *Edwin Drood*, was unfinished. He wrote two historical novels, *Barnaby Rudge*, based on the Gordon Riots of eighteenth century London, and *A Tale of Two Cities*, on the French Revolution. *A Christmas Carol in Prose* is the most famous of his shorter pieces.

Dickens married in 1836 and separated from his wife in 1858. His first visit to the United States, in 1841, resulted in *American Notes*, a work which, together with the American chapters in *Martin Chuzzlewit*, was extremely resented in America. A second visit, in 1867, was a triumphant success. He died at his home at Gadshill on June 9, 1870.

Bibliography

For Dickens' collected work, *The Nonesuch Dickens*, ed. by A. Waugh, W. Dexter, et al., 23 vols., 1937–1938, has been superseded by the *New Oxford Illustrated Dickens*, 1948–1958, and by the definitive Clarendon Dickens series, in progress. Dickens' collected letters, in the Pilgrim Edition under Madeline House and G. Storey, is also in progress, with Vol. 1, 1965, and Vol. 2, 1969. The authorized biography is John Forster's *The Life of Charles Dickens*, 1872–1874, revised by J. W. T. Ley, 1928; but this work should be supplemented by the major biography of Edgar Johnson, *Charles Dickens: His Tragedy and Triumph*, 2 vols., 1953, 1970. Among the still useful earlier studies of Dickens' life are G. K. Chesterton, *Charles Dickens*, 1906; J. W. T. Ley, *The Dickens Circle: The Novelist's Friendships*, 1919; Sir H. F. Dickens, *Memories of my Father*, 1928; and W. H. Bowen, *Charles Dickens and his Family*, 1936. More recent biographical studies include R. J. Cruikshank, *Charles Dickens and Early Victorian England*, 1949; Monroe Engel, *The Maturity of Dickens*, 1959; J. B. Priestly, *Charles Dickens*, 1961; I. Brown, *Dickens in his Time*, 1963; C. Hibbert, *The Making of Charles Dickens*, 1967; A. Wilson, *The World of Charles Dickens*, 1970; Ivor Brown, *Dickens and His World*, 1970; Ivor Brown, *Charles Dickens, 1812–1870*, 1970; Alexander Welsh, *The City of Dickens*, 1971; Joseph Gold, *Charles Dickens: Radical and Moralist*, 1972; John Greaves, *Dickens at Doughty Street*, 1975; and Duane DeVries, *Dickens' Apprentice Years: The Making of a Novelist*, 1976.

Modern Dickens criticism begins around 1940 with the publication of essays by George Orwell and Edmund Wilson, and with Humphrey House's *The Dickens World*, 1941. See Edmund Wilson, *The Wound and the Bow*, 1941;

George Orwell, *Dickens, Dali, and Others*, 1946; Sylvère Monod, *Dickens Romancier*, 1953; J. Hillis Miller, *Charles Dickens: The World of His Novels*, 1958; K. J. Fielding, *Charles Dickens: A Critical Introduction*, 1958, 1965; A. O. J. Cockshut, *The Imagination of Dickens*, 1961; John Gross and Gabriel Pearson, eds., *Dickens and the Twentieth Century*, 1962; Earle Davis, *The Flint and the Flame*, 1963; Mark Spilka, *Dickens and Kafka*, 1963; Robert Garis, *The Dickens Theatre*, 1965; T. Stoehr, *Dickens: The Dreamer's Stance*, 1966; G. H. Ford and L. Lane, eds., *Dickens Critics*, 1967; Harvey Sucksmith, *The Narrative Art of Charles Dickens: The Rhetoric of Sympathy and Irony in His Novels*, 1970; F. R. and Q. D. Leavis, *Dickens: The Novelist*, 1970; Anthony Dyson, *The Inimitable Dickens: A Reading of the Novels*, 1970; George L. Brook, *The Language of Dickens*, 1970, 1973; Herman M. Daleski, *Dickens and the Art of Analogy*, 1970; James R. Kincaid, *Dickens and the Rhetoric of Laughter*, 1971; Michael C. Kotzin, *Dickens and the Fairy Tale*, 1972; N. M. Lary, *Dostoevsky and Dickens: A Study of Literary Influence*, 1973; Garrett Stewart, *Dickens and the Trials of Imagination*, 1974; Fred Kaplan, *Dickens and Mesmerism: The Hidden Springs of Fiction*, 1975; A. L. Zambrano, *Dickens and Film*, 1976; John Romano, *Dickens and Reality*, 1978; and Robert L. Patten, *Charles Dickens and His Publishers*, 1978.

Specialized works include M. Price, ed., *Dickens: A Collection of Critical Essays*, 1967; A. E. Dyson, ed., *Dickens: A Selection of Critical Essays*, 1968; B. N. Schilling, ed., *The Comic World of Dickens*, 1969; Centenary number of *The Dickensian*, Vol. 66, No. 361, May 1960; E. W. F. Tomlin, ed. *Charles Dickens, 1812–1870: A Centenary Volume*, 1970; Robert B. Partlow, Jr., ed., *Dickens Studies Annual*, Vol. I, 1970; John Greaves, *Who's Who in Dickens*, 1972; and Philip Hobsbaum, *A Reader's Guide to Charles Dickens*, 1973. See also John Butt and Kathleen Tillotson, *Dickens at Work*, 1957, which investigates the novelist's methods of publication; and George H. Ford, *Dickens and His Readers*, 1955, 1965, a survey of his contemporary critics and audience.

BLEAK HOUSE

Type of work: Novel
Author: Charles Dickens (1812–1870)
Type of plot: Social criticism
Time of plot: Mid-nineteenth century
Locale: London, Lincolnshire, and Hertfordshire, England
First published: 1852–1853

Bleak House. *a satire on the methods of an English equity court, is based upon an actual case in Chancery, while several of the minor characters are caricatures of well-known literary figures of the day. Although the complicated Lady Dedlock plot which gave* Bleak House *its contemporary popularity is rather thin, the novel as a whole stands up remarkably well.*

Principal Characters

John Jarndyce, the unmarried, aging owner of Bleak House and a party in the famous and protracted Chancery suit of Jarndyce vs. Jarndyce. Generous to a fault, he makes two young cousins, Ada Clare and Richard Carstone, his wards, in the hope that they will fall in love and fill his ancestral home with renewed life. He also takes into his home an orphan, Esther Summerson, as a companion to Ada. He himself falls in love with Esther, but when he learns that she is in love with Allan Woodcourt, a young surgeon, he releases her from her promise to him and gives the couple a new Bleak House of their own. He is loyal to his old friend and is always scrupulously fair, even though he calls his library "The Growlery" and retreats there when the winds of adversity blow on him. Admirable in every way, the head of the Jarndyce family creates rather than preserves a family dignity.

Esther Summerson, the orphan whom John Jarndyce takes into his home and later into his heart. In reality she is the natural daughter of Lady Dedlock and a gallant named Captain Hawdon (who dies and is buried under the name of Nemo). Though part of the story is told by Esther, her ingenuousness makes of her less of a heroine and more of a companion and comforter who goes under various motherly terms of endearment. Although she respects and admires her benefactor, she truly loves the compassionate doctor, Allan Woodcourt, who woos her in spite of her disease-ravaged face, the result of a serious illness incurred while nursing Charley, her maid. Her immediate sympathies are aroused by any homeless beings and by those, as in the case of Caddy Jellyby, whose homes are friendless and loveless. She finally finds happiness with her husband and two daughters.

Ada Clare, John Jarndyce's cousin and ward. She secretly marries Richard Carstone, her cousin, to protect him from the grinding poverty that lawyers and the courts bring upon him. She manages to keep her loyalties and sympathies divided by remaining with her benefactor while extending her love to Carstone. Beautiful and tractable, she displays evenness of disposition and generous motives which make her a tearful heroine.

Richard Carstone, Ada's cousin and husband. Anything suits this young man who has already sold his soul to the case of Jarndyce vs. Jarndyce. He tries medicine, the law, and the army, only to die of disappointment after the suit in Chancery has been settled and he learns that legal costs have eaten up the whole of his inheritance. John Jarndyce provides for Ada and her infant son.

Lady Honoria Dedlock, secretly the mother of Esther Summerson by Captain Hawdon, a rake to whom she was once engaged. When Tulkinghorn, her husband's legal adviser, threatens to inform her husband of her past, she flees from her home and dies, a victim of shame and exposure, at the gate of the cemetery where her lover has been buried under the name of Nemo. Her body is discovered by Esther Summerson.

Sir Leicester Dedlock, an honorable gentleman of prejudice and pride of family, completely unaware of his wife's guilty secret.

Mr. Tulkinghorn, a conniving solicitor who threatens to expose the secret in Lady Dedlock's past. He is murdered by Lady Dedlock's French maid when he refuses to pay her blackmailing demands and threatens her with imprisonment.

Allan Woodcourt, the surgeon who attends Captain Hawdon at the time of his death and who extends his help to Esther Summerson and Richard Carstone as well. He marries Esther after John Jarndyce releases her from her promise to him.

Mrs. Woodcourt, his handsome mother, proud of her Welsh ancestry.

William Guppy, a lawyer's clerk in the firm of Kenge and Carboy, John Jarndyce's solicitors. Attracted to Esther Summerson, he "files a declaration" of his love. Later, discovering that she has lost her beauty as a result of illness, he regrets his proposal and asks her to make a statement, before a witness, that there was never any formal engagement between them. He also meddles, though in a cowardly and humorous fashion, in

Tulkinghorn's intrigue to discover Lady Dedlock's connection with the dead Nemo.

Miss Flite, a Jarndyce relative, half-crazed by the frustrations and delays of the suit in Chancery. Bright, friendly, perceptive of the crushing power of the law, she raises birds for release when the case is settled, and she tries to keep others from her own sad fate.

Miss Barbary, Lady Dedlock's sister and Esther Summerson's aunt and godmother, a good, austere woman.

Mademoiselle Hortense, Lady Dedlock's French maid. She murders Tulkinghorn when he resists her attempt at blackmail.

Inspector Bucket, the police detective who solves the mystery of Tulkinghorn's murder.

Rosa, a village girl also employed as a maid by Lady Dedlock. She is engaged to marry Watt Rouncewell.

Mrs. Rouncewell, the Dedlock housekeeper.

Mr. Rouncewell, her son, the father of Watt Rouncewell.

George Rouncewell, another son, a soldier and later the owner of a shooting gallery in London. He is falsely arrested for the murder of Tulkinghorn.

Watt Rouncewell, the young man engaged to Rosa.

Mrs. Rachael, later **Mrs. Chadband,** a servant to Miss Barbary.

The Reverend Mr. Chadband, her husband, a self-conscious clergyman given to flowery speech.

Mrs. Snagsby, one of his parishioners, a shrew.

Mr. Snagsby, a law-stationer, her mild, hen-pecked husband.

Captain Hawdon, now calling himself **Nemo,** a law writer, the former lover of Lady Dedlock. Dying in a garret over Krook's dingy shop, he is buried in the Potter's Field.

Jo, also called **Toughey,** a street sweeper, befriended by Nemo. Lady Dedlock pays him two half-crowns to point out Nemo's grave.

Krook, the owner of a rag-and-bottle shop and the landlord of Miss Flite and Nemo. He has in his possession a packet of papers belonging to the former Captain Hawdon. This fact has been ferreted out by Tony Jobling, who calls himself Weevle while lodging with Krook, and William Guppy has agreed to reclaim the papers for Lady Dedlock. On the night that the papers are to change hands, Krook, a habitual drunkard, perishes of spontaneous combustion. Apparently the papers are destroyed in the fire.

Mrs. Smallweed, Krook's sister.

Mr. Smallweed, her husband, a superannuated man of unimpaired and irascible mind.

Bartholomew Smallweed, also called **Chickweed,** their grandson, a sponging friend of William Guppy.

Judy Smallweed, Bartholomew's twin sister.

Tony Jobling, a law writer for Mr. Snagsby and a friend of William Guppy. Calling himself **Weevle,** he takes lodgings in Krook's establishment and learns that Krook has in his possession a bundle of Captain Hawdon's papers.

Mrs. Jellyby, a plump, strong-minded woman who neglects her house and family while interesting herself in philanthropic projects, one of which is to settle a colony of English poor in Boorioboola-Gha, on the Niger River in Africa.

Caroline Jellyby, also called **Caddy,** Mrs. Jellyby's oldest daughter. Tired of her mother's endless projects, she marries Prince Turveydrop. A close friend of Esther Summerson, Caddy names her first daughter Esther.

Mr. Jellyby, a mild, miserable man who goes bankrupt.

"Peepy" Jellyby, the Jellybys' weak and neglected son.

Prince Turveydrop, named in honor of the Prince Regent. He marries Caddy Jellyby.

Mr. Turveydrop, Prince Turveydrop's father, a model of deportment and a monster of selfishness.

Harold Skimpole, the sentimental, unworldly recipient of John Jarndyce's bounty, a character thought to have been modeled after Leigh Hunt.

Mrs. Skimpole, his sickly wife.

Arethusa, the "Beauty" daughter, **Laura,** the "Sentiment" daughter, and

Kitty, the "Comedy" daughter, the Skimpole children.

Lawrence Boythorn, John Jarndyce's friend. His character is modeled on that of Walter Savage Landor.

Mr. Gridley, also called **"The Man from Shropshire,"** a farmer's son ruined by a suit in Chancery, frequently jailed for contempt of court. While hiding from the law, he dies in a London shooting gallery.

Bayham Badger, a medical practitioner to whom Richard Carstone is articled for a time. He is proud of his wife's two former husbands.

Mrs. Badger, his wife, who brings glory to her present married state because she is the widow of Captain Swosser, an officer of the Royal Navy, and Professor Dingo, a scientist.

Charlotte Neckett, also called **Charley,** Esther Summerson's devoted maid.

Mr. Kenge, nicknamed **"Conversation"**

Kenge, a member of the law firm of Kenge and Carboy. Through him John Jarndyce first meets Esther Summerson.

Mr. Vholes, Richard Carstone's solicitor. He helps to bring about the young man's ruin.

Mr. Quale, Mrs. Jellyby's partner in her impractical philanthropic schemes.

Miss Wisk, betrothed to Mr. Quale.

Mr. Tangle, a legal authority on the case of Jarndyce vs. Jarndyce.

The Story

The suit of Jarndyce vs. Jarndyce was a standing joke in the Court of Chancery. Beginning with a dispute as to how the trusts under a Jarndyce will were to be administered, the suit had dragged on, year after year, generation after generation, without settlement. The heirs, or would-be heirs, spent their lives waiting. Some, like Tom Jarndyce, blew out their brains. Others, like tiny Miss Flite, visited the Court in daily expectation of some judgment which would settle the disputed estate and bring her the wealth of which she dreamed.

Among those involved in the suit were John Jarndyce, great-nephew of the Tom Jarndyce who had shot himself in a coffee house, and his two cousins, Richard Carstone and Ada Clare. Jarndyce was the owner of Bleak House in Hertfordshire, a country place which was not as dreary as its name. His two young cousins lived with him. He had provided a companion for Ada in the person of Esther Summerson. Esther had suffered an unhappy childhood under the care of Miss Barbary, her stern godmother, and a servant, Mrs. Rachel. The two had told the girl that her mother was a wicked woman who had deserted her. Miss Barbary was now dead, and Mr. Jarndyce had become Esther's benefactor.

Two others who took a strange interest in the Jarndyce estate were Sir Leicester and Lady Dedlock of Chesney Wold, in Lincolnshire. Lord Dedlock had a solicitor named Tulkinghorn, who, like every other reputable lawyer in London, was involved in the Jarndyce suit. One day when Tulkinghorn was in the Dedlock's home, the lawyer presented Lady Dedlock with a document. At the sight of the handwriting on the paper she swooned. Immediately suspicious, Tulkinghorn resolved to trace the handwriting to its source. His search led him to Mr. Snagsby, a stationer, but the best that Snagsby could tell him was that the paper had been copied by a man named Nemo, a lodger in the house of Mr. Krook, a junk dealer. Mr. Tulkinghorn went to the house with Snagsby, only to find Nemo dead of an overdose of opium. Convinced that Nemo was not the dead man's real name, the lawyer could learn nothing of the man's identity or connections.

Esther Summerson soon found an ardent friend and admirer in William Guppy, a clerk in the office of Kenge and Carboy, Jarndyce's solicitors. It was Guppy who first noticed Esther's resemblance to Lady Dedlock. Allan Woodcourt, a young surgeon who had been called to administer to the dead Nemo, requested an inquest. One of the witnesses called was Jo, a crossing sweeper whom Nemo had often befriended. A little later Jo was found with two half-crowns on his person. He explained that they had been given him by a lady he had guided to the gate of the churchyard where Nemo was buried. Jo was arrested, and in the cross-examination which followed, Mr. Guppy questioned the wife of an oily preacher named Chadband and found that the firm of Kenge and Carboy had once had charge of a young lady with whose aunt Mrs. Chadband had lived. Mrs. Chadband was, of course, the Mrs. Rachel of Esther Summerson's childhood. She revealed that Esther's real name was not Summerson, but Hawdon.

The mystery surrounding Esther Summerson began to clear. A French maid who had left Lady Dedlock's service identified her late mistress as the lady who had given two half-crowns to the crossing sweeper. The dead Nemo was promptly proved to have been Captain Hawdon. Years before he and the present Lady Dedlock had fallen in love; Esther was their child. But Miss Barbary, angry at her sister's disgrace, had taken the child and moved to another part of the country. The mother later married Lord Dedlock. She was now overjoyed that the child her unforgiving sister had led her to believe dead was still alive, and she resolved to reveal herself to her.

Mr. Guppy informed Lady Dedlock that a packet of Captain Hawdon's letters was in the possession of the junk dealer, Krook. Fearing that the revelation of these letters would ruin her position, Lady Dedlock asked Guppy to bring them to her, and the wily law clerk agreed. But on the night the letters were to be obtained the drunken Krook exploded of spontaneous combustion, and presumably the letters burned with him.

In the meantime, Richard Carstone, completely obsessed by the Jarndyce case, had abandoned all efforts to establish a career for himself. He lived in a false hope that the Chancery suit would soon be settled, spending the little money he had on an unscrupulous lawyer named Vholes. When Jarndyce remonstrated, Richard thought his cousin's advice prompted by selfish interests. Ada Clare, also worried over Richard's behavior, secretly married him so that her own small fortune might stand between Richard and his folly.

Esther Summerson fell desperately ill of a fever, and when Lady Dedlock heard of the girl's illness she went to her at once and revealed herself. So mother and daughter were finally reunited. As a result of her illness, Esther's beauty was completely destroyed. John Jarndyce, feeling free for the first time to declare his love for a woman so much younger than himself, asked her to marry him, and she accepted.

Tulkinghorn was murdered and several nights later when she knew her secret was about to be revealed to her husband, Lady Dedlock left home. It was discovered that Tulkinghorn had been murdered by the French maid through whom he had learned of Lady Dedlock's connection with the crossing sweeper. The maid had attempted to blackmail the lawyer, and when he threatened her with imprisonment she killed him. Inspector Bucket, who solved the mystery of the murder, also informed Lord Dedlock of his wife's past. The baronet told the detective to employ every means to bring about her return. It was Esther Summerson, however, who found her mother dead at the gate of the churchyard where Captain Hawdon was buried.

Among Krook's effects was a Jarndyce will made at a later date than the one which had been disputed in Chancery for so many years. It settled the question of the Jarndyce inheritance forever. Richard and Ada were declared the heirs, but unfortunately the entire fortune had been eaten up in court costs and the two young people were left to face a life of genteel poverty. Richard did not long survive this final blow. He died, leaving his wife and infant son in the care of John Jarndyce.

Esther became the mistress of her own Bleak House. John Jarndyce, discovering that her true love was young Doctor Woodcourt, released her from her promise to marry him and in his generosity brought the two lovers together. Before her wedding to Doctor Woodcourt, Jarndyce took her to see a country house he had bought at Yorkshire. He had named it Bleak House, and it was his wedding present to the bride and groom. There Esther lived, happy in the love of her husband and her two daughters and in the lasting affection of John Jarndyce, proprietor of that other Bleak House which would always be her second home.

Critical Evaluation

Bleak House, after publication as a serial, first appeared in book form in 1853 at the height of Dickens' career. Preceded by *Martin Chuzzlewit* and followed by *Hard Times,* it comes early in the group of Dickens' great novels of social analysis and protest. A major critical anatomy of mid-nineteenth century England, the novel nevertheless shows some unfortunate signs of serial publication and of the author's concessions to his audience. Pathos, melodrama, and a somewhat strident moralism all reflect weaknesses in the public taste, yet Dickens manages to weave out of these a controlled assessment of the corruption at the heart of his society.

At the center of its intricate plot is the lawsuit of Jarndyce and Jarndyce. To this meager frame Dickens piles sub-plot upon sub-plot, all ultimately interrelated. In one sense, the plot is a series of thin detective stories woven together in such a way as to involve all strata of society. As character after fascinating character appears, each episode is interesting in its own right and, in the masterly resolution, no action or detail remains extraneous.

The third-person narrator of most of *Bleak House* is a sharply ironic commentator on the political, social, and moral evils which abound in the book. There is never any question of the narrator's attitude towards the selfishness and irresponsibility he recounts, but he is not quite so sardonic or homiletic as the narrator of *Hard Times.* The stern attitude of this narrator is both relieved and reinforced by the introduction of a second, first-person narrator,

Esther Summerson. Many critics have seen the dual narration as an aesthetic flaw, but each narrator does contribute a different perspective. Although Esther is a bit simpering and saccharine, she does represent a sympathetic and morally responsible attitude which is rare in the world of *Bleak House*. She is a compassionate insider who adds both a perspective and a model which, if sometimes sentimental, are a corrective to her foul environment.

As the lawsuit of Jarndyce and Jarndyce lumbers to a close after years of litigation, a gallery of characters emerges and each reveals how the moral contagion has spread to his sector. With his talent for caricature, Dickens has created memorable minor characters to flesh out the corrupt world. There is Mr. Chadband, the preacher enamored of his own voice; Mrs. Pardiggle, who would feed the poor Puseyite tracts rather than bacon; Mr. Turveydrop, who is the Model of Deportment and little else; Mrs. Jellyby, who supports noble "causes" while neglecting her own children; Mr. Skimpole, the model of unproductivity. So many of these betray the varieties of egoism and irresponsibility which have left society stagnant and infected. Perhaps the most striking is Krook, the law stationer and small-scale surrogate of the Lord Chancellor, who dies of "spontaneous combustion." Krook is a microcosm of the self-destructive tendency of a diseased society.

However, despite Dickens' talent for plot and character, *Bleak House* is primarily a novel of image and symbol. The first chapter insistently sets the moral tone as it repeats its images of fog and mud which surround the court of Chancery and, by extension, all of English life. As the fog, which surrounds all in a miasma from which there seems no escape, is a symbol of Chancery, the court itself, with its inert, irresponsible, and self-destructive wranglings, is a symbol of the calcified social and economic system strangling English life. The case of Jarndyce and Jarndyce is the perfect model of the social canker. Characters sacrifice their lives to its endless wrangling and forfeit the opportunity to accept individual responsibility and make something of themselves because of the illusory hope of instant riches. When the suit is finally settled, the fortune has been eaten up in court costs—an ironic commentary on the futility of such vain hopes.

People and places, too, in *Bleak House* so consistently have symbolic value that the novel occasionally verges on allegory. The cloudiness and rain which surround Chesney Wold symbolize the hopelessness of the nobility. Even the name of its inhabitants, Dedlock, is a sign of the moral deadlock and immobility of the ruling class. At the other end of the social spectrum, Tom-all-alone's, dirty and disease-ridden, is a symbol of the vulnerability and victimhood of the lowest classes. In gloom of one sort or another, many characters act as detectives searching out the guilty secrets and hypocrisies which permeate this world.

On the more positive side is Bleak House itself where the kindly John Jarndyce, aloof from involvement in the lawsuit, presides over a more orderly and benevolent demesne. But the contagion cannot even be kept from there. Occasionally even the admirable John Jarndyce suffers when the East Wind, a symbol of the agony and frustration outside, blows across the estate. More strikingly, Ada and Richard Carstone bring into their uncle's house the effects of the lawsuit as Richard destroys himself and injures those around him in his obsession with the Chancery case. Richard is another victim of the anachronistic system which destroys those who participate in it, a system which is a symbol of the inertia, complacency, and hypocrisy of the whole society. Finally, that Esther, the housekeeper, contracts smallpox from Jo is a symbol of the interrelatedness of all levels of society. Jo is at the bottom, but his misfortune becomes the misfortune of many as his contagion spreads through the social organism. The implication is that an unfeeling society can create Jo and Tom-all-alone's but it cannot protect itself from its victims.

Dickens offers no programmatic, revolutionary solution. If there is a solution, it is to be found in people like John Jarndyce, Esther Summerson, and Allan Woodcourt. Jarndyce is a figure of the selflessness which is necessary if injustice is to be rectified. Esther Summerson, as her name implies, is a bright antidote to the fog and rain. Her keys, which she shakes regularly, are a sign of her commitment to her domestic duties, an acceptance of responsibility. Dr. Woodcourt is the kind of active man society needs. The marriage of Esther and Woodcourt is a vindication of what they have to offer, as is Jarndyce's generous acceptance of their love. The new Bleak House in which they live is ironically full of the joy and goodness which can reform society. The novel does not offer the easy optimism of radical political solutions, because it is only this revolution in the heart of man which Dickens believes can cure society.

Bibliography

Axton, William F.   "Religious and Scientific Imagery in *Bleak House*," in *Nineteenth-Century Fiction*. XXII (March, 1968), pp. 349–359.

————.   "The Trouble with Esther," in *Modern Language Quarterly*. XXVI (1965), pp. 545–557.

Barnard, Robert.   *Imagery and Theme in the Novels of Dickens*. New York: Humanities Press, 1974, pp. 62–76.

Blount, Trevor.   "Dickens' Slum Satire in *Bleak House*," in *Modern Language Review*. LX (July, 1965), pp. 340–351.

Burke, Alan R.   "The Strategy and Theme of Urban Observation in *Bleak House*," in *Studies in English Literature, 1500–1900*. IX (Autumn, 1969), pp. 659–676.

Cohan, Steven. " 'They Are All Secret': The Fantasy Content of *Bleak House*," in *Literature and Psychology*. XXVI (1976), pp. 79–91.

Coolidge, Archibald. "Dickens' Complex Plots," in *The Dickensian*. LVII (Autumn, 1961), pp. 174–182.

Crompton, Louis. "Satire and Symbolism in *Bleak House*," in *Nineteenth-Century Fiction*. XII (March, 1958), pp. 284–303.

Daleski, Herman M. *Dickens and the Art of Analogy.* New York: Schocken, 1970, pp. 156–190.

Donovan, R.A. "Structure and Idea in *Bleak House*," in *Journal of English Literary History*. XXIX (June, 1962), pp. 175–201.

Dunn, Richard J. "Esther's Role in *Bleak House*," in *The Dickensian*. LXII (September, 1966), pp. 163–166.

Dyson, A.E. *The Inimitable Dickens; A Reading of the Novels.* London: Macmillan, 1970, pp. 154–182.

Johnson, Edgar. "*Bleak House*, The Anatomy of Society," in *Nineteenth-Century Fiction*. VII (September, 1952), pp. 73–89.

Korg, Jacob. *Twentieth Century Interpretations of* Bleak House. Englewood Cliffs, N.J.: Prentice-Hall, 1968.

Manning, Sylvia B. *Dickens as Satirist.* New Haven, Conn.: Yale University Press, 1971, pp. 101–131.

Moers, Ellen. "*Bleak House*: The Agitating Women," in *The Dickensian*. LXIX (1973), pp. 13–24.

Ousby, Ian. "The Broken Glass: Vision and Comprehension in *Bleak House*," in *Nineteenth-Century Fiction*. XXIX (1975), pp. 381–392.

Partlow, Robert B., Jr. *Dickens the Craftsman; Strategies of Presentation.* Carbondale: Southern Illinois University Press, 1970, pp. 115–139.

Pederson, Winifred J. "Jo in *Bleak House*," in *The Dickensian*. LX (Autumn, 1964), pp. 162–167.

Serlin, Ellen. "The Two Worlds of *Bleak House*," in *Journal of English Literary History*. XLIII (Winter, 1976), pp. 551–566.

Stoehr, Taylor. *Dickens: The Dreamer's Stance.* Ithaca, N.Y.: Cornell University Press, 1965, pp. 137–170.

Wilkinson, Ann Y. "*Bleak House*: From Faraday to Judgement Day," in *Journal of English Literary History*. XXXIV (1967), pp. 225–247.

Winslow, Joan D. "Esther Summerson: The Betrayal of the Imagination," in *Journal of Narrative Technique*. VI (1976), pp. 1–13.

Zabel, Morton D. *Craft and Character: Texts, Methods and Vocation in Modern Fiction.* New York: Viking, 1957, pp. 15–49.

Zwerdling, Alex. "Esther Summerson Rehabilitated," in *PMLA*. LXXXVIII (1973), pp. 429–439.

DAVID COPPERFIELD

Type of work: Novel
Author: Charles Dickens (1812–1870)
Type of plot: Sentimental romance
Time of plot: Early nineteenth century
Locale: England
First published: 1849–1850

One of the best-loved novels in the English language, David Copperfield *is a devastating exposé of the treatment of children in the nineteenth century. Admittedly autobiographical, it is a work of art which can be read and reread, chiefly for its gallery of immortalized characters. Though the novel has flaws, it enjoys a kind of freshness and spontaneity stemming from the first-person recounting of events and the sympathetic treatment of characters.*

Principal Characters

David Copperfield, the orphaned hero-narrator whose story of his early years and growing maturity comprises one of the best-known works of fiction in the English language. A posthumous child, extremely sensitive in retrospect, he first experiences cruelty and tyranny when his young widowed mother marries stern Mr. Murdstone, and he quickly forms emotional alliances with the underprivileged and the victimized. His loyalties are sometimes misplaced, as in the case of Steerforth, his school friend who seduces Little Em'ly, but his heart remains sound and generous toward even the erring. As he passes from childhood to disillusioned adolescence, his perceptions increase, though he often misses the truth because he misreads the evidence before him. His trust is all the more remarkable when one considers the recurrence of error which leads him from false friends to false love and on to near catastrophe. Finally, unlike his creator, David finds balance and completion in his literary career, his abiding friendships, and his happy second marriage.

Clara Copperfield, David's childlike but understanding and beautiful mother,

destined to an early death because of her inability to cope with life. Strong in her own attachments, she attributes to everyone motives as good and generous as her own. Misled into a second marriage to an unloving husband, she is torn between son and husband and dies soon after giving birth to another child. Mother and child are buried in the same coffin.

Edward Murdstone, Clara Copperfield's second husband and David's irascible stepfather, who cruelly mistreats the sensitive young boy. Self-seeking to an extreme degree, Murdstone has become a synonym for the mean and low, the calculating and untrustworthy. His cruelty is touched with sadism, and his egoism borders on the messianic.

Jane Murdstone, Edward Murdstone's sister. Like her brother, she is harsh and unbending. Her severe nature is symbolized by the somber colors and metallic beads she wears. Her suspicious mind is shown by her belief that the maids have a man hidden somewhere in the house.

Clara Peggotty, Mrs. Copperfield's devoted servant and David's nurse and friend. Cheerful and plump, she always seems about to burst out of her clothing, and when she moves buttons pop and fly in all directions. Discharged after the death of her mistress, she marries Barkis, a carrier.

Daniel Peggotty, Clara Peggotty's brother, a Yarmouth fisherman whose home is a boat beached on the sands. A generous, kind-hearted man, he has made himself the protector of a niece and a nephew, Little Em'ly and Ham, and of Mrs. Gummidge, the forlorn widow of his former partner. His charity consists of thoughtful devotion as much as material support.

Ham Peggotty, Daniel Peggotty's stalwart nephew. He grows up to fall in love with his cousin, Little Em'ly, but on the eve of their wedding she elopes with James Steerforth, her seducer. Some years later, during a great storm, Ham is drowned while trying to rescue Steerforth from a ship in distress off Yarmouth beach.

Little Em'ly, Daniel Peggotty's niece and adopted daughter, a girl of great beauty and charm and David's first love. Though engaged to marry her cousin Ham, she runs away with James Steerforth. After he discards her, Daniel Peggotty saves her from a life of further shame, and she and her uncle join a party emigrating to Australia.

Barkis, the carrier between Blunderstone and Yarmouth. A bashful suitor, he woos Peggotty by having David tell her that "Barkis is willin'!" This tag-line, frequently repeated, reveals the carter's good and simple nature.

Mrs. Gummidge, the widow of Daniel Peggotty's fishing partner. After he takes her into his home she spends most of her time by the fire, meanwhile complaining sadly that she is a "lone, lorn creetur."

Miss Betsey Trotwood, David Copperfield's great-aunt, eccentric, sharp-spoken, but essentially kind-hearted. Present on the night of David's birth, she has already made up her mind as to his sex and his name, her own. When she learns that the child is a boy, she leaves the house in great indignation. Eventually she becomes the benefactress of destitute and desolate David, educates him, and lives to see him happily married to Agnes Wickfield and established in his literary career.

Richard Babley, called **Mr. Dick,** a mildly mad and seemingly irresponsible man befriended by Miss Trotwood. He has great difficulty in keeping the subject of King Charles the First out of his conversation and the memorial he is writing. Miss Trotwood, who refuses to admit that he is mad, always defers to him as a shrewd judge of character and situation.

Dora Spenlow, the ornamental but helpless "child-wife" whom David loves protectively, marries, and loses when she dies young. Her helplessness in dealing with the ordinary situations of life is both amusing and touching.

Agnes Wickfield, the daughter of Miss Trotwood's solicitor and David's stanch friend for many years. Though David at first admires the father, his admiration is soon transferred to the sensible, generous daughter. She nurses Dora Copperfield at the time of her fatal illness, and Dora on her deathbed advises David to marry Agnes. The delicacy with which Agnes contains her love for many years makes her an appealing figure. Eventually she and David are married, to Miss Trotwood's great delight.

Uriah Heep, the hypocritical villain who, beginning as a clerk in Mr. Wickfield's law office, worms his way into the confidence of his employer, becomes a partner in the firm, ruins Mr. Wickfield, and embezzles Miss Trotwood's fortune. His insistence that he is a very humble person provides the clue to his sly, conniving nature. His villainy is finally uncovered by Wilkins Micawber, whom he has used as a tool, and he is forced to make restitution. After Mr. Wickfield and Miss Trotwood refuse to charge him with fraud, he continues his sharp practices in another section of the country until he is arrested for forgery and imprisoned.

Wilkins Micawber, an impecunious man who is "always waiting for something to turn up" while spending himself into debtors' prison, writing grandiloquent letters, indulging in flowery rhetoric, and eking out a shabbily genteel existence on the brink of disaster. David Copperfield lodges with the Micawbers for a time in London, and to him Mr. Micawber confides the sum of his worldly philosophy: "Annual income twenty pounds; annual expenditure nineteen, nineteen, six—result happiness. Annual income twenty pounds; annual expenditure twenty pounds nought six—result misery." He tries a variety of occupations in the course of the novel and is for a time employed by Uriah Heep, whose villainy he contemptuously unmasks. Miss Trotwood aids him and his family to emigrate to Australia, where he becomes a magistrate. A figure of improvidence, alternating between high spirits and low, well-meaning but without understanding of the ways of the worldly, Mr. Micawber is one of Dickens' great comic creations.

Mrs. Emma Micawber, a woman genteelly born (as she frequently insists) and as mercurial in temperament as her husband, capable of fainting over the prospect of financial ruin at three o'clock and of eating with relish breaded lamb chops and drinking ale, bought with money from two pawned teaspoons, at four. Loyal in nature, she says in every crisis that she will never desert Mr. Micawber.

Master Wilkins and
Miss Emma, the Micawber children.

James Steerforth, David Copperfield's fellow student at Salem House. The handsome, spoiled son of a wealthy widow, he hides his true nature behind pleasing manners and a seemingly engaging disposition. Introduced by David into the Peggotty household at Yarmouth, he succeeds in seducing Little Em'ly and persuading her to elope with him on the eve of her marriage to Ham. Later he tires of her and plans to marry her off to Littimer, the servant who aids him in his amorous conquests. He is drowned when his ship breaks up during a storm off Yarmouth.

Mrs. Steerforth, James Steerforth's mother, a proud, austere woman, at first devoted to her handsome, wayward son but eventually estranged from him.

Rosa Dartle, Mrs. Steerforth's companion. Older than Steerforth but deeply in love with him, she endures humiliation and many indignities because of her unreasoning passion. Her lip is scarred, the result of a wound suffered when Steerforth, in a childish fit of anger, threw a hammer at her.

Littimer, Steerforth's valet, a complete scoundrel. Tired of Little Em'ly, Steerforth plans to marry her to his servant, but the girl runs away in order to escape this degradation.

Miss Mowcher, a pursy dwarf. A hairdresser, she makes herself "useful" to a number of people in a variety of ways. Steerforth avails himself of her services.

Markham and
Grainger, Steerforth's lively, amusing friends.

Francis Spenlow, a partner in the London firm of Spenlow and Jorkins, proctors, in which David Copperfield becomes an articled clerk. During a visit at the Spenlow country place David meets Dora, Mr. Spenlow's lovely but childlike daughter and falls in love with her, but her father opposes David's suit after Miss Trotwood loses her fortune. Mr. Spenlow dies suddenly after a fall from his carriage and Dora is taken in charge by two maiden aunts. Following the discovery that Mr. Spenlow's business affairs were in great confusion and that he died almost penniless, David marries Dora.

Miss Clarissa and
Miss Lavinia Spenlow, Mr. Spenlow's sisters, who take Dora into their home after her father's death.

Mr. Jorkins, Mr. Spenlow's business partner.

Mary Anne Paragon, a servant to David and Dora during their brief married life.

Mr. Tiffey, an elderly, withered-looking clerk employed by Spenlow and Jorkins.

Mr. Wickfield, a solicitor of Canterbury and Miss Trotwood's man of business, brought to ruin by Uriah Heep's scheming and adroit mismanagement of the firm's accounts. He is saved from disaster when Wilkins Micawber exposes Heep's machinations. Mr. Wickfield is a weak, foolish, but high-principled man victimized by a scoundrel who exploits his weaknesses.

Mr. Creakle, the master of Salem House, the wretched school to which Mr. Murdstone sends David Copperfield. Lacking in scholarly qualities, he prides himself on his strict discipline. Years later he becomes interested in a model prison where Uriah Heep and Littimer are among the inmates.

Mrs. Creakle, his wife, the victim of her husband's tyranny.

Miss Creakle, their daughter, reported to be in love with Steerforth.

Charles Mell, a junior master at Salem House, discharged when Mr. Creakle learns that the teacher's mother lives in an almshouse. Emigrating to Australia, he eventually becomes the head of the Colonial Salem-House Grammar-School.

Mr. Sharp, the senior master at Salem House.

George Demple, one of David Copperfield's schoolmates at Salem House.

Thomas Traddles, another student at Salem House. As an unhappy schoolboy he consoles himself by drawing skeletons. He studies law, marries the daughter of a clergyman, and eventually becomes a judge. He, with David Copperfield, acts for Miss Trotwood after Uriah Heep's villainy has been revealed.

Miss Sophy Crewler, the fourth daughter of a clergyman's family, a pleasant, cheerful girl who marries Thomas Traddles. Her husband always refers to her as "the dearest girl in the world."

The Reverend Horace Crewler, a poor clergyman and the father of a large family of daughters.

Mrs. Crewler, his wife, a chronic invalid whose condition mends or grows worse according to the pleasing or displeasing circumstances of her life.

Caroline,
Sarah,
Louisa,
Lucy, and
Margaret, the other Crewler daughters. They and their husbands form part of the family circle surrounding happy, generous Traddles.

Dr. Strong, the master of the school at Canterbury where Miss Trotwood sends her great-nephew to be educated. After Miss Trotwood loses her money, Dr. Strong hires David to help in compiling a classical dictionary.

Mrs. Strong, a woman much younger than her husband.

Mrs. Markleham, the mother of Mrs. Strong. The boys at the Canterbury school call her the "Old Soldier."

Mr. Quinion, the manager of the warehouse of Murdstone and Grinby, where David Copperfield is sent to do menial work after his mother's death. Miserable in these surroundings, David finally resolves to run away and look for his only relative, Miss Betsey Trotwood, in Dover.

Tipp, a workman in the Murdstone and Grinby warehouse.

Mealy Potatoes and
Mick Walker, two rough slum boys who work with David at the warehouse of Murdstone and Grinby.

Miss Larkins, a dark-eyed, statuesque beauty with whom David Copperfield falls in love when he is seventeen. She disappoints him by marrying Mr. Chestle, a grower of hops.

Miss Shepherd, a student at Miss Nettingall's Establishment for Young Ladies

and another of David Copperfield's youthful loves.

Mrs. Crupp, David Copperfield's landlady while he is an articled clerk in the firm of Spenlow and Jorkins. She suffers from "the spazzums" and takes quantities of peppermint for this strange disorder.

Martha Endell, the unfortunate young woman who helps to restore Little Em'ly to her uncle.

Janet, Miss Betsey Trotwood's servant.

Jack Maldon, Mrs. Strong's cousin, a libertine for whom her kind-hearted husband finds employment.

The Story

David Copperfield was born at Blunderstone, in Suffolk, six months after his father's death. Miss Betsey Trotwood, an eccentric great-aunt was present on the night of his birth, but she left the house abruptly and indignantly when she learned that the child was a boy who could never bear her name. David spent his early years with his pretty young mother, Clara Copperfield, and a devoted servant named Peggotty. Peggotty was plain and plump; when she bustled about the house her buttons popped off her dress.

The youthful widow was soon courted by Mr. Murdstone, who proved, after marriage, to be stingy and cruel. When his mother married a second time, David was packed off with Peggotty to visit her relatives at Yarmouth. There her brother had converted an old boat into a seaside cottage, where he lived with his niece, Little Em'ly, and his sturdy young nephew, Ham. Little Em'ly and Ham were David's first real playmates, and his visit to Yarmouth remained a happy memory of his lonely and unhappy childhood. After Miss Jane Murdstone arrived to take charge of her brother's household, David and his mother were never to feel free again from the dark atmosphere of suspicion and gloom the Murdstones brought with them.

One day in a fit of childish terror David bit his stepfather on the hand. He was immediately sent off to Salem House, a wretched school near London. There his life was more miserable than ever under a brutal headmaster named Creakle. But in spite of the harsh system of the school and the bullyings of Mr. Creakle, his life was endurable because of his friendship with two boys whom he was to meet again under much different circumstances in later life—lovable Tommy Traddles and handsome, lordly James Steerforth.

His school days ended suddenly with the death of his mother and her infant child. When he returned home, he discovered that Mr. Murdstone had dismissed

Peggotty. Barkis, the stage driver, whose courtship had been meager but earnest, had taken Peggotty away to become Mrs. Barkis, and David was left friendless in the home of his cruel stepfather.

David was put to work in an export warehouse in which Murdstone had an interest. As a ten-year-old worker in the dilapidated establishment of Murdstone and Grinby, wine merchants, David was overworked and half-starved. He loathed his job and associates such as young Mick Walker and Mealy Potatoes. The youngster, however, met still another person with whom he was to associate in later life. That was Wilkins Micawber, a pompous ne'er-do-well in whose house David lodged. The impecunious Mr. Micawber found himself in debtor's prison shortly afterward. On his release he decided to move with his brood to Plymouth. Having lost these good friends, David decided to run away from the environment he detested.

When David decided to leave Murdstone and Grinby, he knew he could not return to his stepfather. The only other relative he could think of was his father's aunt, Miss Betsey Trotwood, who had flounced indignantly out of the house on the night of David's birth. Hopefully he set out for Dover, where Miss Betsey lived, but not before he had been robbed of all his possessions. Consequently, he arrived at Miss Betsey's home physically and mentally wretched.

David's reception was at first not cordial. Miss Betsey had never forgotten the injustice done her when David was born instead of a girl. However, upon the advice of Mr. Dick, a feeble-minded distant kinsman who was staying with her, she decided to take David in, at least until he had been washed thoroughly. While she was deliberating further about what to do with her bedraggled nephew, she wrote to Mr. Murdstone, who came with his sister to Dover to claim his stepson. Miss Betsey decided she disliked both Murdstones intensely. Mr. Dick solved her problem by suggesting that she keep David.

Much to David's joy and satisfaction, Miss Betsey planned to let the boy continue his education, and almost immediately sent him to a school in Canterbury, run by a Mr. Strong, a headmaster quite different from Mr. Creakle. During his stay at school David lodged with Miss Betsey's lawyer, Mr. Wickfield, who had a daughter, Agnes. David became very fond of her. At Wickfield's he also met Uriah Heep, Mr. Wickfield's cringing clerk, whose hypocritical humility and clammy handclasp filled David with disgust.

David finished school when he was seventeen. Miss Betsey suggested he travel for a time before deciding on a profession. On his way to visit his old nurse, Peggotty, David met James Steerforth and went home with his former schoolmate. There he met Steerforth's mother and Rosa Dartle, a girl passionately in love with Steerforth. Years before, the quick-tempered Steerforth had struck Rosa, who carried a scar as a reminder of Steerforth's brutality.

After a brief visit, David persuaded Steerforth to go with him to see Peggotty and her family. At Yarmouth, Steerforth met Little Em'ly. In spite of the fact that she was engaged to Ham, she and Steerforth were immediately attracted to each other.

At length David told his aunt he wished to study law. Accordingly, he was articled to the law firm of Spenlow and Jorkins. At this time David saw Agnes Wickfield, who told him she feared Steerforth and asked David to stay away from him. Agnes also expressed a fear of Uriah Heep, who was on the point of entering into partnership with her senile father. Shortly after these revelations, by Agnes, David encountered Uriah himself, who confessed he wanted to marry Agnes. David was properly disgusted.

On a visit to the Spenlow home, David met Dora Spenlow, his employer's pretty but childish daughter, with whom he fell instantly in love. Soon they became secretly engaged. Before this happy event, however, David heard some startling news—Steerforth had run away with Little Em'ly.

This elopement was not the only blow to David's happiness. Shortly after his engagement to Dora, David learned from his aunt that she had lost all her money, and from Agnes that Uriah Heep had become Mr. Wickfield's partner. David tried unsuccessfully to be released from his contract with Spenlow and Jorkins. Determined to show his aunt he could repay her, even in a small way, for her past sacrifices, he took a part-time job as secretary to Mr. Strong, his former headmaster.

But the job with Mr. Strong paid very little; therefore David undertook to study for a position as a reporter of parliamentary debates. Even poor simple Mr. Dick came to Miss Betsey's rescue, for Traddles, now a lawyer, gave him a job as a clerk.

The sudden death of Mr. Spenlow dissolved the partnership of Spenlow and Jorkins, and David learned to his dismay that his former employer had died almost penniless. With much study on his part, David became a reporter. At twenty-one he married Dora, who, however, never seemed capable of growing up. During these events, David had kept in touch with Mr. Micawber, now Uriah Heep's confidential secretary. Though something had finally turned up for Mr. Micawber, his relations with David, and even with his own family, were mysteriously strange, as though he were hiding something.

David soon learned what the trouble was, for Mr. Micawber's conscience got the better of him. At a meeting arranged by him at Mr. Wickfield's, he revealed in Uriah's presence and to an assembled company, including Agnes, Miss Betsey, David, and Traddles, the criminal perfidy of Uriah Heep, who for years had robbed and cheated Mr. Wickfield. Miss Betsey discovered that Uriah was also responsible for her own financial losses. With the exposure of the villainous Uriah, partial restitution both for her and for Mr. Wickfield was not long in coming.

His conscience cleared by his exposure of Uriah Heep's villainy, Mr. Micawber proposed to take his family to Australia. There, he was sure something would again turn up. To Australia, too, went Mr. Peggotty and Little Em'ly; she had turned to her uncle in sorrow and shame after Steerforth had deserted her. David watched as their ship put out to sea. It seemed to him the sunset was a bright promise for them as they sailed away to a new life in the new land. The darkness fell about him as he watched.

The great cloud now in David's life was his wife's delicate health. Day after day she failed, and in spite of his tenderest care he was forced to see her grow more feeble and wan. Agnes Wickfield, like the true friend she had always been, was with him on the night of Dora's death. As in his earlier troubles, he turned to Agnes in the days that followed and found comfort in her sympathy and understanding.

Upon her advice he decided to go abroad for a while. But first he went to Yarmouth to put into Ham's hands a last letter from Little Em'ly. There he witnessed the final act of her betrayal. During a storm the heavy seas battered a ship in distress off the coast. Ham went to his death in a stout-hearted attempt to rescue a survivor clinging to a broken mast. The bodies washed ashore by the rolling waves were those of loyal Ham and the false Steerforth.

David lived in Europe for three years. On his return he discovered again his need for Agnes Wickfield's quiet friendship. One day Miss Betsey Trotwood slyly suggested that Agnes might soon be married. Heavy in heart, David went off to offer her his good wishes. When she burst into tears, he realized that what he had hoped was true—her heart was already his. They were married, to match-making Miss Betsey's great delight, and David settled down to begin his career as a successful novelist.

Critical Evaluation

"But, like many fond parents, I have in my heart of hearts a favorite child. And his name is David Copperfield."

This is Charles Dickens' final, affectionate judgment of the work which stands exactly in the middle of his novelistic career, with seven novels before and seven after (excluding the unfinished *The Mystery of Edwin Drood*). When he began the novel, he was in his mid-thirties, secure in continuing success that had begun with *Sketches by Boz* (1836), and *Pickwick Papers* (1836-1837). It was a good time to take stock of his life, to make use of the autobiographical manuscript he had put by earlier. Nor did he try to conceal the personal element from his public, which eagerly awaited each of the nineteen numbers of *David Copperfield*. The novel was issued serially from May, 1849, through November, 1850. Charles Dickens, writer, is readily identified with David Copperfield, writer, viewing his life through the "long Copperfieldian perspective," as Dickens called it.

Although much in the life of the first-person narrator corresponds to Dickens' own life, details are significantly altered. Unlike David, Dickens was not a genteel orphan but the eldest son of living and improvident parents; his own father served as the model for Micawber. Dickens' childhood stint in a shoeblacking factory seems to have been somewhat shorter than David's drudgery in the warehouse of Murdstone and Grinby, wine distributors, but the shame and suffering were identical. Young Charles Dickens failed in his romance with a pretty young girl, but the author Dickens permits David to win his Dora. However, Dickens inflicts upon Dora as Mrs. Copperfield the faults of his own Kate, who, unlike Dora, lived on as his wife until their separation in 1858.

However fascinating the autobiographical details, *David Copperfield* stands primarily on its merits as a novel endowed with the bustling life of Dickens' earlier works but controlled by his maturing sense of design. The novel in its entirety answers affirmatively the question posed by David himself in the opening sentence: "Whether I shall turn out to be the hero of my own life. . . . "

In addition to the compelling characterization of the protagonist, the novel abounds with memorable portrayals. The square face and black beard of Mr. Murdstone, always viewed in conjunction with that "metallic lady" Miss Murdstone, evoke the horror of dehumanized humanity. Uriah Heep's writhing body, clammy skin, and peculiarly lidless eyes suggest a subhuman form more terrifying than the revolting nature of his "umbleness." Above all the figures that crowd the lonely world of the orphan rises the bald head of Wilkins Micawber, flourishing the English language and his quizzing glass with equal impressiveness, confidently prepared in case some opportunity turns up.

Nevertheless, David Copperfield is very definitely the hero of his own story. This is a novel of initiation, organized around the two major cycles of the hero's development, first in childhood, then in early manhood. It focuses steadily upon the testing which will qualify him for full manhood. He makes his own choices, but each important stage of his moral progress is marked by the intervention of Aunt Betsey Trotwood.

To begin with, David is weak simply because he is a child, the hapless victim of adult exploitation. But he is also heir to the moral weakness of his childish mother and his dead father, who was an inept, impractical man. David's birth is, portentously, the occasion of a conflict between his mother's Copperfieldian softness and Aunt Betsey's firmness, displayed in her rigidity of figure and countenance.

From a state of childish freedom, David falls into the Murdstone world. The clanking chains of Miss Murdstone's steel purse symbolize the metaphorical prison which replaces his innocently happy home. Indeed, for David, the world becomes a prison. After his five days of solitary confinement at Blunderstone, he enters the jail-like Salem House School. After his mother's death, he is placed in the grim warehouse, apparently for life. Nor is his involvement with the Micawbers any real escape, for he is burdened with their problems and retains his place in the family even after their incarceration in the King's Bench Prison.

Although David repudiates the tyrannical firmness of which he is a victim, he does not actively rebel, except for the one occasion when he bites Mr.

Murdstone. Instead, like his mother, he indulges his weakness; he submits, fearfully to the Murdstones and Creakle, worshipfully to the arrogant Steerforth. In addition, he escapes into the illusory freedom of fantasy—through books and stories and through the lives of others, which he invests with an enchantment that conceals from him whatever is potentially tragic or sordid.

Nevertheless, David's pliant nature shares something of the resolute spirit of Aunt Betsey, despite her disappearance on the night of his birth. Looking back upon his wretched boyhood, David recalls that he kept his own counsel, and did his work. From having suffered in secret, he moves to the decision to escape by his own act. The heroic flight is rewarded when Aunt Betsey relents and takes him in. Appropriately, she trusses up the small boy in adult clothes and announces her own goal of making him a "fine fellow, with a will of your own," with a "strength of character that is not to be influenced, except on good reason, by anybody, or by anything." The first cycle of testing is complete.

The conventionally happy years in Dover and Canterbury mark an interlude before the second major cycle of the novel, which commences with David's reentry into the world as a young man. Significantly, he at first resumes the docile patterns of childhood. Reunited with Steerforth, he once again takes pride in his friend's overbearing attitude. He allows himself to be bullied by various inferiors. He evades the obligation to choose his own career by entering into a profession which affects him like an opiate. In Dora's childlike charms he recaptures the girlish image of his mother. However, at this point, the firm Aunt Betsey, having cut short his childhood trials, deliberately sets into motion his adult testing with her apparent bankruptcy.

In response to his new challenges, David is forced back upon his childhood resources. At first, he unconsciously imitates Murdstone in trying to mold Dora; but he again rejects tyranny, choosing instead resignation, understanding that she can be no more than his "child-wife." He responds with full sympathy to the tragedy of Little Em'ly's affair with Steerforth, but he is finally disenchanted with the splendid willfulness which had captivated his boyish heart. Most important, he recovers the saving virtue of his childhood, his ability to suffer in secrecy, to keep his own counsel, and to do his work. As his trials pile up—poverty, overwork, disappointment in marriage, his wife's death, and the tribulations of the friends to whom his tender heart is wholly committed—he conquers his own undisciplined heart.

The mature man who emerges from his trials profits from his experiences and heritage. His capacity for secret suffering is, for him as for Aunt Betsey, a source of strength; but his, unlike hers, is joined to the tenderheartedness inherited from his parents. Her distrust of mankind has made her an eccentric. His trusting disposition, though rendering him vulnerable, binds him to mankind.

Although Aunt Betsey sets a goal of maturity before David, Agnes Wickfield is the symbol of the hard-won self-discipline which he finally achieves. She is from the beginning his "better angel." Like him, she is tenderhearted and compliant. Yet, though a passive character, she is not submissive; and she is always in control of herself in even the most difficult human relationships. Moreover, her firmness of character is never distorted by fundamental distrust of mankind. Thus hers is the only influence which David should accept, "on good reason," in his pursuit of the moral goal which Aunt Betsey sets before him.

By the time David has recognized his love for Agnes, he has also attained a strength of character like hers. The appropriate conclusion to his quest for maturity is his union with Agnes—who is from the beginning a model of the self-disciplined person in whom gentleness and strength are perfectly balanced. Furthermore, the home he builds with her is the proper journey's end for the orphaned child who has grasped at many versions of father, mother, family, and home: "Long miles of road then opened out before my mind, and toiling on, I saw a ragged way-worn boy forsaken and neglected, who should come to call even the heart now beating against him, his own." He has outgrown the child-mother, the child-wife, the childhood idols, even the childhood terrors, and he is a mature man ready to accept love "founded on a rock."

In the context of a successful completed quest, the novel ends with a glimpse of the complete man, who writes far into the night to erase the shadows of his past, but whose control of the realities is sufficient in the presence of the woman who is always, symbolically, "near me, pointing upward!"

Bibliography

Bandelin, Carl. "*David Copperfield*: A Third Interesting Penitent," in *Studies in English Literature, 1500–1900*. XVI (1976), pp. 601–611.

Bell, Vereen M. "The Emotional Matrix of *David Copperfield*," in *Studies in English Literature, 1500–1900*. VIII (1968), pp. 633–649.

Brown, Janet H. "The Narrator's Role in *David Copperfield*," in *Dickens Studies Annual*. II (1972), pp. 197–207.

Davis, Earle. *The Flint and the Flame: The Artistry of Charles Dickens*. Columbia: University of Missouri Press, 1963, pp. 157–182.

Donovan, Frank. *Dickens and Youth*. New York: Dodd, Mead, 1968, pp. 24–60.

Dunn, Richard J. "*David Copperfield*: All Dickens Is There," in *English Journal*. LIV (1965), pp. 789–794.

Dyson, A.E. *The Inimitable Dickens; A Reading of the Novels*. London: Macmillan, 1970, pp. 119–153.

Gard, Roger. *"David Copperfield,"* in *Essays in Criticism.* XV (July, 1965), pp. 313–325.

Hardy, Barbara. *The Moral Art of Dickens.* New York: Oxford University Press, 1970, pp. 122–138.

Hornback, Bert G. "Frustration and Resolution in *David Copperfield,"* in *Studies in English Literature, 1500–1900.* VIII (1969), pp. 651–667.

Hughes, Felicity. "Narrative Complexity in *David Copperfield,"* in *Journal of English Literary History.* XLI (1974), pp. 89–105.

Kincaid, James R. "Dickens' Subversive Humor: *David Copperfield,"* in *Nineteenth-Century Fiction.* XXII (March, 1968), pp. 313–329.

————. "The Structure of *David Copperfield,"* in *Dickens Studies.* II (1966), pp. 74–95.

————. "Symbol and Subversion in *David Copperfield,"* in *Studies in the Novel.* I (1969), pp. 196–206.

Kraus, W. Keith. *Charles Dickens*: David Copperfield. New York: Barnes & Noble, 1966.

Lucas, John. *The Melancholy Man: A Study of Dickens' Novels.* London: Methuen, 1970, pp. 166–201.

Manning, Sylvia B. *Dickens as Satirist.* New Haven, Conn.: Yale University Press, 1971, pp. 96–98.

Maugham, William S. *Art of Fiction; An Introduction to Ten Novels and Their Authors.* Garden City N.Y.: Doubleday, 1955, pp. 135–161.

Reed, John R. "Confinement and Character in Dickens' Novels," in *Dickens Studies Annual.* I (1970), pp. 51–54.

Robison, Roselee. "Time, Death and the River in Dickens' Novels," in *English Studies.* LIII (1972), pp. 436–454.

Schilling, Bernard N. *The Comic Spirit; Boccaccio to Thomas Mann.* Detroit: Wayne State University Press, 1965, pp. 98–144.

Spilka, Mark. *"David Copperfield* as Psychological Fiction," in *Critical Quarterly.* I (Winter, 1959), pp. 292–301.

Stone, Harry. "Fairy Tales and Ogres; Dickens' Imagination and *David Copperfield,"* in *Criticism.* VI (1964), pp. 324–330.

Tick, Stanley. "The Memorializing of Mr. Dick," in *Nineteenth-Century Fiction.* XXIV (September, 1969), pp. 142–153.

Worth, George J. "The Control of Emotional Response in *David Copperfield,"* in his *The English Novel in the Nineteenth Century: Essays on the Literary Mediation of Human Values.* Urbana: University of Illinois Press, 1972, pp. 97–108.

GREAT EXPECTATIONS

Type of work: Novel
Author: Charles Dickens (1812–1870)
Type of plot: Mystery romance
Time of plot: Nineteenth century
Locale: England
First published: 1860–1861

From two events, Miss Havisham's desertion by her fiancé on her wedding day, and the youngster Pip's aid to an escaped prisoner, Dickens weaves a story of vindictiveness on the one hand and gratitude on the other. The motives combine to affect the life of young Pip, for Miss Havisham has marked him as an object of her vindictiveness, while the prisoner has sworn to reward the boy. The novel, though resolved on a hopeful note, is primarily gloomy in tone, focusing on the constant pressures placed on the orphan boy, Pip.

Principal Characters

Philip Pirrip, called **Pip,** an orphan and the unwanted ward of his harsh sister, Mrs. Joe. Although seemingly destined for the blacksmith shop, he sees his fortunes improve after he meets a convict hiding in a graveyard. Afterward, through Miss Havisham, he meets Estella, the eccentric old woman's lovely young ward. Thinking Miss Havisham is his benefactor, he goes to London to become a gentleman. Unfortunately for his peace of mind, he forgets who his true friends are. Finally, after Magwitch dies and the Crown confiscates his fortune, Pip understands that good clothes, well-spoken English, and a generous allowance do not make one a gentleman.

Miss Havisham, a lonely, embittered old spinster. When her lover jilted her at the altar, she refused ever to leave her gloomy chambers. Instead, she has devoted her life to vengeance. With careful indoctrination she teaches Estella how to break men's hearts. Just before her death she begs Pip to forgive her cruelty.

Estella, Miss Havisham's ward. Cold, aloof, unfeeling, she tries to warn Pip not to love her, for she is incapable of loving anyone; Miss Havisham has taught her too well. But years later Pip meets her in the garden near the ruins of Satis House, Miss Havisham's former home. She has lost her cool aloofness and found maturity. Pip realizes that they will never part again.

Joe Gargery, Pip's brother-in-law. Even though he is married to the worst of shrews, Mrs. Joe, he manages to retain his gentle simplicity and his selfless love for Pip. After he marries Biddy, he finds the domestic bliss which he so richly deserves.

Mrs. Georgiana Maria Gargery, commonly called **Mrs. Joe,** Pip's vituperative sister, who berates and misuses him and Joe with impunity. When she verbally assails Joe's helper, Orlick, she makes a mortal enemy who causes her death with the blow of a hammer. Later he tries to do the same for Pip.

Abel Magwitch, alias **Mr. Provis,** Pip's benefactor. When Pip helps him, an escaped convict, Magwitch promises to repay the debt. Transported to New South Wales, he eventually makes a large fortune as a sheep farmer. When he returns illegally to England years later, the escaped felon reveals himself as Pip's real patron. Casting off his distaste, Pip finds a real affection for the rough old man and attempts to get him safely out of England before the law apprehends him once more. Recaptured, Magwitch dies in prison.

Mr. Jaggers, a criminal lawyer employed by Magwitch to provide for Pip's future. He is a shrewd man with the ability to size up a person at a glance. To him, personal feelings are unimportant; facts are the only trustworthy things. Although completely unemotional, he deals with Pip and Magwitch honestly throughout their long association.

Herbert Pocket, Miss Havisham's young relative and Pip's roommate in London. Almost always cheerful and uncomplaining, he is constantly looking for ways to improve his prospects. With Pip's aid he is able to establish himself in a profitable business.

John Wemmick, Mr. Jaggers' efficient law clerk. Dry and businesslike in the office, he keeps his social and business life completely separate. As a friend, he proves himself completely loyal to Pip.

Biddy, Joe Gargery's wife after the death of Mrs. Joe. A gentle, loving girl, she is a good wife to him.

Compeyson, a complete villain, the man who jilted Miss Havisham and betrayed Magwitch. He is killed by Magwitch as the two struggle desperately just before the ex-convict is recaptured.

The Aged, John Wemmick's deaf old father. In their neat little home, his chief pleasures are reading the newspaper aloud and listening to his son's nightly firing of a small cannon.

Dolge Orlick, Joe Gargery's surly helper in the blacksmith shop. After an altercation with Mrs. Joe, he attacks her with a hammer. Later he plots to kill Pip, his hated enemy. Only the timely arrival of Herbert Pocket and Startop prevents the crime.

Molly, Mr. Jaggers' housekeeper, a woman of strange, silent habits, with extraordinarily strong hands. A murderess, she is also revealed as Magwitch's former mistress and Estella's mother.

Matthew Pocket, Miss Havisham's distant relative and Pip's tutor during his early years in London. He is also Herbert Pocket's father.

Mrs. Belinda Pocket, a fluttery, helpless woman, the daughter of a knight who had expected his daughter to marry a title.

Alick,
Joe,
Fanny, and
Jane, other children of the Pockets.

Sarah Pocket, another relative of Miss Havisham, a withered-appearing, sharp-tongued woman.

Uncle Pumblechook, a prosperous corn chandler and Joe Gargery's relative. During Pip's childhood he constantly discusses the boy's conduct and offers much platitudinous advice.

Clara Barley, a pretty, winning girl engaged to Herbert Pocket. Magwitch is hidden in the Barley house while Pip is trying to smuggle the former convict out of England.

Old Bill Barley, Clara's father. A former purser, he is afflicted by gout and bedridden.

Mr. Wopsle, a parish clerk who later becomes an actor under the name of Mr. Waldengarver. Pip and Herbert Pocket go to see his performance as Hamlet.

Bentley Drummle, called **The Spider,** a sulky, rich boy notable for his bad manners. He is Pip's rival for Estella's love. After marrying her, he treats her cruelly. Pip meets him while Drummle is being tutored by Mr. Pocket.

Startop, a lively young man tutored by Mr. Pocket.

Mr. Trabb, a village tailor and undertaker.

Trabb's Boy, a young apprentice whose independence is a source of irritation to Pip.

Mr. John (Raymond) Camilla, a toady.

Mrs. Camilla, his wife, Mr. Pocket's sister. She and her husband hope to inherit a share of Miss Havisham's fortune.

Miss Skiffins, a woman of no certain age but the owner of "portable property," who marries John Wemmick.

Clarriker, a young shipping broker in whose firm, Clarriker & Company, Pip secretly buys Herbert Pocket a partnership.

Pepper, also called The Avenger, Pip's servant in the days of his great expectations.

The Story

Little Pip had been left an orphan when he was a small boy, and his sister, much older than he, had grudgingly reared him in her cottage. Pip's brother-in-law, Joe Gargery, on the other hand, was kind and loving to the boy. In the marsh country where he lived with his sister and Joe, Pip wandered alone. One day he was accosted by a wild-looking stranger who demanded that Pip secretly bring him some food, a request which Pip feared to deny. The stranger, an escaped prisoner, asked Pip to bring him a file to cut the iron chain that bound his leg. When Pip returned to the man with a pork pie and file, he saw another mysterious figure in the marsh. After a desperate struggle with the escaped prisoner, the stranger escaped into the fog. The man Pip had aided was later apprehended. He promised Pip he would somehow repay the boy for helping him.

Mrs. Joe sent Pip to the large mansion of the strange Miss Havisham upon that lady's request. Miss Havisham lived in a gloomy, locked house where all clocks had been stopped on the day her bridegroom failed to appear for the wedding ceremony. She often dressed in her bridal robes; a wedding breakfast moldered on the table in an unused room. There Pip went every day to entertain the old lady and a beautiful young girl, named Estella, who delighted in tormenting the shy boy. Miss Havisham enjoyed watching the two children together, and she encouraged Estella in her haughty teasing of Pip.

Living in the grim atmosphere of Joe's blacksmith shop and the uneducated poverty of his sister's home, Pip was eager to learn. One day a London solicitor named Jaggers presented him with the opportunity to go to London and become a gentleman. Pip imagined that his kind backer was Miss Havisham herself. Perhaps she wanted to make a gentleman out of him so he would be fit some day to marry Estella.

In London Pip found a small apartment set up for him, and for a living companion he had a young relative of Miss Havisham, Herbert Pocket. When Pip needed money, he was instructed to go to Mr. Jaggers. Although Pip pleaded with the lawyer to disclose the name of his benefactor, Jaggers advised the eager young man not to make inquiries, for when the proper time arrived Pip's benefactor would make himself known.

Soon Pip became one of a small group of London dandies, among them a disagreeable chap named Bentley Drummle. Joe Gargery came to visit Pip, much to Pip's disturbance, for by now he had outgrown his rural background and he was ashamed of Joe's manners. But Herbert Pocket cheerfully helped Pip to entertain the uncomfortable Joe in their apartment. Plainly Joe loved Pip very much, and after he had gone Pip felt ashamed of himself. Joe had brought word that Miss Havisham wanted to see the young man, and Pip returned with his brother-in-law. Miss Havisham and Estella marked the changes in Pip, and when Estella had left Pip alone with the old lady, she told him he must fall in love with the beautiful girl. She also said it was time for Estella to come to London, and she wished Pip to meet her adopted daughter when she arrived. This request made Pip feel more certain he had been sent to London by Miss Havisham to be groomed to marry Estella.

Estella had not been in London long before she had many suitors. Of all the men who courted her, she seemed to favor Bentley Drummle. Pip saw Estella frequently. Although she treated him kindly and with friendship, he knew she did not return his love.

On his twenty-first birthday Pip received a caller, the man whom Pip had helped in the marsh many years before. Ugly and coarse, he told Pip it was he who had been financing Pip ever since he had come to London. At first the boy was horrified to discover he owed so much to this crude ex-criminal, Abel Magwitch. He told Pip that he had been sent to the colonies where he had grown rich. Now he had wanted Pip to enjoy all the privileges he had been denied in life, and he had returned to England to see the boy to whom he had tried to be a second father. He warned Pip that he was in danger should his presence be discovered, for it was death for a prisoner to return to England once he had been sent to a convict colony. Pip detested his plight. Now he realized Miss Havisham had had nothing to do with his great expectations in life, but he was too conscious of his debt to consider abandoning the man whose person he disliked. He determined to do all in his power to please his benefactor. Magwitch was using the name Provis to hide his identity. Provis told Pip furthermore that the man with whom Pip had seen him struggling long ago in the marsh was his enemy, Compeyson, who had vowed to destroy him. Herbert Pocket, who was a distant cousin of Miss Havisham, told Pip that the lover who had betrayed her on the day of her wedding was named Compeyson.

Pip went to see Miss Havisham to denounce her for having allowed him to believe she was helping him. On his arrival he was informed that Estella was to marry Bentley Drummle. Since Miss Havisham had suffered at the hands of one faithless man, she had reared Estella to inflict as much hurt as possible upon the many men who loved her. Estella reminded Pip that she had warned him not to fall in love with her, for she had no compassion for any human being. Pip returned once more to visit Miss Havisham after Estella had married. An accident started a fire in the old, dust-filled mansion, and although Pip tried to save the old woman she died in the blaze that also badly damaged her gloomy house.

From Provis' story of his association with Compeyson and from other evidence, Pip had learned that Provis was Estella's father; but he did not reveal his discovery to anyone but Jaggers, whose housekeeper, evidently, was Estella's mother. Pip had learned also that Compeyson was in London and plotting to kill Provis. In order to protect the man who had become a foster father to him, Pip with the help of Herbert Pocket arranged to smuggle Provis across the channel to France. There Pip intended to join the old man. Elaborate and secretive as their plans were, Compeyson managed to overtake them as they were putting Provis on the boat. The two enemies fought one last battle in the water, and Provis killed his enemy. He was then taken to jail, where he died before he could be brought to trial.

When Pip fell ill shortly afterward, it was Joe Gargery who came to nurse him. Older and wiser from his many experiences, Pip realized that he need no longer be ashamed of the kind man who had given so much love to him when he was a boy. His sister, Mrs. Joe, had died and Joe had married again, this time very happily. Pip returned to the blacksmith's home to stay awhile, still desolate and unhappy because of his lost Estella. Later Herbert Pocket and Pip set up business together in London.

Eleven years passed before Pip went to see Joe Gargery again. Curiosity led Pip to the site of Miss Havisham's former mansion. There he found Estella, now a widow, wandering over the grounds. During the years she had lost her cool aloofness and had softened a great deal. She told Pip she had thought of him often. Pip was able to foresee that perhaps he and Estella would never have to part again. The childhood friends walked hand in hand from the place which had once played such an enormous part in both their lives.

Critical Evaluation

G. K. Chesterton once observed that all of Dickens' novels could be titled "Great Expectations," for they are full of an unsubstantial yet ardent expectation of everything. Yet, as Chesterton pointed out with irony, the only book to which Dickens gave the actual title was one in which most of the expectations were never realized. To the Victorians, the word *expectations* meant legacy as well as anticipations. In that closed society, one of the few means by which a person born of the lower or lower-middle class could rise dramatically to wealth and high status was through the inheritance of valuables. Consequently, a major theme of the Victorian social novel involved the hero's movement through the class structure. And often the vehicle for that movement was money, either bestowed before death or inherited. Unlike many nineteenth century novels that rely upon the stale plot device of a surprise legacy to enrich the fortunate protagonists, *Great Expectations* probes deeply into the ethical and psychological dangers of advancing through the class system by means of wealth acquired from the toil of others.

Although the story of Pip's expectations dominates the bulk of the novel, he is not the only person who waits to benefit from another's money. His beloved Estella, the ward of Miss Havisham, is wholly dependent upon the caprices of the unstable old woman. Moreover, other characters are the mysterious instrumentalities of legacies. The solicitor Jaggers, who acts as the legal agent for both Miss Havisham and Abel Magwitch, richly benefits from his services. Even his lackey Mr. Wemmick, a mild soul who changes his personality from lamb to wolf to please his employer, earns his living from the legal machinery of the courts. Just as the source of Pip's money is revealed at last to be socially corrupted, so the uses of tainted wealth inevitably bring about corruption.

In *Bleak House* (1852-1853) Dickens had already explored with great skill the ruthless precincts of the law courts. But his next three novels— *Hard Times* (1854), *Little Dorrit* (1855-1857), and *A Tale of Two Cities* (1859)—were not so well sustained and, in spite of memorable scenes, were less popular with the critics and public alike. *Great Expectations* (1860-1861, first published serially in *All the Year Round*) recovered for the author his supremacy with his vast reading audience. Serious, controlled, nearly as complex structurally as *Bleak House,* the novel also reminded Victorian readers of *David Copperfield* (1849-1850). Both are apprenticeship novels that treat the life-education of a hero. *Great Expectations* is somewhat less autobiographical than *David Copperfield,* but it repeats the basic formula of the genre, that of an honest, rather ingenuous but surely likeable young man who, through a series of often painful experiences, learns important lessons about life and himself. These lessons are always designed to reveal the hero's limitations. As he casts off his own weaknesses and better understands the dangers of the world, he succeeds—that is to say, he advances through the class system—and ends up less brash, a chastened but wiser man.

Great Expectations differs from *David Copperfield,* however, in the ways that the hero matures to self-knowledge. Both David and Pip are, in the beginning, young snobs (Pip more than David). Both suffer the traumas of a shattered childhood and troubled adolescence. But David's childhood suffering is fully motivated on the basis of his separation from loved ones. An innocent, he is the victim of evil which he does not cause. Pip, on the other hand, suffers from a childhood nightmare that forms a pattern of his later experience. An orphan like David, he lives with his brutal sister and her husband, the gentle blacksmith Joe Gargery. For whatever abuse he endures from Mrs. Joe, he more than compensates in the brotherly affection of this simple, generous man. Also he wins the loving sympathy of Biddy, another loyal friend. But he is not satisfied. And when he comes upon the convicts in the fog and is terrified, he feels a sense of guilt—misplaced but psychologically necessary—as much for his crimes against his protectors as for the theft of a pork pie. Thereafter, his motives, cloudy as the scene of his childhood terror, are weighted with secret apprehension and guilt. To regain his lost innocence, he must purge himself of the causes of this guilt.

Pip's life-apprenticeship, then, involves his fullest understanding of "crimes" against his loved ones and the ways to redeem himself. The causes of his guilt are, from lesser to greater, his snobbish pride, his betrayal of friends and protectors, and finally his participation in the machinery of corruption.

As a snob, he not only breaks the social mold into which he has been cast, but lords it over the underlings and unfortunates of the class system. Because of his presumed great expectations, he believes himself to be superior to the humbler Joe and Biddy. He makes such a pompous fool of himself that Trabb's boy—that brilliant comic invention, at once naughty boy and honest philosopher—parodies his absurd airs and pretensions. But his snobbery costs him a dearer price than humiliation by an urchin. He falls in love with Estella, like himself a pretender to high social class, only to be rejected in place of a worthless cad, Bentley Drummle. Finally, his fanciful dreams of social distinction are shattered forever when he learns the bitter truth about his benefactor, who is not the highborn Miss Havisham but the escaped convict Magwitch, the wretched stranger of his terror in the fog.

As Pip comes to understand the rotten foundations for his social position, he also learns terrible truths about his own weaknesses. Out of foolish pride he has betrayed his most loyal friends, Joe and Biddy. In a sense, he has even betrayed Miss Havisham. He has mistaken her insanity for mere eccentricity and allowed her to act out her fantasies of romantic revenge. When he tries to confront her with the reality of her life, he is too late. She expires in flames. He is almost too late, in fact, to come to the service of his real benefactor, Magwitch. So disturbed is he with the realization of the convict's sacrifice, that he nearly flees from the old man, now disguised as "Provis," when he is in danger. At best, he can return to Magwitch gratitude, not love. And his sense of guilt grows from his understanding that he cannot ever repay his debt to a man he secretly loathes.

Pip's final lesson is that, no matter how pure might be his motives, he has been one of the instruments of social corruption. In a sense, he is the counterpart to the malcontent Dolge Orlick. Like Orlick, as a youth he had been an apprentice at the forge. But whereas he was fortunate to move upward into society, Orlick, consumed by hatred, failed in every enterprise. In Chapter 53, a climactic scene of the novel, Orlick confronts his enemy and lays to Pip the blame for all of his failures. He even accuses Pip of responsibility for the death of Mrs. Joe. The charge, of course, is paranoiac and false: Orlick is the murderer. Yet, psychologically, Pip can—in his almost hallucinatory terror—accept Orlick's reasoning. As a child, Pip had hated his sister. If he had not been the active instrument of her death, nevertheless he profited from it. Similarly, Pip profited from the hard-earned toil of Magwitch. Indeed, most of the success he had enjoyed, thanks to the astute protection of Mr. Jaggers, had come not as his due but for a price, the payment of corrupted money. Since he had been the ignorant recipient of the fruits of corruption, his psychological guilt is all the greater.

Nevertheless, Pip, though chastened, is not overwhelmed by guilt. During the course of his apprenticeship to life he has learned something about himself, some valuable truths about his limitations. By the end of his career, when his apprenticeship is over and he is a responsible, mature being, he has cast off petty pride, snobbery, and the vexations of corrupted wealth. Although he has lost his innocence forever, he can truly appreciate Herbert Pocket, Joe, and Biddy, who have retained their integrity. When he turns to Estella, also chastened by her wretched marriage to the sadistic Drummle, he has at-least the hope of beginning a new life with her, one founded upon an accurate understanding of himself and the dangers of the world.

Bibliography

Barnard, Robert. "Imagery and Theme in *Great Expectations*," in *Dickens Studies Annual*. I (1970), pp. 238–251.

Bodelson, C.A. "Some Notes on Dickens' Symbolism," in *English Studies*. XL (December, 1959), pp. 420–431.

Crouch, W. George. *Critical Study Guide to Dickens'* Great Expectations. Totowa, N.J.: Littlefield, Adams, 1968.

Dessner, Lawrence J. "*Great Expectations*: 'the ghost of a man's own father,' " in *PMLA*. XCI (1976), pp. 436–449.

Donovan, Frank. *Dickens and Youth*. New York: Dodd, Mead, 1968, pp. 185–196.

Drew, Elizabeth A. *The Novel; A Modern Guide to Fifteen English Masterpieces*. New York: Norton, 1963, pp. 191–207.

Dyson, A.E. *The Inimitable Dickens; A Reading of the Novels*. London: Macmillan, 1970, pp. 228–247.

Hagan, John H., Jr. "The Poor Labyrinth: The Theme of Social Injustice in Dickens' *Great Expectations*," in *Nineteenth-Century Fiction*. IX (December, 1954), pp. 169–178.

Hynes, Joseph A. "Image and Symbol in *Great Expectations*," in *Journal of English Literary History*. XXX (1963), pp. 258–292.

Lelchuk, Alan. "Self, Family, and Society in *Great Expectations*," LXXVIII (1970), pp. 407–426.

Levine, George. "Communication in *Great Expectations*," in *Nineteenth-Century Fiction.* XVIII (September, 1963), pp. 175–181.

Lucas, John. *The Melancholy Man: A Study of Dickens' Novels.* London: Methuen, 1970, pp. 287–314.

Marcus, Phillip L. "Theme and Suspense in the Plot of *Great Expectations*," in *Dickens Studies.* II (Spring, 1966), pp. 57–73.

Marshall, William H. "The Conclusion of *Great Expectations* as the Fulfillment of Myth," in *Personalist.* XLIV (Summer, 1963), pp. 337–347.

Milhauser, Milton. "*Great Expectations*: The Three Endings," in *Dickens Studies Annual.* II (1972), pp. 267–277.

Moynahan, Julian. "The Hero's Guilt; The Case of *Great Expectations*," in *Essays in Criticism.* X (January, 1960), pp. 60–79.

New, William H. "The Four Elements in *Great Expectations*," in *Dickens Studies.* III (1967), pp. 111–121.

Pearce, Richard A. *Stages of the Clown; Perspectives on Modern Fiction from Dostoyevsky to Beckett.* Carbondale: Southern Illinois University Press, 1970, pp. 26–46.

Ricks, Christopher. "*Great Expectations*," in *Dickens and the Twentieth Century.* Edited by J. Gross and G. Pearson. London: Routledge and Kegan Paul, 1962, pp. 199–211.

Shapiro, Charles. *Twelve Original Essays on Great English Novels.* Detroit: Wayne State University Press, 1960, pp. 103–124.

Shores, Lucille P. "The Character of Estella in *Great Expectations*," in *Massachusetts Studies in English.* III (1972), pp. 91–99.

Stone, Harry. "Fire, Hand, and Gate: Dickens' *Great Expectations*," in *Kenyon Review.* XXIV (Autumn, 1962), pp. 662–691.

Tomlin, E.W.F. *Charles Dickens, 1812–1870; A Centennial Volume.* New York: Simon and Schuster, 1969, pp. 109–131, 237–263.

Van Ghent, Dorothy. *The English Novel.* New York: Rinehart, 1953, pp. 125–138.

Winner, Anthony. "Character and Knowledge in Dickens: The Enigma of Jaggers," in *Dickens Studies Annual.* III (1974), pp. 100–121.

HARD TIMES

Type of work: Novel
Author: Charles Dickens (1812–1870)
Type of plot: Social criticism
Time of plot: Mid-nineteenth century
Locale: England
First published: 1854

Dedicated to Thomas Carlyle, this book, based upon personal observations of life in Manchester, was Dickens' first novel of outright social protest. The author's vivid style, unforgettable characterizations, and detailed panoramas equalize the bitterness which sometimes threatens to overpower the narrative. The book remains as important for historical and social reasons as for literary ones.

Principal Characters

Thomas Gradgrind, a retired hardware merchant and the founder of an experimental school where only facts and proved scientific laws are taught. A firm believer that "two and two are four, and nothing over," he is the father of five unhappy fact-finders and the husband of an ailing dispirited woman quite worn out from the facts of life. While he is essentially a kind and good man, his excessive attention to the scientific and the practical and his total neglect of the imaginative and the speculative make him a kind of bumbling ogre. Through Gradgrind's theories and activities Dickens projects his sharp criticism of nineteenth century industry and culture.

Louisa Gradgrind, his older daughter, called **Loo** by her husband, a wealthy, elderly industrialist to whom she was married according to her father's calculated mathematical theories. A sensible young woman, trained to have respect for hard facts by Mr. M'Choakumchild, master of the model school, she has no nonsense about her and therefore makes a proper wife for unsentimental and callous Josiah Bounderby. She cannot wonder, speculate, or love. Her two thwarted rebellions, an attempt in her girlhood to see a circus and a planned elopement from her unhappy marriage, fail because she lacks courage. Resisting the temptation to run away with another man, she returns to her father's house and stays there when she cannot bring herself to return to her husband's bed and board within the time limit he sets.

Thomas Gradgrind, the younger son. Although trained in the same school of hard facts, he is filled with melancholy and a lack of ambition which lead him to a determination to sample life's vices. Loved and protected by his sister, he becomes a drunkard, a sensualist, and finally a thief, stealing one hundred and fifty pounds from his brother-in-law's bank, where he is employed as a clerk. For a time he is able to throw suspicion on an innocent man, but eventually his guilt is revealed. Easily led, he accepts the overtures of cynical James Harthouse, who uses the relationship of weak brother and protective sister as a wedge in his attempted seduction of Louisa. Tom is given another chance to face the facts, something he has rebelled against, when his sister and Sissy Jupe give him an opportunity to flee the country, away from Bounderby's wrath and the law's long arm.

358

Malthus,
Adam Smith, and
Jane, the other Gradgrind children, all victims of their father's harsh training.

Josiah Bounderby, a wealthy industrialist, the friend of Thomas Gradgrind and Louisa's husband. The owner of a Coketown (Manchester) factory, he is exceedingly proud of the fact that he is a self-made man. He advises Mr. Gradgrind against taking Sissy Jupe into his home or allowing her to attend the experimental school. In the end he loses his wife and the respect of his friends—everything but his money.

Cecilia Jupe, called **Sissy,** the daughter of a circus clown. Deserted by her father, she grows up in the Gradgrind home, a companion to Louisa. Unsuccessful in learning facts, she is constantly forced to face them and is turned from her foster home to work in Bounderby's factory. A sensitive, loving girl, she is convinced that her father has not abandoned her, that the Gradgrinds have been generous, that people are generally trustworthy. She proves her own trust by supporting confused Louisa, persuading Harthouse to leave the neighborhood, and helping Tom Gradgrind escape from the law.

James Harthouse, a cynical political aspirant and a shrewd observer of human nature and behavior. Handsome, smooth-spoken, he attempts the seduction of lonely, unloved Louisa. Sissy Jupe saves her friend from folly when she visits the young politician and persuades him the planned elopement would bring unhappiness to all concerned, including himself.

Mrs. Sparsit, born **Powler,** a woman of aristocratic pretensions and closed mind, formerly Bounderby's housekeeper. Deposed from her position of authority after his marriage, she embarrasses the self-made industrialist by producing his respectable mother and thus proving that his story of his rise from rags to riches is a hoax.

Mrs. Pegler, the mother of Josiah Boun-

derby, a figure of mystery after her appearance in Coketown. The truth, finally revealed, is that she had reared her son in modest but comfortable circumstances and given him an education. Ashamed of his real background, the son has paid her a pension to stay away from him so that she cannot disprove his story that he lifted himself from the gutter.

Stephen Blackpool, a poor, honest weaver in Bounderby's factory. The victim of a drunken wife and the factory system, his life is a hard one. During a labor disturbance at the factory he refuses to join the rebellious workers or to side with his employer. Discharged, he leaves Coketown to look for work elsewhere. During his absence he is accused of the robbery committed by Tom Gradgrind. Louisa and Sissy find the miner in an abandoned mine shaft into which he had fallen while returning to prove his innocence. He is brought to the surface alive but severely injured, and he dies soon afterward.

Mrs. Blackpool, his wife, a confirmed drunkard.

Rachel, a worker in Bounderby's factory, hopelessly in love with Stephen Blackpool.

Bitzer, a typical product of Mr. Gradgrind's school. Acting as Bounderby's agent, he tracks down Tom Gradgrind and arrests him, only to lose the culprit when Tom makes his escape with the aid of a circus owner, a performer, a trained dog, and a dancing horse.

Mr. M'Choakumchild, the master of Mr. Gradgrind's model school, also a believer that facts are facts.

Mr. Sleary, the proprietor of a circus troupe. A friend of Sissy Jupe, he helps Tom Gradgrind to flee the country.

E. W. B. Childers, a circus performer billed as "The Wild Huntsman of the North American Prairies." He aids Mr. Sleary in the plan for Tom Gradgrind's escape from Bitzer.

Emma Gordon, Sissy Jupe's friend and a member of the circus troupe.

Master Kidderminster, a young boy with a strangely aged face, the member of the circus troupe who assists E. W. B. Childers in his high-vaulting act.

Josephine Sleary, the lovely daughter of the circus proprietor.

Slackbridge, a trade union organizer.

Lady Scadgers, the eccentric, incredibly fat, bedridden aunt of Mrs. Sparsit.

Signor Jupe, the circus clown who deserts his daughter.

The Story

Thomas Gradgrind, proprietor of an experimental private school in Coketown, insisted that the children under him learn facts and only facts. He felt that the world had no place for fancy or imagination. His own five children were models of a factual education. Never having been permitted to learn anything of the humanities, they were ignorant of literature and any conception of human beings as individuals. Even fairy tales and nursery rhymes had been excluded from their education.

One day, as he walked from the school to his home, Gradgrind was immensely displeased and hurt to find his two oldest children, Louisa and Tom, trying to peek through the canvas walls of a circus tent. Nor did it ease his mind to discover that the two youngsters were not at all sorry for acting against the principles under which they had been reared and educated. Later Gradgrind and his industrialist friend, Mr. Josiah Bounderby, discussed possible means by which the children might have been misled from the study of facts. They concluded that another pupil, Sissy Jupe, whose father was a clown in the circus, had influenced the young Gradgrinds.

Having decided to remove Sissy Jupe from the school, they set out immediately to tell the girl's father. When they arrived at the inn where the Jupes were staying, they found that the clown-father had deserted his daughter. Gradgrind, moved by sentiment, decided to keep the girl in his home and let her be educated at his school, all against the advice of Bounderby, who thought Sissy Jupe would be only a bad influence on the Gradgrind children.

Years passed, and Louisa and young Tom grew up. Gradgrind knew that Bounderby had long wished to marry Louisa. She, educated away from sentiment, agreed to marry Bounderby, who was thirty years her elder. Tom, an employee in Bounderby's bank, was very glad to have his sister marry Bounderby; he wanted a friend to help him if he got into trouble there. In fact, he advised his sister to marry Bounderby for that reason, and she, loving her brother, agreed to help him by marrying the wealthy banker.

Bounderby himself was very happy to have Louisa as his wife. After his marriage he placed his elderly housekeeper in rooms at the bank. Mrs. Sparsit, disliking Louisa, was determined to keep an eye on her for her employer's sake. After the marriage all seemed peaceful at the bank, at the Gradgrind home, and at the Bounderby residence.

In the meantime Gradgrind had been elected to Parliament from his district. He sent out from London an aspiring young politician, James Harthouse, who was to gather facts about the industrial city of Coketown, facts which were to be used in a survey of economic and social life in Britain. In order to facilitate the young man's labors, Gradgrind had given him a letter of introduction to Bound-erby, who immediately told Harthouse the story of his career from street ragamuffin to industrialist and banker. Harthouse thought Bounderby a fool, but he was greatly interested in pretty Louisa. ·

Through his friendship with Bounderby, Harthouse met Tom Gradgrind, who lived with the Bounderbys. Harthouse took advantage of Tom's love for drink to learn more about Louisa. Hearing that she had been subjected to a dehumanizing education, and feeling that she would be easy prey for seduction because of her loveless marriage to the pompous Bounderby, Harthouse decided to test Louisa's virtue.

Before long Harthouse gained favor in her eyes. Neither realized, however, that Mrs. Sparsit, jealous and resenting her removal from the comfortable Bounderby house, spied on them constantly.

Everyone was amazed to learn one day that the Bounderby bank had been robbed. Chief suspect was Stephen Blackpool, an employee whom Bounderby had mistreated. Blackpool, who had been seen loitering in front of the bank, had dis-appeared on the night of the robbery. Suspicion also fell on a Mrs. Pegler, an old woman known to have been in Blackpool's company.

A search for Blackpool and Mrs. Pegler proved fruitless. Bounderby seemed content to wait; he said that the culprits would turn up sooner or later.

The affair between Louisa and Harthouse reached a climax when Louisa agreed to elope with the young man. Her better judgment, however, caused her to return to her father instead of running away with her lover. Gradgrind, horrified to see what his education had done to Louisa's character, tried to make amends for her. The situation was complicated by Mrs. Sparsit. She had learned of the proposed elopement and had told Bounderby. He angrily insisted that Louisa re-turn to his home. Gradgrind, realizing that his daughter had never loved Bound-erby, insisted that she be allowed to make her own choice. Harthouse, giving up all hope of winning Louisa, disappeared.

Mrs. Sparsit returned to act as Bounderby's housekeeper during Louisa's ab-sence and tried to reinstate herself in Bounderby's confidence by tracing down Mrs. Pegler. To her chagrin, Mrs. Pegler turned out to be Bounderby's mother. Bounderby was furious, for his mother disproved his boasts about being a self-made man. Meanwhile Louisa and Sissy Jupe accidentally found Blackpool, who had fallen into a mine shaft while returning to Coketown to prove his innocence of the robbery. After his rescue he told that Tom Gradgrind was the real culprit. When the young man disappeared, his sister and father, with the help of Sissy Jupe, found him and placed him, disguised, in a circus until arrangements could be made for spiriting him out of the country.

Before he could escape, however, Bounderby's agents found Tom and arrested him. With the aid of the circus roustabouts he was rescued and put on a steamer which carried him away from the police and Bounderby's vengeance.

Mrs. Sparsit, who had caused Bounderby all kinds of embarrassment by producing Mrs. Pegler, was discharged from his patronage, much to her chagrin. Bounderby himself died unhappily in a fit a few years later. The Gradgrinds, all of them victims of an education of facts, continued to live unhappily, unable to see the human side of life.

Critical Evaluation

Dickens began as an entertainer (*Pickwick Papers*) but gradually evolved into a moralist and social critic of major significance. In his early works there are heroes and villains; in his later, victims and victimizers. The distinction is important because it measures his development from a writer of fiction to an artist with a tragic vision.

Hard Times is a milestone in Dickens' art: caricature and allegorical names are used here in a form of Swiftian satire so bitter in its contempt and social rage that we almost forget that the same devices are used to create lovable human beings in his other works. Mr. Gradgrind is offensive in a very serious way. His reduction of everything to "facts" constitutes a *gradual grinding* away of the humanity of his pupils and his own children. Louisa marries to obtain advantages for her brother—in itself a noble act; but her blind willingness to set aside personal feelings and needs only makes her more vulnerable to Harthouse's attempts at seduction. It is finally Louisa's responsibility, from the depths of her own denied feelings, to educate Gradgrind to his deficiencies as a father and teacher.

Although Dickens' satirical dismissal of rationalistic Utilitarianism (the doctrine that the greatest good for the greatest number must be the goal of a statistically rigorous and "fact" conscious social reform) is brilliantly effective in the classroom scenes, he does not entirely convince us that Utilitarian education is directly responsible for the dehumanization of England. Dickens wanted to shock the middle-class reformers with the coldness of their ideas. but he himself was curiously limited in his own humanism. Humanitarian that he was, he did not entirely respect the humanity of the very working classes he championed. The portrait of Slackbridge, the trade union organizer, reveals Dickens' contempt of labor as a political force.

Throughout his life Dickens distrusted the people's ability to govern themselves; he always looked to the manufacturers and the aristocracy, the governing classes, to correct or avoid the evils of the society they held in trust. *Hard Times* is a blow at the ideas Dickens felt were preventing the leading classes from meeting their social responsibilities.

Bibliography

Atkinson, F.G.   "*Hard Times*: Motifs and Meanings," in *Use of English*. XIV (Spring, 1963), pp. 165–169.

Barnard, Robert.   *Imagery and Theme in the Novels of Dickens*. New York: Humanities Press, 1974, pp. 77–90.

Batwin, Joseph.   "*Hard Times*: The News and the Novel," in *Nineteenth-Century Fiction*. XXXII (September, 1977), pp. 166–187.

Benn, J. Miriam.   "A Landscape with Figures: Characterization and Expression in *Hard Times*," in *Dickens Studies Annual*. I (1970), pp. 168–182.

Berman, Ronald.   "Human Scale: A Note on *Hard Times*," in *Nineteenth-Century Fiction*. XXII (December, 1967), pp. 288–293.

Brantlinger, Patrick.   "The Case Against Trade Unions in Early Victorian Fiction," in *Victorian Studies*. XIII (September, 1969), pp. 37–52.

Cazamian, Louis.   *The Social Novel in England, 1830–1850: Dickens, Disraeli, Mrs. Gaskell, Kingsley*. Translated by Martin Fido. London: Routledge and Kegan Paul, 1973, pp. 162–173.

Cooperman, Stanley.   "Dickens and the Secular Blasphemy; Social Criticism in *Hard Times, Little Dorrit*, and *Bleak House*," in *College English*. XXII (1960), pp. 156–160.

Crockett, Judith.   "Theme and Metaphor in *Hard Times*," in *Spectrum*. VI (Fall, 1962), pp. 80–81.

Deneau, Daniel P.   "The Brother–Sister Relationship in *Hard Times*," in *The Dickensian*. LX (Autumn, 1964), pp. 173–177.

Donovan, Frank.   *Dickens and Youth*. New York: Dodd, Mead, 1968, pp. 152–159.

Dyson, A.E.   "*Hard Times*: The Robber Fancy," in *The Dickensian*. LXV (May, 1963), pp. 67–79.

————.   *The Inimitable Dickens; A Reading of the Novels*. London: Macmillan, 1970, pp. 183–202.

Ford, George H. and Sylvère Monod.   Hard Times: *An Authoritative Text, Backgrounds, Sources and Contemporary Reactions*. New York: Norton, 1966.

Gray, Paul E.   *Twentieth Century Interpretations of* Hard Times. Englewood Cliffs, N.J.: Prentice-Hall, 1969.

Heck, Edwin J.   "*Hard Times*: The Handwriting on the Factory Wall," in *English Journal*. LXI (1972), pp. 23–27.

Johnson, Alan P.   "*Hard Times*: 'Performance' or 'Poetry,' " in *Dickens Studies*. V (1969), pp. 62–80.

Lodge, David.   *Language of Fiction; Essays in Criticism and Verbal Analy-*

sis of the English Novel. New York: Columbia University Press, 1966, pp. 144–163.

Lougy, Robert E. "Dickens' *Hard Times*: The Romance as Radical Literature," in *Dickens Studies Annual.* II (1972), pp. 237–254.

Manning, Sylvia B. *Dickens as Satirist.* New Haven, Conn.: Yale University Press, 1971, pp. 132–154.

Melada, Ivan. *The Captain of Industry in English Fiction, 1821–1871.* Albuquerque: University of New Mexico Press, 1970, pp. 110–115.

Palmer, William J. "*Hard Times*: A Dickens Fable of Personal Salvation," in *Dalhousie Review.* LII (1972), pp. 67–77.

Sonstroem, David. "Fettered Fancy in *Hard Times*," in *PMLA.* LXXXIV (1969), pp. 520–529.

Voss, A.E. "A Note on Theme and Structure in *Hard Times*," in *Theoria.* XXIII (1964), pp. 35–42.

Winters, Warrington. "Dickens' *Hard Times*: The Lost Childhood," in *Dickens Studies Annual.* II (1972), pp. 217–236.

MARTIN CHUZZLEWIT

Type of work: Novel
Author: Charles Dickens (1812–1870)
Type of plot: Sentimental-mystery romance
Time of plot: Nineteenth century
Locale: England and America
First published: 1843–1844

Despite serious flaws in plotting, tonality, and emphasis, Martin Chuzzlewit *is rich in characterization, Dickensian humor, and dramatic impact. In addition, in the grotesque and unflattering scenes of American life, the writer offers his most outrageous caricatures. The pictures of rude frontier life fade, however, beside his portraits of Mr. Pecksniff, the arch-hypocrite, and the cockney vitality of Mrs. Gamp, perhaps the author's best humorous character.*

Principal Characters

Martin Chuzzlewit (Senior), a rich, eccentric old man descended from a long family line noted for selfishness. He dislikes his fawning relatives and is suspicious that everyone about him is after his fortune. After quarreling with and disinheriting his grandson and namesake whom he had intended to make his heir, he goes to live with Seth Pecksniff in order to prove the motives of that self-styled architect and arch-hypocrite. Having tested young Martin Chuzzlewit by turning him loose to fend for himself in the world and having witnessed many proofs of Pecksniff's duplicity and hypocrisy, he rights the wrongs done to his grandson and abandons Pecksniff to his downward career of drunkenness and beggary.

Martin Chuzzlewit, the title character, a rather wayward and selfish young man brought up in expectation of becoming his grandfather's heir. The two quarrel when Martin falls in love with Mary Graham, his grandfather's companion and ward, and the old man turns his grandson out of the house. Hoping to become an architect, young Martin studies for a time with Seth Pecksniff,

a relative, but after a few hints dropped by old Martin, the young man is rebuffed by Pecksniff. With Mark Tapley, a young hostler, he goes to America. Martin's reactions during this journey show Dickens' singular bias against the "uncivilized" areas, customs, and citizens of the United States. After his return to England Martin seeks an interview with his grandfather, but Pecksniff, with whom the old man is living, turns the humbled young man from his door. Comforted only by the love of Mary Graham, he returns to London. Old Martin Chuzzlewit, no longer the senile man he had seemed to be while residing with Pecksniff, appears in London soon afterward, is reunited with his grandson, and gives his blessing to the marriage of young Martin and Mary Graham.

Anthony Chuzzlewit, old Martin Chuzzlewit's brother, a miserly man of cunning and suspicious nature.

Jonas Chuzzlewit, Anthony Chuzzlewit's son. Eager to inherit his father's wealth, he attempts to poison the old man, but his scheme is discovered beforehand by his father and Chuffey, a faithful clerk. Because old Anthony dies of a broken heart a short time later, Jonas believes himself a murderer. He marries Mercy Pecksniff and treats her brutally. Later he becomes convinced that Montague Tigg, a flashy speculator, has learned his secret. Desperate because Tigg demands hush money, Jonas murders him. His guilt is revealed and he is arrested, but he poisons himself while waiting for a coach to take him off to prison.

George Chuzzlewit, a corpulent, gay bachelor.

Mary Graham, old Martin Chuzzlewit's ward, a girl of great integrity and sweetness. Although his great hope is that she and young Martin Chuzzlewit will fall in love and marry, he tests the young people by telling Mary that she will receive nothing after he is dead and by disinheriting his grandson. Mary remains faithful in her devotion to young Martin through all his hardships and tribulations, until they are finally reunited with old Martin's blessing.

Seth Pecksniff, old Martin Chuzzlewit's cousin, an architect and land surveyor who has never built anything, though he receives large premiums from those who study under him. Young Martin Chuzzlewit becomes one of his apprentices, but Pecksniff turns him away to please the young man's grandfather and to insure his own advancement. In all of his dealings he is completely self-seeking; he performs no generous act, shows no generous motives. Servile, false, conniving, he is a complete hypocrite and a monster of selfishness. He becomes a drunkard and a writer of begging letters to his prosperous relatives.

Charity Pecksniff, called Cherry, his older daughter. Deserted by Augustus Moddle, her betrothed, she becomes her father's shrewish companion in his later years.

Mercy Pecksniff, called **Merry,** a vain, selfish girl who marries her cousin, Jonas Chuzzlewit, partly to spite her sister. The cruel treatment she receives at his hands transforms her into "a model of uncomplaining endurance and self-denying affection." Old Martin Chuzzlewit provides for her after her husband's death.

John Westlock, an apprentice to Seth Pecksniff, who sees through his master, quarrels with him, and leaves him. His departure leaves room for Martin Chuzzlewit in the Pecksniff household. Always a good friend of Tom Pinch, he falls in love with and marries Tom's sister Ruth. His suspicions of Jonas Chuzzlewit's behavior lead also to the discovery of Tigg's murder and the attempted murder of old Anthony Chuzzlewit.

Tom Pinch, Pecksniff's meek, overworked assistant. Left by his grandmother in Pecksniff's care, he is too trusting and too much burdened by a needless sense of obligation to see his master in his true light. Friendship with John Westlock and Martin Chuzzlewit teach him confidence, however, and when Pecksniff forces his attentions on Mary Graham Tom sees Pecksniff for the hypocrite he is. When Pecksniff discharges him, he is hired by an unknown patron, old Martin Chuzzlewit, to catalogue a library, and with the money thus earned he is able to support his sister Ruth.

Ruth Pinch, a governess, Tom Pinch's loyal sister. She marries John Westlock.

Mark Tapley, the merry, self-reliant hostler at the Blue Dragon Inn in Wiltshire. Eager to see more of the world, he goes with Martin Chuzzlewit to America, where they are swindled by land speculators and disillusioned by all that they see and hear. After his return he marries Mrs. Lupin, the landlady of the Blue Dragon and renames the inn the Jolly Tapley, a name that he considers "wery new, conwivial, and expressive."

Mrs. Lupin, landlady of the Blue Dragon Inn, a buxom, beaming widow, later Mrs. Mark Tapley. When they meet after

Mark's return to England, he kisses her often and heartily, but insists that he is really kissing his country after having lived "among the patriots."

Montague Tigg, also known as **Tigg Montague, Esq.,** director of the Anglo-Bengalee Disinterested Loan and Life Insurance Company and a swindler. Having learned of Jonas Chuzzlewit's attempt to poison his father, he blackmails Jonas into buying his worthless stock and persuading Pecksniff to invest his funds as well. Jonas kills him. When news of his death reaches London, another partner, David Crimple, makes off with all the funds.

David Crimple, a former pawnbroker and tapster and secretary of the Anglo-Bengalee Disinterested Loan and Life Insurance Company. His theft of the company funds ruins Pecksniff, who had invested in the enterprise on the advice of Jonas Chuzzlewit.

Dr. John Jobling, a physician employed by Montague Tigg as medical inspector for the insurance company.

Nadgett, Tom Pinch's landlord in London, employed by Montague Tigg as an investigator. He follows his employer and Jonas Chuzzlewit into the country and sees only Jonas returning. Acting on this knowledge, he unmasks Jonas as Tigg's murderer.

Chuffey, Anthony Chuzzlewit's devoted clerk. Old, deaf, and almost blind, he is also shrewd, and he helps to save his employer from Jonas Chuzzlewit's attempt to poison his father.

Sairey Gamp, a Cockney midwife and nurse who displays the same zest at a lying-in or a laying-out. She is fat, husky-voiced, moist-eyed, red-nosed, and overfond of drink, so that she is always surrounded by the odor of spirits. Her fabrications she credits to her completely imaginary friend, Mrs. Harris. She is one of Dickens' great comic characters.

Chevy Slyme, a distant relative of old Martin Chuzzlewit, a dubious character who is "always waiting around the corner." He is a friend of Jonas Chuzzlewit and Montague Tigg.

Mr. Spottletoe, another relative of old Martin Chuzzlewit, also eager for a share of his relative's fortune.

Mrs. Spottletoe, his wife, a woman of a "poetical constitution."

Lewsome, a young surgeon. Under obligations to Jonas Chuzzlewit, he sells Jonas the drugs with which the son makes an attempt on his father's life. After Anthony Chuzzlewit's death, deeply disturbed in his mind while recovering from a serious illness, he confesses to John Westlock his part in the affair and thus helps bring Jonas to justice.

Paul Sweedlepipe, a hairdresser and bird fancier, Sairey Gamp's landlord.

Mrs. Betsey Prig, a Cockney day nurse and Sairey Gamp's bosom friend with whom she often nurses "turn and turn about." They finally quarrel because Betsey dares to doubt the existence of Mrs. Harris.

Mrs. M. Todgers, landlady of the Commercial Boarding House, at which the Pecksniffs stay while in London.

Mr. Jinkins, the oldest resident at Mrs. Todgers' boarding house. His recreation is identifying carriages driving in the parks on Sundays.

Augustus Moddle, a young gentleman living at Mrs. Todgers' boarding house. He is at first smitten by Mercy Pecksniff, but after her marriage to Jonas Chuzzlewit he becomes, rather helplessly, engaged to her sister Charity. On the eve of the wedding he runs away, leaving behind a letter in which he announces his departure for Van Dieman's Land and his determination never to be taken alive if Charity pursues him.

Bailey, the "boots" at Mrs. Todgers' boarding house. He eventually becomes Mr. Sweedlepipe's assistant.

Mr. Fips, the lawyer through whom old Martin Chuzzlewit engages Tom Pinch to catalogue a library.

Mr. Mould, an undertaker whose countenance always seems caught between a look of melancholy and a satisfied smirk.

Mrs. Mould, his wife.

The Misses Mould, their daughters, two plump sisters with cheeks like ripe peaches.

Tacker, Mr. Mould's chief mourner.

Sophia, a girl taught by Ruth Pinch. Mrs. Todgers calls her "a syrup."

Wolf and
Pip, friends and confederates of Montague Tigg.

The Hon. Elijah Pogram, a bombastic Congresssman whom Martin Chuzzlewit meets in New York.

Zephaniah Scadder, a land speculator who, representing the Eden Land Corporation, sells Martin Chuzzlewit fifty acres of land in the backwoods community named Eden.

Major Pawkins, a New York politician who boasts that he is a man of the people.

Mrs. Pawkins, his wife and keeper of a boarding house.

Mr. Bevan, a kind-hearted citizen of Massachusetts who lends Martin Chuzzlewit the money for his return passage to England.

General Fladdock, an American militia officer and a snob.

Lafayette Kettle, a loud-voiced American, secretary of the Watertoast Association of United Sympathizers.

General Cyrus Choke, an officer of the militia, a member of the Eden Land Corporation and the Watertoast Association of United Sympathizers.

Colonel Diver, editor of the New York "Rowdy Journal."

Jefferson Brick, war correspondent of the New York "Rowdy Journal."

Mrs. Brick, his wife, an American "matron."

Cicero, a New York truckman, formerly a slave.

Captain Kedgick, landlord of the National Hotel in New York, in whose hostelry Martin Chuzzlewit stays during his visit to the United States.

Professor Mullit, an American educator, the author of many pamphlets written under the name of Suturb.

Mr. Norris, a wealthy, sentimental abolitionist.

Mrs. Norris, his faded wife.

Miss Toppit, an American woman of literary pretensions.

Mrs. Hominy, another American literary light.

The Story

Selfishness was the quality which set the Chuzzlewits apart from all other men, and the two aged brothers, Martin and Anthony, were not lacking in that strong family trait. From his cradle Jonas Chuzzlewit, Anthony's son, had been taught to think only of money and gain, so that in his eagerness to possess his father's wealth he often grew impatient for the old man to die. Elderly Martin Chuzzlewit suspected the world of having designs on his fortune, with the result that his distrust and lack of generosity turned his grandson, his namesake, into a model of selfishness and obstinacy.

Perhaps old Martin's heart was not as hard as it seemed, for he had taken into his house as his companion and ward an orphan named Mary Graham. Although he told her that she would have a comfortable home as long as he lived but that she could expect nothing at his death, his secret desire was that love might grow between her and his grandson. But when young Martin told him that he had already chosen Mary for his own, he was displeased, afraid that the young couple were acting in their own interests. A disagreement followed, and the old man harshly turned his grandson loose in the world.

Thrown upon his own resources, young Martin decided to become an architect. In a little Wiltshire village, not far from Salisbury, lived Mr. Pecksniff, architect and land surveyor, whose practice it was to train two or three pupils in return for a large premium and exorbitant charges for board and lodging. Mr. Pecksniff thought highly of himself as a moral man, and he had a copybook maxim to quote for every occasion. Although he and Mr. Chuzzlewit were cousins, there had been bad feeling between them in the past. But Mr. Pecksniff saw in Martin a possible suitor for one of his daughters, and he accepted him as a student without payment of the customary fee.

Mr. Pecksniff had never been known to build anything, a fact which took nothing away from his reputation for cleverness. With him lived his two affected daughters, Charity and Mercy, as hypocritical and mean-spirited as their father His assistant was a former pupil named Tom Pinch, a meek, prematurely aged draftsman who looked upon Mr. Pecksniff as a tower of knowledge.

Arriving in Wiltshire, young Martin took the place of John Westlock in Mr. Pecksniff's establishment. Westlock had never been a favorite in the household; his contempt for Mr. Pecksniff was as great as his regard for honest, loyal Tom Pinch. At first Martin treated Tom in a patronizing manner. Tom, accustomed to the snubs and ridicule of Charity and Mercy, returned Martin's slights with simple good-will, and before long the two became close friends.

One day Mr. Pecksniff and his daughters departed suddenly for London, summoned there by Mr. Chuzzlewit. The old man called on them at Mrs. Todgers' shabbily genteel rooming house and accused Martin of deceiving the worthy man who sheltered him. Mr. Pecksniff was pained and shocked to learn that Mr. Chuzzlewit had disowned his grandson, but he was cheered when the visitor hinted at present good-will and future expectations if the architect would send the young man away at once.

Although Mr. Chuzzlewit's proposal was treacherous and his language insulting, Mr. Pecksniff agreed eagerly enough to the conditions imposed. Returning to Wiltshire, he virtuously announced that Martin had ill-treated the best and noblest of men and taken advantage of his own unsuspecting nature. His humble roof, he declared, could never shelter so base an ingrate and impostor.

Homeless once more, Martin made his way to London in hopes of finding employment. As the weeks passed, his small store of money dwindled steadily. At last, when he had nothing left to pawn, he decided to try his fortunes in America. A twenty-pound note in a letter from an unknown sender gave him the wherewithal for his passage. With him on his adventure went Mark Tapley, hostler of the Blue Dragon Inn in Wiltshire, a jolly fellow with a desire to see the world. Martin could not leave London, however, without seeing Mary Graham. He read her a letter he had written to Tom Pinch, in which he asked his friend to show her kindness if the two should ever meet, and he arranged to write to Mary in care of Tom.

As passengers in the steerage Martin and Mark had a miserable voyage to New York. Martin did not care much for the bumptious, tobacco-chewing Americans he met, but he was excited by accounts of the fortunes to be made out West. Taken in by a group of land promoters, he wrote to Mary telling her of his bright prospects.

Old Anthony Chuzzlewit died suddenly in the presence of his son, Mr. Pecksniff, and a faithful clerk, Chuffey. Sairah Gamp was called in to prepare the body for burial. She was a fat, middle-aged cockney woman with a fondness for the bottle and the habit of quoting endlessly from the sayings of Mrs. 'Arris, a friend whom no other of her acquaintances had ever seen. Jonas Chuzzlewit was disturbed by Chuffey's conduct at the funeral. Mrs. Gamp declared that Jonas bore himself in a manner that was filial and fitting.

After the burial Jonas went with Mr. Pecksniff to Wiltshire, for his cautious inquiries had revealed that Mr. Pecksniff was prepared to make a handsome settlement on his daughters when they married, and Jonas was ready to court one or the other. A short time later old Martin Chuzzlewit and Mary Graham arrived to take rooms at the Blue Dragon Inn in the village. There Tom Pinch met Mary and in his humble manner fell deeply in love with her. Only his friendship for Martin kept him from declaring himself.

Mr. Pecksniff had hoped that Jonas would marry Charity, his older daughter, but Mercy was the suitor's choice, much to her sister's dismay. After the ceremony Mr. and Mrs. Jonas Chuzzlewit returned to London, where, before long, he began to treat his bride with ill-humor and brutality. Having some business to transact at the office of the Anglo-Bengalee Disinterested Loan and Life Insurance Company, he discovered that Mr. Montague, the president, was in reality Montague Tigg, a flashy speculator whom Jonas had previously known as an associate of his rascally cousin, Chevy Slyme. Lured by the promise of huge profits, Jonas was persuaded to invest in the company and become a director. Tigg, however, had little trust for his new partner. He told Nadgett, his investigator, to learn whatever he could about Jonas.

Jonas had a guilty secret. Before his father's death he had obtained some poison from a debt-ridden young doctor and had mixed it with old Anthony's medicine. Actually, his father had not taken the dose, but the circumstances, known also to Chuffey, the clerk, would have incriminated Jonas had they been revealed.

This secret, uncovered by Nadgett, gave Tigg a hold over his partner.

In Wiltshire, old Martin Chuzzlewit's condition grew worse. When the invalid's mind seemed to fail, Mr. Pecksniff saw his own opportunity to get control of his kinsman's fortune. Hoping to make his position doubly secure, he planned to marry Mary Graham. But Mary found his wooing distasteful. At last she told Tom Pinch about his employer's unwelcome attentions, and Tom, for the first time, realized that Mr. Pecksniff was a hypocrite and a villain. Having overheard the conversation, Mr. Pecksniff discharged Tom after telling Mr. Chuzzlewit that the young man had made advances to Mary.

Tom went to London to see his sister Ruth. Finding her unhappily employed as a governess, he took her with him to hired lodgings and asked John Westlock, his old friend, to help him in finding work. Before Westlock could go to his assistance, however, an unknown patron hired Tom to catalogue a library.

In America, meanwhile, young Martin and Mark fared badly. They had bought land in Eden, but on their arrival they found nothing more than a huddle of rude cabins in a swamp. Martin fell ill with fever. When he recovered, Mark became sick. While he nursed his friend, Martin had time to realize the faults of his character and the true reason for the failure of his hopes. More than a year passed before the travelers were able to return to England.

John Westlock had also become interested in Jonas Chuzzlewit. He had befriended Lewsome, the young doctor from whom Jonas had secured the poison, and from Mrs. Gamp, who nursed the physician through an illness, he learned additional details to make him suspect the son's guilt in old Anthony's death.

While old Martin seemed in his dotage, his grandson and Mark went to Mr. Pecksniff's house, where Mr. Chuzzlewit was staying. Martin tried to end the misunderstanding between them, but Mr. Pecksniff broke in to say that the grandfather knew the young man for a villain, a deceiver who would not be allowed to wrong the sick old man as long as Mr. Pecksniff lived. Old Martin said nothing. Young Martin and Mark went to London. There they found Tom Pinch and Ruth and heard from John Westlock his suspicions of Jonas Chuzzlewit.

Jonas became desperate when Tigg forced him into a scheme to defraud Mr. Pecksniff. On their journey into Wiltshire, Jonas made plans for disposing of the man he hated and feared. After Mr. Pecksniff had agreed to invest his money in the company, Jonas returned to London, leaving Tigg to handle the transfer of securities. That night, disguised as a workman, he went secretly to the village and assaulted Tigg, who was walking back to his room at the inn. Leaving the body in a wood, he took a coach to London and arrived there at daybreak. But Nadgett, ever on watch, had seen Jonas leave and return, and he followed the murderer when he tried to dispose of the clothing he had worn on his journey.

Old Martin Chuzzlewit, miraculously restored in body and mind, arrived unexpectedly in London for the purpose of righting many wrongs and turning the tables on hypocritical Mr. Pecksniff. Having heard Westlock's story, he went with him to confront Jonas with their suspicions. A few minutes later police officers, led by Nadgett, appeared to arrest Jonas for Tigg's murder. Trapped, the wretched man took the rest of the poison he had obtained from Lewsome.

The next day old Martin met with all concerned. It was he who had hired Tom Pinch, and it was he who now confessed that he had tested his grandson and Mary and found them worthy. When Mr. Pecksniff entered and attempted to shake the hand of his venerable friend, the stern old man struck him to the floor with a cane.

The passing years brought happiness to the deserving. Young Martin and Mary were married, followed a short time later by Westlock and Ruth Pinch. Mark Tapley won the mistress of the Blue Dragon Inn. Old Martin, out of pity, befriended Mercy Chuzzlewit. He himself rejoiced in the happiness of his faithful friends. But there was no joy for Mr. Pecksniff. When news of Tigg's murder had reached the city, another partner in that shady enterprise had run away with the company funds. Mr. Pecksniff, ruined, became a drunken old man who wrote begging letters to Martin and Tom and who had little comfort from Charity, the shrewish companion of his later years.

Critical Evaluation

Martin Chuzzlewit was written in serial form soon after Dickens returned from his first American tour. The first few numbers not being well-received, he injected the American material in hopes of warming up his readership. He achieved the desired effect, but at the expense of tonal unity; the American descriptions are farcical at best, and detract from the seriousness of young Martin's interior struggle and enlightenment. Old Martin's simple-minded scheme to test the young lovers mars the work further, as does the *opera buffa* dénouement. Nor does the ideal of womanhood depicted in Ruth Pinch as cheerful companion and competent housewife add much to the general design.

But in other aspects the novel deserves to rank among Dickens' best; the representation of fraud as a social, rather than a merely legal quantity, is an example. The Anglo-Bengalee Disinterested Loan and Life Insurance Company represents that sort of fraud which can be prosecuted; but the kind of fraud practiced by Sairah Gamp upon her employers, by old Martin upon the lovers, by young Martin on his grandfather, by old Martin on Pecksniff, and by Pecksniff on everybody, is more pervasive and less palpable, so finally more damaging to society.

In addition to its thematic unity, the novel deserves recognition as the vehicle for its two paramount characterizations: Mr. Pecksniff and Sairey Gamp. Pecksniff is a paragon of that freedom from scruple which, by a fine command of moralistic rhetoric, cows and cozens people of real conscience like Tom Pinch; by trumpeting his own virtue, he steals a march on more modest natures who seem to onlookers (even to themselves) to acknowledge blame by their silence. As for Mrs. Gamp, that vile, vivid, old carrion-crow—

for all the humor arising from her free-associated speech, her gluttony, and her pietism—she stands in the novel, according to Angus Wilson, as "the repository of female learning, of the secret knowledge shared together by which Victorian women . . . claimed some sacred position in a society made by men to their abasement."

Bibliography

Barnard, Robert.   *Imagery and Theme in the Novels of Dickens.* New York: Humanities Press, 1974, pp. 37–48.

Beasley, Jerry C.   "The Role of Tom Pinch in *Martin Chuzzlewit,*" in *Ariel.* V (1974), pp. 77–89.

Benjamin, Edwin B.   "The Structure of *Martin Chuzzlewit,*" in *Philological Quarterly.* XXXIV (January, 1955), pp. 39–47.

Brogunier, Joseph.   "The Dreams of Montague Tigg and Jonas Chuzzlewit," in *The Dickensian.* LVIII (Autumn, 1962), pp. 165–170.

Burke, Alan R.   "The House of Chuzzlewit and the Architectural City," in *Dickens Studies Annual.* III (1974), pp. 14–40.

Carolan, Katherine.   "Dickens' American Secretary and *Martin Chuzzlewit,*" in *Dickens Studies Newsletter.* VII (1976), pp. 109–110.

Coolidge, Archibald.   "Dickens' Complex Plots," in *The Dickensian.* LVII (Autumn, 1961), pp. 174–182.

Daleski, Herman M.   *Dickens and the Art of Analogy.* New York: Schocken, 1970, pp. 79–115.

Dyson, A.E.   *The Inimitable Dickens; A Reading of the Novels.* London: Macmillan, 1970, pp. 71–95.

————.   "*Martin Chuzzlewit*: Howls the Sublime," in *Critical Quarterly.* IX (Autumn, 1967), pp. 234–253.

Gold, Joseph.   *Charles Dickens: Radical Moralist.* Minneapolis: University of Minnesota Press, 1972, pp. 130–146.

————.   " 'Living in a Wale': *Martin Chuzzlewit,*" in *Dickens Studies Annual.* II (1972), pp. 150–162.

Greaves, John.   *Who's Who in Dickens.* New York: Taplinger, 1972.

Guerard, Albert J.   "*Martin Chuzzlewit*: The Novel as Comic Entertainment," in *Mosaic.* IX (1976), pp. 107–129.

Hannaford, Richard.   "Irony and Sentimentality: Conflicting Modes in *Martin Chuzzlewit,*" in *Victorian Newsletter.* XLVI (1974), pp. 26–28.

Hardy, Barbara.   "The Change in Heart in Dickens' Novels," in *Victorian Studies.* V (September, 1961), pp. 49–67.

————. "*Martin Chuzzlewit*," in *Dickens and the Twentieth Century*. Edited by J. Gross and G. Pearson. London: Routledge and Kegan Paul, 1962, pp. 107–120.

————. *The Moral Art of Dickens*. New York: Oxford University Press, 1970, pp. 100–121.

Kincaid, James R. *Dickens and the Rhetoric of Laughter*. Oxford: Clarendon Press, 1971, pp. 105–131.

Lucas, John. *The Melancholy Man: A Study of Dickens' Novels*. London: Methuen, 1970, pp. 113–137.

Manning, Sylvia B. *Dickens as Satirist*. New Haven, Conn.: Yale University Press, 1971, pp. 71–86.

Phillips, George L. "Dickens and the Chimney-Sweepers," in *The Dickensian*. LIX (Winter, 1963), pp. 28–44.

Shereikes, Robert. "Selves at the Center: The Theme of Isolation in Dickens' *Martin Chuzzlewit*," in *Dickens Studies Newsletter*. VII (1976), pp. 38–42.

Steig, Michael. "*Martin Chuzzlewit*: Pinch and Pecksniff," in *Studies in the Novel*. I (Summer, 1969), pp. 181–188.

Wall, Stephen. "Dickens' Plot of Fortune," in *Review of English Literature*. VI (January, 1965), pp. 56–67.

OUR MUTUAL FRIEND

Type of work: Novel
Author: Charles Dickens (1812–1870)
Type of plot: Domestic romance
Time of plot: Mid-nineteenth century
Locale: London
First published: 1864–1866

This late novel, one of Dickens' longest, shows the author's creative powers on the wane; the plot is plagued by too-numerous subplots, excessive coincidences, labored humor, and trick turns of events. The sympathetic portrait of the Jew, Riah, is interesting and is seen by some critics as an atonement for prejudices aroused by the villainy of Fagin in Oliver Twist. *The novel contains many powerful descriptions of the Thames, which is painted as a mysterious and sinister background for scenes of murder and villainy.*

Principal Characters

John Harmon, also known as **Julius Handford** and **John Rokesmith.** After his father's death he returns to England from South Africa, where he has lived for some years. On his arrival George Radfoot, a fellow passenger on the homeward voyage, lures him into a waterfront inn, drugs him, robs him, and throws him into the Thames. Revived by the cold water, Harmon swims to shore. He takes the name of Julius Handford. Meanwhile Radfoot has quarreled with a confederate, who murders him and throws his body into the river. When the body, wearing Harmon's clothes, is found, the dead man is identified as John Harmon. Discovering in the meantime that Bella Wilfer, whom he is supposed to marry according to the terms of his father's will, is a mercenary woman, Harmon decides to keep his identity a secret. As John Rokesmith he becomes the secretary to the man who has inherited his father's fortune and takes lodgings in the Wilfer home. When Bella finally realizes that love is more important than money, he marries her. After a year of happiness he reveals his true identity and accepts his inheritance.

Nicodemus Boffin, also called **Noddy** and **The Golden Dustman,** the illiterate, good-hearted confidential clerk who inherits the Harmon fortune after John Harmon's supposed death. When Mrs. Boffin learns John Rokesmith's true identity, her husband, at Harmon's request, agrees to keep the secret. Also at Harmon's suggestion, Boffin behaves with increasing evidence of greed until Bella Wilfer sees what avarice can lead to. Pestered by a blackmailer over the will, he finally shows that the fortune is really his and then generously hands it over to Harmon.

Henrietta Boffin, his cheerful, simple, affectionate wife, a childless woman who lavishes love on everyone around her.

Bella Wilfer, the young woman John Harmon is directed to marry. A beautiful girl from a poor home, she is taken in by the Boffins, who try to give her the advantages she would have enjoyed as Harmon's wife. In time her selfishness is overcome by her natural affections. She makes Harmon a fine wife and bears him a child.

Silas Wegg, a mean-spirited ballad-monger and fruit seller, an ugly person whom illiterate Boffin hires to read to him. A prying rascal, he discovers a will in which the elder Harmon bequeathed his fortune to the Crown. He tries to blackmail Boffin, but he is foiled and tossed out into a garbage cart.

Mr. Venus, a dusty, good-willed taxidermist. He becomes Wegg's accomplice in the scheme to blackmail Boffin, but he later repents, reveals the whole plot, and wins the heart of Pleasant Riderhood.

Mortimer Lightwood, a bright, cautious solicitor who handles Boffin's affairs and reports on the developments of the Harmon case.

Eugene Wrayburn, his reckless, intelligent, and sprightly partner, who falls in love with Lizzie Hexam, the daughter of a Thames riverman. When she rejects him, he follows her to the country and is nearly murdered by a rival. Lizzie marries him finally and nurses him back to health.

Lizzie Hexam, a lovely, courageous, illiterate young woman. Oppressed by her father's death, her brother's rejection of her and the unwelcome courtship of a half-demented, jealous suitor, she moves out of London and finds work in a paper mill. In the end she marries Eugene Wrayburn, whom she nurses back to health after the young barrister has been injured in a murderous attack made by his rival.

Charlie Hexam, her selfish brother, a young man who rejects his father, his sister, and his schoolmaster in his cold-hearted effort to gain "respectability."

Gaffer Hexam, Lizzie's crude father, the riverman who pulls John Harmon's supposed body out of the Thames. After he dies accidentally he is slandered by his ex-partner, who accuses him of Harmon's murder.

Bradley Headstone, a schoolmaster, a pompous man who falls insanely in love with Lizzie, tries to murder Eugene Wrayburn, and take Rogue Riderhood to his watery death.

Roger Riderhood, nicknamed **Rogue,** a brutal man who for the sake of the reward accuses Gaffer Hexam of John Harmon's murder. Later he becomes Bradley Headstone's accomplice in the attempted murder of Eugene Wrayburn. He and Headstone drown during a scuffle.

Pleasant Riderhood, Rogue Riderhood's daughter, an unlicensed pawnbroker and Mr. Venus' sweetheart, whom she marries after rejecting him a number of times.

Fanny Cleaver, called **Jenny Wren,** a shrewd, pretty, but crippled maker of dolls' dresses and Lizzie Hexam's friend.

M. Cleaver, called **Mr. Dolls,** Fanny's spiritless, drunken father.

Mr. Riah, an old, generous-hearted Jew, the friend of Fanny Cleaver and Lizzie Hexam.

Alfred and
Sophronia Lammle, two charming scoundrels who marry for money, learn that neither has any, and decide to prey on prominent members of society. They are forced to go abroad when their debts become pressing.

John Podsnap, a leader of society and a pompous and smug epitome of Philistinism.

Mrs. Podsnap, his majestic wife, the female counterpart of her husband.

Georgiana Podsnap, their warm, shy, silly daughter, the prey of the Lammles.

Mr. Fledgeby, whom his friends call **Fascination Fledgeby** behind his back, Georgiana's suitor. A mean, stupid, miserly dandy, he is encouraged in his social pretensions by the predatory Lam-

mles. He hides his sharp business practices under a fictitious money brokerage
firm, Pubsey and Co. Mr. Riah is his
business agent.

Hamilton and
Anastatia Veneering, two shallow social
climbers who have a new home, new
furniture, new friends, a new baby. A
former clerk in the firm of Chicksey and
Stabbles, he is now a partner. He spends
money liberally in order to get himself
elected to Parliament.

Mrs. Wilfer, Bella Wilfer's austere,
shrewish mother.

Reginald Wilfer, nicknamed **The
Cherub,** Bella's affectionate, seedy, cher-
ubic father.

Lavinia Wilfer, their younger daughter,
a sharp, spirited girl.

George Sampson, Lavinia Wilfer's dull
suitor, over whom she exercises tight
control.

Melvin Twemlow, a poor but "connected" friend of the Veneerings.
Though he lives over a livery stable, he
is accepted in society because he is Lord
Snigsworth's first cousin.

Betty Higden, an old, impoverished independent person who cares for displaced
children; she is a friend of the Boffins.

Emma Peecher, a pedantic, warm, primitive young woman in love with Bradley
Headstone.

Lady Tippins, a foolish woman, a friend
of the Veneerings, who keeps a list of
her nonexistent lovers.

Mr. Sloppy, a foundling taken in by
Betty Higden. He is adopted by the
Boffins.

The Reverend Frank Milney, the humble
young curate who marries Lizzie Hexam
and Eugene Wrayburn.

Mrs. Margaretta Milney, his wife, a
woman of practical mind and brisk
energy.

Mrs. Sprodgkin, one of Mr. Milney's
parishioners. She makes his life miserable
by her constant questions about who
begot whom and other matters in the
Bible.

Young Blight, Mortimer Lightwood's
office boy.

The Story

Young John Harmon, returning to England to marry Bella Wilfer, was supposedly murdered soon after he left the ship, and a body discovered later was
identified as his. Actually, Harmon had not died, but, fearing for his life, he
assumed first one disguise, as Handford, and then another as John Rokesmith.

Under the latter disguise Harmon went to work as secretary to Mr. Boffin, an
employee who had inherited all of the elder Harmon's wealth, under the strange
terms of the dead man's will, after young John Harmon had been pronounced
dead. Living with the Boffins was Bella Wilfer, the young woman whom Harmon
was to have married before he was reported dead. Mr. Boffin, who was illiterate,
had also another employee, a street peddler named Wegg, who read to Mr. Boffin
such books as the latter saw fit.

Mr. and Mrs. Boffin were not at all easy in their new position of wealth. They
both felt that the son and disinherited daughter of old Harmon should have enjoyed the fortune which had come to them. So strongly did the old couple feel in
this matter that they tried to find a little orphan whom they could raise, in hopes

that the boy would be like little John Harmon as they remembered him. They had also taken in Bella Wilfer because she had been engaged to young Harmon, for they wished to give her the advantages she would have had as John Harmon's wife.

Bella Wilfer was not, however, a very likeable young woman. Mercenary in her ways, she repelled Rokesmith's love and declared that her looks and her position with the Boffins made her eligible for a much finer match than a mere secretary to a rich man. Mr. Boffin agreed with her, and after a bitter scene, in which he charged Rokesmith with impudence, he discharged his secretary. Bella changed her attitude, however, when she saw how money and wealth had changed the easy-going Mr. Boffin into a miserly, avaricious old curmudgeon. She refused to stay any longer with the Boffins and returned to the penurious life of her father's home.

Meanwhile Mr. Boffin was having troubles with Wegg, the man who read to him. Mrs. Boffin had established Wegg in a comfortable house in which the Boffins and old Harmon had lived. Inspired by some books about misers which he had been reading to the illiterate Mr. Boffin, Wegg searched diligently for possible items of value that old Harmon might have secreted in his house. While searching, Wegg found a will dated later than that which had given the fortune to Mr. Boffin. The later will provided that only a small portion of the money was to go to Mr. Boffin and that the rest was to be given to the Crown.

Wegg, with the assistance of a friendly taxidermist named Venus, plotted to blackmail Mr. Boffin. They showed him the will, but without allowing him to handle it, and then told him that if he would divide the fortune into three equal parts, one for each of them, they would not make known the existence of the later will. Mr. Boffin was forced to agree.

In the meantime Mr. Boffin had offered a reward to anyone giving information about the murderer of young Harmon and had placed the matter in the hands of Mortimer Lightwood, a lawyer. Lightwood's only clue was Handford, whom he had seen when the body was dragged from the Thames and identified as young Harmon's. For a time Lightwood thought that the murderer might have been a notorious waterside character suspected of killing people, robbing them, and then turning in the bodies to collect rewards for finding the corpses in the river. But Harmon himself, disguised as Rokesmith, secured an affidavit from the informer against the waterman, the affidavit stating that the informant had given false information in order to revenge himself on the waterman for an insult.

After Bella Wilfer returned to her father's home, much chastened upon observing the change his fortune had made in Mr. Boffin, she felt that she now could marry only a man she loved, rather than any man who could provide her with a fortune. When Rokesmith came to see her, apparently penniless, she accepted his suit. Their marriage proved a happy one, for Rokesmith found a job which kept them in modest comfort. Both were happy when their child was born.

One day Lightwood met Rokesmith and Bella on the street and immediately identified Rokesmith as Handford, who had been mysteriously present at the identification of Harmon's body. That evening the police came to arrest Rokesmith, who was then forced to admit his real identity as young Harmon. As it turned out, the corpse identified as Harmon's had really been that of his would-be murderer, who had been killed by thieves. The mistake had occurred because the would-be murderer had put on Harmon's clothes after drugging him.

Harmon had to admit his real identity to his wife, and more besides. He had been struck by Bella's mercenary attitude and had taken the Boffins into his confidence, for Mrs. Boffin had early guessed who he really was. Mr. Boffin had only pretended to become a miser and to hate Rokesmith, for the single purpose of showing Bella the kind of person she might easily become if she continued in her mercenary views. The success of their scheme was proved by her return to her father's home and her subsequent marriage to Rokesmith, whom she had believed to be a poor secretary.

The Boffins, anxious for young Harmon to have the bulk of his father's fortune, had turned over the estate to him; Bella was really the rich woman she had at one time wished to be.

There was still the matter of Wegg and Venus, the two blackmailers who were in possession of old Harmon's later will, which gave the fortune to the Crown. This situation was easily settled. In return for aid in winning a girl he loved, Venus turned evidence for Mr. Boffin and young Harmon. His aid was actually not necessary, for Mr. Boffin himself was in possession of an even later will, which he had kept secret only because of its insulting language in speaking of young Harmon and his sister. The later will also gave the fortune to Mr. Boffin and his wife, but they once again gave the estate to young Harmon and his family. As for Wegg, a servant took him out of the house and dropped him into a wagon loaded with garbage.

Critical Evaluation

Critics generally view *Our Mutual Friend* as a work grand in conception but flawed in execution. It is Dickens' last finished work; he was ill during its writing, and its defects are of a kind that suggests a weakening of creative force. The main plot is over-buttressed with subplots, several of dubious relevance; some of the coincidences strain belief; a good deal of the humor falls flat; and a kind of ironical shorthand replaces the splendiferous verbiage of other works. Bella's "inexhaustible baby," for example, becomes abbreviated to "the Inexhaustible." But it is not, as some reviewers hold, merely old material reworked. Dickens' artistic purpose might have been weakened, but it was not dead; the chief symbol of the work is truly inspired, and the figure of the heroine's character attains a roundness and complexity unique in this author's vast canon.

The great symbol is Noddy Boffin's dustheaps. This equation of money with dirt, and the quest of money with the sifting of rubbish, pervades the work. The comical figure Wegg cuts in his lantern-lit scavenging on the dust-heaps finds a sinister echo in Lizzie Hexam's father at his grisly occupation on the river, and a refined, though equally precise, reverberation in the economic maneuverings of the Lammles and the Veneerings. At every level of society, people of all ages are shown in the act of hunting for money. The heroine herself does so to a marked degree. That all this feverish activity for filthy lucre is just so much rummaging among rags and bones is the message of the work. The peculiar force of the dustheaps as a symbol resides in its absurdity, the high ironic comedy that clings to the activity of digging through refuse to find nonexistent gold, especially surreptitiously. It is as if the whole society were being not chastised, but made to appear mad.

The character of the heroine, Bella Wilfer, is a splendid creation, better even than her antecedent, Estella, of *Great Expectations*. Edith Dombey might be beautiful and yet bad; Estella might be cold, yet sorry for her coldness; but never before had Dickens created a woman who could change her mind, evaluate, and redirect her own behavior. If there is any salvation for the society depicted in *Our Mutual Friend,* it lies in the courage and flexibility of mind that she shows in recognizing her folly and turning from it.

Bibliography

Baker, Robert S.   "Imagination and Literacy in Dickens' *Our Mutual Friend*," in *Criticism*. XVIII (1976), pp. 57–72.

Barnard, Robert.   "The Choral Symphony: *Our Mutual Friend*," in *Review of English Literature*. II (July, 1961), pp. 89–99.

Friedman, Stanley.   "The Motif of Reading in *Our Mutual Friend*," in *Nineteenth-Century Fiction*. XXVIII (1973), pp. 38–61.

Kennedy, G.W. "Naming and Language in *Our Mutual Friend*," in *Nineteenth-Century Fiction*. XXVIII (1973), pp. 165–178.

Knoepflmacher, Ulrich C.   *Laughter and Despair; Readings in Ten Novels of the Victorian Age*. Berkeley: University of California Press, 1971, pp. 137–167.

Lanham, Richard A.   "*Our Mutual Friend*: The Birds of Prey," in *Victorian Newsletter*. XXIV (Fall, 1963), pp. 6–12.

McMaster, R.D.   "Birds of Prey: A Study of *Our Mutual Friend*," in *Dalhousie Review*. XL (Summer, 1960), pp. 372–381.

Shea, F.X.   "Mr. Venus Observed: The Plot Change in *Our Mutual Friend*," in *Papers in Language and Literature*. IV (1968), pp. 170–181.

_____.   "No Change of Intension in *Our Mutual Friend*," in *The Dickensian*. LXIII (January, 1967), pp. 37–40.

ERNEST (CHRISTOPHER) DOWSON

Born: Lee, Kent, England (August 2, 1867)
Died: Catford, England (February 23, 1900)

Principal Works

POEMS: *Verses*, 1896; *Decorations*, 1899.
PLAY: *The Pierrot of the Minute*, 1897.
NOVELS (WITH ARTHUR MOORE): *A Comedy of Masks*, 1893; *Adrian Rome*, 1899.
SHORT STORIES: *Dilemmas*, 1895.

Ernest Dowson, perhaps the most typical and certainly the best remembered of the minor poets of the 1890's, came from a not undistinguished family. His great-uncle, Alfred Domett, the author of some poems now completely forgotten, had been Prime Minister of New Zeland; his father, who has been described as possessing "a taste for literature," was financially able to live on the French Riviera for his poor health. Dowson thus spent a great part of his youth in France and knew the language well, a fact that had its effect on his poetry. He matriculated at Queen's College, Oxford, but left in 1887 without taking a degree. It was during his university years, in all probability, that he was converted to Roman Catholicism.

After leaving Oxford, Dowson settled in London, where he joined the young poets who founded the "Rhymers' Club," the last surviving member of which seems to have been W. B. Yeats. According to those who knew him, Dowson drank heavily and was happiest in the slums of London and Paris. Many of his evenings were spent in a Polish restaurant in London, because he had fallen hopelessly in love with the proprietor's daughter—who subsequently married a waiter. His last years were passed mostly in France. Having returned to London, miserably poor, ill, and living in squalor, he was found by an equally impoverished friend, who took him to a bricklayer's cottage at Catford. Dowson died there after a few weeks.

Like most of the minor poets of the period, Dowson was much influenced by the French poetry of the Symbolist and "decadent" schools, his knowledge of French making this poetry easily accessible. Particularly important was the influence of Paul Verlaine's *Fêtes Galantes* (1869). The eighteenth-century artificialities that Verlaine created fascinated Dowson; his little verse-play, *The Pierrot of the Minute*, reads like an expansion of one of the French poems. Very like Verlaine also are the melancholy and the resignation that pervade Dowson's work. Here all is an autumnal twilight; nothing is worth striving for; "a little while and night shall come," repeated in different words, is the refrain.

Dowson showed great skill in handling the artificial French poetic forms then much in vogue, and his translations of Verlaine are admirable. And he wrote at least one poem that has survived, "Cynara," with its long Latin title taken from Horace (Bk. IV, Ode I). In spite of the vast change in taste during the last half-century, this poem still finds a place in anthologies. With its gentle, haunting music, its refrain "I have been faithful to thee, Cynara! in my fashion," its mood of weariness and of satiety, it is a perfect poem of the 1890's.

Bibliography

The Poems of Ernest Dowson, 1905, contains a memoir by Arthus Symons. V. G. Plarr, *Ernest Dowson, 1887–1897*, 1914, contains reminiscences, letters and a bibliography. A more recent study is Mark Longaker, *Ernest Dowson*, 1944. See also Holbrook Jackson, *The Eighteen Nineties*, 1913; and Osbert Burdett, *The Beardsley Period*, 1925. See further, Thomas B. Swann, *Ernest Dowson*, 1964; Frank Kermode, "Amateur of Grief," *New Statesman*, LXV (1963), 865–866; and John J. Duff, "Ernest Dowson and the Failure of Decadence," *University Review* (1967), 45–49.

THE POETRY OF DOWSON

Author: Ernest Christopher Dowson (1867–1900)
Principal published works: Verses, 1896; *The Pierrot of the Minute*, 1897; *Decorations*, 1899

Essay-Review

If a choice had to be made of the most typical member of the tragic and wasted generation of the "yellow Nineties," that choice would almost inevitably be Ernest Dowson, for in so many ways did his short life fit into what came to be the established pattern of the period. His unhappy love affair with the daughter of a Polish restaurateur, conversion to Roman Catholicism, alcoholism, and early death—all these details, plus the publication of only two small volumes of poems and a verse play, give us, in the career of one man, a portrait of the age. His photograph, taken while he was at Oxford, shows us a shy, limp figure, marked by unusually large eyes that seem fixed in the dreamlike stare of a somnambulist; the drawing by Rothenstein is of a man so dim as to resemble Max Beerbohm's Enoch Soames.

The fantastic decade, variously known as "the yellow Nineties" and "the Beardsly Period," was, above all, the period of the minor poet. After the giants of the Victorian Age had left the scene, there was no one to take their places, and English poetry suffered a sharp decline. By 1895, Tennyson, Browning, and Arnold were dead; Swinburne had been incarcerated in Putney under the watchful eye of Watts-Dunton; and the Pre-Raphaelite Movement had spent its force. To be sure, Kipling had, in 1886 and 1892, published his two most famous volumes of poems; but Kipling was the precise opposite of "the poet's poet"; he was, in spite of his great gifts, a popular writer who had little influence on contemporary literature. The really outstanding talent of the period, that of A. E. Housman with his *A Shropshire Lad* of 1896, was not to be widely recognized until many years later. Thus the stage was occupied only by these minor figures: Dowson, John Gray, Francis Thompson, Lionel Johnson, Arthur Symons, who seem in retrospect, as perhaps do the minor poets of any period, to have been conventionally grouped.

A consideration of the work of any of these minor poets always leads to a consideration of the influence upon it of French poetry and particularly that of Paul Verlaine. Two aspects of Verlaine's work are to be noted here. In 1869 he had published his *Fêtes galantes* and in 1874 his *Romances sans paroles*. The first of these was an evocation of the eighteenth century, the formal gardens of Versailles where, in the twilight of an autumn evening, the Abbés and shepherdesses, Pierrot and Columbine, stroll along the paths between the clipped yews:

> Their short vests, silken and bright,
> Their long pale silken trains,

> Their elegance of delight,
> Twine soft blue silken chains.
>
> And the mandolines and they,
> Faintlier breathing, swoon
> Into the rose and grey
> Ecstasy of the moon.

It is the world of brocaded coats and elaborately curled wigs, depicted so superbly by Beardsley in his illustration for Pope's *The Rape of the Lock*, that Verlaine sought to reanimate and that Dowson used as the background of his slight verse drama, *The Pierrot of the Minute*, which is a Verlaine poem expanded into a colloquy in rhyming couplets between Pierrot and a Moon Maiden. Quite appropriately, the volume was provided with five illustrations by Beardsley. The scene is laid in the Parc du Petit Trianon, in the twilight, and the opening lines give a fair impression of the style:

> My journey's end! This surely is the glade
> Which I was promised: I have well obeyed!
> A clue of lilies I was bid to find,
> Where the green alleys most obscurely wind;
> Where tall oaks darkliest canopy o'erhead,
> And moss and violet make the softest bed....

This passage is reminiscent of Verlaine's "Nuit du Walpurgis Classique" with its delightful description of a garden by Lenôtre: "correct, ridicule et charmant." Dowson knew French well, having traveled much in France, and Verlaine was one of his favorite poets. This little play is obviously intended to be an airy trifle, yet it is suffused with an atmosphere of gentle melancholy, and this is the atmosphere that pervades all of Dowson's work.

Verlaine's *Romances sans paroles* (*Songs without Words*) had an even greater influence on the English poetry of the 1890's than did his eighteenth century fantasies. In his famous "Art poétique" he had proclaimed the doctrine of "music before everything" and that of the "nuance," the last fine shade that joins "the dream to the dream and the flute to the horn." In accordance with this theory, he wrote some of his most famous pieces: "La lune blanche," "Il pleure dans mon coeur," for example, in which the subject of the poem is reduced to a minimum, and the verses become quite literally a song without words. Dowson did indeed compose a "Chanson sans paroles," which begins

> In the deep violet air,
>   Not a leaf is stirred;
>   There is no sound heard
> But afar, the rare,
>   Trilled voice of a bird.

The poem then proceeds in the same manner as do the poems of Verlaine. Further, Dowson translated four of Verlaine's poems. Although he modestly gave them the group title of "After Paul Verlaine," they are excellent translations, so akin were the minds of the two poets. But translating Verlaine was a standard gesture of the period: both Gray and Symons produced versions of the Frenchman's poems; and Wilde, who copied everyone, imitated him shamelessly.

The Roman Church, aware of the embarrassing dearth of Anglo-Saxon religious writers in modern times, has sought to include Dowson in its list of Catholic poets. A Roman Catholic he certainly became. How sincere his conversion may have been is, of course impossible to judge because first, there is a vast difference between being a Roman Catholic poet and being merely a Roman Catholic and a poet; second, "aesthetic Catholicism" was an important part of the attitude of the period. Again we recall Enoch Soames, who described himself as a "Catholic diabolist," thereby showing how well Beerbohm had caught the mood of the period. Johnson and Gray were both converts, the latter eventually entering the priesthood; even Wilde died in the arms of the Church. And had not Verlaine, as a result of his prison experience, returned to the faith, to write a series of humble yet beautiful religious poems? Since the poets of this period sought to turn their backs upon the contemporary world, since the doctrine of "art for art's sake" was supreme, quite naturally the Roman Church, with its vast antiquity, its continuity from the Middle Ages, its elaborate ritual, exercised an enormous appeal. Dowson, in his few religious poems, is the perfect example of the "aesthetic Catholic." He did not write of an overwhelming religious experience, as did Francis Thompson in "The Hound of Heaven," the one really great religious poem of this period; in such verses as "Nuns of the Perpetual Adoration," "Benedictio Domini," and "Carthusians," he was haunted by the withdrawn peace of the religious life, its remoteness from the "voice of London, inarticulate,/Hoarse and blaspheming." Of the Carthusians he asks:

> Through what long heaviness, assayed in what strange fire,
>   Have these white monks been brought into the way of peace,
> Despising the world's wisdom and the world's desire,
>   Which from the body of this death bring no release?

This poem forms a natural and interesting contrast with Arnold's "Stanzas from the Grande Chartreuse," written more than a generation earlier. To Arnold, the Carthusian monks were a relic of an age that was dead, an age that he could wistfully admire but which he could not embrace. To Dowson, these monks represented quietude, an escape from an age that he found intolerable.

But though he sang always in a minor, autumnal key, Dowson wrote at least one poem which all anthologies of English poetry include: his famous "Cynara," or, to give it the full, sonorous Latin title, the quotation from the author's favorite Horace, "Non sum qualis eram bonae sub regno Cynarae." The gentle melancholy, the haunting refrain, "I have been faithful to thee, Cynara! in my fashion," have made this short poem a permanent part of our literature. The weariness, the satiety that were so much a part of the mood of the 1890's are there; yet somehow the poem rises above being merely a period piece and attains, if certainly not to the first, at least to the second rank of high poetry.

Arthur Symons, who knew Dowson well, makes several telling points in his study of the poet. Symons calls him "a child, clamouring for so many things, all impossible." Francois Coppée had said much the same about Verlaine, describing him as a child whom life had wounded cruelly. But Symons continues with the further shrewd observation that Dowson's experiences in the low-life of London and Paris would have made great poets out of many men—as was true of Villon—but that for Dowson they did very little. "He sang," as Symons points out, "one tune over and over, and no one listened to him." It is, perhaps, this very evenness of tone, this constant air of gentle resignation, that keep him in the background of poetry. In fact, it is this singing of one tune again and again that causes the poetry of the 1890's to pall. For some reason, difficult to understand, no really great poetry came out of these broken and tragic lives. Again we think of Villon and of what he brought from the underworld of Paris and the lodgings of Fat Margot, "within this brothel where we keep our state." The 1890's on the contrary, were the age of the minor poet, "the idle singer of an empty day."

GEORGE ELIOT
Marian or Mary Ann Evans

Born: Near Nuneaton, England (November 22, 1819)
Died: Chelsea, London, England (December 22, 1880)

Principal Works

NOVELS: *Scenes from Clerical Life*, 1858 *(The Sad Fortunes of the Reverend Amos Barton, Mr. Gilfil's Love Story,* and *Janet's Repentance)*; *Adam Bede,* 1859; *The Mill on the Floss,* 1860; *Silas Marner,* 1861; *Romola,* 1863; *Felix Holt, Radical,* 1866; *Middlemarch,* 1871–1872; *Daniel Deronda,* 1876.

NOVELLA: *The Lifted Veil,* 1859.

POEMS: *How Lisa Loved the King,* 1867; *The Spanish Gypsy,* 1868; *The Legend of Jubal,* 1870.

ESSAYS: *The Impressions of Theophrastus Such,* 1879.

TRANSLATION: Strauss's *Life of Jesus,* 1846.

George Eliot was a pen name used by Marian or Mary Ann Evans. She was born on November 22, 1819, at Arbury Farm, Warwickshire, in the parish of Chivers Coton, and was baptized at what has since become the famous Shepperton Church. Her mother was Christina Pearson. Her father was Robert Evans, a carpenter, builder, and agent. Part of her early life was spent at Griff, an ancient red brick house of considerable charm. She attended numerous schools, at one of which she became an intimate friend of Miss Lewis, with whom she exchanged letters for years and who did much to deepen her strong sense of religion. Thus at the age of seventeen she already had an excellent background of education when her mother's death in 1836 and her sister's marriage made it necessary that she return home to look after the house for her father. Meanwhile, however, she continued her study with lessons in Greek, Latin, Italian, and German. She was also an accomplished musician, though shy of appearing in public. When her father gave up his duties on the estate, he re-moved in 1841 to Coventry. Here at twenty-two she came under a new and liberal influence. Among her new circle of friends were Mr. and Mrs. Charles Bray and Charles Hennell. Both men were writers, Bray having already published *The Philosophy of Necessity* in 1841. Hennell was the author of *An Inquiry Concerning the Origin of Christianity* (1838). Such influences caused the girl to question the evangelical beliefs which had always been such a strong and wholesome influence on her life. In fact, her liberal attitude and her refusal to attend church caused a temporary rift with her stern father. However, a reconciliation was effected and she returned to church, continuing to live with him until his death in 1849, upon which she inherited a small income for life.

Thus far she had spent two years translating David Friedrich Strauss's *Life of Jesus*, which was published in 1846 with the author's preface. Printed anonymously, the volume is said to have brought its author only twenty pounds. After her father's death she traveled for a time on the Continent, spending about a year in Geneva. Upon her return to England she accepted a position as assistant editor of the *Westminster Review* (1850–1853). During this period her distinguished circle of friends included James A. Froude, John Stuart Mill, Thomas Carlyle, Harriet Martineau, Herbert Spencer, and George Henry Lewes. The last of this group was serving then as the editor of *The Leader*. Evans was strongly attracted to Lewes, who was not living with his mentally ill wife at the time. Flying in the face of public opinion, these two formed a union which they regarded as the same as a marriage, despite the lack of legal sanction—an arrangement which lasted until Lewes' death in 1878.

Meanwhile she continued her scholastic pursuits, working mostly on translations and on articles for *The Leader*, the *Westminster Review*, and the *Saturday Review*. Her first attempt at fiction was *The Sad Fortunes of The Reverend Amos Barton*, the first story in her *Scenes from Clerical Life*. First published in *Blackwood's Magazine* upon the insistence of Lewes, who recognized their merit, these short novels later appeared in two volumes in 1858. Once started on fiction, Marian Evans had at last found her proper métier. In 1859 she published *Adam Bede* under the pen name of George Eliot, which she continued to use in all her later writings. The next year marked the publication of the three-volume edition of *The Mill on the Floss*, which she had first named *Sister Maggie*. By this time George Eliot had joined the ranks of the successful and popular novelists: *Silas Marner*, *Romola*, and *Felix Holt, Radical* were avidly read by a large and eager public. Her works were admired by Dickens, Bulwer-Lytton, Trollope, Mrs. Gaskell, Reade, and Thackeray.

The Mill on the Floss, *Adam Bede*, and *Silas Marner* were skillfully written pictures of provincial life, in some instances drawn from the author's own observations, background, and family. During a trip to Italy she had collected the material for *Romola*, a historical novel of the period of Savonarola. Remarkable for its pictures of Florentine life, its outstanding character is Tito Melema. *Felix Holt*, her only novel concerned with politics, hardly ranks with the other famous titles. Published in 1868, *The Spanish Gypsy*, a blank-verse poem containing drama and narrative, was intended (said its author) to show doctrines of duty and heredity. Her next novel was *Middlemarch: A Study of Provincial Life*, which marked a return to her earlier locale. Probably based on her early life in Coventry, it draws a remarkable picture of middle-class life in an English town. Her last novel, *Daniel Deronda*, was published in 1876.

Having attained notable success as a writer, she and Lewes could now enjoy scholastic pursuits as they wished. They traveled on the Continent and visited the English universities; they even purchased a home in the country. But this life came to an end with the death of Lewes in 1878. Deeply grieved, she finally finished *The Impressions of Theophrastus Such*, a collection of essays which came out in 1879. She also edited Lewes' unpublished works.

Before Lewes' death, the couple had known J. W. Cross, a New York banker. He had also been of considerable service to the widow in settling her affairs. Mutual ties of sympathy brought the pair together, and they were married in the spring of 1880 at St. George's Hanover Square. After returning to London from a trip to the Continent, Mrs. Cross caught a cold at a concert. She died in London on December 22, 1880.

George Eliot, for under this famous name she is known the world over, has been called the most distinguished English woman novelist. Certainly her novels, and particularly those dealing intimately with English life, reach a high point of wisdom, wit, and human understanding.

Bibliography

The standard edition of George Eliot is The Warwickshire Edition, 25 vols., 1908; included is the authorized *Life, Letters and Journals* [1884–1885] by J. W. Cross. For the most important modern biography see Gordon S. Haight, *George Eliot*, 1968. Older biographical studies of some merit include Sir Leslie Stephen, *George Eliot,* English Men of Letters Series, 1902; J. I. May, *George Eliot*, 1930; Anna T. Kitchel, *George Lewes and George Eliot: A Review of the Records*, 1933; and Anne Freemantle, *George Eliot*, 1933. Modern critical biographies of George Eliot begin in the 1940's with Gordon S. Haight, *George Eliot and John Chapman*, 1940; Gerald Bullett, *George Eliot: Her Life and Books*, 1948; Lawrence and Elizabeth Hanson, *Marian Evans and George Eliot*, 1952; John Holloway, *The Victorian Sage*, 1953; Robert Speaight, *George Eliot*, 1954; Bernard J. Paris, *Experiments in Life: George Eliot's Quest for Values*, 1965; F. W. Kenyon, *The Consuming Flame: The Story of George Eliot*, 1970; Ruby Redinger, *George Eliot: The Emergent Self*, 1975; and Lou-Ann Gaeddert, *All-in-All: A Biography of George Eliot*, 1976.

Early but important criticism on George Eliot includes the essays by Virginia Woolf, *The Common Reader*, 1925; and Lord David Cecil, *Early Victorian Novelists*, 1935. Modern criticism begins with F. R. Leavis, *The Great Tradition*, 1948. See also Joan Bennett, *George Eliot, Her Mind and Art*, 1948; Reva Stump, *Movement and Vision in George Eliot's Novels*, 1959; Barbara Hardy, *The Novels of George Eliot*, 1959; Jerome Thale, *The Novels of George Eliot*, 1959; Richard Stang, ed., *Discussions of George Eliot*, 1960; W. J. Harvey, *The Art of George Eliot*, 1961; David Daiches, *George Eliot*, 1963; Walter Allen, *George Eliot*, 1965; Gordon S. Haight, ed., *A Century of George Eliot Criticism*, 1965; U. C. Knoepflmacher, *George Eliot's Early Novels: The Limits of Realism*, 1969; Barbara Hardy, ed., *Critical Essays on George Eliot*, 1970; George R. Creeger, ed., *George Eliot: A Collection of Critical Essays*, 1970; Calvin Bedient, *Architects of the Self: Eliot, D. H. Lawrence and E. M. Forster*, 1972; William Baker, ed., *Critics on George Eliot*, 1973; Marghanita Laski, *George Eliot and her World*,

1973; Barbara Smalley, *George Eliot and Flaubert: Pioneers of the Modern Novel*, 1974; and Neil Roberts, *George Eliot: Her Beliefs and Her Art*, 1975.

See also Gordon S. Haight, ed., *The George Eliot Letters*, 7 vols., 1954–1955; and Thomas Pinner, ed., *Essays of George Eliot*, 1963. Special studies of George Eliot include Jerome Beaty, *Middlemarch from Notebook to Novel*, 1960; Henry Auster, *Local Habitations: Regionalism in the Early Novels of George Eliot*, 1970; Isadore G. Mudge and M. E. Sears, comps., *A George Eliot Dictionary: The Characters and Scenes of the Novels, Stories, and Poems, Alphabetically Arranged*, 1972; Patrick Swinden, ed., *George Eliot, Middlemarch: A Casebook*, 1972; Ian Adam, ed., *This Particular Web: Essays on Middlemarch*, 1975; and Phyllis Hartnoll, *Who's Who in George Eliot*, 1977.

MIDDLEMARCH

Type of work: Novel
Author: George Eliot (Mary Ann Evans, 1819–1880)
Type of plot: Psychological realism
Time of plot: Nineteenth century
Locale: England
First published: 1871–1872

　Middlemarch is the most comprehensive and sweeping of George Eliot's novels and is usually considered her masterpiece. Structuring the book around four major plotlines—the story of Dorothea Brooke, the story of Lydgate's marriage, the history of Mary Garth, and the fall ofe banker Bulstrode—the author creates a dynamic pattern that encompasses an entire spectrum of life, attitudes, and events in early nineteenth century England.

Principal Characters

Dorothea Brooke (Dodo), the sensitive and well-bred heroine who, in her desire to devote herself to something meaningful, marries an arid clerical scholar, Edward Casaubon. After Casaubon's death Dorothea, against the advice of friends and family, marries Will Ladislaw, an impulsive artist anad political thinker. Dorothea also befriends the progressive young doctor of Middlemarch, Tertius Lydgate.

The Rev. Edward Casaubon, the clergyman at Lowick, near Middlemarch. Casaubon is a gloomy, severe, unimaginative, and unsuccessful scholar who soon destroys Dorothea's enthusiasm. He is so jealous of Dorothea's friendship with his cousin, Will Ladislaw, that he adds a codicil to his will depriving Dorothea of his property should she marry his younger relative.

Will Ladislaw, Casaubon's young cousin, whose English heritage is mixed with alien Polish blood. Ladislaw is forceful, imaginative, energetic, and unconventional. An artist and a liberal, he represents an appropriate object of devotion for Dorothea, although many in Middlemarch are shocked by his views. After marrying Dorothea, he becomes a member of Parliament.

Celia Brooke, called **Kitty,** Dorothea's younger sister, a calm and placid young lady. She has none of Dorothea's aspirations, but a great deal of affection. She marries Sir James Chettam, a staid landowner.

Sir James Chettam, the owner of Freshitt Hall. A conservative gentleman, Sir James loves, first, Dorothea, then Celia, whom he happily weds.

Dr. Tertius Lydgate, a young doctor who comes to Middlemarch to establish a new hospital along progressive lines and to pursue scientific research. His noble career is destroyed by his improvident marriage and consequent debts.

Rosamond Vincy Lydgate, the beautiful, spoiled, and selfish daugher of the mayor of Middlemarch. Once married, she insists on living in a style that her husband, Dr. Lydgate, cannot afford.

Mr. Arthur Brooke, of Tipton Grange, the genial, rambling, and ineffectual uncle of Dorothea and Celia. His vague benevolence leads him to run for Parliament and he is soundly beaten.

Fred Vincy, Rosamond's brother, equally spoiled but less selfish. Although Fred gets into debt as a student and rebels against his family's plans to establish him as a respectable vicar, he later reforms, becomes an industrious farmer, and marries Mary Garth.

Mary Garth, the level-headed, competent daughter of a large, old-fashioned family securely tied to the land. She takes care of her aged, ailing relative, Peter Featherstone, before she marries Fred Vincy, her childhood sweetheart.

Mr. Walter Vincy, the mayor of Middlemarch and a prosperous manufacturer. Mr. Vincy, who loves comfort and genial company, is neither wise nor sympathetic in dealing with the problems his children face.

Mrs. Lucy Vincy, his wife, a warm, sentimental woman who spoils her children and has vast pretentions to social gentility. She objects to Fred's relationship with the simple, commonplace Garths.

Mr. Nicholas Bulstrode, the enormously pious, evangelical, wealthy banker of Middlemarch. Bulstrode uses his public morality and his money to control events in Middlemarch; however, the questionable connections and the shady early marriage that built up his fortune are eventually revealed.

Mrs. Harriet Vincy Bulstrode, his wife and the sister of Mayor Vincy. Although she seems to care only for social prestige, she loyally supports her husband after his disgrace.

Peter Featherstone, the wealthy aged owner of Stone Court. He tries to give his fortune to Mary Garth while she is nursing him during his final illness, but she refuses. His capricious will, cutting off all his grasping relatives, brings to Middlemarch strangers who precipitate Bulstrode's disgrace.

The Rev. Camden Farebrother, the vicar of St. Botolph's, a genial and casual clergyman. An expert whist-player and a friend of Lydgate, he is also, unsuccessfully, in love with Mary Garth.

The Rev. Humphrey Cadwallader, of Freshitt and Tipton, another genial clergyman who is particularly fond of fishing.

Mrs. Elinor Cadwallader, his wife, a talkative woman always acquainted with the latest scandal.

Caleb Garth, Mary's father, a stalwart and honest surveyor, land agent, and unsuccessful builder. He pays Fred Vincy's debts.

Susan Garth, his loyal, devoted wife, who educates her children with scholarly care and insight.

Mrs. Selina Plymdale, a Middlemarch gossip, friendly with the Vincys and the Bulstrodes.

Ned Plymdale, her son, a disappointed suitor of Rosamond Vincy.

Borthrop Trumbull, a florid auctioneer and cousin to old Featherstone.

John Raffles, an old reprobate and blackmailer who enters Middlemarch because he has married the mother of Featherstone's unexpected heir and periodically appears to get money. Just before he dies he reveals Bulstrode's sordid past.

Joshua Rigg, an enigmatic man who inherits Featherstone's house and money. He must adopt Featherstone's name as well.

Mr. Tyke, an evangelical clergyman, supported by Bulstrode and Lydgate for the post of chaplain at the new hospital.

Naumann, a German artist and a friend of Will Ladislaw.

Mrs. Jane Waule, the widowed, avaricious sister of Peter Featherstone.

Solomon Featherstone, her wealthy and equally avaricious brother.

Jonah Featherstone, another of Peter's disappointed brothers.

Mrs. Martha Cranch, a poor sister of Peter Featherstone, also neglected in his will.

Tom Cranch, her unintelligent and un-enterprising son.

Ben Garth, the active, athletic son of the Garths.

Letty Garth, the Garths' very bright younger daughter.

Alfred Garth, the son for whose engineering career the Garths are saving the money they use to pay Fred Vincy's debts.

Christy Garth, the Garths' oldest son, who becomes a scholar and tutor.

Mrs. Farebrother, the mother of the Reverend Mr. Camden.

Miss Henrietta Noble, her pious, understanding sister.

Miss Winifred Farebrother, Camden's sister, who idolizes him.

The Dowager Lady Chettam, Sir James's stiff and formal mother.

Arthur Chettam, the child of Sir James and Celia.

Sir Godwin Lydgate, of Quallingham in the north of England, Lydgate's distant and distinguished cousin. Rosamond appeals to him for money, but is denied.

Tantripp, Dorothea's faithful and under-standing maid.

Mme. Laure, a French actress whom Lydgate once loved.

Dr. Sprague and
Dr. Minchin, conservative Middlemarch physicians.

Mr. Wrench, at first physician to the Vincys, replaced by the more competent and progressive Lydgate.

Mr. Standish, the local lawyer who represents Peter Featherstone.

Mr. Mawmsey, a Middlemarch grocer.

Mrs. Mawmsey, his wife, a Middlemarch gossip.

Harry Toller, a local brewer.

Miss Sophy Toller, his daughter, who finally marries Ned Plymdale.

Edwin Larcher, a local businessman.

Mrs. Larcher, his wife, a local gossip.

Mr. Bambridge, a horse dealer who swindles Fred Vincy.

Mr. Horrock, his friend.

Mr. Hawley, a local citizen who frequently comments on people and events.

Mr. Chichely, another local citizen.

Dagley, an insolent farmer on Arthur Brooke's land.

Pinkerton, Mr. Brooke's political opponent in the election for Parliament.

The Story

Dorothea Brooke and her younger sister, Celia, were young women of good birth, who lived with their bachelor uncle at Tipton Grange near the town of Middlemarch. So serious was Dorothea's cast of mind that she was reluctant to keep jewelry she had inherited from her dead mother, and she gave all of it to her sister. Upon reconsideration, however, she did keep a ring and bracelet.

At a dinner party where Edward Casaubon, a middle-aged scholar, and Sir James Chettam both vied for her attention, she was much more attracted to the serious-minded Casaubon. Casaubon must have had an inkling that his chances with Dorothea were good, for the next morning he sought her out. Celia, who did not like his complexion or his moles, escaped to other interests.

That afternoon Dorothea, contemplating the wisdom of the scholar, was walking and by chance encountered Sir James; he, in love with her, mistook her silence for agreement and supposed she might love him in return.

When Casaubon made his proposal of marriage by letter, Dorothea accepted him at once. Mr. Brooke, her uncle, thought Sir James a much better match; Dorothea's acceptance merely confirmed his bachelor views that women were difficult to understand. He decided not to interfere in her plans, but Celia felt that the event would be more like a funeral than a marriage, and frankly said so.

Casaubon took Dorothea, Celia, and Mr. Brooke to see his home so that Dorothea might order any necessary changes. Dorothea, intending in all things to defer to Casaubon's tastes, said she would make no changes in the house. During the visit Dorothea met Will Ladislaw, Casaubon's second cousin, who seemed to be hardly in sympathy with his elderly cousin's marriage plans.

While Dorothea and her new husband were traveling in Italy, Tertius Lydgate, an ambitious and poor young doctor, was meeting pretty Rosamond Vincy, to whom he was much attracted. Fred Vincy, Rosamond's brother, had indicated that he expected to come into a fine inheritance when his uncle, Mr. Featherstone, should die. Vincy, meanwhile, was pressed by a debt he was unable to pay.

Lydgate became involved in petty local politics. When the time came to choose a chaplain for the new hospital of which Lydgate was the head, the young doctor realized that it was to his best interest to vote in accordance with the wishes of Nicholas Bulstrode, an influential banker and founder of the hospital. A clergyman named Tyke received the office.

In Rome, Ladislaw encountered Dorothea and her middle-aged husband. Dorothea had begun to realize too late how pompous and incompatible she found Casaubon. Seeing her unhappiness, Ladislaw first pitied and then fell in love with his cousin's wife. Unwilling to live any longer on Casaubon's charity, Ladislaw announced his intention of returning to England and finding some kind of gainful occupation.

When Fred Vincy's note came due, he tried to sell a horse at a profit but the animal turned out to be vicious. Caleb Garth, who had signed his note, now stood to lose a hundred and ten pounds because of Fred's inability to raise the money. Fred fell ill, and Lydgate was summoned to attend him. Lydgate used his professional calls to further his suit with Rosamond.

Dorothea and her husband returned from Rome in time to hear of Celia's engagement to Sir James Chettam. Will Ladislaw included a note to Dorothea in a letter he wrote to Casaubon. This attention precipitated a quarrel which was followed by Casaubon's serious illness. Lydgate, who attended him, urged him to give up his studies for the time being. To Dorothea, Lydgate confided that Casaubon had a weak heart and must be guarded from all excitement.

Meanwhile all the relatives of old Mr. Featherstone were waiting impatiently for his death, but he hoped to circumvent their desires by giving his fortune to Mary Garth, daughter of the man who had signed Fred Vincy's note. When she refused it, he fell into a rage and died soon afterward. When his will was read, it was learned he had left nothing to his relatives; most of his money was to go to a Joshua Riggs, who was to take the name of Featherstone, and a part of his fortune was to endow the Featherstone Almshouses for old men.

Plans were made for Rosamond's marriage with Lydgate. Fred Vincy was ordered to prepare himself finally for the ministry, since he was to have no inheritance from his uncle. Mr. Brooke, having gone into politics, enlisted the help of Ladislaw in publishing a liberal paper. Mr. Casaubon had come to dislike Ladislaw intensely after his cousin had rejected further financial assistance, and he had forbidden Ladislaw to enter his house.

Casaubon died suddenly. A codicil to his will gave Dorothea all of his property as long as she did not marry Ladislaw. This strange provision caused Dorothea's friends and relatives some concern because if publicly given out, it would appear that Dorothea and Ladislaw had been indiscreet.

Mr. Brooke, on the advice of his Tory friends, gave up his liberal newspaper and thus cut off his connection with Ladislaw. The latter realized that Dorothea's family was in some way trying to separate him from Dorothea but he refused to be disconcerted about the matter. He resolved to stay on in Middlemarch until he was ready to leave. When he heard of the codicil to Casaubon's will, he was more than ever determined to remain so that he could eventually disprove the suspicions of the village concerning him and Dorothea.

Meanwhile Lydgate and Rosamond had married, and the doctor had gone deeply in debt to furnish his house. When he found that his income did not meet his wife's spendthrift habits, he asked her to help him economize. He and his wife began to quarrel. His practice and popularity decreased.

A disreputable man named Raffles appeared in Middlemarch. Raffles knew that Ladislaw's grandfather had amassed a fortune as a receiver of stolen goods and that Nicholas Bulstrode, the highly respected banker, had once been the confidential clerk of Ladislaw's ancestor. More than that, Bulstrode's first wife had been his employer's widow. Upon money inherited from her, money which should have gone to Ladislaw's mother, Bulstrode had built his own fortune.

Already blackmailed by Raffles, Bulstrode reasoned that the scoundrel would tell Ladislaw the whole story. To forestall trouble, he sent for Ladislaw and offered him an annuity of five hundred pounds and liberal provision in his will. Ladislaw, feeling that his relatives had already tainted his honor, refused, unwilling to be associated in any way with the unsavory business. Deciding to leave Middlemarch, Ladislaw went to London without the assurance that Dorothea loved him.

Lydgate drifted deeper into debt. When he wished to sell what he could and take cheaper lodgings, Rosamond managed to make him hold on, to keep up the pretense of prosperity a little longer. At the same time Bulstrode gave up his interest in the new hospital and withdrew his financial support.

Faced at last with the seizure of his goods, Lydgate went to Bulstrode and asked for a loan. The banker advised him to seek aid from Dorothea and abruptly ended the conversation. But when Raffles, in the last stages of alcoholism, returned to Middlemarch and Lydgate was called in to attend him, Bulstrode, afraid the doctor would learn the banker's secret from Raffles' drunken ravings, changed his mind and gave Lydgate a check for a thousand pounds. The loan came in time to save Lydgate's goods and reputation. When Raffles died, Bulstrode felt at peace at last. But it soon became common gossip that Bulstrode had given money to Lydgate and that Lydgate had attended Raffles in his final illness. Bulstrode and Lydgate were publicly accused of malpractice in Raffles' death. Only Dorothea took up Lydgate's defense. The rest of the town was busy with gossip over the affair. Rosamond was anxious to leave Middlemarch to avoid public disgrace. Bulstrode also was anxious to leave town after his secret, which Raffles had told while drunk in a neighboring village, became known. But he became ill and his doctors would not permit him to leave his bed.

Dorothea, sympathetic with Lydgate, determined to give her support to the hospital and to try to convince Rosamond that the only way Lydgate could recover his honor was by remaining in Middlemarch. Unfortunately, she came upon Will Ladislaw, to whom poor Rosamond was pouring out her grief. Afraid Rosamond was involved with Ladislaw, Dorothea left abruptly. Angered at the false position Rosamond had put him in, Ladislaw explained that he had always loved Dorothea, but from a distance. When Dorothea forced herself to return to Lydgate's house on the following morning, Rosamond told her of Ladislaw's declaration. Dorothea realized she was willing to give up Casaubon's fortune for Ladislaw's affection.

In spite of the protests of her family and friends, they were married several weeks later and went to London to live. Lydgate and Rosamond lived together with better understanding and prospects of a happier future. Fred Vincy became engaged to Mary Garth, with whom he had long been in love. For a time Dorothea's family disregarded her, but they were finally reconciled after Dorothea's son was born and Ladislaw was elected to Parliament.

Critical Evaluation

Modestly subtitled "A Study in Provincial Life," George Eliot's *Middlemarch* has long been recognized as a work of great psychological and moral penetration. Indeed, the novel has been compared with Tolstoy's *War and Peace* and Thackeray's *Vanity Fair* for its nearly epic sweep and its perspective of early nineteenth century history. Yet these comparisons are partly faulty. Unlike *War and Peace, Middlemarch* lacks a philosophical bias, a grand *Weltanschauung* that oversees the destinies of nations and generations. And unlike *Vanity Fair,* Eliot's novel is not neatly moralistic. In fact, much of *Middlemarch* is morally ambiguous, in the modern sense of the term. Eliot's concept of plot and character derives from psychological rather than philosophical or social necessity. This is another way of saying that *Middlemarch,* despite its Victorian trappings of complicated plot and subplot, its slow development of character, accumulated detail concerning time and place, its social density is—in many other respects—a "modern" novel that disturbs as well as comforts the reader.

At the height of her powers, George Eliot published *Middlemarch* in eight books, from December 1871 to December 1872, eight years before her death. She had already achieved a major reputation with *Adam Bede* (1859), *The Mill on the Floss* (1860), and *Silas Marner* (1861). But her most recent fiction, *Felix Holt, Radical* (1866), and *The Spanish Gypsy* (1868), both inferior to her best writing, had disappointed her public. *Middlemarch,* however, was received with considerable excitement and critical acclaim. Eliot's publisher, Blackwood, was so caught up with the action, as he received chapters of her novel by mail, that he wrote back to her asking questions about the fates of the characters, as though they were real people with real histories. As a matter of fact, Eliot researched the material for her novel scrupulously. Her discussion of the social climate in rural England directly before the passage of the Reform Bill of 1832 is convincingly detailed; she accurately describes the state of medical knowledge during Lydgate's time; and she treats the dress, habits, and speech of Middlemarch impeccably, creating the metaphor of a complete world, a piece of provincial England that is a microcosm of the greater world beyond.

Yet the theme of the novel itself revolves around the slenderest of threads: the mating of "unimportant" people. This theme, which engages the talents of other great writers as well—Jane Austen, Thomas Hardy, Henry James, D. H. Lawrence—allows George Eliot scope to examine the whole range of human nature. She is concerned with the mating of lovers, because they are most vulnerable in love, most nearly the victims of their romantic illusions. Each of the three sets of lovers in *Middlemarch*—Dorothea Brooke/Edward Casaubon/Will Ladislaw; Rosamond Vincy/Tertius Lydgate; and Mary Garth/Fred Vincy—mistake illusion for reality. Eventually all come to understand themselves better, whether or not they are completely reconciled with their mates. Each undergoes a sentimental education, a discipline of the spirit that teaches the heart its limitations.

Paradoxically, the greater capacity Eliot's characters have for romantic self-deception, the greater is their suffering and subsequent tempering of spirit. Mary Garth, plain, witty, honest, is too sensible to arouse our psychological curiosity to the same degree that we are interested in the proud Dorothea, rash Ladislaw, pathetic Casaubon, ambitious Lydgate, or pampered Rosamond. Mary loves simply, directly. Fred, her childhood sweetheart, is basically a good lad who must learn from his own misfortunes the lessons of thrift and perseverance. He "falls" in class, from that of an idle landowner to one of a decent but socially inferior manager of property. In truth, what he seems to lose in social prominence he more than recovers in the development of his moral character. Moreover, he wins as a mate the industrious Mary, who will strengthen his resolve and make of him an admirable provider like her father Caleb.

Dorothea, on the other hand, more idealistic and noble-hearted than Mary, chooses the worst possible mate as her first husband. Edward Casaubon, thirty years her senior, is a dull pedant, cold, hopelessly ineffectual as a scholar, absurd as a lover. Despite his intellectual pretensions, he is too timid, fussy, and dispirited ever to complete his masterwork, "A Key to All Mythologies." Even the title of his project is an absurdity. He conceals as long as possible his "key" from Dorothea, fearing that she will expose him as a sham. Yet it is possible that she might have endured the disgrace of her misplaced affection were Casaubon only more tender, reciprocating her own tenderness and self-sacrifice. But Casaubon, despotic to the last, tries to blight her spirit when he is alive and, through his will, to restrict her freedom when he is dead.

Dorothea's second choice of a mate, Will Ladislaw is very nearly the opposite of Casaubon. A rash, sometimes hypersensitive lover, he is capable of intense affection, above all of self-sacrifice. He is a worthy suitor for Dorothea, who finds greatness in his ardor, if not his accomplishments. Yet Will, allowing for his greater vitality, is after all a logical successor to Casaubon. Dorothea had favored the elderly scholar because he was unworldly, despised by the common herd. In her imagination he seemed a saint of intellect. In time she comes to favor Will because he is also despised by most of the petty-minded bigots of Middlemarch, because he has suffered from injustice; and because he seems to her a saint of integrity. A Victorian St. Theresa, Dorothea is passive, great in aspiration rather than deed. Psychologically she requires a great object for her own self-sacrifice, and therefore chooses a destiny that will allow her the fullest measure of heroism.

Tertius Lydgate, quite the opposite, is a calculating, vigorous, ambitious young physician who attempts to move others to his own iron will. His aggressive energy contrasts with Dorothea's passiveness. However, like her, he is a victim of romantic illusion. He believes that he can master, through his intelligence and determination, those who possess power. Nevertheless, his choice of a mate, Rosamond Vincy, is a disastrous miscalculation. Rosamond's fragile beauty conceals a petulant, selfish will equal to his own. She dominates him through her own weakness rather than strength of character. Insensitive except to her own needs, she offers no scope for Lydgate's sensitive intelligence. In his frustration, he can only battle with himself. He comes to realize that he is defeated not only in his dreams of domestic happiness but in his essential judgment of the uses of power.

For George Eliot, moral choice does not exist in a sanctified vacuum; it requires an encounter with power. To even the least sophisticated dwellers in Middlemarch, power is represented by wealth and status. As the widow Mrs. Casaubon, Dorothea's social prestige rests upon her personal and inherited fortune. When she casts aside her estate under Casaubon's will to marry Ladislaw, she loses also a great measure of status. At the same time, she acquires moral integrity, a superior virtue for Eliot. Similarly, when Mary Garth rejects Mr. Featherstone's dying proposition to seize his wealth before his relatives make a shambles of his will, she chooses morally, justly, and comes to deserve the happiness that she eventually wins. As for Lydgate, whose moral choices are most nearly ambiguous, he returns Bulstrode's bribe to save himself from a social embarrassment, but his guilt runs deeper than mere miscalculation. He has associated himself, first through his choice of Tyke instead of the worthier Farebrother as vicar, with Bulstrode's manipulation of power. Lydgate's moral defeat is partial, for at least he understands the extent of his compromise with integrity. Bulstrode's defeat is total, for he loses both wealth and social standing. As for Middlemarch, that community of souls is a small world, populated with people of good will and bad, mean spirits and fine, and is the collective agent of moral will. After all, it is the town that endures, the final arbiter of moral judgment in a less than perfect world.

Bibliography

Adam, Ian. *George Eliot.* New York: Humanities, 1969, pp. 21–28, 45–52, 71–77, 97–104.

Anderson, Quentin. "George Eliot in *Middlemarch*," in *The Pelican Guide to English Literature*, Volume VI. Edited by Boris Ford. New York: Penguin Books, 1958, pp. 274–293. Reprinted in *George Eliot: A Collection of Critical Essays.* Edited by George R. Creeger. Englewood Cliffs, N.J.: Prentice-Hall, 1970, pp. 141–160. Also reprinted in *A Century of George Eliot Criticism.* Edited by Gordon S. Haight. Boston: Houghton Mifflin, 1965, pp. 313–324.

Armstrong, Isobel. "*Middlemarch*: A Note on George Eliot's 'Wisdom,' " in *Critical Essays on George Eliot.* Edited by Barbara Hardy. New York: Barnes & Noble, 1970, pp. 116–132.

Beaty, J. Middlemarch *from Notebook to Novel: A Study of George Eliot's Creative Method.* Urbana: University of Illinois Press, 1960.

Blake, Kathleen. "*Middlemarch* and the Woman Question," in *Nineteenth-Century Fiction.* XXXI (December, 1976), pp. 285–312.

Carroll, David R. "Unity Through Analogy: An Interpretation of *Middlemarch*," in *Victorian Studies.* II (1959), pp. 305–316.

Coles, Robert. *Irony in the Mind's Life: Essays on Novels by James Agee, Elizabeth Bowen, and George Eliot.* Charlottesville: University Press of Virginia, 1974, pp. 154–204.

Daiches, David. *George Eliot:* Middlemarch. Great Neck, N.Y.: Barron's, 1963.

Ferris, Sumner J. "*Middlemarch*: George Eliot's Masterpiece," in *From Jane Austen to Joseph Conrad: Essays Collected in Memory of James T. Hillhouse.* Edited by Robert C. Rathburn and Martin Steinman. Minneapolis: University of Minnesota Press, 1958, pp. 194–207.

Hagan, John. "*Middlemarch*: Narrative Unity in the Story of Dorothea Brooke," in *Nineteenth-Century Fiction.* XVI (June, 1961), pp. 17–31.

Hardy, Barbara. "*Middlemarch* and the Passions," in *This Particular Web: Essays on* Middlemarch. Edited by Ian Adam. Toronto: University of Toronto Press, 1975, pp. 3–21.

Harvey, W.J. "The Intellectual Background of the Novel: Casaubon and Lydgate," in Middlemarch: *Critical Approaches to the Novel.* Edited by Barbara Hardy. New York: Oxford University Press, 1967, pp. 25–37. Reprinted in *The Victorian Novel: Modern Essays in Criticism.* Edited by Ian Watt. New York: Oxford University Press, 1971, pp. 311–323.

Jones, R.T. *George Eliot.* Cambridge: Cambridge University Press, 1970, pp. 57–96.

Kettle, Arnold. *An Introduction to the English Novel*, Volume I. London: Hutchinson, 1951, pp. 171–190.

Kitchel, Anna Theresa. *Quarry for* Middlemarch. Berkeley: University of California Press, 1950.

Knoepflmacher, Ulrich Camillus. *Laughter and Despair: Readings in Ten Novels of the Victorian Era.* Berkeley: University of California Press, 1971, pp. 168–201.

Liddell, Robert. *The Novels of George Eliot.* New York: St. Martin's, 1977, pp. 123–161.

Lyons, Richard S. "The Method of *Middlemarch*," in *Nineteenth-Century Fiction.* XXI (June, 1966), pp. 35–47.

Roberts, Neil. *George Eliot: Her Beliefs and Her Art.* Pittsburgh: University of Pittsburgh Press, 1975, pp. 145–182.

Schorer, Mark.   "Fiction and the 'Matrix of Analogy,' " in *Kenyon Review.* XI (Autumn, 1949), pp. 539–559. Reprinted in *A Century of George Eliot Criticism.* Edited by Gordon S. Haight. Boston: Houghton Mifflin, 1965, pp. 270–278.

──────.   "The Structure of the Novel: Method, Metaphor and Mind," in *Middlemarch: Critical Approaches to the Novel.* Edited by Barbara Hardy. New York: Oxford University Press, 1967, pp. 12–24.

Stallknecht, Newton P.   "Resolution and Independence: A Reading of *Middlemarch*," in *Twelve Original Essays on Great English Novels.* Edited by Charles Shapiro. Detroit: Wayne State University Press, 1960, pp. 125–152.

Thale, Jerome,   *The Novels of George Eliot.* New York: Columbia University Press, 1959, pp. 106–120.

Willey, Frederick.   "Appearance and Reality in *Middlemarch*," in *Southern Review.* V (1969), pp. 419–435.

Williams, Raymond.   *The English Novel: From Dickens to Lawrence.* London: Chatto and Windus, 1970, pp. 87–94.

THE MILL ON THE FLOSS

Type of work: Novel
Author: George Eliot (Mary Ann Evans, 1819–1880)
Type of plot: Domestic realism
Time of plot: Nineteenth century
Locale: England
First published: 1860

George Eliot probably identified with Maggie Tulliver, the heroine of The Mill on the Floss, *and that gives the novel much of its immediacy and charm, especially in the early chapters. Like Eliot, Maggie is a girl of deep sensitivity, intellectual capacity, and spiritual longings. But, unlike her creator, Maggie can never realize those inclinations and talents in the provincial, male-dominated environment that surrounds and finally destroys her.*

Principal Characters

Maggie Tulliver, the impetuous and generous young heroine. Regarded as wild and gipsy-like by most of her respectable relatives, the sensitive and imaginative Maggie does not fit into the provincial society in and near St. Ogg's on the River Floss. She worships her brother Tom, who judges her harshly and thinks her unreliable. She loves Philip Wakem, the crippled son of her father's worst enemy, but must promise never to see him. Despite her feeling for Philip and her love for her cousin, Lucy Deane, Maggie is strongly attracted to her cousin's fiancé, Stephen Guest. Stephen persuades her to go boating, but they neglect their destination and are forced to spend the night on a freighter that rescues them. Almost everyone in St. Ogg's, her brother included, thinks Maggie responsible and regards her as an evil and designing woman. In the final scene, during a flood, Maggie takes a boat to rescue Tom, who is at the family mill. The two are reconciled before the raging river drowns them.

Tom Tulliver, Maggie's brother. Although never quick at school, Tom assumes financial responsibility for the family when he is only sixteen, after the father has lost his mill and home through a series of lawsuits. Tom pledges to follow his father in having nothing to do with the Wakem family. He works hard and, through his industry and careful investments in partnership with Bob Jakin, pays off his father's debts and eventually gets the mill back. Somewhat priggish, Tom judges others severely, but he is also generous to his mother and sister.

Edward Tulliver, the father of Maggie and Tom and the owner of Dorlcote Mill, near St. Ogg's on the River Floss. An emotional and hot-tempered man, Tulliver engages in several lawsuits which, in addition to other financial reverses, cause him to lose his mill. Tulliver must swallow his pride and work in the mill as the hated Wakem's manager. When Tom finally earns the money to pay off his father's debts, Tulliver meets Wakem and thrashes him. The exertion produces Tulliver's second stroke and he dies. He is always partial to his clever and imaginative daughter Maggie.

Mrs. Elizabeth Tulliver (Bessy), Edward's wife, proud of her birth as a Dodson and grieved that her husband's temper and improvidence cause her to lose her home and furnishings. She is dependent on the advice and opinions of her more prosperous sisters. Her pleading visit to Wakem inadvertently causes him to plan to buy the mill when Tulliver is bankrupt. Regarding Maggie as wild and unladylike, she is partial to her son Tom.

Philip Wakem, a lawyer's son, humpbacked as the result of a childhood accident. An excellent scholar and a talented artist, he loves Maggie from the time he first meets her, for she does not judge him by his infirmity. He hopes to marry Maggie despite family objections and her temporary attraction to Stephen Guest.

Lucy Deane, Maggie's blonde and pretty cousin. She and Maggie go to boarding school together and become great friends. Maggie confesses her feeling for Philip Wakem to Lucy. At the end, Lucy understands that Maggie was essentially blameless in the boating escapade with Stephen Guest and she forgives Maggie. She marries Stephen after Maggie is dead.

Stephen Guest, the handsome son of the wealthiest and most socially prominent family in St. Ogg's. Although engaged to Lucy, he is so attracted to Maggie that he pleads with her to marry him. After the boating trip, when Maggie is in disgrace, he goes off to Holland.

Mrs. Jane Glegg, the sister of Mrs. Tulliver. She is wealthy, parsimonious, and the proudest of the Dodson sisters. Although she dislikes Maggie, she defends her after the episode with Stephen Guest.

Mrs. Sophy Pullet, another of the Dodson sisters. She is wealthy and sentimental, crying copiously at every misfortune.

Mrs. Susan Deane, another Dodson sister, the pale and ailing mother of Lucy.

She and Tulliver die about the same time.

Mr. Deane, her husband, who has worked his way up in the prosperous firm of Guest and Co., bankers, ship owners, and tradesmen. Although rather pompous about his achievements, he helps Tom get established in his firm.

Mrs. Gritty Moss, Mr. Tulliver's sister, a kind, poor woman with eight children. She has Maggie's ardent nature, although she lacks her niece's intelligence.

Mr. Moss, her husband, an unsuccessful farmer.

Mr. Glegg, husband of Jane Glegg, a wealthy, retired, prudent gentleman who had made a fortune in the wool business.

Mr. Pullet, husband of Sophy Pullet, a tiny, wealthy gentleman farmer who sucks lozenges throughout all family discussions.

Bob Jakin, Tom Tulliver's boyhood friend. He becomes Tom's partner in numerous investments.

John Wakem, the father of Philip and a lawyer in St. Ogg's. Although he does not hate Mr. Tulliver initially, Tulliver's frequent insults cause him to enjoy the family's downfall. His love for his son, however, later leads him to approve of the possibility of Philip's marrying Maggie.

The Rev. Walter Stelling, the owner of King's Lorton, the school attended by Tom Tulliver and Philip Wakem. He regards Tom as hopelessly stupid.

Luke Moggs, the head miller at Dorlcote Mill, fond of Maggie and entirely loyal to the Tullivers.

Mr. Riley, a local auctioneer, surveyor, and engineer who dies, leaving Mr. Tulliver with his debts.

The Rev. Dr. Kenn, rector of St. Ogg's, a clergyman sympathetic toward Maggie.

Mrs. Kenn, his wife, who runs a charity bazaar in St. Ogg's.

Mr. Poulter, the village schoolmaster.

Mr. Pivart, the owner of land near Dorlcote Mill who wishes to irrigate his land and is sued unsuccessfully by Mr. Tulliver.

Mr. Dix, another gentleman unsuccessfully sued by Mr. Tulliver.

Mr. Furley, the gentleman who owns

the mortgage on Mr. Tulliver's land and transfers it to lawyer Wakem.

Mr. Gore, a scheming lawyer.

Mr. Jetsome, the young manager of the mill under Wakem after Tulliver dies. While drunk, he is pitched off his horse and severely injured.

Prissy Jakin, Bob Jakin's tiny "Dutch doll" wife.

Mrs. Jakin, Bob's massive mother.

The Story

Dorlcote Mill stood on the banks of the River Floss near the village of St. Ogg's. Owned by the ambitious Mr. Tulliver, it provided a good living for him and his family, but he dreamed of the day when his son Tom would climb to a higher station in life.

Mrs. Tulliver's sisters, who had married well, criticized Mr. Tulliver's unseemly ambition and openly predicted the day when his air castles would bring himself and his family to ruin. Aunt Glegg, richest of the sisters, held a note on his property, and when he quarreled with her over his plans for Tom's education, Mr. Tulliver determined to borrow the money and repay her.

For Tom, who had inherited the placid arrogance of his mother's people, life was not difficult. He was resolved to be just in all his dealings and to deliver punishment to whomever it was due. His sister Maggie grew up with an imagination beyond her years of understanding. Her aunts predicted she would come to a bad end, because she was tomboyish, dark-skinned, dreamy, and indifferent to their wills. Frightened by ill luck in her attempts to please her brother Tom, her cousin Lucy, and her mother and aunts, Maggie ran away, determined to live with the gypsies. But she was glad enough to return. Her father scolded her mother and Tom for abusing her. Her mother was sure Maggie would come to a bad end because of the way Mr. Tulliver humored her.

Tom's troubles began when his father sent him to study at Mr. Stelling's school. Having little interest in spelling, grammar, or Latin, Tom found himself wishing he were back at the mill, where he might dream of someday riding a horse like his father's and giving orders to people around him. Mr. Stelling was convinced that Tom was not only obstinate but also stupid. Returning home for the Christmas holidays, Tom learned that Philip Wakem, son of a lawyer who was his father's enemy, would also enter Mr. Stelling's school.

Philip Wakem was a cripple, and so Tom was not able to beat him up as he should have liked at first. Philip could draw, and he knew Latin and Greek. After they overcame their initial reserve, the two boys became useful to one another. Philip admired Tom's arrogance and self-possession, and Tom needed Philip's knowledge to help him in his studies. But their fathers' quarrel kept a breach between them. Tom felt that Philip needed to be watched, that he was the son of a rascal.

When Maggie came to visit Tom, she met Philip, and the two became close friends. Then, after Maggie had been sent away to school with her cousin Lucy, Mr. Tulliver became involved in a lawsuit. Because Mr. Wakem defended the opposition, Mr. Tulliver said his children should have as little as possible to do with Philip.

Mr. Tulliver lost his suit and stood to lose all his property as well. In order to pay off Aunt Glegg, he had borrowed money on his household furnishings. Now he hoped Aunt Pullet would lend him the money to pay the debt against which his household goods stood forfeit. He could no longer afford to keep Maggie and Tom in school. Then Mr. Tulliver learned that Mr. Wakem had bought up his debts, and the discovery brought on a stroke. Tom made Maggie promise never to speak to Philip Wakem again. Mrs. Tulliver wept because her household things were to be put up at auction. In the ruin which followed, Tom and Maggie rejected the scornful offers of help from their aunts.

Bob Jakin, a country lout with whom Tom had fought as a boy, turned up to offer Tom partnership with him in a venture where Tom's education would help Bob's native business shrewdness. But both were without capital. For the time being Tom took a job in a warehouse and studied bookkeeping each night.

Mr. Wakem bought the mill but permitted Mr. Tulliver to act as its manager for wages. It was Wakem's plan eventually to turn the mill over to his son. Tulliver, not knowing what else to do, stayed on as an employee of his enemy, but he asked Tom to sign a statement in the Bible that he would wish the Wakems evil as long as he lived. Against Maggie's entreaties, Tom signed his name. Finally Aunt Glegg gave Tom some money which he invested with Bob Jakin. Slowly Tom began to accumulate funds to pay off his father's debts.

Meanwhile Maggie and Philip had been meeting secretly in the glades near the mill. One day he asked Maggie if she loved him. She put him off. Later, at a family gathering, she betrayed her feeling for Philip in a manner which aroused Tom's suspicions. He made her swear on the Bible not to have anything more to do with Philip, and then he sought out Philip and ordered him to stay away from his sister.

Shortly afterward Tom showed his father his profits. The next day Mr. Tulliver thrashed Mr. Wakem and then suffered another stroke, from which he never recovered.

Two years later Maggie, now a teacher, went to visit her cousin, Lucy Deane, who was also entertaining young Stephen Guest in her home. One difficulty Lucy foresaw was that Philip, who was friendly with both her and Stephen, might absent himself during Maggie's visit. Stephen had already decided that Lucy was to be his choice for a wife, but at first sight he and Maggie were attracted to one another. Lucy, blind to what was happening, was pleased that her cousin Maggie and Stephen were becoming good friends.

Maggie asked Tom's permission to see Philip Wakem at a party Lucy was giving. Tom replied that if Maggie should ever consider Philip as a lover, she must expect never to see her brother again. Tom stood by his oath to his father. He felt his dignity as a Tulliver, and he believed Maggie was apt to follow the inclination of the moment without giving consideration to the outcome. He was right. Lacking the iron will which marked so many of her relatives, Maggie loved easily and without restraint.

Meanwhile Lucy's father had promised to try to buy back the mill for Tom. Learning of this plan, Philip hoped to persuade his father to sell the mill. For this service Philip felt sure Tom would forget his old hatred.

At a dance Stephen Guest tried to kiss Maggie. She evaded him and the next day avoided Philip Wakem as well. She felt she owed it to Lucy not to allow Stephen to fall in love with her, and she felt that she owed it to her brother not to marry Philip.

She was carried along by the tide. Her relatives would not let her go back into teaching, for Tom's good luck continued and he repossessed his father's mill. Both Stephen and Philip urged her to marry them without the knowledge of each other's aims. Certainly, Lucy did not suspect Stephen's growing indifference to her.

One day Stephen took Maggie boating and tried to convince her to run away with him and be married. She refused his offer. Then the tide carried them beyond the reach of shore and they were forced to spend the night in the boat.

Maggie dared the wrath and judgment of her relatives when she returned and attempted to explain to Lucy and the others what had happened. They refused to listen to her. Tom turned her away from the mill house, with the word that he would send her money but that he never wished to see her again. Mrs. Tulliver resolved to go with Maggie, and Bob Jakin took them in.

Maggie slowly began to realize what ostracism meant, for one by one people deserted her. Only Aunt Glegg and Lucy offered any sympathy. Stephen wrote to her in agony of spirit, as did Philip. Maggie wanted to be by herself. She wondered if there could be love for her without pain for others.

That autumn a terrible flood ravaged St. Ogg's. Knowing that Tom was at the mill, Maggie attempted to reach him in a boat. The two were reunited and Tom took over the rowing of the boat. But the full force of the flood overwhelmed them and they drowned, together at the end as they had been when they were children.

Critical Evaluation

Shortly after George Eliot published *Adam Bede* in 1858, she began to work on a new novel under the tentative title "Sister Maggie." As the book was taking shape, she considered other possible titles—"The House of

Tulliver," "The Tulliver Family," "The Tullivers"—before her editor, Blackwood, suggested *The Mill on the Floss,* a title she approved with some reservations. She objected at first that the "mill is not strictly on the Floss, being on its small tributary" and that the title "is of rather laborious utterance." Having voiced her usual nice concern for precise details and delicacy of style, she allowed that Blackwood's title was "the only alternate so far as we can see." On March 21, 1860, she completed the book, vacationed in Rome with her husband George Henry Lewes, and awaited the news of the critics' reception, which proved to be almost wholly favorable. With satisfaction Eliot wrote: "From all we can gather, the votes are rather on the side of 'The Mill' as a better book than 'Adam.' "

It is certainly the more poignant novel. Although both fictions have as their setting the Warwickshire background that George Eliot remembered from her youth, *The Mill on the Floss* is less genially picturesque, more concerned with psychological truth. *Adam Bede* concludes, probably contrary to the author's best artistic judgment, with a happy marriage for Adam and Dinah. But Tom and Maggie Tulliver die in the flood, their fate unmitigated by sentimentality. Indeed, much of the novel's power derives from the consistent play of tragic forces that appear early and unify the whole work.

As a boy, Tom entrusts his pet rabbits to his sister Maggie's care. Preoccupied, she allows the creatures to die. Tom upbraids her bitterly, in spite of her tearful protestations, but finally forgives her. This childhood pattern of close sibling affection, followed by deep hurt and estrangement, then by reconciliation, becomes the structural pattern of the novel. Although Henry James admired the design of *The Mill on the Floss,* he criticized the conclusion for its melodrama. As a matter of fact, the conclusion is implicit in the story from the beginning. The flood that carries to their doom the beloved brother and sister is not so much an accidental catastrophe. Rather, it is symbolic of the tide that sweeps away two passionate souls divided in conflict yet united by the closest bonds of affection.

Tom Tulliver, like his father, has a tenacious will that is not always under control of his reason. Even as a child, he is fiercely although honorably competitive. He is slow to forgive injury. Robust and vigorous, he despises weakness in others. As a youth, he insults Philip Wakem by drawing attention to the hunchback's physical deformity. And when Maggie demeans, as Tom mistakenly believes, the good name of the Tulliver family through her foreshortened "elopement" with Stephen Guest, he scorns her as a pariah. Yet Tom's tempestuous nature is also capable of generosity. To redeem his father's good name and restore Dorlcote Mill to the family, he disciplines himself to work purposefully. To this end, he sacrifices his high spirits, his love of strenuous excitement, indeed any opportunities for courtship and marriage. He dies as he had lived and labored, the provider of the Tulliver family.

His sister Maggie, many of whose sprightly qualities are drawn from George

Eliot's memories of her own childhood, is psychologically the more complex character. Whereas Tom is sturdily masculine, Maggie is sensitive, introspective, tenderly feminine. Quick to tears—to the modern reader perhaps too effusive in her emotions—she cannot control her sensibilities, just as her brother cannot hold his temper. As a youngster, she has much of the tomboy in her. She is energetic and, unlike the typical Victorian girl, fights for her place in the world. Intelligent, diligent, earnest, she would make better use of Mr. Stelling's classical schooling than her brother; but girls of her time rarely had the opportunity to advance in education. So she must content herself, although secretively restive, with the narrow place Victorian society allows for girls of her class. Like Dorothea Brooke in *Middlemarch,* she is attracted to a scholarly but fragile lover, Philip. Her sympathetic nature completes what is lacking in the young man's disposition—courage and self-esteem. And in turn he offers her a sense of artistic dedication for which she yearns.

Some astute critics of *The Mill on the Floss* have objected to Maggie's other suitor, Stephen Guest, who is Lucy Deane's fiancé. For Lucy, a more typical Victorian heroine, sweet but passive, the impetuous Stephen would be a satisfactory mate. According to Sir Leslie Stephen, Maggie, in her passion for Lucy's betrothed, throws herself away upon a "low creature." His daughter, Virginia Woolf, repeated Sir Leslie's judgment in describing Stephen's "courseness." But a modern view of the character does not support such hostile interpretations. Stephen is neither low nor coarse. Instead he is an ardent lover who rouses in Maggie a sexual response that she does not feel, in spite of her tender empathy, for Philip. Maggie's torment is to be torn between her promises to Philip (who certainly loves and needs her) and her deeper feelings for Stephen. On one hand, she senses the call of duty and propriety; on the other, she feels the sweep of wild emotion. She masters her feelings, betrays her needs as a woman, and returns to Philip.

For the same reason that some critics refuse to accept Maggie as a mature woman with normal sexual responses, some readers are troubled by the apparent change in her character as she grows from child to adult. So vital, charming, and convincing is the portrait of Maggie the girl, that readers may wish to cherish her youthful image. But Maggie the woman does not really change. Within the prudish conventions of the Victorian novel, George Eliot can only suggest her heroine's psychological and moral development. Nevertheless, she conveys a sense of Maggie's greater sexual vulnerability because of her "highly strung, hungry nature." When she renounces Stephen, she renounces her own happiness. From that point, her tragedy is inevitable. The provincial gossips of St. Ogg's cast her off. Her beloved brother rejects her. To be sure, her mother, Lucy, and Philip have faith in her to the last. But Maggie, characteristically, determines: "I must not, cannot seek my own happiness by sacrificing others." Thus, the flood waters that carry Maggie and her brother downstream cleanse their guilts, unite them as when they were children, innocent with hope. Finally in their death as in their life, Eliot tells us, they are "not divided."

Bibliography

Adam, Ian. *George Eliot.* New York: Humanities, 1969, pp. 12–18, 37–41, 63–68, 88–94.

Auerbach, Nina. "The Power of Hunger: Demonism and Maggie Tulliver," in *Nineteenth-Century Fiction.* XXX (September, 1975), pp. 150–171.

Buckler, William E. "Memory, Morality, and the Tragic Vision in the Early Novels of George Eliot," in *The English Novel in the Nineteenth Century: Essays on the Literary Mediation of Human Values.* Edited by George Goodin. Urbana: University of Illinois Press, 1972, pp. 149–159.

Buckley, Jerome Hamilton. *Season of Youth: The Bildungs-roman from Dickens to Golding.* Cambridge, Mass.: Harvard University Press, 1974, pp. 95–115.

Carroll, David R. "An Image of Disenchantment in the Novels of George Eliot," in *Review of English Studies.* XI (1960), pp. 29–41.

Colby, Robert Alan. *Fiction with a Purpose: Major and Minor Nineteenth Century Novels.* Bloomington: Indiana University Press, 1967, pp. 213–255.

Drew, Elizabeth A. *The Novel: A Modern Guide to Fifteen English Master-pieces.* New York: Norton, 1963, pp. 127–140.

Ermarth, Elizabeth. "Maggie Tulliver's Long Suicide," in *Studies in English Literature, 1500–1900.* XIV (1974), pp. 587–601.

Goldfarb, Russell M. "Robert P. Warren's Tollivers and George Eliot's Tullivers," in *University Review.* XXXVI (1970), pp. 209–213.

————. "Warren's Tollivers and Eliot's Tullivers, II," in *University Review.* XXXVI (1970), pp. 275–279.

Hagan, John. "A Reinterpretation of *The Mill on the Floss*," in *PMLA.* LXXXVII (1972), pp. 53–63.

Haight, Gordon S. "Introduction," in *The Mill on the Floss* (Riverside edition). Boston: Houghton Mifflin, 1961, pp. v-xix. Reprinted in *A Century of George Eliot Criticism.* Edited by Gordon S. Haight. Boston: Houghton Mifflin, 1965, pp. 339–348.

Hardy, Barbara. "*The Mill on the Floss*," in *Critical Essays on George Eliot.* Edited by Barbara Hardy. New York: Barnes & Noble, 1970, pp. 42–58.

Higdon, David Leon. "Failure of Design in *The Mill on the Floss*," in *Journal of Narrative Technique.* III (1973), pp. 183–192.

Jones, R.T. *George Eliot.* Cambridge: Cambridge University Press, 1970, pp. 19–30.

Knoepflmacher, Ulrich Camillus. *George Eliot's Early Novels.* Berkeley: University of California Press, 1968, pp. 162–220.

————. *Laughter and Despair: Readings in Ten Novels of the Victorian Age.* Berkeley: University of California Press, 1971, pp. 109–136.

Levine, George. "Intelligence as Deception: *The Mill on the Floss*," in *PMLA.* LXXX (September, 1965), pp. 402–409. Reprinted in *George Eliot: A Collection of Critical Essays.* Edited by George R. Creeger. Englewood Cliffs, N.J.: Prentice-Hall, 1970, pp. 107–123.

Liddell, Robert. *The Novels of George Eliot.* New York: St. Martin's, 1977, pp. 51–71

Molstad, David. "*The Mill on the Floss* and *Antigone*," in *PMLA.* LXXXV (1970), pp. 527–531.

Paris, Bernard J. *A Psychological Approach to Fiction: Studies in Thackeray, Stendhal, George Eliot, Dostoevsky, and Conrad.* Bloomington: Indiana University Press, 1974, pp. 165–189.

————. "Toward a Revaluation of George Eliot's *The Mill on the Floss*," in *Nineteenth-Century Fiction.* XI (June, 1956), pp. 18–31.

Roberts, Neil. *George Eliot: Her Beliefs and Her Art.* Pittsburgh: University of Pittsburgh Press, 1975, pp. 85–106.

Thale, Jerome. *The Novels of George Eliot.* New York: Columbia University Press, 1959, pp. 36–57.

Williams, Ioan. *The Realist Novel in England: A Study in Development.* London: Macmillan, 1974, pp. 178–182.

EDWARD FITZGERALD

Born: Near Woodbridge, England (March 31, 1809)
Died: Merton, Norfolk, England (June 14, 1883)

Principal Works

BELLES-LETTRES: *Euphranor: A Dialogue on Youth,* 1851.

TRANSLATIONS: *Six Dramas of Calderón,* 1853; *The Rubáiyát of Omar Khayyám,* 1859 (revised 1868, 1872, 1879); Aeschylus' *Agamemnon,* 1865; Sophocles' *Oedipus Rex* and *Oedipus at Colonus,* 1880–1881.

Born in Suffolk on March 31, 1809, into a prosperous family originally named Purcell, Edward FitzGerald was able, after his graduation from Trinity College, Cambridge, to devote his life to study, literary dabbling, and the pursuits of a country gentleman. In his Suffolk home he took up the study of Greek, Spanish, and Persian. He became the friend of Tennyson, Thackeray, and Carlyle; but was the object of a bitter poem by Browning occasioned by a slurring reference on FitzGerald's part to Mrs. Browning's death and her novel in verse, *Aurora Leigh.*

FitzGerald's translations—or rather, free adaptations—from the Greek and Spanish are of no literary interest. It was his version of the eleventh century Persian philosopher, scientist, and poet Omar that made him famous. Following his usual method, he adapted rather than translated, until the result was almost an original poem. At first the book had no sale; but in 1860 it was accidentally discovered by Rossetti, who showed it to Swinburne and others. Its reputation rapidly spread; revised versions were published; and by the end of the century it was the most quoted poem in English. Its haunting music and its facile Epicureanism made it popular among a generation that had wearied of Victorian moralizing. It has become trite through excessive quotation, yet some of its lines have become part of every man's literary heritage. FitzGerald died at Merton, England, on June 14, 1883.

Bibliography

The Letters and Literary Remains of Edward FitzGerald were edited by William A. Wright, 7 vols., 1902–1903. A recent edition of the letters was edited by J. M. Cohen, 1960. The standard biography is Thomas Wright, *The Life of Edward FitzGerald,* 2 vols., 1904. See also Arthur C. Benson, *Edward FitzGerald,* 1905; Morley Adams, *Omar's Interpreter: A New Life of Edward FitzGerald,* 1909; Alfred M. Terhune, *The Life of Edward FitzGerald,* 1947; Peter DePolmay, *The Paradox of Edward FitzGerald,* 1950; and Arthur J. Arberry, *The Romance of the Rubáiyát,* 1959.

THE RUBÁIYÁT OF OMAR KHAYYÁM

Type of work: Philosophical poem
Translator: Edward FitzGerald (1809–1883)
First published: 1859

Essay-Review

> Awake! for Morning in the Bowl of Night
> Has flung the Stone that puts the Stars to Flight:
> And Lo! the Hunter of the East has caught
> The Sultan's Turret in a Noose of Light.

Thus did Edward FitzGerald, a shy dilettante living in the Victorian Age, open the first edition of what he called his "transmutation" of the quatrains of Omar Khayyám, a Persian mathematician and poet of the eleventh century. So striking are these opening lines, which flash like the rays of the morning sun, it seems almost incredible that anyone could read them and not wish to continue; but FitzGerald's poem, unsigned and privately printed, mouldered in bookshops for years, even though the price dropped to a penny a copy. Not until Dante Gabriel Rossetti stumbled on the poem, realized its worth, and began quoting from it in the proper literary circles did *The Rubáiyát* start its upward climb to great popularity. Fearful that its epicurian flavor would prove too spicy for prudish Victorians, FitzGerald did not allow his name to be associated with the poem during his lifetime. Only the fifth edition, published six years after his death in 1883, gives him credit for taking Omar's random verses and turning them into a poem that has shape, vitality, and a lyrical frivolity. Even after the poem had become famous, a theory was seriously advanced that it was all symbolical, that when Omar mentioned "Wine" he really meant "the Divinity." Such a theory seems as hard to swallow as the one which makes a religious allegory out of the "Song of Solomon." FitzGerald finally won out over the Victorians; by 1900 admirers of *The Rubáiyát* had become a cult. Not so lucky had been Omar himself, for he too had to run counter to a trend: the ancient Persians believed that poetry must have mysticism to be of value; *The Rubáiyát* was so worldly that it told them bluntly to eat, drink, and be just as merry as possible. Thus Omar died unpraised and not until more than seven centuries later, when he was "reincarnated" in FitzGerald, did the world hail his philosophy.

Following the opening quatrain, *The Rubáiyát* quickly establishes that philosophy, for as soon as the cock crows some people standing in front of a tavern demand that the door be opened so that they may drink their wine immediately. Such is the theme of the poem: life is short; therefore, you must put no dependence in Tomorrow or the Hereafter, but must seize on Today with all its sensory pleasures. FitzGerald plays variations on this theme for more than a hundred quatrains, and among these are some of the most-quoted stanzas in English literature; for instance, those concerned with "the Bird of Time," with the celebrated "Book of Verses underneath the Bough," with the "batter'd Caravanserai," with "so red the Rose," and with the "Moving Finger." But *The Rubáiyát* is not haphazardly thrown together. It flows smoothly from the praising of wine to the disparagement of logic and wisdom; then from the spoofing of the ordinary conception of Divinity to the finality of death, that simple end to revelry.

One of the most interesting sections, though not the most lyrical, is the group of related stanzas dealing with the Potter and the Pots. Some of the Pots are "loquacious Vessels" and what they say reveals a thought-provoking if somewhat skeptical attitude toward life, the Creator, and death. The first vessel complains that surely the earth will not be molded into a figure and then broken or trampled back to earth again. A second says that since a "peevish Boy" would not break a bowl from which he had drunk with pleasure, the Potter will certainly not in wrath destroy what He created. Then follow these stanzas:

> After a momentary silence spake
> Some Vessel of a more ungainly Make:
>   "They sneer at me for leaning all awry;
> What! did the Hand then of the Potter shake?"
>
> Whereat someone of the loquacious Lot—
> I think a Súfi pipkin—waxing hot—
>   "All this of Pot and Potter—Tell me, then,
> Who is the Potter, pray, and who the Pot?"
>
> "Why," said another, "Some there are who tell
> Of one who threatens he will toss to Hell
>   The luckless Pots he marr'd in making—Pish!
> He's a Good Fellow, and 'twill all be well."

FitzGerald (or Omar) cannot be taken seriously as a destroyer of faith or as a radical philosopher. He is too light-hearted to be accused of inducing corruption. And when *The Rubáiyát* is looked at closely, one becomes aware that there are really no new ideas here; it has all been said before. Certainly this poem and Gray's "Elegy Written in a Country Churchyard" are highly dissimilar, but in one respect they are alike: both FitzGerald and Gray have taken a series of platitudes, strung them together, and created tremendously effective poems because the words and music blend together so appropriately. Gray's music is slow and stately, a funeral march; FitzGerald sings like a skylark that has become tipsy from eating fermented cherries:

> You know, my Friends, with what a brave Carouse
> I made a Second Marriage in my house;
>   Divorced old barren Reason from my Bed,
> And took the Daughter of the Vine to Spouse.

The meter of these lines is plain iambic pentameter, but somehow the unrhymed third line makes each stanza spill into the next, as one might pour wine rapidly from one cup to another. The alliteration and the adroit use of internal part-rhyme (such as "barren Reason") increase the musical effect. And FitzGerald's diction is so fresh, so pert, that *The Rubáiyát* may never become dated, may always sound as if it were written yesterday or (more in the FitzGerald spirit) Today.

In any long poem there are bound to be passages that come as a letdown; *The Rubáiyát* is no exception. A goodly number of its stanzas can be passed over without loss to the reader and even some of the better and best ones are repetitive. In spite of these minor objections *The Rubáiyát* glitters with joy, especially so when one considers it as a product of the Victorian Age, which took itself so seriously. Two fine poets of that era have written poems in which they give their ideas on death. Tennyson's death-poem is, of course, the simple and moving "Crossing the Bar"; in "Prospice" Browning envisions the end of life as a last battle to be won, a fighting-through to heaven. Measured against these two great poems, the final stanza of *The Rubáiyát* may seem flippant, but its very flippancy makes it equally as memorable:

> And when like her, oh Sáki, you shall pass
> Among the Guests Star-scatter'd on the Grass,
>   And in your joyous errand reach the spot
> Where I made One—turn down an empty Glass!

Bibliography

Adams, Morley. *Omar's Interpreter: A New Life of Edward FitzGerald.* London: Priory Press Hampstead, 1911, pp. 141–150.

Bagley, F.R. "Omar Khayyám and FitzGerald," in *Durham University Journal.* XXVIII (1967), pp. 81–93.

Cadbury, William. "FitzGerald's *Rubáiyát* as a Poem," in *Journal of English Literary History.* XXXIV (1967), pp. 541–563.

De Polnay, Peter. *Into an Old Room: A Memoir of Edward FitzGerald.* New York: Creative Age Press, 1949, pp. 207–256.

Draper, John W. "FitzGerald's Persian Local Color," in *West Virginia University Philological Papers.* XIV (1963), pp. 26–56.

Fairchild, Hoxie Neale. *Religious Trends in English Poetry: Volume IV, 1830–1880.* New York: Colgate University Press, 1957, pp. 421–425.

Jewett, Iran B. Hassani. *Edward FitzGerald.* Boston: Twayne, 1967, pp. 73–111.

Richardson, Joanna. *Edward FitzGerald.* London: Longmans, Green, 1960.

Shojai, D.A. "The Structure of FitzGerald's *Rubáiyát of Omar Khayyám*," in *Papers of the Michigan Academy of Science, Arts, and Letters.* LII (1967), pp. 369–382.

Sonstroem, David. "Abandon the Day: FitzGerald's *Rubáiyát of Omar Khayyám*," in *Victorian Newsletter.* XXXVI (1969), pp. 10–13.

Terhune, Alfred McKinley. *The Life of Edward FitzGerald, Translator of* The Rubáiyát of Omar Khayyám. New Haven, Conn.: Yale University Press, 1947, pp. 204–232.

Yohannan, John D. "The Fin de Siecle Cult of FitzGerald's *Rubáiyát of Omar Khayyám*," in *Review of National Literatures.* II (1971), pp. 74–91.

THOMAS HARDY

Born: Higher Bockhampton, England (June 2, 1840)
Died: Dorchester, England (January 11, 1928)

Principal Works

NOVELS: *Desperate Remedies*, 1871; *Under the Greenwood Tree*, 1872; *A Pair of Blue Eyes*, 1873; *Far from the Madding Crowd*, 1874; *The Hand of Ethelberta*, 1876; *The Return of the Native*, 1878; *The Trumpet-Major*, 1880; *A Laodicean*, 1881; *Two on a Tower*, 1882; *The Mayor of Casterbridge*, 1886; *The Woodlanders*, 1887; *Tess of the d'Urbervilles*, 1891; *Jude the Obscure*, 1895; *The Well-Beloved*, 1897.

SHORT STORIES: *Wessex Tales*, 1888; *A Group of Noble Dames*, 1891; *Life's Little Ironies*, 1894; *A Changed Man*, 1913.

POEMS: *Wessex Poems*, 1898; *Poems of the Past and the Present*, 1901; *Time's Laughingstocks*, 1909; *Satires of Circumstance*, 1914; *Moments of Vision*, 1917; *Late Lyrics and Earlier*, 1922; *Human Shows, Far Phantasies, Songs and Trifles*, 1925; *Winter Words*, 1928; *Collected Poems*, 1931.

PLAYS: *The Dynasts: A Drama in Three Parts*, 1903, 1906, 1908; *The Famous Tragedy of the Queen of Cornwall*, 1923.

MISCELLANEOUS: *Life and Art*, 1925; *Letters: Transcribed from the Original Autographs in the Colby College Library*, 1954.

About three miles east of Dorchester, in Dorset, England, there is a hamlet known as Higher Bockhampton. In a thatched-roof cottage which still stands at one end of this hamlet, Thomas Hardy was born on June 2, 1840. The place of his birth is important, for it is the center of a region he learned to know and love—a region he called "Wessex" and wrote about in all his books.

The first of these books was published in 1871 when Hardy was nearly thirty-one years old and was still lacking in literary training and experience. His entire schooling had been confined to eight years between the ages of eight and sixteen. For five years he had worked as an apprentice in the drafting office of a Dorchester architect, John Hicks. When Hardy was twenty-one he went to London and found employment with Arthur Blomfield, a successful metropolitan architect, and remained with him for five years. But Gothic churchs and old manor houses never succeeded in crowding books out of the central place in Hardy's affections. During his years in London, he tried his hand at composing verses, and when he discovered that editors showed no readiness to publish his poems, he turned at the age of twenty-seven to novel-writing.

Hardy called his first attempt at fiction *The Poor Man and the Lady*. He sent his manuscript to Alexander Macmillan, the London publisher, who replied encouragingly but found too many faults in the work to be willing to print it. Hardy thereupon tried a second publisher, Chapman & Hall, and was fortunate enough to have his manuscript placed in the hands of their reader, George Meredith, the novelist. Meredith had an interview with Hardy and advised him to suppress *The Poor Man* (because of the vehemence of its social satire) and to write another novel "with more plot." Hardy took Meredith's advice and wrote *Desperate Remedies*, which was published anonymously and at his own expense in 1871. This was the beginning of a quarter-century's activity as one of the most successful and influential novelists that England has produced.

Like *Desperate Remedies*, Hardy's next novel, *Under the Greenwood Tree*, was published anonymously. In 1872 he was invited to contribute a story for serialization in *Tinsleys' Magazine* and this novel, *A Pair of Blue Eyes* (1873), was the first to carry his name. When *Far from the Madding Crowd* was serialized in the *Cornhill Magazine* in 1874, the acclaim from critics as well as from the general public was cordial enough to encourage Hardy to do three things: he discarded further use of anonymity, he gave up all further practice as an architect, and in September, 1874, he married.

In the twenty years that followed, Hardy turned out ten more full-length novels, besides numerous short stories and articles. His fourteenth and last novel, *Jude the Obscure*, resulted in such an outcry that Hardy, always oversensitive to criticism, shrank from further attempt to find expression in fiction and returned to his first love, poetry. In 1898 he surprised the world by publishing *Wessex Poems*, and throughout the next thirty years he produced volume after volume of verse until, by the time of his death, he had composed nearly a thousand poems. In addition to this achievement in metrical composition, Hardy wrote a gigantic dramatic epic on the Napoleonic wars which he called *The Dynasts* (published in three parts, 1904, 1906, 1908).

As stated above, Hardy's success with *Far from the Madding Crowd* enabled him to marry. He had met Emma L. Gifford, the young lady who became his wife, when he had gone to Cornwall in 1870 to supervise the restoration of a dilapidated church. Ten years after this marriage, he built a house near Dorchester, and from 1885 on, his address remained "Max Gate." He had no children. Mrs. Hardy died in 1912 and was buried in the country churchyard beside the Stinsford parish church which Hardy had attended as a boy. He had these words carved on her tombstone: "This for remembrance." The reader interested in the significance of this inscription should examine Hardy's poignant "Poems of 1912–1913" in his volume, *Satires of Circumstance, Lyrics and Reveries*.

In 1914 Hardy married again. Florence Emily Dugdale, who had helped him with research on *The Dynasts*, became the second Mrs. Hardy. When Hardy died, on January 11, 1928, burial in the Poets' Corner in Westminster Abbey was offered, but there were many people who felt that an author whose heart had always been with Wessex folk among Wessex scenes ought not to have that heart carried off to alien soil. Hardy's heart was accordingly buried in the grave of his first wife at Stinsford, while his ashes were deposited next to those of Charles Dickens in Westminster Abbey.

In the course of the three decades that followed Hardy's death, there came to be general critical agreement that his literary output was of very uneven quality. Some of his novels are excellent, others are mediocre, or worse; and many of his poems have seemed harsh and unmusical, even to modern ears attuned to the discordant. But a reading of Hardy's best novels and a study of his best poems will show the same gifted author at work in both. There is the same attentive eye for nature in all seasons and in her moods, the same tender, sympathetic heart, and the same sorrowing mind. In studying this record of Hardy's earlier years, the reader should avoid making the all-too-common mistake of thinking that his novels were all written from a single, unchanging point of view. Hardy grew and developed, his philosophy of life matured, and the novels show this development. *Far from the Madding Crowd*, and *The Return of the Native* are the most "fatalistic" (to use an overworked word that needs strict definition); *The Mayor of Casterbridge*, in which Hardy quotes "Character is Fate," marks a distinct shift in his viewpoint; and *The Woodlanders, Tess of the d'Urbervilles*, and *Jude the Obscure* are all three written by an older author with a riper social outlook and a clearer understanding of the causes of human unhappiness. The reader who grasps this immense advance on Hardy's part over the fragile charm of *Under the Greenwood Tree* will have no difficulty in understanding why, when John Dewey was asked to name, among books published in the last fifty years, the twenty-five which he regarded as the most influential, he put *Tess of the d'Urbervilles* first among English novels, or why Henry C. Duffin, when appraising the entire literary career of the Wessex author, called *Jude the Obscure* "the greatest of Hardy's novels."

Bibliography

For balanced judgment Carl J. Weber's *Hardy of Wessex: His Life and Literary Career*, 1940, is still the outstanding critical biography among the great quantity of Hardy studies. Other important biographies include Florence Hardy, *The Early Life of Thomas Hardy, 1840–1891*, 1928; Florence Hardy, *The Later Years of Thomas Hardy, 1892–1928*, 1930; Evelyn Hardy, *Thomas Hardy: A Critical Biography*, 1954; Irving Howe, *Thomas Hardy*, 1968; J. I. M. Stewart, *Thomas Hardy: A Critical Biography*, 1971; J. Hollis Miller, *Thomas Hardy: His Career as a Novelist*, 1971; F. E. Halliday, *Thomas Hardy: His Life and Work*, 1972; Robert Gittings, *Young Thomas Hardy* 1975; Desmond Hawkins, *Thomas Hardy*, 1976; Norman Page, *Thomas Hardy*, 1977; and Lance St. John Butler, *Thomas Hardy*, 1978.

Among the earlier but still useful critical studies see Lascelles Abercrombie, *Thomas Hardy: A Critical Study*, 1912; J. W. Beach, *The Technique of Thomas Hardy*, 1922; Ernest Brennecke, *Thomas Hardy's Universe*, 1924; H. B. Grimsditch, *Character and Environment in the Novels of Thomas Hardy*, 1925; Mary Ellen Chase, *Thomas Hardy: From Serial to Novel*, 1927; Samuel C. Chew, *Thomas Hardy: Poet and Novelist*, 1928; A. S. McDowell, *Thomas Hardy:*

A Critical Study, 1931; and Lord David Cecil, *Hardy the Novelist*, 1946. Modern Hardy studies began in the late 1940's with H. C. Webster, *On a Darkling Plain*, 1947; and Albert J. Guerard, *Thomas Hardy: The Novels and Stories*, 1949. See also Carl J. Weber, *Hardy in America*, 1952; J. Hollis Miller, *Thomas Hardy, Distance and Desire*, 1970; Perry Meisel, *Thomas Hardy: The Return of the Repressed—A Study of the Major Fiction*, 1972; Dale Kramer, *Thomas Hardy: The Forms of Tragedy*, 1974; F. B. Pinion, *Thomas Hardy and the Modern World*, 1974; Margaret Drabble, ed., *The Genius of Thomas Hardy* (a collection of essays), 1976; and F. B. Pinion, *Budmouth Essays on Thomas Hardy*, 1976.

For poetry studies see Sameul L. Hynes, *The Pattern of Hardy's Poetry*, 1961; Kenneth Marsden, *The Poems of Thomas Hardy: A Critical Interpretation*, 1969; J. O. Bailey, *The Poetry of Thomas Hardy: A Handbook and Commentary*, 1971; Chester A. Garrison, *The Vast Venture: Hardy's Epic-Drama The Dynasts*, 1972; Donald Davie, *Thomas Hardy and English Poetry*, 1972; Tom Paulin, *Thomas Hardy: The Poetry of Perception*, 1975; and James Richardson, *Thomas Hardy: The Poetry of Necessity*, 1977.

Among the useful specialized studies see Herman Lea, *Thomas Hardy's Wessex*, 1913; the Thomas Hardy Centennial Issue of *The Southern Review*, V (1940), which contains articles on Hardy by Allen Tate, Jacques Barzun, and other critics; Carl J. Weber, *The First Hundred Years of Thomas Hardy, 1840–1940: A Centenary Bibliography of Hardiana*, 1942; Carl J. Weber, *Hardy Letters*, 1954; Reginald G. Cox, ed., *Thomas Hardy: The Critical Heritage*, 1970; Frank R. Southerington, *Hardy's Vision of Man*, 1971; Merryn Williams, *Thomas Hardy and Rural England*, 1972; Glenda Leeming, *Who's Who in Thomas Hardy*, 1975; J. T. Laird, *The Shaping of Tess of the d'Urbervilles*, 1975; R. P. Draper, ed., *Hardy, The Tragic Novels: A Casebook*, 1975; and Lance St. John Butler, ed., *Thomas Hardy after Fifty Years* (collection of articles), 1978.

THE DYNASTS

Type of work: Verse drama
Author: Thomas Hardy (1840–1928)
Type of plot: Historical epic
Time of plot: 1806–1815
Locale: Europe
First published: 1903–1908

Written in a variety of verse forms as well as poetic prose, The Dynasts *is a vast, panoramic drama of the years of Napoleon's domination of Europe. Hardy's intention is to depict mankind as powerless against the forces of Destiny. Both the drastic switching of points of view and settings—from extraterrestrial space to emperors' courts to cottagers' firesides—and the array of allegorical spectators who comment on the events of the drama, make the alarms and skirmishes of man seem trivial.*

Principal Characters

Napoleon Bonaparte, portrayed by Hardy as a man driven by an inscrutable fate and conscious of his ability to master Europe. He is a great leader, at times impatient with his subordinates' abilities. Above all, he wants to found a new dynasty to rank with the established royal families of Europe. Disappointed in his negotiations with Tsar Alexander for the hand of a Russian princess, he turns to the defeated Emperor Francis of Austria, who gives him the hand of Marie Louise for his second wife after Napoleon has divorced the unfortunate Empress Josephine because of her failure to provide an heir. Even though defeated by the Austrians and Prussians at Leipzig, Napoleon does not lose his sense of destiny. Exiled to Elba, he returns for the famous Hundred Days, only to be defeated a second time at Waterloo. His efforts are finally compared by the Spirit of Years, who sees all of history, to the struggles of an insect upon a leaf. Napoleon fluttered many lives and caused great slaughter, all for nothing.

Josephine, Napoleon's first wife, who cannot believe it is truly her fault that she bears no children, even though Napoleon points to bastard children as proof of his own potency in the marriage bed. Despite her protests and tears, for she truly loves her husband, Josephine is forced to consent to make way for Marie Louise.

Marie Louise, Princess of Austria and a pawn of circumstances and politics. She is married to Napoleon to help save Austria from conquest. Eventually she bears a son to Napoleon, though almost at the sacrifice of her own life. When Napoleon is defeated and exiled to Elba, Marie Louise and her small son, styled the King of Rome, go to her native Austria for asylum.

George III, King of England. He is shown first, in 1805, as a robust monarch watching preparations being made along the English coast to meet the expected French invasion. Later King George is shown at the age of seventy-two, shortly before his death, at the mercy of his physicians, who bleed him, drug him, and give him cold-water treatments in cruel, though well-meaning, fashion.

From the state of a monarch he is reduced to the condition of a pathetic mental case who stands as a living symbol between the Prince Regent and the British throne.

Tsar Alexander of Russia, portrayed as a self-seeking monarch who looks down on Napoleon as an upstart, despite the friendship he expresses for Napoleon and the French at the famous meeting between Alexander and Napoleon on a raft in the middle of the River Niemen.

The Emperor Francis of Austria, a monarch forced, against his judgment as a father, to deliver up Marie Louise as Napoleon's second wife. This alliance is concluded after Napoleon has dictated bitter terms following the defeat of the Austrian and Russian forces at Austerlitz.

Sir William Pitt, the energetic Prime Minister of England, who struggles to save his country and Europe from Napoleon. In 1805, Pitt works manfully against isolationist members of the Parliament to provide for the defense of England. Later he works even harder to enlist the Continent against Napoleon. Weakened in health, he continues his political struggles, even though George III refuses to permit a coalition government.

Charles James Fox, Prime Minister after Sir William Pitt. Fox tries to negotiate with Napoleon, even to warning Bonaparte of an attempt at assassination. Unfortunately for Fox, his sincere efforts at negotiation are used by Napoleon to screen his plotting against Prussia.

Lord Horatio Nelson, the famous British Admiral who defeated the naval forces of Napoleon at the Battle of Trafalgar and thus saved his country from invasion. A man of great courage and hardihood, he paces the deck of his flagship in a bright uniform until cut down by a musket shot during the battle.

Admiral Villeneuve, Napoleon's naval planner, who works against the odds of poor ships and equipment to forge a fighting navy for his master. When his best efforts meet defeat at Trafalgar, he stabs himself to death at an inn.

The Immanent Will, the force Thomas Hardy saw as the power or energy behind the workings of the universe. Because it is blind and uncreative in any rational sense, Hardy terms the force It, rather than He.

The Spirit of Years, the oldest of the allegorical spirits introduced by Hardy to give "The Dynasts" a sense of panorama and perspective. The Spirit of Years is the leader among the other spirits, chastening them and dampening their enthusiasms when necessary.

The Spirit of Pities, a spirit of the universal spirit of human nature. This allegorical figure is an idealized human spectator, the chief commentator for the author on the events described.

The Spirit Sinister, a savage allegorical spirit who rejoices in the carnage and the evil displayed during the Napoleonic era.

The Spirit Ironic, an allegorical spirit who comments on the irony, sometimes tragic, sometimes humorous, as the events of the drama unfold.

The Story

The Spirit of Years, Shade of Earth, Spirit Sinister, Spirit Ironic, Spirit of Pities, and their accompanying choruses, forgathered somewhere above the earth to watch the larger movements of men in western Europe in 1805. The design of the Immanent Will manifested itself at the time in Napoleon's preparations for the invasion of England.

Sir William Pitt, in England, contended with isolationist members of Parliament in order to secure proper defense against the invasion. Meanwhile Napoleon went to Milan to be crowned King of Italy. The spirits made light of the chicanery and pomp that attended the coronation. The Spirit of Pities descended to earth and disturbed Napoleon by reminding him of his original intention of championing liberty.

At sea, a Pyrrhic victory of the French and Spanish over the English prevented the support required for the planned invasion. On the south coast of England the Phantoms of Rumor caused great disturbance. A fleet of fishing craft was mistaken for the invasion fleet, and civilians fled from the coastal towns as signal fires flared upon the cliffs and hills.

When Napoleon learned that his admiral, Villeneuve, had returned to Cadiz, he discarded his invasion plan and moved eastward against Austria and Russia, countries which Pitt had enlisted in the English cause. The Spirit of Years remarked that the ensuing campaign would be a model in tactics for all time.

At Ulm, Napoleon defeated the Austrians, who had hoped in vain that the English fleet would hold the French forces in northern France. In London, Pitt, unsuccessful in gaining permission from the king to form a coalition government, visibly declined in health under his terrible burden.

Villeneuve was ordered out of Cadiz. The British under Nelson met the French and Spanish off Trafalgar and defeated them. Nelson was killed in the engagement; Villeneuve subsequently ended his own life in an inn at Rennes.

Napoleon defeated the Austrians and Russians at Austerlitz. Then, hearing of the English victory at Trafalgar, he declared his intention of closing all continental ports to English ships. He dictated peace terms to Emperor Francis of Austria while attendant Austrian officers stood by in disgust at the sight of a nobody dictating to true royalty. In Paris the Spirit of Rumor commented on the way Napoleon was uprooting old dynasties and founding new ones.

Pitt having died and King George III being mentally ill, England, in the person of Charles James Fox, negotiated with Napoleon for peace; but the emperor used the negotiations as a screen for his real plans. He marched on Prussia and defeated the Germans at the Battle of Jena. In Berlin he decreed that all British ships were barred from continental ports. Next, Napoleon and Tsar Alexander of Russia met at the River Niemen, where the two drew up a Franco-Russian alliance. During this meeting Napoleon expressed the desire to cement his various alliances with blood ties. The Spirit of Years remarked ironically that Napoleon was one of the few men who could see the working of the Immanent Will.

Napoleon invaded Spain as a friend to help the Spanish gain Portugal. The Spanish Bourbons abdicated and Napoleon's brother, Joseph, was proclaimed king. When Bourbon partisans enlisted English aid, an English invasion fleet sailed for Portugal.

Back in Paris, Napoleon told his wife, Josephine, that he wished a divorce. Josephine had borne the emperor no children and he was anxious to perpetuate the dynasty he had founded. The British invasion of the Iberian Peninsula drew the emperor to Spain to direct the campaign there. Preparation for war in Austria caused Napoleon next to invade that country and to defeat its forces at Wagram. The British, under the Duke of Wellington, held their own against the French in Spain. At that point the Spirit Sinister reminded the Spirit Ironic not to sneer for fear Immanent Will would cut short the comedy that was taking place.

A British force was sent to the Scheldt, but the expedition ended disastrously when the army was decimated by miasmal fever. Napoleon, fearful of assassination and still anxious to perpetuate his line, negotiated with the Russians for the hand of a Russian princess, and with the Austrians for the hand of Princess Marie Louise. The tsar accepted the offer, but Napoleon had already arranged, through Metternich, for a marriage with the Austrian princess, Marie Louise. The marriage was performed in the conspicuous absence of many high clergy, and the Russians, incensed, prepared for war. In the meantime the British in Spain under the Duke of Wellington gained a decisive victory at Albuera.

In due time Marie Louise gave birth to Napoleon's heir. The insane King of England died after hearing of British successes in Spain. On the continent war became imminent between France and Russia.

Again on the banks of the Niemen, Napoleon received an evil portent when he was thrown from his horse. The Spirit of Pities foresaw misery for the French Grand Army in the Russian campaign. Wellington in Spain defeated the French at Salamanca. Napoleon gained a costly victory over the Russians at Borodino, and the French entered Moscow to find the city deserted and in flames. There followed a general retreat by the French across snow-covered Russian steppes to Lithuania. Thousands perished from the cold or were killed by harassing Russian cavalry. Napoleon deserted his army and raced back to Paris in order to arrive there before the news of his failure in Russia. His chief task now was to hold his empire together.

As the British continued their successes in Spain, Austria joined the allies. Napoleon met defeat at the hands of the Austrians and Prussians at Leipzig. The allies invaded France. Napoleon, forced to abdicate, was exiled to Elba, an island in the Mediterranean. Marie Louise and the infant King of Rome went to Austria to stay. The Bourbons reassumed the throne of France and a congress to deliberate on general peace in Europe met in Vienna.

Napoleon escaped from Elba and returned to Paris at the head of an army he had picked up on his way. The allies outlawed Napoleon and prepared to overthrow him again.

A private ball in Brussels was broken up by the news that the French army was nearing the Belgian frontier. Almost overnight, Napoleon had organized and put into the field a large army. But he failed to separate the British and Prussians in Belgium, and he was brought to utter defeat on the fields south of Waterloo. The Hundred Days were ended.

The Spirit of Years pointed out to the Spirits assembled that the human beings below them behaved as though they were in a dream, as though they were puppets being drawn by strings manipulated by Immanent Will. The Spirit of Years pointed to Napoleon in defeat and compared him to a tiny insect on an obscure leaf in the chart of the Ages. When the Spirit of Pities asked for what purpose the events below had taken place, the Spirit of Irony answered that there was no purpose, for only a dumb thing turned the crank which motivated and directed human behavior.

Critical Evaluation

The Dynasts represents Hardy's most ambitious attempt to portray his philosophic fatalism. An epic-drama written for "mental performance," it combines the skills of Hardy, the novelist with those of Hardy, the poet. Hardy's ability to tell a story is nowhere more apparent than here, and his drama, with its scenes of battle, court life, and common life, anticipates the great motion picture spectacles of such directors as D. W. Griffith. At the same time there are powerful lines and much extremely competent verse which make the stuff of poetry.

Unlike the great Victorian long poems, Hardy's poetic drama deals with recent events. As in his novels, Hardy is concerned with the plight of the common man in an indifferent world. But, unlike in his novels, he is concerned also with potentates, whose will often seems to control the lives of common men and women. This, however, is an illusion, for even the great are moved by the Immanent Will, an impassive, unmotivated force, which at one point is described as having "films or brain-tissue" which "pervade all things." In his final defeat, Napoleon himself comes to acknowledge that he has always "passively obeyed" this Will. His gradual physical deterioration symbolizes his spiritual decay.

The Dynasts is also implicitly antiwar in its vivid portrayal of the carnage that always accompanies war. It is a democratic drama, holding up parliamentary government as preferable to rule by monarchical fiat. And it is a very English work, portraying even the typical English xenophobia. In spite of the gloom that pervades *The Dynasts,* there are moments of humor, and Hardy permits the Chorus of the Spirit of Pities to have the last, semi-hopeful word.

Bibliography

Bailey, J.O. *Thomas Hardy and the Cosmic Mind: A New Reading of* The Dynasts. Chapel Hill: University of North Carolina Press, 1956.

Carpenter, Richard C. *Thomas Hardy*. New York: Twayne, 1964, pp. 185–201.

Chakravarty, Amiya C. The Dynasts *and the Post-War Age in Poetry*. London: Oxford University Press, 1938.

Church, Richard. "Thomas Hardy as Revealed in *The Dynasts*," in *Essays by Divers Hands; Being the Transactions of the Royal Society of Literature*, Volume XXIX. Edited by E.V. Rieu. New York: Oxford University Press, 1958, pp. 1–17.

Clifford, Emma. "The Impressionistic View of History in *The Dynasts*," in *Modern Language Quarterly*. XXII (March, 1961), pp. 21–31.

Dean, Susan. *Hardy's Poetic Vision in* The Dynasts: *The Diorama of a Dream*. Princeton, N.J.: Princeton University Press, 1977.

Dobrée, Bonamy. "*The Dynasts*," in *Southern Review*. VI (Summer, 1940), pp. 109–124.

Duffin, Henry C. *Thomas Hardy: A Study of the Wessex Novels, Poems and* The Dynasts. Manchester, England: Manchester University Press, 1937.

Gittings, Robert. *Thomas Hardy's Later Years*. Boston: Little, Brown, 1978, pp. 106–116.

Hynes, Samuel. *The Pattern of Hardy's Poetry*. Chapel Hill: University of North Carolina Press, 1961, pp. 152–174.

Laird, John. "Hardy's *The Dynasts*," in his *Philosophical Incursions Into English Literature*. London: Cambridge University Press, 1946, pp. 187–204.

Mantripp, J.C. "Thomas Hardy's *The Dynasts*," in *Holborn Review*. LXX (April, 1928), pp. 157–168.

May, Charles E. "The Hero in Thomas Hardy's *The Dynasts*," in *Research Studies*. XL (1972), pp. 251–259.

Newbolt, Henry. "Notes on *The Dynasts*," in his *My World as in My Time*. London: Faber and Faber, 1932, pp. 282–299.

Orel, Harold. *Thomas Hardy's Epic Drama: A Study of* The Dynasts. Lawrence: University of Kansas Press, 1963.

Sherman, George W. *The Pessimism of Thomas Hardy*. Rutherford, N.J.: Fairleigh Dickinson University Press, 1976, pp. 289–403.

Stewart, Agnes. "*The Dynasts*: A Psychological Interpretation," in *English Review*. XXXVIII (May, 1924), pp. 666–680.

Thoules, Priscilla. *Modern Poetic Drama*. Oxford: Blackwell, 1934, pp. 115–125.

Wain, John. "Introduction," in The Dynasts: *An Epic-Drama of the War With Napoleon*. New York: St. Martin's, 1965, pp. v–xix.

Waldock, A.J.A. *Thomas Hardy and* The Dynasts. Sydney: Australian English Association, 1933. Reprinted in *James, Joyce and Others*. London: Williams and Norgate, 1937, pp. 53–78.

Whitmore, C.E. "Mr. Hardy's *Dynasts* as Tragic Drama," in *Modern Lan-*

guage Notes. XXXIX (December, 1924), pp. 455–460.

Wilson, K.G. "Hardy's *The Dynasts*: Some Problems of Interpretations," in *Colby Library Quarterly.* XII (1976), pp. 181–190.

Wing, George. *Thomas Hardy.* New York: Grove, 1963, pp. 80–85.

Wright, Walter F. *The Shaping of* The Dynasts. Lincoln: University of Nebraska Press, 1967.

THE POETRY OF HARDY

Author: Thomas Hardy (1840–1928)
First published: Wessex Poems and Other Verses, 1898; *Poems of the Past and the Present*, 1901; *Time's Laughingstocks and Other Verses*, 1909; *Satires of Circumstance*, 1914; *Moments of Vision*, 1917; *Late Lyrics and Earlier*, 1922; *Human Shows, Far Phantasies: Songs and Trifles*, 1925; *Winter Words*, 1928

Essay-Review

It is frequently said of Thomas Hardy that he turned to the writing of poetry as a result of his anger and disappointment at the shortsighted and discouraging critical response to his last novel, *Jude the Obscure*, which appeared in 1895. The truth of the matter appears to be that he had always preferred writing poetry to writing novels, and that he had written poetry before he presented himself to the reading public as a novelist and short story writer. He returned to his first love and decided to publish his poems only after he had established for himself a firm reputation as a novelist. Some of the verses which he included in his first volume of poems, *Wessex Poems*, had been composed more than thirty years before. He was then fifty-eight years old, and for the next thirty years he devoted himself exclusively to writing or rewriting his poems until his death in 1928.

His *Collected Poems* retains almost a thousand poems which had appeared in eight preceding volumes of verse. This number testifies to his affection for and dedication to poetry, but it is too large an output to allow him to maintain consistent excellence. A few, relative to the large total, must be deemed outright failures, deficient either because of metrical inconsistency or inappropriateness, eccentric, excessive inversion, awkward diction, or an imagery and idea of embarrassing sentimentality. At the other end of the spectrum of his achievement, however, there are a few poems, again relatively speaking, which are extremely successful and claim the right to a permanent place in the ideal anthology of great and memorable poems in the English language. These poems, together with the large number which are at least interesting and competent, constitute a respectable body of work worthy of attention and high regard.

As might be expected, Hardy's poetry complements and intensifies the unhappy vision of life depicted in most of his novels. Hardy protested in an introductory note to his final volume of poems, *Winter Words*, that he had not attempted to present a "harmonious philosophy" in that book or in any of his earlier poetic work. Despite these protestations, however, there can be no question that an easily discernible, special "Hardyesque" vision of life emerges from his poetry as well as from his prose. Cast in the form of imaginative art, it may not have the rigidity or discipline of what we call philosophy, but it offers, nevertheless, a very consistent, even relentless view of life as a series of adventures in frustration and defeat. Man as an individual, man as a creature of society and the cosmos, is simply acting out the whims and dictates of an inexorable life force, a blind, indifferent, neutral Immanent Will. Though the Will (variously called Fate, Chance, Hap, Destiny, and Necessity) is ostensibly neutral about man's fate, the general reality is that man usually becomes "time's laughstock," his efforts to achieve love and dignity and significance simply create "satires of circumstance." These concepts emerge so clearly and triumphantly from his novels and poems because, while they may be few and schematic, they were for him matters of fundamental, abiding concern, and he used them constantly as the basis and the framework of his vision.

The themes and the vision which emerge from the poetry are almost wholly clouded and pessimistic. This was the way Hardy himself summed up the consensus of many reviews of his poetical work ("Apology," *Late Lyrics and Earlier*) a judgment which he deemed "odd." But the real oddity is that he should think this judgment strange because there can be little question that the corpus of his work is in general and quite consistently dark and pessimistic. Hardy contended that the alleged pessimism was in truth a way of questioning and exploring the nature of reality, a first step, as he called it, toward the betterment of man's soul and body. To this end he quoted in his defense a line from an earlier poem, "In Tenebris":

If a way to the Better there be, it exacts a full look at the Worst:

a perspective which he labeled, perhaps in desperation, "evolutionary meliorism." To point a way to the Better may have been his intention, but the fact is that he succeeded all too well in giving us a full look at the Worst; in his poetry there is very little, indeed only the barest hint scattered here and there, about the way to the Better. What little there is stresses the conjectural "if" in his poetical statements and the many qualifications which abound in his prose clarification. In his poetry there is very little of loving-kindness operating through scientific or any other kind of knowledge, and what free will we can see apparently works to the detriment of all, victor and victim alike.

In form, the poetry is fairly conventional. Hardy frequently exploited the forms of folk tradition: popular ballads, hymns, country songs, but there are many sonnets, couplets, dramatic monologues, narratives, and conversational anecdotes. Most are poems with a plot; that is, Hardy develops his theme through a highly concentrated, epitomized dramatic situation. This method has the value of establishing a distance between Hardy the man and Hardy the poet. The poem may actually be the outpouring of Hardy's secret heart, but the externalized narrative or dramatic situation presents the theme in a way that detaches it from Hardy himself. The poems which are narrative monologues or dialogues, and there are many, are not concerned with the creation of character. They are concerned with presenting a view of the world, Hardy's "dramatic truth" for which the speakers or their situation are more or less the actors. There are a few (relatively speaking again) "philosophical" poems which deal directly and explicitly with Hardy's thesis. They represent only a small proportion of the total poetic production but they have attracted a disproportionate amount of attention precisely because their didactic and abstract quality, stripped of character and situation, reveals Hardy's viewpoint so clearly and starkly. Actually, they are like footnotes that clarify a text; if we want a fair characterization of the bulk of Hardy's poems we must not take the footnotes for the text.

The meters in many of the poems are not skillfully handled, especially in some poems which we know were of early composition. To the modern ear, there is a vaguely anachronistic quality about some of these poems, much of it sounding "poetical" in an old-fashioned way. There is some use of dialect terms, some word-coinages, a few obsolete words. On occasion, Hardy attracted too much attention to these words—most of them making for clumsy, gnarled lines—by inverting normal syntax for the sake of the regularity of his meter or to meet the demands of a rhyme. These inversions contribute to the artificial and contrived quality of his unsuccessful poems.

The basic theme of these varied forms and meters is the cruel irony of a universe which does not, and apparently cannot, answer man's desire, indeed, his hunger, for order, justice, equity, or even a rationale for his suffering. The forces or phenomena which oppose and frustrate man can be identified from the various forms—narratives, situations, characters, settings—through which this basic theme is illustrated and dramatized.

In Hardy's world time erodes and corrodes the promise of youth, talent, hope, beauty, freshness, enthusiasm, and vibrancy. Love, in time, wastes away simply by being. Dreams grow weak and vague in time and soon lose their ability to inspire. If they survive, it is only to stand in mocking contrast to the disappointing reality outside. The body weakens; eyes dim; beauty vanishes in time, and too soon: death.

Death always seems to come too early or too late to provide whatever relief it may have offered; or it takes away the wrong person, meaning the good, and spares the ne'er-do-well.

Sex is a powerful force which victimizes all; which betrays unmarried girls into bearing illegitimate children; which compels them to betray the men they love; which distracts young men from their rightful careers and rightful destinies; which breaks up families, defies the security of traditional mores, and frequently leads to crime.

Love is fleeting, short-lived, and vulnerable; easily swayed, tempted, diverted, betrayed or betraying. Love is best at a distance, whether of time or in space, best when unconsummated and only dreamed of. When realized, it withers. It is a trap for women who must marry the wrong man and yearn for another, and who must therefore live in spiritual infidelity.

Society is viewed either as a system of tradition or security that is rapidly disappearing, or as the embodiment of outmoded ideas which destroy true lovers whose natural passions have betrayed them into defying the code. The rich girl may love the poor boy who loves her, but they are doomed to part because of the class system of society.

War is senseless, vicious, and inhumane. Invariably it is fought bravely but in ignorance by its victims, leaving wives, illegitimate children, and betrayal behind. The settings for these poems are Greek wars, Roman wars, colonial wars, Continental wars, world wars, culminating in the bitter "Christmas: 1924."

Nature is generally seen as a powerful, blind force, an unknowing, well-intentioned, but blundering Mother, herself helpless in the grip of the heedless, inexorable Immanent Will. In the sense of the physical world about us, it is most often described as barren and bleak, shivering in the cold rain or snow or sleet, an outer weather to reflect the inner weather of the broken, desolate heart. If the scene is the beauty of spring or summer it is only to provide a mocking background to grief or to warn of the winter or death which lurks in or just behind the innocent beauty of the scene.

The setting for these experiences in frustration is frequently a graveyard, a sad, haunted house, an empty, crumbling church, or a desolate moor. Occasionally, we confront the whirling rapids of a river, suitable for a suicide or a killing. Sometimes it is a tavern where riotous drinking and dancing are betraying a young girl into straying, or a young wife into adultery.

Hardy's is a poetry of action and drama, rarely a poetry of mere description. It is not often a poetry of song, but a poetry which moves at the pace of thoughtful speech or spoken thought. If we follow a division of poetry which Hardy himself once made, we may say that his poetry falls roughly into four categories: (1) passionate poems—his ballads and narratives of ballad-like incident, (2) sentimental poems—his poems of recollection and nostalgia, poems about love and lovers, (3) meditative poems—his introspective, first-person monologues, (4) fanciful poems—his poems of philosophical dialogues with Nature and such Powers or his poems of conversations with ghosts. For the most part, in these poems, Nature complains, God argues, and Man questions. But these poems, like most of Hardy's poems, are designed to give dramatic identities and significances to the abstract idea that man, nature, and the universe are in the hands of the Immanent Will which operates powerfully but blindly, quite indifferent to the individual fate or destiny.

GERARD MANLEY HOPKINS

Born: Stratford, Essex, England (June 11, 1844)
Died: Dublin, Ireland (June 8, 1889)

Principal Works

POEMS: *Poems of Gerard Manley Hopkins, Now First Published, with Notes by Robert Bridges*, 1918; *Complete Poems*, 1947.

LETTERS: *The Letters of Gerard Manley Hopkins to Robert Bridges*, 1935; *The Correspondence of Gerard Manley Hopkins and Richard Watson Dixon*, 1935; *Further Letters*, 1937.

MISCELLANEOUS: *Notebooks and Papers of Gerard Manley Hopkins*, 1936.

In his lifetime few others than his teacher and confessor, R. W. Dixon, and Coventry Patmore, friend and correspondent, knew of the genius Gerard Manley Hopkins. Neither the *Dictionary of National Biography* nor the eleventh edition of the *Encyclopedia Britannica* makes space for one of the most highly praised of modern poets. A quick glance at his life, however, makes one wonder how he or his poems ever became known.

A precocious child, Hopkins, born at Stratford on June 11, 1844, was reared and educated in Highgate where Dixon may have first recognized the talents of this sensitive soul, although the famous correspondence did not begin until nearly twenty years later. Always inward, and an eager reader, Hopkins won a prize for a poem in 1859. He later won a prize for a poem "A Vision of Mermaids" (1862) which was reprinted in *Poems* accompanied by a Blakelike sketch. His interest and ability in music, especially composition, were early manifest.

From 1863 to 1867, Hopkins attended Oxford, where he met Robert Bridges, later Poet Laureate and collector of Hopkins' poems. Here he was converted to Catholicism, at which time he reputedly burned all his poems, most of which must have been reproduced later if content is any guide. He is said to have studied also under John Henry Newman, later Cardinal, in a Jesuit school in Birmingham.

After his novitiate he taught classics at Stonyhurst, Lancashire Catholic College, and later he was Professor of Greek, Royal University of Ireland. He seems to have started writing again in 1875 with the poem "The Wreck of the *Deutschland*," a lament for the death of five nuns who were going into exile. Certainly his voluminous letter writing began at this time and continued until his death in Dublin on June 8, 1889, of typhoid.

Modern critics have given Hopkins credit for introducing the offbeat "sprung" rhythm into poetry, although there is evidence to show that such innovation began with the Elizabethan and metaphysical poets. Even so, Hopkins possessed the finest ear for extremely sensitive alliteration, assonance, and dissonance of any recent poet. His concept of poetry as "inscape," internal landscape, is most revealing and useful; this is a principle the New Critics have used to support the view that a poem is an entity, capable of arousing within each reader a complete emotional response. In a sense even Dadaism arose from such an idea, a kind of surrealistic, highly personal response. Hopkins' themes, mystical and exalted, show the man's great genius and intensity, and his religious leanings indicate that he was ecstatic in the spirit of the great Spanish poets of the Renaissance.

As a theorist he is often thought of as a poet's poet, and his explanations sometimes surpass his verse in sheer imaginative power. Like Melville, Hopkins wrote for another generation than his own; like Thoreau, he marched to the rhythm of a different and distant drum.

Bibliography

The standard edition of the *Poems* is edited by W. H. Gardner and N. H. Mackenzie, 4th edition, 1967. C. C. Abbott has edited *The Letters of Gerard Manley Hopkins to Robert Bridges, and the Correspondence of Gerard Manley Hopkins and Richard Watson Dixon*, 2 vols., 1955. For biography and criticism see G. F. Lahey, *Gerard Manley Hopkins*, 1930; E. E. Phare, *The Poetry of Gerard Manley Hopkins: A Survey and Commentary*, 1933; John Pick, *Gerard Manley Hopkins: Priest and Poet*, 1942; W. A. M. Peters, *Gerard Manley Hopkins: A Critical Study*, 1948; W. H. Gardner, *Gerard Manley Hopkins, 1844–1889*, 2 vols., 1949; and Geoffrey Grigson, *Gerard Manley Hopkins*, 1955. See also Herbert Read, *In Defence of Shelley and Other Essays*, 1936; F. R. Leavis, *New Bearings in English Poetry*, 1938; David Daiches, *Poetry and the Modern World*, 1940; and J. G. Southworth, *Sowing the Spring: Studies in English Poets from Hopkins to MacNeice*, 1940. There are two excellent collections of critical studies by various hands: *Immortal Diamonds: Studies in Gerard Manley Hopkins*, edited by Norman Weyand, 1949, and *Gerard Manley Hopkins [by] the Kenyon Critics*, 1949. Also see *A Hopkins Reader*, edited and with an introduction by John Pick, 1953; Todd K. Bender, *Gerard Manley Hopkins: The Classical Background and Critical Reception of His Work*, 1966; and Elisabeth W. Schneider, *The Dragon in the Gate: Studies in the Poetry of G. M. Hopkins*, 1968.

THE POETRY OF HOPKINS

Author: Gerard Manley Hopkins (1844–1889)
Principal published works: Poems of Gerard Manley Hopkins, Now First Published, with Notes by Robert Bridges, 1918; *Complete Poems,* 1947

Essay-Review

Twenty-nine years elapsed from the time the poet Robert Bridges first published his edition of Gerard Manley Hopkins' *Poems* to publication of the definitive collection edited by the great Hopkins scholar, W. H. Gardner. Within that time Hopkins had been firmly established as an important if not a major British poet, not of his age but of the present. Undoubtedly, many of the conflicts over his life and work will have been resolved by the hundredth anniversary of the year Bridges first presented a small number of Hopkins' poems in important anthologies (1893).

Certain it is that the interest when this brilliant genius was in vogue, during the decade after 1918, has changed to something more deeply critical and scholarly. The letters, notebooks, and essays as well as the complete poems—no one now believes the best of the poet's work was destroyed—are now available to all, and hardly a year passes without the appearance of a volume of criticism or biography of the extremely paradoxical G. M. Hopkins.

Of utmost importance in understanding the very powerful poetry of this often misunderstood poet is his eclecticism, his wide knowledge and deep insights. While it is true that the preponderance of criticism has dwelt on Hopkins' innovations in rhythm-rhyme and imagery ("instress" and "inscape" summarize the two main facets), his whole poetic output indicates that he followed in the great European poetic tradition from Homer to Matthew Arnold. Hopkins' greatest poems are unique in powerful rhythmic effect, equal to or surpassing that of any other poet of like output; historically speaking, his poems prove that the genius of our language lies in stress-rhythms (often "sprung") of our oldest traditional poetry, at least as important as syllabic meters in effect. His poetic diction, his use of common idiom as well as ingenious coinages, is without exact parallel. His ear for language was so acute, though highly individual, that he helped restore poetry as an oral-aural art, a fact the late Dylan Thomas so brilliantly demonstrated.

The lack of bulk, the slender volume of three hundred pages encompassing less than two hundred poems or fragments, makes arbitrary the distinction of whether Hopkins was a major poet. Certainly he is a classic in a very special sense. His central vision was deeply Christian, Jesuit, even mystical, often ecstatic though intellectually controlled. One of his greatest poems, "The Wreck of the *Deutschland*," was inspired as much by the "happy memory of five Franciscan Nuns" as their tragic death in 1875 by drowning. By his own account, the thirty-one-year-old theologian, deeply affected by the newspaper account of these nuns, exiled by the Falk Laws, who drowned in the Thames on a ship carrying them from Germany to America, responded to his rector's suggestion that a commemorative poem should be written of this event. Hopkins was eager to try a new rhythm which had been haunting his ear, as he puts it. In spite of Robert Bridges' disapproval, he kept the rhythmic "oddnesses" because the technique was irrevocably bound to the sentiment he wanted to express, the sprung rhythm or "expressional rhythm . . . a vital fusion of the internal rhythm of thought-and-emotion and the external rhythm of sounds," as Gardner describes this phenomenon. As a threnody the poem is unique. An invocation to God to master rebellious feelings, a narrative of the tragic event, an elegy of one nun's heroism, a meditation on God's beneficence, a plea for intercession—all these and other arguments within the poem demanded a flexibility and felicity of form. The result is one of the great poems in English or any language. Stanza thirty-two, a poem of praise to a merciful God, will illustrate these subtleties:

> I admire thee, master of the tides,
>   Of the Yore-flood, of the year's fall;
> The recurb and the recovery of the gulf's sides,
>   The girth of it and the wharf of it and the wall;
> Stanching, quenching ocean of a motionable mind;
> Ground of being, and granite of it: past all
>   Grasp God, throned behind
> Death with a sovereignty that heeds but hides, bodes but abides.

While no one definition of "inscape" or "instress" will suffice, this stanza contains both: the former is seeing of the internal and fundamental, significant form or nature of, say, the ocean in motion; and the latter would include the access to God's grace and a celebration of this, though the rhythmic expression is also implied.

Perhaps the searching eye and the recording ear are best illustrated in Hopkins' most famous lyric, "Pied Beauty." Here the poet as painter and musician is displayed, showing his deep concern for bringing to bear in a poem all the senses:

> Glory be to God for dappled things—
>   For skies of couple-colour as a brinded cow;
>   For rose-moles all in stipple upon trout that swim;
> Fresh-firecoal chestnut-falls; finches' wings;
>   Landscape plotted and pieced-fold, fallow, and plough;
>   And áll trádes, their gear and tackle and trim.
> All things counter, original, spare, strange;
>   Whatever is fickle, freckled (who knows how?)
>   With swift, slow; sweet, sour; adazzle, dim;
> He fathers-forth whose beauty is past change:
>   Praise him.

Here are rhythmic contrasts, dramatic juxtapositions, unique word manipulations, a compelling meter as dappled and iridescent as the things described.

Another facet of Hopkins' talent, one of his most pronounced achievements, was his variation on the sonnet form, a revolt against the stilted structures and concepts of Victorian poesy. This is not to say he wrote loosely or without thought; quite the contrary is true, for his critical writings reveal the depth of his study and experimentation. Ascetic by habit and temperament, he elevated the form to a new lyricism by breaking with or modifying many old systems and establishing his own.

"The Starlight Night," a well-known sonnet not too revolutionary, illustrates the nervous counterpointed rhythms, the startling pauses, the jarring sound clashes, the harmonic word fusion among many other interesting poetic, semantic, and linguistic devices:

> Look at the stars! look, look up at the skies!
>   O look at all the fire-folk sitting in the air!
>   The bright boroughs, the circle-citadels there!
> Down in dim woods the diamond delves! the elves'-eyes!
> The grey lawns cold where gold, where quickgold lies!
>   Wind-beat whitebeam! airy abeles set on a flare!
>   Flake-doves sent floating forth at a farmyard scare!—
> Ah well! is it all a purchase, all is a prize.
>
> Buy then! bid then!—What?—Prayer, patience, alms, vows.
> Look, look: a May-mess, like an orchard boughs!
>   Look! March-bloom, like on mealed-with-yellow sallows!
> These are indeed the barn; withindoors house
> The shocks. This piece-bright paling shuts the spouse
>   Christ home, Christ and his mother and all his hallows.

This sonnet also illustrates Hopkins' childlike joy in fairy lore, his deep love of nature, and a metaphysical rapture over God's munificence, a simple joy born of a deep religion. In the *Deutschland* poem Hopkins is critical of man's questioning of God's ways, but his later poems show this questioning in his own lack of balance—a conflicting of personal desires, private impulses, and his theology. This unrest is perhaps best expressed in the priest-poet's sonnet "Peace" (1879):

> When will you ever, Peace, wild wood-dove, shy wings shut,
> Your round me roaming end, and under be my boughs?
> When, when, Peace, will you, Peace? I'll not play hypocrite
> To own my heart: I yield you do come sometimes; but
> That piecemeal peace is poor peace. What pure peace allows
> Alarms of wars, the daunting wars, the death of it?
>
> O surely, reaving Peace, my Lord should leave in lieu
> Some good! And so he does leave Patience exquisite,
> That plumes to Peace thereafter. And when Peace here does house
> He comes with work to do, he does not come to coo,
>   He comes to brood and sit.

Here he seems to have found some measure of this peace through virtuous acts, selfless serving of an often thankless mankind.

As most critics point out, Hopkins combined in his interesting person a depth of humanity with a height of mystical insight, with a whole spectrum of emotions and attitudes infused. Most of the contradictions in his nature, the ambiguities within his poetry, can be resolved by a thorough reading not only of his poems, but of his letters, diaries, and essays.

Bibliography

Bergonzi, Bernard. *Gerard Manley Hopkins.* New York: Macmillan, 1977.

Bridges, Robert. "Preface to Notes," in *The Poems of Gerard Manley Hopkins.* London: Oxford University Press, 1918. Reprinted in *Hopkins: A Collection of Critical Essays.* Edited by Geoffrey H. Hartman. Englewood Cliffs, N.J.: Prentice-Hall, 1966, pp. 71–75.

Daiches, David. *New Literary Values.* Edinburgh: Oliver and Boyd, 1936, pp. 23–51.

Deutsch, Babette. *Poetry in Our Time.* New York: Columbia University Press, 1956, pp. 286–311.

Durrell, Lawrence. *A Key to Modern British Poetry.* Norman: University of Oklahoma Press, 1952, pp. 164–177.

Fulweiler, Howard W. "Gerard Manley Hopkins," in *Victorian Poetry.* XIV (1976), pp. 227–231.

Grigson, Geoffrey. *Gerard Manley Hopkins.* London: Longmans, Green, 1962.

Hartman, Geoffrey H. *The Unmediated Vision: An Interpretation of Wordsworth, Hopkins, Rilke, and Valery.* New Haven, Conn.: Yale University Press, 1954, pp. 47–68. Reprinted in *Hopkins: A Collection of Critical Essays.* Edited by Geoffrey H. Hartman. Englewood Cliffs, N.J.: Prentice-Hall, 1966, pp. 117–130.

Jones, A.R. "G.M. Hopkins: Victorian," in *The Major Victorian Poets: Reconsiderations.* Edited by Isobel Armstrong. Lincoln: University of Nebraska Press, 1969, pp. 299–318.

Leavis, F.R. *New Bearings in English Poetry.* London: Chatto and Windus, 1932, pp. 159–193. Reprinted in *Hopkins: A Collection of Critical Essays.* Edited by Geoffrey H. Hartman. Englewood Cliffs, N.J.: Prentice-Hall, 1966, pp. 17–36.

Lees, Francis Noel. *Gerard Manley Hopkins.* New York: Columbia University Press, 1966.

————. "Gerard Manley Hopkins," in *The Pelican Guide to English Liter-*

ature, Volume VI: From Dickens to Hardy. Edited by Boris Ford. Harmondsworth, England: Penguin, 1958, pp. 371–384.

MacKenzie, Norman H. *Hopkins.* Edinburgh: Oliver and Boyd, 1968.

Miller, J. Hillis. *The Disappearance of God: Five Nineteenth-Century Writers.* Cambridge, Mass.: Harvard University Press, 1963, pp. 276–317. Reprinted in *Hopkins: A Collection of Critical Essays.* Edited by Geoffrey H. Hartman. Englewood Cliffs, N.J.: Prentice-Hall, 1966, pp. 89–116.

Peters, W.A.M. *Gerard Manley Hopkins: A Critical Essay Towards the Understanding of His Poetry.* London: Oxford University Press, 1948.

Pick, John. *Gerard Manley Hopkins: Priest and Poet.* New York: Oxford University Press, 1966.

Read, Herbert. *Form in Modern Poetry.* London: Sheed and Ward, 1932, pp. 44–55.

Russell, Jeremy. *A Critical Commentary on Gerard Manley Hopkins' Poems.* London: Macmillan, 1971.

Wain, John. *Preliminary Essays.* London: Macmillan, 1957, pp. 103–114.

Warren, Austin. *Rage for Order.* Chicago: University of Chicago Press, 1948, pp. 52–65. Reprinted in *Hopkins: A Collection of Critical Essays.* Edited by Geoffrey H. Hartman. Englewood Cliffs, N.J.: Prentice-Hall, 1966, pp. 168–177.

GEORGE MEREDITH

Born: Portsmouth, England (February 12, 1828)
Died: Box Hill, Surrey, England (May 18, 1909)

Principal Works

NOVELS: *The Shaving of Shagpat,* 1856; *Farina,* 1857; *The Ordeal of Richard Feverel,* 1859; *Evan Harrington,* 1861; *Sandra Belloni, or Emilia in England,* 1864; *Rhoda Fleming,* 1865; *Vittoria,* 1867; *The Adventures of Harry Richmond,* 1871; *Beauchamp's Career,* 1876; *The Egoist,* 1879; *The Tragic Comedians,* 1880; *Diana of the Crossways,* 1885; *Lord Ormont and His Aminta,* 1894; *One of Our Conquerors,* 1891; *The Amazing Marriage,* 1895; *Celt and Saxon,* 1910 (unfinished).

SHORT STORIES: *The Tale of Chloe,* 1879; *The Case of General Ople and Lady Camper,* 1890.

POEMS: *Poems,* 1851; *Modern Love,* 1862; *Poems and Lyrics of the Joy of Earth,* 1883; *Ballads and Poems of Tragic Life,* 1887; *A Reading of Earth,* 1888; *A Reading of Life,* 1901; *Last Poems,* 1909.

ESSAY: *On the Idea of Comedy and the Uses of the Comic Spirit,* 1897 (first separate publication).

A highly original writer, perhaps too original and idiosyncratic ever to be very popular, George Meredith has always been one of those unfortunate writers whose work is more praised than read. He did not receive much popular attention until he was past fifty, and after that, though he received most of the honors his fellow writers could award, he never attracted the general reader as Dickens, Thackeray, or Trollope did. An age in which the ability to invent a lively plot was highly valued was not likely to be much pleased by a novelist who, like his equally neglected contemporary Henry James, was almost exclusively interested in the subtle depiction of human motivation. Meredith's style also gave the common reader trouble: it was epigrammatic and involved, totally unlike the swift narrative flow of the prose of Dickens or Thackeray. In his poetry Meredith again refused to conform to popular taste; his diction was often rough, his syntax obscure, in contrast to the melodic sweetness of the popular Tennysonian tradition.

His style, however, is admirably suited to his purposes. He considered it the purpose of art to correct the excesses of men in society and to bring them closer to the ideal of the golden mean. His novels usually expose the flaws in human beings so that the reader may eliminate them in himself. His celebrated lecture, *On the Idea of Comedy and the Uses of the Comic Spirit,* delivered in 1877 but not published separately until 1897, is one of the great expressions of the moral value of literature. To this end he developed a style that is leisurely yet challenging, designed to penetrate to the hidden motivations of character by pithy thrusts and subtle implications. His poetry, too, is highly metaphoric; Meredith's nimble mind is too impatient always to make the transitions from image to image clear, and the result is a colorful, affecting style that sometimes cannot fully bear the thought of the poem. His observations of nature are fresh and vivid, and his poetry generally tries to reconcile the forces of passion and intellect.

The son of a naval outfitter, Meredith was born at Portsmouth, England, on February 12, 1828. He received a good early education but was forced to support himself rather than go to college, and he took to journalism in order to secure a reasonably steady income. In 1849 he married Mrs. Mary Ellen Nicholls, a widow almost seven years his senior. The daughter of Thomas Love Peacock, she was a talented and witty woman who was quite unsuited to the even more talented and witty Meredith. The marriage was unhappy; after 1858, when Mrs. Meredith went to Capri with another man, unreconcilable. After her death in 1861 Meredith told the psychological history of their estrangement in the brilliant lyric sequence, *Modern Love*. In 1864 he married Marie Vulliamy, and two years later he served as a war correspondent in the Austro-Italian War of 1866. On his return to England he edited the *Fort-nightly Review* and worked as a publisher's reader. A careful and sensitive critic, he gave needed encouragement to Thomas Hardy and George Gissing.

Meanwhile Meredith was slowly gaining a reputation as a novelist. His first important novel, *The Ordeal of Richard Feverel*, had little success, though it is a fine study of the emotional growth of a young man. The complex characterization and the delicately shaded style of *Evan Harrington* and *Beauchamp's Career* attracted a small but growing group of readers, but it was not until his comic masterpiece, *The Egoist*, appeared in 1879 that he received much popular attention. *Diana of the Crossways*, published in 1885, was his first novel to have a great popular success.

In the same year his second wife died. Meredith's own health was poor. Although a spinal ailment confined him to a wheelchair, he became in his last years the intellectual leader of his time. To his home at Box Hill, just outside of London, came aspiring young men, and Meredith, grown dogmatic and certain, was free with his literary advice. Following the death of Tennyson in 1892, Meredith was made president of the Society of Authors, thereby becoming the titular head of English letters. In 1905 he was awarded the Order of Merit and the medal of the Royal Society of Literature. At his death, on May 18, 1909, at Box Hill, he was England's most honored author and the last of the great Victorians.

Meredith's technique as a novelist is to use the point of view not of an onlooker, but of a particular character. In this way, he can describe the peculiar emotion of the character and, with his powerfully figurative style, catch the interest of the reader. As a result, his characters are extremely complex and varied. His heroines are particularly well drawn and are perhaps the finest since Shakespeare.

Bibliography

The fiction, poetry, and letters of George Meredith have been collected in the Memorial Edition edited by G. M. Trevelyan, 29 vols., 1909–1912. There are several separate collections of letters: *Letters*, edited by W. M. Meredith, 2 vols., 1912; *Letters to Edward Clodd and C. K. Shorter*, edited by T. J. Wise, 1913; and *Letters to Alice Meynell*, 1923. For a modern edition see *Letters*, edited by C. L. Cline, 3 vols., 1970.

The major modern biography of Meredith is Lionel Stevenson, *The Ordeal of George Meredith*, 1953. Among the earlier biographical studies are Richard Curle, *Aspects of George Meredith*, 1908; Constantin Photiades, *George Meredith: sa vie, son imagination, son art, sa doctrine*, 1911 (translated 1913); J. H. E. Crees, *George Meredith: A study of His Works and Personality*, 1918; S. M. Ellis, *George Meredith: His Life and Friends in Relation to His Work*, 1920; René Galland, *George Meredith: les cinquante premières années*, 1923; J. B. Priestley, *George Meredith*, 1926; Mary Sturge Gretton, *The Writings and Life of George Meredith*, 1926; R. E. Sencourt, *The Life of George Meredith*, 1929; and A. H. Able, *George Meredith and Thomas Love Peacock*, 1933. More recent critical biographies include Siegfried Sassoon, *Meredith*, 1948; Gillian Beer, *Meredith: A Change of Masks*, 1970; and Diane Johnson, *The True History of the First Mrs. Meredith and Other Lives*, 1973.

Early but still useful critical studies of George Meredith include G. M. Trevelyan, *The Poetry and Philosophy of George Meredith*, 1906; E. J. Bailey, *The Novels of George Meredith*, 1907; James Moffatt, *George Meredith: A Primer to the Novels*, 1909; and Joseph Warren Beach, *The Comic Spirit in George Meredith*, 1911. More recent criticism is by Sir Osbert Sitwell, *The Novels of George Meredith and Some Notes on the English Novel*, 1947; W. F. Wright, *Art and Substance in George Meredith*, 1953; V. S. Prichett, *George Meredith and English Comedy*, 1970; I. M. Williams, comp., *Meredith: The Critical Heritage*, 1971; Ian Fletcher, ed., *Meredith Now: Some Critical Essays*, 1971; Judith Wilt, *The Readable People of George Meredith*, 1975; and Maurice McCullen and Lewis Sawin, *A Dictionary of the Characters in George Meredith's Fiction*, 1977.

THE POETRY OF MEREDITH

Author: George Meredith (1828–1909)
First published: Poems, 1851; *Modern Love*, 1862; *Poems and Lyrics of the Joy of Earth*, 1883; *Ballads and Poems of Tragic Life*, 1887; *A Reading of Earth*, 1888; *A Reading of Life*, 1901; *Last Poems*, 1910

Essay-Review

In six principal volumes published from 1862 to 1901, George Meredith wrote about 130 poems which make up his main collection, exclusive of the very early poems, some translations, and numerous epitaphs and occasional poems. His best work was published in 1883 as *Poems and Lyrics of the Joy of Earth*, and in 1888, *A Reading of Earth*. The poems of both volumes chiefly explain Meredith's nearly pagan faith in man as a part of natural process, and celebrate, often in terms of regeneration myths, the natural vitality and renewal which comes to men when they forego selfishness and live at one with nature.

> Enter these enchanted woods,
>   You who dare.
> Nothing harms beneath the leaves
> More than waves a swimmer cleaves.
> Toss your heart up with the lark,
> Foot at peace with mouse and worm,
>   Fair you fare.
> Only at a dread of dark
> Quaver, and they quit their form:
> Thousand eyeballs under hoods
>   Have you by the hair.
> Enter these enchanted woods,
>   You who dare.

This, the first stanza of "The Woods of Westermain," expresses Meredith's belief that nature is essentially mysterious, "enchanted," and beneficent. Nature becomes a source of terror only to the man who has lost a sense of his dependence on nature. The man who is guilty of over-weening pride in intellect, who feels superior to nature, is cut off from Mother Earth and so conceives her to be brutish and even fearful. Meredith's attitude toward nature is remarkably advanced for his time. He accepts natural process—both in the way it limits men and also as a creative, evolutionary force—not in the Darwinian sense, nor in the way Tennyson sometimes conceived of science as a possible saving force, but rather in a "mythological" or even "pagan" sense. Man's scientific dominion over nature counts less for Meredith than man as being a part of nature. A man lives a single span of life, and nature provides him with that life. And though the individual dies, as each Spring "dies" in winter, man and nature are continually reborn and renewed within the great cycle of being. Because of this root belief, and because it provides a viewpoint which is essentially one of joy, and because according to it a man's false pride and sense of superiority can be ridiculed, Meredith's "philosophy" is profoundly comic.

Influenced in his early poetry by the Keatsian tradition of Tennyson and even by the "Spasmodic School" of, notably, Richard H. Horne's "Orion," Meredith came under the influence of Swinburne, whose friend he was, and then, breaking away from aestheticism, developed his own, highly characteristic and often unique style which Douglas Bush has called "a bright, muscular idiom." His style is very compressed, his thought often overly convoluted, even tangled. His metaphors, rich in visual observation and sly analogies, come thick and fast and do not normally form a single developing "conceit" or extended metaphor. For these reasons—complexity of thought, ambiguity of expression—Meredith's poetry was greeted by the reading public with some acclaim but more bewilderment. In his verbal tricks, his syncopated rhythms, his compression of language and often confusing use of metaphor, Meredith's poetry bears comparison to that of another contemporary who has been acclaimed as a great innovator, Gerard Manley Hopkins.

> Carols nature, counsel men.
> Different notes as rook from wren
> Hear we when our steps begin,
> And the choice is cast within,
> Where a robber raven's tale
> Urges passion's nightingale.

Such a passage invites a certain amount of study and puzzling out; it will not become clear until the whole poem is studied, but the real point is to assess the immediate effect of the lines. The changing rhythms, the double alliteration, the close rhyming, are intended to produce a mysterious and somehow incantatory effect, as Meredith celebrates, and often preaches, the mysterious influence of nature on the inner man. Unlike Wordsworth, however, Meredith never really abstracts nature, does not perceive behind the concrete forms a quasi-platonic "idea" or ideal. Rather, he finds the deeper meaning within the forms of nature itself. It is in this sense that he has been called "pagan."

The same strong cadence marks "Hard Weather," in which Meredith sings of how storms serve to brace men, to force on them an awareness of nature's vitality. "Contention is the vital force," he chants, and he indicates how such a notion as "the survival of the fittest" can be viewed not with alarm but accepted as a principle of growth:

> Earth yields the milk, but all her mind
> Is vowed to thresh for stouter stock.
> Her passion for old giantkind,
> That scaled the mount, uphurled the rock,

> Devolves on them who read aright
> Her meaning and devoutly serve.

To "read aright" requires the use of brains, believes Meredith. He decries sentimentality as well as crass naturalistic groveling in the gutter. "More brains, more brains," he once cried, testifying to his faith in man's ability to perceive rationally his destiny and being in nature, and so to bring himself into accord with nature, unified then in "blood, brain and spirit."

Meredith finds in Greek legend a character who symbolizes man's communion with nature. Melampus, the physician, preserved some snakes from death, and so was granted the power to understand the language of birds. The theme is not unrelated to that of spiritual renewal in Coleridge's *The Rime of the Ancient Mariner*:

> Of earth and sun they are wise, they nourish their broods,
>   Weave, build, hive, burrow and battle, take joy and pain
> Like swimmers varying billows: never in woods
>   Runs white insanity fleeing itself: all sane
> The woods revolve: as the tree its shadowing limns
>   To some resemblance in motion, the rooted life
> Restrains disorder: you hear the primitive hymns
>   Of earth in woods issue wild of the web of strife.

"The Day of the Daughter of Hades," a remarkable poem which celebrates the renewal of spring, is based on the myth of Persephone's return from Hades. Persephone's daughter, Skiagenia, accompanies her mother, spends a day with an earthling, and chants of the joy of earth's fecundity. She understands earth better than earthlings do because she is a daughter of Hades, of darkness. This mysterious linking of life and death, the earth and underground, is the poem's deepest meaning, and again Meredith's vision here is not unrelated to D. H. Lawrence's belief in the deeply-rooted instinctual life.

To accept the good of nature, pain and death must also be accepted, and Meredith had to struggle to keep his faith in earth despite personal loss, ill health, and discouragement. "A Faith on Trial" records this struggle, but *Modern Love*, published in 1862, is the key poem to an understanding of the tragic side of Meredith's vision of life. This sequence is closer in kind to the other dramatic monologues which Meredith wrote, such as "Juggling Jerry" and "The Old Chartist." His first wife, the daughter of Thomas Love Peacock, had deserted him in 1858 and died in 1861. *Modern Love* dramatizes the bitter psychological warfare of a couple who lose their early romantic and somewhat illusory love and proceed to subtly cut up each other and themselves. The wife finally commits suicide. Meredith's conclusion is typically philosophical and humane:

> Then each applied to each that fatal knife,
> Deep questioning, which probes to endless dole.

> Ah, what a dusty answer gets the soul
> When hot for certainties in this our life!—
> In tragic hints here see what evermore
> Moves dark as yonder midnight ocean's force,
> Thundering like ramping hosts of warrior horse,
> To throw that faint thin line upon the shore!

And, again:

> I see no sin:
> The wrong is mixed. In tragic life, God wot,
> No villain need be! Passions spin the plot:
> We are betrayed by what is false within.

Nature can be harsh, but never wantonly cruel. Only men, in their illusions and pride, can be cruel. Nature, "read aright," disciplines the unruly passions, brings solace, gives strength. Meredith's renewed faith in Earth is intensely felt and is conveyed not infrequently with great eloquence and energy in poems remarkable both for vigor of thought and compressed, rhythmically exciting verse.

Bibliography

Armstrong, Martin. "The Poetry of George Meredith," in *North American Review*. CCXIII (1921), pp. 354–361.

Austin, Deborah. "Meredith on the Nature of Metaphor," in *University of Toronto Quarterly*. XXVII (1957), pp. 96–102.

Baker, Ernest A. *The History of the English Novel*, Volume VIII. New York: Barnes & Noble, 1950, pp. 287–299.

Beach, Joseph Warren. *The Concept of Nature in Nineteenth-Century English Poetry*. New York: Macmillan, 1936, pp. 470–499.

Bogner, Delmar. "The Sexual Side of Meredith's Poetry," in *Victorian Poetry*. VIII (1970), pp. 107–125.

Chambers, Edmund Kerchever. "Meredith's Nature Poetry," in *A Sheaf of Studies*. London: Oxford University Press, 1942, pp. 84–91.

Clutton-Brock, Arthur. "George Meredith," in *More Essays on Books*. London: Methuen, 1921, pp. 35–46.

Crees, J.H.E. *George Meredith: A Study of His Works and Personality*. Oxford: Blackwell, 1928, pp. 70–84.

Crum, Ralph B. *Scientific Thought in Poetry*. New York: Columbia University Press, 1931, pp. 207–227.

Eaker, J. Gordon. "Meredith's Human Comedy," in *Ninteenth-Century Fiction*. V (March, 1951), pp. 267–272.

Edgar, Pelham. "The Poetry of George Meredith," in *Living Age.* CCLV (1907), pp. 744–751.

Evans, B. Ifor. *English Poetry in the Later Nineteenth Century.* London: Methuen, 1933, pp. 162–177.

Gretton, Mary Sturge. *The Writings and Life of George Meredith, A Centenary Study.* London: Oxford University Press, 1926, pp. 174–191.

Kelvin, Norman. *A Troubled Eden: Nature and Society in the Works of George Meredith.* Stanford, Calif.: Stanford University Press, 1961, pp. 114–164.

Priestley, J.B. *George Meredith.* New York: Macmillan, 1926, pp. 86–111.

Quiller-Couch, Arthur Thomas. "The Poetry of George Meredith," in his *Studies in Literature.* Cambridge: Cambridge University Press, 1937, pp. 158–177. Reprinted in his *Cambridge Lectures.* New York: Dutton, 1944, pp. 259–273.

Ridley, M.R. "Meredith's Poetry," in his *Second Thoughts: More Studies in Literature.* London: Dent, 1965, pp. 146–171.

Robertson, Leo C. "Meredith the Poet," in *English Review.* XLIV (1927), pp. 463–471.

Stuart-Young, J.M. "The Poetry of George Meredith," in *Poetry Review.* XVIII (1926), pp. 173–176.

Tinker, Chauncey Brewster. "Meredith's Poetry," in *Essays in Retrospect.* New Haven, Conn.: Yale University Press, 1948, pp. 83–89.

Trevelyan, George Macaulay. *The Poetry and Philosophy of George Meredith.* London: Archibald Constable, 1907.

Vivante, Leone. "George Meredith, 1828–1909," in *English Poetry and Its Contribution to the Knowledge of a Creative Principle.* London: Faber and Faber, 1950, pp. 248–261.

Weygandt, Cornelius. *The Time of Tennyson: English Victorian Poetry as It Affected America.* New York: Appleton-Century, 1936, pp. 181–191.

Wolf, William. "The Poetry of George Meredith," in *Poetry Review.* XLIV (1953), pp. 464–466.

JOHN STUART MILL

Born: London, England (May 20, 1806)
Died: Avignon, France (May 8, 1893)

Principal Works

PHILOSOPHICAL, POLITICAL, AND SCIENTIFIC ESSAYS: *A System of Logic*, 1843; *Pr.nciples of Political Economy*, 1848; *On Liberty*, 1859; *Thoughts on Parliamentary Reform*, 1859; *Considerations on Representative Government*, 1861; *Utilitarianism*, 1863; *Auguste Comte and Positivism*, 1865; *England and Ireland*, 1868; *The Subjection of Women*, 1869; *On the Irish Land Question*, 1870; *Three Essays on Religion*, 1874.

AUTOBIOGRAPHY: *Autobiography*, 1873.

The intellectual leader of a liberal movement that profoundly influenced Western political thought, John Stuart Mill was also a fine literary stylist. His prose style is clear and balanced, admirably suited to bear the weight of his political and social thinking. He developed the Utilitarian movement, started by his father, James Mill, into a political force for humanitarian social developments. His *The Subjection of Women* was an early blow in the fight for women's rights, and his *On Liberty* remains, with Milton's *Areopagitica* (1644), a classic defense of individuality against authoritarianism in all its forms.

Mill, born in London on May 20, 1806, is also a classic example of the precocious child; he himself always insisted that he had no more than average ability, but merely profited from an earlier start than most children. Under the tutelage of his father, Mill acquired an immense background of knowledge. At his earliest recollection he knew Greek; Latin came harder because it was started later. At eleven he began to write a history of Rome; at twelve he began the serious study of logic. By the age of fourteen he was solidly grounded in mathematics, political theory, economics, and history, as well as logic and the classical languages. In 1823 he started as clerk in the India House, a firm in which he eventually succeeded his father as director. But the education his father had given him had excluded emotional development, and in 1826 Mill had a great spiritual crisis. He became aware of his own emotional needs and eventually, particularly through the study of Wordsworth, he was able to resolve his difficulties. After this crisis he saw the need for humanizing the laissez-faire doctrines of the Utilitarians until they met emotional as well as economic human needs.

In 1830 he met Mrs. Taylor, an invalid for whom he developed, with the full knowledge of her intellectually inferior husband, what was apparently a platonic attachment. He married her, after the death of her husband, twenty-one years later. He edited the *London Review*, the organ of Utilitarian thought, from 1835 to 1840 and gave early recognition to Tennyson. *A System of Logic* was a great work in the development of scientific, empirical thinking. He was elected to the House of Commons for a term lasting from 1865 to 1868; he worked for a way to have minority opinions heard more, for he always feared that democracies could become tyrannous. His *Autobiography*, a sensitive record of his emotional and intellectual development, appeared in the year of his death at Avignon, France, on May 8, 1873.

Bibliography

The Collected Works is under the general editorship of F. E. Priestley. Most of the essential details of Mill's life are presented in his *Autobiography*, re-edited by Harold J. Laski in 1944. There are also a collection of *Letters*, edited by H. S. R. Elliot, 2 vols., 1910; and *The Earlier Letters*, edited by Francis E. Mineka, 1963. For biographical and critical studies see W. L. Courtney, *The Life of John Stuart Mill*, 1889; H. K. Garner, *John Stuart Mill and the Philosophy of Mediation*, 1919; Emery Neff, *Carlyle and Mill*, 1924; C. L. Street, *Individualism and Individuality in the Social Philosophy of John Stuart Mill*, 1940; and Michael St. John Packe, *The Life of John Stuart Mill*, 1954. For an earlier study see A. Bain, *John Stuart Mill: A Personal Criticism*, 1882. For articles by various hands see Jerome Schneewind, ed., *A Collection of Critical Essays*, 1968. For background studies of his life and work see also Leslie Stephen, *The English Utilitarians*, Vol. III, 1900; James Seth, *English Philosophers and Schools of Philosophy*, 1912; and Rudolf Metz, *A Hundred Years of British Philosophy*, 1938.

ON LIBERTY

Type of work: Philosophical essay
Author: John Stuart Mill (1806–1873)
First published: 1859

Essay-Review

John Stuart Mill, the English Utilitarian, here concerns himself with the problem of defining the limits of the power of the state in interfering with the liberty of persons. The result is one of the most important statements in the history of Western democracy. The essay is distinguished by its clarity and the orderly arrangement of its persuasive argument. Throughout the book can be discerned Mill's interest in the happiness and rights of men everywhere and his serious concern lest that happiness be threatened by governmental power unwisely used. Mill states concisely that:

> The object of this Essay is to assert one very simple principle, as entitled to govern absolutely the dealings of society with the individual in the way of compulsion and control, whether the means used be physical force in the form of legal penalties, or the moral coercion of public opinion. That principle is, that the sole end for which mankind are warranted, individually or collectively, in interfering with the liberty of action of any of their number, is self-protection. That the only purpose for which power can be rightfully exercised over any member of a civilized community, against his will, is to prevent harm to others.

Another statement of the author's intention is found in the last chapter, "Applications," in which Mill states that two maxims together form "the entire doctrine" of the essay. The first maxim is "that the individual is not accountable to society for his actions, in so far as these concern the interests of no person but himself," and the second is "that for such actions as are prejudicial to the interests of others, the individual is accountable, and may be subjected either to social or to legal punishment, if society is of the opinion that the one or the other is requisite for its protection."

It would be an error of interpretation of Mill's intention to suppose that he is explicitly objecting to all efforts of government to improve the condition of its citizens. What Mill objects to is the restriction of human liberty for the sake of human welfare; he has nothing against welfare itself. On the contrary, as a Utilitarian, he believes that a right act is one which aims at the greatest happiness of the greatest number of persons; and it is precisely because the restriction of human liberty is so destructive to human happiness that he makes a plea for a judicious use of restrictive power, justifying it only when it is used to prevent harm, or unhappiness of whatever sort, to others than the person being restricted.

Restricting a man's liberty for his own good, for his happiness, is not morally justifiable. Mill permits, even encourages, "remonstrating" and "reasoning" with a person who is determined to act against his own best interests, but he does not approve of using force to keep him from it.

After reviewing some of the acts which a person may rightfully be compelled to do—such as to give evidence in court, to bear a fair share of the common defense, and to defend the helpless—Mill asserts that society has no right to interfere when a man's acts concern, for the most part, only himself. This statement means that a man must be free in his conscience, thought, and feeling, and that he must have freedom of opinion and sentiment on all subjects. This latter freedom involves freedom of the press. In addition, each man should be free to do what he likes and to enjoy what he prefers—provided what he does is not harmful to others. Finally, each man should be free to unite with others for any purpose—again, provided no one is harmed by this action.

Certainly this theme is pertinent, for at any time there is either the present or the possible danger of government interference in human affairs. Mill admits that his principal thesis has the "air of a truism," but he goes on to remind the reader that states have often felt justified in using their power to limit the liberty of citizens in areas which Mill regards as sacrosanct. In the context of Mill's philosophic work, *On Liberty* remains one of his most important essays, sharing honors with his *Utilitarianism*.

In perhaps the most carefully articulated part of his argument, in Chapter II, "On the Liberty of Thought and Discussion," Mill considers what the consequences of suppressing the expression of opinion would be if the suppressed opinion were true; and then, having countered a series of objections to his arguments against suppression, he continues by considering what the consequences of suppressing opinion would be if the opinion were false.

Suppressing true opinion is clearly wrong, particularly if the opinion is suppressed on the ground that it is false. Silencing the expression of opinion on the ground that the opinion is false is a sign of an assumption of infallibility. A moment's thought shows that the assumption may be mistaken, and that suppressing opinion may very well make discovery of error impossible.

In response to the objection that it is permissible to suppress opinion, even true opinion, because the truth always triumphs, Mill answers that the idea that truth always wins out is a "pleasant falsehood" proved false by experience. To the objection that at least we no longer put men to death for expressing their opinions, Mill counters with the argument that other kinds of persecution continue to be practiced, destroying truth and moral courage.

If the opinion suppressed be false, Mill continues, the prevailing and true opinion, lacking opposition, becomes a dead dogma. When ideas are not continually met by opposing ideas they tend to become either meaningless or groundless, or both. Beliefs which at one time had force and reasons behind them may come to be nothing but empty words.

The argument in favor of freedom of opinion and the press closes with the claim that most opinions are neither wholly true nor wholly false, but mixtures of the two; and that only in free discussion can the difference be made out.

In order to reinforce his central contention—that it is always wrong to hinder the freedom of an individual when what he does is not harmful to others—Mill devotes a chapter to an argument designed to show that development of individuality is essential to man's happiness. Since there is nothing better than happiness, it follows that individuality should be fostered and guaranteed. Mill supports Baron Wilhelm von Humboldt's injunction that every human being aim at "individuality of power and development," for which there are two prerequisites: "freedom and the variety of situations."

There is a refreshing pertinence to Mill's discussion of the value of individuality. We are reminded of Emerson's defense of nonconformism when we read that "Originality is the one thing which unoriginal minds cannot feel the use of," and "He who lets the world, or his own portion of it, choose his plan of life for him, has no need of any other faculty than the ape-like one of imitation." Mill argues that only if uncustomary acts are allowed to show their merits can anyone decide which mode of action should become customary; and, in any case, the differences among men demand that differences of conduct be allowed so that each man can become what is best for him.

In his discussion of the harm that results from a state's interference with the rights of an individual to act in ways that concern only himself, Mill reviews some of the consequences of religious intolerance, prohibition, and other attempts to restrict liberty for the common good. In each case, he argues, the result is not only failure to achieve the goal of the prohibitive act, but some damage to the character of the state and its citizens.

As if he were writing for our times, Mill closes by saying that "... a State which dwarfs its men, in order that they may be more docile instruments in its hands even for beneficial purposes—will find that with small men no great thing can be accomplished. ..."

WILLIAM MORRIS

Born: Walthamstow, England (March 24, 1834)
Died: Hammersmith, England (October 3, 1896)

Principal Works

POEMS: *The Defence of Guenevere, and Other Poems,* 1858; *The Life and Death of Jason,* 1867; *The Earthly Paradise,* 1868–1870; *Love Is Enough* (a morality), 1872; *Aeneid of Virgil* (a translation), 1875; *Three Northern Love Songs,* 1875; *Sigurd the Volsung,* 1876; *The Odyssey* (a translation), 1887; *Poems by the Way,* 1891.

PROSE ROMANCES: *The Dream of John Ball,* 1888; *The House of the Wolfings,* 1889; *The Roots of the Mountains,* 1890; *The Story of the Glittering Plain,* 1890; *News from Nowhere,* 1891; *The Wood Beyond the World,* 1894; *Child Christopher,* 1895; *The Well at the World's End,* 1896; *The Water of the Wondrous Isles,* 1897; *The Story of the Sundering Flood,* 1898.

The artist, poet, manufacturer, and socialist William Morris was the eldest son and third child of a bill broker father and a music teacher mother. As a boy he freely ranged through the primeval Epping Forest adjacent to his home and thus fed his romantic imagination and sharpened his naturally keen powers of observation. His formal education began at a neighborhood private school and terminated in 1856, after four years at Exeter College, Oxford. At Oxford he formed a lifelong friendship with the painter Edward Burne-Jones. For almost a year after his graduation, Morris served as an apprentice in an architect's office. He then turned to painting and, in partnership with Burne-Jones, set up a studio in London.

At Oxford, Morris had been one of the originators of the *Oxford and Cambridge Magazine,* and to it he had contributed poems, essays, and tales. He continued to write poetry and in 1858 published *The Defence of Guenevere and Other Poems.* Despite its excellence, Morris' poetry always was a supplement to his regular work of drawing, painting (both oil and water-color), modeling, illuminating, and designing. In 1857 he became acquainted with Jane Burden, whom he married in April, 1859. After his marriage Morris gradually abandoned painting (his latest pictures are dated 1862) and concentrated on reëstablishing designing and decoration as one of the five arts. He supervised the building of his own home, Red House, in which his theory of decoration was freely applied; and he formed a manufacturing and decorating firm which continued until 1874. In addition to decorating churches, the firm dealt in furniture, embroideries, jewelry, carpets, tapestries, and the like.

After several years of virtual inactivity as a poet, Morris in 1867 published the epic *Life and Death of Jason.* The twenty-five intricately and beautifully connected narrative poems modeled after Chaucer and known as *The Earthly Paradise* were published in three volumes in 1868–1870. Becoming interested in both the Icelandic sagas and in moral, social, and political doctrine, he sought new ways of artistic expression and turned increasingly to the Middle Ages as his symbol of the essentials to which the practice of both life and art must return so that new beginnings may be made. He translated the Icelandic *Three Northern Love Songs* (1874) and Virgil's *Aeneid* (1875) and composed his longest poem *Sigurd the Volsung and the Fall of the Nibelungs* (1876). In accord with his theory, he taught himself the trade of dying wools, silks, and cottons, and became active in the Democratic Federation and later in the Socialist League. He lectured extensively and published several volumes of addresses and other prose writings, *A Dream of John Ball* (1888) being the most remarkable of these. Finally, since an immediate socialist revolution was not forthcoming, he resolved that socialists must educate people toward its accomplishment in the distant future. To depict his ideal, he turned again to the remote past and produced numerous romances such as *The Well at the World's End* (1896). Meanwhile, however, he produced his masterpiece of Utopian fiction, *News from Nowhere* (1890), a romantic pastoral of future communism. Among other activites of his later life was the establishing of the Kelmscott Press in 1890, one of whose early books was Morris' own volume, *Poems by the Way* (1891).

In 1895 Morris' health began to decline, and he died on October 3, 1896. In literature, as in his amazingly numerous other endeavors (both aesthetic and social), the great effect of William Morris was to arouse the artistic sense and to initiate new beginnings.

Bibliography

The best edition is *The Collected Works of Morris*, with introductions by May Morris, 24 vols., 1910–1915, reprinted 1966, and its supplement, *William Morris, Writer, Socialist*, edited by May Morris, 2 vols., 1936, reprinted 1966. Briefer editions include *Selected Writings and Designs*, 1962; and *A Choice of William Morris's Verse*, edited by G. Grigson, 1968. Philip Henderson edited *The Letters of William Morris to His Family and Friends*, 1950.

Important early studies include J. W. Mackail, *The Life of Morris*, 2 vols., 1899; and A. Clutton-Brock, *William Morris: His Work and Influence*, 1914. Among the many modern biographical and critical work are M. Grennan, *Morris: Medievalist and Revolutionary*, 1945; E. Meynell, *Portrait of Morris*, 1947; E. P. Thompson, *William Morris, Romantic to Revolutionary*, 1955, R. P. Arnot, *William Morris: The Man and the Myth*, 1964; Paul R. Thompson, *The Work of William Morris*, 1967; and Henderson's *William Morris: His Life, Work and Friends*, 1967.

See also W. B. Yeats, "The Happiest of the Poets," *Ideas of Good and Evil*, 1903; G. B. Shaw, *William Morris as I Knew Him*, 1936; Douglas Bush, *Mythology and Romantic Tradition*, 1937; and C. S. Lewis, *Rehabilitations and Other*

Essays, 1939.

For additional material see W. E. Fredeman, *Pre-Raphaelitism: A Bibliocritical Study*, 1965.

THE DEFENCE OF GUENEVERE AND OTHER POEMS

Type of work: Poetry
Author: William Morris (1834–1896)
First published: 1858

Essay-Review

The Defence of Guenevere and Other Poems, the first collection of poems published by William Morris, is one of the three or four principal expressions of Pre-Raphaelitism in poetry. Although Morris had just turned twenty-four when the volume appeared, it epitomizes his qualities and foreshadows his artistic attainment. Swinburne, his contemporary, wrote concerning it: "Such things as are in this book are taught and learned in no school but that of instinct." It was Swinburne's opinion that no other literary work had ever shown more distinctly the mark of native character and that the poetry was entirely original. He saw Morris as "not yet a master," but "assuredly no longer a pupil." Not unmindful of certain technical faults and an occasional hint of confusion, Swinburne nevertheless went on to say that Morris' volume was incomparable in its time for "perception and experience of tragic truth" and that no other contemporary poet had a "touch of passion at once so broad and so sure."

Swinburne may have overstated the case for the originality of the poems; Morris shows strong influences of Malory and Froissart, though more in regard to selection of subject matter than in its interpretation. His Arthurian poems reveal a genuine passion and exceptional beauty, especially in passages such as the vibrant, breath-taking narrative description which opens the title poem. Yet, despite their freshness and strong feeling, these poems are in what may be designated the tapestry tradition, whereas those poems derived more clearly from Froissart than from Malory—among them "Sir Peter Harpdon's End," "Concerning Geoffrey Teste Noire," and the grim "Haystack in the Floods"—attest to Morris' realization that, even in the Middle Ages, the tourney was not the only aspect of war.

Although Morris had a lifelong passion for beauty, a passion kept by his vigorous nature from any Victorian effeminacy, he had a need for certain harsh or stark elements which are already present in these poems but which he did not fully employ until, after discovering the Icelandic sagas, he wrote some of his greatest poetry in *Sigurd the Volsung*. The touches of this later power evident in this first volume of his poems are the stark descriptions such as these lines from "Concerning Geoffrey Teste Noire:"

> I think 'twas Geoffrey smote him on the brow
>   With some spiked axe; and while he totter'd, dim
>
> About the eyes, the spear of Alleyne Roux
>   Slipped through his camaille and his throat; well, well!

And when Sir Peter Harpdon's wife Alice, upon hearing of her husband's death, cries:

> I am much too young to live,
> Fair God, so let me die,

we recognize in the cry a kind of Shakespearean poignancy. Among the many other qualities of this first book of poems is the apparent simplicity of a lyric like "Golden Wings," which attains deep sincerity as it smoothly reflects early memories in a manner distinctly Morris' own. There is also the plain perfection of the little poem, "Summer Dawn," in which, departing momentarily from the dreams and histories of long-past lives and battles, Morris speaks simply in his own voice of his desire for communion in nature.

Morris, while studying medieval romances and admiring them for their curious intrinsic beauty, became convinced that if we could move backward through time to the age of the sea kings, we should find the essential characteristics of the race to be exactly like those of today. Admittedly, he found the Middle Ages much more ignorant, cruel, and savage than the ages preceding or following; nevertheless, he concluded that people of those times must have thought about particular things and issues just as modern men and women do. Why then, he asked, should we not study all possible facets of this terrible society?

Morris gives us some brief, sudden, and flashing pictures of that far-off time. The title poem presents a queen about to be burned at the stake; then, at the sound of a horse's hoofs, she knows that her lover is coming to her rescue. One of the most powerful of these pictures is presented in "The Haystack in the Floods." Not revealing either how the tragedy began or how it ended, the poem opens with the haunting questions:

> Had she come all the way for this
> To part at last without a kiss?
> Yea, had she borne the dirt and rain
> That her own eyes might see him slain
> Beside the haystack in the floods?

We are at first told just enough about the woman Jehane to make us wonder about her character and to know that as she rides along she is miserable. Her lover Robert, who rides some distance ahead of her with a few armed men, is confronted by his adversary Godmar and numerous armed men. At first she fears for her own safety rather than Robert's:

> My God! my God! I have to tread
> The long way back without you; then
> The court at Paris; those six men;
> The gratings of the Chatelet;
> The swift Seine on some rainy day
> Like this, and people standing by,

> And laughing, while my weak hands try
> To recollect how strong men swim.

In her despair she contemplates accepting Godmar, the man whom she hates. Robert, whose men refuse to fight against the heavy odds, charges the enemy and is captured, disarmed, and bound. When after long hesitation Jehane refuses to come willingly to his castle, Godmar and his men brutally murder Robert before her eyes. The poem ends with an uncertainty about her fate. Does she go mad? Will she be taken back and burned at the castle from which she has escaped? The reader may even suspect that she is feigning madness and that before the castle is reached she will selfishly yield to Godmar, who may then retain her until he tires of her. Having given us this glimpse of medieval passion, selfishness, suffering, and cruelty, Morris ends the poem, after Godmar's men had beaten Robert's brains out, on this note:

> Then Godmar turned again and said:
> So, Jehane, the first fitte is read!
> Take note, my lady, that your way
> Lies backward to the Chatelet!
> She shook her head and gazed awhile
> At her cold hands with a rueful smile,
> As though this thing had made her mad.
> This was the parting that they had
> Beside the haystack in the floods.

Another grim, moving poem, a Browningesque monologue called "The Judgement of God," supplies a second example of the same device.

Other noteworthy poems in the book are "The Little Tower," "The Wind," "The Eve of Crecy," "In Prison," and "The Blue Closet." All extremely original, they display a wide range in idea and theme. In their ability to make us understand the feelings of pain, terror, or heroic effort at particular movements in the lives of people, they all have a high psychological quality. For example, Guenevere's natural and horrible soliloquy, revealing that she has wondered how the fire would quiver yards above her head, in its startlingly true psychology improves upon the narrative of the original story. Especially in his use of monologue and dialogue, Morris successfully demonstrates that the poet can best revive the past not by detailed description of things but by faithful expression of the feelings of persons who lived long ago.

Without exaggeration, William Morris's *Defence of Guenevere* may be called an outstanding first volume of poetry. However, not unlike the early volumes of most poets, it did not make any particular impact upon the reading public when it appeared in 1858. This lack of widespread acclaim for the volume may have been a factor in Morris' withdrawing for some time from the writing of poetry. Another factor, of course, was his feeling that writing poetry was neither particularly notable nor difficult and that it had no precedence over the new and exciting experiments in tapestry-weaving and dyeing in which he was already engaged. Morris was content with the appreciation accorded the volume by a few of his friends, among them Burne-Jones and Dante Gabriel Rossetti—to the latter of whom it was dedicated.

Bibliography

Berneri, Marie Louise. "Utopias of the Nineteenth Century," in *Journey Through Utopia*. Boston: Beacon Press, 1951, pp. 207–292.

Calhoun, Blue. *The Pastoral Vision of William Morris.* Athens: University of Georgia Press, 1975.

Clutton-Brock, Arthur. *William Morris: His Work and Influence.* New York: Holt, n.d.

Dahl, Curtis. "Morris's *The Chapel in Lyoness*, an Interpretation," in *Studies in Philology*. LX (July, 1954), pp. 482–491.

Faulkner, Peter. *William Morris and W.B. Yeats.* Dublin: Dolmen Press, 1962.

————. *William Morris: The Critical Heritage.* London: Routledge and Kegan Paul, 1973.

Grigson, Geoffrey. "William Morris," in his *The Contrary View*. London: Rowman and Littlefield, 1974, pp. 77–97.

Henderson, Philip. *William Morris.* London: Longmans, Green, 1952.

McAlindon, T. "The Idea of Byzantium in William Morris and W.B. Yeats," in *Modern Philology*. LXIV (May, 1967), pp. 307–319.

Noyes, Alfred. *William Morris.* London: Macmillan, 1908.

Parrott, Thomas M. "William Morris," in his *Companion to Victorian Literature*. New York: Scribner's, 1955, pp. 222–227.

Pater, Walter H. "Aesthetic Poetry," in his *Essays on Literature and Art*. London: Rowman and Littlefield, 1973, pp. 95–102.

Perrine, Laurence. "Morris's Guenevere: An Interpretation," in *Philological Quarterly*. XXXIX (1960), pp. 234–241.

Robson, W.W. "Pre-Raphaelite Poetry," in *British Victorian Literature*. Edited by S.K. Kumar. New York: New York University Press, 1969, pp. 172–191.

Saintsbury, George E. "Notes on Six Poets," in his *Last Vintage*. New York: Methuen, 1950, pp. 239–241.

Thompson, Francis. "Pre-Raphaelite Morris," in his *Literary Criticism*. New York: Dutton, 1948, pp. 198–203.

Tinker, Chauncey. "William Morris as Poet," in his *Essays in Retrospect.* New Haven, Conn.: Yale University Press, 1948, pp. 62–74.

Yeats, William Butler. "The Happiest of the Poets," in his *Essays and Introductions.* New York: Macmillan, 1961, pp. 53–64.

Young, George M. *Daylight and Champagne.* Chester Springs, Pa.: Dufour, 1948, pp. 60–66.

JOHN HENRY NEWMAN

Born: London, England (February 21, 1801)
Died: Birmingham, England (August 11, 1890)

Principal Works

THEOLOGICAL TRACTS AND STUDIES: *Tract XXXVIII*, 1834; *Tract XLI*, 1834; *Tract XC*, 1841; *Lectures on the Prophetical Office of the Church*, 1837; *Lectures on Justification*, 1838; *An Essay on the Development of Christian Doctrine*, 1845; *An Essay in Aid of a Grammar of Assent*, 1870; *Causes of the Rise of Arianism*, 1872; *Stray Essays on Controversial Points*, 1890.

AUTOBIOGRAPHY: *Apologia pro Vita Sua*, 1864 (*History of My Religious Opinons*).

NOVELS: *Loss and Gain*, 1848; *Callista: A Sketch of the Third Century*, 1856.

POEMS: *Verses on Religious Subjects*, 1853; *The Dream of Gerontius*, 1866; *Verses on Various Occasions*, 1868.

ESSAYS ON EDUCATION: *Discourses on the Scope and Nature of University Education*, 1852; *Lectures and Essays on University Subjects*, 1859; *The Idea of a University Defined*, 1873.

John Henry Newman, who was to be the outstanding figure in nineteenth century English theology, was born in London on February 21, 1801, the oldest son of John Newman, a banker. After private schooling at Ealing, young Newman entered Trinity College, Oxford, in 1817. Before this time, however, he had felt, at age fifteen, a strong call to religion, almost a conversion to deeply religious ways. This force was so great that he changed from a course in law to the study of divinity in 1820.

Graduated in 1820, he was made a fellow of Oriel College the next year. By 1831 Newman was made select preacher before the college, having been ordained an Anglican deacon in 1824. While returning from a visit to Italy in 1832, he wrote his most famous hymn, "Lead, Kindly Light." In July, 1833, he heard John Keble preach his famous sermon on the weaknesses of English government in matters of religion. Profoundly moved by this strong appeal, he and several others prepared and published a series of theological tracts called *Tracts for the Times*, (1833–1841). These publications marked the real beginning of the Oxford Movement, later called Tractarianism from the name of the series. Newman and his friends wanted a more secure and severe basis of doctrine for the Church of England; they felt that the Church had fallen from the high ideals and disciplines of the past, and they advocated a return to the more authoritative faith of previous eras.

In 1836 Newman became editor of the *British Critic* and was able to exert considerable influence in his praise of the "middle life" of the Anglican faith as opposed to the extremes of other religions. About the same time he began to see the firmness of the Catholic position, and learned to admire its principle of authority. In his last tract, *Tract XC*, published in 1841, Newman displayed his weakening opposition to Catholicism, and after retiring as editor he wrote *An Essay on the Development of Christian Doctrine*, a work defending the Catholic Church from a historical standpoint. In September of 1843 he resigned his living at St. Mary's Anglican Church at Oxford, and two years later he was admitted into the Catholic Church.

He was ordained a priest, in Rome, in 1847, and in the next year he returned to England, finally settling at Edgbaston Oratory in Birmingham, where he remained for most of the last forty years of his life. In 1851 he was appointed rector of the newly created Catholic University of Ireland, in Dublin, where he wrote his justly famous series of lectures, *Discourses on the Scope and Nature of University Education*, later revised as *The Idea of a University Defined*. He resigned his rectorship and returned to Edgbaston in 1858.

The great work of Newman's life resulted from an attack made on his sincerity by Charles Kingsley, who had slanderously attacked Newman's integrity. In his *Apologia pro Vita Sua*, published in 1864, Newman answered all attacks and by his obvious sincerity and brilliant writing in this religious autobiography turned the tide of public opinion in his favor. With the general approbation of the English people he continued setting up religious schools. In 1870 he produced *An Essay in Aid of a Grammar of Assent*, a delicately reasoned defense of religious belief which greatly increased his reputation. This reputation was so favorable that when Pope Leo XIII offered Newman a cardinal's hat in February of 1879, most Englishmen were pleased by the honor conferred. He became Cardinal Newman on May 12, 1879. After his return from Rome he resided at Edgbaston until his death on August 11, 1890.

Since his time Newman has stood for sincerity and devotion in religious matters. The extent to which his works are still published is sure evidence of his influence, and there are many Newman Societies established in his honor. The depth of his religious conviction may also be found in his one great poem, *The Dream of Gerontius*, written while his ever-failing health was in a precarious state. This deep and moving poem shows that had Newman chosen, he could have been one of the leading poets of the nineteenth century as well as an outstanding theologian.

Bibliography

John Henry Newman edited the Uniform Edition of his writings, 1869–1881. There are numerous editions of single and selected works. One useful and representative volume is *Newman, Prose and Poetry*, selected by Geoffrey Tillotson, Reynard Library series, 1957. The *Letters and Diaries*, under the general editorship of Charles S. Dessain are in progress, 1961–(about 30 vols., Vol. XXII, 1972). The standard biographies are Anne Mozley, *The Life and Correspondence of John Henry Newman*, 1892; and Wilfrid Ward, *The Life of John Henry Cardinal Newman*, 2 vols., 1912. The most recent biography is Meriol Trevor, Vol. I, *Newman: The Pillar of the Cloud*, Vol. II, *Newman: Light in Winter*, 1962. See also William Barry, *Newman*, 1904; J. C. May, *Cardinal Newman*, 1930; C. F. Harrold, *John Henry Newman*, 1945; and Thomas Vargish, *Newman: The Contemplation of Mind*, 1970. A more specialized study is J. J. Reilly, *Newman as a Man of Letters*, 1927. For an introduction to the story of the Oxford Movement see also W. G. Hutchinson, ed., *The Oxford Movement: Being a Selection from Tracts of the Times*, 1906—an edition containing eighteen of the tracts, including Nos. XXXVIII and XC, by Newman; T. B. Kittredge, *The Influence of Newman on the Oxford Movement*, 1914; H. L. Stewart, *A Century of Anglo-Catholicism*, 1929; A. H. T. Clarke, "The Passing of the Oxford Movement," *Nineteenth Century and After*, LXXI (1912), 133–147, 341–346; and E. G. Selwyn, "The Future of the Oxford Movement," *ibid.*, 532–546.

APOLOGIA PRO VITA SUA

Type of work: Autobiography
Author: John Henry Newman (1801–1890)
First published: 1864

Essay-Review

This long essay, also known as *History of My Religious Opinions*, is the famous reply written by John Henry Newman in answer to the attack made upon him by Charles Kingsley (1819–1875). The years 1833 to 1841 had seen the publication of the *Tracts for the Times*, to which Newman had been a contributor; these tracts, which gave their name to the "Tractarian Movement" or "Oxford Movement," were the spearhead of the great theological controversy of the middle years of the century. Newman and his friends were eager to return the Anglican Church to something like its position during past centuries; they valued tradition and hierarchy; they wished to go back to the severe, authoritarian faith of the past, from which they believed the Church of England had lapsed. In a word, they were the "High Church" party; and some idea of the rift that was created within the Church can be gleaned from Trollope's Barchester novels. In 1845, Newman left the Anglican Church for the Roman; two years later he was ordained priest in that communion.

In January, 1864, Kingsley, an Anglican clergyman of what was known as the "Broad Church" party and a popular novelist, attacked Newman in a magazine article, in which he stated that "Truth, for its own sake, has never been a virtue with the Roman clergy. Father Newman informs us that it need not, and on the whole ought not to be. . . ." To this article, Newman replied in a pamphlet in February of that year, whereupon Kingsley wrote still another pamphlet entitled "What, then, does Dr. Newman mean?" in which he accused Newman of having "gambled away" his reason, of having a "morbid" mind, and of not caring about "truth for its own sake." It was in answer to this pamphlet that *Apologia pro Vita Sua* was written.

Newman divided his work into chapters, each dealing with a crucial period in his life. The first gives the story of his youth and his education up to his thirty-second year, by which time he was a Fellow of Oriel College, Oxford, and had been ordained in the Anglican Church. By his own account, he emerges as an extraordinarily precocious lad, preoccupied at a very early age with religious questions. He resembled, indeed, the hero of his own novel *Loss and Gain*—which phrase might be applied as a description of his career. The modern reader will smile at Newman's decision, reached at the age of fifteen, that celibacy was the only course for him; yet his prodigious intellect shines through his very modest account of his youth. He tells us of his reading; but the real influences were his friends Hurrell Froude and the older John Keble (1792–1866). It was Froude, with his love for tradition and for the external beauty of the Roman Church, who began to soften Newman's insular dislike of that institution.

The year 1830 was a momentous one for Newman. The revolution that deposed Charles X of France distressed him; the Whig victory in England distressed him even more. He had a violent hatred of Liberalism, and everywhere it seemed triumphant. The "Tractarian Movement" was largely a counterattack. Newman himself claimed that the movement had begun to stir as far back as 1828, when he was Vicar of St. Mary's, Oxford; but the date of its beginning is usually set in July of 1833, when Keble preached a famous sermon at Oxford against the errors of the Whig government in Church policy. The *Tracts for the Times*, written by Newman and his friends, stated their position. As Newman saw it, the Whigs must be opposed and the Church of England returned to the position of authority it had held during the early seventeenth century. He considered himself as belonging to neither the "High" nor the "Low" Church party; he was merely anti-Liberal. He explained his position as based on: (1) dogma (he had no use for "religion as a mere sentiment"; there must be positive beliefs); (2) a visible Church with sacraments and rites and the Episcopal system; (3) anti-Romanism. Such was the general point of view of the Oxford Movement. Newman, incidentally, had very little to say about ritual, usually associated with the High Church position. He was interested in theology, not liturgics.

Newman admitted frankly that in the vast amount of writing he did during these years he had attempted to refute many of the tenets of Romanism. What he was seeking for himself was a basis in reason for his beliefs; for the Anglican Church, he was seeking a theology of its own that would make it more than a *via media*. These investigations led him to a consideration of the common heritage of Romanism and Anglicanism and to the question of how much of the Roman belief could be accepted by an Anglican. He began to be convinced that in English history the real objection to Rome had been political rather than theological; that Romanism and Anglicanism had, after all, not been so far apart as was generally believed. Inevitably, he began to find a difference between Roman dogmas, which he could accept, and Roman practice, which he often could not. He confessed that, for a long time, the stumbling block had been the Roman veneration of the Virgin and prayers to the saints. But he was obviously drawing closer to Rome.

It was Tract XC, published in 1841, that brought the storm on Newman's head and led to his final break with the Church of England. In this tract he examined the question of how far the Thirty-Nine Articles, on which the Church rests, were capable of a Roman interpretation. Immediately he was accused of everything from "traducing the Reformation" to planning to build a monastery near Oxford. He himself was feeling grave doubts about Anglicanism, derived mainly from his reading on the abstruse doctrines of the Monophysites. When he could no longer conscientiously maintain his clerical position, he resigned his living of St. Mary's in September 1843. As he explained, he had spent the years from 1835 to 1839 trying, in his writings, to benefit the Church of England at the expense of the Church of Rome and the years from 1839 to 1843 trying to benefit the Church of

England without prejudice to the Church of Rome. In 1843 he began to despair of the Church of England.

The years between 1843 and 1845 were spent, according to Newman, in retirement. He had now reached the crossroads but was as yet unable to make his final decision. He had already retracted the "hard things" he had said against Rome, the things he had felt compelled to say in defense of the Anglican Church. He made a point of seeing no Roman Catholics; his struggle was purely an inward one. Though he still felt that the Church of England was a branch of the true Church, though he still deplored the "Mariolatry" of Rome, he was convinced that Rome was more in accord with the early Church. His horror of Liberalism also played its part; he very genuinely felt that the spirit of Liberalism was the spirt of Antichrist. As he now saw the situation, on the one hand there was Liberalism leading inevitably to atheism; on the other, Anglicanism leading to Rome. He still remained in lay communion with the Church of England during this difficult period, but more and more often he found himself asking this question: "Can I be saved in the English Church?" When he was compelled to answer in the negative, he made the great decision and was received into the Roman Communion in 1845. Two years later he was ordained priest.

In the concluding section of the essay Newman defended himself against the jibes that were hurled at him after his conversion. It was said that by submitting to Rome he had abdicated his power of personal judgment and that he was now compelled to accept dogmas which might, at any moment, be changed. His reply was that the Roman doctrines were not difficult for him, that historically the Church had not suppressed freedom of intellect. He felt that an infallible Church had been intended by the Creator to preserve religion—especially in an age of increasing skepticism. Lastly—and this is the most famous part of the essay—he advanced the idea that a conflict between authority and private judgment is beneficial to the man whose ideas are being tested.

Though the *Apologia* won Newman a resounding victory over Kingsley, the work is not easy reading. The difficulty does not lie in the style, for Newman's prose is direct and lucid. But he wrote for readers who were familiar with Church history and with theological problems, so that most readers in our age of religious ignorance and indifference lack the knowledge to grasp many of his arguments. It is difficult today to understand his dilemma. Yet the *Apologia* remains a powerful and sincere work. Some, naturally, have seen in Newman, as Kingsley must have done, only a man whose habit of mind made him take refuge in an authoritarian Church which would solve his spiritual problems for him. Others, taking the opposite view, would agree with Ramon Fernandez: "In him intelligence and faith act as mutual brakes and yet no attentive reader can accuse him of the slightest artifice."

WALTER PATER

Born: London, England (August 4, 1839)
Died: Oxford, England (July 30, 1894)

Principal Works

ESSAYS AND STUDIES: *Studies in the History of the Renaissance*, 1873; *Appreciations, with an Essay on Style*, 1889; *Plato and Platonism*, 1893; *Miscellaneous Studies*, 1895.
NOVELS: *Marius the Epicurean*, 1885; *The Child in the House*, 1894.
TALES AND SKETCHES: *Imaginary Portraits*, 1887.

Walter (Horatio) Pater was born in London on August 4, 1839. Having attended King's School in Canterbury and graduated B.A. from Queen's College, Oxford, he was made Fellow of Brasenose College, Oxford, from which he received his M.A. degree in 1865. With this college he was connected in some capacity during most of the rest of his life. During vacations, however, he often traveled on the Continent. He died at Oxford after a brief illness, on July 30, 1894.

Much of Pater's literary output consisted of critical essays on aesthetic subjects, most of which were collected in such works as *Studies in the History of the Renaissance* and *Appreciations, with an Essay on Style.* Critics have spoken of his sensual approach to art, and some are bothered by a certain subjective impressionism in his criticism. Pater also wrote a few romances, the most famous of which is *Marius the Epicurean.* There is a relation between these romances and his critical works because in the romances he seems to advocate that life itself be approached as an art. Through elaborate sentences with delicate shadings he worked continually for perfection of expression in his prose style. Although Pater spent most of his life in academic seclusion, he had a profound influence on a group of perceptive younger artists and critics.

Bibliography

Pater's works are collected in the New Library Edition of the *Works of Walter Pater*, 10 vols., 1910. The *Letters* were edited by Lawrence Evans, 1971. The standard bibliography is C. A. and H. W. Stonehill, *Bibliographies of Modern Authors*, Series 2, 1925. The best biographies are Thomas Wright, *The Life of Walter Pater*, 2 vols., 1907; and A. C. Benson's *Walter Pater*, English Men of Letters Series, 1906, which includes a critical bibliography. Other critical works include Helen H. Young, *The Writings of Walter Pater: A Reflection of British Philosophical Opinion From 1860 to 1890*, 1933; R. C. Child, *The Aesthetic of Walter Pater*, 1940; R. V. Johnson, *Walter Pater: A Study of His Critical Outlook*, 1961; and Gordon McKenzie, *The Literary Character of Walter Pater*,

1967. Short critical articles are T. S. Eliot, "Arnold and Pater," in *Selected Essays*, 1932; G. G. Hough, "Walter Pater" in *The Last Romantics*, 1949; Geoffrey Tillotson, "Arnold and Pater: Critics Historical, Aesthetic, and Otherwise," in *Criticism and the Nineteenth Century*, 1951; R. V. Johnson, "Pater and the Victorian Anti-Romantics," *Essays in Criticism*, IV (1954), 42–57; and Lord David Cecil's published lecture, *Walter Pater: The Scholar-Artist*, 1955.

THE RENAISSANCE

Type of work: Essays in art appreciation and criticism
Author: Walter Pater (1839–1894)
First published: 1873

Essay-Review

In the preface to *The Renaissance*, originally titled *Studies in the History of the Renaissance*, Pater writes, "The subjects of the following studies ... touch what I think the chief points in that complex, many-sided movement." The subjects themselves are the French, Italian, and German writers, painters, and sculptors, ranging from the thirteenth to the eighteenth century, in whose lives and in whose works Pater finds represented the many sides, the divergent attitudes and aims, of the Renaissance.

Pater's method is impressionistic. The task of the aesthetic critic, he says, is first to realize distinctly the exact impression which a work of art makes upon him, then to determine the source and conditions—the "virtue"—of that impression, and finally to express that virtue so that the impression it has made on him may be shared by others. *The Renaissance* is largely the record of the impressions induced in the refined temperament of Walter Pater by the art he studies.

The Renaissance, for Pater, was "not merely the revival of classical antiquity which took place in the fifteenth century ... but a whole complex movement, of which that revival of classical antiquity was but one element or symptom." Accordingly, in the first chapter, he finds the roots of the movement in thirteenth century France, illustrated in the prose romances, *Li Amitiez de Ami et Amile* and *Aucassin et Nicolette*. It is in their "spirit of rebellion and revolt against the moral and religious ideas of the time" that these tales prefigure that later "outbreak of the reason and the imagination," the high Renaissance of fifteenth century Italy.

One important part of that later Renaissance, says Pater, was the effort made by fifteenth century Italian scholars "to reconcile Christianity with the religion of ancient Greece." Pico della Mirandola typified that effort, both in his writings and in his life; he was "reconciled indeed to the new religion, but still [had] a tenderness for the earlier life." Lacking the historic sense, Pico and his contemporaries sought in vain, as Pater saw it, a reconciliation based on allegorical interpretations of religious belief; "the Renaissance of the fifteenth century was ... great, rather by what it designed ... than by what it actually achieved."

In discussing Boticelli, Pater acknowledges that he is a painter, of secondary rank, not great as Michelangelo and Leonardo are great. Nonetheless his work has a distinct quality, "the result of a blending in him of a sympathy for humanity in its uncertain condition ... with his consciousness of the shadow upon it of the great things from which it shrinks." He is a forcible realist and a visionary painter as well. Part of his appeal to Pater is simply in this, that "he has the freshness, the uncertain and diffident promise which belong to the earlier Renaissance"—that age which Pater called "perhaps the most interesting period in the history of the mind."

The chapter titled "Luca della Robbia" is as much about sculpture in general as it is about Luca. The limitation of sculpture, says Pater, is that it tends toward "a hard realism, a one-sided presentment of mere form." The Greeks countered this tendency by depicting the type rather than the individual, by purging the accidental until "their works came to be like some subtle extract or essence, or almost like pure thoughts or ideas." But this method sacrificed *expression*. Michelangelo "with a genius spiritualised by the reverie of the middle age," offset the tendency of sculpture towards realism by "leaving nearly all his sculpture in a puzzling sort of incompleteness, which suggests rather than realises actual form." Luca della Robbia and other fifteenth century Tuscan sculptors achieved "a profound expressiveness" by working in low relief earthenware, the subtle delineation of line serving as the means of overcoming the special limitation of sculpture.

In "The Poetry of Michelangelo" we find out less about the poetry itself than we do about Pater's impressions of it. No one, says Pater, need be reminded of the strength of Michelangelo's work. There is, however, another and equally important quality of his work, and that Pater refers to variously as "charm," "sweetness," and "a lovely strangeness." It is in a "brooding spirit of life," achieved only through an idealization of life's "vehement sentiments," that this quality of sweetness resides. There were, says Pater, two traditions of the ideal which Michelangelo might have followed: that of Dante, who idealized the material world, and that of Platonism. It was the Platonic tradition that molded Michelangelo's verse; "Michelangelo is always pressing forward from the outward beauty . . . to apprehend the unseen beauty . . . that abstract form of beauty, about which the Platonists reason." Yet the influence of Dante is there too, in the sentiment of imaginative love. To Pater, Michelangelo was "the last . . . of those on whom the peculiar sentiment of the Florence of Dante and Giotto descended: he is the consummate representative of the form that sentiment took in the fifteenth century." In this sentiment is another source of his "grave and temperate sweetness."

The fifteenth century witnessed two movements: the return to antiquity represented, says Pater, by Raphael and the return to nature represented by Leonardo da Vinci. In Leonardo the return to nature took on a special coloring, for Leonardo's genius was composed not only of a desire for beauty but also of a curiosity which gave to his paintings "a type of subtle and curious grace." His landscapes, as in the background of his masterpiece, *La Gioconda*, partake of the *"bizarre* of *recherché."* One of the most famous passages in the book is Pater's description of *La Gioconda*. Pater sees in the Mona Lisa the image of archetypal woman: "All the thoughts and experience of the world have etched and moulded" her features.

In "The School of Giorgione" (which did not appear in the first edition), Pater propounds his famous dictum that "All art constantly aspires towards the condition of music." The "condition of music" is a complete fusing, an interpenetration, of matter and form. The other arts achieve perfection in the degree that they approach or approximate this condition. Giorgione and others of the Venetian school are representative of the aspiration towards perfect identification of matter and form in their realization that "painting must be before all things decorative." Their subjects are from life, but "mere subject" is subordinated to "pictorial design," so that matter is interpenetrated by form.

In the chapter on Joachim du Bellay, Pater turns from Italy to France, to the theories and the elegant verse of the *Pleiad*. Du Bellay wrote a tract in which he sought "to adjust the existing French culture to the rediscovered classical culture." In this tract, says Pater, the Renaissance became aware of itself as a systematic movement. The ambition of the *Pleiad* was to combine the "music of the measured, scanned verse of Latin and Greek poetry" with "the music of the rhymed, unscanned verse of Villon and the old French poets."

The longest chapter of *The Renaissance* is devoted to Johann Joachim Winckelmann, a German scholar in the study of antiquity. His importance, for Pater, is chiefly that he influenced Goethe: "Goethe illustrates a union of the Romantic spirit . . . with Hellenism . . . that marriage . . . of which the art of the nineteenth century is the child." The Hellenic element, characterized by "breadth, centrality, with blitheness and repose," was made known to Goethe by Winckelmann. Winckelmann stands, then, as a link between antiquity (and the Renaissance) and the modern, post-Enlightenment world.

The most celebrated part of the book—and indeed of Pater's entire body of writing—is the conclusion to *The Renaissance*. Here he utters the famous, and frequently misinterpreted, dicta: "Not the fruit of experience, but experience itself, is the end" and "To burn always with this hard, gemlike flame, to maintain this ecstasy, is success in life." These statements must be seen in the context of Pater's conception of the nature of human existence.

For Pater reality is human experience. It consists not in the objective, material world but in the impressions of color, odor, and texture which that world produces in the observer's mind. Each impression endures for but a single moment and then is gone. Life is made up of the succession of these momentary impressions, and life itself is brief.

Not to make the most of these moments, not to experience them fully, is to waste a lifetime. "What we have to do," says Pater, "is to be for ever curiously testing new opinions and courting new impressions." Given the brevity of our lives and given as well the brevity of the very impressions which constitute our lives, "we shall hardly have time to make theories about the things we see and touch." Hence, "not the fruit of experience, but experience itself, is the end."

This emphasis on experience also leads Pater to distinguish among kinds of experience, and the highest kind, he says, is the great passions (themselves a kind of wisdom) we gain from art. "For art comes to you proposing frankly to give nothing but the highest quality to your moments as they pass"—a life constituted of such moments will indeed "burn always" with a "hard, gemlike flame."

Pater omitted the conclusion from the second edition of the book, fearing "it might possibly mislead some of those young men into whose hands it might fall." Having explained his beliefs more fully in *Marius the Epicurean* and having altered the conclusion slightly, he restored it to later editions.

CHRISTINA ROSSETTI

Born: London, England (December 5, 1830)
Died: London (December 29, 1894)

Principal Works

POEMS: *Goblin Market and Other Poems*, 1862; *The Prince's Progress and Other Poems*, 1866; *Sing Song*, 1872; *A Pageant and Other Poems*, 1881; *Verses*, 1893; *New Poems*, 1896.

DEVOTIONAL STUDIES: *Speaking Likenesses*, 1874; *Seek and Find*, 1879; *Called Be the Saints*, 1881; *Letter and Spirit*, 1882; *Time Flies*, 1885; *The Face of the Deep*, 1892.

Christina (Georgina) Rossetti, born in London on December 5, 1830, was the sister of Dante Gabriel Rossetti, and the youngest child of a Neapolitan political refugee who had settled in England and who became, eventually, Professor of Italian at King's College, University of London. She began to write poetry very early in her life, and when she was seventeen a small volume of her work was printed at her grandfather's private press. A year later, in 1848, one of her lyrics was published in *The Athenaeum*. When Dante Gabriel Rossetti founded the Pre-Raphaelite magazine, *The Germ*, in 1850, she became one of its frequent contributors, using the pseudonym Ellen Alleyn. Twelve years later her first volume, *Goblin Market and Other Poems*, appeared publicly. She continued to write until the end of her life, but only four more volumes, including her poems for children, were published during her lifetime.

Although her creative life extended over a long period, her output, in terms of quantity, was not extensive for two reasons. The first had to do with the form of the poetry she wrote and the fact that she was essentially a composer of brief lyrics. Like precious gems, they were small but clear and of exceeding value; but since she wrote only when she felt the possibility of perfection, her work was understandably limited. The other reason for her small poetic output was her extreme religious devotion. As she grew older she turned more and more from her poetry to the writing of her religious prose, expending her creative energy on this less artistic genre. Yet it cannot be said that her religious interests worked against her poetry, for the poetry itself is imbued completely with her religious feelings. Some lyrics, such as "Three Enemies," "Weary in Well-Doing," and "A Better Resurrection," are specifically religious in theme and subject matter. In all she wrote, at the root if not in stalk and branch, is her religious preoccupation.

This preoccupation was dominant in her personality as well. Sickly most of her life, and an actual invalid during her last years, she turned more and more from the world until she became almost a complete recluse. In her youth she had refused two different suitors because they did not conform to her Church of England beliefs and had chosen instead to remain with her equally devout mother. Having channeled all of her emotional energies into her religion, nevertheless in the end she was tormented by doubt, not of her beliefs but of her own worthiness. It was in this spirit that she cried out, "My life is like a faded leaf/My harvest dwindled to a husk," taking no consolation in the fact that the pure freshness of some of her lyrics will remain green for centuries. She died in London on December 29, 1894.

Bibliography

The standard edition of the *Poetical Works* was edited by William Michael Rossetti, 1904 (rev. ed., 1924). The most important study is Lona M. Packer, *Christina Rossetti*, 1963. For further biography and criticism see H. T. M. Bell, *Christina Rosetti: A Biographical and Critical Study*, 1898; Justine de Wilde, *Christina Rossetti, Poet and Woman*, 1923; M. F. Sandars, *The Life of Christina Rossetti*, 1930; Dorothy M. Stuart, *Christina Rossetti*, English Men of Letters Series, 1930; Fredegond Shove, *Christina Rossetti: A Study*, 1931; Eleanor W. Thomas, *Christina Georgina Rossetti*, 1931; and Georgina Battiscombe, *Christina Rossetti*, 1965. For background studies of the Rossetti family and the period see also R. D. Waller, *The Rossetti Family, 1824–1854*, 1932; and Frances Winwar, *Poor Splendid Wings: The Rossettis and Their Circle*, 1933. Virginia Woolf has an essay on Christina Rossetti in *The Common Reader, Second Series*, 1932. See also Winston Weather, "Christina Rossetti: The Sisterhood of Self," *Victorian Poetry*, III (Spring 1965), 81–89.

THE POETRY OF CHRISTINA ROSSETTI

Author: Christina Rossetti (1830–1894)
Principal published works: Goblin Market and Other Poems, 1862; *The Prince's Progress and Other Poems*, 1866; *Sing Song*, 1872; *A Pageant and Other Poems*, 1881; *Verses*, 1893; *New Poems*, 1896

Essay-Review

The sister of Dante Gabriel Rossetti, one of the founders of the Pre-Raphaelite Brotherhood, Christina Rossetti began writing poetry in her early teens. Her verse, always simple, pure, direct, never lost some of the childlike and direct quality evident in her earliest work. Indeed, she later wrote a nursery rhyme book (*Sing Song*), full of pleasant and sharp little rhymes for children. She even included a rhymed alphabet, containing six or eight onomatopoetic references for each letter. Her skill and facility in light verse can be seen in the lines like the following from "An Alphabet":

> K is a King, or a Kaiser still higher;
> K is a Kitten, or quaint Kangaroo.
> L is a Lute or a lovely-toned Lyre
> L is a Lily all laden with dew.

Her deftness in children's verse and in slight lyrics lasted throughout her poetic career.

Christina Rossetti is, however, far better remembered for her religious or devotional poetry. Living in partial seclusion with her family (primarily with her mother until the latter's death in 1886), Christina Rossetti saw little of the London around her but lived intensely within her own private world of religious contemplation and meditation. Her poetry, the product of inward contemplation rather than a weapon for a public cause like that of the Pre-Raphaelites, was most frequently devotional. Her themes were faith and the peace of the eternal spiritual life.

Her religion was not theological or doctrinal, however, in the manner of many Victorians, for she concentrated on simple faith and applied her simple and pure lyrics to celebration of that faith. In this simple faith, Jesus was the object of much of her devotion; she wrote a number of poems on the incidents in His life and used Good Friday and the Resurrection as a subject for several of her best poems. In devoting her poems, the products of her faith, to Jesus, she idealized the peace that the individual could find in his dedication to Christianity and the life of the spirit. She seemed, often, to picture herself as humble and unworthy, to long for the peace of eternal rest without ever being sure she could obtain it. She made religion a haven, frequently in her poetry presenting religion as a resting place from the cares of a troubled life. This theme, along with her simple diction, is evident in the following passage from "I Do Set My Bow in the Cloud":

> Then tell me: is it not enough
> To feel that, when the path is rough
> And the sky dark and the rain cold,
> His promise standeth as of old?
> When heaven and earth have past away
> Only His righteous word shall stay,
> And we shall know His will is best.
> Behold: He is a haven-rest,
> A sheltering-rock, a hiding place,
> For runners steadfast in the race;
> Who, toiling for a little space,
> Had light through faith when sight grew dim,
> And offered all their world to Him.

This passage illustrates many of Miss Rossetti's frequent attitudes: the darkness and difficulty of this world, usually portrayed in wintry images; the sense of God's promise to man emanating through all human experience; the idea of the "sheltering-rock," the haven of faith in which the poor human being could "hide"; the sense that religious faith, without question, is more important for man than are any of his own attempts to see and understand the world about him.

In her devotional poetry she frequently presents simple images of nature through which she demonstrates her devotion. Flowers, the coming of spring and hope, the simple natural details of the world around her, form the pattern of images through which her faith is conveyed. The fields and the meadows, like her simple reflections, all demonstrate the power of God and man's necessary faith in the mercy and forgiveness of Christ. The most common symbol in her poetry is the rose. Standing for a kind of spiritual beauty, an emanation of the spirit of Christ, the rose figures centrally in her work. Roses are, in a poem like "Three Nuns," the flowers planted in paradise, the sure indications of the existence of divine love. The rose is also, in this and other poems, the symbol of purity, of a virginal and spiritual beauty that emanates from the divine. In addition, the rose is often solitary, blooming alone in a dark and wintry landscape. As a figure of solitary beauty, the rose becomes an emblem for faith and virtue in the midst of a dark and corrupt world.

Christina Rossetti's faith was not simply a private matter. In her poetry she demonstrated a great deal of concern for her family and her small circle of friends, and she included them in her poetic requests for the blessings of a merciful Christ. Many of her poems mark family occasions: birthday greetings, valentines to her mother, hopes that her talented brothers could find the peace and rest latent in the true faith. Sometimes she questions her worthiness for salvation, although she generally concludes that Christ is sufficiently merciful to receive her in paradise. In these poems she often comments on the vanity of worldy ambition and the folly of man's pride. Although she humbly includes her own inclination to judge others as one of the most damning of sins, she often speaks out against those less faithful to the divine spirit than she, giving her work qualities of precision and sharpness.

Not all of Christina Rossetti's verse is religious or devotional. She can be light and witty; some of her early epigrams have the flavor of Jane Austen's quiet, civilized, cutting comments. She also wrote a few satirical poems, like one called "The P.R.B." which begins:

> The two Rossettis (brothers they)
> And Holman Hunt and John Millais,
> With Stephens chivalrous and bland,
> And Woolner in a distant land—
> In these six men I awestruck see
> Embodied the great P.R.B.
> D.G. Rossetti offered two
> Good pictures to the public view;
> Unnumbered ones great John Millais,
> And Holman more than I can say
> William Rossetti, calm and solemn,
> Cuts up his brethren by the column.

Some of this sharpness and directness also appears in the poems she wrote about neighboring farm girls. These poems sometimes begin with a simple characterization or a simple account of the circumstances in which the farm girl lived. From this point, the writer goes on, as in "Margery," to demonstrate that the unhappy girl should not have been so obvious in letting her boyfriend know that she loved him, or she may urge the simple farmer to speak up and tell his love. These poems have a direct, homely quality of easy and unpretentious diction. If they frequently add a didactic tag that spoils them for modern ears, the moral is also kept in the language and the area of concern in the poem. Wit and homely common sense distinguished much of Christina Rossetti's nonreligious poetry, an indication that her observation of the world around her was as sharp, though restrained, as her allegiance to the world of spirit was thorough and genuine.

Praised in her own time for the clarity and sweetness of her diction as well as for the purity of her faith, Christina Rossetti was widely read, although not widely imitated, for she introduced little in the way of technical innovation or a new area of poetic subject matter. Faith is often more bitter in the twentieth century, and the simplicity of her faith seems remote and unworldly to many contemporary readers. Yet the simplicity of her diction and the ability to state a perception with ease and grace and point are still qualities that endear this writer to many modern readers. Although her public is not wide, it is faithful and appreciative.

Bibliography

Battiscombe, Georgina. *Christina Rossetti.* London: Longmans, Green, 1965, pp. 16–36.

Bellas, Ralph A. *Christina Rossetti.* New York: Twayne, 1977, pp. 21–98.

Bowra, C.M. "Christina Rossetti," in his *The Romantic Imagination.* Cambridge, Mass.: Harvard University Press, 1949, pp. 245–270.

Cary, Elisabeth Luther. "Christina Rossetti: Her Poetry," in her *The Rossettis: Dante Gabriel and Christina.* New York: Putnam's, 1900, pp. 251–275.

Curran, Stuart. "The Lyric Voice of Christina Rossetti," in *Victorian Poetry.* IX (Autumn, 1971), pp. 287–299.

de la Mare, Walter. "Christina Rossetti," in *Essays by Divers Hands, Being the Transactions of the Royal Society of Literature of the United Kingdom,* Volume VI. Edited by G.K. Chesterton. London: Milford, 1926, pp. 79–116.

Dombrowski, Theo. "Dualism in the Poetry of Christina Rossetti," in *Victorian Poetry.* XIV (1976), pp. 70–76.

Evans, B. Ifor. "Christina Georgina Rossetti," in his *English Poetry in the Later Nineteenth Century.* London: Methuen, 1933, pp. 65–80.

Fairchild, Hoxie Neale. "Christina Rossetti," in his *Religious Trends in English Poetry, Volume IV: 1830–1880: Christianity and Romanticism in the Victorian Era.* New York: Columbia University Press, 1957, pp. 302–316.

Gosse, Edmund. "Christina Rossetti," in *Century Magazine.* XLVI (June, 1893), pp. 211–217. Reprinted in his *Critical Kit-Kats.* New York: Dodd, Mead, 1903, pp. 135–157.

Hueffer, Ford Madox. "Christina Rossetti," in *Fortnightly Review.* XCV (March, 1911), pp. 422–429. Reprinted as "Christina Rossetti and Pre-Raphaelite Love," in his *Ancient Lights.* London: Chapman and Hall, 1911, pp. 54–69. Also reprinted in his *Memories and Impressions: A Study in Atmospheres.* New York: Harper, 1911, pp. 60–77.

More, Paul Elmer. "Christina Rossetti," in *Atlantic Monthly.* XCIV (December, 1904), pp. 815–821. Reprinted in his *Shelburne Essays.* New York: Putnam's, 1905, pp. 124–142.

Packer, Lona Mosk. *Christina Rossetti.* Berkeley: University of California Press, 1963.

Reilly, Joseph J. "Christina Rossetti: Poet of Renunciation," in his *Dear Prue's Husband and Other People.* New York: Macmillan, 1932, pp. 144–161.

Robb, Nesca Adeline. "Christina Rossetti," in her *Four in Exile.* London: Hutchinson's, 1948, pp. 82–119.

Robson, W.W. "Pre-Raphaelite Poetry," in *British Victorian Literature: Recent Evaluations*. Edited by S.K. Kumar. New York: New York University Press, 1969, pp. 172–191.

Stevenson, Lionel. "Christina Rossetti," in his *The Pre-Raphaelite Poets*. Chapel Hill: University of North Carolina Press, 1972, pp. 78–122.

Stuart, Dorothy Margaret. *Christina Rossetti.* London: Oxford University Press, 1931, pp. 1–18.

Swann, Thomas Burnett. *Wonder and Whimsy: The Fantastic World of Christina Rossetti.* Francestown, N.H.: Marshall Jones, 1960, pp. 32–91.

Symons, Arthur. "Christina G. Rossetti: 1830–1894," in *The Poets and the Poetry of the Nineteenth Century*, Volume IX. Edited by Alfred H. Miles. New York: Dutton, 1907, pp. 1–16.

Thomas, Eleanor Walter. *Christina Georgina Rossetti.* New York: Columbia University Press, 1931, pp. 120–212.

Walker, Hugh. "The Turn of the Century: New Influences," in his *The Literature of the Victorian Era*. Cambridge: Cambridge University Press, 1910, pp. 501–508.

Waugh, Arthur. "Christina Rossetti, December 5, 1830; December 5, 1930," in *Nineteenth Century*. CVIII (December, 1930), pp. 787–798.

Weathers, Winston. "Christina Rossetti: The Sisterhood of Self," in *Victorian Poetry*. III (Spring, 1965), pp. 81–89.

Woolf, Virginia. "I Am Christina Rossetti," in *Nation and Athenaeum*. XLVIII (December 6, 1930), pp. 322–324. Reprinted in her *The Second Common Reader*. New York: Harcourt, Brace, 1932, pp. 257–265.

DANTE GABRIEL ROSSETTI

Born: London, England (May 12, 1828)
Died: Birchington, England (April 9, 1882)

Principal Works

POEMS: *Poems*, 1870; *Ballads and Sonnets*, 1881; *Collected Works*, 1886.
TRANSLATIONS: *Early Italian Poets*, 1861 (retitled *Dante and His Circle*, 1874).

Dante Gabriel Rossetti was born in London, May 12, 1828, the son of Gabriele Rossetti, a political refugee from Naples, and the brother of Christina, the poet, and of William Michael Rossetti, later to be the historian of the Pre-Raphaelites. He attended King's College School in London and then various art schools, finally becoming a pupil of Ford Madox Brown. It was in 1848 that Rossetti, Millais, and Holman Hunt founded the Pre-Raphaelite Brotherhood that was to be a storm center in English art for many years. In 1850 they began their magazine, *The Germ*, in which Rossetti published some of his early poems. The paintings of the group were bitterly attacked by Dickens and by the conventional critics; it was only through the influence of Ruskin, then the aesthetic dictator of art and culture, that the public finally accepted the Pre-Raphaelites and their work.

In 1851 Rossetti became engaged to Elizabeth Siddall, whose peculiar beauty had fascinated him and who had become his model; but they were not married until 1860. She was consumptive; their marriage was unhappy because of Rossetti's increasing indifference, and in 1862 she died of an overdose of laudanum, probably a suicide. Then followed the melodramatic gesture of Rossetti's burying the only manuscript of his poems in her coffin and the gruesome sequel of their exhumation in 1869.

Very early, Rossetti came under the influence of Percy's *Reliques* (1765), the poems of Scott, and various medieval romances; and these influences, plus the avowed medievalism of the Pre-Raphaelites, gave to his poetry its special tone. He excelled in the imitation or adaption of the border ballads; his "Sister Helen" has been considered one of the best literary ballads of the nineteenth century. To the stark language of the old poems he added the luxuriant coloring and mysticism of the Pre-Raphaelites. His sonnet-sequence, "The House of Life," inspired by his love for Elizabeth Siddall and Jane Morris, has also been highly praised. Pre-Raphaelite poetry is out of fashion now, being considered overly-decorated and artificial; yet at the time it was a relief from the didacticism of much Victorian verse.

After 1868 Rossetti became subject to fits of melancholia aggravated by the attack on him in 1871 by Robert Buchanan, in an anonymous essay, "The Fleshly School of Poetry." His failing eyesight eventually made him abandon painting for poetry. His last years were made bearable only through the devoted attention of his brother. He died April 9, 1882, at Birchington, near Margate.

Bibliography

Biographical and critical studies of Rossetti are extensive, and there are numerous collections of his letters. Of particular interest is *D. G. Rossetti's Family Letters*, edited by William M. Rossetti, 1895, who also edited *Pre-Raphaelite Diaries and Letters*, 1900, and *Rossetti Papers, 1862–1870*, 1903. The definitive edition of the *Letters* is that of Oswald Doughty and John R. Wahl, eds., 4 vols., 1965–1967. Biographical and critical studies include William M. Rossetti, *Ruskin, Rossetti: Pre-Raphaelitism*, 1899; F. G. Stephens, *D. G. Rossetti*, 1894; A. C. Benson, *Rossetti*, in the English Men of Letters Series, 1904; Evelyn Waugh, *Rossetti: His Life and Work*, 1928; R. L. Mégroz, *Dante Gabriel Rossetti*, 1929; Viola Hunt, *The Wife of Rossetti*, 1932; Frances V. Winwar, *Poor Splendid Wings*, 1933; *idem, The Rossettis and Their Circle*, 1934; William Gaunt, *The Pre-Raphaelite Tragedy*, 1942; O. Doughty, *A Victorian Romantic: D. G. Rossetti*, 1949; Gordon Hough, *The Last Romantics*, 1949; J. Heath-Stubbs, *The Darkling Plain*, 1950; and Rosalie Glynn Grylls, *Portrait of Rossetti*, 1964. See also W. Stacy Johnson, "D. G. Rossetti as Painter and Poet," *Victorian Poetry*, III (1965), 9–18.

THE POETRY OF DANTE GABRIEL ROSSETTI

Author: Dante Gabriel Rossetti (1828–1882)
Principal published works: Poems, 1870; *Ballads and Sonnets*, 1881; *Collected Works*, 1886

Essay-Review

Some glimpse into Rossetti's ideas on poetry can be obtained from the statement made, at almost the end of his life, to Hall Caine, that when, as a youth, he had first encountered early English ballad literature, he had said to himself, "There lies your line." He read the collections made by Thomas Percy (1765) and by Sir Walter Scott (1802–1803) as well as Scott's original poetry, and he spent many hours in the British Museum poring over medieval romances in a search for words to use in poems that he planned to write.

He began his career, however, as a painter, and entered literature through the coterie which called itself the Pre-Raphaelite Brotherhood. This loosely-knit group, formed in 1848 by Rossetti, Holman Hunt, and J. E. Millais, had as its artistic goal the return to the "fidelity to nature" of Italian painters prior to Raphael. Thus both as painter and as poet Rossetti was directed towards the past. The new group soon needed a periodical through which the members could make their views known; so, in 1850, they founded *The Germ*. Its life was short—only four numbers appeared—but in it some of Rossetti's early work was printed.

Surely no manuscript in all of English literature had a stranger or more macabre history than did Rossetti's first volume of poems. When, on a February night of 1862, he returned to his home to find his wife dead from an overdose of laudanum, he was so conscience-stricken by the possibility that her death had been suicide that he resolved on the melodramatic gesture of placing the manuscript in her coffin under her famous red-gold hair. Even his brother William, who knew that for some of the poems no other copies existed, while for others there were but imperfect copies, was sufficiently influenced by the tension-charged atmosphere to approve the act. The manuscript contained some of Rossetti's most famous poems: "The Blessed Damozel," "Jenny," "Sister Helen" (first titled "The Witch"), and "Love's Nocturn." But further melodrama was to come. In October, 1869, Rossetti, who now wished to publish the poems and had even advertised their appearance, had the grave opened and the manuscript disinterred by C. A. Howell and Dr. Llewellyn Williams. For this exhumation, which he somewhat lamely tried to justify, Rossetti has been much criticized, one biographer even calling him a "changeable widower rifling his dead wife's grave at the dictate of literary ambition."

The pieces that Rossetti included in this first volume can be divided, at least roughly, into three classes: "medieval" poems, love poems, and sonnets for pictures. By the first category is meant those verses employing medieval settings or imitations of medieval techniques. Rossetti derived his literary medievalism from two sources, the romance and the ballad. From the romance he obtained the colorful background of knights, ladies, and castles found in "The Staff and Scrip"; from the ballad he got the terse, tragic story as well as such devices as the refrain and the question and answer method of narration. These two technical devices, which were common enough in the traditional border ballads, Rossetti—as well as the other Pre-Raphaelite poets—developed into artistic elements of considerable effectiveness. From the simple refrain of the old ballads they created what has been called the "incremental" refrain—that is, a refrain which, by changing with the progress of the narrative and its emotional pattern, helps to build up the climax of the story. The trick is best seen in "Sister Helen," which has been considered one of the best literary ballads of the nineteenth century. This poem adds to the starkness of the traditional ballad modern psychological insights. Usually, however, Rossetti tended to overlay the simplicity of the old ballads with the luxuriant detail so dear to the Pre-Raphaelites.

Another side of Rossetti's medievalism appears in his three translations from Villon, one of which, the "Ballad of Dead Ladies," is perhaps the most famous short piece of translation in English.

Rossetti's love poetry, both of this time and later, presents a difficult problem. To understand the work of any poet, one must know something of his life; and this statement is particularly true of Rossetti. Even on the surface, his love poems are not easy reading, for they are densely woven, at times enigmatic. The mystery turns on his attitude toward his dead wife, Elizabeth Siddall, and on the circumstances of her death. It is now fairly well agreed among Rossetti biographers that her death was an act of suicide, and that the suspicion—or even the knowledge—of this fact haunted Rossetti for the rest of his life and was responsible for the gloom of his later years. Some critics even go so far as to say that he never wrote a good poem or painted a good picture after 1862. On the other hand, it seems also true that his brief marriage, after a prolonged engagement, was unhappy. It has been customary to say that these passionate, even sensuous, love poems were inspired by Elizabeth or that they expressed a yearning for a reunion with her; but in recent years it has been claimed that the real inspiration of the poems was Jane Burden, who married William Morris in 1859. She, it is said, was the woman Rossetti really loved. Having married Elizabeth out of a sense of duty and having seen Jane become the wife of one of his best friends, he poured his frustrated love for Jane into "The Stream's Secret" and the sonnet sequence "The House of Life." So anxious was he, according to the proponents of this theory, to conceal the autobiographical aspects of these poems that he deliberately falsified the dates of composition so as to throw readers off the scent. Since all the facts, even after so many years, have never been made public, the matter must remain conjectural.

Rossetti's poetry was, on its publication, generally well received by critics. But a storm was brewing. In 1871 there appeared in the *Contemporary Review* an article, over an assumed name, called "The Fleshly School of Poetry." Twenty years earlier, Rossetti, along with the other Pre-Raphaelites, had been attacked for his paintings; now he was to be attacked for his poetry. The writer of this article was one Robert Buchanan, an almost unknown Scotsman. The whole situation was complicated by personal feuds and animosities. But the (to us) almost unbelievable prudery of Victorian England made Rossetti peculiarly vulnerable to this kind of attack. His poems were, for those days, extremely frank; his sonnet "Nuptial Sleep" and especially "Jenny," the description of a prostitute, with such lines as

> Your silk ungirdled and unlac'd
> And warm sweets open to the waist,

were genuinely shocking to the contemporary reading public. Also, Rossetti's well-known friendship with Swinburne, the real *enfant terrible* of the period, added to the suspicions of the Victorian public. It is certainly true that Rossetti's love poems were far more sensuous than nineteenth century poetry had been used to. But Buchanan's attack hurt Rossetti deeply and increased his tendency toward melancholia.

Both as poet and painter Rossetti exercised a considerable influence over the artistic taste of the subsequent decades. He and the other Pre-Raphaelites were in part responsible for the "aesthetic movement" of the 1880's and 1890's, the chief ornament of which was Oscar Wilde. Perhaps the most important contribution of Rossetti as a poet was his part in shattering the prudery that had strangled so much of Victorian literature.

Bibliography

Benson, Arthur C.   *Rossetti.* London: Macmillan, 1926, pp. 78–145.

Buchanan, Robert.   "The Fleshly School of Poetry: Dante Gabriel Rossetti," in *Notorious Literary Attacks.* Edited by Albert Mordell. New York: Boni and Liveright, 1926, pp. 185–213.

Cooper, Robert M.   *Lost on Both Sides: Dante Gabriel Rossetti—Critic and Poet.* Athens: Ohio University Press, 1970.

Doughty, Oswald.   *Dante Gabriel Rossetti.* London: Longmans, Green, 1957.

Hardesty, William H.   "Rossetti's Lusty Women," in *Cimarron Review.* XXXV (1976), pp. 20–24.

Holberg, Stanley M.   "Rossetti and the Trance," in *Victorian Poetry.* VIII (Winter, 1970), pp. 299–314.

Hough, Graham.   *The Last Romantics.* London: Duckworth, 1949, pp. 67–82.

Howard, Ronnalie Roper.   *The Dark Glass: Vision and Technique in the Poetry of Dante Gabriel Rossetti.* Athens: Ohio University Press, 1972.

Johnson, Wendell Stacy. "D.G. Rossetti as Painter and Poet," in *Victorian Poetry*. III (1965), pp. 9–18. Reprinted in *Pre-Raphaelitism: A Collection of Critical Essays*. Edited by James Sambrook. Chicago: University of Chicago Press, 1974, pp. 220–229.

Johnston, Robert D. *Dante Gabriel Rossetti*. New York: Twayne, 1969.

Lucas, F.L. *Ten Victorian Poets*. Cambridge: Cambridge University Press, 1940, pp. 99–114.

McGann, Jerome J. "Rossetti's Significant Details," in *Victorian Poetry*. VII (1969), pp. 41–54. Reprinted in *Pre-Raphaelitism: A Collection of Critical Essays*. Edited by James Sambrook. Chicago: University of Chicago Press, 1974, pp. 230–242.

Megroz, R.L. *Dante Gabriel Rossetti: Painter Poet of Heaven in Earth*. New York: Scribner's, 1929, pp. 141–318.

Pittman, Philip. "The Strumpet and the Snake: Rossetti's Treatment of Sex as Original Sin," in *Victorian Poetry*. XII (1974), pp. 45–54.

Prince, Jeffrey R. "D.G. Rossetti and the Pre-Raphaelite Conception of the Special Moment," in *Modern Language Quarterly*. XXXVII (1976), pp. 349–369.

Trombly, Albert E. "Rossetti Studies: Craftsmanship," in *South Atlantic Quarterly*. XVIII (July, 1919), pp. 211–221.

Vogel, Joseph F. *Dante Gabriel Rossetti's Versecraft*. Gainesville: University of Florida Press, 1971.

Warner, Janet. "D.G. Rossetti: Love, Death, and Art," in *Hartford Studies in Literature*. IV (1972), pp. 228–240.

Williamson, Audrey. *Artists and Writers in Revolt: The Pre-Raphaelites*. Cranbury, N.J.: Art Alliance Press, 1977, pp. 37–61.

JOHN RUSKIN

Born: London, England (February 8, 1819)
Died: Brantwood, Coniston, England (January 20, 1900)

Principal Works

ART CRITICISM: *Modern Painters*, Vols. I–V, 1843–1860; *The Seven Lamps of Architecture*, 1849; *Pre-Raphaelitism*, 1850; *The Stones of Venice*, Vols. I–III, 1851–1853; *Lectures on Art*, 1870; *Aratra Pentelici*, 1871; *The Eagle's Nest*, 1872; *Ariadne Florentina*, 1873–1876; *Val d'Arno*, 1874; *Mornings in Florence*, 1875–1877; *St. Mark's Rest: The History of Venice*, 1877–1884; *The Bible of Amiens*, 1880–1885; *Lectures on Landscape*, 1898.

SOCIAL CRITICISM: *The Construction of Sheepfolds*, 1851; *Unto This Last*, 1860, 1862; *Munera Pulveris*, 1862; *Sesame and Lilies*, 1865; *The Ethics of the Dust*, 1866; *The Crown of Wild Olive*, 1866; *Time and Tide*, 1867; *Fors Clavigera*, 1871–1884.

NATURE STUDIES: *Proserpina*, 1875–1886; *Love's Meinie*, 1873–1878; *Deucalion*, 1875–1883.

NOVELLA: *The King of the Golden River*, 1851.

AUTOBIOGRAPHY: *Praeterita*, 1885–1889.

During his lifetime John Ruskin acted in several capacities as a man of letters, writing as an aesthetician, an art historian, a poet, a writer of a fairy tale, and as the author of works on reform and economics. Born in London, February 8, 1819, he was the only child of parents who could and did lavish upon him a great deal of wealth and affection. In addition to study at King's College, in London, and at Christ Church College, Oxford, he traveled extensively through Europe. As early as 1837–1838 he wrote a series of articles on "The Poetry of Architecture" for *London's Architectural Magazine*. A defense of Turner's painting led him to write the voluminous *Modern Painters*, which appeared volume by volume from 1843 to 1860. The work became a treatise on art in general, a defense of painting being done at the time, and a formulation of the five categories Ruskin believed conveyed by art: power, imitation, truth, beauty, and relation.

In 1848 Ruskin married Euphemia Chalmers Gray, then nineteen years old, for whom he had written his novel fairy tale, *The King of the Golden River*, in 1841. The marriage was unsuccessful and was annulled in 1854, with Miss Gray later marrying Millais, the artist, in the following year. Millais and other Pre-Raphaelite artists were friends of Ruskin, who supported their movement, especially in *The Stones of Venice*. After 1857 Ruskin became interested in writing as a social reformer, his most famous works in this vein being *Unto This Last*. As a reformer Ruskin also helped found the Working Men's College in London in 1854, and he gave lessons in drawing and lectured to groups at that institution.

During the 1860's Ruskin wrote much and lectured, despite mental illness. One important book of this period was *Sesame and Lilies*, a collection of essays on aesthetic topics addressed primarily to young people. From 1870 to 1890 he wrote and traveled between increasingly severe attacks of mental illness, and the last decade of his life has been described, because of his condition, as a living death. He died at Brantwood, Coniston, England, on January 20, 1900.

Bibliography

The *Works* of Ruskin have been edited by E. T. Cook and Alexander Wedderburn, 39 vols., 1903–1912; this includes an extensive bibliography. A useful selection is P. C. Quennell's edition of *Selected Writings*, 1952. The *Diaries* were edited by Joan Evans and J. H. Whitehouse, 3 vols., 1956–1959; the *Letters to Lord and Lady Mount-Temple* by J. L. Bradley, 1964. The most thorough biography is E. T. Cook, *The Life of John Ruskin*, 2 vols., 1911. Three briefer biographical studies are Frederick Harrison, *John Ruskin*, English Men of Letters Series, 1902; A. Williams-Ellis, *The Exquisite Tragedy: An Intimate Life of John Ruskin*, 1928; and P. C. Quennell, *Ruskin: The Portrait of a Prophet*, 1949. A valuable handbook is R. H. Wilenski, *John Ruskin: An Introduction to Further Study of His Life and Work*, 1933. Advanced readers may consult H. A. Ladd, *The Victorian Morality of Art: An Analysis of Ruskin's Esthetic*, 1932. A provocative essay on Ruskin appears in Virginia Woolf, *The Captain's Death Bed and Other Essays*, 1950. Also important is John D. Rosenberg, *The Darkening Glass: A Portrait of Ruskin's Genius*, 1961.

THE STONES OF VENICE

Type of work: Art history and criticism
Author: John Ruskin (1819–1900)
First published: 1851–1853

Essay-Review

In the three volumes of *The Stones of Venice*, John Ruskin traces the development, apex, and decline of three architectural expressions, Byzantine, Gothic, and Renaissance, and relates their growth and deterioration to the rise and fall of the Venetian state. He shows that the virtue and piety that marked Venice at her most flourishing found expression in Gothic architecture and that as this faith declined, her corruption was expressed in Renaissance architecture. The architecture expressed not only the morality of the state but also the morality of the individual architect and common workmen who designed the buildings and did the labor. Ruskin believed that the artistic expression of any nation is clear and direct evidence of its moral and spiritual condition; thus when Ruskin states that since the fading of the Gothic tradition there has been no architectural growth in all of Europe, he is also commenting on the spiritual poverty of his own time.

In the first volume, *The Foundations*, he traces the history of Venice. For nine hundred years the Venetians had struggled to bring power and order out of anarchy. They succeeded in doing so largely because they possessed a childlike religious spirit that dignified even their business transactions and brought them peace, energy, and, whenever necessary, heroes. The geographical location of the city and the nature of its maritime activities were crucial, for here the superstitious, energetic, northern barbarian and the spiritual Arab met and clashed. Here the three pre-eminent architectures of the world—Roman, Lombardic, and Arabian, each expressing a different religious view—flourished separately and blended into one another. For this reason Ruskin calls the Ducal Palace the central building of the world.

According to Ruskin, in order to appreciate or judge any architecture, one must first establish canons of judgment. To do so, one must understand the basic requirements and structure of any building. When speaking of buildings, parts of buildings or decorations, Ruskin consistently uses words such as moral, immoral, virtuous, corrupt, terms that normally are applied to people or actions. His descriptions are such that he makes buildings come alive, as indeed they were to him, visible manifestations of the souls of their builders. As a result he speaks of the three virtues required of a building as being: to act well, or do properly what was intended; to speak well, that is, record fact, feelings, history; to look well, present a pleasing appearance. He feels that the second virtue is an individual matter, depending on the character of the observer and his mood, but that the first and third are matters which can be weighed and judged according to a known standard. We should admire in architectural construction an admirable human intelligence whose work may be imperfect, but whose feelings are deep and true and honest and show delight in God's work. He then describes brilliantly the construction of the parts of a building—foundation, wall veil, cornice, roof, and apertures—and explains with great clarity not only how a part is constructed, but, more important, why. The why involves not only logical practical considerations, but geographical, moral and spiritual ones as well; all these observations testify to the wide scope of Ruskin's perception and historical sense. After describing the practical construction of a building, he considers the decoration. To judge decoration, one must determine the rightness of the material in terms of function and treatment and its placement with regard to the whole. Ornament should not take for its subject human work, such as figures taken from agriculture, sailing or manufacture, for that is too self-centered. Ornament should express delight in God's work; thus, we may use the abstract lines in nature, moving from the lower to the higher through the whole range of systematized inorganic and organic forms; that is, earth, water, fire, air, animal organisms, and man. An ornament should be so fitted to its place and service that if it were lifted out and placed elsewhere, it would not be satisfactory or complete. The architect must govern his ornament and so design it that simple workmen will be able to accomplish his intention. It is his duty not to try to improve upon nature but to explain it and express his own soul.

In the second volume, *Sea-Stories*, Ruskin describes the Byzantine Period and the Gothic, and concludes with a careful, elaborate detailing of the Ducal Palace. He describes three churches, Torcello, Murano, and St. Marks. Torcello lies to the northeast of Venice, in the marshes. It was an early church built by people fleeing their pillaged homeland. Thus it was built in haste but with effective simplicity, expressive, Ruskin feels, of the great faith they placed in God. It admits an unusual amount of sun and light for such a building, a psychological need, Ruskin points out, in a people fleeing the darkness of oppression. The pulpit is built with simplicity but is sturdy and functional, and Ruskin ponders the effect of the pulpit on congregations. Such a pulpit inspires confidence, whereas many modern pulpits distract the congregations by being too ornate or raising fears that the entire structure will presently collapse.

Murano, built in the tenth century, furnishes a particularly fine study in proportion and the use of color. The apse is heptagonal on the outside and constructed with mathematical precision. Inside, the placement of the shafts with respect to one another, to the nave and the aisles, reflects subtle, true harmony.

St. Marks was constructed in the Byzantine style during the eleventh century and underwent Gothic additions during the fourteenth century. Its peculiarity is adroit incrustation, brick covered with precious materials. This practice saved materials, expense, and weight, and it required that cutting must be shallow, so that the ornamentation had to be done with care and simplicity rather than with crude force. Also, shallow design permitted delicate shading of color. Beauty,

Ruskin thought, is a legitimate offering to God, and the entirety of St. Marks, with its rich colors, mosaics, paintings, and inscriptions is one great book of Common Prayer, the poor man's Bible. Color is one of God's most divine gifts to man and one which the most thoughtful men value highly; thus, Venice was most colorful during the time of her early, earnest religion. Ruskin says that no style of architecture can be exclusively ecclesiastical. Wherever Christian church architecture has been good and lovely, it has been the perfect development of the common dwelling house architecture of the period. A style fit for a church, he felt, is no less fit for a dwelling, and no form was ever brought to perfection where it was not used for both purposes. Once St. Marks has been judged as a work of art, it must be judged for its fitness as a place of worship. If a church is too beautiful, it will divert the attention of intelligent persons from religion to admiration. Thus, Ruskin believed that effective religious art lies between barbarous idol-fashioning on one side and magnificent craftsmanship on the other.

Ruskin lists six moral elements of the Gothic style: savageness or rudeness, love of nature, love of change, disturbed imagination, obstinacy, and generosity. Gothic is the most rational of forms in that it can fit itself to all services; it is also restless, unquiet, tender, and reverent. Its most striking outward feature is the pointed arch. The Ducal Palace, originally Byzantine, was superseded by Gothic, begun in 1301, and later united with Renaissance in 1423, the year in which not only the architecture of Venice began to decline, but Venice herself.

In the third volume, *The Fall*, Ruskin discusses the moral nature of the Central Renaissance, which is corrupt, its two main immoral elements being pride and infidelity. It is a cold, inhuman form, incapable of glowing or stooping. It is highly trained and erudite and meant only for man's worship, not, as was the Gothic, for the common man or for the praise of God. Thus Ruskin stressed again forcibly his belief that a fault in feeling induces a fault in style. It was a self-centered, pleasure-seeking, and hypocritical age in that it named one god but dreamed about pagan gods, meanwhile dreading none.

Ruskin deplored machine-like work. He felt one should never encourage the production of anything in which invention has no major share. Imitation or copying should be done only for the sake of preservation. He believed that a truly religious painter or architect would more often than not be rude and simple. And the work of such a man should not be scorned for lack of perfection because the demand for perfection implies a complete misunderstanding of the ends of art. No man, said Ruskin, ever stopped until he reached a point of failure, and so imperfection is essential; it is a sign of life, of change and progress. One of the chief elements of power in all good architecture is the acceptance of rude and uncultivated energy in the workmen. He believed that many people possess, even unsuspected by themselves, talent that is wasted from sheer lack of use. Because people cannot truly express themselves in the form of an earlier age, Ruskin hoped, through the work of common people, for a rebirth of true and expressive art throughout Europe.

Bibliography

Crow, G.   *Ruskin.* London: Duckworth, 1936, pp. 67–73.

Evans, Joan.   *John Ruskin.* New York: Oxford University Press, 1955, pp. 159–166, 185–189.

Harrison, Frederick.   *John Ruskin.* New York: Macmillan, 1902, pp. 65–77.

Hewison, Robert.   *John Ruskin: The Argument of the Eye.* London: Thames and Hudson, 1976, pp. 132–137, 176–177.

Landow, George P.   *The Aesthetic and Critical Theories of John Ruskin.* Princeton, N.J.: Princeton University Press, 1971, pp. 56–60, 276–280.

Mather, Marshall.   *John Ruskin: His Life and Teaching.* London: Frederick Warne, 1900, pp. 57–62.

Meynell, Mrs.   *John Ruskin.* New York: Dodd, Mead, 1900, pp. 98–116.

Quennell, Peter.   *John Ruskin.* London: Longmans, Green, 1956, pp. 11–14.

————.   *John Ruskin: The Portrait of a Prophet.* New York: Viking, 1949, pp. 66–74.

Stein, Richard L.   *The Ritual of Interpretation: The Fine Arts as Literature in Ruskin, Rossetti, and Pater.* Cambridge, Mass.: Harvard University Press, 1975, pp. 69–118.

Wilenski, R.H.   *John Ruskin: An Introduction to Further Study of His Life and Work.* London: Faber and Faber, 1933, pp. 235–239, 307–310.

Wingate, Ashmore.   *Life and Writings of John Ruskin.* Folcroft, Pa.: Folcroft, 1973, pp. 82–89.

————.   *Life of John Ruskin.* London: Walker Scott, 1910, pp. 82–89.

ALGERNON CHARLES SWINBURNE

Born: London, England (April 5, 1837)
Died: London (April 10, 1909)

Principal Works

POEMS: *Poems and Ballads,* 1866 [*Laus Veneris*]; *Songs Before Sunrise,* 1871; *Poems and Ballads: Second Series,* 1878; *Songs of the Springtides,* 1880; *Tristram of Lyonesse,* 1882; *A Midsummer Holiday,* 1884; *Poems and Ballads: Third Series,* 1889; *The Tale of Balen,* 1896.

PLAYS: *The Queen Mother,* 1860; *Rosamond,* 1860; *Atalanta in Calydon,* 1865; *Chastelard,* 1865; *Bothwell,* 1874; *Erechtheus,* 1876; *Mary Stuart,* 1881; *Marino Faliero,* 1885; *Locrine,* 1887.

CRITICISM: *William Blake,* 1868; *Essays and Studies,* 1875; *A Note on Charlotte Brontë,* 1877; *A Study of Shakespeare,* 1880; *A Study of Victor Hugo,* 1886; *A Study of Ben Jonson,* 1889; *Studies in Prose and Poetry,* 1894; *The Age of Shakespeare,* 1908.

Swinburne's fame as a poet rests on several claims: his dexterity in manipulation of verse; his subject matter, which often glorified the life of the senses or argued for the necessity of social change; and certain oddities in his actual career. In all of these claims, we can see a man at odds with his age and yet drawing strength from his surroundings since they incited him to his protests.

Swinburne was descended from English nobility. The mother of the future revolutionary poet was the daughter of the Earl of Ashburnham, and his father was Admiral Charles Henry Swinburne. Algernon Charles Swinburne enjoyed fully the advantages of his background. From his mother he acquired a literary taste, a love of the French and Italian languages and literatures, and a thorough knowledge of the Bible. He was also able to read such critical writers as Victor Hugo and W. S. Landor, both advocates of republicanism and both objects of Swinburne's hero worship. From a grandfather in Northumberland, Swinburne learned hatred of monarchy and disapproval of the hereditary privileges of the House of Lords.

Born in London, April 5, 1837, Swinburne early discovered his poetic vocation. Acquaintance in childhood with Wordsworth and Samuel Rogers confirmed his intent by the time he was fifteen. The next decade brought Swinburne the companionship and encouragement of the leading literary figures of the period: Tennyson, Ruskin, and among the Pre-Raphaelites, William Morris, Edward Burne-Jones, and Dante Gabriel Rossetti. Swinburne's youthful claims to attention led Burne-Jones to welcome him thus: "We have hitherto been three, and now there are four of us." Swinburne modeled for some of Rossetti's paintings and had the painter's personal direction in his writings. Further, his affiliation with the Pre-

Raphaelite movement drew attention to his work, which early struck his contemporaries as clever, audacious, and erudite. From *Atalanta in Calydon* and *Chastelard*, published in 1865, Swinburne's place in public awareness was important, and remained so for about fifteen years.

Swinburne's themes—glorification of the senses and the assertion of man's dignity—are but two aspects of his central impatience with restraint; the only restraint that Swinburne ever welcomed was that imposed by rather elaborate and even archaic poetical forms. In *Poems and Ballads* he scandalized his times with outspoken endorsement of sensuality; in *Songs Before Sunrise* he stirred them deeply with apostrophes to the insurgent republicans of Italy. In these years he was also a prose propagandist for the Pre-Raphaelites and a defender of his own literary practices. Against a charge made by the *Saturday Review* that with colors intense and violent he effected an "audacious counterfeiting of strong and noble passion by mad, intoxicated sensuality," Swinburne protested against a literary age which "has room only for such as are content to write for children and girls."

The revolt in Swinburne's own life had to be curbed. In 1879 Theodore Watts-Dunton took Swinburne from London to save him from the effects of acute alcoholic dysentery. Although the move to Putney and simplicity probably extended Swinburne's life, it took the essential fire from his writings. He relinquished the idea of political freedom; he turned from poetry to literary criticism more and more; he was capable, as the young Swinburne with his impassioned seriousness would not have been, of composing parodies on the work of prominent Victorian poets like Tennyson, Rossetti, and himself. The prose of his last years is far removed from his Pre-Raphaelite struggles and contemporary politics; he took up his early enthusiasm for the drama of Elizabethan England, of which he wrote brilliantly in criticism which scholarship finds subject to correction.

Upon his death in London, April 10, 1909, Swinburne was buried near his family at Bonchurch, Isle of Wight—his family from which, at every phase of his career, he had been sharply separated.

Swinburne has been described as a man more "elf-like than human." He was just over five feet tall and thin; he had a massive head thatched with shaggy red hair. His bizarre appearance brought him failure in love and, it can be believed gave him reason for heightening heretical behavior which led to his removal from Eton and Oxford, behavior that later led him to refuse a degree from the great university that had ejected him. It is not surprising that he welcomed the onslaught of Darwinism; nor did the poet of the senses and political action find admirable Robert Browning's optimism and Tennyson's aspirations toward immortality. Here again, as might be expected, he departed from his era's canons of taste and created his own philosophy and forms.

Bibliogrphy

The definitive edition is *The Complete Works of Algernon Charles Swinburne*, edited by Edmund Gosse and T. J. Wise, 20 vols., 1925–1927. The same editors published a separate edition of the *Letters*, 2 vols., 1919. The standard biography is Edmund Gosse, *The Life of Algernon Charles Swinburne*, 1917, a work supplemented by Sir Herbert Grierson, *Swinburne*, 1953. See also T. E. Welby, *Swinburne: A Critical Study*, 1914; Harold Nicolson, *Swinburne*, 1926; Georges Lafourcade, *La Jeunesse de Swinburne*, 1928; Samuel C. Chew, *Swinburne*, 1929; Georges Lafourcade, *Swinburne: A Literary Biography*, 1932; C. K. Hyder, *Swinburne's Literary Career and Fame*, 1933; Humphrey Hare, *Swinburne: A Biographical Approach*, 1949; and John A. Cassidy, *Algernon C. Swinburne*, 1964. See also *Swinburne: The Critical Heritage*, edited by Clyde K. Hyder, 1970; and John D. Rosenberg, "Swinburne," *Victorian Studies*, XI (December, 1967), 131–152. Swinburne's letters were edited by Cecil Lang, 6 Vols., 1959–1962.

ATALANTA IN CALYDON

Type of work: Poem
Author: Algernon Charles Swinburne (1837–1909)
Type of plot: Classical tragedy
Time of plot: Remote antiquity
Locale: Ancient Greece
First published: 1865

Atalanta in Calydon, typical of the Victorian treatment of Greek tragedy, first attracted critical notice to Swinburne's works. Although criticized for using excessive intensity and too violent colors in his poetry, Swinburne needed these elements to describe successfully the passionate and soul-searching nature of his characters' fateful existence. As in the case of his other poetic dramas, Atalanta in Calydon *was intended for reading rather than stage presentation.*

Principal Characters

Œneus (ē'nōos), King of Calydon. He has neglected his sacrifice to Artemis, goddess of the hunt. The wild boar sent by Artemis into Calydon, in punishment, is the object of the fateful hunt. Finally, after much tragedy, Œneus rules alone in Calydon.

Althæa (ăl·thē'ə), his wife, a woman of strong will. To avert a prophecy that her new-born son would live and prosper until the brand on the hearth was consumed, she extinguished the brand and hid it. Years later, after her son has slain her brothers, she returns the brand to the fire to be consumed. After her son's death, she dies of sorrow.

Meleager (mə·lē'gĕr), the son of Œneus and Althæa. Strong and valiant, he is afflicted with great pride and lacks a proper submission to fate. He slays the boar and gives the spoils of the hunt to Atalanta. This results in a fight in which Meleager, protecting Atalanta, kills his uncles. He dies hoping his name will live among men.

Atalanta (ă·tə·lăn'tə), an Arcadian maiden of great beauty and a priestess of Artemis. She joins the hunt, and Meleager, though strongly warned against an infatuation, falls in love with her. Her laugh of pleasure on being given the spoils of the hunt is misinterpreted as a taunt by the Calydonians, who attack her. At last, hailing Meleager's greatness, she returns to Arcadia.

Toxeus (tŏk'sōos) and
Plexippus (plĕk·sĭ'pəs), Althæa's brothers, who are slain by Meleager.

Leda (lē'də), Althæa's sister.

The Chorus, whose philosophizing on life and love, and comments on the action, illuminate the poem.

The Story

Œneus, father of Meleager, had offended Artemis, goddess of the hunt, by offering sacrifices to all the gods except her. As a punishment for his negligence Artemis had sent into Calydon a wild boar that ravaged the land and the crops.

Althæa, embittered by the curse, refused to pay homage to Artemis and raged against the gods. Althæa was a woman of strong will and determination. Years before, when her son Meleager was born, she had had a strange dream concerning his birth. In the dream three spinning women, the Fates, had visited Althæa and had promised for Meleager strength, good fortune, and a bounteous life until the brand on the hearth burned out. On hearing the last part of the prophecy, Althæa had sprung from her bed, grasped the burning brand, and beaten and trampled the heat from it with her bare hands and feet. Then, to guard Meleager's life, she had hidden the brand.

Again she had dreamed that the heatless brand burst into flame as a bud bursts into flower: and with this strange phenomenon Death had come to blow charred ash from the brand into her breast, but there Love had quenched the flame. The omen presaged for Althæa the security of her family: but in spite of her great pride she was not unmindful of the lots which the gods might cast for mortals. These thoughts were in her mind as she went to arm Meleager for the boar hunt. Never had there been born so strong a man of royal birth as Meleager.

The Chorus, reviewing the life span of man, summed up this existence as a passing between a sleep and a sleep.

The warriors of Arcadia were to join the Calydonians in the hunt, and Meleager and Althæa discussed the qualities and characteristics of these men, among them the valiant sons of Leda, Althæa's sister. Meleager described Toxeus and Plexippus, Althæa's brothers, as undoing their deeds with too much talk. Althæa counseled her son against too great pride in earthly accomplishments and advised him to submit his soul to fate. The Chorus admonished Meleager to follow his mother's counsel.

Meleager, recounting the many tumultuous battles he had experienced, pointed out to his mother that in all these frays he had never seen evidence of the infallible gods to whom she and the Chorus would have him submit.

Œneus reported the coming of the Arcadians and said that among them was a woman armed for the hunt. Although Œneus wished to have this woman shown great respect because of her favor from the gods, he warned Meleager against becoming infatuated with her beauty. Althæa, recalling the prophecies of the Fates regarding Meleager's career, added to her husband's warning against earthly love. Again imploring her son to give himself to fate, she told him that he would not die as ordinary men die and that his death would be her death as well. Meleager declared his boundless love for his mother and expressed respect for her teaching. Ever faithful to Zeus, the sole determiner of things, he prepared for the hunt.

The Chorus, philosophizing on Love, saw her blind as a flame, covered by earth for hiding, and fronted by laughter to conceal the tears of desire. According to the portent of the Chorus, man and maid would go forth; the maid's name, Fate; the man's, Death. The Chorus lamented also the meagerness of life's span. This futility, an evil blossom born of sea foam and blood froth, had come into existence with Aphrodite, goddess of love. Before, there had been joy upon the earth, but

Aphrodite's influence had resulted in suffering, evil, and devastation.

In the hunt, as predicted, Meleager met the Arcadian maiden. She was Atalanta, the virgin priestess of Artemis, whom Œneus had neglected in his sacrifices and who had sent the wild boar to ravage Calydon. Atalanta invoked Artemis to favor Meleager that he might be victorious in the hunt. Meleager, confessing his love for Atalanta, was taunted by his uncles, Toxeus and Plexippus, for his woman-tonguedness. Althæa pleaded for peace among her kinsmen lest words become snakes and poison them against each other.

The hunt proceeded. According to a message sent by Œneus to Althæa, the expedition demanded energy, courage, and hunting strategy. The boar, crazed by the chase and by the numerous wounds inflicted, charged Meleager, who with all daring and skill slew the animal, thereby ridding Calydon of its curse. Althæa offered praise to the gods. A messenger who had brought the message to Althæa added that pride in earthly accomplishments would bring about destruction.

The Chorus, chanting a song of thanksgiving to the gods, was hushed by the messenger, who ordered them to change their songs to wails of pity because Toxeus and Plexippus had been slain.

Althæa, lamenting the death of her brothers, found comfort in the thought that Meleager would avenge them. The messenger questioned whether her son should slay himself. When Althæa threatened him for his ambiguity, the messenger bluntly informed her that Meleager had slain his uncles.

After the boar had been killed, Toxeus and Plexippus requested that the head and the hide be kept as a monument in Calydon: but Meleager, enamoured of Atalanta, gave her the spoils of the hunt. Pleased with this token of his devotion, Atalanta laughed. The Calydonians construed her reaction as a taunt and sought to destroy her. In furious fighting to protect the maiden, Meleager killed his uncles. Althæa recalled her brothers' kindnesses in their childhood, anticipated her sister's scorn for Meleager's crime, and accepted her fate as a victim of many curses.

The Chorus, endeavoring to comfort Althæa in the loss of her brothers, was rebuked. Had Toxeus and Plexippus died in sacrifice or battle, Althæa maintained, their lives would not have been in vain; but knowing that they had been slain by her son, she could never become reconciled to their deaths or to his crime.

In Meleager's deed, caused by excessive earthly pride and undue desire for attainment, Althæa sensed her error in taking the burning brand from the fire at the time of his birth. Stoically she thrust the brand into the fire that it might be consumed at last. Althæa suffered with torment and anguish as the Chorus described the burning, which resulted in Meleager's death after his return from the hunt.

Meleager reviewed his existence without remorse and besought Œneus and Althæa not to let his name die among men. He described his passing as an empty night harvest in which no man gathers fruit. Althæa died of sorrow. Atalanta, hailing Meleager's greatness, returned to Arcadia. Œneus ruled alone in Calydon.

Critical Evaluation

Swinburne adhered so closely to the principles of Greek drama in *Atalanta in Calydon* that what he achieved must be likened to a reproduction Greek statue clothed in English. His model was most likely Ovid's version of the Atalanta myth in *Metamorphoses,* elaborated and embellished within conventions of form, theme, and meter in the Greek drama. Nevertheless, the degree to which Swinburne succeeded in his imitation Greek drama is almost without parallel, as his first critics pointed out.

Atalanta and Meleager, gears in the machinations of Artemis' revenge upon Œneus, enact a drama of love and death which fulfills the Fates's prophecy to Althæa. Swinburne's characters embody and exemplify themes— love, fate, revenge, and death—but without conveying effect, because Swinburne's poem is pessimistic, sentimental, and didactic, rather than tragic. It is only in the choruses that Swinburne conveys effect, notably when the Chorus sings "We have seen thee, O love, thou art fair." Here, love is seen accompanied by a bridal couple, Fate and Death: Swinburne defines the rose by showing the thorn.

The success of *Atalanta in Calydon* as imitation is also the poem's limitation. It does not transcend imitation, remaining a distinctly literary play in a literary context; but that was Swinburne's interpretation of "art for art's sake," a doctrine which flourished in the Victorian literary circles of Rossetti and the Pre-Raphaelites.

T. S. Eliot, in his essay "Swinburne as Poet," described Swinburne's aesthetics as diffuse and uprooted: using words in a way which mixed image, sound, and idea for rhetorical purposes only—words *as* words and not related to objects in the world. This quality in Swinburne's poetry may be seen particularly in the chorus "Before the beginning of years," which follows Althæa's speech on the Fates's prophecy.

Atalanta in Calydon represents a high point of artifice in the pre-Raphaelite movement. Rather than an imitation of life, as Aristotle defined the drama in *The Poetics,* Swinburne's *Atalanta in Calydon* is an imitation of art.

Bibliography

Bowra, C.M.   *The Romantic Imagination.* Cambridge, Mass.: Harvard University Press, 1957, pp. 221–244.

Cassidy, John A.   *Algernon C. Swinburne.* New York: Twayne, 1964, pp. 85–92.

Chew, Samuel C.   *Swinburne.* Boston: Little, Brown, 1929, pp. 59–65.

Fletcher, Ian.   *Swinburne.* London: Longmans, 1973, pp. 32–38.

Fuller, Jean Overton.   *Swinburne: A Critical Biography.* London: Chatto and Windus, 1968, pp. 94–103.

Jordan, John O. "The Sweet Face of Mothers: Psychological Patterns in *Atalanta in Calydon*," in *Victorian Poetry*. XI (1973), pp. 101–114.

Lougy, Robert E. "Thematic Imagery and Meaning in *Atalanta in Calydon*," in *Victorian Poetry*. IX (1971), pp. 17–34.

McGann, Jerome J. *Swinburne: An Experiment in Criticism*. Chicago: University of Chicago Press, 1972, pp. 95–107.

Mathews, Richard. "Heart's Love and Heart's Division: The Quest for Unity in *Atalanta in Calydon*," in *Victorian Poetry*. IX (1971), pp. 35–48.

Nicholson, Harold. *Swinburne*. New York: Macmillan, 1926, pp. 73–92.

Welby, T. Earle. *A Study of Swinburne*. Port Washington, N.Y.: Kennikat, 1968, pp. 177–184.

Wilson, F.A.C. "Swinburne and Kali: The Confessional Element in *Atalanta in Calydon*," in *Victorian Poetry*. XI (1973), pp. 215–228.

Wymer, Thomas. "Swinburne's Tragic Vision in *Atalanta in Calydon*," in *Victorian Poetry*. IX (1971), pp. 1–16.

POEMS AND BALLADS

Author: Algernon Charles Swinburne (1837–1909)
First published: First Series 1866; Second Series, 1878; Third Series, 1889

Essay-Review

Poems and Ballads, published in three series, contains the major part of Swinburne's great lyric poetry. Whether the First Series of these remarkable poems brought him fame or notoriety is a debatable question. One critic called him the most immoral of all English poets and pointed to *Poems and Ballads: First Series* as the most obscene book of poetry in the English language. Other critics, like George Meredith and John Ruskin, were fascinated by Swinburne's rich melodies and technical virtuosity. These two opinions of Swinburne reflect the most striking qualities of *Poems and Ballads:* the poems are an open revolt against Victorian prudery, and they are among the most technically perfected poems in English. To the reader of 1866, they were unlike anything hitherto published in England; thus while the critics loudly and indignantly denounced the volume, the public avidly bought it.

Swinburne's major themes in the 1866 volume are sex, freedom, sadism, masochism, and the beauty of evil and of things corrupt or decaying. Influenced by the growing interest in the Marquis de Sade and Charles Baudelaire, Swinburne presents his themes without equivocation. Few poems before 1866 celebrated the pleasures of physical love with the straightforwardness of "Les Noyades," in which the sexual act is public and intensified by impending death, or "Fragoletta," in which the act is given overtones of psychological maladjustment. Such sexual deviations are used by Swinburne for their ability to shock the prudish reader. In the 1866 volume, for example, sexual maladjustments run all the way from homosexuality in the group of poems called "Hermaphroditus" and in "Sappho," to incest in "Phaedra," and finally to sexual flagellation in such poems as "A Match." The reasons for such a concern, however, may be far greater than merely the desire to shock. Swinburne was celebrating the human body itself, the sexual pleasure that alone remained after the soul was eliminated. In this sense, his use of the shocking was both a way to jar the apathetic public and to point toward a new religion.

This paganism is especially evident in "Laus Veneris," Swinburne's rehandling of the Tannhäuser legend. In this poem the tragedy is that the knight who has renounced Christ believes in Him and the lover who has embraced Venus does not believe in her. Another poem that glorifies this pagan outlook is "Hymn to Proserpine," in which the speaker, a pagan of A.D. 313 when Christianity was proclaimed to be the state religion, bitterly laments the passing of pagan sensuality and predicts an eventual collapse of Christianity.

The glorification of sensuality, however, leads Swinburne into still another characteristic theme: if sexual ecstasy is truly to be the height of human existence, mankind must be free from all restraints. In the bitter "St. Dorothy" the chaste virgin and her lover die horrible deaths because they are trapped by the restraints of Christianity; and in "The Masque of Queen Barsabe" (a "miracle play" about David, Bathsheba, and Nathan) the prophet is forced to admit that the adulterous queen is right. Related to this desire for sexual freedom is Swinburne's adoration of the prostitute. In "Dolores," the peak of Swinburne's masochistic eroticism, the prostitute is "Our Lady of Pain," a semi-goddess who gives the worshipper an excessive pleasure of suffering. "Faustine," addressed to another prostitute, revels in the pleasure of damnation, a pleasure that only a masochist could enjoy. Sadistic love is the theme of "Satia Te Sanguine" ("Satiate thyself with blood") and "The Leper," in which the lover has the sadistic pleasure of coldly watching his beloved while she is slowly consumed by a fatal disease.

Sensuality, however, would lack much of its charm to Swinburne if it were a permanent state; thus he places it within a world that is characterized above all by the passing of time. "Ilicet" ("Let us go") is a lament for this passing of time, and "The Triumph of Time," as its title implies, laments the mutability of human existence and the inevitable ending to love. "Before Parting" and "Before Dawn" are further laments for the ending of love. Related to these poems are the two eulogies, "In Memory of Walter Savage Landor" and "To Victor Hugo," both of which rather sentimentally note the transience of human life. In contrast to the sentimentality of these eulogies are the two grotesque ballads "After Death" and "The Bloody Son," which present realistic pictures of death. But this view is the exception in Swinburne's poetry; the number of poems which have a yearning to die far outnumber the realistic ones. In "The Garden of Proserpine," for example, the weariness of life is contrasted with the peaceful rest of death, and in "Hendecasyllabics" the speaker seeks rest from "the long decline of roses."

The Second Series of *Poems and Ballads* marks a change in Swinburne's thought. No longer is he the outspoken rebel against Victorian conventionality. His tone has changed from nervous ranting and "naughty" excitement to a calm, sad strain, almost of lamentation. During the twelve years between the two series, Swinburne's friends—Rossetti, Meredith, and Jowett—had brought his attention to Elizabethan drama, and in the 1878 volume he published the lyrics that this study had produced.

Instead of the eroticism of 1866, the Second Series is obsessed with death, so much so that well over half of the fifty-five poems are either eulogies or laments. The theme of death can, in fact, be divided into three parts, each of which Swinburne describes: the death of famous men, the death of youth, and the death of nature. Some of the most remarkable poems in this volume are on the deaths of famous men: Barry Cornwall, Charles Baudelaire (the author of the very influential *Les Fleurs du Mal*), Théophile Gautier (one of Swineburne's favorite contemporaries), and Victor Hugo (the leading exponent of French Romanticism). In these poems Swinburne's concern is twofold: in each he laments the passing of a great poet, to him the crown of existence, and the defeat of a struggling, vivacious man by a force over which he has no control. This last concern partly relates him to the then growing movement of Naturalism, especially as interpreted by Zola, as well as to his own sense of futility that had already appeared in the 1866 volume. A second part of the theme of death deals with the death of nature and is the theme of what many people think is the best poem in the volume—"A Forsaken Garden." Here Swinburne laments the mutability of life and the decay that characterizes nature. Other poems related to this theme are "At a Month's End", "The Year of the Rose", and "Four Songs of Four Seasons"; in each, the poet observes the decay and death that are part of the world of nature. Finally there is a group of lyrics in which Swinbure laments the death or the passing of youth and with youth the passing of love. "A Wasted Vigil" and "Age and Song," for example, show the inevitable decay of youth itself which, being caught up in the world of nature, must die even as nature dies.

The Second Series also reveals Swinburne's increased dependence upon and appreciation for Continental poetry, especially the mature poetry of Baudelaire and Gautier. More and more Swinburne concentrates on the sharply defined image or symbol as developed by these poets and takes his emphasis from the melodious line. But it is in the Third Series of *Poems and Ballads*, published in 1889, that Swinburne most shows the fruits of this influence. During 1879 he was so near death that his friends thought there was no hope for him, but Theodore Watts-Dunton rescued him and by caring for him with almost parental control nursed him back to health. The Third Series reflects this encounter with death and the reconciliation of the rebel to the middle class.

By far the least remarkable of the three volumes, the 1889 *Poems and Ballads* introduced a thread of patriotism that was hardly noticeable in Swinburne's work before this time. "The Commonweal," for example, extols the jubilee of Queen Victoria, an attitude that would have been inconceivable in the young Swinburne, and "The Armada" is an almost Tennysonian exaltation of English sea power. Also, there is now a more obvious attempt to rely on literary experiences rather than his own experiences for the source of his poetry. Especially striking are the echoes of Browning's "Caliban upon Setebos" in "Caliban on Ariel" and of D. G. Rossetti's "Sister Helen" in "The Weary Wedding."

The most interesting poems in this otherwise mediocre volume are those lyrics capturing through fleeting but precise symbols moments that are as ephemeral but profound as those captured in words by Verlaine and Mallarmé. In these poems—"In Time of Mourning," for example, "The Interpreters," "The Recall," or "By Twilight"—Swinburne grasped the poetic vision that was fundamental to the French *Symbolistes* and would be of utmost importance in twentieth century lyrical poetry.

In the three series of *Poems and Ballads* Swinburne shows a profundity of thought expressed in a depth of emotion, a combination that easily accounts for his widespread influence on the poets who followed him. There are few forms of versification, however difficult, that do not appear in these pages. In his translations of François Villon and in his recreations of the early English ballad, he shows that translation and the meager ballad could be the vehicles of great art. In the sestinas and sonnets he shows that he has mastered the most difficult rhyme patterns. In fact, he shows a mastery in technical matters that is perhaps unmatched in English poetry. All in all, *Poems and Ballads* is one of the most unusual and most outstanding works of nineteenth century poetry, a publication that mocked its contemporaries with such art that it became a seminal work in the formation of the poetic theory of the following age.

Bibliography

Cassidy, John A.   *Algernon C. Swinburne.* New York: Twayne, 1964.

Chew, Samuel C.   *Swinburne.* Boston: Little, Brown, 1929.

Dobree, Bonamy.   "Introduction," in *Poems of Algernon Charles Swinburne.* London: Penguin, 1961.

Eliot, T.S.   *Selected Essays.* New York: Harcourt, Brace, 1950, pp. 281–285.

Fletcher, Ian.   *Swinburne.* London: Longmans, 1973.

Fuller, Jean Overton.   *Swinburne: A Critical Biography.* London: Chatto and Windus, 1968, pp. 71–300.

Greenberg, Robert A.   "Swinburne and the Redefinition of Classical Myth," in *Victorian Poetry.* XIV (1976), pp. 175–195.

McGann, Jerome J.   " 'Ave Atque Vale': An Introduction to Swinburne," in *Victorian Poetry.* IX (1971), pp. 145–164.

————.   *Swinburne: An Experiment in Criticism.* Chicago: University of Chicago Press, 1972.

Nicholson, Harold.   *Swinburne.* New York: Macmillan, 1926, pp. 1–180.

Peters, Robert L.   "Algernon Charles Swinburne and the Use of Integral Detail," in *Victorian Studies.* V (1962), pp. 289–302.

Welby, T. Earle.   *A Study of Swinburne.* Port Washington, N.Y.: Kennikat, 1968.

Williamson, Audrey.   *Artists and Writers in Revolt: The Pre-Raphaelites.* Cranbury, N.J.: Art Alliance Press, 1977, pp. 161–181.

ALFRED, LORD TENNYSON

Born: Somersby, England (August 6, 1809)
Died: Near Haslemere, England (October 6, 1892)

Principal Works

POEMS: *Poems, Chiefly Lyrical*, 1830; *Poems*, 1832; *Poems*, 1842 (2 vols.); *The Princess*, 1847; *In Memoriam*, 1850; *Maud and Other Poems*, 1855; *Idylls of the King*, 1859–1885; *Enoch Arden and Other Poems*, 1864; *The Holy Grail and Other Poems*, 1869; *Ballads and Other Poems*, 1880; *Tiresius and Other Poems*, 1885; *Locksley Hall Sixty Years After*, 1886; *Demeter and Other Poems*, 1889; *The Death of Œnone*, 1892.
PLAYS: *Queen Mary*, 1875; *Harold*, 1876; *The Cup*, 1884; *The Falcon*, 1884; *Becket*, 1884; *The Promise of May*, 1886; *The Foresters*, 1892.

"Man comes and tills the field and lies beneath."
Thus in one crisp, true line is life summed up by Tennyson. And between his birth on August 6, 1809, and his death on October 6, 1892, no poet in the whole range of English literature ever tilled the field of poetry with more diligence and versatility than Alfred, fourth son of the Rev. G. C. Tennyson, rector of the parish at Somersby in Lincolnshire, where the boy was born. Tennyson's output began at the age of six, with blank verse scribbled on a slate, and culminated some seventy-five years later, with the much-quoted "Crossing the Bar." In between came poetry that is sometimes magnificent, often vapid and mawkish, but always characteristic of an age alternately self-confident and self-conscious, the age of Victoria.
Somersby was a quiet village containing less than a hundred inhabitants. Tennyson's father was talented (a dabbler in poetry, painting, architecture, and music), and his mother, whose maiden name was Elizabeth Fytche, was noted for her gentleness and sweet disposition. In this setting Tennyson's talent developed early. While he was attending Louth Grammar school he broke into print with *Poems by Two Brothers*, a collection which actually contained the works of three members of a talented family—Alfred, Frederick, and Charles. This juvenile volume shows the influence of Byron, whom Alfred admired so greatly that when he heard of his death he took a lonely, sad walk and carved into the sandstone, "Byron is dead."
In 1828 Tennyson went to Trinity College, Cambridge. There he took an interest in politics and became a member of The Apostles, a club of young literary men. Among these friends was Arthur Henry Hallam, whose later death, at the age of twenty-three, so affected Tennyson that he published nothing for ten years. Hallam is elegized in *In Memoriam*, a loose collection of philosophical lyrics that seems to be groping for, but never quite reaching, the handhold of faith. At Cambridge Tennyson won the chancellor's medal for his poem, "Timbuctoo," and

it was there he brought out in 1830 his first important volume, *Poems, Chiefly Lyrical.* Although some of the reviews of this book were unkind, perhaps justifiably so, and although the influence of another Romantic poet, Keats, is very evident, the volume marked the beginning of a career almost unmatched in popularity afforded a poet during his lifetime.

Two years later came another volume, which included "The Lady of Shalott" and "The Lotus Eaters," two poems in the smooth, melancholy tone of Tennyson at his best. Then came Hallam's death and the ten years of silence. Hallam was Tennyson's close friend and the fiancé of his sister Emily; when Tennyson heard the news of his unexpected death in Vienna, he was dreadfully shocked and shaken. Later he began working on *In Memoriam,* a labor that lasted for seventeen years. Not until 1842 did Tennyson publish again, bringing out two volumes, one of which contained "Morte d'Arthur," the beginning of a series on the Arthurian legends which became *Idylls of the King.* Also in 1842 appeared "Locksley Hall," one of Tennyson's most popular poems.

The auspicious year for Tennyson was 1850. After unwise speculation had left him penniless and two bouts with nervous prostration had damaged his health, his affairs took a threefold upsurge: he married Emily Sellwood, he published *In Memoriam,* and he was appointed Poet Laureate to succeed Wordsworth. Outstanding among his "official" poems as laureate is his "Ode on the Death of the Duke of Wellington," a stiff but moving tribute. The laureateship became the first step toward elevation to the peerage, an honor bestowed on him by an admiring queen. Tennyson had twice refused this honor (tendered to him first through Gladstone and then through Disraeli), but he accepted it in 1883, becoming Baron of Aldworth and Farrington. Even before he became a peer, Tennyson's popularity had been great (for example, ten thousand copies of the first series of *Idylls of the King,* published in 1859, were sold within a few weeks), but now this tall, gaunt man, the idealized figure of a poet, became almost a living legend. So popular was he, that after his death there set in a natural reaction against his sentimentality and "Victorianism." But poems like "The Lotus Eaters," "Tithonus," and "Ulysses" still ring strong and true.

Tennyson's life was quiet, unhurried. Most of it he spent at his home, Farringford, on the Isle of Wight and, after 1867, at Blackdown in Surrey, where he lived in a house which he named Aldworth. In this later period he tried his hand at poetic dramas, *Queen Mary, Harold,* and *Becket.* Only the latter became a success on the stage. In 1889, *Demeter and Other Poems* came out, twenty thousand copies of which were sold within a week. On his eightieth birthday, Tennyson received tributes from all over the world. And though the end was not far away, he still had the strength to write a romantic play, *The Foresters,* a drama on the Robin Hood theme, which was produced at Daly's Theatre in New York in 1892.

Tennyson died at eighty-three at his home, Aldworth House, and was buried in the Poets' Corner of Westminster Abbey. To many readers Tennyson, not Shakespeare, seems more fittingly called the Swan of English literature. The name seems too gentle for the oftentimes fierce Elizabethan, but very appropriate for Tennyson, who experimented widely in the technique of poetry and whose best poems glide with the grace and beauty of a swan moving slowly across an unruffled lake.

Bibliography

The standard edition is *The Works of Lord Tennyson*, edited by Hallam Tennyson, 9 vols., 1908–1910. More recent editions are *Poems of Tennyson*, edited by Jerome H. Buckley, 1958; and *Poems*, edited by Christopher Ricks, 1969, probably the definitive edition. The most recent and informing of the many Tennyson biographies is Sir Charles Tennyson, *Alfred Tennyson*, 1949. See also Arthur Waugh, *Alfred, Lord Tennyson*, 1894; Hallam Tennyson, *Alfred, Lord Tennyson: A Memoir*, 2 vols., 1898; A. C. Benson, *Alfred Tennyson*, 1904; T. R. Lounsbury, *The Life and Times of Tennyson*, 1915; A. C. Bradley, *A Commentary on Tennyson's "In Memoriam,"* 1929; T. S. Eliot, " 'In Memoriam,' " in *Essays Ancient and Modern*, 1936; H. G. Nicolson, *Tennyson, Aspects of His Life, Character, and Poetry*, 1949; Jerome H. Buckley, *Tennyson: The Growth of a Poet*, 1960; Joanna Richardson, *The Pre-eminent Victorian: A Study of Tennyson*, 1962; and Ralph W. Rader, *"Maud": The Biographical Genesis*, 1963. A useful short work is J. B. Steane, *Tennyson*, 1966.

THE IDYLLS OF THE KING

Type of work: Poem
Author: Alfred, Lord Tennyson (1809–1892)
Type of plot: Chivalric romance
Time of plot: Fifth century
Locale: England
First published: Separately, 1859–1885

Divided into twelve sections, each symbolic of one month of the year, these poems present to the reader the span of a man's life, extending from the coming of Arthur to his death. Filled with mystic and spiritual meanings, Tennyson's stories of the Knights of the Round Table are rich in allegorical significance and beauty of narrative.

Principal Characters

King Arthur, of Camelot. His birth is shrouded in great mystery, and he is reared by Merlin the magician. He receives his magic sword Excalibur from the Lady of the Lake, and marries Guinevere. With his Round Table knights he drives out the enemy and unifies his kingdom. He rules wisely and is successful until his Round Table fellowship diminishes in the knights' quest for the Holy Grail. Exposure of Guinevere's infidelity with Lancelot proves thoroughly demoralizing, and in a traitorous revolt Arthur is mortally wounded. After his last remaining faithful knight returns Excalibur to the Lady of the Lake, three maidens come in a barge to the shore to carry Arthur away as mysteriously as he had come.

Guinevere, Arthur's beloved Queen and his inspiration. She falls in love with the courtly, gay Lancelot, whom Arthur had sent to bring her from her father's home. Much later, when her guilty love is exposed, she goes to a nunnery, where she remains until her death.

Lancelot, a knight of the Round Table. His lifelong love for Guinevere is a source of great misery. He is loved by another woman, whom he cannot love

in return. At last, the scandal with Guinevere revealed, he leaves Camelot and dies a monk.

Gareth, a knight of the Round Table and Arthur's sister's youngest son. His first quest is on behalf of a lady who is disdainful of her untried knight. Victorious in his quest, he wins her approval and her hand.

Geraint, a knight of the Round Table. Married to Enid, he jealously keeps her away from the court and as a result of his absence from Camelot his valor is doubted. Enid's reticence on this subject convinces him that she loves another knight, but at last she is able to prove her love. They go to Camelot, where Guinevere welcomes Enid to the court.

Balan, a knight of the Round Table. Returning from a mission for Arthur, he hears mad shrieks and rushes against the knight making them, who is in fact his unrecognized brother.

Balin, Balan's mad brother and a knight of the Round Table. Disillusioned on discovering the intimacy of Guinevere and his idol Lancelot, he leaves hanging on a tree the shield Guinevere had given him. Without the shield he is unrecognized by his brother, and in the struggle between them Balin kills Balan and is crushed by his own horse.

Gawain, a knight of the Round Table. He falls in love with Elaine of Astolat, who rejects him because she loves Lancelot. Later he promises to help Pelleas with Ettarre, who has rejected Pelleas' love. At her castle he tells her he has killed Pelleas, and he becomes intimate with her.

Pelleas, a knight of the Round Table. Suspicious on hearing nothing from Gawain, he steals into Ettarre's castle and finds the lovers in bed together. He places his naked sword across their throats and rushes madly away. After hearing about the scandal of Lancelot and Guinevere, he returns to Camelot, where his rudeness to the Queen foreshadows the ruin of the Round Table.

Galahad, the youngest and purest of the knights of the Round Table. To him the Holy Grail appears in all its splendor, but the experience proves fatal to him.

Percivale, the only other knight of the Round Table pure enough, according to Arthur's gloomy prediction, to see the Holy Grail.

Bors, a knight of the Round Table. He reports back to Arthur that he has seen the Holy Grail.

Tristram, a knight of the Round Table. He and Lancelot, equally guilty in loving other men's wives, fight in a tournament which Tristram wins. He then goes to Isolt of Cornwall, whom he loves. Her husband finds the lovers together and kills Tristram.

Modred, the real Judas among the knights of the Round Table. Malevolent and opportunistic, he traps Lancelot and Guinevere. He heads the revolt which ends in Arthur's death.

Bedivere, Arthur's last remaining knight of the Round Table. Reluctant to throw Excalibur into the lake, he falsely reports to Arthur that he has done so, but is sent back again. When he finally brings the report that an arm reached from the lake to take the sword, Arthur knows that Bedivere has truly done his bidding.

Merlin, the magician who reared Arthur. Tricked by the wanton Vivien into teaching her his magic powers, he is enchanted by her and left forever a prisoner in a hollow tree.

Kay, a surly knight and Arthur's seneschal.

Lynette, the disdainful lady won by Gareth.

Enid, the faithful wife of Geraint.

Vivien, a vain and coquettish woman of the court. Unsuccessful in her efforts to seduce Arthur, she goes to work on Merlin.

Elaine, the lily maid of Astolat. In love with but rejected by Lancelot, she is loved by Gawain, whom she rejects. At last she dies of grief and, according to her dying wish, is sent floating in a boat to Camelot, where Arthur and Lancelot find her. There she is buried.

Ettarre, loved by Pelleas, whom she rejects, and by Gawain, to whom she succumbs.

Isolt of the White Hands, Tristram's bride, whom he leaves.

Isolt of Cornwall, the wife of King Mark and loved by Tristram.

King Mark of Cornwall, the husband of Isolt of Cornwall and the slayer of Tristram.

Ygerne, the mother of Arthur.

Gorloïs, the first husband of Ygerne and possibly Arthur's father.

King Uther. He overcomes Gorloïs in battle and immediately forces the widow Ygerne to marry him. Thus he is possibly Arthur's father.

Bellicent, the daughter of Gorloïs and Ygerne and the mother of Gareth.

Morning Star, the first knight overcome by Gareth on Lynette's behalf.

Death, Gareth's fourth opponent in his quest. Death proves to be a mere boy, forced by his brothers to assume a fearful disguise.

Earl Yniol, the impoverished father of Enid.

King Pellam, whose refusal to pay his yearly tribute to Arthur is the occasion for Balan's leaving the court, thus neglecting the care of his mad brother.

Lavaine, the brother of Elaine of Astolat.

The Story

THE COMING OF ARTHUR

Gorloïs and Ygerne had borne one daughter, Bellicent. King Uther overcame Gorloïs in battle and forced the widow to marry him immediately. Shortly afterward King Uther died. Ygerne's son, Arthur, was born at a time when he could have been the son of Gorloïs or the son of Uther born too soon.

The birth of Arthur was shrouded in great mystery. Merlin the magician reared the prince until it was time for him to take over Uther's kingdom and to receive from the Lady of the Lake the magic sword, Excalibur. After the marriage of Arthur and Guinevere, the king and his loyal members of the Round Table, in twelve battles, drove the enemy out of the kingdom.

GARETH AND LYNETTE

Bellicent, Arthur's sister, allowed her youngest son to join his two brothers in King Arthur's court on the condition that Gareth serve as a kitchen knave under the surly directions of Sir Kay the seneschal. When the young boy presented himself to King Arthur, Gareth made the king promise to give him the first quest which came along without revealing his identity. One day Lynette came to the court asking for Sir Lancelot to save her sister from wicked knights who held her captive. King Arthur sent Gareth questing with Lynette, who grumbled disdainfully at the kitchen knave ordered to serve her.

The first knight Gareth overcame was the Morning Star. Lynette still sneered at the knave. After Gareth had defeated another knight, Lynette began to relent. When he conquered a third strong knight, she allowed him to ride at her side. Next Gareth encountered a terrible knight, Death, who proved to be a mere boy forced by his brothers to assume a fierce appearance. Gareth returned to the Round Table victorious and married Lynette.

THE MARRIAGE OF GERAINT AND GERAINT AND ENID

Geraint, on a quest for Guinevere, came to the impoverished castle of Earl Yniol and his daughter Enid, a girl whose faded brocades spoke of former wealth and family pride. There Geraint learned that the rejected suitor of Enid had caused the ruin of Yniol. The earl gave Geraint Enid for his wife.

Geraint, fearing that the sin of the Queen's love for Lancelot would taint Enid's love, went to his own castle and there idled away the hours in company with his wife until neighbors began to gossip that Geraint had lost his courage. Enid feared to tell her lord about the gossip, and Geraint, observing her strange attitude, decided that she had fallen in love with some knight of the Round Table. One morning, bidding Enid to don her faded brocade gown, Geraint set out with his wife after ordering her not to speak to him. Riding ahead of Geraint, Enid encountered men who would attack her husband, and each time she broke his command by warning him of his danger. After a while Enid was able to prove her love to her suspicious husband. They returned to Camelot, where Guinevere warmly welcomed Enid to the court.

Balin and Balan

Balan left the care of Balin, his mad brother, and went on a mission to quell King Pellam, who had refused to pay his yearly tribute to King Arthur. With his brother gone, Balin was left alone in his gloomy moods. He worshipped the purity of Lancelot and the faithfulness of Guinevere until one day he saw his two idols speaking familiarly in the garden. Disillusioned, Balin fled to the woods. There he met Vivien, a wanton woman of the court, who further poisoned his mind against Lancelot and Guinevere. He left hanging on a tree the shield Guinevere had given him years before. Hearing Balin's mad shrieks among the trees, Balan rushed at Balin, whom he did not recognize without the shield of Guinevere. In the struggle Balin killed Balan and then was crushed by his own horse.

Vivien

Vain and coquettish Vivien set out to ensnare the most chivalric man in all the kingdom, King Arthur, but her wiles failed to win the attention of a king whose mind could harbor no evil thoughts. Vivien then turned to Merlin, who she knew possessed a magic spell. She tried to charm the magician with her beauty, pretending to love the ancient, bearded man, but he knew that she was not to be trusted. When she asked him to teach her the spell, he refused. But Vivien was not to be denied. At last, tricked by her beauty, Merlin taught her his magic powers. She enchanted him and caused him to disappear forever, a prisoner in a hollow tree.

Lancelot and Elaine

Lancelot in disguise went to Astolat where he left his shield with Elaine and rode off with her brother Lavaine to the tournaments. Lancelot won the jousts; then, wounded, he fled before anyone could discover who he was. King Arthur sent Gawain to search for the winner of the tournament. Gawain rode to Astolat, where he lingered because he had fallen in love with Elaine. She told him that she loved the knight who had left his shield with her. When Gawain saw the shield, he identified it as that of Lancelot.

Elaine nursed Lancelot back to health in the hope that he would return her love. Recovered, he sadly told her that he could never marry any woman. After he had gone, Elaine became ill and finally died in her grief. Her dying wish was to be put into a boat and sent to Camelot, in her hand a letter to Lancelot.

In Camelot Guinevere coldly rejected Lancelot, for Gawain had told of the affair between Lancelot and Elaine. When the body of Elaine floated to Camelot, King Arthur and Lancelot found the beautiful maiden in her boat, the letter in her hand.

Lancelot authorized a fitting burial for the lily maid. He unhappily lamented his hopeless love for the Queen, not knowing that he would die a monk.

THE HOLY GRAIL

One day while Sir Galahad, the youngest and purest of all the knights, sat in Merlin's chair, the Holy Grail descended upon the Round Table in a flash and then was gone. When the knights swore to go on a quest for the Holy Grail, King Arthur gloomily predicted that the search would end in disaster for many of his knights because none was pure enough, save Galahad or Percivale, to see the holy vessel.

To Galahad the Grail appeared in all its splendor. Percivale, who followed him, also saw the holy sign. Sir Bors returned to King Arthur to report that he had viewed the Grail; but Lancelot had seen only a sign of it. Some of the other knights never returned to the Round Table from their perilous quest.

PELLEAS AND ETTARRE

Pelleas had given Ettarre a trophy he had won in a tournament, but she, scorning the young knight, barred him from her court. Gawain, meeting Pelleas in his despair, offered to help him. After telling the knight to hide in the forest, Gawain went to Ettarre and told her he had killed Pelleas. As the days passed, Pelleas became impatient. One night, stealing into the castle, he found Gawain and Ettarre sleeping together and placed his naked sword across the throats of the sleeping lovers. Then in a mad rage he rode through the forest until he met Percivale, who accidentally revealed to Pelleas the scandal about Lancelot and Guinevere. Disillusioned, the young knight returned to the Round Table, where his rude manner to the Queen foreshadowed evil to Lancelot and Guinevere. Sir Modred saw that the ruin of the Round Table was near at hand.

THE LAST TOURNAMENT

To a tournament at Camelot came Tristram, who had left his bride, Isolt of the white hands. Her name was the same as that of his beloved, Isolt, the wife of King Mark of Cornwall. Lancelot, laboring under the guilt of his sinful love for Guinevere, decided to fight with the similarly guilty Tristram, who won the tournament. Tristram then went to Isolt of Cornwall. King Mark was away on a hunting trip. He returned unexpectedly, found the lovers together, and killed Tristram.

In the north a knight rebelled against King Arthur's rule and charged that the Round Table was a thing of falseness and guilt where harlots and adulterers lived disguised as ladies and knights. King Arthur rode to quell the revolt and the guilty man was killed; but King Arthur was heavy in heart when he returned to Camelot.

GUINEVERE

Fearing exposure of her love for Lancelot, Guinevere asked him to leave Camelot. On the night of their farewell Modred trapped the lovers together, and

Guinevere, feeling that she was shamed forever, went to Almesbury and took refuge in a nunnery. There she recalled how Lancelot had brought her from her father's home to marry Arthur, how she had thought Arthur cold and had fallen in love with the courtly, gay Lancelot.

King Arthur went to Almesbury. To Guinevere he spoke of his pride in the marvelous truths which the Round Table had upheld, and which Guinevere had inspired. Now all was lost, but he forgave Guinevere before he went off to fight against Modred and his traitor knights.

Filled with remorse, Guinevere asked the nuns to accept her in their order. There she gave her services until they made her abbess. After three years in that rank she died.

THE PASSING OF ARTHUR

In Modred's revolt King Arthur was wounded. As he lay dying he told Sir Bedivere to cast the sword Excalibur into the lake. When Bedivere finally brought to King Arthur the tale that amid flashing and strange sights an arm reached out from the lake to receive the sword, King Arthur knew that Bedivere had truly sent Excalibur back to the Lady of the Lake. Next King Arthur told Bedivere to carry him to the shore. There three maidens came in a barge to take King Arthur away. As Bedivere stood weeping, King Arthur assured him that the old order of the Round Table must pass to give way to something new.

So King Arthur passed, in the manner of his legendary beginning, back across the waters to Avalon, but many men believed that some day he would return to his people in their need. Bedivere watched on the shore until the wintry dawn broke bringing a new year.

Critical Evaluation

As England's poet laureate from 1850 until his death in 1892, Alfred Lord Tennyson spoke to a complex and paradoxical age. His widely varied poetry made the author of *Idylls of the King* the most representative poet of the Victorian age. Writing sometimes with the optimism of his contemporary Robert Browning, sometimes with the brooding melancholy of Matthew Arnold, Tennyson wrote of the demands of love and duty, of the conflict between the public and private selves.

Tennyson's own life, particularly the early days, was one of tension and conflict. Born in 1809, he began writing poetry at an early age, stimulated perhaps by his wide reading and by a desire to escape the morbid atmosphere of his home. His father, the rector of Somersby, was a man of erratic behavior, sometimes kind, but more often melancholy and harsh toward his family. Even after Tennyson left home his life was not easy; he suffered from poverty, the lack of public recognition of his poetry, and the death of his friend, Arthur Hallam—events which must be at least partially responsible for the introspective quality of much of the early poetry. The last section of *Idylls of the King,* "Morte d'Arthur," was written during this period of his life.

But most of the poem was written after 1850. This is the great year of Tennyson's life, when *In Memoriam* was published and he was made poet laureate. With public recognition came financial security, and the opportunity to marry Emily Sellwood, his fiancée of fourteen years. But if the main part of *Idylls of the King* took shape after the bitter conflicts (at least the external ones) were past, many of the themes of the early poetry recur in the mature work. Contrasting motifs that surface in the early lyrics (the passive acceptance of the sensual life in "The Lotus-Eaters," the ultimate rejection of that subjective world in "Palace of Art") come together in many of the later poems, including *Idylls of the King.* In "The Coming of Arthur," for example, the young king sees Guinevere, falls in love with her, but rides on to duty and to battle.

The decision and the conflict seem typically Victorian. The years 1837 to 1901 (Victoria's reign ends neatly just as the new century begins) saw change and reform in England. The Chartist Movement of the 1840's and the various Reform Bills (in 1867, 1884, 1885) were real if not entirely effectual attempts to right the wrongs of a world irreparably altered by the Industrial Revolution. For many Victorians, and certainly for Tennyson, a sense of duty was as real and immediate a part of life as love and pleasure.

But there was often a paradoxically introspective quality about the literature of this age of social action. New developments in science and their religious and philosophical implications turned writers away from the outer world and inward to the self as they tried to discover through meditation and reflection the values and the God that, in J. Hillis Miller's sense of the word, seemed to be "disappearing." Tennyson read widely in the sciences, in astronomy and geology, while he was a student at Cambridge. He knew Lyell's *Principles of Geology,* an unsettling precursor of Darwin and the Theory of Evolution. Undoubtedly this reading reinforced his early predilection for subjectivity—an attitude that would always be at war with the demands of the public role of poet laureate.

A problem that arises when analyzing these tensions in *Idylls of the King* is that Tennyson's epic (like the earlier *In Memoriam*) was written over a long period of time. The question must be asked: are the twelve idylls separate, fragmentary, or is there a unifying theme—or set of themes? Taken from a chronological point of view the problem is even more difficult here than in *In Memoriam,* which was written over a period of about sixteen years. Although "The Coming of Arthur" was conceived in 1833, the first idylls (four in number) were not completed and published until 1859; expanded versions followed in 1869, 1871, and 1872. The complete work did not appear until 1885, seven years before the poet's death. Thus the reader is dealing with a poem that was written over a period of fifty years, begun when the poet was twenty-four and finished when he was seventy-four.

There is, of course, one obvious unifying theme—the Arthurian legend which Tennyson derived mainly from Malory's *Morte d'Arthur*. But just as *In Memoriam* transcends its original theme (Tennyson's sense of personal loss at the death of Hallam), *Idylls of the King* becomes more than a retelling of an ancient romance. Written in the Victorian spirit, the poem speaks not only of the mystique of the Round Table, but of man in and out of society, of what was and what might have been.

The plot centers not on one man, but on a vision of the better world that Arthur and his good knights would create. Tennyson's tale is not of a man who would be king, but of a man who must be king—of a society that is destined to be born, come to fruition, and finally to die because of perfidy from within.

A number of the idylls are concerned with the sharp contrast between the high ideal and the actuality. In "Vivien" Merlin is enticed by the vixenish Vivien into giving up a magic formula known to the magician alone. Merlin sometimes sees Vivien without illusion, but at other times allows himself to be ensnared by her false but charming façade. Even the wise Merlin must be reminded that the world is not always as it seems, that in life exists the potentiality of death, in love the possibility of deceit, and in all idealistic endeavors the opportunity for treachery.

This knowledge of the good in evil, the evil in good, appears throughout the poem. The search for the grail, for instance, is a highly idealistic mission. Through the quest for the cup from which Christ drank and the various tests of character to determine whether he would succeed, the quester is strengthened and purified; he returns a better knight. But the vision can only come to a few; despite the noble motives that initiate the adventure, the end result is the weakening of Cameliard because of the absence of her leaders.

Ultimately, it is not the search for the grail, but Guinevere's guilty love for Lancelot that becomes the catalyst for Cameliard's destruction. But it is only one of a flood of incidents. Many events in the poem lead to the defeat of the Round Table; many perfidies—Tristan's, Gawain's, Modred's—destroy the ideal society. Like the period in which it was written, *Idylls of the King* cannot be interpreted simplistically. The problem it examines is perhaps the basic modern and Victorian dilemma: what is to become of society, and more importantly, what is to become of man, destined to exist simultaneously within himself and among others.

Bibliography

Adicks, Richard.   "The Lily Maid and the Scarlet Sleeve, White and Red in Tennyson's *Idylls*," in *University Review*. XXXIV (October, 1967), pp. 65–71.

Battenhouse, Henry M. *Poets of Christian Thought; Evaluations from Dante to T.S. Eliot.* New York: Ronald Press, 1947, pp. 99–105.

Brashear, William R. "Tennyson's Tragic Vitalism: *Idylls of the King,*" in *Victorian Poetry.* VI (Spring, 1968), pp. 29–49.

Culler, A. Dwight. *The Poetry of Tennyson.* New Haven, Conn.: Yale University Press, 1977, pp. 214–241.

Eggers, J. Phillip. *King Arthur's Laureate: A Study of Tennyson's* Idylls of the King. New York: New York University Press, 1971.

Engelberg, Edward. "The Beast Image in Tennyson's *Idylls of the King,*" in *Journal of English Literary History.* XXII (1955), pp. 287–292.

Hellstrom, Ward. *On the Poems of Tennyson.* Gainesville: University of Florida Press, 1972, pp. 89–134.

Joseph, Gerhard. *Tennysonian Love: The Strange Diagonal.* Minneapolis: University of Minnesota Press, 1969, pp. 145–150, 163–187.

Kaplan, Fred. "Woven Paces and Weaving Hands: Tennyson's Merlin as Fallen Artist," in *Victorian Poetry.* VII (1969), pp. 285–298.

Kincaid, James R. *Tennyson's Major Poems, the Comic and Ironic Patterns.* New Haven, Conn.: Yale University Press, 1975, pp. 150–213.

Kissane, James D. *Alfred Tennyson.* New York: Twayne, 1970, pp. 99–119.

Kozicki, Henry. "Tennyson's *Idylls of the King* as Tragic Drama," in *Victorian Poetry.* IV (Winter, 1966), pp. 15–20.

Legris, Maurice. "Structure and Allegory in Tennyson's *Idylls of the King,*" in *Humanities Association Bulletin.* XVI (1965), pp. 37–44.

Librach, Ronald S. "Myth and Romance in *Idylls of the King,*" in *Dalhousie Review.* LV (1975), pp. 511–525.

Priestly, F.E.L. *Language and Structure in Tennyson's Poetry.* London: Andre Deutsch, 1973, pp. 125–136.

Reed, John R. *Perception and Design in Tennyson's* Idylls of the King. Athens: Ohio University Press, 1969.

Rosenberg, John D. *The Fall of Camelot; A Study of Tennyson's* Idylls of the King. Cambridge, Mass.: Belknap Press, 1973.

Ryals, Clyde de L. *From the Great Deep; Essays on* The Idylls of the King. Athens: Ohio University Press, 1967.

————. "The Moral Paradox of the Hero in *The Idylls of the King,*" in *Journal of English Literary History.* XXX (1963), pp. 53–69.

Shaw, W. David. "The Idealist's Dilemma in *Idylls of the King,*" in *Victorian Poetry.* V (Spring, 1967), pp. 41–53.

————. *Tennyson's Style.* Ithaca, N.Y.: Cornell University Press, 1976, pp. 192–223, 326–330.

Slinn, E. Warwick. "Deception and Artifice in *Idylls of the King*," in *Victorian Poetry*. XI (1973), pp. 1–14.

Solomon, Stanley J. "Tennyson's Paradoxical King," in *Victorian Poetry*. I (November, 1963), pp. 258–271.

Turner, Paul. *Tennyson*. London: Routledge and Kegan Paul, 1976, pp. 29–32, 149–170.

Wilkenfield, R.B. "Tennyson's Camelot: The Kingdom of Folly," in *University of Toronto Quarterly*. XXXVII (1968), pp. 281–294.

IN MEMORIAM

Type of work: Elegy
Author: Alfred, Lord Tennyson (1809–1892)
First published: 1850

Essay-Review

In Memoriam A.H.H., Obiit MDCCCXXXIII, unquestionably one of the greatest elegies of English literature, records the intellectual, emotional, religious, and aesthetic changes Tennyson underwent throughout a sixteen-year period following the early and tragic death of his closest friend, Arthur Henry Hallam, in Vienna, on September 15, 1883. The year *In Memoriam* was first published, 1850, was also the year Tennyson married Emily Sellwood and succeeded Wordsworth as Poet Laureate.

In Memoriam as truly represents the chief Victorian conflict of science and faith as any work of its era; and Tennyson's attempt to reconcile the religious doubts arising from his personal sorrow and the effects of pre-Darwinian theories of evolution was hailed by thinkers of his time as an intellectual landmark. The cyclic change, the turn from private grief and despair to the larger public vision and concern for wider, social issues, that can be found in this poem reflects Tennyson's growing acceptance and reconciliation with the problems of his age.

It appears that Tennyson did not conceive publishing the one hundred thirty-one lyrics of *In Memoriam* until late in the 1840's, when he brought them together as one poem, arranging them so as to reflect in the three-year time scheme of the poem the sixteen-year period of his life which they actually represent. Since these lyrics were written over a long time span, they vary considerably in the tone and mood of reaction to Hallam's death, thus dramatizing lyrically Tennyson's psychological condition. Though many organizational schemes have been offered, the most generally accepted one views the poem as illustrating a movement from initial grief (I-XXVII); to philosophic doubt and despair (XXVIII-LXXVII); to rising hope (IXXVIII-CIII); to affirmation of faith (CIV-CXXXI). But the actual growth is more subtle than this scheme and requires close attention to repeated images, such as the two yew tree poems or the two visits to Hallam's house.

The "Prologue," dated 1849, and addressed to "Strong Son of God, immortal Love," expresses the poet's conviction that faith, not knowledge, leads to a harmonious union of the intellectual and the spiritual. The first section then relates the poet's nearly complete self-absorption in grief, but even here we notice a change, evident for example in the difference between "I held it truth" (I) to "I hold it true" (XXVII). Though Love provides a "higher life" for man hereafter, few can find immediate comfort for present loss in this promise of future tranquility. Nevertheless, the poet affirms his belief that " 'Tis better to have loved and lost/Than never to have loved at all." This acceptance of his experience despite its accompanying sorrow comes only after intervening poems reveal the true depth of his despair; his identification, for instance, with the yew tree, a symbol of death, shows the poet's marked conviction that he, like the yew tree which is not subject to seasonal changes, is imprisoned in grief and can merely endure in "stubborn hardihood."

This fellowship with "Sorrow" (III) induces an intellectual despair and alienates him from comforting Love.

> "The stars," she whispers, "blindly run;
> A web is woven across the sky;
> From out waste places comes a cry,
> And murmurs from the dying sun. . . ."

In one sense this conception of the universe as a blindly run mechanism is the central intellectual conflict of the poem. In his deep melancholy, Tennyson questions not only the justice of Hallam's tragic death, but also the justice of the entire creation.

Like a passenger of a "helmless bark" Tennyson moves alternately from numbed despair to self-awareness (IV), and finds composing poetry an anodyne for pain (V). Poems IX-XVII constitute a group unified by the poet's meditation upon the return from Italy by ship of Hallam's body. A "calmer grief" now pervades his heart (XI).

The pain of grief "slowly forms the firmer mind" (XVIII), but locked in his heart remain the deeper sorrows that words cannot relieve (XX). He writes not to parade his emotions publicly, but because he must (XXI).

The second section commences with the first Christmas celebration some three months after Hallam's death. The Poet hears the bells' message of "peace and goodwill" but almost wishes never to hear them again. Yet even in his despondency, the bells recall his happy youth, and, touching pain with joy, ease his misery. In the renewal of "old pastimes in the hall" they make a "vain pretense" (XXX), but find consolation in the thought of an afterlife for the dead, though what that afterlife may be "remaineth unrevealed" (XXXI).

The second yew tree poem illustrates a lightening of his burden, for he now sees the tree with "fruitful cloud," subject to change like his grief. The group of poems from XI to XLVIII represents Tennyson's attempt to resolve the question about after life and also the possibility of a reunion with Hallam. These speculations are not meant to solve the problems, he tells us (XLVIII), but were "Short swallow-flights of song" which soothed his mind.

In LIV Tennyson expresses the vague "trust that somehow good/Will be the final goal of ill." But the two following poems call in doubt this qualified optimism, so that all he can permit himself is to "faintly trust the larger hope" (LV). In his agitated state of mind the poet views Nature "red in tooth and claw" (LVI). The remaining portion of this section deals with the former relationship of the poet with Hallam.

The third section opens with the second Christmas and finds the poet with the sense of the abiding presence of his friend. His subdued grief allows him to treasure their friendship.

> Which masters Time indeed, and is
> Eternal, separate from fears.

Tennyson contemplates the possibility of a visitation by Hallam and experiences a "mystic trance" in XCV, when "The dead man touch'd" him "from the past." The third section concludes with a four-poem series relating to the Tennyson family's removal from Somersby, with its pleasant and sorrowful associations.

With the fourth and final section the poet turns from the past and his personal grief to the future of mankind; this change is signaled by the famous lyric "Ring out, wild bells" (CVI). Tennyson resolves not to allow sorrow to alienate him from society (CVIII). Hallam's qualities emerge clearly for the first time; in a series of poems Tennyson praises his friend, particularly for his attributes of leadership and dedication to social good.

Tennyson draws an important distinction in CXIV of the difference between knowledge and wisdom; with wisdom man does not fear death since wisdom is "of the soul," while knowledge must learn to submit to wisdom and "know her place." "Acknowledging "Love" as his "lord and king," Tennyson proclaims that "all is well" (CXXVII). His optimism is buttressed by his knowledge that Hallam

> O'erlook'st the tumult from afar,
> And smilest, knowing all is well.

As the elegy draws to a close the poet more strongly feels the certainty of cosmic design: "That all, as in some piece of art,/Is toil coöperant to an end." (CXXVIII). He feels more confident of Hallam's omnipresence: "Thy voice is on the rolling air;/I hear thee where the waters run" (CXXX). His love, though founded on their previous earthly relationship, is "vaster passion" now that Hallam's presence is spiritual and diffused through "God and Nature." The elegy concludes with the poet's self-confident assertion of the permanence of the "living will" which purifies our "deeds" and of the "faith" in truths not to be "proved" until our deaths.

In the "Epilogue" Tennyson celebrates the marriage of his friend, Edward Lushington, to the poet's sister.

Bibliography

Battenhouse, Henry M. *Poets of Christian Thought; Evaluations from Dante to T.S. Eliot.* New York: Ronald Press, 1947, pp. 90–99.

Boyd, John D. "The Principle of Analogy and the Immortality Question in Tennyson's *In Memoriam*," in *University of Toronto Quarterly*. XLV (1976), pp. 123–138.

Bradley, A.C. *A Commentary on Tennyson's* In Memoriam. London: Macmillan, 1901.

Culler, A. Dwight. *The Poetry of Tennyson*. New Haven, Conn.: Yale University Press, 1977, pp. 149–189.

Gransden, K.W. *Tennyson:* In Memoriam. London: Edward Arnold, 1964.

Grant, Stephen A. "The Mystical Implications of *In Memoriam*," in *Studies in English Literature, 1500–1900*. II (Autumn, 1962), pp. 481–495.

Hellstrom, Ward. *On the Poems of Tennyson*. Gainsville: University of Florida Press, 1972, pp. 26–67.

Hunt, John D. "The Symbolist Vision in *In Memoriam*," in *Victorian Poetry*. VIII (Autumn, 1970), pp. 187–198.

Johnson, E.D.H. "*In Memoriam*: The Way of A Poet," in *Victorian Studies*. II (1958), pp. 139–148.

Kincaid, James R. *Tennyson's Major Poems, the Comic and Ironic Patterns*. New Haven, Conn.: Yale University Press, 1975, pp. 80–109.

Kissane, James D. *Alfred Tennyson*. New York: Twayne, 1970, pp. 66–78.

Kozicki, Henry. " 'Meaning' in Tennyson's *In Memoriam*," in *Studies in English Literature, 1500–1900*. XVII (Autumn, 1977), pp. 673–694.

McSweeney, Kerry. "The Pattern of Natural Consolation in *In Memoriam*," in *Victorian Poetry*. XI (1973), pp. 87–99.

Mason, Michael. "*In Memoriam*: The Dramatization of Sorrow," in *Victorian Poetry*. X (1972), pp. 161–177.

Mattes, Eleanor B. In Memoriam, *the Way of a Soul: A Study of Some Influences That Shaped Tennyson's Poems*. New York: Exposition Press, 1951.

Moore, Carlisle. "Faith, Doubt and Mystical Experience in *In Memoriam*," in *Victorian Studies*. VII (December, 1963), pp. 155–169.

Rosenberg, John D. "The Two Kingdoms of *In Memoriam*," in *Journal of English and Germanic Philology*. LVIII (1959), pp 228–240.

Ross, Robert H. In Memoriam: *An Authoritative Text, Backgrounds and Sources, Criticism*. New York: Norton, 1974.

Ryals, Clyde de L. "The 'Heavenly Friend': The 'New Mythus' of *In Memorium*," in *The Personalist*. XLIII (1962), pp. 383–402.

Shaw, W. David. *Tennyson's Style*. Ithaca, N.Y.: Cornell University Press, 1976, pp. 132–167.

Shmiefsky, Marvel. "*In Memoriam*: Its Seasonal Imagery Reconsidered," in *Studies in English Literature, 1500–1900.* VII (Autumn, 1967), pp. 721–739.

Sinfield, Alan. *The Language of Tennyson's* In Memoriam. New York: Barnes & Noble, 1971.

Taaffe, James G. "Circle Imagery in Tennyson's *In Memoriam*," in *Victorian Poetry*. I (April, 1963), pp. 123–131.

Turner, Paul. *Tennyson*. London: Routledge and Kegan Paul, 1976, pp. 114–131.

Zuckermann, Joanne P. "Tennyson's *In Memoriam* as Love Poetry," in *Dalhousie Review*. LI (1971), pp. 202–217.

POEMS

Type of work: Dramatic idylls
Author: Alfred, Lord Tennyson (1809–1892)
First published: 1842

Essay-Review

This volume of Tennyson's poetry contains, with the exception of the songs of *The Princess* and certain lyrics of *In Memoriam*, some of the best poetry he ever wrote. In this 1842 volume is reprinted, often with considerable revision, the earlier poetry of 1830 and 1832 publications which critics had treated, with some justice, harshly. These revisions may be studied with some profit, for they illustrate how Tennyson was developing artistic consciousness during the famous "ten years silence" which followed the death of his best friend, Arthur Henry Hallam, in 1833. In this period Tennyson published few poems but worked steadily revising his early poems and wrote much of *In Memoriam* as well as the new poems, first published in 1842. Since these new poems were composed after Hallam's death, many reflect the various moods the poet experienced as a result of his loss.

Of the poems revised and republished, perhaps of all of Tennyson's poems, "The Lady of Shalott" is best known. In this poem we see the characteristic Tennysonian landscape and the portrait of the isolated lady, as well as the handling of meter and special attention to the sounds of words for which the poet is known. Although landscapes may vary with the mood the poems portray in other Tennyson poems, nature usually harmonizes with and conveys the subject's psychological state, as in *In Memoriam*. Here, however, nature and human activity in the real world from which the lady is withdrawn contrast with the isolation; the lady of the poem finds herself drawn out of her contemplative life into the real world. Ordinarily in a Tennyson poem the landscape echoes the melancholy isolation and spiritual vacuum of the person, but in "The Lady of Shalott" the Keatsian richness of the sensuous detail emphasizes the variety and motion of the world outside the tower where the lady weaves secondhand images of that reality in her "magic web."

It is the movement, the progress of daily life, of barges passing by on the river and people traveling to Camelot, that the lady perceives as a "shadow," a reflection of life in her magic mirror. Knowing that she cannot look upon real life because she suffers under a mysterious curse, she abandons herself to isolation until she grows tired of mere "shadow" and looks out upon "bold Sir Lancelot." Dying, she floats down the river to Camelot, where her arrival mystifies the citizens.

Another characteristic poem is "Mariana in the South." As in "The Lady of Shalott," a natural landscape serves as background for a dramatically conceived feminine portrait, but in "Mariana in the South" nature corresponds to the person's mood; we understand Mariana's psychological state through her responses to nature. Her spiritual condition seems to reflect the barren dryness of the "empty-river bed" and of "shallows on a distant shore" and in the blinding light and oppressive heat of the southern landscape. Alone she worships her beauty at her "secret shrine," the mirror; deserted by her lover she lives "forgotten, and love forlorn." She finds promise of relief only in the "black shadow" of death which hovers over her house.

In "Œnone," Tennyson retells the classical legend of Paris and the golden apple, but the poet approaches it from the point of view of Œnone, the mountain nymph deserted by Paris for Helen. Weary with life, Œnone now sings alone on the mountain in Ida. She tells of the contest in which Paris spurns power, "self-reverence, self-knowledge, self-control" and accepts "the fairest and most loving wife in Greece" in return for awarding the prize to "Idalian Aphrodite." The poem ends with Œnone's dim foresight of the Trojan War and the destruction of a civilization which will accompany her own death.

One of Tennyson's most famous poems, "The Palace of Art," is according to the poet's statement a "sort of allegory. . . . of a soul." This soul "did love beauty only" in all its forms, "knowledge" for its "beauty" alone, and failed to recognize "That Beauty, Good, and Knowledge are three sisters." The narrator constructs for his soul "a lordly pleasure-house" where it can live apart from the world of men. The soul lives grandly in its magnificent structure, full of sights and sounds of nature, beautiful paintings, a complete paradise for the aesthetic soul. But after three years of intense pleasure, self-absorption, and gratification, the soul discovers despair, confusion, self-scorn, and doubts wrought by alienation and pride. For a year the soul dwells in this state until, throwing off its "royal robes," it retreats to a "cottage in the vale," where it can "mourn and pray." The soul requests that the palace not be destroyed so that it may return, purged of guilt, ready to admit Love.

Tennyson evidently felt this conflict of life and art very strongly, and one wonders if in "The Palace" he actually resolved the conflict since the palace remains standing and the soul wishes to return. When Tennyson abandons himself to the claims of art, as he does in "The Lotos-Eaters," his poetry achieves a quality many readers prefer. "The Lotos-Eaters" describes the emotional disengagement from life, from toil and strain, from fatherland and family, of Ulysses and his men in the land of lotus eaters. The men tire of their struggle and "swear an oath" to remain in that pleasant environment rather than renew their voyage homeward.

If "The Lotos-Eaters" shows Tennyson at his best in one area, "Ulysses" represents as well as any other poem in the collection his convinction that man's life must be dedicated to action and involvement. This stately blank verse monologue dramatizes Ulysses as an old man dissatisfied with idleness and yearning to "drink/Life to the lees." Not content to rest with memories of his glorious past, Ulysses leaves his kingdom to his son Telemachus and sails out to a newer world with his old comrades. Some greater task, "Some work of noble note, may yet be done."

"The Two Voices," a dialogue between "a still small voice" and the narrator of the poem, represents a dilemma the speaker feels about suicide. The "voice" offers a dozen or more reasons why death is preferable to life, but the narrator counters each argument. Finally a second voice whispers, "Be of better cheer" and promises a "hidden hope." The speaker suddenly perceives the abiding presence of "love," the ultimate design and end of creation manifest in "Nature's living motion."

"Locksley Hall" presents a narrator returned to the scene of his youthful experiences with his "cousin Amy," whom he had loved and lost to another. He reminisces how in his youth he had optimistically felt at one with his age and envisioned a glorious future for the world. Amy and he loved each other until Amy, "servile" and a "puppet to a father's threat," married another man. The speaker sees Amy's fine nature coarsened by contact with her husband; he reflects bitterly on her unfaithfulness. He realizes that he "must mix with action" to prevent his withering in despair, and he wishes to immerse himself in the progress of his "wondrous Mother-Age." Yet the disillusionment he suffered has left him with a jaundiced eye and he contemplates an escape to "Summer isles of Eden" where there will be "enjoyment more than in this march of mind." Throwing off this romantic dream, however, the speaker resolves to take inspiration from the spirit of his age:

> Forward, forward let us range,
> Let the great world spin for ever down the ringing grooves of change.
>
> Thro' the shadow of the globe we sweep into the younger day;
> Better fifty years of Europe than a cycle of Cathay.

Bibliography

Buckley, Jerome H. *Tennyson: The Growth of a Poet*. Cambridge, Mass.: Harvard University Press, 1960.

Colville, Derek. *Victorian Poetry and the Romantic Religion*. Albany: State University of New York Press, 1970, pp. 167–230.

Culler, A. Dwight. *The Poetry of Tennyson*. New Haven, Conn.: Yale University Press, 1977.

Francis, Elizabeth A. "Tennyson's Political Poetry, 1852–1855," in *Victorian Poetry*. XIV (1976), pp. 113–123.

Golffing, Francis. "Tennyson's Last Phase: The Poet as Seer," in *Southern Review*. II (1966), pp. 264–285.

Johnson, E.D.H. *The Alien View of Victorian Poetry*. Princeton, N.J.: Princeton University Press, 1952, pp. 3–68.

Johnson, Wendell S. *Sex and Marriage in Victorian Poetry*. Ithaca, N.Y.: Cornell University Press, 1975, pp. 110–184.

Killham, John. *Critical Essays on the Poetry of Tennyson.* New York: Barnes & Noble, 1960.

Kincaid, James R. *Tennyson's Major Poems: The Cosmic and Ironic Patterns.* New Haven, Conn.: Yale University Press, 1975.

Korg, Jacob. "The Pattern of Fatality in Tennyson's Poetry," in *Victorian Newsletter.* XIV (1958), pp. 8–11.

Kozicki, Henry. "Philosophy of History in Tennyson's Poetry to the 1842 *Poems,*" in *Journal of English Literary History.* XLII (1975), pp. 88–106.

Pettigrew, John. *Tennyson: The Early Poems.* London: Edward Arnold, 1970.

Preyer, Robert. "Alfred Tennyson: The Poetry and Politics of Conservative Vision," in *Victorian Studies.* IX (June, 1966), pp. 325–352.

————. "Tennyson as an Oracular Poet," in *Modern Philology.* LV (1958), pp. 239–251.

Priestly, F.E.L. *Language and Structure in Tennyson's Poetry.* London: Andre Deutsch, 1973.

Ryals, Clyde de L. *Theme and Symbol in Tennyson's Poems to 1850.* Philadelphia: University of Pennsylvania Press, 1964.

Shaw, W. David. *Tennyson's Style.* Ithaca, N.Y.: Cornell University Press, 1976.

Simpson, Richard. "Mr. Tennyson's Poetry," in *Richard Simpson as Critic.* Edited by David Carroll. London: Routledge and Kegan Paul, 1977, pp. 285–318.

Sonn, Carl R. "Poetic Vision and Religious Certainty in Tennyson's Earlier Poetry," in *Modern Philology.* LVII (1959), pp. 83–93.

Sypher, F. J. "Politics in the Poetry of Tennyson," in *Victorian Poetry.* XIV (1976), pp. 101–112.

Tennyson, Sir Charles. "The Dream in Tennyson's Poetry," in *Virginia Quarterly Review.* XL (Spring, 1964), pp. 228–248.

Turner, Paul. *Tennyson.* London: Routledge and Kegan Paul, 1976.

Walton, James. "Tennyson's Patrimony: From *The Outcast* to *Maud,*" in *Texas Studies in Literature and Language.* XI (Spring, 1969), pp. 733–750.

Waterston, Elizabeth H. "Symbolism in Tennyson's Minor Poems," in *University of Toronto Quarterly.* XX (July, 1951), pp. 369–380.

Wilson, Charles. "Mirror of a Shire: Tennyson's Dialect Poems," in *Durham University Journal.* LII (December, 1959), pp. 22–28.

THE PRINCESS

Type of work: Narrative poem
Author: Alfred, Lord Tennyson (1809–1892)
First published: 1847

Essay-Review

First published in 1847, *The Princess* underwent numerous major changes in its later editions; in the third edition of 1850, the poet added the six intercalary songs in addition to partial revisions of the "Prologue" and "Epilogue." The fourth edition, published in 1851, saw the introduction of the passages relating to the "weird seizures" of the Prince. Reasons for these changes may be Tennyson's almost immediate dissatisfaction with the work and his desire to clarify public misunderstandings of it or his reaction to the rather unfavorable reception of the poem by contemporary critics. Indeed, the poem today is generally regarded as one of Tennyson's ambitious but lesser works, owing chiefly to the mixed style and the shifting tone of the poem, as well as the somewhat transitory nature of his subject, women's rights.

The Princess begins as a light mock-heroic work and ends with a "serious message"; it begins seemingly not seriously concerned with women's rights and ends equivocally with the poet's almost avoiding the issue. Tennyson himself sensed this apparent disunity of the poem and writes in the "Conclusion": "I moved as in a strange diagonal,/And maybe neither pleased myself nor them." Tennyson's ambivalence about his subject and his failure to sustain the comic approach constitute a major blemish for some modern critics, but though the narrative itself is disparaged, few critics deny the power, beauty, and simplicity of the intercalary lyrics of this poem. Several of these are judged among the finest of his poems, and for grace and precision and music, only a small number of English lyrics may favorably compare.

In the "Prologue" the poet and five other college companions join their friend, Walter Vivian, on his father's estate. Here they view the exhibition of the neighboring Institute, of which Walter's father is patron. A book of family history relating the courage of a female ancestor inspires Lilia, Walter's sister, to speak out for women's rights, particularly their education. Walter tells how at college the seven friends told chain-stories to pass away the time; Lilia suggests that they tell such a story now. Walter agrees and adds that Lilia be the heroine, "Grand, epic, homicidal," and the poet, who will begin the story, be the hero. The seven-part story which follows is narrated by each of the seven friends; between each part the ladies present sing one of the six songs.

The young Prince, whose family suffers from a curse laid down by a sorcerer, finds that the Princess to whom he was once betrothed as a child now rejects him and wishes to "live alone/Among her women." He begs the King, his father, to be allowed to investigate this puzzle, but the King, of a warlike masculine nature, replies that they will settle this dispute by war. Driven by an inner voice, the Prince rides off to the southern kingdom of the Princess, accompanied by his two friends Cyril and Florian. At a town near the palace where the girls had established their women's college, the Prince obtains women's clothes for Cyril, Florian, and himself, and together they enter the college disguised, bearing a letter of introduction from Gama, the King and father of the Princess.

In the second narrative the college portress leads the still disguised males to Princess Ida, who greets them as new students and explains the rules to them: they must not for three years correspond with home, leave the boundaries of the college grounds, or converse with men. Ida tells them they must give up "convention" and work now for the freedom of women. She seems surprised that the males praise so highly the Prince, her former suitor. Next they encounter Psyche, Florian's sister, and Ida's favorite tutor. They admire Aglaîa, Psyche's daughter, while Psyche lectures them on the history of feminine slavery. Finally Psyche recognizes her brother beneath his disguise, and nearly betrays them until her natural affection overcomes her duty to Ida. Melissa, the daughter of Blanche, who is Ida's other favorite, also learns their identity but refuses to reveal their secret.

In the third section Ida invites the men to travel with her. but before their departure the Prince has his first seizure, the curse-inflicted malady of his family. Recovering, the Prince as his own mock-ambassador tries to acquaint Ida with his passion for her and with her unnatural attitude toward men; he alludes to her missing "what every woman counts her due,/'Love, children, happiness.' " Ida reiterates her dedication to her ideals, claiming that while children may die, "great deeds" cannot.

In the fourth section a maid sings "Tears, idle tears," but Ida is unmoved by its sentiment of love. The Prince replies with his song, "O Swallow," a love song; Ida, however, spurns his "mere love poem," saying she admires only art addressed to "great ends." At this point Cyril sings a bawdy song which discloses their true identity. The women flee in panic, and Ida in her haste falls into the river. The Prince rescues her but is captured by her retinue and experiences his second seizure.

In the fifth section, the Prince and his companions, released by the Princess out of gratitude, stumble into the camp of the Prince's father. Gama, the Prince, and the King argue how to win Ida's hand; the King favors aggression, but Gama and the Prince suggest peaceful means. Taunted as a coward, the Prince agrees to a tournament where he will face Arac, Ida's brother, who champions women's rights. Again he falls into a trance and is unable to distinguish shadow and substance. Awakening, he finds the tournament ready to begin; fighting Arac, he is wounded and falls into a deep coma.

The sixth part opens with the Prince in a mystic trance. Ida in her triumph sings "Our enemies have fallen," then opens the palace as a hospital for the wounded. Her foolish insistence upon ascetic withdrawal and her unnatural contempt for men is evident; as she gazes upon the wounded Prince, however, she begs the King to allow her to care for his son. She embraces Psyche, whom she had dismissed as a traitor, and disbands the college despite Blanche's objections.

In the final part the palace has become a hospital with the maidens nursing the sick. Ida is heartsick because of the frustration of her ideals, but she finds "peace" aiding the wounded men. The Prince lies in a delirious state tended by Ida; as she cares for him she begins to love him, casts off her "falser self," and kisses the Prince. He succumbs to his love for her and falls into a blissful sleep. That night he awakes to find her reading poems to him; these are two of the best lyrics of the poem, "Now sleeps the crimson petal," and "Come down, O Maid." In the latter poem love is described as being of the "valley," not of mountain heights where Ida's idealism had carried her.

Ida admits her lack of humility, her desire to achieve "power" more than "truth," yet she still regrets the collapse of her idealistic plans to help women achieve status. The Prince, respecting her idealism, replies that they will work together for her goal. He says that women are not "undevelopt" men, that they should join with man in love; from this union the man gains "sweetness" and "moral height," the woman "mental breadth," without losing "the childlike in the larger mind." Either sex alone is "half itself," and together in marriage each "fulfils/Defect in each." The Prince attributes to Ida his rebirth into a better life, his losing doubt and "haunting sense of hollow shows."

The narrative closes and the framework returns with the poet's explanation of the feud which arose between the mockers (the men) and the realists (the women). To satisfy both he proposed his "strange diagonal" and perhaps pleased neither.

Bibliography

The Princess

Assad, Thomas J. "Tennyson's 'Tears, Idle Tears,' " in *Tulane Studies in English.* XIII (1963), pp. 71–83.

Bergonzi, Bernard. "Feminism and Femininity in *The Princess,*" in *The Major Victorian Poets.* Edited by Isobel Armstrong. Lincoln: University of Nebraska Press, 1969, pp. 35–50.

Brooks, Cleanth. "The Motivation of Tennyson's Weeper," in *Critical Essays on the Poetry of Tennyson.* Edited by John Killham. London: Routledge and Kegan Paul, 1960, pp. 177–185.

Collins, Winston. "*The Princess*: The Education of the Prince," in *Victorian Poetry.* XI (1973), pp. 285–294.

Culler, A. Dwight. *The Poetry of Tennyson.* New Haven, Conn.: Yale University Press, 1977, pp. 129–148.

Danzig, Allan. "Tennyson's *The Princess*: A Definition of Love," in *Victorian Poetry*. IV (Spring, 1966), pp. 83–89.

Dietrich, Manfred. "Unity and Symbolic Structure in Tennyson's *The Princess*," in *English Studies in Canada*. II (1976), pp. 182–202.

Goslee, David F. "Character and Structure in Tennyson's *The Princess*," in *Studies in English Literature, 1500–1900*. XIV (1974), pp. 563–573.

Gunter, Garland O. "Symbols of Individuation in Tennyson's *The Princess*," in *A Festschrift for Professor Marguerite Roberts*. Richmond, Va.: University of Richmond Press, 1976, pp. 74–86.

Harrison, James. "The Role of Anachronism in *The Princess*," in *English Studies in Canada*. I (1975), pp. 304–316.

Johnson, Wendell S. *Sex and Marriage in Victorian Poetry*. Ithaca, N.Y.: Cornell University Press, 1975, pp. 124–135.

Joseph, Gerhard. *Tennysonian Love: The Strange Diagonal*. Minneapolis: University of Minnesota Press, 1969, pp. 76–103, 105–110.

Killham, John. *Tennyson and* The Princess*: Reflections of an Age*. London: Athlone Press, 1958.

Kincaid, James R. *Tennyson's Major Poems, the Comic and Ironic Patterns*. New Haven, Conn.: Yale University Press, 1975, pp. 58–79.

Kissane, James D. *Alfred Tennyson*. New York: Twayne, 1970, pp. 93–99.

Kozicki, Henry. "The 'Medieval Ideal' in Tennyson's *The Princess*," in *Criticism*. XVII (1975), pp. 121–130.

Mantell, Deborah B. "*The Princess*: Tennyson's Eminently Shakespearian Poem," in *Texas Studies in Literature and Language*. XX (Spring, 1978), pp. 48–67.

Milhauser, Milton. "Tennyson's *Princess* and *Vestiges*," in *PMLA*. LXIX (1954), pp. 337–343.

Priestly, F.E.L. *Language and Structure in Tennyson's Poetry*. London: Andre Deutsch, 1973, pp. 80–92.

Ryals, Clyde de L. "The 'Weird Seizures' in *The Princess*," in *Texas Studies in Literature and Language*. IV (Summer, 1962), pp. 268–275.

Sait, James E. "Tennyson's *The Princess* and *Queen Mary*: Two Examinations of Sex and Politics," in *Durham University Journal*. XXXVII (1976), pp. 70–78.

Story, Kenneth. "Theme and Image in *The Princess*," in *Tennessee Studies in Literature*. XX (1975), pp. 50–59.

Turner, Paul. *Tennyson*. London: Routledge and Kegan Paul, 1976, pp. 100–113.

Wajid, R.A.   "Tennyson's 'Tears, Idle Tears,' " in *Rutgers University Studies in English*. V (1971), pp. 31–35.

Walton, James.   "Tennyson's Patrimony: From *The Outcast* to *Maud*," in *Texas Studies in Literature and Language*. XI (Spring, 1969), pp. 748–749.

"Tears, Idle Tears"

Assad, Thomas J.   "Tennyson's 'Tears, Idle Tears,' " in *Tulane Studies in English*. XIII (1963), pp. 71–83.

Brooks, Cleanth.   "The New Criticism: A Brief for the Defense," in *American Scholar*. XIII (Summer, 1944), pp. 286–293.

————.   *The Well Wrought Urn*. New York: Reynal and Hitchcock, 1947, pp. 153–162.

Empson, William.   "Thy Darling in an Urn," in *Sewanee Review*. LV (Autumn, 1947), pp. 691–692.

Hough, Graham G.   " 'Tears, Idle Tears,' " in *Critical Essays on the Poetry of Tennyson*. Edited by John Killham. New York: Barnes & Noble, 1960, pp. 186–191.

Ransom, John C.   "The Tense of Poetry," in *Southern Review*. I (Autumn, 1935), pp. 221–222.

Spitzer, Leo.   " 'Tears, Idle Tears' Again," in *Critical Essays on the Poetry of Tennyson*. Edited by John Killham. New York: Barnes & Noble, 1960, pp. 192–203.

Wajid, R.A.   "Tennyson's 'Tears, Idle Tears,' " in *Rutgers University Studies in English*. V (1971), pp. 31–35.

Wimsatt, W.K., Jr. and M.C. Beardsley.   "The Affective Fallacy," in *Sewanee Review*. LVII (Winter, 1949), pp. 46–47.

OSCAR WILDE

Born: Dublin, Ireland (October 15, 1856)
Died: Paris, France (November 30, 1900)

Principal Works

PLAYS: *Vera, or the Nihilists,* 1882; *The Duchess of Padua,* 1884; *A Florentine Tragedy,* 1885; *Lady Windermere's Fan,* 1892; *Salome,* 1893; *A Woman of No Importance,* 1893; *An Ideal Husband,* 1895; *The Importance of Being Earnest,* 1895.

NOVEL: *The Picture of Dorian Gray,* 1891.

TALES AND SKETCHES: *The Happy Prince and Other Tales,* 1888; *Lord Arthur Savile's Crime,* 1891; *A House of Pomegranates,* 1891.

POEMS: *Poems,* 1881; *The Sphinx,* 1894; *The Ballad of Reading Gaol,* 1898.

ESSAYS AND STUDIES: *Intentions,* 1891; *The Soul of Man Under Socialism,* 1891; *De Profundis,* 1905.

One of the most famous of Irish expatriates, Oscar (Fingal O'Flahertie Wills) Wilde, second son of Sir William Robert Wills Wilde and Jane Francisca Elgee Wilde, best known as "Speranza" of political fame, was born in Dublin, October 15, 1856. Early noted for his brilliance and sloth, characteristics he carried with him throughout life, he won prizes at the Portora Royal School in Ennis Killen, and later in Trinity College, Dublin. But it was in London that he first distinguished himself, although he had acquired fame at Magdalen College, Oxford, for his prize-winning poem "Ravenna" (1878) and as the most famous student of a famous master, John Ruskin.

As the leader of the Art-for-Art's-Sake school of aesthetics, Wilde was associated with his famous symbols: a peacock feather, sunflowers, dados, blue china, long hair, and velveteen breeches. A slight stigma was attached to his name even before his graduation from Oxford in 1878, but Wilde preached the doctrine that he did not care what was said as long as he was talked about. He was lampooned in cartoons, in novels, and even in comic opera; but he remained for years the center of attention, the lion of the hour, the most sought after of many famous talkers. His talents were conceded to be great by Shaw, Harris, Whistler, and, of course, Wilde himself. Even his early effusions in such magazines as *Month, The Catholic Mirror,* and the *Irish Monthly* were considered witty, artistic, and accomplished.

In a sense, his fortune was made in America where he lectured in the early 1880's and where his first play, *Vera,* was produced with fair success. His outrageous affectations and witty sayings and paradoxes were eagerly followed by everyone. Certainly this triumphant tour prepared England better to accept his later and best works. In 1884 his marriage to Constance Lloyd allayed somewhat the scabrous gossip of his deprecators. In fact, there seems little evidence for his homosexuality at this time. Only through hearsay and the later Wilde apologia, *De Profundis*, published posthumously in 1905, is there evidence of the depths of degradation to which he later sank. In direct contrast was his delicate language; no one ever heard him utter an oath or make an off-color remark.

Wilde's picture of the successive stages of degradation in man was openly presented in the character of Dorian Gray, who remained young outwardly while his pact with evil allowed his portrait to take on his many sins. Later Wilde's drama *Salome* aroused Philistines everywhere. Some of his poems, read at his famous trials, also caused much tongue-wagging which finally culminated in the Marquis of Queensberry's attack and Wilde's ill-advised slander suit against Lord Alfred Douglas' father. The reversal of this libel case caused Oscar Wilde to spend two years (1895–1897) in the Old Bailey and Reading Gaol, an experience which he immortalized in his famous poem. Much comment has been made on this work, regarded by many as a notable statement against man's inhumanity to man.

Many of the unsavory aspects of Wilde's personal life have been forgotten, but his witty paradoxes remain alive, especially in the plays, for his real reputation rests on his witty comedies of manners. *Lady Windermere's Fan* is a kind of moral tract with the fan used to turn public feeling from a compromising situation; in this case the mother takes on the sins of the daughter in order to prevent the daughter from making a mistake in decorum. As in all the plays, the epigrams are more noteworthy than the plot, especially in *The Importance of Being Earnest*, his last, best, and most popular drama. A *Woman of No Importance* protests the double standard, while *An Ideal Husband* suggests the old ways are best: the way to have an ideal husband is to be an ideal, old-fashioned wife. None of these plays can stand beside the work of Congreve or even Sheridan, but they keep the stream of comedy flowing from the eighteenth century into the twentieth century of Maugham and Coward.

After his release from prison, Wilde lived out a miserable few years on the Continent, estranged from his wife, cut off from his friends, always short of funds. During this time he wrote (and rewrote previously published works) under the assumed name of Sebastian Melmoth. He died at the Hôtel d'Alcace in Paris on November 30, 1900, his death still shrouding the mystery, revulsion, and untruth which colored most of his life and a great deal of his legend.

Bibliography

Wilde's *Works* were published in 14 vols. in 1908. Richard Aldington edited the *Selected Works*, 1946. Vyvyan Holland edited the *Works* in 1966, and Rupert Hart-Davis the *Letters* (complete) in 1962. The standard bibliography is R. E. Cowan and William Andrews Clark, Jr., *The Library of William Andrews Clark: Wilde and Wildeiana*, 5 vols., 1922–1931. For years the standard biography was Frank Harris, *Oscar Wilde; His Life and Confessions*, 2 vols., 1916, which also contains *Memories of Oscar Wilde* by G. B. Shaw; but this work is now super-seded by Hesketh Pearson, *Oscar Wilde: His Life and Wit*, 1946. V. B. Holland has made a unique contribution to biographical data in *Son of Oscar Wilde*, 1954. See also H. Montgomery Hyde, *Oscar Wilde: The Aftermath*, 1963. Critical works include Vincent O'Sullivan, *Aspects of Wilde*, 1936; Frances Winwar, *Oscar Wilde and the Yellow 'Nineties*, 1942; Edouard Roditi, *Oscar Wilde*, 1947; George Woodcock, *The Paradox of Oscar Wilde*, 1949; St. John Ervine, *Oscar Wilde: A Present Time Appraisal*, 1951; and Richard Ellman, *Oscar Wilde: A Collection of Critical Essays*, 1969. An important brief study is Eric Bentley's essay in *The Playwright as Thinker*, 1946. Other critical articles are the chapter on Wilde in Archibald Henderson, *Interpreters of Life and the Modern Spirit*, 1911; Hugh Kingsmill, "The Intelligent Man's Guide to Wilde," *Fortnightly Review*, CL (1938), 296–303; A. H. Nethercot, "Oscar Wilde and the Devil's Advocate," *Publications of the Modern Language Association*, LIX (1944), 833–850; and Edouard Roditi, "Oscar Wilde's Poetry as Art History," *Poetry*, LXVII (1945), 322–337.

THE IMPORTANCE OF BEING EARNEST

Type of work: Drama
Author: Oscar Wilde (1856–1900)
Type of plot: Comedy of manners
Time of plot: Late nineteenth century
Locale: London and Hertfordshire
First presented: 1895

A play built on a pun and plotted around a misunderstanding over the name Ernest, this comic masterpiece is an attack on earnestness; that is, the Victorian solemnity of a false seriousness which results in priggishness, hypocrisy, and so-called piety.

Principal Characters

Algernon Moncrief, called **Algy,** a young man of fashion, considerable worldly charm, and a confirmed Bunburyist; that is, he uses an imaginary sick friend's name and condition as an excuse to leave London when he finds his aristocratic aunt, Lady Bracknell, too domineering or her dinner parties too dull. He delights in the artificial, the trivial, the faddish, and he employs them for his own amusement, the only thing about which, as he insists, he is ever serious. Out for a jape, he poses as John Worthing's fictitious brother Ernest in order to court his friend's ward, Cecily Cardew. Though genuinely in love, he never abandons his pose of reckless pretense or his cynically amusing observations on country and city life, manners, fashions, and relatives.

John Worthing, J.P., called **Jack,** Algernon Moncrief's friend, who poses as Ernest in order to win the hand of Algy's cousin, the Hon. Gwendolen Fairfax, Lady Bracknell's daughter. Also a Bunburyist, he has invented a fictitious brother Ernest, a reprobate who is always getting into scrapes, as an excuse for his frequent visits to London. Jack is serious about most things, especially love. He was a foundling, brought up by a wealthy

man who made Jack the guardian of his benefactor's granddaughter, Cecily Cardew. When Jack proposes to Gwendolyn he arouses Lady Bracknell's displeasure because he cannot trace his family tree. All he knows is that he had been found abandoned in a leather bag left at Victoria Station. Finally his parentage is traced, and he learns that he is the long-lost son of Lady Bracknell's sister, that Algy is his younger brother, and that his Christian name really is Ernest. This last fact is the most pleasing, for Gwendolyn could not possibly love him under any other name.

Lady Augusta Bracknell, Algernon Moncrief's aunt, a strong-willed woman of fashion who lives only by society's dictates. The hostess at numerous dinner parties to which her nephew is always invited but which he seldom attends, she dominates the lives of all about her in the same compulsive fashion that makes her move only in the best circles. Although Jack Worthing is an eligible young bachelor of means, she rejects his suit of Gwendolyn and advises him to find some acceptable relatives as quickly as possible. Although witty in her pronouncements, she never deviates into good sense about the artificial world she inhabits with other snobs and pretenders, but her sense of social superiority is punctured when she learns that her daughter's rejected suitor is her own nephew.

The Hon. Gwendolyn Fairfax, Lady Bracknell's daughter, in love with Jack Worthing, whose name she believes to be Ernest. Although she moves in the same conventional snobbish social world with her mother, her outlook is whimsical and rebellious. Determined to marry the man of her choice, she is pleased to discover that Worthing, his parentage revealed, can offer her not only the right name and devotion but also family connections and wealth. She accommodates herself to her good fortune.

Cecily Cardew, an eighteen-year-old girl given to romantic dreams and a diary of fictitious events. She is the ward of Jack Worthing, who had been adopted by her eccentric grandfather. Lovely, determined, rusticated, she is seemingly without guile, but she is in reality as poised as her newly discovered friend, Gwendolyn Fairfax. The dupe of her guardian's story that he has a wicked brother named Ernest in the city, she is charmed and won when that supposed roué, as

impersonated by Algy Moncrief, appears in the country. She is also pleased that the man she intends to marry is named Ernest. After learning the truth, she decides that she still loves him, in spite of his having such a name as Algernon.

Miss Letitia Prism, the forgetful authoress of a sentimental three-volume romance, the governess of Cecily Cardew and, earlier, of Jack Worthing. Bent on marriage herself, she contrives to keep her charge's mind on the serious business of learning inconsequentials. In the end she is revealed as the absent-minded nurse who twenty-eight years before had placed the infant Ernest Moncrief in a leather handbag deposited in the cloakroom at Victoria station and the manuscript of her novel in a perambulator.

The Rev. Frederick Chasuble, D.D., an Anglican clergyman who is amenable to performing any rite for anyone at any time, in much the same way that he fits one sermon into many contexts. Delightful in his metaphorical allusions, he meets his match in Miss Prism, whose allusions contain direct revelation of matrimonial intent.

The Story

Algernon Moncrieff, nephew of the aristocratic Lady Bracknell, was compelled by necessity to live a more or less double life, or he would have been completely at the mercy of his Aunt Augusta. To escape from her incredibly dull dinner parties, he had emulated that lady's husband by inventing a wholly fictitious friend named Bunbury, whose precarious state of health required Algy's absence from London whenever his aunt summoned him to attendance.

Algy's friend, Jack Worthing, was also forced by circumstances into a similar subterfuge for quite a different reason. He had under his care a young ward named Cecily Cardew, who lived at Jack's country place in Hertfordshire under the admirable tutelage of a stern governess, Miss Prism. Jack thought it necessary to preserve a high moral tone in the presence of Cecily and her governess. To escape from this atmosphere of restraint, he invented an imaginary brother named Ernest, who was supposed to be quite a reprobate, and whose name and general mode of behavior Jack took over during his frequent trips to London.

To complicate matters, Jack had fallen in love with Gwendolen Fairfax, the daughter of Algy's aunt, Lady Bracknell. Moreover, Gwendolen had fallen in love with him, particularly with his name, Ernest, of which she was very fond. When Lady Bracknell learned "Ernest's" intentions toward Gwendolen, she naturally wanted to know something of his family history. But since "Ernest" could supply nothing more definite than the fact that he had been found in a leather bag at the Victoria Railway Station, and that his true parentage was quite unknown, Lady Bracknell refused to consider his marriage to her daughter.

Jack realized that the time had come to put an end to Ernest. He even went so far as to appear at the manor house in Hertfordshire in deep mourning for his brother Ernest. But his friend Algy, "Bunburying" as usual, had preceded him, posing as Ernest. Cecily took an immediate interest in Algy, the supposed brother of her guardian. When Jack and Algy came face to face, Jack promptly announced that his brother Ernest had been unexpectedly called back to London and was leaving at once. But Algy, having fallen in love with Cecily, refused to leave. Cecily, in turn, confessed that it had always been her dream to love someone whose name was Ernest.

Algy, realizing that his hopes of marrying Cecily depended on his name, decided to have himself rechristened Ernest, and to that effect he called upon the local clergyman, the Reverend Canon Chasuble, D.D. But Jack had preceded him with a like request. Dr. Chasuble had an engagement for two christenings at five-thirty that afternoon.

In the meantime Gwendolen arrived at the manor house. Because of the mix-up in names, both Gwendolen and Cecily believed that they were in love with the same man, the non-existent Ernest.

When Jack and Algy appeared together, the real identities of the two pretenders were established. Both girls became furious. At first Jack and Algy upbraided each other for their mutual duplicity, but they finally settled down to tea and consoled themselves by vying with one another to see who could eat the last muffin on the plate. Cecily and Gwendolen at last decided to forgive their suitors, after Algy had admitted that the purpose of his deception was to meet Cecily, and Jack maintained that his imaginary brother was an excuse to go to London to see Gwendolen. Both girls agreed that in matters of grave importance—such as marriage—style and not sincerity was the vital thing.

Lady Bracknell, arriving in search of her daughter, discovered her nephew engaged to Cecily. Afraid that the girl, like her guardian, might possibly have only railway station antecedents, Lady Bracknell demanded to know Cecily's origin. She was informed that Cecily was the granddaughter of a very wealthy man and the heiress to one hundred and thirty thousand pounds. When she willingly gave her consent to the marriage, Jack refused to allow the match, pointing out that Cecily could not marry without his consent until she came of age, and that according to her grandfather's will she would not come of age until she was thirty-five. However, he said he would give his consent the moment Lady Bracknell approved of his marriage to Gwendolen.

There were, however, some objections to Jack as a suitable husband for Gwendolen, the main one being the question of his parentage. But the mystery was cleared up to Lady Bracknell's satisfaction by the revelation that Miss Letitia Prism, Cecily's governess, was the nurse who had left Lord Bracknell's house with a perambulator containing a male infant which she had placed in a leather handbag and left in the cloakroom of the Victoria Station. The infant was the son of Lady Bracknell's sister, a circumstance which made Jack Algy's older brother. Jack's Christian name still had to be determined. It turned out to be—Ernest. The Reverend Chasuble was relieved of his two christenings that afternoon, and Gwendolen was happy that she was actually going to marry a man named Ernest.

Critical Evaluation

Oscar Wilde, the leading spokesman for the so-called Yellow Nineties, stood at the end of the nineteenth century and jeered at his Victorian forefathers. All their sacred values—name, position, and money—are ridiculed in his most popular work, *The Importance of Being Earnest*. Turning on a play of words, the drama also satirizes the idea of earnestness. If there were any virtue to which the Victorians attached the greatest significance, it was that of earnestness. To work hard, to be sincere, frank, and open with a high degree of seriousness was a social ideal which underpinned their whole notion of society and religion. Wilde not only satirized hypocrisy and sham virtue, but also mocked its authentic representation.

If the play has any heroes at all, they are Algernon Moncrieff and Jack Worthing, the two dandies; neither are what they seem. The polar opposites of earnestness, placing no value on sincerity or work, they create "night identities" to live out their instinctual life which is forbidden in society. Algy invents a sick friend and goes "Bunburying," while Jack assumes the identity of his nonexistent brother, "Ernest," for his London escapades. It is while they are engaged in such masquerades that they feel themselves to be real and authentic. It is only when they take on their social identities, Jack as the warden of Cecily Cardew, and Algy as the nephew of the fearsome Lady Augusta Bracknell, that they are unreal and hypocritical. The play, however, does not pursue the serious implications of these circumstances and dissolves into a comic farce where Jack and Algy struggle to convince everyone, even Miss Letitia Prism, that they are their social identities, in order to win Cecily and Gwendolen, two empty-headed Victorian maidens. They fall victim, in fact, to the attractions of earnestness and are appropriately rewarded.

Bibliography

Beerbohm, Sir Max. *Around Theatres.* New York: British Book Centre, 1953, pp. 188–191.

Bentley, Eric. *The Play: A Critical Anthology.* Englewood Cliffs, N.J.: Prentice-Hall, 1951, pp. 210–213.

————. *The Playwright as Thinker.* New York: Reynal & Hitchcock, 1946, pp. 172–177. Reprinted in *Oscar Wilde: A Collection of Essays.* Edited by Richard Ellman. Englewood Cliffs, N.J.: Prentice-Hall, 1969, pp. 111–115.

Braybrooke, Patrick. *Oscar Wilde: A Study.* Folcroft, Pa.: Folcroft, 1970, pp. 21–40.

Brown, J.M. *Seeing More Things.* New York: McGraw, 1948, pp. 209–220.

Ericksen, Donald H. *Oscar Wilde.* New York: Twayne, 1977, pp. 145–152.

Foster, Richard. "Wilde as Parodist: A Second Look at *The Importance of Being Earnest,*" in *College English.* XVIII (1956), pp. 18–23.

Ganz, Arthur. "The Meaning of *The Importance of Being Earnest,*" in *Modern Drama.* VI (1963), pp. 42–52.

Hankin, St. John. "Wilde as a Dramatist," in *Oscar Wilde: A Collection of Critical Essays.* Edited by Richard Ellmann. Englewood Cliffs, N.J.: Prentice-Hall, 1969, pp. 61–72.

Kronenberger, Louis. *Thread of Laughter; Chapters on English Stage Comedy from Jonson to Maugham.* New York: Knopf, 1952, pp. 222–225.

Nassaar, Christopher S. *Into the Demon Universe: A Literary Exploration of Oscar Wilde.* New Haven, Conn.: Yale University Press, 1974, pp. 129–145.

Nethercot, Arthur H. "Prunes and Miss Prism," in *Modern Drama.* VI (1963), pp. 112–116.

Parker, David. "Oscar Wilde's Great Farce: *The Importance of Being Earnest,*" in *Modern Language Quarterly.* XXXV (1974), pp. 173–186.

Partridge, E.B. "The Importance of Not Being Earnest," in *Bucknell Review.* IX (1960), pp. 16–23.

Reinert, Otto. "The Courtship Dance in *The Importance of Being Earnest,*" in *Modern Drama.* I (February, 1959), pp. 256–257.

————. "Satiric Strategy in *The Importance of Being Earnest,*" in *College English.* XVIII (1956), pp. 14–18.

San Juan, Epifanio, Jr. *The Art of Oscar Wilde.* Princeton, N.J.: Princeton University Press, 1967, pp. 180–196.

Shaw, G.B. *Plays and Players: Essays on the Theatre.* New York: Oxford University Press, 1952, pp. 17–25.

Shewan, Rodney. *Oscar Wilde: Art and Egotism.* New York: Macmillan, 1977, pp. 186–193.

Spininger, Dennis J. "Profiles and Principles: The Sense of the Absurd in *The*

Importance of Being Earnest," in *Papers on Language and Literature.* XII (1976), pp. 49–72.

Stone, Geoffrey.   "Serious Bunburyism: The Logic of *The Importance of Being Earnest*," in *Essays in Criticism.* XXVI (1976), pp. 28–41.

Toliver, Harold E.   "Wilde and the Importance of 'Sincere and Studied Triviality,' " in *Modern Drama.* V (1963), pp. 389–399.

Vortriede, Werner.   "A Dramatic Device in *Faust* and *The Importance of Being Earnest*," in *Modern Language Notes.* LXX (1955), pp. 584–585.

THE PICTURE OF DORIAN GRAY

Type of work: Novel
Author: Oscar Wilde (1856–1900)
Type of plot: Fantasy
Time of plot: Late nineteenth century
Locale: England
First published: 1891

Although Oscar Wilde wrote that there is no such thing as a moral or unmoral book, Dorian Gray *is definitely a moral fable. In a rich blend of incredibly sensuous description, allegory, and symbolism, Wilde tells the fantastic tale of a young man who abandons himself to a life of vice. As Dorian's spirit deteriorates into ugliness and corruption, his body shows no sign of decay, since all the outward effects of aging and hard living are assumed by a magic portrait of him, painted when he was still pure and virtuous.*

Principal Characters

Dorian Gray, a handsome young man who, while visiting the studio of an artist friend who is painting his portrait, idly wishes that the portrait would grow old while he himself remained young looking. Later, having treated a young girl cruelly, he notices the first sign of alteration in the portrait. Alarmed, he decides to repent and to marry the girl; but he learns that she has killed herself. He now gives himself over entirely to a life of corruption, under the tutelage of an evil friend. His crimes include murder. At last he decides to destroy the hideous portrait, which has been long locked away. He stabs it with a knife. Hearing a cry, the servants find lying before a portrait of their handsome master a withered, wrinkled body with a knife in its breast.

Lord Henry Wotton, a witty, degenerate man who deliberately tempts Dorian into a life of debauchery.

Basil Hallward, Dorian's artist friend who paints his portrait. He asks Lord Wotton never to meet Dorian, saying that the older man's influence would be evil; but Dorian comes to the studio while Lord Wotton is there, and the friendship begins. Hallward and Dorian become estranged; but on his thirty-eighth birthday Dorian shows Hallward the altered portrait and then, angry because he has betrayed himself, kills Hallward.

Alan Campbell, a young chemist whom Dorian blackmails into disposing of Hallward's body with fire and chemicals. Campbell later commits suicide under strange circumstances.

Sibyl Vane, a young actress who knows Dorian only as "Prince Charming." Dorian treats her cruelly, and she kills herself.

James Vane, her brother. He has sworn revenge against "Prince Charming," but he hestitates to kill Dorian, who looks years too young to be the man who ruined his sister eighteen years before. Assured that Dorian is in fact that man, he follows him to his country house and is accidentally shot and killed during a hunt on the estate.

THE PICTURE OF DORIAN GRAY by Oscar Wilde. Published by The Viking Press, Inc.

The Story

One day, in his London studio, Basil Hallward was putting a few last finishing touches on a portrait of his handsome young friend, Dorian Gray. Lord Henry Wotton, a caller, indolently watched the painter at work. In reply to his friend's admiration for the painting, the artist explained that Dorian was his ideal of youth. For this reason he asked Lord Henry never to meet Dorian because the older man's influence on the boy would be absolute and evil.

While they were talking, Dorian himself came to the studio, and he and Lord Henry met, much against Hallward's wishes. Half seriously, half jokingly, Sir Henry began to exert his influence on Dorian. Hallward signed the portrait and announced it was finished. When Lord Henry offered to buy the picture, the painter said it was not his property, that it belonged to Dorian, to whom he was presenting it. Looking at his portrait, after listening to Lord Henry's witty conversation, Dorian grew sad. He would become old and wrinkled, he said, while the picture would remain the same. He wished, instead, that the portrait might grow old while he remained forever young. He said he would give his soul to keep his youth.

Dorian and Lord Henry became close friends. One of the gifts Lord Henry gave the boy was a book about a young man who attempted to realize in his brief lifetime all the passions of man's history. Dorian made the book a pattern for his own life, and the first lesson from its pages was the lesson of love. In a third-rate theater he saw Sibyl Vane, a young actress who played the role of Juliet with such sincerity and charm that he fell in love with her on the spot. After he had met her, Dorian dreamed of taking her away from the cheap theatrical troupe and making her a great actress who would thrill the world. One night he took Lord Henry to watch her performance. That night Sibyl was listless and wooden, so uninspired in her acting that the audience hissed her. When Dorian went to her dressing room after the final curtain, she explained that before meeting him she had thought acting her only reality. Now, she said, Dorian's love had taught her what reality actually was, and she could no longer act. Dorian coldly and cruelly told her she had killed his love and he never intended to see her again.

In the meantime, Hallward had delivered the painting to Dorian. When the young man returned to his home after the theater that night he saw that the appearance of his portrait had changed. There was a new, faint line of cruelty about the mouth. Looking at his own features in a mirror, he found no such line on his own lips. His wish had evidently been granted. He would remain young and untouched—the portrait would take on an appearance of experience and age.

Disturbed, he resolved to reform, to see no more of Lord Henry, to ask Sibyl Vane's forgiveness and marry her. Accordingly, he wrote her a passionate letter declaring his love. Before he could post the letter, however, Lord Henry visited him the next morning, bringing the news that Sibyl had killed herself in her dressing room the night before.

After his friend had gone, forgetting all his good resolutions Dorian decided on a life of sensation and pleasure. The portrait only was to bear the burden of his shame. That night he attended the opera with Lord Henry. The next day, when Basil Hallward attempted to reason with him over scandalous reports beginning to circulate, Dorian refused to show any emotion over Sibyl's suicide. His part in her tragic story would never be revealed, for she had known him only as Prince Charming. Before he left, Hallward asked to see his painting. Dorian refused to show it. In sudden rage, he shouted that he never wished to see Hallward again. Later he hung the portrait in an old schoolroom upstairs, locked the door, and put the key where only he could find it.

London continued to gossip about the friendship of Lord Henry and Dorian Gray. The young man was suspected of strange vices, and gentlemen walked out of their club rooms when he entered them. He was invited to fewer balls and parties at country houses. Many of his former friends refused to recognize him when they met. It was reported he had been seen in low dives with drunken sailors and thieves. Meanwhile Dorian's features did not change; only the portrait reflected his life of crime and debauchery. For Dorian's life, like that of the hero in the book Lord Henry had given him, became a frenzied quest for fresh experiences and new sensations. In turn, he became interested in religious rituals, perfumes, music, jewels. He frequented opium dens. He had sordid affairs with women. His features in the portrait became the terrible record of his life.

On the eve of Dorian's thirty-eighth birthday, Basil Hallward visited him again. Though the two had been estranged for years, Hallward came in a last attempt to persuade Dorian to change his dissolute ways. He was still unable to believe many of the stories he had heard about Dorian. With a bitter laugh, Dorian said that Hallward should see what he had truly become. He took Hallward to the schoolroom and unveiled the portrait. The artist was horrified, for only by signature could he identify his own handiwork. In anger that he had betrayed his true self to his former friend, Dorian seized a knife which lay nearby and stabbed Hallward in the neck and back.

Dorian relocked the door and went down to the drawing-room. Because Hallward had intended to leave for Paris that night, Dorian knew the painter would not be missed for some time. Removal of the body, he decided, was not enough. He wanted it completely destroyed. Suddenly he thought of Alan Campbell, a young chemist who had once been his intimate. By threatening the young scientist with exposure for some secret crime, Dorian forced Campbell to destroy the body with fire and chemicals. After that night, the hands of the portrait were smeared with blood.

Late one night, commonly dressed, Dorian visited an opium den. As he was leaving the place, a drunken woman addressed him as Prince Charming. A sailor followed him out. The sailor was James Vane, Sibyl's brother, who had sworn revenge on his sister's betrayer. The sailor would have killed Dorian but for the fact that he looked so young. Sibyl had committed suicide eighteen years before, and Dorian seemed no more than twenty years old. When Vane, convinced that

Dorian could not have known his sister, returned to the den, the woman told him that Dorian Gray had ruined her many years before, and that he had not changed in appearance since then.

Some time later, at his country home, Dorian saw James Vane watching him outside a window. During a hunt on the estate Vane was accidentally shot and killed. In the meantime, Alan Campbell had committed suicide under strange circumstances, and Basil Hallward's disappearance was being investigated.

Back in London, Dorian, having decided to destroy the picture which stood as an awful record of his guilt, went to the old schoolroom. The portrait now had an appearance of cunning and triumph. Using the knife with which he had murdered Basil Hallward, Dorian stabbed the frightful portrait. The servants in the house heard a horrible cry of agony. When they forced open the locked door of the room, they found, hanging on the wall, a fine portrait of their master as he had always looked. On the floor was a dead body, withered, wrinkled, in evening dress, with a knife in its breast. Only by his jewelry did they recognize Dorian Gray, who, in his desperate attempt to kill his conscience, had killed himself.

Critical Evaluation

The Picture of Dorian Gray is a curious offspring of the traditional novel form. Wilde called the novel "all conversation and no action." Further, his habit of crossing richly sensual description with starkly realistic glimpses of London "low life" gives the novel aspects of both romance and realism, although there are good reasons why *The Picture of Dorian Gray* is almost always considered a Romantic product.

In spite of its hybrid characteristics, *The Picture of Dorian Gray* continues to be a favorite seller, and has been through more reprints than anything else Wilde wrote. Dorian's bisexual appetite was a subject still scandalously taboo in the 1890's, and the novel was used as evidence against Wilde when he was tried for his homosexual activities. Stuart Mason's *Art and Morality* gives a detailed summary of the heated controversy surrounding the original publication of the book.

The lasting appeal of *The Picture of Dorian Gray,* however, may rather be attributed to the number of successful levels, all well-constructed and interlocking, on which the story operates. The most literal reading the novel offers is that of a detective story. (Wilde admired Sir Arthur Conan Doyle's Sherlock Holmes stories.) Vane functions as the detective in pursuit of the guilty man, and as avenger for his sister's death. A second level of meaning focuses on the idea of spiritual struggle, since Dorian's story hinges, like Faust's, on the fulfillment of the wish that youth be eternal. When Dorian tries to rid himself of guilt, he violates the terms of the "contract," thus calling back into operation the normal laws of life, and the damned man is forced to shoulder his own guilt as he and his portrait exchange roles.

The emphasis on psychological awareness of the self which the novel's dialogue reflects, opens up a third level of interpretation. Intensely conscious of themselves, Wilde's characters take a Jamesian interest in analyzing their own psychological states, to the point of narcissism. This is accompanied by negation and the constant turning away from one another. Dorian's experience leads him to the final negation that "ugliness is the only reality," and so he annihilates himself.

Bibliography

Baker, H.A., Jr. "Tragedy of the Artist; *The Picture of Dorian Gray*," in *Nineteenth-Century Fiction*. XXIV (December, 1969), pp. 349–355.

Beebe, Maurice. *Ivory Towers and Sacred Founts; The Artist as Hero in Fiction from Goethe to Joyce*. New York: New York University Press, 1964, pp. 114–171.

Braybrooke, Patrick. *Oscar Wilde: A Study*. Folcroft, Pa.: Folcroft, 1970, pp. 101–112.

Ericksen, Donald H. *Oscar Wilde*. New York: Twayne, 1977, pp. 96–117.

Gordon, Jan B. "Hebraism, Hellenism and *The Picture of Dorian Gray*," in *Victorian Newsletter*. XXXIII (Spring, 1968), pp. 36–38.

————. "Parody as Initiation: The Sad Education of Dorian Gray," in *Criticism*. IX (1967), pp. 355–371.

Keefe, Robert. "Artist and Model in *The Picture of Dorian Gray*," in *Studies in the Novel*. V (1973), pp. 63–70.

Laver, James. *Oscar Wilde*. London: Longmans, Green, 1968, pp. 15–18.

Nassaar, Christopher S. *Into the Demon Universe: A Literary Exploration of Oscar Wilde*. New Haven, Conn.: Yale University Press, 1974, pp. 37–72.

Pappas, John J. "The Flower and the Beast: A Study of Oscar Wilde's Antithetical Attitudes Toward Nature and Man in *The Picture of Dorian Gray*," in *English Literature in Transition (1880–1920)*. XV (1972), pp. 37–48.

Portnoy, William E. "Wilde's Debt to Tennyson in *Dorian Gray*," in *English Literature in Transition (1880–1920)*. XVII (1974), pp. 259–261.

Poteet, L.J. "Dorian Gray and the Gothic Novel," in *Modern Fiction Studies*. XVII (Summer, 1971), pp. 239–248.

Roditi, Edouard. *Oscar Wilde*. Norfolk, Conn.: New Directions, 1947, pp. 113–124. Reprinted in *Oscar Wilde: A Collection of Critical Essays*. Edited by Richard Ellman. Englewood Cliffs, N.J.: Prentice-Hall, 1969, pp. 47–55.

San Juan, Epifanio, Jr.   *The Art of Oscar Wilde.* Princeton, N.J.: Princeton University Press, 1967, pp. 49–73.

Shewan, Rodney.   *Oscar Wilde: Art and Egotism.* New York: Macmillan, 1977, pp. 112–130.

THE POETRY OF WILDE

Author: Oscar Wilde (1854–1900)
First published: Poems, 1881; *The Sphinx*, 1894; *The Ballad of Reading Gaol*, by "C.3.3," 1898; *The Poems of Oscar Wilde*, 1906

Essay-Review

Oscar Wilde's first literary reputation was made by his poems; the later success of his lectures, essays, stories, and plays obscured his reputation as a poet until the notoriety surrounding his last poem and last piece of writing, *The Ballad of Reading Gaol.* The most important volume is his *Poems* of 1881, the others being the Newdigate Prize poem, "Ravenna"; *The Sphinx*, published in 1894, and *The Ballad of Reading Gaol*, which appeared in 1898. The poems collected from periodicals by Robert Ross were added to the unpublished works to make up the modest collected edition of 1906. Wilde's poetry may be divided by form into long and short poems or by content into those which spiritualize bodily sensations and those which represent spiritual matters in terms of physical sensation.

The long poems of Oscar Wilde cover the twenty years between "Ravenna" and *The Ballad of Reading Gaol.* Their chief use is not to tell a simple fable like those found in Wilde's short stories, but chiefly to celebrate a situation. There is a similar static quality in the short poems where the lack of argument induces a hortatory opening and a fading or frenzied close. "Ravenna," as is proper in a poem intended to win a prize in late nineteenth century Oxford, is written in modified early eighteenth century couplets, in which the favorite words seem to be "O," "yon" and "adieu," giving the poet a declamatory stance to excite energy, a post from which he can observe Ravenna's scenery, and a pathetic resolution. The success of the poem is the succession of enameled portraits of flowers and other pastoral properties needed to construct the contrast between the Italian and English landscapes which is the matter of the poem, all expressed without one false note in the verse or a sincere one in the expression:

> So runs the perfect cycle of the year.
> And so from youth to manhood do we go,
> And fall to weary days and locks of snow.

It is something of a shock to find Oscar Wilde and Rudyard Kipling publishing short poems entitled "Ave Imperatrix" within a year of each other. Kipling's seven stanzas were "Written on the Occasion of the Attempt to Assassinate Queen Victoria in March 1882"; the "Queen" in his poem is obviously Victoria; Wilde's "Queen" is England, but his tone expresses similar jingoistic rejoicing in imperial power and some of the geographical references are identical, particularly when Wilde brings in Afghanistan (strictly Kipling territory) as evidence of imperial might. After many apostrophes ("O wasted dust! O senseless clay!") Wilde shoulders the White Man's Burden and grants that heavy losses in the Pathan wars are necessary to the destiny of his "Imperatrix": "Up the steep road must England go." But he cannot help regretting the loss of many fine young men. A similar public stance is held in poems like "To Milton" and "Louis Napoleon." But Wilde soon tired of these Miltonic and Wordsworthian imitations and imitated instead Rossetti in his Roman Catholic sonnets and Swinburne in his nature pieces.

Wilde's sincerity or his most deeply felt pose is contained in the long poems which glorify a naked pantheism that seems to place the sunny Italian body in the fresh fields of England. In that respect all but the last of his poems is a refinement of the first, "Ravenna," and the last, *The Ballad of Reading Gaol*, is a contradiction of such pieces as "Ave Imperatrix." His best known short poem is "Helas," which prefaces the 1881 volume and is usually regarded, like *The Picture of Dorian Gray*, as a form of Wilde's artistic credo. It begins with an anticipation of Lord Henry Wotton's training of Dorian:

> To drift with every passion till my soul
> Is a stringed lute on which all winds can play. . . .

It ends with the unanswered question that haunts all Wilde's work:

> . . . lo! with a little rod
> I did but touch the honey of romance
> And must I lose a soul's inheritance?

Of the sonnets which make up the bulk of the short poems, those at the graves of Shelley and Keats are effective memorials, but the more characteristic and interesting are the "Impressions" and similar poems in the three sections titled "Wind Flowers," "Flowers of Gold," and "The Fourth Movement," in which Wilde is painting in clear, rich, and sophisticated color combinations. The best known of these "etudes in color" is "Symphony in Yellow," among the previously uncollected poems in the 1906 volume.

There are five long poems in the 1881 volume: "The Garden of Eros," "The Burden of Itys," "Charmides," "Panthea," and "Humanitad." Each is written in approximately the same stanza form of six lines, a quatrain plus a couplet, of varying pentameter and quadrameter meter. All five poems have the flowers, colors, and classical allusions and material of Tennyson's "Œnone," and many echoes of a golden treasury of English verse; but their most characteristic feature is the length to which Wilde could prolong the combined bookish and natural sensations, as he was later to prolong sensation and sensibility in *The Ballad of Reading Gaol*. The easiest to follow is "Charmides" because it tells the legend of the Athenian youth who made love to the naked statue of Athena one long night and was drowned by the goddess the next day for his presumption; in the second section his body is washed ashore on the Greek coast and an Oread, who falls in love with the dead youth, is also slain by Athena; in the third section the girl and the youth are revived by Proserpine and consummate their love in a passionate scene in Hades.

"The Garden of Eros" begins with English flowers, passes to classical myth, surveys English poetry as culminating in Dante Gabriel Rossetti, and concludes the June night of the poem with a return to the beauty of the flowers, all described in fresh images of striking sensuality:

> Mark how the yellow iris wearily
> Leans back its throat, as though it would be kissed
> By its false chamberer, the dragon-fly.

"The Burden of Itys" follows the same pattern, an invocation to the classic gods of field and forest to visit English fields and repeat their bacchanals:

> O that some antique statue for one hour
> Might wake to passion. . . .

But the dream passes with the dawn. "Panthea" begins in the usual English pastoral setting, enumerates such attractive myths as those of Ganymede and Endymion, contrasts the lot of the poet's race to the gods'—"O we are born to late"—and reaches at last the consolation that in the end death will unite the past in "passions Hymeneal" with the earth which then becomes the "Kosmic Soul" of the conclusion. "Humanitad" is as personal a poem in its way as *The Ballad of Reading Gaol*: beginning in winter the poem laments the poet's inability to respond to the approaching spring as he used to because he is now too experienced in passion and wise to the ways of the world. In the search for a meaning to life—

> O for one grand unselfish life
> To teach us what is Wisdom! . . .
> To make the Body and the Spirit one . . .

he looks past modern Italy to ancient Greece, to Wordsworth, and finally to Christ, at which point he resolves the dilemma by deciding to come down from his own Cross: "That which is purely human, that is Godlike, that is God."

The sexual fantasies of "Charmides" are more evident in "The Sphinx" and in *Salome*. "The Sphinx" is a sequence of thirteen short poems in four-line stanzas which begin and end with an invocation to the Sphinx imagined by the poet to be brooding at him from a corner of his room. He asks the Sphinx about her lovers and supplies a long catalogue of possibilities before he decides that Ammon filled the role; then he remembers the present state of the Sphinx and tells her to assemble the ruins of her old lovers and to leave him, as the dawn enters, because she awakens in him "each bestial sense . . . foul dreams of sensual life." This effect is certainly borne out in the poem, where Wilde's sense of color and form becomes fully tactile, passionate, and ultimately preposterous. One doubts whether in Wilde's time poetry could go further without becoming obscene. His jail sentence put a stop to this kind of poetry and produced his last work.

The Ballad of Reading Gaol like "Charmides," tells a narrative of the hanging of a murderer for killing the woman he loved; the paradox of his fate and the correspondence Wilde saw to his own is, together with the realism, the source of the energy which carries the poem through six sections and contains more than one hundred six-line stanzas. In spite of repetitions induced by the stanzas Wilde kept adding to the poem, the ballad rhythm is rarely monotonous and the use of color even more startling than it was in Wilde's earlier verse: "little tent of blue," "scarlet coat," "yellow hole," "purple throat," "teeth of flame."

The first three sections narrate the six weeks spent by the subject of the elegy waiting to "swing"; the fourth describes the execution and in intimate and graphic detail shows its effect on the prisoners; the fifth section contains Wilde's reflection on the execution and on the meaning of prison as a place for repentance, a subject he covered more fully but equally indefinitely in *De Profundis*; the sixth section is a brief envoi or epilogue which repeats the central line of the poem: "all men kill the thing they love." This line, most often quoted of Wilde's verse, poignantly reminds the reader of the poet's own misplaced affections that destroyed his career as a public figure.

THE TWENTIETH CENTURY

Literary Forms

Criticism: Eliot's "Tradition and the Individual Talent"; Empson's *Seven Types of Ambiguity*; Hulme's *Romanticism and Classicism*; Lawrence's *Studies in Classic American Literature*; Richards' *Principles of Literary Criticism*

Drama: Comedy: Shaw's *Major Barbara, Man and Superman*; Wilde's *The Importance of Being Earnest*

   Absurd Comedy: Beckett's *Endgame, Waiting for Godot*

   Tragedy: Eliot's *Murder in the Cathedral*; Pinter's *The Caretaker*

Lyric Poetry: by Auden, Eliot, Graves, Hardy, Hopkins, Lawrence, Larkin, Owen, Thomas

   Elegy: Auden's "In Memory of W. B. Yeats"; Owen's "Anthem for Doomed Youth"

   Religious and Philosophical Verse: Eliot's *Four Quartets*; Hopkins' "The Windhover"; Thomas' "There Was a Saviour"; Yeats's "Byzantium"

Satiric Poetry: Eliot's "The Love Song of J. Alfred Prufrock"; Graves's "The Naked and the Nude"; Hardy's "Ah, Are You Digging on My Grave?"; Yeats's "Crazy Jane Talks with the Bishop"

Novel: Conrad's *The Secret Agent*; Ford's *The Good Soldier*; Forster's *A Passage to India*; Joyce's *Ulysses*; Lawrence's *Women in Love*; Woolf's *To the Lighthouse*

Short Stories and Novellas: Conrad's *Heart of Darkness*; Joyce's "The Dead"; Lawrence's "The Prussian Officer"; Mansfield's "The Garden Party"

Thematic Characteristics

Reaction against Victorian values of progress, moral earnestness, and social responsibility, often viewed negatively as smugness and moral hypocrisy; particular opposition to Victorian puritanism. Twentieth-century emphasis instead upon individual freedom to experiment in life in a diversity of ways

Cultural fragmentation: Social, moral, and religious institutions of the Victorians were seen to collapse or at least to fragment, so that no single unifying ethic appeared to have universal force. Among alternative systems of values, twentieth century writers accepted, variously, Marxism, Freudianism, Existentialism, and Absurdism (see William Y. Tindall's *Forces in Modern British Literature*, 1956)

Marxist theories, influencing a wide spectrum of leftist writers from Fabian socialists to Communists, advocated a thoroughgoing reconstruction of society to eliminate capitalism; important especially during the 1930's, leftist writers were critical of laissez-faire economics, democratic institutions, and imperialism, while they supported the struggle of the masses. Reaction to Marxism, beginning in the late 1930's and continuing throughout the century, centered around opposition to totalitarianism (see George Lukacs' *The Historical Novel*, 1962)

Freudian/Jungian psychology, most influential during the 1920's but continuing throughout the century, centered around depth analysis of the unconscious; emphasis upon motivation, upon the irrational and the instinctive; exploration of psychological symbols expressed in actions or dreams. Also, anti-Freudians, who rejected the principles of depth analysis (see Leon Edel, *The Modern Psychological Novel: 1900–1950*, 1955)

Existentialism, most influential during the late 1940's and the 1950's but continuing throughout the century, emphasized the importance of individual freedom to make moral choices, to define the self, in the absence of universally-accepted norms to serve as patterns of behavior. Also, reaction to existentialism among writers who favored traditional religious and cultural values

Absurdism, most influential as a literary type of drama and fiction during the 1950's and 1960's but continuing throughout the century, emphasized (as did Dadaism during the 1920's) the meaningless aspects of institutions and values; nihilism, often treated humorously, in which life, void of significance, is viewed as both terrible and comic (see David T. Hesla's *The Shape of Chaos*, 1972)

Naturalism, most influential during the first two decades but continuing throughout the twentieth century, emphasized the determinism of heredity and environment upon character; "scientific" study of individuals affected by their social conditioning. Also, realism as a literary means of capturing verisimilitude; by the accumualtion of details, life is presented as it "really" is

Technological and scientific discoveries result in cultural shock, with the perception of vast changes in the traditional patterns of life; changes also derive from the new social sciences, with increased understanding of sociological, psychological, political, and economic pressures upon the individual

Imagism, most influential during the second two decades of the twentieth century, emphasized the sharp, clear image in poetry and rejected sentimental effusivess

Symbolism, deriving from the late-nineteenth and early twentieth century French Symbolists, emphasized the use of symbolic representations of objects or ideas taken from a variety of sources, including dreams, mythic and religious archetypes, and visionary and mystic states of consciousness; interpretation of the symbols sometimes definite, sometimes ambiguous

Impressionism, most influential during the second decades but continuing throughout the twentieth century, emphasized the isolation of significant impressions; stream-of-consciousness techniques in fiction reveal the moment-by-moment flux of impressions, the "interior monologues" of the subconscious mind (see Melvin Friedman, *Stream of Consciousness: A Study in Literary Method*, 1955)

W. H. AUDEN

Born: York, England (February 21, 1907)
Died: Vienna, Austria (September 28, 1973)

Principal Works

POEMS: *Poems*, 1930; *The Orators*, 1932; *The Dance of Death*, 1933; *Poems*, 1934; *Look, Stranger*, 1936; Spain, 1937; *Another Time*, 1940; *The Double Man*, 1941; *For the Time Being*, 1944; *Collected Poetry*, 1945; *The Age of Anxiety*, 1947; *Some Poems*, 1947; *Collected Shorter Poems, 1930–1944*, 1950; *Nones*, 1951; *The Shield of Achilles*, 1955; *The Old Man's Road*, 1956; *About the House*, 1965; *City without Wall, and Other Poems*, 1969.

PLAYS: *The Dog Beneath the Skin*, 1935 (with Christopher Isherwood); *The Ascent of F6*, 1936; *On the Frontier*, 1939 (with Christopher Isherwood).

ESSAYS AND STUDIES: *The Enchaféd Flood*, 1950; *The Dyer's Hand, and Other Essays*, 1962; *The Orators: An English Study*, 1966; *Secondary Worlds*, 1968; *A Commonplace Book*, 1971.

TRAVEL SKETCHES AND IMPRESSIONS: *Letter from Iceland*, 1937 (with Louis MacNeice); *Journey to a War*, 1939 (with Christopher Isherwood).

W(ystan) H(ugh) Auden was born in York, England, on February 21, 1907, the third son of George Augustus Auden, a distinguished physician. After preparing at Gresham's School, Holt, he took his degree at Christ Church College in Oxford University. He taught for five years in a boys' school in Malvern before he became one of a group of young poets which included Stephen Spender, Louis MacNeice, and his childhood friend, Christopher Isherwood. Socially and politically in revolt, dabbling in Marxism and experimenting in poetry, this group seemed the most promising among the younger writers of the time. After spending 1928 and 1929 in Germany with Isherwood, Auden returned to England to publish his first book of verse, *Poems*, in 1930. The prose and verse of *The Orators*, two years later, made it clear that his was a substantial and promising talent. Combining sharp satire and delight in word play with seeming obscurity and private references, his poetry called for action against the depressed condition of England of the 1930's. Another book of verse, *The Dance of Death*, was followed in 1935 by *The Dog Beneath the Skin*, an experimental play written in collaboration with Isherwood. This was also the year of his marriage to Erika Mann, journalist and eldest daughter of novelist Thomas Mann.

Another collaborative verse drama, *The Ascent of F6*, appeared in 1936. In this work, as in the previous one, Auden and Isherwood combined experimental techniques with a concern over social and political problems. Another volume of poetry, *Look, Stranger*, appeared in the same year. Like so many other writers, Auden found his sympathies lay on the side of the Loyalists in the Spanish Civil

War. He went to Spain, and when he returned in 1937 from service there as an ambulance driver, his increasing reputation was further enlarged by the award of the King's Poetry Medal. *Letters from Iceland*, which he published with Mac-Neice in 1937, *Spain*, of the same year, and *On the Frontier*, another collaboration with Isherwood, showed the deepening, maturing effect of his experiences upon his work. With Isherwood he traveled to China in 1938 to view another war. Their impressions were recorded in the prose volume, *Journey to a War*, which was issued the next year.

In 1939 Auden and Isherwood came to the United States, where Auden was to live and later gain citizenship. *Selected Poems, Another Time*, and *New Year Letter* further consolidated Auden's reputation as the first poet of the generation that came after that of T. S. Eliot. *For the Time Being* and *The Age of Anxiety* showed how Auden's genius had matured and how he could still be technically a virtuoso, daring and spectacular, though his view of life had deepened, shifting from Marxist to Anglo-Catholic. His later volumes, *Nones* in 1951 and *The Shield of Achilles* in 1955, revealed the same mastery of his medium. A Guggenheim Fellow in 1942 and 1945, he successfully combined the artistic and the academic life when he served as assosicate professor of English at the University of Michigan in 1950 and occupied a professorship at Smith College in 1953. In 1954 he was elected to membership in the American Academy of Arts and Letters, from which he also received an award for poetry. He was appointed Professor of Poetry at Oxford University in 1956. In addition to the libretto of Stravinsky's *The Rake's Progress* (1951), he published *The Enchaféd Flood*, a work of literary criticism, and two books on Kierkegaard. He also edited selected works of Tennyson and Henry James as well as one volume of Greek literature and three of English poetry. Auden died in 1973.

Bibliography

There is a biographical study of Auden, Charles Osborne, *W. H. Auden: The Life of a Poet*, 1979. The basic critical study is Richard Hoggard, *Auden: An Introductory Essay*, 1951. An important earlier study is Francis Scarfe, *Auden and After*, 1942. See also Cecil Day Lewis, *A Hope for Poetry*, 1934; Stephen Spender, *The Destructive Element*, 1935; Louis MacNeice, *A Hope for Poetry*, 1936; and J. G. Southworth, *Sowing the Spring*, 1940; Richard Hoggart, *W. H. Auden* (Writers and Their Work) No. 93, 1958; A. Alvarez, *The Shaping Spirit: Studies in Modern English and American Poetry* (American title, *Stewards of Excellence*), 1958; and Monroe K. Spears, *The Poetry of W. H. Auden*, 1963.

For articles in periodicals see also Stephen Spender, "The Importance of W. H. Auden," *London Mercury*, XXXIX (1939), 613–619; Delmore Schwartz, "The Two Audens," *Kenyon Review*, I (1939), 34–45; Randall Jarrell, "Freud to Paul: Stages in Auden's Ideology," *Partisan Review* (1945), 437–457; Joseph Warren Beach, "The Poems of Auden and the Prose Diathesis," *Virginia Quarterly Review*, XXV (1949), 365–483; Monroe K. Spears, "Late Auden: The Satirist as

Lunatic Clergyman" and "The Dominant Symbols of Auden's Poetry," *Sewanee Review*, LIX (1951), 50–74 and 392–425; Edward Callan, "The Development of W. H. Auden's Poetic Theory since 1940," *Twentieth Century Literature* IV (1958), 79–91; and George T. Wright, "A General View of Auden's Poetry," *Tennessee Studies in Literature*, X (1965), 43–64.

THE POETRY OF AUDEN

Author: W(ystan) H(ugh) Auden (1907–1973)
Principal published works: Poems, 1930; *The Orators,* 1932; *The Dance of Death,*
1933; *Poems,* 1934; *Look, Stranger,* 1936; *Spain,* 1937; *Another Time,* 1940;
The Double Man, 1941; *For the Time Being,* 1944; *Collected Poetry,* 1945; *The
Age of Anxiety,* 1947; *Nones,* 1951; *The Shield of Achilles,* 1955; *The Old
Man's Road,* 1956; *Homage to Clio,* 1960; *About the House,* 1965; *City With-
out Walls and Other Poems,* 1969; *Epistle to a Godson and Other Poems,* 1972

Essay-Review

W. H. Auden, is, like his contemporary T. S. Eliot, the product of both the
English and the American traditions. Auden was raised in the industrial midlands of England and educated at Oxford during the bleak 1930's. There he became one of a group of young poets, including C. Day Lewis, Louis MacNeice,
Stephen Spender, and Christopher Isherwood, who directed their writing toward
a search for meaning in a world which seemed to them empty and mechanical.

Growing up during the great depression, when unemployment was at a peak in
England, Auden and his contemporaries, in sympathy with the problems of the
working class, looked to Marxism as a possible solution to social conditions and to
Sigmund Freud and George Walther Groddeck for answers to the spiritual barrenness resulting from these conditions. Auden's continual search for meaning
and faith during this period led him away from these ideas to the orthodox Christianity of theologians like Reinhold Niebuhr and Søren Kierkegaard. The most
complete expression of his Christianity is his Christmas Oratorio, *For the Time
Being,* possibly his finest, most cohesive work.

Auden's acceptance of Christianity coincided approximately with his move to
New York, just before the outbreak of World War II. His more recent work combines American images, rhythms, and colloquialism with English ones, but his
poetry is almost always universal rather than regional.

Auden's wide reading is reflected in the development of his technique and his
philosophy. In the inaugural address delivered when he became Professor of Poetry at Oxford in 1956 he named Thomas Hardy as his first real model; the
younger poet found in his master's work an expression of the disillusionment he
himself felt. Hardy wrote of an apparently meaningless universe, governed by
chance, and Auden found men going through life as a ritual in which there is no
meaning. The soldiers of "Which side am I supposed to be on?" are "aware of
our rank and alert to obey orders," but they have no idea of what they fight for.
Like Hardy, Auden often speaks in abstract tones, and he may have acquired his

fondness for experimenting with verse forms from the late-Victorian poet.

William Blake's concern for the mistreated laboring class and the paradoxical religious views expressed in *The Marriage of Heaven and Hell* are reflected in Auden's poetry. Blake's *Songs of Innocence* and *Songs of Experience* also suggest the form of many of the poems in "Songs and other musical pieces" in Auden's *Collected Poetry*. Especially reminiscent of Blake is:

> Now the leaves are falling fast,
> Nurses flowers will not last;
> Nurses to the graves are gone,
> And the prams go rolling on.

Auden's rhythms also reflect his interest in Anglo-Saxon and Middle English verse. *The Age of Anxiety*, "a Baroque Eclogue," is written almost entirely in the old alliterative four-stress line, which is used also in the lines of the Voices of the Desert in *For the Time Being*. The colloquial style of William Butler Yeats's later poetry also influenced some of Auden's work. Critics have pointed out the similarity between Yeats's "September 1913" and Auden's "September 1, 1939":

> I sit in one of the dives
> On Fifty Second Street
> Uncertain and afraid
> As the clever hopes expire
> Of a low dishonest decade.

It is difficult to assess the effect of T. S. Eliot on Auden: the latter is reported to have told his Oxford tutor that Eliot was the only poet to be seriously considered by the prospective writer. The social criticism of *The Waste Land* and *The Hollow Men* was certainly an inspiration to the young poet who felt the same cultured barrenness that Eliot had described. Auden has adopted a few of Eliot's symbols: the desert is a recurrent image of the present civilization for both men.

A particularly striking similarity between Eliot and Auden is their acceptance of Anglo-Catholic Christianity. However, Eliot writes in *Ash Wednesday* and *Four Quartets* of a contemplative ideal, while Auden preaches the necessity for human relationships and mutual concern. His view is well expressed in these lines from *For the Time Being*:

> Space is the Whom our loves are needed by,
> Time is our choice of How to love and Why.

Several related themes run throughout Auden's work. He sees man as an individual isolated in society: a "lonely." "Musée des Beaux Arts" emphasizes this separation. Suffering, Auden says, "takes place while someone else is eating or opening a window or just walking dully along":

> In Brueghel's *Icarus*, for instance; how everything turns away
> Quite leisurely from the disaster; the ploughman may,
> Have heard the splash, the forsaken cry,
> But for him it was not an important failure . . . .

The Wanderer is another recurrent figure in Auden's poetry. The isolated man searches sometimes aimlessly, for meaning in life. An early poem, "Doom is Dark and Deeper Than Any Sea Dingle," whose title comes from a Middle English poem translated by Auden, describes the strange impulse which drives a man away from home to wander "a stranger among strangers." Man's quest is portrayed more elaborately in *The Age of Anxiety*, in the section called "The Seven Stages." The four characters, three men and a woman, travel, sometimes together, sometimes separately, through different scenes, passing through the pitfalls of modern culture and their own dreams, but they lack the courage to cross the desert which is the final stage. They cannot take the "leap of faith" in which Auden found the end to his own quest. Only Rosetta, who possesses the vestiges of her Jewish heritage, has roots and conviction enough to allow her to face the future; whatever happens, she believes that peace lies in reconciliation with her earthly and heavenly fathers. Malin, the Air Force officer, expresses the paradoxes which confront the prospective Christian and the tension which is an integral part of Auden's faith:

> For the others, like me, there is only the flash
> Of negative knowledge. . . .

In both his pre-Christian and Christian poems Auden writes of love as the saving force for mankind, but both humanistic and Christian love in his poetry are extremely impersonal. Concern for others is a familiar theme, but there are almost no descriptions of personal relationships. Even the so-called love lyric, "Lay Your Sleeping Head My Love," is strangely abstract.

Auden is a highly skilled technician. His volume of collected poems includes sonnets, lyrical songs, colloquial meditations, and complex medieval and Renaissance stanza forms like the sestina. His long poems—*The Sea and The Mirror*, in which he discusses the place of the artist in society, using the characters from Shakespeare's *The Tempest*, and *For the Time Being*—contain passages of excellent prose. This virtuosity, one of the poet's greatest assets, is also a defect; verbal tricks intended to produce striking effects succeed only in seeming slick and insincere in some of his work. Many a potentially good poem is marred by the intrusion of a too clever phrase or forced aural effects. Nevertheless, Auden's skill makes his best work inimitable. In the elegiac "In Memory of William Butler Yeats" he interweaves imagery from several of Yeats's own poems and uses three rather different styles of his own to produce one of the finest elegies of the twentieth century. In the concluding lines of this poem one will find Auden's concept of the function of the poet.

Auden has adopted a long, free verse line for many of his more recent poems including parts of *The Shield of Achilles* and "In Praise of Limestone," a "moral landscape" published in 1951. His limestone hill is not the habitat of "saints-to-be" or of "intendant Caesars"; the water-carved stone attracts the men of imagination who see statues, vineyards, in the natural formations, those who climb "arm in arm, but never, thank God, in step."

Bibliography

Bahlke, George W. *The Later Auden: From* "New Year Letter" *to* About the House. New Brunswick, N.J.: Rutgers University Press, 1970.

Beach, Joseph Warren. *The Making of the Auden Canon.* Minneapolis: University of Minnesota Press, 1957.

————. "The Poems of Auden and the Prose Diathesis," in *Virginia Quarterly Review.* XXV (Summer, 1949), pp. 369–383.

Blair, John G. *The Poetic Art of W.H. Auden.* Princeton, N.J.: Princeton University Press, 1965.

Cox, R.G. "The Poetry of W.H. Auden," in *The Modern Age: The Pelican Guide to English Literature*, Volume VII. Edited by Boris Ford. Harmondsworth, England: Penguin, 1961, pp. 373–393.

Davison, Dennis. *W.H. Auden.* London: Evans, 1970.

Day Lewis, Cecil. *A Hope for Poetry.* Oxford: Blackwell, 1934.

Dewsmap, Terence. *The Poetry of W.H. Auden.* New York: Monarch Press, 1965.

Everett, Barbara. *Auden.* Edinburgh: Olmer and Boyd, 1966.

Fuller, John. *A Reader's Guide to W.H. Auden.* London: Thames and Hudson, 1970.

Greenberg, Herbert. *Quest for the Necessary: W.H. Auden and the Dilemma of Divided Consciousness.* Cambridge, Mass.: Harvard University Press, 1968.

Hoggart, Richard. *Auden: An Introductory Essay.* London: Chatto and Windus, 1951.

————. *W.H. Auden.* London: Longmans, 1957.

Nelson, Gerald. *Changes of Heart: A Study of the Poetry of W.H. Auden.* Berkeley: University of California Press, 1969.

Replogle, Justin. *Auden's Poetry.* Seattle: University of Washington Press, 1969.

Scarfe, Francis. *W.H. Auden.* Monaco: Lyrebird Press, 1949.

Sitwell, Edith. *Aspects of Modern Poetry.* London: Duckworth, 1934, pp. 238–245.

Spears, Monroe K., Editor. *Auden: A Collection of Critical Essays.* Englewood Cliffs, N.J.: Prentice-Hall, 1964.

————. *The Poetry of W.H. Auden: The Disenchanted Island.* New York: Oxford University Press, 1963.

Spender, Stephen. "Five Notes on W.H. Auden's Writing," in *Twentieth Century.* III (July, 1932), pp. 13–15.

————. "The Importance of W.H. Auden," in *London Mercury.* XXXIX (April, 1939), pp. 613–618.

Stall, John E. *W.H. Auden; A Reading.* Muncie, Ind.: Ball State University, 1970.

Wright, George T. *W.H. Auden.* New York: Twayne, 1969.

SAMUEL BECKETT

Born: Dublin, Ireland (1906)

Principal Works

NOVELS: *Murphy*, 1938; *Molloy*, 1951; *Malone Meurt*, 1951 (*Malone Dies*) *L'innommable*, 1953; *Watt*, 1953; *Unnamable*, 1958; *How It Is*, 1961.

SHORT STORIES: *More Pricks Than Kicks*, 1934; *Têtes-Mortes*, 1967; *No's Knife* (Collected Shorter Prose, 1945–1966), 1967.

PLAYS: *En Attendant Godot*, 1952 (*Waiting for Godot*); *All That Fall*, 1957; *Endgame*, 1958; *Krapp's Last Tape*, 1960; *Happy Days*, 1961.

POEMS: *Whoroscope*, 1930; *Echo's Bones and Other Precipitates*, 1936

Samuel Beckett, one of the most controversial and difficult writers of the twentieth century, was born in Dublin in 1906. He was educated at the Portora Royal School at Enniskillen, better remembered as Oscar Wilde's school, and received a B.A. in French and Italian from Trinity College, Dublin, in 1927. He spent the next three years as lecturer in English at the École Normale Supérieur in Paris. During this period his first book, a long poem characteristically entitled *Whoroscope*, was published. He returned to Trinity as lecturer in French in 1930 and took his M.A. there. The years 1932–1936 were spent in England or traveling extensively on the Continent. He began writing more intensively, and a long essay on Proust was followed by a collection of short stories entitled *More Pricks Than Kicks* in 1934 and one of poems called *Echo's Bones* in 1936. During these years Beckett was secretary to and a close literary associate of the man who probably influenced him most, James Joyce. In 1929 he assisted Eugene Jolas in editing a collection of critical essays on Joyce, somewhat pompously and puzzlingly entitled *Our Exagmination Round His Factification for Incamination of Work in Progress*, and later, in Paris, he worked with Joyce on a French translation of the "Anna Livia Plurabelle" section of *Finnegans Wake* (1939).

In 1937 Beckett settled in his adopted land, France, for good. His first two novels, *Murphy*, written in Paris before the war, and *Watt*, written in unoccupied Vaucluse during the hostilities, were the last two works he was to write in English.During 1945–1946 he worked as an interpreter and storekeeper at the Irish Red Cross Hospital at St. Lô, and was decorated for his services there. He returned to Paris in 1947 to write a trilogy in French, *Molloy*, *Malone Dies*, and *L'innommable*. In 1952 he published his dramatic masterpiece, the baffling *Waiting for Godot*, which was enthusiastically received by Paris critics and audiences, and ran for over three hundred performances. Beckett's own translation has met with a mixed but chiefly enthusiastic response on the American and English stages.

Waiting for Godot, a "tragicomedy" with only five characters and almost liter-

558   SAMUEL BECKETT

ally no action, has been called the crystallization of all Beckett's work. The two tramps standing by the roadside, waiting for the unknown, mysterious Godot who never comes, share the spiritual misery and hopelessness, if not the physical deformity, of most of the characters in his novels. Although the dramatic structure of this work prevents it from seeming quite as formless as the novels, which are largely composed of incidents without any logical connection, it shares their taut, poetic language, stream-of-consciousness technique, static quality, and highly personal and therefore extremely difficult symbolism. And, like them, this "bible of pessimism" is often surprisingly, indeed inexplicably, funny. It is no mere coincidence that Beckett's writings, which by the postwar period had been purged of their Irishness and rather conceited wit, are best known and appreciated in France. He shares with Sartre and Camus an intense sense of the pervasiveness of misery, solitude, paralysis of will, and, above all, the horror of nothingness. His obscure and difficult style is peculiarly suited to the portrayal of a world where, amidst obscenity and occasional blasphemy, the characters create their personal hells in the prisons of their own dark minds. If Beckett deserves to be ranked, as he sometimes is, in importance and originality with Kafka and Joyce, it is because, like them, he works to perfect a literary style suited to the probing of the innermost recesses of the human mind. His lastest play, *Endgame*, continues in this vein.

Bibliography

An early introductory study is M. Nadeau, "Samuel Beckett, L'humour et le neant," *Mercure de France*, CCCXII (1951), 693–697. The underlying meanings of his work are discussed with considerable insight by Niall Montgomery in *New World Writing*, V (1954), 324–337; this article includes a bibliography. Recent books on Beckett have been numerous: Ruby Cohn, *Samuel Beckett: The Comic Gamut*, 1962; Frederick J. Hoffman, *Samuel Beckett: The Language of Self*, 1962; Hugh Kenner, *Samuel Beckett: A Critical Study*, 1962; Richard N. Coe, *Samuel Beckett*, 1964; John Fletcher, *The Novels of Samuel Beckett*, 1964; Nathan A. Scott, *Samuel Beckett*, 1965; Martin Esslin, ed., *Samuel Beckett: A Collection of Critical Essays*, 1965; Lawrence E. Harvey, *Samuel Beckett, Poet and Critic*, 1970; and Michael Robinson, *The Long Sonata of the Dead*, 1970. A recent biography is *Samuel Beckett*, 1978, by Dierdre Bair. See also Edith Kern, "Drama Stripped for Inaction: Beckett's *Godot*," *Yale French Studies*, XIV (1954), 41–47; Vivian Mercier, "Beckett and the Search for Self," *New Republic*, CXXXIII (September 19, 1955), 20–21, and "Savage Humor," *Commonweal*, LXVI (1957), 188+; Anon., "Puzzling About Godot," *London Times Literary Supplement*, LV (February 10, 1956), 84; Kenneth Rexroth, "The Point Is Irrelevance," *Nation*, CLXXXII (1956), 325–328; Horace Gregory, "Beckett's Dying Gladiators," *Commonweal*, LXV (1956), 88–92; Herbert Gold, "Beckett: Style and Desire," *Nation*, CLXXXIII (1956), 397–399; Ray Biggs and William Barrett, "Samuel Beckett's World in Waiting," *Saturday Review*, XL (June 8, 1957), 14–16; and Warren Lee, "The Bitter Pill of Samuel Beckett," *Chicago Review*, X (1957), 77–87.

MERCIER AND CAMIER

Type of work: Novel
Author: Samuel Beckett (1906–   )
Time of plot: The present
Locale: A vaguely Irish city, village, and countryside
First published: 1975

Essay-Review

Mercier and Camier is a rarity in the field of publishing: a book that the author did *not* want published. In 1947, Samuel Beckett withdrew it from his Parisian publisher, and for twenty-four years had refused to permit its publication, claiming that it was only a working draft, an experiment in new fictional technique. In 1970, his French publishers finally convinced Beckett that he should publish an authoritative version; three years later, the author's own English translation was finally completed. The slender volume is an important and valuable addition to the Beckett canon for two reasons: it marks the shift in Beckett's writing from English to French, and it introduces the vagabond vaudevillian couple, a device which became extremely successful in later prose and dramatic work. In addition, Beckett scholars will find recurrent themes and techniques in this novel that are found in all of his major works: *Malloy, Malone Dies, The Unnamable, Waiting for Godot*, and *Endgame*.

The essence of the work defies reduction and over-simplification in either plot or theme, but its basic vision of the human condition is constant. Life is presented as a journey or as waiting. The narrator of *Mercier and Camier* makes it clear in the first paragraph that this journey will not be the heroic and successful Grail Quest of a medieval knight, nor even the journey of an adventurer such as Gulliver or Robinson Crusoe; he details all the dangers and sufferings that the two protagonists will *not* have to meet. In addition, their goal is obscure: the Grail has vanished, is no longer remembered; rituals as well as heroes have been reduced to insignificance. Only the traditional wasteland of the quest remains, in the form of labyrinths and mazes of cities, empty fields, bogs, and ruins. Man as heroic Knight Errant, as adventurer-explorer, has here given way to man as nonheroic, unpretentious tramp-wanderer, stripped not only of glory, but of most of his humanity. Mercier and Camier, like other Beckett "heroes," stumble along as pathetic, almost transparent nonbeings; their journey is predestined to failure. The reader realizes that they will not progress, but will instead pursue their certain circular path until it is interrupted finally by insanity, suicide, or anguishing despair and *ennui*. This disintegrated condition of man and of his quest underlies the majority of Beckett's major work.

As Mercier and Camier proceed on their intermittent, often delayed journey toward their unknown goal, the reader encounters more of the familiar Beckett themes. The two main characters find themselves progressively alienated from society, God, nature, and even from the basic necessities of life—possessions, clothes, food, sex—and finally from each other. Their alienation from society is evident as Mercier abandons his wife and family, blaming himself for participating in his children's conception, and Camier destroys all that connects him with his job in society. Most dramatically, they seal their separation from society by brutally beating a policeman to death. Their alienation from God and nature is equally clear. Early in the novel, Mercier curses God; nature itself is hostile to them, as the almost continual rain, wind, and darkness disheartens them, making their journey more difficult. When they do leave the city for the countryside, they find only fields and hedges that all seem the same, or the desolation of bogs and ruins, landscapes with nothing to offer man except a place to die.

Typically, Beckett reduces the necessities of his heroes to the bare minimum. Mercier and Camier have only a few essentials: a rucksack, an umbrella, a bicycle, and a raincoat; before leaving the city, they lose all but the latter, which they abandon as useless. Later, in a vague hope that their lost possessions might be important, they return to the city only to discover them useless or irrevocably lost. Functions such as eating and sex are also stripped to the minimum: food becomes an occasional snack, while sex is reduced to the level of the mechanical copulation of the dogs in the first scene.

In the midst of this alienation, Mercier and Camier still have the consolation of each other's friendship, although, like Didi and Gogo, it is a blend of love and recoil. Because of a failure of communication at first, they almost never get together. When they separate for an afternoon, Camier realizes that he basically dreads Mercier's return and the burden of friendship. As they leave on their last journey, their isolation from each other is emphasized as each one walks on the far side of the road from the other. Only when physical and mental strength vanish and touching is necessary for survival do they go arm in arm. But a final breakdown in communication occurs the next morning, and, without speaking, with Chaplinesque courtesy, each bids farewell to the other, as they go their way in total alienation. Their quest to escape loneliness, meaninglessness, and darkness, has been in vain.

The total meaninglessness and pain and absurdity of life is stated many times. "One does what one can, but one can do nothing. Only squirm and wriggle, to end up in the evening where you were in the morning." Suicide seems, at first, a desirable solution; accidental death, even more appealing. However, Mercier later states that they might as well accept "this preposterous penalty and placidly await the executioner." Beckett's nonheroes face the existentialist position, but they refuse to impose meaning on it, realizing that to do so would only be to impose a known fiction upon chaos.

Technically, *Mercier and Camier* is an interesting experiment. Beckett here works out the dialogue form which is used so successfully in *Waiting for Godot*, using puns, rhythm, *non sequiturs*, and vaudeville routines between the heroes to create warmth, humor, and humanity. Traditional elements of the novel—character, setting, clock time, causal plot—all disintegrate as this story moves on. Beckett also establishes the device of resurrecting "heroes" from other works, as in the case of the appearance of Watt in the concluding scenes. Experimentally most interesting is Beckett's use of the narrator to underscore themes of the journey. The narrator fluctuates between an objective yet sympathetic view of his main characters, and a stance of ironic detachment. Likewise, Beckett's use of plot structure and setting follows a similar course. Structurally, the interspersing of short summaries of the action after every two chapters serves to mock that "action," while the many fragmented references only serve to emphasize the triviality of what has occurred. Just as time in the heroes' lives is wasted, so repetitious and irrelevant incidents in the plot accumulate.

In addition, Beckett creates a sense of fragmentation by having the narrator alienate the reader from characters such as the policeman, and even Mercier and Camier, and dropping constant reminders that the heroes' world is artificial rather than real. This occurs most forcefully in the conversation between Mercier and Camier in which they declare that it would take two fat volumes apiece to recount their lives. Beckett's narrator thus ironically undercuts his own tale, which recounts *both* their adventures in a padded 123 pages. Neither characters nor narrator know where they are headed; Beckett refuses to control or guide them as an omniscient author, to consider them as real human beings. Their predicament is thus parallel to the situation, as the author sees it, of man in this world: that of a lost creature deprived of his belief in an all-knowing God who orders and makes meaningful his life and universe.

Bibliography

Abbott, H. Porter. *The Fiction of Samuel Beckett.* Berkeley: University of California, 1973, pp. 75–91.

Auster, Paul. "*Mercier and Camier,*" in *Commentary.* LX (July, 1975), p. 39.

Blair, Deirde. "*Mercier and Camier,*" in *New York Times Book Review.* (March 9, 1975), p. 19.

Brater, Enoch. "*Mercier and Camier,*" in *New Republic.* CLXXII (March 8, 1975), p. 25.

Cohn, Ruby. "Inexhaustible Beckett: An Introduction," in *Samuel Beckett: A Collection of Criticism.* Edited by Ruby Cohn. New York: McGraw-Hill, 1975, pp. 5–6.

Fletcher, John. *The Novels of Samuel Beckett.* New York: Barnes & Noble, 1970, pp. 110–118.

Kilroy, Thomas. "*Mercier and Camier,*" in *Times Literary Supplement.* (December 13, 1974), p. 1405.

Mayoux, Jean-Jacques. *Samuel Beckett.* London: Longmans, 1974, p. 19.

Updike, John. "*Mercier and Camier,*" in *New Yorker.* LI (September 1, 1975), p. 62.

THE UNNAMABLE

Type of work: Novel
Author: Samuel Beckett (1906–   )
Time of plot: The present
Locale: A street in Paris
First published: 1958

Essay-Review

The Unnamable is the third novel of Samuel Beckett's postwar trilogy—*Molloy* and *Malone Dies* were its predecessors—written in French and translated into English by the writer himself. The three are connected in theme if not in narrative sequence, for each is related to some aspect of a central subject, the search for self. Together, they illustrate that revolutionary concern for technical innovation which is reshaping the conception and form of the novel in our time. Perhaps the best way to define Samuel Beckett's method in fiction is to say that it derives from the philosophical doctrine of solipsism, the idea that the world is created in the act of perceiving it. Since these novels do not depend for their effect on sustained narrative interest or rounded development of character, they raised certain problems in connection with the nature of reality in fiction and the structure of the novel.

A classic age in the novel may be described as one in which the writer feels no *conscious* need to make an assault on his medium. The older novelists found no formidable problem involved in the business of getting a story told; they simply began at the beginning, carried their people through a series of events leading up to a climax, and brought the whole to a satisfactory conclusion. They also had at hand a language appropriate to their view of reality and shared in common with their readers. And they made a virtue of necessity in their treatment of time. But no such ready-made formula exists for the modern writer, who after Proust, Joyce, and Virginia Woolf is no longer likely to see environment as the great shaping force of character or reality as an apprehension of experience through the physical senses. The problem of reality in fiction has been complicated even further by every intellectual development of the past hundred years. After Newton, Bergson, and Einstein, the novel could no longer ignore the scientific necessity of new concepts of time and space; after Darwin, the biological necessity; after Freud, the psychological necessity of man's own thwarting and distorted personality. In the face of influences like these, the modern novelist has been forced to find new techniques and new styles to clothe his vision of reality. He struggles with form and language, twists and turns them into new shapes, in his effort to capture and convey the nature of experience, as Virginia Woolf put it, "with as little mixture of the alien and external as possible."

It was Bergson who first pointed in the direction away from the calendar sense in fiction, with his theory of the fluid nature of reality and his emphasis upon intuition rather than upon reason as a means of sensing its duration. The direct influence of Bergson on writers like Proust, Woolf, and Beckett is still debatable, but the fact remains that the modern writer has claimed for fiction the doctrine that reality is a never static process of creation which reason can apprehend only through arbitrary concepts that stand for but do not actually represent experience, that every present moment encloses the past and anticipates the future, and that memory charts the course of personality in the stream of time. The Bergsonian view makes time a relative matter, and here is suggested all the modern consciousness of retrospect and anticipation. It gives the writer his inescapable vision of man in the flux of time and the stream carrying him away in the moment of perception; arouses his need to find some vital link, some emerging pattern, in impressions and incidents that are always in the process of becoming; and directs his search for whatever is permanent in the midst of change.

One result of these activities in the modern novel has been the progressive breakdown of distinctions formerly existing between poetry and prose, in an effort to give to fiction the naked moment of perception and insight which in earlier literary periods was the function of poetry alone. Another has been to create for imaginative prose a variety of patterns which have this one thing in common: the individual approaches to the technique of the novel and the end effects have little relation to what we recognize as the traditional novel form.

Both results are clearly apparent in the novels of Samuel Beckett. It is interesting to find that almost every critic, discussing his work, has fallen back on terms associated with poetry in order to express his precise quality. The objects that function less in his writing—the crutches, hats, sucking stones, sticks, and shoes—bear little relevance to any situation by which the fate of character will be decided, for the fate of the Beckett hero has been determined before the story begins. Objects exist in these novels as they do in poetry, for contemplation, for symbolism, for the functioning of the poetic consciousness. There is no story in the conventional sense; in fact, Beckett has emptied his novel of situation and plot as a means for revealing character or resolving conflict. All that we have is that view of reality, not directly apprehended by the senses, which Virginia Woolf once described as "what remains over when the skin of the day has been cast into the hedge." This kind of reality, more common in the lyric poem than in the novel, allows us to accept Molloy as a man pursued in strange fashion by a figure named Moran, who in the end changes from a creature of hallucinated action and moral rigidity to a helpless paralytic like Molloy himself, or Malone as an old man, apparently dying in some institution, who eats food pushed through the door by some agent never seen, who uses his stick to count his few possessions, and who makes up a story about a man named Macmann. These figures are real because their sufferings and degradations and small comforts are real; the tensions of their self-revelations belong to the moods and insights of poetry, not to a story of conflict unfolding in horizontal time.

Thus it is not surprising to find that the hero of Beckett's novel—unnamed even though he seems to refer to himself as Mahood or as Worm—is completely isolated from the world of normal contacts, a victimized stylite confined in a large jar on a pedestal outside a restaurant on what seems to be a street in Paris. He is without arms or legs and a collar keeps him from moving his head. His position is that of the foetus in the womb, and the view of experience he presents is one that spans the life of man from birth to senescence and the grave. "Where now? Who now? When now? Unquestioning," he begins. The real world appears as shapes and shadows dimly seen. Some he recognizes. There is the restaurant proprietress who feeds him and uses the pedestal on which his jar is perched to display her menus. Sometimes Malone passes by, but always in silence. Alone, sentient, the Unnamable meditates on suffering, on death, on original sin, trying to find in these matters the answers to the questions he has posed at the beginning. He uncovers some truths about the body, the soul, the nature of anguish and compassion, but with no hope except a kind of comic disgust with human frailty and a realization of all that is inescapable. Yet the end of this novel in the form of a dramatic monologue is not despairing as the words flow on and the Unnamable feels that

> perhaps it's a dream, all a dream, that would surprise me, I'll wake, in the silence, and never sleep again, it will be I, or dream, dream again, dream of a silence, a dream silence, full of murmurs, I don't know, that's all words, never wake, all words, there's nothing else, you must go on, that's all I know, they're going to stop, I know that well, I can feel it, they're going to abandon me, it will be the silence, for a moment, a good few moments, or it will be mine, the lasting one, that didn't last, that still lasts, it will be I, you must go on, I can't go on, you must go on, I'll go on, you must say words, as long as there are any, until they find me, until they say me, strange pain, strange sin, you must go on, perhaps it's done already, perhaps they have said me already, perhaps they have carried me to the threshold of my story, before the door that opens on my story, that would surprise me, if it opens, it will be I, it will be the silence, where I am, I don't know, I'll never know, in the silence you don't know, you must go on, I can't go on, I'll go on.

It is as unsatisfactory to explain what Beckett's novels are "about" as it is to extract the "meaning" of a poem. Paraphrase is not enough, for it can never convey the quality of what he says or how he says it. He has been compared to Joyce, to Kafka, to Céline, to Sartre, yet he stands closer to the poets who have given us in brooding flashes their tormented and tragic vision of life. A writer extracting comedy from the spectacle of human indignity and despair, a visionary aware of strange contentment beyond the demands of self, and a writer whose prose is capable of great poetic effect, Samuel Beckett must be counted among the writers who have something serious to say; and he is adding to the dimensions of the novel by the lyrical, contemplative nature of his communication.

Bibliography

Abbott, H. Porter. *The Fiction of Samuel Beckett.* Berkeley: University of California Press, 1973, pp. 110–112, 124–137.

Alvarez, Alfred. *Samuel Beckett.* New York: Viking, 1973, pp. 57–65.

Barnard, G.C. *Samuel Beckett: A New Approach.* London: J.M. Dent, 1970, pp. 57–66.

Blanchot, Maurice. "Where Now? Who Now?," in *On Contemporary Literature.* Edited by Richard Kostelanetz. New York: Avon Books, 1969, pp. 249–254. Also in *Evergreen Review,* II (Winter, 1959), pp. 224–229.

Chambers, Ross. "Samuel Beckett and the Padded Cell," in *Meanjin Quarterly.* XXI (April, 1962), pp. 451–462.

Cohn, Ruby. *Samuel Beckett: The Comic Gamut.* New Brunswick, N.J.: Rutgers University Press, 1962, pp. 114–168.

Cornwell, Ethel J. "Samuel Beckett: The Flight from Self," in *PMLA.* LXXXVIII (January, 1973), pp. 41–51.

Fletcher, John. *The Novels of Samuel Beckett.* New York: Barnes & Noble, 1970, pp. 179–194.

Glicksberg, Charles I. *The Self in Modern Literature.* University Park: Pennsylvania State University Press, 1963, pp. 129–133.

Hassan, Ihab. *The Literature of Silence.* New York: Knopf, 1968, pp. 162–168.

Hoffman, Frederick J. *Samuel Beckett: The Language of Self.* Carbondale: Southern Illinois University Press, 1962, pp. 132–137.

Karl, Frederick. "Waiting for Beckett: Quest and Request," in *The Contemporary English Novel.* New York: Farrar, Straus, 1962, pp. 19–39.

Oates, Joyce Carol. "The Trilogy of Samuel Beckett," in *Renascence.* XIV (Spring, 1962), pp. 160–165.

Peake, Charles. "The Labours of Poetical Excavation," in *Beckett: The Shape Changer.* Edited by Katherine Worth. London: Routledge and Kegan Paul, 1975, pp. 50–58.

Pilling, John. *Samuel Beckett.* London: Routledge and Kegan Paul, 1976, pp. 26–68.

Rickels, Milton. "Existential Themes in Beckett's *Unnamable,*" in *Criticism.* IV (Spring, 1962), pp. 134–147.

Robinson, Michael. *The Long Sonata of the Dead.* London: Rupert Hart-Davis, 1969, pp. 191–207.

Tindall, William Y.   *Samuel Beckett*. New York: Columbia University Press, 1964, pp. 29–32.

Webb, Eugene.   *Samuel Beckett: A Study of His Novels*. Seattle: University of Washington Press, 1973, pp. 72–150.

WAITING FOR GODOT

Type of work: Drama
Author: Samuel Beckett (1906–   )
Type of plot: Tragi-comedy
Time of plot: The present
Locale: A country road
First presented: 1952

In this comedy of the absurd, antic yet philosophically troubling, Beckett views the human condition through symbolism that has its roots in Freudian psychology, the Christian myth, and Existentialism. The two tramps vacillate between hope and despair; they are obsessed by uncertainty and dominated by the absurd.

Principal Characters

Vladimir (Didi) (vlȧ·dē·mēr′; dē·dē′) and
Estragon (Gogo) (ĕs·trȧ·gōn′; gô·gō′), two tramps. In this play action is unimportant; the characters remain undeveloped as the tramps wait impatiently for Godot, who remains a mysterious entity, possibly a local land owner but also a symbol of man's spiritual seeking. They gnaw carrots, rest their tired feet, and engage in other simple activities while their conversations reveal the helplessness of their situation. Throughout the play there is every suggestion that the two live estranged from a state of grace which is hoped for but never realized. Often considering suicide, they are caught in a calm of inactivity between hope and despair in their longing for salvation, which is linked somehow with Godot. When the play ends, the two are still waiting for the promised appearance of Godot.

Pozzo (pō·zō′), a materialist. A rich, boisterous tyrant, he is obviously an ex-pounder of Nietzschean doctrines and materialistic concepts. Pozzo admits that Lucky has taught him all the beautiful things he knows, but now his servant has become unbearable and is driving him mad. At first he drives his servant with a rope; however, when he reappears, blinded in symbolic fashion by his own worldly successes and romantic pessimism, he must be led by his mute servant.

Lucky (lü·kē′), Pozzo's servant. Born a peasant, he gives the impression of a new proletarian, the symbol of modern man's belief in the promises and miracles of science. Lucky first appears driven by Pozzo at the end of a rope. Ordered to think for the group, he delivers the wildest, most brilliantly sustained monologue of the play. When he next appears, he is leading the blind Pozzo, but he is mute.

A Boy, a messenger from Godot.

The Story

Estragon tried to take off his boot but failed. Vladimir agreed with him that it sometimes appeared that there was nothing one could do. They were glad to be reunited after a night apart. With Vladimir's help, Estragon succeeded in removing his painful boot. Vladimir, also in pain, could not laugh in comfort; he tried smiling instead but it was not satisfactory.

Vladimir mused on the one gospel account that said Christ saved one of the thieves. Estragon wanted to leave. They could not leave because they were waiting for Godot. They became confused about the arrangements and wondered if they were waiting at the right time, in the right place, and on the right day. They quarreled briefly but were, as always, reconciled.

They considered hanging themselves but decided that it would be safer to do nothing until they heard what Godot said. They did not know what they had asked Godot for. They concluded they had forgone their rights.

Vladimir gave Estragon a carrot, which he ate hungrily. They decided that although they were not bound to Godot, they were in fact unable to act.

Pozzo entered, driving Lucky, who was laden with luggage, by a rope around his neck. Estragon and Vladimir mistook him for Godot but accepted him as Pozzo. Although he attempted to intimidate them, he was glad of their company. After ordering Lucky to bring him his stool and his coat, he gave Lucky the whip. Lucky obeyed automatically. Vladimir and Estragon protested violently against Pozzo's treatment of Lucky. Pozzo deflected their outburst and the subject was dropped.

After smoking a pipe Pozzo rose. He then decided he did not want to leave, but his pride almost prevented him from reseating himself. The tramps wanted to know why Lucky never put down the luggage. Pozzo said that Lucky was trying to make him keep the fellow. When Pozzo added that he would sell Lucky rather than throw him out, Lucky wept; but when Estragon tried to dry his tears, Lucky kicked him away. Then Estragon wept. Pozzo philosophized on this and said that Lucky had taught him all the beautiful things he knew, but that the fellow had now become unbearable and was driving Pozzo mad. Estragon and Vladimir then abused Lucky for mistreating his master.

Pozzo broke into a monologue on the twilight, alternating between the lyrical and the commonplace and ending with the bitter thought that everything happened in the world when one was least prepared. He decided to reward Estragon and Vladimir for praising him by making Lucky entertain them. Lucky executed a feeble dance which Estragon mocked but failed to imitate.

Estragon stated that there had been no arrivals, no departures, and no action, and that everything was terrible. Pozzo next decided that Lucky should think for them. For this Vladimir replaced Lucky's derby hat. Lucky's thought was an incoherent flood of words which resembled a dissertation on the possible goodness of God, the tortures of hell fire, the prevalence of sport, and the vacuity of suburbs. He desperately upset his listeners, who attacked him and silenced him by seizing his hat. Having restored Lucky to his position as carrier, Pozzo and the tramps said many farewells before he and Lucky finally left.

The Boy called to Vladimir and Estragon. He came with a message from

Godot, who would come the next evening. The Boy, a goatherd, said that Godot was kind to him, but that he beat his brother, a shepherd. Vladimir asked the Boy to tell Godot only that he had seen them.

By the time the Boy left, night had fallen. Estragon decided to abandon his boots to someone else. Vladimir protested and Estragon said that Christ had gone barefoot. Once again they considered and rejected the idea of separating. They decided to leave for the night. They stayed where they were.

The following evening the boots were still there and the tree had grown some leaves. The tramps had spent the night separately. Vladimir returned first. When Estragon came back he said he had been beaten again and Vladimir felt that he could have prevented such cruelty. Vladimir began to talk of the previous day, but Estragon could remember nothing but being kicked. Then they were overwhelmed by the thought of the whispering voices of the dead around them. They tried to break their silence but succeeded only in part. By a great effort Estragon recalled that the previous day had been spent chattering inanities. He reflected that they had spent fifty years doing no more than that.

They discovered that the boots left behind by Estragon had been exchanged for another old pair. After finding Lucky's hat, which assured them that they had returned to the right place, they started a wild exchange of the three hats, shifting them from hand to hand. Finally Vladimir kept Lucky's hat and Estragon kept his own.

Once more Estragon decided to leave. To distract him, Vladimir suggested that they "play" Pozzo and Lucky. Puzzled, Estragon left, but he returned almost immediately because some people were coming. Vladimir was jubilant, convinced that Godot was arriving. They tried to hide, but there was nowhere for them to go. Finally Lucky entered with Pozzo, who was now blind. Lucky fell and dragged Pozzo with him. Pozzo cried for help. Vladimir passionately wished to act while there was the opportunity—to do one good thing as a member of the human race, a species that appalled him. Pozzo was terrified, and Vladimir also fell in his attempts to raise him. Estragon fell too while trying to lift Vladimir. As they fought and argued on the ground, they called Pozzo "Cain" and "Abel." When he responded to both names they concluded that he was all humanity. Suddenly they got up without difficulty.

Pozzo prepared to leave, but Vladimir wanted Lucky to sing first. Pozzo explained that Lucky was dumb. They wanted to know when he had been afflicted. Angry, Pozzo said that all their lives were merely momentary and time did not matter. He left with Lucky.

While Estragon slept, the Boy entered to say that Godot would come, not that night but the next. The message for Godot was that the Boy had seen Vladimir. The Boy left and Estragon awoke. He immediately wanted to leave. Vladimir insisted that they could not go far because they must return the next night in order to wait for Godot, who would punish them if they did not wait.

Estragon and Vladimir remarked that only the tree in the landscape was alive and considered hanging themselves again. Instead, they decided that if Godot did not come to save them the next night, they would hang themselves. At last the tramps decided to go. They remained immobile.

Critical Evaluation

Waiting for Godot (En Attendant Godot) is a landmark in modern drama. When it premiered in Paris, its originality stunned audiences: no one had seen or heard anything like it before. Initially, some were disgusted; some were puzzled; and some were wildly enthusiastic. But within a short time, audiences came to the theater prepared for a wholly new dramatic experience and went away with praises for Samuel Beckett, then a playwright manqué. The play ran for more than three hundred performances in Paris, other productions were mounted in London and major cities on the Continent, and it was widely translated and performed around the world. After a disastrous United States premiere in Miami, *Waiting for Godot* went on to a successful New York run, suggesting that the play was best received by an audience of sophisticated intellectuals.

Nevertheless, audience enthusiasm has not been matched by unalloyed critical acclaim. To be sure, many critics as well as eminent playwrights have paid high tribute to the play. But several other critics, like some members of the first-night audience in Paris, have been repelled or baffled by *Waiting for Godot,* their reactions most often stemming from a misunderstanding of the play. In order to avert such misunderstanding, it is necessary to examine two crucial aspects of the play: its language and its philosophical orientation.

First of all, the language of the play is intimately connected to Beckett's own background in language studies and literary influences. Beckett was born in Dublin, Ireland, and took his A.B. degree in French and Italian at Trinity College. After teaching English in Paris for two years, he returned to Trinity to teach and complete his M.A. in French. Next, he traveled in England and on the Continent, and he wrote poems, short stories, and novels—in English. He at last settled permanently in Paris, except for a brief hiatus during World War II, and began writing in French in the late 1940's. (*Waiting for Godot* was thus originally written in French but translated into English by Beckett himself.)

Of equal importance, during Beckett's first sojourn in Paris (1928-1930), was his meeting with James Joyce, a meeting which launched a long and mutually satisfying friendship between the two Irish expatriates and language experts. The influence of Joyce on Beckett's work is evident in the language play in *Waiting for Godot,* for puns, allusions, and linguistic "tricks" abound.

Great effort has been expended, for instance, in trying to decipher the word "Godot," both as character and as concept. Beckett himself has declined to explain, but critics, undeterred, continue to speculate. The most common view sees Godot as God with the "-ot" as a diminutive suffix. The French title *En Attendant Godot* seems to lend support to this interpretation. Another suggestion is the analogy between Godot and Charlot (both utilizing the diminutive suffix), the latter an affectionate nickname for the Charlie Chaplin character in a derby hat, the kind of hat which plays a significant part in the stage business of *Waiting for Godot*. Some readings inevitably deteriorate into the preposterous—that Godot represents De Gaulle, for example. But the most likely explanation involves an allusion to a highly obscure source: Honore de Balzac's comedy, *Le Faisseur* (also known as *Mercadet*). Balzac's play revolves around a character—named Godeau—who strongly influences the action of the play but who never appears on stage. The parallels between the Balzac work and *Waiting for Godot* are too close to attribute to mere coincidence, for Beckett, like Joyce, has a marked fondness for the esoteric literary allusion. It is possible, of course, to circumvent these literary contortions and simply view Godot as the objectification of a state of being: the *waiting,* bracketed by birth and death, which we call life.

In addition, Beckett plays other word games in *Waiting for Godot*. Estragon, for instance, begins a sentence which Vladimir then finishes. Yet the overwhelming monotony of the dialogue, reflecting the monotony in the characters' lives, is reminiscent of the exercise drills in old language texts of the "La plume de ma tante est sur la table" variety, further suggesting the debasement of language and the consequent breakdown of communication. (This point is a major preoccupation of another modern playwright, Eugene Ionesco.) And the *non sequiturs* which emerge from rapid-fire exchanges in the dialogue echo the music-hall comedians in the heyday of vaudeville. Thus Beckett's penchant for word play reveals the influence of his language training, of his friend James Joyce, and of his conviction that language in the modern world is both necessary and impotent.

The philosophical orientation of *Waiting for Godot* is another matter, however, for the years of Beckett's residence in France coincided with a period of great ferment in Existential philosophy, most of it centered in Paris. Beckett is not a formal or doctrinaire Existentialist, but he could hardly avoid being affected by Existentialism, for such ideas were part of his cultural milieu. There is no systematically Existential point of view in *Waiting for Godot*—as there is in, say, the plays of Jean-Paul Sartre and the novels of Albert Camus. Yet a generally Existential view of the human condition comes through very clearly in the play. Vladimir and Estragon, Lucky and Pozzo are psychically isolated from one another; despite physical proximity, they are alienated and lonely, as indicated by their failure to communicate meaningfully. And in that state of mind, each despairs, feeling helpless in the face of an immutable destiny. But, unlike the formal Existentialists, Estragon and Vladimir hope, and it is that hope which sustains them through their monotonous and immobile existence. Thus, they wait. They wait for Godot, who will surely bring them words of comfort and advice, and who will intervene to alter their destinies. By maintaining this hope, by waiting for Godot to come, Vladimir and Estragon elude the inevitable Existential logic which postulates hopelessness followed by a sense of futility, reducing humankind to absurdity. In this way, Vladimir and Estragon attain truly heroic proportions; they endure.

Beckett's play has been criticized, even by Estragon, because, as the tramp puts it, "Nothing happens." But in fact, a great deal does happen: there is a lot of action, much coming and going. However, action in this sense is quite superficial, for all of it is meaningless. Yet that very action assumes a rhythm and a pattern which constitute the structure of the play. The repetitious movements and dialogue reinforce the quasi-Existential theme of the play: that life is a meaningless and monotonous performance of endlessly repeated routine. The pattern established in the first act is recapitulated in the second act, with only slight variation. Obviously the action in *Waiting for Godot* is not the action of conventional drama, but it is this unique fusion of theme and structure which accounts for the startling originality of the play and which rightly earns Beckett a place as one of the few genuine innovators in modern drama.

Bibliography

Alvarez, Alfred. *Samuel Beckett.* New York: Viking, 1973, pp. 76–86.

Ashomore, Jerome. "Philosophical Aspects of *Godot*," in *Symposium.* XVI (Winter, 1962), pp. 296–306.

Barnard, G.C. *Samuel Beckett: A New Approach.* London: J.M. Dent, 1970, pp. 89–100.

Brereton, Geoffrey. *Principles of Tragedy.* Miami: University of Miami Press, 1968, pp. 244–265.

Chadwick, C. "*Waiting for Godot*: A Logical Approach," in *Symposium.* XIV (Winter, 1960), pp. 252–257.

Cohn, Ruby. *Samuel Beckett: The Comic Gamut.* New Brunswick, N.J.: Rutgers University Press, 1962, pp. 208–225.

Dukore, Bernard F. "The Other Pair in *Waiting for Godot*," in *Drama Survey.* VII (Winter, 1968–1969), pp. 133–137.

Esslin, Martin. *The Theatre of the Absurd.* Garden City, N.Y.: Doubleday, 1961, pp. 13–27.

Fletcher, John. "Bailing Out the Silence," in *Beckett: A Study of His Plays.* Edited by John Fletcher and John Spurling. New York: Hill and Wang, 1972, pp. 55–68.

Flood, Ethelbert. "A Reading of Beckett's *Godot*," in *Culture*. XXII (September, 1961), pp. 257–262.

Gilliat, Penelope. "Beckett," in *Unholy Fools*. New York: Viking, 1973, pp. 20–23.

Glicksberg, Charles I. *The Self in Modern Literature*. University Park: Pennsylvania State University Press, 1963, pp. 117–121.

Guicharnaud, Jacques. "Existence on Stage," in *On Contemporary Literature*. Edited by Richard Kostelanetz. New York: Avon Books, 1969, pp. 262–285.

Harvey, Lawrence E. "Art and the Existential in *En Attendant Godot*," in *PMLA*. LXXV (March, 1960), pp. 137–145.

Hayman, Ronald. *Samuel Beckett*. New York: Frederick Ungar, 1973, pp. 7–37.

Hoffman, Frederick J. *Samuel Beckett: The Language of Self*. Carbondale: Southern Illinois University Press, 1962, pp. 138–161.

Hooker, Ward. "Irony and Absurdity in the Avant-Garde Theatre," in *Kenyon Review*. XXII (Summer, 1960), pp. 436–454.

Karl, Frederick R. "Waiting for Becket: Quest and Request," in *A Reader's Guide to the Contemporary English Novel*. New York: Farrar, Straus, 1962, pp. 19–39.

Kenner, Hugh. *Samuel Beckett: A Critical Study*. Berkeley: University of California, 1968, pp. 133–139, 146–155, 185–186.

Mathews, Honor. *The Primal Curse*. New York: Schocken, 1967, pp. 154–168.

Michalyi, Gabor. "Beckett's *Godot* and the Myth of Alienation," in *Modern Drama*. IX (December, 1966), pp. 277–282.

O'Casey, Sean. "Not Waiting for Godot," in *Blasts and Benedictions*. New York: St. Martin's Press, 1967, pp. 51–52.

Rechtien, Brother John, S.M. "Time and Eternity Meet in the Present," in *Texas Studies in Literature and Language*. VI (Spring, 1964), pp. 5–21.

Robinson, Michael. *The Long Sonata of the Dead*. London: Rupert Hart-Davis, 1969, pp. 245–260.

Scott, Nathan A. *Samuel Beckett*. New York: Hillary House, 1965, pp. 83–94, 100–101, 105–111.

Styan, J.L. *The Dark Comedy*. Cambridge: Cambridge University Press, 1962, pp. 218–234.

Webb, Eugene. *The Plays of Samuel Beckett*. Seattle: University of Washington Press, 1972, pp. 26–41.

Wellworth, George. "Samuel Beckett: Life in the Void," in *The Theatre of Protest and Paradox.* New York: New York University Press, 1964, pp. 37–51.

RUPERT BROOKE

Born: Rugby, England (August 3, 1887)
Died: The Aegean Sea (April 29, 1915)

Principal Works

POEMS: *Poems*, 1911; *1914 and Other Poems*, 1915, *Collected Poems*, 1915; *Complete Poems*, 1932.
LETTERS: *Letters from America*, 1916.
ESSAY: *John Webster*, 1916.

Rupert Brooke, the most popular English poet of the period of World War I, was born at the famous Public School of Rugby, where his father was an Assistant Master. After attending Rugby, Brooke went up to King's College, Cambridge, in 1909. At the University he immediately plunged into all of the intellectual activities there and became the center of a brilliant group. All who knew him at Cambridge remembered his great personal charm and amazing good looks, for he was considered one of the handsomest Englishmen of his time. It was during this period that he joined the Fabian Society, the socialistic group to which belonged many intellectuals, including H. G. Wells and Sidney and Beatrice Webb.

In 1909 he took his classical tripos and then spent some time in Munich, returning to the village of Grantchester near Cambridge. Here he leased the Old Vicarage, the site of one of his most famous poems, "The Old Vicarage, Grantchester," which he wrote in Germany and which he originally planned to call "The Sentimental Exile." While living at Grantchester, he wrote extensively and published his first volume of poems in 1911.

In 1913 he embarked on a long journey that took him across the United States and Canada and eventually to the South Seas where he spent some time in Samoa and Tahiti. It was in this, at that time unspoiled, Pacific paradise, that he wrote some of his best-known poems, including "Tiare Tahiti" and "The Great Lover."

Hardly had Brooke returned to England than World War I broke out. In spite of his early socialistic leanings, he enlisted at once in the Royal Naval Division and took part in the futile attempt to defend Antwerp. In February of 1915 he sailed with the Mediterranean Expeditionary Force for the Dardanelles. But in Egypt he had a sunstroke, from which he recovered, only to die of blood poisoning on a French hospital ship in the Aegean Sea. He was buried on the island of Scyros, Greece.

Brooke began writing poetry while a student at Rugby, under the encouragement of St. John Lucas, and during his undergraduate years he acquired a reputation as a promising younger poet. He became associated with the group known as "the Georgians," which included such men as Gibson, Abercrombie, De la Mare, Thomas, Hodgson, and Drinkwater, who were striving to return English poetry to the language and feelings of everyday life after the artificiality of the 1890's. Brooke himself was much influenced by the Metaphysical poets of the seventeenth century, particularly Marvell. The influence of this metaphysical "wit" is best seen in "Tiare Tahiti," with its half-playful, half-serious handling of Platonic images.

The poems by which Brooke became famous were, however, the five sonnets, *1914*, written at Christmas of that year. To many readers, these were the best expression of the high patriotism with which England entered the war, and Brooke himself became the symbol of the youth of England fallen on the battlefields. But with the anti-war reaction of the 1920's there was a corresponding reaction against Brooke; he came to be regarded as a "war poet," which he really was not, and his once great popularity faded away.

Brooke cannot be called a great poet, and he belonged to a school that is out of fashion today. Their work is too close to us to be historically interesting; it seems merely dated. Yet in spite of the great change in poetic taste since 1915, the poems of the Georgians and of Brooke still have something to offer, and they deserve a careful reëxamination.

Bibliography

The definitive biography of Brooke is that of Christopher Hassall, 1964. See also *Brooke, Letters*, edited by Sir Geoffrey Keynes, 1968. The *Collected Poems* contains a well-known critical essay by George Woodberry and a biographical note by Margaret Lavington. See also John Drinkwater, *Rupert Brooke: An Essay*, 1916; Edward Marsh, *Brooke: A Memoir*, 1918; Walter de la Mare, Rupert Brooke and the Intellectual Imagination, 1919; Bernard Bergonzi, *Heroes Twilight: A Study of the Literature of the Great War*, 1965; and Robert H. Ross, *The Georgian Revolt*, 1967.

THE POETRY OF BROOKE

Author: Rupert Brooke (1887–1915)
Principal published works: Poems, 1911; *1914 and Other Poems*, 1915; *Collected Poems*, 1915

Essay-Review

In World War I, when news of Rupert Brooke's death reached England, John Drinkwater wrote that there had not been a sadder loss to poetry since Shelley's death, a judgment that seemed borne out by the sale of 58,000 copies of the *Collected Poems* by 1921. There was also the legend, rapidly crystallized, of the "great lover," the handsomest Englishman of his day, famed for his charm. So much had he become the symbol of the youth of England, now decimated by the war, that the strange proposal was made to fix the church clock at Grantchester permanently at "ten to three" as a memorial to his best-loved poem. Yet of this reputation, once so splendid, little remains today, and there are few readers of his poems. The reason is to be found in the radical change that has overtaken English poetry since World War I and sent it along roads far different from those that Rupert Brooke knew.

For the literary historian, 1915 was an interestingly crucial year in English poetry: it saw the publication in England of Brooke's *Collected Poems* and in America of T. S. Eliot's "The Love Song of J. Alfred Prufrock," which appeared in the Chicago magazine, *Poetry*. So utterly unalike are Brooke's war sonnets and Eliot's ironic dramatic monologue that it is as difficult to reconcile their publication in the same year as to remember that Brooke was only a year older than Eliot, and that, had it not been for the war, he could easily have lived into the 1960's. Brooke marked the end, as Eliot did the beginning, of a literary age.

The short-lived group known as "the Georgians" was not a poetic school as the term is understood in France; it was a loosely knit group whose members had in common only a reaction against the false medievalism of the late nineteenth century and the artificiality of the 1890's. It was a return to actuality in subject matter and an employment of the tone and accent of natural speech. The preciosity of the generation of Wilde and Dowson had to be removed from English poetry; the vigor of the common language of men had to be restored, as Wordsworth had found necessary a century earlier. More than anything, there was need for fresh air after the incense-laden atmosphere of the Aesthetic Movement. There was a rediscovery of the beauty of the English countryside and of the sheer joy of living, after the elaborately cultivated world weariness and disillusionment of the 1890's. The influence of France, which had been dominant in England, was cast off; there was a return to the mainstream of English poetry. The Georgians were perhaps the last Romantics, as they were also the last to be what we usually think of as typically English.

Brooke went through an early apprentice period during which he was much influenced by the "decadents," particularly Dowson, an experience natural enough for a man of his generation, before he found his own voice and his own style. The late George Woodberry, in his celebrated essay that serves as an introduction to the *Collected Poems*, suggested that Brooke excelled in three aspects of poetry: the dramatic sonnet, the narrative idyll, and the "mélange." By the dramatic sonnet, Woodberry meant a sonnet in which "there is a tragic reversal or its equivalent"; that is, the last line of the poem suddenly reverses the mood that has been carefully built up for thirteen lines. The idyll derives from Milton's early poems, even to the use of seven and eight-syllable rhyming couplets and glimpses of the English countryside with its flowers and trees and streams. By the "mélange" Woodberry meant such poems as "The Great Lover," in which the poet, having garnered experience, re-creates it in language without particular regard for the value of the experience. The poem is a compilation of physical objects and sensations, held together only by a slender thread of association.

There was also at work on Brooke another influence: that of the Metaphysical poets; and it may be well to remind the present generation that it was not T. S. Eliot alone who rediscovered these figures from the early seventeenth century. Brooke was much interested in them while an undergraduate at Cambridge, for he was an omnivorous reader. Christopher Hassall has aptly pointed out that the greater influence on Brooke's poetry came from Marvell rather than from Donne, for it was in Marvell's poetry that gravity becomes transformed into humor and levity into seriousness. This is the tone of many of Brooke's later poems and particularly of his famous, "The Old Vicarage, Grantchester." Hassall maintains quite rightly that Brooke would have been wiser had he allowed the original title of "The Sentimental Exile" to remain, as it expressed more precisely the intended mood of the poem and would have cleared it of the charge of excessive sentimentality that has been brought against it. Clearly, the gravity is making fun of itself in the contrast between the stiff, regulated world of prewar Germany, symbolized by tulips, and the "unofficial" blooming roses of the Vicarage near Cambridge where Brooke had lived.

The two great experiences in Brooke's short life were his visit to the South Seas and the World War of 1914. The first of these came in 1913 after a complicated and unhappy love affair which has been called by his biographer "a deep sleep." The islands of the Pacific, then relatively unspoiled, provided a background, incredibly lush and exuberant, against which the poet's imagination could operate. That Brooke had always been a nature poet is obvious enough; in Tahiti, nature was so prodigal of its beauty that the pinks and carnations and lilacs of the Old Vicarage seemed tame and colorless. It was in this tropical atmosphere that Brooke wrote what is usually considered to be his finest prewar poem, "Tiare Tahiti," in which the sensuous world of the South Seas is combined with Platonic "ideas" treated half-playfully, half-seriously, a marriage of tropical images and metaphysical wit.

It is easy to understand the popularity of Brooke's early poems among young readers of both his own and later generations. They are frankly the work of a young man, deeply in love with life and candidly expressing the joys and the sorrows of his first encounter with the world, its beauty, and its grief. The poems are written in a language that is easy, natural, even colloquial, very beautiful as that term used to be understood. They lost their appeal when the whole attitude of youth changed as one of the results of the shattering explosion of World War I. To the more recent generations of young people, in whose toughened, cynical minds there seems to be little room for youth, these poems have nothing to say.

To read the biography of any Englishman of Brooke's generation is a haunting experience, for behind all the gaiety and brilliance of Georgian society loomed the dark shadow that was to engulf so many of these doomed young men. Brooke's brief part in the war is too well known to need repetition. Because of his charm, his good looks, his poetic promise, he soon became a symbol for the youth of England that was being slaughtered in the trenches.

It is a strange irony that the very qualities of Brooke's poetry that was written during the war are the very ones that have achieved the destruction of his once great reputation. Other war poets, particularly Wilfred Owen, have survived; Brooke has been rejected. The difference is that Brooke's death came early in the conflict, only eight months after its outbreak, when hopes were still high and when the horror of the trenches of Flanders had not yet turned poetry away from a celebration of heroism to a furious hatred of everything connected with the war. Later, the cynical disillusionment of the post-Armistice years completed the cycle. A public that remembered the appalling slaughter in France and that had read such books as *All Quiet on the Western Front* was very different from the reading public of 1915.

And yet—again ironically—Brooke did not glorify war. He accepted and rejoiced in the necessity of dying for his country; he paid tribute to those who had fallen. Further, his war poetry is small in bulk, consisting only of "1914," a sequence of five sonnets. These were written at Christmas of that year, when the war was but a few months old. For these poems he has been saddled with the reputation of being a "war poet" in the worst sense of the term. A contemporary critic, for example, has called these sonnets "decadent and puerile," a statement that is both unfair and inaccurate, for it assumes Brooke's ability to foresee the situation of 1918. What he might have felt, what he might have written, had he survived a few more years or had he seen the eventual battlefields of France, we, of course, cannot know; he might, had he lived, have written poems as bitter as those of Siegfried Sassoon or Wilfrid Owen. But because of his early death, he did become a symbol; and when the post-war reaction set in, he suffered accordingly. The symbol had lost its value.

Brooke's last years were crucial for English poetry. At the very moment when the Georgians were planning their annual anthology, there stood among them the tall figure of T. E. Hulme, who was preparing the dynamite that was to blow their whole poetic practice to bits. Hulme was one of those enigmatic, behind-the-scenes figures who occasionally turn up and are later recognized as having had far more influence than was apparent at the time. He, also, was killed in the war; his own poems, five in number, are undistinguished examples of the Imagist school. But just as Eliot supplied the model that later poetry was to copy all too faithfully, Hulme supplied the intellectual program. It was he who so violently attacked anything that savored of the "romantic" and who prophesied "a period of dry, hard, classical verse." Hulme and Eliot apparently never met, yet here were two forces working in the same direction. Clearly, the kind of poetry written by the Georgians was doomed; it could not survive the change in the intellectual climate that occurred after the war. Brooke, in spite of the youthful cynicism of some of his early poems, was a romantic in both senses of the word. At times he had premonitions of the type of poetry that is so fashionable today: the use of the deliberately "nonpoetic" in subject and detail. So much has taste changed that it is now hard to realize that his sonnet "A Channel Passage" distressed his friends to the point that he was urged not to publish it. Yet its description of sea sickness is mild enough by modern standards.

By no stretch of the term can Brooke be called a great poet. What he might have become, had he not belonged to that tragic generation of Englishmen, we cannot know. His charm—and he undeniably has poetic charm—lies in a youthful exuberance, a boyishness, a love of life, an ability to laugh at himself. And his poetry has this advantage, noted in Hassall's biography: the Georgians were the last poets to attempt to bridge the gap between poet and reader, to attempt to draw the reader to them. The "dry, hard, classical verse" predicted by Hulme, with its tortured syntax, private references, deliberate obscurity, may present a greater intellectual challenge but it has lost its readers.

Bibliography

Bergonzi, Bernard. *Heroes' Twilight: A Study of the Literature of the Great War.* New York: Coward-McCann, 1966, pp. 32–59.

De La Mare, Walter John. *Pleasures and Speculations.* London: Faber and Faber, 1940, pp. 172–199.

Hynes, Samuel Lynn. *Edwardian Occasions: Essays on English Writing in the Early Twentieth Century.* New York: Oxford, 1972, pp. 144–152.

Johnston, John H. *English Poetry of the First World War: A Study of the Evolution of Lyric and Narrative Form.* Princeton, N.J.: Princeton University Press, 1964, pp. 25–36.

Knight, G.W. "Rupert Brooke," in *Promise of Greatness: The War of 1914–1918.* Edited by George Andrew Panichas. New York: Day, 1968, pp. 488–502.

Pearsall, Robert Brainard. *Rupert Brooke: The Man and Poet.* Amsterdam: Rodopi, 1974.

Rogers, Timothy. "Rupert Brooke: Man and Monument," in *English.* XVII (1968), pp. 79–84.

————. *Rupert Brooke: A Reappraisal and Selection.* London: Routledge and Kegan Paul, 1971, pp. 180–190.

Ross, Robert H. *The Georgian Revolt, 1910–1922.* Carbondale: Southern Illinois Press, 1965, pp. 92–96.

Ward, Alfred Charles. "Rupert Brooke and the Soldier Poets," in *Twentieth Century Literature, 1901–1940.* London: Longmans, 1940, pp. 166–172.

Weygandt, Cornelius. *Time of Yeats: English Poetry of Today Against an American Background.* New York: Appleton, 1937, pp. 363–385.

Woodberry, George Edward. "Introduction," in *The Collected Poems of Rupert Brooke.* New York: Dodd, Mead, 1939, pp. 3–14.

JOSEPH CONRAD
Jósef Teodor Konrad Nalecz Korzeniowski

Born: Berdyczew, Poland (December 3 or 6, 1857)
Died: Bishopsbourne, England (August 3, 1924)

Principal Works

NOVELS: *Almayer's Folly*, 1895; *An Outcast of the Islands*, 1896; *The Nigger of the "Narcissus,"* 1897; *Lord Jim*, 1900; *The Inheritors*, 1901 (with Ford Madox Hueffer [Ford]); *Romance*, 1903 (with F. M. Hueffer [Ford]); *Nostromo*, 1904; *The Secret Agent*, 1907; *Under Western Eyes*, 1911; *Chance*, 1914; *Victory*, 1915; *The Shadow-Line*, 1917; *The Arrow of Gold*, 1919; *The Rescue*, 1920; *The Rover*, 1923; *The Nature of a Crime*, 1924 (with F. M. Hueffer [Ford]); *Suspense*, 1925 (unfinished).

SHORT STORIES AND TALES: *Tales of Unrest*, 1898 ("Karain: A Memory," "The Idiots," "An Outpost of Progress," "The Return," "The Lagoon"); *Typhoon*, 1902; *Youth: A Narrative, and Two Other Stories*, 1902 (*Heart of Darkness* and "The End of the Tether"); *Typhoon and Other Stories*, 1903 ("Amy Foster," "Falk," "Tomorrow"); *A Set of Six*, 1908 ("The Informer," "Gaspar Ruiz," "The Brute," "An Anarchist," "The Duel," "Il Conde"); *'Twixt Land and Sea*, 1912 ("A Smile of Fortune," "The Secret Sharer," "Freya of the Seven Isles"); *Within the Tides*, 1915 ("The Planter of Malata," "The Partner," "The Inn of the Two Witches," "Because of the Dollars"); *Tales of Hearsay*, 1925 ("The Warrior's Soul," "Prince Roman," "The Tale," "The Black Mate"); *The Sisters*, 1928; *The Complete Short Stories of Joseph Conrad*, 1933.

PLAYS: *One Day More*, 1917; *The Secret Agent*, 1921; *Laughing Anne*, 1923.

AUTOBIOGRAPHY: *The Mirror of the Sea*, 1906; *Some Reminiscences*, 1912 [*A Personal Record*].

ESSAYS AND STUDIES: *Notes on Life and Letters*, 1921; *Notes on My Books*, 1921; *Last Essays*, 1926.

LETTERS: *Joseph Conrad: Life and Letters*, edited by Gérard Jean-Aubry, 1927; *Joseph Conrad's Letters to His Wife*, 1927; *Conrad to a Friend*, edited by Richard Curle, 1928; *Letters from Joseph Conrad, 1895–1924*, edited by Edward Garnett, 1928; *Lettres françaises de Joseph Conrad*, edited by Gérard Jean-Aubry, 1929; *Letters of Joseph Conrad to Marguerite Poradowska*, edited by John A. Gee and Paul J. Sturm, 1940.

Joseph Conrad, one of the finest novelists and stylists of modern English literature, was born Teodor Jósef Konrad Nalecz Korzeniowski at Berdyczew, in the Ukraine region of Poland, then under Russian rule, on December 3 or 6, 1857. The tradition of both families of Conrad's parentage—of his father, Apollo Nalecz Korzeniowski, a Polish writer, translator, patriot, and nationalist, and of his mother, Ewelina Bobrowska—both of them deriving from the "land-tilling gentry" of the old Poland with connections in the Almanach de Gotha, had for many years been ardently nationalistic, dedicated to the liberation of their country from the occupation of the three powers, Russia, Prussia, and Austria, who had overrun and divided her by the "crime of partition" in the late eighteenth century. In this cause three of Conrad's uncles had died or been exiled to Siberia, and his own father was in 1862 arrested for his activities in the secret Polish National Committee and sentenced to deportation in Russia. Apollo Korzeniowski took his wife and six-year-old son with him into that exile; and when both his parents died as a result of their hardship, Conrad was left an orphan in 1869. Under the guardianship of his uncle Tadeusz Bobrowski, he lived in Kiev and Cracow, attended the St. Anne High School in Cracow, then studied under a tutor, Mr. Pulman, of the University of Cracow, was given the freedom of that city in honor of his father, went on a vacation trip in 1873 with his tutor to Germany, Switzerland, and Italy, saw the sea for the first time from the Lido at Venice, and at the age of seventeen determined to leave his tragic homeland and seek his fortunes in western Europe.

From 1874 to 1878 he lived in southern France, at Marseilles, where he had gone by way of the Vienna Express "as a man might get into a dream." At Marseilles the adventurous and romantic inclinations of his nature found their first outlet. He frequented the *légitimiste* circles of the banker Delestang and his wife, to whom he had carried letters of introduction; and it was as an employee of the banking and shipping firm of Delestang that he entered the French marine service and had his apprenticeship at sea, first on the *Mont-Blanc* to the West Indies late in 1874, again on the *Mont-Blanc* to Martinique in 1875, then on the schooner *St.-Antoine* to the West Indies in 1876–1877. With several young Marseilles friends he also bought a small *tartane*, the *Tremolino*, in which he seems to have engaged in smuggling activities of some kind, possibly on behalf of the Carlists who were attempting to restore Don Carlos to the throne of Spain. He may also have become involved in a romantic relation with a lady of the Carlist circles in Marseilles, as the novel *The Arrow of Gold* suggests, but this matter remains unverified. What appears certain, from a recently discovered letter written by his uncle Tadeusz Bobrowski on March 24, 1879, is that the young Conrad became involved in serious debts in Marseilles and Monte Carlo, that his affairs in France ended in fiasco and serious personal difficulties, and that in these straits he made an attempt on his life. Bobrowski, and later Conrad himself, attempted to disguise this situation with the long-familiar story of a duel with the expatriate American, J. M. K. Blunt, a rival for the favors of "Rita de Lastaola." When he found himself wounded, deserted by his embarrassed Marseilles friends, and faced with the reproof of his guardian uncle who had hastened from Poland to Marseilles to see his disgraced nephew, Conrad determined to redeem himself by taking to the sea in earnest. He found a berth as a common seaman on a British freighter, the *Mavis*, carrying cargoes to the Eastern Mediterranean; and on June 18, 1878, he stepped for the first time on English soil at Lowestoft, "alone in the world," knowing little English, but now at last committed to a seaman's career.

From 1878 to 1894 Conrad spent sixteen years in the British Merchant Service or under various Eastern flags. His voyages took him to the Mediterranean, to Australia, to the Indian Ocean, to India, to Malaya, Sumatra, Java, Borneo, the Philippines, the coasts of China and Indochina, and around the world. He gained third mate status in 1880, first mate papers in 1883, and his master's papers in 1886, and he achieved his "first command" on the ship *Otago* in 1888–1889. In 1890 he made a harrowing and fateful journey up the Congo in the employ of the Société Anonyme Belge pour le Commerce du Haut-Congo, experiencing there illnesses and mental distress from which he suffered the rest of his life. His last berth was on the *Adowa* early in 1894, and when he returned to London on January 14, 1894, his career as a seaman was over, though he did not yet know it and tried for another six years to return to the stabler life of ships and sea-voyages.

It was at this point that he took up once more the manuscript of a tale he had been writing in the ships and ports of his journeys for five years, the story of a defeated Dutchman he had once known in a remote jungle country of Borneo. By agonized and persistent labor he finished the manuscript, sent it to a London publisher (T. Fisher Unwin), and in 1895 found, to his "perpetual surprise," his first book, *Almayer's Folly*, printed and bound in his hands and a career in literature opening to him. In 1896 he married an Englishwoman, Jessie George. In 1898 his first son, Borys, was born; a second, John Alexander, followed in 1906. He had been naturalized as a British subject in 1886; and now he found himself wholly identified with English life as citizen, author, family man, and professional writer.

Though the art and stylistic mastery of Conrad's books was early recognized by some of his most distinguished contemporaries, Henry James, George Gissing, H. G. Wells, Stephen Crane, and Cunninghame Graham among them, success in any practical or popular sense was many years in coming to him. But his working life now became wholly dedicated to authorship, and his last twenty-nine years saw his books appear in continuous succession. His first novels, *Almayer's Folly* and *An Outcast of the Islands*, were tales of Eastern kingdoms and of European exiles who had met their fate in them; but with *The Nigger of the "Narcissus"* in 1897 he turned to his own memories of the sea and wrote his first masterpiece of style and dramatic narration. "Youth," his first notable short story, told of his first discovery of the East; "Heart of Darkness," a sovereign masterwork of moral and symbolic drama, dealt with his Congo journey of 1890; *Typhoon* showed his descriptive powers at their highest; and with *Lord Jim*, in 1900, he achieved his first long novel of classic dimensions in the tale of a dishonored English seaman seeking the recovery of his honor and self-respect in the East.

After collaborating on two minor novels with Ford Madox Hueffer [Ford], Conrad now turned to his most prodigious fear of imaginative creation in the long novel *Nostromo*, a complex drama of civil strife and rival moralities in the South American republic of Costaguana; and the subject of political intrigue or tragedy was to be carried further in *The Secret Agent* and in *Under Western Eyes*, two novels of the "international evil" and Russian danger which he saw as a threat to the stability of Europe and her traditional institutions. *Chance* was his attempt at a modern drama of social persecution and alienation. *Victory* brought his central subject of disillusioned skepticism and the test it imposes on character to its most concise symbolic terms. *The Shadow-Line* treated the experience of his "first command" on the *Otago* in 1888–1889. The minor novel, *The Arrow of Gold*, revived the memory of his Marseilles years and Carlist adventures of 1874–1878. Two works of autobiography had punctuated these fictions: *The Mirror of the Sea* in 1906, and *Some Reminiscences* (later retitled *A Personal Record*) in 1912. Conrad had also written continuously in the shorter forms, and while many of these stories are distinctly minor, some of them achieve his keenest powers of atmospheric and symbolic narrative—"Amy Foster," "Falk," "The Brute," "Il Conde," "Freya of the Seven Isles," and notably the brilliant tale which is a key-story among his works, "The Secret Sharer." His last two completed novels, *The Rescue* and *The Rover*, though personally and thematically significant, show a marked decline in his qualities; and *Suspense* (posthumously published in 1925), which followed *The Rover* as a tale of Napoleonic France, was left half finished when Conrad died suddenly of a heart attack at Oswalds, his last English home, at Bishopsbourne, near Canterbury, on August 3, 1924. He was buried at Canterbury.

Conrad's widest fame perhaps attaches to his tales of the sea and of the East, and he is likewise celebrated as a writer of romantic and heroic subjects. To both these designations he came to object, and his finest work in fact corrects them. For Conrad is basically a tragic novelist, as he is also essentially a moral and psychological realist whose profounder themes are concerned with problems of guilt and honor, with the tests of conscience and moral justice, and with the secret recriminatory and retributive processes of the human personality. Inclined to the moral and historical pessimism of a constitutional skepticism, he was at the same time impelled toward the principles of that "human solidarity" he insistently invoked as a standard of action and moral commitment; and his characteristic tales show a drama of character forced out of the illusions, isolation, self-deception, or nihilism of the private or uncommitted temperament into the larger moral coherence of society and of humanity. And while some of his richest writing comes in his descriptive and atmospheric art, his greater powers appear when he makes the form and structure of his tales, as well as their stylistic detail and analysis, convey the processes of character, of conscience, and of moral justice. It was for this purpose that he advanced out of impressionism into dramatic and moral realism, out of a richly sensuous art into an art of structural intricacy and analytical capacities. His finest novels and tales show him to be an artist scarcely surpassed in his English generation for the probity of his moral vision, the originality of his plotting and construction, and the searching accuracy of his style. When he wrote his artistic credo in the "Preface" to *The Nigger of the "Narcissus"* in 1897, he not only defined the moral idea to which he addressed himself—"the solidarity in mysterious origin, in toil, in joy, in hope in uncertain fate, which binds men to each other and all mankind to the visible world"—but also specified the "task" to which he dedicated his talent: "My task which I am trying to achieve is, by the power of the written word, to make you hear, to make you feel—it is, before all, to make you *see*. That—and no more, and it is everything." By his loyalty to those two principles Conrad made himself a master not only of moral vision but of an art which at its best defines one of the most austere aesthetic purposes in modern fiction, and sets a standard in the novel of the twentieth century.

Bibliography

Joseph Conrad's work has been collected in various editions and collections. Those published in New York include the Sun Dial Edition, 1920–1921; the Concord, 1923; the Canterbury, 1924; the Memorial, 1925, and the Malay, 1927. The Uniform Edition, 22 vols., London, 1923–1928, is complete except for *The Nature of a Crime* and the plays. The Collected Edition, 1946 ff., is a reprint. One-volume selections include *A Conrad Argosy*, edited by William McFee, 1942; *The Conrad Reader*, edited by A. J. Hoppé, 1946 (reprinted as *The Conrad Companion*, 1948); and *The Portable Conrad*, edited by Morton Dauwen Zabel, 1947, 1957.

A recent biography is Frederick R. Karl, *Joseph Conrad: The Three Lives*, 1979. The definitive biography is Jocelyn Baines, *Joseph Conrad: A Critical Biography*, 1960; see also Gérard Jean-Aubry's *Vie de Conrad*, 1947, translated by Helen Sebba as *The Sea Dreamer: A Definitive Biography of Joseph Conrad* 1957. Important source material is contained also in G. Jean-Aubry, *Joseph Conrad: Life and Letters*, 1927, and in other collections of letters previously cited. For biographical information see also (Mrs.) Jessie Conrad, *Joseph Conrad as I Knew Him*, 1926, and *Joseph Conrad and His Circle*, 1935; Richard Curle, *The Last Twelve Years of Joseph Conrad*, 1928; Gustav Morf, *The Polish Heritage of Joseph Conrad*, 1930; John Dozier Gordan, *Joseph Conrad: The Making of a Novelist*, 1940; and J. H. Retinger, *Conrad and His Contemporaries*, 1941. (See also Jocelyn Baines, "The Affair in Marseilles," *London Magazine*, IV (November, 1957), 41–46, and "The Young Conrad in Marseilles," *London Times Literary Supplement*, LVI (December 6, 1957), 748.

Among the critical studies, Gordan's *Joseph Conrad* is also important for its account of Conrad's sources. The field of Conrad criticism is extensive. Among the earlier studies are the following: Richard Curle, *Joseph Conrad: A Study*, 1914; Wilson Follett, *Joseph Conrad: A Short Study*, 1915; Hugh Walpole, *Joseph Conrad*, 1916; Ruth M. Stauffer, *Joseph Conrad: His Romantic Realism*, 1922; Ernst Bendz, *Joseph Conrad: An Appreciation*, 1923; and Ford Madox Ford, *Joseph Conrad: A Personal Remembrance*, 1924. Later studies, written after Conrad's death, include Arthur Symons, *Notes on Joseph Conrad*, 1925; R. L. Mégroz, *Joseph Conrad's Mind and Method*, 1931; William W. Bancroft, *Joseph Conrad: His Philosophy of Life*, 1933; Edward Crankshaw, *Joseph Conrad: Some Aspects of the Art of the Novel*, 1936; Josef Ujejski, *Joseph Conrad*,

1939; M. C. Bradbrook, *Joseph Conrad: Poland's English Genius*, 1941; Albert Guerard, Jr., *Joseph Conrad*, 1947; Walter F. Wright, *Romance and Tragedy in Joseph Conrad*, 1949; Oliver Warner, *Joseph Conrad*, 1951; Douglas Hewitt, *Conrad: A Reassessment*, 1952; Paul L. Wiley, *Conrad's Measure of Man*, 1954; E. H. Visiak, *The Mirror of Conrad*, 1955; Thomas Moser, *Joseph Conrad: Achievement and Decline*, 1957; Richard Curle, *Joseph Conrad and His Characters*, 1957; Ludwick Krzyzanowski, ed., *Joseph Conrad: Centennial Essays*, 1960; and John A. Palmer, *Joseph Conrad's Fiction: A Study in Literary Growth*, 1968.

Some notably important short essays or studies include Henry James, "The New Novel," in *Notes on Novelists*, 1914; H. L. Mencken, "Joseph Conrad," in *A Book of Prefaces*, 1917; "Hommage à Joseph Conrad," with essays by André Gide, Paul Valéry, H. R. Lenormand, G. Jean-Aubry, André Maurois, André Chevrillon, Edmond Jaloux, Ramon Fernandez, and others, *Nouvelle Revue Française*, Nouvelle Série, CXXXV (December 1, 1924), 649–806; Joseph Warren Beach, "Conrad: Impressionism," in *The Twentieth Century Novel*, 1932; Thomas Mann, "Joseph Conrad's *The Secret Angent*," in *Past Masters and Other Papers*, 1933; E. M. Forster, "Joseph Conrad: A Note," in *Abinger Harvest*, 1936; V. S. Pritchett, "A Pole in the Far East," in *The Living Novel*, 1947; Morton Dauwen Zabel, Introduction to *The Portable Conrad*, 1947, 1957; *idem*, "Conrad: Chance and Recognition," "The East and the Sea," "The Threat to the West," "Conrad in His Age," in *Craft and Character*, 1957; F. R. Leavis, "Joseph Conrad," in *The Great Tradition*, 1949; and Dorothy van Ghent, "On *Lord Jim*," in *The English Novel: Form and Function*, 1953. Introductions written for the following novels are also of critical importance: Morton Dauwen Zabel, *The Nigger of the "Narcissus,"* Harper Modern Classics, 1950; *Under Western Eyes*, New Directions edition, 1951; and *Lord Jim*, Houghton Mifflin Riverside Editions, 1958; Robert Penn Warren, *Nostromo*, Modern Library edition, 1951; and Robert B. Heilman, *Lord Jim*, Rinehart Editions, 1957.

The Joseph Conrad Number of *Modern Fiction Studies*, I (February, 1955), contains a selected checklist of Conrad criticism with an index to studies of the separate works, 30–45. A more complete study of this kind is *Joseph Conrad at Mid-Century: Editions and Studies, 1895–1955*, by Kenneth A. Lohf and Eugene P. Sheehy, 1957.

HEART OF DARKNESS

Type of work: Short story
Author: Joseph Conrad (Józef Teodor Konrad Korzeniowski, 1857–1924)
Type of plot: Symbolic romance
Time of plot: Late nineteenth century
Locale: The Belgian Congo
First published: 1902

> *Both an adventure story and the account of a philosophical and moral quest, this tale takes the reader on a symbolic journey into the blackness central to the heart and soul of man. A vagueness at its core has detracted little from the story's power and continued popularity.*

Principal Characters

Marlow, the narrator and impartial observer of the action, who becomes the central figure when the story is interpreted psychologically. He makes a trip into the center of Africa which becomes, symbolically, a journey toward the essential meaning of life. After talking with Kurtz, with whom he identifies himself, he is able to see deeply into his own being.

Mr. Kurtz, manager of an inland trading station in the Belgian Congo. After having arrived in the Congo with high ideals and a self-imposed mission to civilize the natives, he is instead converted by them to savagery. His awareness of his downfall and his conviction that evil is at the heart of everything is revealed in a long talk which he has with Marlow.

The District Manager, an avowed enemy of Mr. Kurtz. His only interest is in collecting as much ivory as possible, and he is totally unaware of the central darkness.

A Russian Traveler, an admirer and disciple of Mr. Kurtz, but one who thought Kurtz lived before his time.

Kurtz's Fiancée, whom Marlow allows to retain her belief in Kurtz's goodness and power.

The Story

A group of men were sitting on the deck of the cruising yawl, *The Nellie*, anchored one calm evening in the Thames estuary. One of the seamen, Marlow, began reflecting that the Thames area had been, at the time of the invading Romans, one of the dark and barbarous areas of the earth. Dwelling on this theme, he then began to tell a story of the blackest, most barbarous area of the earth that he had experienced.

Through his aunt's connections, Marlow had once secured a billet as commander of a river steamer for one of the trading companies with interests in the Belgian Congo. When he went to Belgium to learn more about the job, he found that few of the officials of the company expected him to return alive. In Brussels he also heard of the distinguished Mr. Kurtz, the powerful and intelligent man who was educating the natives and at the same time sending back record shipments of ivory.

The mysterious figure of Mr. Kurtz fascinated Marlow. In spite of the ominous hints that he gathered from various company officials, he became more and more curious about what awaited him in the Congo. During his journey, as he passed along the African coast, he reflected that the wilderness and the unknown seemed to seep right out to the sea. Many of the trading posts and stations the ship passed were dilapidated and looked barbaric. Finally, Marlow arrived at the seat of the government at the mouth of the river. Again, he heard of the great distinction and power of Mr. Kurtz who had, because of his plans to enlighten the natives and his success in gaining their confidence, an enormous reputation. Marlow also saw natives working in the hot sun until they collapsed and died. Marlow had to wait for ten impatient days at the government site because his work would not begin until he reached the district manager's station, two hundred miles up the river. At last the expedition left for the district station.

Marlow arrived at the district station to find that the river steamer had sunk a few days earlier. He met the district manager, a man whose only ability seemed to be the ability to survive. The district manager, unconcerned with the fate of the natives, was interested only in getting out of the country; he felt that Mr. Kurtz's new methods were ruining the whole district. The district manager reported also that he had not heard from Kurtz for quite some time, but had received disquieting rumors about his being ill.

Although he was handicapped by a lack of rivets, Marlow spent months supervising repairs to the antiquated river steamer. He also overheard a conversation which revealed that the district manager was Kurtz's implacable enemy, who hoped that the climate would do away with his rival.

The steamer was finally ready for use, and Marlow, along with the district manager, sailed to visit Kurtz at the inner station far up the river. The journey was difficult and perilous; the water was shallow; there were frequent fogs. Just as they arrived within a few miles of Kurtz's station, natives attacked the vessel with spears and arrows. Marlow's helmsman, a faithful native, was killed by a long spear when he leaned from his window to fire at the savages. Marlow finally blew the steamboat whistle and the sound frightened the natives away. The district manager was sure that Kurtz had lost control over the blacks. When they docked, they met an enthusiastic Russian traveler who told them that Kurtz was gravely ill.

While the district manager visited Kurtz, the Russian told Marlow that the sick man had become corrupted by the very natives he had hoped to enlighten. He still had power over the natives, but instead of his changing them, they had debased him into an atavistic savage. Kurtz attended native rituals, had killed frequently in order to get ivory, and had hung heads as decorations outside his hut. Later Marlow met Kurtz and found that the man had, indeed, been corrupted by the evil at the center of experience. Marlow learned, from the Russian, that Kurtz had ordered the natives to attack the steamer, thinking that, if they did so, the white men would run away and leave Kurtz to die among his fellow savages in the wilderness. Talking to Marlow, Kurtz showed his awareness of how uncivilized he had become, how his plans to educate the natives had reversed. He gave Marlow a packet of letters for his fiancée in Belgium and the manuscript of an article, written sometime earlier, in which he urged efforts to educate the natives.

The district manager and Marlow took Kurtz, now on a stretcher, to the river steamer to take him back home. The district manager contended that the area was now ruined for collecting ivory. Kurtz, full of despair and the realization that devouring evil was at the heart of everything, died while the steamer was temporarily stopped for repairs.

Marlow returned to civilization and, about a year later, went to Belgium to see Kurtz's fiancée. She still thought of Kurtz as the splendid and powerful man who had gone to Africa with a mission, and she still believed in his goodness and power. When she asked Marlow what Kurtz's last words had been, Marlow lied and told her that Kurtz had asked for her at the end. In reality, Kurtz, who had seen all experience, had in his final words testified to the horror of it all. This horror was not something, Marlow felt, that civilized ladies could, or should, understand.

Critical Evaluation

Criticism of Conrad's work in general and *Heart of Darkness* in particular has been both extensive and varied. Many critics concern themselves with Conrad's style; others focus on the biographical aspects of his fiction; some see the works as social commentaries; some are students of Conrad's explorations into human psychology; many are interested in the brooding, shadowy symbolism and philosophy that hovers over all the works. It is easy to see, therefore, that Conrad is a distinctively complex literary genius. E. M. Forster censured him as a vague and elusive writer who never quite clearly discloses the philosophy that lies behind his tales. Such a censure ignores Conrad's notion about the way some fiction can be handled. Partly as Conrad's mouthpiece, the narrator of *Heart of Darkness* states in the first few pages of the novel:

> The yarns of seamen have a direct simplicity, the whole meaning of which lies within the shell of a cracked nut. But Marlow was not typical (if his propensity to spin yarns be excepted), and to him the meaning of an episode was not inside like a kernel but outside, enveloping the tale which brought it out only as a glow brings out a haze, in the likeness of one of

those misty halos that sometimes are made visible by the spectral illumination of moonshine.

The mention of the narrator brings up one of the most complex and intriguing features of *Heart of Darkness*: its carefully executed and elaborately conceived point of view. For one can detect (if careful in his reading) that the novel is in truth two narratives, inexorably woven together by Conrad's masterful craftsmanship. The outer frame of the story—the immediate setting—involves the unnamed narrator who is apparently the only one on the *Nellie* who is profoundly affected by Marlow's tale, the inner story which is the bulk of the entire novella. Marlow narrates, and the others listen passively. The narrator's closing words show his feeling at the conclusion of Marlow's recounting of the events in the Congo:

> Marlow ceased, and sat apart, indistinct and silent, in the pose of a meditating Buddha. Nobody moved for a time. "We have lost the first of the ebb," said the Director suddenly. I raised my head. The offing was barred by a black bank of clouds, and the tranquil waterway leading to the uttermost ends of the earth flowed sombre under an overcast sky—seemed to lead into the heart of an immense darkness.

Since Marlow's narrative is a tale devoted primarily to a journey to the mysterious dark continent (the literal heart of darkness, Africa), a superficial view of the tale is simply that it is essentially an elaborate story involving confrontation with exotic natives, treacherous dangers of the jungle, brutal savagery, and even cannibalism. But such a view ignores larger meanings with which the work is implicitly concerned: namely, social and cultural implications; psychological workings of the cultivated European left to the uncivilized wilderness; and the richly colored fabric of symbolism that emerges slowly but inevitably from beneath the surface.

Heart of Darkness can also be examined for its social and cultural commentaries. It is fairly obvious that a perverted version of the "White Man's Burden" was the philosophy adopted by the ivory hunters at the Inner Station. Kurtz's "Exterminate the brutes!" shows the way a white man can exploit the helpless savage. The futile shelling from the gunboat into the jungle is also vividly portrayed as a useless, brutal, and absurd act perpetrated against a weaker, more uncivilized culture than the one that nurtured Kurtz.

Here the psychological phenomena of Marlow's tale emerge. Kurtz, a man relieved of all social and civilized restraints, goes mad after committing himself to the total pursuit of evil and depravity. And his observation "The horror! the horror!" suggests his final realization of the consequences of his life. Marlow realizes this too and is allowed (because he forces restraint upon himself) to draw back his foot from the precipice of madness. The experience leaves Marlow sober, disturbed, meditative, and obsessed with relating his story in much the same way Coleridge's Ancient Mariner must also relate his story.

On a symbolic level the story is rich; a book could easily be written on this facet of the novel. An arbitrary mention of some of the major symbols must suffice here: the Congo River that reminded Marlow early in his youth of a snake as it uncoiled its length into the darknes of Africa and furnished him with an uncontrollable "fascination of the abomination"; the symbolic journey into man's own heart of darkness revealing blindingly the evil of man's own nature and his capacity for evil; the irony of the quest when the truth is revealed not in terms of light but in terms of darkness (the truth brings not light but rather total darkness). The entire symbolic character of the work is capsuled at the end of Marlow's tale when he is forced to lie to Kurtz's intended spouse in order to preserve her illusion; the truth appears to Marlow as an inescapable darkness and the novel ends with the narrator's own observation of darkness.

Heart of Darkness is one of literature's most sombre fictions. It explores the fundamental questions about man's nature: his capacity for evil; the necessity for restraint; the effect of physical darkness and isolation on a civilized soul; and the necessity of relinquishing pride for one's own spiritual salvation. E. M. Forster's censure of Conrad may be correct in many ways, but it refuses to admit that through such philosophical ruminations Conrad has allowed generations of readers to ponder humanity's own heart of darkness.

Bibliography

Andreas, Osborn. *Joseph Conrad: A Study in Non-Conformity.* New York: Philosophical Library, 1959, pp. 46–54.

Baines, Jocelyn. *Joseph Conrad: A Critical Biography.* New York: McGraw-Hill, 1960, pp. 223–230.

Berthoud, Jacques. *Joseph Conrad: The Major Phase.* New York: Cambridge University Press, 1978, pp. 41–63.

Collins, Harold R. "Kurtz, the Cannibals, and the Second-Rate Helmsman," in *Western Humanities Review.* VIII (1954), pp. 299–310. Reprinted in *Joseph Conrad's* Heart of Darkness: *Backgrounds and Criticisms.* Edited by Leonard Dean. Englewood Cliffs, N.J.: Prentice-Hall, 1960, pp. 149–159.

Crews, Frederick C. "Conrad's Uneasiness—and Ours," in *Out of My System: Psychoanalysis, Ideology, and Critical Method.* New York: Oxford University Press, 1975, pp. 41–62.

Daleski, Herman M. *Joseph Conrad, The Way of Dispossession.* New York: Holmes and Meier, 1977, pp. 51–76.

Dowden, Wilfred S. "The Light and the Dark: Imagery and Thematic Development in Conrad's *Heart of Darkness*," in *Rice Institute Pamphlet*. XLIV (1958), pp. 33–51. Reprinted in *Conrad's* Heart of Darkness *and the Critics*. Edited by Bruce Harkness. San Francisco: Wadsworth, 1960, pp. 137–145.

Evans, Robert O. "Conrad's Underworld," in *Modern Fiction Studies*. II (1956), pp. 56–62. Reprinted in *The Art of Joseph Conrad: A Critical Symposium*. Edited by Robert W. Stallman. East Lansing: Michigan State University Press, 1960, pp. 171–178. Also reprinted in *Conrad's* Heart of Darkness *and the Critics*. Edited by Bruce Harkness. San Francisco: Wadsworth, 1960, pp. 137–145.

Feder, Lillian. "Marlow's Descent into Hell," in *Nineteenth Century Fiction*. IX (1955), pp. 280–292. Reprinted in *The Art of Joseph Conrad: A Critical Symposium*. Edited by Robert W. Stallman. East Lansing: Michigan State University Press, 1960, pp. 162–170. Also reprinted in *Heart of Darkness*. Edited by Robert Kimbrough. New York: Norton, 1963, pp. 186–189.

Guerard, Albert J. *Conrad the Novelist*. Cambridge, Mass.: Harvard University Press, 1958, pp. 33–48. Reprinted in *Joseph Conrad's* Heart of Darkness: *Backgrounds and Criticisms*. Englewood Cliffs, N.J.: Prentice-Hall, 1960, pp. 166–177. Also reprinted in *Conrad's* Heart of Darkness *and the Critics*. Edited by Bruce Harkness. San Francisco: Wadsworth, 1960, pp. 111–119. Also reprinted in *Modern British Fiction: Essays in Criticism*. Edited by Mark Schorer. New York: Oxford University Press, 1961, pp. 110–118. Also reprinted in *Heart of Darkness*. Edited by Robert Kimbrough. New York: Norton, 1963, pp. 168–176. Also reprinted in *The Personal Voice*. Edited by Albert J. Guerard. Philadelphia: Lippincott, 1964, pp. 464–474.

Gurko, Leo. *Joseph Conrad: Giant in Exile*. New York: Macmillan, 1962, pp. 148–163. Reprinted in *Heart of Darkness*. Edited by Robert Kimbrough. New York: Norton, 1963, pp. 218–223.

Haugh, Robert F. *Joseph Conrad: Discovery in Design*. Norman: University of Oklahoma Press, 1957, pp. 35–55. Reprinted in *Heart of Darkness*. Edited by Robert Kimbrough. New York: Norton, 1963, pp. 163–167.

Hewitt, Douglas. *Conrad: A Reassessment*. Cambridge: Bowes and Bowes, 1952, pp. 31–39. Reprinted in *Conrad's* Heart of Darkness *and the Critics*. Edited by Bruce Harkness. San Francisco: Wadsworth, 1960, pp. 103–111.

Karl, Frederick R. *A Reader's Guide to Joseph Conrad*. New York: Noonday, 1960, pp. 133–140.

Krieger, Murray. *The Tragic Vision*. New York: Holt, Rinehart and Winston, 1960, pp. 154–165.

Leavis, F.R. "Joseph Conrad," in *Scrutiny*. X (June, 1941), pp 23–32. Reprinted in *The Great Tradition: George Eliot, Henry James, Joseph Conrad*. London: Chatto and Windus, 1948, pp. 174–182. Reprinted in *Critiques and Essays on Modern Fiction*. Edited by John W. Aldridge. New York: Ronald, 1952, pp. 107–113. Also reprinted in *Modern British Fiction: Essays* *in Criticism.* Edited by Mark Schorer. New York: Oxford University Press, 1961, pp. 88–92.

McClure, John A.   "The Rhetoric of Restraint in *Heart of Darkness*," in *Nineteenth-Century Fiction.* XXXII (December, 1977), pp. 310–326.

Mudrick, Marvin.   "The Originality of Conrad," in *Hudson Review.* XI (1958), pp. 545–553. Reprinted in *Conrad's* Heart of Darkness *and the Critics.* Edited by Bruce Harkness. San Francisco: Wadsworth, 1960, pp. 135–136. Also reprinted in *Heart of Darkness.* Edited by Robert Kimbrough. New York: Norton, 1963, pp. 207–211. Also reprinted in *Conrad: A Collection of Critical Essays.* Edited by Marvin Mudrick. Englewood Cliffs, N.J.: Prentice-Hall, 1966, pp. 37–44.

Reid, Stephen A.   "The 'Unspeakable Rites' in *Heart of Darkness*," in *Modern Fiction Studies.* IX (Winter, 1963–1964), pp. 347–356. Reprinted in *Conrad: A Collection of Critical Essays.* Edited by Marvin Mudrick. Englewood Cliffs, N.J.: Prentice-Hall, 1966, pp. 45–54.

Ridley, Florence H.   "The Ultimate Meaning of *Heart of Darkness*," in *Nineteenth-Century Fiction.* XVIII (1963), pp. 43–53.

Ryf, Robert S.   "Joseph Conrad," in *Six Modern British Novelists.* Edited by George Stade. New York: Columbia University Press, 1974, pp. 145–149.

Singh, Frances B.   "The Colonialistic Bias of *Heart of Darkness*," in *Conradiana.* X (1978), pp. 41–54.

Thale, Jerome.   "Marlow's Quest," in *University of Toronto Quarterly.* XXIV (1955), pp. 351–358. Reprinted in *The Art of Joseph Conrad: A Critical Symposium.* Edited by Robert W. Stallman. East Lansing: Michigan State University Press, 1960, pp. 154–161. Also reprinted in *Joseph Conrad's* Heart of Darkness: *Backgrounds and Criticisms.* Edited by Leonard Dean. Englewood Cliffs, N.J.: Prentice-Hall, 1960, pp. 159–166. Also reprinted in *Heart of Darkness.* Edited by Robert Kimbrough. New York: Norton, 1963, pp. 180–186.

Watt, Ian Pierre.   "Impressionism and Symbolism in *Heart of Darkness*," in *Joseph Conrad: A Commemoration.* Edited by Norman Sherry. New York: Barnes & Noble, 1977, pp. 37–53.

Watts, C.T.   "*Heart of Darkness*: The Covert Murder-Plot and the Darwinian Theme," in *Conradiana.* VII (1975), pp. 137–143.

LORD JIM

Type of work: Novel
Author: Joseph Conrad (Józef Teodor Konrad Korzeniowski, 1857–1924)
Type of plot: Psychological romance
Time of plot: Late nineteenth century
Locale: Ports and islands of the East
First published: 1900

A psychological novel in the setting of an adventure story, Lord Jim *has achieved renown for its breakthrough in narrative technique; the complicated manner in which the story is told has been copied and adapted by many writers. Through this device, Conrad avoids a direct judgment of his protagonist and leaves the reader to evaluate Jim's character.*

Principal Characters

Jim, a British seaman and chief mate of the "Patna." When the ship seems sinking, after striking a submerged derelict, he jumps at the call of the officers who have already abandoned the ship and her pilgrim passengers. The "Patna" does not sink but is discovered by a French gunboat and towed to port. Jim and his three companions are sighted and brought to port separately. After the investigation Jim spends the remainder of his life trying to regain his heroic conception of himself and to prove to men that it was not "he" who jumped. Finally, on the island of Patusan, he earns from the natives the title of Lord Jim and faces up to his death in a heroic manner.

Marlow, an intelligent sea captain and "insatiably curious psychological observer" who sympathizes with Jim and aids him. Narrating most of the story, he says Jim is "one of us," meaning, perhaps, that he is neither maliciously evil nor moderately good.

Captain Brierly, the "unimpeachable professional seaman" and a nautical assessor at the inquiry into the desertion of the "Patna." He identifies himself with Jim in some strange way. Awakened to man's vulnerability, perhaps, he commits suicide on his next voyage.

The French Lieutenant, an unimaginatively brave man who stays aboard the "Patna" for thirty hours while she is being towed to port. He never thinks that he has been heroic.

Stein, a trader who is also a naturalist and a moral philosopher. He gives Jim a chance to have his dream of rehabilitation come true by making him the agent for his enterprises on the island of Patusan.

Chester, a loathsome creature who has been everything but a pirate. He offers Jim a job which would exile him on a guano island for life because, as he says, Jim "is no earthly good for anything else." He mistakes Jim for one of his own kind.

Cornelius, the former unsuccessful agent for Stein on Patusan. He resents Jim and finally aids Brown in causing Jim's destruction.

Gentleman Brown, a renegade who with a cutthroat crew lands on Patusan to get supplies, but remains to rob and plunder. In sympathy, not understanding Brown's deceit, Jim makes a pact with him. Brown's deception results in Jim's death.

Doramin, the leader of Patusan natives with whom Jim makes friends, earning the title of Lord Jim. When Doramin's son is killed because of Jim's misjudgment, Doramin is bound by honor to kill Jim.

Dain Waris, Doramin's son and Jim's friend, killed treacherously by Brown. By his error in judgment Jim is responsible for his friend's death.

The Rajah, the ruler of the natives on Patusan; he unsuccessfully opposes Jim.

Tamb' Itam, the faithful servant of Jim on Patusan.

Kossim, the confidant of the Rajah.

Sherif Ali, a wandering stranger, an Arab half-breed, who invites tribes from the interior to form a third force on Patusan.

The Captain, the German skipper of the "Patna," who abandoned his ship and its load of passengers without remorse.

The Chief Engineer, who swears that he saw the ship go down.

The Second Engineer, who also seems to have no remorse for abandoning the ship.

Captain O'Brien, a large, noisy old man who says that abandoning the "Patna" was a disgrace.

Captain Jones, the first mate serving under Captain Brierly. He finds it hard to explain Brierly's suicide, all the more because he did not like Brierly while the man was alive.

Captain Robinson, an old renegade who has done almost everything from opium smuggling to stealing. Chester takes him in on the guano deal because Robinson has some money.

Jewel, Jim's native wife on Patusan. She finds it difficult to understand his ideals.

The Story

Jim was an outcast, a wanderer. Hired as water clerk in seaports throughout the East, he would keep his job only until his identity became known. Then he would move on. The story of Lord Jim began when he determined to leave home to go to sea. Accordingly, his father obtained a berth for him as an officer candidate and he began his service. Although he loved the sea, his beginning was not heroic. Almost at once he was injured and was left behind in an Eastern port. When he recovered, he accepted a berth as chief mate aboard an ancient steamer, the *Patna*, carrying Moslem pilgrims on their way to Mecca.

The steamer was unseaworthy, her German captain a gross coward, her chief engineer liquor-soaked. One sultry night in the Red Sea the ship struck a floating object. The captain sent Jim to check.

A month later Jim testified in court that when he went to investigate he found the forward hold rapidly filling with sea water. Hearing his report, the captain declared the *Patna* would sink quickly and give orders to abandon ship. At first Jim was determined to stand by his post. At the last minute, on sudden impulse, he jumped to join the other white men in the lifeboat they had launched. The pilgrims were left aboard the sinking vessel.

But the *Patna* had not sunk. A French gunboat overtook the vessel and towed it and the abandoned passengers into port without its chief officers aboard.

Marlow, a white man, sat at the inquiry. Later, he took up the thread of the story as he had learned it from Jim. Something in Jim was fixed to Marlow's memory so that he was forced to recall the event and to tell the story to friends as long as he lived; it became a part of his own life.

It always began the same way. First there had come a cable from Aden telling that the *Patna*, abandoned by its officers, had been towed into port. Then two weeks later the captain, the two engineers, and Jim had come ashore, their boat having been picked up by a steamer of the Dale Line. They were whisked into court at once for the investigation. The captain lost his papers for deserting his ship, and he stormed away declaring that his disgrace did not matter; he would become an American citizen.

The chief engineer went to a hospital. There, raving in delirium tremens, he declared he had seen the *Patna* go down. The *Patna* was full of reptiles when she sank, he declared. He also declared that the space under his bed was crammed with pink toads. The second engineer, his arm broken, was also in the hospital. Neither was called to testify.

Jim, with his recollection of his family and his father's teaching, as well as his own deeply established sense of honor, was a marked man for the rest of his life. Marlow told how he had dinner with Jim during the trial. The boy seemed of a different stamp from the other officers of the *Patna*. Marlow was determined to fathom the boy's spirit, just as Jim was determined to regain his lost moral identity.

Jim told Marlow how the disgraceful affair had happened. After he had investigated the damage, he had felt that the ship could not remain afloat, for her plates were rust-eaten and unable to stand much strain. There were eight hundred passengers and seven boats, and not enough time to get into the boats the few passengers who could be carried to safety. Shortly afterward he discovered the captain and the engineers making ready to desert the ship. They insisted that he join them; the passengers were doomed anyway. The acting third engineer had a heart attack in the excitement and died. Jim never knew when—or why—he had jumped into the lifeboat the other officers had launched. Jim told Marlow how they had agreed to tell the same story. Actually, he and his companions thought that the *Patna* had gone down. Jim said that he had felt relief when he had learned that the passengers were safe. The whole story made sailor-talk in all ports where seamen met and talked. After the inquiry Marlow offered to help Jim, but Jim was determined to become a wanderer, to find out by himself what had happened to his soul.

Jim began his wanderings, to Bombay, to Calcutta, to Penang, Batavia, and the islands of the East. For a time he found work with an acquaintance of Marlow's, but he gave up his job when the second engineer of the *Patna* turned up unexpectedly. Afterward he became a runner for some ship chandlers, but he left them because he had heard one of the owners discussing the case of the *Patna*. He moved on, always toward the East, from job to job.

Marlow continued his efforts to help Jim. He sought out Stein, a trader who owned a number of trading posts on the smaller islands of the East Indies. Stein made Jim his agent at Patusan, an out-of-the-way settlement where he was sure Jim might recover his balance. There, in that remote place, Jim tried to find some answer to his self-hatred. Determined never to leave Patusan, he associated with the natives, and by his gentleness and consideration became their leader. They called him Tuan Jim—Lord Jim. Dain Waris, the son of Doramin, the old native chief, was his friend.

The rumor spread in the ports that Jim had discovered a valuable emerald, and that he had presented it to a native woman. There was a story about a native girl who loved him and who had given him warning when some jealous natives came to murder him.

Marlow followed Jim to Patusan. When Marlow prepared to leave, Jim accompanied him part of the way. He explained to Marlow that at last he felt as though his way had been justified. Somehow, because the simple natives trusted him, he felt linked again to the ideals of his youth. Marlow felt there was a kind of desperateness to his conviction.

The end came when Gentleman Brown, a roving cutthroat, determined to loot Lord Jim's stronghold. He arrived while Jim was away. Led by Dain Waris, the natives isolated Brown and his marauders on a hilltop but were unable to capture them. Lord Jim returned and after a long talk with Brown became convinced that Brown would leave peaceably if the siege were lifted. He persuaded the reluctant natives to withdraw. The vicious Brown repaid Lord Jim's magnanimity by vengefully murdering Dain Waris. Lord Jim went unflinchingly to face native justice when he offered himself to the stern old chieftain as the cause of Dain Waris' death. Doramin shot Jim through the breast.

Marlow, who had watched Jim's life so closely, felt that Jim had at last won back his lost honor.

Critical Evaluation

Critics have said that *Lord Jim,* which was first published as a magazine serial, began as a short story but became a novel because its author lost control of his material. Conrad, however, in a Note to *Lord Jim,* defended his work and claimed its credibility as a novel. Readers and critics alike seemed to feel that Jim's long, tragic story could not logically be told to a group of men sitting on a veranda; yet Conrad claims that men do sit up for hours at night exchanging stories. Besides, he claims that Jim's story is interesting enough to hold the listeners' attention. Conrad also states that his readers, too, should be interested in Jim and the meaning of his experiences; for, as suggested by the motif of the novel, "He is one of us." Because Jim, like all of us, is an enigmatic paradox of strength and weakness, Conrad allows the reader to judge Jim's actions but reminds him that often there is "not the thickness of a sheet of paper between the right and wrong" of something.

The novel often confuses its readers. Shifts in point of view and a seeming disregard for a logical time sequence give the novel a meditative but rambling style. Narrating the first four chapters himself, Conrad first shifts in Chapter Five to Marlow's oral narration and then in Chapter Thirty-Six to a letter written by Marlow. As Jim's story unfolds, however, Conrad also allows other reliable characters to comment on Jim and his actions: the French lieutenant, who saves the *Patna* after Jim deserts it; Stein, who gives Jim another chance to prove himself; and Jewel, the native girl who loves him. Thus Conrad gives his readers the pieces to a gigantic puzzle—the connection between human motivation and human character—but admits that, in spite of one's best efforts toward interpretation, much will remain inscrutable.

Conrad himself says that the central theme of *Lord Jim* is the "acute consciousness of lost honour." Although he admits that Jim may be uncommonly idealistic, he denies that Jim is a figment of cold imagination, for he says that he saw Jim's "form" in an Eastern port. To help the reader understand Jim's desperate preoccupation with his failure to live up to his dreams of himself, Conrad plants several clues to the development of those dreams. In his youth Jim spent his time, Conrad says, reading "light holiday literature," and he imagined himself "always an example of devotion to duty, and as unflinching as a hero in a book." In addition, Jim had been brought up by a minister-father who held absolute ideas of right and wrong and who wrote Jim, just before he joined the *Patna* as chief mate, that one who "gives way to temptation . . . hazards his total depravity and everlasting ruin." That Jim is a dreamer who becomes lost in his own imagination is revealed by the training ship incident in which Jim fails to respond to a cry for help from a wrecked schooner because he was reveling in his dreams of heroism. His inability to face the reality of his failure is seen in his blaming nature for catching him off guard and in his rationalizing that he is saving himself for bigger emergencies. Yet when the crucial emergency comes—that of the *Patna's* crisis—he again fails to act because he imagines the chaos and the screaming desperation of eight-hundred pilgrims fighting for seven lifeboats; instead, he stands as if entranced while the other members of the crew lower their lifeboat and prepare to jump. Jim wants to make it clear that he did not plan to jump, nor did he help to lower the boat. His jumping, then, is to him a subconscious but understandable urge for survival. He tells Marlow: "I had jumped. . . . It seems."

The French lieutenant does not condemn Jim's actions. He blames Jim's youth and natural fear. He believes that "Man is born a coward" but that he does brave deeds to make others believe he is heroic. Jim, he notes, faced a situation in which he thought no one would ever know that he acted cowardly: during the *Patna* crisis it was dark, and Jim thought all the passengers would die. Still, the lieutenant recognizes Jim's self-condemnation: "the honour . . . that is real. . . . And what life may be worth when . . . the honour is gone" is the real question of *Lord Jim*.

Stein diagnoses Jim's problem: "He is romantic. . . . And that is very bad. . . . Very good, too." He sees in Jim the potential found in the tragic hero who has high ideals but who fails as the result of a tragic flaw. Jim's flaw, then, is his excessive imagination and his inability to face the reality of his weakness and his guilt. Not until the end of the novel, when he knows his limitations and accepts his guilt for Dain Waris' death, does he redeem his lost honor by giving his own life unflinchingly in atonement for his error in misjudging Gentleman Brown. For it is Brown who finally makes Jim see man's depravity and the ugliness of reality. Yet in his death Jim remains true to his concept of the hero; he has transcended his guilt and declares that "Nothing can touch me now." Earlier, when Jewel expresses to Marlow her fear that Jim will leave her, Marlow assures her that Jim will not go back to his world because "he is not good enough." Still, in the end Marlow seems to believe in Jim's final heroism and sees him as an "extraordinary success."

Whose evaluation, then, of Jim is accurate? Jim's own, when he feels that he has finally found himself and thus dies willingly, with "a proud and unflinching glance"? Marlow's, when he sees Jim as a fallible creature who looks trustworthy but who fails—until the end—when an emergency arises? Stein's, when he says that a romantic like Jim has no choice but to follow his dream, even if it costs him his life? The French lieutenant's, when he refuses to judge Jim but ironically shows, by his own heroic example, Jim's weakness? Jewel's, when she calls Jim a traitor and refuses to forgive or understand him? The novel itself is puzzling, and Jim remains "inscrutable at heart." Yet it is important that we try to understand the novel and the character of Jim; for, indeed, "He is one of us."

Bibliography

Allen, Walter E. *Six Great Novelists*. London: H. Hamilton, 1955, pp. 165–172.

Andreach, Robert J. *The Slain and Resurrected God: Conrad, Ford, and the Christian Myth*. New York: New York University Press, 1970, pp. 58–66.

Baines, Jocelyn. *Joseph Conrad: A Critical Biography*. New York: McGraw-Hill, 1960, pp. 241–252. Reprinted in *Twentieth Century Interpretations of*

Lord Jim: *A Collection of Critical Essays*. Edited by Robert E. Kuehn. Englewood Cliffs, N.J.: Prentice-Hall, 1969, pp. 35–45.

Berthoud, Jacques. *Joseph Conrad: The Major Phase*. New York: Cambridge University Press, 1978, pp. 64–93.

Cox, C.B. "The Metamorphosis of Lord Jim," in *Critical Quarterly*. XV (1973), pp. 9–31.

Curle, Richard. *Joseph Conrad and His Characters*. London: Heinemann, 1957, pp. 29–65.

Daleski, Herman M. *Joseph Conrad, The Way of Dispossession*. New York: Holmes and Meier, 1977, pp. 77–103.

Drew, Elizabeth A. *The Novel: A Modern Guide to Fifteen English Masterpieces*. New York: Norton, 1963, pp. 156–172.

Epstein, Harry S. "*Lord Jim* as a Tragic Action," in *Studies in the Novel*. V (1973), pp. 229–247.

Guerard, Albert J. *Conrad the Novelist*. Cambridge, Mass.: Harvard University Press, 1958, pp. 126–178. Reprinted in *Twentieth Century Interpretations of* Lord Jim: *A Collection of Critical Essays*. Edited by Robert E. Kuehn. Englewood Cliffs, N.J.: Prentice-Hall, 1969, pp. 82–99.

Haugh, Robert F. *Joseph Conrad: Discovery in Design*. Norman: University of Oklahoma Press, 1957, pp. 56–77.

Hewitt, Douglas. *Conrad: A Reassessment*. Cambridge: Bowes and Bowes, 1952, pp. 31–49. Reprinted in *Conrad: A Collection of Critical Essays*. Edited by Marvin Mudrick. New York: Prentice-Hall, 1966, pp. 55–62.

Karl, Frederick. *A Reader's Guide to Joseph Conrad*. New York: Noonday, 1960, pp. 120–131.

Krieger, Murray. *The Tragic Vision: Variations on a Theme in Literary Interpretation*. New York: Holt, Rinehart and Winston, 1960, pp. 165–179.

Madden, William A. "The Search for Forgiveness in Some Nineteenth Century English Novels," in *Comparative Literature Studies*. III (1966), pp. 139–153.

Marković, Vida E. *The Changing Face: Disintegration of Personality in the Twentieth Century British Novel, 1900–1950*. Carbondale: Southern Illinois University Press, 1970, pp. 3–17.

Miller, Joseph H. "The Interpretation of *Lord Jim*," in *The Interpretation of Narrative: Theory and Practice*. Edited by Morton W. Bloomfield. Cambridge, Mass.: Harvard University Press, 1970, pp. 211–228.

Morf, Gustav. *The Polish Shades and Ghosts of Joseph Conrad*. New York: Twayne, 1976, pp. 143–158.

Perry, John Oliver. "Action, Vision or Voice: The Moral Dilemmas in Conrad's Tale-Telling," in *Modern Fiction Studies*. X (Spring, 1964), pp. 3–14.

Roussel, Royal. *The Metaphysics of Darkness: A Study in the Unity and Development of Conrad's Fiction.* Baltimore: Johns Hopkins University Press, 1971, pp. 80–108.

Saveson, John E. *Joseph Conrad: The Making of a Moralist.* Amsterdam: Rodopi, 1972, pp. 37–53, 65–83, 89–107, 137–161, 165–178.

Tanner, Tony. "Butterflies and Beetles—Conrad's Two Truths," in *Chicago Review.* XVI (Winter–Spring, 1963), pp. 123–140. Reprinted in *Twentieth Century Interpretations of* Lord Jim*: A Collection of Critical Essays.* Edited by Robert E. Kuehn. Englewood Cliffs, N.J.: Prentice-Hall, 1969, pp. 53–67.

Van Ghent, Dorothy. "On *Lord Jim*," in *The English Novel: Form and Function.* New York: Holt, Rinehart and Winston, 1953, pp. 229–244. Reprinted in *Twentieth Century Interpretations of* Lord Jim*: A Collection of Critical Essays.* Edited by Robert E. Kuehn. Englewood Cliffs, N.J.: Prentice-Hall, 1969, pp. 68–81.

Wiley, Paul L. *Conrad's Measure of Man.* Madison: University of Wisconsin Press, 1954, pp. 5–63. Reprinted in *Twentieth Century Interpretations of* Lord Jim*: A Collection of Critical Essays.* Edited by Robert E. Kuehn. Englewood Cliffs, N.J.: Prentice-Hall, 1969, pp. 46–52.

Wright, Walter F. *Romance and Tragedy in Joseph Conrad.* Lincoln: University of Nebraska Press, 1949, pp. 107–123.

T. S. ELIOT

Born: St. Louis, Missouri (September 26, 1888)
Died: London, England (January 4, 1965)

Principal Works

POEMS: *Prufrock and Other Observations*, 1917; *Poems*, 1919; *Ara Vos Prec*, 1920; *The Waste Land*, 1922; *Poems, 1909–1925*, 1925; *The Journey of the Magi*, 1927; *A Song for Simeon*, 1928; *Animula*, 1929; *Ash Wednesday*, 1930; *Marina*, 1930; *Triumphal March*, 1931; *Sweeney Agonistes*, 1932; *Collected Poems, 1909–1935*, 1936; *Old Possum's Book of Practical Cats*, 1939; *Four Quartets*, 1943 ("Burnt Norton," "East Coker," "The Dry Salvages," and "Little Gidding"); *Poems Written in Early Youth*, 1967.

PLAYS: *The Rock: A Pageant Play*, 1934; *Murder in the Cathedral*, 1935; *The Family Reunion*, 1939; *The Cocktail Party*, 1949; *The Confidential Clerk*, 1953; *The Elder Statesman*, 1959.

ESSAYS: *Ezra Pound: His Metric and Poetry*, 1917; *The Sacred Wood*, 1920; *Homage to John Dryden*, 1924; *For Lancelot Andrewes*, 1928; *Dante*, 1929; *Thoughts After Lambeth*, 1931; *John Dryden: The Poet, The Dramatist, The Critic*, 1932; *The Use of Poetry and the Use of Criticism*, 1933; *After Strange Gods*, 1934; *Elizabethan Essays*, 1934; *The Idea of a Christian Society*, 1939; *The Music of Poetry*, 1942; *The Classics and the Man of Letters*, 1942; *Notes Toward the Definition of Culture*, 1948; *Poetry and Drama*, 1951: *The Three Voices of Poetry*, 1954; *On Poetry and Poets*, 1957; *To Criticize the Critic*, 1966.

BIOGRAPHY: *Charles Whibley: A Memoir*, 1931.

The most controversial and influential poet of our time, Nobel Prize winner T(homas) S(tearns) Eliot was born in St. Louis, September 26, 1888, the descendant of a New England family, a branch of which established itself in St. Louis in the 1830's. The poet was educated at Harvard, where he studied under Babbitt and Santayana; later he continued his education in the Harvard Graduate School, the Sorbonne, and Merton College, Oxford. He taught for a time in a school near London, worked in Lloyd's Bank, edited *The Criterion* (a quarterly review), and became a director of the publishing firm of Faber and Faber. In 1927 he became a British subject. From 1932 on he became a familiar figure to American college audiences through several series of lectures.

Although Eliot's first volume of poems appeared in 1917, it was not until 1922 that he achieved celebrity with *The Waste Land*. Seldom has a poem created such a furor. By some it was acclaimed as America's most important modern poem; by others it was denounced as a deliberate hoax. His unusual technique: the elliptical style studded with phrases in foreign tongues, quotations and echoes used for evocative effect, his erudition, were too difficult for most readers. Yet it was soon realized that he had treated an important subject—the aridity of modern life, the horror of a civilization dying of spirtual drought—in a significant way and with a fresh poetic technique. The poem became the Bible of the "lost generation."

Ash Wednesday created equally great consternation, this time among the admirers of the earlier poem. For here Eliot dealt with the most important of all modern questions, that of belief: the dilemma of the modern man who wants to believe and yet who cannot, because of his spiritual dryness, his over-intellectuality. By approaching the problem in the penitential spirit of Lent, by accepting the religious solution ("suffer me not to be separated/ And let my cry come unto Thee"), Eliot antagonized many of his admirers among the secular-minded generation of 1930, who could not believe in his sincerity (*vide* Edmund Wilson in *Axel's Castle*) or who felt that he had betrayed his earlier position. But all had to admit that the poem attained heights of verbal beauty unequaled in any other contemporary verse.

In the twenty years between *The Waste Land* and *Four Quartets*, Eliot had achieved the rank of a major poet. It was no longer possible to consider him as merely a willful obscurantist or to attribute to him, as an early critic did, only "perverse brilliance." Through familiarity, his poetic technique had become better understood. Yet the *Quartets*, in spite of the careful exegesis to which they have been subjected, remain hard reading—more because of the philosophic difficulty of the theme (time and history) than because of the language. Though they are great poetry, their appeal is to a very limited audience, and they well illustrate the extreme demands that the best modern verse makes upon the reader. Much of the difficulty of modern poetry is the result of Eliot's influence; yet until the technique for reading this poetry has become part of the average reader's literary experience, it is probable that Eliot will remain the poet of the few who are willing to make the intellectual effort necessary for the understanding of his work.

Eliot's criticism appeared concurrently with his poetry, and with equally important effect. It has become a commonplace to say that he, quite literally, brought about a revolution in taste. He called attention to long-neglected writers: the metaphysicals, especially Donne; seventeenth century divines; the less familiar Elizabethans; Dryden. Through his influence, Dante, who had become the province of academic specialists, regained popularity. The reputations of the Romantic poets declined. But most important of all, Eliot's criticism was written from the Christian point of view; he, more than anyone else, overturned the secular, humanistic attitude of the 1920's and 1930's. So unfamiliar to most readers was the Anglo-Catholic approach that many of the most acute of them could not believe that he meant what he said. Just as the sincerity of *Ash Wednesday* was doubted, so were the ideas of many of his essays considered as merely a pose. Yet to Eliot, more than any other modern writer, is due the credit for the swing from the intellectual Left to the Right, so that now it is the traditionalists who have the offensive. Even his strongest opponents could not deny his genuine scholarship, his enormous reading, and his careful judgments.

Eliot's most recent work was in the drama. As far back as 1930 he wrote, apropos of the future of poetry: "The ideal medium for poetry, to my mind, and the most direct means of social 'usefulness' for poetry, is the theatre." Beginning with *The Rock*—which was a pageant rather than a drama, and for which he wrote the choruses—Eliot experimented in various ways in an effort to find some effective modern equivalent of the blank verse of the Elizabethans, by means of which the poetic drama might be revitalized. It is perhaps too early to attempt an estimate of the effect that he may have had on the modern theater. Certainly several of his plays—even *Murder in the Cathedral*, in spite of what would hardly seem a popular subject—have had excellent runs on the professional stage, though some of this success may have been due to the author's reputation. It is true that a great poet does not always make a dramatist, and to many readers the plays have seemed the least successful of Eliot's works. Perhaps the plays lack a real sense of the theater; perhaps the poetic drama cannot now be revived. But by breaking with nineteenth century dramatic realism, and yet attempting something more than a mere imitation of Elizabethan tragedy, Eliot demonstrated his importance in contemporary literature.

Bibliography

With the exception of *The Confidential Clerk*, all of Eliot's major work in poetry and the drama appears in *The Complete Poems and Plays of T. S. Eliot*, 1952. Essay collections are *Selected Essays*, 1932, and *Essays, Ancient and Modern*, 1936.

The foundation of all Eliot studies is still F. O. Matthiessen's *The Achievement of T. S. Eliot: An Essay on the Nature of Poetry*, 1935. Other major studies include George Williamson, *The Talent of T. S. Eliot*, 1929; Thomas McGreevy, *Thomas Stearns Eliot: A Study*, 1931; Elizabeth Drew, *T. S. Eliot: The Design of His Poetry*, 1949; Leonard Unger, *The Art of T. S. Eliot*, 1949; H. L. Gardner, *The Art of T. S. Eliot*, 1950; George Williamson, *A Reader's Guide to T. S. Eliot*, 1953; A. Alvarez, *The Shaping Spirit: Studies in Modern English and American Poets*, 1958; David E. Jones, *The Plays of T. S. Eliot*, 1960; and Northrop Frye, *T. S. Eliot*, 1963. There are three collections of critical essays from various sources: *T. S. Eliot: A Selected Critique*, edited by Leonard Unger, 1948; *T. S. Eliot: A Symposium*, edited by Richard March and Tambimuttu, 1948; and *A Collection of Critical Essays on "The Waste Land,"* edited by Jay Martin, 1968.

See also Bonamy Dobree, *The Lamp and the Lute*, 1929; Babette Deutsch, *Poetry in Our Time*, 1956; Morton D. Zabel, "T. S. Eliot in Mid-Career," *Poetry*, XXXVI (1930), 330–337; G. M. Turnell, "Tradition and T. S. Eliot," *Colosseum*, I (1934), 44–54; Theodore Morrison, "Ash Wednesday: A Religious History," *New England Quarterly*, XI (1938), 266–286; Philip Wheelwright, "The Burnt Norton Trilogy," *Chimera*, I (1942), 7–18; Genevieve M. Foster, "The Archetypal Imagery in T. S. Eliot," *Publications of the Modern Language Association*, LX

(1945), 567–587; William Blisset, "The Argument of T. S. Eliot's *Four Quartets*," *University of Toronto Quarterly*, XV (1946), 115–126; T. Weiss, "T. S. Eliot and the Courtyard Revolution," *Sewanee Review*, LIV (1946), 289–307; David Daiches, "Some Aspects of T. S. Eliot," *College English*, IX (1947), 115–122; John Lawlar, "The Formal Achievement of *The Cocktail Party*," *Virginia Quarterly Review*, XXX (1954), 431–451; and Allan Tate, *T. S. Eliot, Sewanee Review*, Special Issue, 1966.

ASH WEDNESDAY

Type of work: Poem
Author: T. S. Eliot (1888–1965)
First published: 1930

Essay-Review

After the publication of *The Waste Land*, in 1922, had established his reputa-. tion as a major poet, T. S. Eliot wrote one important poem, "The Hollow Men" (1925), which seemed at that time to be a postlude to its predecessor but which now appears more as a prelude to *Ash Wednesday*. In any case, it should be read as a connecting link between the two longer poems. Its theme is the emptiness of modern intellectualism, which amounts only to

> Shape without form, shade without colour,
> Paralysed force, gesture without motion.

It is another aspect of the Waste Land, desiccated and meaningless, inhabited only by the empty and futile hollow men.

Ash Wednesday marks an important point in the author's poetic development, for it sprang directly from his acceptance of the Anglo-Catholic faith. This biographical aspect of the poem, even more than its theme, influenced its reception by Eliot's former admirers and caused a schism among them that gave an interesting insight into the modern mind.

The tone of the poem is the humility appropriate to Ash Wednesday, the first day of the penitential season of Lent; its theme is the dilemma of the modern man who wants to believe yet who cannot bring himself to do so because of his dry, sterile intellectuality. This theme is stated in the first of the six parts: the poet, turning his irony upon himself, describes this characteristically modern predicament of a man caught in the web of his own intellectualizing but who can know that he must

> . . . pray that I may forget
> These matters that with myself I too much discuss
> Too much explain,

and that at this stage of religious experience the proper prayer is

> Teach us to sit still.

Throughout this opening section sound the echoes of the Penitential Office: "Turn thou us, O good Lord, and so shall we be turned" as well as of Guido Cavalcanti's poem, "In Exile at Sarzana."

The second part is based on a reminiscence of the Valley of Dry Bones described by Ezekiel, the language of which it echoes. Eliot once said in a lecture that the three white leopards could be taken as representing the World, the Flesh, and the Devil. They have fed on the body of the speaker, but Ezekiel was told to prophesy that these bones should live again, that "I [the Lord] shall put my spirit in you, and ye shall live, and I shall place you in your own land." There is also the figure of the Lady, who seems to play a role analogous to that of Beatrice as an intermediary; she is dressed in white, the color of Faith. The speaker, then, having been stripped of everything, has learned resignation; but through the intercession of the Lady and the prophecy of Ezekiel he has found hope.

The third section, with its description of the spiral stairway, obviously recalls Dante's winding ascent of the Purgatorial Mount. There seems to be no direct connection with any particular canto of the *Purgatorio*, only a linking of the journey of purgation with the penitential spirit of Lent. There is also the glimpse through the window of a scene suggestive of sensual pleasure that distracts the pilgrim from his journey. Dante is again recalled in the fourth section, this time by the Earthly Paradise and the Divine Pageant at the end of the *Purgatorio*. Again there are echoes: of St. Paul's *Epistle to the Ephesians* and of the "Salve Regina."

For the fifth section Eliot made use of a sermon by Lancelot Andrews that he had already quoted in an essay on the Bishop: ". . . the Word of an Infant? The Word and not be able to speak a word?"—an elaborate play upon the word (speech), the Word (the Logos, the most abstruse of Christian doctrines), and the Word made Flesh.

The last section, doubling back upon the opening lines of the poem, suggests a scene in a confessional ("Bless me father") during which the beauty of the natural world intrudes into the mind of the speaker and distracts him from his proper meditation. Thus, the world seeks to draw us back to itself. Then, appropriately, the poem ends with words taken, with one slight change, from the Penitential Office for Ash Wednesday in the Book of Common Prayer:

> And let my cry come unto Thee

Thus, the poem deals with various aspects of a certain stage in religious experience: "Lord, I am not worthy"; it is a poem of spiritual, as Cavalcanti's was one of physical, exile. The dweller in the Waste Land who "cannot drink/there, where trees flower, and springs flow" must find his way back through penitence, with the humble prayer: "Suffer me not to be separated."

This is a simpler poem than *The Waste Land*, though Eliot used much the same technical devices of ellipsis and echoes. It rises to heights of verbal beauty unequaled in any other contemporary verse. Its reception, however, was curious and not without irony. To many readers of the 1920's, Eliot had become the spokesman for the disillusionment of the now famous "lost generation"—a statement that he himself characterized as "nonsense." 1930, with its Marxian enthusiasm for proletarian literature, was probably the high point of the secular humanism of our time; Bertrand Russell's *A Free Man's Worship* was dominant. It was among the adherents to this secular humanism that Eliot's greatest admirers were to be found. For him to become a member of the Anglican Church and to write a poem with a deeply religious theme was to them a grievous shock. Some of them flatly refused to believe in his sincerity; his membership in the Church of England must be a pose, a kind of romantic, aesthetic Catholicism. To others, to whom religion was a retreat from reality, a "failure of nerve," he was a lost leader, a writer whose significant work had ended with "The Hollow Men." Yet it might not be an exaggeration to claim that the publication of *Ash Wednesday* marked the beginning of the swing from the intellectual Left to Right, with the consequent decline of the secular humanist attitude.

Bibliography

Blackmur, R.P. "T.S. Eliot from *Ash Wednesday* to *Murder in the Cathedral*," in *The Double Agent*. New York: Arrow, 1935, pp. 184–218. Reprinted in *T.S. Eliot: A Selected Critique*. Edited by Leonard Unger. New York: Rinehart, 1948, pp. 236–262.

Brooks, Cleanth and Robert Penn Warren. "The Reading of Modern Poetry," in *American Review*. VIII (February, 1937), pp. 442–449.

Chiari, Joseph. *T.S. Eliot, Poet and Dramatist*. London: Vision, 1972, pp. 75–81.

Drew, Elizabeth. *T.S. Eliot, The Design of His Poetry*. New York: Scribner's, 1949, pp. 98–117.

Duncan–Jones, Elsie E. "*Ash Wednesday*," in *T.S. Eliot, A Study of His Writings by Several Hands*. Edited by B. Rajan. London: Dennis Dobson, 1947, pp. 37–56.

Gorman, William J. "Eliot's *Ash Wednesday*," in *Inlander*. XI (November, 1930), pp. 5–10.

Headings, Philip R. *T.S. Eliot*. New York: Twayne, 1964, pp. 70–92.

Kenner, Hugh. *The Invisible Poet: T.S. Eliot*. New York: McDowell, McDowell, Oblensky, 1959, pp. 261–275.

Leavis, F.R. "T.S. Eliot," in *New Bearings in English Poetry*. London: Chatto and Windus, 1932, pp. 75–132. Reprinted in *T.S. Eliot: A Selected Critique*. Edited by Leonard Unger. New York: Rinehart, 1948, pp. 195–215.

Matthiessen, F.O.   *The Achievement of T.S. Eliot.* New York: Oxford University Press, 1959, pp. 114–123.

Morrison, Theodore.   "*Ash Wednesday*: A Religious History," in *New England Quarterly.* XI (June, 1938), pp. 266–286.

Pottle, Frederick A.   *The Idiom of Poetry.* Ithaca, N.Y.: Cornell University Press, 1941, pp. 86–92.

Ross, Malcolm Mackenzie.   "Conclusion: The Firmament Arrested," in *Poetry and Dogma.* New Brunswick, N.J.: Rutgers University Press, 1954, pp. 249–251.

Schneider, Elisabeth.   *T.S. Eliot: The Pattern in the Carpet.* Berkeley: University of California Press, 1975, pp. 108–128.

Seyppel, Joachim.   *T.S. Eliot.* New York: Frederick Ungar, 1972, pp. 71–74.

Smith, Grover.   *T.S. Eliot's Poetry and Plays.* Chicago: University of Chicago Press, 1956, pp. 135–158.

Southam, B.C.   *A Guide to the Selected Poems of T.S. Eliot.* New York: Harcourt, Brace and World, 1968, pp. 111–116.

Spender, Stephen.   *T.S. Eliot.* New York: Viking, 1975, pp. 127–133.

Stein, Arnold.   *Answerable Style.* Minneapolis: University of Minnesota Press, 1953, pp. 132–134.

Tate, Allen.   "On *Ash Wednesday*," in *Reactionary Essays.* New York: Scribner's, 1936, pp. 210–222. Also in his *Collected Essays.* Denver: Alan Swallow, 1959, pp. 341–349. Reprinted in *T.S. Eliot: A Selected Critique.* Edited by Leonard Unger. New York: Rinehart, 1948, pp. 289–295. Also reprinted in *T.S. Eliot: A Collection of Critical Essays.* Edited by Hugh Kenner. Englewood Cliffs, N.J.: Prentice-Hall, 1962, pp. 129–135.

Traversi, Derek.   *T.S. Eliot: The Longer Poems.* New York: Harcourt Brace Jovanovich, 1976, pp. 55–84.

Unger, Leonard.   *T.S. Eliot: Moments and Patterns.* Minneapolis: University of Minnesota Press, 1966, pp. 41–68. Also in *T.S. Eliot: A Selected Critique.* Edited by Leonard Unger. New York: Rinehart, 1948, pp. 349–394.

Ward, David.   *T.S. Eliot Between Two Worlds.* London: Routledge and Kegan Paul, 1973, pp. 148–163.

Williamson, George.   *A Reader's Guide to T.S. Eliot.* New York: Noonday, 1953, pp. 168–185.

Wilson, Edmund.   "T.S. Eliot," in *Axel's Castle.* New York: Scribner's, 1931, pp. 93–131. Reprinted in *T.S. Eliot: A Selected Critique.* Edited by Leonard Unger. New York: Rinehart, 1948, pp. 170–194.

FOUR QUARTETS

Type of work: Poetry
Author: T. S. Eliot (1888–1965)
First published: 1943

Essay-Review

Four Quartets is T. S. Eliot's last book of nondramatic poetry. Written over a period of eight years and published separately, each quartet has the same structure and helps to develop cumulatively the same themes. Eliot has said that transitions in poetry can be similar to those in a symphony or quartet, and these quartets are written in the five-movement sonata form.

The personal and historical significance of the place names which title the poems are the points of departure for the themes developed in the first part of each quartet. The theme of "Burnt Norton"—an old Gloucestershire house—is the nature of time and of personal memories and experience. "East Coker," which is the name of the English village from which Eliot's ancestor left for America in the seventeenth century, is a consideration of the meaning of history and an explanation of the idea of spiritual rebirth. "The Dry Salvages," a group of rocks off the coast of Massachusetts which Eliot knew as a boy, continues the meditations on time and history and includes reflections on human endeavor and further statements on the nature of experience. These themes are all, again, present in "Little Gidding," the name of an Anglican lay community founded by Nicholas Ferrar.

All themes are thus present in each quartet with different emphases, the subsidiary themes are aspects of the major ones and are directly related to them. A difference in these poems from Eliot's earlier verse is that here, although the elements of surprise and rapid transition are still present, the transitional passages are included, whereas in *The Waste Land* they were not. The same symbols also occur in each of the quartets; their multiple and shifting meanings are resolved in "Little Gidding."

In "Burnt Norton" he writes:

> What might have been and what has been
> Point to one end which is always present.

Here there is no placing of experience in time ("do not call it fixity"); it is instead a "stillness." The stillness is the point beyond experience "into the rose-garden." To reach it requires the negation of flesh and spirit. This way of purgation is repeatedly considered and what is required for it is release from desire and com-

---

pulsion. Meaningful experience is both in and out of time, and life is too full of distraction for this end to be often attained. The description of this distraction is a vivid realization of the contemporary predicament:

> Only a flicker
> Over the strained, time-ridden faces
> Distracted from distraction by distraction.

The passage following these lines on suburban Londoners presents "the way down" towards the dark night of the soul, "desiccation of the world of sense." But there are times in the realm of art when the moment can be prolonged

> . . . as a Chinese jar still
> Moves perpetually in its stillness.

A further theme in the quartets, the nature and difficulty of poetic creation, follows in contrast to the image of the jar. The struggle with words which "decay with imprecision" introduces the Word which is subject always to temptation. "Burnt Norton" ends with a repetition of the vision of hidden children laughing in the rose-garden, a motif which occurred in the first movement. Such immediacy is contrasted with the usual bleakness of existence.

Time in "East Coker" involves the consideration of the history of man. This, the most despairing of the quartets, comes closest to complete and unredeemed bitterness. The cyclic nature of life and experience is stressed: fields give way to factories which crumble to dust. The life cycle of man and earth is presented as if in a vision after the poet has gone down the dark lane into the somnolent village. The second section begins with a lyric on November, which is followed by a characteristic reversal:

> That was a way of putting it . . .
> A periphrastic study in a worn-out poetical fashion.

The theme of the bitterness and deception of time mentioned in "Burnt Norton" is expanded here; the wisdom of old men is really folly, and

> The only wisdom we can hope to acquire
> Is the wisdom of humility.

The concrete description, which in these poems always either immediately follows or precedes the abstract thought, is here that of the descent into subways, which were also used as air-raid shelters during World War II. Thus negation and stillness are combined and the necessity for "waiting" is introduced.

The fourth movement is a lyric on the Christian paradox of life in death and death in life. The symbols are those of a hospital with a "wounded surgeon" and "a dying nurse"

> Wherein, if we do well, we shall
> Die of the absolute paternal care.

Fire and roses are multiple symbols of destruction and salvation, purgation and resurrection. After the cold fever of death there is purgatory:

> Of which the flame is roses, and the smoke is briars.

The fifth section despairs of poetic creation, which, at "every attempt/Is a wholly new start" because the difficulties once conquered are no longer those that face the poet. The resolution of this dilemma is similar to that for the soul: "For us there is only the trying." The final section inverts the opening statement: "In my beginning is my end"; the poet concludes, "In my end is my beginning."

The superb pictures of the Mississippi River and the Atlantic Ocean in "The Dry Salvages" show an increase in the music of the verse which is sustained in "Little Gidding." The river is "a strong brown god" and the sea has "Many gods and many voices." The sea time "is not our time"; "time stops and is never ending." The lyric in Section II speaks of the grief of shipwreck and of those things thought "most reliable" which are "therefore the fittest for renunciation." There is no end to this pain, only the possibility of prayer.

The pattern of the past with its content of meaningful experience is seen here in its historical perspective:

> And approach to the meaning restores the experience
> In a different form, beyond any meaning
> We can assign to happiness.

This passage connects with the reference to Krishna from the *Bhagavad Gita* in Section III, one of the many allusions to and quotations of other works in the quartets. The theory of time is drawn from the philosopher Heraclitus and part of the conclusion of "Little Gidding" from Dame Julian of Norwich. The rose and fire symbolism is reminiscent of Dante, and the conception of the dark night of the soul is that of St. John of the Cross. While awareness of these sources adds considerably to the enjoyment of the quartets, Eliot integrates them so completely and so perfectly controls their place in the poetry, placing them where they have such an exact significance, that the poems can be appreciated and understood without knowledge of source or influence.

Section V contains the meaning of the explanation of time's paradoxical aspects:

> But to apprehend
> The point of intersection of the timeless
> With time, is an occupation for the saint.

The images of flowers, sunlight, and music which have recurred throughout these poems symbolize the ordinary man's experiences which, although fragmentary, nevertheless are "hints of grace": "The hint half guessed, the gift half understood, is Incarnation."

The resolution of themes in "Little Gidding" is accomplished by semi-repetitive exposition and some further development. The chapel at Little Gidding is a place "where prayer has been valid." The many allusions to writers and saints and saints who were writers is explained:

> ... the communication
> Of the dead is tongued with fire beyond the language of the living.

The death of the four elements in Section II opens the way to spiritual resurrection. This lyric is followed by the poet's meeting, after an air raid, with a "familiar compound ghost"—the shade of all his past teachers—who tells him of the grief and failure of old age

> ... unless restored by that refining fire
> Where you must move in measure like a dancer.

The historical theme is restated in the relationship of the present and the past as a reconciliation of opposites: "History may be servitude,/History may be freedom." And

> Whatever we inherit from the fortunate
> We have taken from the defeated.

The solution of the dilemma of the burden of divine care for humanity, so bleakly felt in "East Coker," is here seen to be love, which binds us in our desires and alone is able to give the essential release from them.

The end of exploration, of the struggle with words and of all human actions "Will be to arrive where we started/And to know the place for the first time." The moments of personal and historical experience are never lost:

> The moment of the rose and the moment of the yew-tree
> Are of equal duration. A people without history
> Is not redeemed from time, for history is a pattern
> Of timeless moments.

The way of purgation which requires the whole being has led to "complete simplicity" where "the fire and the rose are one."

For all their complexity, *Four Quartets* contains Eliot's most explicit poetry. The poems are specifically Christian, recording the progress of the soul toward salvation. The way in which the themes are at various levels interwoven to augment and illuminate one another, the control of language and rhythm, and the beauty and precision of the images allow some critics to call these quartets Eliot's finest achievement.

Bibliography

Blamires, Harry. *Word Unheard: A Guide Through Eliot's Quartets.* London: Methuen, 1969.

Bradford, Curtis. "Footnotes to 'East Coker,' " in *Sewanee Review.* LII (Winter, 1944), pp. 169–175. Reprinted in *T.S. Eliot: Four Quartets.* Edited by Bernard Bergonzi. Nashville, Tenn.: Aurora, 1970, pp. 57–63.

Chiari, Joseph. *T.S. Eliot, Poet and Dramatist.* London: Vision, 1972, pp. 81–104.

Davie, Donald. "T.S. Eliot: The End of an Era," in *Twentieth Century.* CLIX (April, 1956), pp. 350–362. Reprinted in *T.S. Eliot: A Collection of Critical Essays.* Edited by Hugh Kenner. Englewood Cliffs, N.J.: Prentice-Hall, 1962, pp. 192–206. Also reprinted in *T.S. Eliot: Four Quartets.* Edited by Bernard Bergonzi. Nashville, Tenn.: Aurora, 1970, pp. 153–167.

De Masirevich, Constance. *On the* Four Quartets *of T.S. Eliot.* New York: Barnes & Noble, 1953.

Donoghue, Denis. "T.S. Eliot's *Quartets*: A New Reading," in *Studies.* LIV (Spring, 1965), pp. 41–62. Reprinted in *T.S. Eliot: Four Quartets.* Edited by Bernard Bergonzi. Nashville, Tenn.: Aurora, 1970, pp. 212–238.

Drew, Elizabeth. *T.S. Eliot, The Design of His Poetry.* New York: Scribner's, 1949, pp. 140–200.

Flint, R.W. "The *Four Quartets* Reconsidered," in *Sewanee Review.* LVI (Winter, 1948), pp. 69–81. Reprinted in *T.S. Eliot: Four Quartets.* Edited by Bernard Bergonzi. Nashville, Tenn.: Aurora, 1970, pp. 107–118.

Gardner, Helen. *The Art of T.S. Eliot.* New York: Dutton, 1950, pp. 36–56. Reprinted in *T.S. Eliot: Four Quartets.* Edited by Bernard Bergonzi. Nashville, Tenn.: Aurora, 1970, pp. 119–138.

Harding, D.W. "Little Gidding," in *Scrutiny.* XI (Spring, 1943), pp. 216–219. Reprinted in *T.S. Eliot: A Collection of Critical Essays.* Edited by Hugh Kenner. Englewood Cliffs, N.J.: Prentice-Hall, 1962, pp. 125–128.

Headings, Philip R. *T.S. Eliot.* New York: Twayne, 1964, pp. 119–142, 170–171.

Kenner, Hugh. *The Invisible Poet: T.S. Eliot.* New York: McDowell, McDowell, Oblensky, 1959, pp. 289–323. Reprinted in *T.S. Eliot: Four Quartets.* Edited by Bernard Bergonzi. Nashville, Tenn.: Aurora, 1970, pp. 168–196.

Leavis, F.R. "Eliot's Later Poetry," in *Scrutiny.* XI (Summer, 1942), pp. 60–71. Also in his *Education and the University.* London: Chatto and Windus, 1943, pp. 87–104. Reprinted in *T.S. Eliot: A Collection of Critical Essays.* Edited by Hugh Kenner. Englewood Cliffs, N.J.: Prentice-Hall, 1962, pp. 110–125.

Matthiessen, F.O.   *The Achievement of T.S. Eliot.* New York: Oxford University Press, 1959, pp. 177–197. Reprinted in *T.S. Eliot:* Four Quartets. Edited by Bernard Bergonzi. Nashville, Tenn.: Aurora, 1970, pp. 88–106.

Ross, Malcolm Mackenzie.   "Conclusion: The Firmament Arrested," in *Poetry and Dogma.* New Brunswick, N.J.: Rutgers University Press, 1954, pp. 249–251.

Schneider, Elisabeth.   *T.S. Eliot: The Pattern in the Carpet.* Berkeley: University of California Press, 1975, pp. 168–208.

Seyppel, Joachim.   *T.S. Eliot.* New York: Frederick Ungar, 1972, pp. 91–102.

Smith, Grover.   *T.S. Eliot's Poetry and Plays.* Chicago: University of Chicago Press, 1956, pp. 251–300.

Spender, Stephen.   *T.S. Eliot.* New York: Viking, 1975, pp. 158–167, 169–184.

Stead, C.K.   "The Imposed Structure of the *Four Quartets*," in *The New Poetic.* London: Penguin, 1964, pp. 170–185. Reprinted in *T.S. Eliot:* Four Quartets. Edited by Bernard Bergonzi. Nashville, Tenn.: Aurora, 1970, pp. 197–211.

Sweeney, James Johnson.   "East Coker: A Reading," in *Southern Review.* VI (Spring, 1941), pp. 771–791. Reprinted in *T.S. Eliot: A Selected Critique.* Edited by Leonard Unger. New York: Rinehart, 1948, pp. 395–414. Also reprinted in *T.S. Eliot:* Four Quartets. Edited by Bernard Bergonzi. Nashville, Tenn.: Aurora, 1970, pp. 36–56.

Traversi, Derek.   *T.S. Eliot: The Longer Poems.* New York: Harcourt Brace Jovanovich, 1976, pp. 85–214.

Ward, David.   *T.S. Eliot Between Two Worlds.* London: Routledge and Kegan Paul, 1973, pp. 223–288.

Weitz, Morris.   "T.S. Eliot: Time as a Mode of Salvation," in *Sewanee Review.* LX (Winter, 1952), pp. 48–64. Reprinted in *T.S. Eliot:* Four Quartets. Edited by Bernard Bergonzi. Nashville, Tenn.: Aurora, 1970, pp. 138–152.

Williamson, George.   *A Reader's Guide to T.S. Eliot.* New York: Noonday, 1953, pp. 205–236.

THE WASTE LAND

Type of work: Poem
Author: T. S. Eliot (1888–1965)
First published: 1922

Essay-Review

By the early 1920's the "New Poetry" or the "Poetic Renascence," usually dated from 1912, had spent much of its initial force. The Imagists had come and gone; the reputations of Frost, Masters, and Sandburg had been established. Whatever was original in the new poetry—and, viewed in retrospect, this originality was not nearly so great as it then seemed—had been accomplished. It was time for American poetry to take a new direction.

T. S. Eliot had already published two small volumes in 1917 and 1920, but he had not attracted a great deal of attention—not so much as had Amy Lowell or Vachel Lindsay, for example. In the early editions of Louis Untermeyer's *Modern American Poetry*, a book which was then very influential and which well represented the critical evaluations of that period, he was briefly dismissed as a "brilliant expatriate" whose work lacked "the exaltation which is the very breath of poetry." He was allowed "a certain perverse brilliance"; but his work was finally summed up as merely "mordant light verse; complex and disillusioned *vers de société.*"

The Waste Land first appeared in *The Dial* and, having won that magazine's poetry award for the year, was published in book form in 1922. It may truthfully be said that seldom has a poet created such a sensation in the American literary world. To many readers, it seemed a deliberate hoax; perhaps the appearance, in 1916, of *Spectra*, by "Morgan and Knish," had left some critics with an abiding fear of again being caught out on a limb. The most common charge hurled by those who took the poem seriously was that of willful obscurantism: that the poet was deliberately making his work difficult for his readers when he could have written in a simpler fashion. The eleven pages of notes appended to a poem of but 430 lines only made matters worse; surely Eliot was pulling the reader's leg or he was piling obscurity on obscurity.

The truth of the matter was that the "New Poetry" of 1912 had not prepared the average reader for Eliot's peculiar style. The poets of the preceding decade had expanded the subject matter and vocabulary of poetry and they had substituted free verse for traditional poetic forms; but they had not greatly altered the conventionalities of poetic statement. To put it simply, their verse was not hard to understand, even though its form might be unusual. But Eliot, influenced by the English metaphysicals and the French Symbolists, had broken more sharply with nineteenth century poetry than had any of his contemporaries and had achieved a genuinely new, though very difficult, style. The recent remark of A. Alvarez applies particularly to him: ". . . a great deal of modern poetry seems often as specialized as modern science; both require a degree of single-minded preparedness to which the general public is neither willing nor able to attain."

Eliot's verse has been subjected to such exhaustive critical analysis that the interested reader will find ample exegesis of almost every line, including translations of the phrases in half a dozen foreign languages and identifications of the quotations and echoes of English verse, all of which the poet used for their evocative effect. Eliot himself explained in his notes that the "plan and a good deal of the incidental symbolism of the poem" came from the Grail Legend and Sir James Frazer's *The Golden Bough*. This anthropological material deals with certain vegetation-fertility rites in which the god—Adonis, Attis, Osiris—must be slain each year so that by his death the land can again become fruitful; hence, the prevalence throughout the poem of images of drought and of water: the "dry sterile thunder" contrasted with the rain that restores life to the parched earth. Eliot's theme of sterility is applied to modern civilization, which is dying of spiritual drought.

The poem opens with a picture of this modern world, a picture that is made up of broken fragments of idle conversation.

> What are the roots that clutch, what branches grow
> Out of this stony rubbish?

Nothing can grow from this sterile civilization, from these unreal great cities where the living seem already dead, where "I had not thought death had undone so many"—Dante's exclamation on first seeing the crowds of the Futile, rejected by both Hell and Heaven, for they had lived "without blame and without praise." This is the modern massman. We then are given one of the several sharp contrasts between the past and the present: the deliberately rich description (with its echoes of *Antony and Cleopatra*), perhaps of the Renaissance, set against the equally deliberately banal scene in a pub. In the third section the same device is employed: the vulgar seduction of the typist by the "small house-agent's clerk" (love in the modern world reduced to a meaningless mechanical act) contrasted with the glimpse of Elizabeth and Leicester sailing on Spenser's "sweet Thames." All of this is seen by Tiresias who, Eliot tells us, is "the most important personage in the poem" because, having experienced life as both a man and a woman, he can unite all the characters. In the last section, according to the author's notes, the themes are: "the journey to Emmaus, the approach to the Chapel Perilous, and the present decay of eastern Europe"—that is, the disintegration of secular society which can be saved only by the King who sacrifices himself that his land may revive ("Shall I at least set my lands in order?"), the Risen Christ who, having died for his people, will bring them to a new life. Thus the poem ends on a profoundly religious note.

Just as one critic will write of the irony of the poem and another claim that its method is the obverse of irony, so there are many interpretations of individual lines and, indeed, of whole passages. Yet clearly the "Waste Land" is the modern great city inhabited by those for whom contemporary life provides only "a heap of broken images" and "fear in a handful of dust." It is a civilization dying of spiritual drought. The poem is an enormously complex one, making great demands upon the reader, yet the importance of its theme and the brilliance of its technique give it rank as one of the most significant literary works of our time.

Bibliography

Aiken, Conrad. "An Anatomy of Melancholy," in his *A Reviewer's ABC*. New York: Meridian Books, 1958, pp. 176–181. Reprinted in *T.S. Eliot: The Man and His Work*. Edited by Allen Tate. New York: Delacorte, 1966, pp. 194–202. Also reprinted in *A Collection of Critical Essays on* The Waste Land. Edited by Jay Martin. Englewood Cliffs, N.J.: Prentice-Hall, 1968, pp. 52–58. Also reprinted in *T.S. Eliot:* The Waste Land. Edited by C.B. Cox and Arnold P. Hinchliffe. Nashville, Tenn.: Aurora, 1970, pp. 91–99.

Brooks, Cleanth. "*The Waste Land*: Critique of the Myth," in his *Modern Poetry and the Tradition*. Chapel Hill: University of North Carolina Press, 1939, pp. 136–172. Reprinted in *T.S. Eliot, A Study of His Writings by Several Hands*. Edited by B. Rajan. London: Dennis Dobson, 1947, pp. 7–36. Also reprinted in *T.S. Eliot: A Selected Critique*. Edited by Leonard Unger. New York: Rinehart, 1948, pp. 319–348. Also reprinted in *Storm over* The Waste Land. Edited by Robert E. Knoll. Chicago: Scott, Foresman, 1964, pp. 58–87. Also reprinted in *A Collection of Critical Essays on* The Waste Land. Edited by Jay Martin. Englewood Cliffs, N.J.: Prentice-Hall, 1968, pp. 59–86. Also reprinted in *T.S. Eliot:* The Waste Land. Edited by C.B. Cox and Arnold P. Hinchliffe. Nashville, Tenn.: Aurora, 1970, pp. 128–161.

Craig, David. "The Defeatism of *The Waste Land*," in *Critical Quarterly*. II (1960), pp. 241–252. Reprinted in *Storm over* The Waste Land. Edited by Robert E. Knoll. Chicago: Scott, Foresman, 1964, pp. 122–135. Also reprinted in *T.S. Eliot:* The Waste Land. Edited by C.B. Cox and Arnold P. Hinchliffe. Nashville, Tenn.: Aurora, 1970, pp. 200–215.

Dobrée, Bonamy. "T.S. Eliot," in *The Lamp and the Lute*. Oxford: Clarendon Press, 1929, pp. 107–133.

Drew, Elizabeth. *T.S. Eliot, The Design of His Poetry*. New York: Scribner's, 1949, pp. 58–90.

Gardner, Helen. *The Art of T.S. Eliot*. New York: Dutton, 1950, pp. 86–98.

Headings, Philip R. *T.S. Eliot*. New York: Twayne, 1964, pp. 49–69.

Hough, Graham. "Imagism and Its Consequences," in *Reflections on a Literary Revolution*. Washington, D.C.: Catholic University Press, 1960, pp. 1–40. Reprinted in *Storm over* The Waste Land. Chicago: Scott, Foresman, 1964, pp. 98–121.

Kenner, Hugh. *The Invisible Poet: T.S. Eliot*. New York: McDowell, McDowell, Oblensky, 1959, pp. 145–152. Reprinted in *Storm over* The Waste Land. Edited by Robert E. Knoll. Chicago: Scott, Foresman, 1964, pp. 2–7. Also reprinted in *T.S. Eliot:* The Waste Land. Edited by C.B. Cox and Arnold P. Hinchliffe. Nashville, Tenn.: Aurora, 1970, pp. 168–199.

Kermode, Frank. "A Babylonish Dialect," in *T.S. Eliot: The Man and His Work*. Edited by Allen Tate. New York: Delacorte, 1966, pp. 231–243. Reprinted in *T.S. Eliot:* The Waste Land. Edited by C.B. Cox and Arnold P. Hinchliffe. Nashville, Tenn.: Aurora, 1970, pp. 224–235.

Korg, Jacob. "Modern Art Techniques in *The Waste Land*," in *Journal of Aesthetics and Art Criticism*. XVIII (June, 1960), pp. 456–463. Reprinted in *A Collection of Critical Essays on* The Waste Land. Edited by Jay Martin. Englewood Cliffs, N.J.: Prentice-Hall, 1968, pp. 87–96.

Leavis, F.R. "*The Waste Land*," in *New Bearings in English Poetry* [1932]. Ann Arbor: University of Michigan Press, 1960, pp. 75–91, 112–132. Reprinted in *T.S. Eliot: A Selected Critique*. Edited by Leonard Unger. New York: Rinehart, 1948, pp. 195–215. Also reprinted in *T.S. Eliot: A Collection of Critical Essays*. Edited by Hugh Kenner. Englewood Cliffs, N.J.: Prentice-Hall, 1962, pp. 89–103. Also reprinted in *Storm over* The Waste Land. Edited by Robert E. Knoll. Chicago: Scott, Foresman, 1964, pp. 24–38.

Martin, Jay. "T.S. Eliot's *The Waste Land*," in *A Collection of Critical Essays on* The Waste Land. Edited by Jay Martin. Englewood Cliffs, N.J.: Prentice-Hall, 1968, pp. 1–14.

Matthiessen, F.O. *The Achievement of T.S. Eliot*. New York: Oxford University Press, 1959, pp. 36–41, 46–52. Reprinted in *Storm over* The Waste Land. Edited by Robert E. Knoll. Chicago: Scott, Foresman, 1964, pp. 39–57. Also reprinted in *T.S. Eliot:* The Waste Land. Edited by C.B. Cox and Arnold P. Hinchliffe. Nashville, Tenn.: Aurora, 1970, pp. 108–127.

Patterson, Gertrude. *T.S. Eliot: Poems in the Making*. New York: Barnes & Noble, 1971, pp. 134–168.

Schneider, Elisabeth. *T.S. Eliot: The Pattern in the Carpet*. Berkeley: University of California Press, 1975, pp. 59–91.

Schwartz, Delmore. "T.S. Eliot as the International Hero," in *Partisan Review*. XII (Spring, 1945), pp. 199–206. Reprinted in *T.S. Eliot: A Selected Critique*. Edited by Leonard Unger. New York: Rinehart, 1948, pp. 43–50. Also reprinted in *Storm over* The Waste Land. Edited by Robert E. Knoll. Chicago: Scott, Foresman, 1964, pp. 88–96. Also reprinted in *A Collection of*

Critical Essays on The Waste Land. Edited by Jay Martin. Englewood Cliffs, N.J.: Prentice-Hall, 1968, pp. 97–104.

Scott, Nathan. "T.S. Eliot: A Contemporary Synthesis," in *Rehearsals of Discomposure*. New York: King's Crown Press, 1952, pp. 178–228.

Shapiro, Karl. "The Death of Literary Judgment," in *In Defense of Ignorance*. New York: Random House, 1960, pp. 35–60. Reprinted in *Storm over* The Waste Land. Edited by Robert E. Knoll. Chicago: Scott, Foresman, 1964, pp. 136–154.

Smith, Grover. *T.S. Eliot's Poetry and Plays*. Chicago: University of Chicago Press, 1956, pp. 72–98.

Spender, Stephen. *T.S. Eliot*. New York: Viking, 1975, pp. 100–121.

Traversi, Derek. *T.S. Eliot: The Longer Poems*. New York: Harcourt Brace Jovanovich, 1976, pp. 9–54.

Ward, David. *T.S. Eliot Between Two Worlds*. London: Routledge and Kegan Paul, 1973, pp. 68–141.

Williams, Helen. *T.S. Eliot:* The Waste Land. London: Edward Arnold, 1973.

Williamson, George. *A Reader's Guide to T.S. Eliot*. New York: Noonday, 1953, pp. 118–154.

E. M. FORSTER

Born: London, England (January 1, 1879)
Died: London (June 7, 1970)

Principal Works

NOVELS: *Where Angels Fear to Tread*, 1905; *The Longest Journey*, 1907; *A Room with a View*, 1908; *Howards End*, 1910; *A Passage to India*, 1924; *Maurice*, 1971.

SHORT STORIES: *The Celestial Omnibus and Other Stories*, 1911; *The Eternal Moment and Other Stories*, 1928; *Collected Short Stories*, 1948; (with others) *Fairy Tales for Computers*, 1969.

ESSAYS: *Abinger Harvest—A Miscellany*, 1936; *Two Cheers for Democracy*, 1951.

BIOGRAPHY: *Goldsworthy Lowes Dickinson*, 1934; *Marianne Thornton: A Domestic Biography, 1797–1887*, 1956.

CRITICISM: *Aspects of the Novel*, 1927; *Virginia Woolf*, 1942.

HISTORY AND TRAVEL: *Alexandria: A History and a Guide*, 1922; *Pharos and Pharillon*, 1923; *The Hill of Devi*, 1953.

E[dward] M[organ] Forster, was born in London on January 1, 1879, and educated at Tonbridge School and King's College, Cambridge, where he became friendly with G. Lowes Dickinson. By the time he was twenty he had worked on a novel, although he never finished it. After graduation, he published short stories, some of them appearing in the *Independent Review*. In 1905 he published his first novel, *Where Angels Fear to Tread*, written during his residence in Italy. The novel is laid in that country, and its theme is the impact of a foreign culture on provincial personalities. The next year Forster prepared a school edition of the *Aeneid* (1906). Tonbridge School and Cambridge are the settings for Forster's second novel, *The Longest Journey*, a book dealing with the problem of illusion and reality and the conflict between people who are whole and honest and those who are false and hypocritical. *A Room with a View*, published in 1908, may very well have been conceived five years before. It is a comedy, and like the first novel is laid in Italy.

Forster had returned to England in 1907 and it was there that he finished *A Room with a View*. He also began at this time to lecture at the Working Men's College. In 1910 *Howards End* appeared, felt by many to be Forster's masterpiece. The essential conflict in this novel is embodied in the Schlegel and Wilcox families, the former representing the inner life, the life of art and thought and generous impulses toward man, and the latter representing the outer life, the life of affairs, of telegrams and hurry and anger. Forster here raises the question whether we can reclaim the roots of tradition in the modern world where there is flux even in the hearts of men. His answer is a qualified yes, if men and women are truly perceptive and they are moved by love.

In 1911 Forster made his first trip to India, accompanying G. Lowes Dickinson. During the first World War he did civilian war work in Alexandria and contributed a series of essays to the *Egyptian Mail* which later appeared under the title *Pharos and Pharillon*. He also wrote at this time *Alexandria: A History and Guide*. Back in London after the war, he engaged in literary journalism briefly and in 1921 returned to India, where he served as secretary to the Maharajah of Dewas. His Indian experience provided the background for *Passage to India*, his most celebrated novel and the winner in 1925 of the Femina Vie Heureuse and the James Tait Black Memorial prizes. The novel is a sensitive rendering of the clash of English and Indian temperaments and cultures. Misunderstanding, prejudice, and suspicion poison decent human relationships and work to keep even men of good will apart. Only the elderly Mrs. Moore, a mystic, seems able to penetrate the barriers.

In 1927 Forster was invited to deliver the Clark Lectures at King's College, Cambridge. These were published in the same year as *Aspects of the Novel*, his most substantial and influential volume of criticism. In 1934 he published a life of his friend Dickinson and in 1936 *Abinger Harvest* appeared, a collection of reviews. *The Hill of Devi* deals with his Indian experiences. *Marianne Thornton* is a biography of his great-aunt. Forster was much honored, most recently by Queen Elizabeth II, who conferred upon him the Order of Companions of Honour in 1953. *Maurice*, written in 1913 but never published, appeared posthumously in the autumn of 1971.

Bibliography

The most detailed and comprehensive study of E. M. Forster is Lionel Trilling, *E. M. Forster: A Study*, 1943. For discussion of his earlier writings Rose Macaulay, *The Writings of E. M. Forster*, 1938, is still valuable. More recent studies are H. J. Oliver, *The Art of E. M. Forster*, 1960; John Beer, *The Achievement of E. M. Forster*, 1962; Lawrence Brander, *E. M. Forster: A Critical Study*, 1968; Frederick P. McDowell, *E. M. Forster*, 1969; and P. N. Furbank, *E. M. Forster: A Life*, 1978.

Briefer studies in books include Bonamy Dobrée, *The Lamp and the Lute: Studies in Six Modern Authors*, 1929; Katherine Mansfield, *Novels and Novelists*, 1930; E. B. C. Jones, "E. M. Forster and Virginia Woolf," in *The English Novelists*, edited by Derek Verschoyle, 1936; D. M. Hoare, *Some Studies in the Modern Novel*, 1938; Virginia Woolf, *The Death of the Moth and Other Essays*, 1942; Austin Warren, *Rage for Order: Essays in Criticism*, 1948; Lord David Cecil, *Poets and Story-Tellers*, 1949; and D. S. Savage, *The Withered Branch*, 1950. See also Peter Burra, "The Novels of E. M. Forster," *New Century*, CXVI (1934), 581–594; E. K. Brown, "E. M. Forster and the Contemplative Novel," *University of Toronto Quarterly*, III (1934), 349–361; Montgomery Belgion,

"The Diabolism of E. M. Forster," *Criterion*, XIV (1934), 57–73; F. R. Leavis, "E. M. Forster," *Scrutiny*, VII (1938), 185–202; and H. M. McLuhan, "Kipling and Forster," *Sewanee Review*, LII (1944), 332–343.

THE SHORT STORIES OF E. M. FORSTER

Author: E. M. Forster (1879–1970)
First published: The Celestial Omnibus, 1911; *The Eternal Moment*, 1928

Essay-Review

Whether on business or vacation, a man—say he is middle-aged—leaves an England which is debased, industrial, and unpoetic for a Mediterranean country such as Italy or Greece. What he finds as if by accident in this more primitive, pre-industrial country, in a momentary event which is both in and out of time, a surprising perception wherein he discovers his genuine identity, obliges him quite literally to change his living in accord with the new knowledge of self, or die. Such is the archetypal if not practical situation which lies at the base of the short stories of E. M. Forster. While few of the stories fully correspond to this pattern, it nevertheless furnishes a useful means for perceiving their basic unity. Forster's short stories, written in general immediately before and immediately after his major novels, *Howards End* and *A Passage to India*, do not make claims as imposing as his major fiction and tend in fact to have a stylized period quality which in some cases does not wear well. The stylization may take the form of a brief allegory ("The Other Side of the Hedge"), pre-Orwell doom-predicting science-fiction ("The Machine Stops"), the picaresque tale ("The Road from Colonus"). But certain themes are persistent throughout all the stories, notably the theme of imprisonment ("chains" as a continuing metaphor) and escape, and often the escape is at once mental and geographical. The motif of travel as escape and discovery accords both with Forster's own period of personal travel in these decades and with the general international quality of pre-World War I Europe.

The tone of the earlier collection of stories, *The Celestial Omnibus*, is at once established, and predicted, by the first of these, "The Story of a Panic"—with the exception of the uncollected "Albergo Empedocle," also chronologically the first. In an ironic manner which is not typical of the majority of his stories, Forster recounts through the eyes of a sensitive, intelligent English traveler in Italy the Dionysian epiphany of a boy named Eustace. During a rural outing attended by a representative group of English tourists—a middle-aged female dilettante, a carping aesthete—there suddenly occurs a moment of inexplicable fear; the cause of the fright is unapparent, but its effect is felt as tangibly as if some prehistoric monster had reared its head in a scene of pastoral loveliness. This simile is hardly casual; what has taken place is a resurgence of the primordial power of nature, not that of natural charm so admired by the onlookers, but that of the direct, sensual potency inherent in the countryside. This sudden, unforeseen revelation sets these cultivated and timid souls in a frenzy, except for the boy Eustace, previously scorned by the narrator for his unathletic and brattish nature. One finds here one of the recurrent motifs of the stories: the need to "set one's self right" in youth. As a later story, "The Point of It," remarks at greater length, only through establishing this kind of communion with things as they are, not through the veils men hang about them in youth, before one can be easily lulled into self-deception, can a fundamentally fertile rapport with life be achieved. Forster points out this fact even more clearly through the story's uncommon irony: the narrator, previously unable to see the source of Eustace's corruption within the virtues of his own society, is equally incapable of understanding the boy's exaltation after his conversation. To a "civilized" mind Eustace's wild actions can only be the result of some kind of mental disturbance not the manifestation of the reclamation of man's primitive, direct connection with his world. The incomprehension is reinforced by the secondary action of Eustace's betrayal by his one confrere at the resort, the Italian youth Gennaro; the narrator, in a moment of strategic inspiration appropriate to civilized man, bribes him to return the boy. The scheme backfires, to cause Eustace's liberation and Gennaro's death.

The experience of the world in its direct reality must be, Forster insists, panic; and its peculiar mood can best be described in a work whose situation is deliberately, initially, supernatural, and thus makes the reader aware of the tensions so directly germane to Forster's thesis. In the earlier stories the prototypic example of this effect is "The Celestial Omnibus," which deals, once again, with a boy, but one who, unlike Eustace, already dwells in a state of literature. Significantly, the story is in the third person, and the well-meaning narrator has become now the boy's interlocutor and opposite, the pillar of the community, Mr. Septimus Bons. The boy has discovered, near his home, the Celestial Omnibus, the eternally vital vehicle through time and space which great literature is; his discovery, however, is mocked by his culturally slavish bourgeois parents who hold out his reputed expedition to heaven to Mr. Bons as an example of childish perversity and deceit. When Mr. Bons accepts the boy's challenge and accompanies him on the Celestial Omnibus, the result is predictable: faced with the creators who should be dead, whose workers are symbolically entombed by him in vellum, he falls to his death from the heights while his uncorrupted companion is elevated on the shield of Achilles.

The directly classical allusions aroused by "The Story of a Panic" are continued elsewhere, notably in "Other Kingdom" and "The Curate's Friend." The stories, which complement each other, are located in an English rural milieu, and they involve that settled and clerically infiltrated domain in collision with the antique immersion in a sensuous and vitally transcendent nature. In the first of these, the theme is enunciated by the translated sentence from the *Eclogues*, "Mortal fools, there be gods in these woods." The classical instruction, conducted by the rather fussy narrator of the story, is soon broken into by the property-owner fiancé of one of the pupils, Mr. Harcourt Worters, elated at having added a new meadow to his land. Upon their visiting this place, the Forsterian antithesis is posed: Mr. Worters is anxious to fence in the property, to place his mark upon it, while his betrothed, a rude girl from Ireland whom he is educating, wants to leave the meadow as it is, unbounded. Her spiritual divorce from Worters is physically confirmed when, during a true ecstasy which happens at a picnic in the woods, she forever departs and really makes asses out of the mortals in the woods. The same humorous perversity also appears in "The Curate's Friend," in which a clergyman meets a faun, a reminder of Britain's Roman past, who by casting his clerical acquaintance into a fit of despair causes him for the first time to react in an emotionally honest fashion to his experiences.

If one can speak of a movement from the earlier to the later stories, it is not characterized by an increased complexity but by a greater diversification; the later stories are essentially their predecessors given the flesh and blood of the social environment in which they occur. "The Machine Stops," the first of the tales in *The Eternal Moment*, demonstrates this transition quite well: despite the fantastic setting of the story, in some nameless futurity, its tone, unlike that of "The Celestial Omnibus," is highly practical. We are cast into an England of the future in which the most specifically "realistic" elements of the earlier stories— the human corruption of the natural environment, the elimination of sensual response and individuality—have reached their most extreme expression. The terrible responsibility of intelligence, which cannot escape a confrontation of the tangible facts of existence, has been given up to the machine, which soon becomes the object of a new religious devotion more potent than the well-intentioned Christianity of the curate. Forster affirms what Alexis de Tocqueville had foreseen in 1848: that the tyranny of a modern state, representing the will of the masses and with advanced means at its disposal, would be more terrible and far-reaching than any hitherto seen. The unity that Kuno feels with those who have gone before, and will come after him, on freeing himself from the deranged subterranean labyrinth, is that of man rediscovering his humanity.

Forster's thesis is more substantially, if not more spectacularly, presented in "The Point of It," which picks up a theme already stated in "The Road From Colonus": the impossibility of grasping the source of truth when one has accepted a conventional set of values. In the earlier story, the old man, unlike Oedipus who led his daughter to the place of his disappearance from earth, is prevented by his daughter from accepting the gift of death at the place where he finally experiences a revelation of the real value of classical civilization, a value not to be found in the ruins of Thermopylae or the Parthenon. Forster's picture of Mickey, the hero of "The Point of It," furnishes us with the genesis of such a man, who, by doing good is rewarded by his society and rises in it, though with no benefit to those closest to him. The story begins with an incident which points to a possible source of salvation for Mickey: he permits an invalid acquaintance to overexert himself while rowing against the tide in an estuary. His immediate guilt as soon as the acquaintance dies is still another of Forster's eternal moments, returning to Mickey at intervals through a life of humanitarian actions by which he attempts to atone. Only after his death—by a *tour de force* Forster follows his character's moral progress even after death—does he realize that the conventional guilt was

Short Stories / FORSTER

wrong, that his encouragement to his friend to respond to the situation as such was the only genuine human action in his life. The recognition itself makes for his eternal salvation.

Forster offers an even more enlarged and socially realized description of the same belief in his two final stories, "The Story of the Siren" and "The Eternal Moment." In the first of these the comprehension of a possible source of human revitalization, in a world where Christianity is a mere gesture, comes by means of the siren rising from the eternal sea. The life of the poor fisherman Giuseppe is totally disrupted by his encounter with her, and when he seeks out and marries a woman who has similarly experienced such a vision, he then disrupts the entire life of the village in which he lives, particularly the priest who causes the wife's destruction and the death as well of their unborn child. Nevertheless, like the sea siren whose perpetuation is identifiable with the sea itself, the promise of their child remains forever to be born. This inescapable possibility of reconciliation comes even more poignantly to life in the case of Miss Raby, the spinster novelist in "The Eternal Moment." She returns to the village of Vorta hoping to undo the damage that she had done in popularizing the village in her novel, *The Eternal Moment*. Ironically, even though she discovers the worst effects of civilization to have come to pass in the town, there is a redeeming feature: her rediscovery of the amorous encounter which, she finds, had been the true germ of her novel. Once again Forster has shown how a whole life can be justified by the detailed, if adventitious and unexpected, understanding of a significant moment in the past.

There is a distinctly Dionysian quality of emphasis in these stories of Forster's young manhood, a Nietzschian emphasis, complicated by a characteristic English reticence. As in the major novels, the mystic revelation of culture-bound adults, or the rescue of an intuitive child from uncomprehending elders, is Forster's overwhelming interest. Yet the characters in the short stories are noticeably more maneuverable, flatter and less rounded (to use Forster's terms from his *Aspects of the Novel*) than the people in his longer fictions: they move more in the world of fantasy and allegory where moral values are clear cut and the static civilization of the British Empire, the Industrial Revolution, the increase of knowledge, the defacement of the countryside are unambiguously to be condemned. The stories put starkly the alternatives of sickness and health, both for individuals and their communities. Forster is at one with his novelistic contemporaries Lawrence, Mann, and Proust in repeating again and again in fictional situations the agonized warning that we must "Only Connect."

ROBERT GRAVES

Born: Wimbledon, England (July 26, 1895)

Principal Works

POEMS: *Over the Brazier*, 1916; *Fairies and Fusiliers*, 1917; *Country Sentiment*, 1920; *The Pier Glass*, 1921; *Whipperginny*, 1923; *Mock Beggar Hall*, 1924; *Welchman's Hose*, 1925; *The Marmosite's Miscellany*, 1925; *Poems: 1914–1926*, 1927; *Poems: 1929*, 1929; *Poems: 1926–1930*, 1931; *Collected Poems*, 1938; *No More Ghosts*, 1940; *Poems: 1938–1945*, 1946; *Collected Poems: 1914–1947*, 1948; *Poems and Satires*, 1951; *Collected Poems*, 1955; *New Poems*, 1963; *Poems, 1965–1968*, 1968; *The Green-Sailed Vessel*, 1971.

NOVELS: *My Head! My Head! Being the History of Elisha*, 1925; *I, Claudius*, 1934; *Claudius the God*, 1934; *Count Belisarius*, 1938; *Sergeant Lamb of the Ninth*, 1940 [*Sergeant Lamb's America*]; *Proceed, Sergeant Lamb*, 1941; *Wife to Mr. Milton*, 1943; *The Golden Fleece*, 1944 [*Hercules, My Shipmate*]; *King Jesus*, 1946; *The Islands of Unwisdom*, 1949; *Seven Days in New Crete*, 1949 [Watch the Northwind Rise], 1949; *Homer's Daughter*, 1955; *They Hanged My Saintly Billy*, 1957.

ESSAYS AND STUDIES: *The English Ballad*, 1921; *On English Poetry*, 1922; *The Meaning of Dreams*, 1924; *Poetic Unreason*, 1925; *Contemporary Techniques of Poetry*, 1925; *Another Future of Poetry*, 1926; *Lawrence and the Arabs*, 1927; *John Skelton*, 1927; *Impenetrability, or the Proper Habit of English*, 1926; *Lars Porsena, or the Future of Swearing*, 1927; *A Survey of Modernist Poetry*, 1927 (with Laura Riding); *Mrs. Fisher, or the Future of Humour*, 1928; *The Real David Copperfield*, 1933; *The White Goddess*, 1947; *The Common Asphodel*, 1949; *Occupation: Writer*, 1950; *The Crowning Privilege*, 1955; *Adam's Rib*, 1955; *Oxford Addresses on Poetry*, 1962; *Poetic Craft and Principle*, 1970.

AUTOBIOGRAPHY: *Goodbye to All That*, 1929.

BELLES-LETTRES: *But It Still Goes On*, 1930; *The Greek Myths*, 1955.

TRANSLATIONS: *The Golden Ass*, 1950; *Lives of the Twelve Caesars*, 1957; *The Anger of Achilles* (Homer's *Iliad*), 1959; *The Rubáiyát of Omar Khayyám* (with Omar Ali-Shah), 1967.

Robert (Ranke) Graves came by his literary heritage in part through family tradition; his father, Alfred Perceval Graves (1846–1931), was a gifted Irish poet. Born in Wimbledon, July 26, 1895, the younger Graves was reared in London. He was schooled at Charterhouse and, like most of his generation, fought in World War I. He suffered a head wound which gave him one of his several scars; his broken nose resulted from a mishap at football. (Graves was always athletic and once received an Olympic Games award.) During the war, like Siegfried Sassoon, a fellow officer in the Royal Welch Fusiliers, Graves wrote verse while at the front. His poems, if inferior to those of Sassoon and Wilfred Owen, share with their work a vivid sense of the absolutely unromantic truth of battle. In his auto-biography, *Goodbye to All That*, Graves describes with verve and frankness his wartime experiences. *Fairies and Fusiliers*, though rarely voicing the horror char-acteristic of Owen's verse, exhibits some of its same bitterness; it perhaps differs most in being often ironic. A mild flippancy is detectable throughout Graves's early period.

Discharged after the war, Graves moved with his wife to Wales. Here he wrote two more volumes of poetry. He then decided to take a degree at Oxford and enrolled as an undergraduate of St. John's College. The effect of Oxford life was to subdue some of Graves's high spirits, and in this period he published several books on critical theory and poetic analysis. As he increased in learning, he intro-duced into his own poetry fascinating subtleties drawn from his readings in phi-losophy and psychoanalysis.

In 1926 he was appointed professor of English in the University of Cairo, where he remained but one year. When he and his wife were separated in 1927, Graves went to live in the Balearic Islands. A literary association with the Ameri-can poet Laura Riding, with whom he was to operate at Minorca a small publish-ing enterprise for the better part of a decade, produced the acute but querulous critical study *A Survey of Modernist Poetry*. By this time he had published nine more books of verse and had started his practice of frequently reprinting his col-lected editions. He had already written his biography of Lawrence of Arabia, his monograph on John Skelton (whom at an early stage he had imitated), and his unconventional *Lars Porsena, or the Future of Swearing*.

Graves's first novel, *My Head! My Head! Being the History of Elisha*, is re-markable chiefly for its title. This and his next novel showed him mainly as a facile stylist; but *I, Claudius* and *Claudius the God*, the former a winner of both the Hawthornden Prize and the James Tait Black Memorial Prize, suggest also that besides being one of the most interesting poets of contemporary England, Graves is very nearly the most arresting storyteller. Although he seldom depicts the modern scene, and has no great talent at psychological manipulation of char-acter, he has few masters at the art of romantic narration. *Wife to Mr. Milton* makes a shrewd guess, infuriating to votaries of the author of *Paradise Lost*, about the causes of Milton's marital discord. *King Jesus*, which has infuriated others for reasons of faith, is in many ways both enlightened and enlightening. *Seven Days in New Crete* is a fantasy based on Graves's speculations concerning Cybele, the Great Mother, whose supposedly universal cult in primitive Europe constitutes the subject of his remarkable treatise, *The White Goddess*. *Homer's Daughter* pays the tribute of fiction to Samuel Butler's hypothesis that the *Odys-sey* was composed by a woman.

Bibliography

For critical studies see J. M. Cohen *Robert Graves*, 1960; Douglas T. Day, *Swifter than Reason: The Poetry and Criticism of Robert Graves*, 1963; George

Stade, *Robert Graves*, 1967; and Michael Kirkham, *The Poetry of Robert Graves*, 1969. For articles in books or periodicals see Frank Swinerton, *The Georgian Literary Scene*, 1951 (6th ed.); Nelson Algren, "Sentiment with Terror," *Poetry*, LV (1939), 157–159; Richard Church, "Robert Graves, A Traveller in the Desert," *Fortnightly Review*, CLV (1941), 384–391; Horace Gregory, "Robert Graves: A Parable for Writers," *Partisan Review*, XX (1953), 44–54; and C. M. Bowra, "Greek Myths," *Sewanee Review*, LXIV (1956), 498–507.

THE POETRY OF GRAVES

Author: Robert Graves (1895–   )
First published: Over the Brazier, 1916; *Fairies and Fusiliers,* 1917; *Country Sentiment,* 1920; *The Pier Glass,* 1921; *Whipperginny,* 1923; *Mock Beggar Hall,* 1924; *Welchman's Hose,* 1925; *The Marmosite's Miscellany,* 1925; *Poems: 1914–1926,* 1927; *Poems: 1929,* 1929; *Poems: 1926–1930,* 1931; *Collected Poems, 1938; No More Ghosts,* 1940; *Poems: 1938–1945,* 1946; *Collected Poems: 1914–1947,* 1948; *Poems and Satires,* 1951; *Collected Poems,* 1955; *Collected Poems,* 1959; *More Poems,* 1961; *The Penny Fiddle,* 1962; *New Poems,* 1963; *Man Does, Woman Is,* 1964

Essay-Review

Some poets outlast their periods, others their public. The fact that Robert Graves has done neither is easily explained. During his long career—his first book of verse appeared in 1916—he has never allied himself with any movement or group, never cultivated an eclectic or school style; consequently, he had nothing to lose when critical fashions changed. Also, he has never mistaken current popularity for lasting fame or courted the favor of his readers. A veteran of many hard-fought literary skirmishes, he has battled for only one cause: his own integrity as a poet.

The means by which he has maintained his hard-bitten, roughly achieved literary independence help us in understanding both the tart native flavor of his best verse and the defensive attitude he sometimes assumes toward his poorest.

Graves has often stressed the fact that he is not addicted to any poetic "school." One should not believe, then, that his interest in unusual items of medieval literature makes him automatically a writer of Romantic temper. There is in Graves's poetry, and has been since World War I, a strong element of the satirical, evidence of dissatisfaction with many aspects of the world around him—the times, war, England, even himself. Perhaps even the years he resided outside England seem further evidence of such inner dissatisfaction, the kind that is evident in "To Lucia at Birth," a sonnet written relatively late in life.

The earnest thought, the hope that the individual can resist changes which will make him or her conform to the world, instead of resolutely maintaining individuality, recurs in the last stanza of "At the Savoy Chapel," a poem written on the occasion of his daughter's marriage in 1945.

Despite the ever-recurring satire in the poems directed against the world as it is, in poems as diverse as "Vain and Careless," "Angry Samson," "Sergeant-Major Money," "Down, Wanton, Down," and "The Fallen Tower of Siloam," there is also a touch of true sentiment in Graves's poems. It appears sometimes as if the facade of the poet were stripped away temporarily, so that one can see the man and note that the poet and the man, contrary to the traditions of poetry, are not one and the same. In "Coronation Address," for example, Graves writes in the first person, describing the reactions of a family, particularly the husband's, to the death of Queen Victoria, an incident that may well have a historical basis in the poet's own life. A five-year-old boy brings in the edition of the *Times* telling of the monarch's death, news which sends tears rolling down the father's cheeks. In response to his wife's remark that the Queen was, after all, only a woman, the husband retorts that to honor the king is honorable, but to have a queen to serve is lovely. He adds that he hopes his son, the five-year-old, may someday serve a queen. The poem closes with an admonition to Elizabeth II to think well of her great-great-grandmother, who so earned the love of her subjects.

Graves is really at his best when least abstruse. The simpler, explicit style, the homely yet well-chosen idiom of a poem like "Recalling War," which looks back to World War I from the distance of a score of years, is poetically indicative of the poet at his best. In this poem Graves captures with extraordinary brilliance the attitudes of young men toward war's activity and their attitudes in later years as they remember what happened.

Graves began as a young poet mingling country sentiment and personal war experiences, but over the years the war poems have almost completely disappeared from his collections and his country themes have been reshaped to show the symbolic particularities of things. Meanwhile he has been formulating his own theories on the origin and nature of poetry, as set forth in *The White Goddess*, a highly controversial examination into the sources of poetic being and truth in the buried anthropological past. At least a third of the poems now collected have their roots in his theory of poetic myth, either directly in the love poems or indirectly in his ballad themes and his adaptations from the ancient Gaelic.

One of his attempts to repossess the past, to substitute the White Goddess for Apollo and Zeus as the source of poetic magic far back in the dim beginning of all things, is "To Juan at the Winter Solstice," surely one of the notable poems of the century. The poem contains an array of images and references which bring into relationship the mythology of the seasons, the ancient, doomed heroes of Aegean and Celtic legends, and the Goddess in her persons as mother, lover, and layer-out of the dead, all a part of old fertility myths of predestined death and miraculous rebirth. The same theme is presented in "The White Goddess."

In "Rocky Acres" the images of some secret country of the heart and mind match perfectly the spirit of Robert Graves's best poems. For the landscape of his imagination is no barren land; it shelters and nourishes the poet who shuns the crowd.

How he has made his solitary position a post of strategy and advantage is reflected in the various editions of his *Collected Poems*, especially in the consciousness of man's burdens that we find in "Children of Darkness" and "Trudge, Body," the acceptance of human mortality in "Surgical Ward: Men," the reaching back into the dark corners of racial memory in "To Juan of the Winter Solstice," the outrageous ribaldry of "Ogres and Pygmies" and "Down, Wanton,

Down," the droll foolery of "Mid-Winter Waking," and "Traveller's Curse After Misdirection," the self-mockery of "A Pinch of Salt," and the emotional depths of love revealed in "The Sharp Ridge" and "The Dangerous Gift."

Poems such as these present Graves as a writer of considerable pith and variety, of occasional excellence so beautifully and precisely centered and controlled that his true quality deserves the recognition which criticism has so often withheld in the past. These poems, like all good poetry, offer first the shock of surprise and then take gradual possession of mind and mood. This is the true magic of poetry as Robert Graves conceives it.

Bibliography

Auden, W.H. "A Poet of Honor," in *Shenandoah.* XIII (Winter, 1962), pp. 5–11.

Bold, Alan. "The Poems of Robert Graves," in *Southern Review.* VI (Summer, 1970), pp. 849–852.

Callahan, Patrick J. "Toward Yet Unvisited Harbors," in *Prairie Schooner.* (Summer, 1970), pp. 173–177.

Campbell, Roy. "Contemporary Poetry," in *Scrutinies.* Edited by Edgell Rickword. London: Wishart, 1928, pp. 161–180.

Day, Douglas. *Swifter Than Reason: The Poetry and Criticism of Robert Graves.* Chapel Hill: University of North Carolina Press, 1963.

Elliott, George P. "Poetry Chronicle," in *Hudson Review.* XX (Spring, 1967), pp. 147–149.

Enright, Dennis Joseph. *Conspirators and Poets: Reviews and Essays.* Chester Springs, Pa.: Dufour, 1966, pp. 48–67.

Fraser, G.S. *Vision and Rhetoric: Studies in Modern Poetry.* London: Faber and Faber, 1959, pp. 135–148.

Gaskell, Ronald. "The Poetry of Robert Graves," in *Critical Quarterly.* III (Autumn, 1961), pp. 213–222.

Jarrell, Randall. *Poetry and the Age.* New York: Knopf, 1953, pp. 202–203.

————. *The Third Book of Criticism.* New York: Farrar, Straus and Giroux, 1969.

Johnston, John H. *English Poetry of the First World War.* Princeton, N.J.: Princeton University Press, 1964, pp. 71–112.

Kirkam, Michael. *The Poetry of Robert Graves.* New York: Oxford University Press, 1969.

Mehoke, James S. *Robert Graves: Peace-Weaver.* The Hague: Mouton, 1975, pp. 99–161.

Nemerov, Howard. *Poetry and Fiction.* New Brunswick, N.J.: Rutgers University Press, 1963, pp. 112–117.

Pettet, E.C. "The Poetry of Robert Graves," in *English.* III (1941), pp. 216–220.

Pick, J.B. "The Poet as Cynic: A Discussion of Robert Graves' Poetry," in *Outposts.* XIV (Summer, 1949), pp. 23–25.

Sanders, Peter L. "Robert Graves—A Poet's Quest for Meaning," in *English Journal.* LIX (January, 1970), pp. 23–26.

Schwartz, Delmore. "Graves in Dock: The Case for Modern Poetry," in *New Republic.* CXXXIV (March 19, 1956), pp. 20–21.

Spender, Stephen. "Poetry for Poetry's Sake and Poetry Beyond Poetry," in *Horizon.* LXXVI (April, 1946), pp. 221–238.

Stade, George. *Robert Graves.* New York: Columbia University Press, 1967.

Steiner, George. "The Genius of Robert Graves," in *Kenyon Review.* XXII (Summer, 1960), pp. 340–365.

Thwaite, Anthony. *Contemporary English Poetry.* London: Heinemann, 1961, pp. 125–139.

Trilling, Lionel. *A Gathering of Fugitives; Essays.* Boston: Beacon Press, 1956, pp. 20–30.

Williams, Charles. *Poetry at Present.* Oxford: Clarendon Press, 1930, pp. 194–206.

A. E. HOUSMAN

Born: Fockbury, England (March 26, 1859)
Died: Cambridge, England (April 30, 1936)

Principal Works

POEMS: *A Shropshire Lad*, 1896; *Last Poems*, 1922; *More Poems*, 1936; *Collected Poems*, 1939.

CRITICISM: *The Name and Nature of Poetry*, 1933.

CLASSICAL STUDIES: *Editions of Manilius*, 1903–1931; *Juvenal*, 1905; *Lucan*, 1926.

Despite the title of his most famous volume, A(lfred) E(dward) Housman was born, not in Shropshire, but at Fockbury, in the neighboring county of Worcestershire, March 26, 1859, the son of Edward Housman, a solicitor, and the elder brother of Laurence Housman, author and artist. He was educated st St. John's College, Oxford (1877–81), but failed to take honors in *literae humaniores*. This failure apparently embittered his spirits and temporarily turned him away from an academic career. When he left Oxford, he obtained in 1882 a position in the Patent Office in London and devoted his evenings to classical studies. In 1892 he was offered the Latin professorship at University College, London, which he held until 1911. In that year, against strong competition, he was elected to the Latin professorship at Cambridge, where he became a Fellow of Trinity College and spent the rest of his life.

Although Housman is known to the general public only as a poet, his poetry represented but a small part of his life's work. His main efforts were in classical scholarship, particularly Latin, and in this special world he obtained a formidable reputation. He was especially famous for his biting sarcasm when dealing with the productions of less competent scholars, usually Germans. He denied harboring an animus against that nation; but since, in his highly specialized field, most of the work was done by Germans, they inevitably became the victims of his satire. It was characteristic that he could spend thirty years on a second-rate poet such as Manilius, but one whose work afforded interesting problems in Latin usage and textual criticism.

Of all the poets of modern times, none has won so great a reputation from such a small body of work. The volumes are slender and most of the poems consist of but a few quatrains. That twenty-five years should have elapsed between his first and second books is indicative of his careful workmanship. It has been suggested that the discipline of classical scholarship, as well as the terseness of the Latin language, had an important influence on his own highly compressed style.

Housman himself said that the three great influences on his poetry were Shakespeare's songs, the Scottish border ballads, and the poems of Heine—all three of which achieve their effects with the greatest economy of means. *A Shropshire Lad* represented a reaction against the luxuriance of Victorian poets like Tennyson, Browning, and Swinburne.

Housman always kept his themes and their consequent emotions within a very narrow range. Repeatedly he returned to the same ideas: the passing of spring and of youth, the brevity and tragedy of life. The wind will strip the petals from the flowering trees; the boys and girls, now so brave and young, will all too soon be lying in their narrow beds of clay. It is a bitter, uncompromising, tragic view of life, devoid of hope. To contend against the inexorable tragedy of life is vain, yet a man must make the struggle against hopeless odds—"As I strap on for fighting/ My sword that will not save."

The criticism brought against Housman's poetry was twofold: first, that he over-indulged in certain mannerisms of language, and that he artificially cultivated a tragic attitude. There is some validity in the first charge; to the second, we have his own answer:

Housman was apparently the perfect university don, reserved, withdrawn, immensely erudite. He never married, and he died in Cambridge April 30, 1936.

Bibliography

There is no definitive biography. The *Letters* were edited by Henry Maas, 1971. Memoirs of A. E. Housman appear in two books by his brother, Laurence Housman, *A. E. Housman: Some Poems, Some Letters, and a Personal Memoir*, 1937, and *The Unexpected Years*, 1937. See also Katherine Symons and others, *Alfred Edward Housman: Recollections*, 1936; A. S. F. Gow, *A. E. Housman: A Sketch*, 1936; Percy Withers, *A Buried Life: Personal Recollections of A. E. Housman*, 1940; F. T. Grant Richards, *A. E. Housman, 1897–1936*, 1942; and O. Robinson, *Angry Dust: The Poetry of A. E. Housman*, 1950; G. L. Watson, *A. E. Housman: A Divided Life*, 1957; Norman Marlow, *A. E. Housman: Scholar and Poet*, 1958; and Frank L. Lucas, *The Greatest Problem*, 1960; also Stephen Spender, "The Essential Housman," *Horizon*, I (1940), 295–301; and A. F. Allison, "The Poetry of A. E. Housman," *Review of English Studies*, XIX (1943), 276–284. See also Christopher Ricks, ed., *A. E. Housman: A Collection of Critical Essays*, 1968.

Theodore G. Ehrsam published *A Bibliography of A. E. Housman*, 1941. This was supplemented by Robert Stallman, "An Annotated Bibliography of A. E. Housman: A Critical Study," *Publications of the Modern Language Association*, LX (1945), 463–502. The *Complete Poems* were edited by Tom Burns Haber, 1959; and by John Carter, 1965.

A SHROPSHIRE LAD

Type of work: Poems
Author: A. E. Housman (1859–1936)
First published: 1896

Essay-Review

In 1896, the high point of what has been variously called "the yellow 'nineties" and "the Beardsley period," Victorian poetry was at a low ebb. Tennyson and Browning were both dead; Swinburne had long since retired to Putney. The Pre-Raphaelite movement had subsided. Hardy was still known only as a novelist. Gerard Manley Hopkins was waiting to be discovered. The minor poets seemed stereotyped into two groups; those who, like Wilde, produced "Swinburne and water" and those who wrote frail imitations of the French of Paul Verlaine. The only new and original talent was that of Kipling, who had already published his two most famous volumes. But in spite of Kipling's vigor, the spirit of the age was best represented by *The Yellow Book* and Beardsley's illustrations for *The Rape of the Lock*. It was in this atmosphere of "purple patches and fine phrases" that there appeared *A Shropshire Lad*, a slender volume containing sixty-three short poems—some only eight lines long—written by the Professor of Latin at University College, London.

Twenty-six years later, in a short preface to his second volume, *Last Poems*, Housman gave some hint of the circumstances attending the composition of *A Shropshire Lad*. He said that most of the poems had been written "in the early months of 1895" and under a "continuous excitement." Exactly what he meant by this last phrase has never been quite clear; indeed, his biography, apparently so uneventful, presents some little mystery. Oddly enough for a man who was to become one of the greatest Latinists in the English-speaking world, he did not take honors in his final examinations at Oxford, and as a result he apparently went through a period of depression. But the cause of the "continuous excitement" that resulted in *A Shropshire Lad* remains to be satisfactorily explained.

The reader coming upon the poetry of Housman for the first time will be immediately aware of its extremely narrow range. The poet limited himself to but one theme: the brevity and tragedy of life and the inevitability of death. Spring and youth are beautiful, but they pass quickly, just as the blossoms "stream from the hawthorn on the wind away." Further, a man must expect neither happiness nor justice during the brief span allotted to him; life is cruel and filled with injustice. But at least we know that our misfortunes are the common lot of mankind, for, as he wrote in *Last Poems*,

---

> The troubles of our proud and angry dust
> Are from eternity, and shall not fail.
> Bear them we can, and if we can we must.
> Shoulder the sky, my lad, and drink your ale.

Man has no one but himself to depend on; his own strength must see him through his troubles. He does not have even the hope of immortality—as Horace said, in the ode that Housman translated, "pulvis et umbra sumus—we are dust and dreams." But the grave, when finally won, brings peace: "Turn safe to rest, no dreams, no waking."

The influence of Housman's classical studies upon his own poetry is difficult to measure, and yet it is apparent. Years devoted to the careful editing of texts gave him, if nothing else, a feeling for precise workmanship; the terseness of the Latin language contributed to the characteristic brevity of his poems. Indeed, there is much that might be called "Roman" about his poetry—it could even be claimed that the familiar lines of Catullus,

> Soles occidere et redire possunt:
> Nobis cum semel occidit brevis lux,
> Nox est perpetua una dormienda,
> (Suns may rise and set again.
> For us, when our short light
> Has set, remains no more than sleep
> Through one perpetual night.),

sum up most of what he had to say. Also, it has been observed that the aspect of Roman stoicism which has remained in the imagination of subsequent centuries is the "quality of emotional self-restraint." It is this quality that is apparent in Housman's work and that marks it off sharply from the mass of Victorian poetry. There has been "paganism" enough in some of the late nineteenth century poets; but it took the form either of the wild riot of Maenads, Bassarids, and other mythological fauna so dear to Swinburne or of the soft Epicureanism of FitzGerald's translation of Omar Khayyám. A paganism deriving from Roman stoicism and based on restraint, on acceptance of the inevitable tragedy of life, on the idea that "life is never worth preserving at the cost of dishonor," was something quite different. And it should be remembered that patriotism, expressed in some of these poems, was one of the pagan virtues.

Housman's tragic view of life, his preoccupation with death (particularly with death by hanging), has been criticized by some as artificial. It did not seem plausible that a man whose own existence was so secure could genuinely have viewed life in such grim fashion. But Housman tried to make his readers aware that the tragedies of which he wrote were "not mine, but man's." He was also criticized for cultivating certain mannerisms of language. It is, for example, true that the unfortunate lines describing the football game:

> The goal stands up, the keeper
> Stands up to keep the goal,

sound like an unconscious parody of his own style. But what great poet has not, at least once, unwittingly parodied himself?

Although Housman declared that "the most poetical of all poets is Blake," he elsewhere stated that the great influences on his own work had been Shakespeare's songs, the Border ballads, and the poems of Heine. Poem VIII in *A Shropshire Lad* shows how he used ballad material; in *Last Poems*, the second stanza of "Sinner's Rue" is a translation of Heine's "Am Kreuzweg wird begraben." But the important effect of the three influences was that of compression. He himself felt that "poetry is not the thing said but a way of saying it," and that "to transfuse emotion . . . is the peculiar function of poetry." His own taste was romantic; he derived his critical judgments from Arnold, whose dislike for eighteenth century poetry he shared. Yet the opinions he expressed in his lecture, "The Name and Nature of Poetry" (1933), are sometimes curiously at variance with his practice.

As late as 1922 it was still possible for Holbrook Jackson to list Housman among the minor poets of the 1890's. But today his reputation, resting chiefly on the one hundred and four short poems in his first two volumes, is higher than that of any English poet between the Victorians Tennyson and Browning and the moderns Yeats and Eliot.

Bibliography

Abel, Darrel. "Housman's 'The True Lover,' " in *Explicator.* VIII (1949–1950), item 23.

Andrews, S.G. "Housman's 'The Carpenter's Son,' " in *Explicator.* XIX (1960–1961), item 3.

Bache, William. "Housman's 'To an Athlete Dying Young,' " in *Explicator.* X (1951–1952), item 6.

Bateson, F.W. "The Composition of *A Shropshire Lad* lxiii," in *Housman Society Journal.* I (1974), pp. 3–6.

————. "The Poetry of Emphasis," in *A.E. Housman: A Collection of Critical Essays.* Edited by Christopher Ricks. Englewood Cliffs, N.J.: Prentice-Hall, 1968, pp. 130–145.

Boas, Louise. "Housman's 'The Merry Guide,' " in *Explicator.* III (1944–1945), item 6.

Brooks, Cleanth. "Alfred Edward Housman," in *Anniversary Lectures Under the Auspices of the Gertrude Clarke Whittal Poetry and Literature Fund.* Washington, D.C.: Library of Congress, 1959, pp. 39–56. Reprinted in *A.E.*

Housman: A Collection of Critical Essays. Edited by Christopher Ricks. Englewood, N.J.: Prentice-Hall, 1968, pp. 63–84. Also reprinted in *Literary Lectures Presented at the Library of Congress.* Washington, D.C.: Library of Congress, 1973, pp. 311–330.

————. "Housman's '1887,' " in *Explicator.* II (1943–1944), item 34.

Browne, Robert M.   "The Shropshire Lad as Funeral Orator," in *Quarterly Journal of Speech.* LVII (1971), pp. 134–149.

Combellack, C.R.B.   "Housman's 'To an Athlete Dying Young,' " in *Explicator.* X (1951–1952), item 31.

Connolly, Cyril, F.L. Lucas, Martin Cooper, L.P. Wilkinson and John Sparrow.   "A.E. Housman: A Controversy," in *A.E. Housman: A Collection of Critical Essays.* Edited by Christopher Ricks. Englewood Cliffs, N.J.: Prentice-Hall, 1968, pp. 35–50.

Franklin, Ralph.   "Housman's Shropshire," in *Modern Language Quarterly.* XXIV (1963), pp. 164–171.

Gosse, Edmund.   *More Books on the Table.* London: William Heinemann, 1923, pp. 19–27.

————. *The Making of* A Shropshire Lad. Seattle: The University of Washington Press, 1966.

Haber, Tom Burns.   *A.E. Housman.* New York: Twayne, 1967, pp. 68–100.

Hawkins, Maude.   "Housman's 'The True Lover,' " in *Explicator.* VIII (1949–1950), item 61.

Henry, Nat.   "Housman's 'To an Athlete Dying Young,' " in *Explicator.* XII (1953–1954), item 48.

Kowalczyk, R.L.   "Horatian Tradition and Pastoral Mode in Housman's *A Shropshire Lad,*" in *Victorian Poetry.* IV (1966), pp. 223–235.

Lea, Gordon B.   "Ironies and Dualities in *A Shropshire Lad,*" in *Colby Library Quarterly.* X(1973), pp. 71–79.

Leggett, B.J.   *Housman's Land of Lost Content.* Knoxville: University of Tennessee Press, 1970.

————. "Housman's 'The Recruit,' " in *Explicator.* XXV (1965–1966), item 25.

LeMire, Eugene D.   "The Irony and Ethics of *A Shropshire Lad,*" in *University of Windsor Review.* I (1965), pp. 109–127.

Marlow, Norman.   *A.E. Housman: Scholar and Poet.* London: Routledge & Kegan Paul, 1958, pp. 20–170.

Nitchie, Elizabeth.   "Housman's 'To an Athlete Dying Young,' " in *Explicator.* X (1951–1952), item 57.

Wilson, Edmund. "A.E. Housman," in *A.E. Housman: A Collection of Critical Essays*. Edited by Christopher Ricks. Englewood Cliffs, N.J.: Prentice-Hall, 1968, pp. 14–25.

JAMES JOYCE

Born: Dublin, Ireland (February 2, 1882)
Died: Zurich, Switzerland (January 13, 1941)

Principal Works

NOVELS: *A Portrait of the Artist as a Young Man*, 1916; *Ulysses*, 1922; *Finnegans Wake*, 1939.

SHORT STORIES: *Dubliners*, 1914.

POEMS: *Chamber Music*, 1907; *Pomes Penyeach*, 1927.

PLAY: *Exiles*, 1918.

LETTERS: *Letters of James Joyce*, edited by Stuart Gilbert, 1957.

There was little in James Augustine Aloysius Joyce's family background to indicate that he was to become the most influential novelist of the first half of the twentieth century. His birth in Dublin on February 2, 1882, was the first of the fifteen that marked the union of mild Mary Jane Murray and witty, volatile, improvident John Stanislaus Joyce. Sometime medical student, petty politician, and officeholder, John Joyce managed to send his eldest son to Clongowes Wood College, County Kildare, in September of 1888. Declining family fortunes caused the father to withdraw him in 1891. As a day student, James Joyce continued his classical Jesuit education at Belvedere College in Dublin until 1898. At University College he contributed essays to the college magazine. He was scarcely eighteen when the prominent English *Fortnightly Review* published "Ibsen's New Drama," his perceptive appraisal of the art of the great Henrik Ibsen, in order to read whose plays Joyce had learned Norwegian. On October 31, 1902, he received his degree and a month later left Ireland for the Continent, visiting William Butler Yeats briefly in London on his way.

In Paris, as in Dublin, he found himself unable to attend medical school—he planned to combine medicine with writing. Half a year's poverty there ended when he was summoned home to his dying mother. In the year following her death in August, 1903, he taught school, consorted with lively companions, and wrote. He sent off a manuscript of thirty-six poems entitled *Chamber Music* to be offered to a London publisher, jotted notes for the short story volume *Dubliners*, and began *Stephen Hero*, an autobiographical novel. In this year he had also fallen in love, and on October 8, 1904, he and Nora Barnacle, a straightforward young girl from Galway, left Ireland together for Paris. In Pola and Trieste Joyce worked as a language teacher in the Berlitz school system, barely making enough for themselves and their son Giorgio, born July 27, 1905. In November Joyce sent *Dubliners* to an English publisher, beginning the nine years of rejections and disputes over alleged impropriety and irreligiousness that were to pass before the stories would appear. The year 1907 was marked by the birth of a daughter, Lucia, and the appearance of *Chamber Music*. The form of these finely wrought, musical love lyrics suggested the discipline and simplicity of Ben Jonson; their content recalled the romantic melancholy of the early Yeats.

Brief trips to Dublin in 1909 and 1910 were followed by a third in 1912, to fight for *Dubliners*, which was Joyce's last visit to his native land. *Stephen Hero*, most of it burned in despair in 1907, had been rewritten in a compressed, highly disciplined form as *A Portrait of the Artist as a Young Man*. Through Ezra Pound, American poet and *avant-garde* leader, the novel was accepted early in 1914 for serial publication in the new magazine, *The Egoist*. This success was crowned by the June publication of *Dubliners*. Some reviewers praised the author of the fifteen short stories for realism. Few realized that these polished portrayals of people afflicted with moral paralysis were also freighted with symbolic meanings and religio-mythic references. Having earlier resisted the temptation to call this book *Ulysses at Dublin*, Joyce had in the spring begun a big novel to be called *Ulysses*. In this same year he wrote *Exiles*, a rather static play, strongly influenced by Ibsen, which dealt with the problem of the possibility of complete spiritual freedom between two lovers. The Joyces moved to Zurich in June, 1915. There he continued his teaching, their poverty only a little relieved by funds from friends and relatives. But Joyce's reputation began to grow as both *Dubliners* and *A Portrait of the Artist as a Young Man* were published in New York in 1916. Several critics saw the semi-autobiographical novel as a work of genius, a realistic portrayal, through protagonist Stephen Dedalus, of a young artist's growth, revolt, and dedication against a background of family and religious conflict in politically strife-ridden Ireland. But as with *Dubliners*, fewer critics perceived the pervasive symbolism or the highly allusive, strictly disciplined, and densely textured character of the prose which was an integral part of the novel's meaning. A favorable review upon publication in England was counterbalanced by Joyce's sufferings from glaucoma and Nora's nervous breakdown. In 1917 portions of *Ulysses* appeared in *The Egoist*. A year later it began in serial form in *The Little Review*, only to be halted by court order in 1920 on the grounds of indecency.

In that same year the family moved to Paris, where a year and a half later Shakespeare and Company published *Ulysses* on February 2, 1922, Joyce's birthday. It received one of the most diverse and violent receptions ever accorded a great book. To some, this story of a single day in the lives of Stephen Dedalus and Leopold and Molly Bloom was an obscene picture of base people in a shabby Dublin. To others, these modern events, with their detailed correspondences to those of the *Odyssey*, symbolically elaborated fundamental themes in human experience. Displaying a mastery of a dazzling variety of prose styles, the difficult and erudite novel was on one level the most realistic treatment of a city in literature and on another level an intense exploration in depth of human nature through unforgettable characters whom the reader knew through their very thoughts, sometimes presented only half articulated in their streams of consciousness. By the time a celebrated legal opinion admitted the novel into the United

States in 1933, Joyce had become a *bête noire* to conservatives, a prophet to the *avant-garde*, and an internationally known modern master.

Handicapped by failing sight despite ten serious operations on his eyes, Joyce worked on. Excerpts from *Work in Progress*, later to be titled *Finnegans Wake*, revealed that he had virtually invented a new language. Spiced with borrowings from more than a dozen languages, the words were combined and spelled in such a way as to offer several denotations and connotations in a series of puns and word plays which loaded each individual verbal unit with literal and symbolic meaning. After its appearance in 1939, commentaries gradually explicated the novel for an almost wholly baffled public. They showed that Joyce was trying to compress the history and experience of the race into one night's time through the sleeping, dreaming, and waking experiences of Humphrey Chimpden Earwicker (Everyman), his wife Anna Livia Plurabelle (the great feminine force in life and nature), their twin sons, Shem and Shaun, and their daughter, Issy. More allusive, densely wrought, and demanding than all his previous works together, this novel is still a source of literary debate. Meditating a sequel, *The Reawakening*, Joyce was interrupted in his work by World War II and escaped with his family to Zurich, only to die there as a result of a perforated ulcer on January 13, 1941.

Bibliography

The definitive biography is Richard Ellmann, *James Joyce*, 1959. Also important is *James Joyce*, by Herbert Gorman, 1939. An important study is Stanislaus Joyce, *My Brother's Keeper: James Joyce's Early Years*, 1958. Other books in the critical canon are Stuart Gilbert, *James Joyce's "Ulysses,"* 1930; Louis Golding, *James Joyce*, 1933; Frank Budgen, *James Joyce and the Making of "Ulysses,"* 1934; Harry Levin, *James Joyce: A Critical Introduction*, 1941; Joseph Campbell and H. M. Robinson, *A Skeleton Key to Finnegans Wake*, 1944; Leon Edel, *James Joyce: The Last Journey*, 1947; R. M. Kain: *Fabulous Voyager: James Joyce's Ulysses*, 1947; Alan Parker, *James Joyce*, 1948; W. Y. Tindall, *James Joyce: His Way of Interpreting the Modern World*, 1950; L. A. G. Strong, *The Sacred River*, 1951; John J. Slocum and Herbert Cahoon, *A Bibliography of James Joyce*, 1953; Adaline Glasheen, *A Census of Finnegans Wake*, 1956; Hugh Kenner, *Dublin's Joyce*, 1956; and Marvin Magalaner and R. M. Kain, *Joyce: The Man, The Work, The Reputation*, 1956.

For articles in books see David Daiches, *The Novel and the Modern World*, 1939; *idem*, "James Joyce: The Artist as Exile" in *Forms of Modern Fiction* edited by W. V. O'Connor, 1948; Edmund Wilson, *Axel's Castle*, 1931; *idem*, "The Dream of H. C. Earwicker" in *The Wound and the Bow*, 1947; D. S. Savage, *The Withered Branch*, 1950; and Arland Ussher, *Three Great Irishmen*, 1953.

See also Edwin Muir, "James Joyce: The Meaning of *Ulysses*," *Calendar of Modern Letters*, I (1925), 347–355; Cyril Connolly, "The Position of Joyce," *Life and Letters*, II (1929), 273–290; Joseph Prescott, "James Joyce: A Study in Words," *Publications of the Modern Language Association*, LIV (1939), 304–

315; *idem*, "Homer's *Odyssey* and Joyce's *Ulysses*," *Modern Language Quarterly*, III (1942), 427–444; Ernest Bernbaum, "The Crucial Question Regarding Finnegans Wake," *College English*, VII (1945), 151–154; R. P. Blackmur, "The Jew in Search of a Son," *Virginia Quarterly Review*, XXIV (1948), 300–309; Hugh Kenner, "Baker Street to Eccles Street: The Odyssey of a Myth," *Hudson Review*, I (1949), 481–500; R. G. Kelly, "James Joyce: A Partical Explanation," *Publications of the Modern Language Association*, LXV (1949), 26–39; Edward Duncan, "Unsubstantial Father: A Study of the 'Hamlet' Symbolism in Joyce's *Ulysses*," *University of Toronto Quarterly*, XIX (1950), 126–140; Stanislaus Joyce, "James Joyce: A Memoir," *Hudson Review*, II (1950), 485–515; A. M. Klein, "The Black Panther—A Study of Joyce," *Accent*, X (1950), 139–154; F. J. Thompson, "A Portrait of the Artist Asleep," *Western Review*, XIV (1950), 245–253; Hugh Kenner, "Joyce and Ibsen's Naturalism," *Sewanee Review*, LIX (1951), 75–96; Joseph Prescott, "Notes on Joyce's *Ulysses*," *Modern Language Quarterly*, XIII (1952), 149–162; Richard Ellman, "The Backgrounds of *Ulysses*," *Kenyon Review*, XVI (1954), 337–386, and "The Limits of Joyce's Naturalism," *Sewanee Review*, LXIII (1955), 567–575; and William Empson, "The Theme of *Ulysses*," *Kenyon Review*, XVIII (1956), 26–52.

Additional critical studies have been reprinted in *James Joyce: Two Decades of Criticism*, edited by Seon Givens, 1948. There is also Marvin Magalner, ed., *A James Joyce Miscellany*, 2nd series, 1959, 3rd series, 1962. See further William York Tindall, *A Reader's Guide to James Joyce*, 1959.

FINNEGANS WAKE

Type of Work: Novel
Author: James Joyce (1882–1941)
Time: A cycle of history
Locale: Dublin
First published: 1939

Principal Characters

Finnegan, the title character, whose name is derived from Finn MacCool, for two hundred years the legendary captain of Ireland's warrior heroes; the name change is coined in a Joycean pun ". . . Mister Finn, you're going to be Mister Finnagain." Finnegan, a hod carrier, has fallen from a ladder and is apparently dead. The fall is symbolic of the various falls (with implied corresponding resurrections) of mankind. At the wake, Finnegan's friends become noisy and unrestrained, and in the course of the festivities, at the mention of the Irish word for "whiskey" (usqueadbaugham!), Finnegan sits up, threatening to rise. The mourners soothe him back. With Finnegan's demise, a new day is structured, and the hod carrier is supplanted by a man who has arrived to start life as Finnegan's successor.

Humphrey Chimpden Earwicker, also **Here Comes Everybody** and **Haveth Childer Everywhere.** HCE, the newcomer, is a tavern keeper. In keeping with the metamorphosis, his initials are a carry over from Finnegan's vocation of "hod, cement, and edifice." Another connection between the two men lies in Earwicker's emerging from Howth Castle and Environs, to which locale Finnegan's interment fades in the story. HCE has wandered widely, leaving his progeny along the way, from Troy and Asia Minor, through the lands of the Goths, the Franks, the Norsemen; he has traveled in Britain and Eire; he has Germanic and Celtic manifestations; up

through history he becomes Cromwell. In short, he is Here Comes Everybody and Haveth Childer Everywhere, representing civilization. At present, he is Earwicker, HCE, a sympathetic character, harrowed by relentless fate. In Phoenix Park (the Garden of Eden) he is caught exhibiting himself to several girls. This impropriety and the Dubliners' resentment of HCE as an intruder give rise to rumors that plague Earwicker, as the scandal takes on aspects of troubled times throughout history. The tumult in Earwicker's soul is consistent with the struggles of all battles in the past. The trials and tribulations of HCE continue until ultimately, after a description of the shadows on a windowblind of him and his wife in copulation, HCE turns from his wife. He is now the broken shell of Humpty Dumpty. The hopes of the parents are in the children. The cycle of man is ready to start anew.

Ann, also **Anna Livia Plurabelle,** HCE's wife. Just as Earwicker becomes Adam, Noah, Lord Nelson, a mountain, or a tree, so is ALP (as Ann is referred to generally throughout the book) metamorphosed into Eve, Isis, Iseult, the widow who serves at the wake, a passing cloud, a flowing stream. In this last transformation, as the River Liffey (which flows through Dublin), Ann plays her most important role. At the source, as a brooklet, she is a gay, young girl. Passing her husband's tavern, she is comely, matronly. Flowing on through Dublin, she becomes the haggard cleaning woman, carrying away the filth of the city. She finally moves on to the ocean, from which she rises again in mist to become rain and start again as a mountain stream. As Earwicker's wife, Ann plays the part of the motivator of her husband's energies. She is the housekeeper. She is the mother of his children. Among the various polarities spelled out in the book, Ann is love, opposed to war as depicted by Earwicker.

Kevin, also **Shaun the Postman, Chuff, Jaun,** and **Yawn,** one of their sons. In his domestic role as Kevin, he is the extrovert, the man of action. He is the political orator, the favorite of the people, policeman of the planet, bearer of the white man's burdens. He is the aggressor and the despoiler. As the symbolic Shaun, he is the Postman delivering to mankind the great message discovered and penned by his brother Jerry. Shaun, whose advice is "Collide with man, collude with money," enjoys the rewards of the carrier of good tidings. Shaun is one of the opposites in another polarity stressed by Joyce, the opposites being the principals in the Brother Battle.

Jerry, also **Shem the Penman, Dolph,** and **Glugg,** Kevin's twin brother. As the polar extreme of his brother, Jerry acts on inturned energy. The books he writes are mortifying in that they lose the lines of good and evil; they are rejected by the decent. Erratic in his introversion, he vacillates between vehement action and unselfish forgiveness. His uncontrolled love is as dangerous as his wanton hate. Among the domestic scenes, the personalities of the two boys are shown as

Glugg (Shem) loses to Chuff (Shaun) in their fights for the approval of girls. Also, as Dolph and Kevin working at their lessons, Dolph, the studious one, helps his brother with a problem; Kevin indignantly strikes Dolph, who forgives.

Isobel, HCE and ALP's daughter and sister of the twins. In the domestic scene she behaves as the child of an average family—playing, studying, and brooding on love. Symbolically, Isobel figures in episodes involving Swift and Vanessa, Mark and Iseult. Identifying her with Tristram's Iseult, HCE has illicit desires for Isobel; also, he envisions her as the reincarnation of the wife. These thoughts keep him young.

Among the myriad other characters—local and historical—that are intermingled in this poetic, convoluted account of birth, conflict, death, and resurrection are two significant groups:

Twelve Stately Citizens, who are variously a jury sitting in judgment on HCE, constant customers of Earwicker's tavern, leading mourners at Finnegan's wake, and the twelve signs of the zodiac.

Four Old Men, who are intermittently four senile judges, the four winds, the four recorders of Irish annals, the four phases of the Viconian cycle: theocratic, aristocratic, democratic, and chaotic. This last phase, marked by individualism and sterility, represents the nadir of man's fall. But mankind will rise again in response to the thunderclap, which polysyllabic sound Joyce uses to introduce his story of mankind.

Essay-Review

From that wonderful passage of revelation and recall as Molly Bloom hovers on the edge of sleep in the closing section of *Ulysses*, there was for James Joyce only one short step to the conception of *Finnegans Wake*. *Ulysses*, centering on the events of a specific day and place, presented an exploration of the thoughts and myriad impressions of the waking mind. *Finnegans Wake*, to which Joyce devoted seventeen years of concentrated effort, attempts to create a total world of night-mare fantasies and half-conscious dream sensations experienced in the sleeping mind during an interval which stretches out to enclose all space and time.

Like *Ulysses*, this novel has called into being an extensive literature of criticism and explications, a process of exegesis needed if the majority of readers are fully to understand Joyce's purpose and accomplishment. In the stream-of-consciousness content of *Ulysses*, however, Joyce had kept the edges of thought and imagery bright and sharp; here everything is blurred and muffled by physical sleep sensuously recorded as well as by the kaleidoscopic nature of Joyce's dream world and the shifting identities of his people as the dreamer pursues erotic fancies or is oppressed by feelings of guilt. Baldly stated, *Finnegans Wake* is the story of a man who in the course of a single night dreams of everything that has ever happened in the world. The dream shapes and memories set free in sleep float up from the subconscious not only in accordance with Freud's principles but also in keeping with Jung's, so that the episodes of the novel and the bewildering array of cross references go beyond the experience of the individual to reflect a state of being which may be vaguely referred to as the collective consciousness of the race.

Some facts about the dreamer are easily ascertainable. He is a man, apparently of Danish descent, named Humphrey Chimpden Earwicker, and he keeps a pub, the Bristol, somewhere between Phoenix Park and the River Liffey, in Dublin. To Dubliners his name has always been a matter for joking; in addition to its foreign sound it suggests an insect, the earwig, and he is sometimes referred to as H. C. Earwigger. He has a wife, Ann, and three children—Isobel, a daughter now in her teens, and twin sons, Kevin and Jerry. At some time in the past Earwicker had been involved in a scandal which is never really explained. Apparently he had accosted some young women or exposed himself in Phoenix Park. The true circumstance is never made clear. Although the incident happened a long time ago, Earwicker still fears investigation by the authorities. Now his old feeling of guilt has been renewed by the fact that on a rowdy Saturday evening in the pub Earwicker had drunk too much. There had also been some kind of altercation—possibly a drunk had been forcibly ejected—in which insults were exchanged and stones thrown; and this disturbance had reminded Earwicker of his earlier trouble. When Earwicker went to bed he was still drunk, and the events of the day disturb his troubled sleep. Since he and his wife no longer feel the passion they once had for each other, his dream does not turn toward her but involves his children. His feeling of guilt is again aroused by the incestuous nature of his dream, but the incest taboo intervenes to transform Isobel into Iseult la Belle and Earwicker into Tristram, thus severing the father-daughter relationship. By much the same process the other figures in the dream assume different personalities and meanings. Toward morning Jerry, one of the twins, calls out and the mother goes into another room to comfort the child. Earwicker, only half aware of her going, goes to sleep once more. As the book ends day is breaking and Earwicker and his wife are about to awake.

But to approach Joyce's novel in this fashion, in terms of narrative and character, is to do violence to his structure and style. *Finnegans Wake* is composed of many elements: an exile's memories of Dublin in his youth, theories of modern psychology, the substratum of myth and legend underlying the history of the race, and Joyce's marvelous command of the resources and texture of language. The book takes its structure from the *Principii d'una scienza nuova* by Giovanni Battista Vico, an early eighteenth century Italian philosopher. According to Vico's theory, human societies follow a progression of three distinct cycles, the ages of the gods, of great heroes, of ordinary men. Vico also believed that each cycle created its appropriate institutions and forms of government; autocracy gives place to democracy and democracy at last becomes anarchy before the cycle begins again. In the beginning, however, is Godhead, revealed in lightning and the crash of thunder, which leads man to restrain his brutish acts and appetites.

In the opening paragraphs of *Finnegans Wake* such a polysyllabled thunderclap suggests the Viconian cycle, but it is also associated with the fall of Finnegan the hod carrier. His wake is a noisy affair satisfactorily ended, even though at one stage the corpse, reanimated by the Gaelic word for whiskey, threatens to rise and walk once more. The interment of Finnegan—the Finn MacCool of Irish legend—fades into the landscape of Howth Castle and Environs from which, bearing the same initials, Humphrey Chimpden Earwicker emerges. Like Finnegan, Earwicker is a figure of mythopoeic stature, and in the novel he takes on a more universal significance indicated by his successive appearances as Here Comes Everybody and Haveth Childer Everywhere. His transformations on the universal and spiritual level are the essence of the novel. At the same time he functions on a different level indicated by ambiguous family relationships—as Adam fallen from grace because of the incident in Phoenix Park, as Tristram who loved the two Iseults, as Swift, the Irish dean who loved Stella and Vanessa, as the father of Shaun the Postman (Kevin) and Shem the Penman (Jerry).

Ann the wife also undergoes a transformation in the course of the novel. She becomes identified with the River Liffey, personified as Anna Livia Plurabelle, the stream of life eternally flowing toward the sea, the feminine principle into which all the women in the novel finally merge, just as in the end the river merges with the sea. The stream is time to Earwicker's history, and the Anna Livia Plurabelle sections are not only the finest in the novel but the particular triumph of Joyce's poetic prose.

Joined to these figures are others who function with only slightly less significance in the symbolic texture of the novel: the four old men who act as a kind of chorus but who may be identified at different times as the four apostles, the four points of the compass, the four ancient Irish kingdoms, the Four Masters of Irish legend, the four waves of myth; Shaun the Postman, who is Kevin and also Chuff, Jaun, and Yawn, the practical man who carries on tradition without knowing the nature of the message he bears any more than the postman knows the contents of the letter he delivers; Shem the Penman, also Jerry, Dolph, and Glugg, who is the writer, the maker of tradition. These figures are at all times surrounded by the history of past and present, shapes of legend and symbol in a dream vision which Joyce attempted to convey by a dream language to which he brought all the resources of his logopoeic faculty.

The style of *Finnegans Wake* represents a virtual re-creation of language. In this work Joyce exhibits every variety of style in the range of literature and, in order to achieve his multi-leveled effects, a battery of technical devices—the pun, the play on words, telescoped and portmanteau words, parodies, and connotations, to name only a few of the hundreds employed. Because so much of the understanding of the novel depends on linguistic techniques, its effects are auditory rather than visual. It is a book to be heard as well as to be read, for its structural devices within its cyclic outlines are more those of music than of narrative and drama.

Finnegans Wake is a bold experiment in form, meaning, and style. It is repetitious and irritating in its fragmented episodes and its efforts to push language to the limits of expression. Yet it is a tremendous if imperfect fable of the whole of mankind that carries man backward through the history of his moral and social habits to the mystery of his origin, tells the story of his fall, and affirms the promise of his rebirth. From the unfinished final sentence of the novel to its continuation in the first paragraph, with its images of the flowing river, Adam and Eve, and the circle of Howth Castle and its environs, the cycle runs its never-ending course of life, history, and time.

Bibliography

Adams, Robert Martin. *James Joyce: Common Sense and Beyond.* New York: Random House, 1967, pp. 172–213.

Atherton, James S. *The Books at the Wake: A Study of Literary Allusions in James Joyce's* Finnegans Wake. New York: Viking, 1960.

————. "Sport and Games in *Finnegans Wake*," in *Twelve and a Tilly: Essays on the Occasion of the 25th Anniversary of* Finnegans Wake. Edited by Jack P. Dalton and Clive Hart. Evanston, Ill.: Northwestern University Press, 1965, pp. 52–63.

Begnal, Michael H. and Grace Eckley. *Narrator and Character in* Finnegans Wake. Lewisburg, Pa.: Bucknell University Press, 1975.

Benstock, Bernard. *Joyce Again's Wake.* Seattle: University of Washington Press, 1965.

Burgess, Anthony. *Joysprick: An Introduction to the Language of James Joyce.* London: Deutsch, 1973, pp. 130–178.

————. *Re Joyce.* New York: Norton, 1965, pp. 185–272.

Burgum, Edwin Berry. *The Novel and the World's Dilemma.* New York:

Oxford University Press, 1947, pp. 109–119.

Campbell, Joseph and Henry Morton Robinson. *A Skeleton Key to* Finnegans Wake. New York: Viking, 1961.

Daiches, David. *The Novel and the Modern World.* Chicago: University of Chicago Press, 1939, pp. 147–157.

Goldberg, S.L. *James Joyce.* New York: Grove, 1962, pp. 103–115.

Goldsman, Arnold. *James Joyce.* London: Routledge and Kegan Paul, 1968, pp. 73–102.

Hart, Clive. *Structure and Motif in* Finnegans Wake. London: Faber and Faber, 1962. Partially reprinted in *Joyce: A Collection of Critical Essays.* Edited by William M. Chace. Englewood Cliffs, N.J.: Prentice-Hall, 1974, pp. 130–142.

Jones, William Powell. *James Joyce and the Common Reader.* Norman: University of Oklahoma Press, 1955, pp. 148–158.

Kenner, Hugh. *Dublin's Joyce.* Bloomington: Indiana University Press, 1956, pp. 265–370.

Levin, Harry. *James Joyce: A Critical Introduction.* Norfolk, Conn.: New Directions, 1941, pp. 139–205. Partially reprinted in *Joyce: A Collection of Critical Essays.* Edited by William M. Chace. Englewood Cliffs, N.J.: Prentice-Hall, 1974, pp. 113–129.

Litz, Walton. *Art of James Joyce: Method and Design in* Ulysses *and* Finnegans Wake. London: Oxford University Press, 1961, pp. 76–128.

————. *James Joyce.* New York: Twayne, 1966, pp. 99–111.

Magalaner, Marvin and Richard M. Kain. *Joyce: The Man, the Work, the Reputation.* New York: New York University Press, 1956, pp. 216–258.

Mink, Louis O. "Reading *Finnegans Wake*," in *Southern Humanities Review.* IX (1975), pp. 1–16.

Stewart, J.I.M. *Eight Modern Writers.* Oxford: Oxford University Press, 1963, pp. 465–483.

Tindall, William York. *James Joyce: His Way of Interpreting the Modern World.* New York: Scribner's, 1950, pp. 51–64.

————. *A Reader's Guide to* Finnegans Wake. New York: Farrar, Straus, 1969.

Ussher, Arland. *Three Great Irishmen: Shaw, Yeats, Joyce.* New York: New American Library, 1957, pp. 91–127.

Wilson, Edmund. "The Dream of H.C. Earwicker," in *The Wound and the Bow.* New York: Oxford University Press, 1947, pp. 243–271. Reprinted in *James Joyce: Two Decades of Criticism.* Edited by Seon Givens. New York: Vanguard, 1948, pp. 319–342.

A PORTRAIT OF THE ARTIST AS A YOUNG MAN

Type of work: Novel
Author: James Joyce (1882–1941)
Type of plot: Psychological realism
Time of plot: 1882–1903
Locale: Ireland
First published: 1916

This autobiographical novel follows the emotional and intellectual growth from childhood to young manhood of Stephen Dedalus, who is also the protagonist of the later, more complex Ulysses. *The development of artistic self-awareness necessitates young Stephen's rejection of the values of his upbringing, including blind patriotism and rigid Catholicism. The narration is in the stream-of-consciousness style which Joyce was instrumental in developing.*

Principal Characters

Stephen Dedalus (děd'ə·ləs, dē'də·ləs), a young man who is, like his creator, sensitive, proud, and highly intelligent, but often confused in his attempts to understand the Irish national temperament. He is bewildered and buffeted about in a world of political unrest, theological discord, and economic decline. In this environment he attempts to resolve for himself the problems of faith, morality, and art. At the end, feeling himself cut off from nation, religion, and family, he decides to leave Ireland in order to seek his own fulfillment as an artist, the artificer that his name suggests.

Simon Dedalus, an easy-going, talkative, patriotic Irishman who reveres the memory of Parnell. During his lifetime he has engaged in many activities, as a medical student, an actor, an investor, and a tax gatherer, among others; but he has failed in everything he has tried. Stephen Dedalus' realization that his father is self-deluded and shiftless contributes greatly to the boy's growing disillusionment and unrest. Simon is almost the stereotyped, eloquent Irishman who drinks much more than is good for him.

Mrs. Dedalus, a worn, quiet woman who remains a shadowy background figure in the novel. A woman of deep faith, her son's repudiation of religious belief becomes a source of anxiety and grief adding to her other cares.

Mrs. Dante Riordan, Stephen Dedalus' aunt. An energetic defender of anything Catholic, she despises anyone whose views are opposed to her own. Her special targets are certain Irish patriots, particularly Parnell, and all enemies of priests. Her violent arguments with Simon Dedalus on politics and religion make a profound impression on young Stephen.

Eileen Vance, Stephen Dedalus' childhood love. He is not allowed to play with the little girl because she is a Protestant.

E— C—, called Emma Clery in the "Stephen Hero" manuscript but in this novel more the embodied image of Stephen Dedalus' romantic fancies and fantasies than a real person. She is the girl to whom he addresses his love poems.

Davin, a student at University College and the friend of Stephen Dedalus. He is athletic, emotionally moved by ancient Irish myth, and obedient to the Church. To Stephen he personifies country, religion, and the dead romantic past, the forces in the national life that Stephen is trying to escape.

Lynch, an intelligent but irreverent student at University College. During a walk in the rain Stephen Dedalus tries to explain to Lynch his own views on art. Stephen's explanation of lyrical, epical, and dramatic literary forms helps to illuminate Joyce's own career as a writer.

Cranly, a student at University College. A casuist, he serves as an intellectual foil to Stephen Dedalus. To him Stephen confides his decision not to find his vocation in the Church and the reasons for his inability to accept its rituals or even to believe its teachings.

Father Arnall, a Jesuit teacher at Clongowes Wood School. While Stephen Dedalus is attending Belvedere College, during a religious retreat, Father Arnall preaches an eloquent sermon on the sin of Lucifer and his fall. The sermon moves Stephen so deeply that he experiences a religious crisis, renounces all pleasures of the flesh, and for a time contemplates becoming a priest.

Father Dolan, the prefect of studies at Clongowes Wood School. A strict disciplinarian, he punishes Stephen Dedalus unjustly after the boy has broken his glasses and is unable to study. The beating he administers causes Stephen's first feeling of rebellion against priests.

Uncle Charles, Stephen Dedalus' great-uncle, a gentle, hearty old man employed to carry messages. When Stephen is a small boy, he accompanies Uncle Charles on his errands.

Nasty Roche, a student at Clongowes Wood School. His mocking reference to Stephen Dedalus' name gives Stephen his first impression of being different or alienated.

The Story

When Stephen Dedalus went to school for the first time, his last name soon got him into trouble. It sounded too Latin, and the boys teased him about it. Seeing that he was sensitive and shy, the other boys began to bully him. School was filled with unfortunate incidents for Stephen. He was happy when he became sick and was put in the infirmary away from the other boys. Once, when he was there just before the Christmas holidays, he worried about dying and death. As he lay on the bed thinking, he heard the news of Parnell's death. The death of the great Irish leader was the first date he remembered—October 6, 1891.

At home during the vacation he learned more of Parnell. His father, Simon Dedalus, worshiped the dead man's memory and defended him on every count. Stephen's aunt, Dante Riordan, despised Parnell as a heretic and a rabble-rouser. The fierce arguments that they got into every day burned themselves into Stephen's memory. He worshiped his father, and his father said that Parnell had tried to free Ireland, to rid it of the priests who were ruining the country. Dante insisted that just the opposite was true. A violent defender of the priests, she leveled every kind of abuse against Simon and his ideas. The disagreement between them became a problem which, in due time, Stephen would have to solve for himself.

Returning to school after the holidays, Stephen got in trouble with Father Dolan, one of the administrators of the church school he attended. Because he had broken his glasses, Stephen could not study until a new pair arrived. Father Dolan saw that Stephen was not working, and thinking that his excuse about the glasses was false he gave the boy a beating. The rest of the boys for once were on Stephen's side, and they urged him to complain to the head of the school. With fear and trembling, Stephen went to the head and presented his case. The head understood and promised to speak to Father Dolan about the matter. When Stephen told the boys about his conversation, they hoisted him in their arms like a victorious fighter and called him a hero.

Afterward life was much easier for Stephen. Only one unfortunate incident marked the term. In a spirit of fun, one of his professors announced in class that Stephen had expressed heresy in one of his essays. Stephen quickly changed the offending phrase and hoped that the mistake would be forgotten. After class, however, several of the boys accused him not only of being a heretic but also of liking Byron, whom they considered an immoral man and therefore no good as a poet. In replying to their charges, Stephen had his first real encounter with the problems of art and morality. They were to follow him throughout his life.

On a trip to Cork with his father, Stephen was forced to listen to the oftentold tales of his father's youth. They visited the places his father had loved as a boy. Each night Stephen was forced to cover up his father's drunkenness and sentimental outbursts. The trip was an education in everything Stephen disliked.

At the end of the school year Stephen won several prizes. He bought presents for everyone, started to do over his room, and began an ill-fated loan service. As long as the money lasted, life was wonderful. Then one night, when his money was almost gone, he was enticed into a house by a woman wearing a long pink gown. At sixteen he learned what love was.

Not until the school held a retreat in honor of Saint Francis Xavier did Stephen realize how deeply conscious he was of the sins he had committed with women. The sermons of the priests about heaven and hell, especially about hell, ate into his mind. At night his dreams were of nothing but the eternal torture which he felt he must endure after death. He could not bear to make confession in school. At last he went into the city, to a church where he was unknown. There he opened his unhappy mind and heart to an understanding and wise old priest, who advised him and comforted his soul. After the confession Stephen promised to sin no more, and he felt sure that he would keep his promise.

For a time Stephen's life followed a model course. He studied Aquinas and Aristotle and won acclaim from his teachers. One day the director of the school called Stephen into his office and, after a long conversation, asked him if he had ever thought of joining the order of the Jesuits. Stephen was deeply flattered. Priesthood became his life's goal.

When Stephen entered the university, however, a change came over his thinking. He began to doubt, and the longer he studied, the more confused and doubtful he became.

His problems drew him closer to two of his fellow students, Davin and Lynch and farther away from Emma, a girl for whom he had felt affection since childhood. With Davin and Lynch he discussed his ideas about beauty and the working of the mind. Because he would not sign a petition for world peace, Stephen won the enmity of many of the fellows. They called him anti-social and egotistic. Finally neither the peace movement, the Irish Revival, nor the Church itself could claim his support.

Davin was the first to question Stephen about his ideas. When he suggested to Stephen that in everything Ireland should come first, Stephen answered that to him Ireland was an old sow that ate her offspring.

One day Stephen met Emma at a carnival, and she asked him why he had stopped coming to see her. He answered that he had been born to be a monk. When Emma said that she thought him a heretic instead of a monk, his last link with Ireland seemed to be broken. At least he was not afraid to be alone. If he wanted to find beauty, and to understand beauty, he had to leave Ireland, where there was nothing in which he believed. The prayers of his friends asking that he return to the faith went unanswered. Stephen got together his things, packed, and left Ireland, intending never to return. He did intend, some day, to write a book that would make clear his views on Ireland and the Irish.

Critical Evaluation

A Portrait of the Artist as a Young Man by James Joyce is possibly the greatest example in the English language of the *bildungsroman,* a novel tracing the growth and education of a young man, physically, mentally, and spiritually. Other examples of this genre range from Goethe's *The Sorrows of Young Werther* and Flaubert's *A Sentimental Education* to D. H. Lawrence's *Sons and Lovers.* Published in 1916, the work stands stylistically between the fusion of highly condensed naturalism and symbolism found in *Dubliners* (1914) and the elaborate mythological structure, interior monologues, and stream of consciousness of *Ulysses* (1922). In all three of these works there is a consistent concern for entrapment, isolation, rebellion from home, Church, and nation.

The novel is basically autobiographical, but in the final analysis the variants from, rather than the parallels with, Joyce's own life are of utmost artistic significance. The events of Stephen Dedalus' life are taken from the lives of Joyce, his brother Stanislaus, and his friend Byrne, covering the period between 1885 and 1902. The book begins with the earliest memories of his childhood, recounted in childlike language, and ends when Stephen is twenty-two with his decision to leave his native Dublin in search of artistic development to forge the conscience of his race. In the intervening years, like Joyce, Stephen attends the Jesuit Clongowes Wood School which he must leave because of family financial difficulties, attends a day school in Dublin, has his first sexual experience, his first religious crisis, and finally attends University College where he decides on his vocation as a writer. The dedication to pure art involves for Stephen, and Joyce, a rejection of the claims on him of duty to family, to the Catholic Church, and to Irish nationalism, either of the political type or of the literary type espoused by the writers of the Irish Renaissance. In his characterization of Stephen, however, Joyce eliminates much of himself: his sense of humor; his love of sport; his own graduation from the University before leaving Dublin; his desire to attend medical school in France; his deep concern for his mother's health; his affection for his father; and the life-long liaison he established with Nora Barnacle, who left Ireland with Joyce in 1904. The effect of these omissions is to make a narrower, more isolated character of Stephen than Joyce himself.

Portrait of the Artist as a Young Man is, on one level, an initiation story in which an innocent, idealistic youth with a sense of trust in his elders, slowly is brought to the recognition that this is a flawed, imperfect world, characterized by injustice and disharmony. Stephen finds this fact at home, at school, at church, in relationships with women and friends, and in the past and present history of his nation. Yet his pride prevents him from seeing any shortcomings in himself. In the second portion of the novel he becomes involved in the excesses of carnal lust; in the third portion, in the excesses of penitent piety, which also eventually disgust him. In the fourth section, in which he assumes the motto, *non serviam,* although he sees himself as a pagan worshiper of beauty, he becomes involved in excessive intellectual pride. In the final portion of the novel, Stephen develops his aesthetic theory of the epiphany—the sudden revelation of truth and beauty—through the artistic goals of "wholeness, harmony, and radiance." Thus his final flight from his real home—family, Church, nation—is still part of an almost adolescent rejection of the imperfections of this world and an attempt to replace it with the perfection of form, justice, and harmony of artistic creation.

Stephen Dedalus' very name is chosen to underline his character. His first name links him to Saint Stephen, the first martyr to Christianity and Stephen Dedalus sees himself as a martyr, willing to give up all to the service of art. His last name, Dedalus, is famous from classical antiquity. It was Daedalus, the Athenian exile, who designed the great caste for King Minos of Crete and later designed the famous labyrinth in which the monstrous Minotaur was kept captive. Later, longing to return to his own land, but imprisoned in his labyrinth, Daedalus invented wings for himself and his son, Icarus, to fly from the labyrinth. Stephen, the artist, sees Dublin as the labyrinth from which he must fly in order to become the great artificer Daedalus was. It is important to remember, however, that Daedalus' son, Icarus, ignored his father's instructions on how to use the wings and because of pride and desire to exceed, flew too close to the sun, melting his wings. He plunged into the ocean and drowned. It is only later, in *Ulysses,* that Stephen recognizes himself as "lap-winged Icarus" rather than as Daedalus.

Joyce's technical skill is obvious in the series of interwoven recurrent symbols of the novel. The rose, for instance, which is associated with women, chivalric love, and creativity, appears throughout the novel. Water, also, is found in almost every chapter of the novel: it can be the water which drowns and brings death; it can also be the water which gives life, symbolic of renewal as in baptism and the final choice of escape by sea.

The central themes of *A Portrait of the Artist as a Young Man*—alienation, isolation, rejection, betrayal, the Fall, the search for the father—are developed with amazing virtuosity. This development is the second, following *Dubliners,* of the four major parts in Joyce's cyclical treatment of the life of man which moves, as the great medieval cyclical plays, from Fall to Redemption, from isolation and alienation to acceptance. The later development of Joyce's analysis of the human condition and of the relationship of art to life can be found in *Ulysses* and *Finnegan's Wake.* Joyce himself has emphasized the importance of the word "young" in the title of this work, and his conclusion, in the form of Stephen's diary which illustrates Stephen's own perceptions, words, and style, forces the reader to become more objective and detached in his judgment of Stephen. Knowing that all of Stephen's previous epiphanies have failed, the reader recognizes in these final pages, the human complexity of Stephen's important triumph in escaping from the nets of Ireland but realizes that his triumph is complicated by important losses and sacrifices.

Bibliography

Anderson, Chester G. "Baby Tuckoo: Joyce's 'Features of Infancy,' " in *Approaches to Joyce's* Portrait. Edited by Thomas F. Staley and Bernard Benstock. Pittsburgh: University of Pittsburgh Press, 1976, pp. 135–170.

Brown, Homer Obed. *James Joyce's Early Fiction: The Biography of a Form.* Cleveland: Case Western Reserve University Press, 1972, pp. 108–131.

Burgess, Anthony. *Re Joyce.* New York: Norton, 1965, pp. 48–69.

Daiches, David. *The Novel and the Modern World.* Chicago: University of Chicago Press, 1939, pp. 101–110.

Drew, Elizabeth A. *The Novel: A Modern Guide to Fifteen English Masterpieces.* New York: Norton, 1963, pp. 245–261.

Goldberg, S.L. *The Classical Temper: A Study of James Joyce's* Ulysses. London: Chatto and Windus, 1961, pp. 41–65.

Goldman, Arnold. *James Joyce.* London: Routledge and Kegan Paul, 1968, pp. 4–6, 11–29.

Gorman, Herbert. *James Joyce: His First Forty Years.* New York: Huebsch, 1924, pp. 65–100.

Hoffman, Frederick J. *The Imagination's New Beginning: Theology and Modern Literature.* Notre Dame, Ind.: University of Notre Dame Press, 1967, pp. 22–33, 36–40.

Jack, Jane H. "Art and *The Portrait of the Artist*," in *Essays in Criticism.* V (October, 1955), pp. 354–364. Reprinted in *Joyce's* Portrait: *Criticisms and Critiques.* Edited by Thomas E. Connolly. New York: Meredith, 1962, pp. 156–167.

Kain, Richard M. "Epiphanies of Dublin," in *Approaches to Joyce's* Portrait. Edited by Thomas F. Staley and Bernard Benstock. Pittsburgh: University of Pittsburgh Press, 1976, pp. 91–112.

Karl, Frederick and Marvin Magalaner. *A Reader's Guide to Great Twentieth Century English Novels.* New York: Noonday, 1959, pp. 209–221.

Kenner, Hugh. "The Cubist Portrait," in *Approaches to Joyce's* Portrait. Edited by Thomas F. Staley and Bernard Benstock. Pittsburgh: University of Pittsburgh Press, 1976, pp. 171–184.

————. *Dublin's Joyce.* Bloomington: Indiana University Press, 1956, pp. 109–133. Reprinted in *Joyce: A Collection of Critical Essays.* Edited by William M. Chace. Englewood Cliffs, N.J.: Prentice-Hall, 1974, pp. 29–49.

————. "The *Portrait* in Perspective," in *Kenyon Review.* X (Summer, 1948), pp. 361–381. Reprinted in *James Joyce: Two Decades of Criticism.* Edited by Seon Givens. New York: Vanguard, 1948, pp. 132–174.

Lemon, L.T. "*Portrait of the Artist as a Young Man*: Motif as Motivation and Structure," in *Modern Fiction Studies.* XII (Winter, 1966–1967), pp. 439–450.

Levin, Harry. *James Joyce.* Norfolk, Conn.: New Directions, 1960, pp. 40–61. Reprinted in *Joyce's* Portrait: *Criticisms and Critiques.* Edited by Thomas E. Connolly. New York: Meredith, 1962, pp. 9–24.

Litz, Walton. *James Joyce.* New York: Twayne, 1966, pp. 60–72.

Magalaner, Marvin and Richard M. Kain. *Joyce: The Man, the Work, the Reputation.* New York: New York University Press, 1956, pp. 102–121.

Naremore, James. "Consciousness and Society in *A Portrait of the Artist*," in *Approaches to Joyce's* Portrait. Edited by Thomas F. Staley and Bernard Benstock. Pittsburgh: University of Pittsburgh Press, 1976, pp. 113–134.

Robinson, K.E. "The Stream of Consciousness Technique and the Structure of Joyce's *Portrait*," in *James Joyce Quarterly.* IX (1971), pp. 63–84.

Savage, D.S. *The Withered Branch: Six Studies in the Modern Novel.* London: Spottiswoode, 1950, pp. 160–168.

Stewart, J.I.M. *Eight Modern Writers.* Oxford: Oxford University Press, 1963, pp. 442–450.

Tindall, William York. *A Reader's Guide to James Joyce.* New York: Noonday, 1959, pp. 50–100.

Van Ghent, Dorothy. *The English Novel: Form and Function.* New York: Holt, Rinehartand Winston, 1953, pp. 264–276. Reprinted in *Joyce's* Portrait: *Criticisms and Critiques.* Edited by Thomas E. Connolly. New York: Meredith, 1962, pp. 60–74.

ULYSSES

Type of work: Novel
Author: James Joyce (1882–1941)
Type of plot: Psychological realism
Time of plot: June 16, 1904
Locale: Dublin
First published: 1922

A continuation of the story of Stephen Dedalus told in A Portrait of the Artist as a Young Man, *this major psychological novel is structured around Homeric parallels, so that the incidents, characters, and scenes of a single day in Dublin in 1904 correspond to those of the Odyssean myth.*

Principal Characters

Stephen Dedalus, a proud, sensitive young Irishman, a writer and teacher called **Kinch** (from "kinchin," child) by one of his friends. In his search for the nature and meaning of life, Stephen examines all phases of his existence. History, he says, is a nightmare from which he is trying to awake. As he looks back to his childhood, he can remember only his family's poverty and his father as a patron of taverns. His devotion to Ireland is not the answer to his search; she is an old sow, he believes, that eats her own young. His religion is not enough to make life purposeful. Stephen cannot dismiss his mother's deathbed prayer that he avow his belief, and his inability to comply frets him with remorse. Symbolically, Stephen is Telemachus, the son in search of a father. In effect, he finds a symbolic father in Leopold Bloom, an older man who takes care of Stephen after the young man has been in a street fight with British soldiers. Declining Bloom's invitation to live with him and his wife, Stephen goes out into the darkened street to return to the Tower where he is staying and to his dissolute life among the young men and students he knows.

Leopold Bloom, a Jewish advertising salesman who is, symbolically, Ulysses, the father of Telemachus. Bloom's yearning for a son stems from the long-past death of Rudy, his eleven-day-old son. A patient husband, he is cuckolded by his wife's business manager, but he is carrying on a furtive flirtation of his own. Bloom is Any Man, plodding through the daily routine of living—visiting bars, restaurants, newspaper offices, hospitals, and brothels of Dublin—because he hopes for something out of the ordinary but must be satisfied with the tawdry.

Malachi Mulligan, called **Buck,** a medical student and the friend of Stephen Dedalus. He points up Stephen's attitudes and philosophies, the two young men being opposites, the scientific and the philosophical. Buck, calloused to suffering and death by his medical training, says that death is a beastly thing and nothing else; it simply does not matter. According to Buck, Stephen's religious strain is all mockery; if it were not, Buck says, Stephen could have prayed with his mother. Buck is doubtful that Stephen will ever produce any great writing. The model for Buck Mulligan was the Irish physician and poet, Oliver St. John Gogarty.

Marion Tweedy Bloom, called Molly, whose background differs greatly from her husband's. Brought up in the atmosphere of a military post in Gibraltar, Molly, a lush creature and second-rate concert singer, finds life with her husband and life in Dublin dull. Her escape from the reality of the humdrum comes through love affairs with other men. Her latest lover is Blazes Boylan, a virile younger man. Bloom's suggestion that Stephen Dedalus come to live with them gives Molly a momentary tingle as she contemplates the pleasure of having a still younger man in the house. Molly's thoughts and reverie make up the final section of the book, as she considers the present but finally lapses into reminiscences of a sexual experience of her girlhood. She is Penelope to Bloom's Ulysses.

Blazes Boylan, Molly's lover and the manager of a concert tour she is planning. The business aspect of their meetings does not delude Bloom.

Haines, a young Englishman who lives in the Tower with Stephen Dedalus, Buck Mulligan, and other students and artists. His indulgence in drinking orgies alienates more ascetic Stephen. Because Haines has considerably more money than the other young men, he is frequently the butt of their sarcasm. Haines is an anti-Semite who fears that England may be taken over by German Jews.

Paddy Dignam, Bloom's friend, who dies of a stroke.

Father Coffey, who performs the funeral rites over the body of Paddy Dignam.

Mrs. Breen, a neighbor, to whom Bloom gives the account of the funeral.

Mrs. Purefoy, another neighbor, who, Mrs. Breen reports, is in a maternity hospital. Bloom's visit to the hospital to inquire about her leads to his meeting with Stephen Dedalus, who is drinking with a group of medical students.

Davy Byrnes, a tavern owner whose establishment attracts all types of people who discuss many subjects.

Barney Kiernan, the owner of a bar where Leopold Bloom gets into an argument with a patriotic Irishman and is ejected.

Mr. Deasy, the headmaster of the school where Stephen teaches. Deasy probably assesses Stephen's aptitudes rather exactly when he tells the younger man that he is more a learner than a teacher. In lamenting the influx of Jews in England, Deasy points out to Stephen that Ireland is the only country where Jews have not been persecuted—because she never let them in.

Talbot,
Cochrane,
Armstrong,
Comyn,
Edith,
Ethel, and
Lily, some of Stephen's pupils. Their indifference and ineptness are discouraging to their young teacher, giving rise to Deasy's prognosis of Stephen's career.

Milly, the Blooms' daughter. Her existence does not mitigate Bloom's longing for a son, nor does it lessen Molly's desire for romance and release from tedium.

Gertie MacDowell, a young girl who exhibits herself to Leopold Bloom on Sandymount shore.

Myles Crawford, a newspaper editor.

The Story

Buck Mulligan mounted the stairs of the old Martello tower and prepared to shave himself on that morning of June 16, 1904. A moment later Stephen Dedalus came to the stairhead and stood looking out over Dublin Bay. When

Mulligan spoke of the sea glinting in the morning sunlight, Stephen had a sudden vision of his own mother, to whose deathbed he had been called back from Paris a year before. He remembered how she had begged him to pray for her soul. But stubbornly rebelling against the Jesuit education of his boyhood, he had refused.

After breakfast Stephen and Mulligan went off with Haines, a young Englishman who also lived in the old tower. In spite of the Englishman's attempts to be friendly, Stephen disliked Haines, who was given to night-long drunken sprees. Stephen felt that his own life was growing purposeless and dissolute through his association with Mulligan and other medical students.

Stephen was a teacher at Deasy's school. Because it was a half-holiday, the boys were restless. Irritated by one of his pupils who was unable to do a simple arithmetic problem, Stephen saw in the boy the image of his own awkward youth. He was relieved when he could dismiss the class.

Later he walked alone on the beach. He thought of literature and his student days, of his unhappiness in Dublin, his lack of money, his family sinking into poverty while his hapless father made his daily round of the Dublin pubs. He saw the carcass of a dead dog rolling in the surf. Stephen remembered how a dog had frightened him in his childhood; he was, he thought wryly, not one of the Irish heroes.

Meanwhile Leopold Bloom had crawled out of bed to prepare his wife's breakfast. He was a Jewish advertising salesman, for sixteen years the patient, uncomplaining husband of Marion Tweedy Bloom, a professional singer of mediocre talent. He was vaguely unhappy to know that she was carrying on an affair with Blazes Boylan, a sporting Irishman who was managing the concert tour she was planning.

Munching his own breakfast of pork kidney, Bloom read a letter from his daughter Milly, who was working in a photographer's shop in Mullingar. Her letter reminded Bloom of his son Rudy, who had died when he was eleven days old. Bloom read Milly's letter again, wondering about a young student whom his daughter mentioned. For a moment he was afraid that Milly might grow up like her mother.

Bloom set out on his morning walk. At the post-office he stopped to pick up a letter addressed to Henry Flower, Esq., a letter from a woman who signed herself Martha. Bloom, unhappy at home and under another name, was carrying on a flirtation by mail. Idly he wandered into a church and listened to part of the mass. Later he joined a party of mourners on their way to the funeral of an old friend, Paddy Dignam, who had died suddenly of a stroke. During the service Bloom watched Father Coffey. He thought again of little Rudy and of his own father, a suicide.

The day's business for Bloom was a call at a newspaper office to arrange for the printing of an advertisement. While he was there, Stephen Dedalus also came to the office. The two men saw each other, but they did not speak.

Leaving the newspaper building, Bloom walked across the O'Connell bridge.

He met Mrs. Breen and gave her an account of Dignam's funeral. She told him that Mrs. Purefoy was in the maternity hospital in Holles Street. Bloom walked on, watching the sights of Dublin on a summer day. At last he entered Davy Byrne's pub and ordered a cheese sandwich. Later he went to the National Library to look at some newspaper files. There Stephen, flushed with the drinks he had taken at lunch, was expounding to Buck Mulligan and some literary friends his own ingenious theory of Shakespeare's plays and the second-best bed of Shakespeare's will. Again Bloom and Stephen saw one another but did not speak.

Bloom went to the Ormond Hotel for a late lunch of liver and bacon. Blazes Boylan came into the bar before he went off to keep an appointment with Molly.

Late in that afternoon Bloom got into a brawl in a pub where the talk was all about money Blazes Boylan had won in a boxing match. Escaping from the jeering crowd, Bloom walked along the Sandymount shore and in the dimming twilight watched young Gertie MacDowell. The moon rose. Bloom decided to stop by the hospital to ask about Mrs. Purefoy. As he walked slowly along the strand a cuckoo-clock struck nine in a priest's house he was passing. Bloom suddenly realized that he had been cuckolded again, while he sat dreaming his amorous fantasies on the Dublin beach.

At the National Maternity Hospital he learned that Mrs. Purefoy's baby had not yet been born. There he saw Stephen Dedalus again, drinking with Buck Mulligan and a group of medical students. Bloom was disturbed to find the son of his old friend, Simon Dedalus, in that ribald, dissolute company.

Bloom went with the medical students to a nearby pub, where Stephen and Buck Mulligan began a drunken argument over the possession of the key to the old tower. When the group broke up Stephen and one of the students went on to a brothel in the Dublin slums, Bloom following them slowly. All were drunk by that time. Bloom had a distorted, lurid vision of his wife and Blazes Boylan together. Stephen, befuddled, thought that his dead mother suddenly appeared from the grave to ask him again to pray for her soul. Running headlong into the street, he was knocked down in a scuffle with two British soldiers. After stopping briefly at a cabman's hut, Bloom took Stephen home with him. Stephen, exhausted by his wild night, remained silent and glum while Bloom talked about art and science. Bloom had begged him to spend the night, to leave Mulligan and his wild friends and come to live with the Blooms, but Stephen refused. Stephen took cocoa, then departed. The bells of St. George's Church were ringing as he walked off down the silent street.

Bloom went slowly to bed. As he drifted off to sleep he told Molly firmly that she was to get up and prepare his breakfast in the morning.

Molly Bloom lay awake thinking of Blazes Boylan. She thought of the mysteries of the human body, of people whom she had known, of her girlhood at a military post on Gibraltar. She considered the possibility that Stephen Dedalus might come to live with her and her husband. Stephen was a writer, young, refined, not coarse like Boylan. She heard a far, shrill train whistle. She recalled the lovers she had had, Bloom's courtship, their years together, the rose she wore in her hair the day Bloom had asked her to marry him as they stood close under a Moorish arch. So wakeful, earthy Penelope's thoughts flowed on, while her tawdry Ulysses, Bloom, the far wanderer of a Dublin day, snored in the darkness by her side.

Critical Evaluation

Approaching *Ulysses* for the first time should be done somewhat aggressively. If comprehension lapses—even for pages at a time—it is better to push on. For one thing, it is notoriously a novel to reread. Many elements early in the story make sense only after having read much further along. Bloom's potato talisman, for example, is mentioned in the fourth episode, but remains unexplained until the fifteenth. There are so many such difficulties, and of such variety, that readers sometimes feel lost in random flux. The persistent reader, however, will find that the novel is intensely structured. Joyce later speculated that he had made it perhaps too structured.

Too much or too little, structured it surely is. Although he said he did not want them published, Joyce let out two (very similar) "schemas." These charts indicate for each of the eighteen episodes a title corresponding to an episode in the *Odyssey*; the time of day; a dominant color; a "technic" (the style of the episode: for example, "narrative, young," "catechism, personal," "monologue, male"); a dominant "art" (history, literature, philology); an organ of the body (adding up to a more or less complete person); a dominant symbol (in the first episode: "Hamlet, Ireland, Stephan"); and correspondences between Homeric and Joycean characters. These schemes can be found, in their most complete form, in Richard Ellmann's *Ulysses on the Liffey*.

The schemas have not been an unalloyed blessing to Joycean criticism, for they are sometimes ambiguous or cryptic. However, it is difficult to think of another major author whose critics have been so influenced, indeed dominated, by a single piece of external evidence. The schemas are at least suggestive with regard to three of the more salient (and problematic) aspects of the book. These three, which will be discussed here, are the Homeric parallels, Stephen's theory about Shakespeare and Art, and the episodic structure and use of style.

Shortly after the publication of *Ulysses* the Homeric parallel was lauded by T. S. Eliot as having "the importance of a scientific discovery" and denigrated by Ezra Pound as a more or less gratuitous double-exposure "which any block-head could trace." The schemas and Joyce's notes make clear that he took the parallels very seriously, although "seriousness," for Joyce, is best understood in his word "jocoserious." The elaborate Homeric analogy is, however, surely not, as Eliot thought, merely a backdrop to heighten "the immense panorama of futility that is the modern world."

Ulysses had been Joyce's favorite hero even from his childhood. The quality he was to isolate as unique to the Greek hero was *completeness.* He observed that Ulysses had been a father, a son, a husband, a lover, a soldier who was at first a draft dodger and then a "hawk." Although this is a rather curious ideal, it suggests what may have been Joyce's purpose. The story of Ulysses constitutes such a full representation of a given complex of attitudes and values that Joyce was able to use it as a paradigm for the structure of a modern story. The *Odyssey* itself no doubt had been determined by the structure of Homer's intuitions about the nature of life. These intuitions, we would say, correspond, in the abstract, to Joyce's own. The at times rather wide digressions from Homer's story in Joyce's suggest this kind of sub-stratum "beneath" the Homeric substratum, which determines both in a manner similar to the combinatory processes of mathematical probability.

This ideal "complete" hero "beyond" even Ulysses would be the abstract person, possessor of the "organs of the body" of the schema. The schema supports this general contention in that the distribution of correspondences to Homer is not consistent. Bloom and Stephen are, in fact, only "in general" Ulysses and Telemachus. Correspondences listed on the schema indicate that in the first episode, for example, Stephen is Telemachus, but also Hamlet. In the ninth episode Ulysses is "Jesus, Socrates, Shakespeare"; they are each important there. Furthermore, as has been remarked, Stephen is more like a youthful aspect of Ulysses than like Telemachus, who is almost a minor character in Homer. There is, then, no one-to-one impersonation of Homeric characters. Rather, there is a play of functions pointing to an essential human, the abstract "Ulysses" who belongs not exclusively to Homer, but to the entire tradition of the Ulysses theme.

The ninth episode, *Scylla and Charybdis,* contains Stephen's aesthetic theory. The action is presented as a parable of artistic creation based on Shakespeare's biography. The way the "Ulysses" of the schema functions is rather complex. The schema says that Scylla is "The Rock—Aristotle, Dogma" and Charybdis "The Whirlpool—Plato, Mysticism." "Ulysses," who must sail between these perils, is given as "Socrates, Jesus, Shakespeare." This aspect of "Ulysses" is manifested in Stephen's discourse; Bloom is not even immediately present. The course is the one the artist must take. It in-cludes going between extremes of the inner and outer worlds of his personal experience. There is a struggle between the flux of everyday life and a perma-nent, repeated structure in the artist's Self. This structure is compared to the mole which remains on Stephen's breast although all the molecules of his body have changed, and, in the parable, to a supposed psychological trauma in Shakespeare's youth which determined the structure of his plays and their themes of usurpation, humiliation, and, later, reconciliation. The theory re-capitulates, at the level of the individual artistic psyche, the determinism treated by the novel as historical and sociological.

As to the individual episodes, the schema names a variety of elements of style which make each unique. Joyce told friends that he intended each to be able to stand on its own. Various episodes are sometimes anthologized and read like short stories. *Circe,* episode fifteen, has been produced as a play many times. There is narrational point of view in each episode, but it is clearly never the same. There is abundant exegetical literature for each episode, treating in detail the unity derived of its tone, style, and themes. For this overview, however, it is more important to note that the various episodic styles are part of a second structural principle in the novel.

Total autonomy *and* interdependence combine in the episodic structure; Stephen and Bloom, component elements of the "Ulysses" composite, partake of this combination and therefore avoid becoming mere allegorical types. They are, in fact, complete individuals. This pattern suggests the paradoxical doctrine of the Trinity, where three complete and equal Persons have one Essence. Of the Trinity, Joyce once said that when contemplating one Person, the others slip from view. So it is with Stephen and Bloom; for that matter, any individual episode in *Ulysses* seems capable of absorbing our whole attention. It is, therefore, the overview which leads us best through the myriad captivations of Joyce's odyssey.

Bibliography

Adams, Robert Martin. *Surface and Symbol: The Consistency of James Joyce's* Ulysses. New York: Oxford University Press, 1962.

Blamires, Harry. *The Bloomsday Book: A Guide Through Joyce's* Ulysses. New York: Barnes & Noble, 1966.

Burgess, Anthony. *Re Joyce.* New York: Norton, 1965, pp. 70–176.

Cronin, Anthony. *A Question of Modernity.* London: Martin Secker and Warburg, 1966, pp. 69–81, 86–96. Reprinted in *Joyce: A Collection of Critical Essays.* Edited by William M. Chace. Englewood Cliffs, N.J.: Prentice-Hall, 1974, pp. 84–101.

Daiches, David. *The Novel and the Modern World.* Chicago: University of Chicago Press, 1960, pp. 83–137.

Damon, S. Foster. "The Odyssey in Dublin," in *James Joyce: Two Decades of Criticism.* Edited by Seon Givens. New York: Vanguard, 1948, pp. 203–242.

Ellmann, Richard. Ulysses *on the Liffey.* London: Faber and Faber, 1972. Partially reprinted in *Joyce: A Collection of Critical Essays.* Edited by William M. Chace. Englewood Cliffs, N.J.: Prentice-Hall, 1974, pp. 102–112.

Empson, William. "The Theme of *Ulysses,*" in *Kenyon Review.* XVIII (Winter, 1956), pp. 26–52.

Gilbert, Stuart. *James Joyce's* Ulysses. New York: Vintage, 1955.

Goldberg, S.L. *The Classical Temper: A Study of James Joyce's* Ulysses. New York: Barnes & Noble, 1961. Partially reprinted in *Joyce: A Collection of Critical Essays.* Edited by William M. Chace. Englewood Cliffs, N.J.: Prentice-Hall, 1974, pp. 67–83.

————. *James Joyce.* New York: Grove, 1962, pp. 69–102.

Goldman, Arnold. *James Joyce.* London: Routledge and Kegan Paul, 1968, pp. 30–72.

Kain, Richard M. *Fabulous Voyager: James Joyce's* Ulysses. Chicago: University of Chicago Press, 1947.

Karl, Frederick and Marvin Magalaner. *A Reader's Guide to Great Twentieth Century English Novels.* New York: Noonday, 1959, pp. 221–252.

Kenner, Hugh. *Dublin's Joyce.* Bloomington: Indiana University Press, 1956, pp. 19–26, 158–262.

Levin, Harry. *James Joyce: A Critical Introduction.* New York: New Directions, 1960, pp. 65–135.

Litz, Walton. *The Art of James Joyce: Method and Design in* Ulysses *and* Finnegans Wake. New York: Oxford University Press, 1961, pp. 1–75.

————. *James Joyce.* New York: Twayne, 1966, pp. 77–98.

Maddox, James H., Jr. *Joyce's* Ulysses *and the Assault upon Character.* New Brunswick, N.J.: Rutgers University Press, 1978.

Magalaner, Marvin and Richard M. Kain. *Joyce: The Man, the Work, the Reputation.* New York: New York University Press, 1956, pp. 146–161.

Staley, Thomas F. "Stephen Dedalus and the Temper of the Modern Hero," in *Approaches to* Ulysses: *Ten Essays.* Edited by Thomas F. Staley and Bernard Benstock. Pittsburgh: University of Pittsburgh Press, 1970, pp. 3–28.

Stewart, J.I.M. *Eight Modern Writers.* Oxford: Oxford University Press, 1963, pp. 451–465.

Tindall, William York. *A Reader's Guide to James Joyce.* New York: Noonday, 1959, pp. 123–236.

Toynbee, Phillip. "A Study of James Joyce's *Ulysses*," in *James Joyce: Two Decades of Criticism.* Edited by Seon Givens. New York: Vanguard, 1948, pp. 243–287.

Wilson, Edmund. *Axel's Castle: A Study in the Imaginative Literature of 1870–1930.* New York: Scribner's, 1931, pp. 191–236. Reprinted in *Joyce: A Collection of Critical Essays.* Edited by William M. Chace. Englewood Cliffs, N.J.: Prentice-Hall, 1974, pp. 50-66.

RUDYARD KIPLING

Born: Bombay, India (December 30, 1865)
Died: London, England (January 18, 1936)

Principal Works

POEMS: *Departmental Ditties*, 1886; *Barrack Room Ballads*, 1892; *The Seven Seas*, 1896; *Recessional and Other Poems* 1899; *The Five Nations*, 1903; *The Years Between*, 1919; *Rudyard Kipling's Verse*, 1940.

SHORT STORIES: *In Black and White*, 1888; *Plain Tales from the Hills*, 1888; *Soldiers Three*, 1888; *Under the Deodars*, 1888; *Life's Handicap*, 1891; *Many Inventions*, 1893; *The Day's Work*, 1898; *Traffics and Discoveries*, 1904; *A Diversity of Creatures*, 1917; *Debits and Credits*, 1926; *Limits and Renewals*, 1932.

CHILDREN'S STORIES: *The Jungle Book*, 1894; *The Second Jungle Book*, 1895; *Captains Courageous*, 1897; *Stalky & Co.*, 1899; *Just-So Stories*, 1902; *Puck of Pook's Hill*, 1906; *Rewards and Fairies*, 1910.

NOVELS: *The Light That Failed*, 1890; *The Naulahka: A Story of West and East*, 1892 (with Wolcott Balestier); *Kim*, 1901.

TRAVEL SKETCHES: *Letters of Marque*, 1891; *From Sea to Sea*, 1899; *Letters of Travel*, 1920.

HISTORY: *The Irish Guards in the Great War*, 1923.

AUTOBIOGRAPHY: *Something of Myself*, 1937

Joseph Rudyard Kipling was born in Bombay on December 30, 1865; born at some distance from the center of empire, he was to become one of the chief expressers of the ideas that allowed the English to regard their great power with complacency or optimism. To many contemporary eyes, he justified the "white man's burden"; he also showed how it could be carried with efficiency and dignity.

Kipling was the first child of John Lockwood Kipling, architectural sculptor at the Bombay School of Arts, and Alice Macdonald Kipling. Both parents were children of Methodist ministers and contributed to the Biblical accent in many of Kipling's works. Like many other Anglo-Indian children, Kipling was sent to England for his education. Since he was nearsighted, Kipling could take little part in athletics; instead he spent his spare time writing for and editing the school paper at the United Services College at Westward Ho!, North Devon, the school that is portrayed in *Stalky & Co.* His school journalism led to professional journalism when Kipling returned at seventeen to India to work on the staff of the Lahore *Civil and Military Gazette.* Various assignments for this paper and the Allahabad *Pioneer* gave Kipling the opportunity to travel and provided abundant material for his books, which were then beginning to appear. From the publication of *De-*

partmental Ditties in 1886, the young writer found a wide—some would say a predestined—public for his poetic and narrative impressions of the Indian subcontinent as viewed from a certain distance. It was a distance, later critics have suggested, in which full knowledge and considerable condescension are mingled, in which sympathy and impatience are paradoxically mingled. This, certainly, is the note that is struck in *Plain Tales from the Hills* and it is a note that sounds, with some variations, throughout his work.

Kipling's own life, as a summary indicates, was full of the motion and change that many of his contemporaries regarded as the mark of a notable man. Kipling left India and spent three years of travel that took him to every continent. In the United States he married in 1892 Miss Caroline Starr Balestier of Vermont; there he lived until 1896, when, because of a disagreement with his brother-in-law, the Kiplings went to England to live. Kipling continued to win both great financial rewards and fame by work as a writer, literary and journalistic. He did not, and here he differed from many writers who are taken more seriously by contemporary criticism, turn aside from the chance to cover newsworthy events. Thus, he went as a newspaper correspondent on English naval cruises, made a second visit to America, and went to South Africa to report on the English forces in the Boer War. So great was the popular veneration for Kipling that his checks were preserved rather than cashed, his signature being worth more than the amount of the check. Kipling in his later years continued to mingle writing and action and covered events in World War I.

Kipling's greatest honor lay in the indefatigable public that responded to his vivid, decided insights into the role of beneficent imperialism and, more sensitively, into the differences between cultures brought into startling contact by conquest (e.g., *Kim*, 1901). But he was also the recipient of many specific honors, such as the Doctor of Laws degree from McGill University (1899), the Doctorate of Letters, Oxford (1907), and Cambridge (1908). Further, when in 1907 he became the first Englishman to win the Nobel Prize for Literature, it became apparent that his special sort of greatness was recognized beyond the confines of the English-speaking world. That he failed to become poet laureate on three possible occasions was—twice at least—the result of temporary difficulties rather than a reflection on his eminence; in 1892 he was in disfavor with Victoria, to whom he had referred as "the widow of Windsor," and in 1930 there was concern over Russia's reaction to honors accorded a poet who had once referred to Russia as "the bear that walks as a man."

Kipling died in London, January 18, 1936. He was buried in the Poet's Corner of Westminster Abbey, between Dickens and Hardy, between a writer who had been both popular and great and one who had been chiefly great. As a survey of criticism suggests, it is still an open question whether Kipling was great as well as popular, whether Kipling is—like both Dickens and Hardy—for the ages or interestingly symptomatic of his own times. On the day after Kipling's death, General Sir Ian Hamilton wrote in the London *Observer*: "His death seems to me to place a full stop to the period when war was a romance and the expansion of our Empire a duty." Kipling's whole literary output was a brilliant expression of an attitude later out of favor. He urged action at the expense of refinement of perception and rigorous analysis of the presuppositions on which action rests. He prolonged Carlyle's gospel of work and the hero; he seemed unsympathetic to democracy and many liberal causes, such as the emancipation of women; and his veneration for the signs and tools of material progress has seemed to some persons uncritical. In Kipling's eyes, neither the resolute man nor the steam engine could do wrong.

That the judgment of Kipling is not closed is indicated by the fact that T. S. Eliot could, in 1942, write seriously of Kipling. Eliot points out that Kipling writes transparently, "so that our attention is directed to the object and not to the medium." Kipling had great economy of words, had an "unsurpassed" ability with ballads, and was in "Recessional" a great hymn writer. One might add to this praise the observation that Kipling's energy was poured out in a variety of forms in a way that few more recent writers can imitate. Though *The Light That Failed* was Kipling's only attempt at the conventional novel, he poured out tales for adult readers, tales for children (e.g., *The Jungle Books*, *Just-So Stories*, and *Captains Courageous*), and poetry stirring to persons of differing ages. It is this manly variety that is his distinguishing mark. It is possible to accuse him, as did Richard Le Gallienne, of honoring "everywhere the brute and the bully." But such a judgment overlooks the perceptiveness and even the tenderness that, paradoxically, are interwoven with that which is strikingly typical and topical.

Bibliography

Of the various collected editions of Kipling's work the Burwash Edition, 28 vols., 1941, is definitive. The authorized biography is Charles Edmund Carrington's *The Life of Rudyard Kipling*, 1955. See also W. M. Hart, *Kipling the Story-Writer*, 1918; R. T. Hopkins, *Rudyard Kipling: A Character Study*, 1921; Patrick Braybrooke, *Kipling and His Soldiers*, 1926; G. C. Beresford, *Schooldays with Kipling*, 1936; F. F. Van de Water, *Rudyard Kipling's Vermont Feud*, 1937; Edward Shanks, *Rudyard Kipling: A Study in Literature and Political Ideas*, 1940; Hilton Brown, *Rudyard Kipling: A New Appreciation*, 1945; Rupert Croft-Cooke, *Rudyard Kipling*, 1948; and Bonamy Dobrée, *Rudyard Kipling*, 1951 (revised 1965); also André Maurois, *Prophets and Poets*, 1935; Edmund Wilson, *The Wound and the Bow*, 1941; Eliot L. Gilbert, ed., *Kipling and the Critics*, 1965; Louis L. Cornell, *Kipling in India*, 1967; Bhaskara K. Rao, *Rudyard Kipling's India*, 1967; and Angus Wilson, *The Strange Ride of Rudyard Kipling*, 1978. Lionel Stevenson, "The Ideas in Kipling's Poetry," *University of Toronto Quarterly*, I (1932), Edith Merielees, "Time and Mr. Kipling," *Virginia Quarterly Review*, XI (1935), 37–46, and 467–489; Basil Williams, "Rudyard Kipling," *Nineteenth Century*, CXIX (1937), 291–302.

Two books of selections with critical introductions are *A Choice of Kipling's Verse*, edited by T. S. Eliot, 1942; and *A Choice of Kipling's Prose*, edited by W. Somerset Maugham, 1952.

THE POETRY OF KIPLING

Author: Rudyard Kipling (1865–1936)
First published: Departmental Ditties, 1886; *Barrack-Room Ballads and Other Verses,* 1890; *The Seven Seas,* 1896; *Recessional and Other Poems,* 1899; *The Five Nations,* 1913; *Puck of Pook's Hill,* 1906; *Rewards and Fairies,* 1910; *The Years Between,* 1919; *Sixty Poems,* 1939; *Rudyard Kipling's Verse* (definitive edition), 1940

Essay-Review

Kipling began writing poetry in 1876 at the age of eleven; sixty years later he was generally forgotten, mistrusted, or despised for his popularity that had begun with *Departmental Ditties* fifty years earlier. Kipling's early success led to the Nobel Prize and his rejection of the Order of Merit, to be followed by later obloquy; today he is honestly respected for his short stories but still reluctantly for his verse, in spite of the selection of his poetry edited by T. S. Eliot in 1941. Yet Kipling is remembered most for his poems—"Recessional," "Gunga Din," "Mandalay," "The Land," "Danny Deever," "The 'Mary Gloster' "—and for such quotable lines as these from "The Ladies":

> . . . The Colonel's Lady and Judy O'Grady
> Are sisters under their skins!

The inescapable fact remains that if poetry is memorable speech, Kipling had the gift, used it, and was loved for it. He was the latest and the most prolific of the *popular* poets and perhaps the last in this century. His popularity came from his felicitous handling of the lolloping and hence memorable meters of anapest and dactyl, his wide range of novel, picturesque material, and his clear distinction in each poem between right and wrong. The lack of depth in his perceptions is balanced by the strength of his convictions and emotions. His material gave a voice or at least an echo to the people from whom it was drawn, and his easy superficiality of form and content made those people, generally at an elementary or largely oral level of literacy, read him eagerly and quote him frequently. His well-known "If" is an example of his popular, didactic appeal. This is not the whole of Kipling, but it is essential in the ballad-laureate of Empire.

The sources of Kipling's style are the ballad, the music-hall song, and the Psalms. The last gives him the long, prophetic line in which he sent home the dispatches in verse from the outskirts of the British Empire. Much more of his verse is accompanied by the choruses which perform the same iterative function. The ballads, of which "Sestina of the Tramp-Royal" is typical, are among his simplest and best though not most memorable verse; consider, for example, the quietly noble ballad stanzas of "The Veterans," written for "the gathering of survivors of the Indian Mutiny" in 1907, or the gentle raillery of "The Three-

Decker." Many poems depend on prologues and epilogues set in italics which bring the poem round to a repetition of the opening lines, again for emphasis. The most characteristic feature of his verse is its introduction not so much of clichés like "the White Man's Burden" in a poem of that title (addressed with considerable foresight to America) but of foreign terms. There are too many of these in the Indian poems, in which the Anglo-Indian is showing off to his British cousins: "all along of abbynay, kul, an' hazar-ho"; but a large number of poems stemming from the South African war and the larger number celebrating British regiments use native and military terms easily, such as *kopje* and *voorlooper* in "Two Kopjes." The worst feature of the verse is the hackneyed Cockney that his private soldiers speak; this dialect sounds better in prose.

A curious feature of Kipling's work is that he published in a unique form, most of his volumes combining stories and poems, sometimes with the same titles, such as "The Benefactors." Both are so related in *Puck of Pook's Hill*, which contains ten stories and sixteen poems, that it is a moot point whether his poems can be considered apart from the stories they illustrate (the subtitles often refer to these) or the events they celebrate, as in "The Rowers: 1902: When Germany Proposed that England should help her in a Naval Demonstration to collect debts from Venezuela." At least once his topicality misfired. "The Ballad of the 'Clampherdown' " records the boarding of a cruiser in battle; it was intended to mock the notion of boarding but was taken as Kiplingesque exaltation of the good old days.

The occupations of the folk heroes of Kipling's ballads, from the water-carrier in "Gunga Din" to the ship's engineer in "McAndrew's Hymn" to the Viceroy of India in "One Viceroy Resigns: Lord Dufferin to Lord Landsdowne," are exalted as the cogs of Empire, without his realizing, as George Orwell later pointed out, that an empire exists to preserve and extend an imbalance of trade.

Kipling's first success came when he told inside stories about the Indian Civil Service, for which his father worked, and in the next volume about the Indian Army: the materials were new in literature, the attitudes perhaps necessarily romantic as in the similar pioneer work of Bret Harte. In the first volume, Kipling mocks those who get promotion to the top of the ladder, and in the second he exults in the code and lore of subalterns and privates at the bottom of the scale. When he turns later to English affairs, his preference is not for the artisan but for the traditional yeoman, for the Hobdens of "The Land"; he alternately scolds and praises the leaders and people of England as they falter in or carry out their manifest destiny of guiding mankind, his deepest contempt being reserved for the mob and the inept leaders, as in "The Islanders," whom he blamed when the balance of trade evened and began to shift the other way after World War I. Kipling was born and bred on the British frontier where the issues were simplified, and his poems show his continual interest not only in India but also in South Africa, Canada, Australia, and New Zealand, as in "The Parting of the Columns" and "The Song of the Cities," stanzas on sixteen capitals of the Empire in four continents; he responded to the stimulus at the margin of Empire but found the heart of it, London, too sophisticated for his abilities and too preoc-cupied to heed his strident warnings.

He works mainly in the buffer area between the real center of imperial power and its subjects, often relating Eastern tales but mainly concerned with "the far-flung battle-line" between the civilized and the savage (English and fuzzy-wuzzy) and the "dominion over palm and pine" of "Recessional." But the buffer area is the meeting place of semi-civilized and semi-savage which accounts for the bru-tality of one and the nobility of the other. Orwell has termed this "colonial litera-ture." His phrase is accurate if one remembers that the Roman "colonus" was a military settler on the Roman imperial frontier. Here the distinctions between right and wrong are expressed in physical, not ethical force, though a simple insular ethic lies behind them.

Kipling was always conscious of the greater mass of Empire behind him, whether he was confronting the Indian or the English native, and the greater is always to be imposed on the lesser; he sings the greatness of Empire in many poems. This is frontier-bred psychology always at odds with its environment, whether it be the native civilization surrounding the proconsul or the settled life at "Home." Consequently Kipling's most dated poems show not his glorification of Empire but his continual hectoring of those who do not respond to his own vision of the "far-flung, fenceless prairie" as in "The Native-Born," or the "Never-never country . . . behind the ranges," which in "The Explorer" becomes "God's present to our nation." He is at his best when the glorification is not an oratorio on a set occasion but a lyric like "Mandalay," or when he uses the first person plural as in "The Lesson"—"We have had an Imperial lesson. It may make us an Empire yet."—and not the second person pronoun, as in "The Is-landers"—"then was your shame revealed, At the hands of a little people, few but apt in the field."

Kipling's metier was light journalistic verse; it became awkwardly and stren-uously didactic when he used it as a vehicle for the urgent lessons he was trying to teach the English before it was too late, and his chief enemy was apathy and ignorance about the enormous area and populations under the control of a ruling race on a small and distant island. If the authority of the knowledge he claimed turned to bullying, the sense of inescapable service was often elevated to sacrifice; he rejoices when a British Army Sergeant, "Whatsisname," reforms the Egyptian Army ("Pharoah and the Sergeant"), or when, as in "Two Kopjes," the British Army at last learns how to fight the Boer. Kipling weeps for the young men sent abroad untrained and forgotten, as in his commemoration of the veterans of the charge of the Light Brigade in "The Last of the Light Brigade." His greatest success was "The Absent-Minded Beggar," set to music and making over a quar-ter million pounds for the relief of the dependents of the British Tommy.

Amid the sprawl of his topics over time and space and the hustle of his many meters in hundreds of poems, it is difficult to find any guiding philosophy except a belief in the job well done. He had the pride of his own craft, and several of his best poems illuminate that craft: "The Story of Ung," the dissatisfied Neolithic cave painter; "The Conundrum of the Workshops," in which the Devil insists, "Is it Art?"; the famous "nine and sixty ways of constructing tribal lays" in "In the Neolithic Age." Apart from an occasional lyrical response to nature, as in "The Way Through the Woods" and a frequent response to English history, his poetry is of the world of military and political affairs and sometimes that of other men who know their job: Noah in "A Truthful Song," the smugglers in "A Smuggler's Song," a colonial farmer in "The Settler," the Boer farmer-fighter in "Piet," the Sudanese in "Fuzzy-Wuzzy," the self-made shipping magnate of his dramatic monologue, "The 'Mary Gloster.' " The smaller the object, the sharper is his observation ("The Sergeant's Wedding"); conversely, as the object of his poetic interest enlarged Kipling hated it, as he hates "The People" in "MacDonough's Song." His complementary belief in the competence of the lesser object against the greater mass is rarely defined, but it lies in the body of his own verse, the "tribal lays" in which, as in life, "The Gods of the Copybook Headings" provide all the answers before a man begins his task. From that given base all Kipling had to do was to attack inefficiency and novelty and to glorify the difficult work of the laboring few, Kipling among them, against the many. For his mass he used the British Empire at its apogee; his individual hero is "Thomas Atkins," the British Regular soldier to whom he formally dedicated *Barrack-Room Ballads* and, in spirit, all his work.

Bibliography

Bodelson, C.A. *Aspects of Kipling's Art*. Manchester, England: Manchester University Press, 1963.

Durand, R.A. *A Handbook to the Poetry of Kipling*. London: Hodder, 1917.

Gilmer, H.W. "The Classical Element in the Poems of Rudyard Kipling," in *Classical Weekly*. XIV (1921), pp. 178–181.

Green, Roger L. *Kipling: The Critical Heritage*. New York: Barnes & Noble, 1971, pp. 174–176, 184–191, 259–268.

Hungiville, Maurice. "Epithets and Epitaphs: Rudyard Kipling's Reputation as a Poet," in *Tennessee Studies in Literature*. XX (1975), pp. 138–150.

Rutherford, Andrew. *Some Aspects of Kipling's Verse*. London: Oxford University Press, 1967.

Stevenson, Lionel. "The Ideas in Kipling's Poetry," in *University of Toronto Quarterly*. I (July, 1932), pp. 467–489.

Weygandt, A.M. *Kipling's Reading and Its Influence on His Poetry*. Philadelphia: University of Pennsylvania Press, 1939.

PHILIP LARKIN

Born: Coventry, England (August 9, 1922)

Principal Works

POEMS: *The North Ship*, 1945; *Poems*, 1954; *The Less Deceived*, 1955; *The Whitsun Weddings*, 1964.
NOVELS: *Jill*, 1946 (revised 1964); *A Girl in Winter*, 1947.
ESSAYS: *All What Jazz*, 1969.

Philip Arthur Larkin was educated at King Henry VIII School in Coventry before going up to St. John's College, Oxford University, in 1940, where he took his A.B. during World War II, in 1943, and his M.A. in 1947. After leaving Oxford he held posts in various libraries, becoming librarian at the University of Hull, England, in 1955. Although he is the author of two published novels, *Jill* and *A Girl in Winter*, he is best known and most highly acclaimed because of his poetry. He is one of the generation of writers who reached maturity during the upheavals of World War II; when at Oxford he was a contemporary and a friend of John Wain and Kingsley Amis.

Like the other poets of his generation, Larkin shows in each of his volumes of poetry his awareness of uncertainty as an integral part of our human experience. He accepts that uncertainty, but it does cause, in his poetry if not in his life, a feeling of delusion, a feeling of disillusion, and a longing for adventure. Often he writes about the world of the person who is uncommitted and consciously so.

As a result of his work as a writer, especially as a poet, Philip Larkin has received a number of honors, including election to Britain's Royal Society of Literature. He was awarded the Queen's Gold Medal for poetry in 1965 and has also received an honorary D.Litt. from the University of Belfast, Ireland. His interest in music led to his becoming a correspondent on jazz, with many articles to his credit, for the London *Daily Telegraph*. He also published a series of essays on jazz music, *All What Jazz*, in 1969.

Bibliography

Larkin's poetry is discussed in M. L. Rosenthal, *The Modern Poets: A Critical Introduction*, 1960; J. M. Cohen, *Poetry of This Age, 1908–1958*, 1960; William Van O'Connor, *The New University Wits and the End of Modernism*, 1963; Frederick Grubb, *A Vision of Reality: A Study of Liberalism in Twentieth Century Verse*, 1965; and Roger Fowler, *Essays on Style and Language: Linguistic Approaches to Literary Style*, 1966. James Gindin comments on the novels in *Postwar British Fiction*, 1962.

Among important articles on Larkin are John Wain, "Engagement or Withdrawal: Some Notes on the Work of Philip Larkin," *Critical Quarterly*, VI (1964), 167–178; J. D. Hainsworth, "A Poet of Our Time," *Hibbert Journal*, XLIV (1966), 153–155; and Philip Gardner, "The Wintry Drum: The Poetry of Philip Larkin," *Dalhousie Review*, XLVIII (1968), 88–99.

THE POETRY OF LARKIN

Author: Philip Larkin (1922–)
First published: The North Ship, 1945; *Poems,* 1954; *The Less Deceived,* 1955; *The Whitsun Weddings,* 1964; *High Windows,* 1973

Essay-Review

Where does the mainstream of English poetry lie? Admirers of the contemporary British poet, Philip Larkin, see its source to be Wordsworth, its exponents Thomas Hardy and Edward Thomas, those quiet introverted men who refused to follow any but their own individual bent. It is a stream that moves underground when intensely classical or romantic spirits are abroad—an Eliot or a Dylan Thomas—but which is encouraged into the light by the ironic, contemplative aura of the later Auden. It was in the early 1950's that "The Movement" declared itself again, in Robert Conquest's anthology, *New Lines*; and the British public revealed itself as ready for Wordsworth's "real language of men." Novelists and poets began to take a hard look at changing social patterns: at middle-class mentality, suburban mediocrity, the uncaring anonymity of "I'm all right, Jack." It was a world shorn of metaphor and myth whose poets almost desperately declared themselves as humanists, dedicated to the revelation of "the real person or event." Honesty or the awareness of honesty was their religion.

Philip Larkin was one of the first, along with Kingsley Amis and John Wain, to reflect the new attitudes. He had started off at the beginning of the war as a promising young novelist. His first novel, *Jill*, was published in 1940, when he was twenty-one. It depicts the struggles of a scholarship boy thrust into the upper-class world of Oxford and resolving his problems through fantasy. However, Larkin's 1955 book of poems, *The Less Deceived*, indicated that he had stripped himself of the dream and was forcing himself to become at home in a world essentially alien to the dreamer. He was seeking a way to deal with things as they are, not as they seem; without distortion. Possibly for this reason the first poem in the book, and one that has been much anthologized, is most revealing of his approach and method. It is titled "Lines on a Young Lady's Photograph Album."

With its evocation of a real girl in a real place this poem sets the colloquial, self-mocking tone reminiscent of Hardy's ballads or of Meredith's lyrics. The structure, too, of this poem is as complicated and controlled as Hardy's: a loose iambic stanza of five lines with a consistent rhyme scheme, yet contemporary in its use of half-rhymes and assonances.

In his poem, Larkin is not satisfied merely to record, to photograph, even though he can flick out the exact word to create a picture. He can do more by commenting on the scene and involving the listener in his commentary. A purely "imagist" poet would be content to leave the picture objectively before us, implying only its emotional direction. But Larkin plunges right into exposition, and he goes over the scene again, peeling away leaf after leaf to reveal the frustration.

"Lines on a Young Lady's Photograph Album" reveals his control over his vehicle which is a characteristic of all of Larkin's work. He is an intent craftsman, creating within a set form an amazing variety of rhythmic variations. And he is steadily concerned with the evocative power of assonance and alliteration. This poem is aptly illustrative of Larkin's nostalgic, ironic mood; of his reasonable acceptance of an unsatisfactory world; and of his *angst* which never becomes self-pity. There is, in his best work, a stoicism which keeps the artist apart from the crowd yet not superior to it, as in "Reasons for Attendance" when he looks through a ballroom window at the jiving dancers.

Integrity and honesty are the keynotes in Philip Larkin's volume of poems titled *The Whitsun Weddings*. Here he is willing himself to identify more closely with other men, other houses, other streets and communities. Many of the poems are less introverted, consisting of more objective recording and less private comment. The result is lively, as a newspaper is lively; but one wonders whether the poems in this volume may not be more ephemeral, concrete though they appear. The colloquial tone makes them highly topical, but the sense of timelessness so strong in *The Less Deceived* is somehow missing. Throughout all these later poems it is remarkable to note how often the last line, which in *The Less Deceived* was often a *tour de force* of strength and confidence, has become wearily negative.

The title poem, "The Whitsun Weddings," is the longest and most ambitious. In all eight stanzas the iambic pentameter is skillfully handled; the structure, even the rhymes, seem as natural as everyday speech. Inevitably the tone brings to mind a trenchant, detached observer of the noisy wedding parties: the loud-voiced mothers, an uncle mouthing smut, genteel dress, cheap jewelry. The poem expresses a desperate sense of time spent uselessly. At the end it is no longer merely ironic; it has become a bitter commentary on the meaningless in life. "No exit" faces the poet. Is it that Philip Larkin, who began by assuming a steady unflinching view of the human condition, is now disturbed or terrified by the spectacle of humanity's nakedness? The world that had seemed so interestingly photogenic now forces him to examine its flesh and blood.

Bibliography

Bateson, F.W. "Auden's (and Empson's) Heirs," in *Essays in Criticism.* VII (January, 1957), pp. 76–80.

Bedient, Calvin. *Eight Contemporary Poets.* New York: Oxford University Press, 1974, pp. 69–94.

Brownjohn, Alan. *Philip Larkin.* London: Longmans, 1975, pp. 3–26.

Cox, C.B. "Philip Larkin," in *Critical Quarterly.* I (Spring, 1959), pp. 14–17.

――――――. "Philip Larkin, Anti-Heroic Poet," in *Studies in Literary Imagination.* IX (1976), pp. 155–168.

Davie, Donald. "Landscapes of Larkin," in *Thomas Hardy and British Poetry.* New York: Oxford University Press, 1972, pp. 63–82.

Fraser, G.S. *Essays on Twentieth Century Poets.* Totowa, N.J.: Rowman and Littlefield, 1977, pp. 243–253.

Gardner, Philip. "The Wintry Drum: The Poetry of Philip Larkin," in *Dalhousie Review.* XLVIII (Spring, 1968), pp. 88–99.

Jones, A.R. "The Poetry of Philip Larkin: A Note on Transatlantic Culture," in *Western Humanities Review.* XVI (Spring, 1962) pp. 143–152.

Kuby, Lolette. *An Uncommon Poet for the Common Man: A Study of Philip Larkin's Poetry.* The Hague: Mouton, 1974.

Lodge, David. *The Modes of Modern Writing.* Ithaca, N.Y.: Cornell University Press, 1977, pp. 212–220.

O'Connor, William Van. *The New University Wits and the End of Modernism.* Carbondale: Southern Illinois University Press, 1963, pp. 16–29.

Press, John. *Rule and Energy: Trends in British Poetry Since the Second World War.* London: Oxford University Press, 1963, pp. 97–108.

Rosenthal, M.L. *The New Poets: American and British Poetry Since World War II.* New York: Oxford University Press, 1967, pp. 233–244.

Scofield, Martin. "The Poetry of Philip Larkin," in *Massachusetts Review.* XVII (1976), pp. 370–389.

Thurley, Geoffrey. "The Legacy of Auden: The Poetry of Roy Fuller, Philip Larkin and Peter Porter," in *The Ironic Harvest: English Poetry in the Twentieth Century.* New York: St. Martins, 1974, pp. 137–162.

Thwaite, Anthony. "The Poetry of Philip Larkin," in *The Survival of Poetry: A Contemporary Survey.* Edited by Martin Dodsworth. London: Faber and Faber, 1970, pp. 37–55.

Timms, David. *Philip Larkin.* Edinburgh: Oliver and Boyd, 1973, pp. 1–35, 54–131.

Wain, John. "Engagement, or Withdrawl? Some Notes on the Poetry of Philip Larkin," in *Critical Quarterly.* VI (Summer, 1964), pp. 167–178.

Weatherhead, A. Kingsley. "Philip Larkin of England," in *Journal of English Literary History.* XXXVIII (December, 1971), pp. 616–630.

D. H. LAWRENCE

Born: Eastwood, England (September 11, 1885)
Died: Vence, France (March 2, 1930)

Principal Works

NOVELS: *The White Peacock*, 1911; *The Trespasser*, 1912; *Sons and Lovers*, 1913; *The Rainbow*, 1915; *Women in Love*, 1920; *The Lost Girl*, 1920; *Aaron's Rod*, 1922; *Kangaroo*, 1923; *The Boy in the Bush*, 1924; *The Plumed Serpent*, 1926; *Lady Chatterley's Lover*, 1928; *The Virgin and the Gipsy*, 1930.

POEMS: *Love Poems and Others*, 1913; *Amores*, 1916; *Look! We Have Come Through*, 1917; *New Poems*, 1918; *Bay*, 1919; *Tortoises*, 1921; *Birds, Beasts, and Flowers*, 1923; *Pansies*, 1929; *Nettles*, 1930; *Last Poems*, 1932; *Fire and Other Poems*, 1940.

SHORT STORIES: *The Prussian Officer and Other Stories*, 1914; *England, My England*, 1922; *The Ladybird*, 1923; *St. Mawr*, together with *The Princess*, 1925; *The Woman Who Rode Away*, 1928; *Love Among the Haystacks*, 1930; *The Lovely Lady and Other Stories*, 1933; *A Modern Lover*, 1934.

ESSAYS: *Psychoanalysis and the Unconscious*, 1921; *Fantasia of the Unconscious*, 1922; *Studies in Classic American Literature*, 1923; *Reflections on the Death of a Porcupine*, 1925; *Phoenix*, 1936.

PLAYS: *The Widowing of Mrs. Holyroyd*, 1914; *Touch and Go*, 1920; *David*, 1926; *A Collier's Friday Night*, 1934.

TRAVEL SKETCHES: *Twilight in Italy*, 1916; *Sea and Sardinia*, 1921; *Mornings in Mexico*, 1927; *Etruscan Places*, 1932.

LETTERS: *The Letters of D. H. Lawrence*, edited by Aldous Huxley, 1932.

The passion, conflict, turmoil, and striving that were to mark the brief life and fiery art of D(avid) H(erbert) Lawrence were there before him, clustering about his cradle in the grimy mining town of Eastwood in Nottinghamshire, England. Ten years before his birth on September 11, 1885, a genteel, ambitious school-mistress, Lydia Beardsall, had married an untamed, intensely physical coal miner, John Arthur Lawrence, only to learn in bitterness thereafter that they inhabited different worlds even while they lived in the same house and raised five children. Physically delicate, their sensitive fourth child cleaved to his mother and with her encouragement excelled at school and went on to win a scholarship to Nottingham High School in his twelfth year. After graduation he worked briefly and unhappily as a manufacturer's clerk in 1899 until he suffered a serious attack of pneumonia. After a long convalescence he took a position as a pupil-teacher in the Eastwood British School in 1902. He taught there and then at Ilkeston, Derbyshire, until September, 1906, when he entered Nottingham University (having

two years earlier placed in the First Division of the First Class in the nationwide
King's Scholarship Examination) for a two years' academic program leading to
an Arts degree. Qualified as a teacher two years later, he became junior assistant-
master at Davidson Road School, in Croydon, a suburb of London. He was to
teach there until November, 1911, when he was struck down again by pneumonia.

As early as 1905, however, his literary interests had begun to burgeon. Sharing
the joys of voracious reading with Jessie Chambers, the daughter of a family at
whose home he had spent part of his convalescence five years earlier, he had
begun to experiment with verse and fiction. At the same time he was being torn
by the conflicting emotional demands of Jessie and his mother, which he was to
record so vividly in *Sons and Lovers*. His mother's death, in January, 1911, was
followed in a few weeks by the publication of the novel he had begun with Jessie's
encouragement: *The White Peacock*. The story of a girl and two suitors, narrated
by a character strongly resembling Lawrence, it enunciated many of the themes
he was to treat throughout his career: competition between the over-cerebral,
over-civilized man and the earthy, vital one, as well as the need for truth and
naturalness in the relation between men and men, and men and women. *The
Trespasser*, based on the work of a London friend, Helen Corke, was a very uneven novel of frustrated love which followed a year later. In 1913 Lawrence's
reputation began to grow, for he published not only a book of poems, but the
powerful *Sons and Lovers*, to many his finest novel. Strongly autobiographical, it
relates the growth of a sensitive young man in a coal-mining environment through
emotional turmoil in his relations with a spiritual sweetheart, an earthy one, and
his possessive mother, from whose influence he liberates himself only after her
death.

A year earlier Lawrence's personal life had undergone as great a change as his
professional one. A month after they had met in April, 1912, Lawrence had
eloped with Frieda von Richthofen Weekley, mother of three small children and
wife of a professor of philology at Nottingham University. This was the first move
of the many which were to continue for the rest of Lawrence's life and to take
him around the world. While Frieda and Lawrence lived in poverty on the Continent he continued at work on poems, short stories, a novel, and a play. They
returned to England in 1914, when they were married, to find themselves the
objects of hostility and absurd charges of pro-German sympathies with the outbreak of World War I. An added blow was the reaction to *The Rainbow*, published in 1915. This novel of three generations of people like Lawrence's own,
with its forthright treatment of sexual passion and conflicting values and philosophies, was denounced as obscene by many reviewers, and the entire edition was
destroyed by court order. Poverty stricken, compelled to leave Cornwall by the
military, and badgered by the conscription authorities despite incipient tuberculosis, the Lawrences briefly lived in borrowed apartments in London and cot-
tages in Berkshire before departing for Italy for three years in 1919. The books of
poems which had followed *The Rainbow* were themselves followed by *Women in
Love*, which used some of the same characters as the earlier novel and introduced

clearly recognizable fictional portraits of J. M. Murry, Katherine Mansfield, Bertrand Russell, and Ottoline Morrell as well as Frieda and Lawrence himself. The novel, which showed the influence of the new psychological concepts of Sigmund Freud, seemed to contain a rejection of European culture and to plead for allegiance to a vital and primitive one which would reinfuse life and awareness of fundamental human drives. Besides his preoccupation with what he felt to be healthy and spiritual sexuality, there was throughout the book his vivid intuition about people, his preternatural sensitivity to nature, and his ability to infuse life into whatever he described. Clear too was his belief in the necessity for following instinctual feelings, for blood consciousness, as he called it, rather than sterile cerebral consciousness. This book far overshadowed *The Lost Girl* of the same year, an attempt, after the manner of Arnold Bennett's naturalism, to write a novel that would sell well. His ideas about psychology were elaborated in essay form in *Psychoanalysis and the Unconscious* and *Fantasia of the Unconscious*.

Invited in 1921 to come and live at Taos, New Mexico, by Mabel Dodge Luhan, who was building an artists' colony there, Frieda and Lawrence set out for the American southwest by way of Ceylon, New Zealand, and Australia. Before they reached America, in September 1922, Lawrence was to have absorbed enough material for two novels of Australia. They were preceded by *Aaron's Rod*, which dealt with the attempt of an established man, in the familiar mining environment, to start all over in middle life. In addition to his earlier themes, Lawrence had introduced two new ones: the drive to power and to domination over one's fellows. These studies were amplified by *Kangaroo* in 1923, a novel in which a man much like Lawrence is torn between the claims of Kangaroo, political leader of the Australian miners, and those of his own wife. This idea of the prophet, the leader of an almost-Utopia, was to loom larger with time in Lawrence's own thought and personality. *The Boy in the Bush* of the same year is a rewritten version of a novel by Martin Skinner, an adventure novel of early nineteenth century West Australia.

When the Lawrences arrived in Taos in September, 1922, he found himself as much at harmony as he was ever to be with any place. In Old and New Mexico the plains and mountains, the Indians with their tribal brotherhood and primitivism, all seemed to Lawrence a part of the answer to the problem of European decadence and personal fulfillment. Building, gardening, riding, baking, painting, Lawrence found time too to write verse and begin a novel presenting a modern incarnation of the Aztec god Quetzalcoatl. *The Plumed Serpent* was a violent novel in which both Christianity and sophisticated Europeans bowed before the strength of the blood consciousness of Indian primitivism and the primal instinctive behavior of its representatives. But now a near-fatal tuberculous hemorrhage complicated by malaria showed Lawrence how ill he was. His visa thus unrenewable, Lawrence returned to England and thence to Italy. Here in 1928 he privately printed *Lady Chatterley's Lover*, whose reception, with charges of obscenity and with seizures and threats of prosecution, dwarfed those of his earlier works. With unprecedented frankness of language and accuracy of detail, Lawrence presented the fulfillment of the unsatisfied wife of a maimed aristocrat by an ex-officer, now a game-keeper and a vital Lawrentian hero. *The Virgin and the Gipsy* was also set in England and bore many similarities in tone and character to *Lady Chatterley's Lover.* Lawrence's health steadily worsened, and after a month in a sanatorium, on his insistence he was moved to a villa at Vence, above Cannes. There on March 2, 1930, with Frieda at his side, he died. He left behind him an extraordinarily large body of work for so short a career, nearly all of it strongly marked by his unmistakable literary and philosophical imprint. His body was later reinterred at Taos.

Bibliography

No other writer of modern times has provoked so many slanted biographies or such a mass of controversial criticism. The fullest and most balanced biography is Harry Thornton Moore, *The Intelligent Heart: The Story of D. H. Lawrence*, 1955. Other biographical and personal studies include J. Middleton Murry, *The Son of Woman*, 1931; *idem, Reminiscences of D. H. Lawrence*, 1933; Catherine Carswell, *Savage Pilgrimage*, 1932; Mabel Dodge Luhan, *Lorenzo in Taos*, 1932; Horace Gregory, *Pilgrim of the Apocalypse*, 1933; Frieda Lawrence, *Not I But the Wind*, 1934; E. T., *D. H. Lawrence: A Personal Record*, 1935; Hugh Kingsmill, *The Life of D. H. Lawrence*, 1938; Knud Merrild, *A Poet and Two Painters*, 1939; Richard Aldington, *D. H. Lawrence: Portrait of a Genius But—*, 1950; Harry T. Moore, *The Life and Work of D. H. Lawrence*, 1951; Witter Bynner, *Journey with Genius*, 1951; E. G. Fay, *Lorenzo in Search of the Sun*, 1953; and James C. Cowan, *D. H. Lawrence's American Journey*, 1970.

For criticism see W. Y. Tindall, *D. H. Lawrence and Susan His Cow*, 1939; Anthony West, *D. H. Lawrence*, 1950; William Tiverton, *D. H. Lawrence and Human Existence*, 1951; Dallas Kenmare, *Firebird: A Study of D. H. Lawrence*, 1951; Mark Spilka, *The Love Ethic of D. H. Lawrence*, 1955; Mary Freeman, *D. H. Lawrence: A Basic Study of His Ideas*, 1955; F.R. Leavis, *D. H. Lawrence, Novelist*, 1955; Graham Hough, *The Dark Sun: A Study of D. H. Lawrence*, 1957; and Keith Alldsitt, *The Visual Imagination of D. H. Lawrence*, 1971.

The Achievement of D. H. Lawrence, edited by Frederick J. Hoffman and Harry T. Moore, 1953, is a collection of selected critiques from the great body of Lawrence criticism. See also William White, *D. H. Lawrence: A Check-List, Writings about D. H. Lawrence, 1931–1950*, 1950. *The Collected Letters* were edited by Harry T. Moore, 1962; and the *Complete Poems* by Vivian de Sola Pinto and Warren Roberts, 1964.

A recent study is David Daiches, *D. H. Lawrence*, 1977.

THE PLUMED SERPENT

Type of work: Novel
Author: D. H. Lawrence (1885–1930)
Type of plot: Symbolic romance
Time of plot: Twentieth century
Locale: Mexico
First published: 1926

Colorful in setting and symbolic in theme, The Plumed Serpent *is Lawrence's plea for a restoration of the primitive values of potency and blood unity. The symbols of quest and discovery are the ancient gods of Mexico, Quetzalcoatl and Huitzilopochtli; these dark gods alone can revitalize modern man, for Christianity has failed completely.* The Plumed Serpent *describes a world of male domination, instinctive life, and sexual rebirth.*

Principal Characters

Don Ramón Carrasco (dōn r̄rä·mōn′ kä·r̄räs′kō), a landowner and scholar who is convinced that only the revival of primitive religion can save Mexico. He establishes at his hacienda a meeting place for cultists who worship Quetzalcoatl, the Plumed Serpent. He is denounced by the Church and is seriously wounded when his political and religious enemies attack him. Finally, having desecrated the church at Sayula by burning the holy images, he converts it into a sanctuary of the ancient Aztec gods.

Kate Leslie, the widow of an Irish patriot, who goes to Mexico because she is restless. There she meets Ramón and his followers, saves Ramón's life when he is attacked by his opponents, and falls in love with Cipriano. A product of a culture dominated by technology, she finds strange the masculine, atavistic culture which is Mexico. Her woman's will is no match for the dark primitivism of this savage land and she marries Cipriano in a pagan ceremony conducted by Ramón. Though she wants to return to Ireland, she is impelled to stay with her husband in Mexico.

General Cipriano Viedma (hä·nä·räl sē·pryä′nō byäd′mä), a full-blooded Indian who joins Ramón to revive the ancestral gods. He comes to believe that he is a reincarnation of Huitzilopochtli, Aztec god of war. Kate is unaccountably drawn to him and at last yields to his masculine dominance.

Doña Carlota (dō′nyä kär·lō′tä), Ramón's first wife, a devout Christian who refuses to countenance his heresies. She leaves her husband and goes to Mexico City. Returning to Sayula when Ramón opens the church there as a pagan temple, she protests her husband's blasphemy. Overcome by hysteria, she suffers a stroke and soon dies.

Owen Rhys, Kate's American cousin, who accompanies her to Mexico. He returns to the United States prior to the time Kate becomes embroiled in the ancient god movement at Sayula.

Teresa (tā·rä′sä), Ramón's second wife, the daughter of a local landowner who is deceased. Her manner toward Ramón is passive and submissive.

Mrs. Norris, the widow of a former | Don Ramón.
British ambassador, who invites Kate to | Juana (hwä'nä), a servant at the house
tea. It is at her house that Kate meets | Kate rents in Sayula.

The Story

Kate Leslie was the widow of an Irish patriot. Restless after her husband's death, she had gone to Mexico with Owen Rhys, her American cousin. But Mexico oppressed her. Dark and secretive, the arid land weighed upon her spirit like a sense of doom. She saw it as a country of poverty, brutality, and bloodshed.

Owen and one of his friends took her to a bullfight. It was a distressing experience, for to her that ritual of death was like modern Mexico, vulgar and cruel, without muster or passion. At last, unable to endure the spectacle and the reek of warm blood, she announced that she was returning alone to the hotel. A downpour of rain began as she was leaving the arena and she was forced to wait in the exit tunnel with a crowd whose speech and gestures filled her with alarm. She was rescued from her predicament by a small, authoritative man in uniform who introduced himself as General Cipriano Viedma. A full-blooded Indian, he was impassive and withdrawn, yet vitally alert. While they talked, waiting for the automobile he had summoned to take Kate to her hotel, she felt unaccountably drawn to him.

The next day Mrs. Norris, widow of a former English ambassador, invited Kate and Owen to her house for tea. The general and his friend, Don Ramón Carasco, were among the guests. Don Ramón was a landowner and a distinguished scholar. There were reports of a strange happening near his estate at Sayula. A naked man was supposed to have risen from the Lake of Sayula and told the villagers that Quetzalcoatl and the old gods of Mexico were soon to return to earth. Don Ramón had promised an investigation. The story appealed to Kate's Celtic imagination; she wanted to go to Sayula and see the lake from which the Aztec gods were to be reborn.

Kate and Owen dined with Ramón before his return to Sayula. The guests talked about Mexican politics and the happening at the lake. One impassioned young man declared that only a great miracle, like the return of Quetzalcoatl, could save Mexico. Cipriano seldom spoke but sat, his eyes black and unfathomable, looking from Kate to his host. After dinner he and Kate walked in the garden. In the darkness she felt that he was a man of strange, almost primitive potency and impulses.

When Owen returned to the United States, Kate decided to go to Sayula for a time. There she found an old Spanish house that pleased her. With the house went a servant, Juana, and her two sons and two daughters. Liking the house and its surroundings, Kate rented it for an indefinite stay.

The people of Sayula were restless, filled with a spirit Kate had not seen elsewhere in Mexico. One night she heard drums beating in the village plaza. Men naked to the waist were distributing leaflets printed with a hymn to Quetzalcoatl.

Later the peons began to dance to the savage, insistent rhythms of the drums. In the torchlight the dance looked like a ritual out of old, almost forgotten times, a ritual men remembered in their blood rather than in their minds. Some said that Don Ramón was behind the new cult of Quetzalcoatl that was springing up.

Several weeks after Kate arrived in Sayula, Don Ramón and his wife, Doña Carlota, came to call. Doña Carlota was devoutly pious and eager to be friendly. When Kate visited Jamiltepec, Don Ramón's hacienda, she found soldiers guarding the gates. A drum was beating in the patio. Doña Carlota, hating the sound, told Kate that she was afraid because her husband was involved in the business of Quetzalcoatl. He wished to become a god, she confided, the reincarnation of the Plumed Serpent that the Aztecs had worshipped. Cipriano arrived at the hacienda for supper. That night there was a dance in the patio. Don Ramón promised that the reborn gods would bring new life to the country. The rains began, ending the hot, dry season.

Doña Carlota, refusing to witness her husband's heresies, as she called them, returned to Mexico City. Meanwhile the work of the Men of Quetzalcoatl continued. During one of his visits Cipriano asked Kate to marry him, but she put him off. Don Ramón continued to write and publish his hymns to Quetzalcoatl. Cipriano's soldiers distributed them. After he had been denounced by the clergy Don Ramón had the holy images removed from the church at Sayula and burned.

One day a group of his political and religious enemies, disguised as bandits, attacked Jamiltepec and tried to assassinate Don Ramón. Kate, who happened to be at the hacienda when the raiders appeared, killed one of the attackers and saved Don Ramón's life after he had been seriously wounded. Afterward she stayed much to herself, afraid of her own disturbed emotions. But she was being drawn slowly toward the dark, powerful forces of primitive awareness and power that she found in Don Ramón and Cipriano. The general now believed himself the living Huitzilopochtli, god of war. Fascinated and repelled, Kate yielded at last to his masculine dominance. Don Ramón married them with pagan rites and she became Malintzi, bride of the red-knifed god of battles.

When Don Ramón reopened the church, which he had converted into a sanctuary of the old Aztec gods, Doña Carlota appeared to protest against his blasphemy. Overcome by hysteria and fear of his implacable will, she suffered a stroke and died a short time later. Meanwhile Cipriano had been spreading the new doctrines among his soldiers. On an appointed night he was declared the living Huitzilopochtli, god of the knife, and in the rites of his assumption he sacrificed three of the prisoners captured after the attack on Don Ramón some weeks before.

Don Ramón married again. His bride was Teresa, daughter of a dead landowner of Jalisco. Watching Teresa's passive, female submission to her husband, Kate began to fear the dark potency, the upsurge of blood with which Don Ramón and Cipriano were arousing all Mexico. Men wearing the white and blue serapes of Quetzalcoatl and the red and black serapes of Huitzilopochtli were seen everywhere. When the Church excommunicated the leaders, revolt broke out. The President of Mexico declared the Church outlawed, and the faith of Quetzalcoatl became the official religion of the republic. Kate viewed these happenings with a sense of horror. Because the pride and strength of the old gods seemed to menace her spirit and her womanhood, she decided to return to Ireland.

But in the end she could not go. Cipriano with his black, impassive eyes and dark maleness was stronger than her European sensibility and her woman's will. Afraid of his violence but awed by the strength of a spirit stronger than her own, she felt wanted but not needed. The need, she realized, was her own, not Cipriano's. He had revealed to her the deep, dark, hot life of the senses and the blood, and she was trapped in his primitive world. She could never escape.

Critical Evaluation

Lawrence's belief in the necessity of the superman, which finds its fullest and most unnerving delineation in the characters of Don Ramón and General Cipriano in *The Plumed Serpent,* is an expression of despair in the capacity of a democratic culture to afford man a true equality and nobility. If man is to avoid cataclysm, he must, Lawrence believed, subordinate himself in order to attain spiritual well-being as Kate Leslie does to her husband Cipriano, and to the god-man, Don Ramón, and his religion of pure blood. Lawrence's thought progressed from outrage against the capitalists, who had destroyed his own coal-miner father, as well as English communal life, to the embrace of a philosophy of blood superiority. Like Thomas Carlyle, he began as a champion of individual liberty and with a plea for spiritual rebirth, and ended in fear of the people's growing power and with a call for individual subordination to an irrational, totalitarian idea.

In *The Plumed Serpent* Kate Leslie's adventures in Mexico, her spiritual reawakening, her embrace of the ancient god Quetzalcoatl, and her commitment to Don Ramón's priesthood should probably be read more as a parable than as a theological prescription. Although Lawrence did spend time in both old and New Mexico and was fascinated by the rituals and beliefs of the Indians, he found in the reincarnation of Quetzalcoatl a convenient metaphor for his vituperative attack on modern politics and Christianity. Democracy, he felt—which certainly is not the politics of the Mexico of the novel—succeeds only in "leveling downward," bringing all men to the same grayness, thus destroying individuality. Similarly, he felt Christianity, which he reinterpreted in his brilliant novella, *The Man Who Died,* destroyed the passionate inner life by denying the sanctity of the body and celebrating death.

In contrast, Don Ramón's politics and religion both elevate the individual —at the expense of the majority—and celebrate the passionate, physical life. At the beginning of the novel Kate is presented as an enlightened liberal, the widow of an Irish revolutionary, who is alienated from her own sexual needs as well as ordinary life. Her revulsion at the bull fight typifies her response to all physical reality. When she meets Cipriano, however, she begins to sense her own emptiness and feels an irrational attraction to him. Then, drawn by the seductive rhythms of the Mexican countryside and intrigued by the prophecy of Quetzalcoatl's second coming, Kate refuses to return to the United States with her cousin Owen Rhys. This decision makes her vulnerable for the first time in her life: she is prepared for conversion.

Before Kate can be granted the "light," however, she must negate herself and become subordinate, first to Cipriano and then to Don Ramón. Just as the latter sets up a theocracy with the Mexican state in subjection—the Catholic Church no longer the official religion—in order to save the state, he requires that all his followers give up their individuality to gain their freedom. Kate must, in effect, prostrate herself before Cipriano and his maleness, acknowledging her dependence, her femaleness. When she finally does so, relinquishing her plans to return to Ireland, and admitting her insignificance, Kate affirms the new religion of blood consciousness and personal subordination.

Bibliography

Alldritt, Keith. *The Visual Imagination of D.H. Lawrence.* Evanston, Ill.: Northwestern University Press, 1971, pp. 227–232.

Bedient, Calvin. *Architects of the Self: George Eliot, D.H. Lawrence, and E.M. Forster.* Berkeley: University of California Press, 1972, pp. 147–153.

Clarke, Colin. *River of Dissolution: D.H. Lawrence and English Romanticism.* New York: Barnes & Noble, 1969, pp. 131–147.

Cowan, James C. *D.H. Lawrence's American Journey: A Study in Literature and Myth.* Cleveland: Case Western Reserve University Press, 1970, pp. 99–121.

_____. "The Symbolic Structure of *The Plumed Serpent,*" in *Tulane Studies in English.* XIV (1965), pp. 75–96.

Daleski, Herman M. *The Forked Flame: A Study of D.H. Lawrence.* Evanston, Ill.: Northwestern University Press, 1965, pp. 213–256.

Draper, Ronald P. *D.H. Lawrence.* New York. Twayne, 1964, pp. 103–110.

Freeman, Mary. *D.H. Lawrence: A Basic Study of His Ideas.* Gainesville: University of Florida Press, 1955, pp. 177–188.

Gindin, James. *Harvest of a Quiet Eye: The Novel of Compassion.* Bloomington: Indiana University Press, 1971, pp. 217–221.

Hochman, Baruch. *Another Ego: The Changing View of Self and Society in the Work of D.H. Lawrence.* Columbia: University of South Carolina Press, 1970, pp. 230–254.

Hough, Graham. *The Dark Sun: A Study of D.H. Lawrence.* London: Duckworth, 1956, pp. 118–138.

Howe, Marguerite B. *The Art of the Self in D.H. Lawrence.* Athens: Ohio University Press, 1977, pp. 105–132.

Inniss, Kenneth. *D.H. Lawrence's Bestiary: His Use of Animal Trope and Symbol.* The Hague: Mouton, 1971, pp. 176–188.

Leavis, F.R. *D.H. Lawrence: Novelist.* New York: Knopf, 1956, pp. 67–73.

Lerner, Laurence. *The Truthtellers: Jane Austen, George Eliot, D.H. Lawrence.* New York: Schocken, 1967, pp. 172–180.

Moore, Harry T. "*The Plumed Serpent*: Vision and Language," in *D.H. Lawrence: A Collection of Critical Essays.* Edited by Mark Spilka. Englewood Cliffs, N.J.: Prentice-Hall, 1963, pp. 61–71.

Murry, John Middleton. *Son of Woman: The Story of D.H. Lawrence.* London: Jonathan Cape, 1931, pp. 282–302.

Niven, Alastair. *D.H. Lawrence: The Novels.* New York: Cambridge University Press, 1978, pp. 166–174.

Porter, Katherine Anne. *The Collected Essays and Occasional Writings of Katherine Anne Porter.* New York: Delacorte, 1970, pp. 421–425.

Sagar, Keith. *The Art of D.H. Lawrence.* London: Cambridge University Press, 1966, pp. 159–168.

Sanders, Scott. *D.H. Lawrence: The World of the Five Major Novels.* New York: Viking, 1973, pp. 136–171.

Spilka, Mark. *The Love Ethic of D.H. Lawrence.* Bloomington: Indiana University Press, 1955, pp. 205–219.

Stoll, John E. *The Novels of D.H. Lawrence.* Columbia: University of Missouri Press, 1971, pp. 198–222.

West, Anthony. *D.H. Lawrence.* London: Barker, 1950, pp. 127–131.

Yudhishtar. *Conflict in the Novels of D.H. Lawrence.* Edinburgh: Oliver and Boyd, 1969, pp. 250–266.

THE POETRY OF LAWRENCE

Author: D. H. Lawrence (1885–1930)
First published: Love Poems and Others, 1913; *Amores*, 1916; *Look! We Have Come Through*, 1917; *New Poems*, 1918; *Bay* 1919; *Tortoises*, 1921; *Birds, Beasts, and Flowers*, 1923; *Pansies*, 1929; *Nettles*, 1930; *Last Poems*, 1932; *Fire and Other Poems*, 1940; *The Complete Poems of D. H. Lawrence*, 1964

Essay-Review

In a note to his *Collected Poems* of 1928, D. H. Lawrence explains that he tried to arrange the poems in chronological order "because their personal nature made them, in effect, a biography of inner life and experience." Lawrence's poetry succeeds for just this reason; reading through the volumes, one must agree with the poet, for the poems, rough as they often seem, sometimes even crude and apparently rapidly composed, are everywhere alive; they pulse with the currents and cross currents of their author's tempestuous life and affairs. This effect is remarkable in any body of poems, and Lawrence's are also remarkable for their haunting, incantatory cadences. In other words, the poems are seldom witty or intellectually complex; they do not sustain, nor often require, a great deal of explication or analysis. Perhaps better, they require, even demand, that the reader open himself to them, to the gusts of emotions—anger, bitterness, tenderness, outrage, nostalgia, regret, love—which make up their form and content, and which are artistically controlled and expressed chiefly in haunting though generally a-metrical rhythms.

The poems, up to 1923, revolve around Lawrence's early loves, and his mother, especially. The background of these poems, which are all rhymed, may be supplied easily by anyone familiar with his autobiographical novel, *Sons and Lovers*. Then there is the death of his mother, which completes the volume of rhymed poems and forms, as Lawrence says, the "climax" of the first volume of the collected poems. Chronologically overlapping these poems, which run through the war into 1918, are the unrhymed poems of *Look! We Have Come Through*, poems which deal mainly with the love and torments of his marriage to Frieda, who left a husband and two children to marry Lawrence, and their life in Austria and in England during the war. The poems in *Birds, Beasts and Flowers,* including a number of his most original and powerful verses, are mainly of the Mexico and New Mexico sojourn of 1920–1923, and conclude the first volume. Beyond these, Lawrence's poems, most notably in *Pansies* and *Nettles*, become stridently political and anti-social. Roughhewn and full of disdain, anger, and even hate, often near hysteria, full of preachings and pronouncements, these poems are mostly strident. Then, with last poems like "The Ship of Death," he reaches the apex of his poetic career. Haunting, mysterious, religious, the poem is a unique contribution to modern verse.

It is nearly impossible to illustrate the nature of Lawrence's poetry with short quotations, for the poems build slowly from a perception, an image, to a flash of realized emotion. They are deceptively simple, for the curve of feeling is often very complex. They are organic growths, and the art with which Lawrence can build a poem to a climax is disarming. Details are introduced; they slowly become focused and symbolic as a *persona*, a viewpoint, is established, a conflict—emotional, sexual—is gradually engaged and developed through incremental repetition. Then the full experience blossoms forth, usually directly stated, and the poem, a little drama built out of the countercurrents of image and response, is completed. To quote a line or stanza hardly reveals the process, for it is a process, a chaffing, rhythmic movement building a tension and bringing a release, that is Lawrence's method. There is, therefore, more intensity and significance in the cadences and reiterations of detail than in single images or memorable lines. The poems grow, develop; they are not set pieces at all. Of course, all poems work in some such way, but Lawrence's more purely so, and with the attendant risk of flatness, prosaic-ness, and loss of form.

At his best, however, the accumulating reiteration of line, image, and thought has the effect of a chant or incantation. The poem becomes, as in "The Ship of Death" or in "Bavarian Gentians," a kind of ritual; or, in a sexually symbolic poem like "Snake," it is as if the poet's nerves were laid bare, quivering. In one of his early poems, "The Scent of Irises," Lawrence displays the facility with which he can develop a response, in this case to a jar of iris in the classroom where he was teaching. The iris and his lonely slavery as a schoolteacher take him back to an earlier time, in the country, with a girl. The internal rhyme and alliteration, the way the lines are "rove-over," the strongly cadenced anapestic like rhythm with the beautifully manipulated double stresses, the repetition of syntactic phrases and clauses, may, in their chanting effect and syncopation, remind one of Hopkins or Whitman or Dylan Thomas, and rightfully so. The developing tensions between the girl and the flowers, between sexual blossoming and the reminder, in the last line, of death, illustrates, in part, the manner in which Lawrence characteristically works. There is strife here, between the "you" of the girl and the "me" of the poet; the tone is half-nostalgic, half-bitter. The love and the simultaneous hate vie for precedence with desire and scorn: cross currents of emotion. The "Scent of Irises" is a very typical and compelling poem, as are the better-known "Love on the Farm," "Lightening," and "Monologue of a Mother," all from the early poems.

"Piano," from the last volume of the rhymed poems, *Bay*, is one of Lawrence's best-known poems but is often dismissed with the charge of sentimentality. The poem relates how the poet, listening to a woman sing, is reminded of his mother singing to him as a child, and how that remembrance sweeps his manhood away. The poem is *about* the dominion of mother over even the adult man, and one may say that the poem is *about* a particularly pernicious sentimentality, but the *poem* is not sentimental, for Lawrence has objectified and dramatized the experience.

His tormenting love for Frieda is well expressed in "A Young Wife," from *Look! We Have Come Through*. The experiences reflected in this volume begin in 1912 and extend to the winter of 1916. In the poem the ambivalent feelings, the tension between love and fear, are expressed in images of darkness and night. The darkness becomes a favorite image for Lawrence, as it appears to symbolize or suggest both death and the profound, mysterious, and instinctual inner life. Lawrence, who grew up in the raped countryside of the Midlands, whose father was a victim of the mines, became in "philosophy" a primitivist who felt that modern society had buried man's instinctual, most human self. He advocated a retreat from rationality and a rediscovering of the primitive "blood-consciousness" of emotional and instinctive being. His novel *The Plumed Serpent* depicts a revolution in Mexico, behind which lies the revival of the ancient Indian god Quetzalcoatl, whose "return" is accompanied by rituals which include the shedding of blood. The forms of modern culture were to be swept away; and the original man, including his cruelty, was to be resurrected. In another poem, "Snake," Lawrence vividly describes his horror at seeing a snake emerge from a hole in the ground and drink at the water fountain. He throws a stick at it, signifying modern man's fear of the primitive, the secret, and, by extension, the sexual. Then the poet is disgusted with himself for such a reaction of fear and cowardliness. The snake is described in terms which relate him to the ancient, primitive past, to the mythic. In Lawrence's view it is that modern "voice" of education which must be overcome, so that men can live as men again, and not as machines or as slaves to machines and the bloodless, passionless machine-owners, such as Lady Chatterley's symbolically crippled husband.

Lawrence's movement, in his verse, toward themes dealing with ancient myth and ritual is evidenced by this first stanza from "Middle of the World," one of his last poems, in which he asserts that the sea will never grow old, lose its blueness, or fail to raise its watery hills in the dawn-light as the ship of Dionysos, grape vines decorating its masts and attended by leaping dolphins, sails the waves.

Here is cadenced verse, working very close to prose, but highly poetic in its control, in its patterning of syntax, and the movement of symbolic images. Dionysos is, of course, a symbol and the repository of the life of passion, of instinct, and of freedom from the bindings of rationality. The sea is a symbol of fruition and life.

Lawrence searched the globe for a place where he could feel the ancient pulse of life still beating, but perhaps nowhere did he feel it more than in the burial caves of the ancient Etruscans; the vaults are vividly decorated with images of hunting and of other activities. From the Etruscan caves Lawrence drew the main images and primitive conception of death which informs "The Ship of Death." Perhaps his greatest poem, it was rewritten many times, but the reader will find it fully rewarding simply to read as one poem the many versions. It is a ritual chant in praise of death and man's journey toward obliviousness. In this poem Lawrence refers to the Etruscan belief in a kind of rebirth, when souls will need their tools and crockery, and the ship, which sails to oblivion, sails on through to a new life, where peace is renewed within the heart.

No quotation can communicate the poem. Alternately elegiac and joyful, the cadences subtly modulated to fit the moods, Lawrence here plumbs, as it were, his vision of death and touches on the rock of belief he found in ancient ritual and culture.

"Bavarian Genetians" also depicts an imaginative journey to the underworld, where in the mysterious life in darkness Lawrence chants, in images of Pluto's hell and of Persephone, his mythic sense of death and rebirth in the darkness of lost and legendary time.

THE SHORT STORIES OF D. H. LAWRENCE

Author: D. H. Lawrence (1885–1930)
First published: The Prussian Officer and Other Stories, 1914; *England, My England,* 1922; *The Ladybird,* 1923; *St. Mawr,* together with *The Princess,* 1925; *The Woman Who Rode Away,* 1928; *Love Among the Haystacks,* 1930; *The Lovely Lady and Other Stories,* 1933; *A Modern Lover,* 1934

Essay-Review

A prolific writer of short fiction, D. H. Lawrence often attempted in his stories and novellas to examine on a more limited scale the complex themes of his novels. In addition to the forty-seven stories reprinted in the three-volume *Complete Short Stories of D. H. Lawrence,* two fine autobiographical sketches, "Adolf" and "Rex," have been collected in *Phoenix* (1936), and ten other brief stories appear in *Phoenix II* (1968). Taken as a whole, the stories are remarkable for their range, vigor, and—considering the best—their mastery of form. What Lawrence once said in judgment of the novel, that it is the "one bright book of life," applies as well to his view of the short story. To Lawrence, a good work of fiction must represent the conflicts, the sway of oppositions, that simulate tension in real life. In his stories these tensions either are resolved to create a new poised balance, or they jar out of balance toward a tragic resolution.

Lawrence's greatest stories— "The Woman Who Rode Away," "The Blind Man," "Sun," "The Prussian Officer," "The Rocking-Horse Winner," "Odour of Chrysanthemums," "The Horse-Dealer's Daughter" —generally treat the conflict between one individual or several who stand for vitality, against some other individual or force that stands for sterility or death. In some stories, a character must make an existential decision to reject the narrow, sterile quality of his or her life and resolve instead to choose a full, freely loving, sexually responsive existence. Such a decision, to Lawrence, is always painful, for it requires courage and sometimes the will to renounce comfortable but outmoded moral sentiments. In "The Horse-Dealer's Daughter," for example, Mabel Pervin has suffered sullenly but without complaint the harshness of her drudgery. Although her brothers are full of vitality, exulting in the hard labor of the farm, she toils in suppressed rage, more like a tethered horse than a woman, her passions unawakened. Symbolically, indeed, she resembles a great draught-horse, powerfully sensual, restive, but held in control. Without fully comprehending her condition on the level of consciousness, yet miserable, she wades into a dirty pond to drown herself. At this moment a friend of the family, Dr. Ferguson, spies her, goes into the cold, dismal waters, and rescues her. As though reborn through symbolic baptism, he struggles first nearly to the point of death, then saves the girl and himself from a watery grave. But in rescuing Mabel, he has made possible his own salvation as well. Merely to exist is not enough; to be a vital person, he must also commit himself to love. As Lawrence resolves the moral parable of the story, Dr. Ferguson and

Mabel redeem each other from the death of sterility by choosing passion. In a curious adaptation of the Sleeping Beauty myth, Lawrence restores to life the Prince no less than his Princess.

To be sure, many of Lawrence's finest stories treat mythic archetypes in new, often startling ways. He relates in different forms the myth of Dionysus, the sensual god, as symbolic of the dark, unconscious instincts of the blood that oppose the conscious intellect. For example, in the short novel *The Ladybird*, Count Psanek exerts his mysterious, primitive power to awaken to passion Lady Daphne. In this tale and others, Lawrence also recasts vampire myths to treat themes on the corruption of sensual energy. In "Witch a la Mode," Winifred Varley threatens with her disturbing sensuality her passive lover, Bernard Coutts; and in "The Lovely Lady," Pauline Attenborough seems to retain her beauty despite her advanced age, so long as she can absorb from younger people their vitality.

To Lawrence the urge for vitality often runs counter to the impulse toward death. In the great story "The Prussian Officer," the Captain is obsessed both by hatred and love for his young orderly; inhibited, unable to express his homosexual passion for the youth, the officer turns upon Schöner sadistically to master his spirit. But the youth is also subconsciously drawn to his brutal superior. He murders the Captain as much out of compulsion, the physical need for release of tension, as from a desire for revenge. Once he kills, his ego disintegrates; he goes mad from "brain fever," and is at last united in death with his enemy. In Lawrence's complex myth of love-hatred, the protagonists destroy themselves through deadlocked passion.

In other stories, however, Lawrence allows passion free choice, and fortunate characters reach out for vitality instead of death. These stories are structurally quite simple, with the center of conflict a love triangle involving a woman and two potential lovers, only one of whom is worthy of her affection. In "The Blind Man," for example, Isabel Pervin rejects as a possible lover the clever but sexually timid Bertie Reid and clings instead to her blind husband Maurice, who possesses vital strength. But when Lawrence's characters choose unwisely, when they accept in place of a true life-sustaining quality some material substitute, they certainly destroy themselves. In "The Rocking-Horse Winner" Paul's parents reject their son's freely-offered love, choosing instead the worship of money, a false value that will kill their boy and shatter their hopes. In "Things" the acquisitive Melvilles waste their energy collecting art treasures, but the substance of their lives is empty, valueless.

Many of Lawrence's stories may be understood as moral parables that show how an unwise choice must inevitably lead to ruin. In "The Princess" Dolly Urquhart, spoiled and self-willed, loses her chance for passion. Similarly, Cyril Mersham in "A Modern Lover" and Edward Severn in "The Old Adam," both excessively fastidious, clever, but sexually passive young men, fail their tests of passion. These typically Lawrentian heroes, uncertain about their masculinity, abandon to a more virile rival their claims upon a woman. Other heroes, however, neglect to exercise their free choice for happiness, and they too suffer a defeat. In "England, My England," Egbert passively submits to the urgings of his manipulative father-in-law, Godfrey Marshall, to enlist as a soldier in World War I. When the young man dies in battle, Lawrence views him as much a victim of betrayal as of the mass hysteria that drove so many youths to war. Like Henry James, Lawrence deplores the manipulation of one's free will. In the great novella *The Fox*, Nellie March submits to the love of Henry Grenfel, whose predatory instincts symbolically resemble those of a fox, solely because he dominates her spirit. But his triumph is empty, for she has not chosen freely.

On the other hand, should a character make a conscientious choice, even if the choice is dangerous, Lawrence allows his protagonist a victory. In "The Woman Who Rode Away" —that strangest and most compelling of the short stories—a woman in fact rides away from civilization (a static, barren civilization) into the primitive hinterlands of the Chilchui Indians. There she submits as a human sacrifice to the gods. By acquiescing to a fate that goes beyond mere death, for the purpose of renewing the vital power of a whole Indian nation, she chooses, paradoxically, life. Similarly in "Sun," Juliet transcends her limitations as the product of an effete civilization by passing into the realm of nature. Submitting to the healing force of the sun, as though to a substitute lover, she becomes fully alive— a restored goddess. And in the extraordinary novella *The Man Who Died*, Lawrence extends his parable of transfiguration. A Christ-figure is restored to the flesh, a ritual transcending sterility and death, through the power of sexual passion. As in his novels, Lawrence's short stories treat the themes of a protagonist's choice between vitality and sterility, warmth and coldness, emotion and intellect, the unconscious and the conscious, the instincts of life or of death.

Bibliography

"The Fox"

Boren, James L. "Commitment and Futility in 'The Fox,' " in *University Review*. XXXI (1965), pp. 301–304.

Davis, Patricia C. "Chicken Queen's Delight: D.H. Lawrence's 'The Fox,' " in *Modern Fiction Studies*. XIX (1974), pp. 565–571.

Draper, R.P. *D.H. Lawrence*. New York: Twayne, 1964, pp. 125–126.

Engel, Monroe. "The Continuity of Lawrence's Short Novels," in *Hudson Review*. XI (1958), pp. 203–204. Reprinted in *D.H. Lawrence: A Collection of Critical Essays*. Edited by Mark Spilka. Englewood Cliffs, N.J.: Prentice-Hall, 1963, pp. 93–95.

Fulmer, O. Bryan. "The Significance of the Death of the Fox in D.H. Lawrence's 'The Fox,' " in *Studies in Short Fiction*. V (1968), pp. 275–282.

Goodheart, Eugene. *The Utopian Vision of D.H. Lawrence.* Chicago: University of Chicago Press, 1963, pp. 51–56.

Gregor, Ian. " 'The Fox': A Caveat," in *Essays in Criticism.* IX (1959), pp. 10–21.

Hough, Graham. *The Dark Sun: A Study of D.H. Lawrence.* New York: Macmillan, 1957, pp. 176–177.

Inniss, Kenneth. *D.H. Lawrence's Bestiary: A Study of His Use of Animal Trope and Symbol.* The Hague: Mouton, 1971, pp. 159–163.

Leavis, F.R. *D.H. Lawrence: Novelist.* New York: Knopf, 1956, pp. 320–332.

Moynahan, Julian. *The Deed of Life.* Princeton, N.J.: Princeton University Press, 1963, pp. 196–209.

Pritchard, R.E. *D.H. Lawrence: Body of Darkness.* Pittsburgh: University of Pittsburgh Press, 1973, pp. 140–141.

Pritchard, William H. *Seeing Through Everything: English Writers 1918–1940.* Oxford: Oxford University Press, 1977, pp. 80–82.

Sagar, Keith. *The Art of D.H. Lawrence.* London: Cambridge University Press, 1966, pp. 116–117.

Shields, E.F. "Broken Vision in Lawrence's 'The Fox,' " in *Studies in Short Fiction.* IX (1972), pp. 353–363.

Tedlock, E.W. *D.H. Lawrence: Artist and Rebel.* Albuquerque: University of New Mexico Press, 1963, pp. 116–120.

Vickery, John B. "Myth and Ritual in the Shorter Fiction of D.H. Lawrence," in *Modern Fiction Studies.* V (1959), pp. 78–82. Reprinted in *Myth and Literature: Contemporary Theory and Practice.* Edited by John B. Vickery. Lincoln: University of Nebraska Press, 1966, pp. 310–313.

"The Man Who Died"

Draper, R.P. *D.H. Lawrence.* New York: Twayne, 1964, pp. 144–148.

Eisenstein, Samuel A. *Boarding the Ship of Death: D.H. Lawrence's Quester Heroes.* The Hague: Mouton, 1974, pp. 126–148.

Engel, Monroe. "The Continuity of Lawrence's Short Novels," in *Hudson Review.* XI (1958), pp. 208–209. Reprinted in *D.H. Lawrence: A Collection of Critical Essays.* Edited by Mark Spilka. Englewood Cliffs, N.J.: Prentice-Hall, 1963, pp. 99–100.

Ford, George H. *Double Measure: A Study of the Novels and Stories of D.H. Lawrence.* New York: Holt, Rinehart and Winston, 1965, pp. 104–111.

Goodheart, Eugene. *The Utopian Vision of D.H. Lawrence.* Chicago: University of Chicago Press, 1963, pp. 149–160. Reprinted in *Critics on D.H. Law-*

rence. Edited by W.T. Andrews. Coral Gables, Fla.: University of Miami Press, 1971, pp. 109–116.

Hough, Graham. *The Dark Sun: A Study of D.H. Lawrence.* New York: Macmillan, 1957, pp. 246–257. Reprinted in *D.H. Lawrence: A Collection of Critical Essays.* Edited by Mark Spilka. Englewood Cliffs, N.J.: Prentice-Hall, 1963, pp. 101–111.

Kunkel, Francis L. *Passion and the Passion: Sex and Religion in Modern Literature.* Philadelphia: Westminster Press, 1975, pp. 37–57.

Ledoux, Larry V. "Christ and Isis: The Function of the Dying and Reviving God in 'The Man Who Died,' " in *D.H. Lawrence Review.* V (1972), pp. 132–148.

Murry, John Middleton. *Son of Woman: The Story of D.H. Lawrence.* London: Jonathan Cape, 1931, pp. 349–360.

Nahal, Chaman. *D.H. Lawrence: An Eastern View.* South Brunswick, N.J.: A.S. Barnes, 1970, pp. 216–235.

Panichas, George A. *Adventures in Consciousness: The Meaning of D.H. Lawrence's Religious Quest.* The Hague: Mouton, 1964, pp. 128–135.

Pritchard, R.E. *D.H. Lawrence: Body of Darkness.* Pittsburgh: University of Pittsburgh Press, 1973, pp. 195–197.

Sagar, Keith. *The Art of D.H. Lawrence.* London: Cambridge University Press, 1966, pp. 216–226.

Spilka, Mark. *The Love Ethic of D.H. Lawrence.* Bloomington: Indiana University Press, 1955, pp. 219–231.

Stewart, J.I.M. *Eight Modern Writers.* Oxford: Clarendon Press, 1963, pp. 580–582.

Tedlock, E.W. *D.H. Lawrence: Artist and Rebel.* Albuquerque: University of New Mexico Press, 1963, pp. 216–220.

Widmer, Kingsley. *The Art of Perversity.* Seattle: University of Washington Press, 1962, pp. 200–214.

"The Rocking Horse Winner"

Amon, Frank. "D.H. Lawrence 'The Rocking Horse Winner,' " in *The Achievement of D.H. Lawrence.* Edited by Frederick J. Hoffman and Harry T. Moore. Norman: University of Oklahoma Press, 1953, pp. 231–233. Reprinted in *The Rocking Horse Winner.* Edited by Dominick P. Consolo. Columbus, Oh.: Merrill, 1969, pp. 92–93.

Beauchamp, Gorman. "Lawrence's 'The Rocking Horse Winner,' " in *Explicator.* XXXI (1973), item 32.

Burroughs, William D. "No Defense for 'The Rocking Horse Winner,' " in *College English.* XXIV (1963), p. 323. Reprinted in *The Rocking Horse*

Winner. Edited by Dominick P. Consolo. Columbus, Oh.: Merrill, 1969, pp. 55–56.

Draper, R.P. *D.H. Lawrence.* New York: Twayne, 1964, p. 141.

Goldberg, Michael. "Lawrence's 'The Rocking Horse Winner': A Dickensian Fable?," in *Modern Fiction Studies.* XV (1969), pp. 525–536.

Gordon, Caroline and Allen Tate. *The House of Fiction.* New York: Scribner's, 1960, pp. 343–351. Reprinted in *The Rocking Horse Winner.* Edited by Dominick P. Consolo. Columbus, Oh.: Merrill, 1969, pp. 37–40.

Junkins, Donald. " 'The Rocking Horse Winner': A Modern Myth," in *Studies in Short Fiction.* II (1964), pp. 87–89.

Lamson, Roy, Hallet Smith, Hugh Maclean and Wallace W. Douglas. *The Critical Reader.* New York: Norton, 1962, pp. 542–547. Reprinted in *The Rocking Horse Winner.* Edited by Dominick P. Consolo. Columbus, Oh.: Merrill, 1969, pp. 47–51.

Marks, W.S. "The Psychology of the Uncanny in Lawrence's 'The Rocking Horse Winner,' " in *Modern Fiction Studies.* XI (1966), pp. 381–392. Reprinted in *The Rocking Horse Winner.* Edited by Dominick P. Consolo. Columbus, Oh.: Merrill, 1969, pp. 71–83.

Martin, W.R. "Fancy or Imagination? 'The Rocking Horse Winner,' " in *College English.* XXIV (1962), pp. 64–65. Reprinted in *The Rocking Horse Winner.* Edited by Dominick P. Consolo. Columbus, Oh.: Merrill, 1969, pp. 52–54.

Rohrberger, Mary. *Hawthorne and the Modern Short Story: A Study in Genre.* The Hague: Mouton, 1966, pp. 74–80.

San Juan, Epifanio. "Theme Versus Imitation: D.H. Lawrence's 'The Rocking Horse Winner,' " in *D.H. Lawrence Review.* III (1970), pp. 136–140.

Snodgrass, W.D. "A Rocking Horse: The Symbol, the Pattern, the Way to Live," in *Hudson Review.* XI (1958), pp. 191–200. Reprinted in *The Rocking Horse Winner.* Edited by Dominick P. Consolo. Columbus, Oh.: Merrill, 1969, pp. 26–36.

Tedlock, E.W. *D.H. Lawrence: Artist and Rebel.* Albuquerque: University of New Mexico Press, 1963, pp. 209–210. Reprinted in *The Rocking Horse Winner.* Edited by Dominick P. Consolo. Columbus, Oh.: Merrill, 1969, pp. 69–70.

Turner, Frederick W. "Prancing in to a Purpose: Myths, Horses, and True Selfhood in Lawrence's 'The Rocking Horse Winner,' " in *The Rocking Horse Winner.* Edited by Dominick P. Consolo. Columbus, Oh.: Merrill, 1969, pp. 95–106.

Widmer, Kingsley. *The Art of Perversity.* Seattle: University of Washington Press, 1962, pp. 92–95. Reprinted in *The Rocking Horse Winner.* Edited by Dominick P. Consolo. Columbus, Oh.: Merrill, 1969, pp. 43–46.

"St. Mawr"

Cowan, James C. *D.H. Lawrence's American Journey: A Study in Literature and Myth.* Cleveland: Case Western Reserve University Press, 1970, pp. 81–96.

Draper, R.P. *D.H. Lawrence.* New York: Twayne, 1964, pp. 131–135.

Engel, Monroe. "The Continuity of Lawrence's Short Novels," in *Hudson Review.* XI (1958), pp. 206–208. Reprinted in *D.H. Lawrence: A Collection of Critical Essays.* Edited by Mark Spilka. Englewood Cliffs, N.J.: Prentice-Hall, 1963, pp. 97–99.

Goodheart, Eugene. *The Utopian Vision of D.H. Lawrence.* Chicago: University of Chicago Press, 1963, pp. 56–62.

Goonetilleke, D.C.R. *Developing Countries in British Fiction.* Totowa, N.J.: Rowman and Littlefield, 1977, pp. 174–179.

Hough, Graham. *The Dark Sun: A Study of D.H. Lawrence.* New York: Macmillan, 1957, pp. 179–186.

Inniss, Kenneth. *D.H. Lawrence's Bestiary: A Study of His Use of Animal Trope and Symbol.* The Hague: Mouton, 1971, pp. 168–174.

Kermode, Frank. *D.H. Lawrence.* New York: Viking, 1973, pp. 119–122.

Leavis, F.R. "The Novel as Dramatic Poem: 'St. Mawr,'" in *Scrutiny.* XXXVIII (Spring, 1950), pp. 38–53. Reprinted in *D.H. Lawrence: Novelist.* New York: Knopf, 1956, pp. 48–49, 279–306.

Moore, Harry T. *The Life and Works of D.H. Lawrence.* New York: Twayne, 1951, pp. 225–228.

Nahal, Chaman. *D.H. Lawrence: An Eastern View.* South Brunswick, N.Y.: Barnes, 1970, pp. 112–115.

Poirier, Richard. *A World Elsewhere: The Place of Style in American Literature.* New York: Oxford University Press, 1966, pp. 40–49.

Pritchard, R.E. *D.H. Lawrence: Body of Darkness.* Pittsburgh: University of Pittsburgh Press, 1973, pp. 157–162.

Sagar, Keith. *The Art of D.H. Lawrence.* London: Cambridge University Press, 1966, pp. 151–159.

Smith, Bob L. "D.H. Lawrence's 'St. Mawr': Transposition of Myth," in *Arizona Quarterly.* XXIV (1968), pp. 197–208.

Tedlock, E.W.   *D.H. Lawrence: Artist and Rebel*. Albuquerque: University of New Mexico Press, 1963, pp. 176–179.

Widmer, Kingsley.   *The Art of Perversity*. Seattle: University of Washington Press, 1962, pp. 66–75.

Wilde, Alan.   "The Illusion of 'St. Mawr': Technique and Vision in D.H. Lawrence's Novel," in *PMLA*. LXXIX (1964), pp. 164–170.

LOUIS MACNEICE

Born: Belfast, Ireland (September 12, 1907)
Died: London, England (September 4, 1963)

Principal Works

POEMS: *Blind Fireworks,* 1929; *Poems,* 1935; *The Earth Compels,* 1938; *Autumn Journal,* 1939; *The Last Ditch,* 1940; *Poems: 1925–1940,* 1940; *Plant and Phantom,* 1941; *Springboard: Poems 1941–1944,* 1944; *Holes in the Sky: Poems 1944–1947,* 1948; *Collected Poems, 1925–1948,* 1949; *Ten Burnt Offerings,* 1952; *Autumn Sequel,* 1954; *The Other Wing,* 1954; *Visitations,* 1957; *Eighty-Five Poems,* 1959; *Solstices,* 1961; *The Burning Perch,* 1963; *The Collected Poems of Louis MacNeice,* 1966.

CRITICISM: *Modern Poetry: A Personal Essay,* 1938; *The Poetry of W. B. Yeats,* 1941; *Varieties of Parable,* 1965.

PLAY: *Out of the Picture,* 1937.

RADIO PLAYS: *Christopher Columbus,* 1944; *The Dark Tower,* 1947; *The Mad Islands,* and *The Administrator,* 1964.

AUTOBIOGRAPHY: *The Strings Are False,* 1965.

Louis MacNeice was born in Belfast, Northern Ireland, on September 12, 1907, of parents who had come from the West of Ireland. After a career as poet, classic scholar, and university lecturer, and finally feature writer for the British Broadcasting Company, he died of pneumonia in London, September 4, 1963.

In 1926, MacNeice entered Merton College at Oxford, and he remained there until 1930, when he married and moved to Birmingham, where he was lecturer in Classics until 1936. Next, he went to London and lectured in Greek at the Bedford College for Women. His reputation as a classicist was high, and his translation of the *Agamemnon* of Aeschylus is considered excellent.

At the outbreak of World War II, MacNeice was lecturing at Cornell University in America; subsequently he returned to Britain and made a lasting reputation writing programs for the B.B.C. His verse-plays for radio stand as the most brilliant of that genre. His wartime piece, "Dark Towers," the most memorable of all, was written in collaboration with the British composer Benjamin Britton.

In the 1930's MacNeice was widely recognized as one of the so-called Oxford Group, including W. H. Auden, Stephen Spender, and C. Day Lewis, all poets who had attended Oxford. These poets, reacting to the image of modern society as a "Wasteland," as popularized by T. S. Eliot, were notable for having developed a "new" poetry which eschewed the openly lyrical and "poetic" for an idiom based on colloquial language and a direct, forthright use of statement. Ironic, disillusioned, and nostalgic in turn, the poetry of MacNeice and his fellows offered no concession to those who would look upon the cataclysmic events of their time in any terms but those of the strictest honesty. Yet each of the poets, beyond the toughly intellectual tone of assessment and criticism, was capable of the most human of lyric sentiment.

The Oxford Group committed themselves to the cause of resisting Fascism and, in particular, Generalissimo Franco of Spain. Of the group, MacNeice, while sharing their sympathies, was wary of oversimplifying political matters, and asserted that the artist should beware of committing himself wholly to any political movement. One who knew him well comments on his ability to inspire friendship through silence, as if his deepest life remained an inner one; he was taciturn, highly intelligent, and yet not aloof. The same qualities are revealed in his poetry, which ranges from social commentary through ironic disillusionment to a controlled and quiet lyricism.

His first volume of poems, *Blind Fireworks*, appeared in 1929. It was followed by *Poems* in 1935; *The Earth Compels*, 1938; *Autumn Journal*, 1939; *Letter from Iceland*, in collaboration with Auden, 1937; *Plant and Phantom* appeared in 1941, *Springboard* in 1944, *Holes in the Sky*, 1948, and his *Collected Poems* (1925 to 1948), published in 1949. After that time his notable publications were *Visitations*, 1957, and some selected collections. MacNeice translated Horace and Goethe's *Faust*, as well as the *Agamemnon*.

Generally it is regarded that his poetry suffered in his later years; but his best works, mostly those of the 1930's, are memorable for their control, intelligence, and humanity.

Bibliography

Selected Poems, edited by W. H. Auden in 1964, provides a good introduction to MacNeice's work. For biographical material see MacNeice's unfinished autobiography, *The Strings Are False*, 1965.

Good critical discussions are found in Elton E. Smith, *Louis MacNeice*, 1970; John Press, *Louis MacNeice*, 1965; and Derek Stanford, *Stephen Spender, Louis MacNeice, Cecil Day Lewis: A Critical Essay*, 1969.

See also John Wain, "MacNeice as Critic," *Encounter*, XXVII, No. v (1966), 49–55; William Jay Smith, "The Black Clock: The Poetic Achievement of Louis MacNeice," *The Sounder Few: Essays from the Hollins Critic*, 1971; and G. S. Fraser, *Vision and Rhetoric*, 1959. Additional articles are listed in "Louis MacNeice: A Bibliography," compiled by W. T. McKinnon, *Bulletin of Bibliography*, XXVII (April, 1970, 51–42 +; July, 1970, 79–84).

THE POETRY OF MacNEICE

Author: Louis MacNeice (1907–1963)
Principal published works: Blind Fireworks, 1929; *Poems*, 1935; *The Earth Compels*, 1938; *Autumn Journal*, 1939; *The Last Ditch*, 1940; *Plant and Phantom*, 1941; *Springboard: Poems 1940–1944*, 1944: *Holes in the Sky: Poems 1944–1947*, 1948; *Ten Burnt Offerings*, 1952; *Autumn Sequel: A Rhetorical Poem in XXVI Cantos*, 1954; *Visitations*, 1957; *Eight-five Poems*, 1959; *Solstices*, 1961; *The Collected Poems of Louis MacNeice*, 1967

Essay-Review

Louis MacNeice was associated in the 1930's with Stephen Spender and W. H. Auden and, like them, directed his poetry to recording, and lamenting, the contemporary, metropolitan scene and the breakdown of older values. MacNeice's poems, published steadily since 1929, in later years became more and more preoccupied with the past, the poet's lost youth and, at times, his sense of having lost his freshness as a poet.

At his best, he succeeded in mingling the commonplace and even trivial with an ironically acute insight to produce a memorable portrait of the modern industrial society. The rather forlorn and wistful attempts of metropolitan man to achieve some satisfaction in a generally treadmill life were chronicled by MacNeice in tones of mild sympathy, more detachment, and, sometimes, condescension. The rhythms are very close to prose or speech, the rhyming is often deliberately banal in order to achieve a caustically comic effect, and, occasionally, doggerel is used to express something of the tired, cheapened quality of a wasteland society. One of his best poems is "Sunday Morning," in which his coupling of the once-valued expanding heart of man and the newly banal, vulgar substitution of working with his car on a Sunday morning illustrates a typical kind of rhetoric as well as MacNeice's sense of how the romantic ambitions of the previous, prewar generations have become cheapened and empty of anything but momentary and shallow diversion. Disillusionment is everywhere, but the poet maintains a detached, resigned pose most of the time. In the poem, the car is readied, and the weekenders speed to Hindhead, trying to recapture something of the past and hold firmly to it in the flow of time measured by dull days and dragging weeks. Life thus becomes escape from boredom, meaninglessness, and a march of time which only destroys old dreams. There is no escape.

While, especially in his poems of the 1930's, MacNeice is often highly successful in expressing the sadness and wistful regret of modern men caught between two wars, his verse becomes increasingly tired itself, even tedious, as the rhythms grow stale and prosaic or "talky"; the constant use of comic or merely doggerel rhyme and the undifferentiated tone of slightly supercilious disillusionment, constantly verging on the merely nostalgic, wear thin. The symbols of planned obsolescence and overproduction which in turn signify the hopeless and helpless vulgarity and sterility of "modern life" cease either to surprise or to shock when constantly juxtaposed with older and "higher" thoughts. MacNeice's studied use of the banal ends, at times, in sinking the poetry beneath its own dead weight.

On the other hand, MacNeice's ability to use dance-hall rhythms and clichés to good satiric purpose is evident in "Bagpipe Music." The cleverness of parody and the cliché, like the colloquial idiom, belong strictly to a time and place, and though MacNeice has recorded that time, often effectively, he has lacked the larger gifts of either Spender or the protean, effervescent Auden.

MacNeice constantly counterpoises the older traditions and values with the present state of society. Playing off the old pastoral illusions, in "Nuts in May" he describes the breakdown of the traditional values.

MacNeice's early influence was Edith Sitwell, and then, like Auden, C. D. Lewis and Spender, the war poetry of Sassoon and Owen. The political and moral chaos of the war and the decades following it, the manifestoes of Hulme, Pound, and Eliot for a "harder" and more "classical" poetry, the teeming and dingy metropolis, all lay behind the sort of poetry MacNeice and his friends wrote. It seemed as if all the world had turned a final corner away from the past, and the aestheticism of the 1890's, the pastoral poetry of the Georgians, in fact, the whole Keatsian and Tennysonian tradition seemed no longer a possible idiom in which to express the "new world" of quiet terror, cataclysm, and tenements. Instead, the "new" verse, close to colloquial speech, used the clichés of the shopgirl, the banalities of the popular song, the cadences of jazz, and the dance hall. In such a world, the British Museum seemed an anomaly, where one discovered poor scholars, cranks, and hacks.

A poem similar to "The British Museum Reading Room" is entitled, simply, "Museums," and jokingly expresses MacNeice's conviction that the Past is now only the past, and the museum is where we go to find a tenuous kind of escape or refuge. MacNeice seldom "reaches" for a metaphor or a poetic effect. He uses materials ready at hand, even clichés, and often produces an adroit and truly poignant image of modern life. His tone, at best, is controlled, detached, yet sad and intelligent. He represented an awareness of self and of reality which is so scrupulous as almost to preclude poetry. He had little or none of Spender's romanticism. His materials sometimes failed him, and do so increasingly with the passage of time away from that period when both the poetry and the disillusionment at least had the grace of novelty.

Bibliography

Brown, Terence. "Louis MacNeice and the 'Dark Conceit,'" in *Ariel*. III (1972), pp. 16–24.

————. *Louis MacNeice: Sceptical Vision.* New York: Barnes & Noble, 1975.

————. "MacNeice: Father and Son," in *Time Was Away: The World of Louis MacNeice.* Edited by Terence Brown and Alec Reid. Dublin: Dolmen Press, 1974, pp. 21–34.

Highet, Gilbert. *The Powers of Poetry.* New York: Oxford University Press, 1960, pp. 25–26.

Longley, Michael. "A Misrepresented Poet," in *Dublin Magazine.* VI (1967), pp. 68–74.

McKinnon, William T. *Apollo's Blended Dream: A Study of the Poetry of Louis MacNeice.* London: Oxford University Press, 1971, pp. 39–170.

Montague, John. "Despair and Delight," in *Time Was Away: The World of Louis MacNeice.* Edited by Terence Brown and Alec Reid. Dublin: Dolmen Press, 1974, pp. 123–127.

Moore, D.B. *The Poetry of Louis MacNeice.* Leicester, England: Leicester University Press, 1972.

Press, John. *Louis MacNeice.* London: Longmans, Green, 1965, pp. 23–44.

Scarfe, Francis. *Auden and After: The Liberation of Poetry, 1930–1941.* London: Routledge, 1942, pp. 53–67.

Skelton, Robin. "Celt and Classicist: The Versecraft of Louis MacNeice," in *Time Was Away: The World of Louis MacNeice.* Edited by Terence Brown and Alec Reid. Dublin: Dolmen Press, 1974, pp. 43–53.

Smith, Elton Edward. *Louis MacNeice.* New York: Twayne, 1970.

Smith, William J. "The Black Clock: The Poetic Achievement of Louis Mac-Neice," in *Hollins Critic.* IV (1967), pp. 1–11.

KATHERINE MANSFIELD
Kathleen Mansfield Beauchamp

Born: Wellington, New Zealand (October 14, 1888)
Died: Fontainebleau, France (January 9, 1923)

Principal Works

SHORT STORIES: *In a German Pension*, 1911; *Prelude*, 1918; *Je ne parle pas français*, 1920; *Bliss and Other Stories*, 1920; *The Garden Party and Other Stories*, 1922; *The Doves' Nest and Other Stories*, 1923; *Something Childish and Other Stories*, 1924; *The Aloe*, 1930.

POEMS: *Poems*, 1923.

AUTOBIOGRAPHY: *The Journal of Katherine Mansfield*, 1927; *The Scrapbook of Katherine Mansfield*, 1939.

ESSAYS AND STUDIES: *Novels and Novelists*, 1930.

LETTERS: *The Letters of Katherine Mansfield*, 1929; *Katherine Mansfield's Letters to John Middleton Murry, 1913–1922*, 1951.

One of the great shapers of the modern short story, Katherine Mansfield was a colonial who had escaped to the cosmopolitanism of London and the Continent, only to find some of the richest sources of her art in the New Zealand from which she had fled. Born Kathleen Beauchamp in Wellington on October 14, 1888, she was the third daughter of Harold Beauchamp, a banker later to be knighted. At the age of five Kathleen went to school outside Wellington at Karori. Imaginative and withdrawn, she did not respond well to formal education and discipline, but by the time the Beauchamps were entered in the Wellington College for Girls in 1897, she had already won a composition prize with an entry prophetically called "A Sea Voyage." By 1900, in still another school, Kathleen had developed an interest in the cello and in a boy prodigy, Arnold Trowell, from whose father she took lessons. Kathleen first saw London in 1903, where her father had taken her and her sisters to be educated at Queen's College, Harley Street. She studied desultorily there, taking lessons at the Royal Academy of Music, and developing her art, watching and observing while, concomitantly, her hypersensitivity and incipient neuroticism increased. Immersed in *fin de siècle* atmosphere and the writings of Wilde, Pater, Verlaine, and others, she became secretly engaged to Arnold Trowell, who was giving increasingly successful concerts. Her distraction at the knowledge of his waning ardor was made desperate by her father's summons home in 1906.

Back in New Zealand, but in rebellion against being there, she had decided by the spring of 1907 that writing, not music, was her forte, and she began to work earnestly at short stories and verse. But neither the publication of three of her stories in *The Native Companion*, a Melbourne monthly, nor a six-week trip into the bush could make her forget her aim. She gained it in July of 1908 when she secured her father's reluctant consent and, with a £100 yearly allowance, returned to England. At first she lived at an unmarried ladies' hostel and then at the Trowells'. But she was soon in despair, for Arnold no longer loved her, and besides she found herself in financial straits, unable to live comfortably even when she supplemented her allowance by touring with an opera company and working as a movie extra. In March, 1909, funereally dressed, she contracted a hasty marriage with George Bowden, a young musician, only to leave him a few days later. Mrs. Beauchamp joined her and, finding her pregnant but not by her husband, took her to Woerishofen, Bavaria. There her child was stillborn and the decline in her health began.

When she returned to England in 1910, A. R. Orage published some of her work, signed "Katherine Mansfield," in *The New Age*. Collected with other stories, it was published as *In a German Pension* in 1911. The next year saw her fateful meeting with John Middleton Murry, already a rising literary journalist. Soon they began to live together, impecunious and unable to marry until 1918, when Bowden divorced her. Despite illness, insecurity, and depression, she continued to write, temporarily exhilarated by the visit of her young brother Leslie, on his way to the front in the summer of 1915. His death in action shortly thereafter brought heartbreak which no amount of work and travel in France and England could assuage. Her thoughts turned to her homeland. Embodied in "Prelude," among other stories, they appeared under the imprint of the Hogarth Press, founded by her friends, Leonard and Virginia Woolf. Other work of hers had previously appeared in *Signature*, which she had begun with Murry and D. H. Lawrence.

Her sufferings in France during the winter of 1917–1918, where she had sought a milder climate than that of England, made it clear that she, like her great predecessor and master, Chekhov, was the victim of what was to be incurable tuberculosis. Virtually an invalid by the end of the war, she was in lonely separation from Murry, who was in London earning a living as editor of *The Athenaeum*, to which she contributed. *Bliss and Other Stories*, published in 1920, helped her growing reputation, but her personal exigencies were becoming desperate. Like her friend D. H. Lawrence, Katherine Mansfield found her last years filled with continuous unsuccessful trips from one place to another in search of health. But she did not possess Lawrence's inner certitude, so that there was the corollary travail of a fruitless spiritual pilgrimage as well. By 1922, when she published *The Garden Party and Other Stories*, her work was appearing in America as well as England. X-ray treatments in Paris seemed for a time to help her wasted lungs, but finally, in the last phase of her desperate search, she entered the Gurdjieff Institute for the Harmonic Development of Man at Fontainebleau. As her wasted body grew even more debilitated under an unfavorable physical environment, her questing spirit grew calmer. There her last and fatal hemorrhage occurred on January 9, 1923, the year in which *The Doves' Nest and Other Sto-*

ries confirmed her place as one of the most accomplished experimentalists and shapers of the modern short story.

Katherine Mansfield's work was intensely autobiographical, and throughout her career her protagonists often approximated her own age, interests, and temperament. Her favorite themes were family relationships, parental and marital, most often somberly treated. Excelling at the portrayal of children, she was able at her best to enter into the souls of her characters and turn them outward for her reader to see and understand. Her technique, much of it revolutionary in her own time, was marked by the use of the stream-of-consciousness method, skillful shifts in point of view from one character to another, and evocation of mood through poetically appropriate gesture and detail. Almost lyrical, her art bypassed conventional narration, ellipsizing naturalistic detail and de-emphasizing the traditional plot structure to produce, like James Joyce and Virginia Woolf, works of art which conveyed the greater truth found in the portrayal of the essence of character and experience itself.

Bibliography

Katherine Mansfield's short stories have been collected in chronological sequence in *The Short Stories of Katherine Mansfield*, 1945. The standard biography is Anthony Alpers, *Katherine Mansfield: A Biography*, 1953, a work containing much new material not found in Ruth E. Mantz and John Middleton Murry, *The Life of Katherine Mansfield*, 1933. Francis Carco, *Souvenirs sur Katherine Mansfield*, 1934, contains reminiscences by a French writer upon whom Katherine Mansfield modeled several of her characters.

The basic critical study is Sylvia Berkman, *Katherine Mansfield: A Critical Study*, 1951. See also Saralyn Daly, *Katherine Mansfield*, 1965; and Marvin Magalaner, *The Fiction of Katherine Mansfield*, 1971. For briefer criticism see André Maurois *Prophets and Poets*, 1935; A. Sewell, *Katherine Mansfield: A Critical Essay*, 1936; David Daiches, *The Novel in the Modern World*, 1939; L. E. Rillo, *Katherine Mansfield and Virginia Woolf*, 1944; John Middleton Murry, *Katherine Mansfield and Other Literary Portraits*, 1949; Katherine Anne Porter, *The Days Before*, 1952; Louis Gillet, "Katherine Mansfield," *Revue des Deux Mondes*, VII Période, XXIV (1924), 929–942; Edward Wagenknecht, "Katherine Mansfield," *English Journal*, XVII (1928), 272–284; Sidney Cox, "The Fastidiousness of Katherine Mansfield," *Sewanee Review*, XXXIX (1931), 158–169; Gerard Jean-Aubry, "Katherine Mansfield, *Revue de Paris*, XXXVIII An, V (1931), 57–72; and Arnold Whitridge, "Katherine Mansfield," *Sewanee Review*, XLVIII (1940), 256–272.

THE SHORT STORIES OF KATHERINE MANSFIELD

Author: Katherine Mansfield (Kathleen Mansfield Beauchamp, 1888–1923)
First published: In a German Pension, 1911; *Prelude,* 1918; *Je ne parle pas français,* 1920; *Bliss and Other Stories,* 1920; *The Garden Party and Other Stories,* 1922; *The Doves Nest and Other Stories,* 1923; *Something Childish and Other Stories,* 1924; *The Aloe,* 1930

Essay-Review

Katherine Mansfield effected a revolution in the short story causing it to be based on a consistent reliance upon a functional language, concentrating on a single moment in time, eliminating a strongly plotted action line, and using imagery and metaphor to expand the moment and give it significance beyond itself. The form that Mansfield used moved the short story away from the formulistic in England and established it as an art whose aesthetic value was sufficient to place it beside the other and older literary genres.

Mansfield used language to express the non-verbal, as the painter uses color, texture, and line, as the musician uses notes in time patterns. The results of her efforts were the presentation of moments as metaphors, embodying total meaning. All fictional techniques became functional in the total design and created it. A plot line that could be charted—rising action, climax, falling action—gave way in a Mansfield story to a line that did not rise very much and then stopped somewhere and remained hovering. Interest in the story lay not on what happened, but on why it happened. In a Mansfield story nothing is apparent, everything implied. Objects, characters, incidents and their positioning in the design make a tangential point. The structure creates a metaphor; the metaphor reveals the meaning.

Most studies of Katherine Mansfield approach her work chronologically, in terms of developmental patterns, making the point that her skill developed over the thirteen years of her writing career. But that statement is not true. As a craftsman, Mansfield's development was quick. Masterful short stories occur at the beginning of her career as at the end, and lesser stories occur alongside better ones in all of her volumes of collected stories.

Mansfield writes of childhood joys and fears, of adolescent pleasures and pains, of adult aspirations and failures, and of the memories and final knowledge of the aged. But statements of theme are abstractions, existing in a realm outside of the concrete, in a vacuum of unreality. The reality is a person living in the reader's mind, put there by a feeling caught and transmitted in such a way that the reader knows the individual as real, living, but always mortal. From the early "How Pearl Button Was Kidnapped" to the later "The Wrong House" the child exists in life knowing, whether consciously or unconsciously, violence and death, and the aged face death, holding on to life. The symbolic journey to the sea that Pearl Button takes in the arms of the gypsy earth mother is a movement toward both life and death. The sea symbolizes natural order and movements in life at the same time that it connotes a dark oblivion, a return to a deep sleep, the security born of the subconscious knowledge of darkness. Where "How Pearl Button Was Kidnapped," a story about a child, is flooded in light and color, "The Wrong House," a story of an aged woman, is a study in darkness. But the darkness is not absolute. Mrs. Bean calls for a lamp and picks up again the pattern of her life, though she knows, with a knowledge deep and abiding but nonverbalized, that she is at the point of death.

A New Zealand story, "The Wind Blows" exhibits the typical structure of a Mansfield story and uses all the characteristic devices. The plot line is almost nonexistent. An adolescent girl, Matilda, wakes up one morning, nervous and tense. While the wind blows outside, she readies herself to go to her music lesson. Before she gets away she has a small argument with her mother. She has her music lesson, goes home, meets her brother, and goes for a walk with him to the sea. They stand together and watch a ship in the water. Then she imagines a time in the future when she and her brother will be leaving their home on just such a ship.

The story begins *in medias res*. There is no formal introduction, no formal setting of scene, just, "Suddenly—dreadfully—she wakes up." The positioning of words in the sentence, the punctuation, the harsh consonants grouped together suggest the jarring quality of the awakening and the anxiety it creates. But more than this; the very act of awakening sets the area of thematic concern. The tension created in the first sentence of the story is carried over into an interior monologue. Short sentences filled with repetitive phrases continue the abrupt movement, beating out the anxiety pattern. The wind that she hears outside is emphasized by the use of the present participle in the verb forms. The wind is "shaking," "rattling," "banging," things around outside, causing her bed on the inside to tremble. Although no mention is made of her physical actions, it is clear that she rises from the bed and goes to the window to look outside. Everything she sees is described in terms of the movement of the wind which reflects the tension within her: "It is all over." Her inability to define the pronoun reference indicates that her anxiety feelings are undifferentiated, as they will remain for her, but not for the reader, for the story proceeds to locate the specific area of anxiety and to comment on it. That Matilda does not dare to look in the mirror is a significant detail in the pattern that will be established, making credible and acceptable her fantasy which ends the story.

Outside she is stung and beaten by the wind and the dust it carries. She hears the roar of the trees and the sea sob: "Ah!...Ah!... Ah-h!" The cry appears to come also from within her. But the piano teacher's drawing room is quiet; it is a haven from within and without. The picture hanging over Mr. Bullen's piano is a romanticized image of a dark and tragic woman who is draped in white. The woman sits on a rock with her knees crossed and her chin in her hands. The picture is an idealized version of Matilda—the image she would not have seen in the mirror, had she looked at it. Close to Mr. Bullen, her fingers tremble; her heart beats loudly; she identifies the source: "It's the wind." When he speaks kindly to her she feels she must cry. She leans her head on his shoulder and he comforts her.

Back in her room, she believes that her bed is frightening, lying there "sound asleep." Then her brother calls to her to come take a walk. They stand together and she looks at herself and her brother in the mirror, noticing their excited eyes and hot lips. "Ah," she thinks, "they know those two in the glass." They walk, blown by the wind. On the water she sees a big, black steamer cutting through the waves. The ship is making for an open gate between two pointed rocks. The imagery here recalls the picture of the tragic woman in the piano studio. The ship is a vehicle to carry Matilda away from the wind. Then she imagines that she and her brother are on board the ship, and she sees them as she had seen the mirror images. They are older; the wind is down; they are being carried away over the tumbling water. Then the ship disappears and with it her vision, leaving the wind.

In this story, the wind, as major metaphor, becomes a concrete objectification of Matilda's anxieties. The trembling and frightened bed, the idealized image of womanhood expressed in the picture, the mirror images are symbols functioning within the major metaphor, delineating the area of anxiety: the sexual stirrings of adolescence.

In the multipersonal point of view which Mansfield made peculiarly her own, a narrator hovers just outside the consciousness of the characters, shifting from one to another and sometimes to a composite consciousness, causing readers to become familiar not only with a central character or characters but also with a host of minor characters. This method, of course, enlarges the scope of the stories and is the viewpoint used in almost half of her short fiction including the masterful New Zealand stories involving the Burnell family as well as the excellent and frequently anthologized "The Man Without a Temperament" and "The Daughters of the Late Colonel."

Mansfield's ability to assume various voices consistent with the various characters makes it possible for her to begin characterization and delineate the situation in very little space. The opening paragraph of "The Man Without a Temperament" introduces Robert Salesby and quickly catches his tension and detachment as he stands turning his ring upon his finger and pursing his lips as if he is about to whistle— " but he did not whistle—only turned the ring—turned the ring on his pink, freshly washed hands." Robert's inner frustrations, reflected in the rhythmic repetitive patterns, his posture, poised for action but in arrested movement, his strength, held in check by sheer will power, are contrasted with the weakness and languidity of his wife who moves with light, dragging steps and whose hand, "like a leaf," falls on his shoulder.

The tension created by the relative positions of these two characters is never released but is emphasized continuously, not only by their every action and thought but also by the thoughts and behavior of the people around them, by the hotel setting, and by the landscape itself. The spinster top-knots as grey and speckled as their drink and food, the sexually frustrated American woman playing up to the great purple plant, the marvelously fecund honeymoon couple making love to each other across the table, the sterile hotel cluttered with useless objects contrasted with the total sensuality of the plants in full bloom, serve as a backdrop against which the drama of the Salesbys is played.

"The Daughters of the Late Colonel" begins in a composite consciousness, where Mansfield enters the minds of the two sisters simultaneously, a device which serves to emphasize their likenesses at the same time that it provides motivation for their behavior, for the fact that there are two of them is important thematically. They have been able to indulge each other's vagaries, to cleave to one another for comfort, to join together in a common concern to appease their father. They eat together, shop together, sleep together, and, at the end, choose each other, for they know nothing else and they are fearful. But, if they are alike in some ways, they are different in others and so a hovering narrator enters the minds of both Constantia and Josephine to delineate the differences. And the hovering narrator enters the minds or stays just outside the minds of the other characters to show their responses to the two sisters and their positions in the household. "Proud young Kate," the servant girl, sees them as two old tabbies to be controlled to her advantage, slapped down in the same way as she slaps down the "white, terrified blancmange" on the table. Nurse Andrews uses them to provide a leisurely interlude between jobs and takes advantage of their hesitations. Their nephew, Cyril, provides a note of normalcy for the absurd household, but even he tries to get away as quickly as he can. Only Colonel Pinner, their father, remains a mystery, outside of the scope of the hovering narrator, and it is right that he should. He is a reality in the minds of his daughters and whether that reality conforms to an objective reality is never revealed.

One of Mansfield's best stories, "Prelude" describes a move the Burnell family makes from one house to another. As is usual in Mansfield stories, "Prelude" begins *in medias res*. The Burnell women are in the buggy. A few pieces of furniture, still to be moved, stand on the walk, Lottie and Kezia beside them, as there is no room for them in the buggy. It is decided to leave the children with a neighbor, Mrs. Samuel Josephs, until they can be brought later by the grocery man in his wagon. Left behind, Lottie and Kezia have lunch with the Samuel Josephs children, and later Kezia explores the empty house. That night she and Lottie are driven to their new home. It is the first time either of the children has been out at night. When they arrive they find the family assembled in the dining room for dinner. Shortly afterwards the children are sent to bed. Then, later, the adults retire. The next day is spent in getting the house arranged and in exploring the garden. Linda, the children's mother, is half an invalid, and the work of the house falls to Linda's sister, Beryl, and their mother, Mrs. Fairchild. Stanley, Linda's husband, is away at work. One day, when the children are playing with their cousins, Rags and Pip, who live close by, Pat, the handyman, takes them to the pond where he kills a duck for the family dinner. Alice, the maid, cooks it, while she also serves tea to visitors in the drawing room. Later, Linda goes out to view the aloe tree. In the concluding section, Beryl writes a letter to a friend in which she indicates that the family has been living in the new house for a week and that Stanley is bringing two young men home with him for lunch and tennis.

The interest that develops in "Prelude" is not in the outcome of a particular problem. Interest resides, rather, in the complexities of the characters and in the unraveling skeins of motivations, desires, and thoughts, all expressed through the dramatic presentation of experiences juxtaposed one with another, forming a created moment in time that expands to include past and future.

There is no internal evidence in the story fixing the specific date or geographic location, except that it is not Australia. A general time is fixed by the fact that buggies and candles are used, and the mention of certain plants suggests the New Zealand location. But, although setting is not specific, there is a strong feeling of both time and place. There is the time that is measured by the clock and to which the characters respond with daily routines; there is the time of a larger order, that of generations in history; there is time in a grander sense, the time of nature, of the movement of the planets through the heavens, rotating about the sun. A corresponding sense of place is achieved as the family moves through prescribed paths and areas. The family moves from one house to another, from city to country. The characters move from house to garden; they move from family rooms to private rooms, and they move from reality to dream to fantasy in the innermost circle of all.

Time and place are parallel, correspondences being set up and maintained. In the space of one short story, readers see a family for the calendar space of seven days and become familiar with daily routines that measure time like a clock through mealtimes and bedtimes. But readers also see the years of the past merge in the present so that the future is always on the point of becoming one with the present, and sometimes does. The child becomes mother and the mother is child. Generation is followed by generation in one unbroken sequence. The century plant is coming into bloom and will bloom again in another century. A person can know the hot sun of Australia while at the same time he or she occupies a space in another country viewing a scene from a kitchen window. A person can exist at once as child and adult while the past, present, and future integrate and coalesce into another reality.

Like "Prelude," "At the Bay" is organized around time in all its aspects, the design of the story functioning symbolically as part of the overall meaning. The story begins at the moment the sun rises over Crescent Bay, and from the merging images of earth and sea comes the major metaphor of the story. Throughout the narrative the activities of the characters are seen against the background of the rise and fall of the tides of the ocean, and, as in "Prelude," timed with the movement of the sun and the moon through the heavens. Life moves through a path between birth and death and is no more than the rising and setting of the sun; and as the images of sea and earth merge, so life and death are unified. The manifestations of sex, male and female, merge also, so that distinctions disappear.

"At the Bay" was written four years after "Prelude," and the stories, of course, exist separately. But read together they provide a richer experience. "Prelude" serves not only as an introduction to the Burnell household but also to presage certain themes suggested in the earlier story but developed more fully in the later. Foreshadowed events are realized. Linda's baby is born; Beryl's lover appears; Kezia grows in her knowledge to the point that feelings are translated into words; some of Stanley's ambitions are realized. But alongside of the development are also some of the static qualities of life. Stanley still worries about his journey into the city; Kezia still plays with her food; Linda still spends her time in the garden; Mrs. Fairchild still minds the children. There are the same three meals a day, the same gametimes and bedtimes, all governed by the passage of the sun across the heavens, the sun that in its movement illuminates the human drama, revealing the struggle and the contentment, the pleasure and the pain, the birth and the death as one ongoing process.

Other than a volume of poems, Mansfield's fictional writings are entirely in the form of the short story. She did write reviews and she kept a journal. After her death, her reviews, journal notes, and many letters were published by her husband, John Middleton Murray, in volumes dating from 1929 to 1954. These non-fictional writings reveal that Mansfield was a conscious artist who had constructed not only a coherent aesthetic but also a body of criticism based on that aesthetic and further that her search for form grew out of her knowledge that short fiction must create a total interrelated world, recognizable both in its scale and context.

Bibliography

"At the Bay"

Alpers, Antony. *Katherine Mansfield: A Biography.* New York: Knopf, 1953, pp. 316–322.

Berkman, Sylvia. *Katherine Mansfield: A Critical Study.* New Haven, Conn.: Yale University Press, 1951, pp. 168–169.

Brewster, Dorothy and Angus Burrell. *Modern Fiction.* New York: Columbia University Press, 1934.

Corin, Fernand. "Creation of Atmosphere in Katherine Mansfield's Stories," in *Revue des Langues Vivantes.* XXII (1956), pp. 65–78.

Daly, Saralyn. *Katherine Mansfield.* New York: Twayne, 1965, pp. 92–99.

Hubbell, George S. "Katherine Mansfield and Kezia," in *Sewanee Review.* XXXV (1927), pp. 332–333.

Kempton, Kenneth. *Short Stories for Study.* Cambridge, Mass.: Harvard University Press, 1953, pp. 280–282.

Kleine, Don W. "An Eden for Insiders: Katherine Mansfield's New Zealand," in *College English.* XXVII (1965), pp. 205–206.

Magalaner, Marvin. *The Fiction of Katherine Mansfield.* Carbondale: Southern Illinois University Press, 1971, pp. 38–45.

Stegner, Wallace, Richard Snowcroft and Boris Ilyin. *The Writers Art.* Boston: Heath, 1950, pp. 74–77.

Walsh, William. *A Manifold Voice: Studies in Commonwealth Literature.* London: Chatto and Windus, 1970, pp. 176–180.

"Bliss"

Armstrong, Martin. "The Art of Katherine Mansfield," in *Fortnightly Review.* CXIII (1923), p. 484–490.

Berkman, Sylvia. *Katherine Mansfield: A Critical Study.* New Haven, Conn.: Yale University Press, 1951.

Brewster, Dorothy and Angus Burrell. *Modern Fiction.* New York: Columbia University Press, 1934, pp. 374–377.

Daly, Saralyn. *Katherine Mansfield.* New York: Twayne, 1965, pp. 82–88.

Eliot, Thomas E. *After Strange Gods.* London: Faber, 1934, pp. 35–36.

Foff, Arthur and Daniel Knapp. *Story: An Introduction to Prose Fiction.* Belmont, Calif.: Wadsworth, 1964, pp. 70–75.

Heilman, Robert B. *Modern Short Stories: A Critical Anthology.* New York: Harcourt, Brace, 1950, pp. 207–209.

Lawrence, Margaret. *The School of Femininity.* New York: Stokes, 1963

Magalaner, Marvin. *The Fiction of Katherine Mansfield.* Carbondale: Southern Illinois University Press, 1971, pp. 74–86.

Murry, John M. *Katherine Mansfield and Other Literary Portraits.* London: Peter Nevill, 1949.

Nebeker, Helen E. "The Pear Tree: Sexual Implications in Katherine Mansfield's 'Bliss,' " in *Modern Fiction Studies.* XVIII (1973), pp. 545–551.

Orvis, Mary B. *The Art of Writing Fiction.* New York: Prentice-Hall, 1948.

Van Kramendonk, A.G. "Katherine Mansfield," in *English Studies.* XII (April, 1930), pp. 56–57.

Ward, Alfred C. *Aspects of the Modern Short Story.* London: University of London Press, 1924, pp. 287–289.

Wright, Celeste T. "Katherine Mansfield's Dog Image," in *Literature and Psychology.* X (1960), pp. 80–81.

"The Doll's House"

Daly, Saralyn. *Katherine Mansfield.* New York: Twayne, 1965, pp. 100–101.

Delaney, Paul. "Short and Simple Annals of the Poor: Katherine Mansfield's 'The Doll's House,' " in *Mosaic.* X (1976), pp. 7–17.

Hubbell, George S. "Katherine Mansfield and Kezia," in *Sewanee Review.* XXXV (1927), pp. 334–335.

Kleine, Don W. "An Eden for Insiders: Katherine Mansfield's New Zealand," in *College English.* XXVII (1965), pp. 204–206.

Lawrence, Margaret. *The School of Femininity.* New York: Stokes, 1963.

Ryan, Alvan S. " 'The Doll's House,' " in *Insight II: Analyses of British Literature.* Frankfurt, Germany: Hirschgraben, 1964, pp. 247–250.

Singleton, Ralph H. *Instructor's Manual for Two and Twenty: A Collection of Short Stories.* New York: St. Martin's, 1962.

Walsh, William. *A Manifold Voice: Studies in Commonwealth Literature.* London: Chatto and Windus, 1970, pp. 164–168.

"The Fly"

Bateson, F.W. "More on 'The Fly,' " in *Essays in Criticism.* XII (October, 1962), pp. 451–452.

Bateson, F.W. and B. Shahevitch. "Katherine Mansfield's 'The Fly': A Critical Exericse," in *Essays in Criticism.* XII (January, 1962), pp. 39–53.

Berkman, Sylvia. *Katherine Mansfield: A Critical Study.* New Haven, Conn.: Yale University Press, 1951, pp. 137–140.

Boyle, Ted E. "The Death of the Boss: Another Look at Katherine Mansfield's 'The Fly,' " in *Modern Fiction Studies.* XI (Summer, 1965), pp. 183–185.

Copland, R.A. "Katherine Mansfield's 'The Fly,' " in *Essays in Criticism.* XII (July, 1962), pp. 338–341.

Daly, Saralyn. *Katherine Mansfield.* New York: Twayne, 1965, pp. 109–111.

Greenwood, E.B. "Katherine Mansfield's 'The Fly,' " in *Essays in Criticism.* XII (July, 1962), pp. 341–347.

Hagopian, John. "Capturing Mansfield's 'Fly,' " in *Modern Fiction Studies.* IX (Winter, 1963–1964), pp. 385–390.

————. " 'The Fly,' " in *Insight II: Analyses of British Literature.* Edited by John V. Hagopian and Martin Dolch. Frankfurt, Germany: Hirschgraben, 1964, pp. 240–247.

Jolly, R.A. "Katherine Mansfield's 'The Fly,' " in *Essays in Criticism.* XII (July, 1962), pp. 335–338.

Meredith, Robert C. and John D. Fitzgerald. *The Professional Story Writer and His Art.* New York: Crowell, 1963, pp. 411–420.

Michel-Michot, Paulette. "Katherine Mansfield's 'The Fly': An Attempt to Capture the Boss," in *Studies in Short Fiction.* XI (1974), pp. 85–92.

Peltzie, Bernard E. "Teaching Meaning Through Structure in the Short Story," in *English Journal.* LV (September, 1966), pp. 703–709.

Rohrberger, Mary.   *Hawthorne and the Modern Short Story: A Study in Genre.* The Hague: Mouton, 1966, pp. 68–74.

Thomas, J.D.   "Symbol and Parallelism in 'The Fly,'" in *College English.* XXII (January, 1961), pp. 256–262.

"The Garden Party"

Bloom, Edward A.   *The Order of Fiction.* New York: Odyssey, 1964, pp. 176–179.

Brewster, Dorothy and Angus Burrell.   *Modern Fiction.* New York: Columbia University Press, 1934.

Daly, Saralyn.   *Katherine Mansfield.* New York: Twayne, 1965, pp. 99–100.

Davis, Robert M.   "The Unity of 'The Garden Party,'" in *Studies in Short Fiction.* II (1964), pp. 61–65.

Iverson, Anders.   "A Reading of Katherine Mansfield's 'The Garden Party,'" in *Orbis Litterarum.* XXIII (1968), pp. 5–34.

Kleine, Don W.   "An Eden for Insiders: Katherine Mansfield's New Zealand," in *College English.* XXVII (1965), pp. 207–209.

————.   "'The Garden Party': A Portrait of the Artist," in *Criticism.* V (1963), pp. 360–371.

Lawrence, Margaret.   *The School for Femininity.* New York: Stokes, 1963.

Magalaner, Marvin.   *The Fiction of Katherine Mansfield.* Carbondale: Southern Illinois University Press, 1971, pp. 110–119.

O'Connor, Frank.   *The Lonely Voice: A Study of the Short Story.* Cleveland: World, 1963, pp. 138–139.

Taylor, Donald S.   "A Dream—A Wakening," in *Modern Fiction Studies.* IV (1958), pp. 361–362.

Walker, Warren S.   "The Unresolved Conflict in 'The Garden Party,'" in *Modern Fiction Studies.* III (1957), pp. 354–358.

Walsh, William.   *A Manifold Voice: Studies in Commonwealth Literature.* London: Chatto and Windus, 1970, pp. 170–171.

Weiss, Daniel A.   "The Garden Party of Proserpina," in *Modern Fiction Studies.* IV (1958), pp. 363–364.

"Prelude"

Alpers, Antony.   *Katherine Mansfield: A Biography.* New York: Knopf, 1953, pp. 213–219.

Berkman, Sylvia.   *Katherine Mansfield: A Critical Study.* New Haven, Conn.: Yale University Press, 1951, pp. 83–86.

Daly, Saralyn.   *Katherine Mansfield.* New York: Twayne, 1965, pp. 67–73.

Hale, Nancy. "Through the Looking Glass to Reality," in *Saturday Review of Literature*. XLI (November 8, 1958), pp. 39–40.

Hubbell, George S. "Katherine Mansfield and Kezia," in *Sewanee Review*. XXXV (1927), pp. 329–331

Kleine, Don W. "An Eden for Insiders: Katherine Mansfield's New Zealand," in *College English*. XXVII (1965), pp. 205–206.

Magalaner, Marvin. *The Fiction of Katherine Mansfield*. Carbondale: Southern Illinois University Press, 1971, pp. 26–38.

Maurois, André. *Points of View from Kipling to Graham Greene*. Translated by Hamish Miles. New York: Frederick Ungar, 1968, pp. 331–332.

Murry, John M. *Katherine Mansfield and Other Literary Portraits*. London: Peter Nevill, 1949, pp. 12–14.

O'Connor, Frank. *The Lonely Voice: A Study of the Short Story*. Cleveland: World, 1963, pp. 139–140.

GEORGE ORWELL
Eric Hugh Blair

Born: Motihari, India (1903)
Died: London, England (January 23, 1950)

Principal Works

NOVELS: *Burmese Days*, 1934; *A Clergyman's Daughter*, 1935; *Keep the Aspidistra Flying*, 1936; *Coming Up for Air*, 1939; *Nineteen Eighty-Four*, 1949.

SATIRE: *Animal Farm: A Fairy Story*, 1945.

ESSAYS: *Inside the Whale*, 1940; *Critical Essays*, 1946; *Shooting an Elephant*, 1950.

AUTOBIOGRAPHY: *Down and Out in Paris and London*, 1933; *Such, Such Were the Joys*, 1953.

MISCELLANEOUS: *The Road to Wigan Pier*, 1937; *Homage to Catalonia*, 1938.

Eric Hugh Blair was born in 1903 at Motihari in Bengal, India, the son of a Customs and Excise official of Scottish descent. Although his father soon retired on a small pension, the modest family resources were strained to send the boy in 1911 to a fashionable English preparatory school. Accepted at a reduced rate because of the likelihood of his winning a scholarship, he crammed successfully and won one to Eton in 1917. Lonely, imaginative, and insecure among the children of the well-to-do, he studied at Eton until 1921, reading Shaw, Wells, and other advanced writers and doing some writing of his own. Deciding not to try for a scholarship to Cambridge, he took a job in the Indian Imperial Police, intending to choose his own way of life when he would be pensioned off at forty. The five years between 1922 and 1927 which he spent in this service in Burma were unhappy ones. He was torn between opposed feelings: shame, guilt, and outrage at the often brutal workings of colonialism, and inability to feel more than contemptuous sympathy for its native victims.

Returning home on leave in 1927, he quit the service, took his terminal leave pay, and went to Paris to live on it for a year and a half while he wrote short stories and novels which no one published. With his money spent and the depression on, he plummeted down into the depths of poverty, at times seeming to make his plunge an act of expiation for feelings of guilt attaching to his Burma days. By a combination of public charity, a dishwashing job (in Paris), and a few loans, he managed to survive, tasting the bitterness of extreme penury in both Paris and London. The years between 1929 and 1935 saw him supporting himself as a private tutor, a teacher in cheap private schools, and (for a year and a half between 1932 and 1934) a part-time assistant in a Hampstead Heath bookshop. By this time, however, he had been published, as George Orwell, in various magazines such as *The Adelphi*, and in January, 1933, his first book, the autogiographical

Down and Out in Paris and London, had appeared to receive high praise from the critics. His portraits of the people of this nether world and his etchings of the miseries of their surroundings were lit up by the flame of his social consciousness.

In his first novel, *Burmese Days*, he presented a decaying empire, his writing—not illusioned like Kipling's or sympathetic like Forster's—serving him as a purgative for some of his feelings of guilt at having been part of a system he loathed. In *A Clergyman's Daughter*, Orwell drew upon his experience as a schoolteacher, hop-picker, and down-and-outer. This novel, with its amnesiac protagonist, shows the inadequacy of the Church and its philosophy in an acquisitive society. There was now a slight income from his writing (an average of $15 a week from 1930 to 1940) to permit him to escape to Essex, where he kept a pub, a village store, and a flock of hens. In 1936 he married Eileen O'Shaughnessy. In the same year *Keep the Aspidistra Flying* was published. A novel about a young man who escapes from, but finally capitulates to, the advertising industry in order to permit rather unromantic matrimony, it presents a gray, shabby middle-class life dominated by money. Increasingly active as a Socialist by this time, Orwell recorded the experiences of his stay in a depressed area of Britain in *The Road to Wigan Pier*. A choice of the Left Book Club, this documentary study displayed Orwell's strong sympathy for the laboring classes.

By Christmas of 1936 Orwell had decided to go to Spain to do a series of newspaper articles about the Spanish Civil War. When he arrived there, he felt compelled instead to join the military force of the anarchist-affiliated P.O.U.M. organization, fighting on the side of the Loyalists. A bullet through the throat put an end to his service in May, and when the Communists crushed the P.O.U.M. in Barcelona, Orwell barely escaped the country. All this was recorded graphically in clear, vivid prose in *Homage to Catalonia*.

Despite the tuberculosis aggravated by his hardships in Spain, Orwell continued to work, publishing in 1939 *Coming Up for Air*. This novel of a man returning to find the old home town destroyed by gray suburban developments was dominated by the conviction of impending war. When the war came, Orwell served as a sergeant in the Home Guard and as a member of the Indian Service of the B.B.C. In the last year of the war, as his own health further declined, his wife died suddenly from the combined effects of a minor operation and poor nutrition.

Animal Farm, published in 1945, was his most successful single work, a classically-written Swiftian animal story which was on one level a satiric allegory of Stalinism and on another of totalitarianism in general. Now a prominent, successful author and journalist, the ill, tired man went in 1947 to live with his sister and adopted son on the island of Jura, off the west coast of Scotland. He had hoped there to complete a new novel about the totalitarian future he saw, but in 1949 he found it necessary to enter a sanatorium in Gloucestershire. *Nineteen Eighty-Four*, completed in University College Hospital, London, was a horrifying vision of a world in which all the old values were systematically eradicated, language was deliberately made rudimentary to prevent unorthodox thought, and three superstates dominated an enslaved planet. The author's avowed faith in the proletarians was but a feeble flicker against the overpowering gloom of this fictional relation of personal and national horror. By late 1949, when he had married Sonia Bromwell, George Orwell had envisioned another novel. Planned as a new departure into a study of human relationships, it died with him when he succumbed after a tuberculous hemorrhage on January 23, 1950.

Bibliography

The *Collected Essays, Journalism, and Letters* were edited by Sonia and Ian Angus, 4 vols., 1968. There are four interesting and significant biographical and critical studies of Orwell by Laurence Brander, 1954; John Atkins, 1954; Christopher Hollis, 1956; and George Woodcock, *The Crystal Spirit*, 1966. See also Tom Hopkinson, *George Orwell*, 1955 (pamphlet); Kenneth M. Hamilton, "G. K. Chesterton and George Orwell: A Contrast in Prophecy," *Dalhousie Review*, XXXI (1951), 198–205; Charles I. Glicksberg, "The Literary Contribution of George Orwell," *Arizona Quarterly*, X (1954), 234–245; Philip Rieff, "George Orwell and the Post-Liberal Imagination," *Kenyon Review*, XVI (1954), 49–70; Richard J. Vorhees, "George Orwell: Rebellion and Responsibility," *South Atlantic Quarterly*, LIII (1954), 556–565; R. H. Rovere, "George Orwell," *New Republic*, CXXXV (1956), 11–15; Robert F. Gleckner, "1984 or 1948?" *College English*, XVIII (1956), 95–99; and Richard J. Vorhees, "*Nineteen Eighty-Four*: No Failure of Nerve," *ibid.*, 101–102.

NINETEEN EIGHTY-FOUR

Type of work: Novel
Author: George Orwell (Eric Blair, 1903–1950)
Type of plot: Political satire
Time of plot: 1984
Locale: London
First published: 1949

Nineteen Eighty-Four *along with Aldous Huxley's* Brave New World *and Yevgeni Zamyatin's* We, *must be considered one of the three great early anti-Utopian novels, a genre that has become disturbingly popular in contemporary literature. Orwell's vision is especially bleak because it is not simply a flight of fancy, but is, rather, the logical projection of the social, cultural, and historical environment that Orwell observed when writing the book in 1948.*

Principal Characters

Winston Smith, a citizen of Oceania. He is an intelligent man of thirty-nine, a member of the Outer Ring of the Party who has a responsible job in the Ministry of Truth, where he changes the records to accord with the aims and wishes of the Party. He is not entirely loyal, however, for he keeps a secret journal, takes a mistress, and hates Big Brother. Caught in his infidelities to the Party, he is tortured until he is a broken man; he finally accepts his lot, even to loving Big Brother.

Mrs. Smith, Winston's wife, a devoted follower of the Party and active member of the Anti-Sex League. Because she believes procreation a party duty, she leaves her husband when the union proves childless.

Julia, a bold, good-looking girl who, though she wears the Party's red chastity belt, falls in love with Winston and becomes his mistress. She, like her lover, rebels against Big Brother and the Party. Like Winston, too, she is tortured and brainwashed and led to repent her political sins.

O'Brien, a member of the Inner Party. He leads Winston and Julia to conspire against the Party and discovers all their rebellious acts and thoughts. He is Winston's personal torturer and educator, who explains to Winston why he must accept his lot in the world of Big Brother.

Mr. Charrington, a member of the thought police who disguises himself as an old man running an antique shop in order to catch such rebels as Winston and Julia. He is really a keen, determined man of thirty-five.

The Story

In externals, at least, Winston Smith was well adjusted to his world. He drank the bitter victory gin and smoked the vile victory cigarettes. In the morning he did his exercises in front of the telescreen, and when the instructor spoke to him over the two-way television, he bent with renewed vigor to touch the floor. His flat was dingy and rickety, but at thirty-nine he was scarcely old enough to remember a time when housing had been better. He had a fair job at the Ministry of Truth, since he had a good mind and the ability to write newspeak, the official language. He was a member of the outer ring of the Party.

One noon, by giving up his lunch at the ministry, he had a little free time to himself. Going to an alcove out of reach of the telescreen, he furtively took out his journal. It was a noble book with paper of fine quality unobtainable at present. It was an antique, bought on an illicit trip to a second-hand store run by old Mr. Charrington. While it was not illegal to keep a diary, for there were no laws in Oceania, it made him suspect. He wrote ploddingly about a picture he had seen of the valiant Oceania forces strafing shipwrecked refugees in the Mediterranean.

Musing over his writing, Winston found to his horror that he had written a slogan against Big Brother several times. He knew his act was a crime, even if the writing was due to gin; even to think such a slogan was a crime. Everywhere he looked, on stair landings and on store fronts, were posters showing Big Brother's all-seeing face, and citizens were reminded a hundred times a day that Big Brother was watching every move.

At the Ministry of Truth, Winston plunged into his routine. He had the job of rewriting records. If the Party made a wrong prediction on the progress of the war, if some aspect of production did not accord with the published goals of the ninth three-year plan, Winston corrected the record. All published material was constantly changed so that all history accorded with the wishes and aims of the Party.

There was a break in the day's routine for a two-minute hate period. On the big telescreen the face of Goldstein, the enemy of the Party, would appear, and a government speaker would work up the feelings of the viewers. Goldstein supposedly headed a great conspiracy against Oceania, and Winston loudly and dutifully drummed his heels as he took part in the group orgasm of hate.

A bold, dark-haired girl, wearing the red chastity belt, seemed often to be near Winston in the workrooms and in the commissary. He was afraid that she might be a member of the thought police. Seeing her outside the ministry, he decided she was following him. For a time he played with the idea of killing her. One day she slipped a note to him at work; the little paper announced that she loved him.

Winston was troubled. He had been married, but his wife belonged to the Anti-Sex League. For her, procreation was a Party duty. When they produced no children, his wife left him. Now this girl, Julia, spoke of love. Carefully making their conversation look like chance, Winston had a few private words with her in the lunchroom. She quickly named a country rendezvous. Winston met her in a woods, far from a telescreen, and she eagerly took him for a lover. Julia boasted that she had been the temporary mistress of several Party members and that she had no patience with the Anti-Sex League, although she worked diligently for it. She also bought sweets on the black market.

On another visit to Mr. Charrington's antique shop, the proprietor showed Winston an upstairs bedroom still preserved as it was before the Revolution. Although it was madness, Winston rented the room. Thereafter he and Julia had a comfortable bed for their brief meetings. Winston felt happy in the old room; there was no telescreen to spy on them.

Sometimes, while at work, Winston saw O'Brien, a kindly-looking member of the Inner Party. From a chance remark Winston deduced that O'Brien was not in sympathy with all the aims of the Party. When they could, Winston and Julia went to O'Brien's apartment. He assured them that Goldstein was really the head of a conspiracy and that eventually the Party would be overthrown. Julia told him of her sins against Party discipline, and Winston recounted his evidence that the Party distorted facts in public trials and purges. O'Brien then enrolled them in the conspiracy and gave them Goldstein's book to read.

After an exhausting hate week directed against the current enemy, Eurasia, Winston read aloud to the dozing Julia, both comfortably lying in bed, from Goldstein's treatise. Suddenly a voice rang out, ordering them to stand in the middle of the room. Winston grew sick when he realized that a hidden telescreen had spied on their actions. Soon the room was filled with truncheon-wielding policemen. Mr. Charrington came in, no longer a kindly member of the simple proletariat, but a keen, determined man of thirty-five. Winston knew then that Mr. Charrington belonged to the thought police. One of the guards hit Julia in the stomach. The others hurried Winston off to jail.

Winston, tortured for days, was beaten, kicked, and clubbed until he confessed his crimes. He willingly admitted to years of conspiracy with the rulers of Eurasia and told everything he knew of Julia. In the later phases of his torture O'Brien was at his side constantly. O'Brien kept him on a kind of rack with a doctor in attendance to keep him alive. He told Winston that Goldstein's book was a Party production, written in part by O'Brien himself.

Through it all the tortured man had one small triumph; he still loved Julia. Then O'Brien, knowing Winston's fear of rats, brought in a large cage filled with rodents and fastened it around Winston's head. In his unreasoning terror Winston begged him to let the rats eat Julia, instead.

Only one hurdle was left. Winston still hated Big Brother and said so. O'Brien patiently explained that the Party wanted no martyrs, for they strengthened opposition; nor did the leaders want only groveling subjection. Winston must also think right. The proletariat, happy in their ignorance, must never have a leader to rouse them. All Party members must think and feel as Big Brother directed.

When Winston was finally released, he was bald and his teeth were gone. Because he had been purged and because his crime had not been serious, he was even given a small job on a sub-committee. Mostly he sat solitary in taverns and drank victory gin. He even saw Julia once. She had coarsened in figure and her face was scarred. They had little to say to each other.

One day a big celebration was going on in the tavern. Oceania had achieved an important victory in Africa. Suddenly the doddering Winston felt himself purged. He believed. Now he could be shot with a pure soul, for at last he loved Big Brother.

Critical Evaluation

Although *Nineteen Eighty-Four* was published only thirty-odd years ago, it is a much different book today from the book its first readers held. It is no exaggeration to say that much of the book's atmosphere depends on the date of its title, a date sufficiently distant from 1949 (or 1959, or even 1969) to allow for dramatic changes, yet close enough to be ominous, a date which does not immediately cut the reader loose from reality. But what if the reader of Orwell's novel has a calendar on the wall for the year 1984? When 1984 becomes the actual calendar year, and then very quickly just another year past, one essential ingredient of Orwell's novel is irrevocably lost.

It is important to note this metamorphosis, because many critical commentaries on *Nineteen Eighty-Four* have failed to account for or even acknowledge the book's enormous popular appeal, an appeal which is based on the intrinsic fascination of Orwell's "what if" premise, just as *Animal Farm* banks on the age-old appeal of the fable, in which animals behave more or less like men.

It might seem incongruous to speak of the "fascination" of Orwell's premise, since the world of *Nineteen Eighty-Four* is brutal, nightmarish, hopeless. To understand this incongruity, one need only read Orwell's essay on *Gulliver's Travels*, "Politics and Literature" (1946), one of the keys to *Nineteen Eighty-Four*. Swift, Orwell argues at length, is a diseased writer, who "falsifies his picture of the world by refusing to see anything in human life except dirt, folly and wickedness. . . ." Yet, Orwell says, *Gulliver's Travels* has an inexhaustible fascination for him: "If I had to make a list of six books which were to be preserved when all others were destroyed, I would certainly put *Gulliver's Travels* among them."

How does Orwell resolve this apparent contradiction? First, he acknowledges the intrinsic appeal of Swift's imaginary worlds, worlds which—like Orwell's Oceania—are provided with their peculiar customs, with a history, and even with a language. But even this imaginative power would not suffice, Orwell says, to "enable us to enjoy Swift if his world view were truly wounding or shocking." Although Swift's picture of the world is distorted, it is not wholly false: "Swift is not actually inventing anything, he is merely leaving something out." Swift shows a side of life which "we all know about while shrinking from mentioning it."

In an extraordinary passage, Orwell goes on to explain how Swift's vision can fascinate us. He says:

> In the queerest way, pleasure and disgust are linked together . . . A child, when it is past the infantile stage but still looking at the world with fresh eyes, is moved by horror almost as often as by wonder—horror of snot and spittle, of the dogs' excrement on the pavement, the dying toad full of maggots, the sweaty smell of grown-ups, the hideousness of old men, with their bald heads and bulbous noses.

It has been necessary to quote from Orwell's essay on Swift at length in order to clear up a number of misconceptions about *Nineteen Eighty-Four*. Many critics have read the novel as Orwell's final, utterly despairing judgment of mankind, but—as the essay on Swift clearly shows—this reading misses Orwell's intentions. Orwell, like Swift, takes an existing aspect of reality and—experimentally, as it were—makes it whole. Like Swift, he has invented nothing in his grim vision of the totalitarian state; he *has* left something out. The difference, Orwell would say, is that he was conscious of the process, whereas Swift was wholly committed to his "diseased" and partial view.

Again, many critics, while praising Orwell's acute analysis of totalitarianism, have called the novel an artistic failure. The characters, they say, are not fully developed. The structure of the novel is ill-conceived: the entire first part is exposition, and the essential action does not begin until Part Two, a third of the way into the book. Substantial sections peripheral to the action—such as the long excerpt from Goldstein's "book" and the appendix on "The Principles of Newspeak"—are aesthetic disasters.

None of these objections are fair or even relevant, because they all mistakenly assume that Orwell attempted to write a realistic novel and botched the job. In fact, *Nineteen Eighty-Four* should be linked with a deliberately digressive, loosely-structured satiric work like *Gulliver's Travels*. The premise of a not-too-distant future, like Swift's premise of a voyage, enabled Orwell (again, like Swift) to develop simultaneously a number of ideas which preoccupied him without having to tie them neatly together.

If the year 1984 no longer has the resonance it once had, Orwell's novel still has much to offer that has not yet become dated. His analysis of the ruses whereby totalitarian regimes—and sympathetic Western journalists—continually rewrite history is as applicable today as it was in 1949. A recent *National Geographic* article on Shanghai sounds at times very much like the children's history textbook which Winston Smith reads, trying to grasp what life was like before the Revolution. (This excerpt, which describes the "uniform" of the capitalists, including the top hat, is one of many fine comic passages which critical discussions of the novel often neglect.) A *National Geographic* photo shows an old Chinese man reading a Spanish-English newspaper. The caption says that he:

> may have learned his English before World War II, when foreign gunboats kept Shanghai a stronghold of Western trade concessions wrested from a weak imperial government. Those were the days of rampant prostitution and opium addition—days when local peasants were 'shanghaied' for cheap labor abroad, or to crew shorthanded ships.

Like the excerpt from Winston's textbook, this account of "life before the Revolution" uses a partial truth to justify the enormities of a totalitarian regime. Indeed, the recent history of China, in which respected leaders become traitors overnight, to be vilified by schoolchildren, in which diabolical conspiracies are suddenly "discovered" and made to account, like the "Gang of Four," for every imaginable problem, seems to be lifted from the pages of *Nineteen Eighty-Four*.

Nineteen Eighty-Four / ORWELL 729

However, Orwell's political critique is not limited to totalitarian regimes. If Oceania is based in part on the Soviet Union—often with no exaggeration—it was also based on dreary postwar England. Orwell despised the smug acceptance of hierarchy, of manifest inequality and injustice which he saw in the Western democracies. He was aware of the immense, corrupting influence of the media in the West, and his "Newspeak" owes as much to Madison Avenue as it does to *Pravda* and *Tass*. Indeed, the adjective "Orwellian" is not generally used to name a political condition. "Orwellian" usually refers to the frightening potential for surveillance and even for thought-control which is all too real today, in democracies as well as in totalitarian states.

Orwell's aim in *Nineteen Eighty-Four* was not merely to condemn. Like Czeslaw Milosz in *The Captive Mind* (1953), Orwell sought to understand the "why" of totalitarianism. This is the "ultimate secret" which Goldstein's book is about to reveal when Winston stops reading and falls asleep with Julia. When they awake they are arrested, and Winston never finishes the book. The revelation of the secret is left to O'Brien, who tells Winston that the "Party seeks power entirely for its own sake ... Not wealth or luxury or long life or happiness; only power, pure power." Pure power, he soon explains, is the power to make another man suffer. "Obedience is not enough. Unless he is suffering, how can you be sure that he is obeying your will and not his own? Power is inflicting pain and humiliation."

Orwell's little-known but important essay, "Raffles and Miss Blandish" (1944), helps to gloss O'Brien's speech. This essay anticipates many of the ideas which Orwell developed in the last part of *Nineteen Eighty-Four*. Even O'Brien's famous image of the future ("imagine a boot stamping on a human face—forever") is anticipated when Orwell describes a scene from a novel by James Hadley Chase (the author of *No Orchids for Miss Blandish*) in which the hero is "described as stamping on somebody's face, and then, having crushed the man's mouth in, grinding his heel round and round in it."

Orwell's subject in this essay is the "interconnection between sadism, masochism, success-worship, power-worship, and totalitarianism," a neglected subject: "even to mention it is considered somewhat indelicate." Orwell shows how the brutal sadism and masochism of a novel like Chase's *No Orchids for Miss Blandish* is connected with the slavish worship of Stalin or Hitler, as well as with "the efficiency experts who preached 'punch,' 'drive,' 'personality,' " in the 1920's. "It is important to notice," he adds, "that the cult of power tends to be mixed up with a love of cruelty and wickedness *for their own sakes*." In *Nineteen Eighty-Four*, the "ultimate secret" of the Party is simply this: they are sadists, who feel as they inflict pain the same ecstasy that Winston and Julia feel when they make love. Men like O'Brien love cruelty for its own sake, just as Julia loves making love ("the thing in itself," Winston says) for its own sake. Beyond that, Orwell suggests, it is impossible to inquire. He does not offer any psychological or sociological explanation. Some men love cruelty and wickedness, and they never lack victims.

Bibliography

Alldritt, Keith. *The Making of George Orwell: An Essay in Literary History.* New York: St. Martin's, 1969, pp. 150–178.

Atkins, John A. *George Orwell: A Literary Study.* London: J. Calder, 1954, pp. 237–254.

Barr, Alan. "The Paradise Behind *1984*," in *English Miscellany.* XIX (1968), pp. 197–203.

Calder, Jenni. *Chronicles of Conscience: A Study of George Orwell and Arthur Koestler.* Pittsburgh: University of Pittsburgh Press, 1968, pp. 229–253.

Connors, J. " 'Do It to Julia': Thoughts on Orwell's *1984*," in *Modern Fiction Studies.* XVI (Winter, 1970–1971), pp. 463–473.

Dyson, Anthony E. *The Crazy Fabric; Essays in Irony.* New York: St. Martin's, 1965, pp. 197–219.

Elsbree, Langdon. "The Structured Nightmare of *1984*," in *Twentieth Century Literature.* V (October, 1959), pp. 135–141.

Fink, Howard. "Newspeak: The Epitome of Parody Techniques in *Nineteen Eighty-Four*," in *Critical Survey.* V (1971), pp. 155–163.

Harris, Harold J. "Orwell's Essays and *1984*," in *Twentieth Century Literature.* IV (January, 1959), pp. 154–161.

Howe, Irving. *Orwell's Nineteen Eighty-Four: Text, Sources, Criticism.* New York: Harcourt Brace, 1963.

Hynes, Samuel L. *Twentieth Century Interpretations of 1984: A Collection of Critical Essays.* Englewood Cliffs, N.J.: Prentice-Hall, 1971.

Karl, Frederick R. "George Orwell: The White Man's Burden," in *A Reader's Guide to the Contemporary English Novel.* Edited by Frederick R. Karl. New York: Octagon, 1972, pp. 159–161, 163–165.

Kessler, Martin. "Power and the Perfect State: A Study in Disillusionment as Reflected in Orwell's *Nineteen Eighty-Four* and Huxley's *Brave New World*," in *Political Science Quarterly.* LXXII (December, 1957), pp. 565–577.

Knox, George. "The Divine Comedy in *1984*," in *Western Humanities Review.* IX (Autumn, 1955), pp. 371–372.

Kubal, David L. *Outside the Whale: George Orwell's Art and Politics.* Notre Dame, Ind.: Notre Dame University Press, 1972, pp. 43–47, 130–141.

Lee, Robert E. *Orwell's Fiction.* Notre Dame, Ind.: Notre Dame University Press, 1969, pp. 128–157

Lief, Ruth Ann. *Homage to Oceania: The Prophetic Vision of George Orwell.* Columbus: Ohio State University Press, 1969.

Maddison, Michael. "*1984*: A Burnhamite Fantasy?," in *Political Quarterly.* XXXII (January–March, 1961), pp. 71–79.

Malkin, Lawrence. "Halfway to *1984*," in *Horizon.* XII (Spring, 1970), pp. 33–39.

Oxley, B.T. *George Orwell.* New York: Arco, 1969, pp. 112–125.

Ranald, Ralph A. "George Orwell and the Mad World: The Anti-Universe of *1984*," in *South Atlantic Quarterly.* LXVI (Autumn, 1967), pp. 544–553.

Rankin, David. "Orwell's Intention in *1984*," in *English Language Notes.* XII (1975), pp. 188–192.

Smith, Marcus. "The Wall of Blackness: A Psychological Approach to *1984*," in *Modern Fiction Studies.* XIV (Winter, 1968–1969), pp. 423–433.

Steinhoff, William. *George Orwell and the Origins of 1984.* Ann Arbor: University of Michigan Press, 1975.

Thale, Jerome. "Orwell's Modest Proposal," in *Critical Quarterly.* IV (Winter, 1962), pp. 365–368.

WILFRED OWEN

Born: Oswestry, England (March 18, 1893)
Died: Sanbre Canal, France (November 4, 1918)

Principal Works

POEMS: *Poems* (edited by Siegfried Sassoon, 1920); enlarged edition, with a memoir by Edmund Blunden, 1931.

Wilfred Owen was born and raised in the Shropshire countryside made famous by another poet, A. E. Housman. Born in Oswestry, Owen moved to Shrewsbury for a year, and then to Birkenhead where, in 1900, he entered school. In 1911, he matriculated at London University. According to his friend Edmund Blunden, whose *Memoir* (1931) is an affectionate and detailed account of the poet's short life, Owen was a quiet, imaginative boy, not given to sports, whose greatest pleasure was to be read to by his mother. Owen was writing verse by the time he reached London University, and was deep in his earliest love—Keats. He was awarded the Military Cross on October 1, 1918, and killed in action on November 4. His life and poems reveal a young man highly sensitive, idealistic, and given to aestheticism who was transformed by the horrors of trench warfare into a quietly courageous leader of men, a biting social critic, and a poet of hard, tough truthfulness and humanity. He is generally regarded as the greatest English war-poet.

As a boy, Owen read widely, not only Keats, but Dickens, Scott, George Eliot, and Ruskin, for whose work he had great respect, except "that Prophet ... warned us so feebly against the war." He played the piano, studied botany and archaeology, and in August of 1913 became a tutor in English at the Berlitz School, Bordeaux. After some private tutoring he returned to England in 1915 and joined the Artist's Rifles. His friendship, in Bordeaux, with M. Laurent Tailhade was his first contact with a genuine man of letters, for, despite Owen's love of poetry, he had never been part of a literary circle. At the time he contemplated music as a profession, and painting, but was aware that poetry was his first love.

Owen went to war just after Christmas in 1916, with the Lancashire Fusiliers. That spring he fell into a shellhole and suffered a concussion, the effect of which was to affect his nerves so that, on June 26, 1917, he was sent back to Craiglockhart Hospital, Edinburgh, where he met and became close to Siegfried Sassoon, a poet and a sharp critic of the public illusions regarding the war. It was in the long talks with Sassoon that Owen completed his maturity as a poet. Henceforth his poems, for example, "Dulce et Decorum Est," toughened to the task of expressing with both bitterness and deep humanity the conditions, the waste, stupidity, and terror, of war. He once observed that "Tennyson, it seems, was always a great child." The world had changed radically since the war began, and Owen's poetry, like that of Sassoon, Blunden, Rosenburg, and others, had turned sharply away from Victorian and aesthetic models. No one in France, except one captain, knew that Owen was a poet. His letters to his mother are, perhaps, the most vivid record written of the actual conditions of life, or better, of death during the Great War. In them he describes the fetid mud, "three, four, five feet deep," the lonely terror of outpost and reconnaisance duty in No-Man's Land, the sensation of being drenched with the warm blood of a man killed by his side. But with all the horrors and realism of his poems and letters, with all the scornful and bitter criticism of those at home who still regarded the war as a sort of pilgrimage or holy crusade, Owen maintained the selfless pity and love for his fellows that make his poems—and his life—memorable.

Bibliography

A good introduction to Owen's poetry is Edmund Blunden's memoir in *The Poems of Wilfred Owen*, 1931. Harold Owen's *Journey from Obscurity: Wilfred Owen, 1893–1918*, 3 vols., 1963–1965, is an indispensible biographical study. A fine recent edition of Owen's work is *The Collected Poems*, edited by C. Day Lewis, 1963.

See also Dennis S. R. Welland, *Wilfred Owen, A Critical Study*, 1960; Gertrude M. White, *Wilfred Owen*, 1969; I. M. Parsons, "The Poems of Wilfred Owen," *New Criterion*, X (1931), 658–699; Bernard Bergonzi, *Heroes' Twilight: A Study of the Literature of the Great War*, 1965; John H. Johnston, *English Poetry of the First World War*, 1964; and C. M. Bowra, *Poetry and Politics, 1900–1960*, 1966.

For additional material see William White, *Wilfred Owen, 1893–1918: A Bibliography*, 1966.

THE POETRY OF OWEN

Author: Wilfred Owen (1893–1918)
Principal published works: Poems, 1920; *The Poems of Wilfred Owen*, edited by
Edmund Blunden, 1931

Essay-Review

For Wilfred Owen, born and brought up in the Housman country of Shropshire and Shrewsbury, reader of Keats, Tennyson, and Swinburne, a young poet devoted to boyish "loneliness" and the aesthetic cult of Beauty, wounded March 19, 1917, again on May 1, and killed in action November 4, 1918, Beauty was no escape. The horrors of war, in Owen's hands, were transfigured in poems into a terrible beauty.

The war itself did not make Owen a poet, but it did mature his poems, as if overnight; too, the war never completely dissolved his early yearning for a misty, aesthetic Beauty. But the war transformed that Beauty from a literary dream to a stark necessity, held to in the face of the horrors recorded so bluntly, the devastating "Dulce et Decorum Est."

Owen, who published only three poems during his short lifetime, could find cause for elation, within two months of his death, at being accepted "as a peer" by the generally innocuous Georgian poets, those purveyors of sentiment and pictures of the English countryside. But his poetry had before them moved sharply away from both the literary aestheticism of his youth and the either jingoistic or merely homesick poesy which had been the first two reactions to the war which, begun in August, 1914, was to be "over by Christmas."

Just before the outbreak of war, Owen could write in his diary poems about wind murmuring in the leaves and birds singing. Such evidence of a boy's experiments with sound and celebration of youth and a pastoral setting is obviously a young man's conception of poetry, based not on any real experience but probably on an immature reading of Keats, Tennyson and Swinburne. His last known poem, "Smile, Smile, Smile," starkly illustrates how daydreams have turned into nightmares, the disingenuous into the ironic, aestheticism into social protest, beauty and truth into a deeply-felt pity which, while expressed with mature artistic detachment, is nonetheless a product of personal pain, fear, and moral outrage. The soldiers read the hometown paper and think of buying homes after the war. The poem also describes the stupid, callous, mawkish sentiment and blindness of the Home Front.

Siegfried Sassoon, Robert Graves, Edmund Blunden, Isaac Rosenburg, and Owen were the first poets to take another look at the war which had at first been regarded as a kind of sacred crusade. In his study of Owen, D. S. R. Welland writes of how, by about 1915, the emphasis in the anthologies of "war poetry" had shifted righteous nature of the crusade to the knightly crusader. The latter response merely replaced national glorification with self-pity, or, at best, evocations of better times in England. Obviously, neither reaction produced much in the way of an honest, fully human poetry. The old ways died hard.

The third reaction was one of protest, and Sassoon, perhaps, or Rosenburg, was most biting in satirical attack. Sassoon met Owen in a hospital in England, and Owen's mature war poetry dates, roughly, from their long discussions (though to say that Sassoon "made" Owen a poet is a vast distortion). Owen, however, expressed his protest not so much satirically as through a mixture of sarcasm, ironic detachment, and, most importantly, of pity. His verse develops conciseness, becomes hard, direct, colloquial, strongly cadenced. In this respect he was not different than the other poets of the war. In Owen, however, pity for the "poor wretches" is dominant both over pity for himself (based, according to Joseph Cohen, upon the poet's sense of guilt for homosexual repression) and satiric protest at the perpetrated outrage of war, or the naïve, even criminal stupidities mouthed at home. And the pity is rooted not in condescension or gratuitous superiority, but in a profound awareness of human fellowship and fellow suffering.

In "Strange Meeting" the poet meets an enemy he had killed. They meet in Hell, where he had fled to escape the terror of battle in a dream-vision. They must find fellowship in Hell itself, for Earth has become worse. The German is not a fiend, a killer who delights in atrocities and is devoted to crushing freedom and the British Empire, but a man who, like the poet, dreamed and hoped. Neither the dead nor the living indulges in self-pity. The "enemy" refers to the pity the war has distilled, but by "pity" the poet means not for self, but for his fellows, for humanity itself. Indeed, Owen develops finally a viewpoint which is largely characteristic of the poetry of World War II: a poetry not so much of protest but of a recognition of how, in the horror of battle, human fellowship is starkly, and of necessity, thrown into sharp relief. Enforced murder breeds, at last, a kind of gentleness.

Poems like "Apologia pro Poemate Mea" must be understood in this context. Death becomes a joke, and the men laugh in its face, not out of false bravado, but out of a sense of a new awareness of life, death, and fellowship. What seems bravado is, instead, an honest account of actual human response to a living, absurd hell. The death-bound comradeship, both pitiable and defiant of battle comrades, is a theme on which Owen probes the paroxysm of war more deeply and poignantly than any protest alone could. It is the core of his achievement, and his frequently quoted statement that he was not concerned with "Poetry" must be understood in terms of this attitude. Poetry, here, suggests the old illusions, the old "literary" aestheticism, poesy of birds and Greek goddesses and pastoral landscapes. To a large extent it refers to Owen's own youthful effusions and illusions. Now the poetry is in such matters as pity and protest.

In the matter of style, it should be noted that Owen's development away from the vague, vaporous, and pseudo-Keatsian effusions of his youth, his development of a style which is abrupt, chiseled, and colloquially dramatic, corresponds to a general drift in the poetry of the late nineteenth and early twentieth centuries. Parallel developments occur in the poetry of Yeats, and T. E. Hulme (who also was killed in the war). Pater and Pound had called for a more objective, "harder" or "classical" poetry, and this development may be traced in Imagism or, better, in Yeats and Eliot. In Yeats, the line of development is clear from the softly sensuous and evocative "symbolism" of his early poem to the harder and more genuinely symbolic and dramatic specimens of *The Green Helmet and Other Poems*, published in 1910.

But Wilfred Owen, until he met Sassoon in 1917, had had no important contact with the literary world, and his development of terse, "hard" idiom must have been only a natural and necessary way of expressing, without illusions, lies, evasion, and the stark and monumentally un-"Poetic" reality of war.

Owen's experiments with slant and internal rhyme, with nonmetrical cadences and compressions like that of "bloodshod," are significant steps toward a poetry which moves away from the more regular and traditionally "poetic" work of the previous two centuries. Owen influenced, in this respect, later poets like Auden, C. Day Lewis, Stephen Spender, and Louis MacNeice. But it is his individual and searing exposure of both the horror and the pity of war that provides Owen a lasting niche in the history of English poetry. A world changed during his short lifetime. His ability to change with it, and to record the old world's dying anguish, is his unique and memorable achievement.

HAROLD PINTER

Born: London, England (October 10, 1930)

Principal Works

PLAYS: *The Room,* 1957; *The Birthday Party and Other Plays,* 1958; *The Caretaker,* 1960; *A Slight Ache and Other Plays,* 1961; *The Collection* and *The Lover,* 1963; *The Homecoming,* 1965; *Tea Party and Other Plays,* 1967; *Landscape* and *Silence,* 1968.

POEMS: *Poems,* 1968.

MEMOIRS: *Mac,* 1968.

Harold Pinter is a British playwright who has recently become one of the leading practitioners in the dramatic mode known generally as the Theatre of the Absurd. Born in 1930, the son of a Jewish tailor in Hackney, a part of East London, Pinter began his literary career in his teens by writing poetry for the little magazines. At the same time, however, he was studying acting at the Royal Academy of Dramatic Art and the Central School of Speech and Drama. This led to a career in acting. Under the stage name of David Baron, he performed in many parts of Ireland with a Shakespearean company and also did a considerable amount of repertory work in the provinces. Before turning to plays, he started a novel entitled *The Dwarfs,* which he failed to complete. But in 1957, he was actually commissioned to write his first play. He spoke of an idea for a play to a friend of his in the drama department of Bristol University, and the friend was so attracted by the idea that he requested Pinter to write the play. Pinter composed it in four days.

The result of this nimble, almost impulsive feat of composition was a one-act drama called *The Room,* first performed at Bristol University in May of 1957. It was followed shortly by a second one-act play, *The Dumb Waiter,* also written in 1957 but not performed until January 21, 1960, when it was presented at the Hampstead Theatre Club in London. After this came Pinter's first full-length play, *The Birthday Party,* which opened at the Arts Theatre in Cambridge on April 28, 1958. Unsuccessful at first, the play was soon transferred to the Lyric Theatre in Hammersmith, and Pinter himself directed it the following year in Birmingham. After an enthusiastically received performance by the Tavistock Players at the Tower Theatre in Canonbury, London, it was broadcast on television to millions of Britons in the spring of 1960. It crossed the Atlantic in July of the same year, when it was presented by the Actors Workshop in San Francisco.

Besides *The Caretaker,* his second full-length play (and first great public success), Pinter's work for the stage includes a number of other scripts—among them *The Lover* and *The Collection,* two one-act plays performed in Boston during the spring of 1965. In addition, he has written extensively for the screen, radio, and television. On the B.B.C.'s Third Programme, Britons have heard his radio plays *A Slight Ache*, first broadcast on July 29, 1959; *A Night Out*, first presented in March, 1960; and *The Dwarfs*, based on his unfinished novel, first performed on December 2, 1960. On television, they have seen a viewer's version of *A Night Out* (April, 1960), as well as *Night School*, a television play first broadcast in July of 1960. Pinter is the author of the script for *The Pumpkin Eater*, a film released in 1964 with a cast that includes James Mason, Anne Bancroft, and Peter Finch. In 1963 he was awarded an Italian prize for his television scripts, and in 1966 he was made a Commander of the Order of the British Empire.

Bibliography

Important studies of Pinter include Martin Esslin, *The Peopled Wound: The Work of Harold Pinter*, 1970; Katherine H. Burkman, *The Dramatic World of Harold Pinter: Its Basis in Ritual*, 1971; Ronald Hayman, *Harold Pinter*, 1968; Walter Kerr, *Harold Pinter*, 1967; Arlene Sykes, *Harold Pinter*, 1970; L. Gordon, *Strategems to Uncover Nakedness: The Dramas of Harold Pinter*, 1969; Arnold P. Hinchliffe, *Harold Pinter*, 1967; John R. Taylor, *Harold Pinter*, 1969; James R. Hollis, *Harold Pinter: The Poetics of Silence*, 1970; and Herman T. Schroll, *Harold Pinter: A Study of His Reputation, 1958–1969*, 1971.

See also Martin Esslin, *The Theatre of the Absurd*, revised edition, 1969; John Russell Brown, editor, *Modern British Dramatists*, 1968; Louis MacNeice, *Varieties of Parable*, 1965; John Kershaw, *The Present Stage*, 1966; and Allardyce Nicoll, *English Drama: A Modern Viewpoint*, 1968.

THE CARETAKER

Type of work: Drama
Author: Harold Pinter (1930–   )
Time: The present
Locale: A house in west London
First presented: 1960

Essay-Review

    The Caretaker is a dramatic study of the relations among three men in a cluttered, unkempt, crudely furnished room: Aston, the slow-witted tenant, a man in his early thirties; Mick, the landlord, who is Aston's younger brother; and Davies, an old tramp subsisting on the brothers' hospitality. At the beginning of the play, which takes place entirely within the confines of a single room, Aston has rescued Davies from a fight at a nearby café. Because the old man has been fired from his job at this establishment, Aston has brought him to the room. Charitably he gives Davies a chair, a bed, and a little money, and offers him cigarettes, a pair of shoes, and a job as caretaker of the flat—an offer that is repeated by Mick. But Davies' presistent complaints about the arrangements made for him gradually antagonize the brothers, and at the end of the play, in a moment that is almost tragic in impact, Davies is driven out. The power of the play derives from the skill with which Pinter moves his characters toward the inevitability of this final expulsion.

    Davies is established at the outset of the drama as a lonely derelict, at once pathetic and ludicrous. From the moment that Aston ushers him into the room, the audience sees that he is utterly dependent on the kindness and generosity of his host. So simple a convenience as a chair to sit on gives Davies satisfaction, for this is a man deprived of common comforts, dispossessed of the amenities and securities that insulate the life of the average working man. During his job at the café, he says, he could never get a seat during the tea break. But Davies is less often grateful for small favors than dissatisfied with large ones. In spite of his position as a mendicant, he masquerades as a man to be reckoned with. He tells Aston, for example, that the fight at the café started because he refused to empty a bucket of rubbish because he thought the task beneath his position and he resented this affront to his dignity as an old man. He therefore challenged the Scotsman who had given him the order (as he later threatens the innocuous Aston with a knife), but actually he was capable only of saying what he *might* have done to his antagonist had he been younger, or what he *may* do later in revenge. His Falstaffian bravado collapsed in the face of imminent violence, from which Aston saved him just in time. In retrospect, he is forced to admit that the Scotsman could have put him in the hospital with a single punch.

    The incident, even in the retelling, graphically reveals the central paradox in Davies' character: the conflict between his situation and his pretensions. He is a beggar with appalling arrogance, a petty, useless hobo who presumes to be a man of stature and importance. His presumption takes a number of forms. He is fanatically zenophobic, denouncing to Aston the numbers of Poles, Greeks, and Blacks who would crowd him out of a seat at the café; he accepts pipe tobacco only after explaining that he has been recently robbed of a tin of it; he declares that he has dined in the best company, that he abandoned his wife shortly after their marriage because of her slovenly housekeeping. He contends, too, that he has a number of friends who help him, among them a lavatory attendant who gives him soap, and he repeatedly maintains that papers establishing his identity are available in Sidcup, where he intends to go as soon as the weather clears. But as the play proceeds, Davies' claims, his demands, and his cantankerous assertiveness gradually appear for what they are, the threadbare covering of a helpless old man, clutching desperately at the rags of a tattered self-respect. The story about his papers is patently spurious, and even his name is subject to question, for he has been living much of his life, he says, under the pseudonym of Jenkins. He pretends to be a connoisseur of shoes, preferring leather to suede and pointedly expressing his dissatisfaction with the fit of the footwear offered him by Aston, but he must confess that his own shoes are almost entirely worn out. He does not like his bed, which is situated directly under an open window and is consequently exposed in the night to rainy gusts, but he has no other place to sleep and must accept it.

In large part, of course, Davies' character is defined and elicited by the two other figures in the play. Each punctures the old man's noxious presumptuousness in a different way, Aston by his disarming modesty and Mick by his cool, cruelly penetrating tone of sustained mockery. Aston is deceptively mild in appearance and manner. He is thoughtful, quiet, patient, and generous to a fault, qualities which make him seem the perfect putty for Davies' rather heavy-handed manipulation. When Davies rejects the profferred shoes, Aston does not chide his guest for ingratitude; instead, he returns to the room, in the third act, with another pair of shoes. He opens not only his house and purse to Davies, but also his heart; in a long speech at the end of Act II, he unfolds the bleak horror of his past—of his early hallucinations, of the insidious rumor which sent him to a mental institution, of the electric shock treatment he received there, of his discharge, of his present life as a kind of human vegetable. Aston, in fact, is clearly the sort of man who needs the compassion that a personal caretaker would give him, and he seems unconsciously to imply this fact when he offers Davies the job of caretaker; the meaning of the term vacillates between "house janitor" and "sympathetic guardian." Pinter exploits this ambiguity throughout the play. But the ambiguity is especially enriched by the circumstances in which the job offer is made. As a crude, demanding intruder, Davies is fitted to be a caretaker in neither sense. On the contrary, we see from the beginning that as a homeless, destitute old man, he himself requires a caretaker. In Aston, his kindly, unassuming, uncomplaining host, Davies thinks that he has found his man.

But Davies woefully underestimates Aston. The old man shortly discovers that his modest host is perfectly capable of self-assertion when the occasion demands. On the morning after their first night in the room together, Aston charges Davies with jabbering in his sleep, creating a disturbance that awoke Aston. The next morning, when Davies complains that rain and wind came in upon him through the open window as he slept, and he therefore demands that the window be closed, Aston insists that the window shall remain open. Still later, in Act III, Aston reacts sharply when Davies explodes over the treatment he has been getting. After accepting the second pair of shoes which Aston offers him, after churlishly objecting to the color of the laces, Davies goes to sleep. Once more his mutterings awaken Aston, who in turn arouses the old man. When Davies spews out a torrent of abuse at Aston's mental status and draws a knife on him, Aston quietly tells the old man that he smells and that he must leave. Davies can do nothing for the moment except leave. He goes off in a flurry of feckless imprecations.

But if Davies underestimates Aston, his judgment of Mick is doubly inept. From his first encounter with Davies at the end of Act I, Mick is almost ruthlessly in command, supremely confident of his power to strip away every one of Davies' pretensions and to expose him for the selfish, useless parasite he is. Davies, significantly clad only in his underwear, is rummaging in a sideboard drawer when Mick enters the room, surprises him, forces him to the floor, and calmly launches on a cross-examination calculated to drive the old man mad. He taunts Davies by withholding his trousers, all the while questioning him about his name, his bed, his sleep of the night just passed, his reason for being in the room, and his intentions, all the time mockingly pretending that Davies might be a prospective tenant of limitless means. When Aston enters the room with a bag for Davies, Mick takes it and teases Davies with it before letting him have it. It is Mick, too, who restates Aston's offer of the caretaking job, but he defines the duties in flamboyantly elaborate terms. The man he wants, he tells Davies, must be a first-class interior decorator capable of transforming the rudely furnished room into a sumptuously appointed flat. Davies, of course, is compelled to admit that he has no such qualifications; this is only one of the many retractions and evasions to which Mick's merciless questioning drives him. The final blow comes in Act III when Davies turns to Mick for support against Aston, who has just asked Davies to leave. With that astounding presumption which has marked his conduct and attitude from the beginning, Davies expects to displace Aston in Mick's affection, in effect, to gain Mick as a caretaker. But it shortly becomes clear that Mick has no intention of evicting his own brother, for whom he has generously provided living quarters; instead, he tells Davies that Aston can do what he likes with the house. At this point Aston returns and firmly repeats his order that Davies must go. It is a tribute to Pinter's power as a playwright that Davies' plight here is almost tragic. He has proved himself a thoroughly boorish, obnoxious, petulant, cranky, and ungrateful guest, but he somehow holds out sympathy in the final moments of the play. He is no longer ludicrous; he is now desperate and forlorn. The would-be caretaker must roam the world in search of care.

In the light of this ending, the play might be called a comedy-turned-tragedy. It has its moments of laughter, for Pinter has an uncanny gift for reproducing the banalities of ordinary conversation—its trudging pace, its cul-de-sacs, its involutions, its maddening regressions. His dialogue, therefore, is often amusing, as are the ludicrous claims, evasions, and self-deceptions of Davies. But like the climate in so many of Pinter's plays, the atmosphere of *The Caretaker* is subtly, treacherously charged with potential menace. The characters who move about in the room are never directly exposed to the dangers of the outside world, but Davies must sleep with a gas stove above his head (the gas jets make him apprehensive), and with the wind and rain blowing in upon his head. He wants to close the window, to insulate himself from the world outside, but Aston will not let him; and it is into that world that Aston ultimately thrusts him. As the curtain falls on the final act, one is left with the spectacle of a lonely, desolate, dispossessed man, still talking of papers in Sidcup which do not exist.

Bibliography

Anderson, Michael. *Anger and Detachment: A Study of Arden, Osborne, and Pinter.* London: Pitman, 1976, pp. 102–108.

Baker, William and Stephen Ely Tabachnick. *Harold Pinter.* New York: Barnes & Noble, 1973, pp. 70–89.

Boulton, James T. "Harold Pinter: *The Caretaker* and Other Plays," in *Modern Drama.* VI (September, 1963), pp. 131–140. Reprinted in *Pinter: A Collection of Critical Essays.* Edited by Arthur Ganz. Englewood Cliffs, N.J.: Prentice-Hall, 1972, pp. 93–104.

Brown, John Russell. *Theatre Language: A Study of Arden, Osborne, Pinter, and Wesker.* New York: Taplinger, 1972, pp. 55–92.

Burkman, Katherine H. *The Dramatic World of Harold Pinter: Its Basis in Ritual.* Columbus: Ohio State University Press, 1971, pp. 76–87.

Cohn, Ruby. "The World of Harold Pinter," in *Tulane Drama Review.* VI (March, 1962), pp. 55–68. Reprinted in *Pinter: A Collection of Critical Essays.* Edited by Arthur F. Ganz. Englewood Cliffs, N.J.: Prentice-Hall, 1972, pp. 78–92.

Donoghue, Denis. "London Letter: Moral West End," in *Hudson Review.* XIV (Spring, 1961), pp. 93–103.

Dukore, Bernard F. *Where Laughter Stops: Pinter's Tragicomedy.* Columbia: University of Missouri Press, 1976, pp. 25–31.

Esslin, Martin. *The Peopled Wound: The Plays of Harold Pinter.* London: Methuen, 1970, pp. 94–112.

Gabbard, Lucina Paquet. *The Dream Structure of Pinter's Plays: A Psychoanalytic Approach.* Rutherford, N.J.: Fairleigh Dickinson University Press, 1976, pp. 98–116.

Gale, Steven H. *Butter's Going Up: A Critical Analysis of Harold Pinter's Work.* Durham: Duke University Press, 1977, pp. 81–95.

Gassner, John. *Dramatic Soundings.* New York: Crown, 1968, pp. 503–507.

Goodman, Florence J. "Pinter's *The Caretaker*: The Lower Depths Descended," in *Midwest Quarterly.* V (January, 1964), pp. 117–126.

Gordon, Lois G. *Stratagems to Uncover Nakedness: The Dramas of Harold Pinter.* Columbia: University of Missouri Press, 1969, pp. 40–50.

Hayman, Ronald. *Harold Pinter.* New York: Frederick Ungar, 1973, pp. 55–70.

Hinchliffe, Arnold P. *Harold Pinter.* New York: Twayne, 1967, pp. 87–107.

Hollis, James R. *Harold Pinter: The Poetics of Silence.* Carbondale: Southern Illinois University Press, 1970, pp. 77–95.

Kerr, Walter. *Harold Pinter.* New York: Columbia University Press, 1967.

Minogue, Valerie. "Taking Care of the *Caretaker*," in *Twentieth Century.* CLXVIII (September, 1960), pp. 243–248. Reprinted in *Pinter: A Collection of Critical Essays.* Edited by Arthur Ganz. Englewood Cliffs, N.J.: Prentice-Hall, 1972, pp. 72–77.

Pesta, John. "Pinter's Usurpers," in *Drama Survey.* VI (1967–1968), pp. 54–65. Reprinted in *Pinter: A Collection of Critical Essays.* Edited by Arthur Ganz. Englewood Cliffs, N.J.: Prentice-Hall, 1972, pp. 123–135.

Quigley, Austin E. *The Pinter Problem.* Princeton, N.J.: Princeton University Press, 1975, pp. 113–172.

Schiff, Ellen F. "Pancakes and Soap Suds: A Study of Childishness in Pinter's Plays," in *Modern Drama.* XVI (1973).

Simon, John. "Theatre Chronicle," in *Hudson Review.* XIV (1961), pp. 586–592.

Sykes, Alrene. *Harold Pinter.* New York: Humanities Press, 1970.

Taylor, John Russell. *The Angry Theatre: New British Drama.* New York: Hill and Wang, 1969, pp. 336–340.

————. *Harold Pinter.* London: Longmans, Green, 1969.

Trussler, Simon. *The Plays of Harold Pinter.* London: Gollancz, 1974, pp. 76–104.

Walker, Augusta. "Messages from Pinter," in *Modern Drama.* X (1967), pp. 1–10.

Williams, Raymond. *Drama from Ibsen to Brecht.* London: Chatto and Windus, 1968.

Wellwarth, George. *The Theatre of Protest and Paradox: Developments in the Avant-Garde Drama.* New York: New York University Press, 1971.

I. A. RICHARDS

Born: Chesire, England (February 26, 1893)

Principal Works

CRITICISM: *Foundations of Aesthetics* (with C. K. Ogden and J. Wood), 1921; *The Meaning of Meaning* (with C. K. Ogden), 1923; *Principles of Literary Criticism*, 1924; *Science and Poetry*, 1925; *Practical Criticism*, 1929; *Mencius on the Mind*, 1931; *Coleridge on Imagination*, 1934; *Interpretation in Teaching*, 1938; *How to Read a Page*, 1942; *Basic English and Its Uses*, 1943; *Speculative Instruments*, 1955; *So Much Nearer: Essays Toward a World English*, 1968; *Design for Escape: World Education Through Modern Media*, 1968.

POEMS: *Goodbye Earth and Other poems*, 1958; *The Screens and Other poems*, 1960; *Tomorrow Morning, Faustus*, 1962; *Internal Colloquies*, 1971.

Ivor Armstrong Richards, University Professor Emeritus of Harvard University, is one of the most influential figures in twentieth century scholarship. His primary impact comes from the series of volumes written in the 1920's which remain primary texts in fields as diverse as literary criticism and communicology.

Richards is perhaps most famed for his critical trilogy: *Principles of Literary Criticism, Science and Poetry*, and *Practical Criticism*. In the first of these volumes, he stated his basic theory of poetry and of criticism. *Science and Poetry* examined the role of poetry in life and forecast its future, while the final book was an application of the precepts explicated in the first two.

The critical system outlined and applied in the three volumes has often been misunderstood; Richards has been accused of dismissing the imaginative aspect of poetic creation. His interest in the neurological aspects of aesthetic appreciation has been interpreted to mean that the enjoyment of poetry rests solely upon minor interactions of brain waves.

Richards' critical precepts are, in fact, quite different from the coldly scientific position often ascribed to them. He attempted to place the poetic act on a scientifically sound basis. It is important to recall that his work appeared in reaction to Romantic critics, who emphasized the reader's ineffable emotional feelings. Richards denied the validity of such an approach to criticism. Rather, he said, the poem as an art object was a completed whole which communicated experience directly to the reader. A poet was a creator whose organization of experience was more efficient and more meaningful than that of ordinary men.

Richards' influence upon the field of communicology is due to his work with C. K. Ogden in semantics; their book, *The Meaning of Meaning*, was the first serious attempt to explore semantics and its relationship to effective communication.

Bibliography

Important studies of Richards' work are W. H. N. Hotopf, *Language, Thought and Comprehension: A Case Study of the Writings of I. A. Richards*, 1965, and J. P. Schiller, *I. A. Richards' Theory of Literature*, 1969. His contributions to literary criticism are considered in many studies, among them are John Crowe Ransom, *The New Criticism*, 1941; S. E. Hyman, *The Armed Vision*, 1948; D. G. James, *Critiques and Essays in Criticism*, edited by R. W. Stallman, 1950; George Watson, *The Literary Critics: A Study of English Descriptive Criticism*, 1962; Cleanth Brooks and William K. Wimsatt, *Literary Criticism: A Short History*, 1957; Rene Welleck, *Concepts of Criticism*, 1963; Lee T. Lemon, *The Partial Critics*, 1966; and Gerald E. Graff, "The Later Richards and the New Criticism," *Criticism*, IX (1967), 229–242.

PRINCIPLES OF LITERARY CRITICISM

Type of work: Critical treatise
Author: I. A. Richards (1893–   )
First published: 1924

Essay-Review

Although Ivor Armstrong Richards published poetry and drama, his major contributions are in the fields of literary criticism and philology. His first book, *The Foundations of Aesthetics*, published in 1922 and written in collaboration with psychologist C. K. Ogden and art authority James Wood, examined the whole area of aesthetics in an attempt to arrive at the nature of beauty and to offer the authors' own definition of aesthetics. In 1923, Richards and Ogden published *The Meaning of Meaning*, a psychologically oriented pursuit of "meaning" in the arts. But more significant critical pronouncements were made in the next three books: *Principles of Literary Criticism* in 1924, *Science and Poetry* in 1926, and *Practical Criticism* in 1929. All three books treat the question of value in the arts, primarily poetry, and all are concerned with the problem of correct interpretation of art. Their aims are different, however: *Principles of Literary Criticism* spells out the theory; *Science and Poetry* discusses the role and future of literature in life; and *Practical Criticism* applies theory to individual literary works. Richards' last major critical book, *Coleridge on Imagination*, published in 1935, explores several meanings of the concept of imagination and singles out Coleridge's definition as the one most accurate and applicable to twentieth century criticism.

From the early 1930's, as the solution to problems in education and general communication, Richards had been interested in Basic English. In writing *The Meaning of Meaning*, he and Ogden realized that they repeatedly used certain key words which, they discovered, could form a basic language that would permit the expression of any idea. While it was Ogden who published the first Basic word list, Richards actively pursued his own linguistic research in *Basic in Teaching: East and West*, *Interpretation in Teaching*, *How to Read a Page*, and *Basic English and Its Uses*.

Among his critical books, *Principles of Literary Criticism* most directly concerns the deriving of value from the arts, especially the art of poetry. In many ways the basis of all Richards' pronouncements on criticism, it sets forth his fundamental critical and artistic theories.

He begins this complex study by indicating several difficulties which often preclude valid criticism. First of all, there is too much of what Richards calls "experimental aesthetics" in the arts: futile attempts to make human tastes and actions amenable to laboratory examination. Moreover, criticism tends to concentrate on secondary aspects of the arts and thereby ignores the all-important subject of value. And at other times, the very language of criticism causes misunderstandings because of its vague, often deceiving vocabulary. For example, critics often speak of objects of art as if the objects themselves possess qualities, whereas what they should say is that the objects evoke effects in us.

To offset these impediments, Richards insists that valid criticism is contingent upon an understanding of the nature of experience and the formulating of an acceptable theory of valuation and communication in the arts. The first of these topics, experience, is approached purely psychologically. In fact, much of *Principles of Literary Criticism* is comprised of chapters which give the psychological background to particular facets of aesthetic appreciation and communication. In Chapter XI, "A Sketch for a Psychology," Richards reminds us that the mind is the nervous system and is thus a system of impulses which are influenced by various stimuli. Our response to certain stimuli depends upon the needs of the body at a given moment. The basis of aesthetic experience, then, also lies in the impulses which arise in the mind as a result of various stimuli. These stimuli may be either new and independent or associated with former experiences.

Other aspects of experience are discussed throughout the book; for example, the role of memory, of emotion and coenesthesia, and of attitudes. The fine line between the "pleasure-unpleasure" of a sensation is also considered. An important adjunct to the discussion of experience is treated in Chapter XXII, "The Poet's Experience." The difference between the artist and the ordinary man, points out Richards, is first of all in the "range, delicacy, and freedom" of the relationships he can make among facets of his experience. Secondly, it is in the "availability" of the artist's experience: the ability to have a particular state of mind available when needed. Moreover, the artist has a higher degree of what Richards terms vigilance: a more complete, satisfactory organization of the impulses within him. Thus, though we all have experiences and, except for the insane, can organize them to some extent, the poet is more capable of making use of his experience.

After attempting to suggest succinctly the causation, nature, and effect of experience, Richards moves on to the two topics with which he is most concerned, valuation and communication. The arts, he says, are our "storehouses" of recorded values. He admonishes the critic to be concerned with value and morality. His definition of value is explained in Chapter VII, "A Psychological Theory of Value," in which he asserts that anything is valuable that satisfies a desire within us without thwarting an equal or more important desire. Additional value is achieved when any desire is sacrificed to another. Value, then, is defined as the exercise of impulses and the fulfilling of their desires.

Though all men are concerned with values, he who is most concerned is the artist. He is the one preoccupied with recording and perpetuating the experiences he deems most valuable; he is also the one most likely to have valuable experiences to record; finally, he is the one most able to organize or systematize the significant and trivial impulses which are a part of experience. The poet, moreover, lays the basis of morality, for the problem of morality is the problem of obtaining the most value from life. Thus, Richards is opposed to the "Art for Art's sake" theory of poetry, a theory which denies external values in art. He urges the similarity between the world of poetry and the real world and fears that any separation of poetic experience from life results in imbalance, narrowness, and incompleteness in advocators of the aesthetic theory. Value can even determine whether a poem is good or bad. In Chapter XXV, "Badness in Poetry," Richards asserts that art can fail if (1) communication is defective or (2) if the experience communicated is not valuable.

For value in the arts to be perceived by the spectator there must, of course, be effective communication. In Chapter IV, "Communication and the Artist," Richards states that not only are the arts communicative, but they are the "supreme form" of communication, even though the artist may not have communication as his primary goal; he is usually concerned foremost with making the work correct.

By communication, Richards means that under certain conditions individual minds are able to share quite similar experiences. Never is there an actual transference of or participation in the shared experiences, however. Communication, a complicated process, occurs when one mind acting upon its environment influences another mind, and that other mind undergoes an experience that is similar to the experience in the first mind.

If the arts are the supreme form of communication, the artist is faced with the challenge of transmitting his experiences to the reader effectively. To do so, he must maintain a state of normality. For no matter how available his past experience is, the artist must be normal enough to communicate it. Since communication requires responses which are uniform and are initiated by stimuli which can be handled physically, any eccentricity in the artist will be disastrous if it interferes with his responses. His expression in the arts means nothing to his spectators if he is unable to organize his responses.

After probing the nature of experience, the essence of value, and the importance of communication in the arts, Richards turns his attention more specifically to the practicing critic of poetry. The good critic must meet three qualifications: he must be able to experience without eccentricity the state of mind of the work he is criticizing; he must be able to differentiate between experiences by discerning their more subtle features; and he must be adept at judging values. But given these capabilities, the critic is still unable to pass sound judgments on poetry if he is unsure of exactly what poetry is. One of the reasons for so much backward criticism, Richards believes, is that the critic simply does not know what he is judging. He needs a workable definition of poetry, and Richards offers one by defining poetry as a group of experiences which differ only very slightly from a standard experience. Such a definition, he says, is far more meaningful than calling poetry the artist's experience, for the latter implies that only the artist has the experience. In Richard's view the reader's involvement is necessary for completion of the poetic experience.

These four topics,—experience, value, communication, and poetry and the critic—are the major concerns of *Principles of Literary Criticism*. Many other related topics are discussed. Among the most significant for poetry and literary criticism are his treatments of analyzing a poem (XVI), of rhythm and meter in verse (XVII), of allusiveness in modern poetry (XXVIII), and of the creative imagination (XXXII). The book closes with a brief essay on "The Poetry of T. S. Eliot," an appendix which was added to the second edition of the book in 1926.

In his discussion of the imagination, Richards shows his allegiance to Coleridgean theory. He accepts the concept of the imagination as being the synthesizing or balancing of dissimilar qualities. This concept, he concludes, is the heart of poetry and the other arts.

It would be futile to attempt to estimate the influence that *Principles of Literary Criticism* has had on the field of criticism. Let it suffice to say that the book is credited with beginning the whole era of modern criticism. Practically every midtwentieth century critic, from a traditionalist like Lionel Trilling to a New Critic such as Cleanth Brooks, has been influenced by this work because of its penetrating study of experience, value, and communication and its clarification of the definition of poetry.

GEORGE BERNARD SHAW

Born: Dublin, Ireland (July 26, 1856)
Died: Ayot St. Lawrence, England (November 2, 1950)

Principal Works

PLAYS: *Widowers' Houses*, 1893 [1892]*; *Plays, Pleasant and Unpleasant*, 1898 (*Pleasant: Arms and the Man* [1894], *Candida* [1897], *The Man of Destiny* [1897], *You Never Can Tell* [1899]; *Unpleasant: Widowers' Houses, Mrs. Warren's Profession* [1902], *The Philanderer* [1905]); *Three Plays for Puritans*, 1901 (*The Devil's Disciple* [1897], *Caesar and Cleopatra* [1901], *Captain Brassbound's Conversion* [1900]); *Man and Superman*, 1903 [1905]; *John Bull's Other Island*, 1907 (*John Bull's Other Island* [1904], *How He Lied to Her Husband* [1904], *Major Barbara* [1905]); *Press Cuttings,* 1909; *The Doctor's Dilemma*, 1911 (*The Doctor's Dilemma* [1906], *Getting Married* [1908], *The Shewing-up of Blanco Posnet* [1909]); *Misalliance*, 1914 (*Misalliance* [1910], *The Dark Lady of the Sonnets* [1910], *Fanny's First Play* [1911]); *Androcles and the Lion*, 1916 (*Androcles and the Lion* [1913], *Overruled* [1912], *Pygmalion* [1913]); *Heartbreak House*, 1919 (*Heartbreak House* [1920], *Great Catherine* [1913], *Playlets of the War*); *Back to Methuselah*, 1921 [1922]; *Saint Joan*, 1924 [1923]; *The Apple Cart*, 1929; *Too True to Be Good*, 1934 (*Too True to Be Good* [1932], *A Village Wooing* [1934], *On the Rocks* [1933]); *The Simpleton of the Unexpected Isles*, 1936 (*The Simpleton of the Unexpected Isles* [1935], *The Six of Calais* [1934], *The Millionairess* [1936]); *Geneva*, 1939 [1938]; *In Good King Charles's Golden Days*, 1939; *Buoyant Billions*, 1951 [1949].

NOVELS: *Cashel Byron's Profession*, 1886; *An Unsocial Socialist*, 1887; *Love Among the Artists*, 1900; *The Irrational Knot*, 1905; *Immaturity*, 1930.

SHORT STORIES AND TALES: *The Adventures of the Black Girl in Her Search for God*, 1932; *Short Stories, Scraps, and Shavings*, 1934.

ESSAYS AND STUDIES: *The Quintessence of Ibsenism*, 1891; *The Sanity of Art*, 1895; *The Impossibilities of Anarchism*, 1893; *The Perfect Wagnerite*, 1898; *Dramatic Opinions and Essays*, 1906; *Common Sense about the War*, 1914 (reprinted as *What I Really Wrote about the War*, 1931); *The Intelligent Woman's Guide to Socialism and Capitalism*, 1928; *The League of Nations*, 1929; *Major Critical Essays*, 1930; *Our Theatres in the Nineties*, 1932 (3 vols.); *Music in London, 1890–1894*, 1932 (3 vols.); *Essays in Fabian Socialism*, 1932; *Pen Portraits and Reviews*, 1932; *London Music in 1888–1889*, 1937; *Everybody's Political What's What*, 1944.

AUTOBIOGRAPHY: *Shaw Gives Himself Away: An Autobiographical Miscellany*, 1939; *Sixteen Self Sketches*, 1949.

LETTERS: *Letters from George Bernard Shaw to Miss Alma Murray*, 1927; *Ellen*

---

* *Dates of first performances which differ from dates of book publication are set within brackets.*

Terry and Bernard Shaw: A Correspondence, 1931 (with Ellen Terry); *Some Unpublished Letters of George Bernard Shaw*, 1939; *Bernard Shaw and Mrs. Patrick Campbell: Their Correspondence*, 1952.

George Bernard Shaw, dramatist, essayist, and critic, was born of Irish Protestant parents in Dublin on July 26, 1856. From his unsuccessful father and a "wicked uncle" he inherited his Shavian sense of fun and anticlimax and his "superficial blasphemy," from his mother a deep love and knowledge of music, which, with his keen interest in the spoken and written language, was to prove his most enduring love and one of the greatest influences on his work.

In 1876 Shaw left Ireland for good. Though not susceptible to its "Celtic twilight," he was to its natural beauty, the joy of which, he declared, was to remain with him all his life. His work retains what G. K. Chesterton called "the virginity and violence of Ireland. . . . a strange purity and a strange pugnacity." Before he left, he had made his first excursion into print, in a form that was to remain with him to the end a favorite means of expression: a letter to the press. This first one, written to *Public Opinion* in April 1875 on the advent of the famous "firm of American evangelists," Moody and Sankey, deals maturely enough with the unsavory effect on individuals of sudden conversion. True religion is not to be had on the cheap.

In London, where his mother had preceded him, having left her unloved husband to devote herself to music-teaching, young Shaw soon abandoned clerking and turned to literature by writing five novels between 1879 and 1883. All were commercially rejected or unsuccessful; the best are *Love Among the Artists* and *Cashel Byron's Profession*. Written for the most part in an early Shavian prose bearing traces of strained Victorian elegance, they are insufficiently enlivened by the virile colloquialism he later added to form the supple and athletic prose of his prefaces and plays. The genuine Shavian style was developed the hard way, by "a teeming and tumultuous life spent on many platforms, from the British Association to the triangle at the corner of Salmon's Lane in Limehouse." From this vital public speaking experience (1883–1895), Shaw learned both how easy it is to lose an audience and yet how very much people are prepared to take in the way of serious thought and provocative ideas if entertainingly and strategically presented in dialectically dramatic form leavened with humor. He also acquired the great virtue of courtesy in debate and respect for his adversary's opinions, and to this his plays owe much—not least the great Trial Scene in *Saint Joan*, in which he is, if anything, "too fair" to the Inquisition.

An encounter (1882) with Henry George and the reading of Karl Marx had turned his thoughts towards socialism, and while any direct propagation of it is absent from his plays, his faith in it is the backbone of all his subsequent work. As he himself said, an understanding of economics was to him what a knowledge of anatomy was to Michelangelo, and it stood him in good stead not only as a local government councilor in St. Pancras (in North London) but on the Executive Committee of the small but influential Fabian Society, to which he devoted himself selflessly (1884–1911) and for which he edited *Fabian Essays* (1889) and wrote many well-known socialist tracts.

Political and public speaking activities did not prevent Shaw's taking proudly to journalism (he welcomed it as another platform), and it was as "Corno di Bassetto," music critic for the new *Star* newspaper (1888–1890), that he made what was, perhaps, his first indelible mark on the intellectual and artistic consciousness of his times. In this and in his later music criticism for *The World* (1890–1894) and, above all, in his dramatic criticism for the *Saturday Review* (1895–1898), he was in fact attempting, as De Quincey said of Wordsworth, to create the taste by which he was to be appreciated. To this period also belong *The Quintessence of Ibsenism* and *The Perfect Wagnerite*, tributes to fellow "artist-philosophers" and revelatory as much of the author as of their subjects.

The rest of Shaw's life, especially after his marriage (1898) to the wealthy Charlotte Payne-Townshend, is mainly the history of his plays. Those written between 1892 and the end of the century may be said to be the extension of his theater criticism in more directly dramatic form. The first of these, *Widowers' Houses*, was actually begun in 1885 in collaboration with his great friend and fellow-Ibsenite, William Archer, but was finished quite independently in 1892 as the result of the challenge he felt to produce the drama he had been advocating. Into the earliest plays, which include *Mrs. Warren's Profession*, *Arms and the Man*, and *Candida* (one of the first of Shaw's remarkable gallery of marvelous feminine portraits), creeps already the Shavian theme of conversion—from dead system and outworn morality towards a more creatively vital approach to life—and it is further developed in *Three Plays for Puritans* written between 1897 and 1899: *The Devil's Discipline*, *Caesar and Cleopatra*, and *Captain Brassbound's Conversion*. These also develop Shaw's scathing attitude to the routineers and slaves of petty bourgeois morality and his fondness for the exponents of original virtue and for those, true to their own faiths, who live in defiance of accepted codes.

His quest for a new religion or purer ethical approach to life reaches its first apotheosis in the Hell Scene of *Man and Superman*, "a Comedy and a Philosophy" in which Don Juan advocates, against the barren worldliness of Everyman and the more eloquent hedonistic desires of the Devil, the ecstasy of philosophical thought and the true joy of man's unceasing creative evolutionary urge for world betterment as well as for his own self-improvement. This theme was further developed, refined, and possibly enfeebled in *Back to Methuselah*, the longest if not the greatest of all Shaw's attempts, in play and preface, to expound the gospel of Creative Evolution and the Life Force, which he had taken over from Butler and Bergson and to which he added his own more Shavianly socialistic and naturalistically mystical yearnings.

With the turn of the century, Shaw found fame at last, first on the Continent and in the United States, and then, with the important advent in his life of the actor-director-playwright, Granville Barker, in England itself during the Court Theater season of 1904–1907. Notable plays of this "second period" include *John Bull's Other Island*, *Major Barbara*, and *The Doctor's Dilemma*, which with the two more purely disquisitory plays, *Getting Married* and *Misalliance*, testify to the growing encyclopedic range of the Shavian drama. In 1909 Shaw was "investigated" by the Joint Select Committee on Stage Censorship, and he declared all his plays to be "conscientiously immoral." Every advance in thought and conduct is made by immoralists and heretics, and from now on Shaw's attitude to men and affairs, manners and customs, and to current morality becomes ever more astringent, his religious views ever more "catholic and comprehensive," anti-Fundamentalist and non-anthropomorphic. In a long line of plays, from *The Shewing-up of Blanco Posnet* the same year, through *Androcles and the Lion* (his "religious pantomime"), *Heartbreak House*, *Saint Joan*, and onwards to the very end, he is seeking to distill the pure elixir of religion from the muddy faiths of mortal men, desperately trying not to empty out the baby with the dirty bath-water. The stern Shavian morality of complete individual responsibility, self-discipline, heroic effort without thought of reward or "atonement," and unsentimental and non-sexual regard for one's fellow beings is detectable in even a delightful "potboiler" like *Pygmalion*. In *Saint Joan*, whom Eric Bentley has said Shaw would have had to invent had she never existed, is synthesized the aspiring religious greatness of all Shaw's noblest characters and his impassioned devotion to what Bentley calls his "Both/And" view of life.

In 1925 Shaw was awarded the Nobel Prize for literature, but gave away the money to start the Anglo-Swedish Literary Foundation. In 1931 he visited Russia, and in 1932, with Mrs. Shaw, made a world tour which included the United States and a memorable address on political economy at the Metropolitan Opera House. Greater perhaps than any of the plays written in the last years of his life are the two prose works, *The Intelligent Woman's Guide to Socialism and Capitalism*, and *The Adventures of the Black Girl in Her Search for God*. The later plays, except for *The Apple Cart*, have scarcely received adequate public stage presentation, and those such as *Too True to Be Good* and *The Simpleton of the Unexpected Isles* show signs of striking a newer and even more experimental dramatic note altogether.

Shaw sought to be not only a great radical reformer, like Dickens (by whom he was much influenced, not least in his humor and characterization), but a synthesizer of all that was best in the thought of his times as well. His plays, *sui generis*, are richly endowed with striking characterization, colorful situation, and intellectual but dramatic argument. His importance lies in providing a bridge between the old and the new and in showing a way forward that need not be unduly contemptuous of all that is best in what went before. He is the Socratic gadfly that questions all things, yet steadfastly holds fast to that which is good. His clean astringent style is a healthy example to all who would write of serious matters without solemnity (he is the Mozart of literature), and his personal and professional pride in fine workmanship is an inspiration beyond the merely literary to those who study his life and work. Leaving no school and few, if any, avowed disciples, his influence is wide wherever his plays are performed or his works read. And that, in spite of some not unnatural decline in his personal popularity in the British Isles after his death at the age of ninety-four on November 2, 1950, seems to be everywhere.

Bibliography

There are two collected editions of Shaw's *Works*, the limited Ayot St. Lawrence Edition, 30 vols., 1930, and the Standard Edition, 36 vols., 1931 ff. Excellent one-volume collections are the *Complete Plays*, 1931 (enlarged eds., 1934, 1938), and the *Complete Prefaces*, 1934 (enlarged ed., 1938). The authorized biography is Archibald Henderson's monumental *George Bernard Shaw: Man of the Century*, 1956. Stanley Weintraub has edited an "autobiography" from Shaw's autobiographical sketches: *The Playwright Years*, 1970, and *The Crucial Years*, 1971. The best critical study is Eric Bentley's *Bernard Shaw*, 1947 (rev. ed., 1957).

Shaw studies are so extensive that any listing must be highly selective. For biography and criticism see H. L. Mencken, *George Bernard Shaw: His Plays*, 1905; Holbrook Jackson, *George Bernard Shaw*, 1907; G. K. Chesterton, *George Bernard Shaw*, 1909; Julius Bab, *Bernard Shaw*, 1909; John Palmer, *Bernard Shaw: An Epitaph*, 1915; H. C. Duffin, *The Quintessence of Bernard Shaw*, 1920 (enlarged ed., 1939); Edward Shanks, *Bernard Shaw*, 1924; Archibald Henderson, *Table Talk of G.B.S.*, 1925; *idem, Bernard Shaw, Playboy and Prophet*, 1932; J. S. Collis, *Shaw*, 1925; Frank Harris, *Bernard Shaw*, 1931; André Maurois, *Poets and Prophets*, 1935; Hesketh Pearson, *G.B.S.: A Full-Length Portrait*, 1942; *idem, G.B.S.: A Postscript*, 1951; Stephen Winsten, ed., *G.B.S., 90*, 1946; *idem, Days with Bernard Shaw*, 1948; C. E. M. Joad, *Shaw*, 1949; A. C. Ward, *Bernard Shaw*, 1950; Blanche Patch, *30 Years with G.B.S.*, 1951; Desmond MacCarthy, *Bernard Shaw*, 1951; and Louis Kronenberger, ed., *George Bernard Shaw: A Critical Survey*, 1953, an anthology of Shaw criticism written by various hands, 1901–1951.

See also C. L. and V. M. Broad, *A Dictionary to the Plays and Novels of Bernard Shaw*, 1929; X. Heydet, *Shaw-Kompendium* (in German), 1936; and Raymond Mander and Joe Mitchenson, *Theatrical Companion to Shaw: A Pictorial Record of the First Performances of the Plays of George Bernard Shaw*, 1954. Dan H. Laurence has published, *Books and Libraries*, 1976, a bibliographical monograph.

MAJOR BARBARA

Type of work: Drama
Author: George Bernard Shaw (1856–1950)
Time: Early twentieth century
Locale: London
First presented: 1905

Principal Characters

Sir Andrew Undershaft, a munitions tycoon. Believing that poverty is the root of all discontent and, consequently, a threat to capitalism, he uses his power and wealth in an attempt to eliminate it. In a war of ideas with his daughter Barbara, he proves that a donation from a dealer in death—namely, himself—will buy the good graces of the Salvation Army. He then proceeds to fill the void created by her disillusionment by converting her to his own creed.

Barbara, Sir Andrew's daughter. As a major in the Salvation Army, she exercises her moral fervor in the cause of winning the souls of the poor to the Kingdom of God. When her father proves to her that a donation from his deplored and destructive profession can win the favor of the Army, she becomes converted to his creed that it is useless to attempt the salvation of souls until the souls' destroyer, poverty, has been eliminated.

Adolphus Cusins, a professor of Greek,

Barbara's suitor. His intellect, added to Sir Andrew's power and Barbara's moral fervor, completes the trinity that Sir Andrew believes will be the salvation of society.

Lady Britomart Undershaft, Sir Andrew's domineering wife, who abhors what she calls her husband's immorality, though she does not hesitate to capitalize on it.

Stephen Undershaft, Sir Andrew's painfully conventional son.

Sarah Undershaft, Sir Andrew's younger daughter.

Charles Lomax, Sarah Undershaft's vacuous suitor.

Snobby Price,
Rummy Mitchens,
Peter Shirley, and
Bill Walker, frequenters of the Salvation Army headquarters.

Essay-Review

In writing *Major Barbara*, Shaw faced essentially the same problems that had confronted the earliest English dramatists, the authors of the medieval miracle and mystery plays. Like those writers, Shaw considered drama to be only a means, not an end, and like them he used drama as a means of educating the great ignorant public. But the problems confronting Shaw were considerably more formidable than those posed by the dramatization of Biblical stories. Instead of stories which were intrinsically dramatic and which provided ready-made plots, Shaw dramatized themes: philosophical themes, moral themes, social, economic, historic, and even biological themes, most of which were intrinsically non-dramatic and unentertaining. No one but a college sophomore or a genius would have dared inflict on a theater audience, intent only on an evening's entertainment, the doctrines of Nietzsche, Schopenhauer, or, for that matter, Ernest Belfort Box. This is not to deny that earlier dramatists had successfully woven philosophical themes into their plays. But in Shaw's plays the theme is not merely an integral part of the characters and action; as often as not it is a topic of conversation which the characters, sitting in their parlors or standing on the streets, discuss and explore.

Shaw's problem, then, was clear-cut. to create characters who were so interesting and lively that the audience would not mind listening to them preach. For Shaw's characters do preach, and seldom quite so vociferously as in *Major Barbara*.

The subject of *Major Barbara* is salvation of society and salvation of the human soul; the text, blessed are the poor. As might be expected, Shaw's message is paradoxically opposed to the lesson taught by Christian ethics. Shaw believed that the poor were unblessed. Since poverty was obviously the source of sin, no poor man could possibly hope to enter the kingdom of heaven. More important to Shaw, perhaps, was the fact that poverty was also the source of crime. To eliminate poverty, then, was a social as well as a moral imperative.

A play built on such a theme could easily have sunk either into the depths of naturalism or drifted into the zone of platitudinous propaganda. Instead, since Shaw was the author, the play turned out to be outrageously funny. In fact, *Major Barbara* is one of the funniest plays Shaw wrote and therefore one of the most effective.

As in all Shaw's plays, the focus is on a conflict between the forces of conventionality and the power of a superior being—the Shavian hero. Ironically, since Shaw was a Socialist, the hero, Andrew Undershaft, is a multimillionaire capitalist, a manufacturer of munitions. Pitted against him is his daughter Barbara, a major in the Salvation Army. Undershaft is the apostle of Shaw's secular morality. Realizing that poverty breeds social discontent and thus constitutes a threat to capitalism, he uses his immense power to eliminate poverty, at least among his own workers. Barbara he recognizes to be a superior person possessed of true, but misguided, moral energy. She has deluded herself into thinking that the converts she wins through her work in the Salvation Army have truly reformed, that the Army truly wins souls to the kingdom of God. Undershaft undertakes to convert her. On the other hand, Barbara deplores her father's profession, believing that he is dedicated to the destruction rather than the salvation of mankind. She undertakes to convert him.

The battle is one-sided, short, and decisive. Undershaft merely has to show Barbara that he, a dealer in death and destruction, can buy the Army's good graces for the price of a donation. He shows that he and others like him—a distiller, for instance—provide the financial backing without which the Army would collapse. Crushed by her father's cynicism and what she considers the Army's hypocrisy, she turns in her uniform.

The play ends on a note of sardonic optimism. Undershaft's destruction of Barbara's faith is only a preliminary step; he must now convert her to his own creed. This conversion he accomplishes by taking Barbara and the rest of his family on a tour of his factory and Perivale St. Andrews, the town in which his workers live. The town turns out to be a workingman's paradise. Instead of the misery and squalor which Barbara expects, she finds prosperity and sanitation. Realizing at last that it is impossible to save hungry men's souls, she resolves to devote her energies to saving the souls of the well-fed.

Directly involved in this struggle for Barbara's soul is her suitor, Adolphus Cusins, a professor of Greek, who, to please Barbara, neglects his studies to play the bass drum in the Salvation Army band. Cusins is important, too, in the thematic structure of the play because he is the third member of the triumvirate which is to save society. Undershaft, following the tradition of his predecessors in the munitions business, disinherits his own son Stephen and adopts Adolphus as his protégé and heir. To Undershaft's power and Barbara's moral fervor, Adolphus adds intellect. In this combination, presumably, lay Shaw's hope for the salvation of society.

The minor characters serve both to act out the message of the play and to provide much of the humor. They are divided into two classes: rich and poor. The poor class is represented by the rascals and reprobates who frequent Barbara's Salvation Army shelter. Of these, by far the most typical are Snobby Price and Rummy Mitchens, both of whom feign a desire for spiritual sustenance and testify to their conversion to Christianity in return for free meals. The most pathetic is Peter Shirley, who at forty-five has been thrown out of work because he has a streak of gray in his hair. A disciple of Thomas Paine, he swallows his pride to accept a free meal only when he is starving. By far the meanest and funniest is Bill Walker, who comes to the shelter to pommel his girl friend because she deserted him when she was converted. A bully and ruffian, he provides the funniest scene of the play when, after blackening the eye of one of Barbara's young female assistants, he is shamed into an excruciating sense of guilt by Barbara's reproofs. His role as a foil to Undershaft is apparent when Bill tries to atone for the black eye by giving a donation to the Army.

The idle rich are represented by Undershaft's wife, son, younger daughter, and the latter's suitor. Lady Britomart and her son Stephen reek of conventional morality. A typical domineering mother, Lady Britomart abhors her husband's immorality but does not hesitate to capitalize on it, accepting his money to ensure her children's comfortable place in society. Stephen, though cowed at first by his mother, declares his independence toward the end of the play and is rewarded with a career in journalism by his amused father. Charles Lomax, Sarah's suitor, demonstrates the utter frivolity and vacuity of the rich. Although these are stock characters borrowed from Oscar Wilde's drawing-room comedies, they are vigorous and funny.

Shaw's success in creating such thoroughly delightful characters is the key to the success of *Major Barbara*. Without the relief of the humor which each and every character provides, the moralizing and preaching would be tedious. It is by no means certain, however, that Shaw converted anyone to his brand of secular morality by using such a dramatic technique. The play is so amusing that it is difficult to take the theme seriously. But in the process of entertaining his audiences, Shaw was able at least to acquaint them with serious ideas. Surely he did not expect to accomplish more.

Bibliography

Abbott, Anthony S. *Shaw and Christianity*. New York: Seabury Press, 1965, pp. 119–140. Reprinted in *Twentieth Century Interpretations of* Major Barbara*: A Collection of Critical Essays*. Edited by Rose Zimbardo. Englewood Cliffs, N.J.: Prentice-Hall, 1970, pp. 42–57.

Bentley, Eric. "Bernard Shaw, Caesar, and Stalin," in *Antioch Review*. III (March, 1943), pp. 117–124.

Berst, Charles A. *Bernard Shaw and the Art of Drama*. Urbana: University of Illinois Press, 1973, pp. 154–174.

Brée, Germaine. *Literature and Society*. Lincoln: University of Nebraska Press, 1964, pp. 121–141.

Carr, Pat M. *Bernard Shaw*. New York: Frederick Ungar, 1976, pp. 54–62.

Crompton, Louis. "Shaw's Challenge to Liberalism," in *Prairie Schooner*. XXXVII (Fall, 1963), pp. 229–244. Reprinted in *George Bernard Shaw: A Collection of Critical Essays*. Edited by R.J. Kaufmann. Englewood Cliffs, N.J.: Prentice-Hall, 1965, pp. 88–99.

Dukore, Bernard. "The Undershaft Maxims," in *Modern Drama*. IX (May, 1966), pp. 90–100. Reprinted in *Twentieth Century Interpretations of* Major Barbara*: A Collection of Critical Essays*. Edited by Rose Zimbardo. Englewood Cliffs, N.J.: Prentice-Hall, 1970, pp. 58–67.

Fergusson, Francis. *The Idea of a Theater*. Princeton, N.J.: Princeton University Press, 1949, pp. 178–183. Reprinted in *Twentieth Century Interpretations of* Major Barbara*: A Collection of Critical Essays*. Edited by Rose Zimbardo. Englewood Cliffs, N.J.: Prentice-Hall, 1970, pp. 109–115.

Frank, Joseph. "*Major Barbara*: Shaw's 'Divine Comedy,' " in *PMLA*. LXXI (March, 1956), pp. 61–74. Reprinted in *Twentieth Century Interpretations of* Major Barbara*: A Collection of Critical Essays*. Edited by Rose Zimbardo. Englewood Cliffs, N.J.: Prentice-Hall, 1970, pp. 28–41.

Frankel, Charles. "Efficient Power and Inefficient Virtue," in *Great Moral Dilemmas in Literature, Past and Present*. Edited by R.M. McIver. New

York: Harper and Row, 1956, pp. 15–24.

Freedman, Morris. *The Moral Impulse: Modern Drama from Ibsen to the Present.* Carbondale: Southern Illinois University Press, 1967, pp. 45–62.

Hugo, Leon. *Bernard Shaw: Playwright and Preacher.* London: Methuen, 1971, pp. 150–160.

Joran, Robert J. "Theme and Character in *Major Barbara,*" in *Texas Studies in Literature and Language.* XII (1970), pp. 471–480.

Kronenberger, Louis. *The Thread of Laughter.* New York: Knopf, 1952, pp. 250–256.

Lorichs, Sonja. *The Unwomanly Woman in Bernard Shaw's Drama and Her Social and Political Background.* Stockholm: Uppsala University Press, 1973, pp. 61–88.

MacCarthy, Desmond. *Shaw: The Plays.* Newton Abbot, England: David and Charles, 1973, pp. 44–56.

Mayne, Fred. *The Wit and Satire of George Bernard Shaw.* New York: St. Martin's, 1967, pp. 10–15, 42–44, 89–101, 124–126. Reprinted in *Twentieth Century Interpretations of* Major Barbara*: A Collection of Critical Essays.* Edited by Rose Zimbardo. Englewood Cliffs, N.J.: Prentice-Hall, 1970, pp. 89–102.

Meisel, Martin. *Shaw and the Nineteenth Century Theater.* Princeton, N.J.: Princeton University Press, 1963, pp. 290–303. Reprinted in *Twentieth Century Interpretations of* Major Barbara*: A Collection of Critical Essays.* Edited by Rose Zimbardo. Englewood Cliffs, N.J.: Prentice-Hall, 1970, pp. 17–27.

Morgan, Margery M. "*Major Barbara,*" in *Twentieth Century Interpretations of* Major Barbara*: A Collection of Critical Essays.* Edited by Rose Zimbardo. Englewood Cliffs, N.J.: Prentice-Hall, 1970, pp. 68–88. Revised version in *The Shavian Playground: An Exploration of the Art of Bernard Shaw.* London: Methuen, 1972, pp. 134–157.

Stewart, J.I.M. *Eight Modern Writers.* Oxford: Clarendon Press, 1963, pp. 155–163.

Valency, Maurice. *The Cart and the Trumpet: The Plays of George Bernard Shaw.* New York: Oxford University Press, 1973, pp. 247–265.

Whittemore, Reed. "Shaw's Abstract Clarity," in *Tulane Drama Review.* II (November, 1957), pp. 46–57.

Wisenthal, J.L. *The Marriage of Contraries: Bernard Shaw's Middle Plays.* Cambridge, Mass.: Harvard University Press, 1974, pp. 57–86.

Zimbardo, Rose. "Introduction," in *Twentieth Century Interpretations of* Major Barbara*: A Collection of Critical Essays.* Edited by Rose Zimbardo. Englewood Cliffs, N.J.: Prentice-Hall, 1970, pp. 1–15.

SAINT JOAN

Type of work: Drama
Author: George Bernard Shaw (1856–1950)
Time: 1428–1456
Locale: France
First presented: 1923

Principal Characters

Joan of Arc, a farmer's daughter from the village of Domrémy. Joan's imagination is so vivid that her inspirations seem to come to her as visions in which the voices of the saints direct her to raise the siege of Orleans and crown the Dauphin at Rheims. By sheer force of personality and a genius for leadership, the seventeen-year-old Joan does these things. Ignorant of the complexities of politics, Joan is unwilling to defer to the experience and advice of ordinary men. She oversteps herself and is tried by the Inquisition for heresy. Her trial is an eminently fair one by the standards of the age, but Joan condemns herself by insisting that the instructions of her "voices" take precedence over the instructions of the Church. Sentenced to be burned and fearing pain, she recants. When she finds her recantation simply commutes her sentence to perpetual imprisonment, she reaffirms her innocence and is burned. In an Epilogue, Joan's ghost appears and learns that she has been canonized. Her allies and enemies alike bow down and worship her; but when Joan offers to bring herself to life again, they all demur and drift away. Joan wonders when earth shall be ready for God's saints.

The Dauphin, later Charles VII. Although physically weak and bullied by everyone, he is intelligent and more refined than most nobles of his time. Once he is crowned, Charles tells Joan to be content with what she already has won. He warns her he cannot protect her if she fights on. After Joan is executed

Charles himself becomes a successful warrior.

The Inquisitor, Brother John Lemaître (lɔ·mě′tr), a Dominican monk. A mild, elderly, highly intelligent man, he believes that Joan's heresy is the most heinous one of all: the Protestant heresy of believing God speaks directly to an individual through one's conscience. Realizing Joan is innocent of evildoing, he believes she must be sacrificed to the welfare of Christian society.

Peter Cauchon (kō·shän′), Bishop of Beauvais, the co-judge, with the Inquisitor, at Joan's trial. An honest believer in the grossness of Joan's heresy, the Bishop wishes to save Joan's soul and, if possible, her life.

Richard de Beauchamp, Earl of Warwick, the English commandant. Warwick wants Joan put to death because she represents the new spirit of nationalism which threatens the power of his social class.

John de Stogumber, Warwick's chaplain. A bigoted and fanatical English patriot, he howls for Joan's death at her trial. He is so horrified by her execution that, half-mad, he retires to a small country parish and becomes an exemplary priest.

Dunois (dü′nwä′), **Bastard of Orleans,** the rugged and pragmatic commander of the French forces. He admires Joan's military ability, but he abandons her when she ignores his advice.

Brother Martin Ladvenu (läd·v′noō′), a

young priest who takes pity on Joan at her trial and tries to persuade her to save herself.

The Archbishop of Rheims, a member of the Dauphin's court. A rich and worldly administrator, the Archbishop is struck by Joan's saintliness. He tries to warn Joan of the dangerousness of her contempt for all authority.

Gilles de Rais (gĭl də rā′), a flippant and cynical young courtier who affects a blue beard. He is contemptuous of Joan.

Captain la Hire (lä·ēr′), a tough French soldier who becomes fanatically devoted to Joan.

Canon John d'Estivet (dĕs·tĭ·vä′), the prosecutor at Joan's trial, so captious and vindictive that the Inquisitor must repeatedly censure him.

Canon de Courcelles (də koor′sĕl), a young priest who, with de Stogumber,

draws up the indictment against Joan. He is stupid, petty, and contentious.

Robert de Baudricourt (də bōd′r′koōr), a loud-mouthed but weak-willed French gentleman-at-arms. Against his better judgment, he provides Joan an escort to the Dauphin's court.

Bertrand de Poulengy (də poō′lĕn·zhē), a knight under Baudricourt's command. Convinced of Joan's holiness, he escorts her to see the Dauphin.

The Executioner of Rouen, who puts Joan to death.

An English Soldier, who gives Joan a cross of twigs while she is at the stake. For this action he is given each year one day's vacation from Hell.

A Gentleman of 1920, an English priest who, in the Epilogue, announces Joan's elevation to sainthood.

Essay-Review

In 1920, almost five hundred years after she had been burned at the stake as a heretic, sorceress, and witch, Joan of Arc, Maid of Orléans, was canonized; three and one half years later, with the first performance of *Saint Joan* on December 28, 1923, at the Garrick Theatre in New York City, Joan was Shavianized. That is to say, George Bernard Shaw told the world the truth about Joan in terms of the Shavian dramatic dialectic.

Shaw felt that although Joan had been completely rehabilitated, both by the Church and by secular commentators, the true significance of her life and martyrdom was not yet understood; for in exonerating Joan of the crimes for which it had burned her, the Church had whitewashed Joan and condemned itself. Furthermore, the literary interpretations of Joan, ranging from Voltaire's ribald burlesque to Mark Twain's romantic adulation, were misleading and therefore worthless. Shaw believed that he could rectify all these erroneous interpretations. He proceeded to write *Saint Joan*, basing it on the extraordinary premises, first, that Joan was a harbinger of Protestantism and, secondly, that she was a fomenter of nationalism. Within the framework of the play he concludes that Joan had to die because as an independent thinker she threatened the authority of the Church, and as a nationalist she imperiled the power of the feudal lords.

Whether or not these premises and conclusions are valid historically is, of course, conjectural. But such a question is irrelevant since they are valid dramatically. In this play more than in any other, Shaw succeeded in creating characters who lived the theme in addition to preaching it. *Saint Joan* is thus a genuine play, not just a Shavian dialogue.

Joan's defiance of authority is rooted in her good common sense, her insistence on listening to the dictates of her heavenly voices, which she concedes may be figments of her imagination. Convinced that the advice given her by Saint Margaret and Saint Catherine is sensible and practical, she finds the courage to defy bishops, archbishops, and inquisitors. Her nationalism grows out of her almost fanatical zeal to save France from the English and to establish France as an autonomous state dedicated to glorifying God. This zeal, manifested as fervid sincerity and earnestness, enables her to command generals and to crown kings.

Independence, courage, and zeal—these characteristics make Joan a Shavian genius, a superwoman, and the female counterpart of Jack Tanner from *Man and Superman*. Her ability to probe deep into the problems of life and to formulate independent ethical values causes her to be alienated from conventional society. Although Joan is a Shavian genius, she is not a typical one. As a proud, stubborn peasant girl, Joan is profoundly, pathetically human. She can stand as a character without reference to Shaw or his philosophy.

The characterization of Joan is by no means the only original one in the play: the treatment of the minor personages is even less conventional, most notably with the Earl of Warwick, and Cauchon, Bishop of Beauvais. Shaw objected to the traditional interpretation of Warwick and Cauchon as egregious blackguards and set out to rehabilitate them. Within the typically Shavian framework they represent the conservative and reactionary—the established—elements of society who resist and defeat the genius. Within the thematic framework of *Saint Joan*, they represent the power of the Church and of feudalism. Their opposition to Joan is not vindictive; Cauchon, in fact, strives to save her and insures a fair trial for her. Both are forced to resist her because as thinking men they recognize that she threatens their own self-interest within the existing social order. As a feudal lord, Warwick cannot brook Joan's nationalism, which, if unchecked, would diminish his power. As a ruler of the Church, Cauchon cannot tolerate Joan's Protestantism, which, if unchecked, would subvert his authority. Both are reasonable, even virtuous men, and by executing Joan they perform a service to the elements of society which they represent. Far from being villains, they were medieval heroes.

Most of the other characters also represent the conservative elements of society, but they see, for a while at least, the advantage in allying themselves with Joan. To the French, Joan is a new hope for France, a crazy hope, perhaps, but the last hope for driving out the English. Thus Captain Robert de Baudricourt, lord of the province where Joan was born, agrees to furnish her horse and armor as well as an escort to take her to the dauphin. The dauphin, timid and a little silly, a prisoner of his own court, makes Joan his commander-in-chief and succumbs to her efforts to make a man and king of him. The Archbishop of Rheims gives to her enterprise the sanction of the Church. And Dunois, commander of the forces at Orléans, agrees to follow Joan's leadership in a desperate attack across the Loire. Yet all these desert Joan when she has served their purposes. When her plans to complete her mission by driving the English from Paris seem too impractical, too audacious to execute, they withdraw their support, charging her with impudence and pride. By the time Joan has crowned the dauphin at Rheims, they have recovered their conventionality and are embarrassed by their former enthusiasm in accepting a peasant girl's leadership. Therefore they do not move to save Joan when she is captured and sold to Warwick and Cauchon.

This theme of the rejection of the moral genius by the conservative elements of society is recapitulated and generalized in an epilogue. Twenty-five years after her death, on the occasion of her rehabilitation by the Church in 1456, Joan meets again the men who were involved in her career. When a messenger from the Pope appears to announce the canonization of Joan, all, from Cauchon to King Charles, fall to their knees in adoration of the new saint. Yet when Joan acknowledges their praise by asking if she should return from the dead, a living woman, each—except for a common soldier—again rejects her, humbly this time, and disappears. Shaw's message is clear: those who rule society are never ready to accept the moral genius who would change society, even though that genius be a saint.

Bibliography

Bentley, Eric. *Bernard Shaw.* Norfolk, Conn.: New Directions, 1947, pp. 168–172.

Berst, Charles A. *Bernard Shaw and the Art of Drama.* Urbana: University of Illinois Press, 1973, pp. 259–292.

Carr, Pat M. *Bernard Shaw.* New York: Frederick Ungar, 1976, pp. 136–145.

Eastman, Fred. *Christ in the Drama.* New York: Macmillan, 1947, pp. 54–60.

Fielden, John. "Shaw's *Saint Joan* as Tragedy," in *Twentieth Century Literature.* III (July, 1957), pp. 59–67.

Hugo, Leon. *Bernard Shaw: Playwright and Preacher.* London: Methuen, 1971, pp. 195–206.

Irvine, William. *Universe of George Bernard Shaw.* New York: McGraw-Hill, 1949, pp. 320–325.

Lorichs, Sonja. *The Unwomanly Woman in Bernard Shaw's Drama and Her Social and Political Background.* Stockholm: Uppsala University Press, 1973, pp. 155–179.

MacCarthy, Desmond. *Shaw: The Plays.* Newton Abbot, England: David and Charles, 1973, pp. 162–175.

Martz, Louis L. "The Saint as Tragic Hero," in *Tragic Themes in Western Literature*. Edited by Cleanth Brooks. New Haven, Conn.: Yale University Press, 1955, pp. 156–177. Reprinted in *George Bernard Shaw: A Collection of Critical Essays*. Edited by R.J. Kaufmann. Englewood Cliffs, N.J.: Prentice-Hall, 1965, pp. 143–161.

Morgan, Margery M. *The Shavian Playground: An Exploration of the Art of Bernard Shaw*. London: Methuen, 1972, pp. 248–256.

Searle, William. *The Saint and the Skeptics: Joan of Arc in the Work of Mark Twain, Anatole France, and Bernard Shaw*. Detroit: Wayne State University Press, 1976, pp. 99–138.

Solomon, Stanley J. "*Saint Joan* as Epic Tragedy," in *Modern Drama*. VI (February, 1964), pp. 437–449.

Stewart, J.I.M. *Eight Modern Writers*. Oxford: Clarendon Press, 1963, pp. 179–182.

Turco, Alfred, Jr. *Shaw's Moral Vision: The Self and Salvation*. Ithaca, N.Y.: Cornell University Press, 1976, pp. 268–273.

Valency, Maurice. *The Cart and the Trumpet: The Plays of George Bernard Shaw*. New York: Oxford University Press, 1973, pp. 368–391.

Williams, Raymond. *Drama from Ibsen to Brecht*. London: Chatto and Windus, 1968, pp. 252–256.

Wisenthal, J.L. *The Marriage of Contraries: Bernard Shaw's Middle Plays*. Cambridge, Mass.: Harvard University Press, 1974, pp. 172–192.

EDITH SITWELL

Born: Scarborough, England (September 7, 1887)
Died: London, England (December 9, 1964)

Principal Works

POEMS: *Clowns' Houses,* 1918; *The Wooden Pegasus,* 1920; *Façade,* 1922; *The Sleeping Beauty,* 1924; *Troy Park,* 1925; *Rustic Elegies,* 1927; *Gold Coast Customs,* 1929; *Collected Poems,* 1930; *Poems New and Old,* 1940; *Street Songs,* 1942; *Green Song and Other Poems,* 1944; *The Song of the Cold,* 1945; *The Shadow of Cain,* 1947; *The Canticle of the Rose: Poems 1917–1949,* 1949; *Gardeners and Astronomers,* 1953; *Collected Poems,* 1957; *The Outcasts,* 1962; *Music and Ceremonies,* 1963.

NOVEL: *I Live Under a Black Sun,* 1937.

BIOGRAPHY: *Alexander Pope,* 1930; *The English Eccentrics,* 1933; *Victoria of England,* 1936; *Fanfare for Elizabeth,* 1946; *The Queens and the Hive,* 1962.

CRITICISM: *Poetry and Criticism,* 1925; *Aspects of Modern Poetry,* 1936; *A Poet's Notebook,* 1943; *A Notebook on William Shakespeare,* 1948.

AUTOBIOGRAPHY: *Taken Care of,* 1965.

Edith Sitwell, one of the century's foremost poets and a flamboyant exponent of experimentation in verse, was the oldest child of Sir George Sitwell, fourth baronet of Renishaw Park, the family seat for six hundred years. Much of the extravagant personality of Edith and her brothers, Osbert and Sachaverell, is readily understandable to the reader of the memoirs of their fabulous and outrageous father, written by Sir Osbert Sitwell in *Left Hand, Right Hand.*

Educated in secret (as she said), Edith Sitwell first became known in 1916 as the editor of an anthology, *Wheels,* which stridently featured for six years her own work, that of her brothers, and other authors whose voices were to be heard frequently in the 1920's. One of the highlights of the 1925 season in London was the premiere of Sitwell's *Façade,* in which she chanted her early fanciful and rhythmical verse to similarly exciting musical settings provided by William Walton. For the performance Sitwell spoke through an amplifying mask behind a screen, another device to provide artificiality for the exotic occasion. The London Hall was an uproar of Sitwell's admirers and detracters, as the staid English audience itself came close to a performance more appropriate to Paris or Dublin than to London. Twenty-five years later, the work was similarly performed in New York's Museum of Modern Art, but so far had modern taste and Sitwell's reputation advanced, that the last occasion was almost regal in dignity, as befitted its central performer who was given the accolade of Grand Dame of the Cross of the British Empire in 1954.

Sitwell's flair for self-dramatization for a long time made students of literature uneasy about the seriousness of her poetry. Standing six feet in height, she always appeared in extravagant and archaic costumes and headgear, often medieval, spangled with ostentatious rings and necklaces. "I have always had a great affinity for Queen Elizabeth," she said once. "We were born on the same day of the month and about the same hour of the day."

Although her Dadaist stunts were calculated to express her love of being flamboyant and of irritating the stuffy ("Good taste," she claimed, "is the worst vice ever invented"), her interest in poetry was serious as was her talent. Her keenness for verbal experimentation found a fit subject in the extraordinary *Gold Coast Customs* (1929), her own version of Eliot's *The Waste Land* and one of the remarkable poems of that remarkable decade.

For ten years afterwards Sitwell wrote little verse, devoting herself to critical essays and non-fiction, including a biography of Pope, but mainly taking care of a friend, Helen Rootham, through her fatal illness. With the coming of World War II, Sitwell returned to poetry, still with her dazzling technical equipment but now with a rich store of traditional Christian imagery. (Sitwell became a Roman Catholic in 1955.) The agonies of the bombardment of London, and the terror of the atomic bomb evoked from Sitwell some of the most moving poetry ever written about the cruelty of war.

Along with her delight in self dramatization, Sitwell was renowned, from the publication of *Wheels* all through her life, for her championship of younger writers. Dylan Thomas is but one of the best known of the young men whose verbal experimentation she praised and championed early in his career.

Bibliography

Biographical studies include Sitwell's autobiography, *Taken Care Of*, 1965; her brother Osbert's memoirs, *Left Hand, Right Hand*, 5 vols., 1944–1950; her secretary Elizabeth Salter's *The Last Years of a Rebel: A Memoir of Edith Sitwell*, 1967; and John Lehmann's *A Nest of Tigers: Edith, Osbert and Sacheverell Sitwell in Their Times*, 1968. Lehmann and Derek Parker edited *Selected Letters, 1919–1964*, 1970.

For criticism of the work see Ralph J. Mills, Jr., *Edith Sitwell: A Critical Essay*, 1966; Geoffrey Singleton, *Edith Sitwell: The Hymn to Life*, 1960; J. Brophy, *Edith Sitwell: The Symbolist Order*, 1968; Louis Untermeyer, *Lives of the Poets*, 1960; C. M. Bowra, *Edith Sitwell*, 1947; ibid., *Poetry and Politics 1900–1960*, 1966; and Sister M. Jeremy, "Clown and Canticle: The Achievement of Edith Sitwell," *Renascence*, III (Spring, 1951), 135–136. Also of interest are R. L. Megroz, *Three Sitwells: A Biographical and Critical Study*, 1927, reprinted, 1969; and *A Celebration for Edith Sitwell*, edited by José Garcia Villa, 1948.

Additional references may be found in Richard Fifoot, *A Bibliography of Edith, Osbert, and Sacheverell Sitwell*, 1963; and Lois D. Rosenberg, "Edith Sitwell, A Critical Bibliography, 1915–1950," *Bulletin of Bibliography*, XXI, no. 2 (1953), 40–43; XXI, no. 3 (1954), 57–60.

THE POETRY OF EDITH SITWELL

Author: Edith Sitwell (1887–1964)
First published: Clowns' Houses, 1918; *The Wooden Pegasus* 1920; *Façade*, 1922;
   Bucolic Comedies, 1923; *The Sleeping Beauty,* 1924; *Troy Park,* 1925; *Elegy
   on Dead Fashion,* 1926; *Rustic Elegies,* 1927; *Poems Old and New,* 1940;
   Street Songs, 1942; *Green Song and Other Poems,* 1944; *The Song of the Cold,*
   1945; *The Shadow of Cain,* 1947; *Poor Man's Music,* 1950; *Gardeners and
   Astronomers: New Poems,* 1953; *The Collected Poems of Edith Sitwell,* 1954;
   The Queens and the Hive, 1961

Essay-Review

Edith Sitwell achieved notoriety instantly when she and her brothers, Osbert
and Sacheverell, burst upon the London literary scene during the period of World
War I, each of them striving in flamboyant and self-mocking fashion to live ec-
centrically against the grain of a dull industrial world. This early pose was maintained by Edith Sitwell all her life.

Extravagant too were the verses of her earliest period, well suited for the brittle
musical setting given *Façade* by her composer friend, William Walton. The music
was performed with the poet herself chanting her hypnotic and quasinonsensical
lines about Daisy and Lily. Equally absurd but dazzling to the ear is the poem
"Sir Beelzebub."

Only a perceptive few noted, however, that Sitwell's extravagance was serious
and that in her own amusing provocative way she was forging an innovative poetic instrument. When she began to write, she said later, the conventional
rhythms, outworn language, and stale imagery made necessary a new direction
and more immediate effects of sight and sound in poetry. So when she wrote of
the morning light in its "creaking" descent, she was endeavoring to make the
reader hear the morning as well as see it, and thus feel a new dimension to the
dawn. The same deepening of sensuous experience is found in many of her poems
during this period. Trees, for example, are compared to hissing green geese; the
wind is a blue-maned horse that whinnies and neighs. Some of Sitwell's experiments in synesthesia are strained and excessive, but just as often she does achieve
that newness called for by Ezra Pound that is the goal of all good poets. Every
reader of Sitwell's criticism of her own work and of that of others, in essays and
prefaces, instantly recognizes her keen ear and her constant concern with the
relation between sense and sound in poetry, a concern that lay behind all her
experimentation and made her deliberately strain or even break old associational
patterns in her quest for fresh effects.

Edith Sitwell was obviously a student of the later Yeats and of Gerard Manley
Hopkins, but her own work had a different cast and, as the years went by, a
meaning all its own. Though the verbal techniques of *Façade* are clearly on dis-

play in *Gold Coast Customs*, its structure presented ideas and feelings never imagined by dazzled and largely amused audiences of Sitwell's earlier work. Still chic, on one level her re-creation of savagery and cannibalism is obviously part of the 1920's movement that brought primitive art into modern culture, to be found in sculpture and in the early music of Stravinsky and Prokovieff. But like the novelist Conrad, Sitwell shows, as the poem goes on, that the river of darkness flows through London as well as through The Congo. Cannibal feasts become the equivalents of Lady Bamburgher's stupid but fashionable parties, and Sitwell effectively creates a depiction of a spiritual wasteland. The Negro worships a black stone that stands upright on a bone. But Lady Bamburgher's god never lived at all. Unable to live or die, her god suffers as one in a trance, capable of hearing and bearing everything and yet remaining immobile.

The spirit of Blake, perhaps, tries to sing out here above her images of cannibalism new and old. Through most of the 1940's Sitwell devoted herself to criticism and biography (most notably in her volume on Alexander Pope). But World War II challenged her concern, by now become agony, and found a talent that was worthy of the suffering of the time. Christ's image is now fundamental and right in her "Still Falls the Rain," called by C. M. Bowra, among others, one of the most moving, memorable poems in English about the war. From the magnificent ambiguity of the first word "still" as "always" and also as profound quietness, the comparison between man and god both dying forever is evoked in a contemporary hymn that purges finally profound terror through profound pity. In the poem the still-falling rain eventually becomes the blood from Christ's side, still shed for mankind.

More and more, as war's horror increased, Sitwell found herself capable of turning the traditional images of light, of blood, of the rose of love into poems that somehow made the present meaningful through placing it in perspective with the past. Man's inhuman use of technology creates a new ice age in "The Song of the Cold," in which the poet finds the deadly chill in the heart of man himself. In "The Shadow of Cain" the whimsy of *Façade* has become frozen in a new kind of terror.

Hiroshima provided her with a new vision of the cities of Cain, where the sun descended and the earth ascended in a totemic emblem of destruction and loss. Throughout her famous "Three Poems of the Atomic Age," Sitwell evokes the terrible contrast between the old sun that nourished and gave life, and this new one of man's that kills and destroys. Yet the terrible cloud that brilliantly blossoms also evokes the rose, the traditional image of love both physical and spiritual, and through Sitwell's nightmare vision Christ appears in the terrible rain and walks on seas of blood.

The craft that merely seemed so fashionably clever in the 1920's came a long way before its end, unlike many of the lesser talents of that promising day. Though Edith Sitwell's range is not as great as Yeats's, nor is her influence as deep as Eliot's, she nevertheless wrote a body of work that promises to live.

Bibliography

Beach, Joseph Warren. "Baroque: The Poetry of Edith Sitwell," in *New Mexico Quarterly Review*. XIX (1949), pp. 163–176.

Bowra, Cecil Maurice. "The War Poetry of Edith Sitwell," in *Cornhill*. CLXI (July, 1945), pp. 378–387. Reprinted in *A Celebration for Edith Sitwell*. Edited by José García Villa. New York: New Directions, 1948, pp. 20–32.

Brophy, James D. *Edith Sitwell: The Symbolist Order*. Carbondale: Southern Illinois University Press, 1968.

Clark, Kenneth. "On the Development of Miss Sitwell's Later Style," in *Horizon*. XVI (July, 1947), pp. 7–17. Reprinted in *A Celebration for Edith Sitwell*. Edited by José García Villa. New York: New Directions, 1948, pp. 56–67.

Cohen, John Michael. "New Violence Breaks In," in *Poetry of This Age, 1908–1965*. London: Hutchinson's, 1966, pp. 146–175.

Cuffel, Keith D. "The Shadow of Cain: Themes in Dame Edith Sitwell's Later Poetry," in *Personalist*. XLVI (October, 1965), pp. 517–526.

Deutsch, Babette. "The Ghostly Member," in his *Poetry in Our Time: A Critical Survey of Poetry in the English-Speaking World, 1900–1960*. Garden City, N.Y.: Doubleday, 1963, pp. 243–268.

Every, George. "Sons of the Cold," in *Poetry and Personal Responsibility*. London: S.C.M., 1949, pp. 68–73.

Fairchild, Hoxie Neale. "Toward Hysteria," in his *Religious Trends in English Poetry, Volume V: 1880–1920, Gods of a Changing Poetry*. New York: Columbia University Press, 1962, pp. 578–627.

Gilkes, Martin. *A Key to Modern English Poetry*. London: Blackie, 1937, pp. 147–152.

Harrington, David V. "The 'Metamorphosis' of Edith Sitwell," in *Criticism*. IX (1967), pp. 80–91.

Hassan, Ihab. "Edith Sitwell and the Symbolist Tradition," in *Comparative Literature*. VII (Summer, 1955), pp. 240–251.

Lehmann, John. *A Nest of Tigers: Edith, Osbert and Sacheverell Sitwell in Their Times*. London: Macmillan, 1968, pp. 1–12, 87–99, 110–115, 190–197.

Lindsay, Jack. "The Poetry of Edith Sitwell," in *Life and Letters*. LXIV (January, 1950), pp. 39–52. Reprinted as "Introductory Essay," in *Facade and Other Poems, 1920–1935, by Edith Sitwell*. London: Duckworth, 1950, pp. 7–24.

Mégroz, R.L. *The Three Sitwells: A Biographical and Critical Study*. Port Washington, N.Y.: Kennikat, 1969, pp. 109–155, 294–331.

Mills, Ralph J., Jr. "The Poetic Roles of Edith Sitwell," in *Chicago Review.* XIV (Spring, 1961), pp. 33–64. Revised and reprinted as *Edith Sitwell: A Critical Essay.* Grand Rapids, Mich.: William B. Eerdmans, 1966.

Ower, John B. "Cosmic Aristocracy and Cosmic Democracy in Edith Sitwell," in *Contemporary Literature.* XII (1971), pp. 527–553.

————. "Edith Sitwell: Metaphysical Medium and Metaphysical Message," in *Twentieth Century Literature.* XVI (October, 1970), pp. 253–267.

————. "A Golden Labyrinth: Edith Sitwell and the Theme of Time," in *Renascence.* XXVI (1974), pp. 207–217.

Palmer, Herbert. *Post-Victorian Poetry.* London: Dent, 1938, pp. 337–344.

Pinto, Vivian de Sola. "After Eliot," in his *Crisis in English Poetry: 1880–1940.* London: Hutchinson's, 1967, pp. 167–185.

Powell, Dilys. "Edith Sitwell," in *Descent from Parnassus.* New York: Macmillan, 1935, pp. 101–134.

Reed, Henry. "Edith Sitwell," in *Writers of Today*, Volume I. Edited by Denys Val Baker. London: Sidgwick, 1946, pp. 58–71.

Spender, Stephen. "Images in the Poetic World of Edith Sitwell," in *A Celebration for Edith Sitwell.* Edited by José García Villa. New York: New Directions, 1948, pp. 11–19.

Wells, Henry W. *New Poets from Old.* New York: Columbia University Press, 1940, pp. 261–265, 275–279.

STEPHEN SPENDER

Born: London, England (February 28, 1909)

Principal Works

POEMS: *Nine Entertainments*, 1928; *Twenty Poems*, 1930; *Poems*, 1933; *Poems*, 1934; *Vienna*, 1935; *The Still Centre*, 1939; *Ruins and Visions*, 1942; *Poems of Dedication* , 1947; *Returning to Vienna*, 1947; *The Edge of Being*, 1949; *Collected Poems, 1928–1953*, 1955; *The Generous Days*, 1971.

CRITICISM: *The Destructive Element*, 1936; *The Creative Element*, 1954; *The Struggle of the Moderns*, 1963.

PLAYS: *Trial of a Judge*, 1938.

ESSAYS: *Forward from Liberalism*, 1937; *Life and the Poet*, 1942; *Citizens in War and After*, 1945; *Shelley*, 1952; *The Making of a Poem*, 1955; *The Year of the Young Rebels*, 1969.

TRAVEL SKETCHES AND IMPRESSIONS: *European Witness*, 1946; *Learning Laughter*, 1953.

AUTOBIOGRAPHY: *World Within World*, 1951.

SHORT STORIES: *The Burning Cactus*, 1936.

NOVELS: *The Backward Son*, 1940; *Engaged in Writing*, and *The Fool and the Princess*, 2 vols. in one, 1958.

Stephen (Harold) Spender was born on February 28, 1909, in London, the son of an English father, journalist Edwin Harold Spender, and a German-Jewish mother, Violet Schuster Spender. After attending University College, Oxford, which he left in 1931 without taking his degree, he became associated in London with the vocal and promising group of young poets which included Christopher Isherwood, W. H. Auden, Louis MacNeice, and C. Day Lewis. As early as 1928 he had published a book of verse called *Nine Entertainments*, which was followed by *Twenty Poems* two years later. It was not until 1933, however, with the publication of *Poems*, that he began to receive widespread recognition. Critics applauded the lyrical, Shelleyan quality of his poetry which was infused, however, with the Marxist views of the decade. Although he was always an individualist and never a doctrinaire Communist, much of his poetry was based upon a criticism of capitalism and espousal of the cause of the proletariat and revolutionary movements. *Vienna* showed his awareness of the events which were producing the ominous political tensions of Europe, and in 1937, while he was attending the leftist International Writers' Congress in Spain, he found himself in the midst of the Spanish Civil War. A drama, *Trial of a Judge*, was not as successful as his lyric writing had been.

In 1939, the year he published *The Still Centre*, Spender became cofounder with Cyril Connolly of the influential literary magazine, *Horizon*, only to break with Connolly over political policy in 1941. From 1941 through 1944 he served as a member of the London Auxiliary Fire Service, still managing to continue his work, however, and to publish *Ruins and Visions* in 1942. Like many other disillusioned artists and intellectuals, but considerably later than some, he broke with communism after the war, recording his struggle in *The God That Failed*. In postwar years his reputation as a poet has declined somewhat (unlike that of his friend and colleague Auden) while his stature as a critic and prose writer has grown. In 1936 he had published *The Burning Cactus*, a book of short stories, and in 1940 the novel, *A Backward Son*. *World Within World* was a sensitive, reflective, and at times lyrical autobiography which further showed his versatility as a mature man of letters. *Collected Poems, 1928–1953*, which was published in 1955, emphasized the fact that though he might not be a twentieth century Shelley, he is an influential and a major modern poet. In addition to editing three anthologies of English poetry, he has translated two volumes of the work of Rainer Maria Rilke and one of the poetry of Federico García Lorca. Beginning in 1953 he served as co-editor of *Encounter*, and he continues as a prolific poet-critic-editor whose career has in many ways been typical of that of the literary artist of his generation.

Bibliography

For biographical detail the most reliable work is the poet's autobiography, *World Within World*, 1951. Most of the books dealing with English literature of the 1930's contain material on Spender; see in particular Francis Scarfe, "Stephen Spender: A Sensitive," in *Auden and After*, 1942. See also James G. Southworth, "Stephen Spender," *Sewanee Review*, XLV (1937), 272–284; C. I. Glicksberg, "Poetry and the Social Revolution," *Dalhousie Review*, XVII (1938), 493–503; and Willis D. Jacobs, "The Moderate Poetical Success of Stephen Spender," *College English*, XVII (1956), 374–378.

THE POETRY OF SPENDER

Author: Stephen Spender (1909–   )
Principal published works: Nine Entertainments, 1928; *Twenty Poems, 1930*; *Poems*, 1933; *Poems*, 1934; *Vienna*, 1935; *The Still Centre*, 1939; *Ruins and Visions*, 1942; *Poems of Dedication*, 1947; *Returning to Vienna*, 1947; *The Edge of Being*, 1949; *Collected Poems, 1928–1953*, 1955

Essay-Review

Stephen Spender explains in a brief introduction to his *Collected Poems* that the volume does not contain his entire poetic output over a period of twenty-five years, but rather a selection of those poems which he wished to gather together from earlier volumes with an aim "to retrieve as many past mistakes, and to make as many improvements, as possible, without 'cheating.'" He admits that he has altered a few readings here and there in the interest of clarity or aesthetics, but adds that he has retained, in the interest of honesty and truth, certain passages in which he now recognizes youthful imperfections and a few poems which reflect views he no longer holds. As printed, the poems have been grouped to represent roughly his development as a poet, as well as his interest in contemporary history—chiefly the Spanish Civil War and World War II—and in such eternal themes as love and separation. He views his book as "a weeded, though not a tidied up or altered garden."

The volume gives an opportunity for a studied reappraisal of one of a group of English poets who first achieved fame between the two world wars. The members of the Oxford Group, as they have sometimes been called, included W. H. Auden, Christopher Isherwood, Cecil Day Lewis, and Louis MacNeice. Spender dedicates three of his groups of poems to the first three of these poets. Though Spender has written elsewhere of the "teacher-to-pupil" relationship between Auden and himself at Oxford, his later development as a poet has been largely an independent one.

This is not to say, however, that he has followed poetic paths never traveled before. Some of his critics have compared him to Shelley, for the young Spender was also a rebel against the society of his time; and in both poets criticism of their own ears is combined with a vision of a future, better time. Both saw themselves somewhat as prophets of their respective ages. Shelley addressed the West Wind:

> Be through my lips to unawakened earth
>
> The trumpet of a prophecy! O, Wind,
> If Winter comes, can Spring be far behind?

More than a century later Spender exhorted, in "Exiles from Their Land, History Their Domicile":

> Speak with your tongues,
> O angels, fire your guns
> . . . . . .
> And let my words appear
> A heaven-printed world!

   Though some similarities of attitude and theme are to be found in poems of Shelley and Spender, their poetic techniques are as different as the times in which they lived. Spender is as romantically emotional as Shelley: he believes in the unmistakable love of man for his fellow man; he often opposes the darkness of man's life with the bright sun which brings light and warmth into it. But Spender's poems echo twentieth century phrasing, though some lines might be described as Shelleyan, as in the beautiful lyric which begins, "I think continually of those who were truly great."
   At times Spender reminds one of T. S. Eliot (and Auden too), as in "The Uncreating Chaos":

> Shall I never reach
> The fields guarded by stones
> Rare in the stone mountains
> Where the scytheless wind
> Flushes the swayed grasses....

Spender himself has said, however, that he was more influenced by Wilfred Owen than by Eliot. Like Owen, Spender often employs subtle combinations of sound effects, as in the lines quoted above: "Where the scytheless wind/Flushes the swayed grasses." Owen's poetry was principally inspired by World War I, which brought early death to the poet whose pity had been stirred by the suffering and dying which he had witnessed. Spender seems to have been influenced not only by Owen's bitterness against the bloody injustices of the world, but also by what he himself had learned of war during his months in Spain and later in the Battle of Britain and even more directly, perhaps, by the content of certain of Owen's war poems. Compare, for example, Spender's "Two Armies," which describes enemy forces resting at night only a few yards apart,

> When the machines are stilled, a common suffering
> Whitens the air with breath and makes both one
> As though these enemies slept in each other's arms,

with Owen's "Strange Meeting," an unfinished poem in which a soldier dreams he meets in Hell the enemy whom he killed and discovers in that "strange friend" the same hope and pity and compassion that was in his own heart.
   In a critical essay on Auden which Spender published in the *Atlantic Monthly*

(July, 1953), he pointed out that the essential direction of Auden's poetry has been toward a definition of Love. The reader of the *Collected Poems* discovers that, like his slightly older friend and mentor, Spender has written a series of variations on the same theme. In the early poems the love seems often like Whitman's "manly love of comrades," even to the point of suggesting Whitmanesque ambiguities, as in the poem which begins "How strangely this sun reminds me of my love" or another which addresses directly an unnamed "Abrupt and charming mover." One is reminded of Whitman again in the hortatory "Oh young men, oh young comrades," in which the theme of loving comradeship is combined with the call to desert the dusty past, to leave the "great houses where the ghosts are prisoned," and to make a new and better world:

> Oh comrades, step beautifully from the solid wall
> advance to rebuild and sleep with friend on hill
> advance to rebel and remember what you have
> no ghost ever had, immured in his hall.

In other lyrics, as in the lovely sonnet "Daybreak," which describes a couple waking at dawn, first the man, then the woman, one finds both tenderness and the passionate intensity that suffuses so much of the poetry of D. H. Lawrence. But the mixture of desire and revulsion which unpleasantly mars so many of Lawrence's love poems is not in Spender. In Lawrence's "Lightning," for example, a lightning flash reveals to a lover the fear in the face of the woman he is preparing to kiss, and his passion is followed by hatred of both the woman and himself. Contrast with this Spender's "Ice," in which a woman comes "in from the snowing air" and is greeted by a kiss:

> Then my lips ran to her with fire
> From the chimney corner of the room,
> Where I had waited in my chair.
> I kissed their heat against her skin
> And watched the red make the white bloom. . . .

The love of man and woman shows no hectic flush in Spender; the colors are those of radiant health.

Another aspect of love is revealed in Spender's numerous poems about children. Several are about his daughter, but the group titled "Elegy for Margaret" is to or about the niece who died after a long, wasting illness on Christmas Day, 1945. Here, though there are morbid lines which describe the progress of the disease, the whole elegy is filled with pity and sorrow for both the child and her parents; and the final poem, in which he attempts to console his "Dearest and nearest brother," is as moving as anything that Spender has written.

Many of the poems for which Spender is best known were published early in *Poems* (1933). In the *Collected Poems* these are reprinted in a group under the title "Preludes." Here one finds such familiar poems as "The Express" and "The

Landscape near an Aerodrome," both of which illustrate Spender's early interest in enlarging the language of modern poetry through the use of terms drawn from science, machinery, and industry. The first opens:

> After the first powerful, plain manifesto
> The black statement of pistons, without more fuss
> But gliding like a queen, she leaves the station.

The blending of the names of mechanical objects with language more usual in poetry is so skillfully achieved that the train becomes a mighty poem in motion. "The Express" is perhaps the finest train poem since Walt Whitman's portrait of a very different train in "To a Locomotive in Winter."

"The Landscape near an Aerodrome" contains poetic beauty like that in "The Express," but it is weakened by the attempt to combine arresting description with social commentary. The poem begins with the picture of a gliding air liner and then contrasts the quiet descent of the great machine with the scenes of squalor and misery which become clearer to the passengers as they approach the aerodrome. It ends with a sudden, trenchant last line that not only surprises the reader but seems totally uncalled-for by the preceding descriptive lines:

> Then, as they land, they hear the tolling bell
> Reaching across the landscape of hysteria,
> To where, louder than all those batteries
> And charcoaled towers against the dying sky,
> Religion stands, the Church blocking the sun.

Several of the "Preludes" and two or three poems in the next group, "A Heaven-Printed World," belong to the literature of protest of the 1930's and reflect Spender's leftwing politics which he later forswore. These poems, as Spender has said, "did not please the politicians." Notable are "The Funeral," "The Pylons," and "An Elementary School Classroom in a Slum." The last is full of the pity which is deep in Spender's poems, political or otherwise.

The introspective poems in the group called "Explorations" are as a whole less impressive than those in the other groups. Rather hazy and inchoate, these "explorations," when compared with Spender's other poems, lead one to conclude that he is a sensitive but not a cerebral poet.

It has been said that Spender is a humorless poet. He does usually take himself seriously, often too much so; but the gracefully witty conceit in one of his later poems called "Word" refutes the charge against him:

> The word bites like a fish.
> Shall I throw it back free
> Arrowing to that sea
> Where thoughts lash tail and fin?
> Or shall I pull it in
> To rhyme upon a dish?

Bibliography

Daiches, David. *Poetry and the Modern World: A Study of Poetry in England Between 1900 and 1939.* Chicago: University of Chicago Press, 1940, pp. 233–239.

Fremantle, Anne. "Stephen Spender," in *Commonweal.* LIV (May 11, 1951), pp. 119–121.

Hazard, James. "Stephen Spender," in *Wisconsin Studies in Literature.* III (1966), pp. 57–66.

Herzman, Ronald B. "Stephen Spender: The Critic as Poet," in *Notes on Contemporary Literature.* III (1973), pp. 6–7.

Jacobs, Willis D. "The Moderate Poetical Success of Stephen Spender," in *College English.* XVII (April, 1956), pp. 374–379.

Kulkarni, H.B. *Stephen Spender: Poet in Crisis.* Glasgow, Scotland: Blackie & Son, 1970.

Savage, D.S. "The Poet's Perspectives," in *Poetry.* LXIV (June, 1944), pp. 148–158.

Scarfe, Francis. *Auden and After: The Liberation of Poetry, 1930–1941.* London: Routledge, 1942, pp. 35–52.

Seif, Morton. "The Impact of T.S. Eliot on Auden and Spender," in *South Atlantic Quarterly.* LIII (January, 1954), pp. 61–69.

Sellers, W.H. "Spender and Vienna," in *Humanities Association Bulletin.* XVIII (Spring, 1967), pp. 59–68.

————. "Wordsworth and Spender: Some Speculations on the Use of Rhyme," in *Studies in English Literature, 1500–1900.* IV (Autumn, 1965), pp. 641–650.

Southworth, James G. "Stephen Spender," in *Sewanee Review.* XLV (July/September, 1937), pp. 272–283.

Stanford, Derek. *Stephen Spender, Louis MacNeice, Cecil Day Lewis: A Critical Essay.* Grand Rapids, Mich.: Eerdmans, 1969, pp. 11–23.

Weatherhead, A. Kingsley. *Stephen Spender and the Thirties.* Lewisburg, Pa.: Bucknell University Press, 1975.

————. "Stephen Spender: Lyric Impulse and Will," in *Contemporary Literature.* XII (1971), pp. 451–465.

DYLAN THOMAS

Born: Swansea, Wales (October 27, 1914)
Died: New York, N.Y. (November 9, 1953)

Principal Works

POEMS: *18 Poems*, 1934; *Twenty-five Poems*, 1936; *The Map of Love*, 1939; *The World I Breathe*, 1939; *New Poems*, 1943; *Deaths and Entrances*, 1946; *In Country Sleep*, 1952; *Collected Poems, 1934–1952*, 1952.

SHORT STORIES AND SKETCHES: *Adventures in the Skin Trade and Other Stories*, 1955.

AUTOBIOGRAPHY: *Portrait of the Artist as a Young Dog*, 1940.

PLAYS: *The Doctor and the Devils*, 1953; *Under Milk Wood*, 1954.

ESSAYS AND BROADCASTS: *Quite Early One Morning*, 1954.

Dylan (Marlais) Thomas, born in Swansea, Wales, on October 27, 1914, regularly produced and published poetry and short fiction to the age of thirty-five. His last four years were wasted in public readings of earlier works as well as the works of other poets (for the ostensible purpose of earning more but as well to find reassurance in adulation), and new works were produced but occasionally and hurriedly under the pressure of professional commitments. It was during this latter period that Thomas disintegrated psychically to die of acute alcoholism in New York City on November 9, 1953. When the memory of his exuberant personality has dissipated, he will probably be judged the greatest lyric poet of his generation and a fiction writer of original humor and charm.

The total amount of Thomas' work could be contained in one volume; however, he was not so much a slow writer as a careful one, altering some of his poems over two hundred times. He insisted that his work be read at its face value, preferably aloud. (Thomas once said that he wanted to be *read*, not *read into*.) Much of the criticism of the obscurity of his work has been irrelevant for this reason: the reader is not supposed to find answers to anything; rather, he is to allow the words to work on him, which they do tremendously in spite of the many private and esoteric references. While some scholars have traced these to their sources for further enjoyment, the magic of the literature as it stands is the main reward.

Thomas was a tragic figure, a man of effusive good will who dissipated to death in agonies of guilt. While his poetry tortuously worked through to a celebration of the Christian belief, in his prose, as well as in his personal life, he revealed the mind of one who wished to believe, to find faith, but could not, and in not finding it knew life as a nightmare from which there was no escape except death. This was the reason for the number of images depicting horror in his work. If some of it was symbolic, it was because there was nothing in the familiar world that sufficiently expressed the horror that he saw. Extremely sensitive, imbued with an impossible ethical code by his schoolmaster father, he projected his own guilt onto the world at large, its hypocrisy and money-getting, its general inhumanity. Two symptoms of this were his telling the truth beyond the edge of tact and his profligate wastefulness of money, though he was miserable when the first resulted in hurt feelings and the second in poverty.

Thomas was essentially a rural poet, and much of what he had to say was concerned with that world, of its harmony with the rhythm of the earth in its emphasis on birth, marriage, death, rebirth, and a simple faith in God, or else with the lost world of childhood innocence. His readers were of the urban world, however, a world he feared and hated.

Thomas was educated in the Swansea Grammar School in which his father was an English master. The English scholar is often antithetical to works of writers not dead, and Dylan's later scorn of scholars in England and America may indicate that his father belittled his early efforts, just as his antisocial boisterousness indicated an overstrict childhood. However, his early poetry and prose were published frequently in the grammar school literary magazine; and when his first volume, *18 Poems*, appeared, it was received enthusiastically by critics such as Edith Sitwell, though not by the general public, some of whom wrote virulent abuses to the *Sunday Times*. The poetry of this first period was concerned almost entirely with personal problems and was made perhaps deliberately obscure by private imagery and a highly personalized style.

Until World War II Thomas lived in London much of the time. Short but broad, of huge energy, he had experiences that were in many ways those of any proud rural innocent; always scornful of hypocrisy and the unnatural, he found much to reject in the city. At the same time his great warmth and talent made him many friends among its literary leaders. His way of adapting to this life was to mock the conventions with droll acts. During the war he served as an antiaircraft gunner; the sight of the courage and suffering induced his second creative phase, one which revealed poignant feelings for others. When he also read poetry over the B.B.C., he began to have a general public.

With the printing of the *Collected Poems* in 1952 he became a public figure on the basis of his enthusiastic reception by reviewers and critics. His later poetry had begun to reveal the change in his attitude from one of doubt and fear to faith and hope, with love of God gained through love of man and the world of nature. It also was more verbose. It was at this time that he became unbearably dissatisfied with life, expressing this in such poems as "I Have Longed to Move Away." Part of this feeling may have been due to his growing fear of alienation from his Irish-born wife Caitlin and their three children; part of it may have been the effect of his fear of losing his powers and upon which the first fear would be based. In addition, he was miserable as a public figure. Like all provincials, he was anxious before the stranger; although he was deeply appreciated by the audiences he read to, most of these people were interested in the poet of public fame, not in the private man. For a man with a huge capacity and need to love and be loved, this experience may have been devastating. Whatever the causes, Thomas produced mostly fiction and verse plays the last few years of his life. Of these the unfinished *Adventures in the Skin Trade* deals with his urban experiences, *Under Milk Wood* with his village reminiscences. Both of these works were celebrations of innocence, written at a time when the poet said of himself, "I have seen the gates of hell."

Bibliography

There are two biographies: John Ackerman, *Dylan Thomas: His Life and Work*, 1964; and Constantine FitzGibbon, *The Life of Dylan Thomas*, 1965. See also *ibid.*, ed., *Selected Letters*, 1966. The *Poems* have been edited by Daniel Jones, 1971. Highly subjective and often conflicting details are given in two works combining biography and reminiscence: John Malcolm Brinnin, *Dylan Thomas in America*, 1955; and Caitlin Thomas, *Leftover Life to Kill*, 1957. The basic critical studies are Henry Treece, *Dylan Thomas*, 1949; Elder Olson, *The Poetry of Dylan Thomas*, 1954; and Clark Emery, *The World of Dylan Thomas*, 1971. See also *Dylan Thomas: Letters to Vernon Watkins*, edited, with an introduction, by Vernon Watkins, 1957.

The best brief yet comprehensive study of the poetry and prose is John L. Sweeney's Introduction to *Selected Writings of Dylan Thomas*, 1946. See also Francis Scarfe, "Dylan Thomas: A Pioneer," in *Auden and After*, 1942; Babette Deutsch, "Alchemists of the Word," in *Poetry in Our Time*, 1952; M. W. Stearn, "Unsex the Skeleton: Notes on the Poetry of Dylan Thomas," *Sewanee Review*, LII (1944), 424–440; Robert Horan, "In Defense of Dylan Thomas," *Kenyon Review*, VII (1945), 304–310; Anon., "Salute to a Poet," *London Times Literary Supplement*, LI (Nov. 28, 1952), 776; David Daiches, "The Poetry of Dylan Thomas," *College English*, XVI (1954), 1–8; and Henry W. Wells, "Voice and Verse in Dylan Thomas' Play," *College English*, XV (1954), 438–444.

COLLECTED POEMS, 1934–1952

Type of work: Poetry
Author: Dylan Thomas (1914–1953)
First published: 1952

Essay-Review

A poet who is both very complex and very popular is an anomaly, but Thomas is not in this position by virtue of belonging to a particular school of verse, nor by writing in a recognized poetic convention. Nor is he socially or politically committed. His poetry is an affirmation of life: "These poems are written for the love of man and in praise of God, and I'd be a damn' fool if they weren't." The truth of this assertion in the introductory note to his volume of collected verse is shown in every successful poem that he wrote. His early poetry is egocentric; he was writing of his own private feelings in these poems of birth, death, and sex, and the glory he found in these themes was entirely personal. His later poems show a far wider human interest and an increasing concern for mankind.

Throughout his work a unity of vision is apparent. He sees death in birth and resurrection in death. He is aware of the hate in all love and of the power of love to transcend suffering. He comprehends the simultaneous glory and corruption in life and the fact that all forms of life are interdependent and inseparable. "I see the boys of summer" is a dialogue between the young poet who sees the destruction of the future in the present and the adolescent boys living their first passionate and confusing loves. The successive images of light and dark, heat and cold, throughout the poem emphasize this contrast. The poem is filled with pleasure and pain conjoined, and with gain and loss. The polarity of these emotions is explicitly stated in the final, joyful image:

> O see the poles are kissing as they cross.

"If I were tickled by the rub of love" is a difficult poem, to be understood by remembering the comprehensiveness of Thomas' idea of life. In the context of the poem, "tickled" appears to mean completely involved with, or wholly absorbed by, but the term necessarily retains the connotations of amusement and enjoyment. "Rub," as well as having sensual implications, also means doubt, difficulty, or strain. The poet says that if he were "tickled by the rub of love," he would not fear the fall from Eden or the flood; if he were "tickled" by the birth of a child, he would not fear death or war. Desire is spoken of as devilish and is provoked by

> . . . the drug that's smoking in a girl
> And curling round the bud that forks her eye.

This harsh image is followed by a statement of the poet's consciousness that he carries his own old age and death already within him.

> An old man's shank one-marrowed with my bone,
> And all the herrings smelling in the sea,
> I sit and watch the worm beneath my nail
> Wearing the quick away.

The feeling of fear is strong, and neither love, sex, beauty, nor birth is the "rub"; the solution is in wholeness or unity:

> I would be tickled by the love that is:
> Man be my metaphor.

Thomas' poetical development is unusual in that the thought in his later poems is usually not at all obscure. These poems are also less clotted with cosmological allusions; there are fewer esoteric symbols; ideas are developed at greater length, and tension is relaxed. The close attention to rhythm and structure persists, and the evocative power of his language is enhanced. Thomas' genius lay in the brilliant and highly personal use of the words with which his penetrating perception is communicated. This ambiguity of his language parallels the reciprocal nature of his images. He delights in punning and the various meanings of a word or image will often reverberate throughout an entire stanza.

"Poem on his birthday" is a good example of his method. The last poems are often, as this one is, set in the Welsh countryside. The heron is always in his poems a religious or priestly symbol. In the first stanza "herons spire and spear"; in the third, "herons walk in their shroud," and in the ninth he writes of the "druid herons' vows" and of his "tumbledown tongue"—this last a beautifully fused image of the action of the tongue of a pealing bell and the impetuous voice of the poet. In the tenth stanza he speaks of the "nimbus bell" which is a magical goal. By this use of compound images Thomas explores and thoroughly penetrates his subject. All aspects of the experience are involved, and pain, happiness, grief, and joy are equally present in this expression of unified sensibility.

Thomas' inclusive view of the universe is sometimes incoherent in his early poems, sometimes illuminating. One of the finest of his early poems is titled "The force that through the green fuse drives the flower." The symbolism here is not obscure and the emotions are controlled by the form of the poem. The third line of each of the four five-line stanzas has only three or four words and is the main clause of the three-line sentence in which the theme of each stanza is stated. The last two lines of each stanza begin with the words "And I am dumb. . . ." After the dramatic first two lines the short solemn third lines ready the reader for the equally forceful antithesis. The poem ends with a rhyming couplet:

> And I am dumb to tell the lover's tomb,
> How at my sheet goes the same crooked worm.

The theme of the poem is that the forces of nature are the same as those that drive man and that these forces both create and destroy. The careful structure of this poem is typical of Thomas' craftsmanship.

The sonnet sequence "Altarwise by owl-light" is Thomas' most densely symbolic volume. The sonnets contain lines and passages of great beauty, and the overall movement, from horror and suffering toward the idea of the redemption of man by the Resurrection of Christ after the Crucifixion, is clear. But the sequence as a whole requires close reading and an understanding of the poet's cosmology. But in the *Poetry of Dylan Thomas*, Elder Olsen demonstrates that even the poet's difficult first two volumes of verse are rigorously disciplined and symbolically consistent.

In "After the funeral," an elegy for a cousin, Ann Jones, Thomas expresses both his own grief and the character of the dead woman. It is, as the poet points out, written with a magniloquence that exceeds the subject's,

> Though this for her is a monstrous image blindly
> Magnified out of praise....

This manner contrasts so sharply with the humble and suffering woman that the poignancy of the portrait is increased. His grief

> Shakes a desolate boy who slit his throat
> In the dark of the coffin and sheds dry leaves.

The clear-sighted description of the woman after the expression of such grief is very moving:

> I know her scrubbed and sour humble hands
> Lie with religion in their cramp, her thread-bare
> Whisper in a damp word, her wits drilled hollow,
> Her fist of a face died clenched on a round pain.

The sonnet sequence and the elegy give some indication of Thomas' later themes, where religious faith and a concern for mankind are evident.

During the second world war Thomas spent several years in London, where he was deeply moved by German air raids on the city. This reaction is very clear in his fourth volume, *Deaths and Entrances*. The well-known "A refusal to Mourn the Death, by Fire, of a Child in London" is both an affirmation of Christian faith and an expression of cold fury at such a death. The poet feels that the event was too great for grief and that no elegy should be written for the child until the end of the world. Writing of grief at the time would be as if to murder her again:

> I shall not murder
> The mankind of her going with a grave truth.

The child is representative of all mankind and of all London's dead, a view which gives her a certain greatness:

> Deep with the first dead lies London's daughter.

The last line of the poem is ambivalent; it communicates both the irrevocability, finality, and cruelty of death and the Christian belief of the deathlessness of the soul:

> After the first death there is no other.

After the war Thomas was concerned to recapture in his poetry the world of his childhood. The rhythm of these poems is more relaxed and flowing than that of his early work, and the landscapes are glowing and full of color and wonder. These lyrics are poems in praise of the created world. Thomas' skill with words and rhythm evokes the whole Welsh countryside, and his unique imaginative vision makes the places his own. He has here communicated his great reverence and love of life The unified vision of life remains, and Thomas is still aware of the presence of death in life, although this is no longer a cause of anguish as it was in the early poems.

In "Fern Hill," Thomas describes his youth on a farm. He has re-created youthful feeling that the whole world was his; there is an atmosphere of timelessness, a lulling of the consciousness of time's destruction, which the poet in recapturing his youthful feeling has conveyed without negating his manhood's knowledge.

Dylan Thomas was a highly emotional poet whose lyrics express a unified vision of life. His poetry contains many of the aspects of birth and death, fear, grief, joy, and beauty. From the violent, anguished poems of his youth, his power over his "craft or sullen art" increased until he was able to channel his special mode of feeling in ways which enabled him to speak for all men:

> And you shall wake, from country sleep, this dawn and each first dawn,
> Your faith as deathless as the outcry of the ruled sun.

Bibliography

Aivaz, David. "The Poetry of Dylan Thomas," in *Hudson Review*. III (Autumn, 1950), pp. 382–404.

Bayley, John. "Chains and the Poet," in *Dylan Thomas: New Critical Essays*. Edited by Walford Davies. London: Dent, 1972, pp. 56–72.

————. *The Romantic Survival*. New York: Oxford University Press, 1957, pp. 186–228. Reprinted in *Dylan Thomas: A Collection of Critical Essays* Edited by C.B. Cox. Englewood Cliffs, N.J.: Prentice-Hall, 1966, pp. 140–168.

Daiches, David. *Literary Essays*. London: Oliver and Boyd, 1956, pp. 50–61.

Reprinted in *Dylan Thomas: A Collection of Critical Essays*. Edited by C.B. Cox. Englewood Cliffs, N.J.: Prentice-Hall, 1966, pp. 14–24.

Davies, Andrin Talfan. *Dylan: Druid of the Broken Body*. New York: Barnes & Noble, 1966.

Deutsch, Babette. *Poetry in Our Time*. New York: Holt, 1952, pp. 312–347.

Fraser, G.S. "Dylan Thomas," in *Essays on Twentieth Century Poets*. Totowa, N.J.: Rowman and Littlefield, 1977, pp. 182–203.

———. *Vision and Rhetoric*. London: Faber and Faber, 1959, pp. 211–241. Reprinted in *A Casebook on Dylan Thomas*. Edited by John Malcolm Brinnin. New York: Thomas Y. Crowell, 1960, pp. 34–58.

Hardy, Barbara. *The Advantage of Lyric: Essays on Feeling in Poetry*. Bloomington: Indiana University Press, 1977, pp. 112–120.

Horan, Robert. "In Defense of Dylan Thomas," in *Kenyon Review*. VII (Spring, 1945), pp. 304–310.

Jones, Thomas Henry. *Dylan Thomas*. New York: Grove, 1963.

Korg, Jacob. *Dylan Thomas*. New York: Twayne, 1965, pp. 13–153.

Maud, Ralph. *Entrances to Dylan Thomas' Poetry*. Pittsburgh: University of Pittsburgh Press, 1963, pp. 1–118.

Miller, J. Hillis. *Poets of Reality: Six Twentieth Century Writers*. Cambridge, Mass.: Harvard University Press, 1966, pp. 190–216.

Mills, Ralph J., Jr. "Dylan Thomas: The Endless Monologue," in *Accent*. XX (Spring, 1960), pp. 114–136.

Moore, Geoffrey. "Dylan Thomas," in *Kenyon Review*. XVII (Spring, 1955), pp. 258–277.

Moynihan, William T. "Dylan Thomas' 'Hewn Voice,' " in *Texas Studies in Literature and Language*. I (Autumn, 1959), pp. 313–326.

Olson, Elder. *The Poetry of Dylan Thomas*. Chicago: University of Chicago Press, 1954, pp. 1–102. Part reprinted in *A Casebook on Dylan Thomas*. Edited by John Malcolm Brinnin. New York: Thomas Y. Crowell, 1960, pp. 72–79.

Shapiro, Karl. *In Defense of Ignorance*. New York: Random House, 1960, pp. 171–186. Reprinted in *Dylan Thomas: A Collection of Critical Essays*. Edited by C.B. Cox. Englewood Cliffs, N.J.: Prentice-Hall, 1966, pp. 169–180.

Sitwell, Edith. "Dylan Thomas," in *Atlantic Monthly*. CXCIII (February, 1954), pp. 42–45.

Thurley, Geoffrey. *The Ironic Harvest: English Poetry in the Twentieth Century*. New York: St. Martin's Press, 1974, pp. 121–136.

Tindall, William York. *A Reader's Guide to Dylan Thomas*. New York: Noonday, 1962, pp. 3–292.

Treece, Henry. "Is Dylan a Fake?," in *Dylan Thomas*. London: Lindsay Drummond, 1949, pp. 129–135. Reprinted in *A Casebook on Dylan Thomas*. Edited by John Malcolm Brinnin. New York: Thomas Y. Crowell, 1960, pp. 104–109.

Wain, John. "Druid of Her Broken Body," in *Dylan Thomas: New Critical Essays*. Edited by Walford Davies. London: Dent, 1972, pp. 1–20.

————. *Preliminary Essays*. New York: St. Martin's Press, 1957, pp. 180–185. Reprinted in *Dylan Thomas: A Collection of Critical Essays*. Edited by C.B. Cox. Englewood Cliffs, N.J.: Prentice-Hall, 1966, pp. 9–13.

PORTRAIT OF THE ARTIST AS A YOUNG DOG

Type of work: Short stories
Author: Dylan Thomas (1914–1953)
First published: 1940

Essay-Review

If his critics are right in concluding that most of Thomas' best poetry was written in Swansea before he left Wales for London at the age of twenty, it may also be suggested that this collection of short stories set in Swansea and environs laid the foundations for much of the work that was to follow. "One Warm Saturday," the final story in the collection, seems to anticipate the events of Thomas' next book of prose, the unfinished novel, *Adventures in the Skin Trade*, and to use the same surrealistic style. In both the story and the novel the ever-pursued eludes capture by the hero as reality dissolves around him, which may well be the theme of *Portrait of the Artist as a Young Dog.*

But the relationship of these stories to the Thomas canon is not so straightforward. *Adventures in the Skin Trade* is his first prose work; Thomas called it his "Welsh book." It was commissioned by a London publisher and the first chapter appeared in the periodical *Wales* in 1937. The previous year Richard Church had suggested that Thomas write some autobiographical prose tales, and after his marriage in July 1937, he set to work in a very different style and produced "A Visit to Grandpa's," in which the surrealism is muted and the lyrical tone sustained by the young narrator; this story, standing second in *Portrait of the Artist as a Young Dog*, became Thomas' favorite broadcast and reading material. The most interesting feature of the new style of story is the rapid succession of apparently logical but often haphazardly related events, the whole ending in a diminuendo that seems anticlimactic.

The intention of the play of event on the diminutive observer is to record, by means of an episode that largely concerns or happens to others, a stage in the observer's growth, in his development as a "young dog."

The development of the "Dylan Thomas" of the *Portrait* stories into the "young dog" of the final tales is related to the development of the real Thomas as a writer, principally in the latter's use of autobiographical material for prose, poetry, and drama. Thomas delivered the typescript of *Portrait of the Artist as a Young Dog* to his publisher, in lieu of the "Welsh book" in December, 1939. Nine days later, talking to Richard Hughes, he remarked that the people of Laugharne, where he was then living, needed a play of their own. This remark is usually recognized as the origin of *Under Milk Wood*. Some years earlier Thomas had toyed with the notion of another imitation of Joyce, a sort of Welsh *Ulysses* that would cover twenty-four hours in the life of a Welsh village. Thus, from the notions of imitating Joyce and the suggestions of Church and Hughes, together with his development of a distinct prose style (instead of a prose extension of his verse, as in *Adventures in the Skin Trade*) came his best-known prose and drama. The autobiographical base is common to both works and to his poetry.

In real life Fern Hill and Ann Jones provided Gorsehill and Auntie Ann of the first story, "The Peaches," and also the poems "Fern Hill" and "Ann Jones." The fourth story, "The Fight," is a version of Thomas' first meeting with Daniel Jones, the Welsh composer, when they were boys in Swansea. Likewise, Trevor Hughes, his first genuine admirer, became the central character of the eighth story, "Who Do You Wish Was with Us?" and some of Thomas' experiences on the *South Wales Daily Post* are recorded in four of the stories, especially the last two.

The book, although composed of short stories, is given a sense of direction by careful ordering of the sequence and by repeated and cumulative details inside the stories. The ten stories fall into three periods of life: childhood, boyhood, and young manhood. The central character is called "Dylan Thomas," and although this fact is not stressed in each story it is obliquely indicated in most. Other characters reappear in some of the tales, such as his cousin Gwilym Jones and his older colleagues in journalism. But the chief cohesive factor in the collection is not the central character so much as the fact that each story celebrates a visit or an excursion either within the provincial town or just beyond it. Thus the town and its environs become a character in the book, elaborated in the names of its houses, its shops and pubs, and its weather from the warmth of summer evenings on the beach to its wet wintry nights. The locales of the stories, like the seasons of the year, change from story to story and help create the image of the region as a setting for the gallery of minor characters who dominate each story. The hero remains, as he says in "Just Like Little Dogs," a lonely and late-night observer of the odd doings of the townsfolk. The landmarks of the locale become associated with the stories of chance or temporary acquaintances met on his excursions, and these stories generally say that everyone has a skeleton in the kitchen cupboard, as is certainly true of *Under Milk Wood*.

The skeleton is generally a private vice which is not too vicious and may be both comic and pathetic. From the first three stories, "The Peaches," "A Visit To Grandpa's," and "Patricia, Edith and Arnold," we learn that Dylan's Uncle Jim is drinking his pigs away; Cousin Gwilym has his own makeshift chapel and rehearses there his coming ministry; Grandfather Dan dreams he is driving a team of demon horses and has delusions about being buried; the Thomases' maid, Patricia, is involved with the sweetheart of the maid next door.

In the next pair of stories, "The Fight" and "Extraordinary Little Cough," the pains and pleasures of boyhood begin to affect the hero, chiefly in finding a soul-mate, a fellow artist, and also in coming up against the horror of plain viciousness in his companions. The remainder of the stories deal with young manhood and are varied in subject and treatment, from the recital of a tale told to the narrator to the final story in which the narrator for the first time becomes the protagonist, although an ineffectual one.

Most of the stories include an episode set at night, and it seems a pity that the best of Thomas' night stories, the ghostly "The Followers," could not somehow be included now in the present collection.

The stories are arranged in roughly chronological order, culminating in "One Warm Saturday" and "Old Garbo," which show Dylan Thomas' inner way of escape from his home town as reality disappears in a wash of beer and a montage of what-might-have-been. In real life Thomas took to London and drinking to get out of Swansea; by the time he arrived in London he had already discovered how to blur the concrete outlines of provincial life and make its mores jump as he was to do best in *Under Milk Wood.* There is another possible explanation for his ability to see events under the conditions of dream, and that is his Welshness; there is a hint of that in the story, "Where Tawe Flows," titled after the "Great Welsh Novel" which a character named "Mr. Thomas" and three older friends are writing in weekly installments. "Mr. Thomas" is about to leave for London and a career as a freelance journalist. The novel is supposed to be a study of provincial life but the collaborators are only at the second chapter. We do not hear the contribution of "Mr. Thomas" because he has spent the week writing the story of a dead governess turned into a vampire because a cat jumped over her at the moment of her death. One of the foursome offers, instead, the biography of a character named Mary, an account supposed to be realistic but as fantastic as anything the real Mr. Thomas ever wrote.

Portrait of the Artist as a Young Dog accumulates the tensions of provincial life to the breaking point, as does Joyce's *A Portrait of the Artist as a Young Man.* At the end of both books the hero breaks from home as the style becomes distinctly broken. The increasingly nonrealistic style at the end of both books, a formal expression of the whirling thoughts of each young man, could be somehow symptomatic of the breaking of ties with Dublin and Swansea. Since it occurs in both books, and elsewhere, it cannot be explained as Joyce's Irishness or Thomas' Welshness; both are provincials heading for what they consider to be a literary center, Paris or London. In both books the break is long prepared for in the tensions built up, but more obviously in Joyce, from a highly imaginative childhood in the case of both author and hero through the pains of adolescence to the frustrations of university study or journalism on a provincial daily. The tensions recorded in both works are so strong that they expel their subjects far from their place of origin. If we want to know why Joyce died in Zurich or Thomas in New York, the answer is in their own autobiographies of provincial life.

Bibliography

Ackerman, John.   *Dylan Thomas: His Life and Work.* London: Oxford University Press, 1964, pp. 104–113.

Bruns, Gerald L.   "Daedalus, Orpheus, and Dylan Thomas's *Portrait of the Artist*," in *Renascence.* XXV (1973), pp. 147–156.

Davies, Walford. "Imitation and Invention: The Use of Borrowed Material in Dylan Thomas's Prose," in *Essays in Criticism.* XVIII (July, 1968), pp. 275–295.

French, Warren. "Two Portraits of the Artist: James Joyce's *Young Man*: Dylan Thomas's *Young Dog*," in *University Review.* XXXIII (Summer, 1967), pp. 261–266.

Korg, Jacob. *Dylan Thomas.* New York: Twayne, 1965, pp. 168–172.

Phelps, Robert. "In Country Dylan," in *Sewanee Review.* LXIII (Autumn, 1955), pp. 681–687.

Stanford, Derek. *Dylan Thomas: A Literary Study.* New York: Citadel, 1964, pp. 165–168.

VIRGINIA WOOLF

Born: London, England (January 25, 1882)
Died: Lewes, Sussex, England (March 28, 1941)

Principal Works

NOVELS: *The Voyage Out*, 1915; *Night and Day*, 1919; *Jacob's Room*, 1922; *Mrs. Dalloway*, 1925; *To the Lighthouse*, 1927; *Orlando: A Biography*, 1928; *The Waves*, 1931; *The Years*, 1937; *Between the Acts*, 1941.

SHORT STORIES: *Kew Gardens*, 1919; *The Mark on the Wall*, 1919; *Monday or Tuesday*, 1921; *The Haunted House*, 1943.

LITERARY CRITICISM: *Mr. Bennett and Mrs. Brown*, 1924; *The Common Reader*, 1925; *The Common Reader: Second Series*, 1932 [*The Second Common Reader*].

ESSAYS AND STUDIES: *A Room of One's Own*, 1929; *Three Guineas* 1938; *The Death of the Moth*, 1942; *The Moment and Other Essays*, 1947; *The Captain's Deathbed and Other Essays*, 1950; *Granite and Rainbow*, 1958.

BIOGRAPHY: *Flush: A Biography*, 1933; *Roger Fry: A Biography*, 1940.

JOURNALS: *A Writer's Diary*, 1953.

The greatest woman novelist of this century was born Adeline Virginia Stephen in London on January 25, 1882, the daughter of Sir Leslie Stephen, eminent editor, biographer, and critic. The youngest of eight children (four were half-brothers and sisters), Virginia was frail and found her education at home in her father's superb library. Reflections of these early years were to appear in her fiction: the close-knit family group, the brilliant and domineering father, the lovely and conciliating mother, all seen in London or at seasides resembling that of their Cornish summer home. Her mother's death in 1895 was a traumatic shock, but Virginia Stephen continued reading voluminously, studying Greek, and imitating the Elizabethan prose masters. Then, following Sir Leslie's death in 1904, Vanessa, Thoby, Virginia, and Adrian Stephen took a house in the Bloomsbury district. In 1905, however, Virginia suffered the first onslaught of the mental illness which was to recur during World War I. Two years later, after Vanessa's marriage and Thoby's tragic death, Virginia and Adrian took another house among a congenial set which included economist John Maynard Keynes, artist Roger Fry, biographer Lytton Strachey, and others who became associated with the Bloomsbury Group. Reviewing books and publishing essays and criticism, Virginia Stephen worked at her art. In 1912 she married Leonard Woolf, a journalist and political essayist. Sympathetic and protective, he encouraged her in her work.

Three years later, *The Voyage Out* appeared. This story of young Rachel Vinrace's South American voyage was conventional in technique and desultory in plot, but its sensitive treatment of Rachel's maturation, abruptly stopped by death, foreshadowed a rejection of conventional plot and realistic description. *Night and Day*, longer, more sure and solid, dealt specifically with Katherine Hilbery's finding of the right fiancé and generally with a young woman's intellectual and emotional growth in an environment such as Virginia Woolf's own as a girl. Her new goals and experimental methods were indicated in *Monday or Tuesday* in 1921. Its eight sketches ranged from impressionistic creation of moods in short pieces to the use of symbolic imagery in longer ones. Still others attempted to convey through highly suggestive lyrical prose the sound of music and the quality of color. (This arresting book was published by the Hogarth Press. Founded by the Woolfs in 1917, it was to publish all her books as well as work by T. S. Eliot, E. M. Forster, and Sigmund Freud.) *Jacob's Room* used some of the devices of *Monday or Tuesday* in a novel built around the magnetic Jacob Flanders, modeled on Thoby Stephen. Here the author's interest in her characters lies principally in their relationship with Jacob as he grows into manhood and even after his death in World War I. Despite uncertain health, Virginia Woolf continued to produce literary criticism and essays. A number were collected in *The Common Reader: First Series* which appeared in 1925. She ranged from the Greeks to her contemporaries, writing as a sensitive critic who was also a creative artist.

In *Mrs. Dalloway* she explored her characters' streams-of-consciousness as she depicted twelve hours in the inner and outer life of a sensitive woman. Unlike Dorothy Richardson, she revealed the interior monologues of other characters besides the central one; unlike James Joyce, she presented these thoughts so as to avoid any seemingly chaotic effect. In 1927 came her finest achievement, *To the Lighthouse*. Plotless in the ordinary sense, like *Mrs. Dalloway*, this story of the Ramsays was based on her childhood. Rich in image and symbol, it treated her favorite themes of love, marriage, time, and death. She combined experiment and lyricism in "Time Passes," an interlude describing the decay of the summer home in the seven years following Mrs. Ramsay's death. In *Orlando*, a dashing Elizabethan nobleman unaccountably changes into a woman during the Restoration and continues thus into the present. This pleasant fantasy, based on Vita Sackville-West's family, re-emphasized Woolf's interest in the merging flow of time and experience. *A Room of One's Own* discussed fiction and women, protesting against the widespread discrimination women faced. Two years later Virginia Woolf published a novel that some said signalized the end of that form. *The Waves* comprised the impressionistic interior monologues of six characters from early childhood to old age. Separated by italicized lyrical descriptions of a seaside from dawn to dark, the book's sections traced the characters' developing natures, interaction, and relationship to a dominating character named Percival who resembled Jacob Flanders. Here again Virginia Woolf intended recurrent, interrelated images and symbols to impose the unity and coherence which Bennett and Galsworthy sought through conventional plotting, narration, and description.

The Common Reader: Second Series was followed a year later by *Flush*, a pleasant little biography of a spaniel whose mistress, Elizabeth Barrett Browning, dominates the story. *The Years* was not stylized like *The Waves*. This overlong novel emphasized the flow of time by tracing the Pargiters' fortunes from 1880 to the present. *Three Guineas* returned sharply to Virginia Woolf's feminist concerns. *Roger Fry: A Biography*, although a sympathetic memoir, lacked the characteristic incandescence of her prose. Fry's death had deepened the shadows which, cast by ill health and the specter of war, were gathering around her. On March 28, 1941, she left her work table and walked across the fields of her Sussex home into the river Ouse to her death. A note revealed her fear of oncoming incurable madness. *Between the Acts*, a poetically evocative and symbolic book built around a country pageant spanning Britain's history, showed both her weariness and continued intent to expand, here through symbol, the novel's scope. *The Death of the Moth*, *The Moment and Other Essays*, and *The Captain's Deathbed and Other Essays* included new and old essays displaying her characteristic perception. *A Writer's Diary*, published in 1953, is an invaluable record of the inner feelings and creative processes of this modern master. *Virginia Woolf and Lytton Strachey: Letters* (1956) reveals personal aspects of these two gifted Bloomsburyites.

Bibliography

The *Collected Essays* were edited in 4 vols. by Leonard Woolf, 1966–1967. The definitive biography is Quentin Bell, Vol. I, *Virginia Stephen, 1882–1912*, and Vol. II, *Mrs. Woolf, 1912–1941*, 1972. See also Aileen Pippett, *The Moth and the Star: A Biography of Virginia Woolf*, 1955; and Leonard Woolf, *Growing*, 1962, and *Beginning Again*, 1964. The following contain authoritative critical commentary: Winifred Holtby, *Virginia Woolf*, 1932; Ruth Gruber, *Virginia Woolf: A Study*, 1935; David Daiches, *Virginia Woolf*, 1942; E. M. Forster, *Virginia Woolf*, 1942; Joan Bennett, *Virginia Woolf: Her Art as a Novelist*, 1945; R. L. Chambers, *The Novels of Virginia Woolf*, 1947; Bernard Blackstone, *Virginia Woolf: A Commentary*, 1949; James Hafley, *The Glass Roof: Virginia Woolf as Novelist*, University of California English Studies, No. 9, 1954; and David Daiches, *Virginia Woolf*, 1963.

See also Elizabeth N. Monroe, *The Novel and Society*, 1941; Edward Wagenknecht, *Cavalcade of the English Novel*, 1943; E. B. Burgum, *The Novel and the World's Dilemma*, 1947; Lord David Cecil, *Poets and Story-Tellers*, 1949; Elizabeth Bowen, *Collected Impressions*, 1950; D. S. Savage, *The Withered Branch*, 1950; Robert Humphrey, *The Stream of Consciousness in the Modern Novel*, 1954; and J. K. Johnstone, *The Bloomsbury Group*, 1954.

For criticism in magazines see Edwin Muir, "Virginia Woolf," *Bookman*, LXXIV (1931), 362–367; William Troy, "Virginia Woolf: The Poetic Method," *Symposium*, III (1932), 53–63, and "Virginia Woolf: The Poetic Style," *ibid.*, 153–166; J. H. Roberts, "Towards Virginia Woolf," *Virginia Quarterly Review*, X

(1934), 587–612; T. S. Eliot, "Virginia Woolf," *Horizon*, III (1941), 313–316; W. H. Mellers, "Virginia Woolf: The Last Phase," *Kenyon Review*, IV (1942), 381–387; Martin Turnell, "Virginia Woolf," *Horizon*, IV (1942), 44–56; James Southall Wilson, "Time and Virginia Woolf," *Virginia Quarterly Review*, XVIII (1942), 267–276; J. H. Roberts, " 'Vision and Design' in Virginia Woolf," *Publications of the Modern Language Association*, LXI (1946), 835–847; Dayton Kohler, "Time in the Modern Novel," *College English*, X (1948), 15–24; W. Y. Tindall, "Many Leveled Fiction: Virginia Woolf to Ross Lockridge," *College English*, X (1948), 65–71; John Graham, "Time in the Novels of Virginia Woolf," *University of Toronto Quarterly*, XVIII (1949), 186–201; Margaret Church, "Concepts of Time in the Novels of Virginia Woolf and Aldous Huxley," *Modern Fiction Studies*, I (May, 1955), 19–24; and Dean Doner, "Virginia Woolf: The Service of Style," *Modern Fiction Studies*, II (February, 1956), 1–12.

The Virginia Woolf Number of *Modern Fiction Studies*, II (February, 1956) contains a selected checklist of criticisms of Virginia Woolf with an index to studies of her separate works, 36–45.

Current interest in Woolf has resulted in a significant number of recent books on her. Of further interest are her diaries and letters, which continue to appear.

BETWEEN THE ACTS

Type of work: Novel
Author: Virginia Woolf (1882–1941)
Type of plot: Symbolic allegory
Time of plot: June, 1939
Locale: England
First Published: 1941

A work filled with cryptic and portentious symbols, Between the Acts was written during the early years of World War II. A mood of threat and impending doom pervades the novel, reinforced by the planes droning overhead during the pageant. But the true drama lies neither in the destructiveness of war nor in the stark human history played out for the villagers, but, rather, in the lives of the trivial, selfish, frustrated, idealistic people who must face one another between the acts.

Principal Characters

Bartholomew Oliver, retired from civil service and the disgruntled owner of Pointz Hall where a historical pageant is being held.

Giles Oliver, Bartholomew's son, a stockbroker who has longed to be a farmer. Recently on rather chilly terms with his wife, he is engaged in an affair with Mrs. Manresa.

Isa Oliver, Giles's wife, secretly a writer of poetry. She suspects her husband's unfaithfulness and fancies herself in love with Rupert Haines.

Mrs. Lucy Swithin, Bartholomew's widowed sister. In her imagination she lives in England's historic past.

Mrs. Manresa, a cheerful, vulgar, and uninvited guest of the Olivers. She is carrying on an affair with Giles.

William Dodge, an uninvited and unwanted guest brought to the Olivers by Mrs. Manresa. Talking with Isa, he finds solace in his rejection and loneliness, as does she in hers.

Miss La Trobe, the lonely, frustrated writer and director of the historical pageant being presented at Pointz Hall.

Rupert Haines, a married gentleman farmer with whom Isa fancies herself in love.

George and
Caro, grandchildren of Bartholomew.

Eliza Clark,
Albert,
Mrs. Otter, and
Mr. Budge, villagers who act in the pageant

The Story

Pointz Hall was not one of the great English houses mentioned in the guidebooks, but it was old and comfortable and pleasantly situated in a tree-fringed meadow. The house was older than the name of its owners in the county. Although they had hung the portrait of an ancestress in brocade and pearls beside the staircase and kept under glass a watch that had stopped a bullet at Waterloo, the Olivers had lived only a little more than a century in a district where the names of the villagers went back to Domesday Book. The countryside still showed traces of the ancient Britons, the Roman road, the Elizabethan manor house, the marks of the plow on a hill sown in wheat during Napoleon's time.

The owner of the house was Bartholomew Oliver, retired from the Indian Civil Service. With him lived his son Giles, his daughter-in-law Isa, two small grandchildren, and his widowed sister, Mrs. Lucy Swithin. Bartholomew, a disgruntled old man who lived more and more in the past, was constantly snubbing his sister as he had done when they were children. Mrs. Swithin was a woman of careless dress, good manners, quiet faith, and great intelligence. Her favorite book was an *Outline of History*; she dreamed of a time when Piccadilly was a rhododendron forest in which the mastodon roamed. Giles Oliver was a London stockbroker who had wanted to be a farmer until circumstances decided otherwise. A misunderstanding had lately developed between him and his wife Isa, who wrote poetry in secret, suspected that Giles had been unfaithful, and fancied herself in love with Rupert Haines, a married gentleman farmer of the neighborhood. Isa thought that Mrs. Haines had the eyes of a gobbling goose.

On a June morning in 1939, Pointz Hall awoke. Mrs. Swithin, aroused by the birds, read again in the *Outline of History* until the maid brought her tea. She wondered if the afternoon would be rainy or fine, for this was the day of the pageant to raise funds for installing electric lights in the village church. Later she went to early service. Old Bartholomew walked with his Afghan hound on the terrace where his grandson George was bent over a cluster of flowers. When the old man folded his newspaper into a cone to cover his nose and jumped suddenly at the boy, George began to cry. Bartholomew grumbled that his grandson was a crybaby and went back to his paper. From her window Isa looked out at her son and the baby, Caro, in her perambulator that a nurse was pushing. Then she went off to order the fish for lunch. She read in Bartholomew's discarded newspaper the story of an attempted assault on a girl in the barracks at Whitehall. Returning from church, Mrs. Swithin tacked another placard on the barn where the pageant would be given if the day turned out rainy; regardless of the weather, tea would also be served there during the intermission. Mocked again by her brother, she went off to make sandwiches for the young men and women who were decorating the barn.

Giles was expected back from London in time for the pageant. The family had just decided not to wait lunch for him when Mrs. Manresa and a young man named William Dodge arrived unexpectedly and uninvited. They had intended, Mrs. Manresa explained, to picnic in the country, but when she saw the Olivers' name on the signpost she had suddenly decided to visit her old friends. Mrs. Manresa, loud, cheerful, vulgar, was a woman of uncertain background married to a wealthy Jew. William Dodge, she said, was an artist. He was, he declared, a clerk. Giles, arriving in the middle of lunch and finding Mrs. Manresa's showy car at the door, was furious; he and Mrs. Manresa had been carrying on an affair. After lunch, on the terrace, he sat hating William Dodge. Finally Mrs. Swithin took pity on the young man's discomfort and took him off to see her brother's collection of pictures. William wanted to tell her that he was married but his child was not his child, that he was a pervert, that her kindness had healed his wretched day; but he could not speak.

The guests, arriving for the pageant, began to fill the chairs set on the lawn, for the afternoon was sunny and clear. Behind the thick bushes that served as a dressing room, Miss La Trobe, the author and director of the pageant, was giving the last instructions to her cast. She was something of a mystery in the village, for no one knew where she came from. There were rumors that she had kept a tea shop, that she had been an actress. Abrupt, restless, she walked about the fields, used strong language, and drank too much at the local pub. She was a frustrated artist. Now she was wondering if her audience would realize that in her pageant she had tried to give unity to English history, to give something of herself as well.

The pageant began. The first scene showed the age of Chaucer, with pilgrims on their way to Canterbury. Eliza Clark, who sold tobacco in the village, appeared in another scene as Queen Elizabeth. Albert, the village idiot, played her court fool. The audience hoped he would not do anything dreadful. In a play performed before Gloriana, Mrs. Otter of the End House played the old crone who had saved the true prince, the supposed beggar who fell in love with the duke's daughter. Then Miss La Trobe's vision of the Elizabethan age ended and it was time for tea during the intermission.

Mrs. Manresa applauded; she had seen herself as Queen Elizabeth and Giles as the hero. Giles glowered. Walking toward the barn, he came on a coiled snake swallowing a toad, and he stamped on them until his tennis shoes were splattered with blood. Isa tried to catch a glimpse of Rupert Haines. Failing, she offered to show William Dodge the greenhouses. They discovered that they could talk frankly, like two strangers drawn together by unhappiness and understanding.

The pageant began again. This time the scene showed the Age of Reason. Once more Miss La Trobe had written a play within a play; the characters had names like Lady Harpy Harraden, Sir Spaniel Lilyliver, Florinda, Valentine, and Sir Smirking Peace-be-with-you-all, a clergyman. After another brief interval, the cast reassembled for a scene from the Victorian Age. Mr. Budge, the publican, was made up as a policeman. Albert was in the hindquarters of a donkey while the rest of the cast pretended to be on a picnic in 1860. Then Mr. Budge announced that the time had come to pack and be gone. When Isa asked Mrs. Swithin what the Victorians were like, the old woman said that they had been like Isa, William Dodge, and herself, only dressed differently.

The terrace stage had been left bare. Suddenly the cast came running from behind the bushes, each holding up a mirror of some kind in which the men and women in the audience saw themselves reflected in self-conscious poses. The time was the present of June, 1939. Swallows were sweeping homeward in the late light. Above them twelve airplanes flying in formation cut across the sky, drowning out all other sounds. The pageant was over, the audience dispersed. Mrs. Manresa and William Dodge drove away in her car. Miss La Trobe went on to the inn. There she drank and saw a vision and tried to find words in which to express it—to make people see once more, as she had tried to do that afternoon.

Darkness fell across the village and the fields. At Pointz Hall the visitors had gone and the family was alone. Bartholomew read the evening paper and drowsed in his chair. Mrs. Swithin took up her *Outline of History* and turned the pages while she thought of mastodons and prehistoric birds. At last she and her brother went off to bed.

Now the true drama of the day was about to begin, ancient as the hills, secret and primitive as the black night outside. Giles and Isa would quarrel, embrace, and sleep. The curtain rose on another scene in the long human drama of enmity, love, and peace.

Critical Evaluation

Between the Acts was completed without final revision before Virginia Woolf's suicide in 1941; in it she returns to the tightly controlled structure, the classical unities of time and place, used before in *Mrs. Dalloway. Between the Acts* takes place all in a single day, the day of the annual village pageant, and in the house or on the grounds of Pointz Hall.

The title suggests the book's three levels of meaning. *Between the Acts* refers first of all to events, relationships, and conversation taking place between the acts of the village pageant. Second, it refers to that precarious time between the two world wars. Third, the story occurs between the times when Giles and Isa truly communicate. Significantly, the novel's last lines are: "Then the curtain rose. They spoke."

Miss La Trobe, director of the pageant and probably a lesbian, is the one character who has contact with all others; she, with her pageant of English history, provides another unity to the work. She is, as well, a representative of Virginia Woolf's ideal of the androgynous artist, a creator who is "womanmanly."

The impending war, although seldom directly spoken of, is always in the background in the novel, referred to briefly in spectators' conversation and more directly in the sound of airplanes at the end. British civilization, celebrated in the pageant, is what may be lost in the coming battles. The last war had fragmented mankind both socially and psychologically; now the spectators see themselves in the mirrors held by the actors as somewhat fragmented. For a moment, however, Miss La Trobe creates a unity in the audience by means of music; a state of harmony is reached wherein male and female, the one and the many, the silent and the speaking are joined. Such a unity Woolf is always searching for in her art, a way to reconcile opposites.

Bibliography

Alexander, Jean. *The Venture of Form in the Novels of Virginia Woolf.* Port Washington, N.Y.: Kennikat, 1974, pp. 200–220.

Basham, C. *"Between the Acts,"* in *Durham University Journal.* LIII (March, 1960), pp. 87–94. Reprinted in *Critics on Virginia Woolf: Readings in Literary Criticism.* Edited by Jacqueline E.M. Latham. Coral Gables, Fla.: University of Miami Press, 1970, pp. 106–114.

Bazin, Nancy Topping. *Virginia Woolf and the Androgynous Vision.* New Brunswick, N.J.: Rutgers University Press, 1973, pp. 191–222.

Bennett, Joan Frankau. *Virginia Woolf.* Cambridge: Cambridge University Press, 1945, pp. 112–131.

Blackstone, Bernard. *Virginia Woolf.* New York: Harcourt, Brace, 1949, pp. 232–242.

Brewster, Dorothy. *Virginia Woolf.* New York: New York University Press, 1962, pp. 151–160.

Chambers, R.L. *The Novels of Virginia Woolf.* London: Oliver and Boyd, 1947, pp. 46–51.

Daiches, David. *Virginia Woolf.* New York: New Directions, 1963, pp. 121–129.

Fleishman, Avrom. *Virginia Woolf: A Critical Study.* Baltimore: Johns Hopkins, 1975, pp. 202–219.

Guiguet, Jean. *Virginia Woolf and Her Works.* New York: Harcourt, Brace, and World, 1965, pp. 319–329.

Hafley, James. *The Glass Roof: Virginia Woolf as Novelist.* Berkeley: University of California Press, 1954, pp. 146–161.

Johnson, Manly. *Virginia Woolf.* New York: Frederick Ungar, 1973, pp. 103–113.

Kelley, Alice van Buren. *The Novels of Virginia Woolf: Fact and Vision.* Chicago: University of Chicago Press, 1973, pp. 225–250.

Lee, Hermione. *The Novels of Virginia Woolf.* London: Methuen, 1977, pp. 203–225.

Love, Jean O. *Worlds in Consciousness: Mythopoetic Thought in the Novels of Virginia Woolf.* Berkeley: University of California Press, 1970, pp. 222–237.

McLaurin, Allen. *Virginia Woolf: The Echoes Enslaved.* London: Cambridge University Press, 1973, pp. 49–59.

Naremore, James. *The World Without a Self: Virginia Woolf and the Novel.* New Haven, Conn.: Yale University Press, 1973, pp. 219–239.

Schaefer, Josephine O'Brien. *The Three-Fold Nature of Reality in the Novels of Virginia Woolf.* The Hague: Mouton, 1965, pp. 186–199.

Shanahan, Mary Steussy. *"Between the Acts*: Virginia Woolf's Final Endeavor in Art," in *Texas Studies in Literature and Language.* XIV (1972), pp. 123–138.

Snow, Lotus. "Vision of Design: Virginia Woolf's 'Time Passes' and *Between the Acts,"* in *Research Studies.* XLIV (1976), pp. 24–34.

Summerhayes, Don. "Society, Morality, Analogy: Virginia Woolf's World, *Between the Acts,"* in *Modern Fiction Studies.* IX (Winter, 1964), pp. 329–337.

Thakur, N.C. *The Symbolism of Virginia Woolf.* London: Oxford University Press, 1965, pp. 141–164.

Watkins, R. "Survival in Discontinuity: Virginia Woolf's *Between the Acts,"* in *Massachusetts Review.* X (Spring, 1969), pp. 356–376.

Wilkinson, Ann Y. "A Principle of Unity in *Between the Acts,"* in *Criticism.* VIII (Winter, 1966), pp. 52–63. Reprinted in *Virginia Woolf: A Collection of Critical Essays.* Edited by Claire Sprague. Englewood Cliffs, N.J.: Prentice-Hall, 1971, pp. 145–154.

Zorn, Marilyn. "The Pageant in *Between the Acts,"* in *Modern Fiction Studies.* II (February, 1956), pp. 31–35. Reprinted in *Critics on Virginia Woolf: Readings in Literary Criticism.* Edited by Jacqueline E.M. Latham. Coral Gables, Fla.: University of Miami Press, 1970, pp. 117–119.

MRS. DALLOWAY

Type of work: Novel
Author: Virginia Woolf (1882–1941)
Type of plot: Psychological realism
Time of plot: 1920's
Locale: London
First published: 1925

Mrs. Dalloway *traces a single day in the life of two characters, Clarissa Dalloway and Septimus Smith, largely through their impressions, thoughts, and feelings. For Clarissa the day culminates with a successful party; for Septimus it ends in suicide. In the complex psychological relationship between the two, Virginia Woolf suggests provocative ideas about the nature and meaning of life, love, time, and death.*

Principal Characters

Clarissa Dalloway, a woman fifty-two years old and chic, but disconcerted over life and love. The June day in her late middle years is upsetting to Mrs. Dalloway, uncertain as she is about her daughter and her husband's love, her own feelings for them and her former fiancé, lately returned from India. Years before Peter Walsh had offered her agony and ecstasy, though not comfort or social standing, and so she had chosen Richard Dalloway. Now, seeing Peter for the first time in many years, her belief in her motives and her peace of mind are gone. Engaged in preparations for a party, she knows her life is frivolous, her need for excitement neurotic, and her love dead. Meeting her best friend, Sally Seton, also makes her realize that their love was abnormal as is her daughter's for an older woman. Although she knows that her husband's love for her is very real and solid, she feels that death is near, that growing old is cruel, that life can never be innocently good again.

Richard Dalloway, her politician husband, a Conservative Member of Parliament. Never to be a member of the Cabinet or a Prime Minister, Richard is a good man who has improved his character, his disposition, his life. Loving his wife deeply but silently, he is able only to give her a conventional bouquet of roses to show his feeling, a fortunate gift because roses are the one flower she can stand to see cut. Devoted to his daughter, he sees her infatuation as a passing thing, an adolescent emotional outlet. He is gently persuasive among his constituents and colleagues, and in thought and deed a thoroughly good man.

Peter Walsh, a widower lately returned from India to make arrangements for the divorce of a major's wife, a woman half his age whom he plans to marry, again an action to fill the void left by Clarissa. Perceptive and quick to understand motives for unhappiness, Peter sees his return to England as another step in his failure to live without Clarissa. Unnerved by seeing her again, he blurts out his recent history, and he continues the cruel probe all day and that night at her party.

Septimus Warren Smith, a war casualty who commits suicide on the night of Mrs. Dalloway's party and delays the arrival of one of the guests, a doctor. A poet and a brave man, Septimus brings back to England an Italian war bride whom he cannot really love, all feeling having been drained from him by the trauma of war. Extremely sensitive to motives, to Septimus his doctors represent the world's attempt to crush him, to force him into conventionality. Feeling abandoned and unable to withstand even the devotion of his lovely wife, he jumps to his death, a martyr to the cause of individuality, of sensitivity to feelings and beauty.

Lucrezia Smith, called **Rezia,** the Italian wife whom Smith met in Milan and married after the war. Desperately in love with her husband, she tries to give him back his former confidence in human relations, takes him to doctors for consultation, and hopes to prevent his collapse and suicide.

Elizabeth Dalloway, the daughter who has none of her mother's charm or vivacity and all of her father's steady attributes. Judged to be handsome, the sensible seventeen-year-old appears mature beyond her years; her thoughtfulness directly contradicts her mother's frivolity. She is until this day enamored of Miss Kilman, a desperate and fanatical older woman who is in love with Elizabeth but conceals her feeling under the guise of religiosity and strident charity. On the day of the party Elizabeth sees Miss Kilman's desire for power and escapes from the woman's tyranny of power and need. That night Elizabeth blossoms forth in womanly radiance so apparent that her father fails to recognize his conception of a daughter.

Doris Kilman, Elizabeth Dalloway's tutor and friend, an embittered, frustrated spinster whose religious fanaticism causes her to resent all the things she could not

have or be. With a lucid mind and intense spirit, largely given to deep hatreds of English society, she represents a caricature of womanly love and affection, a perversion.

Lady Rosseter, nee **Sally Seton,** the old friend with whom Mrs. Dalloway had believed herself in love when she was eighteen. Sally has always known that Clarissa made the wrong choice and has always been aware of the shallowness of her friend's existence. Mellowed now, Sally and Peter Walsh can see the pattern of life laid out before them at this gay party, and they console each other for loss of girlhood friend and beloved.

Dr. Holmes, Septimus Smith's physician. Brisk and insensitive, he fails to realize the seriousness of his patient's condition. Puzzled because Smith does not respond to prescriptions of walks in the park, music halls, and bromides at bedtime, he sends him to consult Sir William Bradshaw.

Sir William Bradshaw, a distinguished specialist who devotes three-quarters of an hour to each of his patients. Ambitious for worldly position but apathetic as a healer, he shuts away the mad, forbids childbirth, and advises an attitude of proportion in sickness and in health. Because of Septimus Smith's suicide he and his wife arrive late at Mrs. Dalloway's party.

Lady Millicent Bruton, a fashionable Mayfair hostess. A dabbler in charities and social reform, she is sponsoring a plan to have young men and women emigrate to Canada.

Hugh Whitbread, a friend of the Dalloways and a minor official at Court.

The Story

Mrs. Clarissa Dalloway went to make last-minute preparations for an evening party. During her day in the city she enjoyed the summer air, the many sights and people, the general bustle of London. She met High Whitbread, now a court official, a handsome and sophisticated man. She had known Hugh since her youth, and she knew his wife, Evelyn, as well, but she did not particularly care for Evelyn. Other people came down to London to see paintings, to hear music, or to shop. The Whitbreads came down to consult doctors, for Evelyn was always ailing.

Mrs. Dalloway went about her shopping. While she was in a flower shop, a luxurious limousine pulled up outside. Everyone speculated on the occupant behind the drawn curtains of the car. Everywhere the limousine went, it was followed by curious eyes. Mrs. Dalloway, who had thought that the queen was inside, felt that she was right when the car drove into the Buckingham Palace grounds.

The sights and sounds of London reminded Mrs. Dalloway of many things. She thought back to her youth, to the days before her marriage, to her husband, to her daughter Elizabeth. Her daughter was indeed a problem and all because of the horrid Miss Kilman who was her friend. Miss Kilman was something of a religious fanatic, who scoffed at the luxurious living of the Dalloways and felt sorry for Mrs. Dalloway. Mrs. Dalloway hated her. Miss Kilman was not at all like the friend of her own girlhood. Sally Seton had been different. Mrs. Dalloway had really loved Sally.

Mrs. Dalloway wondered what love really was. She had loved Sally, but she had loved Richard Dalloway and Peter Walsh, too. She had married Richard, and then Peter had left for India. Later she learned that he had married someone he met on shipboard. She had heard little about his wife since his marriage. But the day was wonderful and life itself was wonderful. The war was over and she was giving a party.

While Mrs. Dalloway was shopping, Septimus Smith and his wife were sitting in the park. Septimus had married Lucrezia while he was serving in Italy, and she had given up her family and her country for him. Now he frightened her because he acted so queerly and talked of committing suicide. The doctor said that there was nothing wrong with him, nothing wrong physically. Septimus, one of the first to volunteer for war duty, had gone to war to save his country, the England of Shakespeare. When he got back, he was a war hero and he was given a good job at the office. They had nice lodgings and Lucrezia was happy. Septimus began reading Shakespeare again. He was unhappy; he brooded. He and Lucrezia had no children. To Septimus the world was in such horrible condition that it was unjust to bring children into it.

When Septimus began to have visitations from Evans, a comrade who had been killed in the war, Lucrezia became even more frightened and she called in Dr. Holmes. Septimus felt almost completely abandoned by that time. Lucrezia could not understand why her husband did not like Dr. Holmes, for he was so kind, so much interested in Septimus. Finally she took her husband to Sir William Bradshaw, a wealthy and noted psychiatrist. Septimus had had a brilliant career ahead of him. His employer spoke highly of his work. No one knew why he wanted to kill himself. Septimus said that he had committed a crime, but his wife said that he was guilty of absolutely nothing. Sir William suggested a place in the country, where Septimus would be by himself, without his wife. It was not, Sir William said, a question of preference. Since he had threatened suicide, it was a question of law.

In the meantime Mrs. Dalloway returned home. Lady Bruton had invited Richard Dalloway to lunch. Mrs. Dalloway had never liked Millicent Bruton; she was far too clever. Then Peter Walsh came to call, and Mrs. Dalloway was surprised and happy to see him again. She introduced him to her Elizabeth. He asked Mrs. Dalloway if she were happy; she wondered why. When he left, she called out to him not to forget her party. Peter thought, Clarissa Dalloway and her parties! That was all life meant to her. He had been divorced from his wife and had come to England. For him, life was far more complicated. He had fallen in love with another woman, one who had two children, and he had come to London to arrange for her divorce and to get some sort of a job. He hoped Hugh Whitbread would find him one, something in the government.

That night Clarissa Dalloway's party was a great success. At first she was afraid that it would fail. But at last the prime minister arrived and her evening was complete. Peter was there, and Peter met Lady Rossetter. Lady Rossetter turned out to be Sally Seton. She had not been invited, but had just dropped in. She had five sons, she told Peter. They chatted. Then Elizabeth came in and Peter noticed how beautiful she was.

Later, Sir William Bradshaw and his wife entered. They were late, they explained, because one of Sir William's patients had committed suicide. For Septimus Smith, feeling altogether abandoned, had jumped out of a window before they could take him into the country. Clarissa was upset. Here was death, she thought. Although the suicide was completely unknown to her, she somehow felt it was her own disaster, her own disgrace. The poor young man had thrown away his life when it became useless. Clarissa had never thrown away anything more valuable than a shilling into the Serpentine. Yes, once she had stood beside a fountain while Peter Walsh, angry and humiliated, had asked her whether she intended to marry Richard. And Richard had never been prime minister. Instead, the prime minister came to her parties. Now she was growing old. Clarissa Dalloway knew herself at last for the beautiful, charming, inconsequential person she was.

Sally and Peter talked on. They thought idly of Clarissa and Richard, and wondered whether they were happy together. Sally agreed that Richard had improved. She left Peter and went to talk with Richard. Peter was feeling strange. A sort of terror and ecstasy took hold of him, and he could not be certain what it was that excited him so suddenly. It was Clarissa, he thought. Even after all these years, it must be Clarissa.

Critical Evaluation

Mrs. Dalloway comes midway in Virginia Woolf's fiction-writing career, and near the beginning of her experiments with form and technique (just after *Jacob's Room,* her first experimental novel). The book is really two stories—Clarissa Dalloway's and Septimus Smith's—and the techniques by which Woolf united these two narrative strands are unusual and skillful. While writing the novel, Woolf commented in her diary on her new method of delineating character. Instead of explaining the characters' pasts chronologically, she uses a "tunnelling process": "I dig out beautiful caves behind my characters." The various characters appear in the present without explanation; various sense impressions—a squeaky hinge, a repeated phrase, a particular tree—call to their minds a memory and past becomes present. Such an evocation of the past is reminiscent of Proust, but Woolf's method does not involve the ego of the narrator. Woolf's "caves" reveal the past and at the same time give characters' reactions to present events. Woolf is then able to connect the "caves" and also her themes by structural techniques, both spatial and temporal.

Unlike that of James Joyce, Woolf's handling of the stream-of-consciousness method is always filtered and indirect; the narrator is in command, telling the reader, "Clarissa thought" or "For so it had always seemed to her." This ever-present narrative voice generally helps the reader by clarifying the characters' inner thoughts and mediating the commentary of the novel although, at times, it blurs the identity of the speaker. Woolf's use of the "voice" becomes more prominent in *To the Lighthouse* (1927), but disappears in *The Waves* (1931).

The structure of the book seems at first to lack unity, with its disparate characters and various scenes of street life. But Woolf uses many devices, both technical and thematic, to unite those elements. The day (in mid-June, 1923), moving uninterruptedly from the early morning to the late evening, is a single whole. Although the book is not divided into chapters or sections headed by titles or numbers, Woolf notes *some* of the shifts in time or scene by a short blank space in the manuscript. More often, however, the transition from one group of characters to another is accomplished by the remarking of something public, something common to the experience of both, something seen or heard. The world of Clarissa and her friends alternates with the world of Septimus Smith; and the sight of the motor car, the sight and sound of the skywriting plane, the running child, the woman singing, the omnibus, the ambulance, and the clock striking are the transitions connecting those two worlds. Moreover, the striking of the clocks ("first a warning, musical; then the hour, irrevocable") is noted at various other times to mark a shift from one character's consciousness to another within Clarissa's group. The exact time is given periodically, signaling the day's progress (noon comes at almost the exact center of the book) and stressing the irrevocable movement towards death, one of the book's themes. Usually at least two clocks are described as striking—first Big Ben, a masculine symbol; then a few seconds later, St. Margaret's, a feminine symbol, suggesting again the two genders of all existence, united in the echoes of the bells, "the leaden circles."

The main thematic devices used to unify the book are the similarity between Clarissa and Septimus, and the repetition of key words and phrases in the minds of various characters. The likeness between Clarissa and Septimus is most important, as each helps to explain the other, although they never meet. Both are lonely and contemplate suicide. Both feel guilty for their past lives, Septimus because he "cannot feel" the death of Evans, Clarissa because of her rejection of Peter and her tendency to dominate others. Both have homosexual feelings, Septimus for Evans, Clarissa for Sally Seton. More importantly, both want desperately to bring order out of life's chaos. Septimus achieves this momentarily with the making of Mrs. Peters' hat, and Clarissa creates a harmonious unity with her successful party. Septimus understands that the chaos will return and so takes his own life uniting himself with Death, the final order. Septimus' suicide forces Clarissa to see herself in a new and honest way, understanding for the first time her schemings for success. Clarissa "felt somehow very like him"; she does not pity him but identifies with his defiant "embracing" of death.

Certain phrases become thematic because they are so often repeated, gaining richer overtones of meaning at each use, as different characters interpret the phrases differently. "Fear no more," "if it were now to die," the sun, the waves—these are some of the phrases and images appearing over and over, especially in the thoughts of Septimus and Clarissa.

All the disparate strands of the story are joined at Clarissa's party, over which she presides like an artist over his creation. Not inferior to the painter Lily Briscoe as a creator, Clarissa's great talent is "knowing people almost by instinct," and she is able triumphantly to combine the right group of people at her party. Not only Clarissa, but Richard and Peter also come to a new realization about themselves at the party. Richard, who has been unable to verbalize his love for Clarissa, is finally able to tell his daughter Elizabeth he is proud of her. Peter realizes at the end that the terror and excitement he feels in Clarissa's presence indicate his true feeling for her.

The two figures who are given unfavorable treatment—Sir William, the psychiatrist, and Miss Kilman, the religious fanatic—insist on modes of existence inimical to the passionate desire of Clarissa and Septimus for wholeness. Claiming that Septimus "lacks proportion," Sir William nevertheless uses his profession to gain power over others and, as Clarissa understands, makes life "intolerable" for Septimus. Miss Kilman's life is built on evangelical religion; she feels herself better than Clarissa, whom she wants to humiliate. She proudly asserts that she will have a "religious victory," which will be "God's will."

The real action of the story is all within the minds of the characters, but Woolf gives these inner lives a reality and harmony which reveals the excitement and oneness of human existence. Clarissa and Septimus are really two aspects of the same being—the feminine and the masculine—united in Clarissa's ultimate awareness. *Mrs. Dalloway* remains the best introduction to Woolf's characteristic style and themes.

Bibliography

Alexander, Jean. *The Venture of Form in the Novels of Virginia Woolf.* Port Washington, N.Y.: Kennikat, 1974, pp. 85–104.

Bazin, Nancy Topping. *Virginia Woolf and the Androgynous Vision.* New Brunswick, N.J.: Rutgers University Press, 1973, pp. 102–123.

Benjamin, Anna S. "Towards an Understanding of the Meaning of Virginia Woolf's *Mrs. Dalloway,*" in *Wisconsin Studies in Contemporary Literature.* VI (Summer, 1965), pp. 214–227.

Blackstone, Bernard. *Virginia Woolf.* New York: Harcourt, Brace, 1949, pp. 71–98.

Daiches, David. *Virginia Woolf.* New York: New Directions, 1963, pp. 61–78. Reprinted in *Critiques and Essays on Modern Fiction, 1920–1951.* Edited by John W. Aldridge. New York: Ronald Press, 1952, pp. 497–502.

Fleishman, Avrom. *Virginia Woolf: A Critical Study.* Baltimore: Johns Hopkins University Press, 1975, pp. 69–95.

Friedman, Ralph. *The Lyrical Novel: Studies in Hermann Hesse, André Gide, and Virginia Woolf.* Princeton, N.J.: Princeton University Press, 1963, pp. 213–226.

Guiguet, Jean. *Virginia Woolf and Her Works.* New York: Harcourt, Brace, 1965, pp. 227–260.

Hafley, James. *The Glass Roof: Virginia Woolf as Novelist.* Berkeley: University of California Press, 1954, pp. 60–76.

Hawthorn, Jeremy. *Virginia Woolf's* Mrs. Dalloway: *A Study in Alienation.* London: Chatto and Windus, 1975.

Holtby, Winifred. *Virginia Woolf.* London: Wishart, 1932, pp. 137–160.

Johnson, Manly. *Virginia Woolf.* New York: Frederick Ungar, 1973, pp. 52–63.

Karl, Frederick R. and Marvin Magalaner. *A Reader's Guide to Great Twentieth Century English Novels.* New York: Noonday, 1959, pp. 128–149.

Kelley, Alice van Buren. *The Novels of Virginia Woolf: Fact and Vision.* Chicago: University of Chicago Press, 1973, pp. 88–113.

Lee, Hermione. *The Novels of Virginia Woolf.* London: Methuen, 1977, pp. 91–115.

McLaurin, Allen. *Virginia Woolf: The Echoes Enslaved.* London: Cambridge University Press, 1973, pp. 38–44, 66–69, 149–157.

Markovic, Vida E. *The Changing Face: Disintegration of Personality in the Twentieth Century British Novel, 1900–1950.* Carbondale: Southern Illinois University Press, 1970, pp. 54–69.

Mollach, Francis L. "Thematic and Structural Unity in *Mrs. Dalloway*," in *Thoth.* V (Winter, 1964), pp. 62–73.

Moody, A.D. "*Mrs. Dalloway* as Comedy," in *Virginia Woolf.* Edinburgh: Oliver and Boyd, 1963, pp. 19–25. Partly reprinted in *Critics on Virginia Woolf: Readings in Literary Criticism.* Edited by Jacqueline E.M. Latham. Coral Gables, Fla.: University of Miami Press, 1970, pp. 48–51.

Naremore, James. *The World Without a Self: Virginia Woolf and the Novel.* New Haven, Conn.: Yale University Press, 1973, pp. 77–111.

Rackman, Shalom. "Clarissa's Attic: Virginia Woolf's *Mrs. Dalloway* Reconsidered," in *Twentieth Century Literature.* XVIII (1972), pp. 3–18.

Samuelson, Ralph. "The Theme of *Mrs. Dalloway*," in *Chicago Review.* XI (Winter, 1958), pp. 57–76.

Schaefer, Josephine O'Brien. *The Three-Fold Nature of Reality in the Novels of Virginia Woolf.* The Hague: Mouton, 1965, pp. 85–109.

Schlack, Beverly Ann. "A Freudian Look at *Mrs. Dalloway*," in *Literature and Psychology.* XXIII (1973), pp. 49–58.

Thakur, N.C. *The Symbolism of Virginia Woolf.* London: Oxford University Press, 1965, pp. 55–71.

TO THE LIGHTHOUSE

Type of work: Novel
Author: Virginia Woolf (1882–1941)
Type of plot: Psychological realism
Time of plot: c. 1910–1920
Locale: The Isle of Skye in the Hebrides
First published: 1927

> *This major psychological novel, based in part upon the author's own family background, is significant for its impressionistic evocation of setting and character; its effective use of stream-of-consciousness technique; its complex, unified structure; and its advancement of Woolf's theory of androgynous personality.*

Principal Characters

Mr. Ramsay, a professor of philosophy, a metaphysician of high order, an author, and the father of eight. Not really first-rate, as he realized by the time he was sixty, he knew also that his mind was still agile, his ability to abstract strong. Loved by his wife, he is nonetheless offered sympathy and consolation for the things he is not. Lithe, trim, the very prototype of the philosopher, he attracts many people to him and uses their feelings to buoy him in his weaknesses. Not truly a father, his gift for the ironic and sardonic arouses fear and hatred rather than respect among his children. Broken by his wife's and oldest son's deaths, he continues to endure and to sharpen his mind on the fine whetstone of wit.

Mrs. Ramsay, a beautiful woman even in her aging; she is warm, compassionate, and devoted to the old-fashioned virtues of hearth, husband, and children. With an aura of graciousness and goodness about her, ineffable but pervasive, Mrs. Ramsay gathers about her guests, students, friends, and family at their summer home on the Isle of Skye. Loving and tender to her children, polite and pleasant to her guests, she impresses upon them all the sanctity of life and marriage, the elemental virtues. Her love and reverence of life have its effect on all her guests, even an atheistic student of her husband and an aloof poet. Mostly she affects women, especially worshiping Lily Briscoe, with the need to throw oneself into life, not to limit life but to live it, especially through motherhood.

James, the Ramsays' youngest son and his mother's favorite, though the child most criticized by the professor because the boy robs him of sympathy that he desperately needs. Sensitive and austere, James at six and sixteen suffers most the loss of his mother, taken from him at first by a calculating father's demands and later by her death. He and his sister Camilla make a pact of war against their father's tyranny of demands and oversights. Finally, on a trip to the lighthouse, the symbol of what had been denied him by his father, Mr. Ramsay praises his son's seamanship.

Prue, who dies in childbirth,
Andrew, killed in World War I,
Nancy,

Roger,
Rose,
Jasper, and
Camilla, called Cam, the other children of Mr. and Mrs. Ramsay. All the children resent their father and his dominance. Mrs. Ramsay regrets that they must grow up because of the loss of sensitivity and imagination that will come with adulthood.

Lily Briscoe, an artist and friend of the family who more than any other loved and cared for the weeks spent with the Ramsays in the Hebrides. Desperately in need of assurance, Lily has withheld love and affection from others until the summer she spends at the Ramsay cottage where she observes life with its fixed center and raw edges. Completely won over by Mrs. Ramsay, Lily almost gets her chance at life, and had the war not interfered she might have married. She is not really a great artist, but during a visit to the Ramsay home after the war she experiences a moment of fulfilled vision, a feeling of devotion to the oldest cause, of a sense of oneness with all time, of sympathy for the human condition, and she is able to express this fleeting moment in a painting she had begun before Mrs. Ramsay's death.

Augustus Carmichael, a minor poet with one major success, a hanger-on, the only one who does not at first love his hostess but who finally discovers her genius years after her death. Laughed at by all the Ramsay children because of his yellow-tinted beard, the result of taking opium, as they imagine, he soaks up love and life without himself giving anything. His late fame as a poet is a surprise to all who know him.

Minta Doyle and
Paul Rayley, two handsome guests who become engaged through Mrs. Ramsay's quiet management. Minta is like the young Mrs. Ramsay and sends out an aura of love and passion, while Paul, with his good looks and careful dress, is a foil for all affections and strong feelings. But the marriage turns out badly; Minta leads her own life and Paul takes a mistress. No longer lovers, they can afford to be friends.

William Bankes, a botanist, the oldest friend of Professor Ramsay. An aging widower, he first comes to visit with the Ramsays out of a sense of duty, but he stays on enraptured with life. The object of Lily Briscoe's undisguised affections, he appears to Mrs. Ramsay almost willing to become domesticated in spite of his eccentricities and set ways. Nothing comes of this relationship except a broadening of Lily's views on life.

Charles Tansley, Mr. Ramsay's protégé, a boorish young man who eventually is won over to the warmth and love of Mrs. Ramsay. It is his opinionated conviction that women cannot paint or write. Interested in abstract thought, he makes his career in scholarship.

Mrs. McNab, the old charwoman who acts as caretaker of the Ramsay house in the Hebrides during the ten years it stands empty.

Mrs. Bast, the cottager who helps Mrs. McNab get the house ready for the return of the Ramsay family.

George Bast, her son, who catches the rats and cuts the grass surrounding the Ramsay house.

Macalister, the aged Scottish boatman who takes Mr. Ramsay, Cam, and James on an expedition to the lighthouse. He tells the voyagers tales of winter, storm, and death.

The Story

Mrs. Ramsay promised James, her six-year-old son, that if the next day were fair he would be taken on a visit to the lighthouse they could see from the window of their summer home on the Isle of Skye. James, the youngest of Mrs. Ramsay's eight children, was his mother's favorite. The father of the family was a professor of philosophy whose students often thought that he was inspiring and one of the foremost metaphysicians of the early twentieth century: but his own children, particularly the youngest, did not like him because he made sarcastic remarks.

Several guests were visiting the Ramsays at the time. There was young Mr. Tansley, Ramsay's student, who was also unpopular with the children because he seemed to delight in their discomfiture. Tansley was mildly in love with his hostess, in spite of her fifty years and her eight children. There was Lily Briscoe, who was painting a picture of the cottage with Mrs. Ramsay and little James seated in front of it. There was old Mr. Carmichael, a ne'er-do-well who amused the Ramsay youngsters because he had a white beard and a mustache tinged with yellow. There was also William Bankes, an aging widower, and Pure, the prettiest of the Ramsay daughters.

The afternoon went by slowly. Mrs. Ramsay went to the village to call on a sick woman. She spent several hours knitting stockings for the lighthouse keeper's child, whom they were planning to visit. Many people wondered how the Ramsays, particularly the wife, managed to be as hospitable and as charitable as they were, for they were not rich: Mr. Ramsay could not possibly make a fortune by expounding Locke, Berkeley, and Hume to students or by publishing books on metaphysics.

Mr. Carmichael, pretending to read, had actually fallen asleep early after lunch. The children, except for James, who was busy cutting pictures out of a catalogue, had busied themselves in a game of cricket. Mr. Ramsay and Mr. Tansley had passed the time in a pointless conversation. Miss Briscoe had only made a daub or two of paint on her canvas. For some reason the lines of the scene refused to come clear in her painting. She then went for a walk with Mr. Bankes along the shore.

Even the dinner went by slowly. The only occasion of interest to the children, which was one of tension to their mother, came when Mr. Carmichael asked the maid for a second bowl of soup, thereby angering his host, who liked to have meals dispatched promptly. As soon as the children had finished, their mother sent the younger ones to bed. Mrs. Ramsay hoped that Mr. Bankes would marry Lily Briscoe. Lily always became seasick, so it was questionable whether she would want to accompany them in the small sailboat if they should go to the lighthouse the following day. She thought also about the fifty pounds needed to make some necessary repairs on the house.

After dinner Mrs. Ramsay went upstairs to the nursery. James had a boar's skull which his sister detested. Whenever Camilla tried to remove it from the wall and her sight, he burst into a frenzy of screaming. Mrs. Ramsay wrapped the boar's skull in her shawl. Afterward she went downstairs and joined her husband in the library, where they sat throughout the evening, she knitting and Mr. Ramsay reading. Before they went to bed it was agreed that the trip for the next day would have to be canceled. The night had turned stormy.

Night followed night. The trip to the lighthouse was never made that summer, nor did the Ramsays return to their summer home for some years. In the meantime Mrs. Ramsay died quietly in her sleep. Her daughter Prue by now had gotten married and had died in childbirth. The first World War began. Andrew Ramsay enlisted and was sent to France, where he was killed by an exploding shell.

Time passed. The wallpaper in the house came loose from the walls. Books mildewed. In the kitchen a cup was occasionally knocked down and broken by old Mrs. McNab, who came to look after the house from time to time. In the garden the roses and the annual flowers grew wild or died.

Mr. Carmichael brought out a volume of poems during the war. About the time his book appeared, daffodils and violets bloomed on the Isle of Skye. Mrs. McNab looked longingly at a warm cloak left in a closet. She wished the cloak belonged to her.

At last the war ended. Mrs. McNab received a telegram requesting that the house be put in order. For several days the housekeeper worked, aided by two cleaning women, and when the Ramsays arrived the cottage was in order once more. Several visitors came again to share a summer at the cottage. Lily Briscoe returned for a quiet vacation. Mr. Carmichael, the successful poet, also arrived.

One morning Lily Briscoe came down to breakfast and wondered at the quiet which greeted her. No one had been down ahead of her, although she had expected that Mr. Ramsay and the two youngest children, James and Camilla, would have eaten early and departed for the long-postponed sail to the lighthouse, to which the youngsters had not been looking forward with joyful anticipation. Very shortly the three straggled down, all having slept past the time they had intended to arise. After a swift breakfast they disappeared toward the shore, their going watched by Lily Briscoe, who had set up her canvas with the intention of once again trying to paint her picture of the cottage.

The journey to the island where the lighthouse stood was not very pleasant, as the children had expected. They had never really liked their father: he had taken too little time to understand them. He was short and sharp when they did things which seemed foolish to him, though those actions were perfectly comprehensible to his son and daughter. James, especially, expected to be blamed caustically and pointlessly if the crossing were slow or not satisfactory in some other way, for he had been delegated to handle the sheets and the tiller of the boat.

Mr. Ramsay strode down to the beach with his offspring, each carrying a paper parcel to take to the keepers of the lighthouse. They soon set sail and pointed the prow of the sailboat toward the black and white striped pillar of the lighthouse in the hazy distance. Mr. Ramsay sat in the middle of the boat, along with an old

To the Lighthouse / WOOLF

fisherman and his son. They were to take over the boat in case of an emergency, for Mr. Ramsay had little trust in James as a reliable seaman. In the stern sat James himself, nerves tingling lest his father look up from his book and indulge in unnecessary and hateful criticism. But his nervous tension was needless, for within a few hours the little party reached the lighthouse, and, wonderful to relate, Mr. Ramsay sprang ashore like a youngster, smiled back at his children, and praised his son for his seamanship.

Critical Evaluation

Because of its unity of theme and technique, *To the Lighthouse* is probably Virginia Woolf's most satisfying novel. In theme, it is her most direct fictional statement about the importance of an androgynous artistic vision: that ideal which is neither masculine nor feminine but partakes of both. The book was almost contemporaneous with her important essay on women and fiction, *A Room of One's Own,* and *Orlando,* her androgynous fictional biography. In *A Room of One's Own* she appeals for androgynous creation, arguing that it is fatal for a writer to emphasize gender. For her, the mind which blends female and male themes "is naturally creative, incandescent and undivided." Many of her protagonists and most of the artists in her novels have both traditional "masculine" and "feminine" characteristics: Bernard in *The Waves,* Eleanor in *The Years,* Miss La Trobe in *Between the Acts,* and Lily Briscoe in *To the Lighthouse.* They have androgynous *consciousness,* even as Orlando completes the *physical* change from male to female.

To the Lighthouse clearly shows the deficiencies of the purely masculine (Mr. Ramsay) and the purely feminine (Mrs. Ramsay) personalities, and, as well, holds up the androgynous vision as a means of unifying the two—in the person of Lily Briscoe, the artist. Mr. Ramsay, a philosopher, has those qualities associated with the empirico-theoretical view, while Mrs. Ramsay employs a mythopoetic vision. Mr. Ramsay is concerned with the discovery of Truth, and his mind functions in a logical, reasoned fashion, moving, as he says, from A to Z, step by step. He worries that he has only so far reached Q. Mrs. Ramsay cares about details, about people's feelings, about her relationship with her husband and children; and her mind jumps and skips with the association of ideas—she can move from A to Z in one leap.

Mr. Ramsay is deficient in the attention he gives to his children and his wife, in concern for important financial details, in awareness of social and international situations. His character is satirized by Lily who always pictures him as seeing the whole of reality in a phantom kitchen table (the table is a traditional object for philosophic speculation). Mrs. Ramsay too is lacking: she attempts to direct and fashion people's lives (she engineers the engagement of Minta and Paul and tries to match Lily Briscoe and William Bankes);

she does not want her children to grow up; she cannot understand mathematics or history; she too often relies on men and their "masculine intelligence." The dinner scene shows Mrs. Ramsay's main strengths and weaknesses. She orchestrates the whole, directs the conversation, worries about the *Boeuf en Daube,* thinks about the lateness of the hour, makes sure all the guests are involved. Yet she lets her mind wander, looking ahead to the next details. She is the unifier in the first part of the book, but she fails because her vision is too limited; the trip to the lighthouse is not made, and she dies before the Ramsays can return to the island.

Lily Briscoe and her art become the true unifier of the story's disparate elements. During the dinner party, as she remembers Charles Tansley's dictum that "Women can't write, women can't paint," she suddenly envisions the way to give her picture coherence, and she moves the salt cellar to remind herself. But her painting remains incomplete, and, like the trip to the lighthouse, is not accomplished until many years later. Lily, an unmarried professional, embodies both rational (masculine) and imaginative (feminine) characteristics. She analyzes art with William Bankes and still feels emotionally attuned with Mrs. Ramsay. Lily becomes the central figure in the final section; her visions of Mrs. Ramsay and of Mr. Ramsay and the children finally landing at the lighthouse enable her to complete her work, uniting the rational and the imaginative into the androgynous whole which the painting symbolizes.

The novel's structure is thematically as well as technically brilliant. The work has three parts; the first, entitled "The Window," takes place about 1910, the last, entitled "The Lighthouse," about 1920. The middle section is entitled "Time Passes" and narrates the intervening time period. The window in the first section functions as a symbol of the female principle, as the narrator returns again and again to Mrs. Ramsay in her place near the open window. Mrs. Ramsay is the center and unifier of the family, and even as different characters participate in various activities, their thoughts and glances return to Mrs. Ramsay. The reddish-brown stocking she is knitting is another emblem of her unifying power. But, like the trip to the lighthouse and Lily's painting, it is not completed in the first section. The thoughts of different characters are narrated by means of interior monologue, and Woolf makes skillful use of the theory of association of ideas. Mrs. Ramsay's mind is most often viewed, however, and she is the most real of the characters.

Early in the novel, the lighthouse, in its faraway light-giving aspects, functions as a female symbol. Mrs. Ramsay identifies herself with the lighthouse: "she was stern, she was searching, she was beautiful like that light." In the last section, however, the lighthouse becomes a masculine principle; when seen from nearby it is a "tower, stark and straight . . . barred with black and white." But the male and female aspects become joined in that section as well; James thinks, "For nothing was simply one thing. The other Lighthouse was true too." So James and Cam come to understand their father as well as their dead mother. The line that Lily Briscoe draws in the center of her picture—perhaps her image of the lighthouse—enables her to complete her painting, uniting both the masculine and the feminine.

The center section, "Time Passes," is narrated from the viewpoint of the house itself, as the wind over the years peels wallpaper; rusts pots; brings mildew, dust, spider webs, and rats. Important events in the lives of the Ramsays are inserted into this poetic interlude prosaically by means of square brackets.

To the Lighthouse is a difficult work, but each successive reading brings new insights into Woolf's techniques and themes.

Bibliography

Alexander, Jean. *The Venture of Form in the Novels of Virginia Woolf.* Port Washington, N.Y.: Kennikat, 1974, pp. 104–126.

Bazin, Nancy Topping. *Virginia Woolf and the Androgynous Vision.* New Brunswick, N.J.: Rutgers University Press, 1973, pp. 124–138.

Blackstone, Bernard. *Virginia Woolf.* New York: Harcourt, Brace, 1949, pp. 99–130.

Cohn, Ruby. "Art in *To the Lighthouse*," in *Modern Fiction Studies.* VIII (Summer, 1962), pp. 127–136. Reprinted in *Virginia Woolf: A Collection of Criticism.* Edited by Thomas S.W. Lewis. New York: McGraw-Hill, 1975, pp. 63–72.

Daiches, David. *Virginia Woolf.* New York: New Directions, 1963, pp. 79–96. Partly reprinted in *Critics on Virginia Woolf: Readings in Literary Criticism.* Edited by Jacqueline E.M. Latham. Coral Gables, Fla.: University of Miami Press, 1970, pp. 70–71. Reprinted in *Twentieth Century Interpretations of* To the Lighthouse*: A Collection of Critical Essays.* Edited by Thomas A. Vogler. Englewood Cliffs, N.J.: Prentice-Hall, 1970, pp. 58–69.

Drew, Elizabeth. *The Novel: A Modern Guide to Fifteen English Masterpieces.* New York: Norton, 1963, pp. 262–279. Partly reprinted in *Twentieth Century Interpretations of* To the Lighthouse*: A Collection of Critical Essays.* Edited by Thomas A. Vogler. Englewood Cliffs, N.J.: Prentice-Hall, 1970, pp. 100–101.

Edel, Leon J. *The Psychological Novel, 1900–1950.* Philadelphia: J.B. Lippincott, 1955, pp. 195–201.

Fleishman, Avrom. *Virginia Woolf: A Critical Study.* Baltimore: Johns Hopkins University Press, 1975, pp. 96–134.

Friedman, Ralph. *The Lyrical Novel: Studies in Hermann Hesse, André Gide, and Virginia Woolf.* Princeton, N.J.: Princeton University Press, 1963, pp. 226–243.

Guiguet, Jean. *Virginia Woolf and Her Works.* New York: Harcourt, Brace, 1965, pp. 248–260. Reprinted in *Twentieth Century Interpretations of To the Lighthouse: A Collection of Critical Essays.* Edited by Thomas A. Vogler. Englewood Cliffs, N.J.: Prentice-Hall, 1970, pp. 82–94.

Hafley, James. *The Glass Roof: Virginia Woolf as Novelist.* Berkeley: University of California Press, 1954, pp. 77–92.

Holtby, Winifred. *Virginia Woolf.* London: Wishart, 1932, pp. 137–160.

Johnson, Manly. *Virginia Woolf.* New York: Frederick Ungar, 1973, pp. 66–76.

Karl, Frederick R. and Marvin Magalaner. *A Reader's Guide to Great Twentieth Century English Novels.* New York: Noonday, 1959, pp. 128–149.

Kelley, Alice van Buren. *The Novels of Virginia Woolf: Fact and Vision.* Chicago: University of Chicago Press, 1973, pp. 114–143.

Leaska, Mitchell A. *Virginia Woolf's* Lighthouse*: A Study in Critical Method.* New York: Columbia University Press, 1970, pp. 47–164.

Lee, Hermione. *The Novels of Virginia Woolf.* London: Methuen, 1977, pp. 116–137.

Love, Jean O. *Worlds in Consciousness: Mythopoetic Thought in the Novels of Virginia Woolf.* Berkeley: University of California Press, 1970, pp. 161–179, 180–194.

McLaurin, Allen. *Virginia Woolf: The Echoes Enslaved.* London: Cambridge University Press, 1973, pp. 177–206.

Naremore, James. *The World Without a Self: Virginia Woolf and the Novel.* New Haven, Conn.: Yale University Press, 1973, pp. 112–150.

Proudfit, S.W. "Lily Briscoe's Painting: A Key to Personal Relationships in *To the Lighthouse*," in *Criticism.* XIII (Winter, 1971), pp. 26–38.

Richter, Harvena. *Virginia Woolf: The Inward Voyage.* Princeton, N.J.: Princeton University Press, 1970, pp. 180–187, 211–215, 219–226.

Schaefer, Josephine O'Brien. *The Three-Fold Nature of Reality in the Novels of Virginia Woolf.* The Hague: Mouton, 1965, pp. 110–136. Partly reprinted in *Critics on Virginia Woolf: Readings in Literary Criticism.* Edited by Jacqueline E.M. Latham. Coral Gables, Fla: University of Miami Press, 1970, pp. 72–78.

Seltzer, Alvin J. *Chaos in the Novel: The Novel in Chaos.* New York: Schocken, 1974, pp. 120–140.

Thakur, N.C. *The Symbolism of Virginia Woolf.* London: Oxford University Press, 1965, pp. 72–88.

WILLIAM BUTLER YEATS

Born: Sandymount, Ireland (June 13, 1865)
Died: Roquebrune, France (January 28, 1939)

Principal Works

POEMS: *Mosada: A Dramatic Poem*, 1886; *The Wanderings of Oisin*, 1889; *Poems*, 1895; *The Wind Among the Reeds*, 1899; *In the Seven Woods*, 1903; *The Green Helmet and Other Poems*, 1910; *Responsibilites*, 1914; *The Wild Swans at Coole*, 1917; *Michael Robartes and the Dancer*, 1920; *Later Poems*, 1922; *The Cat and the Moon and Certain Poems*, 1924; *The Tower*, 1928; *The Winding Stair*, 1933; *Collected Poems*, 1933; *The King of the Great Clock Tower*, 1934; *A Full Moon in March*, 1935; *New Poems*, 1938; *Last Poems and Plays*, 1940; *Collected Poems*, 1949.

PLAYS: *The Countess Kathleen*, 1892; *The Land of Heart's Desire*, 1894; *The Shadowy Waters*, 1900; *Cathleen ni Houlihan*, 1902; *Where There Is Nothing*, 1902; *The Hour Glass*, 1903; *The Pot of Broth*, 1904; *The King's Threshold*, 1904; *Deirdre*, 1907; *The Unicorn from the Stars and Other Plays*, 1908 (with Lady Gregory); *Plays for an Irish Theatre*, 1911; *Four Plays for Dancers*, 1921; *Wheels and Butterflies*, 1934; *Collected Plays*, 1934; *The Herne's Egg*, 1938; *Collected Plays*, 1952.

SHORT STORIES AND TALES: *The Celtic Twilight*, 1893; *Stories of Red Hanrahan*, 1904.

MEMOIRS: *Reveries Over Childhood and Youth*, 1915; *Four Years*, 1921; *The Trembling of the Veil*, 1922; *Autobiographies*, 1926; *Estrangement*, 1926; *Reflections from a Diary Kept in 1909*, 1926; *The Death of Synge and Other Passages from an Old Diary*, 1928; *Dramatis Personae*, 1936.

ESSAYS: *Ideas of Good and Evil*, 1903; *Discoveries*, 1907; *Poetry and Ireland*, 1908 (with Lionel Johnson); *Synge and the Ireland of His Time*, 1911; *The Cutting of an Agate*, 1912; *Essays*, 1924; *A Vision*, 1925.

LETTERS: *Letters on Poetry to Dorothy Wellesley*, 1940; *Letters to Katharine Tynan*, 1953.

TRANSLATIONS: Sophocles' *King Oedipus*, 1928; *Oedipus at Colonus*, 1934.

William Butler Yeats was born at Sandymount, near Dublin, on June 13, 1865. His father, John Butler Yeats, was an artist of considerable merit who had given up a moderately lucrative law practice in order to devote himself to painting; his mother was a frail, beautiful woman who nurtured in her son a deep love for the "west country" of Ireland that was to last all his life. His early childhood and later vacations were spent there, among the green hills and lakes of Sligo which were to become, in such poems as "The Lake Isle of Innisfree," a symbol of his imaginative escape from the disappointments and unpleasant realities of life.

Much of Yeats's early life was spent in London, but between 1880 and 1887 the family was in Dublin, years which had a lasting effect on the impressionable young poet. Stimulated by his father, who loved to read aloud, Yeats discovered Shakespeare, the Romantic poets, and the Pre-Raphaelites, explored popular works on Eastern mysticism, became interested in Irish myths and folklore, and, perhaps most important, met the poets and intellectuals of the Irish Literary Revival, many of whom were to remain lifelong friends. During the period he made several attempts at poetic drama, but the plays were highly imitative and hopelessly cluttered with magic islands and timid shepherds. Back in London, Yeats embarked on a serious study of Irish folk tales in the British Museum and published his first major poem, *The Wanderings of Oisin*, in 1889. Although the poem is superficially reminiscent of Spenser, Shelley, and his friend William Morris, the Gaelic theme and unorthodox rhythms are characteristic of Yeats's quest for a fresh tradition and an individual style.

There is, however, little that is imitative in poetic plays such as *The Countess Kathleen* and *The Land of Heart's Desire*, or in the lyrics that accompanied the former. The continued use of Irish themes evident in these volumes is indicative of an important and complex aspect of Yeats's early development. In common with the other writers of the nationalistic Irish Literary Revival, he wished to create a literature that was purely Irish in tone and subject matter. As part of the same general movement, he strove to reawaken in his people a sense of the glory and significance of Ireland's historical and legendary past. Furthermore, the remoteness of these Celtic themes was consistent with Yeats's aesthetic theory, later repudiated in part, of the separation of art from life. Finally, Irish folklore offered an answer to his search for a personal and individual mythology, for he found there a treasury of symbols hitherto unused in English poetry. Yeats's tendency to make mythical figures into private symbols was encouraged by his contacts with such Symbolist poets as Arthur Symons and Mallarmé, and by his undisciplined but enthusiastic dabbling in such esoteric subjects as "hermetic" philosophy, astrology, and spiritualism. *The Secret Rose* (1897) and *The Wind Among the Reeds* are representative of Yeats's work at this time, and while the clues to the meaning of the poems in these volumes is not always readily accessible to the uninitiated reader, they reveal a major step forward in terms of artistic skill and emotional maturity.

In spite of Yeats's theoretic dissociation from contemporary Irish life and politics, he could not escape his environment, the less so because he was in love, and was to be for two decades, with the beautiful and fiery actress and nationalist, Maud Gonne. In 1899 he and Isabella Augusta, Lady Gregory, founded the Irish National Theatre Society, which presently became the famous Abbey Theatre of Dublin. During the first decade of the twentieth century, working alongside Lady Gregory and J. M. Synge, Yeats wrote several plays for the Abbey, the best of which is a patriotic propaganda piece, *Cathleen ni Houlihan*, and the tragedy *Deirdre*. In the poetry of this period, too, Yeats reacted against what he considered the sentimentality and divorce from reality of his earlier work. As the legendary past became less important, in order to rescue his imagination from abstractions and bring it closer to actuality, he pressed everything into his poetry: the theater, patriotism, contemporary controversies.

The Green Helmet characteristically shows a tremendous advance in precision of imagery and syntax, as well as an increased use of personal and contemporary themes. Yet along with the substitution of a hard, dry manner and lively, homely detail for the dreamy vagueness of the early poetry, the symbolism which he was evolving becomes more and more esoteric and obscure. In 1917, having had proposals of marriage rejected by both Maud Gonne and her daughter Iseult, Yeats precipitously married Miss Georgie Hyde-Lees. The marriage was on the whole a success; one of its curious by-products was their joint experiment in spiritualism and "automatic writing," begun by his wife as a game to distract Yeats from personal worries. From the renewed interest in the occult and the mystical which arose out of these investigations Yeats developed a system of symbols by means of which he hoped to express his philosophy of life and art. This symbolism, which Yeats discusses in detail in *A Vision*, privately printed in 1925, is extremely complex, but while it provided the poet with a device which gave unity to his ideas on history, art, and human experience, its difficulties need not be a barrier to an understanding of his poems. It is probably enough for the average reader to recognize in the gyre, or ascending spiral, and the phases of the moon, Yeats's theories regarding the cyclical natures of both human nature and history.

For the aging Yeats this concept of the cyclical character of history was in a sense his defense against time. The poems of his later years are dominated by the figure of the poet, withdrawn from the "blood and mire" of life into the eternal realm of art, smiling with "tragic joy" at the cycles of life and death, creation and destruction, which mark human existence. But Yeats could not, either in his life or in his art, consistently maintain this withdrawal. In 1923 he was made a senator of the new Irish Free State, a post he entered into with enthusiasm, if not always tact. Some of Yeats's last poems, such as the "Crazy Jane" group, are a harsh, almost bitter glorification of the physical and even the sensual. As he says in "The Circus Animal's Desertion" from *Last Poems*, he "must lie down where all the ladders start,/In the foul rag-and-bone shop of the heart." The period after 1923, when Yeats was awarded the Nobel Prize in Literature, saw the production of some of his best and most exciting poetry. On January 28, 1939, his mind still alert and active, Yeats died at Roquebrune, on the French Riviera.

No sparse biographical outline can adequately characterize the complex personality of William Butler Yeats. He was fascinated by strange and supernatural phenomena but scorned the wonders of modern science; he was by nature inclined towards mysticism, but found little that attracted him in Christianity; he was an ardent patriot who dissociated himself as far as possible from the revolutionary course his country was following; he was a disciple of the doctrine of the separation of life from art. He was all these, yet his poetry had its basis in his own quick response to life, and was indeed a criticism *of* life. Yeats himself was aware of the contradictions in his nature and in life, and throughout his career he sought for a philosophical and artistic system that would resolve the conflict between his vision of what art should be and the recognition of what life is. Perhaps he found it, but it was in many ways too private, too personal a vision to be communicated. Yeats is not always an easy poet to read; however, his compact, intellectually intense, but supremely lyrical poetry deserves the careful attention it demands.

Bibliography

There is no collected edition of Yeats. The definitive edition of the poems is *The Collected Poems of William Butler Yeats*, 2 vols., 1949, incorporating revisions made by the poet before his death. For those interested in a reading of the texts an indispensable work is *The Variorum Edition of the Poems of William Butler Yeats*, edited by George Daniel Peter Allt and Russell K. Alspach, 1957. A revised edition of the *Collected Plays* was published in 1952. There is also *Collected Prose* edited by John P. Frayne, Vol. I, *First Reviews and Articles, 1880–1896*, 1970. There are two bibliographies: A. J. H. Symons, *A Bibliography of William Butler Yeats*, 1924, and Allan Wade, *A Bibliography of the Writings of William Butler Yeats*, 1953.

The Yeats bibliography is extensive. The best and most recent study is Harold Bloom, *William Butler Yeats*, 1970. Also valuable is Joesph Hone, *The Life of William Butler Yeats*, 1942. For biography and criticism see also Forrest Reid, *W. B. Yeats: A Critical Study*, 1915; C. L. Wrenn, *William Butler Yeats: A Literary Study*, 1920; J. H. Pollock, *William Butler Yeats*, 1935; J. P. O'Donnell, *Sailing to Byzantium: A Study of the Later Style and Symbolism of William Butler Yeats*, 1939; Lennox Robinson, *William Butler Yeats: A Study*, 1939; Louis Mac-Neice, *The Poetry of William Butler Yeats*, 1941 (rev. ed. 1967); V. K. N. Menon, *The Development of W. B. Yeats*, 1942; Peter Ure, *Towards a New Mythology*, 1946; Richard Ellman, *Yeats: The Man and the Masks*, 1948; and *The Identity of Yeats*, 1950; A. N. Jeffares, *W. B. Yeats: Man and Poet*, 1949; Donald Stauffer, *Golden Nightingale*, 1949; T. R. Henn, *Lonely Tower*, 1950; Vivienne Koch: *William Butler Yeats: The Tragic Phase*, 1951; Virginia Moore, *The Unicorn: William Butler Yeats' Search for Reality*, 1954; Frank Kermode, *Romantic Images*, 1957; and John R. Moore, *Masks of Love and Death* (plays), 1971.

For briefer studies in books and periodicals see, further, Cornelius Weygandt, *The Time of Yeats*, 1937; Arland Ussher, *Three Great Irishmen*, 1952; R. P. Blackmur, "The Later Poetry of W. B. Yeats," *Southern Review*, II (1936), 339–362; Morton Dauwen Zabel, "Yeats at Thirty and Seventy," *Poetry*, XLVII (1936), 268–277; Cleanth Brooks, "The Vision of W. B. Yeats," *Southern Review*, IV (1938), 116–142; W. K. Tindall, "The Symbolism of W. B. Yeats," *Accent*, V (1945), 203–212; D. S. Savage, "The Aestheticism of W. B. Yeats," *Kenyon Review*, VII (1945), 118–134; Harold H. Watts, "Yeats and Lapsed Mythology," *Renascence*, III (1951), 107–112; Peter Allt, "Yeats, Religion, and History," *Sewanee Review*, LX (1952), 624–658; Robert M. Admas, "Now That My

Ladder's Gone—Yeats Without Myth," *Accent*, XIII (1953), 140–152; Richard Ellman, "The Art of Yeats: Affirmative Capability," *Kenyon Review*, XV (1953), 357–385; T. R. Henn, "W. B. Yeats and the Irish Background," *Yale Review*, XLII (1953), 351–364; Hugh Kenner, "The Sacred Book of the Arts," *Sewanee Review*, LXIV (1956), 574–590; and Peter Ure, "Yeats' Supernatural Songs," *Review of English Studies*, VII (1956), 38–51.

The Permanence of Yeats, edited by James Hall and Martin Steinmann, 1950, is a collection of essays by various hands. The special Yeats Issue of the *Southern Review*, VII (Winter, 1942), was devoted entirely to studies of Yeats as poet and mystic.

THE AUTOBIOGRAPHY OF WILLIAM BUTLER YEATS

Type of work: Memoirs and journals
Author: William Butler Yeats (1865–1939)
First published: Reveries over Childhood and Youth, 1915; *Four Years,* 1921;
The Trembling of the Veil, 1922; *Autobiographies,* 1926; *Estrangement,* 1926;
Reflections from a Diary Kept in 1909, 1926; *The Death of Synge and Other
Passages from an Old Diary,* 1928; *Dramatis Personae,* 1936

Essay-Review

Yeats's *Autobiography* is important for several reasons, not the least of which is
that it serves as an illuminating background to the work of perhaps the greatest
twentieth century English poet. Yeats's poetry is about people: imaginary people
(Michael Robartes, Crazy Jane), people of Irish legend (Cuchulain, Fergus), people of Irish history (Parnell, Robert Emmet), people to whom Yeats was related
(the Middletons, the Pollexfens), people Yeats knew (Maud Gonne, Lady Gregory). All these, and many more, are celebrated in his poems. The main figure in
the poems is, of course, "I, the poet William Yeats."

The poems themselves are not important as autobiography, for the people in
them exist in art, not in life. There is a "Yeats country" just as there is a
"Faulkner country," but whereas Faulkner changed the names (Oxford, Mississippi becoming "Jefferson"), Yeats did not. In the "Yeats country" Michael
Robartes is as real as Maud Gonne, Cuchulain is as alive as Lady Gregory. Yet
we are always aware that many of Yeats's people are taken from real life, and in
the *Autobiography* we are afforded an extraordinary view into that life. We read
about the places Yeats made famous: Sligo, Coole, Ballylee. We meet the Yeats
family and Irish peasants, poets of the 1890's, patriots and revolutionaries, spir-
itualists, and Swedish royalty. We are presented with the real life equivalent of
the "Yeats country" of the *Collected Poems,* and we see it through the eyes and
through the memory of the poet himself.

The first section of the *Autobiography,* "Reveries over Childhood and Youth,"
begins with Yeats's earliest memories and concludes with the publication of his
first book of poems, *The Wanderings of Oisin and Other Poems* (1889). The chief
locales are Sligo, London, and Dublin.

As a very young child Yeats stood in awe of his sea-captain grandfather,
William Pollexfen, but it was his father, John Butler Yeats, whose influence was
dominant throughout his childhood and adolescence. The elder Yeats, a none-too-
successful painter and an opinionated skeptic, influenced his son in several ways.
He fostered his interest in literature by reading to him from the works of James
Fenimore Cooper, Walter Scott, Chaucer, Shelley, Thoreau, and many other writers, and in the theater by taking him to see Henry Irving in *Hamlet.* Until he was
nearly twenty Yeats seems to have shared most of his father's opinions (and they

were generally outspoken ones) about art, education, and politics. It was only after he had begun to study psychical research and mystical philosophy that he finally was able to break away from his father's influence. But in some respects his father's influence was never broken; John Butler Yeats's hatred for abstractions, for example, was one opinion his son held to all his life, and it greatly influenced the younger Yeats's attitudes towards politics, art, and life itself. Moreover, Yeats was always conscious of being an artist's son and aware, therefore, that he must follow a career that would be the whole end of life in itself rather than a means to becoming well off and living pleasantly. The work which Yeats took as the all and end of life was, of course, his poetry.

In this section we read of many things: Yeats's early interest in natural science (which he later grew to hate); his lack of scholarship and his resultant lack of anything like a systematic formal education; the influence on him of the Fenian leader, John O'Leary; and his continuing interest in legends of the Irish heroes, in stories of ghosts and omens, and in peasant tales of all kinds. It was only natural that Yeats was later to collect these stories (as in *The Celtic Twilight*, 1893), for he was never to forget his mother and a fisherman's wife telling each other stories such as Homer himself might have told.

Most of all, this section of the *Autobiography* is a portrait of the artist as a young man. At first Yeats merely played the roles of sage, magician, poet. Sometimes he was Hamlet, or Byron's Manfred, or Shelley's Alastor; at other times he was Byron himself. Then he began to write poems in admiring imitation of Shelley and Spenser. All of his early work was derivative: the well-known poem, "The Lake Isle of Innisfree," for example, was heavily indebted to his acquaintance with Thoreau's *Walden*. It was not until years afterward that he began, deliberately, to reshape his style by discarding traditional metaphors, employing looser rhythms, communicating emotion that he described as "cold." But for now there was nothing "cold" about his emotion. Very much under the influence of his father's belief that only passionate poetry is important, he filled his early lyrics with imagery and color, a heritage from the Romantic poets.

The longest section of the *Autobiography*, "The Trembling of the Veil," deals with the period between 1887 and the turn of the century. On the one hand, this section is a record of his friendships during these years. Nearly all of the famous literary figures of the 1890's are here: W. E. Henley, Oscar Wilde, William Morris, Lionel Johnson, Ernest Dowson, Shaw, George Russell ("A. E."), John Synge, Arthur Symons, Aubrey Beardsley, Max Beerbohm, William Sharp ("Fiona Mcleod"), Paul Verlaine—Yeats knew them all. On the other hand, the section is a record of the coming to maturity of Yeats's own work and its chief importance is perhaps that it gives us insights into the development of his theories of poetry.

He did not forsake his interest in emotion, but he began to write poems combining personal feeling with larger patterns of myth and symbol. His interest in myth and symbol, an understanding of which is essential to an understanding of his mature poetry, led him into a series of esoteric studies. He was associated with the Theosophist Madame Blavatsky; he experimented with the evocative power of symbols under the direction of Macgregor Mathers and later in conjunction with his uncle, George Pollexfen. He eventually realized that he had found only a variety of images. He had been searching for a tradition—for the centrality of a tradition—but he had hit upon its opposite: fragmentation.

Yeats envied Dante for having had a unified culture out of which to write. "Unity of Culture," a unity stemming from a universally accepted mythology, is precisely what, in Yeats's view, the modern world lacks. Symbolism he saw as the language of mythology. For years Yeats was occupied with the attempt to regain, in Ireland, that "Unity of Culture" which would make the language of symbolism intelligible. He hoped to find his mythology in peasant legendry. He hoped to encourage a national literature, one above politics and all temporal disputes, which would draw upon such a mythology. Finally he came to realize that his dream of a modern nation returned to Unity of Culture, was false. When this dream failed, he inevitably turned inward. Lacking a traditional mythology, he created one of his own, compounded from a complex variety of sources. He adopted myths and symbols from Christianity, from paganism, from the Orient, from Theosophy, and from Irish folklore. Perhaps his most important source was his own life: the people he knew became symbolic personages figuring in a private mythology. Consequently, as we read anecdotes about Synge, Lady Gregory, Maud Gonne, or John O'Leary, we come face to face with the real-life counterparts of some of the chief inhabitants of the "Yeats country."

In the third section of the *Autobiography*, "Dramatis Personae, 1896–1902," the chief "Personae" are Edward Martyn, Arthur Symons, George Moore, and above all, Lady Gregory. This section recounts the struggles of a small group of people to found in Ireland a native and national theater. But most of all it serves as Yeats's graceful and grateful tribute to Lady Gregory, his patron, collaborator, and friend. She encouraged him in his work and lent him money. Of even greater influence in the development of his art, as Yeats recalled years later, were the times he stayed at Coole, Lady Gregory's home, where Yeats spent the summers of twenty years. Among the trees and by the lake at Coole, Yeats was to do much of his greatest work, and the place itself, which he said he knew better than any spot on earth, became, like the people he knew, a familiar and important part of the world of his *Collected Poems*.

The *Autobiography* is far from being a complete account of Yeats's life. The first three sections cover the years 1865 to 1902, but Yeats was to live until 1939, and to do nearly all of his important work during the remaining years. Of the last three sections of the book, two ("Estrangement" and "The Death of Synge") are but fragmentary extracts from a diary Yeats kept in 1909. "Estrangement" is a collection of scattered and, at times, half-formed ideas about art, and is not, in the true sense of the word, autobiography. "The Death of Synge" is also largely a series of reveries about art; those reveries, in particular, which were induced by his friend's death. The final section of the book, "The Bounty of Sweden," (written in 1925), is a genial account of his trip to Stockholm in 1923 to receive the Nobel Prize.

THE POETRY OF YEATS

Author: William Butler Yeats (1865–1939)
Principal published works: Mosada: A Dramatic Poem, 1886; *The Wanderings of Oisin,* 1889; *Poems,* 1895; *The Wind Among the Reeds,* 1899; *In the Seven Woods,* 1903; *The Green Helmet and Other Poems,* 1910; *Responsibilities,* 1914; *The Wild Swans at Coole,* 1917; *Mic* 1920; *Later Poems,* 1922; *The Cat and the Moon and Certain Poems,* 1924; *The Tower,* 1928; *The Winding Stair,* 1933; *Collected Poems,* 1933; *The King of the Great Clock Tower,* 1934; *A Full Moon in March,* 1935; *New Poems,* 1938; *Last Poems and Plays,* 1940; *Collected Poems,* 1949

Essay-Review

The conflict that the antimonies between dream and action caused in the mind of William Butler Yeats could not be resolved in the verse tradition of the Aesthetic Movement of the 1880's. This was the poetry, together with that of Shelley and Keats and the plays of Shakespeare, with which he was most familiar. It was also the tradition to which he was closest in time. As he did not have a background of coherent culture on which to base his poetry, nor a personally satisfying faith, Yeats throughout his life had to create his own systems of thought—create, in fact, the convention in which he was to write.

In the introduction to *A Vision,* he said: "I wished for a system of thought that would leave my imagination free to create as it chose and yet make all it created, or could create, part of the one history, and that the soul's." His search for reality in belief and feeling was aided by his knowledge that the Romantic poets expressed faith in the power of the imagination. This knowledge also strengthened his conviction that the problems of human existence would never be solved by science and that answers would have to come from quite different disciplines: therefore, both his philosophy and his actions were of paramount importance to him in the writing of poetry.

Yeats spent many years in the study of the occult: spiritualism, magic, mysticism, and theosophy. His feelings for Ireland and for the Pre-Raphaelites led him, early in his life, to the study and use of ancient Irish myths. His hopes of independence for Ireland and his periodic identification with Irish nationalism, also a part of the fabric of his verse, were influenced by his passion for Maud Gonne and his friendship with his patron, Lady Gregory. He believed the system expounded in *A Vision* was revealed to him by his wife's power as a medium. Thus for Yeats, as for all poets, the pattern of his relationships, interests, beliefs, and loyalties was the material of his poetry. However, great poetry is always the expression of one man's personality in such a way that it is generally or universally meaningful. Magic, nationalism, and myth partly formed Yeats's complex personality, and his prose writings in these areas are undoubtedly esoteric. Although it was through these studies that Yeats was able to write as he did, it is not through them that the reader appreciates his poetry. All Yeats's poetry can be enjoyed and understood when carefully read, without reference to any of his prose. Yeats, in fact, took care to make his work understandable, and one of the most interesting aspects in the study of his poetry is his lifelong preoccupation with clarity, simplicity and exactness.

This clarity was the goal toward which he worked throughout his career. For Yeats, symbol was the means by which the natural and the supernatural could be fused and the antimonies be resolved. Writing in many *personae*, he worked toward this unified expression of reality, with the result that the continuous development of his powers and his ultimate success are both rare and exciting achievements. Yeats's dedication to his art was such that to the end of his life his conscious goals were always in advance of the poems he had completed.

Yeats was a lyric poet, but his belief in and practice of "active virtue"—that is, following a discipline that one has forged oneself—makes his verse essentially dramatic. His first volumes of poetry express the sensibility of the Aesthetic Movement; the lyrics are slight and the emotion, incompletely realized, often expresses his indecision between the life of dream and that of action. Twilight and longing predominate in these poems.

In his fourth volume, *In the Seven Woods*, published in 1903, Yeats began to find his true voice. Emotion is particularized and he has started to speak with authority. His technique is more sure and his tone more varied. In "Adam's Curse," in which the poet discusses the labor of writing poetry with a woman whom he loves, he uses common words and speech idioms which firmly link the poem to reality:

> Better go down upon your marrow-bones
> And scrub a kitchen pavement or break stones
> Like an old pauper, in all kinds of weather;
> For to articulate sweet sounds together
> Is to work harder than all these.

In his verse plays of this period Yeats was beginning deliberately to eschew abstraction and to introduce more direct and bold speech into his work. His 1910 volume, *The Green Helmet and Other Poems*, shows this technique in his lyric verse, which is becoming more dramatic and assertive. In "No Second Troy" the use of Greek myth approximates a reconciliation between dream and reality.

The 1914 volume, *Responsibilities*, shows an increase in force. Here Yeats uses other voices, or *personae*, of beggars, fools, and hermits to present his ideas. At that time he was encouraged further in his progress toward exactness of expression and the use of only the most meaningful images by his contact with Ezra Pound, who insisted that Yeats remove all abstractions from his verse. He appears to have learned quickly and well from the younger poet, and in subsequent poems he is able to integrate completely his theories of history and personality, and his feelings of despair for Ireland. He also learned to pare his images so that they are totally relevant to his emotion:

> Things fall apart, the centre cannot hold;
> Mere anarchy is loosed upon the world,
> The blood-dimmed tide is loosed, and everywhere
> The ceremony of innocence is drowned.

The Tower, published in 1928, contains several of Yeats's finest poems. One of the most brilliant and complex of these is "Sailing to Byzantium." The dazzling civilization of Byzantium which had successfully withstood the power of Rome as Yeats would probably have liked Ireland to withstand that of England, became for him the symbol of eternal art and of the fusion of the creator with the work of art. The reconciliation of youth and age, passion and intellect, is effected by the symbolic representation of the wisdom of the inspired soul in a supernatural form. In this poem, natural birds sing of the cycle of human life and the created birds of Byzantium, of the cycle of history. The glory of the old and of the young is here presented with a single steady vision, and the conflict between them has been resolved:

> This is no country for old men. The young
> In one another's arms, birds in the trees
> —Those dying generations—at their song,
> The salmon-falls, the mackerel-crowded seas,
> Fish, flesh, or fowl, commend all summer long
> Whatever is begotten, born, and dies.

He continues:

> An aged man is but a paltry thing,
> A tattered coat upon a stick, unless
> Soul clap its hands and sing, and louder sing. . . .

The poet has sailed to Byzantium that he may thus sing. His soul after death will not take "bodily form from any natural thing" but will be one of the singing birds of metal and enamel that the goldsmiths make to amuse the Emperor,

> Or set upon a golden bough to sing
> To lords and ladies of Byzantium
> Of what is past, or passing, or to come.

Another unified vision of life which is not dependent upon the supernatural is communicated in the poem "Among School Children." The mastery of technique which gives "Sailing to Byzantium" its *tour de force* brilliance, enables Yeats in this poem to communicate the feeling of peace after storm. The poet visits a convent school where the children see him as an old man, and as the children stare in mild curiosity, he is reminded of the "Ledaean body" of a woman he had loved, and this vision causes him to feel so joined in sympathy with her that he can visualize her as she must have been as a child:

> For even daughters of the swan share
> Something of every paddler's heritage.

The vision of the childhood of the woman who caused him much pain leads him to the thought that women would not think motherhood worth while if they could see their progeny at sixty. His suggestion that mothers as well as nuns worship images returns the poem to the convent school setting. In the last stanza of the poem Yeats, by a unifying image of continuity and completeness, reconciles the opposing forces of age and youth at the level of reality.

The poems written in the three years before Yeats's death at seventy-four show no diminution of power. He was still intent on his search for unity and reality of expression. In "The Circus Animals' Desertion," he reviews his poetic output and says that until he was an old man the machinery of his poetry was still in evidence:

> My circus animals were still on show,
> Those stilted boys, that gilded chariot.

He lists his old themes: the Irish myths, his lost love, and his preoccupation with the theater, and he tells how he dramatized his love in his plays. He faces his own delight in dreams which he feared would inhibit him from reality: "This dream itself had all my thought and love." He speaks of the *personae* in which he wrote and of the characters of Irish history:

> Players and painted stage took all my love
> And not those things they were the emblems of.

The reversal and resolution of these ideas comes in the last verse where he evaluates the use of images in his poetry by questioning their origin and finding that they indeed had their bases in reality.

Thus his adolescent faith in the imagination had been justified, and he could join the ranks of those whom he admired and who had fused the subjective and objective self into a meaningful whole: "The antithetical self comes to those who are no longer deceived, whose passion is reality."

The philosophy that Yeats so carefully constructed was the basis for a personal vision of life, which by unswerving dedication to craftsmanship and constantly renewed emotional and intellectual vitality he presented in his poetry in all its varied facets and with always increasing significance.

Bibliography

Beum, Robert. *The Poetic Art of William Butler Yeats.* New York: Frederick Ungar, 1969.

―――――. "Yeats's Octaves," in *Texas Studies in Language and Literature.* III (Spring, 1961), pp. 89–96.

Drew, Elizabeth and John L. Sweeney. "W.B. Yeats," in *Directions in Modern Poetry.* New York: Norton, 1940, pp. 148–171.

Ellmann, Richard. *The Identity of Yeats.* New York: Oxford University Press, 1964, pp. 39–61. Reprinted in *William Butler Yeats: A Collection of Criticism.* Edited by Patrick J. Keane. New York: McGraw-Hill, 1973, pp. 81–99.

Fraser, George Sutherland. "W.B. Yeats," in *Essays on Twentieth Century Poets.* Totowa, N.J.: Rowman and Littlefield, 1977, pp. 11–28.

Henn, T.R. "Yeats and the Picture Galleries," in *Southern Review.* I (Winter, 1965), pp. 57–75.

Jeffares, A. Norman. *The Poetry of W.B. Yeats.* Great Neck, N.Y.: Barron's Educational Series, 1961.

Kenner, Hugh. *Gnomon.* New York: Ivan Obolensky, 1958, pp. 9–29. Reprinted in *Yeats: A Collection of Critical Essays.* Edited by John Unterecker. Englewood Cliffs, N.J.: Prentice-Hall, 1967, pp. 10–22.

Loftus, Richard J. "Yeats and the Easter Rising: A Study in Ritual," in *Arizona Quarterly.* XVI (Summer, 1960), pp. 168–177.

Nist, John. "In Defense of Yeats," in *Arizona Quarterly.* XVIII (1962), pp. 58–65.

Parkinson, Thomas. "The Modernity of Yeats," in *Southern Review.* V (1969), pp. 922–934.

Rajan, Balachandra. *William Butler Yeats: A Critical Introduction.* London: Hutchinson's, 1965, pp. 7–93, 107–192.

Rosenthal, M.L. "Introduction," in *Selected Poems and Two Plays of William Butler Yeats.* New York: Collier, 1962, pp. xv–xxxix.

Saul, George Brandon. *Prolegomena to the Study of Yeats's Poems.* Philadelphia: University of Pennsylvania Press, 1957.

Tate, Allen. "Yeats' Romanticism," in *Collected Essays.* Denver, Colo.: Alan Swallow, 1959, pp. 227–236. Reprinted in *Yeats: A Collection of Critical Essays.* Edited by John Unterecker. Englewood Cliffs, N.J.: Prentice-Hall, 1967, pp. 155–162.

Tindall, William York. *William Butler Yeats.* New York: Columbia University Press, 1966.

Unterecker, John.   *A Reader's Guide to William Butler Yeats.* New York: Noonday, 1959.

Ussher, Arland.   *Three Great Irishmen: Shaw, Yeats, Joyce.* New York: New American Library, 1957, pp. 50–90.

Warren, Austin.   *Rage for Order.* Chicago: University of Chicago Press, 1948, pp. 66–83.

Watkins, Vernon.   "W.B. Yeats—The Religious Poet," in *Texas Studies in Language and Literature.* III (Winter, 1962), pp. 475–498.

Winters, Yvor.   *The Poetry of William Butler Yeats.* Denver: Alan Swallow, 1960.

ALPHABETICAL LIST OF TITLES

835

AUTHOR AND TITLE INDEX